Highlights From
125 Years
of
THE
Atlantic

Edited by
Louise Desaulniers

Atlantic
Subscriber
Edition

The Atlantic Monthly
wishes to thank the following for permission to reprint material included in this volume:

Kathryn Seely Adams for "Our Dissolving Ethics" by James Truslow Adams. N. J. Berrill for his "Detectives of Time." Paul Brooks for his "Warning: The Chain Saw Cometh." Raymond Carver for his "Cathedral." Dr. Robert Coles for his "Children of Affluence." William L. Copithorne for his "From Us to You." Curtis Brown Ltd. for "Wartime Journey" by Jan Struther. J. M. Dent & Sons Ltd. Publishers, the Trustees for the Copyrights of the late Dylan Thomas, and New Directions Publishing Corporation for "In Country Sleep" from COLLECTED POEMS by Dylan Thomas. Copyright 1947, 1952 by Dylan Thomas. Mrs. John Dos Passos for "U.S.A. Revisited" by John Dos Passos. Doubleday & Co., Inc. — and Methuen and Co., Ltd for "Off Stage and On" from IF MEMORY SERVES by Sacha Guitry. Copyright 1935 by The Atlantic Monthly Company. — and William Heinemann Ltd. Publishers for "Mademoiselle O" from NABOKOV'S DOZEN by Vladimir Nabokov. Copyright 1942 by The Atlantic Monthly Company. — and Raines & Raines for "Looking for the Buckhead Boys" copyright © 1969 by The Atlantic Monthly Company from EYE-BEATERS, BLOOD, VICTORY, MADNESS, BUCKHEAD AND MERCY by James Dickey. Bergen Evans for an amended version of his "Nursery Crimes." Herbert Gold and his agent, James Brown Associates, Inc. for "Reviewmanship and the I-Wrote-A-Book Disease." Copyright © 1970 by Herbert Gold. Goulding-Elliott-Greybar Productions, Inc. for "The Day the Computers Got Waldon Ashenfelter" by Bob Elliott and Ray Goulding. Harper & Row, Publishers, Inc. for abridgement of "Old Times on the Mississippi" from pp. 32–43 in LIFE ON THE MISSISSIPPI by Mark Twain. — and Joan Daves for "Letter from Birmingham Jail-April 16, 1963" from WHY WE CAN'T WAIT (1964) by Martin Luther King, Jr. Copyright © 1963 by Martin Luther King, Jr. (published in *The Atlantic Monthly* under the title "The Negro Is Your Brother.") — for "Death of a Pig" in THE SECOND TREE FROM THE CORNER by E. B. White. Copyright 1947 by E. B. White. And to Hamish Hamilton Ltd. who published the book in 1954. Mary Hemingway and Alfred Rice for "Two Tales of Darkness." Copyright © 1957 by Ernest Hemingway. John Hersey for his "Peggety's Parcel of Shortcomings." Historical Society of Saratoga Springs for "Clichés on the Air" by Frank Sullivan. Holt, Rinehart and Winston, Publishers, the Estate of Robert Frost and Jonathan Cape Ltd. for "Birches," "The Road Not Taken," and "The Sound of Trees" by Robert Frost, from THE POETRY OF ROBERT FROST edited by Edward Connery Latham. Copyright 1916, © 1969 by Holt, Rinehart and Winston. Copyright 1944 by Robert Frost. Houghton Mifflin Company for "The Summit of the Years" from WORKS by John Burroughs. Copyright renewed 1941 by Julian Burroughs. — and Hamish Hamilton Ltd. and Helga Greene for "Writers in Hollywood" by Raymond Chandler, with brief deletions from pages 116–125 of RAYMOND CHANDLER SPEAKING by Dorothy Gardiner and Kathrine Sorley Walker. Copyright © 1962 by the Helga Greene Literary Agency. Bruce Jackson for his "White-Collar Pill Party." Alexander R. James, Literary Executor, for "Remarks at the Peace Banquet" by William James. The trustees for the Estate of Rufus Jones, Girard Trust Bank, Trustee and Mary Hoxie Jones for "The Mystic's Experience of God" by Rufus Jones. Tracy Kidder for his "Railroads: Aboard the Ghost Trains." Alfred A. Knopf and Faber and Faber Ltd. for "Banjo Boomer" from OPUS POSTHUMOUS by Wallace Stevens. Copyright © 1957 by Elsie Stevens and Holly Stevens. Leonard Labaree for "Fiddlers' Luck" by Robert Haven Schauffler. Stanley Kunitz for his "The Wellfleet Whale." J. B. Lippincott and McIntosh, McKee & Dodds, Inc. for "The Parents at Country Day" from HOW TO PROTECT YOURSELF AGAINST WOMEN AND OTHER VICIS-SITUDES (Under the title "Problems for Parents") by Charles W. Morton. Copyright 1951 by Charles W. Morton. Little, Brown and Company in association with the Atlantic Monthly Press for "Sing: A Song of Sixpence" from THE FORGOTTEN ONE" and Other True Tales of the South Seas by James Norman Hall. Copyright 1925 by James Norman Hall. — "My Horse Buck" from Chapter XV of THE MUSTANGS by J. Frank Dobie. Copyright 1952 by J. Frank Dobie. — in association with the Atlantic Monthly Press for "The Aesthetics of Eating," excerpts from ANDRE SIMON'S FRENCH COOK BOOK by André Simon. Copyright 1938. © 1966 by André L. Simon. — for eight poems by Emily Dickinson from POEMS by Emily Dickinson, edited by Martha Dickinson Bianchi and Alfred Leete Hampson. Copyright 1929 by Martha Dickinson Bianchi. Copyright © 1957 by Mary L. Hampson. — in association with the Atlantic Monthly Press, excerpts from THE GOOD SOCIETY by Walter Lippmann. Copyright 1937. © 1965 by Walter Lippmann. Macmillan Publishing Co., Inc. — and Ernest Benn Limited for "Universities and Their Function" from AIMS OF EDUCATION AND OTHER ESSAYS by Alfred North Whitehead. Copyright 1929 by Macmillan Publishing Co., Inc. Renewed 1957 by Evelyn Whitehead. — and the Trustees of the Tagore Estate and Macmillan London and Basingstroke for "To the Watcher" (or "Fruit-Gathering") from COL-LECTED POEMS AND PLAYS by Rabindranath Tagore. Copyright 1916 by Macmillan Publishing Co., Inc., renewed 1944 by Rabindranath Tagore. Macmillan London and Basingstoke and the Royal Economic Society for a condensation of John Maynard Keynes's "The World's Economic Outlook" to be published in THE COLLECTED WRITINGS OF JOHN MAYNARD KEYNES. Mary Manning for her "The Dublin Social Scene." Robert Manning for his "Hemingway in Cuba." Mercantile Safe Deposit & Trust Company, Trustee of Estate for Henry Louis Mencken, for "Newspaper Morals." Harold Ober Associates Incorporated for "Canadian Spring" copyright © 1962 by Sheila Burnford, and for "The Nature of the Artist" © 1961 by Catherine Drinker Bowen. Isidor I. Rabi for his "The Cost of Secrecy." Random House, Inc. — and the Estate of Gertrude Stein for "The Winner Loses: A Picture of Occupied France," from SELECTED WRIT-INGS OF GERTRUDE STEIN by Gertrude Stein, edited by Carl Van Vechten. Copyright 1946 by Random House, Inc. — and Faber and Faber Ltd. for "Loneliness" from EPISTLE TO A GODSON AND OTHER POEMS by W. H. Auden. Copyright © 1972 by W. H. Auden. John Savles for his "Breed." Charles Scribner's Sons and The Society of Authors as the literary representative of the Estate of John Galsworthy for "Two Looks" from CARAVAN by John Galsworthy. Copyright 1925 by Charles Scribner's Sons. Elaine A. Steinbeck and Elizabeth Otis for "How Mr. Hogan Robbed a Bank" by John Steinbeck. Richard Stern for his "Dr. Cahn's Visit." James C. Thomson, Jr. for his "How Could Vietnam Happen? An Autopsy." Mrs. James Thurber and Hamish Hamilton Ltd. London for "The Porcupines in the Artichokes" from LAN-TERNS & LANCES published by Harper & Row, New York, copyright © 1960 by James Thurber, and by Hamish Hamilton Ltd., London, copyright © 1959 by James Thurber. John Updike for his "Augustine's Concubine." Vanguard Press, Inc. for "Int'l Jet Set Hits Watkins Glen" from INNOCENT BYSTANDER: The Scene from the '70s by L.E. Sissman. Copyright © 1975 by L.E. Sissman. The Viking Press, Laurence Pollinger Ltd., and the Estate of the late Mrs. Frieda Lawrence for "Mercury" from PHOENIX: THE POSTHUMOUS PAPERS OF D. H. LAWRENCE edited by Edward D. McDonald. Copyright 1927 by D. H. Lawrence, Copyright 1936 by Frieda Lawrence, Copyright © 1964 by The Estate of the late Frieda Lawrence Ravagli. All rights reserved. A. Watkins, Inc. for "Confessions of a Novelist" by Edith Wharton. Copyright 1933 by Edith Wharton, renewed 1961 by William R. Tyler. Andrew Ward for his "The Trouble with Architects." Edward Weeks for his "How Big is One?"

EDITOR'S NOTE

How does one capture the shape and essence of more than a century's history in an hour-long documentary? How does one fit 125 years of a magazine into a 670-page book? When I began my task I did so with a bit of trepidation, awe, but with a thirty-five-year association with the subject, and a determination to present *The Atlantic* as the vibrant and entertaining magazine it was and is.

The Atlantic was founded as a magazine devoted to literature, art, and politics, and as it grew in age, its horizons expanded with the concerns of the times. Education, science, the total environment became as much a part of its essence as the poetry and fiction of its founders had been. The literature of ideas was balanced against the literature of the imagination, and it is this balance that the editors have successfully and consistently maintained throughout the 125 years.

I invite you to share with me the excitement of Philip Hubert's prediction in 1889 that future reporters and editors would dictate to a machine instead of to a secretary; of Henry Pritchett's suggestion in 1905 that students play a part in university administration; of Margaret Deland's paper on the New Woman as seen in 1910; of Della Cyrus' courageous challenge to the American family in 1946; of Bruce Jackson's timely reporting of the middle-class, adult drug scene in 1966; of Robert Coles's theory of "entitlement" as seen by the wealthy class in 1977. This is but a sample of the literature of ideas; the literature of the imagination runs a star-studded course from Edward Everett Hale to John Updike to Raymond Carver, from Walt Whitman to W. H. Auden to Stanley Kunitz.

The limits of space and chronology have compelled me to omit some of our noted creative writers. Articles of nonfiction have been cut; the fiction and poetry selections have been allowed to run as originally written.

I am most grateful to Roy M. Green, the magazine's circulation director, for the opportunity to put together this volume of treasures gleaned from the century and a quarter of *The Atlantic*'s writings. To Roy I dedicate this book.

Louise Desaulniers

CONTENTS

EDITORS OF THE ATLANTIC

James Russell Lowell	1857 – 1861
James Thomas Fields	1861 – 1871
William Dean Howells	1871 – 1881
Thomas Bailey Aldrich	1881 – 1890
Horace Elisha Scudder	1890 – 1898
Walter Hines Page	1898 – 1899
Bliss Perry	1899 – 1909
Ellery Sedgwick	1909 – 1938
Edward Weeks	1938 – 1966
Robert Manning	1966 – 1980
William Whitworth	1981 –

THE AUTOCRAT OF THE BREAKFAST-TABLE
by Oliver Wendell Holmes

THIS business of conversation is a very serious matter. There are men that it weakens one to talk with an hour more than a day's fasting would do. There are men of *esprit* who are excessively exhausting to some people. They are the talkers that have what may be called *jerky* minds. Their thoughts do not run in the natural order of sequence. They say bright things on all possible subjects, but their zigzags rack you to death. After a jolting half-hour with one of these jerky companions, talking with a dull friend affords great relief. It's like taking the cat in your lap after holding a squirrel.

What a comfort a dull but kindly person is, to be sure, at times! A ground-glass shade over a gas-lamp does not bring more solace to our dazzled eyes than such a one to our minds.

I really believe some people save their bright thoughts, as being too precious for conversation. What do you think an admiring friend said the other day to one that was talking good things, — good enough to print? "Why," said he, "you are wasting merchantable literature, a cash article, at the rate, as nearly as I can tell, of fifty dollars an hour." The talker took him to the window and asked him to look out and tell what he saw.

"Nothing but a very dusty street," he said, "and a man driving a sprinkling-machine through it."

"Why don't you tell the man he is wasting that water? What would be the state of the highways of life, if we did not drive our *thought-sprinklers* through them with the valves open, sometimes?

"Besides, there is another thing about this talking, which you forget. It shapes our thoughts for us; — the waves of conversation roll them as the surf rolls the pebbles on the shore. Let me modify the image a little. I rough out my thoughts in talk as an artist models in clay. Spoken language is so plastic, — you can pat and coax, and spread and shave, and rub out, and fill up, and stick on so easily, when you work that soft material, that there is nothing like it for modelling. Out of it come the shapes which you turn into marble or bronze in your immortal books, if you happen to write such. Or, to use another illustration, writing or printing is like shooting with a rifle; you may hit your reader's mind, or miss it; — but talking is like playing at a mark with the pipe of an engine; if it is within reach, and you have time enough, you can't help hitting it."

I want to make a literary confession now, which I believe nobody has made before me. You know very well that I write verses sometimes, because I have read some of them at this table. (The company assented, — two or three of them in a resigned sort of way, as I thought, as if they supposed that I had an epic in my pocket, and was going to read half a dozen books or so for their benefit.) — I continued. Of course I write some lines or passages which are better than others; some which, compared with the others, might be called relatively excellent. It is in the nature of things that I should consider these relatively excellent lines or passages as absolutely good. So much must be pardoned to humanity. Now I never wrote a "good" line in my life, but the moment after it was written it seemed a hundred years old. Very commonly I had a sudden conviction that I had seen it somewhere. Possibly I may have sometimes unconsciously stolen it, but I do not remember that I ever once detected any historical truth in these sudden convictions of the antiquity of my new thought or phrase. I have learned utterly to distrust them, and never allow them to bully me out of a thought or line.

This is the philosophy of it. (Here the number of the company was diminished by a small secession.) Any new formula which suddenly emerges in our consciousness has its roots in long trains of thought; it is virtually old when it first makes its appearance among the recognized growths of our intellect.

Literary life is full of curious phenomena. I don't know that there is anything more noticeable than what we may call *conventional reputations*. There is a tacit understanding in every community of men of letters that they will not disturb the popular fallacy respecting this or that electro-gilded celebrity. There are various reasons for this forbearance: one is old; one is rich; one is good-natured; one is such a favorite with the pit that it would not be safe to hiss him from the manager's box. The venerable augurs of the literary or scientific temple may smile faintly when one of the tribe is mentioned; but the farce is in general kept up as well as the Chinese comic scene of entreating and imploring a man to stay with you, with the implied compact between you that he shall by no means think of doing it. A poor wretch he must be who would wantonly sit down on one of these bandbox reputations. A Prince-Rupert's-drop, which is a tear of unannealed glass, lasts indefinitely, if you keep it from meddling hands; but break its tail off, and it explodes and resolves itself into powder. These celebrities I speak of are the Prince-Rupert's-drops of the learned and polite world. See how the papers treat them! What an array of pleasant kaleidoscopic phrases, that can be arranged in ever so many charming patterns, is at their service! How kind the "Critical Notices"

— where small authorship comes to pick up chips of praise, fragrant, sugary, and sappy — always are to them! Well, life would be nothing without paper-credit and other fictions; so let them pass current. Don't steal their chips; don't puncture their swimming-bladders; don't come down on their pasteboard boxes; don't break the ends of their brittle and unstable reputations, you fellows who all feel sure that your names will be household words a thousand years from now.

1858
CHESUNCOOK
by Henry David Thoreau

STRANGE that so few ever come to the woods to see how the pine lives and grows and spires, lifting its evergreen arms to the light, — to see its perfect success; but most are content to behold it in the shape of many broad boards brought to market, and deem *that* its true success! But the pine is no more lumber than man is, and to be made into boards and houses is no more its true and highest use than the truest use of a man is to be cut down and made into manure. There is a higher law affecting our relation to pines as well as to men. A pine cut down, a dead pine, is no more a pine than a dead human carcass is a man. Can he who has discovered only some of the values of whalebone and whale oil be said to have discovered the true use of the whale? Can he who slays the elephant for his ivory be said to have "seen the elephant"? These are petty and accidental uses; just as if a stronger race were to kill us in order to make buttons and flageolets of our bones; for everything may serve a lower as well as a higher use. Every creature is better alive than dead, men and moose and pine-trees, and he who understands it aright will rather preserve its life than destroy it.

Is it the lumberman, then, who is the friend and lover of the pine, stands nearest to it, and understands its nature best? Is it the tanner who has barked it, or he who has boxed it for turpentine, whom posterity will fable to have been changed into a pine at last? No! no! it is the poet; he it is who makes the truest use of the pine — who does not fondle it with an axe, nor tickle it with a saw, nor stroke it with a plane — who knows whether its heart is false without cutting into it — who has not bought the stumpage of the township on which it stands. All the pines shudder and heave a sigh when *that* man steps on the forest floor. No, it is the poet, who loves them as his own shadow in the air, and lets them stand. I have been into the lumber-yard, and the carpenter's shop, and the tannery, and the lampblack-factory, and the turpentine clearing; but when at length I saw the tops of the pines waving and reflecting the light at a distance, high over all the rest of the forest, I realized that the former were not the highest use of the pine. It is not their bones or hide or tallow that I love most. It is the living spirit of the tree, not its spirit of turpentine, with which I sympathize, and which heals my cuts.

1859
MY DOUBLE; AND HOW HE UNDID ME
by Edward Everett Hale

IT is not often that I trouble the readers of the "Atlantic Monthly." I should not trouble them now, but for the importunities of my wife, who "feels to insist" that a duty to society is unfulfilled, till I have told why I had to have a double, and how he undid me. She is sure, she says, that intelligent persons cannot understand that pressure upon public servants which alone drives any man into the employment of a double. And while I fear she thinks, at the bottom of her heart, that my fortunes will never be remade, she has a faint hope, that, as another Rasselas, I may teach a lesson to future publics, from which they may profit, though we die. Owing to the behaviour of my double, or, if you please, to that public pressure which compelled me to employ him, I have plenty of leisure to write this communication.

I am, or rather was, a minister, of the Sandemanian connection. I was settled in the active, wide-awake town of Naguadavick, on one of the finest water-powers in Maine. We used to call it a Western town in the heart of the civilization of New England. A charming place it was and is. A spirited, brave young parish had I; and it seemed as if we might have all "the joy of eventful living" to our hearts' content.

Alas! how little we knew on the day of my ordination, and in those halcyon moments of our first housekeeping! To be the confidential friend in a hundred families in the town, — cutting the social trifle, as my friend Haliburton says, "from the top of the whipped-syllabub to the bottom of the sponge-cake, which is the foundation," — to keep abreast of the thought of the age in one's study, and to do one's best on Sunday to interweave that thought with the active life of an active town, and to inspirit both and make both infinite by glimpses of the Eternal Glory, seemed such an exquisite forelook into one's life! Enough to do, and all so real and so grand! If this vision could only have lasted!

The truth is, that this vision was not in itself a delusion, nor, indeed, half bright enough. If one could only have been left to do his own business, the vision would have accomplished itself and brought out new paraheliacal visions, each as bright as the original. The misery was and is, as we found out, I and Polly, before long, that, besides the vision, and besides the usual human and finite failures in life, (such as breaking the old pitcher that came over in the "Mayflower," and putting into the fire the Alpenstock with which her father climbed Mont Blanc,) — besides these, I say, (imitating the style of Robinson Crusoe,) there were pitchforked in on us a great rowen-heap of humbugs, handed down from some unknown seed-time, in which we were expected, and I chiefly, to fulfil certain public functions before the community, of the character of those fulfilled by the third row of supernumeraries who stand behind the Sepoys in the spectacle of the "Cataract of the Ganges." They were the duties, in a word, which one performs as member of one or another social class or subdivision, wholly distinct from what one does as A. by himself A. What invisible power put these functions on me, it would be very hard to tell. But such power there was and is. And I had not been at work a year before I found I was living two lives, one real and one merely functional, — for two sets of people, one my parish, whom I loved, and the other a vague public, for whom I did not care two straws. All this was in a vague notion, which everybody had and has, that this second life would eventually bring out some great results, unknown at present, to somebody somewhere.

Crazed by this duality of life, I first read Dr. Wigan on the "Duality of the Brain," hoping that I could train one side of my head to do these outside jobs, and the other to do my intimate and real duties. For Richard Greenough once told me, that, in studying for the statue of Franklin, he found that the left side of the great man's face was philosophic and reflective, and the right side funny and smiling. If you will go and look at the bronze statue, you will find he has repeated this observation there for posterity. The eastern profile is the portrait of the statesman Franklin, the western of Poor Richard. But Dr. Wigan does not go into these niceties of this subject, and I failed. It was then, that, on my wife's suggestion, I resolved to look out for a Double.

I was, at first, singularly successful. We happened to be recreating at Stafford Springs that summer. We rode out one day, for one of the relaxations of that watering-place, to the great Monsonpon House. We were passing through one of the large halls, when my destiny was fulfilled! I saw my man!

He was not shaven. He had on no spectacles. He was dressed in a green baize roundabout and faded blue overalls, worn sadly at the knee. But I saw at once that he was of my height, five feet four and a half. He had black hair, worn off by his hat. So have and have not I.

He stooped in walking. So do I. His hands were large, and mine. And — choicest gift of Fate in all — he had, not "a strawberry-mark on his left arm," but a cut from a juvenile brickbat over his right eye, slightly affecting the play of that eyebrow. Reader, so have I! — My fate was sealed!

A word with Mr. Holley, one of the inspectors, settled the whole thing. It proved that this Dennis Shea was a harmless, amiable fellow, of the class known as shiftless, who had sealed his fate by marrying a dumb wife, who was at that moment ironing in the laundry. Before I left Stafford, I had hired both for five years. We had applied to Judge Pynchon, then the probate judge at Springfield, to change the name of Dennis Shea to Frederic Ingham. We had explained to the Judge, what was the precise truth, that an eccentric gentleman wished to adopt Dennis under this new name into his family. It never occurred to him that Dennis might be more than fourteen years old. And thus, to shorten this preface, when we returned at night to my parsonage at Naguadavick, there entered Mrs. Ingham, her new dumb laundress, myself, who am Mr. Frederic Ingham, and my double, who was Mr. Frederic Ingham by as good right as I.

Oh, the fun we had the next morning in shaving his beard to my pattern, cutting his hair to match mine, and teaching him how to wear and how to take off gold-bowed spectacles! Really, they were electroplate, and the glass was plain (for the poor fellow's eyes were excellent). Then in four successive afternoons I taught him four speeches. I had found these would be quite enough for the supernumerary-Sepoy line of life, and it was well for me they were. For though he was good-natured, he was very shiftless, and it was, as our national proverb says, "like pulling teeth" to teach him. But at the end of the next week he could say, with quite my easy and frisky air, —

1. "Very well, thank you. And you?" This for an answer to casual salutations.

2. "I am very glad you liked it."

3. "There has been so much said, and, on the whole, so well said, that I will not occupy the time."

4. "I agree, in general, with my friend the other side of the room."

At first I had a feeling that I was going to be at great cost for clothing him. But it proved, of course, at once, that, whenever he was out, I should be at home. And I went, during the bright period of his success, to so few of those awful pageants which require a black dress-coat and what the ungodly call, after Mr. Dickens, a white choker, that in the happy retreat of my own dressing-gowns and jackets my days went by as happily and cheaply as those of another Thalaba. And Polly declares there was never a year when the tailoring cost so little. . . .

I launched him by sending him to a meeting of the Enlightenment

Board. The Enlightenment Board consists of seventy-four members, of whom sixty-seven are necessary to form a quorum. One becomes a member under the regulations laid down in old Judge Dudley's will. I became one by being ordained pastor of a church in Naguadavick. You see you cannot help yourself, if you would. At this particular time we had had four successive meetings, averaging four hours each, — wholly occupied in whipping in a quorum. At the first only eleven men were present; at the next, by force of three circulars, twenty-seven; at the third, thanks to two days' canvassing by Auchmuty and myself, begging men to come, we had sixty. Half the others were in Europe. But without a quorum we could do nothing. All the rest of us waited grimly for our four hours, and adjourned without any action. At the fourth meeting we had flagged, and only got fifty-nine together. But on the first appearance of my double, — whom I sent on this fatal Monday to the fifth meeting, — he was the *sixty-seventh* man who entered the room. He was greeted with a storm of applause! The poor fellow had missed his way, — read the street signs ill through his spectacles, (very ill, in fact, without them,) — and had not dared to inquire. He entered the room, — finding the president and secretary holding to their chairs two judges of the Supreme Court, who were also members *ex officio,* and were begging leave to go away. On his entrance all was changed. *Presto,* the by-laws were amended, and the Western property was given away. Nobody stopped to converse with him. He voted, as I had charged him to do, in every instance, with the minority. I won new laurels as a man of sense, though a little unpunctual, — and Dennis, *alias* Ingham, returned to the parsonage, astonished to see with how little wisdom the world is governed. He cut a few of my parishioners in the street; but he had his glasses off, and I am known to be near-sighted. Eventually he recognized them more readily than I.

I "set him again" at the exhibition of the New Coventry Academy; and here he undertook a "speaking part," — as, in my boyish, worldly days, I remember the bills used to say of Mlle. Céleste. We are all trustees of the New Coventry Academy; and there has lately been "a good deal of feeling" because the Sandemanian trustees did not regularly attend the exhibitions. It has been intimated, indeed, that the Sandemanians are leaning towards Free-Will, and that we have, therefore, neglected these semi-annual exhibitions, while there is no doubt that Auchmuty last year went to Commencement at Waterville. Now the head master at New Coventry is a real good fellow, who knows a Sanskrit root when he sees it, and often cracks etymologies with me, — so that, in strictness, I ought to go to their exhibitions. But think, reader, of sitting through three long July days in that Academy chapel, following the programme from:

TUESDAY MORNING. *English Composition.* "SUNSHINE." Miss Jones.

round to

Trio on Three Pianos. Duel from the Opera of "Midshipman Easy." *Marryatt.*

coming in at nine, Thursday evening! Think of this, reader, for men who know the world is trying to go backward, and who would give their lives if they could help it on! Well! The double had succeeded so well at the Board, that I sent him to the Academy. (Shade of Plato, pardon!) He arrived early on Tuesday, when, indeed, few but mothers and clergymen are generally expected, and returned in the evening to us, covered with honors. He had dined at the right hand of the chairman, and he spoke in high terms of the repast. The chairman had expressed his interest in the French conversation. "I am very glad you liked it," said Dennis; and the poor chairman, abashed, supposed the accent had been wrong. At the end of the day, the gentlemen present had been called upon for speeches, — the Rev. Frederic Ingham first, as it happened; upon which Dennis had risen, and had said, "There has been so much said, and, on the whole, so well said, that I will not occupy the time." The girls were delighted, because Dr. Dabney, the year before, had given them at this occasion a scolding on impropriety of behavior at lyceum lectures. They all declared Mr. Ingham was a love, — and *so* handsome! (Dennis is good-looking.) Three of them, with arms behind the others' waists, followed him up to the wagon he rode home in; and a little girl with a blue sash had been sent to give him a rosebud. After this *début* in speaking, he went to the exhibition for two days more, to the mutual satisfaction of all concerned. Indeed, Polly reported that he had pronounced the trustees' dinners of a higher grade than those of the parsonage. When the next term began, I found six of the Academy girls had obtained permission to come across the river and attend our church. But this arrangement did not long continue.

After this he went to several Commencements for me, and ate the dinners provided; he sat through three of our Quarterly Conventions for me, — always voting judiciously, by the simple rule mentioned above, of siding with the minority. And I, meanwhile, who had before been losing caste among my friends, as holding myself aloof from the associations of the body, began to rise in everybody's favor. "Ingham's a good fellow, — always on hand"; "never talks much, — but does the right thing at the right time"; "is not as unpunctual as he used to be, — he comes early, and sits through to the end." "He has got over his old talkative habit, too. I spoke to a friend of his about it once; and I think Ingham took it kindly," etc., etc.

This voting power of Dennis was particularly valuable at the quarterly meetings of the Proprietors of the Naguadavick Ferry. My wife inherited from her father some shares in that enterprise, which is not yet fully developed, though it doubtless will become a very valuable property. The law of Maine then forbade stockholders to appear by proxy at such meetings. Polly disliked to go, not being, in fact, a "hens'-rights hen," and transferred her stock to me. I, after going once, disliked it more than she. But Dennis went to the next meeting, and liked it very much. He said the armchairs were good, the collation good, and the free rides to stockholders pleasant. He was a little frightened when they first took him upon one of the ferry-boats, but after two or three quarterly meetings he became quite brave.

Thus far I never had any difficulty with him. Indeed, being of that type which is called shiftless, he was only too happy to be told daily what to do, and to be charged not to be forthputting or in any way original in his discharge of that duty. He learned, however, to discriminate between the lines of his life, and very much preferred these stockholders' meetings and trustees' dinners and Commencement collations to another set of occasions, from which he used to beg off most piteously. Our excellent brother, Dr. Fillmore, had taken a notion at this time that our Sandemanian churches needed more expression of mutual sympathy. He insisted upon it that we were remiss. He said, that, if the Bishop came to preach at Naguadavick, all the Episcopal clergy of the neighborhood were present; if Dr. Pond came, all the Congregational clergymen turned out to hear him; if Dr. Nichols, all the Unitarians; and he thought we owed it to each other, that, whenever there was an occasional service at a Sandemanian church, the other brethren should all, if possible, attend. "It looked well," if nothing more. Now this really meant that I had not been to hear one of Dr. Fillmore's lectures on the Ethnology of Religion. He forgot that he did not hear one of my course on the "Sandemanianism of Anselm." But I felt badly when he said it; and afterwards I always made Dennis go to hear all the brethren preach, when I was not preaching myself. This was what he took exceptions to, — the only thing, as I said, which he ever did except to. Now came the advantage of his long morning-nap, and of the green tea with which Polly supplied the kitchen. But he would plead, so humbly, to be let off, only from one or two! I never excepted him, however. I knew the lectures were of value, and I thought it best he should be able to keep the connection.

Polly is more rash than I am, as the reader has observed in the outset of this memoir. She risked Dennis one night under the eyes of her own sex. Governor Gorges had always been very kind to us; and when he gave his great annual party to the town, asked us. I confess I hated to go. I was deep in the new volume of Pfeiffer's "Mystics," which Haliburton had just sent me from Boston. "But how rude," said Polly, "not to return the Governor's civility and Mrs. Gorges's, when they will be sure to ask why you are away!" Still I demurred, and at last she, with the wit of Eve and of Semiramis conjoined, let me off by saying, that, if I would go in with her, and sustain the initial conversations with the Governor and the ladies staying there, she would risk Dennis for the rest of the evening. And that was just what we did. She took Dennis in training all that afternoon, instructed him in fashionable conversation, cautioned him against the temptations of the supper-table, — and at nine in the evening he drove us all down in the carry-all. I made the grand star-*entrée* with Polly and the pretty Walton girls, who were staying with us. We had put Dennis into a great rough top-coat, without his glasses, — and the girls never dreamed, in the darkness, of looking at him. He sat in the carriage, at the door, while we entered. I did the agreeable to Mrs. Gorges, was introduced to her niece, Miss Fernanda, — I complimented Judge Jeffries on his decision in the great case of D'Aulnay *vs.* Laconia Mining Co., — I stepped into the dressing-room for a moment, — stepped out for another, — walked home, after a nod with Dennis, and tying the horse to a pump; — and while I walked home, Mr. Frederic Ingham, my double, stepped in through the library into the Gorges's grand saloon.

Oh! Polly died of laughing as she told me of it at midnight! And even here, where I have to teach my hands to hew the beech for stakes to fence our cave, she dies of laughing as she recalls it, — and says that single occasion was worth all we have paid for it. Gallant Eve that she is! She joined Dennis at the library-door, and in an instant presented him to Dr. Ochterlong, from Baltimore, who was on a visit in town, and was talking with her, as Dennis came in. "Mr. Ingham would like to hear what you were telling us about your success among the German population." And Dennis bowed and said, in spite of a scowl from Polly, "I'm very glad you liked it." But Dr. Ochterlong did not observe, and plunged into the tide of explanation, — Dennis listening like a prime-minister, and bowing like a mandarin, — which is, I suppose, the same thing. Polly declared it was just like Haliburton's Latin conversation with the Hungarian minister, of which he is very fond of telling. "*Quæne sit historia Reformationis in Ungariâ?*" quoth Haliburton, after some thought. And his *confrère* replied gallantly, "*In seculo decimo tertio,*" etc., etc., etc.; and from *decimo tertio** to the nineteenth century and a half lasted till the oysters came. So was it that before Dr. Ochter-long came to the "success," or near it, Governor Gorges came to Dennis and asked him to hand Mrs. Jeffries down to supper, a request which he heard with great joy.

* Which means, "In the thirteenth century," my dear little bell-and-coral reader. You have rightly guessed that the question means, "What is the history of the Reformation in Hungary?"

Polly was skipping round the room, I guess, gay as a lark. Auchmuty came to her "in pity for poor Ingham," who was so bored by the stupid pundit, — and Auchmuty could not understand why I stood it so long. But when Dennis took Mrs. Jeffries down, Polly could not resist standing near them. He was a little flustered, till the sight of the eatables and drinkables gave him the same Mercian courage which it gave Diggory. A little excited then, he attempted one or two of his speeches to the judge's lady. But little he knew how hard it was to get in even a *promptu* there edgewise. "Very well, I thank you," said he, after the eating elements were adjusted; "and you?" And then did not he have to hear about the mumps, and the measles, and arnica, and belladonna, and chamomile-flower, and dodecathem, till she changed oysters for salad, — and then about the old practice and the new, and what her sister said, and what her sister's friend said, and what the physician to her sister's friend said, and then what was said by the brother of the sister of the physician of the friend of her sister, exactly as if it had been in Ollendorff? There was a moment's pause, as she declined Champagne. "I am very glad you liked it," said Dennis again, which he never should have said, but to one who complimented a sermon. "Oh! you are so sharp, Mr. Ingham! No! I never drink any wine at all, — except sometimes in summer a little currant spirits, — from our own currants, you know. My own mother, — that is, I call her my own mother, because, you know, I do not remember," etc., etc., etc.; till they came to the candied orange at the end of the feast, — when Dennis, rather confused, thought he must say something, and tried No. 4, — "I agree, in general, with my friend the other side of the room," — which he never should have said but at a public meeting. But Mrs. Jeffries, who never listens expecting to understand, caught him up instantly with, "Well, I'm sure my husband returns the compliment; he always agrees with you, — though we do worship with the Methodists; — but you know, Mr. Ingham," etc., etc., etc., till the move was made up-stairs; — and as Dennis led her through the hall, he was scarcely understood by any but Polly, as he said, "There has been so much said, and, on the whole, so well said, that I will not occupy the time."

His great resource the rest of the evening was, standing in the library, carrying on animated conversations with one and another in much the same way. Polly had initiated him in the mysteries of a discovery of mine, that it is not necessary to finish your sentences in a crowd, but by a sort of mumble, omitting sibilants and dentals. This, indeed, if your words fail you, answers even in public extempore speech, — but better where other talking is going on. Thus, — "We missed you at the Natural-History Society, Ingham." Ingham replies, — "I am very gligloglum, that is, that you were mmmmm." By gradually dropping the voice, the interlocutor is compelled to supply the answer. "Mrs. Ingham, I hope your friend Augusta is better." Augusta has not been ill. Polly cannot think of explaining, however, and answers, — "Thank you, Ma'am; she is very rearason wewahwewoh," in lower and lower tones. And Mrs. Throckmorton, who forgot the subject of which she spoke, as soon as she asked the question, is quite satisfied. Dennis could see into the card-room, and came to Polly to ask if he might not go and play all-fours. But, of course, she sternly refused. At midnight they came home delighted, — Polly, as I said, wild to tell me the story of victory; only both the pretty Walton girls said, — "Cousin Frederic, you did not come near me all the evening."

We always called him Dennis at home, for convenience, though his real name was Frederic Ingham, as I have explained. When the election-day came round, however, I found that by some accident there was only one Frederic Ingham's name on the voting-list; and, as I was quite busy that day in writing some foreign letters to Halle, I thought I would forego my privilege of suffrage, and stay quietly at home, telling Dennis that he might use the record on the voting-list and vote. I gave him a ticket, which I told him he might use, if he liked to. That was that very sharp election in Maine which the readers of the "Atlantic" so well remember, and it had been intimated in public that the ministers would do well not to appear at the polls. Of course, after that, we had to appear by self or proxy. Still, Naguadavick was not then a city, and this standing in a double queue at town-meeting several hours to vote was a bore of the first water; and so, when I found that there was but one Frederic Ingham on the list, and that one of us must give up, I staid at home and finished the letters, (which, indeed, procured for Fothergill his coveted appointment of Professor of Astronomy at Leavenworth,) and I gave Dennis, as we called him, the chance. Something in the matter gave a good deal of popularity to the Frederic Ingham name; and at the adjourned election, next week, Frederic Ingham was chosen to the legislature. Whether this was I or Dennis, I never really knew. My friends seemed to think it was I; but I felt, that, as Dennis had done the popular thing, he was entitled to the honor; so I sent him to Augusta when the time came, and he took the oaths. And a very valuable member he made. They appointed him on the Committee on Parishes; but I wrote a letter for him, resigning, on the ground that he took an interest in our claim to the stumpage in the minister's sixteenths of Gore A, next No. 7, in the 10th Range. He never made any speeches, and always voted with the minority, which was what he was sent to do. He made me and himself a great many good friends, some of whom I did not afterwards recognize as quickly as Dennis did my parishioners. On one or two occasions, when there was wood to saw at home, I kept him at home; but I took those occasions to go to Augusta myself. Finding myself often in his vacant seat at these times, I watched the proceedings with a good deal of care; and once was so much excited that I delivered my somewhat celebrated speech on the Central School-District question, a speech of which the "State of Maine" printed some extra copies. I believe there is no formal rule permitting strangers to speak; but no one objected.

Dennis himself, as I said, never spoke at all. But our experience this session led me to think, that, if, by some such "general understanding" as the reports speak of in legislation daily, every member of Congress might leave a double to sit through those deadly sessions and answer to roll-calls and do the legitimate party-voting, which appears stereotyped in the regular list of Ashe, Bocock, Black, etc., we should gain decidedly in working-power. As things stand, the saddest State prison I ever visit is that Representatives' Chamber in Washington. If a man leaves for an hour, twenty "correspondents" may be howling, "Where was Mr. Pendergrast when the Oregon bill passed?" And if poor Pendergrast stays there! Certainly, the worst use you can make of a man is to put him in prison!

I know, indeed, that public men of the highest rank have resorted to this expedient long ago. Dumas's novel of the "Iron Mask" turns on the brutal imprisonment of Louis the Fourteenth's double. There seems little doubt, in our own history, that it was the real General Pierce who shed tears when the delegate from Lawrence explained to him the sufferings of the people there, — and only General Pierce's double who had given the orders for the assault on that town, which was invaded the next day. My charming friend, George Withers, has, I am almost sure, a double, who preaches his afternoon sermons for him. This is the reason that the theology often varies so from that of the forenoon. But that double is almost as charming as the original. Some of the most well-defined men, who stand out most prominently on the background of history, are in this way stereoscopic men, who owe their distinct relief to the slight differences between the doubles. All this I know. My present suggestion is simply the great extension of the system, so that all public machine-work may be done by it.

But I see I loiter on my story, which is rushing to the plunge. Let me stop an instant more, however, to recall, were it only to myself, that charming year while all was yet well. After the double had become a matter of course, for nearly twelve months before he undid me, what a year it was! Full of active life, full of happy love, of the hardest work, of the sweetest sleep, and the fulfilment of so many of the fresh aspirations and dreams of boyhood! Dennis went to every school-committee meeting, and sat through all those late wranglings which used to keep me up till midnight and awake till morning. He attended all the lectures to which foreign exiles sent me tickets begging me to come for the love of Heaven and of Bohemia. He accepted and used all the tickets for charity concerts which were sent to me. He appeared every-where where it was specially desirable that "our denomination," or "our party," or "our class," or "our family," or "our street," or "our town," or "our county," or "our State," should be fully represented. And I fell back to that charming life which in boyhood one dreams of, when he supposes he shall do his own duty and make his own sacri-fices, without being tied up with those of other people. My rusty San-skrit, Arabic, Hebrew, Greek, Latin, French, Italian, Spanish, German, and English began to take polish. Heavens! how little I had done with them while I attended to my *public* duties! My calls on my parishioners became the friendly, frequent, homelike sociabilities they were meant to be, instead of the hard work of a man goaded to desperation by the sight of his lists of arrears. And preaching! what a luxury preaching was when I had on Sunday the whole result of an individual, personal week, from which to speak to a people whom all that week I had been meeting as hand-to-hand friend! I never tired on Sunday, and was in condition to leave the sermon at home, if I chose, and preach it ex-tempore, as all men should do always. Indeed, I wonder, when I think that a sensible people, like ours, — really more attached to their clergy than they were in the lost days, when the Mathers and Nortons were noblemen, — should choose to neutralize so much of their ministers' lives, and destroy so much of their early training, by this undefined passion for seeing them in public. It springs from our balancing of sects. If a spirited Episcopalian takes an interest in the alms-house, and is put on the Poor Board, every other denomination must have a minister there, lest the poor-house be changed into St. Paul's Cathe-dral. If a Sandemanian is chosen president of the Young Men's Li-brary, there must be a Methodist vice-president and a Baptist secre-tary. And if a Universalist Sunday-School Convention collects five hundred delegates, the next Congregationalist Sabbath-School Con-ference must be as large, "lest 'they' — whoever *they* may be — should think 'we' — whoever *we* may be — are going down."

Freed from these necessities, that happy year, I began to know my wife by sight. We saw each other sometimes. In those long mornings, when Dennis was in the study explaining to map-peddlers that I had eleven maps of Jerusalem already, and to school-book agents that I would see them hanged before I would be bribed to introduce their textbooks into the schools, — she and I were at work together, as in those old dreamy days, — and in these of our log-cabin again. But all this could not last, — and at length poor Dennis, my double, over-tasked in turn, undid me.

It was thus it happened. — There is an excellent fellow, — once a minister, — I will call him Isaacs, — who deserves well of the world till he dies, and after, — because he once, in a real exigency, did the right

thing, in the right way, at the right time, as no other man could do it.
In the world's great football match, the ball by chance found him
loitering on the outside of the field; he closed with it, "camped" it,
charged it home, — yes, right through the other side, — not disturbed, not frightened by his own success, — and breathless found
himself a great man, — as the Great Delta rang applause. But he did
not find himself a rich man; and the football has never come in his
way again. From that moment to this moment he has been of no use,
that one can see, at all. Still, for that great act we speak of Isaacs
gratefully and remember him kindly; and he forges on, hoping to
meet the football somewhere again. In that vague hope, he had arranged a "movement" for a general organization of the human family
into Debating-Clubs, County Societies, State Unions, etc., etc.; with a
view of inducing all children to take hold of the handles of their
knives and forks, instead of the metal. Children have bad habits in that
way. The movement, of course, was absurd; but we all did our best to
forward, not it, but him. It came time for the annual county-meeting
on this subject to be held at Naguadavick. Isaacs came round, good
fellow! to arrange for it, — got the town-hall, got the Governor to
preside, (the saint! — he ought to have triplet doubles provided him
by law,) and then came to get me to speak. "No," I said, "I would not
speak, if ten Governors presided. I do not believe in the enterprise. If
I spoke, it should be to say children should take hold of the prongs of
the forks and the blades of the knives. I would subscribe ten dollars,
but I would not speak a mill." So poor Isaacs went his way, sadly, to
coax Auchmuty to speak, and Delafield. I went out. Not long after, he
came back, and told Polly that they had promised to speak, — the
Governor would speak, — and he himself would close with the quarterly report, and some interesting anecdotes regarding Miss Biffin's
way of handling her knife and Mr. Nellis's way of footing his fork.
"Now if Mr. Ingham will only come and sit on the platform, he need
not say one word; but it will show well in the paper, — it will show that
the Sandemanians take as much interest in the movement as the Ar-
menians or the Mesopotamians, and will be a great favor to me." Polly,
good soul! was tempted, and she promised. She knew Mrs. Isaacs was
starving, and the babies, — she knew Dennis was at home, — and she
promised! Night came, and I returned. I heard her story. I was sorry.
I doubted. But Polly had promised to beg me, and I dared all! I told
Dennis to hold his peace, under all circumstances, and sent him down.

It was not half an hour more before he returned, wild with excitement, — in a perfect Irish fury, — which it was long before I understood. But I knew at once that he had undone me!

What happened was this. — The audience got together, attracted by
Governor Gorges's name. There were a thousand people. Poor Gorges

was late from Augusta. They became impatient. He came in direct
from the train at last, really ignorant of the object of the meeting. He
opened it in the fewest possible words, and said other gentlemen were
present who would entertain them better than he. The audience were
disappointed, but waited. The Governor, prompted by Isaacs, said,
"The Honorable Mr. Delafield will address you." Delafield had forgotten the knives and forks, and was playing the Ruy Lopez opening at
the chess-club. "The Rev. Mr. Auchmuty will address you." Auchmuty
had promised to speak late, and was at the school-committee. "I see
Dr. Stearns in the hall; perhaps he will say a word." Dr. Stearns said
he had come to listen and not to speak. The Governor and Isaacs
whispered. The Governor looked at Dennis, who was resplendent on
the platform; but Isaacs, to give him his due, shook his head. But the
look was enough. A miserable lad, ill-bred, who had once been in
Boston, thought it would sound well to call for me, and peeped out,
"Ingham!" A few more wretches cried, "Ingham! Ingham!" Still Isaacs
was firm; but the Governor, anxious, indeed, to prevent a row, knew I
would say something, and said, "Our friend Mr. Ingham is always
prepared, — and though we had not relied upon him, he will say a
word, perhaps." Applause followed, which turned Dennis's head. He
rose, fluttered, and tried No. 3: "There has been so much said, and,
on the whole, so well said, that I will not longer occupy the time!" and
sat down, looking for his hat; for things seemed squally. But the people cried, "Go on! go on!" and some applauded. Dennis, still confused,
but flattered by the applause, to which neither he nor I are used, rose
again, and this time tried No. 2: "I am very glad you liked it!" in a
sonorous, clear delivery. My best friends stared. All the people who
did not know me personally yelled with delight at the aspect of the
evening; the Governor was beside himself, and poor Isaacs thought he
was undone! Alas, it was I! A boy in the gallery cried in a loud tone,
"It's all an infernal humbug," just as Dennis, waving his hand, commanded silence, and tried No. 4: "I agree, in general, with my friend
the other side of the room." The poor Governor doubted his
senses, and crossed to stop him, — not in time, however. The same
gallery-boy shouted, "How's your mother?" — and Dennis, now completely lost, tried, as his last shot, No. 1, vainly: "Very well, thank you;
and you?"

I think I must have been undone already. But Dennis, like another
Lockhard, chose "to make sicker." The audience rose in a whirl of
amazement, rage, and sorrow. Some other impertinence, aimed at
Dennis, broke all restraint, and, in pure Irish, he delivered himself of
an address to the gallery, inviting any person who wished to fight to
come down and do so, — stating, that they were all dogs and cowards
and the sons of dogs and cowards, — that he would take any five of

them single-handed. "Shure, I have said all his Riverence and the Misthress bade me say," cried he, in defiance; and, seizing the Governor's cane from his hand, brandished it, quarter-staff fashion, above his head. He was, indeed, got from the hall only with the greatest difficulty by the Governor, the City Marshal, who had been called in, and the Superintendent of my Sunday-School.

The universal impression, of course, was, that the Rev. Frederic Ingham had lost all command of himself in some of those haunts of intoxication which for fifteen years I have been laboring to destroy. Till this moment, indeed, that is the impression in Naguadavick. This number of the "Atlantic" will relieve from it a hundred friends of mine who have been sadly wounded by that notion now for years; — but I shall not be likely ever to show my head there again.

No! My double has undone me.

We left town at seven the next morning. I came to No. 9, in the Third Range, and settled on the Minister's Lot. In the new towns in Maine, the first settled minister has a gift of a hundred acres of land. I am the first settled minister in No. 9. My wife and little Paulina are my parish. We raise corn enough to live on in summer. We kill bear's meat enough to carbonize it in winter. I work on steadily on my "Traces of Sandemanianism in the Sixth and Seventh Centuries," which I hope to persuade Phillips, Sampson, & Co. to publish next year. We are very happy, but the world thinks we are undone.

1860
BARDIC SYMBOLS
by Walt Whitman

I

ELEMENTAL drifts!
Oh, I wish I could impress others as you and the waves have just been
 impressing me!

II

As I ebbed with an ebb of the ocean of life,
As I wended the shores I know,
As I walked where the sea-ripples wash you, Paumanok,
Where they rustle up, hoarse and sibilant,
Where the fierce old mother endlessly cries for her castaways,
I, musing, late in the autumn day, gazing off southward,
Alone, held by the eternal self of me that threatens to get the better of
 me and stifle me,

Was seized by the spirit that trails in the lines underfoot,
In the ruin, the sediment, that stands for all the water and all the land
    of the globe.

III

Fascinated, my eyes, reverting from the south, dropped, to follow
    those slender windrows,
Chaff, straw, splinters of wood, weeds, and the sea-gluten,
Scum, scales from shining rocks, leaves of salt-lettuce, left by the tide.

IV

Miles walking, the sound of breaking waves the other side of me,
Paumanok, there and then as I thought the old thought of likenesses,
These you presented to me, you fish-shaped island,
As I wended the shores I know,
As I walked with that eternal self of me, seeking types.

V

As I wend the shores I know not,
As I listen to the dirge, the voices of men and women wrecked,
As I inhale the impalpable breezes that set in upon me,
As the ocean so mysterious rolls toward me closer and closer,
At once I find, the least thing that belongs to me, or that I see or
    touch, I know not;
I, too, but signify a little washed-up drift, — a few sands and dead
    leaves to gather,
Gather, and merge myself as part of the leaves and drift.

VI

Oh, baffled, lost,
Bent to the very earth, here preceding what follows,
Terrified with myself that I have dared to open my mouth,
Aware now, that, amid all the blab whose echoes recoil upon me, I
    have not once had the least idea who or what I am,
But that before all my insolent poems the real me still stands
    untouched, untold, altogether unreached,
Withdrawn far, mocking me with mock-congratulatory signs and
    bows,
With peals of distant ironical laughter at every word I have written or
    shall write,
Striking me with insults, till I fall helpless upon the sand!

VII

Oh, I think I have not understood anything, — not a single object, —
    and that no man ever can!

VIII

I think Nature here, in sight of the sea, is taking advantage of me to
    oppress me,
Because I was assuming so much,
And because I have dared to open my mouth to sing at all.

IX

You oceans both! You tangible land! Nature!
Be not too stern with me, — I submit, — I close with you, —
These little shreds shall, indeed, stand for all.

X

You friable shore, with trails of debris!
You fish-shaped island! I take what is underfoot:
What is yours is mine, my father!

XI

I, too, Paumanok,
I, too, have bubbled up, floated the measureless float, and been
    washed on your shores.

XII

I, too, am but a trail of drift and debris, —
I, too, leave little wrecks upon you, you fish-shaped island!

XIII

I throw myself upon your breast, my father!
I cling to you so that you cannot unloose me, —
I hold you so firm, till you answer me something.

XIV

Kiss me, my father!
Touch me with your lips, as I touch those I love!
Breathe to me, while I hold you close, the secret of the wondrous
    murmuring I envy!
For I fear I shall become crazed, if I cannot emulate it, and utter
    myself as well as it.

XV

Sea-raff! Torn leaves!
Oh, I sing, some day, what you have certainly said to me!

XVI

Ebb, ocean of life! (the flow will return,) —
Cease not your moaning, you fierce old mother!

Endlessly cry for your castaways! Yet fear not, deny not me, —
Rustle not up so hoarse and angry against my feet, as I touch you, or
    gather from you.

XVII

I mean tenderly by you, —
I gather for myself, and for this phantom, looking down where we
    lead, and following me and mine.

XVIII

Me and mine!
We, loose windrows, little corpses,
Froth, snowy white, and bubbles,
Tufts of straw, sands, fragments,
Buoyed hither from many moods, one contradicting another,
From the storm, the long calm, the darkness, the swell,
Musing, pondering, a breath, a briny tear, a dab of liquid or soil,
Up just as much out of fathomless workings fermented and thrown,
A limp blossom or two, torn, just as much over waves floating, drifted
    at random,
Just as much for us that sobbing dirge of Nature,
Just as much, whence we come, that blare of the cloud-trumpets, —
We, capricious, brought hither, we know not whence, spread out
    before you, — you, up there, walking or sitting,
Whoever you are, — we, too, lie in drifts at your feet.

1861

PAUL REVERE'S RIDE
by Henry Wadsworth Longfellow

LISTEN, my children, and you shall hear
Of the midnight ride of Paul Revere,
On the eighteenth of April, in Seventy-Five:
Hardly a man is now alive
Who remembers that famous day and year.

He said to his friend, — "If the British march
By land or sea from the town to-night,
Hang a lantern aloft in the belfry-arch
Of the North-Church-tower, as a signal-light, —
One if by land, and two if by sea;
And I on the opposite shore will be,

Ready to ride and spread the alarm
Through every Middlesex village and farm,
For the country-folk to be up and to arm."

Then he said good-night, and with muffled oar
Silently rowed to the Charlestown shore,
Just as the moon rose over the bay,
Where swinging wide at her moorings lay
The Somersett, British man-of-war:
A phantom ship, with each mast and spar
Across the moon, like a prison-bar,
And a huge, black hulk, that was magnified
By its own reflection in the tide.

Meanwhile, his friend, through alley and street
Wanders and watches with eager ears,
Till in the silence around him he hears
The muster of men at the barrack-door,
The sound of arms, and the tramp of feet,
And the measured tread of the grenadiers
Marching down to their boats on the shore.

Then he climbed to the tower of the church,
Up the wooden stairs, with stealthy tread,
To the belfry-chamber overhead,
And startled the pigeons from their perch
On the sombre rafters, that round him made
Masses and moving shapes of shade, —
Up the light ladder, slender and tall,
To the highest window in the wall,
Where he paused to listen and look down
A moment on the roofs of the town,
And the moonlight flowing over all.

Beneath, in the churchyard, lay the dead
In their night-encampment on the hill,
Wrapped in silence so deep and still,
That he could hear, like a sentinel's tread,
The watchful night-wind, as it went
Creeping along from tent to tent,
And seeming to whisper, "All is well!"
A moment only he feels the spell
Of the place and the hour, the secret dread
Of the lonely belfry and the dead;

For suddenly all his thoughts are bent
On a shadowy something far away,
Where the river widens to meet the bay, —
A line of black, that bends and floats
On the rising tide, like a bridge of boats.

Meanwhile, impatient to mount and ride,
Booted and spurred, with a heavy stride,
On the opposite shore walked Paul Revere.
Now he patted his horse's side,
Now he gazed on the landscape far and near,
Then impetuous stamped the earth,
And turned and tightened his saddle-girth;
But mostly he watched with eager search
The belfry-tower of the old North Church,
As it rose above the graves on the hill,
Lonely, and spectral, and sombre, and still.

And lo! as he looks, on the belfry's height,
A glimmer, and then a gleam of light!
He springs to the saddle, the bridle he turns,
But lingers and gazes, till full on his sight
A second lamp in the belfry burns!

A hurry of hoofs in a village-street,
A shape in the moonlight, a bulk in the dark,
And beneath from the pebbles, in passing, a spark
Struck out by a steed that flies fearless and fleet:
That was all! And yet, through the gloom and the light,
The fate of a nation was riding that night;
And the spark struck out by that steed, in his flight,
Kindled the land into flame with its heat.

It was twelve by the village-clock,
When he crossed the bridge into Medford town.
He heard the crowing of the cock,
And the barking of the farmer's dog,
And felt the damp of the river-fog,
That rises when the sun goes down.

It was one by the village-clock,
When he rode into Lexington.
He saw the gilded weathercock
Swim in the moonlight as he passed,

And the meeting-house windows, blank and bare,
Gaze at him with a spectral glare,
As if they already stood aghast
At the bloody work they would look upon.

It was two by the village-clock,
When he came to the bridge in Concord town.
He heard the bleating of the flock,
And the twitter of birds among the trees,
And felt the breath of the morning-breeze
Blowing over the meadows brown.
And one was safe and asleep in his bed
Who at the bridge would be first to fall,
Who that day would be lying dead,
Pierced by a British musket-ball.

You know the rest. In the books you have read
How the British regulars fired and fled, —
How the farmers gave them ball for ball,
From behind each fence and farmyard-wall,
Chasing the red-coats down the lane,
Then crossing the fields to emerge again
Under the trees at the turn of the road,
And only pausing to fire and load.

So through the night rode Paul Revere;
And so through the night went his cry of alarm
To every Middlesex village and farm, —
A cry of defiance, and not of fear, —
A voice in the darkness, a knock at the door,
And a word that shall echo forevermore!
For, borne on the night-wind of the Past,
Through all our history, to the last,
In the hour of darkness and peril and need,
The people will waken and listen to hear
The hurrying hoof-beat of that steed,
And the midnight-message of Paul Revere.

1862
BATTLE HYMN OF THE REPUBLIC
by Julia Ward Howe

MINE eyes have seen the glory of the coming of the Lord:
He is trampling out the vintage where the grapes of wrath are stored;
He hath loosed the fateful lightning of His terrible swift sword:
> His truth is marching on.

I have seen Him in the watch-fires of a hundred circling camps,
They have builded Him an altar in the evening dews and damps;
I can read His righteous sentence by the dim and flaring lamps:
> His day is marching on.

I have read a fiery gospel writ in burnished rows of steel:
"As ye deal with my contemners, so with you my grace shall deal;
Let the Hero, born of woman, crush the serpent with his heel,
> Since God is marching on."

He has sounded forth the trumpet that shall never call retreat;
He is sifting out the hearts of men before His judgment-seat:
Oh, be swift, my soul, to answer Him! be jubilant, my feet!
> Our God is marching on.

In the beauty of the lilies Christ was born across the sea,
With a glory in his bosom that transfigures you and me:
As he died to make men holy, let us die to make men free,
> While God is marching on.

1863
BARBARA FRIETCHIE
by John Greenleaf Whittier

Up from the meadows rich with corn,
Clear in the cool September morn,

The clustered spires of Frederick stand
Green-walled by the hills of Maryland.

Round about them orchards sweep,
Apple- and peach-tree fruited deep,

Fair as a garden of the Lord
To the eyes of the famished rebel horde,

On that pleasant morn of the early fall
When Lee marched over the mountain-wall, —

Over the mountains winding down,
Horse and foot, into Frederick town.

Forty flags with their silver stars,
Forty flags with their crimson bars,

Flapped in the morning wind: the sun
Of noon looked down, and saw not one.

Up rose old Barbara Frietchie then,
Bowed with her fourscore years and ten;

Bravest of all in Frederick town,
She took up the flag the men hauled down;

In her attic-window the staff she set,
To show that one heart was loyal yet.

Up the street came the rebel tread,
Stonewall Jackson riding ahead.

Under his slouched hat left and right
He glanced: the old flag met his sight.

"Halt!" — the dust-brown ranks stood fast.
"Fire!" — out blazed the rifle-blast.

It shivered the window, pane and sash;
It rent the banner with seam and gash.

Quick, as it fell, from the broken staff
Dame Barbara snatched the silken scarf;

She leaned far out on the window-sill,
And shook it forth with a royal will.

"Shoot, if you must, this old gray head,
But spare your country's flag," she said.

A shade of sadness, a blush of shame,
Over the face of the leader came;

The nobler nature within him stirred
To life at that woman's deed and word:

"Who touches a hair of yon gray head
Dies like a dog! March on!" he said.

All day long through Frederick street
Sounded the tread of marching feet:

All day long that free flag tossed
Over the heads of the rebel host.

Ever its torn folds rose and fell
On the loyal winds that loved it well;

And through the hill-gaps sunset light
Shone over it with a warm good-night.

Barbara Frietchie's work is o'er,
And the Rebel rides on his raids no more.

Honor to her! and let a tear
Fall, for her sake, on Stonewall's bier.

Over Barbara Frietchie's grave
Flag of Freedom and Union, wave!

Peace and order and beauty draw
Round thy symbol of light and law;

And ever the stars above look down
On thy stars below in Frederick town!

1864
PROSPICE
by Robert Browning

FEAR death? — to feel the fog in my throat,
  The mist in my face,
When the snows begin, and blasts denote
  I am nearing the place,

The power of the night, the press of the storm,
    The post of the foe;
Where he stands, the Arch Fear in a visible form,
    Yet the strong man must go:
For the journey is done and the summit attained,
    And the barriers fall,
Though a battle's to fight ere the guerdon be gained,
    The reward of it all.
I was ever a fighter, so — one fight more,
    The best and the last!
I would hate that Death bandaged my eyes, and forbore,
    And bade me creep past.
No! let me taste the whole of it, fare like my peers
    The heroes of old,
Bear the brunt, in a minute pay glad life's arrears
    Of pain, darkness, and cold.
For sudden the worst turns the best to the brave,
    The black minute 's at end,
And the elements' rage, the fiend-voices that rave,
    Shall dwindle, shall blend,
Shall change, shall become first a peace, then a joy,
    Then a light, then thy breast,
O thou soul of my soul! I shall clasp thee again,
    And with God be the rest!

———————————

1865
THE PLACE OF ABRAHAM LINCOLN IN HISTORY
by George Bancroft

THE funeral procession of the late President of the United States has passed through the land from Washington to his final resting place in the heart of the prairies. Along the line of more than fifteen hundred miles his remains were borne, as it were, through continued lines of the people; and the number of mourners and the sincerity and unanimity of grief were such as never before attended the obsequies of a human being; so that the terrible catastrophe of his end hardly struck more awe than the majestic sorrow of the people. The thought of the individual was effaced; and men's minds were drawn to the station which he filled, to his public career, to the principles he represented, to his martyrdom.

Why has the President been struck down, and why do the people mourn? We think we pay the best tribute to his memory, and the most fitting respect to his name, if we ask after the relation in which he stands to the history of his country and his fellow men.

Buchanan, who took the presidential chair in 1857, had no traditional party against him; he owed his nomination to confidence in his moderation and supposed love of Union. He might have united the whole North and secured a good part of the South. Constitutionally timid, on taking the oath of office he betrayed his own weakness and foreshadowed the forthcoming decision of the Supreme Court. Under the wing of the Executive, Chief Justice Taney gave his famed disquisition. The delivery of that opinion was an act of revolution. The truth of history was scorned; the voice of passion was put forward as the rule of law; doctrines were laid down which, if they are just, give a full sanction to the rebellion which ensued. The country was stung to the quick by the reckless conduct of a body which it needed to trust and which now was leading the way to the overthrow of the Constitution and the dismemberment of the Republic.

At the same time Buchanan, in selecting the members of his cabinet, chose four of the seven from among those who were prepared to sacrifice the country to the interests of slavery. In time of peace the finances were willfully ill-administered, and in the midst of wealth and credit the country was saved from bankruptcy only by the patriotism of the city of New York, against the treacherous intention of the Secretary of the Treasury. Cannon and muskets and military stores were sent in numbers where they could most surely fall into the hands of the coming rebellion; troops of the United States were placed under disloyal officers and put out of the way; the navy was scattered abroad. And then, that nothing might be wanting to increase the agony of the country, an attempt to force the institution of slavery on the people of Kansas, who refused it, received the encouragement and aid of Buchanan.

The position of Abraham Lincoln, on the day of his inauguration, was apparently one of helpless debility. A bark canoe in a tempest on mid-ocean seemed hardly less safe. The vital tradition of the country on slavery no longer had its adequate expression in either of the two great political parties, and the Supreme Court had uprooted the old landmarks and guides. The men who had chosen him President did not constitute a consolidated party and did not profess to represent either of the historic parties which had been engaged in the struggles of three quarters of a century. They were a heterogeneous body of men, of the most various political attachments in former years, and on many questions of economy held the most discordant opinions. Scarcely knowing each other, they did not form a numerical majority of the whole country, were in a minority in each branch of Congress except from the willful absence of members, and could not be sure of their own continuance as an organized body. They did not know their own position and were startled by the consequences of their success.

The new President himself was, according to his own description, a man of defective education, a lawyer by profession, knowing nothing of administration beyond having been master of a very small post office, knowing nothing of war but as a captain of volunteers in a raid against an Indian chief, repeatedly a member of the Illinois legislature, once a member of Congress. He spoke with ease and clearness, but not with eloquence. He wrote concisely and to the point, but was unskilled in the use of the pen. He had no accurate knowledge of the public defenses of the country, no exact conception of its foreign relations, no comprehensive perception of his duties. The qualities of his nature were not suited to hardy action. His temper was soft and gentle and yielding, reluctant to refuse anything that presented itself to him as an act of kindness, loving to please and willing to confide, not trained to confine acts of good will within the stern limits of duty. He was of the temperament called melancholic, scarcely concealed by an exterior of lightness of humor, having a deep and fixed seriousness, jesting lips, and wanness of heart. And this man was summoned to stand up directly against a power with which Henry Clay had never directly grappled, before which Webster at last had quailed, which no President had offended and yet successfully administered the government, to which each great political party had made concessions, to which in various measures of compromise the country had repeatedly capitulated, and with which he must now venture a struggle for the life or death of the nation.

The credit of the country had not fully recovered from the shock it had treacherously received in the former Administration. A part of the navy yards were intrusted to incompetent agents or enemies. The social spirit of the city of Washington was against him, and spies and enemies abounded in the circles of fashion. Every executive department swarmed with men of treasonable inclinations, so that it was uncertain where to rest for support. The army officers had been trained in unsound political principles. The chief of staff of the highest general officers, wearing the mask of loyalty, was a traitor at heart.

The country was ungenerous toward the Negro, who in truth was not in the least to blame, who was impatient that such a strife should have grown out of his condition and wished that he were far away. On the side of prompt decision the advantage was with the Rebels; the President sought how to avoid war without compromising his duty; and the Rebels, who knew their own purpose, won incalculable advantages by the start which they thus gained. The country stood aghast, and would not believe in the full extent of the conspiracy to shatter it in pieces; men were uncertain if there would be a great uprising of the people. The President and his cabinet were in the midst of an enemy's country and in personal danger, and at one time their connections with the North and West were cut off; and that very moment was chosen by the trusted chief of staff of the lieutenant general to go over to the enemy.

Everyone remembers how this state of suspense was terminated by the uprising of a people who now showed strength and virtues which they were hardly conscious of possessing.

In some respects Abraham Lincoln was peculiarly fitted for his task in connection with the movement of his countrymen. He was of the Northwest; and this time it was the Mississippi River, the needed outlet for the wealth of the Northwest, that did its part in asserting the necessity of Union. He was one of the mass of the people; he represented them, because he was of them; and the mass of the people, the class that lives and thrives by self-imposed labor, felt that the work which was to be done was a work of their own: the assertion of equality against the pride of oligarchy, of free labor against the lordship over slaves, of the great industrial people against all the expiring aristocracies of which any remnants had tided down from the Middle Ages. He was of a religious turn of mind, without superstition, and the unbroken faith of the mass was like his own. As he went along through his difficult journey, sounding his way, he held fast by the hand of the people and "tracked its footsteps with even feet." "His pulse's beat twinned with their pulses." He committed faults, but the people were resolutely generous, magnanimous, and forgiving; and he in his turn was willing to take instructions from their wisdom.

The measure by which Abraham Lincoln takes his place, not in American history only, but in universal history, is his Proclamation of January 1, 1863, emancipating all slaves within the insurgent states. It was indeed a military necessity, and it decided the result of the war. It took from the public enemy one or two million bondmen and placed between one and two hundred thousand brave and gallant troops in arms on the side of the Union. A great deal has been said in time past of the wonderful results of the toil of the enslaved Negro in the creation of wealth by the culture of cotton; and now it is in part to the aid of the Negro in freedom that the country owes its success in its movement of regeneration — that the world of mankind owes the continuance of the United States as the example of a Republic. The death of President Lincoln sets the seal to that Proclamation, which must be maintained. It cannot but be maintained. It is the only rod that can safely carry off the thunderbolt. He came to it perhaps reluctantly; he was brought to adopt it, as it were, against his will, but compelled by inevitable necessity. He disclaimed all praise for the act, saying reverently, after it had succeeded, "The nation's condition God alone can claim."

And what a futurity is opened before the country when its institutions become homogeneous! From all the civilized world the nations will send hosts to share the wealth and glory of this people. It will receive all good ideas from abroad; and its great principles of personal equality and freedom: freedom of conscience and mind, freedom of speech and action, freedom of government through ever-renewed common consent, will undulate through the world like the rays of light and heat from the sun. With one wing touching the waters of the Atlantic and the other on the Pacific, it will grow into a greatness of which the past has no parallel; and there can be no spot in Europe or in Asia so remote or so secluded as to shut out its influence.

1866

RECONSTRUCTION
by Frederick Douglass

THE assembling of the Second Session of the Thirty-ninth Congress may very properly be made the occasion of a few earnest words on the already much-worn topic of reconstruction.

Seldom has any legislative body been the subject of a solicitude more intense, or of aspirations more sincere and ardent. There are the best of reasons for this profound interest. Questions of vast moment, left undecided by the last session of Congress, must be manfully grappled with by this. No political skirmishing will avail. The occasion demands statesmanship.

Whether the tremendous war so heroically fought and so victoriously ended shall pass into history a miserable failure, barren of permanent results, — a scandalous and shocking waste of blood and treasure, — a strife for empire, as Earl Russell characterized it, of no value to liberty or civilization, — an attempt to re-establish a Union by force, which must be the merest mockery of a Union, — an effort to bring under Federal authority States into which no loyal man from the North may safely enter, and to bring men into the national councils who deliberate with daggers and vote with revolvers, and who do not even conceal their deadly hate of the country that conquered them; or whether, on the other hand, we shall, as the rightful reward of victory over treason, have a solid nation, entirely delivered from all contradictions and social antagonisms, based upon loyalty, liberty, and equality, must be determined one way or the other by the present session of

Congress. The last session really did nothing which can be considered final as to these questions. The Civil Rights Bill and the Freedmen's Bureau Bill and the proposed constitutional amendments, with the amendment already adopted and recognized as the law of the land, do not reach the difficulty, and cannot, unless the whole structure of the government is changed from a government by States to something like a despotic central government, with power to control even the municipal regulations of States, and to make them conform to its own despotic will. While there remains such an idea as the right of each State to control its own local affairs, — an idea, by the way, more deeply rooted in the minds of men of all sections of the country than perhaps any one other political idea, — no general assertion of human rights can be of any practical value. To change the character of the government at this point is neither possible nor desirable. All that is necessary to be done is to make the government consistent with itself, and render the rights of the States compatible with the sacred rights of human nature.

The arm of the Federal government is long, but it is far too short to protect the rights of individuals in the interior of distant States. They must have the power to protect themselves, or they will go unprotected, in spite of all the laws the Federal government can put upon the national statute-book.

Slavery, like all other great systems of wrong, founded in the depths of human selfishness, and existing for ages, has not neglected its own conservation. It has steadily exerted an influence upon all around it favorable to its own continuance. And today it is so strong that it could exist, not only without law, but even against law. Custom, manners, morals, religion, are all on its side everywhere in the South; and when you add the ignorance and servility of the ex-slave to the intelligence and accustomed authority of the master, you have the conditions, not out of which slavery will again grow, but under which it is impossible for the Federal government to wholly destroy it, unless the Federal government be armed with despotic power, to blot out State authority, and to station a Federal officer at every cross-road. This, of course, cannot be done, and ought not even if it could. The true way and the easiest way is to make our government entirely consistent with itself, and give to every loyal citizen the elective franchise, — a right and power which will be ever present, and will form a wall of fire for his protection.

One of the invaluable compensations of the late Rebellion is the highly instructive disclosure it made of the true source of danger to republican government. Whatever may be tolerated in monarchical and despotic governments, no republic is safe that tolerates a privileged class, or denies to any of its citizens equal rights and equal means to maintain them.

It remains now to be seen whether we have the needed courage to have that cause [for rebellion] entirely removed from the Republic. At any rate, to this grand work of national regeneration and entire purification Congress must now address itself, with full purpose that the work shall this time be thoroughly done.

If time was at first needed, Congress has now had time. All the requisite materials from which to form an intelligent judgment are now before it. Whether its members look at the origin, the progress, the termination of the war, or at the mockery of a peace now existing, they will find only one unbroken chain of argument in favor of a radical policy of reconstruction.

The people themselves demand such a reconstruction as shall put an end to the present anarchical state of things in the late rebellious States, — where frightful murders and wholesale massacres are perpetrated in the very presence of Federal soldiers. This horrible business they require shall cease. They want a reconstruction such as will protect loyal men, black and white, in their persons and property; such a one as will cause Northern industry, Northern capital, and Northern civilization to flow into the South, and make a man from New England as much at home in Carolina as elsewhere in the Republic. No Chinese wall can now be tolerated. The South must be opened to the light of law and liberty, and this session of Congress is relied upon to accomplish this important work.

The plain, common-sense way of doing this work is simply to establish in the South one law, one government, one administration of justice, one condition to the exercise of the elective franchise, for men of all races and colors alike. This great measure is sought as earnestly by loyal white men as by loyal blacks, and is needed alike by both. Let sound political prescience but take the place of an unreasoning prejudice, and this will be done.

1867
MR. HARDHACK ON THE DERIVATION
OF MAN FROM THE MONKEY
by Edwin Percy Whipple

I CAN stand it no longer, sir. I have been seething and boiling inwardly for a couple of years at this last and final insult which science has put upon human nature, and now I must speak, or, if you will, explode. And how is it, I want to know, that the duty of hurling imprecations at this infernal absurdity has devolved upon me? Don't we employ a professional class to look after the interests of the race? — paid, sir, by me and you to proclaim that men — ay, and women too — are at the top of things in origin, as well as in nature and destiny? What's the use of their asserting, Sunday after Sunday, that man was made a little lower than the angels, when right under their noses are a set of anatomical miscreants who contend that he is only a little higher than the monkeys? And the thing has now gone so far, that you are a fossilized old fogy, in this day of scientific light, if you repudiate your relationship with any fossilized monstrosity which, from the glass case of a museum, mocks at you with a grin a thousand centuries old. To exalt a man's soul above his skeleton, is now to be behind the age. All questions of philosophy, sir, are fast declining into a question of bones, — and blasted dry ones they are!

Now you can't keep company with monkeys without insensibly getting be-monkeyed. Your mind feeds on them until its thoughts take their shape and nature. Huxley must have pretty thoroughly assimilated monkey before he recognized his ancestor in one. The poor beast himself may have made no pretensions to the honor, until he was mentally transformed into Huxley, entered into the substance of Huxley's mind, became inflamed with Huxley's arrogance. This is the true explanation, not perhaps of the origin of species, but of the origin of the theory of the origin; and I should like to thunder the great truth into the ears of all the scientific societies now talking monkey with the self-satisfied air of great discoverers. Yes, sir, and I should also be delighted to insinuate that this progress of monkey into man was not so great an example of "progressive development" as they seem inclined to suppose, and didn't require the long reaches of prehistoric time they consider necessary to account for the phenomenon. Twenty years would be enough, in all conscience, to effect *that* development.

Thus I tell you, sir, it isn't monkey that rises anatomically into man, but rather man that descends mentally into monkey. Why, nothing is more common than to apply to us human beings the names of animals, when we display weaknesses analogous to their habitual characters. But this is metaphor, not classification; poetry, not science. Thus I, Solomon Hardhack, was called a donkey the other day by an intimate friend. Thought it merely a jocose reference to my obstinacy, and did not knock him down. Called the same name yesterday by a comparative anatomist. Thought it an insulting reference to my understanding, and did. But suppose that, in respect both to obstinacy and understanding, I had established, to my own satisfaction, a similarity between myself and that animal, do you imagine that I would be donkey enough to take the beast for my progenitor? Do you suppose that I would go even further, and, having established with the donkey a relation of descent, be mean enough to generalize the whole human race into participation in my calamity? No, sir, I am not sufficiently a man of science to commit that breach of good manners. Well, then, my proposition is, that nobody who reasons himself into a development from the monkey has the right to take mankind with him in his induction. His argument covers but one individual, — himself. As for the Hardhacks, they at least beg to be excused from joining him in that logical excursion, and insist on striking the monkey altogether out from their genealogical tree.

And speaking of genealogical trees, do the adherents of this mad theory realize the disgrace they are bringing on the most respectable families! There is not an aristocracy in Europe or America that can stand it one moment, for aristocracy is based on the greatness of forefathers. In America, you know, nobody is aristocratic who cannot count back at least to his great-grandfather, who rode in a carriage, or — drove one. As for the Hardhacks, I may be allowed to say, though I despise family pride as much as any man, that they came in with the Conqueror, and went out with the Puritans. But if this horrible Huxleian theory be true, the farther a person is from his origin, the better; antiquity of descent is no longer a title to honor; and a man must pride himself in looking forward to his descendants rather than back to his ancestors. And what comfort is this to me, an unmarried man? With a monkey in the background, how can even a Hapsburg or a Guelf put on airs of superiority? How must he hide his face in shame to think, that, as his line lengthens into an obscure antiquity, the foreheads of his house slope, and their jaws project; that he has literally been all his life aping aristocracy, instead of being the real thing; and that, when he has reached his true beginning, his only consolation must be found in the fact that his great skulking, hulking, gibbering baboon of an ancestor rejoices, like himself, in the possession of "the third lobe," "the posterior cornu of the lateral ventricle," and "the hippocampus minor." Talk about radicalism, indeed! Why, I, who am considered an offence to my radical party for the extremes to which I run, cannot think of this swamping of all the families in the world without a thrill of horror and amazement! It makes my blood run cold to imagine this infernal Huxley pertly holding up the frontispiece of his book in the faces of the haughty nobility and gentry of his country, and saying, "Here, my friends, are drawings of the skeletons of gibbon, orang, chimpanzee, gorilla; select your ancestors; you pays your money and has your choice." I don't pretend to know anything about the temper of the present nobility and gentry of England; but if the fellow should do this thing to me, I would blow out of his skull everything in it which allied him with the apes, — taking a specially grim vengeance on "the posterior cornu of the lateral ventricle," — as sure as my name's Hardhack, and as sure as there's any explosive power in gunpowder.

And in this connection, too, I should like to know how the champions of this man-monkey scheme get over a theological objection. Don't start, sir, and say I am unscientific. I am not going to introduce Christianity, or monotheism, or polytheism, or fetichism, but a religion which you know was before them all, and which consisted in the worship of ancestors. If you are in the custom of visiting in good society, you will find that that is a form of worship which has not yet altogether died out, but roots itself in the most orthodox creeds. Now you must admit that the people who worshipped their ancestors were the earliest people of whose religion we have any archæological record, and therefore a people who enjoyed the advantage of being nearer the ancestors of the race than any of the historical savages to whom you can appeal. I put it to you if this people, catching a glimpse of the monkey at the end of their line, if the monkey was really there, would have been such dolts as to worship it? Worship ancestors, when ancestors are known to have been baboons!

I don't pretend to know whether a "third lobe" is in my head or not, but I do know that Solomon Hardhack is there, and as long as he has possession of the premises, you will find written on his brow, "No monkeys need apply!"

1868
HAWTHORNE
IN THE BOSTON CUSTOM-HOUSE
[Extracts from Nathaniel Hawthorne's Letters]

BOSTON, *July* 3,1839. — I do not mean to imply that I am unhappy or discontented; for this is not the case. My life only is a burden in the same way that it is to every toilsome man, and mine is a healthy weariness, such as. needs only a night's sleep to remove it. But henceforth forever I shall be entitled to call the sons of toil my brethren, and shall know how to sympathize with them; seeing that I likewise have risen at the dawn, and borne the fervor of the midday sun, nor turned my heavy footsteps homeward till eventide. Years hence, perhaps, the experience that my heart is acquiring now will flow out in truth and wisdom.

August 27. — I have been stationed all day at the end of Long Wharf, and I rather think that I had the most eligible situation of anybody in Boston. I was aware that it must be intensely hot in the midst of the city; but there was only a short space of uncomfortable heat in my region, half-way towards the centre of the harbor; and almost all the time there was a pure and delightful breeze, fluttering and palpitating, sometimes shyly kissing my brow, then dying away, and then rushing upon me in livelier sport, so that I was fain to settle my straw hat more tightly upon my head. Late in the afternoon there was a sunny shower, which came down so like a benediction, that it seemed ungrateful to take shelter in the cabin or to put up an umbrella. Then there was a rainbow, or a large segment of one, so exceedingly brilliant, and of such long endurance, that I almost fancied it was stained into the sky, and would continue there permanently.

February 7, 1840. — What beautiful weather this is! — beautiful, at least, so far as sun, sky, and atmosphere are concerned, though a poor, wingless biped is sometimes constrained to wish that he could raise himself a little above the earth. How much mud and mire, how many pools of unclean water, how many slippery footsteps, and perchance heavy tumbles, might be avoided, if we could but tread six inches above the crust of this world! Physically, we cannot do this; our bodies cannot; but it seems to me that our hearts and minds may keep themselves above moral mud-puddles and other discomforts of the soul's pathway.

February 11. — I have been measuring coal all day on board of a black little British schooner, in a dismal dock at the north end of the city. Most of the time, I paced the deck to keep myself warm, for the wind (northeast, I believe) blew up through the dock as if it had been the pipe of a pair of bellows. The vessel lying deep between two wharves, there was no more delightful prospect on the right hand and on the left than the posts and timbers, half immersed in the water, and covered with ice which the rising and falling of successive tides had left upon them, so that they looked like immense icicles. Across the water, however, not more than half a mile off, appeared the Bunker Hill Monument; and, what interested me considerably more, a church-steeple, with the dial of a clock upon it, whereby I was enabled to measure the march of the weary hours. At last came the sunset, with delicate clouds, and a purple light upon the islands; and I blessed it, because it was the signal of my release.

March 15. — I pray that in one year more I may find some way of escaping from this unblest Custom-House; for it is a very grievous thraldom. I do detest all offices, — all, at least, that are held on a political tenure. And I want nothing to do with politicians. Their hearts wither away, and die out of their bodies. Their consciences are turned to India-rubber, or to some substance as black as that, and which will stretch as much. One thing, if no more, I have gained by

my Custom-House experience, — to know a politician. It is a knowledge which no previous thought or power of sympathy could have
taught me, because the animal, or the machine rather, is not in nature.

March 28. — I do think that it is the doom laid upon me of murdering
so many of the brightest hours of the day at the Custom-House, that
makes such havoc with my wits; for here I am again trying to write
worthily, ... yet with a sense as if all the noblest part of man had
been left out of my composition, or had decayed out of it, since my
nature was given to my own keeping. . . . . Never comes any bird of
Paradise into that dismal region. A salt, or even a coal ship, is ten
million times preferable; for there the sky is above me, and the fresh
breeze around me, and my thoughts, having hardly anything to do
with my occupation, are as free as air.

Nevertheless, you are not to fancy that the above paragraph gives a
correct idea of my mental and spiritual state. . . . . It is only once in a
while that the image and desire of a better and happier life makes me
feel the iron of my chain; for, after all, a human spirit may find no
insufficiency of food fit for it, even in the Custom-House. And with
such materials as these, I do think and feel and learn things that are
worth knowing, and which I should not know unless I had learned
them there, so that the present portion of my life shall not be quite left
out of the sum of my real existence. . . . . It is good for me, on many
accounts, that my life has had this passage in it. I know much more
than I did a year ago. I have a stronger sense of power to act as a man
among men. I have gained worldly wisdom, and wisdom also that is
not altogether of this world. And when I quit this earthly cavern
where I am now buried, nothing will cling to me that ought to be left
behind. Men will not perceive, I trust, by my look, or the tenor of my
thoughts and feelings, that I have been a custom-house officer.

April 19. . . . . What a beautiful day was yesterday. My spirit rebelled
against being confined in my darksome dungeon at the Custom-
House. It seemed a sin, — a murder of the joyful young day, — a
quenching of the sunshine. Nevertheless, there I was kept a prisoner
till it was too late to fling myself on a gentle wind, and be blown away
into the country. . . . . When I shall be again free, I will enjoy all things
with the fresh simplicity of a child of five years old. I shall grow young
again, made all over anew. I will go forth and stand in a summer
shower, and all the worldly dust that has collected on me shall be
washed away at once, and my heart will be like a bank of fresh flowers
for the weary to rest upon. . . . .

6 *P.M.* — I went out to walk about an hour ago, and found it very

pleasant, though there was a somewhat cool wind. I went round and across the Common, and stood on the highest point of it, where I could see miles and miles into the country. Blessed be God for this green tract, and the view which it affords, whereby we poor citizens may be put in mind, sometimes, that all His earth is not composed of blocks of brick houses, and of stone or wooden pavements! Blessed be God for the sky, too, though the smoke of the city may somewhat change its aspect; but still it is better than if each street were covered over with a roof.

May 19. . . . . Lights and shadows are continually flitting across my inward sky, and I know neither whence they come nor whither they go; nor do I inquire too closely into them. It is dangerous to look too minutely into such phenomena. It is apt to create a substance where at first there was a mere shadow. . . . . If at any time there should seem to be an expression unintelligible from one soul to another, it is best not to strive to interpret it in earthly language, but to wait for the soul to make itself understood; and were we to wait a thousand years, we need deem it no more time than we can spare. . . . . It is not that I have any love of mystery, but because I abhor it, and because I have often felt that words may be a thick and darksome veil of mystery between the soul and the truth which it seeks. Wretched were we, indeed, if we had no better means of communicating ourselves, no fairer garb in which to array our essential being, than these poor rags and tatters of Babel. Yet words are not without their use, even for purposes of explanation; but merely for explaining outward acts and all sorts of external things, leaving the soul's life and action to explain itself in its own way.

What a musty disquisition I have scribbled! I would not read it over for sixpence.

May 30. . . . . On board my salt vessels and colliers there are many things happening, many pictures which in future years, when I am again busy at the loom of fiction, I could weave in; but my fancy is rendered so torpid by my ungenial way of life, that I cannot sketch off the scenes and portraits that interest me, and I am forced to trust them to my memory, with the hope of recalling them at some more favorable period. For these three or four days I have been observing a little Mediterranean boy, from Malaga, not more than ten or eleven years old, but who is already a citizen of the world, and seems to be just as gay and contented on the deck of a Yankee coal-vessel as he could be while playing beside his mother's door. It is really touching to see how free and happy he is, — how the little fellow takes the whole wide world for his home, and all mankind for his family. He talks Spanish, — at least, that is his native tongue; but he is also very intelligible in English, and perhaps he likewise has smatterings of the speech of other countries, whither the winds may have wafted this little sea-bird. He is a Catholic, and, yesterday being Friday, he caught some fish and fried them for his dinner, in sweet oil; and really they looked so delicate, that I almost wished he would invite me to partake. Every once in a while he undresses himself and leaps overboard, plunging down beneath the waves, as if the sea were as native to him as the earth. Then he runs up the rigging of the vessel, as if he meant to fly away through the air. I must remember this little boy, and perhaps I may make something more beautiful of him than these rough and imperfect touches would promise.

Salem, October 4. — Union Street [Family Mansion]. . . . . Here I sit, in my old, accustomed chamber, where I used to sit in days gone by. . . . . Here I have written many tales, — many that have been burned to ashes, many that doubtless deserved the same fate. This claims to be called a haunted chamber, for thousands upon thousands of visions have appeared to me in it; and some few of them have become visible to the world. If ever I should have a biographer, he ought to make great mention of this chamber in my memoirs, because so much of my lonely youth was wasted here, and here my mind and character were formed, and here I have been glad and hopeful, and here I have been despondent. And here I sat a long, long time, waiting patiently for the world to know me, and sometimes wondering why it did not know me sooner, or whether it would ever know me at all, — at least, till I were in my grave. And sometimes it seemed as if I were already in the grave, with only life enough to be chilled and benumbed. But oftener I was happy, — at least, as happy as I then knew how to be, or was aware of the possibility of being. By and by the world found me out in my lonely chamber, and called me forth, — not indeed with a loud roar of acclamation, but rather with a still, small voice; and forth I went, but found nothing in the world that I thought preferable to my old solitude till now. . . . . And now I begin to understand why I was imprisoned so many years in this lonely chamber, and why I could never break through the viewless bolts and bars; for if I had sooner made my escape into the world, I should have grown hard and rough, and been covered with earthly dust, and my heart might have become callous by rude encounters with the multitude. . . . . But living in solitude till the fulness of time was come, I still kept the dew of my youth and the freshness of my heart. . . . . I used to think that I could imagine all passions, all feelings and states of the heart and mind; but how little did I know! . . . . Indeed, we are but shadows —

we are not endowed with real life, and all that seems most real about us is but the thinnest substance of a dream — till the heart be touched. That touch creates us, — then we begin to be, — thereby we are beings of reality and inheritors of eternity.

1869
THE TRUE STORY OF LADY BYRON'S LIFE
by Harriet Beecher Stowe

THE true history of Lord and Lady Byron has long been perfectly understood in many circles in England, but the facts were of a nature that could not be made public. While there was a young daughter living, whose future might be prejudiced by its recital, and while there were other persons on whom the disclosure of the real truth would have been crushing as an avalanche, Lady Byron's only course was the perfect silence in which she took refuge, and those sublime works of charity and mercy to which she consecrated her blighted earthly life.

But the time is now come when the truth may be told. No person in England, we think, would as yet take the responsibility of relating the true history which is to clear Lady Byron's memory. But, by a singular concurrence of circumstances, all the facts of the case, in the most undeniable and authentic form, were at one time placed in the hands of the writer of this sketch, with authority to make such use of them as she should judge best. Had this melancholy history been allowed to sleep, no public use would have been made of them; but the appearance of a popular attack on the character of Lady Byron calls for a vindication, and the true story of her married life will, therefore, now be related.

Lord Byron has described, in one of his letters, the impression left upon his mind by a young person whom he met one evening in society, and who attracted his attention by the simplicity of her dress, and a certain air, of singular purity and calmness, with which she surveyed the scene around her. On inquiry, he was told that this young person was Miss Milbanke, an only child, and one of the largest heiresses in England.

Some idea of the course which their acquaintance took, and of the manner in which he was piqued into thinking of her is given in [his poem *Don Juan*].

The result of the enkindling of Byron's nobler feelings was an offer of marriage, which she [Miss Millbanke], though at the time deeply interested in him, declined with many expressions of friendship and interest. In fact, she already loved him, but had that doubt of her power to be to him all that a wife should be, which would be likely to arise in a mind so sensitively constituted and so unworldly. They however continued a correspondence as friends; on her part the interest continually increased, on his the transient rise of better feelings was choked and overgrown by the thorns of base, unworthy passions.

From the height at which he might have been happy as the husband of a noble woman, he fell into the depths of a secret adulterous intrigue with a blood relation [his half-sister, Augusta], so near in consanguinity that discovery must have been utter ruin and expulsion from civilized society.

From henceforth, this damning guilty secret became the ruling force in his life, holding him with a morbid fascination, yet filling him with remorse and anguish and insane dread of detection. Two years after his refusal by Miss Milbanke, his various friends, seeing that for some cause he was wretched, pressed marriage upon him; and so he determined to marry, and, in an hour of reckless desperation, sat down and wrote proposals to two ladies. One was declined. The other, which was accepted, was to Miss Milbanke. He had sent the letter in mere recklessness; he had not seriously expected to be accepted, and the discovery of the treasure of affection which he had secured was like a vision of lost heaven to a soul in hell.

But, nevertheless, in his letters written about the engagement, there are sufficient evidences that his self-love was flattered at the preference accorded him by so superior a woman and one who had been so much sought. He mentions with an air of complacency that she has employed the last two years in refusing five or six of his acquaintance; that he had no idea she loved him, admitting that it was an old attachment on his part; he dwells on her virtues with a sort of pride of ownership. There is a sort of childish levity about the frankness of these letters, very characteristic of the man who skimmed over the deepest abysses with the lightest jests. Before the world, and to his intimates, he was acting the part of the successful *fiancé*, conscious all the while of the deadly secret that lay cold at the bottom of his heart.

When he went to visit Miss Milbanke's parents, as her accepted lover, she was struck with his manner and appearance; she saw him moody and gloomy, evidently wrestling with dark and desperate thoughts, and anything but what a happy and accepted lover should be. She sought an interview with him alone, and told him that she had observed that he was not happy in the engagement, and magnanimously added that, if on review he found he had been mistaken in the nature of his feelings, she would immediately release him, and they should remain only friends.

Overcome with the conflict of his feelings, Lord Byron fainted away.
Miss Milbanke was convinced that his heart must really be deeply involved in an attachment with reference to which he showed such
strength of emotion, and she spoke no more of a dissolution of the
engagement.

There is no reason to doubt that Byron was, as he relates in his
Dream, profoundly agonized and agitated, when he stood before
God's altar, with the trusting young creature whom he was leading to a
fate so awfully tragic.

The moment the carriage doors were shut upon the bridegroom
and the bride, the paroxysm of remorse and despair — unrepentant
remorse and angry despair — broke forth upon her gentle head.

"You might have saved me from this, madam! you had all in your
own power when I offered myself to you first. Then you might have
made me what you pleased; but now you will find that you have married a *devil!*"

In Miss Martineau's Sketches, recently published, is an account of
the termination of this wedding journey, which brought them to one
of Lady Byron's ancestral country-seats, where they were to spend the
honeymoon.

Miss Martineau says: —

"At the altar she did not know that she was a sacrifice; but before
sunset of that winter day she knew it, if a judgment may be formed
from her face and attitude of despair when she alighted from the
carriage on the afternoon of her marriage-day. It was not the traces of
tears which won the sympathy of the old butler who stood at the open
door. The bridegroom jumped out of the carriage and walked away.
The bride alighted, and came up the steps alone, with a countenance
and frame agonized and listless with evident horror and despair. The
old servant longed to offer his arm to the young, lonely creature, as an
assurance of sympathy and protection. From this shock she certainly
rallied, and soon. The pecuniary difficulties of her new home were
exactly what a devoted spirit like hers was fitted to encounter. Her
husband bore testimony, after the catastrophe, that a brighter being, a
more sympathizing and agreeable companion, never blessed any man's
home. When he afterward called her cold and mathematical, and
over-pious, and so forth, it was when public opinion had gone against
him, and when he had discovered that her fidelity and mercy, her
silence and magnanimity, might be relied on, so that he was at full
liberty to make his part good, as far as she was concerned.

"Silent she was even to her own parents, whose feelings she magnanimously spared. She did not act rashly in leaving him, though she
had been most rash in marrying him."

Not all at once did the full knowledge of the dreadful reality into which she had entered come upon the young wife. She knew vaguely, from the wild avowals of the first hours of their marriage, that there was a dreadful secret of guilt, that Byron's soul was torn with agonies of remorse, and that he had no love to give to her in return for a love which was ready to do and dare all for him. Yet bravely she addressed herself to the task of soothing and pleasing and calming the man whom she had taken "for better or for worse."

The most dreadful men to live with are those who alternate between angel and devil. The buds of hope and love called out by a day or two of sunshine are frozen again and again till the tree is killed.

But there came an hour of revelation, — an hour when, in a manner which left no kind of room for doubt, Lady Byron saw the full depth of the abyss of infamy which her marriage was expected to cover, and understood that she was expected to be the cloak and the accomplice of this infamy.

Many women would have been utterly crushed by such a disclosure; some would have fled from him immediately, and exposed and denounced the crime. Lady Byron would neither leave her husband nor betray him, nor yet would she for one moment justify his sin; and hence came two years of convulsive struggle.

Lord Byron argued his case with himself and with her, with all the sophistries of his powerful mind. He repudiated Christianity as authority, asserted the right of every human being to follow out what he called "the impulses of nature." Subsequently he introduced into one of his dramas the reasoning by which he justified himself in incest.

These two years, in which Lady Byron was with all her soul struggling to bring her husband back to his better self, were a series of passionate convulsions.

During this time, such was the disordered and desperate state of his worldly affairs, that there were ten executions for debt levied on their family establishment; and it was Lady Byron's fortune each time which settled the account.

Toward the last she and her husband saw less and less of each other, and he came more and more decidedly under evil influences and seemed to acquire a sort of hatred of her.

Lady Byron once said significantly to a friend who spoke of some causeless dislike in another: "My dear, I have known people to be hated for no other reason than because they impersonated conscience."

THE ENGLISH GOVERNESS AT THE SIAMESE COURT

by Anna Leonowens

IN 1825 a royal prince of Siam (his birthright wrested from him by an elder half-brother and his life imperilled) took refuge in a Buddhist monastery and assumed the yellow garb of a priest. Finally in 1851, at the age of 45, he emerged from his cloister, and was crowned, with the title of Somedtch-Phra Paramendr Maha Mongkut (duke, and royal bearer of the great crown).

For twenty-five years had the true heir to the throne of the Phrabatts (the Golden-footed), patiently biding his time, lain perdu in his monastery, diligently devoting himself to the study of Sanskrit, Bali, theology, history, geology, chemistry, and especially astronomy.

In the Oriental tongues this progressive king was eminently proficient; and toward priests, preachers, and teachers, of all creeds, sects, and sciences, an enlightened exemplar of tolerance. It was likewise his peculiar vanity to pass for an accomplished English scholar, and to this end he maintained in his palace at Bangkok a private printing establishment, with fonts of English type, which he was at no loss to keep in "copy." Perhaps it was the printing-office which suggested, quite naturally, an English governess for the *élite* of his wives and concubines, and their offspring, — in number amply adequate to the constitution of a royal school, and in material most attractively fresh and romantic. Happy thought! Wherefore, behold me, just after sunset on a pleasant day in April, 1862, on the threshold of the outer court of the Grand Palace, accompanied by my own brave little boy, and escorted by a compatriot.

A flood of light sweeping through the spacious Hall of Audience displayed a throng of noblemen in waiting. None turned a glance, or seemingly a thought, on us, and, my child being tired and hungry, I urged Captain B____ to present us without delay. At once we mounted the marble steps, and entered the brilliant hall unannounced. Ranged on the carpet were many prostrate, mute, and motionless forms, over whose heads to step was a temptation as drolly natural as it was dangerous. His Majesty spied us quickly, and advanced abruptly, petulantly screaming, "Who? who? who?"

Captain B____ (who, by the by, is a titled nobleman of Siam) introduced me as the English governess, engaged for the royal family. The king shook hands with us, and immediately proceeded to march up and down in quick step, putting one foot before the other with mathematical precision, as if under drill. "Forewarned, forearmed,"

my friend whispered that I should prepare myself for a sharp cross-
questioning as to my age, my husband, children, and other strictly
personal concerns. Suddenly his Majesty, having cogitated sufficiently
in his peculiar manner, with one long final stride halted in front of us,
and, pointing straight at me with his forefinger, asked, "How old shall
you be?"

Scarcely able to repress a smile at a proceeding so absurd, and with
my sex's distaste for so serious a question, I demurely replied, "One
hundred and fifty years old."

Had I made myself much younger, he might have ridiculed or assailed me; but now he stood surprised and embarrassed for a few
moments, then resumed his quick march, and at last, beginning to
perceive the jest, coughed, laughed, coughed again, and then in a
high, sharp key asked, "In what year were you borned?"

Instantly I "struck" a mental balance, and answered, as gravely as I
could, "In 1788."

At this point the expression of his Majesty's face was indescribably
comical. Captain B____ slipped behind a pillar to laugh; but the king
only coughed, with a significant emphasis that startled me, and addressed a few words to his prostrate courtiers, who smiled at the carpet, — all except the prime minister, who turned to look at me. But
his Majesty was not to be baffled so: again he marched with vigor, and
then returned to the attack with *élan*.

"How many years shall you be married?"

"For several years, your Majesty."

He fell into a brown study; then suddenly rushed at me, and demanded triumphantly: —

"Ha! How many grandchildren shall you now have? Ha! ha! How
many? How many? Ha! ha! ha!"

Of course we all laughed with him; but the general hilarity admitted
of a variety of constructions.

Then suddenly he seized my hand, and dragged me, *nolens volens,*
my little Louis holding fast by my skirt, through several sombre passages along which crouched duennas, shrivelled and grotesque, and
many youthful women, covering their faces, as if blinded by the splendor of the passing Majesty. At length he stopped before one of the
many-curtained recesses and, drawing aside the hangings, disclosed a
lovely, childlike form. He stooped and took her hand (she naïvely
hiding her face), and placing it in mine, said: "This is my wife, the
Lady T. She desires to be educated in English. She is as renowned for
her talents as for her beauty, and it is our pleasure to make her a good
English scholar. You shall educate her for me."

I replied that the office would give me much pleasure; for nothing

could be more eloquently winning than the modest, timid bearing of
that tender young creature in the presence of her lord. She laughed
low and pleasantly as he translated my sympathetic words to her, and
seemed so enraptured with the graciousness of his act that I took my
leave of her with a sentiment of profound pity.

He led me back by the way we had come; and now we met many
children, who put my patient boy to much childish torture for the
gratification of their startled curiosity.

"I have sixty-seven children," said his Majesty, when we had returned to the Audience Hall. "You shall educate them; and as many of
my wives, likewise, as may wish to learn English. And I have much
correspondence in which you must assist me. And, moreover, I have
much difficulty for reading and translating French letters; for French
are fond of using gloomily deceiving terms. You must undertake; and
you shall make all their murky sentences and gloomily deceiving propositions clear to me. And, furthermore, I have by every mail many
foreign letters whose writing is not easily read by me. You shall copy
on round hand, for my readily perusal thereof."

Nil desperandum; but I began by despairing of my ability to accomplish tasks so multifarious. I simply bowed, however, and so dismissed
myself for that evening.

When next I "interviewed" the king, I was accompanied by the pre-
mier's sister, a fair and pleasant woman, whose whole stock of English
was, "Good morning, sir"; and with this somewhat irrelevant greeting,
a dozen times in an hour, though the hour were night, she relieved
her pent-up feelings, and gave expression to her sympathy and regard
for me. We found his Majesty in a less genial mood than at my first
reception. He approached us coughing loudly and repeatedly, a sufficiently ominous fashion of announcing himself. He then approached
me, and said, in a loud and domineering tone, —

"It is our pleasure that you shall reside within this palace with our
family."

I replied that it would be quite impossible for me to do so; that,
being as yet unable to speak the language, and the gates being shut
every evening, I should feel like an unhappy prisoner in the palace.

"Where do you go every evening?" he demanded.

"Not anywhere, your Majesty. I am a stranger here."

"Then why you shall object to the gates being shut?"

"I do not clearly know," I replied, with a secret shudder at the idea
of sleeping within those walls; "but I am afraid I could not do it. I beg
your Majesty will remember that in your gracious letter you promised
me 'a residence adjoining the royal palace,' not within it."

He turned and looked at me, his face growing almost purple with rage. "I do not know I have promised. I do not know former condition. I do not know anything but you are our servant; and it is our pleasure that you must live in this palace, and *you shall obey*." Those last three words he fairly screamed.

I trembled in every limb, and for some time knew not how to reply. At length I ventured to say: "I am prepared to obey all your Majesty's commands, within the obligation of my duty to your family; but beyond that I can promise no obedience."

"You *shall* live in palace," he roared, — "you shall live in palace. I will give woman slaves to wait on you. You shall commence royal school in this pavilion on Thursday next. That is the best day for such undertaking, in the estimation of our astrologers."

With that, he addressed, in a frantic manner, commands, unintelligible to me, to some of the old women about the pavilion. I turned and saw the king beckoning and calling to me. I bowed to him profoundly, but passed on through the brass door.

But kings who are not mad have their sober second thoughts like other rational people. His Golden-footed Majesty presently repented him of his arbitrary "cantankerousness," and in due time, my ultimatum was accepted.

His Majesty was the most capricious of kings as to his working moods, — busy when the average man should be sleeping, sleeping while letters, papers, despatches, messengers, mailboats waited. More than once had we been aroused at dead of night by noisy female slaves, and dragged in hot haste and consternation to the Hall of Audience, only to find that his Majesty was, not at his last gasp, as we had feared, but simply bothered to find in Webster's Dictionary some word that was to be found nowhere but in his own fertile brain.

Before my arrival in Bangkok it had been his not uncommon practice to send for a missionary at midnight, have him beguiled or abducted from his bed, and conveyed by boat to the palace, some miles up the river, to inquire if it would not be more elegant to write *murky* instead of *obscure*, or *gloomily dark* rather than *not clearly apparent*. And if the wretched man should venture to declare his honest preference for the ordinary over the extraordinary form of expression, he was forthwith dismissed with irony, arrogance, or even insult, and without a word of apology for the rude invasion of his rest.

His Majesty usually passed his mornings in study or dictating or writing English letters and despatches. His breakfast, though a repast sufficiently frugal for Oriental royalty, was served with awesome forms. In an antechamber adjoining a noble hall, rich in grotesque carvings and gildings, a throng of females waited, while his Majesty sat at a long table, near which knelt twelve women before great silver trays laden with twelve varieties of viands, — soups, meats, game, poultry, fish, vegetables, cakes, jellies, preserves, sauces, fruits, and teas. Each tray, in its order, was passed by three ladies to the head wife or concubine, who removed the silver covers, and at least seemed to taste the contents of each dish; and then, advancing on her knees, she set them on the long table before the king.

But his Majesty was notably temperate in his diet, and by no means a gastronome. In his long seclusion in a Buddhist cloister he had acquired habits of severe simplicity and frugality, as a preparation for the exercise of those powers of mental concentration for which he was remarkable. At these morning repasts it was his custom to detain me in conversation, relating to some topic of interest derived from his studies, or in reading or translating. He was more systematically educated, and a more capacious devourer of books and news, than perhaps any man of equal rank in our day. But much learning had made him morally mad; his extensive reading had engendered in his mind an extreme scepticism concerning all existing religious systems. In inborn integrity and steadfast principle he had no faith whatever, and he honestly pitied the delusion that pinned its faith on human truth and virtue.

Ah! if this man could but have cast off the cramping yoke of his intellectual egotism, and been loyal to the free government of his own true heart, what a demigod might he not have been, among the lower animals of Asiatic royalty!

When the sweet, bright little princess, Somdetch Chowfa Chandrmondol (who was so dear to me by her pet name of Fâ-ying), was seized with cholera on the night of the 13th of May, 1863, his Majesty wrote to me: —

"My dear Mam:

"Our well-beloved daughter, your favorite pupil, is attacked with cholera, and has earnest desire to see you, and is heard much to make frequent repetition of your name. I beg that you will favor her wish. I fear her illness is mortal, as there has been three deaths since morning. She is best beloved of my children.

"I am your afflicted friend,

"S. P. P. Maha Mongkut."

In a moment I was in my boat. I entreated, I flattered, I scolded, the rowers. How slow they were! how strong the opposing current! And when at last I stood panting at the door of my Fâ-ying's chamber — too late! even Dr. Campbell (the surgeon of the British consulate) had come too late.

An attendant hurried me to the king, who, reading the heavy tidings in my silence, covered his face with his hands and wept passionately. Strange and terrible were the tears of such a man. What could I say? What could I do but weep with him; and then steal quietly away, and leave the king to the father?

1871
OUR WHISPERING GALLERY
Extracts from Charles Dickens' Letters
by James T. Fields

LET us speak to-day of the younger Dickens. How well I recall the bleak winter evening in 1842 when I first saw the handsome, glowing face of the young man who was even then famous over half the globe! He came bounding into the Tremont House, fresh from the steamer that had brought him to our shores, and his cheery voice rang through the hall, as he gave a quick glance at the new scenes opening upon him in a strange land on first arriving at a Transatlantic hotel. "Here we are!" he shouted, as the lights burst upon the merry party just entering the house, and several gentlemen came forward to greet him. Ah, how happy and buoyant he was then!

After Dickens left Boston, he went on his Amercan travels, gathering up materials, as he journeyed, for his "American Notes." He was accompanied as far as New York by a very dear friend, to whom he afterwards addressed several most interesting letters. The friend was also an intimate and dear associate of mine, and his children have kindly placed at my disposal the whole correspondence.

Here is a letter dated from Niagara, and I know you will relish his allusion to oysters with wet feet, and his reference to the squeezing of a Quaker.

CLIFTON HOUSE, NIAGARA FALLS,
29th April, 1842.

MY DEAR FELTON: I have long suspected that oysters have a rheumatic tendency. Their feet are always wet; and so much damp company in a man's inside cannot contribute to his peace. But whatever the cause of your indisposition, we are truly grieved and pained to hear of it, and should be more so, but that we hope from your account of that farewell dinner, that you are all right again. . . .

To say anything about this wonderful place would be sheer nonsense. It far exceeds my most sanguine expectations, though the impression on my mind has been, from the first, nothing but beauty and peace. I haven't drunk the water. Bearing in mind your caution, I have devoted myself to beer, whereof there is an exceedingly pretty fall in this house.

One of the noble hearts who sat for the Cheeryble Brothers is dead. If I had been in England, I would certainly have gone into mourning for the loss of such a glorious life. His brother is not expected to survive him. I am told that it appears from a memorandum found among the papers of the deceased, that in his lifetime he gave away in charity £600,000, or three millions of dollars!

What do you say to my *acting* at the Montreal Theatre? I am an old hand at such matters, and am going to join the officers of the garrison in a public representation for the benefit of a local charity. We shall have a good house, they say. I am going to enact one Mr. Snobbington in a funny farce called A Good Night's Rest. I shall want a flaxen wig and eyebrows; and my nightly rest is broken by visions of there being no such commodities in Canada. I wake in the dead of night in a cold perspiration, surrounded by imaginary barbers, all denying the existence or possibility of obtaining such articles. If ____ had a flaxen head, I would certainly have it shaved, and get a wig and eyebrows out of him, for a small pecuniary compensation.

By the by, if you could only have seen the man at Harrisburg, crushing a friendly Quaker in the parlor door! It was the greatest sight I ever saw. I had told him not to admit anybody whatever, forgetting that I had previously given this honest Quaker a special invitation to come. The Quaker would not be denied, and H. was stanch. When I came upon them, the Quaker was black in the face, and H. was administering the final squeeze. The Quaker was still rubbing his waistcoat with an expression of acute inward suffering, when I left the town. I have been looking for his death in the newspapers almost daily.

Do you know one General G.? He is a weazen-faced warrior, and in his dotage. I had him for a fellow-passenger on board a steamboat. I had also a statistical colonel with me, outside the coach from Cincinnati to Columbus. A New England poet buzzed about me on the Ohio, like a gigantic bee. A mesmeric doctor, of an impossibly great age, gave me pamphlets at Louisville. I have suffered much, very much.

You and Dr. Howe MUST come to New York. On the 6th of June, you must engage yourselves to dine with us at the "Carlton"; and if we don't make a merry evening of it, the fault shall not be in us.

Mrs. Dickens unites with me in best regards to Mrs. Felton and your little daughter, and I am always, my dear Felton,

Affectionately your friend,
CHARLES DICKENS.

When Dickens arrived in Montreal he had, it seems, a busy time of it, and I have often heard of his capital acting in private theatricals while in that city.

MONTREAL,
Saturday, 21st May, 1842 .

MY DEAR FELTON: — The wig and whiskers are in a state of the highest
preservation. The play comes off next Wednesday night, the 25th. What
would I give to see you in the front row of the centre box, your spectacles
gleaming not unlike those of my dear friend Pickwick. I would give something (not so much, but still a good round sum) if you could only stumble
into that very dark and dusty theatre in the daytime (at any minute between twelve and three), and see me with my coat off, the stage manager
and universal director, urging impracticable ladies and impossible gentlemen on to the very confines of insanity, shouting and driving about, in my
own person, to an extent which would justify any philanthropic stranger in
clapping me into a strait-waistcoat without further inquiry, endeavoring to
goad H. into some dim and faint understanding of a prompter's duties,
and struggling in such a vortex of noise, dirt, bustle, confusion, and inextricable entanglement of speech and action as you would grow giddy in
contemplating. We perform A Roland for an Oliver, A Good Night's Rest,
and Deaf as a Post. This kind of voluntary hard labor used to be my great
delight. The *furor* has come strong upon me again, and I begin to be once
more of opinion that nature intended me for the lessee of a national theatre, and that pen, ink, and paper have spoiled a manager.

About those joints of yours, I think you are mistaken. They *can't* be stiff.
At the worst they merely want the air of New York, which, being impreg-
nated with the flavor of last year's oysters, has a surprising effect in rendering the human frame supple and flexible in all cases of rust.

A terrible idea occurred to me as I wrote those words. The oyster-cellars,
— what do they do when oysters are not in season? Is pickled salmon
vended there? Do they sell crabs, shrimps, winkles, herrings? The oyster-
openers, — what do *they* do? Do they commit suicide in despair, or wrench
open tight drawers and cupboards and hermetically sealed bottles for practice? Perhaps they are dentists out of the oyster season. Who knows?

Affectionately yours,
CHARLES DICKENS.

Here is the first letter to his friend after Dickens arrived home again
in England. It is delightful, through and through.

LONDON, 1 DEVONSHIRE TERRACE, YORK GATE,
REGENT'S PARK, Sunday, July 31, 1842.

MY DEAR FELTON: — Of all the monstrous and incalculable amount of
occupation that ever beset one unfortunate man, mine has been the most
stupendous since I came home. The dinners I have had to eat, the places I
have had to go to, the letters I have had to answer, the sea of business and
of pleasure in which I have been plunged, not even the genius of an ——
or the pen of a —— could describe.

Wherefore I indite a monstrously short and wildly uninteresting epistle to the American Dando; but perhaps you don't know who Dando was. He was an oyster-eater, my dear Felton. He used to go into oyster-shops, without a farthing of money, and stand at the counter eating natives, until the man who opened them grew pale, cast down his knife, staggered backward, struck his white forehead with his open hand, and cried, "You are Dando! ! !" He has been known to eat twenty dozen at one sitting, and would have eaten forty, if the truth had not flashed upon the shopkeeper. For these offences he was constantly committed to the House of Correction. During his last imprisonment he was taken ill, got worse and worse, and at last began knocking violent double-knocks at Death's door. The doctor stood beside his bed, with his fingers on his pulse. "He is going," says the doctor. "I see it in his eye. There is only one thing that would keep life in him for another hour, and that is — oysters." They were immediately brought. Dando swallowed eight, and feebly took a ninth. He held it in his mouth and looked round the bed strangely. "Not a bad one, is it?" says the doctor. The patient shook his head, rubbed his trembling hand upon his stomach, bolted the oyster, and fell back — dead. They buried him in the prison yard, and paved his grave with oyster-shells.

We are all well and hearty, and have already begun to wonder what time next year you and Mrs. Felton and Dr. Howe will come across the briny sea together. To-morrow we go to the seaside for two months. I am looking out for news of Longfellow, and shall be delighted when I know that he is on his way to London and this house.

On board that ship coming home I established a club, called the United Vagabonds, to the large amusement of the rest of the passengers. This holy brotherhood committed all kinds of absurdities, and dined always, with a variety of solemn forms, at one end of the table, below the mast, away from all the rest. The captain being ill when we were three or four days out, I produced my medicine-chest and recovered him. We had a few more sick men after that, and I went round "the wards" every day in great state, accompanied by two Vagabonds, habited as Ben Allen and Bob Sawyer, bearing enormous rolls of plaster and huge pairs of scissors. We were really very merry all the way, breakfasted in one party at Liverpool, shook hands, and parted most cordially. . . . .

Affectionately

Your faithful friend,
C.D.

P.S. I have looked over my journal, and have decided to produce my American trip in two volumes. I have written about half the first since I came home, and hope to be out in October. This is "exclusive news," to be communicated to any friends to whom you may like to intrust it, my dear F.

HOW SANTA CLAUS CAME TO SIMPSON'S BAR

by Bret Harte

IT had been raining in the valley of the Sacramento. The North Fork had overflowed its banks and Rattlesnake Creek was impassable. The few boulders that had marked the summer ford at Simpson's Crossing were obliterated by a vast sheet of water stretching to the foothills. The up stage was stopped at Grangers; the last mail had been abandoned in the *tules*, the rider swimming for his life. "An area," remarked the "Sierra Avalanche," with pensive local pride, "as large as the State of Massachusetts is now under water."

Nor was the weather any better in the foothills. The mud lay deep on the mountain road; wagons that neither physical force nor moral objurgation could move from the evil ways into which they had fallen, encumbered the track, and the way to Simpson's Bar was indicated by broken-down teams and hard swearing. And farther on, cut-off and inaccessible, rained upon and bedraggled, smitten by high winds and threatened by high water, Simpson's Bar on the eve of Christmas day, 1862, clung like a swallow's nest to the rocky entablature and splintered capitals of Table Mountain, and shook in the blast.

As night shut down on the settlement, a few lights gleamed through the mist from the windows of cabins on either side of the highway now crossed and gullied by lawless streams and swept by marauding winds. Happily most of the population were gathered at Thompson's store, clustered around a red-hot stove, at which they silently spat in some accepted sense of social communion that perhaps rendered conversation unnecessary. Indeed, most methods of diversion had long since been exhausted on Simpson's Bar; high water had suspended the regular occupations on gulch and on river, and a consequent lack of money and whiskey had taken the zest from most illegitimate recreation. Even Mr. Hamlin was fain to leave the Bar with fifty dollars in his pocket, — the only amount actually realized of the large sums won by him in the successful exercise of his arduous profession. "Ef I was asked," he remarked somewhat later, — "ef I was asked to pint out a purty little village where a retired sport as didn't care for money could exercise hisself, frequent and lively, I'd say Simpson's Bar; but for a young man with a large family depending on his exertions, it don't pay." As Mr. Hamlin's family consisted mainly of female adults, this remark is quoted rather to show the breadth of his humor than the exact extent of his responsibilities.

Howbeit, the unconscious objects of this satire sat that evening in the listless apathy begotten of idleness and lack of excitement. Even the sudden splashing of hoofs before the door did not arouse them. Dick Bullen alone paused in the act of scraping out his pipe, and lifted his head, but no other one of the group indicated any interest in, or recognition of, the man who entered.

It was a figure familiar enough to the company, and known in Simpson's Bar as "The Old Man." A man of perhaps fifty years; grizzled and scant of hair, but still fresh and youthful of complexion. A face full of ready, but not very powerful sympathy, with a chameleon-like aptitude for taking on the shade and color of contiguous moods and feelings. He had evidently just left some hilarious companions, and did not at first notice the gravity of the group, but clapped the shoulder of the nearest man jocularly, and threw himself into a vacant chair.

"Jest heard the best thing out, boys! Ye know Smiley, over yar, — Jim Smiley, — funniest man in the Bar? Well, Jim was jest telling the richest yarn about —"

"Smiley's a ——— fool," interrupted a gloomy voice.

"A particular ——— skunk," added another in sepulchral accents.

A silence followed these positive statements. The Old Man glanced quickly around the group. Then his face slowly changed. "That's so," he said reflectively, after a pause, "certingly a sort of a skunk and suthin of a fool. In course." He was silent for a moment as in painful contemplation of the unsavoriness and folly of the unpopular Smiley. "Dismal weather, ain't it?" he added, now fully embarked on the current of prevailing sentiment. "Mighty rough papers on the boys, and no show for money this season. And to-morrow's Christmas."

There was a movement among the men at this announcement, but whether of satisfaction or disgust was not plain. "Yes," continued the Old Man in the lugubrious tone he had, within the last few moments, unconsciously adopted, — "yes, Christmas, and to-night's Christmas eve. Ye see, boys, I kinder thought — that is, I sorter had an idee, jest passin like you know — that may be ye'd all like to come over to my house to-night and have a sort of tear round. But I suppose, now, you wouldn't? Don't feel like it, may be?" he added with anxious sympathy, peering into the faces of his companions.

"Well, I don't know," responded Tom Flynn with some cheerfulness. "P'r'aps we may. But how about your wife, Old Man? What does *she* say to it?"

The Old Man hesitated. His conjugal experience had not been a happy one, and the fact was known to Simpson's Bar. His first wife, a delicate, pretty little woman, had suffered keenly and secretly from the jealous suspicions of her husband, until one day he invited the whole Bar to his house to expose her infidelity. On arriving, the party found the shy, *petite* creature quietly engaged in her household duties, and retired abashed and discomfited. But the sensitive woman did not easily recover from the shock of this extraordinary outrage. It was with difficulty she regained her equanimity sufficiently to release her lover from the closet in which he was concealed and escape with him. She left a boy of three years to comfort her bereaved husband. The Old Man's present wife had been his cook. She was large, loyal, and aggressive.

Before he could reply, Joe Dimmick suggested with great directness that it was the "Old Man's house," and that, invoking the Divine Power, if the case were his own, he would invite who he pleased, even if in so doing he imperilled his salvation. The Powers of Evil, he further remarked, should contend against him vainly. All this delivered with a terseness and vigor lost in this necessary translation.

"In course. Certainly. Thet's it," said the Old Man with a sympathetic frown. "Thar's no trouble about *thet*. It's my own house, built every stick on it myself. Don't you be afeard o' her, boys. She *may* cut up a trifle rough, — ez wimmin do, — but she'll come round." Secretly the Old Man trusted to the exaltation of liquor and the power of courageous example to sustain him in such an emergency.

As yet, Dick Bullen, the oracle and leader of Simpson's Bar, had not spoken. He now took his pipe from his lips. "Old Man, how's that yer Johnny gettin' on? Seems to me he didn't look so peart last time I seed him on the bluff heavin' rocks at Chinamen. Didn't seem to take much interest in it. Thar was a gang of 'em by yar yesterday, — drownded out up the river, — and I kinder thought o' Johnny, and how he'd miss 'em! May be now, we'd be in the way ef he wus sick?"

The father, evidently touched not only by this pathetic picture of Johnny's deprivation, but by the considerate delicacy of the speaker, hastened to assure him that Johnny was better and that a "little fun might 'liven him up." Whereupon Dick arose, shook himself, and saying, "I'm ready. Lead the way, Old Man: here goes," himself led the way with a leap, a characteristic howl, and darted out into the night. As he passed through the outer room he caught up a blazing brand from the hearth. The action was repeated by the rest of the party, closely following and elbowing each other, and before the astonished proprietor of Thompson's grocery was aware of the intention of his guests, the room was deserted.

The night was pitchy dark. In the first gust of wind their temporary torches were extinguished, and only the red brands dancing and flitting in the gloom like drunken will-o'-the-wisps indicated their whereabouts. Their way led up Pine-Tree Cañon, at the head of which a broad, low, bark-thatched cabin burrowed in the mountain-side. It was the home of the Old Man, and the entrance to the tunnel in which he worked when he worked at all. Here the crowd paused for a moment, out of delicate deference to their host, who came up panting in the rear.

"P'r'aps ye'd better hold on a second out yer, whilst I go in and see thet things is all right," said the Old Man, with an indifference he was far from feeling. The suggestion was graciously accepted, the door opened and closed on the host, and the crowd, leaning their backs against the wall and cowering under the eaves, waited and listened.

For a few moments there was no sound but the dripping of water from the eaves, and the stir and rustle of wrestling boughs above them. Then the men became uneasy, and whispered suggestion and suspicion passed from the one to the other. "Reckon she's caved in his head the first lick!" "Decoyed him inter the tunnel and barred him up, likely." "Got him down and sittin' on him." "Prob'ly bilin suthin to heave on us: stand clear the door, boys!" For just then the latch clicked, the door slowly opened and a voice said, "Come in out o' the wet."

The voice was neither that of the Old Man nor of his wife. It was the voice of a small boy, its weak treble broken by that preternatural hoarseness which only vagabondage and the habit of premature self-assertion can give. It was the face of a small boy that looked up at theirs, — a face that might have been pretty and even refined but that it was darkened by evil knowledge from within, and dirt and hard experience from without. He had a blanket around his shoulders and had evidently just risen from his bed. "Come in," he repeated, "and don't make no noise. The Old Man's in there talking to mar," he continued, pointing to an adjacent room which seemed to be a kitchen from which the Old Man's voice came in deprecating accents. "Let me be," he added, querulously to Dick Bullen who had caught him up, blanket and all, and was affecting to toss him into the fire, "let go o' me, you d—d old fool, d' ye hear?"

Thus adjured, Dick Bullen lowered Johnny to the ground with a smothered laugh, while the men, entering quietly, ranged themselves around a long table of rough boards which occupied the centre of the room. Johnny then gravely proceeded to a cupboard and brought out several articles which he deposited on the table. "Thar's whiskey. And crackers. And red herons. And cheese." He took a bite of the latter on his way to the table. "And sugar." He scooped up a mouthful *en route* with a small and very dirty hand. "And terbacker. Thar's dried appils too on the shelf, but I don't admire 'em. Appils is swellin'. Thar," he concluded, "now wade in, and don't be afeard. *I* don't mind the old woman. She don't b'long to *me*. S'long."

He had stepped to the threshold of a small room, scarcely larger than a closet, partitioned off from the main apartment, and holding in its dim recess a small bed. He stood there a moment looking at the company, his bare feet peeping from the blanket, and nodded.

"Hello, Johnny! You ain't goin' to turn in agin, are ye?" said Dick.

"Yes, I are," responded Johnny, decidedly.

"Why, wot's up, old fellow?"

"I'm sick."

"How sick?"

"I've got a fever. And childblains. And roomatiz," returned Johnny, and vanished within. After a moment's pause, he added in the dark, apparently from under the bedclothes, — "And biles!"

There was an embarrassing silence. The men looked at each other, and at the fire. Even with the appetizing banquet before them, it seemed as if they might again fall into the despondency of Thompson's grocery, when the voice of the Old Man, incautiously lifted, came deprecatingly from the kitchen.

"Certainly! Thet's so. In course they is. A gang o' lazy drunken loafers, and that ar Dick Bullen's the orneriest of all. Didn't hev no more *sabe* than to come round yar with sickness in the house and no provision. Thet's what I said: 'Bullen,' sez I, 'it's crazy drunk you are, or a fool,' sez I, 'to think o' such a thing.' 'Staples,' I sez, 'be you a man, Staples, and 'spect to raise h—ll under my roof and invalids lyin' round?' But they would come, — they would. Thet's wot you must 'spect o' such trash as lays round the Bar."

A burst of laughter from the men followed this unfortunate exposure. Whether it was overheard in the kitchen, or whether the Old Man's irate companion had just then exhausted all other modes of expressing her contemptuous indignation, I cannot say, but a back door was suddenly slammed with great violence. A moment later and the Old Man reappeared, haply unconscious of the cause of the late hilarious outburst, and smiled blandly.

"The old woman thought she'd jest run over to Mrs. McFadden's for a sociable call," he explained, with jaunty indifference, as he took a seat at the board.

Oddly enough it needed this untoward incident to relieve the embarrassment that was beginning to be felt by the party, and their natural audacity returned with their host. I do not propose to record the convivialities of that evening. The inquisitive reader will accept the statement that the conversation was characterized by the same intellectual exaltation, the same cautious reverence, the same fastidious delicacy, the same rhetorical precision, and the same logical and coherent discourse somewhat later in the evening, which distinguish similar gatherings of the masculine sex in more civilized localities and under more favorable auspices. No glasses were broken in the absence of any; no liquor was uselessly spilt on floor or table in the scarcity of that article.

It was nearly midnight when the festivities were interrupted. "Hush," said Dick Bullen, holding up his hand. It was the querulous voice of Johnny from his adjacent closet: "O dad!"

The Old Man arose hurriedly and disappeared in the closet. Presently he reappeared. "His rheumatiz is coming on agin bad," he explained, "and he wants rubbin'." He lifted the demijohn of whiskey from the table and shook it. It was empty. Dick Bullen put down his tin cup with an embarrassed laugh. So did the others. The Old Man examined their contents and said hopefully, "I reckon that's enough; he don't need much. You hold on all o' you for a spell, and I'll be back"; and vanished in the closet with an old flannel shirt and the whiskey. The door closed but imperfectly, and the following dialogue was distinctly audible: —

"Now, sonny, whar does she ache worst?"

"Sometimes over yar and sometimes under yer; but it's most powerful from yer to yer. Rub yer, dad."

A silence seemed to indicate a brisk rubbing. Then Johnny:

"Hevin' a good time out yer, dad?"

"Yes, sonny."

"To-morrer 's Chrismiss, — ain't it?"

"Yes, sonny. How does she feel now?"

"Better. Rub a little furder down. Wot's Chrismiss, anyway? Wot's it all about?"

"O, it's a day."

This exhaustive definition was apparently satisfactory, for there was a silent interval of rubbing. Presently Johnny again:

"Mar sez that everywhere else but yer everybody gives things to everybody Chrismiss, and then she jist waded inter you. She sez thar's a man they call Sandy Claws, not a white man, you know, but a kind o' Chinemin, comes down the chimbley night afore Chrismiss and gives things to chillern, — boys like me. Put's 'em in their butes! Thet's what she tried to play upon me. Easy now, pop, whar are you rubbin' to, — thet's a mile from the place. She jest made that up, didn't she, jest to aggrewate me and you? Don't rub thar. . . . Why, dad?"

In the great quiet that seemed to have fallen upon the house the sigh of the near pines and the drip of leaves without was very distinct. Johnny's voice, too, was lowered as he went on, "Don't you take on now, fur I'm gettin' all right fast. Wot's the boys doin' out thar?"

The Old Man partly opened the door and peered through. His guests were sitting there sociably enough, and there were a few silver coins and a lean buckskin purse on the table. "Bettin' on suthin, —

some little game or 'nother. They're all right," he replied to Johnny, and recommenced his rubbing.

"I'd like to take a hand and win some money," said Johnny, reflectively, after a pause.

The Old Man glibly repeated what was evidently a familiar formula, that if Johnny would wait until he struck it rich in the tunnel he'd have lots of money, etc., etc.

"Yes," said Johnny, "but you don't. And whether you strike it or I win it, it's about the same. It's all luck. But it's mighty cur'o's about Chrismiss, — ain't it? Why do they call it Chrismiss?"

Perhaps from some instinctive deference to the overhearing of his guests, or from some vague sense of incongruity, the Old Man's reply was so low as to be inaudible beyond the room.

"Yes," said Johnny, with some slight abatement of interest, "I've heerd o' *him* before. Thar, that'll do, dad. I don't ache near so bad as I did. Now wrap me tight in this yer blanket. So. Now," he added in a muffled whisper, "sit down yer by me till I go asleep." To assure himself of obedience, he disengaged one hand from the blanket and grasping his father's sleeve, again composed himself to rest.

For some moments the Old Man waited patiently. Then the unwonted stillness of the house excited his curiosity, and without moving from the bed, he cautiously opened the door with his disengaged hand, and looked into the main room. To his infinite surprise it was dark and deserted. But even then a smouldering log on the hearth broke, and by the upspringing blaze he saw the figure of Dick Bullen sitting by the dying embers.

"Hello!"

Dick started, rose, and came somewhat unsteadily toward him.

"Whar's the boys?" said the Old Man.

"Gone up the cañon on a little *pasear*. They're coming back for me in a minit. I'm waitin' round for 'em. What are you starin' at, Old Man," he added with a forced laugh; "do you think I'm drunk?"

The Old Man might have been pardoned the supposition, for Dick's eyes were humid and his face flushed. He loitered and lounged back to the chimney, yawned, shook himself, buttoned up his coat and laughed. "Liquor ain't so plenty as that, Old Man. Now don't you git up," he continued as the Old Man made a movement to release his sleeve from Johnny's hand. "Don't you mind manners. Sit jest whar you be; I'm goin' in a jiffy. Thar, that's them now."

There was a low tap at the door. Dick Bullen opened it quickly, nodded "Good night" to his host and disappeared. The Old Man would have followed him but for the hand that still unconsciously grasped his sleeve. He could have easily disengaged it: it was small, weak, and emaciated. But perhaps because it *was* small, weak, and emaciated, he changed his mind, and, drawing his chair closer to the bed, rested his head upon it. In this defenceless attitude the potency of his earlier potations surprised him. The room flickered and faded before his eyes. reappeared, faded again, went out, and left him — asleep.

Meantime Dick Bullen, closing the door, confronted his companions. "Are you ready?" said Staples. "Ready," said Dick; "what's the time?" "Past twelve," was the reply; "can you make it? — it's nigh on fifty miles, the round trip hither and yon." "I reckon," returned Dick, shortly. "Whar's the mare?" "Bill and Jack's holdin' her at the crossin'." "Let 'em hold on a minit longer," said Dick.

He turned and re-entered the house softly. By the light of the guttering candle and dying fire he saw that the door of the little room was open. He stepped toward it on tiptoe and looked in. The Old Man had fallen back in his chair, snoring, his helpless feet thrust out in a line with his collapsed shoulders, and his hat pulled over his eyes. Beside him, on a narrow wooden bedstead, lay Johnny, muffled tightly in a blanket that hid all save a strip of forehead and a few curls damp with perspiration. Dick Bullen made a step forward, hesitated, and glanced over his shoulder into the deserted room. Everything was quiet. With a sudden resolution he parted his huge mustaches with both hands and stooped over the sleeping boy. But even as he did so a mischievous blast, lying in wait, swooped down the chimney, rekindled the hearth, and lit up the room with a shameless glow from which Dick fled in bashful terror.

His companions were already waiting for him at the crossing. Two of them were struggling in the darkness with some strange misshapen bulk, which as Dick came nearer took the semblance of a great yellow horse.

It was the mare. She was not a pretty picture. From her Roman nose to her rising haunches, from her arched spine hidden by the stiff *machillas* of a Mexican saddle, to her thick, straight, bony legs, there was not a line of equine grace. In her half-blind but wholly vicious white eyes, in her protruding under lip, in her monstrous color, there was nothing but ugliness and vice.

"Now, then," said Staples, "stand cl'ar of her heels, boys, and up with you. Don't miss your first holt of her mane, and mind ye get your off stirrup *quick*. Ready!"

There was a leap, a scrambling struggle, a bound, a wild retreat of the crowd, a circle of flying hoofs, two springless leaps that jarred the earth, a rapid play and jingle of spurs, a plunge, and then the voice of Dick somewhere in the darkness, "All right!"

"Don't take the lower road back onless you're hard pushed for time! Don't hold her in down hill! We'll be at the ford at five. G'lang! Hoopa! Mula! GO!"

A splash, a spark struck from the ledge in the road, a clatter in the rocky cut beyond, and Dick was gone.

Sing, O Muse, the ride of Richard Bullen! Sing, O Muse of chivalrous men! the sacred quest, the doughty deeds, the battery of low churls, the fearsome ride and grewsome perils of the Flower of Simpson's Bar! Alack! she is dainty, this Muse! She will have none of this bucking brute and swaggering, ragged rider, and I must fain follow him in prose, afoot!

It was one o'clock, and yet he had only gained Rattlesnake Hill. For in that time Jovita had rehearsed to him all her imperfections and practised all her vices. Thrice had she stumbled. Twice had she thrown up her Roman nose in a straight line with the reins, and, resisting bit and spur, struck out madly across country. Twice had she reared, and rearing, fallen backward; and twice had the agile Dick, unharmed, regained his seat before she found her vicious legs again. And a mile beyond them, at the foot of a long hill, was Rattlesnake Creek. Dick knew that here was the crucial test of his ability to perform his enterprise, set his teeth grimly, put his knees well into her flanks, and changed his defensive tactics to brisk aggression. Bullied and maddened, Jovita began the descent of the hill. Here the artful Richard pretended to hold her in with ostentatious objurgation and well-feigned cries of alarm. It is unnecessary to add that Jovita instantly ran away. Nor need I state the time made in the descent; it is written in the chronicles of Simpson's Bar. Enough that in another moment, as it seemed to Dick, she was splashing on the overflowed banks of Rattlesnake Creek. As Dick expected, the momentum she had acquired carried her beyond the point of balking, and holding her well together for a mighty leap, they dashed into the middle of the swiftly flowing current. A few moments of kicking, wading, and swimming, and Dick drew a long breath on the opposite bank.

The road from Rattlesnake Creek to Red Mountain was tolerably level. Either the plunge in Rattlesnake Creek had dampened her baleful fire, or the art which led to it had shown her the superior wickedness of her rider, for Jovita no longer wasted her surplus energy in wanton conceits. Once she bucked, but it was from force of habit; once she shied, but it was from a new freshly painted meetinghouse at the crossing of the county road. Hollows, ditches, gravelly deposits, patches of freshly springing grasses flew from beneath her rattling hoofs. She began to smell unpleasantly, once or twice she coughed slightly, but there was no abatement of her strength or speed. By two o'clock he had passed Red Mountain and begun the descent to the plain. Ten minutes later the driver of the fast Pioneer coach was over-taken and passed by a "man on a Pinto hoss," — an event sufficiently notable for remark. At half past two Dick rose in his stirrups with a great shout. Stars were glittering through the rifted clouds, and be-yond him, out of the plain, rose two spires, a flagstaff and a straggling line of black objects. Dick jingled his spurs and swung his *riata*, Jovita bounded forward, and in another moment they swept into Tuttleville and drew up before the wooden piazza of "The Hotel of All Nations."

What transpired that night at Tuttleville is not strictly a part of this record. Briefly I may state, however, that after Jovita had been handed over to a sleepy ostler, whom she at once kicked into unpleas-ant consciousness, Dick sallied out with the bar-keeper for a tour of the sleeping town. Lights still gleamed from a few saloons and gam-bling-houses; but, avoiding these, they stopped before several closed shops, and by persistent tapping and judicious outcry roused the pro-prietors from their beds, and made them unbar the doors of their magazines and expose their wares. Sometimes they were met by curses, but oftener by interest and some concern in their needs, and the interview was invariably concluded by a drink. It was three o'clock before this pleasantry was given over, and with a small waterproof bag of india-rubber strapped on his shoulders Dick returned to the hotel. But here he was waylaid by Beauty, — Beauty opulent in charms, af-fluent in dress, persuasive in speech, and Spanish in accent! In vain she repeated the invitation in "Excelsior," happily scorned by all Al-pine-climbing youth, and rejected by this child of the Sierras, — a re-jection softened in this instance by a laugh and his last gold coin. And then he sprang to the saddle and dashed down the lonely street and out into the lonelier plain, where presently the lights, the black line of houses, the spires, and the flagstaff sank into the earth behind him again and were lost in the distance.

The storm had cleared away, the air was brisk and cold, the outlines of adjacent landmarks were distinct, but it was half past four before Dick reached the meeting-house and the crossing of the county road. To avoid the rising grade he had taken a longer and more circuitous road, in whose viscid mud Jovita sank fetlock deep at every bound. It was a poor preparation for a steady ascent of five miles more; but Jovita, gathering her legs under her, took it with her usual blind, unreasoning fury, and a half-hour later reached the long level that led to Rattlesnake Creek. Another half-hour would bring him to the creek. He threw the reins lightly upon the neck of the mare, chir-ruped to her, and began to sing.

Suddenly Jovita shied with a bound that would have unseated a less practised rider. Hanging to her rein was a figure that had leaped from the bank, and at the same time from the road before her arose a shadowy horse and rider. "Throw up your hands," commanded this second apparition, with an oath.

Dick felt the mare tremble, quiver, and apparently sink under him. He knew what it meant and was prepared.

"Stand aside, Jack Simpson, I know you, you d—d thief. Let me pass or —"

He did not finish the sentence. Jovita rose straight in the air with a terrific bound, throwing the figure from her bit with a single shake of her vicious head, and charged with deadly malevolence down on the impediment before her. An oath, a pistol-shot, horse and highwayman rolled over in the road, and the next moment Jovita was a hundred yards away. But the good right arm of her rider, shattered by a bullet, dropped helplessly at his side.

Without slackening his speed he shifted the reins to his left hand. But a few moments later he was obliged to halt and tighten the saddle-girths that had slipped in the onset. This in his crippled condition took some time. He had no fear of pursuit, but looking up he saw that the eastern stars were already paling, and that the distant peaks had lost their ghostly whiteness, and now stood out blackly against a lighter sky. Day was upon him. Then completely absorbed in a single idea, he forgot the pain of his wound, and mounting again dashed on toward Rattlesnake Creek. But now Jovita's breath came broken by gasps, Dick reeled in his saddle, and brighter and brighter grew the sky.

Ride, Richard; run, Jovita; linger, O day!

For the last few rods there was a roaring in his ears. Was it exhaustion from loss of blood, or what? He was dazed and giddy as he swept down the hill, and did not recognize his surroundings. Had he taken the wrong road, or was this Rattlesnake Creek?

It was. But the brawling creek he had swam a few hours before had risen, more than doubled its volume, and now rolled a swift and resistless river between him and Rattlesnake Hill. For the first time that night Richard's heart sank within him. The river, the mountain, the quickening east swam before his eyes. He shut them to recover his self-control. In that brief interval, by some fantastic mental process the little room at Simpson's Bar and the figures of the sleeping father and son rose upon him. He opened his eyes wildly, cast off his coat, pistol, boots, and saddle, bound his precious pack tightly to his shoulders, grasped the bare flanks of Jovita with his bared knees, and with a shout dashed into the yellow water. A cry rose from the opposite bank as the head of a man and horse struggled for a few moments against the battling current, and then were swept away amidst uprooted trees and whirling drift-wood.

The Old Man started and woke. The fire on the hearth was dead, the candle in the outer room flickering in its socket, and somebody was rapping at the door. He opened it, but fell back with a cry before the dripping, half-naked figure that reeled against the doorpost.

"Dick?"

"Hush! Is he awake yet?"

"No, — but Dick? —"

"Dry up, you old fool! Get me some whiskey *quick!*" The Old Man flew and returned with — an empty bottle! Dick would have sworn, but his strength was not equal to the occasion. He staggered, caught at the handle of the door, and motioned to the Old Man.

"Thar's suthin' in my pack yer for Johnny. Take it off. I can't."

The Old Man unstrapped the pack and laid it before the exhausted man.

"Open it, quick!"

He did so with trembling fingers. It contained only a few poor toys, — cheap and barbaric enough, goodness knows, but bright with paint and tinsel. One of them was broken; another, I fear, was irretrievably ruined by water; and on the third — ah me! there was a cruel spot.

"It don't look like much, that's a fact," said Dick, ruefully. . . . "But it's the best we could do. . . . Take 'em, Old Man, and put 'em in his stocking, and tell him — tell him, you know — hold me, Old Man —" The Old Man caught at his sinking figure. "Tell him," said Dick, with a weak little laugh, — "tell him Sandy Claus has come."

And even so, bedraggled, ragged, unshaven, and unshorn, with one arm hanging helplessly at his side, Santa Claus came to Simpson's Bar and fell fainting on the first threshold. The Christmas dawn came slowly after, touching the remoter peaks with the rosy warmth of ineffable love. And it looked so tenderly on Simpson's Bar that the whole mountain, as if caught in a generous action, blushed to the skies.

MARJORIE DAW

by Thomas Bailey Aldrich

I

Dr. Dillon to Edward Delaney, Esq., at The Pines, near Rye, N.H.

August 8, 187-.

MY DEAR SIR: I am happy to assure you that your anxiety is without reason. Flemming will be confined to the sofa for three or four weeks, and will have to be careful at first how he uses his leg. A fracture of this kind is always a tedious affair. Fortunately, the bone was very skilfully set by the surgeon who chanced to be in the drug-store where Flemming was brought after his fall, and I apprehend no permanent inconvenience from the accident. *Flemming is doing perfectly well physically;* but I must confess that the irritable and morbid state of mind into which he has fallen causes me a great deal of uneasiness. He is the last man in the world who ought to break his leg. You know how impetuous our friend is ordinarily, what a soul of restlessness and energy, never content unless he is rushing at some object, like a sportive bull at a red shawl; but amiable withal. He is no longer amiable. His temper has become something frightful. Miss Fanny Flemming came up from Newport, where the family are staying for the summer, to nurse him; but he packed her off the next morning in tears. He has a complete set of Balzac's works, twenty-seven volumes, piled up by his sofa, to throw at Watkins whenever that exemplary serving-man appears with his meals. Yesterday I very innocently brought Flemming a small basket of lemons. You know it was a strip of lemon-peel on the curbstone that caused our friend's mischance. Well, he no sooner set his eyes upon these lemons, than he fell into such a rage as I cannot describe adequately. This is only one of his moods, and the least distressing. At other times he sits with bowed head regarding his splintered limb, silent, sullen, despairing. When this fit is on him — and it sometimes lasts all day — nothing can distract his melancholy. He refuses to eat, does not even read the newspapers; books — except as projectiles for Watkins — have no charms for him. His state is truly pitiable.

Now, if he were a poor man, with a family dependent on his daily labor, this irritability and despondency would be natural enough. But in a young fellow of twenty-four, with plenty of money and seemingly not a care in the world, the thing is monstrous. If he continues to give way to his vagaries in this manner, he will end by bringing on an inflammation of the fibula. It was the fibula he broke. I am at my wits' end to know what to prescribe for him. I have anæsthetics and lotions, to make people sleep and to soothe pain; but I've no medicine that will make a man have a little common-sense. That is beyond my skill, but maybe it is not beyond yours. You are Flemming's intimate friend, his *fidus Achates*. Write to him, write to him frequently, distract his mind, cheer him up, and prevent him from becoming a confirmed case of melancholia. Perhaps he has some important plans disarranged by his present confinement. If he has you will know, and will know how to advise him judiciously. I trust your father finds the change beneficial? I am, my dear sir, with great respect, etc.

II

EDWARD DELANEY TO JOHN FLEMMING, WEST 38TH STREET, NEW YORK.

August 9, —.

MY DEAR JACK: I had a line from Dillon this morning, and was rejoiced to learn that your hurt is not so bad as reported. Like a certain personage, you are not so black and blue as you are painted. Dillon will put you on your pins again in two or three weeks, if you will only have patience and follow his counsels. Did you get my note of last Wednesday? I was greatly troubled when I heard of the accident.

I can imagine how tranquil and saintly you are with your leg in a trough! It's deuced awkward, to be sure, just as we had promised ourselves a glorious month together at the seaside; but we must make the best of it. It is unfortunate, too, that my father's health renders it impossible for me to leave him. I think he has much improved; the sea air is his native element; but he still needs my arm to lean upon in his walks, and requires some one more careful than a servant to look after him. I cannot come to you, dear Jack, but I have hours of unemployed time on hand, and I will write you a whole post-office full of letters if that will divert you. Heaven knows, I haven't anything to write about. It isn't as if we were living at one of the beach houses; then I could do you some character studies, and fill your imagination with hosts of sea-goddesses, with their (or somebody else's) raven and blond manes hanging down their shoulders. You should have Aphrodite in morning wrapper, in evening costume, and in her prettiest bathing suit. But we are far from all that here. We have rooms in a farmhouse, on a cross-road, two miles from the hotels, and lead the quietest of lives.

I wish I were a novelist. This old house, with its sanded floors and high wainscots, and its narrow windows looking out upon a cluster of pines that turn themselves into æolian-harps every time the wind blows, would be the place in which to write a summer romance. It should be a story with the odors of the forest and the breath of the sea in it. It should be a novel like one of that Russian fellow's — what's his name? — Tourguénieff, Turguenef, Toorguniff, Turgénjew, — nobody knows how to spell him. (I think his own mother must be in some doubt about him.) Yet I wonder if even a Liza or an Alexandra Paulovna could stir the heart of a man who has constant twinges in his leg. I wonder if one of our own Yankee girls of the best type, haughty and *spirituelle*, would be of any comfort to you in your present deplorable condition. If I thought so, I would rush down to the Surf House and catch one for you; or, better still, I would find you one over the way.

Picture to yourself a large white house just across the road, nearly opposite our cottage. It is not a house, but a mansion, built, perhaps, in the colonial period, with rambling extensions, and gambrel roof, and a wide piazza on three sides, — a self-possessed, high-bred piece of architecture, with its nose in the air. It stands back from the road, and has an obsequious retinue of fringed elms and oaks and weeping willows. Sometimes in the morning, and oftener in the afternoon, when the sun has withdrawn from that part of the mansion, a young woman appears on the piazza with some mysterious Penelope web of embroidery in her hand, or a book. There is a hammock over there, — of pineapple fibre, it looks from here. A hammock is very becoming when one is eighteen, and has gold hair, and dark eyes, and a blue illusion dress looped up after the fashion of a Dresden china shepherdess, and is *chaussée* like a belle of the time of Louis Quatorze. All this splendor goes into that hammock, and sways there like a pond-lily in the golden afternoon. The window of my bedroom looks down on that piazza, — and so do I.

But enough of this nonsense, which ill becomes a sedate young attorney taking his vacation with an invalid father. Drop me a line, dear Jack, and tell me how you really are. State your case. Write me a long, quiet letter. If you are violent or abusive, I'll take the law to you.

III
JOHN FLEMMING TO EDWARD DELANEY.

August 11, —.

YOUR letter, dear Ned, was a godsend. Fancy what a fix I am in, — I, who never had a day's sickness since I was born. My left leg weighs three tons. It is embalmed in spices and smothered in layers of fine linen, like a mummy. I can't move. I haven't moved for five thousand years. I'm of the time of Pharaoh.

I lie from morning till night on a lounge, staring into the hot street. Everybody is out of town enjoying himself. The brown-stone-front houses across the street resemble a row of particularly ugly coffins set up on end. A green mould is settling on the names of the deceased, carved on the silver door-plates. Sardonic spiders have sewed up the key-holes. All is silence and dust and desolation. — I interrupt this a moment, to take a shy at Watkins with the second volume of César Birotteau. Missed him! I think I could bring him down with a copy of Sainte-Beuve or the Dictionnaire Universel, if I had it. These small Balzac books somehow don't quite fit my hand. But I shall fetch him yet. I've an idea Watkins is tapping the old gentleman's Château Yquem. Duplicate key of the wine-cellar. Hibernian swarries in the front basement. Young Cheops up stairs, snug in his cerements. Watkins glides into my chamber, with that colorless, hypocritical face of his drawn out long like an accordion; but I know he grins all the way down stairs, and is glad I have broken my leg. Was not my evil star in the very zenith when I ran up to town to attend that dinner at Delmonico's? I didn't come up altogether for that. It was partly to buy Frank Livingstone's roan mare Margot. And now I shall not be able to sit in the saddle these two months. I'll send the mare down to you at The Pines, — is that the name of the place?

Old Dillon fancies that I have something on my mind. He drives me wild with lemons. Lemons for a mind diseased! Nonsense. I am only as restless as the devil under this confinement, — a thing I'm not used to. Take a man who has never had so much as a headache or a toothache in his life, strap one of his legs in a section of water-spout, keep him in a room in the city for weeks, with the hot weather turned on, and then expect him to smile and purr and be happy! It is preposterous. I can't be cheerful or calm.

Your letter is the first consoling thing I have had since my disaster, a week ago. It really cheered me up for half an hour. Send me a screed, Ned, as often as you can, if you love me. Anything will do. Write me more about that little girl in the hammock. That was very pretty, all that about the Dresden china shepherdess and the pond-lily; the imagery a little mixed, perhaps, but very pretty. I didn't suppose you had so much sentimental furniture in your upper story. It shows how one may be familiar for years with the reception-room of his neighbor, and never suspect what is directly under his mansard. I supposed your loft stuffed with dry legal parchments, mortgages and affidavits; you take down a package of manuscript, and lo! there are lyrics and sonnets and canzonettas. You really have a graphic descriptive touch, Edward Delaney, and I suspect you of short love-tales in the magazines.

I shall be a bear until I hear from you again. Tell me all about your pretty *inconnue* across the road. What is her name? Who is she? Who's her father? Where's her mother? Who's her lover? You cannot imagine how this will occupy me. The more trifling the better. My imprisonment has weakened me intellectually to such a degree that I find your epistolary gifts quite considerable. I am passing into my second childhood. In a week or two I shall take to india-rubber rings and prongs of coral. A silver cup, with an appropriate inscription, would be a delicate attention on your part. In the mean time, write!

IV

EDWARD DELANEY TO JOHN FLEMMING.

August 12, —.

THE sick pasha shall be amused. *Bismillah!* he wills it so. If the story-teller becomes prolix and tedious, — the bow-string and the sack, and two Nubians to drop him into the Piscataqua! But, truly, Jack, I have a hard task. There is literally nothing here, — except the little girl over the way. She is swinging in the hammock at this moment. It is to me compensation for many of the ills of life to see her now and then put out a small kid boot, which fits like a glove, and set herself going. Who is she, and what is her name? Her name is Daw. Only daughter of Mr. Richard W. Daw, ex-colonel and banker. Mother dead. One brother at Harvard, elder brother killed at the battle of Fair Oaks nine years ago. Old, rich family, the Daws. This is the homestead, where father and daughter pass eight months of the twelve; the rest of the year in Baltimore and Washington. The New England winter too many for the old gentleman. The daughter is called Marjorie, — Marjorie Daw. Sounds odd at first, doesn't it? But after you say it over to yourself half a dozen times, you like it. There's a pleasing quaintness to it, something prim and violet-like. Must be a nice sort of girl to be called Marjorie Daw.

I had mine host of The Pines in the witness-box last night, and drew the foregoing testimony from him. He has charge of Mr. Daw's vegetable-garden, and has known the family these thirty years. Of course I shall make the acquaintance of my neighbors before many days. It will be next to impossible for me not to meet Mr. Daw or Miss Daw in some of my walks. The young lady has a favorite path to the sea-beach. I shall intercept her some morning, and touch my hat to her. Then the princess will bend her fair head to me with courteous surprise not unmixed with haughtiness. Will snub me, in fact. All this for thy sake, O Pasha of the Snapt Axle-tree! . . . How oddly things fall out! Ten minutes ago I was called down to the parlor, — you know the kind of parlors in farm-houses on the coast, a sort of amphibious parlor, with sea-shells on the mantel-piece and spruce branches in the chimney-place, — where I found my father and Mr. Daw doing the antique polite to each other. He had come to pay his respects to his new neighbors. Mr. Daw is a tall, slim gentleman of about fifty-five, with a florid face and snow-white mustache and side-whiskers. Looks like Mr. Dombey, or as Mr. Dombey would have looked if he had served a few years in the British Army. Mr. Daw was a colonel in the late war, commanding the regiment in which his son was a lieutenant. Plucky old boy, backbone of New Hampshire granite. Before taking his leave, the colonel delivered himself of an invitation as if he were issuing a general order. Miss Daw has a few friends coming, at 4 P.M., to play croquet on the lawn (parade-ground) and have tea (cold rations) on the piazza. Will we honor them with our company? (or be sent to the guard-house.) My father declines, on the plea of ill-health. My father's son bows with as much suavity as he knows, and accepts.

In my next I shall have something to tell you. I shall have seen the little beauty face to face. I have a presentiment, Jack, that this Daw is a *rara avis!* Keep up your spirits, my boy, until I write you another letter, — and send me along word how's your leg.

v

EDWARD DELANEY TO JOHN FLEMMING.

August 13, —.

THE party, my dear Jack, was as dreary as possible. A lieutenant of the navy, the rector of the Episcopal church at Stillwater, and a society swell from Nahant. The lieutenant looked as if he had swallowed a couple of his buttons, and found the bullion rather indigestible; the rector was a pensive youth, of the daffydowndilly sort; and the swell from Nahant was a very weak tidal wave indeed. The women were much better, as they always are; the two Miss Kingsburys of Philadelphia, staying at the Seashell House, two bright and engaging girls. But Marjorie Daw!

The company broke up soon after tea, and I remained to smoke a cigar with the colonel on the piazza. It was like seeing a picture to see Miss Marjorie hovering around the old soldier, and doing a hundred gracious little things for him. She brought the cigars and lighted the tapers with her own delicate fingers, in the most enchanting fashion. As we sat there, she came and went in the summer twilight, and seemed, with her white dress and pale gold hair, like some lovely phantom that had sprung into existence out of the smoke-wreaths. If she had melted into air, like the statue of the lady in the play, I should have been more sorry than surprised.

It was easy to perceive that the old colonel worshipped her, and she him. I think the relation between an elderly father and a daughter just blooming into womanhood the most beautiful possible. There is in it a subtle sentiment that cannot exist in the case of mother and daughter, or that of son and mother. But this is getting into deep water.

I sat with the Daws until half past ten, and saw the moon rise on the sea. The ocean, that had stretched motionless and black against the horizon, was changed by magic into a broken field of glittering ice. In the far distance, the Isles of Shoals loomed up like a group of huge bergs drifting down on us. The Polar Regions in a June thaw! It was exceedingly fine. What did we talk about? We talked about the weather — and *you!* The weather has been disagreeable for several days past, — and so have you. I glided from one topic to the other very naturally. I told my friends of your accident; how it had frustrated all our summer plans, and what our plans were. Then I described you; or, rather, I didn't. I spoke of your amiability; of your patience under this severe affliction; of your touching gratitude when Dillon brings you little presents of fruit; of your tenderness to your sister Fanny, whom you would not allow to stay in town to nurse you, and how you heroically sent her back to Newport, preferring to remain alone with Mary, the cook, and your man Watkins, to whom, by the way, you were devotedly attached. If you had been there, Jack, you wouldn't have known yourself. I should have excelled as a criminal lawyer, if I had not turned my attention to a different branch of jurisprudence.

Miss Marjorie asked all manner of leading questions concerning you. It did not occur to me then, but it struck me forcibly afterwards, that she evinced a singular interest in the conversation. When I got back to my room, I recalled how eagerly she leaned forward, with her full, snowy throat in strong moonlight, listening to what I said. Positively, I think I made her like you!

Miss Daw is a girl whom you would like immensely, I can tell you that. A beauty without affectation, a high and tender nature, — if one can read the soul in the face. And the old colonel is a noble character, too.

I am glad the Daws are such pleasant people. The Pines is an isolated place, and my resources are few. I fear I should have found life here rather monotonous before long, with no other society than that of my excellent sire. It is true, I might have made a target of the defenceless invalid; but I haven't a taste for artillery, *moi.*

VI

JOHN FLEMMING TO EDWARD DELANEY.

August 17, —.

FOR a man who hasn't a taste for artillery, it occurs to me, my friend, you are keeping up a pretty lively fire on my inner works. But go on. Cynicism is a small brass field-piece that eventually bursts and kills the artilleryman.

You may abuse me as much as you like, and I'll not complain; for I don't know what I should do without your letters. They are curing me. I haven't hurled anything at Watkins since last Sunday, partly because I have grown more amiable under your teaching, and partly because

Watkins captured my ammunition one night, and carried it off to the library. He is rapidly losing the habit he had acquired of dodging whenever I rub my ear, or make any slight motion with my right arm. He is still suggestive of the wine-cellar, however. You may break, you may shatter Watkins, if you will, but the scent of the Roederer will hang round him still.

Ned, that Miss Daw must be a charming person. I should certainly like her. I like her already. When you spoke in your first letter of seeing a young girl swinging in a hammock under your chamber window, I was somehow strangely drawn to her. I cannot account for it in the least. What you have subsequently written of Miss Daw has strengthened the impression. You seem to be describing a woman I have known in some previous state of existence, or dreamed of in this. Upon my word, if you were to send me her photograph, I believe I should recognize her at a glance. Her manner, that listening attitude, her traits of character, as you indicate them, the light hair and the dark eyes, — they are all familiar things to me. Asked a lot of questions, did she? Curious about me? That is strange.

You would laugh in your sleeve, you wretched old cynic, if you knew how I lie awake nights, with my gas turned down to a star, thinking of The Pines and the house across the road. How cool it must be down there! I long for the salt smell in the air. I picture the colonel smoking his cheroot on the piazza. I send you and Miss Daw off on afternoon rambles along the beach. Sometimes I let you stroll with her under the elms in the moonlight, for you are great friends by this time, I take it, and see each other every day. I know your ways and your manners! Then I fall into a truculent mood, and would like to destroy somebody. Have you noticed anything in the shape of a lover hanging around the colonial Lares and Penates? Does that lieutenant of the horse-marines or that young Stillwater parson visit the house much? Not that I am pining for news of them, but any gossip of the kind would be in order. I wonder, Ned, you don't fall in love with Miss Daw. I am ripe to do it myself. Speaking of photographs, couldn't you manage to slip one of her *cartes-de-visite* from her album, — she must have an album, you know, — and send it to me? I will return it before it could be missed. That's a good fellow! Did the mare arrive safe and sound? It will be a capital animal this autumn for Central Park.

Oh — my leg? I forgot about my leg. It's better.

VII
EDWARD DELANEY TO JOHN FLEMMING.

August 20, —.

You are correct in your surmises. I am on the most friendly terms with our neighbors. The colonel and my father smoke their afternoon cigar together in our sitting-room or on the piazza opposite, and I pass an hour or two of the day or the evening with the daughter. I am more and more struck by the beauty, modesty, and intelligence of Miss Daw.

You ask me why I do not fall in love with her. I will be frank, Jack: I have thought of that. She is young, rich, accomplished, uniting in herself more attractions, mental and personal, than I can recall in any girl of my acquaintance; but she lacks the something that would be necessary to inspire in me that kind of interest. Possessing this unknown quantity, a woman neither beautiful nor wealthy nor very young could bring me to her feet. But not Miss Daw. If we were shipwrecked together on an uninhabited island, — let me suggest a tropical island, for it costs no more to be picturesque, — I would build her a bamboo hut, I would fetch her bread-fruit and cocoanuts, I would fry yams for her, I would lure the ingenuous turtle and make her nourishing soups, but I wouldn't make love to her, — not under eighteen months. I would like to have her for a sister, that I might shield her and counsel her, and spend half my income on thread-laces and camel's-hair shawls. (We are off the island now.) If such were not my feeling, there would still be an obstacle to my loving Miss Daw. A greater misfortune could scarcely befall me than to love her. Flemming, I am about to make a revelation that will astonish you. I may be all wrong in my premises and consequently in my conclusions; but you shall judge.

That night when I returned to my room after the croquet party at the Daws', and was thinking over the trivial events of the evening, I was suddenly impressed by the air of eager attention with which Miss Daw had followed my account of your accident. I think I mentioned this to you. Well, the next morning, as I went to mail my letter, I overtook Miss Daw on the road to Rye, where the post-office is, and accompanied her thither and back, an hour's walk. The conversation again turned on you, and again I remarked that inexplicable look of interest which had lighted up her face the previous evening. Since then, I have seen Miss Daw perhaps ten times, perhaps oftener, and on each occasion I found that when I was not speaking of you, or your sister, or some person or place associated with you, I was not holding her attention. She would be absent-minded, her eyes would wander away from me to the sea, or to some distant object in the landscape; her fingers would play with the leaves of a book in a way that convinced me she was not listening. At these moments if I abruptly changed the theme, — I did it several times as an experiment, — and dropped some remark about my friend Flemming, then the sombre blue eyes would come back to me instantly.

Now, is not this the oddest thing in the world? No, not the oddest.

The effect, which you tell me was produced on you by my casual mention of an unknown girl swinging in a hammock, is certainly as strange. You can conjecture how that passage in your letter of Friday startled me. Is it possible, then, that two people who have never met, and who are hundreds of miles apart, can exert a magnetic influence on each other? I have read of such psychological phenomena, but never credited them. I leave the solution of the problem to you. As for myself, all other things being favorable, it would be impossible for me to fall in love with a woman who listens to me only when I am talking of my friend!

I am not aware that any one is paying marked attention to my fair neighbor. The lieutenant of the navy — he is stationed at Rivermouth — sometimes drops in of an evening, and sometimes the rector from Stillwater; the lieutenant the oftener. He was there last night. I should not be surprised if he had an eye to the heiress; but he is not formidable. Mistress Daw carries a neat little spear of irony, and the honest lieutenant seems to have a particular facility for impaling himself on the point of it. He is not dangerous, I should say; though I have known a woman to satirize a man for years, and marry him after all. Decidedly, the lowly rector is not dangerous; yet, again, who has not seen Cloth of Frieze victorious in the lists where Cloth of Gold went down?

As to the photograph. There is an exquisite ivorytype of Marjorie, in passe-partout, on the drawing-room mantel-piece. It would be missed at once, if taken. I would do anything reasonable for you, Jack; but I've no burning desire to be hauled up before the local justice of the peace, on a charge of petty larceny.

P.S. — Enclosed is a spray of mignonette, which I advise you to treat tenderly. Yes, we talked of you again last night, as usual. It is becoming a little dreary for me.

VIII
Edward Delaney to John Flemming.

August 22, —.

Your letter in reply to my last has occupied my thoughts all the morning. I do not know what to think. Do you mean to say that you are seriously half in love with a woman whom you have never seen, — with a shadow, a chimera? for what else can Miss Daw be to you? I do not understand it at all. I understand neither you nor her. You are a couple of ethereal beings moving in finer air than I can breathe with my commonplace lungs. Such delicacy of sentiment is something I admire without comprehending. I am bewildered. I am of the earth earthy, and I find myself in the incongruous position of having to do with mere souls, with natures so finely tempered that I run some risk of shattering them in my awkwardness. I am as Caliban among the spirits!

Reflecting on your letter, I am not sure it is wise in me to continue this correspondence. But no, Jack; I do wrong to doubt the good sense that forms the basis of your character. You are deeply interested in Miss Daw; you feel that she is a person whom you may perhaps greatly admire when you know her: at the same time you bear in mind that the chances are ten to five that, when you do come to know her, she will fall short of your ideal, and you will not care for her in the least. Look at it in this sensible light, and I will hold back nothing from you.

Yesterday afternoon my father and myself rode over to Rivermouth with the Daws. A heavy rain in the morning had cooled the atmosphere and laid the dust. To Rivermouth is a drive of eight miles, along a winding road lined all the way with wild barberry-bushes. I never saw anything more brilliant than these bushes, the green of the foliage and the red of the coral berries intensified by the rain. The colonel drove, with my father in front, Miss Daw and I on the back seat, I resolved that for the first five miles your name should not pass my lips. I was amused by the artful attempts she made, at the start, to break through my reticence. Then a silence fell upon her; and then she became suddenly gay. That keenness which I enjoyed so much when it was exercised on the lieutenant was not so satisfactory directed against myself. Miss Daw has great sweetness of disposition, but she can be disagreeable. She is like the young lady in the rhyme, with the curl on her forehead,

> "When she is good,
> She is very, very good,
> And when she is bad, she is horrid!"

I kept to my resolution, however; but on the return home I relented, and talked of your mare! Miss Daw is going to try a side-saddle on Margot some morning. The animal is a trifle too light for my weight. By the by, I nearly forgot to say Miss Daw sat for a picture yesterday to a Rivermouth artist. If the negative turns out well, I am to have a copy. So our ends will be accomplished without crime. I wish, though, I could send you the ivorytype in the drawing-room; it is cleverly colored, and would give you an idea of her hair and eyes, which of course the other will not.

No, Jack, the spray of mignonette did not come from me. A man of twenty-eight doesn't enclose flowers in his letters — to another man. But don't attach too much significance to the circumstance. She gives sprays of mignonette to the rector, sprays to the lieutenant. She has even given a rose from her bosom to your slave. It is her jocund nature to scatter flowers, like Spring.

If my letters sometimes read disjointedly, you must understand that I never finish one at a sitting, but write at intervals, when the mood is on me.

The mood is not on me now.

IX
EDWARD DELANEY TO JOHN FLEMMING.

August 23, —.

I HAVE just returned from the strangest interview with Marjorie. She has all but confessed to me her interest in you. But with what modesty and dignity! Her words elude my pen as I attempt to put them on paper; and, indeed, it was not so much what she said as her manner; and that I cannot reproduce. Perhaps it was of a piece with the strangeness of this whole business, that she should tacitly acknowledge to a third party the love she feels for a man she has never beheld! But I have lost, through your aid, the faculty of being surprised. I accept things as people do in dreams. Now that I am again in my room, it all appears like an illusion, — the black masses of shadow under the trees, the fire-flies whirling in Pyrrhic dances among the shrubbery, the sea over there, Marjorie sitting on the hammock!

It is past midnight, and I am too sleepy to write more.

Tuesday Morning. — My father has suddenly taken it into his head to spend a few days at the Shoals. In the mean while you will not hear from me. I see Marjorie walking in the garden with the colonel. I wish I could speak to her alone, but shall probably not have an opportunity before we leave.

X
EDWARD DELANEY TO JOHN FLEMMING.

August 28, —.

YOU were passing into your second childhood, were you? Your intellect was so reduced that my epistolary gifts seemed quite considerable to you, did they? I rise superior to the sarcasm in your favor of the 11th instant, when I notice that five days' silence on my part is sufficient to throw you into the depths of despondency.

We returned only this morning from Appledore, that enchanted island, — at four dollars per day. I find on my desk three letters from you! Evidently there is no lingering doubt in *your* mind as to the pleasure I derive from your correspondence. These letters are undated, but in what I take to be the latest are two passages that require my consideration. You will pardon my candor, dear Flemming, but the conviction forces itself upon me that as your leg grows stronger your head becomes weaker. You ask my advice on a certain point. I will give it. In my opinion you could do nothing more unwise than to address a note to Miss Daw, thanking her for the flower. It would, I am sure, offend her delicacy beyond pardon. She knows you only through me; you are to her an abstraction, a figure in a dream, — a dream from which the slightest shock would awaken her. Of course if you enclose a note to me and insist on its delivery, I shall deliver it; but I advise you not to do so.

You say you are able, with the aid of a cane, to walk about your chamber, and that you purpose to come to The Pines the instant Dillon thinks you strong enough to stand the journey. Again I advise you not to. Do you not see that, every hour you remain away, Marjorie's glamour deepens and your influence over her increases? You will ruin everything by precipitancy. Wait until you are entirely recovered; in any case, do not come without giving me warning. I fear the effect of your abrupt advent here — under the circumstances.

Miss Daw was evidently glad to see us back again, and gave me both hands in the frankest way. She stopped at the door a moment, this afternoon, in the carriage; she had been over to Rivermouth for her pictures. Unluckily the photographer had spilt some acid on the plate, and she was obliged to give him another sitting. I have an impression that something is troubling Marjorie. She had an abstracted air not usual with her. However, it may be only my fancy. . . . I end this, leaving several things unsaid, to accompany my father on one of those long walks which are now his chief medicine, — and mine!

XI
EDWARD DELANEY TO JOHN FLEMMING.

August 29, —.

I WRITE in great haste to tell you what has taken place here since my letter of last night. I am in the utmost perplexity. Only one thing is plain, — *you* must not dream of coming to The Pines. Marjorie has told her father everything! I saw her for a few minutes, an hour ago, in the garden; and, as near as I could gather from her confused statement, the facts are these: Lieutenant Bradly — that's the naval officer stationed at Rivermouth — has been paying court to Miss Daw for some time past, but not so much to her liking as to that of the colonel, who it seems is an old friend of the young gentleman's father. Yesterday (I knew she was in some trouble when she drove up to our gate) the colonel spoke to Marjorie of Bradly, — urged his suit, I infer. Marjorie expressed her dislike for the lieutenant with characteristic frankness, and finally confessed to her father — well, I really do not know what she confessed. It must have been the vaguest of confessions, and must have sufficiently puzzled the colonel. At any rate, it exasperated him. I suppose I am implicated in the matter, and that the colonel feels bitterly towards me. I do not see why: I have carried no messages between you and Miss Daw; I have behaved with the greatest discretion. I can find no flaw anywhere in my proceeding. I do not see that anybody has done anything, — except the colonel himself.

It is probable, nevertheless, that the friendly relations between the two houses will be broken off. "A plague o' both your houses," say you. I will keep you informed, as well as I can, of what occurs over the way. We shall remain here until the second week in September. Stay where you are, or, at all events, do not dream of joining me. ... Colonel Daw is sitting on the piazza looking rather ferocious. I have not seen Marjorie since I parted with her in the garden.

XII

EDWARD DELANEY TO THOMAS DILLON, M.D., MADISON SQUARE, NEW YORK.

August 30, —.

MY DEAR DOCTOR: If you have any influence over Flemming, I beg of you to exert it to prevent his coming to this place at present. There are circumstances, which I will explain to you before long, that make it of the first importance that he should not come into this neighborhood. His appearance here, I speak advisedly, would be disastrous to him. In urging him to remain in New York, or to go to some inland resort, you will be doing him and me a real service. Of course you will not mention my name in this connection. You know me well enough, my dear doctor, to be assured that, in begging your secret co-operation, I have reasons that will meet your entire approval when they are made plain to you. My father, I am glad to state, has so greatly improved that he can no longer be regarded as an invalid. With great esteem, I am, etc., etc.

XIII

EDWARD DELANEY TO JOHN FLEMMING.

August 31, —.

YOUR letter, announcing your mad determination to come here, has just reached me. I beg of you to reflect a moment. The step would be fatal to your interests and hers. You would furnish just cause for irritation to R. W. D.; and, though he loves Marjorie tenderly, he is capable of going to any lengths if opposed. You would not like, I am convinced, to be the means of causing him to treat *her* with severity. That would be the result of your presence at The Pines at this juncture. Wait and see what happens. Moreover, I understand from Dillon that you are in no condition to take so long a journey. He thinks the air of the coast would be the worst thing possible for you; that you ought to go inland, if anywhere. Be advised by me. Be advised by Dillon.

XIV
TELEGRAMS

September 1, —.

1. — *To Edward Delaney.*
Letter received. Dillon be hanged. I think I ought to be on the ground.

J. F.

2. — *To John Flemming.*
Stay where you are. You would only complicate matters. Do'not move until you hear from me.

E. D.

3. — *To Edward Delaney.*
My being at The Pines could be kept secret. I must see her.

J. F.

4. — *To John Flemming.*
Do not think of it. It would be useless. R. W. D. has locked M. in her room. You would not be able to effect an interview.

E. D.

5. — *To Edward Delaney.*
Locked her in her room. Good God. That settles the question. I shall leave by the twelve-fifteen express.

J. F.

On the 2d of September, 187-, as the down express due at 3.40 left the station at Hampton, a young man, leaning on the shoulder of a servant whom he addressed as Watkins, stepped from the platform into a hack, and requested to be driven to "The Pines." On arriving at the gate of a modest farmhouse, a few miles from the station, the young man descended with difficulty from the carriage, and, casting a hasty glance across the road, seemed much impressed by some peculiarity in the landscape. Again leaning on the shoulder of the person Watkins, he walked to the door of the farmhouse and inquired for Mr. Edward Delaney. He was informed by the aged man who answered his knock, that Mr. Edward Delaney had gone to Boston the day before, but that Mr. Jonas Delaney was within. This information did not appear satisfactory to the stranger, who inquired if Mr. Edward Delaney had left any message for Mr. John Flemming. There *was* a letter for Mr. Flemming, if he were that person. After a brief absence the aged man reappeared with a letter.

XV

EDWARD DELANEY TO JOHN FLEMMING.

September 1, —.

I am horror-stricken at what I have done! When I began this correspondence I had no other purpose than to relieve the tedium of your sick-chamber. Dillin told me to cheer you up. I tried to. I thought you entered into the spirit of the thing. I had no idea, until within a few days, that you were taking matters *au sérieux*.

What can I say? I am in sackcloth and ashes. I am a Pariah, a dog of an outcast. I tried to make a little romance to interest you, something soothing and idyllic, and, by Jove! I have done it only too well! My father doesn't know a word of this, so don't jar the old gentleman any more than you can help. I fly from the wrath to come — when you arrive! For O, dear Jack, there isn't any colonial mansion on the other side of the road, there isn't any piazza, there isn't any hammock, — there isn't any Marjorie Daw!!

1874

A REBEL'S RECOLLECTIONS
by George Cary Eggleston

IT is impossible to say precisely when the conviction became general in the South that we were to be beaten. We schooled ourselves from the first to think that we should ultimately win, and the habit of thinking so was too strong to be easily broken by adverse events. And yet I think we must have known from the beginning of the campaign of 1864 that the end was approaching, and that it could not be other than a disastrous one. We knew very well that General Lee's army was smaller than it ever had been before. We knew, too, that there were no reinforcements to be had from any source. The conscription had put every man worth counting into the field already, and the little army that met General Grant in the Wilderness represented all that remained of the Confederate strength in Virginia. In the South matters were at their worst, and we knew that not a man could come thence to our assistance. Lee mustered a total strength of about sixty-six thousand men, when we marched out of winter-quarters and began in the Wilderness that long struggle which ended nearly a year later at Appomattox. With that army alone the war was to be fought out, and we had to shut our eyes to facts very resolutely, that we might not see how certainly we were to be crushed. And we did shut our eyes so successfully as to hope in a vague, irrational way for the impossible, to the very end.

In the Wilderness we held our own against every assault, and the visible punishment we inflicted upon the foe was so great that hardly any man in our army expected to see a Federal force on our side of the river at daybreak next morning. We thought that General Grant was as badly hurt as Hooker had been on the same field, and confidently expected him to retreat during the night. When he moved by his left flank to Spottsylvania instead, we understood what manner of man he was, and knew that the persistent pounding, which of all things we were least able to endure, had begun. When at last we settled down in the trenches around Petersburg, we ought to have known that the end was rapidly drawing near. We congratulated ourselves instead upon the fact that we had inflicted a heavier loss than we had suffered, and buckled on our armor anew.

If General Grant had failed to break our power of resistance by his sledge-hammer blows, it speedily became evident that he would be more successful in wearing it away by the constant friction of a siege. Without fighting a battle he was literally destroying our army. The sharp-shooting was incessant, and the bombardment hardly less so, and under it all our numbers visibly decreased day by day. During the first two months of the siege my own company, which numbered about a hundred and fifty men, lost sixty, in killed and wounded, an average of a man a day; and while our list of casualties was greater than that of many other commands, there were undoubtedly some companies and regiments which suffered more than we. The reader will readily understand that an army already weakened by years of war, with no source from which to recruit its ranks, could not stand this daily waste for any great length of time. We were in a state of atrophy for which there was no remedy except that of freeing the negroes and making soldiers of them, which Congress was altogether too loftily sentimental to think of for a moment.

There was no longer any room for hope except in a superstitious belief that Providence would in some way interfere in our behalf, and to that very many betook themselves for comfort. This shifting upon a supernatural power the task we had failed to accomplish by human means rapidly bred many less worthy superstitions among the troops. The general despondency, which amounted almost to despair, doubtless helped to bring about this result, and the great religious "revival" contributed to it in no small degree. I think hardly any man in that army entertained a thought of coming out of the struggle alive. The only question with each was when his time was to come, and a sort of gloomy fatalism took possession of many minds. Believing that they must be killed sooner or later, and that the hour and the manner of their deaths were unalterably fixed, many became singularly reckless, and exposed themselves with the utmost carelessness to all sorts of unnecessary dangers.

"I'm going to be killed pretty soon," said as brave a man as I ever knew, to me one day. "I never flinched from a bullet until to-day, and now I dodge every time one whistles within twenty feet of me."

I tried to persuade him out of the belief, and even got for him a dose of valerian with which to quiet his nerves. He took the medicine, but assured me that he was not nervous in the least.

"My time is coming, that's all," he said; "and I don't care. A few days more or less don't signify much." An hour afterwards the poor fellow's head was blown off as he stood by my side.

One such incident — and there were many of them — served to confirm a superstitious belief in presentiments which a hundred failures of fulfillment were unable to shake. Meantime the revival went on. Prayer-meetings were held in every tent. Testaments were in every hand, and a sort of religious ecstasy took possession of the army. The men had ceased to rely upon the skill of our leaders or the strength of our army for success, and not a few of them hoped now for a miraculous interposition of supernatural power in our behalf.

Men in this mood make the best of soldiers, and at no time were the fighting qualities of the Southern army better than during the siege. Under such circumstances men do not regard death, and even the failure of any effort they were called upon to make wrought no demoralization among troops who had persuaded themselves that the Almighty held victory in store for them, and would give it them in due time. We persisted, as I have said, in vaguely hoping and trying to believe that success was still to be ours, and to that end we shut our eyes to the plainest facts, refusing to admit the truth which was everywhere evident, namely, that our efforts had failed, and that our cause was already in its death struggles. But we must have known all this, nevertheless, and our diligent cultivation of an unreasonable hopefulness served in no sensible degree to raise our spirits.

When at last the beginning of the end came, in the evacuation of Richmond and the effort to retreat, everything seemed to go to pieces at once. The best disciplinarians in the army relaxed instead of tightening their reins. The best troops became disorganized, and hardly any command marched in a body. Companies were mixed together, parts of each being separated by detachments of others. Flying citizens in vehicles of every conceivable sort accompanied and embarrassed the columns. Many commands marched heedlessly on without orders, and seemingly without a thought of whither they were going. Others mistook the meaning of their orders, and still others had instructions which it was impossible to obey in any case.

At Amelia Court House we should have found a supply of provisions. General Lee had ordered a train load to meet him there, but the interests of the starving army had been sacrificed to the convenience or the cowardice of the President and his personal following. The train had been hurried on to Richmond and its precious cargo of food thrown out there, in order that Mr. Davis and his people might retreat rapidly and comfortably from the abandoned capital. Then began the desertion of which we have heard so much. Up to that time, as far as I can learn, if desertions had occurred at all they had not become general; but now that the government, in flying from the foe, had cut off our only supply of provisions, what were the men to do? Many of them wandered off in search of food, with no thought of deserting at all. Many others followed the example of the government, and fled; but a singularly large proportion of the little whole stayed and starved to the last.

And it was no technical or metaphorical starvation which we had to endure, either, as a brief statement of my own experience will show. The battery to which I was attached was captured near Amelia Court House, and within a mile or two of my home. Seven men only escaped, and as I knew intimately everybody in the neighborhood, I had no trouble in getting horses for these to ride. Applying to General Lee in person for instructions, I was ordered to march on, using my own judgment, and rendering what service I could in the event of a battle. In this independent fashion I marched, with much better chances than most of the men had to get food, and yet during three days and nights our total supply consisted of one ear of corn to the man, and we divided that with our horses.

The end came, technically, at Appomattox, but of the real difficulties of the war the end was not yet. The trials and the perils of utter disorganization were still to be endured.

Outrages of every kind were of daily enactment, and there was no remedy. There was no State, county, or municipal government in existence among us. We had no courts, no justices of the peace, no sheriffs, no officers of any kind invested with a shadow of authority, and there were not men enough in the community, at first, to resist the marauders, comparatively few of the surrendered soldiers having found their way home as yet. Those districts in which the Federal armies were stationed were peculiarly fortunate. The troops gave protection to the people, and the commandants of posts constituted a government able to enforce order, to which outraged or threatened people could appeal. But these favored sections were only a small part of the whole. The troops were not distributed in detached bodies over the country, but were kept in considerable masses at strategic points, lest a guerrilla war should succeed regular hostilities; and so the greater part of the country was left wholly without law, at a time when law was most imperatively needed.

It is difficult to comprehend, and impossible to describe, the state of uncertainty in which we lived at this time. We had surrendered at discretion, and had no way of discovering or even of guessing what terms were to be given us. We were cut off almost wholly from trustworthy news, and in the absence of papers were unable even to rest conjecture upon the expression of sentiment at the North. Rumors we had in plenty, but so many of them were clearly false that we were forced to reject them all as probably untrue.

I think nobody in my neighborhood believed the rumor of Mr. Lincoln's assassination until it was confirmed by a Federal soldier whom I questioned upon the subject one day, a week or two after the event. When we knew that the rumor was true, we deemed it the worst news we had heard since the surrender. We distrusted President Johnson more than any one else. Regarding him as a renegade Southerner, we thought it probable that he would endeavor to prove his loyalty to the Union by extra severity to the South, and we confidently believed he would revoke the terms offered us in Mr. Lincoln's amnesty proclamation; wherefore there was a general haste to take the oath and so to secure the benefit of the dead president's clemency before his successor should establish harsher conditions.

We should have regarded Mr. Lincoln's death as a calamity, even if it had come about by natural means; and coming as it did through a crime committed in our name, it was a disaster.

1875
OLD TIMES ON THE MISSISSIPPI
by Mark Twain

WHEN I was a boy, there was but one permanent ambition among my comrades in our village on the west bank of the Mississippi River. That was, to be a steamboatman. We had transient ambitions of other sorts, but they were only transient. When a circus came and went, it left us all burning to become clowns; now and then we had a hope that if we lived and were good, God would permit us to be pirates. These ambitions faded out, each in its turn; but the ambition to be a steamboatman always remained.

Once a day a cheap, gaudy packet arrived upward from St. Louis,

and another downward from Keokuk. Before these events had transpired, the day was glorious with expectancy; after they had transpired,
the day was a dead and empty thing. Not only the boys, but the whole
village, felt this. After all these years I can picture that old time to
myself now, just as it was then: the white town drowsing in the sunshine of a summer's morning; the streets empty, or pretty nearly so;
one or two clerks sitting in front of the Water Street stores, with their
splint-bottomed chairs tilted back against the wall, chins on breasts,
hats slouched over their faces, asleep — with shingle shavings enough
around to show what broke them down; a sow and a litter of pigs
loafing along the sidewalk, doing a good business in water-melon rinds
and seeds; two or three lonely little freight piles scattered about the
levee; a pile of skids on the slope of the stone-paved wharf, and the
fragrant town drunkard asleep in the shadow of them; two or three
wood flats at the head of the wharf, but nobody to listen to the peaceful lapping of the wavelets against them; the great Mississippi, the
majestic, the magnificent Mississippi, rolling its mile-wide tide along,
shining in the sun; the dense forest away on the other side; the point
above the town, and the point below, bounding the river glimpse and
turning it into a sort of sea, and withal a very still and brilliant and
lonely one. Presently a film of dark smoke appears above one of those
remote points; instantly a negro drayman, famous for his quick eye
and prodigious voice, lifts up the cry, "S-t-e-a-m-boat a-comin'!" and
the scene changes! The town drunkard stirs, the clerks wake up, a
furious clatter of drays follows, every house and store pours out a
human contribution, and all in a twinkling the dead town is alive and
moving. Drays, carts, men, boys, all go hurrying from many quarters
to a common centre, the wharf.

Assembled there, the people fasten their eyes upon the coming boat
as upon a wonder they are seeing for the first time. And the boat *is*
rather a handsome sight, too. She is long and sharp and trim and
pretty; she has two tall, fancy-topped chimneys, with a gilded device of
some kind swung between them; a fanciful pilot-house, all glass and
gingerbread, perched on top of the texas deck behind them; the pad-
dle-boxes are gorgeous with a picture or with gilded rays above the
boat's name; the boiler deck, the hurricane deck, and the texas deck
are fenced and ornamented with clean white railings; there is a flag
gallantly flying from the jack-staff; the furnace doors are open and
the fires glaring bravely; the upper decks are black with passengers;
the captain stands by the big bell, calm, imposing, the envy of all; great
volumes of the blackest smoke are rolling and tumbling out of the
chimneys — a husbanded grandeur created with a bit of pitch pine
just before arriving at a town; the crew are grouped on the forecastle;

the broad stage is run far out over the port bow, and an envied deck-hand stands picturesquely on the end of it with a coil of rope in his hand; the pent steam is screaming through the gauge-cocks; the captain lifts his hand, a bell rings, the wheels stop; then they turn back, churning the water to foam, and the steamer is at rest. Then such a scramble as there is to get aboard, and to get ashore, and to take in freight and to discharge freight, all at one and the same time; and such a yelling and cursing as the mates facilitate it all with! Ten minutes later the steamer is under way again, with no flag on the jack-staff and no black smoke issuing from the chimneys. After ten more minutes the town is dead again, and the town drunkard asleep by the skids once more.

My father was a justice of the peace, and I supposed he possessed the power of life and death over all men and could hang anybody that offended him. This was distinction enough for me as a general thing; but the desire to be a steamboatman kept intruding, nevertheless. I first wanted to be a cabin-boy, so that I could come out with a white apron on and shake a table-cloth over the side, where all my old comrades could see me; later I thought I would rather be the deck-hand who stood on the end of the stage-plank with the coil of rope in his hand, because he was particularly conspicuous. But these were only daydreams — they were too heavenly to be contemplated as real possibilities.

By and by one of our boys went away. He was not heard of for a long time. At last he turned up as apprentice engineer or "striker" on a steamboat. This thing shook the bottom out of all my Sunday-school teachings. That boy had been notoriously worldly, and I just the reverse; yet he was exalted to this eminence, and I left in obscurity and misery. There was nothing generous about this fellow in his greatness. He would always manage to have a rusty bolt to scrub while his boat tarried at our town, and he would sit on the inside guard and scrub it, where we could all see him and envy him and loathe him. And whenever his boat was laid up he would come home and swell around the town in his blackest and greasiest clothes, so that nobody could help remembering that he was a steamboatman; and he used all sorts of steamboat technicalities in his talk, as if he were so used to them that he forgot common people could not understand them. He would speak of the "labboard" side of a horse in an easy, natural way that would make one wish he was dead. And he was always talking about "St. Looy" like an old citizen; he would refer casually to occasions when he "was coming down Fourth Street," or when he was "passing by the Planter's House," or when there was a fire and he took a turn on the brakes of "the old Big Missouri;" and then he would go on and lie about how many towns the size of ours were burned down there that day.

This fellow had money, too, and hair oil. Also an ignorant silver watch and a showy brass watch chain. He wore a leather belt and used no suspenders. If ever a youth was cordially admired and hated by his comrades, this one was. No girl could withstand his charms. He cut out every boy in the village. When his boat blew up at last, it diffused a tranquil contentment among us such as we had not known for months. But when he came home the next week, alive, renowned, and appeared in church all battered up and bandaged, a shining hero, stared at and wondered over by everybody, it seemed to us that the partiality of Providence for an undeserving reptile had reached a point where it was open to criticism.

This creature's career could produce but one result, and it speedily followed. Boy after boy managed to get on the river. The minister's son became an engineer. The doctor's and the postmaster's sons became "mud clerks;" the wholesale liquor dealer's son became a barkeeper on a boat; four sons of the chief merchant, and two sons of the county judge, became pilots. Pilot was the grandest position of all. The pilot, even in those days of trivial wages, had a princely salary — from a hundred and fifty to two hundred and fifty dollars a month, and no board to pay. Two months of his wages would pay a preacher's salary for a year. Now some of us were left disconsolate. We could not get on the river — at least our parents would not let us.

So by and by I ran away. I said I never would come home again till I was a pilot and could come in glory. But somehow I could not manage it. I went meekly aboard a few of the boats that lay packed together like sardines at the long St. Louis wharf, and very humbly inquired for the pilots, but got only a cold shoulder and short words from mates and clerks. I had to make the best of this sort of treatment for the time being, but I had comforting daydreams of a future when I should be a great and honored pilot, with plenty of money, and could kill some of these mates and clerks and pay for them.

Months afterward the hope within me struggled to a reluctant death, and I found myself without an ambition. But I was ashamed to go home. I was in Cincinnati, and I set to work to map out a new career. I packed my valise, and took passage on an ancient tub called the *Paul Jones,* for New Orleans. For the sum of sixteen dollars I had the scarred and tarnished splendors of her main saloon principally to myself, for she was not a creature to attract the eye of wiser travelers.

When we presently got under way and went poking down the broad Ohio, I became a new being, and the subject of my own admiration. I was a traveler! A word never had tasted so good in my mouth before.

I had an exultant sense of being bound for mysterious lands and distant climes which I never have felt in so uplifting a degree since.

We reached Louisville in time — at least the neighborhood of it. We stuck hard and fast on the rocks in the middle of the river and lay there four days. I was now beginning to feel a strong sense of being a part of the boat's family, a sort of infant son to the captain and younger brother to the officers. There is no estimating the pride I took in this grandeur, or the affection that began to swell and grow in me for those people. I could not know how the lordly steamboatman scorns that sort of presumption in a mere landsman. I particularly longed to acquire the least trifle of notice from the big stormy mate, and I was on the alert for an opportunity to do him a service to that end. It came at last. The riotous powwow of setting a spar was going on down on the forecastle, and I went down there and stood around in the way — or mostly skipping out of it — till the mate suddenly roared a general order for somebody to bring him a capstan bar. I sprang to his side and said: "Tell me where it is — I'll fetch it!"

If a rag-picker had offered to do a diplomatic service for the Emperor of Russia, the monarch could not have been more astounded than the mate was. He even stopped swearing. He stood and stared down at me. It took him ten seconds to scrape his disjointed remains together again. Then he said impressively: "Well, if this don't beat hell!" and turned to his work with the air of a man who had been confronted with a problem too abstruse for solution.

I crept away, and courted solitude for the rest of the day. I did not go to dinner; I stayed away from supper until everybody else had finished. I did not feel so much like a member of the boat's family now as before. However, my spirits returned, in installments, as we pursued our way down the river. I was sorry I hated the mate so, because it was not in (young) human nature not to admire him. He was huge and muscular, his face was bearded and whiskered all over; he had a red woman and a blue woman tatooed on his right arm, — one on each side of a blue anchor with a red rope to it; and in the matter of profanity he was perfect. When he was getting out cargo at a landing, I was always where I could see and hear. He felt all the sublimity of his great position, and made the world feel it, too. When he gave even the simplest order, he discharged it like a blast of lightning, and sent a long, reverberating peal of profanity thundering after it. I could not help contrasting the way in which the average landsman would give an order, with the mate's way of doing it. If the landsman should wish the gang-plank moved a foot farther forward, he would probably say: "James, or William, one of you push that plank forward, please;" but put the mate in his place, and he would roar out: "Here, now, start that gang-plank for'ard! Lively, now! *What*'re you about! Snatch it!

snatch it! There! there! Aft again! aft again! Don't you hear me? Dash it to dash! are you going to *sleep* over it! *'Vast* heaving. 'Vast heaving, I tell you! Going to heave it clear astern? WHERE're you going with that barrel! *for'ard* with it 'fore I make you swallow it, you dash-dash-dash-*dashed* split between a tired mud-turtle and a crippled hearse-horse!"

I wished I could talk like that.

When the soreness of my adventure with the mate had somewhat worn off, I began timidly to make up to the humblest official connected with the boat — the night watchman. He snubbed my advances at first, but I presently ventured to offer him a new chalk pipe, and that softened him. So he allowed me to sit with him by the big bell on the hurricane deck, and in time he melted into conversation. He could not well have helped it, I hung with such homage on his words and so plainly showed that I felt honored by his notice. He told me the names of dim capes and shadowy islands as we glided by them in the solemnity of the night, under the winking stars, and by and by got to talking about himself.

He seemed over-sentimental for a man whose salary was six dollars a week — or rather he might have seemed so to an older person than I. But I drank in his words hungrily, and with a faith that might have moved mountains if it had been applied judiciously. What was it to me that he was soiled and seedy and fragrant with gin? What was it to me that his grammar was bad, his construction worse, and his profanity so void of art that it was an element of weakness rather than strength in his conversation? He was a wronged man, a man who had seen trouble, and that was enough for me.

As he mellowed into his plaintive history his tears dripped upon the lantern in his lap, and I cried, too, from sympathy. He said he was the son of an English nobleman — either an earl or an alderman, he could not remember which, but believed he was both; his father, the nobleman, loved him, but his mother hated him from the cradle; and so while he was still a little boy he was sent to "one of them old, ancient colleges" — he couldn't remember which; and by and by his father died and his mother seized the property and "shook" him, as he phrased it. After his mother shook him, members of the nobility with whom he was acquainted used their influence to get him the position of "lob-lolly-boy in a ship;" and from that point my watchman threw off all trammels of date and locality and branched out into a narrative that bristled all along with incredible adventures; a narrative that was so reeking with bloodshed and so crammed with hair-breadth escapes and the most engaging and unconscious personal villainies, that I sat speechless, enjoying, shuddering, wondering, worshiping.

It was a sore blight to find out afterwards that he was a low, vulgar,

ignorant, sentimental, half-witted humbug, an untraveled native of the
wilds of Illinois, who had absorbed wildcat literature and appropriated
its marvels, until in time he had woven odds and ends of the mess into
this yarn, and then gone on telling it to fledgelings like me, until he
had come to believe it himself.

1876

AN ODE FOR THE FOURTH OF JULY, 1876
by James Russell Lowell

. . .

FLAWLESS his heart and tempered to the core
Who, beckoned by the forward-leaning wave,
First left behind him the firm-footed shore,
And, urged by every nerve of sail and oar,
Steered for the Unknown which gods to mortals gave,
Of thought and action the mysterious door,
Bugbear of fools, a summons to the brave:
Strength found he in the unsympathizing sun,
And strange stars from beneath the horizon won,
And the dumb ocean pitilessly grave:
High-hearted surely he;
But bolder they who first off-cast
Their moorings from the habitable Past
And ventured chartless on the sea
Of storm-engendering Liberty:
For all earth's width of waters is a span,
And their convulsed existence mere repose,
Matched with the unstable heart of man,
Shoreless in wants, mist-girt in all it knows,
Open to every wind of sect or clan,
And sudden-passionate in ebbs and flows.

They steered by stars the elder shipmen knew,
And laid their courses where the currents draw
Of ancient wisdom channeled deep in law,
The undaunted few
Who changed the Old World for the New,
And more devoutly prized
Than all perfection theorized
The more imperfect that had roots and grew.
They founded deep and well,

Those danger-chosen chiefs of men
Who still believed in Heaven and Hell,
Nor hoped to find a spell,
In some fine flourish of a pen,
To make a better man
Than long-considering Nature will or can,
Secure against his own mistakes,
Content with what life gives or takes,
And acting still on some fore ordered plan,
A cog of iron in an iron wheel,
Too nicely poised to think or feel,
Dumb motor in a clock-like commonweal.
They wasted not their brain in schemes
Of what man might be in some bubble-sphere,
As if he must be other than he seems
Because he was not what he should be here,
Postponing Time's slow proof to petulant dreams:
Yet herein they were great
Beyond the incredulous lawgivers of yore,
And wiser than the wisdom of the shelf,
That they conceived a deeper-rooted state,
Of hardier growth, alive from rind to core,
By making man sole sponsor of himself.

God of our fathers, Thou who wast,
Art, and shalt be when the eye-wise who flout
Thy secret presence shall be lost
In the great light that dazzles them to doubt,
We, sprung from loins of stalwart men
Whose strength was in their trust
That Thou would'st make thy dwelling in their dust
And walk with them a fellow-citizen
Who build a city of the just,
We, who believe Life's bases rest
Beyond the probe of chemic test,
Still, like our fathers, feel Thee near,
Sure that, while lasts the immutable decree,
The land to Human Nature dear
Shall not be unbeloved of Thee.

THE AMERICAN CONGRESS
After Its First Century
by James A. Garfield

CONGRESS has always been and must always be the theater of contending opinions; the forum where the opposing forces of political philosophy meet to measure their strength; where the public good must meet the assaults of local and sectional interests; in a word, the appointed place where the nation seeks to utter its thought and register its will.

Now, more than ever before, the people are responsible for the character of their Congress. If that body be ignorant, reckless, and corrupt, it is because the people tolerate ignorance, recklessness, and corruption. If it be intelligent, brave, and pure, it is because the people demand those high qualities to represent them in the national legislature. Congress lives in the blaze of "that fierce light which beats against the throne." The telegraph and the press will to-morrow morning announce at a million breakfast tables what has been said and done in Congress to-day. Now, as always, Congress represents the prevailing opinions and political aspirations of the people. The wildest delusions of paper money, the crudest theories of taxation, the passions and prejudices that find expression in the senate and house, were first believed and discussed at the firesides of the people, on the corners of the streets, and in the caucuses and conventions of political parties.

The most alarming feature of our situation is the fact that so many citizens of high character and solid judgment pay but little attention to the sources of political power, to the selection of those who shall make their laws.

There have always been, and always will be, bad men in all human pursuits. There was a Judas in the college of the apostles, an Arnold in the army of the Revolution, a Burr in our early politics; and they have had successors in all departments of modern life. But it is demonstrable, as a matter of history, that on the whole the standard of public and private morals is higher in the United States at the present time than ever before; that men in public and private stations are held to a more rigid accountability, and that the average moral tone of Congress is higher to-day than at any previous period of our history. It is certainly true that our late war disturbed the established order of society, awakened a reckless spirit of adventure and speculation, and greatly multiplied the opportunities and increased the temptations to evil. The disorganization of the Southern States and the temporary disfranchisement of its leading citizens threw a portion of their representation in Congress, for a short time, into the hands of political adventurers, many of whom used their brief hold on power for personal ends, and thus brought disgrace upon the national legislature. And it is also true that the enlarged sphere of legislation so mingled public duties and private interests that it was not easy to draw the line between them. From that cause also the reputation, and in some cases the character, of public men suffered eclipse. But the earnestness and vigor with which wrong-doing is everywhere punished is a strong guaranty of the purity of those who may hold posts of authority and honor. Indeed, there is now danger in the opposite direction, namely, that criticism may degenerate into mere slander, and put an end to its power for good by being used as the means to assassinate the reputation and destroy the usefulness of honorable men. It is as much the duty of all good men to protect and defend the reputation of worthy public servants as to detect and punish public rascals.

In a word, our national safety demands that the fountains of political power shall be made pure by intelligence, and kept pure by vigilance; that the best citizens shall take heed to the selection and election of the worthiest and most intelligent among them to hold seats in the national legislature; and that when the choice has been made, the continuance of their representative shall depend upon his faithfulness, his ability, and his willingness to work.

Congress must always be the exponent of the political character and culture of the people; and if the next centennial does not find us a great nation, with a great and worthy Congress, it will be because those who represent the enterprise, the culture, and the morality of the nation do not aid in controlling the political forces which are employed to select the men who shall occupy the great places of trust and power.

1878
A FIGHT WITH A TROUT
by Charles Dudley Warner

TROUT-FISHING in the Adirondacks would be a more attractive pastime than it is, but for the popular notion of its danger. The trout is a retiring and harmless animal, except when he is aroused and forced into a combat, and then his agility, fierceness, and vindictiveness become apparent. No one who has studied the excellent pictures representing men in an open boat exposed to the assaults of long, enraged trout, flying at them through the air with open mouth, ever ventures with his rod upon the lonely lakes of the forest without a certain terror, or ever reads of the exploits of daring fishermen without a feeling of admiration for their heroism. Most of their adventures are thrilling, and all of them are in narration more or less unjust to the trout; in fact, the object of them seems to be to exhibit, at the expense of the trout, the shrewdness, the skill, and the muscular power of the sportsman. My own simple story has few of these recommendations.

We had built our bark camp one summer, and were staying on one of the popular lakes of the Saranac region. It would be a very pretty region if it were not so flat; and if the margins of the lakes had not been flooded by dams at the outlets, which have killed the trees and left a rim of ghastly dead-wood — like the swamps of the under-world pictured by Doré's bizarre pencil; and if the pianos at the hotels were in tune. It would be an excellent sporting region also (for there is water enough) if the fish commissioners would stock the waters; and if previous hunters had not pulled all the hair and skin off from the deer's tails.

We had been hearing for weeks of a small lake in the heart of the virgin forest, some ten miles from our camp, which was alive with trout, unsophisticated, hungry trout; the inlet to it was described as *stiff* with them. In my imagination I saw them lying there in ranks and rows, each a foot long, three tiers deep, a solid mass. The lake had never been visited, except by stray sable-hunters in the winter, and was known as the Unknown Pond. I determined to explore it, fully expecting, however, that it would prove to be a delusion, as such mysterious haunts of the trout usually are. Confiding my purpose to my guide Luke, we secretly made our preparations, and stole away from the shanty one morning at day-break. Each of us carried a boat, a pair of blankets, a sack of bread, pork, and maple-sugar; while I had my case of rods, creel, and book of flies; and Luke had an axe and the kitchen utensils. We think nothing of loads of this sort in the woods.

Five miles, through a tamarack swamp, brought us to the inlet of Unknown Pond, upon which we embarked our fleet, and paddled down its vagrant waters. They were at first sluggish, winding among *triste* fir-trees, but gradually developed a strong current. At the end of three miles a loud roar ahead warned us that we were approaching rapids, falls, and cascades. We paused. The danger was unknown. We had our choice of shouldering our loads and making a *détour* through the woods, or of "shooting the rapids." Naturally we chose the more dangerous course. Shooting the rapids has often been described, and I will not repeat the description here. It is needless to say that I drove my frail bark through the boiling rapids, over the successive waterfalls, amid rocks and vicious eddies, and landed, half a mile below, with whitened hair and a boat half full of water; and that the guide was upset, and boat, contents, and man were strewn along the shore.

After this common experience we went quickly on our journey, and a couple of hours before sundown reached the lake. If I live to my dying day, I never shall forget its appearance. The lake is almost an exact circle, about a quarter of a mile in diameter. The forest about it was untouched by axe, and unkilled by artificial flooding. The azure water had a perfect setting of evergreens, in which all the shades of the fir, the balsam, the pine, and the spruce were perfectly blended, and at intervals on the shore in the emerald rim blazed the ruby of the cardinal flower. It was at once evident that the unruffled waters had never been vexed by the keel of a boat. But what chiefly attracted my attention and amused me was that the water boiled with the breaking trout. I studied the surface for some time to see upon what sort of flies they were feeding, in order to suit my cast to their appetites; but they seemed to be at play rather than feeding, leaping high in the air in graceful curves and tumbling about each other as we see them in the Adirondack pictures.

It is well known that no person who regards his reputation will ever kill a trout with anything but a fly. It requires some training on the part of the trout to take to this method. The uncultivated, unsophisticated trout, in unfrequented waters, prefers the bait; and the rural people, whose sole object in going a-fishing appears to be to catch fish, indulge them in their primitive taste for the worm. No sportsman, however, will use anything but a fly, except he happens to be alone.

While Luke launched my boat and arranged his seat in the stern, I prepared my rod and line. The rod is a bamboo, weighing seven ounces, which has to be spliced with a winding of silk thread every time it is used; this is a tedious process, but by fastening the joints in this way a uniform spring is secured in the rod; no one devoted to high art would think of using a socket joint. My line was forty yards of untwisted silk upon a multiplying reel. The "leader" — I am very particular about my leaders — had been made to order from a domestic animal with which I had been acquainted. The fisherman requires as good a cat-gut as the violinist. The interior of the house cat, it is well known, is exceedingly sensitive; but it may not be so well known that the reason why some cats leave the room in distress when a pianoforte is played is because the two instruments are not in the same key, and the vibration of the chords of the one are in discord with the cat-gut of the other. On six feet of this superior article I fixed three artificial flies: a simple brown hackle, a gray body with scarlet wings, and one of my own invention, which I thought would be new to the most experienced fly-catcher. The trout-fly does not resemble any known species of insect. It is a "conventionalized" creation, as we say of ornamentation. The theory is that fly-fishing being a high art, the fly must not be a tame imitation of nature, but an artistic suggestion of it. It requires an artist to construct one; and not every bungler can take a bit of red flannel, a peacock's feather, a flash of tinsel thread, a cock's plume, a section of a hen's wing, and fabricate a tiny object that will not look like any fly, but still will suggest the universal conventional fly.

I took my stand in the centre of the tipsy boat, and Luke shoved off and slowly paddled towards some lily pads, while I began casting, unlimbering my tools as it were. The fish had all disappeared. I got out perhaps fifty feet of line, with no response, and gradually increased it to one hundred. It is not difficult to learn to cast, but it is difficult to learn not to snap off the flies at every throw. Of this, however, we will not speak.

I continued casting for some moments, until I became satisfied that there had been a miscalculation. Either the trout were too green to know what I was at, or they were dissatisfied with my offers. I reeled in, and changed the flies (that is, the fly that was not snapped off). After studying the color of the sky, of the water, and of the foliage, and the moderated light of the afternoon, I put on a series of beguilers, all of a subdued brilliancy, in harmony with the approach of evening. At the second cast, which was a short one, I saw a splash where the leader fell, and gave an excited jerk. The next instant I perceived the game, and did not need the unfeigned "dam" of Luke to convince me that I had snatched his felt hat from his head and deposited it among the lilies.

Discouraged by this, we whirled about and paddled over to the inlet, where a little ripple was visible in the tinted light. At the very first cast I saw that the hour had come. Three trout leaped into the air. The danger of this manœuvre all fishermen understand; it is one of the commonest in the woods; three heavy trout taking hold at once, rushing in different directions, smash the tackle into flinders. I evaded this catch, and threw again.

I recall the moment. A hermit thrush on the tip of a balsam uttered his long, liquid, evening note. Happening to look over my shoulder I saw the peak of Marcy gleam rosy in the sky (I can't help it that Marcy is fifty miles off, and cannot be seen from this region; these incidental touches are always used). The hundred feet of silk swished through the air and the tail fly fell as lightly on the water as a three-cent piece (which no slamming will give the weight of a ten) drops upon the contribution plate. Instantly there was a rush, a swirl; I struck; and "Got him by — !" Never mind what Luke said I got him by. "Out on a fly!" continued that irreverent guide, but I told him to back water and make for the centre of the lake.

The trout, as soon as he felt the prick of the hook, was off like a shot, and took out the whole of the line with a rapidity that made it smoke. "Give him the butt!" shouted Luke. It is the usual remark in such an emergency. I gave him the butt, and, recognizing the fact and my spirit, the trout at once sunk to the bottom and sulked. It is the most dangerous mood of a trout, for you cannot tell what he will do next. We reeled up a little, and waited five minutes for him to reflect. A tightening of the line enraged him, and he soon developed his tactics. Coming to the surface, he made straight for the boat, faster than I could reel in, and evidently with hostile intentions. "Look out for him!" cried Luke, as he came flying in the air. I evaded him by dropping flat in the bottom of the boat, and when I picked my traps up he was spinning across the lake as if he had a new idea; but the line was still fast. He did not run far. I gave him the butt again, a thing he seemed to hate, even as a gift; in a moment the evil-minded fish, lashing the water in his rage, was coming back again, making straight for the boat as before.

Luke, who was used to these encounters, having read of them in the writings of travelers he had accompanied, raised his paddle in self-defense. The trout left the water about ten feet from the boat and came directly at me, with fiery eyes, his speckled sides flashing like a meteor. I dodged, as he whisked by with a vicious slap of his bifurcated tail, and nearly upset the boat. The line was of course slack, and the danger was that he would entangle it about me and carry away a leg. This was evidently his game. But I untangled it, and only lost a breast button or two by the swiftly moving string. The trout plunged into the water with a hissing sound, and went away again with all the line on the reel. More butt. More indignation on the part of the captive.

The contest had now been going on for half an hour, and I was getting exhausted. We had been back and forth across the lake, and round and round the lake; what I feared was that the trout would start up the inlet and wreck us in the bushes. But he had a new fancy, and began the execution of a manœuvre which I had never read of. Instead of coming straight towards me he took a large circle, swimming rapidly and *gradually contracting his orbit*. I reeled in, and kept my eye on him. Round and round he went, narrowing his circle. I began to suspect the game, which was to twist my head off. When he had reduced the radius of his circle to about twenty-five feet, he struck a tremendous pace through the water. It would be false modesty in a sportsman to say that I was not equal to the occasion. Instead of turning round with him as he expected, I stepped to the bow, braced myself, and let the boat swing. Round went the fish, and round we went like a top. I saw a line of Mt. Marcys all round the horizon. The rosy tint in the west made a broad band of pink along the sky above the tree-tops. The evening star was a perfect circle of light, a hoop of gold in the heavens. We whirled and reeled, and reeled and whirled. I was willing to give the malicious beast butt and line and all, if he would only go the other way for a change.

When I came to myself, Luke was gaffing the trout at the boat-side. After we had got him in and dressed him, he weighed three-quarters of a pound. Fish always lose by being "got in and dressed." It is best to weigh them while they are in the water. The only really large one I ever caught got away with my leader when I first struck him. He weighed ten pounds.

1879
BUYING A HORSE
by William Dean Howells

I F one has money enough, there seems no reason why one should not go and buy such a horse as he wants. This is the commonly accepted theory, on which the whole commerce in horses is founded, and on which my friend proceeded.

He was about removing from Charlesbridge, where he had lived many happy years without a horse, further into the country, where there were charming drives and inconvenient distances, and where a horse would be very desirable, if not quite necessary. But as a horse seemed at first an extravagant if not sinful desire, he began by talking vaguely round, and rather hinting than declaring that he thought somewhat of buying. The professor to whom he first intimated his purpose flung himself from his horse's back to the grassy border of the sidewalk where my friend stood, and said he would give him a few points. "In the first place, don't buy a horse that shows much daylight under him, unless you buy a horse-doctor *with* him; get a short-legged horse; and he ought to be short and thick in the barrel," — or words to that effect. "Don't get a horse with a narrow forehead: there are horse-fools as well as the other kind, and you want a horse with room for brains. And look out that he's *all right forward*."

"What's that?" asked my friend, hearing this phrase for the first time.

"That he isn't tender in his forefeet, — that the hoof isn't contracted," said the professor, pointing out the well-planted foot of his own animal.

"What ought I to pay for a horse?" pursued my friend, struggling to fix the points given by the professor in a mind hitherto unused to points of the kind.

"Well, horses are cheap, now; and you ought to get a fair family horse — You want a family horse?"

"Yes."

"Something you can ride and drive both? Something your children can drive?"

"Yes, yes."

"Well, you ought to get such a horse as that for a hundred and twenty-five dollars."

This was the figure my friend had thought of; he drew a breath of relief. "Where did you buy your horse?"

"Oh, I always get my horses" — the plural abashed my friend — "at the Chevaliers'. If you throw yourself on their mercy, they'll treat you well. I'll send you a note to them."

"Do!" cried my friend, as the professor sprang upon his horse, and galloped away.

My friend walked home encouraged; his purpose of buying a horse had not seemed so monstrous, at least to this hardened offender. He now began to announce it more boldly; he said right and left that he wished to buy a horse, but that he would not go above a hundred. This was not true, but he wished to act prudently, and to pay a hundred and twenty-five only in extremity. He carried the professor's note to the Chevaliers', who duly honored it, understood at once what my friend wanted, and said they would look out for him. They were sorry he had not happened in a little sooner, — they had just sold the very horse he wanted. I may as well say here that they were not able to find him a horse, but that they used him with the strictest honor, and that short of supplying his want they were perfect.

In the mean time the irregular dealers began to descend upon him, as well as amateurs to whom he had mentioned his wish for a horse, and his premises at certain hours of the morning presented the effect of a horse-fair, or say rather a museum of equine bricabrac. At first he blushed at the spectacle, but he soon became hardened to it, and liked the excitement of driving one horse after another round the block, and deciding upon him. To a horse, they had none of the qualities commended by the professor, but they had many others which the dealers praised. These persons were not discouraged when he refused to buy, but cheerfully returned the next day with others differently ruinous. They were men of a spirit more obliging than my friend has found in other walks. One of them, who paid him a prefatory visit in his library, in five minutes augmented from six to seven hundred and fifty pounds the weight of a pony-horse, which he wished to sell. ("What you want," said the Chevaliers, "is a pony-horse," and my friend, gratefully catching at the phrase, had gone about saying he wanted a pony-horse. After that, hulking brutes of from eleven to thirteen hundred pounds were every day brought to him as pony-horses.) The same dealer came another day with a mustang, in whom was no fault, and who had every appearance of speed, but who was only marking time, as it is called in military drill, I believe, when he seemed to be getting swiftly over the ground; he showed a sociable preference for the curbstone in turning corners, and was condemned, to be replaced the next evening by a pony-horse that a child might ride or drive, and that especially would not shy. Upon experiment, he shied half across the road, and the fact was reported to the dealer. He smiled compassionately. "What did he shy *at?*"

"A wheelbarrow."

"Well! I never see the hoss *yet* that *wouldn't* shy at a wheelbarrow."

The dealers had a jargon of their own, in which my friend became an expert. They did not say that a horse weighed a thousand pounds, but ten hundred; he was not worth a hundred and twenty-five dollars, but one and a quarter; he was not going on seven years old, but was coming seven. There are curious facts, by the way, in regard to the age of horses which are not generally known. A horse is never of an even age: that is, he is not six, or eight, or ten, but five, or seven, or nine years old; he is sometimes, but not often, eleven; he is *never* thirteen; his favorite time of life is seven, and he rarely gets beyond it, if on sale. My friend found the number of horses brought into the world in 1871 quite beyond computation. He also found that most hard-working horses were sick or ailing, as most hard-working men and women are; that perfectly sound horses are as rare as perfectly sound human beings, and are apt, like the latter, to be vicious.

He began to have a quick eye for the characteristics of horses, and could walk round a proffered animal and scan his points with the best. "What," he would ask, of a given beast, "makes him let his lower lip hang down in that imbecile manner?"

"Oh, he's got a parrot-mouth. Some folks like 'em." Here the dealer would pull open the creature's flabby lips, and discover a beak like that of a polyp; and the cleansing process on the grass or trousers would take place.

Of another, "What makes him trot in that spread-out, squatty way, behind?" he demanded, after the usual tour of the block.

"He travels wide. Horse men prefer that."

In the course of long talks, which frequently took the form of warnings, my friend became wise in the tricks practiced by all dealers. One of these, a device for restoring youth to an animal nearing the dangerous limit of eleven, struck him as peculiarly ingenious. You pierce the forehead, and blow into it with a quill; this gives an agreeable fullness, and erects the drooping ears in a spirited and mettlesome manner, so that a horse coming eleven will look for a time as if he were coming five.

I pass over an unprofitable interval in which he abandoned himself to despair, and really gave up the hope of being able ever to buy a horse. During this interval he removed from Charlesbridge to the country, and found himself, to his self-scorn and self-pity, actually reduced to hiring a livery horse by the day. But relief was at hand. The carpenter who had remained to finish up the new house after my friend had gone into it bethought himself of a firm in his place who brought on horses from the West, and had the practice of selling a horse on trial, and constantly replacing it with other horses till the purchaser was suited. This seemed an ideal arrangement, and the carpenter said that he *thought* they had the very horse my friend wanted.

The next day he drove him up, and upon the plan of successive exchanges till the perfect horse was reached my friend bought him for one and a quarter, the figure which he had kept in mind from the first. He bought a phaeton and harness from the same people, and when the whole equipage stood at his door he felt the long-delayed thrill of pride and satisfaction. The horse was of the Morgan breed, a bright bay, small and round and neat, with a little head tossed high, and a gentle yet alert movement. He was in the prime of youth, of the age of which every horse desires to be, and was just coming seven. My friend had already taken him to a horse-doctor, who for one dollar had gone all over him, and pronounced him sound as a fish, and complimented his new owner upon his acquisition. It all seemed too good to be true. As Billy turned his soft eye on the admiring family group, and suffered one of the children to smooth his nose while another held a lump of sugar to his dainty lips, his amiable behavior restored my friend to his peace of mind and his long-lost faith in a world of reason.

One evening after tea, the young gentleman who was about to drive Billy out, stung by the reflection that he had not taken blackberries and cream twice, ran into the house to repair the omission, and left Billy, as usual, unhitched at the door. During his absence, Billy caught sight of his stable, and involuntarily moved towards it. Finding himself unchecked, he gently increased his pace; and when my friend, looking up from the melon-patch which he was admiring, called out, "Ho, Billy! Whoa, Billy!" and headed him off from the gap, Billy profited by the circumstance to turn into the pear orchard. The elastic turf under his unguided hoof seemed to exhilarate him; his pace became a trot, a canter, a gallop, a tornado; the reins fluttered like ribbons in the air; the phaeton flew ruining after. In a terrible cyclone the equipage swept round the neighbor's house, vanished, reappeared, swooped down his lawn, and vanished again. It was incredible.

My friend stood transfixed among his melons. He knew that his neighbor's children played under the porte-cochère on the other side of the house which Billy had just surrounded in his flight, and probably . . . My friend's first impulse was not to go and see, but to walk into his own house, and ignore the whole affair. But you cannot really ignore an affair of that kind. You must face it, and commonly it stares you out of countenance. Commonly, too, it knows how to choose its time so as to disgrace as well as crush its victim. His neighbor had people to tea, and long before my friend reached the house the host and his guests were all out on the lawn, having taken the precaution to bring their napkins with them.

At the foot of a stone-wall four feet high lay the phaeton, with three wheels in the air, and the fourth crushed flat against the axle; the willow back was broken, the shafts were pulled out, and Billy was gone.

Some half-grown boys got the phaeton right-side up, and restored its shafts and cushions, and it limped away with them towards the carriage-house. Presently another half-grown boy came riding Billy up the hill. Billy showed an inflated nostril and an excited eye, but physically he was unharmed, save for a slight scratch on what was described as the off hind-leg; the reader may choose which leg this was.

"The worst of it is," said a guest, "that you never can trust 'em after they've run off once."

"Have some tea?" said the host to my friend.

"No, thank you," said my friend, in whose heart the worst of it rankled; and he walked home embittered by his guilty consciousness that Billy ought never to have been left untied. But it was not this self-reproach; it was not the mutilated phaeton; it was not the loss of Billy, who must now be sold; it was the wreck of settled hopes, the renewed suspense of faith, the repetition of the tragical farce of buying another horse, that most grieved my friend.

My friend remained grieving over his own folly and carelessness, with a fond hankering for the poor little horse he had lost, and the belief that he should never find such another.

"Look here," said his neighbor, finding him in this low state, "why don't you get a horse of the gentleman who furnishes mine?" This had been suggested before, and my friend explained that he had disliked to make trouble. His scruples were lightly set aside, and he suffered himself to be entreated. The fact was he was so discouraged with his attempt to buy a horse that if any one had now given him such a horse as he wanted he would have taken it.

One sunny, breezy morning his neighbor drove my friend over to the beautiful farm of the good genius on whose kindly offices he had now fixed his languid hopes.

The possessor of this luscious realm at once took my friend's case into consideration; he listened, the owner of a hundred horses, with gentle indulgence to the shapeless desires of a man whose wildest dream was *one* horse. At the end he said, "I see; you want a horse that can take care of himself."

"No," replied my friend, with the inspiration of despair. "I want a horse that can take care of me."

The good genius laughed, and turned the conversation. The three had a glass of sherry; from time to time something was casually murmured about Frank. My friend felt that he was in good hands, and left the affair to them. It ended in a visit to the stable, where it appeared that this gentleman had no horse to sell among his hundred which exactly met my friend's want, but that he proposed to lend him Frank while a certain other animal was put in training for the difficult office he required of a horse. One of the men was sent for Frank, and in the mean time my friend was shown some gaunt and graceful thoroughbreds, and taught to see the difference between them and the plebeian horse. But Frank, though no thoroughbred, eclipsed these patricians when he came. He had a little head, and a neck gallantly arched; he was black and plump and smooth, and though he carried himself with a petted air, and was a dandy to the tips of his hooves, his knowing eye was kindly. He turned it upon my friend with the effect of understanding *his* case at a glance.

Frank was not merely not coming seven or nine, but his age was an even number, — he was sixteen; and it was his owner's theory, which Frank supported, that if a horse was well used he was a good horse till twenty-five.

The truth is that Frank looked like a young horse; he was a dandy without any of the ghastliness which attends the preservation of youth in old beaux of another species. When my friend drove him in the rehabilitated phaeton he felt that the turn-out was stylish, and he learned to consult certain eccentricities of Frank's in the satisfaction of his pride. One of these was a high reluctance to be passed on the road. Frank was as lazy a horse — but lazy in a self-respectful, æsthetic way — as ever was; yet if he heard a vehicle at no matter how great distance behind him (and he always heard it before his driver), he brightened with resolution and defiance, and struck out with speed that made competition difficult. If my friend found that the horse behind was likely to pass Frank, he made a merit of holding him in. If they met a team, he lay back in his phaeton, and affected not to care to be going faster than a walk, any way.

One of the things for which he chiefly prized Frank was his skill in backing and turning. He is one of those men who become greatly perturbed when required to back and turn a vehicle; he cannot tell (till too late) whether he ought to pull the right rein in order to back to the left, or *vice versa;* he knows, indeed, the principle, but he becomes paralyzed in its application. Frank never was embarrassed, never confused. My friend had but to say, "Back, Frank!" and Frank knew from the nature of the ground how far to back and which way to turn. He has thus extricated my friend from positions in which it appeared to him no earthly power could relieve him.

In going up hill Frank knew just when to give himself a rest, and at what moment to join the party in looking about and enjoying the prospect. He was also an adept in scratching off flies, and had a precision in reaching an insect anywhere in his van with one of his rear hooves which few of us attain in slapping mosquitoes. This action sometimes disquieted persons in the phaeton, but Frank knew perfectly well what he was about, and if harm had happened to the people under his charge my friend was sure that Frank could have done anything short of applying arnica and telegraphing to their friends.

The summer passed, and in the comfort of Frank's possession my friend had almost abandoned the idea of ever returning him to his owner. He had thoughts of making the loan permanent, as something on the whole preferable to a purchase. The drives continued quite into December, over roads as smooth and hard as any in June, and the air was delicious. The first snow brought the suggestion of sleighing; but that cold weather about Christmas dispersed these gay thoughts, and restored my friend to virtue. Word came from the stable that Frank's legs were swelling from standing so long without going out, and my friend resolved to part with an animal for which he had no use. I do not praise him for this; it was no more than his duty; but I record his action in order to account for the fact that he is again without a horse, and now, with the opening of the fine weather, is beginning once more to think of buying one.

But he is in no mood of arrogant confidence. He has satisfied himself that neither love nor money is alone adequate to the acquisition: the fates also must favor it. The horse which Frank's owner has had in training may or may not be just the horse he wants. He does not know; he humbly waits; and he trembles at the alternative of horses, mystically summoned from space, and multitudinously advancing upon him, parrot-mouthed, pony-gaited, tender for'a'd, and traveling wide behind.

———————————

1880
THE EXAMINATION SYSTEM IN EDUCATION
by Willard Brown

WHILE it is true that the recent great increase in the number and in the thoroughness of written examinations in our schools and colleges has had good effect in increasing the total work of students, and in raising the minimum qualifications for graduation, it may also be true that bad results have followed which are capable of correction, and which may be readily seen in the mental characteristics of many of our students. The intellectual indifference of the students and recent graduates of the foremost English and American universities has become too noteworthy to be longer passed by, and this indifference seems to be greatest where the examination system has been most developed. In the schools, colleges, and universities of the highest reputation in England and America, the scholar, from entrance until graduation, sees before him an examination paper, and to pass this the competition of his teachers drives him to the utmost. In the foremost preparatory schools of America he is scarcely taught to appreciate the significance of his studies, save in view of the coming examination for college, and for independent work he has neither time nor encouragement. His final struggle for entrance to college, and especially to Harvard or Yale, is a weary, distasteful trial of multitudes of examination papers, in order to obtain the speed and knack in answering which are necessary to success. If he has entered a small college from a school in which there has been no such mechanical drill, in independent growth and love of study he is probably in advance of his contemporary who has entered Harvard from a high-pressure fitting school.

We will suppose now that the preparatory school has been left behind, and that the student is in Oxford or Harvard. In the former university the majority of students give the main portion of their time to athletic sports and society, considering the taking of a degree as a necessary evil, which is to be undergone for the benefit of parents, and which is to be attained with as little trouble as possible. Of the remaining minority nearly all are ambitious workers, but such is the severity of the examinations that they also, like the majority, work only to pass, but with honors.

At Harvard there are long annual and mid-year examinations in each subject, while shorter ones occur frequently. The course is hard, requiring rather more work than at Oxford for a moderate standing. But this work is mainly in view of coming examinations, and is exerted to pass only, or to attain high rank, according to the ambition of the student; and if a man of ability works for himself alone, and is careless of rank, he is looked upon by his fellow students as rather eccentric. To succeed well in the numerous examinations the student must cultivate excessive docility and receptivity of intellect, and bend himself to the whim of the instructor. For years his study has been one struggle to please examiners, to adapt his nature to passing examinations, and the consequence is the development mainly of memory and ability in mechanical working in examinations. The examination papers are usually made so long that the student must write at his utmost speed to answer all the questions, and a very slow writer can seldom obtain high rank. In an examination, for example, in philosophy, the questions are so numerous, that the student has no time to reason long about them; and in truth he has little need of so reasoning, as these same questions have been answered by the professor in his lectures, and the student has only to thrust into his examination book an epitome of what the professor has before given. In mathematics, to be sure, there is more room for original work, but in the classics and in most studies the examinations are like those in philosophy, and here memory, the ability to express another's thoughts in your own words, rapid penmanship, and physical energy are the principal desiderata for success.

As success in the majority of examinations does not require that the student should be an original or broad thinker, it is not surprising that the majority of recent graduates of Harvard lack on graduation that training in independent thought which is so necessary to true culture. There is an indisposition among the majority of students to engage deeply on broad general questions of the day, whence comes the well-known phrase, "Harvard indifference." The creative era of the college is not the present. . . .

Harvard has been dwelt upon at length only because she is the most advanced of American colleges in this system; but Yale is advancing close upon, if indeed she is not already up to, Harvard in the development of the system, and this age, which worships organization for its own sake, without considering its ultimate tendency, is driving our smaller colleges also in the same direction.

Three changes would greatly improve this condition: fewer examinations in school and college, and these as far as possible in original work performed at the student's leisure; greater freedom for students, both as regards their choice of study and attendance at recitations; and a different method of appointing college instructors. Education should be a training to promote insight, power of thought, and facility in acquiring knowledge. To obtain such a training examinations should be means, not ends. For example, instead of the student in political economy, history, philosophy, or mathematics being obliged to work, as now, with an examination, perhaps of catch questions, ever in view, the examination might consist in original essays in the first three subjects, and the performance of a paper of great severity in the last, all being done at the student's leisure and with such assistance as he can get from books. Here is a training similar to that in actual life; the best qualities in mind are brought out, while recitations can furnish the students with practice in answering questions, and the instructor with opportunity of guiding the students and correcting their errors. Such work will also be far more interesting than that under the present system, and consequently greater industry will exist among the students.

Closely allied with this change is that demanding greater freedom for the student. At Oxford the non-honor men have no choice in what their course shall be, and they are compelled to attend lectures. The honor men can indeed choose their general course, but must hear such lectures within that course as their tutors command. It is, however, an indication of the weakness of the system that during a student's last six months he is usually excused from lectures, on the plea that he wishes to work. In American colleges both the course of study and the attendance are generally compulsory, though there are a few exceptions, like Johns Hopkins University and Harvard. In the latter university, though perfect freedom does not yet exist, great advances have recently been made. Compulsion deprives the student of that training in self-dependence which is necessary to his best work; and though I do not under-value that sturdy training in industry which compulsion involves, still if the compulsion were made less immediate, the prudence of the student would act in place of the daily pressure which is now placed upon him.

The appointment of instructors in English and American universities depends at present on their success in passing examinations. In England the Fellows (whence the tutors are chosen) are selected by competitive examination, and in America it is generally useless for a graduate to expect a tutorship who has not, in college, achieved high rank. Those, therefore, get positions who have subjected themselves to the highest pressure of the examination system, and though some of these instructors are men who possess, besides the ability to pass a good examination, other qualities which cause them to be able teachers, it may also happen that some possess little besides ability in passing examinations.

It must never be forgotten that college training is a training for life. Our professors may sneer at the shallow arguments of our sturdy politicians, but what matters it if they neither possess nor help students to acquire our politicians' rough strength? In England and America the best thinkers on education favor this reform; at Harvard, recently, a powerful but ineffectual attempt was made in the faculty to induce a vote in its favor; and the attention now given in this country and England to the principles of education must before long bring about changes similar to those which I have indicated.

1881

SOME PERSONAL RECOLLECTIONS OF CARLYLE

by Henry James, Sr.

THOMAS CARLYLE is incontestably dead at last, by the acknowledgment of all newspapers. I had, however, the pleasure of an intimate intercourse with him when he was an infinitely deader man than he is now, or ever will be again, I am persuaded, in the remotest *seculum seculorum*. I undoubtedly felt myself at the time every whit as dead (spiritually) as he was, and, to tell the truth, I never found him averse to admit my right of insight in regard to myself. But I could never bring him, much as he continually inspired me so to do, to face the philosophic possibility of this proposition in regard to himself.

I cherish the most affectionate esteem for his memory, and could freely say or do nothing to wound the sentiment in any honest human breast. At the same time, I cannot doubt that the proper effect of much that I have to say will be to lower the estimation many persons have formed of Carlyle as a man of ideas. This estimate of Carlyle, *as a man of ideas,* always struck me as unfounded in point of fact. I think his admirers, at least his distant admirers, generally mistook the claim he made upon attention. They were apt to regard him as eminently a man of thought, whereas his intellect, as it seemed to me, except where his prejudices were involved, had not got beyond the stage of instinct. They insisted upon finding him a philosopher, but he was only and consummately a man of genius. They had the fatuity to deem him a great teacher, but he never avouched himself to be anything else than a great critic.

I intend no disparagement of Carlyle's moral qualities in saying that he was almost sure finally to disappoint one's admiration. I merely mean to say that he was without that breadth of humanitary sympathy which one likes to find in distinguished men; that he was deficient in spiritual as opposed to moral force. He was a man of great simplicity and sincerity in his personal manners and habits, and exhibited even an engaging sensibility to the claims of one's physical fellowship. But he was wholly impenetrable to the solicitations both of your heart and your understanding.

I think he felt a helpless dread and distrust of you instantly that he found you had any positive hope in God or practical love to man. His own intellectual life consisted so much in bemoaning the vices of his race, or drew such inspiration from despair, that he couldn't help regarding a man with contempt the instant he found him reconciled to the course of history. Pity is the highest style of intercourse he allowed himself with his kind. He compassionated all his friends in the measure of his affection for them. "Poor John Sterling," he used always to say, "poor John Mill, poor Frederic Maurice, poor Neuberg, poor Arthur Helps, poor little Browning, poor little Lewes," and so on; as if the temple of his friendship were a hospital, and all its inmates scrofulous or paralytic.

Especially did Carlyle conceive that no one could be actively interested in the progress of the species without being intellectually off his balance, and in need of tenderness from all his friends. His own sympathy went out freely to cases of individual suffering, and he believed that there was an immense amount of *specific* divine mercy practicable to us. But as to any sympathy with human nature itself and its inexorable wants, or any belief in a breadth of the divine mercy commensurate with those wants, I could never discern a flavor of either in him. He would have been the last man formally to deny the divine existence and providence, but that these truths had any human virtue, any living efficacy to redeem us out of material and spiritual penury, I don't think he ever dreamt of such a thing. That our knowledge of God was essentially expansive; that revelation contemplated its own spiritual enlargement and fulfillment in the current facts of human history, in the growth and enlargement of the human mind itself — all this he took every opportunity to assure you was the saddest bosh. "Poor John Mill," he exclaimed one night, — "poor John Mill is writing away there in the Edinburgh Review about what he calls the Philosophy of History! As if any man could ever know the road he is going, when once he gets astride of such a distracted steed as that!"

Carlyle had very much of the narrowness, intellectual and moral, which one might expect to find in a descendant of the old Covenanting stock, bred to believe in God as essentially inhuman, and in man, accordingly, as exposed to a great deal of divine treachery and vindictiveness, which were liable to come rattling about his devoted ears the moment his back was turned. I have no idea, of course, that this grim ancestral faith dwelt in Carlyle in any acute, but only in chronic, form. He did not actively acknowledge it, but it was latent in all his intellectual and moral personality, and made itself felt in that cynical, mocking humor and those bursts of tragic pathos which set off all his abstract views of life and destiny.

Too much cannot be said of Carlyle in personal respects. He was a man of even a genial practical morality, an unexceptionable good neighbor, friend, and citizen. But in all larger or human regards he was a literalist of the most unqualified pattern, incapable of uttering an inspiring or even a soothing word in behalf of any struggling manifestation of human hope. It is true, he abused every recognized guide of the political world with such hearty good-will that many persons claimed him at once as an intelligent herald of the new or spiritual divine advent in human nature. But the claim was absurdly unfounded. He was an amateur prophet exclusively, — a prophet "on his own hook," or in the interest of his own irritable cuticle, without a glimmer of sympathy with the distinctively public want, or a gleam of insight into its approaching divine relief; a harlequin in the guise of Jeremiah, who fed you with laughter in place of tears, and put the old prophetic sincerity out of countenance by his broad, persistent winks at the by-standers over the foot-lights.

It always appeared to me that Carlyle valued truth and good as a painter does his pigments, not for what they are in themselves, but for the effects they lend themselves to in the sphere of production. Indeed, he always exhibited a contempt so characteristic as to be comical for every one whose zeal for truth or good led him to question existing institutions with a view to any practical reform. He himself was wont to question established institutions and dogmas with the utmost license of skepticism, but he obviously meant nothing beyond the production of a certain literary surprise, or the enjoyment of his own æsthetic power. Nothing maddened him so much as to be mistaken for a reformer, really intent upon the interests of God's righteousness upon the earth, which are the interests of universal justice. This is what made him hate Americans, and call us a nation of bores, that we took him at his word, and reckoned upon him as a sincere well-wisher to his species. He hated us, because a secret instinct told him that our exuberant faith in him would never be justified by closer knowledge; for no one loves the man who forces him upon a premature recognition of himself.

Alas! poor Yorick!

The main intellectual disqualification, then, of Carlyle, in my opinion, was the absoluteness with which he asserted the moral principle in the human bosom, or the finality which his grim imagination lent to the conflict of good and evil in men's experience. He never had the least idea, that I could discover, of the true or intellectually educative nature of this conflict, as being purely ministerial to a new and final evolution of *human nature itself* into permanent harmony with God's spiritual perfection. He never expressed a suspicion that out of this conflict would one day emerge a positive or faultless life of man, which would otherwise have been impracticable; just as out of the conflict of alkali and acid emerges a neutral salt which would otherwise be invisible. On the contrary, he always expressed himself to the effect that the conflict was absolutely *valid in itself;* that it constituted its own end, having no other result than to insure to good men the final dominion of evil men, and so array heaven and hell in mere chronic or fossil antagonism.

Of course this is only saying in other words that Carlyle was without any sense of a *universal* providence in human affairs. He supposed that God Almighty literally saw with our eyes, and had therefore the same sympathy for strong men that we ourselves have, and the same disregard for feeble men. And he conceived that the world was governed upon the obvious plan of giving strong men sway, and hustling weak men out of sight. In the teeth of all the prophets who have ever prophesied, he held that the race *is* always to the swift, the battle always to the strong. Long before Mr. Darwin had thought of applying the principle of natural selection to the animal kingdom, Carlyle, not in words but in fact, had applied it to the spiritual kingdom, proclaiming as fundamental axioms of the divine administration, *Might makes right* and *Devil take the hindmost.* He thought the divine activity in the world exceptional, not normal, occasional, not constant; that God worked one day out of seven, and rested the remaining six; thus, that he had a much nearer relation to holiday persons like Plato, or Shakespeare, or Goethe, than he has to every-day people like the negro, the prison convict, the street-walker. In this shallow way the great mystery of godliness, which the angels desire to look into, became to his eyes as flat as any pancake; Deity himself being an incomparable athlete, or having an enormous weight of selfhood, so that all his legitimate children are born to rule. Ruler of men, this was Carlyle's most rustical ideal of human greatness; rule on the one hand, obedience on the other, this was his most provincial ideal of human society or fellowship, and he never dreamt of any profounder key to the interpretation of our earthly destiny. The strong man to grow ever more strong, the feeble man to grow ever more feeble, until he is finally extinguished, that was his very pedantic and puerile conception of the rest that remains to the people of God. The glorification of force, ability, genius, "that is the one condition," he always said, "in my poor opinion, of any much-talked-of millennial felicity for this poor planet, — the only thing which will ever rescue it from being the devil's churchyard and miserable donkey pasture it now for the most part turns out to be."

TOM'S HUSBAND
by Sarah Orne Jewett

I SHALL not dwell long upon the circumstances that led to the marriage of my hero and heroine; though their courtship was, to them, the only one that has ever noticeably approached the ideal, it had many aspects in which it was entirely commonplace in other people's eyes. While the world in general smiles at lovers with kindly approval and sympathy, it refuses to be aware of the unprecedented delight which is amazing to the lovers themselves.

But, as has been true in many other cases, when they were at last married, the most ideal of situations was found to have been changed to the most practical. Instead of having shared their original duties, and, as school-boys would say, going halves, they discovered that the cares of life had been doubled. This led to some distressing moments for both our friends; they understood suddenly that instead of dwelling in heaven they were still upon earth, and had made themselves slaves to new laws and limitations. Instead of being freer and happier than ever before, they had assumed new responsibilities; they had established a new household, and must fulfill in some way or another the obligations of it. They looked back with affection to their engagement; they had been longing to have each other to themselves, apart from the world, but it seemed that they never felt so keenly that they were still units in modern society. Since Adam and Eve were in Paradise, before the devil joined them, nobody has had a chance to imitate that unlucky couple. In some respects they told the truth when, twenty times a day, they said that life had never been so pleasant before; but there were mental reservations on either side which might have subjected them to the accusation of lying. Somehow, there was a little feeling of disappointment, and they caught themselves wondering — though they would have died sooner than confess it — whether they were quite so happy as they had expected. The truth was, they were much happier than people usually are, for they had an uncommon capacity for enjoyment. For a little while they were like a sail-boat that is beating and has to drift a few minutes before it can catch the wind and start off on the other tack. And they had the same feeling, too, that any one is likely to have who has been long pursuing some object of his ambition or desire. Whether it is a coin, or a picture, or a stray volume of some old edition of Shakespeare, or whether it is an office under government or a lover, when it is fairly in one's grasp there is a loss of the eagerness that was felt in pursuit. Satisfaction, even after one has dined well, is not so interesting and eager a feeling as hunger.

My hero and heroine were reasonably well established to begin with:

they each had some money, though Mr. Wilson had most. His father had at one time been a rich man, but with the decline, a few years before, of manufacturing interests, he had become, mostly through the fault of others, somewhat involved; and at the time of his death his affairs were in such a condition that it was still a question whether a very large sum or a moderately large one would represent his estate. Mrs. Wilson, Tom's step-mother, was somewhat of an invalid; she suffered severely at times with asthma, but she was almost entirely relieved by living in another part of the country. While her husband lived, she had accepted her illness as inevitable, and had rarely left home; but during the last few years she had lived in Philadelphia with her own people, making short and wheezing visits only from time to time, and had not undergone a voluntary period of suffering since the occasion of Tom's marriage, which she had entirely approved. She had a sufficient property of her own, and she and Tom were independent of each other in that way. Her only other step-child was a daughter, who had married a navy officer, and had at this time gone out to spend three years (or less) with her husband, who had been ordered to Japan.

It is not unfrequently noticed that in many marriages one of the persons who choose each other as partners for life is said to have thrown himself or herself away, and the relatives and friends look on with dismal forebodings and ill-concealed submission. In this case it was the wife who might have done so much better, according to public opinion. She did not think so herself, luckily, either before marriage or afterward, and I do not think it occurred to her to picture to herself the sort of career which would have been her alternative. She had been an only child, and had usually taken her own way. Some one once said that it was a great pity that she had not been obliged to work for her living, for she had inherited a most uncommon business talent, and, without being disreputably keen at a bargain, her insight into the practical working of affairs was very clear and far-reaching. Her father, who had also been a manufacturer, like Tom's, had often said it had been a mistake that she was a girl instead of a boy.

Such executive ability as hers is often wasted in the more contracted sphere of women, and is apt to be more a disadvantage than a help. She was too independent and self-reliant for a wife; it would seem at first thought that she needed a wife herself more than she did a husband. Most men like best the women whose natures cling and appeal to theirs for protection. But Tom Wilson, while he did not wish to be protected himself, liked these very qualities in his wife which would have displeased some other men; to tell the truth, he was very much in love with his wife just as she was. He was a successful collector of almost everything but money, and during a great part of his life he had been an invalid, and he had grown, as he laughingly confessed, very old-womanish. He had been badly lamed, when a boy, by being caught in some machinery in his father's mill, near which he was idling one afternoon, and though he had almost entirely outgrown the effect of his injury, it had not been until after many years. He had been in college, but his eyes had given out there, and he had been obliged to leave in the middle of his junior year, though he had kept up a pleasant intercourse with the members of his class, with whom he had been a great favorite. He was a good deal of an idler in the world. I do not think his ambition, except in the case of securing Mary Dunn for his wife, had ever been distinct; he seemed to make the most he could of each day as it came, without making all his days' works tend toward some grand result, and go toward the upbuilding of some grand plan and purpose. He consequently gave no promise of being either distinguished or great. When his eyes would allow, he was an indefatigable reader; and although he would have said that he read only for amusement, yet he amused himself with books that were well worth the time he spent over them.

The house where he lived nominally belonged to his step-mother, but she had taken for granted that Tom would bring his wife home to it, and assured him that it should be to all intents and purposes his. Tom was deeply attached to the old place, which was altogether the pleasantest in town. He had kept bachelor's hall there most of the time since his father's death, and he had taken great pleasure, before his marriage, in refitting it to some extent, though it was already comfortable and furnished in remarkably good taste. People said of him that if it had not been for his illness, and if he had been a poor boy, he probably would have made something of himself. As it was, he was not very well known by the towns-people, being somewhat reserved, and not taking much interest in their every-day subjects of conversation. Nobody liked him so well as they liked his wife, yet there was no reason why he should be disliked enough to have much said about it.

After our friends had been married for some time, and had outlived the first strangeness of the new order of things, and had done their duty to their neighbors with so much apparent willingness and generosity that even Tom himself was liked a great deal better than he ever had been before, they were sitting together one stormy evening in the library, before the fire. Mrs. Wilson had been reading Tom the letters which had come to him by the night's mail. There was a long one from his sister in Nagasaki, which had been written with a good deal of ill-disguised reproach. She complained of the smallness of the income of her share in her father's estate, and said that she had been assured by American friends that the smaller mills were starting up everywhere, and beginning to do well again. Since so much of their money was invested in the factory, she had been surprised and sorry to find by Tom's last letters that he had seemed to have no idea of putting in a proper person as superintendent, and going to work again. Four per cent. on her other property, instead of eight, which she had been told she must soon expect, would make a great difference to her. A navy captain in a foreign port was obliged to entertain a great deal, and Tom must know that it cost them much more to live than it did him, and ought to think of their interests. She hoped he would talk over with their mother (who had been made executor, with Tom, of his father's will) what was best to be done.

Tom laughed a little, but looked disturbed. His wife had said something to the same effect, and his mother had spoken once or twice in her letters of the prospect of starting the mill again. He was not a bit of a business man, and he did not feel certain, with the theories which he had arrived at of the state of the country, that it was safe yet to spend the money which would have to be spent in putting the mill in order. "They think that the minute it is going again we shall be making money hand over hand, just as father did when we were children," he said. "It is going to cost us no end of money before we can make anything. Before father died he meant to put in a good deal of new machinery, I remember. I don't know anything about the business myself, and I would have sold out long ago if I had had an offer that came anywhere near the value. The larger mills are the only ones that are good for anything now, and we should have to bring a crowd of French Canadians here; the day is past for the people who live in this part of the country to go into the factory again. Even the Irish all go West when they come into the country, and don't come to places like this any more."

"But there are a good many of the old work-people down in the village," said Mrs. Wilson. "Jack Towne asked me the other day if you weren't going to start up in the spring.".

Tom moved uneasily in his chair. "I'll put you in for superintendent, if you like," he said, half angrily, whereupon Mary threw the newspaper at him; but by the time he had thrown it back he was in good humor again.

"Do you know, Tom," she said, with amazing seriousness, "that I believe I should like nothing in the world so much as to be the head of a large business? I hate keeping house, — I always did; and I never did so much of it in all my life put together as I have since I have been married. I suppose it isn't womanly to say so, but if I could escape from the whole thing I believe I should be perfectly happy. If you get rich when the mill is going again, I shall beg for a housekeeper, and shirk everything. I give you fair warning. I don't believe I keep this house half so well as you did before I came here."

Tom's eyes twinkled. "I am going to have that glory, — I don't think you do, Polly; but you can't say that I have not been forbearing. I certainly have not told you more than twice how we used to have things cooked. I'm not going to be your kitchen-colonel."

"Of course it seemed the proper thing to do," said his wife, meditatively; "but I think we should have been even happier than we have if I had been spared it. I have had some days of wretchedness that I shudder to think of. I never know what to have for breakfast; and I ought not to say it, but I don't mind the sight of dust. I look upon housekeeping as my life's great discipline;" and at this pathetic confession they both laughed heartily.

"I've a great mind to take it off your hands," said Tom. "I always rather liked it, to tell the truth, and I ought to be a better house-keeper, — I have been at it for five years; though housekeeping for one is different from what it is for two, and one of them a woman. You see you have brought a different element into my family. Luckily, the servants are pretty well drilled. I do think you upset them a good deal at first!"

Mary Wilson smiled as if she only half heard what he was saying. She drummed with her foot on the floor and looked intently at the fire, and presently gave it a vigorous poking. "Well?" said Tom, after he had waited patiently as long as he could.

"Tom! I'm going to propose something to you. I wish you would really do as you said, and take all the home affairs under your care, and let me start the mill. I am certain I could manage it. Of course I should get people who understood the thing to teach me. I believe I was made for it; I should like it above all things. And this is what I will do: I will bear the cost of starting it, myself, — I think I have money enough, or can get it; and if I have not put affairs in the right trim at the end of a year I will stop, and you may make some other arrangement. If I have, you and your mother and sister can pay me back."

"So I am going to be the wife, and you the husband," said Tom, a little indignantly; "at least, that is what people will say. It's a regular Darby and Joan affair, and you think you can do more work in a day than I can do in three. Do you know that you must go to town to buy cotton? And do you know there are a thousand things about it that you don't know?"

"And never will?" said Mary, with perfect good humor. "Why, Tom, I can learn as well as you, and a good deal better, for I like business, and you don't. You forget that I was always father's right-hand man after I was a dozen years old, and that you have let me invest my money and some of your own, and I haven't made a blunder yet."

Tom thought that his wife had never looked so handsome or so happy. "I don't care, I should rather like the fun of knowing what people will say. It is a new departure, at any rate. Women think they can do everything better than men in these days, but I'm the first man, apparently, who has wished he were a woman."

"Of course people will laugh," said Mary, "but they will say that it's just like me, and think I am fortunate to have married a man who will let me do as I choose. I don't see why it isn't sensible: you will be living exactly as you were before you married, as to home affairs; and since it was a good thing for you to know something about housekeeping then, I can't imagine why you shouldn't go on with it now, since it makes me miserable, and I am wasting a fine business talent while I do it. What do we care for people's talking about it?"

"It seems to me that it is something like women's smoking: it isn't wicked, but it isn't the custom of the country. And I don't like the idea of your going among business men. Of course I should be above going with you, and having people think I must be an idiot; they would say that you married a manufacturing interest, and I was thrown in. I can foresee that my pride is going to be humbled to the dust in every way," Tom declared in mournful tones, and began to shake with laughter. "It is one of your lovely castles in the air, dear Polly, but an old brick mill needs a better foundation than the clouds. No, I'll look around, and get an honest man with a few select brains for agent. I suppose it's the best thing we can do, for the machinery ought not to lie still any longer; but I mean to sell the factory as soon as I can. I devoutly wish it would take fire, for the insurance would be the best price we are likely to get. That is a famous letter from Alice! I am afraid the captain has been growling over his pay, or they have been giving too many little dinners on board ship. If we were rid of the mill, you and I might go out there this winter. It would be capital fun."

Mary smiled again in an absent-minded way. Tom had an uneasy feeling that he had not heard the end of it yet, but nothing more was said for a day or two. When Mrs. Tom Wilson announced, with no apparent thought of being contradicted, that she had entirely made up her mind, and she meant to see those men who had been overseers of the different departments, who still lived in the village, and have the mill put in order at once, Tom looked disturbed, but made no opposition; and soon after breakfast his wife formally presented him with a handful of keys, and told him there was meat enough in the house for dinner; and presently he heard the wheels of her little phaeton rattling off down the road. I should be untruthful if I tried to persuade any one that he was not provoked; he thought she would at least have waited for his formal permission, and at first he meant to take another horse, and chase her, and bring her back in disgrace, and put a stop to the whole thing. But something assured him that she knew what she was about, and he determined to let her have her own way. If she failed, it might do no harm, and this was the only ungallant thought he gave her. He was sure that she would do nothing unlady-like, or be unmindful of his dignity; and he believed it would be looked upon as one of her odd, independent freaks, which always had won respect in the end, however much they had been laughed at in the beginning. "Susan," said he, as that estimable person went by the door with the dust-pan, "you may tell Catherine to come to me for orders about the house, and you may do so yourself. I am going to take charge again, as I did before I was married. It is no trouble to me, and Mrs. Wilson dislikes it. Besides, she is going into business, and will have a great deal else to think of."

"Yes, sir; very well, sir," said Susan, who was suddenly moved to ask so many questions that she was utterly silent. But her master looked very happy; there was evidently no disapproval of his wife; and she went on up the stairs, and began to sweep them down, knocking the dust-brush about excitedly, as if she were trying to kill a descending colony of insects.

Tom went out to the stable and mounted his horse, which had been waiting for him to take his customary after-breakfast ride to the post-office, and he galloped down the road in quest of the phaeton. He saw Mary talking with Jack Towne, who had been an overseer and a val-ued workman of his father's. He was looking much surprised and pleased.

"I wasn't caring so much about getting work, myself," he explained; "I've got what will carry me and my wife through; but it'll be better for the young folks about here to work near home. My nephews are want-ing something to do; they were going to Lynn next week. I don't say but I should like to be to work in the old place again. I've sort of missed it, since we shut down."

"I'm sorry I was so long in overtaking you," said Tom, politely, to his wife. "Well, Jack, did Mrs. Wilson tell you she's going to start the mill? You must give her all the help you can."

"'Deed `I will," said Mr. Towne, gallantly, without a bit of astonishment.

"I don't know much about the business yet," said Mrs. Wilson, who had been a little overcome at Jack Towne's lingo of the different rooms and machinery, and who felt an overpowering sense of having a great deal before her in the next few weeks. "By the time the mill is ready, I will be ready, too," she said, taking heart a little; and Tom, who was quick to understand her moods, could not help laughing, as he rode alongside. "We want a new barrel of flour, Tom, dear," she said, by way of punishment for his untimely mirth.

If she lost courage in the long delay, or was disheartened at the steady call for funds, she made no sign; and after a while the mill started up, and her cares were lightened, so that she told Tom that before next pay day she would like to go to Boston for a few days, and go to the theatre, and have a frolic and a rest. She really looked pale and thin, and she said she never worked so hard in all her life; but nobody knew how happy she was, and she was so glad she had married Tom, for some men would have laughed at it.

"I laughed at it," said Tom, meekly. "All is, if I don't cry by and by, because I am a beggar, I shall be lucky." But Mary looked fearlessly serene, and said that there was no danger at present.

It would have been ridiculous to expect a dividend the first year, though the Nagasaki people were pacified with difficulty. All the business letters came to Tom's address, and everybody who was not directly concerned thought that he was the motive power of the reawakened enterprise. Sometimes business people came to the mill, and were amazed at having to confer with Mrs. Wilson, but they soon had to respect her talents and her success. She was helped by the old clerk, who had been promptly recalled and reinstated, and she certainly did capitally well. She was laughed at, as she had expected to be, and people said they should think Tom would be ashamed of himself; but it soon appeared that he was not to blame, and what reproach was offered was on the score of his wife's oddity. There was nothing about the mill that she did not understand before very long, and at the end of the second year she declared a small dividend with great pride and triumph. And she was congratulated on her success, and everyone thought of her project in a different way from the way they had thought of it in the beginning. She had singularly good fortune: at the end of the third year she was making money for herself and her friends faster than most people were, and approving letters began to come from Nagasaki. The Ashtons had been ordered to stay in that region, and it was evident that they were continually being obliged to entertain more instead of less. Their children were growing fast too, and constantly becoming more expensive. The captain and his wife had already begun to congratulate themselves secretly that their two sons would in all probability come into possession, one day, of their uncle Tom's handsome property.

For a good while Tom enjoyed life, and went on his quiet way serenely. He was anxious at first, for he thought that Mary was going to make ducks and drakes of his money and her own. And then he did not exactly like the looks of the thing, either; he feared that his wife was growing successful as a business person at the risk of losing her womanliness. But as time went on, and he found there was no fear of that, he accepted the situation philosophically. He gave up his collection of engravings, having become more interested in one of coins and medals, which took up most of his leisure time. He often went to the city in pursuit of such treasures, and gained much renown in certain quarters as a numismatologist of great skill and experience. But at last his house (which had almost kept itself, and had given him little to do besides ordering the dinners, while faithful old Catherine and her niece Susan were his aids) suddenly became a great care to him. Catherine, who had been the main-stay of the family for many years, died after a short illness, and Susan must needs choose that time, of all others, for being married to one of the second hands in the mill. There followed a long and dismal season of experimenting, and for a time there was a procession of incapable creatures going in at one kitchen door and out of the other. His wife would not have liked to say so, but it seemed to her that Tom was growing fussy about the house affairs, and took more notice of those minor details than he used. She wished more than once, when she was tired, that he would not talk so much about the housekeeping; he seemed sometimes to have no other thought.

In the first of Mrs. Wilson's connection with manufacturing, she had made it a rule to consult Tom on every subject of importance; but it had speedily proved to be a formality. He tried manfully to show a deep interest which he did not feel, and his wife gave up, little by little, telling him much about her affairs. She said that she liked to drop business when she came home in the evening; and at last she fell into the habit of taking a nap on the library sofa, while Tom, who could not use his eyes much by lamp-light, sat smoking or in utter idleness before the fire. When they were first married his wife had made it a rule that she should always read him the evening papers, and afterward they had always gone on with some book of history or philosophy, in which they were both interested. These evenings of their early married life had been charming to both of them, and from time to time one would say to the other that they ought to take up again the habit of reading together. Mary was so unaffectedly tired in the evening that Tom never liked to propose a walk; for, though he was not a man of peculiarly social nature, he had always been accustomed to pay an occasional evening visit to his neighbors in the village. And though he had little interest in the business world, and still less knowledge of it, after a while he wished that his wife would have more to say about what she was planning and doing, or how things were getting on. He thought that her chief aid, old Mr. Jackson, was far more in her thoughts than he. She was forever quoting Jackson's opinions. He did not like to find that she took it for granted that he was not interested in the welfare of his own property; it made him feel like a sort of pensioner and dependent, though, when they had guests at the house, which was by no means seldom, there was nothing in her manner that would imply that she thought herself in any way the head of the family. It was hard work to find fault with his wife in any way, though, to give him his due, he rarely tried.

But, this being a wholly unnatural state of things, the reader must expect to hear of its change at last, and the first blow from the enemy was dealt by an old woman, who lived near by, and who called to Tom one morning, as he was driving down to the village in a great hurry (to post a letter, which ordered his agent to secure a long-wished-for ancient copper coin, at any price), to ask him if they had made yeast that week, and if she could borrow a cupful, as her own had met with some misfortune. Tom was instantly in a rage, and he mentally condemned her to some undeserved fate, but told her aloud to go and see the cook. This slight delay, besides being killing to his dignity, caused him to lose the mail, and in the end his much-desired copper coin. It was a hard day for him, altogether; it was Wednesday, and the first days of the week having been stormy the washing was very late. And Mary came home to dinner provokingly good-natured. She had met an old school-mate and her husband driving home from the mountains, and had first taken them over her factory, to their great amusement and delight, and then had brought them home to dinner. Tom greeted them cordially, and manifested his usual graceful hospitality; but the minute he saw his wife alone he said in a plaintive tone of rebuke, "I should think you might have remembered that the girls are unusually busy to-day. I do wish you would take a little interest in things at home. The girls have been washing, and I'm sure I don't know what sort of a dinner we can give your friends. I wish you had thought to bring home some steak. I have been busy myself, and couldn't go down to the village. I thought we would only have a lunch."

Mary was hungry, but she said nothing, except that it would be all right, — she didn't mind; and perhaps they could have some canned soup.

She often went to town to buy or look at cotton, or to see some improvement in machinery, and she brought home beautiful bits of furniture and new pictures for the house, and showed a touching thoughtfulness in remembering Tom's fancies; but somehow he had an uneasy suspicion that she could get along pretty well without him when it came to the deeper wishes and hopes of her life, and that her most important concerns were all matters in which he had no share. He seemed to himself to have merged his life in his wife's; he lost his interest in things outside the house and grounds; he felt himself fast growing rusty and behind the times, and to have somehow missed a good deal in life; he felt that he was a failure. One day the thought rushed over him that his had been almost exactly the experience of most women, and he wondered if it really was any more disappointing and ignominious to him than it was to women themselves. "Some of them may be contented with it," he said to himself, soberly. "People think women are designed for such careers by nature, but I don't know why I ever made such a fool of myself."

Having once seen his situation in life from such a stand-point, he felt it day by day to be more degrading, and he wondered what he should do about it; and once, drawn by a new, strange sympathy, he went to the little family burying-ground. It was one of the mild, dim days that come sometimes in early November, when the pale sunlight is like the pathetic smile of a sad face, and he sat for a long time on the limp, frostbitten grass beside his mother's grave.

But when he went home in the twilight his step-mother, who just then was making them a little visit, mentioned that she had been looking through some boxes of hers that had been packed long before and stowed away in the garret. "Everything looks very nice up there," she said, in her wheezing voice (which, worse than usual that day, always made him nervous); and added, without any intentional slight to his feelings, "I do think you have always been a most excellent house-keeper."

"I'm tired of such nonsense!" he exclaimed, with surprising indignation. "Mary, I wish you to arrange your affairs so that you can leave them for six months at least. I am going to spend this winter in Europe."

"Why, Tom, dear!" said his wife, appealingly. "I couldn't leave my business any way in the" —

But she caught sight of a look on his usually placid countenance that was something more than decision, and refrained from saying anything more.

And three weeks from that day they sailed.

1883
AN AFTER-BREAKFAST TALK
by Oliver Wendell Holmes

BETWEEN the author's just right to his time and the claims which a kind heart makes it impossible not to listen to, many writers who have gained the ear of the public, and who pass for amiable and well-disposed persons, in this country, as doubtless in others, have found themselves not a little perplexed. The late meeting of those interested in the subject, of which many of our readers may not have heard, seems to have adjusted these conflicting interests in a manner which, it may be hoped, will prove satisfactory to all concerned. It only remains to carry out the provisions which, after long deliberation, were unanimously agreed upon as expressing the sense of the meeting. Some extracts from the minutes of the proceedings have been put in my hands by the secretary, and are here reproduced, being now printed for the first time. It is hoped that they will be generally read by the two classes of persons to whom their provisions more especially apply, namely, authors and their visitors and correspondents.

Abstract of the Record of Proceedings of The Association of Authors for Self-Protection, at a Meeting held at Washington, September 31, 1882

PREAMBLE

Whereas there is prevalent in the community an opinion that he or she who has written and published a book belongs thenceforward to everybody but himself or herself, and may be called upon by any person for any gratuitous service for which he or she is wanted; and Whereas we believe that some rights do still remain to authors (meaning by that term writers of both sexes), notwithstanding the fact of such writing and publication; and Whereas we have found it impossible to make a stand in our individual capacity against the various forms of tyranny which have grown out of the opinion above mentioned, we do hereby unite and constitute ourselves a joint body for the purpose and by the title above named.

OF THE PROPERTY OF AUTHORS

This does not consist, for the most part, of what is called real, or of what is called personal, estate, but lies chiefly in that immaterial and intangible possession known in its general expression as *time,* or in special portions, as days, hours, minutes, and seconds. If the author is fortunate enough to own the piece of mechanism commonly called a clock, his timepiece will be found to mark and measure sixty seconds to the minute, sixty minutes to the hour, and twenty-four hours to the day, and *no more,* like the timepieces of other owners; which fact is contrary to the apparent belief of many of his visitors and correspondents.

OF THE PERSONS OF AUTHORS

It is not to be considered that authorship entirely changes the author to a being of a different nature. He or she is entitled to the common kind of consideration which belongs to humanity in general. Bodily defects and infirmities are not fit subjects for public comment, especially in the case of women, to whom the *spretæ injuria formæ* is an unforgivable offense. And so of all the ordinary decencies of life; the author is to be considered as having the same rights as the general public.

OF VISITS OF STRANGERS TO AUTHORS

Visits of Curiosity or Admiration. These are not always distinguishable from each other, and may be considered together. The stranger should send up his card, if he has one; if he has none, he should, if admitted, at once announce himself and his object, without circumlocution, as thus: "My name is M. or N. from X. or Y. I wish to see and take the hand of a writer whom I have long admired for his," etc., etc. *Here the Author should extend his hand, and reply in substance as follows:* "I am pleased to see you, my dear sir, and very glad that anything I have written has been a source of pleasure or profit to you." The visitor has now had what he says he came for, and, after making a brief polite acknowledgment, should retire, unless, for special reasons, he is urged to stay longer.

Visits of Interviewers. The interviewer is a product of over-civilization, who does for the living what the undertaker does for the dead, taking such liberties as he chooses with the subject of his mental and conversational manipulations, whom he is to arrange for public inspection. The interview system has its legitimate use; is often a convenience to politicians, and may even gratify the vanity and serve the interests of an author. In its abuse it is an infringement of the liberty of the private citizen, to be ranked with the edicts of the Council of Ten, the Decrees of the Star-Chamber, the Lettres de Cachet, and the visits of the Inquisition. The Interviewer, if excluded, becomes an enemy, and has the columns of a newspaper at his service, in which to revenge himself. If admitted, the Interviewed is at the mercy of the Interviewer's memory, if he is the best meaning of men; of his inaccuracy, if he is careless; of his malevolence if he is ill-disposed; of his prejudices, if he has any; and of his sense of propriety, at any rate.

In consideration of the possible abuses arising from the privilege granted to, or rather usurped by, the irresponsible individuals who exercise the function of domiciliary inspection, it is proposed to place the whole business under legal restrictions, in accordance with the plan here sketched for consideration, and about to be submitted to the judgment of all our local governments.

— A licensed corps of Interviewers, to be appointed by the municipal authorities. — Each Interviewer to wear in a conspicuous position a Number and a Badge, for which the following emblems and inscriptions are suggested: Zephyrus with his lips at the ear of Boreas, who holds a speaking-trumpet; signifying that what is said by the Interviewed in a whisper will be shouted to the world by the Interviewer through that brazen instrument. For mottoes, either of the following: *Fœnum habet in cornu; Hunc tu, Romane, caveto.* — No person to be admitted to the Corps of Interviewers without a strict preliminary examination. — The candidate to be proved free from color-blindness and amblyopia, ocular and mental strabismus, double refraction of memory, kleptomania, mendacity of more than average dimensions, and tendency to alcoholic endosmosis. — His moral and religious character to be vouched for by three orthodox clergymen of the same belief, and as many deacons who agree with them and with each other. — All reports to be submitted to the Interviewed, and the proofs thereof to be corrected and sanctioned by him before being given to the public.

Until the above provisions are carried into effect, no record of an alleged Interview to be considered as anything more than the untrustworthy gossip of an irresponsible impersonality.

OF UNKNOWN CORRESPONDENTS

Of *Autograph-Seekers.* The increase in the number of applicants for autographs is so great that it has become necessary to adopt positive regulations to protect the Author from the exorbitant claims of this class of virtuosos. The following propositions were adopted without discussion: —

— No author is under any obligation to answer any letter from an unknown person applying for his autograph. If he sees fit to do so, it is a gratuitous concession on his part.

— No stranger should ask for more than one autograph.

— No stranger should request an author to copy a poem, or even a verse. He should remember that he is one of many thousands; that a thousand fleas are worse than one hornet, and that a mob of mosquitoes will draw more blood than a single horse-leech.

— Every correspondent applying for an autograph should send a *card* or *blank paper,* in a *stamped envelope* directed to himself (or herself). If he will not take the trouble to attend to all this, which he can just as well do as make the author do it, he must not expect the author to make good his deficiencies. [Accepted by acclamation.]

— Sending a stamp does not constitute a claim on an author for an answer. [Received with loud applause.] The stamp may be retained by the author, or, what is better, devoted to the use of some appropriate charity, as, for instance, the Asylum for Idiots and Feeble-Minded Persons.

— No stranger should expect an author to send him or her his photograph. These pictures cost money, and it may not be convenient to an impecunious celebrity to furnish them to the applicants, who are becoming singularly numerous.

   — *Albums.* An album of decent external aspect may, without impropriety, be offered to an author, with the request that he will write his name therein. It is not proper, as a general rule, to ask for anything more than the name. The author may, of course, add a quotation from his writings, or a sentiment, if so disposed; but this must be considered as a work of supererogation, and an exceptional manifestation of courtesy.

   — *Bed-quilt Autographs.* It should be a source of gratification to an author to contribute to the soundness of his reader's slumbers, if he cannot keep him awake by his writings. He should therefore cheerfully inscribe his name on the scrap of satin or other stuff (provided always that it be sent him *in a stamped and directed envelope*), that it may take its place in the patch-work mosaic for which it is intended.

Letters of Admiration. These may be accepted as genuine, unless they contain specimens of the writer's own composition, upon which a critical opinion is requested, in which case they are to be regarded in the same light as medicated sweetmeats: namely, as meaning more than their looks imply. Genuine letters of admiration, being usually considered by the recipient as proofs of good taste and sound judgment on the part of his unknown correspondent, may be safely left to his decision as to whether they shall be answered or not.

Questioning Letters. These are commonly fraudulent in their nature, their true intent being to obtain an autograph letter in reply. They should be answered, if at all, by a clerk or secretary; which will be satisfactory to the correspondent, if he only wishes for information, and will teach him not to try to obtain anything by false pretences, if his intent was what it is, for the most part, in letters of this kind.

Letters asking Advice. An author is not of necessity a competent adviser on all subjects. He is expected, nevertheless, to advise unknown persons as to their health of body and mind, their religion, their choice of a profession; on matrimony, on education, on courses of reading; and, more especially, to lay down a short and easy method for obtaining brilliant and immediate success in a literary career. These applicants, if replied to at all, should be directed to the several specialists who are competent to answer their questions. Literary aspirants commonly send a specimen of their productions in prose or verse, oftenest the latter. They ask for criticism, but they want praise, which they very rarely deserve. If a sentence can be extracted from any letter written them which can help an advertisement, the publisher of their little volume will get hold of it. They demoralize kind-hearted authors by playing on their good-nature, and leading them to express judgments not in conformity with their own standards. They must be taught the lesson that authors are not the same thing as editors and publishers, whose business it is to examine manuscripts intended for publication, and to whom their applications should be addressed.

— No stranger whose letter has been answered by an Author should consider himself (or herself) as having *opened a correspondence* with the personage addressed. Once replied to, he (or she) should look upon himself (or herself) as done with, unless distinctly requested or encouraged to write again.

Invitations. An Author cannot and must not be expected to accept most of the invitations he is constantly receiving. The fact of noted authorship should be considered equivalent to a perpetual previous engagement. A formal answer to an invitation shall discharge him from further duty, and he shall not be taxed to contribute in prose or verse to occasions in which he has no special interest, or any other, unless so disposed.

—*Private letters of Authors.* No private letter of any Author, and no extract from such letter, shall be printed without his permission, or without giving him the opportunity of *correcting the proof,* as in the case of any other publication of what he has written. If any letter, or extract from a letter, of an Author is printed in violation of these obvious rights and duties, the Author shall not be held responsible for any statement such letter or extract may be alleged to contain; and those who publish any such alleged statement as having been made by the Author in question shall be considered as taking part in the original violation of confidence, unless they defend the Author against all unfavorable inferences drawn from said letter or extract.

Of *Books sent to Authors.* An Author is not bound to read any book sent him by a stranger. He is not under any obligation to express his opinion of any book so sent, whether said opinion is to be used as a Publisher's advertisement or not. An acknowledgment, with thanks, is to be reckoned a discharge of all obligations to the sender.

Of *Remembering introduced Strangers.* Strangers who have had an introduction to an Author have no right to expect that their faces will be remembered by him as well as they remember his. This is especially true of persons of the female sex who are youthful and comely, and for this reason have a certain resemblance to each other. If such youthful and comely individuals identify the Author before he shows, by the usual mark of courtesy, that he recognizes them, they need not think themselves intentionally slighted, but may address him freely, and he will not take offence at being spoken to before speaking.

The above rules are to be considered applicable only to strangers having no special claim upon the author.

The Association may be found fault with for passing these resolves, some of which may sound harshly in the ears of certain readers, who have not acted in accordance with their precepts. But it must be remembered that it is almost a question of life and death with Authors. This cannot be considered too strong an expression, when we remember that Pope was driven to exclaim, a century and a half ago, —

> "Fatigued, I said,
> Tie up the knocker; say I'm *sick,* I'm *dead.*"

In obtaining and giving to the public this abstract of the Proceedings of the Association, I have been impelled by the same feelings of humanity which led me to join the Society for the Prevention of Cruelty to Animals, believing that the sufferings of Authors are as much entitled to sympathy and relief as those of the brute creation.

1884
WOLFE ON THE PLAINS OF ABRAHAM
by Francis Parkman

THE siege of Quebec, begun in June, 1759, by General Wolfe, with an inadequate force, was protracted till August without the slightest apparent prospect of success. At the end of July, Wolfe met a terrible rebuff in a desperate attempt to scale the heights of Montmorenci; and the French, elated by their victory, flattered themselves with the hope that the enemy would soon sail homeward in despair.

Meanwhile, a deep cloud fell on the English. Since the siege began Wolfe had passed with ceaseless energy from camp to camp, animating the troops, observing everything and directing everything; but now the pale face and tall, lean form were seen no more, and the rumor spread that the general was dangerously ill. He had in fact been seized by an access of the disease that had tortured him for some time past, and fever had followed. His quarters were at a French farmhouse in the camp at Montmorenci; and here, as he lay in an upper chamber, helpless in bed, his singular and most unmilitary features haggard with disease and drawn with pain, no man could less have looked the hero. But as the needle, though quivering, points always to the pole, so, through torment and languor and the heats of fever, the mind of Wolfe dwelt on the capture of Quebec.

By the end of August, he was able for the first time to leave the house, and on the 2d of September, a vessel was sent to England with his last dispatch to Pitt. It begins thus: "The obstacles we have met with in the operations of the campaign are much greater than we had reason to expect or could foresee; not so much from the number of the enemy (though superior to us) as from the natural strength of the country, which the Marquis of Montcalm seems wisely to depend upon."

Some days later, he wrote to the Earl of Holderness: "The Marquis of Montcalm has a numerous body of armed men (I cannot call it an army) and the strongest country, perhaps, in the world. Our fleet blocks up the river above and below the town, but can give no manner of aid in an attack upon the Canadian army. We are now here [off Cap Rouge] with about thirty-six hundred men, waiting to attack them when and wherever they can best be got at. I am so far recovered as to do business, but my constitution is entirely ruined, without the consolation of doing any considerable service to the state, and without any prospect of it."

Perhaps he was as near despair as his undaunted nature was capable of being. In his present state of body and mind, he was a hero without the light and cheer of heroism. He flattered himself with no illusions, but saw the worst and faced it all. He seems to have been entirely without excitement. The languor of disease, the desperation of the chances, and the greatness of the stake may have wrought to tranquilize him. His energy was doubly tasked, to bear up his own sinking frame and to achieve an almost hopeless feat of arms.

On the 10th of September the English naval commanders held a council on board the flagship, in which it was resolved that the lateness of the season required the fleet to leave Quebec without delay. Wolfe then went to the admiral, told him that he had found a place where the heights could be scaled, that he would send up a hundred and fifty picked men to feel the way, and that if they gained a lodgment at the top the other troops should follow; if, on the other hand, the French were there in force to oppose them, he would not sacrifice the army in a hopeless attempt, but embark them for home.

Wolfe's army was greatly weakened. Since the end of June, his loss in killed and wounded was more than eight hundred and fifty, including two colonels, two majors, nineteen captains, and thirty-four sub-alterns; and to these were to be added a greater number disabled by disease.

The squadron of Admiral Holmes, above Quebec, had now increased to twenty-two vessels, great and small. One of the last that went up was a diminutive schooner, armed with a few swivels, and jocosely named the Terror of France. She sailed by the town in broad daylight, the French, incensed at her impudence, blazing at her from all their batteries; but she passed unharmed, anchored by the admiral's ship, and saluted him triumphantly with her swivels.

Wolfe's first move towards executing his plan was the critical one of evacuating the camp at Montmorenci. This was accomplished on the 3d of September. Montcalm sent a strong force to fall on the rear of the retiring English. Monckton saw the movement from Point Levi, embarked two battalions in the boats of the fleet, and made a feint of landing at Beauport. Montcalm recalled his troops to repulse the threatened attack, and the English withdrew from Montmorenci unmolested; some to the Point of Orleans, others to Point Levi. On the night of the 4th a fleet of flatboats passed above the town with the baggage and stores. On the 5th Murray, with four battalions, marched up to the river Etechemin, and forded it under a hot fire from the French batteries at Sillery. Monckton and Townshend followed with three more battalions, and the united force of about thirty-six hundred men was embarked on board the ships of Holmes, where Wolfe joined them on the same evening.

These movements of the English filled the French commanders with mingled perplexity, anxiety, and hope. Vaudreuil grew confident. Yet he was ceaselessly watchful. So was Montcalm; and on the night of the 2d, he snatched a moment to write to Bourlamaque from his headquarters in the stone house by the river of Beauport: "The night is dark; it rains; our troops are dressed in their tents, and on the alert; I in my boots; my horses saddled. In fact, this is my usual way. I wish you were here, for I cannot be everywhere, though I multiply myself, and have not taken off my clothes since the 23d of June." On the 11th of September, he wrote his last letter to Bourlamaque, and probably the last that his pen ever traced: "I am overwhelmed with work, and should often lose temper, like you, if I did not remember that I am paid by Europe for not losing it. Nothing new since my last. I give the enemy another month, or something less, to stay here." The more sanguine Vaudreuil would hardly give them a week.

Meanwhile, no precaution was spared. The force under Bougainville, above Quebec, was raised to three thousand men. He was ordered to watch the shore as far as Jacques Cartier, and follow with his main body every movement of Holmes's squadron. There was little fear for the heights near the town. They were thought inaccessible. Montcalm himself believed them safe, and had expressed himself to that effect some time before. "We need not suppose," he wrote to

Vaudreuil, "that the enemy have wings;" and again, speaking of the very place where Wolfe afterwards landed, "I swear to you that a hundred men posted there would stop their whole army." He was right. A hundred watchful and determined men could have held the position long enough for reinforcements to come up.

The hundred men were there. Thus all was vigilance; for while the French were strong in the hope of speedy delivery, they felt that there was no safety till the tents of the invader had vanished from their shores and his ships from their river. "What we knew," says one of them, "of the character of M. Wolfe, that impetuous, bold, and intrepid warrior, prepared us for a last attack before he left us."

Wolfe had been very ill on the evening of the 4th. The troops knew it, and their spirits sank; but after a night of torment he grew better, and was soon among them again, rekindling their ardor, and imparting a cheer that he could not share. He examined the river and the shores as far as Point aux Trembles; till at length, landing on the south side a little above Quebec, and looking across the water with a telescope, he descried a path that ran with a long slope up the face of the woody precipice, and saw at the top a cluster of tents. They were those of Captain de Vergor's guard at the Ance du Foulon, now called Wolfe's Cove. As he could see but ten or twelve of them, he thought that the guard could not be numerous, and might be overpowered.

The morning of the 7th was fair and warm, and the vessels of Holmes, their crowded decks gay with scarlet uniforms, sailed up the river to Cap Rouge. A lively scene awaited them, for here were the headquarters of Bougainville, and here lay his principal force, while the rest watched the banks above and below. The cove into which the little river runs was guarded by floating batteries; the surrounding shore was defended by breastworks; and a large body of regulars, militia, and mounted Canadians in blue uniforms moved to and fro, with restless activity, on the hills behind. When the vessels came to anchor, the horsemen dismounted and formed in line with the infantry; then, with loud shouts, the whole rushed down the heights to man their works at the shore. That true Briton, Captain Knox, looked on with a critical eye from the gangway of his ship, and wrote that night in his diary that they had made a ridiculous noise. "How different," he exclaims, "how nobly awful and expressive of true valor, is the customary silence of the British troops!"

In the afternoon the ships opened fire, while the troops entered the boats and rowed up and down, as if looking for a landing place. It was but a feint of Wolfe to deceive Bougainville as to his real design. A heavy easterly rain set in on the next morning, and lasted two days without respite. All operations were suspended, and the men suffered greatly in the crowded transports. Half of them were therefore landed on the south shore, where they made their quarters in the village of St. Nicolas, refreshed themselves, and dried their wet clothing, knapsacks, and blankets.

For several successive days the squadron of Holmes was allowed to drift up the river with the flood tide and down with the ebb, thus passing and repassing incessantly between the neighborhood of Quebec on the one hand and a point high above Cap Rouge on the other; while Bougainville, perplexed and always expecting an attack, followed the ships to and fro along the shore by day and by night, till his men were exhausted with ceaseless forced marches.

At last the time for action came. On Wednesday, the 12th, the troops at St. Nicolas were embarked again, and all were told to hold themselves in readiness. Wolfe, from the flagship Sutherland, issued his last general orders: "The enemy's force is now divided; great scarcity of provisions in their camp, and universal discontent among the Canadians. Our troops below are in readiness to join us, all the light artillery and tools are embarked at the Point of Levi, and the troops will land where the French seem least to expect it. The first body that gets on shore is to march directly to the enemy, and drive them from any little post they may occupy; the officers must be careful that the succeeding bodies do not by any mistake fire on those who go before them. The battalions must form on the upper ground with expedition, and be ready to charge whatever presents itself. When the artillery and troops are landed, a corps will be left to secure the landing place, while the rest march on and endeavor to bring the Canadians and French to a battle."

Wolfe had thirty-six hundred men and officers with him on board the vessels of Holmes, and he now sent orders to Colonel Burton at Point Levi to lead to his aid all who could be spared from that place and the Point of Orleans. They were to march along the south bank after nightfall, and wait farther orders at a designated spot convenient for embarkation. Their number was about twelve hundred, so that the entire force destined for the enterprise was at the utmost forty-eight hundred. With these, Wolfe meant to climb the heights of Abraham in the teeth of an enemy who, though much reduced, were still twice as numerous as their assailants.

Admiral Saunders lay with the main fleet in the Basin of Quebec. This excellent officer, whatever may have been his views as to the necessity of a speedy departure, aided Wolfe to the last with unfailing energy and zeal. It was agreed between them that while the general made the real attack the admiral should engage Montcalm's attention by a pretended one. As night approached the fleet ranged itself along the Beauport shore; the boats were lowered, and filled with sailors, marines, and the few troops that had been left behind; while ship signaled to ship, cannon flashed and thundered, and shot ploughed the beach, as if to clear a way for assailants to land. In the gloom of the evening the effect was imposing. Montcalm, who thought that the movements of the English above the town were only a feint, that their main force was still below it, and that their real attack would be made there, was completely deceived, and massed his troops in front of Beauport to repel the expected landing. But while in the fleet of Saunders all was uproar and ostentatious menace, the danger was ten miles away, where the squadron of Holmes lay tranquil and silent at its anchorage off Cap Rouge.

It was less tranquil than it seemed. All on board knew that a blow would be struck that night, though only a few high officers knew where. Colonel Howe, of the light infantry, called for volunteers to lead the unknown and desperate venture, promising, in the words of one of them, "that if any of us survived we might depend on being recommended to the general." As many as were wanted, twenty-four in all, soon came forward. Thirty large *bateaux* and some boats belonging to the squadron lay moored alongside the vessels, and late in the evening the troops were ordered into them, the twenty-four volunteers taking their place in the foremost. They held in all about seventeen hundred men. The rest remained on board the ships.

Bougainville could discern the movement, and like Montcalm thought it was he who was to be attacked. The tide was still flowing, and, the better to deceive him, the vessels and boats were allowed to drift upward with it for a little distance, as if to land above Cap Rouge.

The day had been fortunate for Wolfe. Two deserters came from the camp of Bougainville, with information that, at ebb tide on the next night, he was to send down a convoy of provisions to Montcalm. The necessities of the camp at Beauport and the difficulties of transportation by land had before compelled the French to resort to this perilous means of conveying supplies; and their boats, drifting in darkness under the shadows of the northern shore, had commonly passed in safety. Wolfe saw at once that, if his own boats went down in advance of the convoy, he could turn the intelligence of the deserters to good account.

He was still on board the Sutherland. Every preparation was made and every order given; it only remained to wait the turning of the tide.

Towards two o'clock the tide began to ebb, and a fresh wind blew down the river. Two lanterns were raised into the maintop shrouds of the Sutherland. It was the appointed signal. The boats cast off and fell down with the current, those of the light infantry leading the way. The vessels with the rest of the troops had orders to follow a little later.

To look for a moment at the chances on which this bold adventure hung: first, the deserters told Wolfe that provision boats were ordered to go down to Quebec that night; secondly, Bougainville countermanded them; thirdly, the sentries posted along the heights were told of the order, but not of the countermand; fourthly, Vergor, at the Ance du Foulon, had permitted most of his men, chiefly Canadians from Lorette, to go home for a time and work at their harvesting, on condition, it is said, that they should afterwards work in a neighboring field of his own; fifthly, he kept careless watch and went quietly to bed; sixthly, the battalion of Guienne, ordered to take post on the Plains of Abraham, had, for reasons unexplained, remained encamped by the St. Charles; and lastly, when Bougainville saw Holmes's vessels drift down the stream, he did not tax his weary troops to follow them, thinking that they would return as usual with the flood tide. But for these conspiring circumstances New France might have lived a little longer, and the fruitless heroism of Wolfe would have passed with countless other heroisms into oblivion.

For full two hours the procession of boats, borne on the current, steered silently down the St. Lawrence. The stars were visible, but the night was moonless and sufficiently dark. The general was in one of the foremost boats, and near him was a young midshipman, John Robison, afterwards professor of natural philosophy in the University of Edinburgh. He used to tell in his later life how Wolfe, probably to relieve the intense strain of his thoughts, repeated Gray's Elegy in a Country Churchyard to the officers about him, and among the rest, the verse which his own fate was soon to illustrate: —

"The paths of glory lead but to the grave."

"Gentlemen," he said, as his recital ended, "I would rather have written those lines than take Quebec." None were there to tell him that the hero is greater than the poet.

As they neared their destination the tide bore them in towards the shore, and the mighty wall of rock and forest towered in darkness on their left. Suddenly the challenge of a French sentry rang out of the gloom: —

"Qui vive?"

"France," answered a Highland officer of Fraser's regiment from one of the boats of the light infantry. He had served in Holland, and spoke French fluently.

"À quel régiment?"

"De la Reine," replied the Highlander. He knew that a part of that corps was with Bougainville. The sentry, expecting the convoy of provisions, was satisfied, and did not ask for the password.

Soon after, the foremost boats were passing the heights of Samos, when another sentry challenged them, and they could see him through the darkness running down to the edge of the water, within range of a pistol shot. In answer to his questions the same officer replied in French, "Provision boats. Don't make a noise; the English will hear us." In fact, the sloop of war Hunter was anchored in the stream, not far off. Again the sentry let them pass. In a few moments they rounded the lofty headland above the Ance du Foulon. There was no sentry there. The strong current swept the boats of the light infantry a little below the intended landing place. They disembarked on a narrow strand at the foot of heights as steep as a hill covered with trees can be. The twenty-four volunteers led the way, climbing with what silence they might, closely followed by a much larger body. When they reached the top they saw in the dim light a cluster of tents not far off, and immediately made a dash at them. Vergor leaped from bed and tried to escape, but was shot in the heel and captured. His men, taken by surprise, made little resistance. One or two were caught, and the rest fled.

The main body of troops waited in their boats by the edge of the strand. The heights near by were cleft by a great ravine, choked with forest trees; and in its depths ran a little brook called Ruisseau St. Denis, which, swollen by the late rains, fell plashing in the stillness over a rock. Other than this no sound could reach the strained ear of Wolfe but the gurgle of the tide and the cautious climbing of his advance parties, as they mounted the steeps at some little distance from where he sat listening. At length, from the top came a sound of musket shots, followed by loud huzzas, and he knew that his men were masters of the position. The word was given; the troops leaped from the boats and scaled the heights, some here, some there, clutching at trees and bushes, their muskets slung at their backs. Tradition still points out the place near the mouth of the ravine where the foremost reached the top. Wolfe said to an officer near him, "You can try it, but I don't think you'll get up." He himself, however, found strength to drag himself up with the rest. The narrow, slanting path on the face of the heights had been made impassable by trenches and abatis; but all obstructions were soon cleared away, and then the ascent was easy. In the gray of the morning the long file of red-coated soldiers moved quickly upward, and formed in order on the plateau above.

Before many of them had reached the top, cannon were heard close on the left. It was the battery at Samos firing on the boats in the rear and the vessels descending from Cap Rouge. A party was sent to silence it, which was soon effected; and the more distant battery at Sillery was next attacked and taken. As fast as the boats were emptied they returned for the troops left on board the vessels, and for those waiting on the southern shore under Colonel Burton.

The day broke in clouds and threatening rain. The British battalions were drawn up along the crest of the heights. No enemy was in sight, though a body of Canadians had sallied from the town and moved along the strand towards the landing place, whence they were quickly driven back. Wolfe had achieved the most critical part of his enterprise; yet the success that he coveted placed him in imminent danger. On one side was the garrison of Quebec and the army of Beauport, and Bougainville was on the other. Wolfe's alternative was victory or ruin; for, if he should be overwhelmed by a combined attack, retreat would be hopeless. His feelings no man can know, but it would be safe to say that hesitation or doubt had no part in them.

He went to reconnoitre the ground, and soon came to the Plains of Abraham; so called from Abraham Martin, a pilot, known as Maître Abraham, who had owned a piece of land here in the early times of the colony. The Plains were a tract of grass, tolerably level in most parts, patched here and there with cornfields, studded with clumps of bushes, and forming a part of the high plateau at the eastern end of which Quebec stood. On the south, it was bounded by the declivities along the St. Lawrence; on the north, by those along the St. Charles, or rather along the meadows through which that lazy stream crawled like a writhing snake. At the place that Wolfe chose for his battle-field the plateau was less than a mile wide.

Thither the troops advanced, marched by files till they reached the ground, and then wheeled to form their line of battle, which stretched across the plateau and faced the city.

Quebec was not a mile distant, but they could not see it; for a ridge of broken ground intervened, called Buttes à Neveu, about six hundred paces off. The first division of troops had scarcely come up when, about six o'clock, this ridge was suddenly thronged with white uniforms. It was the battalion of Guienne, arrived at the eleventh hour from its camp by the St. Charles. Some time after, there was hot firing in the rear. It came from a detachment of Bougainville's command, attacking a house where some of the light infantry were posted. The assailants were repulsed, and the firing ceased. Light showers fell at intervals, besprinkling the troops as they stood patiently waiting the event.

Montcalm had passed a troubled night. Through all the evening the cannon bellowed from the ships of Saunders, and the boats of the fleet hovered in the dusk off the Beauport shore, threatening every moment to land. Troops lined the entrenchments till day, while the general walked the field that adjoined his headquarters till one in the morning, accompanied by the Chevalier Johnstone and Colonel Poulariez. Johnstone says that he was in great agitation, and took no rest all night. At daybreak, he heard the sound of cannon above the town, where the battery at Samos was firing on the English ships. He had sent an officer to the quarters of Vaudreuil, which were much nearer Quebec, with orders to bring him word at once should anything unusual happen; but no word came, and about six o'clock he mounted and rode thither with Johnstone. As they advanced, the country behind the town opened more and more upon their sight, till at length, when opposite Vaudreuil's house, they saw across the St. Charles, more than a mile away, the red coats of British soldiers on the heights beyond.

"This is a serious business," Montcalm said, and sent off Johnstone at full gallop to bring up the troops from the centre and left of the camp. Those of the right were in motion already, doubtless by the governor's order. Vaudreuil came out of the house. Montcalm stopped for a few words with him; then set spurs to his horse, and galloped over the bridge of the St. Charles to the scene of danger. He rode with a fixed look, uttering not a word.

The army followed in such order as it might, crossed the bridge in hot haste, passed under the northern rampart of Quebec, entered at the Palace Gate, and pressed on in headlong march along the quaint, narrow streets of the warlike town: troops of Indians in scalp-locks and war paint, a savage glitter in their deep-set eyes; bands of Canadians, whose all was at stake, — faith, country, and home; the colony regulars; the battalions of Old France, a torrent of white uniforms and gleaming bayonets. They swept on, poured out upon the plain, some by the gate of St. Louis and some by that of St. John, and hurried, breathless, to where the banners of Guienne still fluttered on the ridge.

Montcalm was amazed at what he saw. He had expected a detachment, and he found an army. Full in sight before him stretched the lines of Wolfe: the close ranks of the English infantry, a silent wall of red, and the wild array of the Highlanders, with their waving tartans and bagpipes screaming defiance. Vaudreuil had not come; but not the less was felt the evil of a divided authority and the jealousy of the rival chiefs. Montcalm waited long for the forces he had ordered to join him from the left wing of the army. He waited in vain. Neither did the garrison of Quebec come to the aid of Montcalm. He sent to Ramsay, its commander, for twenty-five field-pieces which were on the Palace battery. Ramsay would give him only three, saying that he wanted them for his own defense. There were orders and counter-orders, misunderstanding, haste, delay, perplexity.

Montcalm and his chief officers held a council of war. He felt that there was no time to lose, for he imagined that Wolfe would soon be reinforced, which was impossible; and he believed that the English were fortifying themselves, which was no less an error. His men were ready for the fray, and he resolved to attack before their ardor cooled. He spoke a few words to them in his keen, vehement way. "I remember very well how he looked," a Canadian, then a boy of eighteen, used to say in his old age. "He rode a black or dark bay horse along the front of our lines, brandishing his sword, as if to excite us to do our duty. He wore a coat with wide sleeves, which fell back as he raised his arm, and showed the white linen of the wristband."

The English waited the result with a composure which, if not quite real, was at least well feigned. It was towards ten o'clock, when, from a hillock on the right of the line, Wolfe saw that the crisis was near. The French on the ridge had gathered themselves into three bodies; regulars in the centre, regulars and Canadians on right and left. Two fieldpieces which had been dragged up the height fired on them with grape-shot, and the troops, rising from the ground, formed to receive them. In a few moments more they were in motion. They came on rapidly, uttering loud shouts, and firing as soon as they were within range. Their ranks, ill ordered at the best, were farther confused by a number of Canadians, who had been interspersed among the regulars, and who, after hastily firing, threw themselves on the ground to reload. The British advanced a few rods; then halted and stood still. When the French were within forty paces, the word of command rang out, and a crash of musketry answered all along the line. The volley was delivered with remarkable precision. In the battalions of the centre, which had suffered least from the enemy's bullets, the simultaneous explosion was afterwards said by French officers to have sounded like a cannon shot. Another volley followed, and then a furious clattering fire, that lasted but a minute or two. When the smoke rose, a miserable sight was revealed: the ground cumbered with dead and wounded, the advancing masses stopped short and turned into a frantic mob, shouting, cursing, gesticulating. The order was given to charge. Then over the field rose the British cheer, joined with the fierce yell of the Highland slogan. Some of the corps pushed forward with the bayonet; some advanced firing. The clansmen drew their broadswords and dashed on, keen and swift as bloodhounds. At the English right, though the attacking column was broken to pieces, a fire was still kept up; chiefly, it seems, by sharpshooters from the bushes and cornfields, where they had lain for an hour or more. Here Wolfe himself led the charge, at the head of the Louisbourg grenadiers. A shot shattered his wrist. He wrapped his handkerchief about it, and kept on. Another shot struck him, and he still advanced, when a third lodged in his breast. He staggered, and sat on the ground. Lieutenant Brown, of the grenadiers, one Henderson, a volunteer in the same company, and a private soldier, aided by an officer of artillery who ran to join them, carried him in their arms to the rear. He begged them to lay him down. They did so, and asked if he would have a surgeon. "There's no need," he answered; "it's all over with me." A moment after, one of them cried out, "They run! See how they run!" "Who run?" Wolfe demanded, like a man roused from sleep. "The enemy, sir. Egad, they give way everywhere." "Go, one of you, to Colonel Burton," returned the dying man: "tell him to march Webb's regiment down to Charles River, to cut off their retreat from the bridge." Then, turning on his side, he murmured, "Now, God be praised, I will die in peace;" and in a few moments his gallant soul had fled.

Montcalm, still on horseback, was borne with the tide of fugitives towards the town. As he approached the walls, a shot passed through his body. He kept his seat; two soldiers supported him, one on each side, and led his horse through the St. Louis Gate. On the open space within, among the excited crowd, were several women, drawn, no doubt, by eagerness to know the result of the fight. One of them recognized him, saw the streaming blood, and shrieked, "Oh, mon Dieu! mon Dieu! le Marquis est tué!" "It's nothing, it's nothing," replied the death-stricken man. "Don't be troubled for me, my good friends." ("Ce n'est rien, ce n'est rien. Ne vous affligez pas pour moi, mes bonnes amies.")

1885
A STORY OF ASSISTED FATE
by Frank R. Stockton

IN a general way I am not a superstitious man, but I have a few ideas, or notions, in regard to fatality and kindred subjects of which I have never been able entirely to dispossess my mind; nor can I say that I have ever tried very much to do so, for I hold that a certain amount of irrationalism in the nature of a man is a thing to be desired. By its aid he clambers over the wall which limits the action of his intellect, and if he be but sure that he can get back again no harm may come of it, while he is the better for many pleasant excursions.

My principal superstitious notion, and indeed the only one of importance, is the belief that whatever I earnestly desire and plan for will happen. This idea does not relate to things for which people fight hard, or work long, but to those events for which we sit down and wait. It is truly a pleasant belief, and one worthy to be fostered if there can be found any ground for it. I do not exercise my little superstition

very often, but when I do I find things happen as I wish; and in cases
where this has not yet occurred there is plenty of time to wait.

I am not a very old person, being now in my twenty-eighth year, but
my two sisters, who live with me, as well as most of my acquaintances,
look upon me, I think, as an older man. This is not due to my experience in the world, for I have not gone out a great deal among my
fellow-men, but rather to my habits of reading and reflection, which
have so matured my intellectual nature that the rest of me, so to
speak, has insensibly stepped a little faster to keep pace with it. Grace
Anna, indeed, is two years older than I, yet I know she looks up to me
as a senior quite as much as does Bertha, who is but twenty-four.

These sisters had often laughingly assured me that the one thing I
needed was a wife, and, although I never spoke much on the subject,
in the course of time I began to think a good deal about it, and the
matter so interested my mind that at last I did a very singular thing. I
keep a diary, in which I briefly note daily events, especially those
which may, in a degree, be considered as epochs. My book has a page
for every day, with the date printed at the top thereof; not a very
desirable form, perhaps, for those who would write much on one day
and very little the next, but it suits me well enough, for I seldom enter
into details. Not many months ago, as I sat alone, one evening, in my
library, turning over the leaves of this diary, I looked ahead at the
pages intended for the days of the year that were yet to come, and the
thought entered my mind that it was a slavish thing to be able to note
only what had happened, and not to dare to write one word upon the
blank pages of the next month, or the next, or even of to-morrow. As
I turned backward and forward these pages devoted to a record of the
future the desire came to me to write something upon one of them. It
was a foolish fancy, perhaps, but it pleased me. I would like a diary,
not only of what had been, but of what was to be. I longed to challenge fate, and I did it. I selected a page, not too far ahead and in
a good time of the year, — it was September 14th, — and on it I
wrote, —

> "This day came into my life
> She who is to be my wife."

When I had made this strange entry I regarded it with satisfaction. I
had fully come to the conclusion that it was due to my position as the
owner of a goodly estate that I should marry. I had felt that at some
time I must do something in this matter. And now a thing was done,
and a time was fixed. It is true that I knew no woman who was at all
likely, upon the day I had selected, or upon any other day, to exercise

a matrimonial influence upon my life. But that made no difference to me. I had taken my fate into my own hands, and I would now see what would happen.

It was then early in July, and in a little more than two months the day which I had made a very momentous one to me would arrive. I cannot say that I had a positive belief that what I had written would occur on the 14th of September, but I had a very strange notion that, as there was no reason why it should not be so, it would be so. At any rate, who could say it would not be so? This sort of thing was not a belief, but to all intents and purposes it was just as good.

It was somewhat amusing even to myself, and it would probably have been very amusing to any one else acquainted with the circumstances, to observe the influence that this foundationless and utterly irrational expectation had upon me. To the great delight of my sisters, I began to attend to matters in which formerly I had taken little interest. I set two men at work upon the grounds about the house, giving my personal supervision to the removal of the patches of grass in the driveway, which led under the oaks to the door. Here and there I had a panel of fence put in better order, and a dead apple-tree, which for some time had stood on the brow of a hill in view of the house, was cut down and taken away.

"If any of our friends think of visiting us," said Bertha, "they ought to come now, while everything is looking so trim and nice."

"Would you like that?" asked Grace Anna, looking at me.

"Yes," I replied. "That is, they might begin to come now."

At this both my sisters laughed.

"Begin to come!" cried Bertha. "How hospitable you are growing!"

The summer went on, and I kept good faith with my little superstition. If either of us should desert the other, it should not be I who would do it. It pleased me to look forward to the event which I had called up out of the future, and to wait for it — if perchance it should come.

One morning my sister Bertha entered my library, with a letter in her hand and a very pleasant expression on her face. "What do you think?" she said. "We are going to have a visit! — just as the paint is dry on the back porch, so that we can have tea there in the afternoon."

"A visit!" I exclaimed, regarding her with much interest.

"Yes," continued Bertha. "Kitty Watridge is coming to stay with us. I have written and written to her, and now she is coming."

"Who is she?" I asked.

Bertha laughed. "You haven't forgotten the Watridges, have you?"

No, I had not forgotten them; at least, the only one of them I ever knew. Old Mr. Watridge had been a friend of my late father, a cheerful and rather ruddy man, although much given to books. He had been my friend, too, in the days when he used to come to us; and I remember well that it was he who started me on a journey along the third shelf from the top, on the east wall of the library, through The World Displayed, in many volumes, by Smart, Goldsmith, and Johnson; and thence to some New Observations on Italy, in French, by two Swedish gentlemen, in 1758; and so on through many other works of the kind, where I found the countries shown forth on their quaint pages so different from those of the same name described in modern books of travel that it was to me a virtual enlargement of the world. It had been a long time since I had seen the old gentleman, and I felt sorry for it.

"Is Mr. Watridge coming?" I asked.

"Of course not," said Bertha. "That would be your affair. And besides, he never leaves home now. It is only Kitty, his youngest daughter, my friend."

I had an indistinct recollection that Mr. Watridge had some children, and that they were daughters, but that was all I remembered about them. "She is grown?" I asked.

"I should think so," answered Bertha, with a laugh. "She is at least twenty."

If my sister could have known the intense interest which suddenly sprung up within me she would have been astounded. A grown-up, marriageable young lady was coming to my house, in September! My next question was asked hurriedly: "When will she be here?"

"She is coming next Wednesday, the 16th," answered Bertha, referring to her letter.

"The 16th!" I said to myself. "That is two days after my date."

"What kind of a lady is she?" I asked Bertha.

"She is lovely, — just as lovely as she can be."

I now began to feel a little disappointed. If she were lovely, as my sister said, and twenty, with good Watridge blood, why did she not come a little sooner? It was truly an odd thing to do, but I could not forbear expressing what I thought. "I wish," I said, somewhat abstractedly, "that she were coming on Monday instead of Wednesday."

Bertha laughed heartily. "I was really afraid," she said, "that you might think there were enough girls already in the house. But here you are wanting Kitty to come before she is ready. Grace Anna!" she cried to my elder sister, who was passing the open door, "he isn't put out a bit, and he is in such a hurry to see Kitty that he thinks she should come on Monday."

It was impossible to chide my sisters for laughing at me, and I could not help smiling myself. "It is not that I am in a hurry to see her," I observed, "for I do not know the young lady at all; but I consider Monday a more suitable day than Wednesday for her arrival."

"It is odd," replied Bertha, "that you should prefer one day to another."

"Is there any reason why it does not suit you to have her come on Wednesday?" asked Grace Anna. "Her visit might be deferred a day or two."

Of course I could give no reason, and I did not wish the visit deferred.

"It's just because he's so dreadfully systematic!" cried Bertha. "He thinks everything ought to begin at the beginning of the week, and that even a visit should make a fair start on Monday, and not break in unmethodically."

My elder sister was always very considerate of my welfare and my wishes, and had it been practicable I believe that she would have endeavored in this instance to make our hospitality conform to what appeared to be my love of system and order. But she explained to me that, apart from the awkwardness of asking the young lady to change the day which she had herself fixed, without being able to give any good reason therefor, it would be extremely inconvenient for them to have their visitor before Wednesday, as an earlier arrival would materially interfere with certain houshold arrangements.

I said no more, but I was disappointed; and this feeling grew upon me, for the reason that during the rest of the day and the evening my sisters talked a great deal about their young friend, and I found that, unless they were indeed most prejudiced judges, — which in the case of Grace Anna, at least, I could never believe, — this young person who was coming to us must be possessed of most admirable personal qualities. She was pretty; she had excellent moral sentiments, a well-cultured intellect, and a lovable disposition. These, with the good blood, — which, in my opinion, was a most important requisite, — made up a woman in every way fitted to enter my life in a matrimonial capacity. If, without any personal bias, I had been selecting a wife for a friend, I could not have expected to do better than this. That such a young person should come within the range of my cognizance on the wrong day would be, to say the least, a most annoying occurrence. Why did I not select the 16th, or she the 14th? A fate that was two days slow might as well be no fate at all. My meeting with the girl would have no meaning. I must admit that the more I thought about this girl the more I wished it should have a meaning.

During the night, or perhaps very early in the morning, a most felicitous idea came into my mind. I would assist my fate. My idea was this: On Monday I would drive to Mr. Watridge's house. It was a pleasant day's journey. I would spend Tuesday with him, and, returning on Wednesday, I could bring Miss Kitty with me. Thus all the necessary conditions would be fulfilled. She would come into my life on the 14th, and I would have opportunities of knowing her which probably would not occur to me at home. Everything would happen as it should; only, instead of the lady coming to me, I should go to her.

As I expected, my project, when I announced it at the breakfast table, was the occasion of much mirth, especially on the part of Bertha. "I never saw anything like it!" she cried. "You want to see Kitty even more than I do. I should never have thought of such a thing as going for her two days in advance."

"As it would have been impossible for you to do so," said I, "I can easily conceive that you would not have allowed the idea to enter your mind."

Grace Anna, however, looked upon my plan with much favor, and entered into its details with interest, dwelling particularly on the pleasure Mr. Watridge would derive from my visit.

I looked forward with great pleasure to the little journey I was about to make. The distance, from Eastover, my residence, to Mr. Watridge's house was some twenty-five miles, — a very suitable day's drive in fine weather. The road led through a pleasant country, with several opportunities for pretty views; and about half-way was a neat tavern, standing behind an immense cherry-tree, where a stop could be made for rest and for a midday meal. I had a comfortable, easy-cushioned buggy, well provided with protective appurtenances in case of rain or too much sunshine; and my sisters and myself were of the opinion that, under ordinary circumstances, no one would hesitate between this vehicle and the crowded stage-coach, which was the only means of communication between our part of the country and that in which the Watridge estate lay.

I made an early start on Monday morning, with my good horse, Dom Pedro; named by my sister Bertha, but whether for the Emperor of Brazil, or for a social game of cards which we generally played when we had two or three visitors, and therefore there were too many of us for whist, I do not know. I arrived at my destination towards the close of the afternoon, and old Mr. Watridge was delighted to see me. We spent a pleasant hour in his library, waiting for the return of his two daughters, who were out for a walk. It must be admitted that it was with considerable emotional perturbation that I beheld the entrance into that room of Miss Kitty Watridge. She came in alone; her sister, who was much older, being detained by some household duties, connected, probably, with my unexpected arrival. This, with the action of Mr. Watridge in presently excusing himself for a time, gave me an opportunity, more immediate than I had expected, for an uninterrupted study of this young lady, who had become to me so important a person.

I will not describe Kitty, her appearance, nor her conversation, but will merely remark that before we were joined by her father and sister I would have been quite willing, so far as I was concerned, to show her the entry in my diary.

It may be that a man heavily clad with the armor of reserve and restraint sinks more quickly and deeper than one not so encumbered, when he finds himself suddenly in a current of that sentiment which now possessed me. Be that as it may, my determination was arrived at before I slept that night: Kitty Watridge had entered into my life on the 14th of September, and I was willing to accept her as my wife.

As the son of an old comrade on the part of the father, and as the brother of two dear friends on the part of the daughters, I was treated with hearty cordiality by this family, and the next day was a most pleasing and even delightful one to me, until the evening came. Then a cloud, and a very heavy one, arose upon my emotional horizon. I had stated how I purposed to make the little journey of Miss Kitty to our house more comfortable and expeditious than it would otherwise be, and Mr. Watridge had expressed himself very much pleased with the plan; while Kitty had declared that it would be charming, especially when compared with travel by stage-coach, of which the principal features, in her idea of it, appeared to be mothers, little children, and lunch baskets. But, after dinner, Miss Maria, the elder daughter, remarked very quietly, but very positively, that she did not think it would do — that is the phrase she used — for me to drive her sister to Eastover. She gave no reasons, and I asked none, but it was quite evident that her decision was one not to be altered.

"It would be far better," she said, "not to change our original plan, and for Kitty, as well as her trunk, to go by the stage. Mrs. Karcroft is going the whole of the way, and Kitty will be well taken care of."

Miss Maria was the head of the house; she had acted for many years as the maternal director of her sister; and I saw very soon that what the other two members of the family might think upon the subject would matter very little. The father, indeed, made at first some very vigorous dissent, urging that it would be a shame to make me take that long drive home alone, when I had expected company; and although Kitty said nothing, I am sure she looked quite disappointed. But neither words nor looks availed anything. Miss Maria was placid, but very firm, and under her deft management of the conversation the subject was soon dismissed as settled.

"I am very sorry," observed the old gentleman to me, when the ladies had bidden us good-night, "that Kitty cannot take advantage of your invitation, which was a very kind one, and to which I see not the slightest objection. My daughter Maria has very peculiar ideas sometimes, but as she acts as a sort of mother here we don't like to interfere with her."

"I would not have you do so for the world," answered I.

"You are very good, very good!" exclaimed Mr. Watridge; "and I must say I think it's a confounded shame that you and Kitty cannot take that pleasant drive together. Suppose you go with her in the stage, and let me send a man to Eastover with your horse and vehicle."

"I thank you very kindly, sir," I replied, "but it will be better for me to return the way I came; and your daughter will have a companion, I understand."

"Nobody but old Mrs. Karcroft, and she counts for nothing as company. You had better think of it."

I would not consent, however, to make any change in my arrangements; and, shortly after, I retired.

I went to bed that night a very angry man. When I prepared a plan or scheme with which no reasonable fault could be found, I was not accustomed to have it thwarted, or indeed even objected to. I was displeased with Mr. Watridge because he allowed himself to be so easily influenced, and I was even dissatisfied with Kitty's want of spirit, though of course she could not have been expected to exhibit an eagerness to accompany me. But with that horrible old maid, Miss Maria, I was truly indignant. There frequently arises in the mind an image which forcibly connects itself with the good or bad qualities of a person under our contemplation, and thus Miss Maria appeared to me in the character of a moral pepper-box. Virtue is like sugar or cream, — good in itself, and of advantage to that with which it is suitably mingled; but Miss Maria's propriety was the hottest and most violent sort of pepper, extremely disagreeable in itself, and never needed except in the case of weak moral digestion. Her objections were an insult to me. I went to sleep thinking of a little pepper cruet which I would like to have made of silver for my table, to take the place of the owl or other conventional pattern, which should be exactly like Miss Maria, — hard and unimpressionable without, hollow within, and the top of its head perforated with little holes. At breakfast I endeavored to be coldly polite, but it must have been easy for the family to perceive that I was very much offended. I requested that my horse and buggy should be made ready as soon as possible. While I was waiting for it on the porch, where Mr. Watridge had just left me, Miss Kitty came out to me. This was the first time I had been alone with her since the preceding afternoon, when we had had a most charming walk through the orchard and over the hills to a high point, where we had stayed until we saw the sun go down.

"It seems a real pity," she observed very prettily, and in a tone which touched me, "that you should be driving off now by yourself, while in about an hour I shall start from the same place."

"Miss Kitty," said I, "would you like to go with me?"

She hesitated for a moment, looked down, and then looked up, and said, "So far as I am concerned, I think — I mean I know — that I should like very much to go with you. But you see" — and then she hesitated again.

"Say no more, I pray you!" I exclaimed. I would not place her in the unpleasant position of defending, or even explaining, the unwarrantable interference of a relative. "If you really wish to accompany me," I continued, warmly shaking her hand, for my buggy was now approaching, "I am entirely satisfied, and nothing more need be said. It is, in a measure, the same as if you were going with me. Good-by."

A moment before I was depressed and morose. Now I was exuberantly joyful. The change was sudden, but there was reason for it. Kitty wished to go with me, and had come to tell me so!

Mr. Watridge and his elder daughter now appeared in the doorway, and as I took leave of the latter I am sure she noticed a change in my manner. I said no more to her than was absolutely necessary, but the sudden cheerfulness which had taken possession of me could not be repressed even in her presence.

The old gentleman accompanied me to the carriage-block. "I don't want to bore you about it," he said, "but I really am sorry you are going away alone."

I felt quite sure, from several things Mr. Watridge had said and done during my visit, that he would be well pleased to see his younger daughter and myself thrown very much into the company of each other, and to have us remain so, indeed, for the rest of our lives. And there was no reason why he should not desire it. In every way the conditions of such a union would be most favorable.

"Thank you very much," I returned; "but the pleasure of having your daughter at my house will make me forget this little disappointment."

He looked at me with glistening eyes. Had I boldly asked him, "Will you be my father-in-law?" no more favorable answer could have come from his lips than I now saw upon his countenance.

"Good fortune be with you!" were his last words as I drove away.

I do not suppose anything of the kind could be more delightful than my drive that morning. Miss Kitty had said that she would like to be my companion, and I determined to have her so in imagination, if not in fact. The pleasures of fancy are sometimes more satisfactory than those of reality, for we have them entirely under our control. I chose now to imagine that Miss Kitty was seated by my side, and I sat well to the right, that I might give her plenty of room. In imagination I conversed with her, and she answered me as I would have her. Our remarks were carefully graduated to the duration of our acquaintance and the seemly progress of our intimacy. I wished to discover the intellectual status of the fair young creature who had come into my life on the 14th of September. I spoke to her of books, and found that her reading had been varied and judicious. She had read Farrar's Life of Christ, but did not altogether like it; and while she had much enjoyed Froude's Cæsar, she could have wished to believe the author as just as he endeavored to make his hero appear. With modern romance she had dealt but lightly, rather preferring works of history and travel, even when pervaded with the flavor of the eighteenth century. But we did not always speak of abstract subjects; we were both susceptible to the influences of nature, and my companion enjoyed as much as I did the bright sunshine tempered by a cooling breeze, the clear sky with fair white clouds floating along the horizon, and the occasional views of the blue and distant mountains, their tops suffused with warm autumnal mists. After a time I asked her if I might call her Kitty, and glancing downward, and then up, with the same look she had given me on the porch, she said I might. This was very pleasant, and was not, in my opinion, an undue familiarity, which feature I was very careful to eliminate from our companionship. One act, however, of what might be termed super-friendly kindness, I intended to propose, and the contemplation of its probable acceptance afforded me much pleasure. After our quiet luncheon in the shaded little dining-room of the Cherry-Tree Inn, and when she had rested as long as she chose, we would begin our afternoon journey, and the road, before very long, would lead us through a great pine wood. Here, rolling over the hard, smooth way, and breathing the gentle odor of the pines, she would naturally feel a little somnolent, and I intended to say to her that if she liked she might rest her head upon my shoulder, and doze. If I should hear the sound of approaching wheels I would gently arouse her; but as an interruption of this kind was not likely to occur, I thought with much satisfaction of the pleasure I should have in the afternoon, when this fancy would be appropriate. To look upon the little head gently resting on that shoulder, which, when our acquaintance had more fully developed, I would offer her as a permanent possession, would be to me a preconnubial satisfaction of a very high order.

When about a mile from the Cherry-Tree Inn, and with my mind filled with these agreeable fancies, an accident happened to me. One of the irons which connected the shafts to the front axle broke, and the conditions of my progress became abruptly changed. The wheel at that end of the axle to which a shaft was yet attached went suddenly forward, and the other flew back and grated against the side of the buggy, while both wheels, instead of rolling in the general course of the vehicle, were dragged in a sidewise direction. The disconnected shaft fell upon the legs of Dom Pedro, who, startled by the unusual sensation, forsook his steady trot, and broke into a run. Thus, with the front wheels scraping the road, the horse attached but by a single shaft, I was hurried along at an alarming pace. Pull as I might, I could not check the progress of Dom Pedro; and if this state of affairs had continued for more than the few moments which it really lasted, the front wheels would have been shattered, and I do not know what sad results might have ensued. But the other shaft broke loose, the reins were rudely torn from my hands, and the horse, now free from attachment to the vehicle, went clattering along the road, the shafts bobbing at his heels; while the buggy, following the guidance of the twisted front axle, ran into a shallow ditch at the side of the road, and abruptly stopped.

Unhurt, I sprang out, and my first thought was one of joy that the Kitty who had been by my side was an imaginary one. Had the real Kitty been there, what might not have happened to her! A dozen possible accidents crowded themselves on my mind, and I have no doubt my countenance expressed my feelings.

There was nothing to be done but to take my valise and the whip from the buggy, and walk on to the inn, where I found the landlord in the act of saddling a horse, to come and see what had happened to me. Dom Pedro had arrived with a portion of the shafts attached to him, the rest having been kicked away. The accident occasioned considerable stir at the inn; but as I never care to discuss my personal affairs any further than is necessary, it was soon arranged that after I had lunched I would borrow a saddle from the landlord, and ride Dom Pedro home, while the broken buggy would be brought to the inn, where I would send for it the next day. This plan did not please me, for I was not fond of equestrianism, and Dom Pedro was rather a hard trotter; but there was nothing better to do. Had I not taken this road, which was much more agreeable although rather longer than the high road, I might have been picked up by the stage which was conveying Miss Kitty to my house.

While I was yet at my meal there arrived at the inn a young man, who shortly afterward entered the room, and informed me that, having heard of my accident, he came to offer me a seat in the buggy in which he was traveling. He was going my way, and would be glad of a companion. This invitation, given as it was by a well-appearing young man of pleasing manners, was, after a little consideration, accepted by me. I would much prefer to ride a dozen miles in a buggy with a stranger than on horseback alone.

The drive of the afternoon was very different from what I had expected it to be, but it was not devoid of some pleasant features. My companion was sociable and not too communicative; and although he annoyed me very much by giving me the entirely uncalled-for information that if I had had short straps from the ends of the shafts to the axle, which no well-ordered buggy should be without, the accident would not have occurred, I passed this by, and our conversation became more general, and to me more acceptable. The young man was going to Harnden, a village not far from my house, where he appeared to have some business, and he assured me that he would not object in the least to go a little out of his way and set me down at my door.

We reached Eastover quite late in the afternoon, and I perceived, from the group on the porch, that Miss Kitty had arrived. All three of the ladies came down to meet me, evidently very much surprised to see me in a strange vehicle. When I had alighted, and was hastily explaining to my sisters the cause of this change of conveyance, I was surprised to see Miss Kitty shaking hands with the young man, who was standing by his horse's head. My elder sister, Grace Anna, who had also noticed this meeting, now approached the pair, and was introduced to the gentleman. In a few moments she returned to me, who had been regarding the interview with silent amazement.

"It is Harvey Glade," she said, — "Kitty's cousin. We should invite him to stay here to-night."

I cannot conceive of anything which more quickly than these words would have snuffed out the light which had illumined the vision of my house with Kitty in it; but it was impossible for me to forget that I was a gentleman and the master of Eastover, and, instantly causing my perception of these facts to take precedence of my gathering emotions, I stepped up to Miss Kitty, and, asking to be introduced to her cousin, I begged him to make my house his home during his stay in the neighborhood.

This invitation was accepted, as I supposed it would be when I made it; yet I must own that I did not expect Mr. Glade to remain at my house for a week. Of course his presence prevented the execution of any of my plans regarding the promotion of my intimacy with Kitty; but although the interruption caused me much vexation, I maintained the equanimity due to my position, and hoped each day that the young man would take his leave. Towards the end of his visit I became aware, through the medium of my sisters, to whom I had left in a great degree the entertainment of our guests, that young Glade was actually engaged to be married to Kitty. She had told them so herself. This statement, which chilled to the verge of frigidity my every sensibility, was amplified as follows: The young people had been attached to each other for some time, but the visits of Glade having been discouraged by Miss Kitty's family they had not seen each other lately, and there had been no positive declaration of amatory sentiment on the part of either; this protracted sojourn in my house had given the young man all the opportunity he could desire, and the matter was settled so definitely that there was no reason to suppose that the better judgment of her elders would cause the young woman to change her mind.

Here was a fine ending to my endeavors to assist my fate. Instead of so doing, I had assisted the fate of Mr. Harvey Glade, in whose welfare I had no interest whatever. He had not known that Miss Kitty was coming to my house; he had not even been aware, until he met her at Eastover, that I was acquainted with her family. Had it not been for my endeavors to promote my own fortune in the direction of the lady, he would have had no opportunity to make her his own; and they probably would not have seen each other again, unless he had happened to call upon her as the mistress of Eastover. Instead of aiding Miss Kitty to enter my life on the 14th of September, I had ushered her into his life on the 16th of that month.

For a week after the departure of our guests — the young man went first — I found myself in a state of mental depression from which the kindly efforts of my sisters could not arouse me. Not only was I deeply chagrined at what had occurred, but it wounded my self-respect to think that my fate, which had been satisfactorily pursuing the course I had marked out for it, should have been thus suddenly and disastrously turned aside. I felt that I must confess myself conquered. It was an unusual and a difficult thing for me to do this, but there was no help for it. I took out my diary, and turned to the page whereon I had challenged fate. That entry must be erased. I must humble myself, and acknowledge it untrue.

At the moment that I dipped the pen in the inkstand there was a knock at the door, and Grace Anna entered.

"I have just had a letter," she said, "from dear Jane Wiltby, who married your old schoolfellow, Dr. Tom. I thought you would like to hear the news it contains. They have a little girl, and she is to be named for me."

"How old is it?" I asked, with indifferent interest.

"She was born on the 14th of September," said Grace Anna.

I sat erect, and looked at my sister, — looked at her without seeing her. Thoughts, like clouds upon the horizon brightened by the rays of dawn, piled themselves up in my mind. Dr. Tom, the companion of my youth, ever my cherished friend! Jane, woman above women! Grace Anna!

I laid down the pen, and, leaving the momentous and prognostic entry just as I had written it, I closed my diary, and placed it in my desk.

He who cannot adapt himself to the vagaries of a desired fate, who cannot place himself upon the road by which he expects it to come, and who cannot wait for it with cheerful confidence is not worthy to be assistant arbiter of his destiny.

1886
SALEM CUPBOARDS
by Eleanor Putnam

THERE were cupboards in Salem. Whether they are there still, or have been built up, or pulled down, or swept away, in the march of modern improvement, I know not, but in my childhood there were cupboards in Salem.

They were, moreover, real cupboards; no after-thoughts, built across the end of an entry here, or the corner of a room there, — places into which to huddle umbrellas and overcoats, or to hustle mending and children's litter out of the sight of visitors. Salem cupboards were always intentional. The builder understood his responsibility, and acted accordingly. The housewife regarded her cupboards as the inner and most sacred portion of her trust. It was no light task even to keep the keys always counted and polished. As for losing one, or forgetting which was which, that would indicate a mind so utterly frivolous that one could hardly conceive of it.

The genuine, old-time Salem housekeeper realized that there was a conscience in her work. She took her cupboards seriously. To her there was nothing trivial about them. To do her duty by her cupboards was one of the most inviolable principles of her sober and decorous life.

It took no ordinary brain to keep watch and ward over these cupboards. They were many in number. They were confusing as to size and shape. They possessed the charm of the unexpected. One never knew quite when or where one should chance upon them. They were tall and narrow beside the fireplace, or low and chubby above it; they lurked behind the wainscoting, like Polonius back of the arras. One of them was to be reached only by a stepladder; another jolly pair occupied crannies under two deep window-seats. In one house was a cupboard which pretended to be solid wall, but was really a deep recess for the concealment of firearms; and in yet another was a narrow closet about which hung the horror of an old Ginevra-like legend of smothering to death.

There was literally no end to the number and variety of Salem cupboards. They possessed a charm quite their own, and this charm was felt to the utmost by the children, who were only occasionally allowed to view the treasures kept under strict lock and key by the high priestesses of these sacred nooks and shrines.

Foremost in the memory of delightful Salem cupboards stands the dining-room closet of a second-cousin of ours, whom I will call cousin Susan. She was a widow of some fifty odd years, and kept house for a bachelor brother, who was a retired sea-captain. She was a round, trim, black-eyed woman, greatly afflicted with rheumatism, for which reason she always walked with a cane. The cane was of some dark, foreign wood, highly polished, and the top was carved to resemble a falcon's head, with shining eyes of yellow glass.

Cousin Susan believed very sincerely in the old-time maxim that "children should be seen, and not heard," and she had rather an alarming way at times of saying "Tut, tut!" But she was really fond of young people, and whenever we went to see her she would say seductively, —

"I wonder, now, if we could find anything nice in cousin Susan's dining-room cupboard."

And truly that person who failed to do so must have been hard to please; for, in our eyes at least, that cupboard held a little of everything that was rare and delightful.

A most delicious odor came forth when the door was opened: a hint of the spiciness of rich cake, a tingling sense of preserved ginger, and a certain ineffable sweetness which no other closet ever possessed, and which I know not how to describe. It might well have proceeded from the walls and shelves of the cupboard itself, for they were indeed emblems of purity.

The china here, as in all genuine Salem cupboards, was chiefly of the honest old blue Canton ware. There were shining piles of those plates which, while they are rather heavy to handle, always surprise one by being so thin at the edges. There were generous teacups like small bowls, squat pitchers with big noses, and a tureen whose cover had the head of a boar for a handle. And in all this the blue was dull and deep in tint, with a certain ill-defined, vaporous quality at the edges of the lines, and the white of the cool greenish tinge of a duck's egg. You can buy blue Canton today, but it is not old blue Canton. Such china is matchless now, but in this cupboard there were shelves of it.

Cousin Susan possessed also another set of china, which she valued far above her blue. It was a pure, thin white ware, delicately fluted at the edges and decorated with little raised lilac sprigs. It was used only upon occasions of solemn company tea-drinkings, and cousin Susan always washed it herself in her little cedar dish-tub. We children considered this china so choice and desirable that a bit of a broken saucer,

which included one of the pale, tiny sprays, was cherished far above
our real doll's dishes.

At the left hand of cousin Susan's shelves of china was a little cupboard with a diamond-paned glass door. This was the *sanctum sanctorum,* — a cupboard within a cupboard; and here, as one might have
expected, were stored the choicest treasures of all. It was not the domestic preserve closet. Cousin Susan was thrifty, and had good store
of home-made dainties, but they were kept in the cool seclusion of a
dark cellar store-room. This little glass cupboard held the stock of
foreign sweetmeats: the round-shouldered blue jars, inclosed in a network of split bamboo, which contained the fiery, amber ginger; the flat
boxes of guava jelly, hot curry powders, chilli sauce, and choleric Ben-
gal chutney. Here were two miniature casks of tamarinds, jolly and
black, cousin Susan's favorites. She had a certain air of disapproval
toward most of these strange conserves. "They were not good for little
people," she averred; and indeed she always maintained that these
ardent sweetmeats were fitter for the delectation of rude men than for
the delicate palates of gentlewomen. Of tamarinds, however, cousin
Susan did approve. Properly diluted with cool water, they made what
she called a "very pretty drink." She was fond of sending a glass to any
neighbor who was ill and feverish, and she was always following our
cousin the sea-captain about with a blue china bowl of the mixture,
begging him to partake of it.

"Susan, I hate tamarind-water," our cousin would protest.

"It will cool your blood, William," his sister would urge.

"But I don't want my blood cool. I want it warm," the captain would
reply.

As a general thing, however, cousin Susan came off triumphant.
The captain grumblingly partook of his dose, and was always most
generous in sharing it with us children. The beautiful little brown
stones also fell to our lot, and we hoarded the useless things with great
care, although it seemed to us a great oversight on the part of nature
that tamarind seeds did not have holes through them, that one might
string them as beads.

Cousin Susan's cupboard also contained stronger waters than tamarind, for side by side sat two corpulent cut-glass decanters, of which
one was half filled with madeira wine, and the other with honest rum.
A variety of sweet cakes was near by, to be served with the wine to any
chance visitor. There were black fruit cake in a japanned box; "hearts
and rounds" of rich yellow pound cake; and certain delicate but inane
little sponge biscuit, of which our cousin spoke by the older-fashioned
name of diet — or, as she chose to pronounce it, "dier" — bread. She
always called the sponge cakes "little dier breads." Pound and fruit
cakes were forbidden to our youth, but we might have our ladylike fill

of "dier breads," and also of delightful seed-cakes, which were cut in the shape of an oak-leaf, and were marvels of sugary thinness.

These seed-cakes, by the bye, were kept in a jar which deserves at least a passing mention. It was, I suppose, some two or three feet high, though it looked to me then much higher. It was of blue-and-white china, and was fitted with a cover of dull silver. Tradition stated that some seafaring ancestor had brought it home from Calcutta, filled with rock-candy. What was done with so large a supply of this confection I never knew. In those days choice sugar-plums were not as plenty as they have since become; possibly at the time "black-jacks" and "gibraltars" were unknown, and this was Salem's only candy. At all events, it is somewhere recorded that the ship Belisarius brought from Calcutta "ten thousand seven hundred and sixty-seven pounds" of this same rocky and crystalline dainty. The fact of such a quantity of candy had for us children a superb and opulent significance. Even now a stick of sparkling rock-candy has power to call up cousin Susan's dining-room cupboard, its sweet, curious perfume, the quaint old silver and blue china, and the huge turkey-feather fan, with its wreath of brilliant painted flowers, which hung on the inside of the door.

Out of the shadows of the past comes another memory, the picture of that strange old Salem homestead which has been made known to fame as the House of the Seven Gables. Some alterations have done away with two of the gables, but the old house is otherwise unchanged. In the days of my childhood its mistress was a lonely woman, about whom hung the mystery of one whose solitude is peopled by the weird visions that opium brings. We regarded her with something of awe, and I have wondered, in later days, what strange and eldritch beings walked with her about those shadowy rooms, or flitted noiselessly up and down the fine old staircase.

The House of the Seven Gables was no open and joyous dwelling, where children loved to flock and run about at will. We never paid a visit there except with some grown person, and then sat throughout our stay, dangling our legs from our high chairs, and studying the quaintly stiff array of ornaments upon the lofty mantel. There were three covered Delft jars, two vases of flowers, and at either end a flask-shaped china vase. Between these taller articles were set shallow cups of painted china. Except in the flowers which filled the two middle vases, I never knew the arrangement of the mantel to differ.

A large jar stood on the floor directly beneath the mantel, and ranged firmly about the room were several Dutch apple-tree chairs, with others of old-fashioned severity. On the right of the mantel was a delightful cupboard, whose tall, arched door often stood open, displaying a beautiful collection of old cut glass. We children used to describe this cupboard as "hollow," it being, in fact, shaped like an apse. It had six semi-circular shelves, all of rich dark wood, against which the rows of splendid old glass glittered most bravely. There were graceful pitchers, shallow dishes, odd bowls, and flagons almost without number. On the floor of the cupboard a vast china punch-bowl was flanked by jars and vases each more enchanting than the other. I believe there was no truly housewifely dame in Salem who did not adore and envy this wealth of crystal, but although we children admired it, it did not inspire us with any deeper feelings. It did not appeal to the youthful imagination.

Equally far removed, and even more splendid, was the chest of family silver, which we were sometimes allowed to behold. How little did we think, as we viewed in admiring silence the fine heavy tankards, candlesticks, old two-tined silver forks, and antique porringers, that the fate of this haughty collection was to be sold for mere old silver, and hustled without respect or reverence to a fiery death in the silver-smith's crucible! Sadly changed since that day is the House of the Seven Gables. The family silver is melted; the antique furnishings are scattered; and gone, one knows not whither, the beautiful old glass, the glory of that tall, dark, "hollow" cupboard, and the pride of that strange mistress, who dreamed such dreams and saw such eerie visions in her great lonely chamber above-stairs.

1887
LOW TIDE ON GRAND-PRÉ
by Bliss Carman

THE sun goes down, and over all
These barren reaches by the tide
Such unelusive glories fall,
I almost dream they yet will bide
Until the coming of the tide.

And yet I know that not for us,
By any ecstasy of dream,
He lingers to keep luminous
A little while the grievous stream,
Which frets, uncomforted of dream, —

A grievous stream, that to and fro
Athrough the fields of Acadie
Goes wandering, as if to know
Why one beloved face should be
So long from home and Acadie!

Was it a year or lives ago
We took the grasses in our hands,
And caught the summer flying low
Over the waving meadow lands,
And held it there between our hands?

The while the river at our feet —
A drowsy inland meadow stream —
At set of sun the after-heat
Made running gold, and in the gleam
We freed our birch upon the stream.

There down along the elms at dusk
We lifted dripping blade to drift,
Through twilight scented fine like musk,
Where night and gloom a while uplift,
Nor sunder soul and soul adrift.

And that we took into our hands —
Spirit of life or subtler thing —
Breathed on us there, and loosed the bands
Of death, and taught us, whispering,
The secret of some wonder-thing.

Then all your face grew light, and seemed
To hold the shadow of the sun;
The evening faltered, and I deemed
That time was ripe, and years had done
Their wheeling underneath the sun.

So all desire and all regret,
And fear and memory, were naught;
One to remember or forget
The keen delight our hands had caught:
Morrow and yesterday were naught!

The night has fallen, and the tide . . .
Now and again comes drifting home,
Across these aching barrens wide,
A sigh like driven wind or foam:
In grief the flood is bursting home!

1888
ECONOMY IN COLLEGE WORK
by John Trowbridge

SOME years ago a one-study college was established west of the Mississippi. Its cardinal principle consisted in taking one subject at a time, and in finishing it before taking up another. We are tempted, living in the shade of an old university, to laugh at this experiment in education, and to point to the experience of many hundred years in universities older than ours as a reason for not following in the track of the one-study college.

I hear some one exclaim, "Would you take away the mental freshness which a student gets in turning from subject to subject, and confine him to one subject until he becomes a dull specialist?" Many remember the intense relish with which they turned, while in college, from Greek to fine arts, or from mathematics to the classics, and are tempted to argue that this relish led to a better assimilation than if they had been kept on one diet for a prolonged period. The truth is that most of us sentimentalize in regard to our early education, and are apt to think that all should take a course which may have awakened intellectual curiosity for the first time in our special case. Thus the classical man would have all men study Greek, because he, having studied it assiduously, has obtained the grip which it should be one of the primary objects of education to acquire. If he had studied physical science, which offers an ample field for intellectual effort, with as much persistence as he had Greek, the classical man might have become an advocate of science instead of the classics.

There are certain studies which are so nearly related that intellectual effort in one immediately aids one in another. Thus Latin and Greek can be studied together with philological profit. French can be studied with French history; German with German history; political economy with history; chemistry alone, or in conjunction with English; Spanish with Spanish history; philosophy with history; physics alone; Semitics with ancient history; fine arts and music with English, or fine arts and music as a let-up with any of the severer studies; mathematics with English; Romance philology with its suitable language. Thus having twelve subjects, three of these could be pursued in the nine months of each college year, and in four years the whole twelve could be accomplished, — if a student wished to take all the subjects enumerated. (While seeking information upon this subject, I asked a professor in the United States Military Academy at West Point how many subjects were pursued there during the week, and he replied, "Three, — mathematics, mathematics, mathematics." No one who has met a graduate of West Point can deny that he has a grip on the subject of the calculus which few college men obtain.)

Can there be two true solutions to the problem of running the human engine so as to produce the most telling effect?

If the college year is blocked out into periods of three months, during which a student pursues only one subject, the odium of specializing too early in education is escaped. During these terms or periods of three months, I would have the student become thoroughly imbued with his subject. If it be German, he should get his news through a daily German newspaper; he should attend a German *seminar,* where German subjects are discussed in German; he should read German novels, play German games, puzzle out jokes in the Fliegende Blätter; in short, should surround himself with as perfect a German atmosphere as is possible. If he is studying physics, he should give his days to the laboratory, his nights to the theory of the subject; he should look up a physical subject in a library; he should attend a physical seminar, where physical subjects are discussed.

During the past thirty years a remarkable group of young mathematicians have grown up in the English universities. This group of men, who in English parlance have a grip upon the subject of mathematics and mathematical physics, have obtained this grip by assiduously devoting themselves to doing riders or problems. This work admits of no rival occupation. The questions set require the exertion of the entire intellectual man for a long period; and it was largely by this prolonged and specialized exertion that the English mathematician won such mastery.

We are all spendthrifts of physical and intellectual exertion. But with strong images in the brain, and with a method of excitation to which constant and prolonged use has accustomed us, we are not far from the plane of genius.

1889

THE NEW TALKING-MACHINES
by Philip G. Hubert, Jr.

THE first idea of a genuine talking-machine appears to belong to Thomas A. Edison, who, in 1875, took out patents upon a device intended to reproduce complex sounds, such as those of the human voice. Of the thousands of persons who in that year visited the small room in the Tribune building, in New York, where the first phonograph was for months on exhibition, very few were found to hope much for the invention. It was apparently a toy of no practical value; its talking was more or less of a caricature upon the human voice, and only when one knew what had been said to the phonograph could its version be understood.

The defects of the early phonograph were so great that Edison found it impossible to interest capitalists in perfecting it. It reproduced singing and whistling with wonderful accuracy, but as a talker it was merely a curiosity. As such it was exhibited throughout the country, and the few hundreds then made soon found their way into college laboratories and museums. Edison went to work at his electric light.

More than a score of times, during the last ten years, he has said to me, "I wish I had leisure to work at my phonograph. When I get rich I will astonish the world with it." Two years ago he found himself in a position to take it up again, and he has devoted nearly two years to the task of making the phonograph of commercial use. He believes that he has succeeded.

The new phonograph takes up, with its table, about the space occupied by a sewing-machine, and might at first be taken for one. Underneath the table is an electric battery or a treadle, according to the power used in moving the cylinder. The wax cylinders, or phonograms, as they are called, are two inches in diameter, and vary in length from one to ten inches, according to the amount of talking which is to be engraved upon them. The smallest size is about that of a napkin ring, and will be sufficient for an ordinary business letter of two or three hundred words. The wax surface is highly polished; when it has been through the apparatus, the marks or engraving upon it can be seen only with a glass. When a message is to be recorded, one of these phonograms is slipped over the permanent steel cylinder, which is set in motion, and the diaphragm, carrying its stylus on the under side, is lowered toward the wax surface until a slight grating sound announces that it touches. Then the talking may begin. It is not necessary to talk louder than in an ordinary conversation, but distinct articulation is required. For reproduction, the stylus is raised, and the "follower" or sounding-spring is brought into contact with the wax. The amount of talking upon a cylinder depends, of course, upon the speed of the talker; one page of this magazine might easily be recorded upon a cylinder ten inches long. The exact value of the reproduction, both in the phonograph and the graphophone, is still, according to my own experience in a score of tests, something of a lottery. With a phone at my ear, I have heard Mr. Edison's phonograph read off a page of Nicholas Nickleby so clearly that not one word in twenty was lost; the phonograph's voice was as distinct and as loud as that of a telephone in good working order.

When it comes to music, the present achievements are wonderful. The phonograph will reproduce any kind of music — singing, the piano, violin, cornet, oboe, etc. — with a beauty of tone and accuracy which will astonish the musician. It is possible, also, to magnify musical sounds without distorting them, as often happens where speech is concerned. The phonograph itself cannot cost more than fifty dollars, and the wax cylinders used upon them scarcely more than writing-paper. Once a cylinder has been "engraved," or has had a message recorded upon it, it can be passed through the phonograph any number of times, apparently without deterioration. Mr. Edison has some phonograms, containing pages of Nicholas Nickleby, which have been read out thousands of times by the phonograph, and no indications of wear are audible. Finally, bear in mind that having once obtained a good phonogram, it can be multiplied *ad infinitum* at nominal cost, and what a wonderful prospect opens before us! The duplication of a phonogram is as simple as it is perfect. The wax phonogram is placed in a bath, and coated with nickel by electric deposition. When the nickel plate is sufficiently thick, it is stripped off, giving an exact mould, a die representing every minute indentation of the original wax. In order to make a second or a thousandth wax fac-simile, wax sheets can be pressed against the nickel die. Edison estimates that novels of the length of Nicholas Nickleby could be sold in phonogram shape for a few cents. A good reader would first have to read the whole book to the phonograph and the multiplication of the resulting phonograms would then be simply a matter of detail. So also with music, — songs, piano pieces, symphonies, operas. There seems to be no reason why a play cannot be reproduced so as to give infinite pleasure. The length of the phonograph's message is limited only by the size of the phonograms. Edison estimates that Nicholas Nickleby can be transcribed upon six cylinders, six inches in diameter by twelve inches in length. But some one will soon discover a method of recording the phonographic message upon an endless roll, so that the man who cannot sleep at night will be able to have the machine read to him hour after hour without the trouble of changing cylinders.

As a saving in the time given up to writing, the phonograph promises to far outstrip the typewriter. The business man can dictate to the phonograph as fast as he can talk, and the wax cylinder, inclosed in a suitable box, can be sent off by mail to read out its message perhaps thousands of miles away. Or else, as is now done in Mr. Edison's laboratory in Orange, N.J., the typewriter girl can print out upon paper what her employer has dictated to the phonograph. For the reporter, the editor, and the author who can dictate, a device has been adapted to the phonograph which causes it to stop its message at every tenth word, and to continue only when a spring is touched. Thus, the editor can dictate his article to the phonograph as he does now to his stenographer, and when the printer at the case gets the resulting phonogram the instrument will dictate to him in short sentences. If he cannot set up the sentence at one hearing, it will repeat its ten words. If he is satisfied, it reads out ten words more.

I really see no reason why the newspaper of the future should not come to the subscriber in the shape of a phonogram. It would have to begin, however, with a table of contents, in order that one might not have to listen to a two hours' speech upon the tariff question in order to get at ten lines of a musical notice. But think what a musical critic might be able to do for his public! He might give them whole arias from an opera or movements from a symphony, by way of proof or illustration. The very tones of an actor's or singer's voice might be reproduced in the morning notice of last night's important dramatic or musical event. It has been remarked, by the way, that business letters and orders by phonograph would not be so binding as when put in black and white upon paper. A little wax cylinder covered with microscopic dots would not be considered as good evidence in court. But if the speaker's voice, inflection, accent, were so reproduced that witnesses could swear to the personality, would it not suffice?

Mr. Edison says that by the beginning of 1890 the phonograph will be far less of a curiosity than the telephone is now. For the last year it has been the same story, — the phonographs would be ready for sale next month. It was so a year ago, and it may be so a year from now. But these many delays, which have made people rather skeptical as to the doings of the phonograph, do not make the wonders already achieved less wonderful, or warrant any doubts as to the vast possibilities which the little device contains.

1890
THE UNITED STATES LOOKING OUTWARD
by A. T. Mahan

WERE our sea frontier as strong as it now is weak, passive self-defense, whether in trade or war, would be but a poor policy, so long as this world continues to be one of struggle and vicissitude. All around us now is strife; "the struggle of life," "the race of life," are phrases so familiar that we do not feel their significance till we stop to think about them. Everywhere nation is arrayed against nation; our own no less than others. What is our protective system but an organized warfare? Are our people, however, so unaggressive that they are likely not to want their own way in matters where their interests turn on points of disputed right, or so little sensitive as to submit quietly to encroachment by others, in quarters where they have long considered their own influence should prevail?

Our self-imposed isolation in the matter of markets, and the decline of our shipping interest in the last thirty years, have coincided singularly with an actual remoteness of this continent from the life of the rest of the world. The writer has before him a map of the North and South Atlantic oceans, showing the direction of the principal trade routes and the proportion of tonnage passing over each; and it is curious to note what deserted regions, comparatively, are the Gulf of Mexico, the Caribbean Sea, and the adjoining countries and islands.

When the Isthmus is pierced this isolation will pass away, and with it the indifference of foreign nations. From wheresoever they come and whithersoever they afterward go, all ships that use the canal will pass through the Caribbean. Whatever the effect produced upon the prosperity of the adjacent continent and islands by the thousand wants attendant upon maritime activity, around such a focus of trade will centre large commercial and political interests. To protect and develop its own, each nation will seek points of support and means of influence in a quarter where the United States has always been jealously sensitive to the intrusion of European powers.

It has been said that, in our present state of unpreparedness, a trans-isthmian canal will be a military disaster to the United States, and especially to the Pacific coast. When the canal is finished the Atlantic seaboard will be neither more nor less exposed than it now is; it will merely share with the country at large the increased danger of foreign complications with inadequate means to meet them.

The military needs of the Pacific States, as well as their supreme importance to the whole country, are yet a matter of the future, but of a future so near that provision should immediately begin. To provide this, three things are needful: First, protection of the chief harbors by fortifications and coast-defense ships, which gives defensive strength, provides security to the community within, and supplies the bases necessary to all military operations. Secondly, naval force, the arm of offensive power, which alone enables a country to extend its influence outward. Thirdly, it should be an inviolable resolution of our national policy that no European state should henceforth acquire a coaling position within three thousand miles of San Francisco, — a distance which includes the Sandwich and Galapagos islands and the coast of Central America. For fuel is the life of modern naval war; it is the food of the ship; without it the modern monsters of the deep die of inanition.

THE NEXT STAGE IN DEVELOPMENT OF PUBLIC PARKS
by Alpheus Hyatt

A CRITICISM often made upon public museums and gardens in all parts of the world is that they fail to give any rational explanation of the interesting and instructive laws which govern the relations of animals to their surroundings. A short paragraph in a printed guidebook, perhaps, names the country to which a group of interesting forms belongs, and adds a few words about their habits; but no notice is taken of the wonderful adaptations of their structures to the work they have to do, and the effective parts they perform in the great drama of existence.

Natural history is beginning to be taught everywhere, and intelligent teachers often take their pupils to museums, even making excursions some distance by rail for that purpose. Whether persons regard this tendency as desirable or the reverse is not a question that one need consider. The fact cannot be safely denied that throughout the civilized world the study of natural history has been introduced into private and public schools. The benefit of this policy is shown by the constantly increasing demand for instruction of this kind, and the yearly increase in the number of pupils and teachers who visit museums. Zoological gardens would be very much more useful to them if they were integral parts of the educational system of the city in which they were situated. This connection could be acknowledged by definite privileges of admission to the collections free of expense on certain convenient days, together with other concessions, if necessary, to secure the fullest use of these privileges.

Books have occupied, and perhaps always will occupy, a very important place in education, but those used in the schools have long been considered unsatisfactory by many of the best teachers. They recognize that printed pages cannot convey knowledge in sufficiently definite and impressive form unless used in connection with pictures, or models, or, preferably, the things themselves. In other words, the visual element in education is becoming more and more important every day, and in many of the finest European and American schools objective methods are extensively used. Teachers, however, are not specialists, and cannot keep their knowledge abreast of the always advancing lines of research, especially in natural history.

Public museums and gardens should therefore aim to supply, as has already been done in some European countries, loan and consulting collections for the use of teachers. It does not require prophetic insight to predict that these institutions will some day be required to do for the public much the same service as that now performed by libraries, but their circulating medium for the diffusion of knowledge will be things themselves, and not books. Natural objects are nature's books, the only ones that hold within themselves the infinite sources of knowledge, and never need reissue in improved editions.

1892
AGRIPPINA
by Agnes Repplier

SHE is sitting on my desk, as I write, and I glance at her with deference, mutely begging permission to begin. But her back is turned to me, and expresses in every curve such fine and delicate disdain that I falter and lose courage at the very threshold of my task. I have long known that cats are the most contemptuous of creatures, and that Agrippina is the most contemptuous of cats. I should like to explain to her, if I dared, that my desk is small, littered with many papers, and sadly overcrowded with the useful inutilities which affectionate friends delight in giving me at Christmas time. Sainte-Beuve's cat, I am aware, sat on his desk, and roamed at will among those precious manuscripts which no intrusive hand was ever permitted to touch; but Sainte-Beuve probably had sufficient space reserved for his own comfort and convenience. I have not; and Agrippina's beautifully ringed tail flapping across my copy distracts my attention and imperils the neatness of my penmanship. Even when she is disposed to be affable, turns the light of her countenance upon me, watches with attentive curiosity every stroke I make, and softly, with curved paw, pats my pen as it travels over the paper, — even in these halcyon moments, though my self-love is flattered by her condescension, I am aware that I should work better and more rapidly if I denied myself this charming companionship.

But in truth it is impossible for a lover of cats to banish these alert, gentle, and discriminating little friends, who give us just enough of their regard and complaisance to make us hunger for more. M. Fée, the naturalist, who has written so admirably about animals, and who understands, as only a Frenchman can understand, the delicate and subtle organization of a cat, frankly admits that the keynote of its character is independence. It dwells under our roof, sleeps by our fire, endures our blandishments, and apparently enjoys our society, without for one moment forfeiting its sense of absolute freedom, without acknowledging any servile relation to the human creature who shelters it. "The cat," says M. Fée, "will never part with its liberty; it will neither be our servant, like the horse, nor our friend, like the dog. It consents to live as our guest; it accepts the home we offer and the food we give; it even goes so far as to solicit our caresses, but capriciously, and when it suits its humor to receive them."

Rude and masterful souls resent this fine self-sufficiency in a domestic animal, and require that it should have no will but theirs, no pleasure that does not emanate from them. They are forever prating of the love and fidelity of the dog, of the beast that obeys their slightest word, crouches contentedly for hours at their feet, is exuberantly grateful for the smallest attention, and so affectionate that its demonstrations require to be curbed rather than encouraged. All this homage is pleasing to their vanity; yet there are people, less magisterial perhaps, or less exacting, who believe that true friendship, even with an animal, may be built up on mutual esteem and independence; that to demand gratitude is to be unworthy of it; and that obedience is not essential to agreeable and healthy intercourse. A man who owns a dog is, in every sense of the word, its master; the term expresses accurately their mutual relations. But it is ridiculous when applied to the limited possession of a cat. I am certainly not Agrippina's mistress, and the assumption of authority on my part would be a mere empty dignity. If I call Agrippina, she does not come; if I tell her to go away, she remains where she is; if I try to persuade her to show off her one or two little accomplishments, she refuses, with courteous but unswerving decision. She has frolicsome moods, in which a thimble, a shoe-buttoner, a scrap of paper, or a piece of string will drive her wild with delight; she has moods of inflexible gravity, in which she stares solemnly at her favorite ball rolling over the carpet, without stirring one lazy limb to reach it. "Have I seen this foolish toy before?" she seems to be asking herself with musing austerity; "and can it be possible that there are cats who run after such frivolous trifles? Vanity of vanities, and all is vanity, save only to lie upon the hearth-rug, and be warm, and 'think grave thoughts to feed a serious soul.' " In such moments of rejection and humiliation, I comfort myself by recalling the words of one too wise for arrogance. "When I play with my cat," says Montaigne, "how do I know whether she does not make a jest of me? We entertain each other with mutual antics; and if I have my own time for beginning or refusing, she, too, has hers."

This is the spirit in which we should approach a creature so reserved and so utterly self-sufficing; this is the only key we have to that natural distinction of character which repels careless and unobservant natures. When I am told that Agrippina is disobedient, ungrateful, cold-hearted, perverse, stupid, treacherous, and cruel, I no longer strive to check the torrent of abuse. I know that Buffon said all this, and much more, about cats, and that people have gone on repeating it

ever since, principally because these spirited little beasts have remained just what it pleased Providence to make them, have preserved
their primitive freedom through centuries of effete and demoralizing
civilization.

1893
OF A DANCING-GIRL
by Lafcadio Hearn

NOTHING is more silent than the beginning of a Japanese
banquet; and no one, except a native, who observes the
opening scene could possibly imagine the tumultuous
ending.

The robed guests take their places, quite noiselessly and without
speech, upon the kneeling-cushions. The lacquered services are laid
upon the matting before them by maidens whose bare feet make no
sound. For a while there are only smiling and flitting, as in dreams.
You are not likely to hear any voices from without, as a banqueting-
house is usually secluded from the street by spacious gardens. At last
the master of ceremonies, host or provider, breaks the hush with the
consecrated formula, *"O-somatsu degozarimasu ga! — dōzo o-hashi!"*
whereat all present bow silently, take up their *hashi* (chopsticks), and
fall to. But hashi, deftly used, cannot be heard at all. The maidens
pour warm *saké* into the cup of each guest without making the least
sound; and it is not until several dishes have been emptied, and several cups of saké absorbed, that tongues are loosened.

Then, all at once, with a little burst of laughter, a number of young
girls enter, make the customary prostration of greeting, glide into the
open space between the ranks of the guests, and begin to serve the
wine with a grace and dexterity of which no common maid is capable.
They are pretty; they are clad in very costly robes of silk; they are
girdled like queens; and the beautifully dressed hair of each is decked
with fresh flowers, with wonderful combs and pins, and with curious
ornaments of gold. They greet the stranger as if they had always
known him; they jest, laugh, and utter funny little cries. These are the
geisha, or dancing-girls, hired for the banquet.

Samisen — guitars of three strings — tinkle. The dancers withdraw
to a clear space at the farther end of the banqueting-hall, always vast
enough to admit of many more guests than ever assemble upon common occasions. Some form the orchestra, under the direction of a
woman of uncertain age; there are several samisen, and a tiny drum
played by a child. Others, singly or in pairs, perform the dance. It may

be swift and merry, consisting wholly of graceful posturing, — two girls dancing together with such coincidence of step and gesture as only years of training could render possible. But more frequently it is rather like acting than like what we Occidentals call dancing, — acting accompanied with extraordinary waving of sleeves and fans, and with a play of eyes and features, sweet, subtle, subdued, wholly Oriental.

There are more voluptuous dances known to geisha, but upon ordinary occasions and before refined audiences they portray beautiful old Japanese traditions, like the legend of the fisher Urashima, beloved by the Sea God's daughter; and at intervals they sing ancient Chinese poems, expressing a natural emotion with delicious vividness by a few exquisite words. And always they pour the wine, — that warm, pale yellow, sleepy wine which fills the veins with soft contentment, making a faint sense of ecstasy, through which, as through some poppied sleep, the commonplace becomes wondrous and blissful, and the geisha Maids of Paradise, and the world much sweeter than, in the natural order of things, it could ever possibly be.

The banquet, at first so silent, slowly changes to a merry tumult. The company break ranks, form groups; and from group to group the girls pass, laughing, prattling, — still pouring saké into the cups which are being exchanged and emptied with low bows. Men begin to sing old samurai songs, old Chinese poems. One or two even dance. A geisha tucks her robe well up to her knees; and the samisen strike up the quick melody, *"Kompira funé-funé."* As the music plays, she begins to run lightly and swiftly in a figure of 8, and a young man, carrying a saké bottle and cup, also runs in the same figure of 8. If the two meet on a line, the one through whose error the meeting happens must drink a cup of saké. The music becomes quicker and quicker, and the runners run faster and faster, for they must keep time to the melody; and the geisha wins. In another part of the room, guests and geisha are playing *ken.* They sing as they play, facing each other, and clap their hands, and fling out their fingers at intervals with little cries; and the samisen keep time.

Now, to play ken with a geisha requires a perfectly cool head, a quick eye, and much practice. Having been trained from childhood to play all kinds of ken, — and there are many, — she generally loses only for politeness, when she loses at all. The signs of the most common ken are a Man, a Fox, and a Gun. If the geisha makes the sign of the Gun, you must instantly, and in exact time to the music, make the sign of the Fox, who cannot use the Gun. For if you make the sign of the Man, then she will answer with the sign of the Fox, who can bewitch the Man, and you lose. And if she makes the sign of the Fox first, then you should make the sign of the Gun, by which the Fox can be killed. But all the while you must watch her bright eyes and supple hands. These are pretty; and if you suffer yourself, just for one fraction of a second, to think how pretty they are, you are bewitched and vanquished.

Notwithstanding all this apparent comradeship, a certain rigid decorum between guest and geisha is invariably preserved at a Japanese banquet. However flushed with wine a guest may have become, you will never see him attempt to caress a girl; he never forgets that she appears at the festivities only as a human flower, to be looked at, not to be touched. The familiarity which foreign tourists in Japan frequently permit themselves with geisha or with waiter-girls, though endured with smiling patience, is considered by native observers an evidence of extreme vulgarity.

For a time the merriment grows; but as midnight draws near, the guests begin to slip away, one by one, unnoticed. Then the din gradually dies down, the music stops; and at last the geisha, having escorted the latest of the feasters to the door, with laughing cries of *Sayōnara*, can sit down alone to break their long fast in the deserted hall.

Such is the geisha's rôle. But what is the mystery of her? What are her thoughts, her emotions, her secret self? What is her veritable existence beyond the night circle of the banquet lights, far from the illusion formed around her by the mist of wine? Is she always as mischievous as she seems while her voice ripples out with mocking sweetness the words of an ancient song?

Always in the dwelling which a band of geisha occupy, there is a strange image placed in the alcove. Sometimes it is of clay, rarely of gold, most commonly of porcelain. It is reverenced: offerings are made to it, sweetmeats and rice-bread and wine; incense smoulders in front of it, and a lamp is burned before it. It is the image of a kitten erect, one paw outstretched as if inviting, — whence its name, "the Beckoning Kitten." It is the *genius loci:* it brings good fortune, the patronage of the rich, the favor of banquet-givers. Now, they who know the soul of the geisha aver that the semblance of the image is the semblance of herself, — playful and pretty, soft and young, lithe and caressing, and cruel as a devouring fire.

Worse, also, than this they have said of her: that in her shadow treads the God of Poverty, and that the Fox-Women are her sisters; that she is the ruin of youth, the waster of fortunes, the destroyer of families; that she knows love only as the source of the follies which are her gain, and grows rich upon the substance of men whose graves she has made; that she is the most consummate of pretty hypocrites, the most dangerous of schemers, the most insatiable of mercenaries, the most pitiless of mistresses. This cannot all be true. Yet thus much is true, — that, like the kitten, the geisha is by profession a creature of prey.

The geisha is only what she has been made in answer to foolish human desire for the illusion of love mixed with youth and grace, but without regrets or responsibilities: wherefore she has been taught, besides ken, to play at hearts. Now, the eternal law is that people may play with impunity at any game in this unhappy world except three, which are called Life, Love, and Death. Those the gods have reserved to themselves, because nobody else can learn to play them without doing mischief. Therefore, to play with a geisha any game much more serious than ken, or at least *go,* is displeasing to the gods.

The girl begins her career as a slave, a pretty child bought from miserably poor parents under a contract, according to which her services may be claimed by the purchasers for eighteen, twenty, or even twenty-five years. She is fed, clothed, and trained in a house occupied only by geisha; and she passes the rest of her childhood under severe discipline. She is taught etiquette, grace, polite speech; she has daily lessons in dancing; and she is obliged to learn by heart a multitude of songs with their airs. Also she must learn games, the service of banquets and weddings, the art of dressing and looking beautiful. Whatever physical gifts she may have are carefully cultivated. Afterwards she is taught to handle musical instruments: first, the little drum (*tsudzumi*), which cannot be sounded at all without considerable practice; then she learns to play the samisen a little, with a plectrum of tortoise-shell or ivory. At eight or nine years of age she attends banquets, chiefly as a drum-player. She is then the most charming little creature imaginable, and already knows how to fill your wine-cup exactly full, with a single toss of the bottle and without spilling a drop, between two taps of her drum.

Thereafter her discipline becomes more cruel. Her voice may be flexible enough, but lacks the requisite strength. In the iciest hours of winter nights, she must ascend to the roof of her dwelling-house, and there sing and play till the blood oozes from her fingers and the voice dies in her throat. The desired result is an atrocious cold. After a period of hoarse whispering, her voice changes its tone and strengthens. She is ready to become a public singer and dancer.

In this capacity she usually makes her first appearance at the age of twelve or thirteen. If pretty and skillful, her services will be much in demand, and her time paid for at the rate of twenty to twenty-five *sen* per hour. Then only do her purchasers begin to reimburse themselves for the time, expense, and trouble of her training; and they are not apt to be generous. For many years more all that she earns must pass into their hands. She can own nothing, not even her clothes.

At seventeen or eighteen she has made her artistic reputation. She has been at many hundreds of entertainments, and knows by sight all the important personages of her city, the character of each, the history of all. Her life has been chiefly a night life; rarely has she seen the sun rise since she became a dancer. She has learned to drink wine without ever losing her head, and to fast for seven or eight hours without ever feeling the worse. She has had many lovers. To a certain extent she is free to smile upon whom she pleases; but she has been well taught, above all else, to use her power of charm for her own advantage. She hopes to find somebody able and willing to buy her freedom.

At this point of her career we may leave the geisha: thereafter her story is apt to prove unpleasant, unless she dies young. Should that happen, she will have the obsequies of her class, and her memory will be preserved by divers curious rites.

Some time, perhaps, while wandering through Japanese streets at night, you hear sounds of music, a tinkling of samisen floating through the great gateway of a Buddhist temple, together with shrill voices of singing girls; which may seem to you a strange happening. And the deep court is thronged with people looking and listening. Then, making your way through the press to the temple steps, you see two geisha seated upon the matting within, playing and singing, and a third dancing before a little table. Upon the table is an *ihai*, or mortuary tablet; in front of the tablet burns a little lamp, and incense in a cup of bronze; a small repast has been placed there, fruits and dainties, — such a repast as, upon festival occasions, it is the custom to offer to the dead. You learn that the *kaimyō* upon the tablet is that of a geisha; and that the comrades of the dead girl assemble in the temple on certain days to gladden her spirit with songs and dances. Then whosoever pleases may attend the ceremony free of charge.

1894
THE CITY ON THE HOUSETOPS
by James K. Paulding

ABOVE the narrow, crowded streets of the tenement-house district there is a city of housetops, which alone enjoys the pure air and the sunlight, and turns its face upward to the sky. This city of the housetops has a life of its own, distinct from that of the city down below there between the squares of tall houses. Even in the winter this life does not cease altogether, but in the summer it expands, until it includes most of the leisure existence of the tenement dwellers in the neighborhood. The families living in a house have a common right to the roof, and the communistic ideal of sharing all things together comes nearest to realization there. As a matter of fact, the families living in the lower stories of a house visit but little the aerial city. The city of the street has superior attractions for them, lying as it does at their door or before their window; and if the house has a high "stoop," they will take their station here, and watch for the flotsam and jetsam that the tide of human travel brings sooner or later to their feet.

It is a less depraved taste that brings people, of a summer evening, to the starlit precincts of the city on the housetops. One is not secure there from occasional bickerings; but the presence of night is more appreciable, there is opportunity for closer intimacy, the disturbance from the street reaches one only in faint gusts, and there is less grating of the merely individual upon the consciousness of the universal. Do not suppose I mean that the people who prefer the street are really depraved! But we roof-dwellers cannot help looking down a little upon those of our neighbors who are either in continual fear of fire, or dislike the fatigue of climbing five flights of stairs.

The principal structures of the city on the housetops are the chimneys, skylights, and little hutlike out-buildings bearing resemblance to the deck-cabins on some ships, which shelter the stairway leading to the house below, and permit, when the door is left open, a draught of air to penetrate the hallways. Many of the housetops are surrounded by a high wooden fence with projecting poles from which the clothes-lines are suspended. Here and there one finds an improvised roof-garden, its green shrubs and potted plants occupying a corner between high brick walls. The city abounds in good views. The Brooklyn Bridge is in sight, its long, low arch between the great Gothic piers spanning an arc in the sky, firm and distinct, — an imperial roadway by day, studded with stars at night. High buildings and church spires lift their heads on all sides, and flags are streaming from a score of poles. Thick columns and thin spirals of smoke ascend from hundreds of chimneys. Over there is the river: in faint outline one can see the sharp bow of a ship, with a piece of the rigging; the smoke of a steam-boat or tug hangs like a dusky cloud across the face of the tall buildings on the Brooklyn shore; the hoarse whistles of the ferryboats announce each arrival and departure. At sunset, distant windows catch the reflection of the sun's rays, and gleam as if the interior of the house were ablaze.

During the day, the women and children, except for the occasional presence of a painter, a carpenter, or a roof-mender, have the city on the housetops to themselves. A periodical visitor is the line-man, a young fellow who mounts the gaunt poles from which the clotheslines are suspended to the windows opposite, climbing up by means of the big iron nails which serve as pegs upon which to tie the lines. His lusty shout of "Line up!" informs the neighbors that now is the time to get their lines attached. His acquaintance is a large one, and his social function important. Resort to these clothesline poles is sometimes had by small boys in search of a temporary retreat before an irritated relative. The little boys fly their kites; and this is one of the gayest, most delightful amusements to all who really understand what amusement is. Sometimes one undertakes, perversely enough, to act for itself, and then it frequently gets caught and tangled up in a telegraph wire, where it hangs limp and forlorn, like some gigantic wounded bird of prey. But when it sails clear and free, with a graceful streamer in its wake, there is no sight more gracious and encouraging.

During the dinner hour, and in midsummer through the early hours of the afternoon, when the sun is scorching the tin roofs with its rays, the city on the housetops is deserted. But let a thunder shower come up and cool off the burning roofs, then after it is over the people will return to enjoy the momentary freshness. I have seen some little boys make their appearance, on a hot day in August, in the very midst of a thunder shower, and fully prepared to enjoy it. There were three of them, and they were guiltless of a garment amongst them. They took their shower bath with delight, and chased one another about among the chimneys and clotheslines, with the lightning flashes playing around them. Their gambol ended only when the storm ceased, and they disappeared, by this time shivering, down the hatchway.

Late in the afternoon is the grandfathers' hour. Old men, the day's labor at an end, come up to the city on the housetops to smoke their pipes and enjoy an hour of peace before descending into the close, often crowded rooms where the night must be spent. One hears from every direction the factory whistles proclaiming the cessation of work for another breathing-space, and down below the streets are filled with a long, black procession of men and women returning from the labor of the day. From one of the open windows of a tall tenement in the opposite street come the plaintive strains of an old violin, into which a young fellow seeks to infuse poetry. His efforts are a little primitive, but now and then such things as Little Annie Rooney or a few bars of Comrades struggle to recognition.

Then the evening comes; and in summer this is the fashionable hour for the denizens of the housetops. It is less stifling up there than in the houses, or in the streets below. Often there is a breeze, generally from the south, with a whiff of the ocean in its breath. Then the scene on the housetops becomes animated. Whole families are encamped there; there is singing, stories are told, sometimes there is dancing. Musical instruments are not at all rare, and the accordion is chief among them. Now and then the merriment of separate parties becomes extinct; all pause to listen to a single voice that rises high and distinct above the hubbub. Sometimes it is a hymn of the synagogue, caroled forth upon the night by a boy's quavering voice; sometimes it is an air from an operetta, delivered in stentorian tones by a "professional" man singer. The applause, when the performance is over, comes from every roof in the neighborhood. Sometimes a burst of mad melody, full of the weird cadence and passionate abandon that characterize the dance-music of the peasantry of eastern Europe, awakens sad memories or passionate longing in an immigrant lately come from some far-off country.

Late into the night the merriment lasts; and then, when good-nights have been said, only about one half of the company descend to take their rest indoors. The others roll themselves in sheets and blankets, and prepare for a night under the stars. A thunder shower coming up in the middle of the night disperses them, and there is a great noise of scuffling and running, as each one awakes to take up his bed and walk with it. Between two and three o'clock of a fine morning, the moon looks down upon a bivouac of shrouded motionless figures, and the city on the housetops is turned into a shining necropolis. Little children and women sleep thus in the open air, sometimes on the roof, sometimes on their own fire-escape; but the majority of the out-of-door sleepers are young men, accustomed all their lives, many of them, to hard bunks and uneasy surroundings. The glow of a cigar or a cigarette from one of these shapeless heaps of bedding might disturb the night's slumber of an apprehensive person. Dawn comes to awaken them early, for the most part, but it is no uncommon sight to see their outstretched forms when the sun already rides high in the sky. Other men and women pass in and out among them without disturbing them; and when they awake and open their arms to the day, no complicated toilet awaits them; they are half clothed already, and a few instinctive touches do the rest.

Do not shake your head, and reflect sadly upon the low, uncivilized state of these primitive beings, O cultivated reader! Circumstances do not always admit of daintiness, but you will do wrong to assume, on this account, that refinement is absent from the soul. Volumes are written every year concerning the overcrowding of the poor, and it is commonly taken for granted that this overcrowding leads to immorality and vice. Vice, to be sure, is not excluded from the city on the housetops, but neither is it excluded from the comfortable homes of the rich.

MARS
by Percival Lowell

LET us review, now, the chain of reasoning by which we have been led to regard it probable that upon the surface of Mars we see the effects of local intelligence: we find, in the first place, that the broad physical conditions of the planet are not antagonistic to some form of life; secondly, that there is an apparent dearth of water upon the planet's surface, and therefore, if beings of sufficient intelligence inhabited it, they would have to resort to irrigation to support life; thirdly, that there turns out to be a network of markings covering the disc precisely counterparting what a system of irrigation would look like; and, lastly, that there is a set of spots placed where we should expect to find the lands thus artificially fertilized, and behaving as such constructed oases should. All this, of course, may be a set of coincidences, signifying nothing; but the probability seems the other way. As to details of explanation, any we may adopt will undoubtedly be found, on closer acquaintance, to vary from the actual Martian state of things; for any Martian life must differ markedly from our own.

To be shy of anything resembling himself is part and parcel of man's own individuality. Like the savage who fears nothing so much as a strange man, like Crusoe who grows pale at the sight of footprints not his own, the civilized thinker instinctively turns away from the thought of mind other than the one he himself knows. It is simply an instinct like any other, the projection of the instinct of self-preservation. We ought, therefore, to rise above it, and, where probability points to other things, boldly accept the fact provisionally, as we should the presence of oxygen, or iron, or anything else.

We must be just as careful not to run to the other extreme, and draw deductions of purely local outgrowth. To talk of Martian beings is not to mean Martian men. Even on this earth man is of the nature of an accident. He is the survival of by no means the highest physical organism. He is not even a high form of mammal. Mind has been his making. For aught we can see, some lizard or batrachian might just as well have popped into his place in the race, and been now the dominant creature of this earth. Under different physical circumstances he would have been certain to do so. Amid the physical surroundings that exist on Mars, we may be practically sure other organisms have been evolved which would strike us as exquisitely grotesque. What manner of beings they may be we have no data to conceive.

How diverse, however, they doubtless are from us will appear from such definite deduction as we are able to make from the physical differences between Mars and our earth. For example, the mere difference of gravity on the surface of the two planets is much more far-reaching in its effect than might at first be thought. Gravity on the surface of Mars is only a little more than one third what it is on the surface of the earth. This would work in two ways to very different conditions of existence from those to which we are accustomed. To begin with, three times as much work, as for example in digging a canal, could be done by the same expenditure of muscular force. If we were transported to Mars, we should be pleasingly surprised to find all our manual labor suddenly lightened threefold. But, indirectly, there might result a yet greater gain to our capabilities; for if Nature chose, she could afford there to build her inhabitants on three times the scale she does on earth, without their ever finding it out except by interplanetary comparison.

As we all know, a very large man is much more unwieldy than a very small one. An elephant refuses to hop like a flea; not because he considers it undignified to do so, but simply because he cannot take the step. If we could, we should all jump straight across the street, instead of painfully paddling through the mud. Our inability to do so depends partly on the size of the earth, and partly on the size of our own bodies, but not at all on what it at first seems entirely to depend on, the size of the street.

To see this, let us consider the very simplest case, that of standing erect. To this every-day feat opposes itself the weight of the body simply, a thing of three dimensions, height, breadth, and thickness, while the ability to accomplish it resides in the cross-section of the muscles of the knee, a thing of only two dimensions, breadth and thickness. Consequently, a person half as large again as another has about twice the supporting capacity of that other, but about three times as much to support. Standing therefore tires him out more quickly. If his size were to go on increasing, he would at last reach a stature at which he would no longer be able to stand at all, but would have to lie down.

Now apply this principle to a possible inhabitant of Mars, and suppose him to be constructed three times as large as a human being in every dimension. If he were on earth, he would weigh twenty-seven times as much as the human being, but on the surface of Mars, since gravity there is only about one third of what it is here, he would weigh but nine times as much. The cross-section of his muscles would be nine times as great. Therefore the ratio of his supporting power to the weight he must support would be the same as ours. Consequently, he would be able to stand with no more fatigue than we experience. Now consider the work he might be able to do. His muscles, having length, breadth, and thickness, would all be twenty-seven times as effective as ours. He would prove twenty-seven times as strong as we, and could accomplish twenty-seven times as much. But he would further work upon what required, owing to decreased gravity, but one third the effort to overcome. His effective force, therefore, would be eighty-one times as great as man's, whether in digging canals or in other bodily occupation. As gravity on the surface of Mars is really a little more than one third that at the surface of the earth, the true ratio is not eighty-one, but about fifty; that is, a Martian would be, physically, fifty-fold more efficient than a man.

Something more we may deduce about the characteristics of possible Martians, dependent upon Mars itself, a result of the age of the world they would live in.

A planet may in a very real sense be said to have a life of its own, of which what we call life may or may not be a detail. It is born, has its fiery youth, its sober middle age, its palsied senility, and ends at last in cold incapability of further change, its death. The speed with which it runs through its gamut of change depends upon its size; for the larger the body, the longer it takes to cool, and with it loss of heat means loss of life. It takes longer to cool because it has relatively more inside than outside, and it is through its outside that its inside cools. Now, inasmuch as time and space are not, as some philosophers have from their too mundane standpoint supposed, forms of our intellect, but essential attributes of the universe, the time taken by any process affects the character of the process itself, as does also the size of the body undergoing it. The changes brought about in a large planet by its cooling are not, therefore, the same as those brought about in a small one. Physically, chemically, and, to our present end, organically, the two results are quite diverse. So different, indeed, are they that unless the planet have at least a certain size it will never produce what we call life, meaning our particular chain of changes or closely allied forms of it, at all.

Whatever the particular planet's line of development, however, in its own line it proceeds to greater and greater degrees of evolution, till the process is arrested by the planet's death. The point of development attained is, as regards its capabilities, precisely measured by the planet's own age, since the one is but a symptom of the other.

Now, in the special case of Mars, we have before us the spectacle of an old world, a world well on in years, a world much older relatively than the earth, halfway between it and the end we see so sadly typified by our moon, a body now practically past possibility of change. His continents are all smoothed down; his oceans have all dried up. If he ever had a *jeunesse orageuse,* it has long since been forgotten.

Mars being thus old himself, we know that evolution on his surface must be similarly advanced. This only informs us of its condition relative to the planet's capabilities. Of its actual state our data are not definite enough to furnish much deduction. But from the fact that our own development has been comparatively a recent thing, and that a long time would be needed to bring even Mars to his present geological condition, we may judge any life he may support to be not only relatively, but really, more advanced than our own.

From the little we can see, such appears to be the case. The evidence of handicraft, if such it be, points to a highly intelligent mind behind it. Irrigation, unscientifically conducted, would not give us such truly wonderful mathematical fitness in the several parts to the whole as we there behold. A mind of no mean order would seem to have presided over the system we see, — a mind certainly of considerably more comprehensiveness than that which presides over the various departments of our own public works. Quite possibly, such Martian folk are possessed of inventions of which we have not dreamed, and with them electrophones and kinetoscopes are things of a bygone past, preserved with veneration in museums as relics of the clumsy contrivances of the simple childhood of their kind. Certainly, what we see hints at the existence of beings who are in advance of, not behind us, in the race of life.

For answers to such problems we must look to the future. That Mars seems to be inhabited is not the last, but the first word on the subject. More important than the mere fact of the existence of living beings there is the question of what they may be like. Whether we ourselves shall live to learn this cannot, of course, be foretold.

If astronomy teaches anything, it teaches that man is but a detail in the evolution of the universe, and that resemblant though diverse details are inevitably to be expected in the host of orbs around him. He learns that though he will probably never find his double anywhere, he is destined to discover any number of cousins scattered through space.

1896
WINTER
by Harriet Monroe

EARTH bears her sorrow gladly, like a nun,
Her young face glowing through the icy veil.
The storms that threaten her, the winds that rail,
Kindle a deeper color. She has won
Graces that please the high-enthronèd sun;
Across her soft white robes that drift and trail
He casts his lordly purples, lest she quail

With the dead year, and deem that all is done.
She leadeth on through desolate sad days,
A smile upon her lips, a triumph-song
Shut in her heart. Be glad! so singeth she;
Glad of the solitude, the silent ways, —
Yea, of the pain: so shall thy soul grow strong
For the brave spring that comes to set us free.

1897
MUNICIPAL ADMINISTRATION:
The New York Police Force
by Theodore Roosevelt

I N New York, in the fall of 1894, Tammany Hall was overthrown by a coalition composed partly of the regular Republicans, partly of anti-Tammany Democrats, and partly of Independents. Under the last head must be included a great many men who in national politics habitually act with one or the other of the two great parties, but who feel that in municipal politics good citizens should act independently. The tidal wave, which was running high against the Democratic party, was undoubtedly very influential in bringing about the anti-Tammany victory; but the chief factor in producing the result was the widespread anger and disgust felt by decent citizens at the corruption which under the sway of Tammany had honeycombed every department of the city government.

The center of corruption was the police department. No man not intimately acquainted with both the lower and the humbler sides of New York life — for there is a wide distinction between the two — can realize how far this corruption extended. Except in rare instances, where prominent politicians made demands which could not be refused, both promotions and appointments towards the close of Tammany rule were almost solely for money, and the prices were discussed with cynical frankness. There was a well-recognized tariff of charges, ranging from two or three hundred dollars for appointment as a patrolman, to twelve or fifteen thousand dollars for promotion to the position of captain. The money was reimbursed to those who paid it by an elaborate system of blackmail. This was chiefly carried on at the expense of gamblers, liquor sellers, and keepers of disorderly houses; but every form of vice and crime contributed more or less, and a great many respectable people who were ignorant or timid were blackmailed under pretense of forbidding or allowing them to violate obscure ordinances, and the like.

In May, 1895, I was made president of the newly appointed police board, whose duty it was to cut out the chief source of civic corruption in New York by cleansing the police department. We could not accomplish all that we should have liked to accomplish, for we were shackled by preposterous legislation, and by the opposition and intrigues of the basest machine politicians. Nevertheless, we did more to increase the efficiency and honesty of the police department than had ever previously been done in its history.

Besides suffering, in aggravated form, from the difficulties which beset the course of the entire administration, the police board had to encounter — and honest and efficient police boards must always encounter — certain special and peculiar difficulties. It is not a pleasant thing to deal with criminals and purveyors of vice. It is very rough work, and it cannot always be done in a nice manner. The man with the night stick, the man in the blue coat with the helmet, can keep order and repress open violence on the streets; but most kinds of crime and vice are ordinarily carried on furtively and by stealth, perhaps at night, perhaps behind closed doors. It is possible to reach them only by the employment of the man in plain clothes, the detective. Now the function of the detective is primarily that of the spy, and it is always easy to arouse feeling against a spy. It is absolutely necessary to employ him. Ninety per cent of the most dangerous criminals and purveyors of vice cannot be reached in any other way. But the average citizen who does not think deeply fails to realize the need for any such employment. In a vague way he desires vice and crime put down; but, also in a vague way, he objects to the only possible means by which they can be put down.

The Tammany officials of New York, headed by the comptroller, made a systematic effort to excite public hostility against the police for their warfare on vice. The lawbreaking liquor seller, the keeper of disorderly houses, and the gambler had been influential allies of Tammany, and head contributors to its campaign chest. Naturally Tammany fought for them; and the effective way in which to carry on such a fight was to portray with gross exaggeration and misstatement the methods necessarily employed by every police force which honestly endeavors to do its work.

Tammany found its most influential allies in the sensational newspapers. Of all the forces that tend for evil in a great city like New York, probably no other is so potent as the sensational press. To sustain law and order is humdrum, and does not furnish material for flaunting woodcuts; but if the editor will stoop, and make his subordinates stoop, to raking the gutters of human depravity, to upholding the wrongdoer and assailing what is upright and honest, he can make money. The man who is to do honorable work in any form of civic

politics must make up his mind to treat the assaults of papers like
these with absolute indifference, and to go his way unheeding. He will
have to make up his mind to be criticized also, sometimes justly, and
more often unjustly, even by decent people; he must not be thin-
skinned.

In administering the police force, we found, as might be expected,
that there was no need of genius, nor indeed of any very unusual
qualities. What was required was the exercise of the plain, ordinary
virtues, of a rather commonplace type, which all good citizens should
be expected to possess. Common sense, common honesty, courage,
energy, resolution, readiness to learn, and a desire to be as pleasant
with everybody as was compatible with a strict performance of duty, —
these were the qualities most called for. We soon found that, in spite
of the widespread corruption which had obtained in the New York
police department, most of the men were desirous of being honest.
Although not possessing the stamina to war against corruption when
the odds seemed well-nigh hopeless, they welcomed the change to a
system under which they were rewarded for doing well, and punished
for doing ill.

Our methods for restoring order and discipline were simple, and
hardly less so were our methods for securing efficiency. We made
frequent personal inspections, especially at night, going anywhere, at
any time. In this way we soon got an idea of whom among our upper
subordinates we could trust and whom we could not. We then proceeded to punish those who were guilty of shortcomings, and to reward those who did well, refusing to pay any heed whatever to anything except the man's own character and record. A very few
promotions and dismissals sufficed to show our subordinates that at
last they were dealing with superiors who meant what they said, and
that the days of political "pull" were over while we had the power. The
effect was immediate. The decent men took heart, and those who were
not decent feared longer to offend. The *morale* of the entire force
improved steadily.

A similar course was followed in reference to the relations between
the police and citizens generally. There had formerly been much complaint of the brutal treatment by police of innocent citizens. This was
stopped peremptorily by the obvious expedient of dismissing from the
force the first two or three men who were found guilty of brutality.
On the other hand, we made the force understand that in the event of
any emergency requiring them to use their weapons against either a
mob or an individual criminal, the police board backed them up without reservation. If a mob threatened violence, we were glad to have
the mob hurt. If a criminal showed fight, we expected the officer to
use any weapon that was requisite to overcome him on the instant. All

that the board required was to be convinced that the necessity really existed. We did not possess a particle of that maudlin sympathy for the criminal, disorderly, and lawless classes which is such a particularly unhealthy sign of social development; and we were determined that the improvement in the fighting efficiency of the police should keep pace with the improvement in their moral tone.

To break up the system of blackmail and corruption was less easy. It was not at all difficult to protect decent people in their rights, and this result was effected at once. But the criminal who is blackmailed has a direct interest in paying the blackmailer, and it is not easy to get information about it. Nevertheless, we put a complete stop to most of the blackmail by the simple process of rigorously enforcing the laws, not only against crime, but against vice.

It was the enforcement of the liquor law which caused most excitement. In New York, the saloon-keepers have always stood high among professional politicians. Nearly two thirds of the political leaders of Tammany Hall have been in the liquor business at one time or another. The saloon is the natural club and meeting-place for the ward heelers and leaders, and the bar-room politician is one of the most common and best recognized factors in local government. The influence the saloon-keepers wield in local politics has always been very great, and until our board took office no man ever dared seriously to threaten them for their flagrant violations of the law. On the other hand, a corrupt police captain, or the corrupt politician who controlled him, could always extort money from a saloon-keeper by threatening to close his place and let his neighbor's remain open. Gradually the greed of corrupt police officials and of corrupt politicians grew by what it fed on, until they began to blackmail all but the very most influential liquor sellers; and as liquor sellers were numerous and the profits of the liquor business great, the amount collected was enormous.

During the year after we took office, the number of arrests for violation of the Sunday liquor law sank to about one half of what they had been during the last year of the Tammany rule; and yet the saloons were practically closed, whereas under Tammany most of them had been open. We adopted no new methods, save in so far as honesty could be called a new method. We did not enforce the law with unusual severity; we merely enforced it against the man with a pull just as much as against the man without a pull. We refused to discriminate in favor of influential lawbreakers.

In reorganizing the force the board had to make, and did make, more promotions, more appointments, and more dismissals in its two years of existence than had ever before been made in the same length of time. We were so hampered by the law that we were not able to dismiss many of the men who should have been removed, but we did turn out two hundred men; more than four times as many as ever had been turned out in a similar period before. All of them were dismissed after formal trial, and after having been given full opportunity to be heard in their own defense. We appointed about seventeen hundred men all told, — again more than four times as many as ever before, — for we were allowed a large increase of the police force by law. We made one hundred and thirty promotions; more than had been made in the six preceding years. All this work was done in strictest accord with what we have grown to speak of as the principles of civil service reform.

The result of our labors was of value to the city, for we gave the citizens better protection than they had ever before received, and at the same time cut out the corruption which was eating away civic morality. We showed conclusively that it was possible to combine both honesty and efficiency in handling the police. We were attacked with the most bitter animosity by every sensational newspaper and every politician of the baser sort, not because of our shortcomings, but because of what we did that was good. We enforced the laws as they were on the statute books, we broke up blackmail, we kept down the spirit of disorder and repressed rascality, and we administered the force with an eye single to the welfare of the city. In doing this we encountered, as we had expected, the venomous opposition of all men whose interest it was that corruption should continue, or who were of such dull morality that they were not willing to see honesty triumph at the cost of strife.

Our experience with the police department taught one or two lessons which are applicable to the whole question of municipal reform. Very many men put their faith in some special device, some special bit of legislation or some official scheme for getting good government. In reality good government can come only through good administration, and good administration only as a consequence of a sustained — not spasmodic — and earnest effort by good citizens to secure honesty, courage, and common sense among civic administrators. If they demand the impossible, they will fail; if they do not demand a good deal, they will get nothing. But though they should demand much in the way of legislation, they should make their special effort for good administration. A bad law may seriously hamper the best administrator, and even nullify most of his efforts; but a good law is of no value whatever unless well administered.

THE END OF THE WAR, AND AFTER
by Walter Hines Page

IT is reason for universal congratulation that the war is ended (for it seems safe to assume that it is ended) so early and so happily, — for us, for the Spanish colonies, and, in spite of her present humiliation, for Spain herself; for the result makes for civilization. There was never a doubt that it would end with an American victory; but that the victory would be so easily and so cheaply won was not foreseen. Nor were the incidental benefits foreseen; for there are incidental benefits as great as the main result itself. Unforeseen, also, were the new obligations that have been imposed on us.

The danger to our successful management of Cuba and Porto Rico, or even of the Philippine Islands, consists, not in their distance from our shores, but in their difference of population and institutions from ours. They cannot be converted into American states by any statutes, and no laws can change their character. Nor is there any need that they should now or ever be converted into American states. We are committed to two duties: we have by conquest taken upon ourselves a solemn obligation to the people of the conquered islands to insure stable government, and the nature of our institutions forbids that we should set up any form of government except one that at the earliest possible moment shall become self-government. Even if we wished we could not shirk these responsibilities. We cannot leave the people of these islands either to their own fate, or to the mercy of the now defeated and disorganized Spanish rule, or yet to the mercy of any predatory nation that might seize them. We are become responsible for their development.

The main result of the war, the freedom of Cuba from Spanish misrule, has been achieved, but the full fruits of it will ripen more slowly than most men at first supposed. Sympathy with the Cuban insurgents had led many persons to regard them as capable at once of self-government; but the conduct of a part of them during the war has confirmed the judgment of those men who knew them best, — that the removal of Spanish rule will not immediately nor easily lead to the self-government of Cuba. The complete conquest of the island by civilization will be accomplished through American industry and commerce, which will now follow American arms. In his proclamation concerning the government of Santiago, the President indicated the proper course to pursue: local government to be permitted, to be required, in fact; the United States to maintain military control so long as military control is necessary for the security of life and property, but to relax it, and at last to give it up, when a competent local government has been created and tested. If the Cubans do not at first show capacity for self-government, the certain increase of American influence and even of American population in the island will greatly hasten its coming. The engineer will follow the soldier.

And the same plan whereby local self-government will be built up in Cuba will apply, with modifications, to Porto Rico. One island will become an independent territory under our guardianship; the other will be directly ceded to us. But the essential elements of their government under our tutelage must be the same, for the moral obligations that we have assumed are the same, and there is but one great principle of government that we can adhere to. How much territory it may be wise to retain in the Philippine Islands it is impossible to foresee; but the principle that should govern our action is clear. We want no "colonies," can indeed have no "colonies," in the continental sense; but we must fulfill every obligation to Spain's conquered subjects that our conduct of the war in Asiatic waters has put upon us, without regard to the colonizing ambitions of the European nations.

The war, then, brings within the sphere of English-speaking civilization two of the most valuable of the Antilles; incidentally the Hawaiian Islands, and perhaps a part of the Philippine group: and these results can be only good. But in achieving them we have achieved other results quite as great, and no less great because they were unexpected.

We have recovered our own national feeling. Four months ago, we were a great mass of people rather than a compact nation conscious of national strength and unity. By forgetting even for this brief time our local differences, we have welded ourselves into a conscious unity such as the Republic has not felt since its early days. Not only have the North and the South forgotten that they were ever at war, — for time and industry had already wellnigh brought this result, — but the Pacific states are nearer to the rest of the Union than they ever were before, and the great middle West is no longer estranged from the seaboard. We can work out our own problems and build our own future with a steadier purpose.

1899

THE BATTLE WITH THE SLUM
by Jacob A. Riis

THE battle with the slum began the day civilization recognized in it her enemy. It was a losing fight until conscience joined forces with fear and self-interest against it. When common sense and the golden rule obtain among men as a rule of practice, it will be over. The two have not always been classed together, but here they are plainly seen to be allies. Justice to the individual is accepted in theory as the only safe groundwork of the commonwealth. When it is practiced in dealing with the slum, there will shortly be no slum. All that is required is that it shall not be left to itself. When a man is drowning, the thing to do is to pull him out of the water; later there will be time for talking it over.

The slum complaint had been chronic in all ages, but the great changes which the nineteenth century saw, the new industry, political freedom, brought on an acute attack which threatened to become fatal. Too many of us had supposed that, because our commonwealth was built on universal suffrage, it would be proof against the complaints that harassed older states; but in fact there was extra hazard in that. Having solemnly resolved that all men are created equal and have certain inalienable rights, among them life, liberty, and the pursuit of happiness, we shut our eyes and waited for the formula to work. It was as if a man with a cold should take the doctor's prescription to bed with him, expecting it to cure him. The formula was all right, but merely repeating it worked no cure. When after a hundred years we opened our eyes, it was upon sixty cents a day as the living wage of the workingwoman in our cities; upon knee pants at forty cents a dozen for the making; upon the Potter's Field taking tithe of our city life, ten per cent each year for the trench, truly the Lost Tenth of the slum. Our country had grown great and rich; through our ports was poured food for the millions of Europe. But in the back streets multitudes huddled in ignorance and want. The foreign oppressor had been vanquished, the fetters stricken from the black man at home; but his white brother, in his bitter plight, sent up a cry of distress that had in it a distinct note of menace. Political freedom we had won; but the problem of helpless poverty, grown vast with the added offscourings of the Old World, mocked us, unsolved. Liberty at sixty cents a day set presently its stamp upon the government of our cities, and it became the scandal and the peril of our political system.

So the battle began. Three times since the Civil War the slum confronted us in New York with its challenge. In the darkest days of the great struggle it was the treacherous mob; later on, the threat of the cholera, which found swine foraging in the streets as the only scavengers and a swarming host — little above the hog in its appetites and in the quality of the shelter afforded it — peopling the back alleys. Still later the mob, caught looting the city's treasury with its idol, the thief Tweed, at its head, had, drunk with power and plunder, insolently defied the outraged community to do its worst. There were meetings and protests. The rascals were turned out for a season; the archthief died in jail. There are other fights to be fought in that war, other victories to be won, and it is slow work. It was nearly ten years after the great robbery before decency got the upper grip in good earnest. That was when the civic conscience awoke in 1879.

In that year the slum was arraigned in the churches. The sad and shameful story was told of how it grew and was fostered by avarice that saw in the homeless crowds from over the sea only a chance for business and exploited them to the uttermost, making sometimes a hundred per cent on the capital invested — always most from the tenants of which "nothing was expected" save that they pay the usurious rents — how Christianity, citizenship, human fellowship, shook their skirts clear of the rabble that was only good enough to fill the greedy purse, and how the rabble, left to itself, improved such opportunities as it found after such fashion as it knew; how it ran elections merely to count its thugs in, and fattened at the public crib; and how the whole evil thing had its root in the tenements, where the home had ceased to be sacred — those dark and deadly dens in which the family ideal was tortured to death and character was smothered, in which children were "damned rather than born" into the world, thus realizing a slum kind of foreordination to torment, happily brief in many cases. The Tenement House Committee long afterward called the worst of the barracks "infant slaughterhouses," and showed, by reference to the mortality lists, that they killed one in every five babies born in them.

The story shocked the town into action. Plans for a better kind of tenement were called for, and a premium was put on every ray of light and breath of air that could be let into it. Money was raised to build model houses, and a bill to give the health authorities summary powers in dealing with tenements was sent to the legislature. The landlords held it up until the last day of the session, when it was forced through by an angered public opinion. The power of the cabal was broken. The landlords had found their Waterloo. Many of them got rid of their property, which in a large number of cases they had never seen, and tried to forget the source of their ill-gotten wealth. Light and air did find their way into the tenements in a halfhearted fashion, and we began to count the tenants as "souls." That is one of our milestones in the history of New York. They were never reckoned so before; no one ever thought of them as "souls." So, restored to human fellowship, in the twilight of the air shaft that had penetrated to their dens, the first Tenement House Committee was able to make them out "better than the houses" they lived in, and a long step forward was taken. The Mulberry Bend, the wicked core of the "bloody Sixth Ward," was marked for destruction, and all slumdom held its breath to see it go. With that gone, it seemed as if the old days must be gone too, never to return. There would not be another Mulberry Bend. As long as it stood, there was yet a chance. The slum had backing, as it were.

The civic conscience was not very robust yet, and required many and protracted naps. It slumbered fitfully, waking up now and then with a start, while the politicians did their best to lull it back to its slumbers. I wondered often, in those years of delay, if it was just plain stupidity that kept the politicians from spending the money which the law had put within their grasp; for with every year that passed a million dollars that could have been used for small park purposes was lost.

Today we can count the months to the time when every child who knocks shall find a seat in our schools. We have a school census to tell us of the need. In that most crowded neighborhood in all the world, where the superintendent lately pleaded in vain for three new schools, five have been built, the finest in this or any other land — great, light, and airy structures, with playgrounds on the roof — and all over the city the like are going up. The briefest of our laws, every word of which is like the blow of a hammer driving the nails home in the coffin of the bad old days, says that never one shall be built without its playground. So the boy is coming to his rights.

The streets are cleaned; the slum has been washed. Even while I am writing, a bill is urged in the legislature to build in every senatorial district in the city a gymnasium and a public bath. It matters little whether it passes at this session or not. The important thing is that it is there. The rest will follow. A people's club is being organized to crowd out the saloon that has had a monopoly of the brightness and the cheer in the tenement streets too long. The labor unions are bestirring themselves to deal with the sweating curse, and the gospel of less law and more enforcement sits enthroned at Albany. Theodore Roosevelt will teach us again Jefferson's forgotten lesson, that "the whole art of government consists in being honest."

Of free soup there is an end. It was never food for free men. Our experience has taught us a new reading of the old word that charity covers a multitude of sins. It does. Uncovering some of them has kept us busy since our conscience awoke, and there are more left. The worst of them all, that awful parody on municipal charity, the police station lodging room, is gone after twenty years of persistent attack upon the foul dens — years during which they were arraigned, condemned, indicted by every authority having jurisdiction. The stale beer dives went with them, and the grip of the tramp on our throat has been loosened.

One after another, the outworks of the slum have been taken. The higher standards now set up on every hand, in the cleaner streets, in the better schools, in the parks and the clubs, in the settlements, and in the thousand and one agencies for good that touch and help the lives of the poor at as many points, will tell at no distant day and react upon the homes and upon their builders. Philanthropy is not sitting

idle and waiting. It is building tenements on the humane plan that lets
in sunshine and air and hope. It is putting up hotels deserving of the
name for the army that just now had no other home than the cheap
lodging houses which Inspector Byrnes fitly called "nurseries of
crime." These are standards from which there is no backing down,
and they are here to stay, for they pay. That is the test. Not charity,
but justice — that is the gospel which they preach.

1900

TUPPENNY TRAVELS IN LONDON
by Kate Douglas Wiggin

IF one really wants to know London, one must live there for years
and years.

This sounds like a reasonable and sensible statement, yet the
moment it is made I retract it, as quite misleading and altogether too
general.

We have a charming English friend who has not been to the Tower
since he was a small boy, and begs us to conduct him there on the very
next Saturday. Another has not seen Westminster Abbey for fifteen
years, because he attends church at St. Dunstan's-in-the-East. Another
says that he should like to have us "read up" London in the red-
covered Baedeker, and then show it to him, properly and systematically.

We think we get a kind of vague apprehension of what London
means from the top of a bus better than anywhere else. We often set
out on a fine morning, Salemina and I, and travel twenty miles in the
day, though we have to double our twopenny fee several times to
accomplish that distance.

We never know whither we are going, and indeed it is not a matter
of great moment (I mean to a woman) where everything is new and
strange, and where the driver, if one is fortunate enough to be on a
front seat, tells one everything of interest along the way, and instructs
one regarding a different route back into town.

We have our favorite buses, of course; but when one appears, and
we jump on while it is still in motion, as the conductor seems to prefer,
and pull ourselves up the corkscrew stairway, — not a simple matter in
the garments of sophistication, — we have little time to observe more
than the color of the lumbering vehicle.

We like the Cadbury's Cocoa bus very much; it takes you by St.
Mary-le-Strand, Bow-Bells, the Temple, Mansion House, St. Paul's,
and the Bank.

If you want to go and lunch, or dine frugally, at the Cheshire Cheese, eat black pudding and drink pale ale, sit in Dr. Johnson's old seat, and put your head against the exact spot on the wall where his rested, — although the traces of this form of worship are all too apparent, — then you jump on a Lipton's Tea bus, and are deposited at the very door. All is novel, and all is interesting, whether it be the crowded streets of the East End traversed by the Davies' Pea-Fed Bacon buses, or whether you ride to the very outskirts of London, through green fields and hedgerows, by the Ridge's Food or Nestlé's Milk route.

There are trams, too, which take one to delightful places, though the seats on top extend lengthwise, after the old "knifeboard pattern," and one does not get so good a view of the country as from the "garden seats" on the roof of the omnibus; still there is nothing we like better on a warm morning than a good outing on the Vinolia tram that we pick up in Shaftesbury Avenue. There is a street running from Shaftesbury Avenue into Oxford Street, which was once the village of St. Giles, one of the dozens of hamlets swallowed up by the great maw of London, and it still looks like a hamlet, although it has been absorbed for many years. We constantly happen on these absorbed villages from which, not a century ago, people drove up to town in their coaches.

If you wish to see another phase of life, go out on a Saturday evening, from nine o'clock on to eleven, starting on a Beecham's Pill bus, alighting occasionally to stand with the crowd in the narrower thoroughfares. It is a market night, and the streets will be a moving mass of men and women buying at the hucksters' stalls. Everything that can be sold at a stall is there: fruit, vegetables, meat, fish, crockery, tinware, children's clothing, cheap toys, boots, shoes, and sunbonnets, all in reckless confusion. The venders cry their wares in stentorian tones, vying with one another to produce excitement and induce patronage, while gas jets are streaming into the air from the roofs and flaring from the sides of the stalls; children crying, children dancing to the strains of an accordion, children quarreling, children scrambling for the refuse fruit. In the midst of this spectacle, this din and uproar, the women are chaffering and bargaining quite calmly, watching the scales to see that they get their full pennyworth or sixpennyworth of this or that.

To the student of faces, of manners, of voices, of gestures; to the person who sees unwritten and unwritable stories in all these groups of men, women, and children, the scene reveals many things: some comedies, many tragedies, a few plain narratives (thank God!), and now and then — only now and then — a romance. As to the dark alleys and tenements on the fringe of this glare and brilliant confusion, this Babel of sound and ant-bed of moving life, one can only surmise and pity and shudder; close one's eyes and ears to it a little, or one could never sleep for thinking of it, yet not too tightly lest one sleep too soundly, and forget altogether the seamy side of things.

One can hardly believe that there is a seamy side when one descends from his traveling observatory a little later, and stands on Westminster Bridge, or walks along the Thames Embankment. The lights of Parliament House gleam from a hundred windows, and in the dark shadows by the banks thousands of colored disks of light twinkle and dance and glow like fairy lamps, and are reflected in the silver surface of the river. That river, as full of mystery and contrast in its course as London itself, — where is such another?

If you care to go to any particular place or reach that place by any particular time, you must not, of course, look at the most conspicuous signs on the tops and ends of the chariots as we do; you must stand quietly at one of the regular points of departure and try to decipher, in a narrow horizontal space along the side, certain little words that show the route and destination of the vehicle. They say that it can be done, and I do not feel like denying it on my own responsibility. Old Londoners assert that they are not blinded or confused by Pears' Soap in letters two feet high, scarlet on a gold ground, but can see below in fine print, and with the naked eye, such legends as Tottenham Court Road, Westbourne Grove, St. Pancras, Paddington, or Victoria. It is certainly reasonable that the omnibuses should be decorated to suit the inhabitants of the place rather than foreigners, and it is perhaps better to carry a few hundred stupid souls to the wrong station daily than to allow them to cleanse their hands with the wrong soap, or quench their thirst with the wrong (which is to say the unadvertised) beverage.

The conductors do all in their power to mitigate the lot of unhappy strangers, and it is only now and again that you hear an absent-minded or logical one call out, "Castoria! All the w'y for a penny!"

If you have determined to make a certain train from a certain station, and do not care for any other, no matter if it should turn out to be just as interesting, then never take a Lipton's Tea bus, for it is the most unreliable of all. If it did not sound so learned, and if I did not feel that it must have been said before, it is so apt, I should quote Horace and say, "Omnibus hoc vitium est." There is no bus unseized by the Napoleonic Lipton. Do not ascend one of them supposing for a moment that by paying fourpence and going to the very end of the route you will come to a neat tea station, where you will be served with the cheering cup. Never; nor with a draught of Cadbury's cocoa nor Nestlé's milk, although you have jostled along for nine weary miles in company with their blatant recommendations to drink nothing else, and though you may have passed other buses with the same highly colored names glaring at you until they are burned into the gray matter of your brain, to remain there as long as the copybook maxims you penned when you were a child.

These pictorial methods doubtless prove a source of great financial gain; of course it must be so, or they would never be prosecuted; but although they may allure millions of customers, they will lose two in our modest persons. When Salemina and I go into a café for tea we ask the young women if they serve Lipton's, and if they say yes, we take coffee. This is self-punishment indeed (in London!), yet we feel that it may have a moral effect; perhaps not commensurate with the physical effect of the coffee upon us, but these delicate matters can never be adjusted with absolute exactitude.

Sometimes when we are to travel on a Pears' Soap bus we buy beforehand a bit of pure white Castile, cut from a shrinking, reserved, exclusive bar with no name upon it, and present it to some poor woman when we arrive at our journey's end. We do not suppose that so insignificant a protest does much good, but at least it preserves one's individuality and self-respect.

On one of our excursions our English friend Hilda Mellifica accompanied us, and we alighted to see the place where the Smithfield martyrs were executed, and to visit some of the very old churches in that vicinity. We found hanging in the vestibule of one of them something quite familiar to Hilda, but very strange to our eyes: "A Table of Kindred and Affinity, wherein whosoever are related are forbidden in Scripture and our Laws to Marry Together."

Salemina was very quiet that afternoon, and we accused her afterward of being depressed because she had discovered that, added to the battalions of men in England who had not thus far urged her to marry them, there were thirty persons whom she could not legally espouse even if they did ask her!

"The Table of Kindred and Affinity is all too familiar to me," sighed Hilda, "because we had a governess who made us learn it as a punishment. I suppose I could recite it now, although I haven't looked at it for ten years. We used to chant it in the nursery schoolroom on wet afternoons."

Here Hilda chanted softly, there being no one in the old churchyard: —

"A woman may not marry with her Grandfather | Grandmother's Husband, Husband's Grandfather || Father's Brother | Mother's Brother | Father's Sister's Husband || Mother's Sister's Husband | Husband's Father's Brother | Husband's Mother's Brother || Father | Step-Father | Husband's Father || Son | Husband's Son | Daughter's Husband || Brother | Husband's Brother | Sister's Husband || Son's

Son | Daughter's Son | Son's Daughter's Husband || Daughter's Daughter's Husband | Husband's Son's Son | Husband's Daughter's Son || Brother's Son | Sister's Son | Brother's Daughter's Husband || Sister's Daughter's Husband | Husband's Brother's Son | Husband's Sister's Son."

"It seems as if there were nobody left," I said disconsolately, "save perhaps your Second Cousin's Uncle, or your Enemy's Dearest Friend."

"That's just the effect it has on one," answered Hilda. "We always used to conclude our chant with the advice: —

"And if there is anybody, after this, in the universe | left to | marry || marry him as expeditiously | as you | possibly | can || Because there are very few husbands omitted from this table of | Kindred and | Affinity || And it behooveth a maiden to snap them up without any delay | willing or unwilling | whenever and | wherever found."

As we jog along, or walk, by turns, we come to Buckingham Street, and looking up at Alfred Jingle's lodgings say a grateful word of Mr. Pickwick. We tell each other that much of what we know of London and England seems to have been learned from Dickens.

Deny him the right to sit among the elect, if you will; talk of his tendency to farce and caricature; call his humor low comedy, and his pathos bathos, — although you shall say none of these things in my presence unchallenged; but the fact remains that every child, in America at least, knows more of England, — its almshouses, debtors' prisons, and law courts, its villages and villagers, its beadles and cheap-jacks and hostlers and coachmen and boots, its streets and lanes, its lodgings and inns and landladies and roast beef and plum pudding, its ways, manners, and customs, — knows more of these things and a thousand others from Dickens's novels than from all the histories, geographies, biographies, and essays in the language. Where is there another novelist who has so peopled a great city with his imaginary characters that there is hardly room for the living population, as one walks along the ways?

Oh, these streets of London! There are other more splendid shades in them, — shades that have been there for centuries, and will walk beside us so long as the streets exist. One can never see these shades, save as one goes on foot, or takes that chariot of the humble, the omnibus. I should like to make a map of literary London somewhat after Leigh Hunt's plan, as projected in his essay on the World of Books; for to the booklover "the poet's hand is always on the place, blessing it." One can no more separate the association from the partic-ular spot than one can take away from it any other beauty.

"Fleet Street is always Johnson's Fleet Street" (so Leigh Hunt says); "the Tower belongs to Julius Cæsar, and Blackfriars to Suckling, Vandyke, and the Dunciad. . . . I can no more pass through Westminster without thinking of Milton, or the Borough without thinking of Chaucer and Shakespeare, or Gray's Inn without calling Bacon to mind, or Bloomsbury Square without Steele and Akenside, than I can prefer brick and mortar to wit and poetry, or not see a beauty upon it beyond architecture in the splendor of the recollection."

1901
HUNTING BIG REDWOODS
by John Muir

THE Big Tree (*Sequoia gigantea*) is nature's forest masterpiece, and, as far as I know, the greatest of living things. It belongs to an ancient stock, as its remains in old rocks show, and has a strange air of other days about it, a thoroughbred look inherited from the long ago, the auld lang syne of trees. Once the genus was common, and with many species flourished in the now desolate Arctic regions, the interior of North America, and in Europe; but in long eventful wanderings from climate to climate only two species have survived the hardships they had to encounter, the *gigantea* and *sempervirens:* the former now restricted to the western slopes of the Sierra, the other to the Coast Mountains, and both to California, excepting a few groves of redwood which extend into Oregon.

The Pacific coast in general is the paradise of conifers. Here nearly all of them are giants, and display a beauty and magnificence unknown elsewhere. The climate is mild, the ground never freezes, and moisture and sunshine abound all the year. Nevertheless, it is not easy to account for the colossal size of the sequoias. The largest are about three hundred feet high and thirty feet in diameter. Who of all the dwellers of the plains and prairies and fertile home forests of round-headed oak and maple, hickory and elm, ever dreamed that earth could bear such growths? Sequoias are trees that the familiar pines and firs seem to know nothing about, lonely, silent, serene, with a physiognomy almost godlike, and so old that thousands of them still living had already counted their years by tens of centuries when Columbus set sail from Spain, and were in the vigor of youth or middle age when the star led the Chaldean sages to the infant Saviour's cradle. As far as man is concerned, they are the same yesterday, today, and forever, emblems of permanence.

Excepting the sugar pine, most of its neighbors with pointed tops seem to be forever shouting "Excelsior!" while the Big Tree, though soaring above them all, seems satisfied, its rounded head poised lightly as a cloud, giving no impression of trying to go higher. Only in youth does it show, like other conifers, a heavenward yearning, keenly aspiring with a long quick-growing top. Indeed, the whole tree, for the first century or two, or until a hundred to a hundred and fifty feet high, is arrowhead in form, and compared with the solemn rigidity of age, is as sensitive to the wind as a squirrel tail. The lower branches are gradually dropped as it grows older, and the upper ones thinned out, until comparatively few are left. These, however, are developed to great size, divide again and again, and terminate in bossy rounded masses of leafy branchlets, while the head becomes dome-shaped. Then, poised in fullness of strength and beauty, stern and solemn in mien, it glows with eager, enthusiastic life, quivering to the tip of every leaf and branch and far-reaching root, calm as a granite dome — the first to feel the touch of the rosy beams of the morning, the last to bid the sun good night.

Perfect specimens, unhurt by running fires or lightning, are singularly regular and symmetrical in general form, though not at all conventional, showing infinite variety in sure unity and harmony of plan. The immensely strong, stately shafts, with rich purplish-brown bark, are free of limbs for a hundred and fifty feet or so, though dense tufts of sprays occur here and there producing an ornamental effect, while long parallel furrows give a fluted, columnar appearance. The limbs shoot forth with equal boldness in every direction, showing no weather side. On the old trees the main branches are crooked and rugged, and strike rigidly outward, mostly at right angles from the trunk, but there is always a certain measured restraint in their reach which keeps them within bounds. No other Sierra tree has foliage so densely massed or outlines so finely, firmly drawn and so obediently subordinate to an ideal type. A particularly knotty, angular, ungovernable-looking branch, five to eight feet in diameter and perhaps a thousand years old, may occasionally be seen pushing out from the trunk, as if determined to break across the bounds of the regular curve; but, like all the others, as soon as the general outline is approached, the huge limb dissolves into massy bosses of branchlets and sprays, as if the tree were growing beneath an invisible bell glass against the sides of which the branches were molded, while many small varied departures from the ideal form give the impression of freedom to grow as they like.

Except in picturesque old age, after being struck by lightning and broken by a thousand snowstorms, this regularity of form is one of the Big Tree's most distinguishing characteristics. Another is the simple sculptural beauty of the trunk and its great thickness as compared with its height and the width of the branches; many of them being from eight to ten feet in diameter at a height of two hundred feet from the ground and seeming more like finely modeled and sculptured architectural columns than the stems of trees, while the great strong limbs are like rafters supporting the magnificent dome head.

The root system corresponds in magnitude with the other dimensions of the tree, forming a flat, far-reaching, spongy network, two hundred feet or more in width, without any taproot; and the instep is so grand and fine, so suggestive of endless strength, it is long ere the eye is released to look above it. The natural swell of the roots, though at first sight excessive, gives rise to buttresses no greater than are required for beauty as well as strength, as at once appears when you stand back far enough to see the whole tree in its true proportions.

The bark of full-grown trees is from one to two feet thick, rich cinnamon brown, purplish on young trees and shady parts of the old, forming magnificent masses of color with the underbrush and beds of flowers. Toward the end of winter the trees themselves bloom, while the snow is still eight or ten feet deep. The pistillate flowers are about three eighths of an inch long, pale green, and grow in countless thousands on the ends of the sprays. The staminate are still more abundant, pale yellow, a fourth of an inch long, and when the golden pollen is ripe they color the whole tree and dust the air and the ground far and near.

The cones are bright grass green in color, about two and a half inches long, one and a half wide, and are made up of thirty or forty strong closely packed rhomboidal scales, with four to eight seeds at the base of each. The seeds are extremely small and light, being only from an eighth to a fourth of an inch long and wide, including a filmy surrounding wing, which causes them to glint and waver in falling and enables the wind to carry them considerable distances from the tree.

The faint lisp of snowflakes, as they alight, is one of the smallest sounds mortal can hear. The sound of falling sequoia seeds, even when they happen to strike on flat leaves or flakes of bark, is about as faint. Very different are the bumping and thudding of the falling cones. Most of them are cut off by the Douglas squirrel and stored for the sake of the seeds, small as they are. In the calm Indian summer these busy harvesters with ivory sickles go to work early in the morning, as soon as breakfast is over, and nearly all day the ripe cones fall in a steady pattering, bumping shower. Unless harvested in this way, they discharge their seeds and remain on the tree for many years. In fruitful seasons the trees are fairly laden. On two small specimen branches, one and a half and two inches in diameter, I counted four hundred and eighty cones. No other California conifer produces nearly so many seeds, excepting perhaps its relative, the redwood of the Coast Mountains. Millions are ripened annually by a single tree, and the product of one of the main groves in a fruitful year would suffice to plant all the mountain ranges of the world.

The dense tufted sprays make snug nesting places for birds, and in some of the loftiest, leafiest towers of verdure thousands of generations have been reared, the great solemn trees shedding off flocks of merry singers every year from nests like the flocks of winged seeds from the cones.

The Big Tree keeps its youth far longer than any of its neighbors. Most silver firs are old in their second or third century, pines in their fourth or fifth, while the Big Tree, growing beside them, is still in the bloom of its youth, juvenile in every feature, at the age of old pines, and cannot be said to attain anything like prime size and beauty before its fifteen hundredth year, or, under favorable circumstances, become old before its three thousandth. Many, no doubt, are much older than this. On one of the Kings River giants, thirty-five feet and eight inches in diameter, exclusive of bark, I counted upwards of four thousand annual wood rings, in which there was no trace of decay after all these centuries of mountain weather.

There is no absolute limit to the existence of any tree. Their death is due to accidents, not, as of animals, to the wearing out of organs. Only the leaves die of old age — their fall is foretold in their structure — but the leaves are renewed every year, and so also are the other essential organs, wood, roots, bark, buds. Most of the Sierra trees die of disease. Thus the magnificent silver firs are devoured by fungi, and comparatively few of them live to see their three hundredth birth year. But nothing hurts the Big Tree. I never saw one that was sick or showed the slightest sign of decay. It lives on through indefinite thousands of years, until burned, blown down, undermined, or shattered by some tremendous lightning stroke. No ordinary bolt ever seriously hurts sequoia. In all my walks I have seen only one that was thus killed outright.

I have seen silver firs, two hundred feet high, split into long peeled rails and slivers down to the roots, leaving not even a stump; the rails radiating like the spokes of a wheel from a hole in the ground where the tree stood. But the sequoia, instead of being split and slivered, usually has forty or fifty feet of its brash knotty top smashed off in short chunks about the size of cordwood, the beautiful rosy-red ruins covering the ground in a circle a hundred feet wide or more. I never saw any that had been cut down to the ground, or even to below the branches, except one in the Stanislaus Grove, about twelve feet in diameter, the greater part of which was smashed to fragments, leaving only a leafless stump about seventy-five feet high. It is a curious fact that all the very old sequoias have lost their heads by lightning.

The great age of these noble trees is even more wonderful than their huge size, standing bravely up, millennium in, millennium out, to all that fortune may bring them; triumphant over tempest and fire and time, fruitful and beautiful, giving food and shelter to multitudes of small fleeting creatures dependent upon their bounty.

To the dwellers of the plain, dependent on irrigation, the Big Tree is a tree of life, a never failing spring, sending living water to the lowlands all through the hot, rainless summer as it stores and dispenses the bounty of the mountain clouds. For every grove cut down a stream is dried up. Therefore all California is crying, "Save the trees of the fountains!" Nor, judging by the signs of the times, is it likely that the cry will cease until the salvation of all that is left of *Sequoia gigantea* is sure.

1902
LI WAN, THE FAIR
by Jack London

"THE sun sinks, Canim, and the heat of the day is gone!"

So called Li Wan to the man whose head was hidden beneath the squirrel-skin robe, but she called softly, as though divided between the duty of waking him and the fear of him awake. For she was afraid of this big husband of hers, who was like unto none of the men she had known.

The moose meat sizzled uneasily, and she moved the frying-pan to one side of the red embers. As she did so she glanced warily at the two Hudson Bay dogs dripping eager slaver from their scarlet tongues and following her every movement. They were huge, hairy fellows, crouched to leeward in the thin smoke-wake of the fire to escape the swarming myriads of mosquitoes. As Li Wan gazed down the steep to where the Klondike flung its swollen flood between the hills, one of the dogs bellied its way forward like a worm, and with a deft, catlike stroke of the paw dipped a chunk of hot meat out of the pan to the ground. But Li Wan caught him out of the corner of her eye, and he sprang back with a snap and a snarl as she rapped him over the nose with a stick of firewood.

"Nay, Olo," she laughed, recovering the meat without removing her eye from him. "Thou art ever hungry, and for that thy nose leads thee into endless troubles."

But the mate of Olo joined him, and together they defied the woman. The hair on their backs and shoulders bristled in recurrent waves of anger, and the thin lips writhed and lifted into ugly wrinkles, exposing the flesh-tearing fangs, cruel and menacing. Their very noses serrulated and shook in brute passion, and they snarled as wolves snarl, with all the hatred and malignity of the breed impelling them to spring upon the woman and drag her down.

"And thou, too, Bash, fierce as thy master and never at peace with the hand that feeds thee! This is not thy quarrel, so that be thine! and that!"

As she cried, she drove at them with the firewood, but they avoided the blows and refused to retreat. They separated and approached her from either side, crouching low and snarling. Li Wan had struggled with the wolf-dog for mastery from the time she toddled among the skin-bales of the tepee, and she knew a crisis was at hand. Bash had halted, his muscles stiff and tense for the spring; Olo was yet creeping into striking distance.

Grasping two blazing sticks by the charred ends, she faced the brutes. The one held back, but Bash sprang, and she met him in mid-air with the flaming weapon. There were sharp yelps of pain and swift odors of burning hair and flesh as he rolled in the dirt and the woman ground the fiery embers into his mouth. Snapping wildly, he flung himself sidelong out of her reach and in a frenzy of fear scrambled for safety. Olo, on the other side, had begun his retreat, when Li Wan reminded him of her primacy by hurling a heavy stick of wood into his ribs. Then the pair retreated under a rain of firewood, and on the edge of the camp fell to licking their wounds and whimpering and snarling by turns.

Li Wan blew the ashes off the meat and sat down again. Her heart had not gone up a beat, and the incident was already old, for this was the routine of life. Canim had not stirred during the disorder, but instead had set up a lusty snoring.

"Come, Canim!" she called. "The heat of the day is gone and the trail waits for our feet."

The squirrel-skin robe was agitated and cast aside by a brown arm. Then the man's eyelids fluttered and drooped again.

"His pack is heavy," she thought, "and he is tired with the work of the morning."

A mosquito stung her on the neck, and she daubed the unprotected spot with wet clay from a ball she had convenient to hand. All morning, toiling up the divide and enveloped in a cloud of the pests, the man and woman had plastered themselves with the sticky mud, which, drying in the sun, covered their faces with masks of clay. These masks, broken in divers places by the movement of the facial muscles, had constantly to be renewed, so that the deposit was irregular of depth and peculiar of aspect.

Li Wan shook Canim gently but with persistence till he roused and sat up. His first glance was to the sun, and after consulting the celestial timepiece he hunched over to the fire and fell to ravenously on the meat. He was a large Indian, fully six feet in height, deep-chested and heavy-muscled, and his eyes were keener and vested with greater intelligence than the average of his kind. The lines of will had marked his face deeply, and this, coupled with a sternness and primitiveness, advertised a native indomitability, unswerving of purpose and prone, when thwarted, to sullen cruelty.

"To-morrow, Li Wan, we shall feast." He sucked a marrow-bone clean and threw it to the dogs. "We shall have *flapjacks* fried in *bacon grease,* and *sugar,* which is more toothsome" —

"*Flapjacks?*" she cried, mouthing the word curiously.

"Ay," Canim answered with superiority; "and I shall teach you new ways of cookery. Of these things I speak, you are ignorant, and of many more things besides. You have lived your days in a little corner of the earth and know nothing. But I" — he straightened himself and looked at her pridefully — "I am a great traveler, and have been all places, even among the white people, and I am versed in their ways, and in the ways of many peoples. I am not a tree, born to stand in one place always and know not what there be over the next hill; for I am Canim, The Canoe, made to go here and there and to journey and quest up and down the length and breadth of the world."

She bowed her head humbly. "It is true. I have eaten fish and meat and berries all my days, and lived in a little corner of the earth. Nor did I dream the world was so large until you stole me from my people, and I cooked and carried for you on the endless trails." She looked up at him suddenly. "Tell me, Canim, does this trail ever end?"

"Nay," he answered. "My trail is like the world; it never ends. My trail *is* the world, and I have traveled it since the time my legs could carry me, and I shall travel it until I die. My father and my mother may be dead, but it is long since I looked upon them, and I do not care. My tribe is like your tribe. It stays in the one place, — which is far from here, — but I care naught for my tribe, for I am Canim, The Canoe!"

"And must I, Li Wan, who am weary, travel always your trail until I die?"

"You, Li Wan, are my wife, and the wife travels the husband's trail wheresoever it goes. It is the law. And were it not the law, yet would it be the law of Canim, who is lawgiver unto himself and his."

She bowed her head again, for she knew no other law than that man was the master of woman.

"Be not in haste," Canim cautioned her, as she began to strap the meagre camp outfit to her pack. "The sun is yet hot, and the trail leads down and the footing is good."

She dropped her work obediently and resumed her seat.

Canim regarded her with speculative interest. "You do not squat on your hams like other women, " he remarked.

"No," she answered. "It never came easy. It tires me, and I cannot take my rest that way."

"And why is it your feet point not straight before you?"

"I do not know, save that they are unlike the feet of other women."

A satisfied light crept into his eyes, but otherwise he gave no sign.

"Like other women, your hair is black; but have you ever noticed that it is soft and fine, softer and finer than the hair of other women?"

"I have noticed," she answered shortly, for she was not pleased at such cold analysis of her sex deficiencies.

"It is a year, now, since I took you from your people," he went on, "and you are nigh as shy and afraid of me as when first I looked upon you. How does this thing be?"

Li Wan shook her head. "I am afraid of you, Canim, you are so big and strange. And further, before you looked upon me, even, I was afraid of all the young men. I do not know — I cannot say — only, it seemed, somehow, as though I should not be for them, as though" —

"Ay," he encouraged, impatient at her faltering.

"As though they were not my kind."

"Not your kind?" he demanded slowly. "Then what is your kind?"

"I do not know, I" — She shook her head in a bewildered manner. "I cannot put into words the way I felt. It was strangeness in me. I was unlike other maidens who sought the young men slyly. I could not care for the young men that way. It would have been a great wrong, it seemed, and an ill deed."

"What is the first thing you remember?" Canim asked with abrupt irrelevance.

"Pow-Wah-Kaan, my mother."

"And naught else before Pow-Wah-Kaan?"

"Naught else."

But Canim, holding her eyes with his, searched her secret soul and saw it waver.

"Think, and think hard, Li Wan!" he threatened.

She stammered, and her eyes were piteous and pleading, but his will dominated her and wrung from her lips the reluctant speech.

"But it was only dreams, Canim, ill dreams of childhood, shadows of things not real, visions such as the dogs, sleeping in the sun warmth, behold and whine out against."

"Tell me," he commanded, "of the things before Pow-Wah-Kaan, your mother."

"They are forgotten memories," she protested. "As a child I dreamed awake, with my eyes open to the day, and when I spoke of the strange things I saw I was laughed at, and the other children were afraid and drew away from me. And when I spoke of the things I saw to Pow-Wah-Kaan, she chided me and said they were evil; also she beat me. It was a sickness, I believe, like the falling sickness that comes to old men; and in time I grew better and dreamed no more. And now — I cannot remember" — She brought her hand in a confused manner to her forehead, "They are there, somewhere, but I cannot find them, only" —

"Only," Canim repeated, holding her.

"Only one thing. But you will laugh at its foolishness, it is so unreal."

"Nay, Li Wan. Dreams are dreams. They may be memories of other lives we have lived. I was once a moose. I firmly believe I was once a moose. What of the things I have seen in dreams, and heard?"

Strive as he would to hide it, a growing anxiety was manifest, but Li Wan, groping after the words with which to paint the picture, took no heed.

"I see a snow-tramped space among the trees," she began, "and across the snow the sign of a man where he has dragged himself heavily on hand and knee. And I see, too, the man in the snow, and it seems I am very close to him when I look. He is unlike real men, for he has hair on his face, much hair, and the hair of his face and head is yellow like the summer coat of the weasel. His eyes are closed, but they open and search about. They are blue like the sky, and look into mine and search no more. And his hand moves, slow, as from weakness, and I feel" —

"Ay," Canim whispered hoarsely. "You feel" —

"No, no!" she cried in haste. "I feel nothing. Did I say 'feel'? I did not mean it. It could not be that I should mean it. I see, and I see only, and that is all I see — a man in the snow, with eyes like the sky and hair like the weasel. I have seen it many times, and always it is the same — a man in the snow" —

"And do you see yourself?" he asked, leaning forward and regarding her intently. "Do you ever see yourself and the man in the snow?"

"Why should I see myself? Am I not real?"

His muscles relaxed and he sank back, an exultant satisfaction in his eyes which he turned from her so that she might not see.

"I will tell you, Li Wan," he spoke decisively; "you were a little bird in some life before, a little moose-bird, when you saw this thing, and the memory of it is with you yet. It is not strange. I was once a moose, and my father's father afterward became a bear — so said the shaman, and the shaman cannot lie. Thus, on the Trail of the Gods, we pass from life to life, and the gods know only and understand. Dreams and the shadows of dreams be memories, nothing more, and the dog, whining asleep in the sun warmth, doubtless sees and remembers things gone before. Bash, there, was a warrior once. I do firmly believe he was once a warrior."

Canim tossed a bone to the brute and got upon his feet. "Come, let us begone. The sun is yet hot, but it will get no cooler."

"And these white people, what are they like?" Li Wan made bold to ask.

"Like you and me," he answered, "only they are less dark of skin. You will be among them ere the day is dead."

Canim lashed the sleeping-robe to his one hundred and fifty pound pack, smeared his face with wet clay, and sat down to rest till Li Wan had finished loading the dogs. Olo cringed at sight of the club in her hand, and gave no trouble when the bundle of forty pounds and odd was strapped upon him. But Bash was aggrieved and truculent, and could not forbear to whimper and snarl as he was forced to receive the burden. He bristled his back and bared his teeth as she drew the straps tight, the while throwing all the malignancy of his nature into the glances shot at her sidelong and backward. And Canim chuckled and said, "Did I not say I believed he was once a very great warrior?"

"These furs will bring a price," he remarked as he adjusted his head-strap and lifted his pack clear of the ground. "A very big price. The white men pay well for such goods, for they have no time to hunt and are soft to the cold. Soon shall we feast, Li Wan, as you have feasted never in all the lives before."

She grunted acknowledgment and gratitude for her lord's condescension, slipped into the harness, and bent forward to the load.

"The next time I am born, I would be born a white man," he added, and swung off down the trail which dived into the gorge at his feet.

The dogs followed close at his heels, and Li Wan brought up the rear. But her thoughts were far away, across the Ice Mountains to the east, to the little corner of the earth where her childhood had been lived. Ever as a child, she remembered, she had been looked upon as strange, as one with an affliction. Truly she had dreamed awake and been scolded and beaten for the remarkable visions she saw, till, after a time, she had outgrown them. But not utterly. Though they troubled her no more waking, they yet came to her in her sleep, grown woman that she was, and many a night of nightmare was hers, filled with fluttering shapes, vague and meaningless. The talk with Canim had excited her, and down all the twisted slant of the divide she harked back to the mocking fantasies of her dreams.

"Let us take breath," Canim said, when they had tapped midway the bed of the main creek.

He rested his pack on a jutting rock, slipped the head-strap, and sat down. Li Wan joined him, and the dogs sprawled panting on the ground beside them. At their feet rippled the glacial drip of the hills, but it was muddy and discolored, as soiled by some commotion of the earth.

"Why is this?" Li Wan asked.

"Because of the white men who work in the ground. Listen!" He held up his hand, and they heard the ring of pick and shovel and the sound of men's voices. "They are made mad by *gold,* and work without ceasing that they may find it. *Gold?* It is yellow and comes from the ground, and is considered of great value. It is also a measure of price."

But Li Wan's roving eyes had called her attention from him. A few yards below, and partly screened by a clump of young spruce, the tiered logs of a cabin rose to meet its overhanging roof of dirt. A thrill ran through her, and all her dream phantoms roused up and stirred about uneasily.

"Canim," she whispered in an agony of apprehension. "Canim, what is that?"

"The white man's tepee, in which he eats and sleeps."

She eyed it wistfully, grasping its virtues at a glance and thrilling again at the unaccountable sensations it aroused. "It must be very warm in time of frost," she said aloud, though she felt impelled to form strange sounds with her lips.

She longed to utter them, but did not, and the next instant Canim said, "It is called a *cabin.*"

Her heart gave a great leap — these were the sounds, the very sounds! She looked about her in sudden awe. How should she know that strange word before ever she heard it? What could be the matter? And then, with a shock, half of fear and half of delight, she realized that for the first time in her life there had been sanity and significance in the promptings of her dreams.

"*Cabin,*" she repeated to herself. "*Cabin.*" Then an incoherent flood of dream stuff welled up and up till her head was dizzy and her heart seemed bursting. Shadows, and looming bulks of things, and unintelligible associations fluttered and whirled about, and she strove vainly with her consciousness to grasp and hold them. For she felt that there, in that welter of memories, was the key of the mystery; could she but grasp and hold it, all would be clear and plain.

O Canim! O Pow-Wah-Kaan! O shades and shadows, what was that?

She turned to Canim, speechless and trembling; the dream stuff in mad, overwhelming riot. She was sick and fainting, and could only listen to the ravishing sounds which proceeded from the cabin in a wonderful rhythm.

"Hum, fiddle," Canim vouchsafed.

But she did not hear him, for in the ecstasy she was experiencing it seemed at last that all things were coming clear. Now! now! she thought. A sudden moisture swept into her eyes, and the tears trickled down her cheeks. The mystery was unlocking, but the faintness was overpowering her. If only she could hold herself long enough! If only — but the landscape bent and crumpled up, and the hills swayed back and forth across the sky, as she sprang to her feet and screamed, "*Daddy! Daddy!*" Then the sun reeled, and darkness smote her, and she pitched forward limp and headlong among the rocks.

Canim looked to see if her neck had been broken by the heavy pack, grunted his satisfaction, and threw water from the creek upon her. She came to slowly, with choking sobs, and sat up.

"It is not good, the hot sun on the head," he ventured.

And she answered, "No, it is not good, and the pack bore upon me hard."

"We shall camp early, so that you may sleep long and win strength," he said gently. "And if we go now we shall be the quicker to bed."

She said nothing, but tottered to her feet in obedience and stirred up the dogs. Taking the swing of his pace mechanically, she followed him past the cabin scarce daring to breathe. But no sounds issued forth, though the door was open and smoke curling upward from the sheet-iron stovepipe.

They came upon a man in the bend of the creek, white of skin and blue of eye, and for a moment Li Wan saw the other man in the snow. But she saw dimly, for she was weak and tired from what she had undergone. Still, she looked at him curiously, and stopped with Canim to watch him at his work. He was washing gravel in a large pan, with a circular, tilting movement; and as they looked, giving a deft flirt, he flashed up the yellow gold in a broad streak across the bottom of the pan.

"Very rich, this creek," Canim told her, as they went on. "Some time I will find such a creek, and then I shall be a big man."

Cabins and men grew more plentiful, till they came to where the main portion of the creek was spread out before them. It was the scene of a vast devastation. Everywhere the earth was torn and rent as though by a Titan's struggles. Where there were no up-thrown mounds of gravel, great holes and trenches yawned, and chasms where the thick rime of the earth had been peeled to bed-rock. There was no worn channel for the creek, and its waters, dammed up, diverted, flying through the air on giddy flumes, trickling into sinks and low places, and raised by huge water wheels, were used and used again a thousand times. The hills had been stripped of their trees, and their raw sides gored and perforated by great timber slides and prospect holes. And over all, like a monstrous race of ants, was flung an army of men, — mud-covered, dirty, disheveled men, who crawled in and out of the holes of their digging, crept like big bugs along the flumes, and toiled and sweated at the gravel heaps which they kept in constant unrest, — men, as far as the eye could see, even to the rims of the hilltops, digging, tearing, and scouring the face of nature.

Li Wan was appalled at the tremendous upheaval. "Truly, these men are mad," she said to Canim.

"Small wonder. The gold they dig after is a great thing," he replied. "The greatest thing in the world."

For hours they threaded the chaos of greed, Canim eagerly intent, Li Wan weak and listless. She knew she had been on the verge of disclosure, and she felt that she was still on the verge of disclosure; but the nervous strain she had undergone had tired her, and she passively waited for the thing, she knew not what, to happen. From every hand her senses snatched up and conveyed to her innumerable impressions, each of which became a dull excitation to her jaded imagination. Somewhere within her, responsive notes were answering to the things without; forgotten and undreamed-of correspondences were being renewed; and she was aware of it in an incurious way, and her soul was troubled, but she was not equal to the mental exaltation necessary to transmute and understand. So she plodded wearily on at the heels of her lord, content to wait for that which she knew, somewhere, somehow, must happen.

After undergoing the mad bondage of man, the creek finally returned to its ancient ways, all soiled and smirched from its toil, and coiled lazily among the broad flats and timbered spaces where the valley widened to the mouth. Here the "pay" ran out, and men were loath to loiter with the lure yet beyond. And here, as Li Wan paused to prod Olo with her staff, she heard the mellow silver of a woman's laughter.

Before a cabin sat a woman, fair of skin and rosy as a child, dimpling with glee at the words of another woman in the doorway. But the woman who sat shook about her great masses of dark wet hair which yielded up its dampness to the warm caresses of the sun.

For an instant Li Wan stood transfixed. Then she was aware of a blinding flash, and a snap, as though something gave way; and the woman before the cabin vanished, and the cabin, and the tall spruce timber, and the jagged sky line, and Li Wan saw another woman, in the shine of another sun, brushing great masses of black hair and singing as she brushed. And Li Wan heard the words of the song, and understood, and was a child again. She was smitten with a vision, wherein all the troublesome dreams merged and became one, and shapes and shadows took up their accustomed round, and all was clear and plain and real. Many pictures jostled past, strange scenes, and trees, and flowers, and people; and she saw them and knew them all.

"When you were a little bird, a little moose-bird," Canim said, his eyes upon her and burning into her.

"When I was a little moose-bird," she whispered, so faint and low he scarcely heard. And she knew she lied, as she bent her head to the strap and took the swing of the trail.

And such was the strangeness of it, the real now became unreal. The mile tramp and the pitching of camp by the edge of the stream seemed like a passage in a nightmare. She cooked the meat, fed the dogs, and unlashed the packs as in a dream, and it was not until Canim began to sketch his next wandering that she became herself again.

"The Klondike runs into the Yukon," he was saying; "a mighty river, mightier than the Mackenzie, of which you know. So we go, you and I, down to Fort o' Yukon. With dogs, in time of winter, it is twenty sleeps. Then we follow the Yukon away into the west — one hundred sleeps, two hundred, I have never heard. It is very far. And then we come to the sea. You know nothing of the sea, so let me tell you. As the lake is to the island, so the sea is to the land; all the rivers run to it, and it is without end. I have seen it at Hudson Bay; I have yet to see it in Alaska. And then we may take a great canoe upon the sea, you and I, Li Wan, or we may follow the land into the south many a hundred sleeps. And after that I do not know, save that I am Canim, The Canoe, wanderer and far-journeyer over the earth!"

She sat and listened, and fear ate into her heart as she pondered over this plunge into the illimitable wilderness. "It is a weary way," was all she said, head bowed on knee in resignation.

Then it was a splendid thought came to her, and at the wonder of it she was all a-glow. She went down to the stream and washed the dried clay from her face. When the ripples died away she stared long at her mirrored features; but sun and weather had done their work, and, with the roughness and bronze, her skin was not soft and dimpled as a child's. But the thought was still splendid and the glow unabated as she crept in beside her husband under the sleeping-robe.

She lay awake, staring up at the blue of the sky and waiting for Canim to sink into the first deep sleep. When this came about, she wormed slowly and carefully away, tucked the robe around him, and stood up. At her second step, Bash growled savagely. She whispered persuasively to him and glanced at the man. Canim was snoring profoundly. Then she turned, and with swift, noiseless feet sped up the back trail.

Mrs. Evelyn Van Wyck was just preparing for bed. Bored by the duties put upon her by society, her wealth, and widowed blessedness, she had journeyed into the Northland and gone to housekeeping in a cosy cabin on the edge of the diggings. Here, aided and abetted by her friend and companion, Myrtle Giddings, she played at living close to the soil, and cultivated the primitive with refined abandon.

She strove to get away from the generations of culture and parlor selection, and sought the earth-grip her ancestors had forfeited. Likewise she induced mental states which she fondly believed to approximate those of the stone folk, and just now, as she put up her hair for the pillow, she was indulging her fancy with a palæolithic wooing. The details consisted principally of cave dwellings and cracked marrowbones, intersprinkled with fierce carnivora, hairy mammoths, and combats with rude flaked knives of flint; but the sensations were delicious. And as Evelyn Van Wyck fled through the sombre forest aisles before the too arduous advances of her slant-browed, skin-clad wooer, the door of the cabin opened, without the courtesy of knock, and a skin-clad woman, savage and primitive, came in.

"Mercy!"

With a leap that would have done credit to a cave woman, Miss Giddings landed in safety behind the table. But Mrs. Van Wyck held her ground. She noted that the intruder was laboring under a strong excitement, and cast a swift glance backward to assure herself that the way was clear to the bunk, where the big Colt's revolver lay beneath a pillow.

"Greeting, O Woman of the Wondrous Hair," said Li Wan.

But she said it in her own tongue, — the tongue spoken in but a little corner of the earth, and the women did not understand.

"Shall I go for help?" Miss Giddings quavered.

"The poor creature is harmless, I think," Mrs. Van Wyck replied. "And just look at her skin clothes, ragged and trail-worn, and all that. They are certainly unique. I shall buy them for my collection. Get my sack, Myrtle, please, and set up the scales."

Li Wan followed the shaping of the lips, but the words were unintelligible, and then, for the first time, she realized, in a moment of suspense and indecision, that there was no medium of communication between them.

And at the passion of her dumbness she cried out, with arms stretched wide apart, "O Woman, thou art sister of mine!"

The tears coursed down her cheeks as she yearned toward them, and the break in her voice carried the sorrow she could not utter. But Miss Giddings was trembling, and even Mrs. Van Wyck was disturbed.

"I would live as you live. Thy ways are my ways, and our ways be one. My husband is Canim, The Canoe, and he is big and strange, and I am afraid. His trail is all the world, and never ends, and I am weary. My mother was like you, and her hair was as thine, and her eyes. And life was soft to me, then, and the sun warm."

She knelt humbly, and bent her head at Mrs. Van Wyck's feet. But Mrs. Van Wyck drew away, frightened at her vehemence.

Li Wan stood up, panting for speech. Her dumb lips could not articulate her overmastering consciousness of kind.

"Trade? You trade?" Mrs. Van Wyck questioned, slipping, after the manner of the superior peoples, into pigeon tongue.

She touched Li Wan's ragged skins to indicate her choice, and poured several hundreds of gold into the blower. She stirred the dust about and trickled its yellow lustre temptingly through her fingers. But Li Wan saw only the fingers, milk-white and shapely, tapering daintily to the rosy, jewel-like nails; and she placed her own hand alongside, all work-worn and calloused, and wept.

Mrs. Van Wyck misunderstood. "Gold," she encouraged. "Good gold! You trade? You changee for changee?" And she laid her hand again on Li Wan's skin garments.

"How much? You sell? How much?" she persisted, running her hand against the way of the hair so that she might make sure of the sinew-thread seam.

But Li Wan was deaf as well, and the woman's speech was without significance. Dismay at her failure sat upon her. How could she identify herself with these women? For she knew they were of the one breed, blood-sisters among men and the women of men. Her eyes roved wildly about the interior, taking in the soft draperies hanging around, the feminine garments, the oval mirror, and the dainty toilet accessories beneath. And the things haunted her, for she had seen like things before; and as she looked at them her lips involuntarily formed sounds which her throat trembled to utter. Then a thought flashed upon her, and she steadied herself. She must be calm. She must control herself. There must be no misunderstanding this time, or else, — and she shook with a storm of suppressed tears and steadied herself again.

She put her hand on the table. "*Table,*" she clearly and distinctly enunciated. "*Table,*" she repeated.

She looked at Mrs. Van Wyck, who nodded approbation. Li Wan exulted, but brought her will to bear and held herself steady. "*Stove,*" she went on. "*Stove.*"

Then at every nod of Mrs. Van Wyck, Li Wan's excitement mounted. Now stumbling and halting, and again in feverish haste, as the recrudescence of forgotten words was fast or slow, she moved about the cabin, naming article after article. And when she paused, finally, it was in triumph, with body erect and head thrown back, expectant, waiting.

"C-a-t," Mrs. Van Wyck laughingly spelled out in kindergarten fashion. "I — see — the — cat — catch — the — rat."

Li Wan nodded her head seriously. They were beginning to understand at last, these women. The blood flushed darkly under her bronze at the thought, and she smiled and nodded her head still more vigorously.

Mrs. Van Wyck turned to her companion. "Received a smattering of mission education somewhere, I fancy, and has come to show it off."

"Of course," Miss Giddings tittered. "Little fool! We shall lose our sleep with her vanity."

"All the same I want that jacket. If it *is* old, the workmanship is good, — a most excellent specimen." She returned to her visitor. "Changee for changee? You! — changee for changee? How much? Eh? How much, you?"

"Perhaps she'd prefer a dress or something," Miss Giddings suggested.

Mrs. Van Wyck went up to Li Wan and made signs that she would exchange her wrapper for the jacket. And to further the transaction, she took Li Wan's hand and placed it amid the lace and ribbons of the flowing bosom, and rubbed the fingers back and forth that she might feel the texture. But the jeweled butterfly which loosely held the fold in place was insecurely fastened, and the front of the gown fell aside, exposing a firm white breast which had never known the lip-clasp of a child.

Mrs. Van Wyck coolly repaired the mischief; but Li Wan uttered a loud cry, and ripped and tore at her skin-shirt till her own breast showed firm and white as Evelyn Van Wyck's. Murmuring inarticulately and making swift signs, she strove to establish the kinship.

"A half-breed," Mrs. Van Wyck commented. "I thought so from her hair."

Miss Giddings made a fastidious gesture. "Proud of her father's white skin. It's beastly. Do give her something, Evelyn, and make her go."

But the other woman sighed. "Poor creature, I wish I could do something for her."

There was a crunching on the gravel without. Then the cabin door swung wide and Canim stalked in. Miss Giddings saw a vision of sudden death and screamed, but Mrs. Van Wyck faced him composedly.

"What do you want?" she demanded.

"How do," Canim answered suavely and directly, pointing at the same time to Li Wan. "Um my wife."

He reached out to her, but she waved him back.

"Speak, Canim! Tell them I am" —

"Daughter of Pow-Wah-Kaan? Nay, of what is it to them that they should care? Better should I tell them thou art an ill wife, given to creeping from thy husband's bed when sleep is heavy in his eyes."

Again he reached out for her, but she fled away from him to Mrs. Van Wyck, at whose feet she made frenzied appeal, and whose knees she tried to clasp. But the lady stepped back, giving permission with her eyes to Canim. He gripped Li Wan under the shoulders and raised her. She fought with him, in a madness of despair, till his chest was heaving with the exertion and they had reeled about over half the room.

"Let me go, Canim!" she sobbed.

But he twisted her wrist till she ceased to struggle. "The memories of the little moose-bird are over-strong and make trouble," he began.

But she interrupted. "I know! I know! I see the man in the snow, and, as never before, I see him crawl on hand and knee. And I, who am a little child, am carried on his back. And this is before Pow-Wah-Kaan and the time I came to live in a little corner of the earth."

"You know," he answered, forcing her toward the door; "but you will go with me down the Yukon and forget."

"Never shall I forget! So long as my skin is white shall I remember!"

She clutched frantically at the door-post and looked a last appeal to Mrs. Evelyn Van Wyck.

"Then will I teach thee to forget, I, Canim, The Canoe!"

As he spoke, he pulled her fingers clear and passed out with her upon the trail.

1903
LAWN TENNIS
by Arthur Stanwood Pier

THAT tennis is entitled to the place of supremacy among games seems to me no unreasonable claim. First of all and most important: when you are playing tennis, whether in singles or doubles, it is always you and your opponent. You are not looking on, except for the briefest moment; you are not getting any more rest than you wish, you are more often not having as much as you would like.

From the first stroke of the game to the last you are in constant yet always changing opposition to another player. Even in doubles on the strokes that are your partner's you are not a mere spectator; you are running backward, forward, keeping pace with him, seeking the position in which the next ball may be most advantageously received. Your decision must be instant; in the fraction of a second you determine whether you shall drive the ball or toss it into the air, place it on the left or on the right, rush to the net or run back; you must have an instinctive knowledge of what your opponent expects you to do and then, if possible, do something else. Once you have succeeded in outwitting him, the triumph is all yours; you divide the honors with no one. Tennis more than any other game has the qualities that gave the duel its fascination; it is all eager and alive, two men at close quarters, feinting, parrying, thrusting, both alert for an opening to give the final *coup de grace*.

Call to mind some long rally that you have had; remember how on one occasion when your opponent was playing deep in the court you drew him to the net by a ball chopped skillfully just over it; how he returned the stroke, and how you next shot the ball down the side line, thinking to pass him. But he had anticipated the attempt and volleyed cleverly; then, instead of trying the cross court shot that he was waiting for, you tossed the ball high over his head, and while he spun round and raced for it you trotted to the net, prepared to "kill" the lob that he should send in return. And, just as you had hoped, it was a short lob; but instead of killing it, you decided it would be more fun to keep him running, and you turned the ball over into the far-ther corner of his court. He went after it at full speed and lobbed again — it was all he could do, poor fellow — and again the ball fell short, again you had him at your mercy. Nor did you smash the ball this time; instead, you turned it off slowly into the other corner. He sprinted hard and reached it, only to pop it up easily once more. And now you gathered yourself; you saw out of the tail of your eye that he had turned and had already started back desperately toward the far-ther corner; and you landed on that ball with all your might, beat it to the earth, and sent it bounding straight at the place he was leaving. He made a miserable, futile effort to right himself and shift his racket; then you saw him walk slowly after the ball, with his head drooping and his shoulders heaving up about his ears, and you chuckled to yourself with huge approval of your own astute play — "That got his wind, I guess."

There is a human amusement in making your antagonist run back and forth thus earnestly and desperately; but one has a more exalted satisfaction in placing a shot so sudden, swift, and accurate that the opposing player has not time to move. Teasing your man, you feel your power over a particular individual; paralyzing him by a stroke, you experience a moment of omnipotence. "There," you say, "there I sent a ball that nobody could touch." In your sublimity you may even spare a moment's compassion for the poor wretch who stands rooted in astonishment, dazed by the bolt before which champions had been powerless. You say to him condescendingly, "I caught that just right;" you may even intimate, if you are magnanimous, that you do not expect to do the thing every time. But in your heart you are boastfully hopeful, you feel that at last you have found your game, and you believe that you have the man cowed.

And how is it when instead of driving your opponent before you and exhibiting a cleverness that seems really outside yourself, a supernatural precision of eye and arm, you are going down to defeat? Is there any delight in that?

From a wide range of personal experience I would modestly assert that there is. Although you realize that the doom is drawing nearer, although to avert it you put forth your mightiest efforts and only lose in strength and breath while your adversary seems to be renewing his inhuman power, you fight on, hoping even to the last that you may turn the tide and pull out a glorious victory. You make a stroke that spurs you on, you follow it with three that provoke your bitterest self-contempt, and you plant yourself with melodramatic determination in your soul and, doubtless, upon your face. "The Old Guard dies, but never surrenders;" was there no joy for them in their supreme, superb annihilation? It makes after all little difference to you emotionally whether your fight against odds is a winning or a losing one, so long as it is the best fight that you can put forward. To be in the thick of it, battering away undaunted, is the fun. Even if your opponent so far overmatches you that the outcome is hardly in question, you may have as good a time as if you stood to win; for you go in resolved to break down his cool assurance, to make him show his best efforts, to unmask and damage his strategy and gain his respect; and while you are striving with all your pigmy fury to achieve this, you now and then must pause to admire the overwhelming strokes of his resourceful master hand.

It seems fitting here to consider the theory, often advanced and seldom disputed, that a sport is the better for an element of danger. If this is true, the advocates of tennis must be dumb. Nothing worse than a sprained ankle or a wrenched knee can befall a man on a tennis court; and these, however painful, are not heroic injuries. I once heard an eloquent and distinguished man in the course of a brilliant address declare that the occasional deaths occurring in polo, in football, on the hunting field, are the price the Anglo-Saxon race pays for its position of headship and command. It was an impressive and inspiring oration; and this sentiment was echoed with a great outburst of applause. Yet it does not bear cool scrutiny. The football player will tell you that, once in the game, the possibility of injury does not occur to him; the polo player will say the same; after you have taken the first jump, danger in the hunting field does not beset you. Where there is no consciousness of danger, there is no bravery. In the heat of battle no man is a poltroon. Yes, but to take the first jump, to go into the game, it is urged; does not that compel and develop a man's courage? Only if he is physically unfit or dangerously ignorant; under other circumstances to enter a sport in which there is an element of peril is as natural as to go to bed when one is sleepy or to eat when one is hungry.

It is not the element of danger in a game which trains one to fortitude and courage; it is the element of opposition, purely. The injuries and deaths that sometimes take place in our rougher sports should not be viewed as glorifying; they are deplorable calamities, with no mitigation. It seems to me beyond debate that the game which is entirely harmless in its play, which does not imperil, is the best of all games.

Certainly of them all tennis is the most universal; small boys, girls, women, men of three generations play it, and the crack has not very much more enjoyment out of it than the duffer. So long as a player feels within him possibilities of growth he enjoys the game; and even when these fail, even when he realizes that he is slipping backward, he clings on, light-heartedly contesting every inch of the decline with some one of his contemporaries. "If I cannot keep pace with the advancing battalion, I shall not head those who are in retreat," cries your optimist; and so — because tennis players are generally optimists — you will see on any warm summer day veterans urging their old limbs upon the grassy courts, crouching in their play with racket held stiffly, trotting with little, timorous steps, poking at the ball with the gesture of uncertain vision; and you watch them awhile and think perhaps in the pride of your youth, "There can't be much fun in that." And then, while you are looking on, they begin to wrangle about some point; they are suspicious as to whether or not that ball actually did strike the line; and such verbal vitality as those four old men will then display, congregating at the net, wagging their heads, and finally examining the ball itself for traces of whitewash! You do not doubt any longer that their tennis is something of extreme moment to them; and you wonder if with your own occasional slipshod indifference to your rights on doubtful points you do not show an unworthy slight regard for a noble game.

In fact, I think that a match between old men deeply in earnest is a spectacle more inspiring to one's humanity than a tournament of champions. I do not mean that I would rather watch it; I do not deny that for a spectator in ordinary mood it is a slumberous proceeding. Yet if one is in an idle, reflective, kindly frame of mind, there is nothing so cheering to one's faith, so soothing to one's soul, so hopeful and sane and healthy as the sight of these graybeards, — venerable enough when you meet them on the street, and now scampering after a ball with the single-minded passion of a dog or a child. Their squabbles and their laughter are alike pleasant to the ear; and when they stop between sets to rest and draw their asthmatic breath, you look at them admiringly and hope that when you grow old you too may be this kind of fine old boy.

REMARKS AT THE PEACE BANQUET[1]
by William James

I AM only a philosopher, and there is only one thing that a philosopher can be relied on to do. You know that the function of statistics has been ingeniously described as being the refutation of other statistics. Well, a philosopher can always contradict other philosophers. In ancient times philosophers defined man as the rational animal; and philosophers since then have always found much more to say about the rational than about the animal part of the definition. But looked at candidly, reason bears about the same proportion to the rest of human nature that we in this hall bear to the rest of America, Europe, Asia, Africa, and Polynesia. Reason is one of the very feeblest of Nature's forces, if you take it at any one spot and moment. It is only in the very long run that its effects become perceptible. Reason assumes to settle things by weighing them against one another without prejudice, partiality, or excitement; but what affairs in the concrete are settled by is and always will be just prejudices, partialities, cupidities, and excitements. Appealing to reason as we do, we are in a sort of a forlorn hope situation, like a small sand-bank in the midst of a hungry sea ready to wash it out of existence. But sand-banks grow when the conditions favor; and weak as reason is, it has the unique advantage over its antagonists that its activity never lets up and that it presses always in one direction, while men's prejudices vary, their passions ebb and flow, and their excitements are intermittent. Our sand-bank, I absolutely believe, is bound to grow, — bit by bit it will get dyked and break-watered. But sitting as we do in this warm room, with music and lights and the flowing bowl and smiling faces, it is easy to get too sanguine about our task, and since I am called to speak, I feel as if it might not be out of place to say a word about the strength of our enemy.

Our permanent enemy is the noted bellicosity of human nature. Man, biologically considered, and whatever else he may be in the bargain, is simply the most formidable of all beasts of prey, and, indeed, the only one that preys systematically on its own species. We are once for all adapted to the military *status*. A millennium of peace would not breed the fighting disposition out of our bone and marrow, and a function so ingrained and vital will never consent to die without resistance, and will always find impassioned apologists and idealizers.

Not only men born to be soldiers, but non-combatants by trade and nature, historians in their studies, and clergymen in their pulpits, have

---

[1] This banquet was given in Boston on the closing day of the World's Peace Congress, October 7, 1904.

been war's idealizers. They have talked of war as of God's court of justice. And, indeed, if we think how many things beside the frontiers of states the wars of history have decided, we must feel some respectful awe, in spite of all the horrors. Our actual civilization, good and bad alike, has had past wars for its determining condition. Greatmindedness among the tribes of men has always meant the will to prevail, and all the more so if prevailing included slaughtering and being slaughtered. Rome, Paris, England, Brandenburg, Piedmont, — soon, let us hope, Japan, — along with their arms have made their traits of character and habits of thought prevail among their conquered neighbors. The blessings we actually enjoy, such as they are, have grown up in the shadow of the wars of antiquity. The various ideals were backed by fighting wills, and where neither would give way, the God of battles had to be the arbiter. A shallow view, this, truly; for who can say what might have prevailed if man had ever been a reasoning and not a fighting animal? Like dead men, dead causes tell no tales, and the ideals that went under in the past, along with all the tribes that represented them, find to-day no recorder, no explainer, no defender.

But apart from theoretic defenders, and apart from every soldierly individual straining at the leash, and clamoring for opportunity, war has an omnipotent support in the form of our imagination. Man lives *by* habits, indeed, but what he lives *for* is thrills and excitements. The only relief from Habit's tediousness is periodical excitement. From time immemorial wars have been, especially for non-combatants, the supremely thrilling excitement. Heavy and dragging at its end, at its outset every war means an explosion of imaginative energy. The dams of routine burst, and boundless prospects open. The remotest spectators share the fascination. With that awful struggle now in progress on the confines of the world, there is not a man in this room, I suppose, who doesn't buy both an evening and a morning paper, and first of all pounce on the war column.

A deadly listlessness would come over most men's imagination of the future if they could seriously be brought to believe that never again *in saecula saeculorum* would a war trouble human history. In such a stagnant summer afternoon of a world, where would be the zest or interest?

This is the constitution of human nature which we have to work against. The plain truth is that people *want* war. They want it anyhow; for itself; and apart from each and every possible consequence. It is the final bouquet of life's fireworks. The born soldiers want it hot and actual. The non-combatants want it in the background, and always as an open possibility, to feed imagination on and keep excitement going. Its clerical and historical defenders fool themselves when they talk as they do about it. What moves them is not the blessings it has won for us, but a vague religious exaltation. War, they feel, is human nature at its uttermost. We are here to do our uttermost. It is a sacrament. Society would rot, they think, without the mystical blood-payment.

We do ill, I fancy, to talk much of universal peace or of a general disarmament. We must go in for preventive medicine, not for radical cure. We must cheat our foe, politically circumvent his action, not try to change his nature. In one respect war is like love, though in no other. Both leave us intervals of rest; and in the intervals life goes on perfectly well without them, though the imagination still dallies with their possibility. Equally insane when once aroused and under head-way, whether they shall be aroused or not depends on accidental circumstances. How are old maids and old bachelors made? Not by deliberate vows of celibacy, but by sliding on from year to year with no sufficient matrimonial provocation. So of the nations with their wars. Let the general possibility of war be left open, in Heaven's name, for the imagination to dally with. Let the soldiers dream of killing, as the old maids dream of marrying. But organize in every conceivable way the practical machinery for making each successive chance of war abortive. Put peace-men in power; educate the editors and statesmen to responsibility; — how beautifully did their trained responsibility in England make the Venezuela incident abortive! Seize every pretext, however small, for arbitration methods, and multiply the precedents; foster rival excitements and invent new outlets for heroic energy; and from one generation to another, the chances are that irritations will grow less acute and states of strain less dangerous among the nations. Armies and navies will continue, of course, and will fire the minds of populations with their potentialities of greatness. But their officers will find that somehow or other, with no deliberate intention on any one's part, each successive "incident" has managed to evaporate and to lead nowhere, and that the thought of what might have been remains their only consolation.

The last weak runnings of the war spirit will be "punitive expeditions." A country that turns its arms only against uncivilized foes is, I think, wrongly taunted as degenerate. Of course it has ceased to be heroic in the old grand style. But I verily believe that this is because it now sees something better. It has a conscience. It knows that between civilized countries a war is a crime against civilization. It will still perpetrate peccadillos, to be sure. But it is afraid, afraid in the good sense of the word, to engage in absolute crimes against civilization.

SHALL THE UNIVERSITY BECOME A BUSINESS CORPORATION?

by Henry S. Pritchett

TO-DAY, in the United States, two radically different plans for the support and conduct of higher institutions of learning are in process of development: the one that of the private university, the other of the university supported and controlled by the state. The first finds its notable examples mainly amongst the older universities of the East, the second in the universities of the Central and Western states. While these last are younger, their growth has been rapid, not only in the number of instructors and students, but in facilities and income.

In the Eastern States, where the older universities have for a century and more supplied the demands of higher education, no great state institutions have grown up. In the central West, on the other hand, where the state universities were founded just as the railroads were built, to supply not a present but a future want, there are few strong and growing private universities. In fact, there are in almost every Western state private colleges and universities whose development has been practically stopped, and which must in the end become feeders to the great state universities.

There are a few notable exceptions to this rule: the University of Chicago, Northwestern University, and Leland Stanford University. The first two are in the suburbs of Chicago. The reason that they have flourished is not far to seek. They are situated at the seat of the greatest social and industrial centre in America. They occupy an exceptional strategic situation for a great university or for a great school.

As one looks back at the rise of the great Western universities and realizes the wisdom and the far-sightedness displayed by their founders, one is surprised that they should have estimated at such low value the matter of strategic position. In nearly all cases these institutions have been placed in small and isolated villages; rarely have they been founded in connection with the centres of the social, commercial, and industrial life of the various states. The reasoning appears to have been the same as that which governed the location of the state capitals, which were put at the most inconvenient possible points, usually near the geographic centre of the state, without regard to the commercial centre toward which all lines of transportation lead. This was done upon the theory that the innocent lawmakers must be defended from contact with the wicked people of the cities. In the same way it was believed that the student must be protected from the temptations and the distractions which the nearness of a great city might give. Both these assumptions are fallacious, and the history of the past forty years has proved their unwisdom.

The great state universities of the middle West have succeeded, not because of their isolation, but in spite of it, and no one can say how different might have been their history or how much more powerful might be their position in the future had the larger policy been adopted. The only possible chance for success for a new university in an isolated point lies in the possession of an enormous foundation, such as that which was given by Leland Stanford, by which an institution was founded out-of-hand and with free tuition. But even here the limitations of environment will place a practical limit to what endowment may effect.

These two systems of universities rest upon fundamentally different views as to the support of higher education. The one assumes that this support will come by the free gift of citizens of the commonwealth, the other assumes that the support of higher education no less than that of elementary education is the duty of the state. The one system appeals to the generosity of the individual citizen, the other appeals to the sense of responsibility and the patriotism of the whole mass of citizens. The one establishes a set of higher institutions which may or may not be in harmony with the elementary schools of the municipality or of the state; the other establishes a set of institutions which are an integral part of that system, and its crown. The one furnishes a system of instruction in which tuition fees are high and tending constantly to grow higher, the other furnishes a system of instruction practically free. The one had its origin in essentially aristocratic distinctions, whatever may be its present form of development, the other is essentially democratic in both its inception and its development.

Will these two systems — different in ideal, different in inception, different in development, not necessarily antagonistic but contrasted — continue to flourish, if not side by side, at least in contiguous sections of the country?

As far as one can see into the future, both of these systems will continue to live and to flourish, but with few exceptions they will flourish in different sections, not side by side. No one can doubt today that the state university is gaining as a centre of influence in intellectual and national life. There can be no question that it is to be the seat of university education for the greater part of the whole country, including the Central, Western, and Southern states. The private university which seeks to gain power and influence in this region should set itself seriously to the problem of supplementing, not paralleling, the work of the state university. It should ask itself earnestly the question, What is the logical function of the privately endowed university in a commonwealth where higher education is supplied by the state? So far as I have been able to see, little attention has been paid to this question, which nevertheless deserves serious and careful consideration.

No one interested in education can repress a thrill of exultation as he looks forward to the future of the great state universities. They were started at a fortunate intellectual epoch. Their foundation stones were laid when the battle for scientific freedom and scientific teaching had just been won. They were dedicated by the pioneers who founded them in a spirit of intellectual and spiritual freedom. They are essentially and in the broadest and simplest way democratic, and the logical outgrowth of a democratic system of public schools. It is to this real democracy, to the fact that they were founded, not by a few men or by a single man, but by the whole people of the state, that they owe their greatest fortune, and no one looking into the future can doubt that they are to be amongst the most influential, the richest, and most democratic universities of our land, vying with the oldest and most famous institutions of our Eastern States in a rivalry which we may well hope to see the noble rivalry of the scholar rather than a rivalry of riches, of buildings, and of numbers.

The American university, whether supported by private gift or by the state, is conducted under an administrative system which approximates closer and closer as time goes on that of a business corporation. The administrative power is lodged in a small body of trustees or regents, who are not members of the university community. The board of trustees, with the president as its chief executive officer, passes upon the entire policy and administration of the institution. It appoints professors, promotes them, or dismisses them, it engages them to carry out specific pieces of work at specified times, as a business corporation employs its officials; the tenure of office of the professor is at the will of the corporation, as in the tenure of office of a business employee.

Under this arrangement the powers of the president are enormously increased, and the action of the corporation is in nearly all cases his action. He possesses an autocratic power which would not for a moment be tolerated in a European institution. From him the same administrative system reaches down through the institution. Professors employ their assistants for specific duties at specified times; students are required to undertake specific work in a prescribed way and at a fixed time.

It is worth while to note some of the consequences of this administrative attitude upon the life and upon the work of those who make up the university. One of the most direct consequences is that the professor in the American university is charged not only with the work of a scholar, but with a large amount of routine administrative work as well.

Would the American university — whether a private or a state institution — be bettered if its administration were turned over to the faculty instead of being vested, as now, in a board of trustees who do not pretend to be experts in educational methods? Would it be a step forward, for example, to intrust to the faculty the election of the president and of the professors, and to put into their hands the settlement of the larger questions of policy and of expenditure? Ought the university freedom to be extended through the faculty to the student body so as to diminish the pressure of the organization and to enlarge the sphere of freedom both for professor and student? Can scholarship of a high order be developed under pressure? Are we educating our youth away from democratic ideals, not toward them, by the form and tendency of our university administration?

These are fundamental questions which affect our national life and, most directly, our youth.

1906
MAN AND THE ACTOR
by Richard Mansfield

THE more you study mankind, the more you discover that every man is playing a part.

Take, for instance, two men at a club. The one has the reputation of being a good fellow, the other of being a Misanthrope. Both are playing parts for which they pay a price. The jolly good fellow must keep up his jollity at any cost. He shakes hands with every one; he drinks with every one; he slaps people on the back; he has a large fund of anecdotes; he flatters men; he knows when to be silent and when to talk; he never lends money for fear of losing a friend. Otherwise is it with the Misanthrope, — the sour-faced man who sits by himself in a corner of the club reading his magazine. Nobody slaps him on the back, and he slaps nobody. He is short of speech, abrupt in manners; experience has taught him to be suspicious, and he does not thaw readily; but, strange to say, the grip of his hand, once given, is strong; and a tear sparkles in his eye and rolls unseen upon the page of the magazine at the recital of some sorrow. And so the jolly man about town is really the Misanthrope, who acts the good fellow because he knows his world, and the Misanthrope is the child who has been forbidden to show his heart.

If you act well, you will live well. Study your part, and know how to play it. The man who does not study the art of *acting* is at a disadvantage, and thus the greatest philosophers and statesmen have devoted themselves to an art concerning which an eminent writer in New York has inquired whether it was worth while. So universal is the habit of acting that when a man ceases to act we cease to believe in him, and the only creature who can be said to be absolutely natural is a maniac.

But it is surprising to discover how very differently people who have played parts all their lives deport themselves before the footlights. I was acquainted with a lady in London who had been the wife of a peer of the realm, ambassadress at foreign courts, and at one time a reigning beauty. She came to me, longing for a new experience, and implored me to give her an opportunity to appear upon the stage. In a weak moment I consented, and, as I was producing a play, I cast her for a part which I thought she would admirably suit, — that of a society woman. What that woman did and did not do on the stage passes all belief. She became entangled in her train, she could neither sit down nor stand up, she shouted, she could not be persuaded to remain at a respectful distance, but insisted upon shrieking into the actor's ears, and she committed all the gaucheries you would expect from an untrained country wench. But because everybody is acting in private life, every one thinks he can act upon the stage, and there is no profession that has so many critics. Every individual in the audience is a critic, and knows all about the art of acting. But acting is a gift. It is as much an inspiration as the making of great poetry and great pictures. And inspiration only comes to those who permit themselves to be inspired.

Allow yourself to be convinced by the character you are portraying that you *are* the character. If you are to play Napoleon, and you are sincere and determined to be Napoleon, Napoleon will not permit you to be any one but Napoleon, or Richard III Richard III, or Nero Nero, and so on. He would be a poor, miserable pretense of an actor who in the representation of any historical personage were otherwise than firmly convinced, after getting into the man's skin (which means the exhaustive study of all that was ever known about him), that he is living that very man for a few brief hours. And so it is, in another form, with the creation or realization of the author's, the poet's, fancy. In this latter case the actor, the poet actor, sees and creates in the air before him the being he delineates; he makes him, he builds him during the day, in the long hours of the night; the character gradually takes being; he is the actor's genius; the slave of the ring, who comes when he calls him, stands beside him, and envelops him in his ghostly arms; the actor's personality disappears; he is the character. All of you have the right to object to the actor's creation; you may say this is not your conception of Hamlet or Macbeth or Iago or Richard or Nero or Shylock, — but respect his. And who can tell whether he is right or you are right? He has created them with much loving care; therefore don't sneer at them, — don't jeer at them, — it hurts!

The most severe critic can never tell me more, or scold me more than I scold myself. I have never left the stage satisfied with myself. And I am convinced that every artist feels as I do about his work. It is the undoubted duty of the critic to criticise, and that means to blame as well as to praise; and it must be confessed that, taking all things into consideration, the critics of this country are actuated by honesty of purpose and kindliness of spirit, and very often their work is, in addition, of marked literary value. Occasionally we will still meet the man who is anxious to impress his fellow citizens with the fact that he has been abroad, and tinctures all his views of plays and actors with references to Herr Dinkelspiegel or Frau Mitterwoorzer; or who, having spent a few hours in Paris, is forced to drag in by the hair Monsieur Popin or Mademoiselle Fifine. But as a matter of fact, is not the interpretation of tragedy and comedy by the American stage superior to the German and French? — for the whole endeavor in this country has been toward a closer adherence to nature. In France and in Germany the ancient method of declamation still prevails, and the great speeches of Goethe and Schiller and Racine and Corneille are to all intents and purposes intoned. No doubt this sounds very fine in German and French, but how would you like it now in English?

The old-time actor had peculiar and primitive views as to elocution and its uses. I remember a certain old friend of mine, who, when he recited the opening speech in *Richard III*, and arrived at the line "In the deep bosom of the ocean buried," suggested the deep bosom of the ocean by sending his voice down into his boots. Yet these were fine actors, to whom certain young gentlemen, who never saw them, constantly refer. The methods of the stage have completely changed, and with them the tastes of the people. The probability is that some of the old actors of only a few years ago would excite much merriment in their delineation of tragedy. A very great tragedian of a past generation was wont, in the tent scene in *Richard III*, to hold a piece of soap in his mouth, so that, after the appearance of the ghosts, the lather and froth might dribble down his chin! and he employed, moreover, a trick sword, which rattled hideously; and, what with his foam-flecked face, his rolling eyes, his inarticulate groans, and his rattling blade, the small boy in the gallery was scared into a frenzy of vociferous delight!

Yet, whilst we have discarded these somewhat crude methods, we have perhaps allowed ourselves to wander too far in the other direction, and the critics are quite justified in demanding in many cases greater virility and force. The simulation of suppressed power is very useful and very advisable, but *when the firebell rings* the horses have got to come out, and rattle and race down the street, and rouse the town!

The stage is not likely to die of neglect anywhere. But at this moment it cannot be denied that the ship of the stage is drifting somewhat hither and thither. We need a recognized stage and a recognized school. America has become too great, and its influence abroad too large, for us not to have a great and recognized theatre. Consider our speech, and our manner of speech! Consider our voices, and the production of our voices! Consider the pronunciation of words, and the curious use of vowels! Let us say we have an established theatre, to which you come not only for your pleasure, but for your education. Of what immense advantage this would be if behind its presiding officer there stood a board of literary directors, composed of such men as William Winter, Howells, Edward Everett Hale, and Aldrich, and others equally fine, and the presidents of the great universities.

These men might well decide how the American language should be spoken in the great American theatre, and we should then have an authority in this country at last for the pronunciation of certain words. It would finally be decided whether to say fancy or fahncy — dance or dahnce — advertisement or advertysement, and so with many other words; whether to call the object of our admiration "real elegant" — whether we should say "I admire" to do this or that, and whether we should say "I guess" instead of "I think." And the voice! The education of the American speaking voice is, I am sure all will agree, of immense importance. It is difficult to love, or to continue to endure, a woman who shrieks at you; a high-pitched, nasal, stringy voice is not calculated to charm. This established theatre of which we dream should teach men and women how to talk; and how splendid it would be for future generations if it should become characteristic of American men and women to speak in soft and beautifully modulated tones!

As for the practical side of an established theatre, I am absolutely convinced that the national theatre could be established in this country on a practical and paying basis; and not only on a paying basis, but upon a profitable basis. It would, however, necessitate the investment of a large amount of capital. In short, the prime cost would be large, but if the public generally is interested, there is no reason why an able financier could not float a company for this purpose. But under no circumstances must or can a national theatre be made an object of personal or commercial profit. Nor can it be a scheme devised by a few individuals for the exploitation of a social or literary fad. The national theatre must be given by the people to the people, and be governed by the people. Every inducement should be offered to secure the services of the best actors; by actors, I mean actors of both sexes; and those who have served for a certain number of years should be entitled to a pension upon retirement.

The national theatre is a practical possibility. From my personal experience I am convinced that serious effort upon the American stage meets with a hearty endorsement.

1907

THE IMMIGRANT WOMAN
by Frances A. Kellor

WHAT becomes of the ever-increasing number of immigrant women who come to this country? Do they enter the ranks of laborers or of drifters? Do they rise in the scale of human life and friendship, or deteriorate? The labor and vote of immigrant men are so valuable to the business interests of this country, that there is much available information as to what becomes of them, but no corresponding data for immigrant women. The Inter-Municipal Research Committee, in cooperation with others, has set out to gather this information, particularly for the young and unmarried women during their first three years of residence.

Immigrant women, quite as much as immigrant men, belong to the exploited and disinherited group, and though we flatter ourselves that women are better protected than men, immigrant women upon their arrival have no advantage in laws or trade over men, and are at a disadvantage politically. The problem of immigrant women is not entirely that of immigrant men, for two main reasons. First, the labor, housing, and wages of women are more complicated by questions of sex and morality; and second, the field of domestic service, which takes great numbers of them, has an influence unlike that of any other occupation. It is a mistake to attempt to understand or solve the social, industrial, and moral questions arising from immigration without considering the women.

For the year ending June 30, 1905, 301,585 women, nearly one-half of the number of men, came to this country. The great majority of these came here for work. 19 out of every 100 native American women are engaged in gainful occupations; but 32 out of every 100 foreign-born women are so engaged, and the percentage is increasing. By far the greatest number are found in domestic service. The household industry is literally dependent upon the immigrant, and a famine of labor would result should this supply be cut off. This is in a scarcely less degree true of the factories.

For the year ending June 30, 1905, 84 per cent of all women entering the port of New York gave domestic service as their occupation; of Philadelphia, 65 per cent; and of Boston, 82 per cent. The last available statistics for Massachusetts show that 16,694 women were engaged in domestic service in Boston, and of this number 80 per cent were foreign-born. In Chicago there are many agencies entirely for foreign women. In New York city there are 169 agencies run for the purpose of distributing immigrant houseworkers, chiefly women.

Notwithstanding the constant increase in immigration, under the present conditions of prosperity, the demand far exceeds the supply. The first problem which faces the immigrant is the need of work which she can do. The American housewife is depending upon the immigrant to solve her domestic problem, while the great number of immigrants come to America to be free, and especially from all badges of servitude. To them America is something beautiful, and represents a great opportunity. Ordinarily they are unskilled and may be willing to be household workers while learning English and American ways and acquiring training; but housewives who are looking to the immigrant as a means of establishing a trained servant class in this country, will be disappointed, for opportunities are open to them to enter any trade, profession, or home for which they fit themselves.

The immigrant then is a transient, not a permanent, domestic worker. The privilege of the American housewife is to train the green immigrant, not for her permanent or even long service, but to give her knowledge, efficiency, culture, and a democratic spirit. When she has acquired these, the power of choice becomes hers, and she leaves for a trade or public house where the conditions are better, hours regular, duties definite, and social isolation and discrimination not so pronounced.

While the number of all nationalities is increasing, there were in 1905, 78,136 women immigrants from Austria-Hungary, — three times as many as came from Ireland, Germany, or England, and nearly seven times as many as from Sweden or Norway. From Russia there were 51,883 women, or more than from Sweden, Germany, and England put together. From Italy 38,761 women, or more than from Germany and Sweden.

The bulk of immigrant women represent races having wide language variations, and not only a different standard of living, but variations from the American social standard — all serious matters where a worker becomes a part of the home. Two civilizations meet in intimate daily contact under one roof. The one often represents experiences, traditions, superstitions, and suspicions of a middle-age progress and opportunity, together with a different language and religion. The other often represents an advanced civilization which has little sympathy with or understanding of the other. The transition of the peasant from Russia or Austria or Hungary to the American home is, at its very best, difficult and perplexing. Even where the worker goes, as many thousands do, into the home of one of her own nationality, who has been here one or more generations, the transition is not an easy one.

The question of difficult adjustment is also complicated by that of limited supply. Few Italian women are found in household work. In New York, where the greatest majority enter, there is but one agency which furnishes Italian girls and that one "only once in a while." The Italian girls are, however, attracted by the light and music and color of the cafés and restaurants, and are entering them to such an extent as to present a grave moral situation. The Italian man is opposed to menial work for women, and the Italian feeling of the "impropriety of their going about unaccompanied" prevents to any degree their isolation as household workers, which would remove the guardianship now maintained.

The home ties of the Jews are proverbially strong, and there also exists a prejudice against personal service. The difference in food and in its preparation is an obstacle to their working in Christian families or for unorthodox Jews. The Jewish girl prefers to return to her home at night, and to marry young, and she is consequently found in the restaurant, hotel, and boarding-house, or in factories and shops. There are more than 75 agencies in New York city run by Jews for the purpose of placing Jewish girls in households, hotels, restaurants, and similar places. They are well patronized, but not so much by girls who have been here several years. Domestic training-schools started for Jewish immigrant girls have failed utterly.

Germans, French, Scandinavians, English, Irish, and Canadians are found in large numbers in domestic work, and are much in demand. The difficulties are that they come in small numbers, and many prefer mills and factories and are quite as much in demand by business men. Housewives can well complain to their husbands that their competition has depleted the homes of its domestic workers. The tendency of the Scandinavians to colonize withdraws many from the cities. The rapid assimilation of American standards and customs and freedom by Germans and Irish makes them train their children for occupations other than housework.

Roughly speaking, there are three classes of immigrants who are coming to America. (1) Those who come because the way is made easy and who do not intend to work. They hope to live off their friends and relations, or marry. They are the drifters. (2) Those who come on promises of high wages and easy work. They mean to work, but at something they like, and they mean to be free. They frequently leave for the shop. (3) Those who have been poor beasts of burden, and are driven to this haven by persecution, taxation, wretchedness, starvation, oppression, and the great desire to better their condition. They are willing to learn, will do anything that comes to hand, and in their generation, barring marriage, rarely leave domestic work or get beyond the factory or sweat-shop door.

Influences are also at work that are changing the moral fibre of the immigrants. Formerly they came for some strong political, religious, or economic reason. They meant to win their way by hard work. They had to suffer many privations in order to come, and they came to stay — to make this their home, and not to earn as much money as possible and then go back and live in ease. Strong characters equal to these privations came, and they made equally good citizens. Now the desire to emigrate is artificially stimulated.

Steamship ticket agents offer cheap rates and present alluring and misleading pictures of ease. Friends and relatives send them the money. Employment agents lure them on and are their only friends and advisers when they arrive.

The agent is frequently foreign-born, works for a fee, and his sympathies are with the immigrant. If the immigrant is too old for the position, the agent starts her American career by teaching her to lie, a step made necessary, in his judgment, by the false standard of age instead of efficiency, on which the employer insists. Next she is told that she can get high wages for what she can do, and so he teaches her a few replies to questions which will make her appear efficient. When discharged for incompetency the agent immediately gets her another place and labels her "experienced." She asks for a "steady job." The agent prefers to place her for a month and then call for her for another patrón, thereby making another fee. She does not know this is his object, but in a short time she likes changing about, and her idea of a steady place becomes half a dozen in a year.

These are only instances of the kind of training given by the agent, for he really continues her education. She visits him frequently, goes to him for advice or when out of work, and sees much of American life as he represents it.

But his influence does not end there. The household worker, unlike any other worker, when she loses her position loses her "home," and it may be at an hour's notice. The immigrant homes will take such a worker in, but these are unknown to the great majority, and the house-worker, if known as such, is barred from most working-girls' clubs, homes, and hotels. So the agent and his boarding-house friend take her in. The boarding-house keepers, anxious for the lodging fee, frequently refuse to let the immigrant girls work anywhere but in hotels and restaurants.

It may be said that domestic service is preferable for immigrant women when they first arrive, especially for races which do not readily assimilate. But both immigrant and American citizen would benefit if some of the following suggestions were carried out:

1. Greater supervision of work, and training by housewives, and a higher home standard, so that the immigrant will realize more quickly its advantages in making her a better citizen.

2. Establishment of training-schools or transition schools for newly arrived immigrants. These schools should offer courses in English, American standards of living, personal hygiene, sanitation, information about rights, wages, conditions of work, etc. Folk dances, games, amusements of their nationalities, to lessen the isolation in a new country, will attract.

3. Friendly visiting of young immigrant workers in their own homes when they first arrive and are looking for work, so that they may become interested in the right kind of work and be directed to fair employers to whom they will make fair representations.

4. Treatment of the immigrant worker as a human being.

5. Protection of young immigrant women who come here, so that they may find honest work. Business men are interested in obtaining laws to prevent the exploitation of their employees and in movements to make them efficient. But in many cases housewives permit, without apparent interest, the exploitation and demoralization of young women who would have become honest workers had they been protected upon arrival.

6. Some provisions for lodging household workers when out of employment.

1908
A RECORD-BREAKING BALLOON VOYAGE
by Henry Helm Clayton

THE Blue Hill Meteorological Observatory, with which I am connected, is renowned throughout the world for its researches concerning the conditions of the upper air. For this reason, when the interested aeronauts of the great nations of Europe began to make arrangements for the first international balloon contest, to be held in America, naturally they sought information from the observatory. The Germans, particularly appreciative of scientific knowledge and the advantages of expert advice, invited the director of the Blue Hill Observatory to go as aide in one of their balloons. Not finding it convenient to go himself, the director asked me to represent the observatory in this voyage. And so it happened that I was to map out the best air-currents for a balloon to take, in order to reach the greatest distance from its starting-point at St. Louis.

Provided with heavy wraps for the balloon voyage, I arrived at St. Louis on October 20, the morning before the race. Most of the aeronauts had come from far distant lands, and some of them had only a limited command of English. Under the inspiration of the Aero Club of St. Louis, many thousands of dollars had been contributed toward the promotion of this unique race; a section of the city's gas-plant had been reserved for the purpose of making a light gas especially for the balloons, and about three hundred soldiers had been detailed from the United States Army to aid in protecting and launching the balloons.

On the afternoon of my arrival, I was called to meet the officials conducting the race and the contestants for the prize. At this meeting, it was decided that whenever any contestant came to the ground voluntarily and landed, the race was over for him; and that the distance should be measured in a straight line from St. Louis to the point of landing.

The morning of the race all the balloons were spread out, each on a large sheet of canvas, with the valve uppermost and the mouth next the gas-main. Next, the various lines were attached: first, a line for operating the valve and allowing the gas to escape when necessary; second, a line for ripping open the top of the balloon and thus letting out all the gas at once. This line was to be used only at the moment of landing. So secure did the pilot of our balloon, the Pommern, feel in its use that the anchor usually carried was dispensed with.

In order to place these ropes properly, a man had to crawl down through the empty balloon and come out at its mouth. After the arrangement of these details, the net to which the basket is attached when in place was quickly spread over the balloon under the skillful guidance of our pilot, Mr. Erbsloeh.

Before noon, all the balloons were ready to receive the supply of gas which was to carry them aloft, and within less than two hours afterward, the gas-main being connected with all the balloons simultaneously, they became swelling globes, some twenty-five or thirty feet in diameter, towering above the ground and gently oscillating in the breeze.

As a check on the movements of the contestants and to provide material for a study of the race afterward, the Aero Club at St. Louis gave each contestant a sealed, self-recording barometer, which traced on a sheet every movement of the balloon in a vertical direction, and thus showed at what height it was sailing at each moment in its course, making it impossible for any contestant to descend to earth without a record of the event. These packages were placed in the baskets of the balloons by the judges themselves, with instructions that they were to be returned with the seal unbroken immediately after landing.

In addition we had recording barometers of our own, thermometers of a delicate kind for recording temperature, and compasses of various sizes and shapes.

The rules of the contest were that the balloons should ascend following one another in rapid succession. We were provided with red envelopes by the committee, with instructions to throw them overboard at the end of each two hours and as near as possible to towns, so that they might more readily be found. We also had a number of blanks placed in envelopes addressed to various newspapers, which we were requested to fill out and throw overboard, giving our position and speed at the time.

A few seconds after four o'clock the order to depart was given. We grasped the hands of our friends in a final farewell, the restraining hands of the soldiers were removed, and slowly the earth began to recede from us. A wild, tumultuous cheer burst from the waiting thousands and I waved my hat in return to the waving hats and handkerchiefs below. The balloon was rising and moving northward without the slightest jar or jolt. Soon the great city of St. Louis lay spread out below us as on a map. The houses and street-cars looked like toys and the men like creeping ants.

The upper currents of the atmosphere in the United States almost always move toward some point between northeast and southeast, usually nearly east. We had discussed our course the previous evening at dinner, and Mr. Erbsloeh agreed to seek this upper current immediately after leaving St. Louis, and to make directly for the Atlantic coast, going south of the lake region. We wished to reach the coast as far north as possible, because in that direction the land stretched to the greatest distance from St. Louis, and it was agreed that we should ascend or descend as was necessary during the voyage in order to find favoring currents.

At the height of about a mile and a quarter, we found a current moving toward the northeast with a speed of about twenty-two miles an hour. Here the ascent of the balloon was checked, and at this level we prepared to spend the night. It was now past sunset. In finding our course, we had crossed the lower Missouri near its mouth and then the Mississippi near the city of Alton, Illinois. The sun had set in a deep haze, a glowing ball of fire, but the adjustments necessary to beginning our journey had prevented much note of this, our first sunset. It was about six P.M. when we passed the twin cities of Alton and Upper Alton, their brilliant electric lights sparkling in the gathering dusk.

We watched these glowing lights amid a silence more profound than any I have ever known. After we left St. Louis, the roar of the city sank to a soft murmur, and then ceased, and now not a sound was to be heard, not even the rustle of the wind, because we were moving with the wind and hence in a dead calm.

As we passed over towns, we threw overboard the notices provided for giving the press information of our progress. In order to cause these notices to be more easily found, I bought a number of small rubber balloons from a peddler on the ground, and at the appointed time a package of notices was attached to one of them and it was set free. The balloon, thus weighted, descended rapidly, and I thought it would serve to attract the attention of any one who passed near it after it had reached the earth.

About 3 A.M., the brilliant lights of a large city brightened the haze of the lower air like a coming dawn. This was Lafayette, Indiana, and we were soon passing over its northern suburbs. Here we crossed the Wabash, moving softly toward the southwest, and soon afterward we had an adventure often enjoyed by balloonists, that of a race with a locomotive, in which, I regret to say, the locomotive won. It was evidently a swift midnight express for the east, and when our courses finally diverged, the train was already several miles ahead of us.

The balloon had now sunk to within three-fourths of a mile of the earth's surface, and the landscape was seen clearly for the first time. We were crossing the headwaters of the Wabash, whose bed was covered with a broad river of fog far more beautiful than the river itself.

The cause of this fog is the great cooling of the surface of the earth by radiation. The air, more transparent than glass, is but little heated by day or cooled at night by radiation, so that, at heights exceeding a half mile, there is very little daily change in its temperature, and it is scarcely more than one degree warmer during the day than at night. On the other hand, the earth's surface is much heated by day and much cooled at night, causing a large daily change in the temperature of the ground and in the air which comes in contact with the ground.

The balloon is like a little earth; it absorbs and radiates heat very powerfully. At night, the balloon is continuously cooling, and we had to throw out ballast at intervals to keep from sinking to the earth on account of the cooling and shrinking of the gas, as well as on account of a slow loss of gas through the envelope of the balloon. This ballast was in the form of little scoopfuls of sand taken from a bag.

On the other hand, when the sun rose that first morning, a dazzling, brilliant orb, the balloon was heated in a surprisingly few minutes. Its gas, expanding and growing lighter, caused us to ascend rapidly, and we were soon again at a height of about eight thousand feet. Had it not been for an opening at the bottom of the gas-bag, made for that purpose, the balloon would have ascended many miles, — in fact until the expanding gas burst the envelope asunder and allowed it to fall to earth a lifeless mass.

All day we were crossing the great state of Ohio, so splendidly cultivated as to be almost a garden, with hardly an interval of waste land from one end to the other. We passed over or near the cities of Dayton, Springfield, Columbus, Newark, and Zanesville. When we reached Columbus it was already past noon, and we were hungry. Reclining in our basket, and shielding ourselves as best we could from the sun, we ate our mid-day meal. At the height of a mile and a half, we found it necessary to shelter our faces to prevent sunburn, although the air around us was but little warmer than that of the previous night, being about forty-five degrees. As the afternoon wore on and the balloon began to cool and sink, we were obliged to throw out much sand, casting it away a scoopful at a time; and just after sunset, it was even necessary to empty two or three bags at once.

We lost our bearing in eastern Ohio; and consequently, shortly after sunset, in order to make inquiries, we allowed our balloon to settle within about two hundred feet of the ground near a lonely farmhouse. The inhabitants of the farm did not see us until we were close upon them, and then consternation reigned supreme. In the barnyard, pigs, chickens, geese, and sheep rushed frantically in every direction for cover. In the midst of this commotion and noise, a woman appeared at the door of the house, and gazing motionless from wonder, fear, or other emotion, could not reply to our oft-repeated inquiry as to the name of the nearest town.

In a brief time we had swept past her little domain on to that of a farmer who responded to our inquiry by the query, "Where did you come from?" and then, "Where are you going?" Before we could get this matter settled to his satisfaction, we were out of hearing; and, passing over a small cluster of houses, we learned from some boys that we were over the town of Otsego, between Zanesville and Port Washington. Freeing ourselves from the boys, who had seized our trail-rope, we now rose several hundred feet, and continued our journey toward the northeast. In the gathering dusk the Ohio River was flowing below us. We crossed about twenty miles north of Wheeling, West Virginia, and at 7.20 P.M. passed over the city of Pittsburg with its glowing furnaces and innumerable lights. Over all this region there was a tinge of smoke indicating the centre of the great coal industries, and making it difficult to see clearly the objects beneath us. We were now traveling northeastward well along the path we had planned to follow from St. Louis. But we were approaching mountains with which neither of us was familiar, and as the balloon was now within a distance of about one thousand feet of the ground, it seemed desirable to rise in order to avoid becoming entangled in the forests on the mountain-side.

We threw over ballast, and rose to a height of about a mile. We were soon crossing the ridges of the Appalachian Mountains which showed dusky gray outlines in the moonlight, while between them lay black, abysmal valleys. There were suggestions of awful precipices and bottomless depths which made me shudder involuntarily as I looked into them, although up to that time I had felt safe and free from fear. About 2 A.M., we saw the brilliant lights of Harrisburg to the north, and passed directly over the city of Carlisle, where long lines of lights stretched at right angles to each other. We were now within about two thousand feet of the ground, and I listened for signs of life, but the sleeping city was as quiet as the dead. We crossed the Susquehanna River near the rapids at a height of less than one thousand feet, and could hear the gurgling murmur of the waters long before they came in view, and after they were lost to sight. We crossed a railroad-siding, where a puffing engine was waiting with a train of cars, and called through our megaphone, hoping to attract the notice of the engineer; but our voices were drowned by the hissing steam. Some factories, or foundries, were passed, where the wheels of industry evidently turn by night as well as by day, for we could hear the throb of engines and the voices of men.

Even before the first signs of dawn appeared in the east, we were hailed with a cheerful "Good-morning" by some early riser, and in response to our inquiries he informed us that we were then thirty-seven miles from Philadelphia, and moving directly toward that city. As we approached Philadelphia, we exchanged morning greetings and bits of information with people below, hearing them as distinctly as if only separated from them by the width of a street. We talked through a megaphone and were easily understood.

Before we reached the centre of the city the warming rays of the rising sun touched the balloon, and we shot upward to a height slightly exceeding two miles, where the temperature was found to be a few tenths of a degree below the freezing point. This manœuvre of the balloon was in accordance with our wishes, because the ocean was now near, and if we were to continue our voyage, for which we had ample gas and provisions, it must be in the direction of New York and New England. At the height of two miles, the State of New Jersey lay spread out below us like a map. Looking eastward we could see the bays and inlets of the shoreline for fully fifty miles on either hand, while the great ocean lay before us glistening in the morning sun with a silver sheen. We did not find a favorable current, so it became evident that we must descend, and Mr. Erbsloeh requested me to pack everything secure because the balloon might strike the earth with a shock.

I pulled the valve-rope and down we came, two miles in a few minutes. When within several hundred yards of the earth's surface, we emptied two bags of sand, checking the downward speed of the balloon; and a few additional scoopfuls of sand thrown overboard brought us into equilibrium within a short distance of the ground, over which we continued to glide rapidly toward the northeast, traversing the state of New Jersey diagonally in about an hour and a half. We crossed the head of a bay and could see the waves of ocean breaking on the shore beyond. It was high time to descend, and selecting an open place in the suburbs of Asbury Park, we opened our valve and approached the ground. Suddenly our flight was arrested. We had encountered some telegraph wires amid which the basket was entangled, while the great mass of the balloon above was tugging to free us. The emptying of two more bags of ballast, a combined push against the wires, and the balloon was free once more, ascending rapidly. It now became necessary to act quickly; the valve was reopened, and in addition, a small hole was torn in the side of the balloon with the ripping-cord. This was effective, and we touched the ground; then with a long vigorous pull of the ripping-cord, the balloon lay to the leeward of the basket, an empty bag, and the race was over. In forty hours we had traversed the greatest distance in a straight line ever traveled by a balloon in America, and had won the race. In an air line from St. Louis, the distance is 872 miles; but in making this distance, since the course was not perfectly straight, we had traveled 932 miles at a speed varying between 17 and 31 miles an hour, and averaging 23.3 miles an hour. In all this distance, we had found it necessary to inquire as to our geographical position only once.

During the forty hours that we were in the air we lived in a basket two and a half by three feet. In these narrow quarters there was not much room for freedom of motion, yet neither of us felt greatly cramped for room. There was no provision for sleep, but we ate our three regular meals in the air just as if we had been on the ground. There was no dressing for breakfast, or dinner, except to exchange our shoes for slippers, and to add or remove wraps, as the temperature demanded. For food we carried such provisions as rolls, mutton chops, mutton stew, fried chicken, eggs, crackers, and sausage. The last we did not taste. It was a concentrated food reserved in case the balloon might drop in some out-of-the way place, where we would be several days in finding our way out to civilization. For drinks we carried some dozen or so bottles of Apollinaris water, a bottle of coffee, a bottle of tea, and two or three bottles of wine.

In making the air a domain for human travel, the conquest of which seems almost in sight, a competitive race like this is a trial of methods, materials, and men to the utmost possibilities; and although the results of one race cannot settle the matter, the results of many races determine the best of these appliances and open the door to new inventions and new methods.

In the distances traveled this balloon race from St. Louis proved to be one of the greatest ever undertaken. Seven of the nine contestants crossed the Allegheny Mountains and landed near the Atlantic coast, while one landed in the region of the Great Lakes about six hundred miles from the starting point.

This result is so impressive that it has aroused the imagination of the American people and set them wondering as to the possibilities of this novel method of navigation. Aero clubs have sprung into existence in almost every large city; the Signal Corps of our army is considering the building of several airships, and Congress will be asked for a large appropriation for further experiments; the officers of our navy are discussing the possibilities of launching flying machines from naval vessels, or of sending up men in captive balloons from the ships for the purpose of reconnoitering, and a horde of inventors are at work on improvements of present appliances and on new machines for navigating the air. It seems safe to predict that the next year or two will witness an enormous activity in this matter in America.

1909
THE MEANING OF THE ELECTION
by Charles A. Conant

THE decision of every presidential election naturally arouses discussion and suggests reflection as to the future of the contending parties, both the victor and the vanquished. Opponents have many times predicted, after a great defeat, the dissolution of the Democratic party, and it was not unusual to hear the dissolution of the Republican party seriously discussed after the second election of Mr. Cleveland. But the Democratic party showed the capacity to survive the Civil War, and it is not likely to be dissolved by a fourth successive defeat while it still has a powerful organization in practically every state of the Union. Every country governed by representative institutions requires at least two parties, and there seems no reason to doubt that both the Republican and Democratic parties will continue to exist under their present names, even if they submit to changes in their creeds and membership.

But no political party can govern long unless it has some vital principle. The Democratic party of Jefferson and Madison had practically achieved its mission before the Civil War. That mission was the reduction to practical legislation of the Declaration of Independence. Equal justice before the law for all men; the severance of the bond between church and state; the abolition of imprisonment for debt; the gradual reduction and final annulment of restrictions upon white manhood suffrage, — these were the mission and the achievements of the Democratic party in the early days of the Republic. Equality of all men before the law had been the arduous mission of the English-speaking race in the Old World during the centuries which began with King John and ended with the Georges. But equality before the law does not in itself mean an equal share in making the law. A share for every man in the government of the state was the achievement of the Democratic party in America, and the Liberal party in England, during the nineteenth century. Along with these achievements in both countries went many measures of social reform.

High hopes were entertained in all civilized countries that equality before the law, and equality in making the law, would bring about the reign of justice and equality of opportunity in all branches of human endeavor. But with the enormous increase of wealth arising from machine production emerged a new problem, only vaguely apprehended during the early conflict for purely political rights. This is the problem of economic equality, — the right of every man to his full share in the increased national resources of the race. This problem has not been solved by the achievement of political equality, but is likely to be the most fiercely contested political problem of the next generation. In so far as the Democratic party is able to present a solution of it which will bear the test of experience, and will increase the ratio of well-being dealt out to the average man, it is likely to find a mission and an opportunity.

On the other side, however, will always be arrayed the interests of those who have against those who have not. In their ranks will eventually be found men of achievement, of foresight, and of constructive power. From them, whatever their views of social questions, will come creative ideas for the development of the economic resources of the nation, for the extension of its political power and its economic opportunities in all quarters of the world. Up to the time of the intervention of the United States in Cuba these international problems had attracted little attention. The economic unrest which ultimately gave birth to the so-called "tariff reform" movement in Great Britain had already driven the British government to the extension of empire over India, Egypt, Australia, and many islands of the sea. The controlling motive behind these extensions of power was essentially economic, the necessity for markets for English goods, which should not be closed by discriminating taxes or the open hostility of competing powers.

The first to enter on a great scale the field of manufacture, England was for a time not only ahead of her rivals, but almost without rivals;

but, within the past generation, France, Germany, Belgium, and other countries have overtaken her in the field of production, and like her they have entered upon the struggle for control of the world's markets. The United States was late in appreciating the necessity for entering upon this contest. Her entrance came indeed almost as if by accident, with the sinking of a few ill-equipped Spanish ships in the Bay of Manila on the first day of May, 1898. The country awoke, almost by magic, to the necessity of participation in international policies. Within two years Secretary Hay revealed the vital interest of this country in the markets of the Orient, by securing from the Powers the promise of an open door for the trade of all in Manchuria.

By an almost instant alignment, according to individual interest, temperament, or breadth of historic view, the country became divided into two schools — those who believed in the consolidation and extension of national influence, whatever the cost, and those who believed in casting aside such opportunities, in order to remain a self-centred and isolated nation. It was natural that the party in power at the time should accept the new responsibilities, while the party out of power should urge their rejection. This might have been true, even if the party in power at the time of Dewey's victory had been the Democratic party.

It has been the Republican party, however, which has had imposed upon it by events the duty of construction, of organization, and achievement in the field of domestic affairs, as well as in the extension of national influence in distant seas. In recent years the wavering and lack of visible aim, which marked to a considerable extent the administrations of Presidents Arthur and Harrison, has given place to a fever of constructive energy such as has rarely been equaled in the history of political parties. To go no further back than the inauguration of President McKinley in 1897, the Republican party has not only added to the sphere of influence of the nation the 8,000,000 people of the Philippines and the 2,000,000 people of Cuba and Porto Rico, but it has acquired an important strip of territory on the Darien Isthmus, and is undertaking, in the building of the Panama Canal, one of the most important engineering achievements of modern times.

At home the Republican party has not only carried out the measures of President Roosevelt for reducing capital to the rank of a servant rather than a master, — a work which the other party might have undertaken, — but it has established the gold standard, has reorganized the army, has added scores of fighting ships to the navy, has modified in favor of labor the doctrine of common employment, has saved thousands of infant and adult lives by meat inspection and the pure-food law, and has planned to save the forests and to regulate immigration.

It is not to be expected, however, that the Republican party will have an uninterrupted lease of power. A victory for the Democratic party might even be possible at the next general election. Meanwhile it is floundering through many counter-currents toward the position of the state-socialist parties of Europe. When it has firmly reached this position, and the conservative element has been substantially eliminated, then the Democratic party may prove again a dangerous competitor for the control of the federal government.

But time is likely to be required for the consummation of this process. It may be doubted if Mr. Bryan is suited by temperament and training for leadership in such policies. In spite of his subsequent declaration for government ownership of railways, there is force in the criticism made by the *New York Journal* in 1901, that "Mr. Bryan, able and patriotic as he is, is not really modern. He lives in the past. He has never been able fully to adapt himself to the economic and social revolution that has changed the face of the world."

In indicating that the Democratic party is likely to find its natural and most profitable course in adopting the policies of state socialism, it is not intended to intimate that these policies will be of a violent character, or outside the range of legitimate political discussion. There is enough to be achieved, if socialistic theories are well-founded, in such fields as old-age pensions and insurance, government operation of public utilities, restrictions upon corporations, the adoption of the income tax, the redistribution of other taxes, and government ownership and operation of the railways, before any such questions can arise as those of distributing private property or carrying out the tenets of abstract socialism.

The democratic idea, therefore, must seek a new manifestation, if the party would survive as a healthy rival of the party of expansion. That democracy has fulfilled its mission in the direction of purely political reforms is the reason for its hesitations, divisions, and defeats on two continents within the last few years. When it has formulated a new and comprehensive programme, — logical and virile from the point of view of a large class of thinkers, — it may be in a position to measure swords again, with courage and enthusiasm, with the party which supports a constructive national policy at home, and a resolute foreign policy abroad. For the moment, the latter party will profit by the divisions and hesitations in the ranks of its opponents, and will receive as recruits from their ranks those who are impatient of any party without a constructive policy, and those who tremble at the signs of the coming of the new order.

THE CHANGE IN THE FEMININE IDEAL
by Margaret Deland

WHEN I planned to write this paper, I thought I would call it "The New Woman"; but the last page of *Puck,* and the first of *Punch,* rose before me; ladies in bloomers, with latch-keys, mothers-in-law and club-women and Suffragettes, made the title impossible. When you come to think of it, it is curious how fatal it is, either to a situation or to an individual, or even to a name, if in an evil moment it becomes funny. And that the New Woman has been funny, I suppose there can be no doubt. Indeed, one can hardly say "The New Woman" with any hope of being taken seriously; although some of us feel that certain conditions of which she is a symptom are serious enough, in all conscience!

However, as I am going to venture to speak of her, I shall begin by mentioning briefly those facts which lead me to conclude that she exists — outside the columns of the jocose newspaper, and not as a mere eccentricity of sex. Of course there have been sporadic "new women," ever since the world began, and they have shocked the old women and amused the men, young and old, just as our new women shock or amuse to-day. When Miriam and her friends took timbrels in their hands and danced out before the children of Israel, declaring that the Lord had triumphed gloriously, for the horse and his rider had been thrown into the sea, no doubt the women who were too fat or too stiff to dance, declared that such things were unknown when they were young; and when Deborah sat under the palm-tree between Ramah and Beth-el in Mount Ephraim and judged Israel, I am sure there were respectable housewives who called her a "very unwomanly woman."

There have always been occasional women who did so-called unwomanly things, that is, unusual things, things generally left to men; there have always been stray women, who have distinguished themselves in art, or politics, or religion, or science; but they were conspicuous, because they were strays. Achieving women are not very conspicuous now, simply because there are more of them. Indeed, the New Woman is almost ceasing to be "new," and that is why she is ceasing to be entirely a joke; for there is something more than a joke in all this curious turning upside-down of traditions and theories in regard to women; something more than a joke in the girl with a latch-key; in the matron who gives her time to civic affairs or to berating officers of the law; in myself here instead of, as a good and contemptuous man said to me once, "making soup."

To my mind there are several things which point to the conclusion that this amusing person, who is called the New Woman, is to be reckoned with as a reality which is not entirely amusing; but I shall mention only two of them: the first is *a prevailing discontent among women;* and the second, *a change in what we might call the "feminine ideal."* Once grant these two things, the discontent and the change, and we find ourselves face to face, not only with the lady herself, but with certain sobering possibilities which accompany her. For that discontent and change are in themselves sobering, is as certain as that they are in themselves hopeful.

II

Of the *prevailing discontent among women* I shall speak very briefly, and I must not go into certain industrial and economic conditions which have forced stern and inevitable discontents upon us all; nor shall I refer to the discontents of foolish or second-rate minds. It is the discontents of the woman of privilege, the woman of sane and sheltered life, which have real significance.

I am sometimes amused to have the response made by some mild-eyed, domestic creature, in her comfortable home, with her little children about her knees, "Why, I don't believe women are discontented. *I'm* not discontented!" and so ending the subject. Yet even this satisfied and sheltered woman can hardly venture outside the warm and narrow circle of her own content, without hearing a shrill feminine chatter and clamor, a more or less petulant criticism of life as it is lived; a demand, — often intelligent but sometimes extremely silly and devoid of any economic basis, — a loud demand for the reconstruction of many things: government, business, the laws of property, the education of children. This contented woman (who has to be told by her husband whether she is a Republican or a Democrat), whose property never troubles her because her dear and honest men-creatures take such affairs from her shoulders, whose children are admirably well and good, — even this happy and contented woman must know that all women are not so satisfied as she. Even while she thanks God that her girls are not as other mothers' girls, she is aware of her neighbor's daughter's discontent.

This young person has gone to college, and when she graduates she is going to earn her own living. She declines to be dependent upon a father and mother amply able to support her. She will do settlement work; she won't go to church; she has views upon marriage and the birth-rate, and she utters them calmly, while her mother blushes with embarrassment; she occupies herself, passionately, with everything except the things that used to occupy the minds of girls.

Restlessness! Restlessness! And as it is with the young woman, so it is with the older woman. Countless Woman's Clubs, largely composed of middle-aged women, have sprung into eager existence in the last twenty years: they are admirable and helpful organizations, but they all express in one way or another the restlessness of growth, a restlessness infinitely removed from the old content of a generation ago.

III

But it is not the various discontents, it is the changing ideals of women, which seem to me most significant, — because the ideals are responsible for the discontents. Of course there were women a generation ago, as in all the generations, who asserted themselves; but they were practically "sports." Now, the simple, honest woman; the shy, respectable, commonplace, dear woman; the woman of ringlets (as it used to be) and many babies; the good housekeeper, the good wife, the good mother — is evolving ideals that are changing her life, and the lives of those people about her.

As for the difference between us and our mothers, of course we all begin by protesting that if we can ever hope to do our duty as well as they did, our consciences will acquit us. Who of us women, in our comfortable living, dare compare ourselves to our mothers? They did not talk about their "rights" or "reforms"; they would have thought interference in municipal questions, and agitation for legislation, most unbecoming and unfeminine. They had, bless their dear hearts! a gentle and ladylike irresponsibility in regard to the world lying in darkness in city halls or legislative chambers — though they gave their pennies toward the saving of souls in dark Africa, with a true, even tender emotion, to which most of us are strangers. No; the mothers of forty or fifty years ago had no theories about improving the world (except the heathen) outside their own respectable doors; but they had strength, and patience, and tenderness, and courage, and *selflessness*.

There is another point of conspicuous difference, and of tremendous social significance, between the woman of yesterday and the woman of to-day. We have come to appreciate the fact that our mothers were unconscientious concerning the right of children *not* to be born. We are beginning — alas, only just beginning — to say that when parents, unable to support a child in physical and moral and intellectual well-being, bring such a child into the world, for the state, or for their unfortunate relations, to support, they are socially criminal. Contrast our mothers' ideas of large families with that! Quantity, not quality, marked the good mother of fifty or sixty years ago. And there are folk to-day — some of them in high places — who still cling to that tradition; but one would like to ask such persons whether the state would have been benefited if, for instance, in a recent notorious murder trial in New York, the principal had been twins? No; maternal instinct, that exquisite blossom of pure animalism, is now striking its roots into spiritual responsibilities, and is becoming divine enough to forbid an undesirable existence.

It is such contrasts as these between the past and the present, that show what a change there is in the ideals of women; but the really important thing is to recognize what it is which is creating the change. There are, it seems to me, two forces at work: one is the sense of individualism, and the other is the sense of social responsibility. Both seem to have been evolved in women in our generation; and each in itself is good.

Let us consider first the impulse of individualism as we see it in the home life. The sudden and very general expansion of the girl's horizon is manifest to everybody. She apes the independence of the boys, and often emphasizes it with an affected and ludicrous swagger; but with that independence, she has grasped at the splendid possibility of physical perfection, which implies a resulting mental strength heretofore classed as masculine. This is fine, and apart from its occasionally æsthetic objectionableness, we all rejoice in it. The day of the interesting feminine invalid is gone, thank Heaven!

Now there is a certain regal word, the only word that can finally compel the soul, the word *ought*. Our girls know how to say, "I want," and "I will," or sometimes, "I must"; but they are not learning to say, "I ought." Instead, the education of to-day too often cries out to them in their colleges: "Look! The heavens and earth and waters that are under the earth are yours! The song that the morning stars sing is for your ears. The eternal tides of life await your adventurous prows. The very winds of God are blowing for your sails!" "You — *you* — YOU — " the higher education cries; "never mind other people; make the most of your own life. Never mind marriage: it is an incident; men have proved it so for themselves; it is just the same for women. Never mind social laws; do what your temperament dictates — art, affairs, enjoyment even. But do your duty to yourself!"

"And," remarks the observer of an older generation, grimly, "*the Devil take the hindermost!*" Then he adds, — the observer is generally he, — he adds, with the candor peculiar to his engaging sex, that, according to his poor way of thinking, he would call the state of mind of the girl who acts on this advice, just plain garden selfishness.

Of course, he is only a man; but certainly some thoughtful women wonder whether these gracious opportunities of learning which are flooding in upon women, are not translated in terms of *self* in the minds of many girls.

The sense of individualism, as it expresses itself in the occupations of women, is one of the most interesting economic facts of our generation, — but it is too large and involved a subject to take up here. I must only say that individualism has taken advantage of certain grim industrial necessities to create the business woman — not the occasional and shrinking figure of a generation or so ago, the "woman in business," who was pitied and smiled at and helped; but an eager, hard-headed, strenuous person, ready to give and take, neither asking nor granting favors; she is, generally speaking, a fine, wholesome, sound person.

But while the voice of woman is crying in the wilderness for self-culture, self-advancement, self-satisfaction, it is crying also for power to act for the public good; and that we call the sense of social responsibility. Women are taking part in many public matters in which a generation ago they were not in the least interested. They are making themselves heard in municipal affairs with no uncertain voice; city housekeeping seems to them a duty; they want clean streets, and decent markets; they see that penal institutions ought to be improved, and that the conditions of labor need investigation and legislation; and they say so, often with an impetuosity so nearly childish that it antagonizes legislators, — or amuses them, which is even worse. But how strenuous, and fine, and courageous it all is!

This sense of social responsibility is expressing itself, first and foremost, in the determination of women to exercise the suffrage. Out of that determination spring, of course, many fine and noble purposes, which would contribute to the general well-being of the race. In the excitement of her high aims, and her dogged intention to have the ballot (even if she upsets the whole kettle of fish, so to speak) a curious thing has happened: she does not apparently realize that she has secured by intelligent influence, and plain unsensational common sense, a large number of rights and privileges without the ballot. But, all the same, she is eager to try her " 'prentice han' " in a government, whose most complicated machinery is the ballot.

Incidentally, she proposes to force upon men the feminine view of morality: "Let me get the reins in my hands," she says, "and I will make men temperate; I will make them pure; I will cut corruption out of their politics. In fact, my vote shall make human nature cease to be human nature!" What the outside, gaping, anxious world thinks of us when we make such statements, we do not stop to hear, — perhaps we would not like it if we did! Curiously enough, however, even while the new woman insists upon the civil equality of men and women which will be secured by woman suffrage, there has come, upon her part, an insistence on their essential difference, which is most unlovely. She has her "Woman's Building" at the World's Fair, her "Woman's Editions" of newspapers, and the exploitation of "Woman's Inventions." Heretofore the work of women in the arts has been simply work, good or bad, as the case may be, and considered irrespective of sex; now, it is classified as "feminine," and loses immeasurably in consequence.

I hope I shall not be thought too dogmatic if I say that I believe there was very general regret among thoughtful women that there should have been a Woman's Building at Chicago in 1893, and that it was on the whole a mortifying and humiliating display. How much better if the few great things — the noble pictures, the valuable inventions, the dignified expressions of any art or science — had been placed among their peers, and not put aside as noticeable because women did them. Such insistence upon sex in work is not only an insult to the work, but to the sex.

1911
TWO LOOKS
by John Galsworthy

THE old Director of the "Yew Trees" Cemetery walked slowly across from his house, to see that all was ready.

He had seen pass into the square of earth committed to his charge so many to whom he had been in the habit of nodding, so many whose faces even he had not known. To him it was the everyday event; yet this funeral, one more in the countless tale, disturbed him — a sharp reminder of the passage of time.

For twenty years had gone by since the death of Septimus Godwin, the cynical, romantic doctor who had been his greatest friend; by whose cleverness all had sworn, of whose powers of fascination all had gossiped! And now they were burying his son!

He had not seen the widow since, for she had left the town at once; but he recollected her distinctly, a tall, dark woman with bright brown eyes, much younger than her husband, and only married to him eighteen months before he died. He remembered her slim figure standing by the grave, at that long-past funeral, and the look on her face which had puzzled him so terribly — a look of — a most peculiar look!

He thought of it even now, walking along the narrow path toward his old friend's grave — the handsomest in the cemetery, commanding from the topmost point the whitened slope and river that lay beyond. He came to its little private garden. Spring flowers were blossoming; the railings had been freshly painted; and by the door of the grave wreaths awaited the new arrival. All was in order.

The old Director opened the mausoleum with his key. Below, seen through a thick glass floor, lay the shining coffin of the father; beneath, on the lower tier, would rest the coffin of the son.

A gentle voice, close behind him, said, —

"Can you tell me, sir, what they are doing to my old doctor's grave?"

The old Director turned, and saw before him a lady well past middle age. He did not know her face, but it was pleasant, with faded rose-leaf cheeks, and silvered hair under a shady hat.

"Madam, there is a funeral here this afternoon."

"Ah! Can it be his wife?"

"Madam, his son; a young man of only twenty."

"His son! At what time did you say?"

"At two o'clock."

"Thank you: you are very kind."

With uplifted hat, he watched her walk away. It worried him to see a face he did not know.

All went off beautifully; but, dining that same evening with his friend, a certain doctor, the old Director asked,

"Did you see a lady with gray hair hovering about this afternoon?"

The doctor, a tall man, with a beard still yellow, drew his guest's chair nearer to the fire.

"I did," he answered.

"Did you remark her face? A very odd expression — a sort of — what shall I call it? — Very odd indeed! Who is she? I saw her at the grave this morning."

The doctor shook his head.

"Not so very odd, I think."

"Come! What do you mean by that?"

The doctor hesitated. Then, taking the decanter, he filled his old friend's glass, and answered, —

"Well, sir, you were Godwin's greatest chum — I will tell you, if you like, the story of his death. You were away at the time, if you remember."

"It is safe with me," said the old Director.

"Septimus Godwin," began the doctor slowly, "died on a Thursday about three o'clock, and I was only called in to see him at two. I found him far gone, but conscious now and then. It was a case of — but you know the details, so I needn't go into that. His wife was in the room, and on the bed at his feet lay his pet dog — a terrier; you may recollect, perhaps, he had a special breed. I hadn't been there ten minutes, when a maid came in, and whispered something to her mistress. Mrs. Godwin answered angrily, 'See him? Go down and say she ought to know better than to come here at such a time!' The maid went, but soon came back. Could the lady see Mrs. Godwin for just a moment? Mrs. Godwin answered that she could not leave her husband. The

maid looked frightened, and went away again. She came back for the
third time. The lady had said she must see Dr. Godwin; it was a matter
of life and death! 'Death — indeed!' exclaimed Mrs. Godwin: 'Shameful! Go down and tell her, if she doesn't go immediately, I will send
for the police!'

"The poor maid looked at me. I offered to go down and see the
visitor myself. I found her in the dining-room, and knew her at once.
Never mind her name, but she belongs to a county family not a
hundred miles from here. A beautiful woman she was then; but her
face that day was quite distorted.

" 'For God's sake, Doctor,' she said, 'is there any hope?'

"I was obliged to tell her there was none.

" 'Then I must see him,' she said.

"I begged her to consider what she was asking. But she held me out
a signet ring. Just like Godwin — wasn't it — that sort of Byronism,
eh?

" 'He sent me this,' she said, 'an hour ago. It was agreed between us
that if ever he sent that, I must come. If it were only myself I could
bear it — a woman can bear anything; but he'll die thinking I couldn't
come, thinking I didn't care — and I would give my life for him this
minute!'

"Now, a dying man's request is sacred. I told her she should see
him. I made her follow me upstairs, and wait outside his room. I
promised to let her know if he recovered consciousness. I have never
been thanked like that, before or since.

"I went back into the bedroom. He was still unconscious, and the
terrier whining. In the next room a child was crying — the very same
young man we buried to-day. Mrs. Godwin was still standing by the
bed.

" 'Have you sent her away?'

"I had to say that Godwin really wished to see her. At that she broke
out: —

" 'I won't have her here — the wretch!'

"I begged her to control herself, and remember that her husband
was a dying man.

" 'But I'm his wife,' she said, and flew out of the room."

The doctor paused, staring at the fire. He shrugged his shoulders,
and went on: "I'd have stopped her fury, if I could! A dying man is
not the same as the live animal, that he must needs be wrangled over!
And suffering's sacred, even to us doctors. I could hear their voices
outside. Heaven knows what they said to each other. And there lay
Godwin with his white face and his black hair — deathly still — fine-
looking fellow he always was! Then I saw that he was coming to! The
women had begun again outside — first, the wife, sharp and scornful;

then the other, hushed and slow. I saw Godwin lift his finger and point it at the door. I went out, and said to the woman, 'Dr. Godwin wishes to see you; please control yourself!'

"We went back into the room. The wife followed. But Godwin had lost consciousness again. They sat down, those two, and hid their faces. I can see them now, one on each side of the bed, their eyes covered with their hands, each with her claim on him, all murdered by the other's presence; each with her torn love. H'm? What they must have suffered, then! And all the time, the child crying — the child of one of them, that might have been the other's!"

The doctor was silent, and the old Director turned toward him his white-bearded, ruddy face, with a look as if he were groping in the dark.

"Just then, I remember," the doctor went on suddenly, "the bells of St. Jude's close by began to peal out for the finish of a wedding. That brought Godwin back to life. He just looked from one woman to the other with a queer, miserable sort of smile, enough to make your heart break. And they both looked at him. The face of the wife — poor thing — was as bitter hard as a cut stone, but she sat there, without ever stirring a finger. As for the other woman — I couldn't look at her. He beckoned to me; but I couldn't catch his words, the bells drowned them. A minute later he was dead.

"Life's a funny thing! You wake in the morning with your foot firm on the ladder — One touch, and down you go! You snuff out like a candle. And it's lucky when your flame goes out, if only one woman's flame goes out too.

"Neither of those women cried. The wife stayed there by the bed. I got the other one away to her carriage, down the street. — And so she was there to-day! That explains, I think, the look you saw."

The doctor ceased; and in the silence the old Director nodded. Yes! That explained the look he had seen on the face of that unknown woman, the deep, unseizable, weird look. That explained the look he had seen on the wife's face at the funeral twenty years ago!

And peering wistfully, he said: —

"She looked — she looked — almost triumphant!"

Then, slowly, he rubbed his hands over his knees, with the secret craving of the old for warmth.

THE SUMMIT OF THE YEARS
by John Burroughs

THE longer I live the more my mind dwells upon the beauty and the wonder of the world. I hardly know which feeling leads, wonderment or admiration. After a man has passed the psalmist's deadline of seventy years, as Dr. Holmes called it, if he is of a certain temperament, he becomes more and more detached from the noise and turmoil of the times in which he lives. The passing hubbub in the street attracts him less and less; more and more he turns to the permanent, the fundamental, the everlasting. More and more is he impressed with life and nature in themselves, and the beauty and the grandeur of the voyage we are making on this planet. The burning questions and issues of the hour are for the new generations, in whom life burns intensely also.

My life has always been more or less detached from the life about me. I have not been a hermit, but my temperament and love of solitude, and a certain constitutional timidity and shrinking from all kinds of strife, have kept me in the by-paths rather than on the great highways of life. My talent, such as it is, is distinctly a by-path talent, or at most, a talent for green lanes and sequestered roadsides; but that which has most interested me in life, Nature, can be seen from lanes and by-paths better even than from the turnpike, where the dust and noise and the fast driving obscure the view or distract the attention. I have loved the feel of the grass under my feet, and the sound of the running streams by my side. The hum of the wind in the tree-tops has always been good music to me, and the face of the fields has often comforted me more than the faces of men.

In my tranquil seclusion I am often on the point of upbraiding myself because I keep so aloof from the struggles and contentions and acrimonious debates of the political, the social, and the industrial world about me. I do not join any of the noisy processions, I do not howl with the reformers, or cry Fire! with the alarmists. I say to myself, What is all this noisy civilization and all this rattling machinery of government for, but that men may all have just the sane and contented life that I am living, and on the same terms that I do. They can find it in the next field, beyond the next hill, in the town or in the country — a land of peace and plenty, if one has peace in his heart and the spirit of fair play in his blood.

Business, politics, government, are but the scaffoldings of our house of life; they are there that I may have a good roof over my head, and a warm and safe outlook into the beauty and glory of the universe, and let them not absorb more time and energy than the home itself. They have absorbed very little of mine, and I fancy that my house of life would have just as staunch walls, and just as many windows and doors, had they not absorbed so much of other men's. Let those who love turmoil arm for turmoil: their very arming will bring it; and let those who love peace disarm for peace: the disarming will hasten it. Those also serve who mind their own business and let others mind theirs.

I know that all this clamor and competition, all this heat and friction and turmoil of the world, are only the result of the fury with which we play the game of our civilization. It is like our college football, which is brutal and killing, and more like war than like sport. Why should I be more than an amused or a pained spectator?

I was never a fighter; I fear that at times I may have been a shirker, but I have shirked one thing or one duty that I might the more heart- ily give myself to another. He also serves who sometimes runs away.

From the summit of the years I look back over my life, and see what I have escaped and what I have missed, as a traveler might look back over his course from a mountain-top, and see where he had escaped a jungle or a wilderness or a desert, and where he had missed a fair field or a fountain, or pleasant habitations. I have escaped the soul-killing and body-wrecking occupations that are the fate of so many men in my time. I have escaped the greed of wealth, the "mania of owning things," as Whitman called it. I have escaped the disappointment of political ambition, of business ambition, of social ambition; I have never been a cog in anybody's wheel, or an attachment to the tail of anybody's kite. I have never lost myself in the procession of parties, or trained with any sect or clique. I have been fortunate in being allowed to go my own way in the world.

It is a question whether in escaping a college education I made a hit or a miss. I am inclined to the opinion that a little systematic training, especially in science, would have been a gain, though the systematic grind in literature which the college puts its students through, I am glad to have escaped. I thank heaven that in literature I have never had to dissect Shakespeare or Milton, or any other great poet, in the class-room, and that I have never had to dissect any animal in the laboratory. I have had the poets in their beautiful and stimulating unity and wholeness, and I have had the animals in the fields and woods in the joy of their natural activities. In my literary career I have escaped trying to write for the public or for editors; I have written for myself. I have not asked, "What does the public want?" I have only asked, "What do I want to say? What have I lived or felt or thought that is my own, and has its root in my inmost being?"

I have few of the aptitudes of the scholar, and fewer yet of the methodical habits and industry of the man of business. I live in books a certain part of each day, but less as a student of books than as a student of life. I go to books and to nature as a bee goes to the flower, for a nectar that I can make into my own honey. My memory for the facts and the arguments of books is poor, but my absorptive power is great.

There is no one, I suppose, who does not miss some good fortune in his life. We all miss congenial people, people who are going our way, and whose companionship would make life sweeter for us. Often we are a day too early, or a day too late, at the point where our paths cross. How many such congenial souls we miss we know not, but for my part, considering the number I have met, I think it may be many.

I have missed certain domestic good fortunes, such as a family of many children (I have only one), which might have made the struggle of life harder, but which would surely have brought its compensations. Those lives are, indeed, narrow and confined which are not blessed with several children. Every branch the tree puts out lays it open more to the storms and tempests of life; it lays it open also to the light and the sunshine, and to the singing and the mating birds. A childless life is a tree without branches, a house without windows.

I missed being a soldier in the armies of the Union during the Civil War, which was probably the greatest miss of my life. I think I had in me many of the qualities that go to the making of a good soldier — love of adventure, keenness of eye and ear, love of camp-life, ability to shift for myself, skill with the gun, and a sound constitution. But the rigidity of the military system, the iron rules, the mechanical unity and precision, the loss of the one in the many — all would have galled me terribly, though better men than I willingly, joyously, made themselves a part of the great military machine.

I got near enough to the firing line during our Civil War, — when Early made his demonstration against the Capital in 1864, and I was a clerk in the Treasury Department, — to know that I much prefer the singing of the birds to the singing of hostile bullets.

War is a terrible business.

II

From youth to age I have lived with nature more than with men. In youth I saw nature as a standing invitation to come forth and give play to myself; the streams were for fishing and swimming, the woods were for hunting and exploring, and for all kinds of sylvan adventure; the fields were for berries and birds' nests, and color, and the delight of the world of grasses; the mountains were for climbing and the prospects and the triumphs of their summits.

The world was good; it tasted good, it delighted all my senses. The seasons came and went, each with its own charms and enticements. I was ready for each and contented with each. The spring was for the delights of sugar-making, and the returning birds — the naked maple woods flooded with the warm creative sunshine, the brown fields slipping off their covering of snow, the loosened rills, the first robin, the first phœbe, the first song sparrow — how all these things thrilled one! The summer was for bare feet, light clothes, freedom from school, strawberries, trout, hay-making, and the Fourth of July. Autumn was for apples, nuts, wild pigeons, gray squirrels, and the great dreamy tranquil days; winter for the fireside, school, games, coasting, and the tonic of frost and snow. How the stars twinkled in winter! how the ice sang, and whooped on the ponds! how the snow sculpturing decked all the farm fences! how the sheeted winds stalked across the hills!

Oh, the eagerness and freshness of youth! How the boy enjoys his food, his sleep, his sports, his companions, his truant days! His life is an adventure, he is widening his outlook, he is extending his dominion, he is conquering his kingdom. How cheap are his pleasures, how ready his enthusiasms! In boyhood I have had more delight on a haymow with two companions and a big dog — delight that came nearer intoxication — than I have ever had in all the subsequent holidays of my life. When youth goes, much goes with it. When manhood comes, much comes with it. We exchange a world of delightful sensations and impressions for a world of duties and studies and meditations. The youth enjoys what the man tries to understand. Lucky is he who can get his grapes to market and keep the bloom upon them, who can carry some of the freshness and eagerness and simplicity of youth into his later years, who can have a boy's heart below a man's head.

The birds have always meant much to me; as a farm-boy they were like a golden thread that knit the seasons together. In early manhood I turned to them with the fondness of youth, reinforced with an impetus obtained from literature. Books, especially the poets, may do this for a man; they may consecrate a subject, give it the atmosphere of the ideal, and lift it up in the field of universal interest. They seem to have done something like that for me in relation to birds. I did not go to books for my knowledge of the birds, except for some technical knowledge, but I think literature helped to endow them with a human interest to me, and relate them to the deeper and purer currents of my life. What joy they have brought me! How they have given me wings to escape the tedious and the deadening! I have not studied them so much as I have played with them, camped with them, gone berrying with them, summered and wintered with them, and my knowledge of them has filtered into my mind almost unconsciously.

The bird as a piece of living nature is what interests me, having vital relations to all out-of-doors, and capable of linking my mind to itself and its surroundings with threads of delightful associations. The live bird is a fellow passenger; we are making the voyage together, and there is a sympathy between us that quickly leads to knowledge. If I looked upon it as something to be measured and weighed and tabulated, or as a subject for laboratory experimentation, my ornithology would turn to ashes in my hands.

The whole of nature, directly or indirectly, goes with him who gives his mind to objects in the open air. The observer of bird-life in the open has heaven and earth thrown in. Well, I need not harp on this string. All lovers of life in the open know what I would say. The book of living nature is unlike other books in this respect: one can read it over and over, and always find new passages and new meanings. It is a book that goes to press new every night, and comes forth fresh every morning.

III

I began by saying how much the beauty and wonder of the world occupies me these later years. How these things come home to me as life draws near the end. I am like a man who makes a voyage and falls so much in love with the ship and the sea that he thinks of little else and is not curious about the new lands before him. I suppose if my mind had dwelt much upon the other world toward which we are headed, and which is the main concern with so many passengers, I should have found less to absorb and instruct me in this. In fact, the hypothetical other world has scarcely occupied me at all, and when it has, I have thought of it as a projection from this, a kind of Brocken shadow cast by our love of life upon futurity. My whole being is so well, so exquisitely attuned to this world, that I have instinctively felt that it was for this world that I was made.

I have never been able to see how I could be adjusted to two worlds unless they were much alike. A better world I have never wanted. I could not begin to exhaust the knowledge and the delights of this one. I have found in it deep beneath deep, worlds within a world — an endless series of beautiful and wonderful forms forever flowing out of itself. From the highest heavens of the telescope, to the minutest organisms of the microscope, all is beautiful and wonderful, and passeth understanding.

1913
TO THE WATCHER
by Rabindranath Tagore

SHE is still a child, my lord. She runs about your palace and plays and tries to make you a plaything of her own.

When her hair tumbles down and her careless garment drags in the dust, she heeds not. When she builds her house with sands and decks her dolls with tinsels, she thinks she is doing great works.

Her elders warn her even not to hold you of small account. She is frightened, and she knows not how to serve you. Suddenly she starts up from her play and reminds herself she must do what she is bid.

She falls asleep when you speak to her, and answers not. And the flower you gave her in the morning slips to the dust from her hand.

When the storm bursts in the evening with a sudden clash and darkness is on land and sky, she is sleepless; her dolls lie scattered on the earth and she clings to you in terror.

We are ever afraid lest she should be guilty of remissness. But smiling you peep at the door of her playhouse, you watch her at her games, and you know her.

You know that the child sitting on dust is your destined bride. You know that all her play will end in love. For her you keep ready a jeweled seat in your house and precious honey in the golden jar.

1914
NEWSPAPER MORALS
by Henry L. Mencken

ASPIRING, toward the end of my nonage, to the black robes of a dramatic critic, I took counsel with an ancient whose service went back to the days of *Our American Cousin*, asking him what qualities were chiefly demanded by the craft.

"The main idea," he told me frankly, "is to be interesting, to write a good story. All else is dross. Of course, I am not against accuracy, fairness, information, learning. If you want to read Lessing and Frey-tag, Hazlitt and Brunetière, go read them: they will do you no harm. It is also useful to know something about Shakespeare. But unless you can make people *read* your criticisms, you may as well shut up your shop. And the only way to make them read you is to give them some-thing exciting."

"You suggest, then," I ventured, "a certain — ferocity?"

"I do," replied my venerable friend. . . . "Knock somebody in the head every day — if not an actor, then the author, and if not the author, then the manager. And if the play and the performance are perfect, then excoriate someone who doesn't think so — a fellow critic, a rival manager, the unappreciative public. But make it hearty; make it hot! . . . You must give a good show to get a crowd, and a good show means one with slaughter in it."

Destiny soon robbed me of my critical shroud, and I fell into a long succession of less æsthetic newspaper berths, from that of police re-porter to that of managing editor, but always the advice of my ancient counselor kept turning over and over in my memory, and as chance offered I began to act upon it, and whenever I acted upon it I found that it worked. What is more, I found that other newspaper men acted upon it too. . . . The primary aim of all of them . . . was to please the crowd, to give a good show; and the way they set about giving that good show was by first selecting a deserving victim, and then putting him magnificently to the torture. This was their method when they were performing for their own profit only, when their one motive was to make the public read their paper; but it was still their method when they were battling bravely and unselfishly for the public good, and so discharging the highest duty of their profession. They lightened the dull days of midsummer by pursuing recreant aldermen with blood-hounds and artillery, by muckraking unsanitary milk-dealers, or by denouncing Sunday liquor-selling in suburban parks — and they fought constructive campaigns for good government in exactly the same gothic, melodramatic way. Always their first aim was to find a concrete target, to visualize their cause in some definite and defiant opponent. And always their second aim was to shell that opponent until he dropped his arms and took to ignominious flight. . . .

Does this confession of newspaper practice involve a libel upon the American people? Perhaps it does — on the theory, let us say, that the greater the truth, the greater the libel. But I doubt if any reflective newspaper man, however lofty his professional ideals, will ever deny any essential part of that truth. He knows very well that a definite limit is set, not only upon the people's capacity for grasping intellectual concepts, but also upon their capacity for grasping moral concepts. . . . He knows that it is hard for the plain people to *think* about a thing, but

easy for them to *feel*. Error, to hold their attention, must be visualized
as a villain, and the villain must proceed swiftly to his inevitable retribution. They can understand that process; it is simple, usual, satisfying; it squares with their primitive conception of justice as a form of
revenge. . . .

It is the merit of the villain, pursued publicly by a *posse comitatus*,
that he makes the public breast the primary seat of heroism, that he
makes every citizen a personal participant in a glorious act of justice.
Wherefore it is ever the aim of the sagacious journalist to foster that
sense of personal participation. The wars that he wages are always
described as the people's wars, and he himself affects to be no more
than their strategist and *claque*. When the victory has once been
gained, true enough, he may take all the credit without a blush; but
while the fight is going on he always pretends that every honest yeo-
man is enlisted, and he is even eager to make it appear that the yeo-
manry began it on their own motion, and out of the excess of their
natural virtue.

I assume here, as an axiom too obvious to be argued, that the chief
appeal of a newspaper, in all such holy causes, is not at all to the
educated and reflective minority of citizens, but frankly to the ignorant and unreflective majority. The truth is that it would usually get a
newspaper nowhere to address its exhortations to the former, for in
the first place they are too few in number to make their support of
much value in general engagements, and in the second place it is
almost always impossible to convert them into disciplined and useful
soldiers. They are too cantankerous for that, too ready with embarrassing strategy of their own. One of the principal marks of an educated man, indeed, is the fact that he does *not* take his opinions from
newspapers — not, at any rate, from the militant, crusading newspapers. On the contrary, his attitude toward them is almost always one of
frank cynicism, with indifference as its mildest form and contempt as
its commonest. He knows that they are constantly falling into false
reasoning about the things within his personal knowledge, — that is,
within the narrow circle of his special education, — and so he assumes
that they make the same, or even worse errors about other things,
whether intellectual or moral. This assumption, it may be said at once,
is quite justified by the facts.

I know of no subject, in truth, save perhaps baseball, on which the
average American newspaper, even in the larger cities, discourses with
unfailing sense and understanding. Whenever the public journals presume to illuminate such a matter as municipal taxation, for example,
or the extension of local transportation facilities, or the punishment of
public or private criminals, or the control of public-service corporations, or the revision of city charters, the chief effect of their effort is

to introduce into it a host of extraneous issues, most of them wholly emotional, and so they contrive to make it unintelligible to all earnest seekers after the truth.

But it does not follow thereby that they also make it unintelligible to their special client, the man in the street. . . . He is not at all responsive to purely intellectual argument, even when its theme is his own ultimate benefit, for such argument quickly gets beyond his immediate interest and experience. But he *is* very responsive to emotional suggestion, particularly when it is crudely and violently made, and it is to this weakness that the newspapers must ever address their endeavors. . . .

In the reform campaigns which periodically rock our large cities, — and our small ones, too, — the newspapers habitually make use of this fact. Such campaigns are not intellectual wars upon erroneous principles, but emotional wars upon errant men: they always revolve around the pursuit of some definite, concrete, fugitive malefactor, or group of malefactors. That is to say, they belong to popular sport rather than to the science of government; the impulse behind them is always far more orgiastic than reflective. For good government in the abstract, the people of the United States seem to have no liking, or, at all events, no passion. . . . What the mob thirsts for is not good government in itself, but the merry chase of a definite exponent of bad government. The newspaper that discovers such an exponent — or, more accurately, the newspaper that discovers dramatic and overwhelming evidence against him — has all the material necessary for a reform wave of the highest emotional intensity. All that it need do is to goad the victim into a fight. Once he has formally joined the issue, the people will do the rest. They are always ready for a man-hunt, and their favorite quarry is the man of politics. If no such prey is at hand, they will turn to wealthy debauchees, to fallen Sunday-school superintendents, to money barons, to white-slave traders, to unsedulous chiefs of police. But their first choice is the boss.

In assaulting bosses, however, a newspaper must look carefully to its ammunition, and to the order and interrelation of its salvos. There is such a thing, at the start, as overshooting the mark, and the danger thereof is very serious. The people must be aroused by degrees, gently at first, and then with more and more ferocity. . . . One fact at a time! If a newspaper printed the whole story of a political boss's misdeeds in a single article, that article would have scarcely any effect whatever, for it would be far too long for the average reader to read and absorb. . . . He cannot read more than three columns of any one subject without tiring: 6,000 words, I should say, is the extreme limit of his appetite. And the nearer he is pushed to that limit, the greater the strain upon his psychic digestion. He can absorb a single capital fact, leaping from a headline, at one colossal gulp; but he could not down a disser-

tation in twenty. And the first desideratum in a headline is that it deal
with a single and capital fact. It must be "McGinnis Steals
$1,257,867.25," not "McGinnis Lacks Ethical Sense."

Moreover, a newspaper article which presumed to tell the whole of a
thrilling story in one gargantuan installment would lack the dynamic
element, the quality of mystery and suspense. . . . The newspaper in
charge of the business must harrow him, tease him, promise him, hold
him. It is thus that his indignation is transformed from a state of being
into a state of gradual and cumulative becoming; it is thus that reform
takes on the character of a hotly contested game, with the issue agree-
ably in doubt. And it is always as a game, of course, that the man in
the street views moral endeavor. Whether its proposed victim be a
political boss, a police captain, a gambler, a fugitive murderer, or a
disgraced clergyman, his interest in it is almost purely a sporting interest. And the intensity of that interest, of course, depends upon the
fierceness of the clash. The game is fascinating in proportion as the
morally pursued puts up a stubborn defense, and in proportion as the
newspaper directing the pursuit is resourceful and merciless, and in
proportion as the eminence of the quarry is great and his resultant
downfall spectacular. A war against a ward boss seldom attracts much
attention, even in the smaller cities, for he is insignificant to begin with
and an inept and cowardly fellow to end with; but the famous war
upon William M. Tweed shook the whole nation, for he was a man of
tremendous power, he was a brave and enterprising antagonist, and
his fall carried a multitude of other men with him. Here, indeed, was
sport royal. . . .

But once such a buccaneer is overhauled and manacled, the show is
over, and the people take no further interest in reform. In place of
the fallen boss, a so-called reformer has been set up. He goes into
office with public opinion apparently solidly behind him: there is every promise that the improvement achieved will be lasting. But experience shows that it seldom is. . . . The mob has been fed, for weeks
preceding the reformer's elevation, upon the blood of big and little
bosses; it has acquired a taste for their chase, and for the chase in
general. Now, of a sudden, it is deprived of that stimulating sport.
The old bosses are in retreat; there are yet no new bosses to belabor
and pursue; the newspapers which elected the reformer are busily
apologizing for his amateurish errors, — a dull and dispiriting business. No wonder it now becomes possible for the old bosses, acting
through their inevitable friends on the respectable side, . . . to start the
rabble against the reformer. . . . How easy to convince it that the reformer is a scoundrel himself, that he is as bad as any of the old
bosses, that he ought to go to the block for high crimes and misde-
meanors! It never had any actual love for him, or even any faith in

him; his election was a mere incident of the chase of his predecessor. No wonder that it falls upon him eagerly, butchering him to make a new holiday!

This is what has happened over and over again in every large American city — Chicago, New York, St. Louis, Cincinnati, Pittsburg, New Orleans, Baltimore, San Francisco, St. Paul, Kansas City. Every one of these places has had its melodramatic reform campaigns and its inevitable reactions. The people have leaped to the overthrow of bosses, and then wearied of the ensuing tedium. . . .

Such is the ebb and flow of emotion in the popular heart — or perhaps, if we would be more accurate, the popular liver. It does not constitute an intelligible system of morality, for morality, at bottom, is not at all an instinctive matter, but a purely intellectual matter: its essence is the control of impulse by an ideational process, the subordination of the immediate desire to the distant aim. But such as it is, it is the only system of morality that the emotional majority is capable of comprehending and practicing; and so the newspapers, which deal with majorities quite as frankly as politicians deal with them, have to admit it into their own system. That is to say, they cannot accomplish anything by talking down to the public from a moral plane higher than its own: they must take careful account of its habitual ways of thinking, its moral thirsts and prejudices, its well-defined limitations. They must remember clearly, as judges and lawyers have to remember it, that the morality subscribed to by that public is far from the stern and arctic morality of professors of the science. On the contrary, it is a mellower and more human thing; it has room for the antithetical emotions of sympathy and scorn; it makes no effort to separate the criminal from his crime. The higher moralities, running up to that of Puritans and archbishops, allow no weight to custom, to general reputation, to temptation; they hold it to be no defense of a ballot-box stuffer, for example, that he had scores of accomplices and that he is kind to his little children. But the popular morality regards such a defense as sound and apposite.

Hence the need of a careful and wary approach in all newspaper crusades, particularly on the political side. . . .

I have written of popular morality copiously, and of newspaper morality very little. But . . . the one is the other. The newspaper must adapt its pleading to its clients' moral limitations, just as the trial lawyer must adapt *his* pleading to the jury's limitations. Neither may like the job, but both must face it to gain a larger end. And that end, I believe, is a worthy one in the newspaper's case quite as often as in the lawyer's, and perhaps far oftener. The art of leading the vulgar, in itself, does no discredit to its practitioner. Lincoln practiced it unashamed, and so did Webster, Clay, and Henry. What is more, these men practiced it with frank allowance for the naïveté of the people they presumed to lead. It was Lincoln's chief source of strength, indeed, that he had a homely way with him, that he could reduce complex problems to the simple terms of popular theory and emotion, that he did not ask little fishes to think and act like whales.

This is the manner in which the newspapers do their work, and in the long run, I am convinced, they accomplish far more good than harm thereby. Dishonesty, of course, is not unknown among them: we have newspapers in this land which apply a truly devilish technical skill to the achievement of unsound and unworthy ends. But not as many of them as perfectionists usually allege. Taking one with another, they strive in the right direction. . . .

The way of ethical progress is not straight. It describes, to risk a mathematical pun, a sort of drunken hyperbola. But if we thus move onward and upward by leaps and bounces, it is certainly better than not moving at all. Each time, perhaps, we slip back, but each time we stop at a higher level.

1915
A GROUP OF POEMS
by Robert Frost

BIRCHES

WHEN I see birches bend to left and right
Across the lines of straighter darker trees,
I like to think some boy's been swinging them.
But swinging doesn't bend them down to stay.
Ice-storms do that. Often you must have seen them
Loaded with ice a sunny winter morning
After a rain. They click upon themselves
As the breeze rises, and turn many-colored
As the stir cracks and crazes their enamel.
Soon the sun's warmth makes them shed crystal shells
Shattering and avalanching on the snow-crust —
Such heaps of broken glass to sweep away
You'd think the inner dome of heaven had fallen.
They are dragged to the withered bracken by the load
And they seem not to break; though once they are bowed
So low for long they never right themselves:
You may see their trunks arching in the woods
Years afterwards, trailing their leaves on the ground

Like girls on hands and knees that throw their hair
Before them over their heads to dry in the sun.
But I was going to say when truth broke in
With all her matter-of-fact about the ice-storm,
(Now am I free to be poetical?)
I should prefer to have some boy bend them
As he went out and in to fetch the cows —
Some boy too far from town to learn baseball,
Whose only play was what he found himself,
Summer or winter, and could play alone.
One by one he subdued his father's trees
By riding them down over and over again
Until he took the stiffness out of them
And not one but hung limp, not one was left
For him to conquer. He learned all there was
To learn about not launching out too soon
And so not carrying the tree away
Clear to the ground. He always kept his poise
To the top branches, climbing carefully
With the same pains you use to fill a cup
Up to the brim, and even above the brim.
Then he flung outward, feet first, with a swish,
Kicking his way down through the air to the ground.
So was I once myself a swinger of birches.
And so I dream of going back to be.
It's when I'm weary of considerations,
And life is too much like a pathless wood
Where your face burns and tickles with the cobwebs
Broken across it, and one eye is weeping
From a twig's having lashed across it open.
I'd like to get away from earth awhile
And then come back to it and begin over.
May no fate willfully misunderstand me
And half grant what I wish and snatch me away
Not to return. Earth's the right place for love:
I don't know where it's likely to go better.
I'd like to go by climbing a birch tree,
And climb black branches up a snow-white trunk
Toward heaven, till the tree could bear no more,
But dipped its top and set me down again.
That would be good both going and coming back.
One could do worse than be a swinger of birches.

THE ROAD NOT TAKEN

Two roads diverged in a yellow wood,
And sorry I could not travel both
And be one traveler, long I stood
And looked down one as far as I could
To where it bent in the undergrowth;

Then took the other, as just as fair,
And having perhaps the better claim
Because it was grassy and wanted wear,
Though as for that the passing there
Had worn them really about the same,

And both that morning equally lay
In leaves no step had trodden black.
Oh, I marked the first for another day!
Yet knowing how way leads on to way
I doubted if I should ever come back.

I shall be telling this with a sigh
Somewhere ages and ages hence:
Two roads diverged in a wood, and I,
I took the one less traveled by,
And that has made all the difference.

THE SOUND OF TREES

I WONDER about the trees:
Why do we wish to bear
Forever the noise of these
More than another noise
So close to our dwelling place?
We suffer them by the day
Till we lose all measure of pace
And fixity in our joys,
And acquire a listening air.
They are that that talks of going
But never gets away;
And that talks no less for knowing,
As it grows wiser and older,
That now it means to stay.
My feet tug at the floor
And my head sways to my shoulder

Sometimes when I watch trees sway
From the window or the door.
I shall set forth for somewhere,
I shall make the reckless choice,
Some day when they are in voice
And tossing so as to scare
The white clouds over them on.
I shall have less to say,
But I shall be gone.

1916
WAR AND THE SEXES
by Ellen Key

THE first year of the war was nearing its close when a middle-aged American woman, visiting in my home, said to me, "Nowhere will the war bring about a more radical change, more unexpected changes, than in the relations between the sexes. What way out will be found by the millions of women who more than ever must give up all hope of realizing their longing for love and children?"

A few months later I had with me another American woman, — this time a young girl, — who put the same question, only with the alteration natural to her age. "What will become of all us young girls who formerly could reasonably expect to marry, but who now see our chances infinitely diminished?"

The answer can only be this: —

After the war, woman's prospects, from the point of view of her natural duty — motherhood — will be dark indeed.

The number of women who will have to dismiss all thought of marriage — already far too large — is destined to become much larger still. The number of those who lead immoral lives and are childless, or who bear illegitimate children, will therefore increase. Others, from a sense of patriotic duty to which appeal has already been made, may marry invalids. How many of these will be disappointed in their most justified wishes for happiness! Those women who have chosen among the men who are rejected from military service quite often have defective children. The possibilities for millions of women who are now at the most favorable age for marriage decrease steadily, for with every day that goes by the number of young men who might return from the war without severe bodily or mental injuries grows less and less — not to mention the millions who will never return. And, lastly, the higher the development of women, the more they chafe under the "patriotic" mandate to bear many children to replace the nation's losses. For they know that, from the point of view of their personal development as well as that of the race, *fewer* but *better* children are to be preferred.

II

A considerable number of plans have already been suggested in Europe to relieve the abnormal sex-conditions, which have, of course, met with much formidable opposition.

Some one in London has conceived the idea of founding a "society for the marrying of wounded heroes" — an appeal to woman's self-sacrifice and patriotism to make the lives of these men bearable and to propagate children who will inherit their fathers' qualities of heroism. These wives, who would, in most cases, have to become the supporters of their families, would, therefore, be paid a man's wages and would, in many cases, also be given a stipend to facilitate their marriage. Moreover, in order to insure suitable mating, it is suggested that recourse be had to selective committees of clergymen and physicians; it is evidently not proposed to let the parties themselves choose. Women who are physically strong will be expected to marry men who need to be carried or pushed in a chair. Blind men, who can still at least enjoy good food, will be married to good cooks, and so forth.

It seems impossible to believe the statement that the society already has hundreds of thousands of female members.

In Germany some one has suggested that the government give invalids an opportunity to own their homes. This would enable the heroes of the war to found families — for it is to be expected that thousands of heroic women who are widowed by the war will remarry these invalids. Another thoughtful German has suggested that the government open a marriage department, partly to further early marriages.

The fact that the battlefields swallow up millions of lives makes the birth-rate a national question and revolutionizes ideas of sexual morality. What was formerly considered a sin — loveless marriages contracted simply for the purpose of having offspring — will perhaps, from the national point of view, come to be considered a duty hereafter. The bearing of children outside of marriage, and perhaps other deviations from the ideal of monogamy, will be practiced openly after the war to a far greater extent than was done secretly by people of Europe before the war. Twenty months of war have already dealt heavier blows to the foundations of "Holy Marriage" than all the "apostles of immorality" were able to compass. That all new forms of sex-relation will not be *officially* sanctioned is self-evident, but they may have the sanction of custom; and this, in some cases, means more than the approval of the State.

Another moral question that was previously discussed — that of birth-prevention — has come up again during the war. In East Prussia the question has been discussed as to whether the law against abortion should be suspended for those women who fell victims to the Russian soldiers. And in France, where many women have, with great suffering, borne the children of their enemies, some people still advocate preventive measures; some one even suggested killing these children, in order to ensure the purity of the race. Surely one cannot go further from the ideals of Christian morality! And though these suggestions have been rejected, the mere fact that they have been discussed proved what this whole war has so clearly shown: that the religion of Europe is no longer that of *Christianity* but that of *nationalism,* and that everything that is considered good for the nation is assumed to be right.

Among the nations so heavily oppressed by the war, it will inevitably be necessary to count on a far greater number of women having to become self-supporting than formerly. This will bring about very radical changes in the community, in economic conditions, in family life, and in the increase of population. Family life, during the next generations, will be more sober, more prosaic. The death of so many men will, to a certain extent, do away with competition between the sexes, but also with marriage. The number of illegitimate children will increase, but they will be better cared for. On the whole, the increase of population will be hindered by woman's inability both to bear and provide for children, and to those who look upon woman as the producer of soldiers, this will seem a misfortune. To those, however, who look upon the matter in a more human way, it will, on the contrary, *become a condition for future development that women resolutely refuse mass production of children,* and more consistently seek to improve the quality of humanity, while they, at the same time, try more energetically to procure the right to have a share in dictating the politics on which the lives of their sons and daughters are so dependent.

1917
INDIVIDUAL LIBERTY AND PUBLIC CONTROL
by Bertrand Russell

SOCIETY cannot exist without law and order, and cannot advance except through the initiative of vigorous innovators. Yet law and order are always hostile to innovations, and innovators are almost always to some extent anarchists. Those whose minds are dominated by fear of a relapse toward barbarism will emphasize the importance of law and order, while those who are inspired by the hope of an advance toward civilization will usually be more conscious of the need of individual initiative. Both temperaments are necessary, and wisdom lies in allowing each to operate freely where it is beneficent. But those who are on the side of law and order, since they are reinforced by custom and the instinct for upholding the *status quo,* have no need of a reasoned defense. It is the innovators who have difficulty in being allowed to exist and work. Each generation believes that this difficulty is a thing of the past, but each generation is tolerant only of *past* innovations. Those of its own day are met with the same persecution as if the principle of toleration had never been heard of.

On any matter of general interest, there is usually in any given community, at any given time, a received opinion, which is accepted as a matter of course by all who give no special thought to the matter. Any questioning of the received opinion arouses hostility, for a number of reasons.

The most important of these is the instinct of conventionality, which exists in all gregarious animals, and often leads them to put to death any markedly peculiar member of the herd. The next most important is the feeling of insecurity aroused by doubt as to the beliefs by which we are in the habit of regulating our lives. Whoever has tried to explain the philosophy of Berkeley to a plain man will have seen in its unadulterated form the anger aroused by this feeling. What the plain man derives from Berkeley's philosophy at a first hearing is an uncomfortable suspicion that nothing is solid, so that it is rash to sit on a chair or to expect the floor to sustain us. Because this suspicion is uncomfortable it is irritating, except to those who regard the whole argument as merely nonsense. And in a more or less analogous way any questioning of what has been taken for granted destroys the feeling of standing on solid ground, and produces a condition of bewildered fear.

A third reason which makes men dislike novel opinions is, that vested interests are bound up with old beliefs. The long fight of the Church against science, from Giordano Bruno to Darwin, is attributable to this motive, among others. The horror of socialism which existed in the remote past was entirely attributable to this cause. But it would be a mistake to assume, as is done by those who seek economic motives everywhere, that vested interests are the principal source of anger against novelties in thought. If this were the case, intellectual progress would be much more rapid than it is. The instinct of conventionality, horror of uncertainty, and vested interests, all militate against the acceptance of a new idea. And it is even harder to think of a new idea than to get it accepted: most people might spend a lifetime in reflection without ever making a genuinely original discovery.

In view of all these obstacles, it is not likely that any society at any time will suffer from a plethora of heretical opinions. Least of all is this likely in a modern civilized society, where the conditions of life are in constant rapid change, and demand, for successful adaptation, an equally rapid change in intellectual outlook. There should, therefore, be an attempt to encourage rather than discourage the expression of new beliefs and the dissemination of knowledge tending to support them. But the very opposite is in fact the case. From childhood upwards, everything is done to make the minds of men and women conventional and sterile. And if, by misadventure, some spark of imagination remains, its unfortunate possessor is considered unsound and dangerous, worthy only of contempt in time of peace and of prison or a traitor's death in time of war. Yet such men are known to have been in the past the chief benefactors of mankind, and are the very men who receive most honor as soon as they are safely dead.

The whole realm of thought and opinion is utterly unsuited to public control: it ought to be as free, and as spontaneous, as is possible to those who know what others have believed. The state is justified in insisting that children shall be educated, but it is not justified in forcing their education to proceed on a uniform plan and to be directed to the production of a dead level of glib uniformity. Education, and the life of the mind generally, is a matter in which individual initiative is the chief thing needed; the function of the state should begin and end with insistence on *some* kind of education, and, if possible, a kind which promotes mental individualism, not a kind which happens to conform to the prejudices of government officials.

II

Questions of practical morals raise more difficult problems than questions of mere opinion. The Thugs of India honestly believe it their duty to commit murders, but the government does not acquiesce. Conscientious objectors honestly hold the opposite opinion, and again the government does not acquiesce. The punishment of conscientious objectors seems clearly a violation of individual liberty within its legitimate sphere.

It is generally assumed without question that the state has a right to punish certain kinds of sexual irregularity. No one doubts that the Mormons sincerely believed polygamy to be a desirable practice, yet the United States required them to abandon its legal recognition, and probably any other Christian country would have done likewise. Nevertheless, I do not think this prohibition was wise. Polygamy is legally permitted in many parts of the world, but is not much practiced except by chiefs and potentates. I think that in all such cases the law should intervene only when there is some injury inflicted without the consent of the injured person.

It is obvious that men and women would not tolerate having their wives or husbands selected by the state, whatever eugenists might have to say in favor of such a plan. In this, it seems clear that ordinary public opinion is in the right, not because people choose wisely, but because any choice of their own is better than a forced marriage. What applies to marriage ought also to apply to the choice of a trade or profession: although some men have no marked preferences, most men greatly prefer some occupations to others, and are far more likely to be useful citizens if they follow their preferences than if they are thwarted by a public authority.

III

We may now arrive at certain general principles in regard to individual liberty and public control.

The greater part of human impulses may be divided into two classes, those which are possessive and those which are constructive or creative. Property is the direct expression of possessiveness; science and art are among the most direct expressions of creativeness. Possessiveness is either defensive or aggressive: it seeks either to retain something against a robber, or to acquire something from a present holder. In either case, an attitude of hostility to others is of its essence.

The whole realm of the possessive impulses, and of the use of force to which they give rise, stands in need of control by a public neutral authority, in the interests of liberty no less than of justice. Within a nation, this public authority will naturally be the state; in relations between nations, if the present anarchy is to cease, it will have to be some international parliament. But the motive underlying the public control of men's possessive impulses should always be the increase of liberty, both by the prevention of private tyranny, and by the liberation of creative impulses. If public control is not to do more harm than good, it must be so exercised as to leave the utmost freedom of private initiative in all ways that do not involve the private use of force. In this respect, all governments have always failed egregiously, and there is no evidence that they are improving.

The creative impulses, unlike those that are possessive, are directed to ends in which one man's gain is not another man's loss. The man who makes a scientific discovery or writes a poem is enriching others at the same time as himself. Any increase in knowledge or good-will is a gain to all who are affected by it, not only to the actual possessor. Force cannot create such things, though it can destroy them; no principle of distributive justice applies to them, since the gain of each is the gain of all. For these reasons, the creative part of a man's activity ought to be as free as possible from all public control, in order that it may remain spontaneous and full of vigor. The only function of the state in regard to this part of the individual life should be to do everything possible toward providing outlets and opportunities.

Huge organizations, both political and economic, are one of the distinguishing characteristics of the modern world. These organizations have immense power, and often use their power to discourage originality in thought and action. They ought, on the contrary, to give the freest scope that is possible without producing anarchy or violent conflict.

The problem which faces the modern world is the combination of individual initiative with the increase in the scope and size of organizations. Unless it is solved, individuals will grow less and less full of life and vigor, more and more passively submissive to conditions imposed upon them. A society composed of such individuals cannot be progressive, or add much to the world's stock of mental and spiritual possessions.

Only personal liberty and the encouragement of initiative can secure these things. Those who resist authority when it encroaches upon the legitimate sphere of the individual are performing a service to society, however little society may value it. In regard to the past, this is universally acknowledged; but it is no less true in regard to the present and the future.

1918

ORDINARY SEAMEN, U.S.N.
by Joseph Husband

FORTY miles north of Chicago, on the high bluffs that overlook Lake Michigan, the Naval Training Station of the Great Lakes stretches a mile back to the railroad tracks from a mile frontage on the shore; and even beyond the tracks the latest additions have crept out on the rolling prairie. Here, covering approximately three hundred acres, the vast camp, with its recent additions to meet the war emergency, houses an average total of 22,000 men — the largest and most complete naval training establishment in the world.

There had been a heavy blizzard in Chicago the first week in January, and when, on the eighth, I walked up from the railroad station to the great brick entrance, the ground was deep with snow. Beyond the iron gates, hundreds of jackies in white trousers and blue pea-coats were piling the snow back from roads and sidewalks. From the entrance a long, straight road stretched almost to the lake. On either side, and back as far as the eye could see, the substantial brick buildings of the station extended in orderly arrangement, like the buildings of a modern university. At the far end the tall, massive clock-tower of the Administration Building rose red against the blue winter sky. High above it, to the right, the slender tapering towers of the wireless caught their swinging cobwebs of wires up four hundred feet against the blue. Below, everywhere, the red brick buildings and the glitter of sun-touched snow in zero air.

In the recruiting building a long line of men already were waiting to swear their loyalty to Uncle Sam's Navy, and merciless hostility to his enemies. One by one we filed into the recruiting-room, where a dozen jackies, in neat uniforms with their yeomen's ratings on their blue sleeves, shamed our motley civilian clothes by contrast. Short and tall, stout and thin, from Texas, Ohio, Colorado, and Minnesota, in cheap "sport suits," sweaters, caps, derbies, every kind of clothing, with broken dress-suit-cases, cord-bound, with paper bundles, and many with hands empty — here was young America in its infinite variety.

To the room where physical examinations were held we were passed along with our identifying papers. Yellow sunshine shone warmly through high windows; there was the moist smell of steam radiators, and the unmistakable and indescribable smell of naked bodies which threw my recollection back to school and college gymnasia. At a desk by the window the surgeon faced the room; two assistants stood beside him; along the side of the room three or four yeomen at tables recorded the results of the examination.

The test was severe, and from our little squad of seventeen, two were cast out for defective eyesight, one for stricture, two for heart trouble, and another for some imperfection of the foot. Weighed, measured, tested for eyesight and color-sight, identified by scars and blemishes, we dressed and then recorded our finger-prints on the voluminous record, which grew as the examination progressed. It was late afternoon and the electric lights were lighted when we finally stood before the desk of the last officer, and, with right hand lifted, touched the Book with our left and swore to follow the flag by sea or land wherever the fate of war might call us.

I had come in my oldest suit, which I planned to throw away as soon as my sailor clothes were issued; and I was a little disappointed to find that I should not get my uniform my first day in camp.

A white hammock, a blue mattress (which also serves as a life-preserver at sea), a white cotton mattress-cover, two thick white blankets, and a large bath-towel were immediately given to me, and these were plainly stenciled with my name in black paint, in letters an inch high. With this cumbersome bundle on one shoulder, and in my hand the ancient satchel that I had brought, containing a few toilet articles, I followed my guide to the barrack designated as my home for the three weeks to come.

The barrack was only half occupied, and I was warmly greeted by the men. The barrack "chief," appointed by the company commander from among the first recruits in the barrack, whose luckless job is to maintain order and neatness among his fellows, without powers of punishment, welcomed me and showed me how to lay my mattress in my hammock, fold my blankets so that my name showed clearly, and hang my towel in an equally exact location on the foot lashings of the hammock.

"Chow!"

It was only half-past four, but Jack is an early riser, retires early, and must be fed accordingly, with breakfast at six-thirty, dinner at eleven-thirty, and supper at four-thirty. Through the open door two of my new comrades suddenly appeared, with a great cylinder swinging between them. Behind them another lugged a huge can, like the old-fashioned milk-can but more complicated in construction, while a fourth carried four long loaves of white bread in his arms.

We sat down at the long table, and my first meal in the Navy was consumed with alacrity. Beans are usually served at one meal a day — big red mealy beans, cooked almost to a soupy consistency. Coffee, tea, and cocoa are served daily, coffee with breakfast and dinner, and tea or cocoa at night; but for some reason unknown to me, all are indiscriminately called "Java." We have meat, usually in a stew, at least twice a day, and always two vegetables with dinner. Bread is provided with every meal, and butter with breakfast. Two or three times a week we have excellent cereal with breakfast, and on the other days soup with dinner. Jam is often served with supper, and we have fresh apples or stewed fruit daily.

II

Our barrack contains a strange assortment of men, but perhaps no stranger than every other barrack in the camp. Here are two Texas boys, who, during the extreme weather of the past few days, have clung tenaciously to the radiators. One was a farmer-boy, another a fireman on a southern railroad. The head bell-boy of a Middle-West hotel swings in a hammock near my own, and on one side of me is a lithe, alert, blond-haired young man of perhaps four and twenty, who in his vicarious career has peddled papers, "ridden the rods," bumming from town to town, driven a motor-truck, won his laurels as a successful prize-fighter, and waited on the table in a city cabaret — of all the men he is one of the most attractive, with a lively humor, a pleasant manner, and a quick sense of fair play. He joined the Navy, he told me, because it "offered him the finest opportunity to make a real man of himself."

Another interesting character is a young Wisconsin farmer-boy. Of French descent, from the old Green Bay settlement, he has developed a rugged American character, the result of the purification and enrichment of the blood of an ancient nation by three generations of labor on our north-western frontier. His bursts of wild laughter and rough horse-play are constantly blended with sentiment when mention is made of the finer things of life, and with a frank affection for those who show their friendship. He was the joint owner of a small farm, which he gave up to join the Navy.

I must not forget to mention the pessimist of our little company. Away for the first time from home, he weathered the early anguish of nostalgia to settle into a fixed atmosphere of constant gloom. It was he who gathered voluminous data regarding supposititious sickness in the camp, although it would be hard to find anywhere so large a number of men in such splendid health. It was he who always told with sour visage the latest camp-gossip if it held bad future omens. I last saw him on the way to the camp hospital, where he was to have his tonsils removed; and I think he was really complacent in contemplation of his discomfort to come.

Of the eastern colleges, Amherst and Harvard are represented in our barrack each by a graduate, and there are a number of boys from various western state universities. A painter, whose good-natured laziness and rotund figure immediately won him the nickname of "Butterfly," a hotel clerk, the assistant purchasing agent of a large automobile company, a carpenter, a bond salesman, and a number of youthful clerks and office-boys complete our numbers. It is interesting to find how many of the recruits are under draft age.

It is still dark with the blackness of five o'clock when the barrack chief calls us in the morning with his "Hit the deck, boys." Five minutes to tumble out into the brilliance of the electric lights flashed on sleeping eyes, fold our blankets, lash up our hammocks, and get out our toilet articles, is all the time allowed. In line we answer to our names, and then a rush to the shower-baths, with much friendly "joshing" and cheering as those hardy ones who turn on the cold water spatter the crowd.

As soon as we are dressed comes the first of our three daily housecleanings. After the entire room is swept out, all the cracks and corners are cleaned with water and a stiff broom, and then dried with a cloth. Then the floor is mopped and dried, and the whole room carefully dusted. The same complete cleansing is at the same time given to the "head" or wash-room, the scullery, and the vestibule; and after dinner and supper the operation is repeated. At least twice a week all the windows are washed, and a weekly scrubbing is administered to our benches and tables.

For four days we cleared the ground immediately about our barracks of the winter's accumulation of snow, which had piled about the buildings in four- or five-foot drifts. With huge improvised sleds, carts, boxes, and every possible kind of receptacle, the forty-eight men in the two barracks beneath our roof loaded the snow and dragged it to a near-by ravine. Under a bright sun shining in a cloudless sky, hundreds of Jackies from the other barracks, like the uniformed students of some great university, dashed up and down the slippery roads with frequent collisions and endless merriment.

Our company commander is a fine big Texan, with a soft southern inflection, a ready smile, and a rigidity of purpose that compels prompt obedience. As likely as not he will appear at five in the morning to catch the laggard riser, or at midnight to check the man on watch in the barrack-room. By day he is our counselor and guide and drill-master. Under his crisp commands the long blue-clad lines tramp back and forth across the snow-packed drill-ground. "Squads right into line, march!" and we swing sharply past him. A dozen other companies are drilling also, under their respective commanders. It is an inspiring scene.

Each evening we sit at the long white-scrubbed pine mess-table and write letters home, read, study, and sew. Then there is laundry work to be done, for we seem to take pride in washing our own clothes, as it will soon be necessary for us to do on shipboard. Occasionally we have an entertainment, which consists of the Y.M.C.A. phonograph with its dozen worn records, an impromptu sparring bout, or, more often, an improvised band with a strange variety of instruments, to which all keep time with tapping feet and cheers for "Dixie" and "Columbia, the Gem of the Ocean." By nine we are ready for our hammocks. Sometimes during the night I wake with a sudden start, and my thoughts carry me far away before sleep comes again. I am sure that there are many such thoughts here, although such things are rarely mentioned.

It was a bright blue morning and the sun was still stalking low behind the trees, when a bugle-note brought me suddenly to a halt. I was passing a turn in the road when it reached me. Everywhere bluecoated men and boys were working; their voices sounded here and there, word-snatches on the breeze. Half a mile away, against the pale western sky, a flagstaff pointed high above the green buildings. Fluttering, a flag was mounting to the peak. I stiffened and a shiver seemed to pass through me, the same emotional shiver that comes when the band goes by. My hand snapped to salute; the flag reached the peak, and the red stripes and star-flecked blue stood out against the sky.

SQUADRONS OF THE AIR
by Charles Bernard Nordhoff

THESE are strenuous days — I have done nothing but fly, eat, and sleep for a fortnight. Our "traveling circus" has been living up to its name — going about from place to place with amazing mobility and speed. I have lived for a week with no baggage but the little bag I carry in my plane. It contains one change of light underwear, one pair of socks, tooth-brush, tooth-paste, tobacco, sponge, soap, towel, shaving things, mirror, a first-aid kit, and a bottle of eau de cologne. With this I can weather a few days anywhere until the baggage-trucks catch up.

Our mobility is marvelous — we can receive our orders at daybreak, breakfast, and land in a place a hundred miles away in an hour and a half. Then a little oil and petrol, and we are ready to bounce something off the local Boche. I could easily write a large calf-bound volume on nothing but my experiences of the past week — one of the most strangely fascinating (in retrospect) of my life, though saddened by the loss of two of our pilots, one an American.

We had no sooner got to this place than we were sent out on a patrol — six of us, with a French lieutenant, a special friend of mine, as flight-commander. None of us had flown before in this sector, and a young American was making his second flight over the lines. The weather was wretched, thick, low-hanging clouds with a fine drizzle of rain — visibility almost zero. While mechanics filled the machine, I pored over my map till I had all necessary landmarks thoroughly in mind. At last the captain glanced at his watch and shouted, *"En voiture!"*

I climbed into my tiny cockpit, loaded my gun with a snap of the lever, wiped the sights free of moisture, and sank back in my seat, while my mechanic adjusted the belt which holds one tight in place. Up went the captain's hand, and almost with a single roar the six motors started. One after another we rushed across the field, rose to the low ceiling of the clouds, and swept back, bunched like a flock of teal. The flight-commander's head, a black leather dot in his cockpit, turned swiftly for a glance back. All there and well grouped; so he headed for the lines, flying so low that we seemed to shave the spires of village churches. Soon the houses ceased to have roofs — we were over the front.

A great battle was raging below us — columns of smoke rose from the towns and the air was rocked and torn by the passage of projectiles. Soon we were far into the German lines; deep coughs came from the air about us as patches of black sprang out. But we were too low and our speed was too great to be bothered by the Boche gunners. Suddenly the clouds broke for an instant, and across the blue hole I saw a dozen Albatrosses driving toward us — German single-seaters, dark ugly brutes with broad short wings and pointed snouts. Our leader saw them too, and we bounded upward three hundred feet, turning to meet them. The rest happened so swiftly that I can scarcely describe it coherently. Out of the tail of my eye I saw our leader dive on an Albatross, which plunged spinning to the ground. At the same instant I bounded upward to the clouds and dropped on a Boche who was attacking a comrade. I could see my gun spitting streams of luminous bullets into the German's fuselage. But suddenly swift incandescent sparks began to pour past me, and a glance backward showed three Albatrosses on my tail. I turned upside down, pulled back, and did a hairpin turn, rising, to get behind them. Not a German machine was in sight — they had melted away as suddenly as they came.

Far off to the south four of our machines were heading back toward the lines. Feeling very lonely and somewhat *de trop*, I opened the throttle wide and headed after them. Just as I caught up, the leader signaled that he was done for, and glided off, with his propeller stopped. Praying that he might get safely across to our side, I fell in behind the second in command. Only four now — who and where was the other? Anxiously I ranged alongside of each machine for a look at its number. As I had feared, it was the American — a hot-headed, fearless boy, full of courage and confidence, but inexperienced and not a skillful pilot. No word of him since. Did he lose the patrol in a sharp turn and get brought down by a prowling gang of Albatrosses, or did he have motor-trouble which forced him to land in the enemy lines? These are the questions we ask ourselves, hoping for the best.

An hour after we landed at our field, a telephone message came, saying that Lieutenant de G—— had landed safely a thousand yards behind the firing-line, with three balls in his motor.

The captain sent for me. "Take my motor-car," he said, "and go fetch de G——. The machine is in plain view on a hill. I am giving you two mechanics, so do your best to save the instruments and machine-gun. The Boche artillery will probably drop shells on the machine before nightfall."

The trip proved rather a thriller, for at this point the old-fashioned picture-book trenchless warfare was in full blast. Picking up de G——, we hid the car in a valley and sneaked forward under an unpleasant fire of shrapnel and high explosives. The unconcerned infantry reserves, chaffing and smoking where they lay hidden in fields of ripe wheat, stiffened our slightly shaky nerves. Poor timid aviators, completely out of their element — I heaved a sigh of relief that came from the very soles of my feet when at last our task was done, and with our cargo safely stowed, we sped out of the valley and back toward the rear. Hats off to the infantry!

Next day two of us went patrolling with the captain — a famous "ace" whose courage and skillful piloting are proverbial and who never asked one of his men to do a thing he hesitated to do himself. He was particularly fond of Americans, and on many occasions had done things for me which showed his rare courtesy and thoughtfulness. None of us dreamed, as he laughed and joked with us at the breakfast-table, that it was his last day of life.

The details of this patrol will always be fresh in my mind. We were flying at about 7000 feet, the three of us, I on the captain's right. At 6000, stretching away into the German lines, there was a beautiful sea of clouds, white and level and limitless. Far back, fifteen miles "*chez Boche,*" a flight of Albatrosses crawled across the sky — a roughly grouped string of dots, for all the world like migrating wildfowl. Suddenly, about seven or eight miles in, a Hun two-seater poked his nose above the clouds, rose leisurely into view, and dove back. I was quite sure that he had not seen us. The captain began at once to rise, turning at the same time to take advantage of the sun, and for a few minutes we wove back and forth, edging in till we were nearly over the spot where the Boche had appeared. At last the Boche emerged from the clouds, seemed to hesitate an instant like a timid fish rising from a bed of seaweed, and headed for the lines, where doubtless he had some reconnaissance to do.

Our position was perfect — in the sun and well above the enemy. The captain banked vertically and plunged like a thunderbolt on the German, I following a little behind and to one side. At 150 yards, streaks of fire poured from his two guns, and as he dove under the German's belly I got into range. Dropping vertically at a speed (I suppose) of 250 miles an hour, with the wind screaming through the wires, I got my sights to bear and pulled the trigger. Faintly above the furious rush of air, I could hear the stutter of my gun and see the bullets streaking to their mark. It was over in a wink of time: as I swerved sharply to the left, I caught a glimpse of the Hun machine-gunner, in a great yellow helmet and round goggles, frantically getting his gun to bear on me. A pull-back and I shot up under his tail, tilted up, and gave him another burst.

But what was this — as I opened the throttle, the engine sputtered and died! I dove steeply at once to keep the propeller turning, realizing in a flash of thought that the long fast dive had made the pressure in my gasoline tank go down. A turn of the little lever put her on the small gravity tank called the "nurse"; but no luck — something was wrong with the valve. Nothing to do but pump by hand, and I pumped like a madman. Seven miles in the enemy lines and dropping like a stone — I was what the French call *très inquiet*. Three thousand feet, two thousand, a thousand — and I pumped on. Five hundred; a splutter from the engine, and at two hundred feet above a ruined village she burst into her full roar, and I drew a breath for the first time in the descent. Crossed the lines three hundred feet up with full throttle and the nose down, and didn't get a bullet-hole!

I was unable to find the others, and as my petrol was low I went home. The rest I have from the other pilot.

The captain apparently had the same trouble as I, for he continued his dive to about 3,000 feet, followed by the other. The German, when last seen, was diving for the ground, so we shall never know whether or not we got him. Rising again above the sea of clouds, the captain attacked the rear man of a patrol of eleven Albatrosses which passed beneath him. Turning over and over aimlessly, the Hun fell out of sight into the clouds. At this moment three Boches dove on the captain from the rear — his machine burst into flames and dove steeply toward our lines. Our remaining pilot, hopelessly outnumbered, extricated himself with difficulty and arrived a few minutes after me, his bus riddled with balls. We found the captain's body, just behind the firing-line. He had been killed by three bullets, but had retained consciousness long enough to get to friendly ground before he died. A splendid officer and a true friend, whom we all mourn sincerely.

II

The past fortnight has been rather stirring for us — constant flying, plenty of fights, and the usual moving about. One gets used to it in time, but at first it is a wrench to a man of my conservative nature and sedentary habits. This time we have struck it rich in a village where soldiers are still welcome. I have a really charming room in the house of the principal family — well-to-do people who own the local factory. Great sunny south windows, running water, and a soft snowy bed, scented with lavender! A day of rest to-day, as they are installing a new motor in my "taxi"; so I am planted at a little table, looking out through my window on a warm peaceful scene of tiled roofs, rustling leaves, and a delicious sky across which float summery clouds. Not a uniform in sight, not a sound of a cannon — the war seems an impossible dream.

The last day at our old field I had a narrow escape. Two of us were flying together up and down the lines at about 4000 feet. The other chap had allowed me to get pretty far in the lead, when I spied, about 2000 feet below me, a strange-looking two-seater, darkly camouflaged, on which I could see no insignia. I dove on him, but not headlong, as the English have a machine on similar lines, and it was not until I was quite close that I made out two tiny black crosses *set in circles of orange*.

By this time the machine-gunner was on the alert, and just as I was going to give him a burst, *flac, flac, flac,* bullets began to pass me from behind. Holes suddenly appeared in my wings; in another moment whoever was shooting would have had me, so I rose steeply in a sharp turn, saw nothing, turned again and again, and finally, disappearing in the distance after the two-seater, I made out two little Pfalz scouts, painted dark green.

My comrade, who was having engine trouble, saw the whole thing. The Boche single-seaters were well behind the larger plane they were protecting, and when I dove at their pal they rose up under my tail and let me have it with their four guns. Only some rotten shooting saved me from being brought down. The hardest thing for a new pilot to learn is the proper combination of dash and wariness: neither produces results alone; both are absolutely essential. One must bear in mind two axioms: first, bring down the enemy; second, don't get brought down yourself.

Our field was deserted: the mechanics were packing to leave, and my machine — old Slapping Sally — stood mournfully in the corner of a hangar. I stowed my belongings in the little locker at my side, had her wheeled out, adjusted my maps, and in five minutes was off on my long trip over unknown country. Our maps are really marvelous. With the compass to check up directions of roads, railroads, canals, and rivers, one can travel hundreds of miles over strange country and never miss a crossroad or a village. If, however, you allow yourself to become lost for an instant, you are probably hopelessly lost, with nothing to do but land and locate yourself on the map.

When I left, there was a gale of wind blowing, with spits of rain; and in fifteen minutes, during which I had covered forty miles, the clouds were scudding past at 300 feet off the ground, forcing me at times to jump tall trees on hills. A bit too thick. Seeing a small aerodrome on my right, I buzzed over and landed, getting a great reception from the pilots, who had never examined one of the latest single-seaters.

In a couple of hours the weather showed signs of improvement, so I shook hands all round and strapped myself in. To satisfy their interest and curiosity, I taxied to the far edge of the field, headed into the wind, rose a yard off the ground, gave her full motor, and held her down to within 30 yards of the spectators, grouped before a hangar. By this time Sally was fairly burning the breeze — traveling every yard of her 135 miles an hour; and as my hosts began to scatter, I let her have her head. Up she went in a mighty bound at 45 degrees, 900 feet in the drawing of a breath. There I flattened her, reduced the motor, did a couple of "Immelman turns" (instead of banking, turn upside-down, and pull back), and waved good-bye. Rather childish, but they were good fellows, and really interested in what the bus would do.

All went well as far as Paris, where I had one of the classic Paris breakdowns. Landed in the suburbs, got a mechanic to work, and had time for a delicious lunch at a small workmen's restaurant. Treated myself to a half bottle of sound Medoc and a villainous cigar with the coffee, and got back just in time to find them testing my motor. The rest of the trip was uneventful. I arrived here in the early afternoon and installed myself for the night in these superb quarters.

III

One of my friends here had the luck, several months ago, to force a Zeppelin to land. A strange and wonderful experience, he says, circling for an hour and a half about the huge air-monster, which seemed to be having trouble with its gas. He poured bullets into it until his supply was exhausted, and headed it off every time it tried to make for the German lines. All the while it was settling, almost insensibly, and finally the Hun crew began to throw things out — machine-guns, long belts of cartridges, provisions, furniture, a motley collection. In the end it landed intact in our lines — a great catch. The size of the thing is simply incredible. This one was at least ninety feet through, and I hesitate to say how many hundred feet long.

Three more of our boys gone, one of them my most particular pal. Strange as it seems, I am one of the oldest members of the squadron left. We buried Harry yesterday. He was the finest type of young French officer — an aviator since 1913; volunteer at the outbreak of war; taken prisoner, badly wounded; fourteen months in a German fortress; escaped, killing three guards, across Germany in the dead of winter, sick and with an unhealed wound; back on the front, after *ten days* with his family, although he need never have been a combatant again. A charming, cultivated, witty companion, one of the most finished pilots in France, and a soldier whose only thought was of duty, his loss is a heavy one for his friends, his family, and his country. For a day and a night he lay in state in the church of a nearby village, buried in flowers sent by half the squadrons of France; at his feet his tunic ablaze with crosses and orders. It was my turn to stand guard the morning his family arrived, and I was touched by the charming simple piety of the countryfolk, who came in an unending stream to kneel and say a prayer for the soul of the departed soldier. Old women with baskets of bread and cheese on their arms brought pathetic little bouquets; tiny girls of seven or eight came in solemnly alone, dropped a flower on Harry's coffin, and knelt to pray on their little bare knees. The French peasants get something from their church that most of us at home seem to miss.

At last the family came — worn out with the long sad journey from their château in middle France. Harry's mother, slender, aristocratic, and courageous, had lost her other son a short time before, and I was nearer tears at her magnificent self-control than if she had broken down like a farmer's wife. Her bearing throughout the long Mass and at the graveside was one of the finest and saddest things I have ever seen in my life. Poor old Harry — I hope he is in a paradise reserved for heroes — for he was one in the truest sense of the word.

IV

I got absolutely lost the other day, for the second time since I have been on the front. I was flying at about 19,000 feet, half a mile above a lovely sea of clouds. I supposed I was directly over the front, but in reality there was a gale of wind blowing, drifting me rapidly *chez Boche.* Three thousand feet below, and miles to the northeast, a patrol of German scouts beat back and forth, a string of dots, appearing and disappearing among the cloudy peaks and cañons. Too strong and too far in their lines to attack, I was alternately watching them and my clock — very cold and bored. Suddenly, straight below me and heading for home at top speed, I saw a big Hun two-seater, with enormous black crosses on his wings. At such a moment — I confess it frankly — there seem to be two individuals in me who in a flash of time conclude a heated argument. Says one, "You're all alone; no one will ever know it if you sail calmly on, pretending not to see the Boche."

"See that Boche," says the other; "you're here to get Germans — go after him."

"See here," puts in the first, who is very clever at excuses, "time's nearly up, petrol's low, and there are five Hun scouts who will drop on you if you dive on the two-seater."

"Forget it, you poor weak-kneed boob!" answers number two heatedly. "Dive on that Hun and be quick about it!"

So I dove on him, obeying automatically and almost reluctantly the imperious little voice. With an eye to the machine-gunner in the rear, I drove down on him almost vertically, getting in a burst point-blank at his port bow, so to speak. Pushing still farther forward on the stick, I saw his wheels pass over me like a flash, ten yards up. Pulled the throttle wide open, but the motor was a second late in catching, so that when I did an Immelman turn to come up under his tail, I was too far back and to one side. As I pulled out of the upside-down position, luminous sparks began to drive past me, and a second later I caught a glimpse of the goggled Hun observer leaning intently over his cockpit as he trained his gun on me.

But beside old Slapping Sally his machine was as a buzzard to a falcon; in a breath I was under his tail, had reared almost vertically, and was pouring bullets into his underbody. "You will shoot me up, will you?" I yelled ferociously — just like a bad boy in a back-yard fight. "Take that, then —" at which dramatic instant a quart of scalding oil struck me in the face, half in the eyes, and half in my open mouth. I never saw the Boche again, and five minutes later, when I had cleaned my eyes out enough to see dimly, I was totally lost. Keeping just above the clouds to watch for holes, I was ten long minutes at 130 miles per hour in getting to the lines, at a place I had never seen before.

Landed at a strange aerodrome, filled Sally up, and flew home 75 miles by map. As usual, everyone had begun the old story of how I was not a bad chap at bottom, and had many noble qualities safely hidden away — when I strolled into the bar. Slight sensation as usual, tinged with a suspicion of mild disappointment.

Almost with regret, I have turned faithful old Slapping Sally over to a newly arrived young pilot, and taken a new machine, the last lingering echo of the *dernier cri* in fighting single-seaters. I had hoped for one for some time, and now the captain has allotted me a brand-new one, fresh from the factory. It is a formidable little monster, squat and broad-winged, armed to the teeth, with the power of two hundred and fifty wild horses bellowing out through its exhausts.

With slight inward trepidations I took it up for a spin after lunch. The thing is terrific — it fairly hurtles its way up through the air, roaring and snorting and trembling with its enormous excess of power. Not half so pleasant as Sally, but a grimly practical little dragon of immense speed and potential destructiveness. At a couple of thousand feet over the field, I shut off the motor and dove to try it out. It fairly took my breath away — behind my goggles my eyes filled with tears; my body rose up in the safety-belt, refusing to keep pace with the machine's formidable speed. In a wink, I was close to the ground, straightened out, and rushing low over the blurred grass at a criminal gait — never made a faster landing. It is a tribute to man's war-time ingenuity, but, for pleasure, give me my old machine.

The psychology of flying would be a curious study, were it not so difficult to get frankly stated data — uninfluenced by pride, self-respect, or sense of morale. It is hard to give reasons, but certainly flying is not an enjoyable sport, like riding or motoring, once the wonder of it has worn off; simply a slightly disagreeable but marvelously fast means of transport. The wind, the noise, the impossibility of conversation, the excessive speed — are all unpleasant features. These are partially redeemed by the never-ceasing wonder of what one sees. One's other senses are useless in the air, but what a feast for the eyes! Whole fruitful domains spread out beneath one, silvery rivers, smoking cities, perhaps a glimpse of the far-off ragged Alps. And when, at 18,000 or 20,000 feet, above a white endless sea of clouds, you float almost unconscious of time and space in the unearthly sunshine of the Universe, there are moments when infinite things are very close.

FIDDLERS' LUCK
by Robert Haven Schauffler

DURING my whole service in France up to the day when I rose from the cot in Base Hospital 14 and began to hobble, I had only one fiddling adventure.

My regiment spent some time in the town of Champlitte, training for the front lines. So far as we were aware, Champlitte possessed but one bathtub. You dropped into the bathing establishment every time you passed that way, and once during the course of several weeks you probably were fortunate enough to find the tub hospitably vacant.

Now, I had known about cleanliness being next to godliness. France showed me that it was but one remove from the divine art of fiddling. One day I stopped in to make the usual tender inquiries after the bathtub's condition. I was informed that it was doing better than was to be expected under the circumstances, and that, if I would honor a chair in the next room for a little bit with my distinguished presence, facilities for cleanliness would soon be at my disposal.

I was ushered into the family parlor. The first thing that I saw on entering was a 'cello. It was suffering from anæmia, recessive gums, and that form of acute St. Vitus's dance in the lumbar regions known as Pernicious Wolf Tone; but it was still a 'cello. Of course I picked it up and began to play.

In rushed madame, clasping her hands as if in ecstasy. In waddled grand'mère, not in any ecstasy, but flying signals of extreme content. In tornadoed a small boy and began to cavort about my chair, like a young puppy, wild with jubilation on being released from long captivity and offered a juicy bone.

I inquired if the bath were ready.

"Ah, monsieur le lieutenant, but first we entreat you to play some more! You cannot know how we have starved for our dear music during these sad years when no one has had the heart to play. But now it is different. Thanks to messieurs les Américains we are about to achieve the victory."

I asked what they wanted to hear, and they wanted the Meditation from *Thaïs,* copious extracts from *Faust,* Massenet's Élégie, the Berceuse from *Jocelyn,* and the Sextette from *Lucia.* These I dutifully rendered, while my audience caressed the music with their eyes. Madame slipped out for a moment and returned with a bottle of her choicest wine. Grand'mère cut me a bunch of delicious grapes from the arbor outside the door.

I was not allowed to bathe until I had given young Antoine, the 'cello's owner, some pointers on how to manipulate his property. While I splashed, the earnest garçon kept running in with eager inquiries about how to bow an arpeggio, how to make the C-string stay at C without sliding down to zero every few moments, and how to gain the rare altitude of the fourth position without slipping into a crevasse.

When all was said and done and bathed, I had much ado to make madame accept compensation for the bath. Regarding the wine and the grapes, she was adamant. Had I not brightened their lives and given them all a foretaste of the peace-time coming? Any moment I wanted to play that 'cello to my friends, Antoine should carry it for me to whatever point I might designate. For it was not meet and right that an officer should bemean his honored uniform by carrying so bulky and plebeian a parcel.

Now it happened that I did want to fiddle elsewhere: for I had found a pianist in almost as singular a fashion as that in which I had found a 'cello. I had found the 'cello on the way to a bath. And I had found the pianist on the way to a dentist.

It all began with the texture and consistency of the A.E.F. bread. This form of the staff of life was durably constructed of ironwood. It was of so firm a substance that only teeth of Bessemer steel fitted with diamond points could have bitten it month in, month out, and remained intact. Mine, being made of merely mortal enamel and a very painful substance they call pulp, rained down fillings like the hail that plagued Egypt, and cried, *"Kamerad!"* and had to be taken to the hospital.

But when they arrived there, the dentist looked sheepish and confessed that all his tools had been sent to France in the heavy freight, and had probably succumbed to the submarines. Unless he hitched my tooth to a wire and the other end of the wire to a bullet, and pulled the trigger and shot the bullet forth into space, he couldn't help my tooth out. I explained that filling, not extraction, — more pulp rather than less, — was my ideal. But he hadn't a single tool, and could not say when he could get his hands on any.

My little affair was urgent, and I could not let the matter rest there. I started forth to find him some of the murderous instruments of his profession. It soon developed that all the local French tooth-doctors were at the front, and, unlike our own, had all their tools with them.

Hold! One of them had been killed in action. Perhaps the widow possessed his outfit. I hastened to the address and found a delightful lady who owned a large and representative memorial collection of dental forceps (from which I involuntarily recoiled), and a charming niece who produced no such effect upon me.

This young woman, indeed, played the piano remarkably handily. I revealed my own weakness for operating upon the 'cello. We accordingly laid our plans with affectionate minuteness as to what we would make happen if a 'cello could be discovered. But it never was, until the day I finally found the bathtub empty.

The very next evening I summoned Antoine with his poor, suffering old bull-fiddle, and mademoiselle and I gave ourselves and the family a concert. We didn't have any music anywhere but in our heads. But we had so much there that we played all the evening without once repeating ourselves. At first she played, like ninety-nine pianists out of a hundred, a bit heavily. But she made me feel like the lord of creation when I murmured in her ear, "Let it be light," and it *was* light. So a pleasant time was had by all.

Like most of her countrywomen, and like most of the English and other peoples who had been at war long enough to find a full outlet for all their pent-up energies and passions, this lady had no prejudice against German music; so we alternated Debussy with Beethoven and Franck with Bach, to everybody's satisfaction. And afterwards, when I took Antoine's 'cello over to the American Officers' Club and played till midnight, there was the same feeling that art is international, and that to cut off German music is no wiser than cutting off your own nose to spite your face.

It was interesting to notice that this feeling grew much more pronounced in my regiment after we had been under fire. As a rule I found that the front-line fighting man had little or no prejudice against German music. He had translated into action, and worked out of his system, that pent-up spleen which so ate into the vitals of the S.O.S. and of the good folks at home.

His idea was somewhat as follows: "Let's lap up everything good that we can get out of the Boches, and enjoy it to the limit! That's the least we can do to get even for the rats and the mud, the forced marches, the hospitals, the cold and the cooties." So he consumed a German tune with the same gusto that he showed in sampling the cigars and schnapps he found in the captured dugout. I consider this a healthier state than being poisoned by the ingrowing morbidness of the lines of communication. Virulence against German music appeared to increase in direct proportion to the agitator's distance from Germany. I remember that it was a telephone girl in the rearest of the rear who based her abhorrence of German music on the original ground that it was bad music. Triumphantly she backed up this contention with the syllogism: —

"Music is goodness.

"The German is not good.

"Therefore the German is not musical."

Naturally I forebore to invert this extraordinary proposition and come back with: —

"Music is goodness.

"The German is musical.

"Therefore the German is good," — for I did not in the least think so myself. I merely inquired of her in the mildest of tones whether

Bach, Beethoven, and Brahms were, then, unmusical. In the engaging manner of so many cornered ladies, she resorted at once to invective. With wrath flashing from her eyes she denounced me as a disgrace to the uniform I wore.

It was clear that my views on the art of music had not made a hit with the telephone girl. I told myself that you can't please anyone with everything any more than you can please everyone with anything. But this philosophical reflection did little toward cheering me. For then and there I saw that, when I stopped shooting the Boches and being shot at by them, and went home, I would have to choose between disliking Beethoven, and being shot at by a considerable body of noncombatants.

This was a painful dilemma. For, in going over the top, it was Beethoven and other Boches of his sort who kept such nice, encouraging tunes going all the time in my head, that they made the whizz-bangs and the blind pigs and the bombs and bullets sound much less dismaying than they might otherwise have sounded. These good Teutonic musicians released more of my energies toward the great end of making more present-day Germans good, that is, dead. It was a droll thing to catch Brahms in the act of helping me kill Germans; for in my interesting solo position as Assistant Regimental Intelligence Officer during an attack, I found no more helpful aide than the composer of the *Triumphlied.*

My chief recollection of music in the trenches is of the wedding hymns which the highly uxorious rats of Verrières sang, as they performed Russian ballets on the corrugated iron of my superterranean dug-out, and while using my face as a spring-board for the high dive. So I am not going to say much of anything about fiddlers' luck at the front, because it was conspicuous by its absence.

Stay! There was one rare specimen of a fiddler, — well, perhaps not exactly a fiddler, — who went into the Meuse-Argonne offensive with us before Montfaucon, sitting on top of his tank with the shells bursting about him at reasonable distances and intervals. All this time he kept twanging a disreputable banjo and singing at the top of a gay and lusty voice — till one of the shells put a sudden and final double-bar to the music.

My beloved Brahms was the best of bunkies and buddies right up to the moment when the Boche sniper in the tree got me through the hip-bone. And he stayed with me during the hours of jolting back on the stretcher, borne by willing but awkward amateurs. And he stayed with me all the time that very elastic Ford ambulance was cavorting back *andante con motor,* through the shell-holes to the field hospital.

It was one of those high-brow ambulances that have no use for low gear. Low, in fact, was burned out. So every time we struck a shell-hole, Henry Ford gave a last gasp and had eventually to be propelled by hand to the crest of the next hill. Those hours might have been an unpleasant experience if it had not been for the Brahms sextettes. Henry might shake me until I was all hip, but, in the words of the ancient song, those darling old comrades (the sextettes) were there by my side.

1921
THE MYSTIC'S EXPERIENCE OF GOD
by Rufus M. Jones

THE revival of mysticism, which has been one of the note-worthy features in the Christianity of our time, has presented us with a number of interesting and important questions. We want to know, first of all, what mysticism really is. Secondly, we want to know whether it is a normal or an abnormal experience. And we want to know whether mystical experiences actually enlarge our sphere of knowledge.

I am not interested in mysticism as an *ism*. It turns out, in most accounts, to be a dry and abstract thing, hardly more like the warm and intimate experience than the color of the map is like the country for which it stands. It is mystical experience, and not mysticism, that is worthy of our study.

According to those who have been there, the experience that we call mystical is charged with the conviction of real, direct contact and commerce with God. It is the almost universal testimony of those who are mystics that they find God through their experience. John Tauler says that, in his best moments of "devout prayer and the uplifting of the mind to God," he experiences "the pure presence of God" in his own soul; but he adds that all he can tell others about the experience is "as poor and unlike it as the point of a needle is to the heavens above us."

There are many different degrees of intensity, concentration, and conviction in the experiences of different individual mystics, and also in the various experiences of the same individual from time to time. There has been a tendency in most studies of mysticism to regard the state of ecstasy as *par excellence* mystical experience. That is, however, a grave mistake. The calmer, more meditative, less emotional, less ecstatic experiences of God are not less convincing and possess greater constructive value for life and character than do ecstatic experiences which presuppose a peculiar psychical frame and disposition. The seasoned Quaker, in the corporate hush and stillness of a silent meeting, is far removed from ecstasy, but he is not the less convinced that he is meeting with God.

Brother Lawrence, a barefooted lay brother of the seventeenth century, according to the testimony of the brotherhood, attained "an unbroken and undisturbed sense of the Presence of God." He was not an ecstatic; he was a quiet, faithful man, who did his ordinary daily tasks with what seemed to his friends "an unclouded vision, an illuminated love, and an uninterrupted joy." Simple and humble though he was, he nevertheless acquired, through his experience of God, "an extraordinary spaciousness of mind."

The more normal, expansive mystical experiences come apparently when the personal self is at its best. Its powers and capacities are raised to an unusual unity and fused together. The whole being, with its accumulated submerged life, *finds itself*. The process of preparing for any high achievement is a severe and laborious one; but nothing seems easier in the moment of success than is the accomplishment for which the life has been prepared. There comes to be formed within the person what Aristotle called "a dexterity of soul," so that the person does with ease what he has become skilled to do. Brother Lawrence finely says: "The most excellent method which I found of going to God was that of *doing my common business* purely for the love of God."

There are many human experiences which carry a man up to levels where he has not usually been before, and where he finds himself possessed of insight and energies that he had hardly suspected were his until that moment. One leaps to his full height when the right inner spring is reached. We are quite familiar with the way in which instinctive tendencies in us, and emotions both egoistic and social, become organized under a group of ideas and ideals into a single system, which we call a sentiment, such as love, or patriotism, or devotion to truth. It forms slowly, and one hardly realizes that it has formed until some occasion unexpectedly brings it into full operation, and we find ourselves able with perfect ease to overcome the most powerful inhibitory and opposing instincts and habits, which, until then, had usually controlled us. We are familiar, too, with the way in which a well-trained and disciplined mind, confronted by a concrete situation, will sometimes, in a sudden flash of imaginative insight, discover a universal law revealed there and then in the single phenomenon. Literary and artistic geniuses supply us with many instances in which, in a sudden flash, the crude material at hand is shot through with vision, and the complicated plot of a drama, the full significance of a character, or the complete glory of a statue stands revealed, as if, to use R. L. Stevenson's illustration, a *geni* had brought it on a golden tray as a gift from another world. Abraham Lincoln, striking off in a few intense minutes his Gettysburg address, as beautiful in style and perfect in form as anything in human literature, is as good an illustration as we need of the way in which a highly organized person, by a kindling flash, has at his hand all the moral and spiritual gains of a lifetime.

The most important mystical experiences occur usually, not at the beginning of the religious life, but rather in the ripe and developed stage of it. They are the fruit of long-maturing processes. Clement's "harmonized man" is always a person who has brought his soul into parallelism with divine currents, has habitually practised his religious insights, and has finally formed a unified central self, subtly sensitive, acutely responsive to the Beyond within him. In such experiences, which may come suddenly or may come as a more gradual process, the whole self operates and masses all the cumulations of a lifetime. They are no more emotional than they are rational and volitional.

I must say a few words about the normality or abnormality of them. Some instances are normal, and some are undoubtedly abnormal. Trance, ecstasy, and rapture are unusual experiences, and, in that sense, not normal occurrences. But it seems hardly sound to call a state abnormal if it has raised the "experient," as a mystic experience often does, into a hundred-horsepower man, and by his influence has turned multitudes of other men and women into more joyous, hopeful, and efficient persons. This question of abnormality and reality is thus not one to be settled off-hand by a superficial diagnosis.

An experience which brings spaciousness of mind, new interior dimensions, ability to stand the universe, — and the people in it, — and capacity to work at human tasks with patience, endurance, and wisdom may quite intelligently be called normal, though to an external beholder it may look like what he usually calls a trance of hysteria, a state of dissociation, or hypnosis by auto-suggestion. The calmer and more restrained stages of mysticism are no more marked with the stigma of hysteria than is love-making, enjoyment of music, devotion to altruistic causes, risking one's life for one's country, or any lofty experience of *value*.

II

Do mystical experiences settle anything? Do they take the experient across the chasm that separates "self" from "other"? Mystical experience undoubtedly feels as if it had objective reference. It comes to the individual with indubitable authority. He is certain that he has found something other than himself. He has an unescapable conviction that he is in contact and commerce with reality beyond the margins of his personal self. "A tremendous muchness is suddenly revealed," as William James once put it.

But mystical experience does not supply concrete information. It does not bring new finite facts, new items that can be used in a description of "the scenery and circumstance" of the realm beyond our sense-horizons. It is the awareness of a Presence, the consciousness of a Beyond.

The most striking effect of such experience is not new fact-knowledge, not new items of empirical information, but new moral energy, heightened conviction, increased caloric quality, enlarged spiritual vision, an unusual radiant power of life. In short, the whole personality, in the case of the constructive mystics, appears to be raised to a new level of life, and to have gained from somewhere many calories of life-feeding, spiritual substance. We are quite familiar with the way in which adrenalin suddenly flushes into the physical system and adds a new and incalculable power to brain and muscle. Under its stimulus a man can carry out a piano when the house is on fire. May not, perhaps, some energy, from some Source with which our spirits are allied, flush our inner being with forces and powers by which we can be fortified to stand the universe and more than stand it!

I believe that mystical experiences do, in the long run, expand our knowledge of God, and do succeed in verifying themselves. Mysticism is a sort of spiritual protoplasm, which underlies, as a basic substance, much that is best in religion, in ethics, and in life itself. It has generally been the mystic, the prophet, the seer, who have spotted out new ways forward in the jungle of our world, or lifted our race to new spiritual levels. Their experiences have in some way equipped them for unusual tasks, have given supplies of energy to them which their neighbors did not have, and have apparently brought them into vital correspondence with dimensions and regions of reality that others miss. The proof that they have found God, or at least a domain of spiritual reality, does not lie in some new stock of knowledge, not in some gnostic secret, which they bring back; it is to be seen rather in the moral and spiritual fruits which test out and verify the experience.

Consciousness of beauty or of truth or of goodness baffles analysis as much as consciousness of God does. These values have no objective standing-ground in current psychology. They have their ground of being in some other kind of world than that of the mechanical order. These experiences of value, which are as real for experience as stone-walls are, make very clear the fact that there are depths and capacities in the nature of the normal human mind which we do not usually recognize, and of which we have scant and imperfect accounts in our textbooks. Our minds, taken in their full range, in other words, have some sort of contact and relationship with an eternal nature of things far deeper than atoms and molecules.

Only very slowly and gradually has the race learned, through finite symbols and temporal forms, to interpret beauty and truth and goodness, which, in their essence, are as ineffable and indescribable as is the mystic's experience of God. Plato often speaks as if he had high moments of experience when he rose to the naked vision of beauty — beauty "alone, separate and eternal," as he says. But, as a matter of fact, however exalted heavenly and enduring beauty may be in its essence, we know *what it is* only as it appears in fair forms of objects, of body, of soul, of actions; in harmonious blending of sounds or colors; in well-ordered or happily combined groupings of many aspects in one unity, which is as it ought to be. Truth and moral goodness always transcend our attainments, and we sometimes feel that the very end and goal of life is the pursuit of that truth or that goodness which eye hath not seen nor ear heard. But whatever truth we do attain, or whatever goodness we do achieve, is always concrete. Truth is just this one more added fact that resists all attempt to doubt it. Goodness is just this simple everyday deed that reveals a heroic spirit and a brave venture of faith in the midst of difficulties.

So, too, the mystic knowledge of God is not some esoteric communication, supplied through trance or ecstasy; it is an intuitive personal touch with God, felt to be the essentially real, the bursting forth of an intense love for Him, which heightens all the capacities and activities of life.

1922
JAZZ: A MUSICAL DISCUSSION
by Carl Engel

JAZZ is upon us, everywhere. To deny the fact is to assume the classic ostrich pose, head buried in the sand, tail-feathers to the sun. To shout alarm hysterically from the housetops, is to exhibit over-confidence in clamorous indignation as a purifier of morals, if it be not wholly to ignore historic precedent.

The situation we are facing is not new. It offers many problems which are grave, yet seemingly not more perplexing than those which have arisen under similar conjunctures, in the past. True it is that the dance to which jazz music has been coupled is not precisely setting an example of modesty and grace. True, also, that certain modern dance-perversions have called up music that is as noxious as the breath of Belial. Only by a bold stretch of fancy can this delirious caterwauling be brought under the head of music proper — or improper; as noise, its significance at times becomes eloquent to the point of leaving little or nothing to the imagination.

However, let us remember that the worst of our present dances are not beginning to approach in barefaced wickedness the almost unbelievable performances of our forefathers, for which we need not seek much further back than the time of the French Revolution, when the 1800 dance-halls of Paris were not enough to hold the whirling pairs, but dancing went on gayly in churches and in cemeteries. And let us admit that the *best* of jazz tunes is something infinitely more original — perhaps even musically better — than the so-called "popular" music that America produced in the "good old days," that golden age which lives only in the mythology of disappointed sinners.

To a great many minds, the word "jazz" implies frivolous or obscene deportment. Let me ask what the word "sarabande" suggests to you? When you hear mention of a "sarabande," you think of Bach's, of Handel's slow and stately airs; you think of noble and dignified strains in *partitas,* sonatas, and operas of the eighteenth century. Yet the sarabande, when it was first danced in Spain, about 1588, was probably far more shocking to behold than is the most shocking jazz to-day. The sarabande seems to have been of Moorish origin. Then, as now, the oriental, the exotic touch, gave dancing an added fillip. When Lady Mary Montagu, writing from Adrianople in 1717, described the dance that she saw in the seraglio of a rich Mussulman, she made allusions which leave no uncertainty as to the exact nature of these proceedings. Something of that character must have belonged to the earliest sarabandes. They were the proud Hidalgo's hoolah-hoolah. Father Mariana, in his book *De Spectaculis,* published in 1609, devoted a whole chapter to an attack on the sarabande, accusing it of having done more harm than the bubonic plague which devastated Europe in the Middle Ages.

Again, we hear it alleged that the moral corruption worked by jazz is vastly more calamitous than was the material havoc wrought by the World War. And yet, as we know, this once objectionable sarabande finally became a matrix wherein the greatest musical composers have cast some of their loftiest and purest inspirations. Dances, popular and no doubt shocking in their day, have furnished the soil for the cyclic growth from which has sprung, by way of the concerto and sonata, the grandest form of absolute music, the orchestral symphony.

II

The term jazz, as applied to music, is rather elastic. It embraces not only the noisy-noisome sort, the jumble-jungle kind, but a type that refines upon and meliorates the racy stuff of wilder species with matter of a distinctly and engagingly musical nature. Good jazz is a composite, the happy union of seemingly incompatible elements. Good jazz is the latest phase of American popular music. It is the upshot of a transformation which started some twenty years ago, and culminated in something unique, unmatched in any other part of the world. Fifteen years ago we had progressed to the insipid "Waltz me around again, Willie," to the Coon-song and Rag-time factories in the back parlors of the West Twentieth streets of New York. With the period of "Everybody's doing it, doing it, doing it," about 1912, we reached the short insistent motive which was to usurp the prerogatives of songfulness.

Then, one fine day, in 1915, we were treated to "The Magic Melody." A young man, gifted with musical talent and unusual courage, had dared to introduce into his tune a modulation which was nothing extraordinary in itself, but which marked a change, a new régime in American popular music. It was just the thing that the popular composer in the making had been warned against by the wise ones as a thing too "high-brow" for the public to accept. They were foolish prophets. The public not only liked it: they went mad over it. And well they might; for it was a relief, a liberation.

"The Magic Melody," by Jerome Kern, was the opening chorus of an epoch. It is not a composition of genius, but it is very ingenious. While it is almost more tuneless than was "Everybody's doing it," — if that be possible, — and largely adheres to the short, insistent phrase, it stands on a much higher musical plane. Its principal claim to immortality is that it introduces a modulation which, at the time it was first heard by the masses, seized their ears with the power of magic. And the masses, for once, showed excellent judgment.

Mr. Kern subsequently proved to be one of the most fertile, tasteful, and characteristic composers of light music. When he tries to be purely melodic, he is apt to fall back upon cheap sentimentalism, tinged with spurious folk-song color. But his little harmonic device had a hue all its own; and popular parlance decided that it was "blue." What the uninitiated tried to define by that homely appellation was, perhaps, an indistinct association of the minor mode and dyspeptic intonation with poor digestion; in reality, it is the advent in popular music of something which the textbooks call ambiguous chords, altered notes, extraneous modulation, and deceptive cadence.

Instead of the traditional sequence of dominant diminished-seventh, and dominant-seventh harmonies — which formed the timeworn transition into the refrain and accompanied the chanted announcement: "When he to her did say," — there sprang up a diversity of the freshest, most unexpected modulations, which fell upon the ear like drops of evening rain upon a parched and sun-baked soil. The various shades of blue, in which untutored harmonists indulged, ranged all the way from faint cerulean to deep indigo. The last could often be more fittingly compared to mud.

Between the earlier "rag" and the "blues," there was this distinction: the rag had been mainly a thing of rhythm, of syncopation; the blues were syncopation relished with spicier harmonies. In addition to these two elements of music, rhythm and harmony, the people — who in the beginning had known but one thing: melody, fastened upon a primitive and weak harmonic structure of "barbershop" chords — the people, I say, who had stepwise advanced from melody and rhythm to harmony, lastly discovered counterpoint. And the result of this last discovery is jazz. In other words, jazz is rag-time, *plus* "Blues," *plus* orchestral polyphony; it is the combination, in the popular music current, of melody, rhythm, harmony, and counterpoint.

III

Each of these four ingredients bears racial features which are unequivocally American. Yet this Americanism is not exclusively a tribal one. The contrapuntal complexity of jazz is something native, born out of the complex, strident present-day American life. Where did you hear, before jazz was invented, such multifarious stirring, heaving, wrestling of independent voices as there are in a jazz orchestra? The saxophone bleats a turgid song; the clarinets turn capers of their own; the violins come forward with an *obbligato;* a saucy flute darts up and down the scale, never missing the right note on the right chord; the trombone lumberingly slides off on a tangent; the drum and xylophone put rhythmic high lights into these kaleidoscopic shiftings; the cornet is suddenly heard above the turmoil, with good-natured brazenness. Chaos in order, — orchestral technic of master craftsmen, — music that is recklessly fantastic, joyously grotesque, — such is good jazz. A superb, incomparable creation, inescapable yet elusive; something it is almost impossible to put in score upon a page of paper.

For jazz finds its last and supreme glory in the skill for improvisation exhibited by the performers. The deliberately scored jazz tunes are generally clumsy, pedestrian. It is not for the plodding, routine orchestrator to foresee the unexpected, to plan the improbable.

Jazz is abandon, is whimsicality in music. A good jazz band should never play, and actually never does play, the same piece twice in the same manner. Each player must be a clever musician, an originator as well as an interpreter, a wheel that turns hither and thither on its own axis without disturbing the clockwork.

Strange to relate, this orchestral improvisation, which may seem to you virtually impossible or artistically undesirable, is not an invention of our age. To improvise counterpoint was a talent that the musicians in the orchestras of Peri and Monteverdi, three hundred years ago, were expected to possess, and did possess, to such a high degree that the skeleton scores of those operas which have come down to us give but an imperfect idea of how this music sounded when performed.

A semblance of this lost, and rediscovered, art is contained in the music of the Russian and Hungarian gypsies. Just as that music is a riotous improvisation, throbbing with a communicative beat, ever restless in mood, so is jazz. Just as the gypsy players are held together by an identical, inexplicable rhythmic spell, following the leader's fiddle in its harmonic meanderings, each instrument walking in a bypath of its own, so is the ideal jazz band constituted — that is, the jazz band made up of serious jazz artists.

Franz Liszt could give a suggestion of gypsy music on the keyboard. He had a way of playing the piano orchestrally. There are few people who can play jazz on the piano. Jazz, as much as the gypsy dances, depends on the many and contrasting voices of a band, united in a single and spontaneous rhythmic, harmonic, and contrapuntal will.

Jazz, fortunately, can be preserved on phonographic records for our descendants. They will form their own estimate of our enormities. If we had such records of what Scarlatti, Couperin, and Rameau did with their figured bases, we should need fewer realizations, restitutions, and renditions by arranger and deranger.

1923
THE ROAD AWAY FROM REVOLUTION
by Woodrow Wilson

IN these doubtful and anxious days, when all the world is at unrest and, look which way you will, the road ahead seems darkened by shadows which portend dangers of many kinds, it is only common prudence that we should look about us and attempt to assess the causes of distress and the most likely means of removing them.

There must be some real ground for the universal unrest and perturbation. It is not to be found in superficial politics or in mere economic blunders. It probably lies deep at the sources of the spiritual life of our time. It leads to revolution; and perhaps if we take the case of the Russian Revolution, the outstanding event of its kind in our age, we may find a good deal of instruction for our judgment of present critical situations and circumstances.

What gave rise to the Russian Revolution? The answer can only be that it was the product of a whole social system. It was not in fact a sudden thing. It had been gathering head for several generations. It was due to the systematic denial to the great body of Russians of the rights and privileges which all normal men desire and must have if they are to be contented and within reach of happiness. The lives of the great mass of the Russian people contained no opportunities, but were hemmed in by barriers against which they were constantly flinging their spirits, only to fall back bruised and dispirited. Only the powerful were suffered to secure their rights or even to gain access to the means of material success.

It is to be noted as a leading fact of our time that it was against "capitalism" that the Russian leaders directed their attack. It was capitalism that made them see red; and it is against capitalism under one name or another that the discontented classes everywhere draw their indictment.

There are thoughtful and well-informed men all over the world who believe, with much apparently sound reason, that the abstract thing, the system, which we call capitalism, is indispensable to the industrial support and development of modern civilization. And yet everyone who has an intelligent knowledge of social forces must know that great and widespread reactions like that which is now unquestionably manifesting itself against capitalism do not occur without cause or provocation; and before we commit ourselves irreconcilably to an attitude of hostility to this movement of the time, we ought frankly to put to ourselves the question, Is the capitalistic system unimpeachable? which is another way of asking, Have capitalists generally used their power for the benefit of the countries in which their capital is employed and for the benefit of their fellow men?

Is it not, on the contrary, too true that capitalists have often seemed to regard the men whom they used as mere instruments of profit, whose physical and mental powers it was legitimate to exploit with as slight cost to themselves as possible, either of money or of sympathy? Have not many fine men who were actuated by the highest principles in every other relationship of life seemed to hold that generosity and humane feeling were not among the imperative mandates of conscience in the conduct of a banking business, or in the development of an industrial or commercial enterprise?

And, if these offenses against high morality and true citizenship have been frequently observable, are we to say that the blame for the present discontent and turbulence is wholly on the side of those who are in revolt against them? Ought we not, rather, to seek a way to remove such offenses and make life itself clean for those who will share honorably and cleanly in it?

The world has been made safe for democracy. There need now be no fear that any such mad design as that entertained by the insolent and ignorant Hohenzollerns and their counselors may prevail against it. But democracy has not yet made the world safe against irrational revolution. That supreme task, which is nothing less than the salvation of civilization, now faces democracy, insistent, imperative. There is no escaping it, unless everything we have built up is presently to fall in ruin about us; and the United States, as the greatest of democracies, must undertake it.

The road that leads away from revolution is clearly marked, for it is defined by the nature of men and of organized society. It therefore behooves us to study very carefully and very candidly the exact nature of the task and the means of its accomplishment.

The nature of men and of organized society dictates the maintenance in every field of action of the highest and purest standards of justice and of right dealing; and it is essential to efficacious thinking in this critical matter that we should not entertain a narrow or technical conception of justice. By justice the lawyer generally means the prompt, fair, and open application of impartial rules; but we call ours a Christian civilization, and a Christian conception of justice must be much higher. It must include sympathy and helpfulness and a willingness to forgo self-interest in order to promote the welfare, happiness, and contentment of others and of the community as a whole. This is what our age is blindly feeling after in its reaction against what it deems the too great selfishness of the capitalistic system.

The sum of the whole matter is this, that our civilization cannot survive materially unless it be redeemed spiritually. It can be saved only by becoming permeated with the spirit of Christ and being made free and happy by the practices which spring out of that spirit. Only thus can discontent be driven out and all the shadows lifted from the road ahead.

Here is the final challenge to our churches, to our political organizations, and to our capitalists — to everyone who fears God or loves his country. Shall we not all earnestly coöperate to bring in the new day?

1924
YOU GET THE PIG
by Dayton Stoddart

ALL of your life you've wanted a pig; and now that at last you've got a place in the country, you decide to have a pig, no matter at what cost. For in addition to the prospect of a curly-tailed pig that will fraternize with the baby, there is the more material prospect of the pig eating the garbage. And the garbage is always a difficult problem in the burying when the soil is rocky and a ledge of shale awaits the pickaxe everywhere.

All the farmers in the countryside have pigs, until you really settle down to the business of getting one. And then the pigs vanish overnight. This farmer had two, but sold them; another gave his away to a friend; and the third had none at all, and never had any. With dying hopes you visit the last prospect, who is deaf, and bellow at him as he rides unconcernedly down a large field on a tractor which snorts and rocks in its job of turning a green pasture into loamy brown. As the prospect blithely ignores your shouts, you notice in the barnyard an enormous sow, prostrate in the mud, exhausted from eating, and with a litter of white pigs of the size of large rats. Like rats they run in and out of the barn, and like kittens they tumble over doorsills and frolic about in and out of holes around the barn. Innocence and quaintness!

Desperately you dash down the field after the deaf one, puffing and snorting as much as the tractor, stumbling over the brown clods of earth in the wake of the plough, and shriek at the farmer. Finally, when you're gasping and no longer can run, after a long canter abreast of the tractor, the farmer emits a distinguishable "H-uuuh?" and stops the engine. In the quiet stillness of the fields you plead nobly for a pig, just *one* pig. Leathery jaws masticating tobacco alone disturb the serenity of his face; and when your argument is finished, exhausting completely your supply of air, he replies laconically, "Too young; two more weeks"; and moves on, leaving you alone and raging, a sorry figure surrounded by derisive acres.

Verbally you wash your hands of all pigs. The baby has other things to interest him; and the garbage can be burned. But the vision of a young pig, slathering delightedly when you approach to feed him, persists. So when a friend arrives with a box two days later, contentment fills your heart. A hatchet rips the boards from the top of the box, and there stands your pig. He's *yours;* you can do with him what you will (if he lets you).

This particular pig is about a foot long, and has, by virtue of the country humor of our friend, a pink-paper rose tied round its neck. Through manipulation the rose rests rakishly on one pink ear. The assembled company look at the pig and murmur how clean and white and cute he looks. The pig surveys them defiantly, with a malevolent gleam in his small red eye.

"How old is he?" asks your wife.

"Two and a half weeks."

"Isn't that a shame! So innocent, and away from its mother."

The conversation is interrupted by the pig, who tumbles out of the box, slides through fumbling, outstretched hands, and gallops down the porch.

"Catch him!" shriek all in chorus.

The pig does not wait to be caught, but eludes his pursuers, wriggles under the rail, and drops twenty feet on some rocks. Cries from the women; curses from the men; moans of sympathy from the baby. Expecting to see a dying pig, you look over the rail; but there goes the pig loping off through the grass, and before the hunt is resumed he has disappeared in a large berry-patch. The assemblage scatters to catch the pig. Thick canes from last year bar the way with vicious thorns, you stumble over a root and land on all fours, scratched into savageness, and come face to face with the pig. His snout is bleeding, also. You gaze stupidly into his face as he squats there, and he does equally as well for you. But, being quicker-witted, he wheels about suddenly, you see the waving white tail, and then all is the darkness of the berry-patches. Before you can regain your feet there are cries of, "I got 'im," rebellious squeals, and the pig is returned to the box.

He must now be fed, and to feed him is a problem. The baby's bottles long since have been discarded, and the pig is too young to eat. A rubber tube is found, and your wife volunteers to feed the pig, having practised previously for a year and a half on the baby. The theory is excellent. On the principle that liquids seek their lowest level, one end of the tube is held up high, dangling from a bowl of milk, the other stuck in the pig's mouth. The pig gurgles, sucks, and laps noisily, but gets little. After most of the milk is on the floor and your wife's dress is hopelessly stained, you reluctantly come to the conclusion that it won't work this way. The bowl is filled up again and you douse the pig's head in it; but though his ears and eyes are bathed in milk, his mouth gets none. And when the problem seems hopeless of solution, it is all ended when Master Pig licks milky fingers, grunts with satisfaction, and is put away in the box for the night.

The next morning the pig is still a novelty and accorded every attention. (The baby alone refuses to join the circle of admirers.) After matutinal inspections have been completed, it finally dawns that the pig must have a pen. Lumber carefully saved for a tool-house, chicken-wire that should be used for the garden, asbestos shingles laid by for a rainy day and leaky roofs, are dragged out from cover and the work begins. And on the slope that curves from the house to the lake, under two walnuts, — pretty things with their rough black bark and plumes of light green leaves, — the pen is constructed. Many things need paint around the house but the can of dark green paint frugally hoarded is flung with a dripping brush on the pen that hides beneath the walnut trees. And stakes soon stick their green heads around the pen for the wire and planks to be nailed on. Indeed, nothing is too much trouble to encompass the comfort of the pig, even carefully shingling a lean-to at one side of the pen. Still, the pen looks tidy when finished: the gray shingles and green pen and green trough and, needless to add, a partly green pig. The trough is small and has the pig's name painted on the end in white letters; it is big enough, at that, for the pig to stand in it while eating. And on the end of the pen near the house is emblazoned in white letters:

NUTTY NELL

The adjective indicated his temperament.

Nell was secure at last. And being adaptable, where affairs gastronomic were concerned, it was but a day or so before he learned to devour coarse flour and water. And then he ate so much flour and water that he had no room for garbage.

It would not do to say that faithfulness and loyalty were among his virtues. Nell tolerated anybody who fed him. But he accepted food only on his own terms. The moment you approached with the pan of food, Nell would try to nudge it from your hand altogether; failing in that, he would stand in the trough, so that you would either have to wait until he was tired of standing there, or simply pour the food on his back. He received it usually on his back. And when he didn't get what he thought was sufficient, he would express his displeasure by grunts and squeals and by pushing the trough around the pen with his nose.

This is surprising, until it becomes noticeable how his neck has grown, and you realize that the pig is no longer a baby pig but growing up. Where formerly the boards met the grass on all sides of the pen in neat lines, now jagged holes appear, where Nell has rooted. And all the stones have been removed by him to the lake side of the pen, and there he stretches out day and night, scorning contemptuously his house with the gray shingles.

Indeed the pen is fast losing its original look. It changes with the pig. One morning you find that the post holding up the pig's house has been rooted out and the house itself has been torn down by the pig. And, with a contemptuous disregard of the family, he has begun to whiff malodorously.

As summer wanes, the pig becomes more blatant and noisome, pushing the tin basin (which has superseded his trough) around his pen. Tin and rocks! What a din! *Zip, crash, bang, boom* — Nell bounces the tin pan from one rock to another, around the pen, showing how *he* feels toward everything. At night, Nell continues his activities. Ofttimes visitors, unaccustomed to country noises, are startled by a loud crash from the direction of the lake. Useless to persuade them that it's only Nell being savage with the basin.

Then, too, while you like children theoretically, there is a constant juvenile flood of visitors to the pig. And just when you are trying to concentrate on some difficult bit of writing, Nell lets loose with a series of inharmonious snout-thumbing grunts, and there are loud howls of delight from Nell's callers.

And while the pen falls to pieces slowly, you wonder idly whether it will last till autumn, when Nell will be reduced to toothsome hams and succulent bacon. You erase one dream fulfilled from your mental calendar, and speculate about a goat. A goat is admirable because of his wise, cynical look, and, moreover, he has undoubtedly a sense of humor that the pig lacks. So you decide that next spring you will certainly buy a goat.

1925

SING:
A Song of Sixpence
by James Norman Hall

SEVERAL years ago while living at Papeete, the capital of Tahiti in French Oceania, I found myself so low in funds that it seemed the part of wisdom to retire for a time to one of the remote country-districts until I could repair my fortunes. On the windward side of the island, thirty-five miles from the town, I found an attractive place about an acre in extent, with a one-room house on it precisely suited to my needs. My verandah overlooked the sea, and a clear mountain-stream flowed through my small domain, so that I had both fresh- and salt-water bathing; but a more important feature than either of these was the cheapness of the rental — $3.00 per month.

The land thereabout was so fertile that I decided to make a vegetable garden. In the tropics gardening would be a delightful occupation, and it might easily prove so profitable that I should never again need to resume my old trade of journalism. So I set to work, hopefully enough, glad of the necessity which had brought me to this decision.

The experience was disillusioning. Millions of tiny red ants carried away most of my seed, and, if any happened to be overlooked by the ants, the moment they sent forth green shoots these were sheared off by land crabs. After three months of patient effort all that I had to show for my toil was two ears of sweet corn (or, better, corncobs, for the rats had eaten off the kernels), three small tomatoes, and one squash. Having estimated my time as worth, at a modest figure, twenty cents an hour, and adding expenditures for seed, garden tools, and so forth, I found that these vegetables cost me $15.50 each.

Nevertheless I resolved to try once more, and ordered from America a fresh supply of seed — a small quantity this time, for my funds were getting low; and furthermore, because of my innumerable enemies I meant to garden on a reduced front. But when I had cleared away the weeds — how marvelously they had flourished meanwhile, without care! — and saw the hosts of ants drawn up in waiting battalions, and the ground perforated like a sieve with the holes of land crabs, and a crab at the entrance of each hole, waving his keen-edged nippers in the air, I lost heart. "It is useless," I thought. "I'd better go back to journalism." Therefore I put away my tools and left Nature to plant whatever she would in my garden plot. She chose, as before, lantana and false tobacco.

That afternoon I was oiling and cleaning my typewriter, which had long been rusting in disuse, when a Chinaman named Hop Sing drove past my door in his dilapidated spring-wagon. He lived a quarter of a mile down the lagoon beach from my place, in a house which he himself had built from the boards of old packing-cases and roofed over with flattened-out biscuit-tins. I knew that he had a vegetable garden, — although he raised only sweet potatoes, watermelons, and a very tough variety of field corn, — so I hailed him, thinking he might find use for my dollar's worth of seed. He stopped, willingly enough, and I brought out to him a small packet each of beans, sweet corn (Golden Bantam), squash, pumpkin, lettuce, and tomato seed, all of the best varieties. Hop grunted expressions of mild interest while I explained what the various packets contained, and, when I had finished, asked: "How much?" "Oh, nothing at all," I replied. "A little present for you." He grasped the back of the seat to steady himself, perhaps, from the shock of receiving a present in that heathen land, and his black eyes glittered a trifle more brightly; but these were the only evidences of emotion — if it may be called emotion — that he displayed.

I forgot Hop Sing forthwith; there were other things to think of, chiefly the precarious state of my finances. Having counted on my garden to furnish food, I had spent my little capital all too freely. Luckily my rent was paid several months in advance, but I had left only 128 francs — a little more than $5.00 American, at the current rate of exchange — and not a penny coming in until I had written something, story, sketch, or what not. The manuscript would have to be sent to America, and even though it should be accepted at once — a remote possibility — I could not hope to receive a cheque for at least three months. How was I to live in the meantime? There were bananas on my place and about fifty coconut palms; but my landlord, a native, reserved the right to both the nuts and the fruit, which was no more than fair, considering the modest rental he asked for house and grounds. The nuts were gathered as they fell and the bananas picked green to send to the Papeete market. I thought of fishing, but, re-membering past experiences, I knew it would be foolish to count on that. I had no better luck at fishing than at gardening. No, I should have to live, somehow, on my 128 francs. That, of course, was impossi-ble, so I resolved not even to try. I kept 28 francs for incidental ex-penses, spent 25 francs for native tobacco, — if I was to write I should have to smoke, — and the remainder for sweet potatoes and tinned beef. When the food was gone — well, I should worry about that when the time came.

Three days later I was on page two of a sketch which I planned to call "Settling Down in Polynesia," a story of some experiences I had had the year before. I had written and rewritten the two pages of my story, vainly trying with each new draft to blacken page three. I was aroused from a mood of profound dejection by a knock at the back door. It was Hop Sing, and with him were his wife, their three small children, and a wizened little man with a scant beard and shaped like an interrogation point. Hop was dressed in a clean cotton undershirt and a pair of dungaree trousers. His wife wore a pyjama-suit of black silk, and her hair was elaborately dressed. She carried one child on her arm, led another by the hand, and had a third, the baby, in a sling at her back. The children were beautifully dressed, and each of them had on a little skullcap of blue silk with flowers and butterflies embroidered on it in gold thread. The ancient wore a coat like a dressing-gown. He was very feeble and got down from the wagon with difficulty. It was pathetic to see the effort it cost him to walk. He would advance his staff a few inches and, grasping it with both hands, make a shuffling hop up to it. Then he would rest for a moment while gathering strength for a new effort. We helped him up the steps and at length all were seated on the verandah, Mrs. Sing sitting sidewise on her chair because of the baby in the sling.

"My fadda-law," said Sing, indicating the old man.

I smiled and nodded.

A rather long silence followed. I felt embarrassed and could think of nothing to say.

"What name you?" he then asked.

I told him. Another interval of silence. I gave my forefinger to the baby on Mrs. Sing's lap. It clasped it gravely and held on. Mrs. Sing smiled. Her father, too, smiled; at least his face wrinkled suddenly, like a pool into which a pebble has been thrown. The small baby in the sling was asleep, its chubby arms sticking straight out. It looked like a doll rather than a real baby. The oldest child, a boy of six or seven, had the curious mature look and the air of profound wisdom common to many Chinese children.

Sing took from his pocket one of the packets of seeds I had given him.

"What name this?" he asked.

"That? Corn, sweet corn — Golden Bantam. Very good. Tahiti corn no good — too tough. This corn fine."

"Where you get?"

"From America," I replied.

He brought forth the other packets.

"All this Melican seed?"

I told him that it was, and the best that could be bought.

He was silent for a moment. Then he said: "Make fine garden now. No have good seed before. Make plenty big tomato now, plenty squash, plenty corn. Bimeby you see."

Thinking of my three tomatoes, about the size of marbles, I was not sanguine about Sing's being plenty big. However, I expressed the hope that they might be. I brought out my seed catalogue and showed him pictures of the various vegetables. He was much interested and exchanged remarks in Chinese with his father-in-law. Meanwhile one of those heavy local showers common at Tahiti in the rainy season broke with violence. The thunder of water on my tin roof was deafening. Soon the cloud melted into pure sunlight, the last of it descending in a fine mist shot through with rainbow lights. Sing then went to his wagon and returned with three huge watermelons. He made a second excursion, bringing this time a live fowl, a bottle of Dubonnet (vin apéritif), and a basket containing seventeen eggs. All of these articles he placed on my kitchen table.

"Littly plesent, you," he said with a deprecatory gesture. Mrs. Sing and her father then rose, and all three shook my hand, bidding me good-bye with smiles and nods. A moment later they drove off, leaving me astonished at this expression of Chinese friendliness.

II

It would be difficult to exaggerate the value to me of their generous gift. Tinned beef is a nourishing food, but I had lost all relish for it during the Great War. As for sweet potatoes, I had eaten so many while knocking about the Pacific on trading schooners that I could hardly endure the sight of them. How welcome, then, was this more palatable food! I planned to have a chicken dinner at once, but on second thought decided not to kill my fowl. Perhaps she would lay, and if I could somehow procure a rooster I might, from that small beginning, raise enough chickens to provide for all my needs. So I staked the hen out in the dooryard, with a string tied to her leg; and, having found several coconuts partly eaten by rats, I broke these open and gave her a good meal. Then, having dined on a six-egg omelet with half a watermelon for dessert, I resumed my work with interest and enthusiasm. All the afternoon the bell of my typewriter rang with the steady persistence of an alarm gong at a railroad crossing, and pages of manuscript fell from my hands like autumn leaves after a heavy frost. By six o'clock that evening I had reached the end of my "Settling Down" story.

I had no time to lose if I were to get it in the north-bound mail. The monthly steamer from New Zealand to San Francisco was due at Papeete on Monday. I decided to go into town to post the manuscript, not being willing to trust the native mail-carrier with so precious a document. A motor-bus ran daily between Papeete and Taravao, a village just beyond my place, but the fare for the round-trip was twenty-four francs. I should need at least ten francs for stamps and expenses in town, so I decided to walk in to Papeete and, if I had enough money left, to ride back. Therefore, having fortified myself with a small glass of Dubonnet and another six-egg omelet, I set out.

It was a beautiful night, dewy and still and fresh, with a full moon rising above the palm trees on the Taravao isthmus. The road wound this way and that around the shoulders of the hills, now skirting the sea, now crossing the mouths of broad valleys where the *hupé* — the night breeze from the interior — blew cool and refreshing. I had glimpses through the trees of lofty precipices festooned with the silvery smoke of waterfalls and, on the left hand, of the lagoon bordered by the barrier reef where great combers, rising to break on the coral, caught the moonlight in lines of white fire. From native houses along the road came snatches of song, a strange mixture of airs, part French, part Tahitian, to the accompaniment of guitars, accordions, and mouth-organs. On verandahs here and there women were busy with their ironing, sitting cross-legged on the floor with a lamp beside them, and far out on the lagoon the lights of the fishermen were already beginning to appear.

I walked briskly along the moonlit road, feeling at peace with the world and with myself. How pleasant it would be, I thought, really to settle down in this remote tropical paradise, to remain here for the rest of my life. Where could I find kindlier people, or a life more suited to one of my indolent habits? If it were true that a man's wealth may be estimated in terms of the things he can do without, then in that sense I might hope soon to achieve affluence. Material possessions added little to the sum of one's happiness, and I could always earn enough at writing to provide for the simple necessities of life.

So I mused, proceeding on my way; but at length, toward midnight, when I had covered about half the distance to Papeete, I found myself again thinking of food. The nourishment stored in my second six-egg omelet had already been absorbed and its energy expended. I had a drink of water from a mountain stream and tightened my belt a notch or two.

"I'll have a good breakfast when I get to town," I thought. For three francs I could buy a large portion of chop suey at one of the Chinese restaurants; that would have to suffice until I returned to the country, which I meant to do at once, as soon as I had posted my manuscript.

At a place where the road followed a lonely strip of beach I came to a thatched hut, and sitting near it, by a fire of driftwood, were an old native man and woman. I stopped for a moment to enjoy the beauty of the scene. The stems of the palm trees were black against the fire-light, which flickered over the faces of the old couple and cast huge shadows behind them. They saw me, and the old man called out, "*Haere mai ta maa!* (Come and eat!)" This is merely a friendly greeting, but evidently they really meant that I should partake of their midnight supper. They were roasting in the coals what appeared to be shellfish and some sort of native vegetable, and an appetizing fragrance filled the air. "Come!" said the old woman in the native tongue. "Try this, it is very good" — and putting several generous portions in a coconut shell she held it up to me.

Good? I should think it was! The meat of the shellfish was as deli-cately flavored as that of the finest lobster, and the vegetable had a mealy, nutlike taste. My hosts seemed delighted at my appetite and urged more food upon me. "Eat! Eat!" said the old man. "We have plenty — enough for a dozen," and he pointed to several buckets filled with uncooked food; so I ate with a will.

"What kind of shellfish are these?" I asked. "Did you get them on the reef?"

"Shellfish! These are not shellfish; they're *tupas.*"

"What!" I exclaimed. *Tupas* are land crabs, and those I was eating with such relish were members of the pestiferous family, countless in number, which had assisted the ants in ruining my garden. I didn't know they were edible, but the old man told me that Tahitians thought them a great delicacy, which they are, in truth. As for the vegetable, it was not a vegetable at all, but a nut, the fruit of the *mapé*, the Pacific chestnut-tree. These trees flourish at Tahiti. They are found along the banks of streams and in moist or swampy places. There was a grove of them on my place, and the ground beneath was littered with nuts that I had never bothered to examine, not knowing that they were of value. I was appalled at thought of the time and effort I had wasted trying to make a garden, when all the while there was an inexhaustible food-supply at hand, to be enjoyed without labor, to be had for the mere taking. But no; the taking of land crabs could not be such a simple matter. I remembered the wariness of those which infested my garden plot. The moment they saw me coming they scurried to their holes and, if I made so much as a move in their direction, dodged down to safety. I had once caught one by digging him out, but that cost me two hours of hard work.

I asked the old man how he caught them and he showed me a method so simple and reasonable that I wondered I had not thought of it. He had a fishpole and line, but instead of a hook at the end of the line he tied there a bunch of green leaves from the hibiscus tree. These leaves and the blossoms of the hibiscus are the principal food of land crabs. We went a little way from the hut to a spot in full moonlight where there were many crab-holes. "Now stand very still," he said. In a moment the crabs, which had scurried away at our approach, came warily up again. He then cast his bait very much as one does in fly-fishing. Immediately several crabs came sidling toward it. They fastened their nippers in the leaves, each of them trying to drag the bundle to his hole. The old man then gave a deft jerk to the line, and the crabs, not being able to disengage their nippers quickly enough, were dragged to his feet. He pounced upon them and threw them into the bucket with the others. I then tried my hand, with such success that I was tempted to forgo my journey to town, but more prudent counsels prevailed. Therefore, having bade farewell to my kindly hosts, I proceeded on my way and reached Papeete at dawn, just as the steamer that was to carry my manuscript to America was entering the harbor. Stamps for the precious parcel cost three francs. I then breathed over it a silent prayer and slipped it into the letter-chute.

III

Papeete is a colorful town, particularly in the early morning when the inhabitants are going to and from the market. Everyone is in the streets then, and the French and Chinese restaurants are filled with people exchanging gossip over their morning coffee. I was walking along the Quai de Commerce looking at the shipping when someone touched my shoulder. It was a bald fat little Chinaman who had evidently been running after me, for he was out of breath and could not speak for a moment. Then he began talking in Chinese-Tahitian, a sort of *bêche-de-mer* that I don't understand. I shook my head. He renewed his efforts, speaking very earnestly and rapidly, and presently I caught the name "Hop Sing."

"Hop Sing?" I said.

"*É! É!* (Yes! Yes!)" he replied, and of a sudden he found some English words. "You know Hop Sing? Hop Sing flen, you?"

"Yes," I said. "I know him. Hop Sing live close me, Papeari."

Papeari is the name of the district where I was living.

The Chinaman's face glowed with pleasure.

"*Maitai! Maitai!* (Good! Good!) Hop Sing send me letta. I know name, you. You give seed; put in gloun, make garden. *Maitai! Maitai!* Hop Sing glad. Me glad. Hop Sing brudda-law me."

"What name you?" I asked.

"Lee Fat. Keep store over there," and he pointed down the street. "When you go back Papeari?"

"Go this morning on motor-bus."

"Goo-bye," the Chinaman said, and rushed away as though he had not a moment to lose. I was surprised at the abrupt leave-taking and stood looking after him, hardly knowing what to make of the encounter, touched at thought of this odd little man chasing me down the street to thank me for the trifling favor I had done his brother-in-law.

It was nearly midday when I arrived at Papeari. While I was paying my fare to the driver, the boy who attended to the distribution of parcels put a box down beside me.

"You've made a mistake," I said. "That isn't mine."

"Yes it is," he replied.

He insisted that it was mine. A Chinaman had brought it just before the bus left the market, he said, and had paid for its carriage to my place. The parcel contained the following articles: one two-pound box of New Zealand chocolates, a large paper bag of lichi nuts, one quart of champagne (Louis Roederer), and a beautiful lacquered box with a gold dragon on the lid. In this box were two silk handkerchiefs and a silk pyjama-suit.

I was tempted to open the champagne at once, that I might drink long life and abundant health to Hop Sing and his brother-in-law, Lee Fat, but I had no ice, and I knew that I could not drink, alone, a quart of champagne without having a headache the following day. So I tied a string to the bottle and lowered it into the cistern to keep cool. Then I went out to attend to my chicken.

She was gone. The string was still tied to the stake, but she had worked her leg out of the noose and vanished. After a long search I found her under the back steps. I reached in, very cautiously, to grasp her. She pecked at my hand and, as I drew her forth, gave utterance to the indignant squawks common to hens when they are sitting. Surely enough, she had laid an egg and was sitting on it; evidently she had been ready to sit when Hop Sing brought her to me. The egg under her was unfertilized, of course, so I took that out. Then I made her a nest of excelsior out of Lee Fat's box, and placed in it the five eggs remaining of Hop Sing's gift. The hen settled down on them with contented cluckings and, when comfortable, closed her eyes as much as to say, "Now then, all I ask is to be fed from time to time, and twenty-one days hence we shall see what we shall see."

IV

It seems to me now that the definite upward trend in the graph of my fortunes began that afternoon when I started land-crab fishing. The results not only flattered my vanity — sadly in need of flattery — but gave me renewed confidence. "At last," I thought, "I am a success at something." I could not eat a tenth of the crabs I had caught, so I made a pen of stakes set closely together and deeply into the ground, and turned the surplus loose inside it. They immediately dug new holes for themselves, but this did not disturb me, for I knew I could easily catch them again. I fished all over my two-acre estate with such success that I had to enlarge the pen several times, and even then, and despite the fact that some of the crabs dug their way out, there were so many inside that the ground was honeycombed with their burrows. It occurred to me that by feeding them regularly on hibiscus leaves and blossoms I might add to their size and increase the delicacy of their flavor. The experiment was highly successful. The crabs thrived upon the regular and abundant food and I thrived upon them. At the time of Hop Sing's visit, what through worry and an uncongenial diet, I was very thin, but within six weeks I had gained fourteen pounds.

Meanwhile, upon the appointed day, my hen stepped out of her nest, followed by five bits of animated fluff. I was quite as proud of them as she was, and doubtless took more credit to myself on that occasion than the facts warranted. I fed both the hen and her brood on a mixture of roasted land-crabs and mapé nuts, and never have I seen chickens grow so rapidly.

It may seem incredible that my bottle of champagne should have remained unbroached during this time, but such is the case. In my interest in crab and chicken farming, I had quite forgotten it; but one day, when my landlord was gathering coconuts in a near-by grove, I asked him to share it with me. He was more than willing, and at the first glass his habitually reserved attitude toward me altered at once. I then learned the reason for this attitude. He told me that his last tenant, an Australian, had not only eaten bananas and coconuts to which he had no right, but had gone away without paying his rent. We drank confusion to this scurvy tenant wherever he might be. Several of my landlord's children had accompanied him to the house, and I shared with them the box of New Zealand chocolates. It was a merry little party, and after much pleasant talk my landlord left me with repeated expressions of good will. The following morning I found on my back verandah a large bunch of bananas and a gunny sack filled with oranges and mangoes, and thereafter I was never without these delicious fruits, gifts from my landlord and his family. Not infrequently Mata, his wife, would send me, by one of the children, baked fish, breadfruit, and mountain plantain wrapped in green leaves, fresh from her native oven. I was overwhelmed with benefits and remembered with deep gratitude that I owed them all to Hop Sing.

His garden was flourishing; all of the seeds I had given him had sprouted and gave promise of a rich harvest under his patient, ceaseless care. He was always at work, and so too was Mrs. Sing, despite the demands on her time made by three small children. Sing was a baker as well as a gardener, and four times per week, after his long day's toil, he made the rounds of the district selling crisp loaves and pineapple tarts to the native population. Invariably, during these excursions, he left something at my gate, either a tart or a loaf of bread or a basket of vegetables, and to my great relief nothing I could do or say served to dry up his fountain of gratitude for my wretched little gift of seed.

Under these circumstances the weeks passed so pleasantly and quickly that steamer day — the third since the posting of my manuscript — was at hand before I realized it. I walked into town once more and waited on the bench for the distribution of the mail. I waited all through the afternoon until everyone in Papeete and its environs had called for their letters. I waited until the sun was sinking behind the mountains of Moorea and the post office was about to close. Then, summoning all my resolution, I mounted the steps and walked toward the delivery window, saying inwardly, "It's useless to ask; I'm quite certain to be disappointed." The girl who presided there went hastily through a small heap of letters.

"Yes, there's one letter," she said. "Fifty centimes postage due."

Having paid this, I had left only a twenty-five-centime piece, the smallest coin in use in French Oceania. But little that mattered. The letter contained a gracious note accepting my manuscript, and a cheque for five hundred dollars!

To those living luxurious lives in the high latitudes five hundred dollars may seem a trifling sum, but to me it was a fortune. With the half of it I could pay the rental for my house and grounds for a period of nearly seven years, and, provided I lived as modestly in the future as I had in the immediate past, the two hundred and fifty remaining would suffice for other expenses for a much longer time. But now, with bright vistas of ease and plenty and peace of mind opening out before me, I found myself perversely considering the possibility of leaving Tahiti. The north-bound steamer to San Francisco was expected in three days' time, and I might never again have enough money for a steamship ticket. I walked the streets long after everyone else was in bed, in an agony of indecision, and at last, as the clock in the cathedral was striking two, the decision was made.

Hop Sing was in town on the day of my departure. He had driven to market with garden produce, and both he and Lee Fat came to see me off. Fat insisted on my accepting a pair of Russian-leather bedroom-slippers and a Chinese fan of blue silk embroidered with gold butter-flies. Sing's parting gift was a basket of tomatoes as large as oranges, and a dozen ears of sweet corn, Golden Bantam — the first fruits from the seeds I had given him.

Adam — "Our General Ancestor," as Milton calls him — was undoubtedly the first husbandman, and a highly successful one during the early part of his career. But, even under the exceptionally favorable conditions prevailing in the Garden of Eden before The Fall, I doubt whether he ever reaped a richer or more varied harvest than I did in my garden at Tahiti. And it all came from a dollar's worth of seed.

1926
OUR DISSOLVING ETHICS
by James Truslow Adams

THE scapegoat is one of the most venerable and widespread of human institutions. The victim may be literally a goat, as among the Children of Israel, or a rat or a monkey or other animal. Not infrequently it is a human being. For example, in Nigeria all persons who during the year have committed incendiarism, witchcraft, theft, adultery, or other crimes, chip in about ten dollars each and buy a young girl, who is then dragged to the river and drowned for the sins of the town. The sense of guilt requires some sort of expiation, and this "cash and carry" system of expiating the sins of an entire community by attributing them to someone else has obvious advantages. It enables one to settle with one's conscience and the social conventions with a minimum of personal inconvenience and mental anguish.

Here in these United States in this post-war period, realizing that all is not right with our world, we have found the scapegoat which permits us to go about our business with a free mind. The name on its collar is "The Younger Generation."

That youth is questioning the validity of our entire system of ethics to an extent that is perturbing to parents and, in a lesser degree, to grandparents may be admitted. But it cannot be so readily argued that the babies born between 1900 and 1910 all received a hypodermic injection of new original sin. For one thing, these youngsters have been fed on a different intellectual fare from that on which their parents were fed. It must not be lost to sight, however, that this fare has been prepared for them by their parents, or at least by their elders. It must also be noted that they are going to college by the tens of thousands annually. The responsibility for what happens to them there intellectually is squarely up to the older generation. The institutions are provided and run by that generation, the young are in great measure sent by it, and the instruction is wholly provided by it.

Let us consider briefly what a few of the ideas are which are familiar to the younger generation and which to a great extent were not so to the youth of the older one. For one thing, we may cite the comparative study of religion. There are only two methods of intellectual approach to any subject, whether religious or scientific. We may rely upon authority — that is, someone else's judgment — or upon our own. From the time that Protestantism rejected the authority of the Catholic Church and insisted upon the right of personal searching and interpretation of the Scriptures the way was opened for the decline in the prestige of authority. Nothing serves more subtly to break down a belief in the theology of Christianity than to find, for example, that the idea of a dying god is common to many religions and many people, and that even the doctrine of transubstantiation and the eating of bread which somehow becomes the body of a god is widespread. The question naturally arises why, if we must reject these doctrines as taught by every religion except Christianity, should we be obliged to accept them as true in that? Religion and theology are very different things. The younger generation is not irreligious. In the truest sense they want a religion, but for them a mere sentence in the Bible can no longer be appealed to as affording a sufficient sanction for an ethical idea or a code of conduct that has no other apparent reason for being.

In another comparative study, that of anthropology, they also find much to make them question current ethics. By a study of the various tribes and races of the world in different times and places the student finds that they all, indeed, have codes and ethics, but that these all vary and have grown out of specific social or economic needs under particular conditions. The institution of the family, for example, and the relations of the sexes have assumed many forms. The whole question is thrown into the intellectual melting pot as one for discussion, and the sanction tends to become not some religious authority but the good of society and the individual. The older generation was taught that God gave certain commands, regarding sexual and other relations, engraved on a tablet of stone, to a Hebrew some thousands of years ago. It is useless to tell that to a young person today and expect it to settle the matter.

If he turns to philosophy he comes in contact with a world, not of fixed ideas, of eternal verities, but a world where all is in a state of flux. It is not that certain "eternal truths" are being attacked in order to substitute others in their places, but that the lasting validity of truths, any truths, is itself under fire. No teacher, perhaps, has been more popular or exerted greater influence than the late William James, and the pragmatism associated with his name is, in the form of its presentation at least, one of the original American contributions to philosophy. Now the essence of pragmatism is that the truth or validity of an idea depends on whether it works in practice.

This philosophy is thoroughly consonant with the American temperament and natural outlook on life. We are not mentally a subtle or an abstract people. If a thing does not work, it is of no use. If it does, that is a sufficient answer to any attack, and it is this pragmatic sanction that, consciously or not, many a thoughtful young person of today is seeking for the new ethics.

Philosophical and scientific ideas are coming to affect the thinking of people, who may never read the books in which they are primarily expressed, with steadily increasing acceleration. It took many generations for the discovery by Copernicus that the earth was not the centre of the universe, but moved round the sun, to affect religious and other ideas. It took something more than a generation for Darwin's theory of evolution to revolutionize all our thinking. Who knows what the influence, not merely in science, but in all social thinking, including ethics, may very soon be of Einstein's theory of relativity? It has already had great influence, in spite of the fact that those of us who are not mathematicians cannot comprehend it. But to be told — to mention only one aspect of his theory — that there is no such thing as a "correct size" of anything, but that for human knowledge the size of anything depends on the relative speed maintained by the observer and the thing observed, is, literally, appalling. This fact brings to us in startling fashion and in mathematical terms the realization that things are not permanent but relative. The theory of relativity is far more of a solvent for the eternal verities than either the Copernican or the Darwinian theory, and its effect, already being felt, is bound to be profound in realms of thought seemingly remote from physics.

II

In a few words, the young generation has a religion, but it is nebulous. It may to some extent serve, at moments when it is felt, as a source of strength, as an aid to being straight and decent. At many times it is not felt. In any case it issues no commands covering specific conduct. It has no decalogue, and the question of what is decent and straight is left open by it. The youngster's ethics, therefore, have no religious sanction which points out any specific rules of conduct. On the other hand, through his anthropological and sociological studies he comes to realize that there are innumerable ways of living and choices of conduct, all of which have been or are thought right and moral by some people, sometime, somewhere. What constitutes right conduct depends, therefore, apparently on conditions and not on any eternal rules. The prevailing temperament of his nation and its most popular philosophy teach him that the only test of validity is "workability" — that if an idea has good results it is good, if it has not it is bad. The world has never been a very satisfactorily organized place, and nowadays, what with the results of the war, our socially developed conscience, and all the conditions of present life, it can hardly be said to look like an outstanding success. Those who have lived long have for the most part become either reconciled or hopeless over the situation. But for the young it is different, fortunately. They see the poverty, the social injustice, the frequent emotional maladjustment between the individual and society, and they do not see, and let us hope that they are right, that such things need always be.

The fact is that the younger generation is simply carrying forward where we leave off. The decay in belief in the Christian theology, the loss of religious sanction for ethics, the development of such comparative studies as religion and anthropology, the pragmatic philosophy, the Freudian psychology of inhibitions and complexes, and the various scientific and mechanical discoveries which have transformed the world, have all been the work of the older generation. We of the older generation have played with ideas and let loose forces the power of which we little dreamed of. We have, indeed, sowed the wind, and it will be those of the younger generation who will reap the whirlwind unless they can control it.

Never has the road been wilder nor the signposts fewer.

1927
MERCURY
by D. H. Lawrence

IT was Sunday, and very hot. The holiday makers flocked to the hill of Mercury, to rise two thousand feet above the steamy haze of the valleys. For the summer had been very wet, and the sudden heat covered the land in hot steam.

Every time it made its ascent, the funicular was crowded. It hauled itself up the steep incline, which toward the top looked almost perpendicular, the steel thread of the rails in the gulf of pine trees hanging like an iron rope against a wall. The women held their breath, and didn't look. Or they looked back toward the sinking levels of the river, steamed and dim, far-stretching over the frontier.

When you arrived at the top, there was nothing to do. The hill was a pine-covered cone, paths wound between the high tree trunks, and you could walk round and see the glimpses of the world all round, all round: the dim far river plain, with a dull glint of the great stream, to westward; southward the black, forest-covered, agile-looking hills, with emerald-green clearings and a white house or two; east the inner valley, with two villages, factory chimneys, pointed churches, and hills beyond; and north the steep hills of forest, with reddish crags and reddish castle ruins. The hot sun burned overhead, and all was in steam.

Only on the very summit of the hill there was a tower, an outlook tower; a long restaurant with its beer garden, all the little yellow tables standing their round discs under the horse-chestnut trees; then a bit of a rock garden on the slope. But the great trees began again in wilderness a few yards off.

The Sunday crowd came up in waves from the funicular. In waves they ebbed through the beer garden. But not many sat down to drink. Nobody was spending any money. Some paid to go up the outlook tower, to look down on a world of vapors and black, agile-crouching hills and half-cooked towns. Then everybody dispersed along the paths, to sit among the trees in the cool air.

There was not a breath of wind. As you lay and looked upward at the shaggy, barbaric middle world of the pine trees, it was difficult to decide whether the pure, high trunks supported the upper thicket of darkness, or whether they descended from it like great cords stretched downward. Anyhow, in between the tree-top world and the earth world went the wonderful clean cords of innumerable proud tree trunks, clear as rain. And as you watched you saw that the upper world was faintly moving, faintly, most faintly swaying, with a circular movement, though the lower trunks were utterly motionless and monolithic.

There was nothing to do. In all the world there was nothing to do, and nothing to be done. Why have we all come to the top of the Merkur? There is nothing for us to do.

What matter! We have come a stride beyond the world. Let it steam and cook its half-baked reality below there. On the hill of Mercury we take no notice. Even we do not trouble to wander and pick the fat blue sourish bilberries. Just lie and see the rain-pure tree trunks like chords of music between two worlds.

The hours pass by, people wander and disappear and reappear. All is hot and quiet. Humanity is rarely boisterous any more. You go for a drink; finches run among the few people at the tables; everybody glances at everybody, but with remoteness.

There is nothing to do but to return and lie down under the pine trees. Nothing to do. But why do anything, anyhow? The desire to do anything has gone. The tree trunks, living like rain, they are quite active enough.

At the foot of the outlook tower there is an old tablet stone with a very much battered Mercury in relief. There is also an altar, or votive stone, both from the Roman times. The Romans are supposed to have worshiped Mercury on this summit. The battered god, with his round sun head, looks very hollow-eyed and unimpressive in the purplish-red sandstone of the district. And no one any more will throw grains of offering in the hollow of the votive stone: also common, purplish-red sandstone, very local and un-Roman.

The Sunday people do not even look. Why should they? They keep passing on into the pine trees. And many sit on the benches, many lie upon the long chairs. It is very hot in the afternoon, and very still.

Till there seems a faint whistling in the tops of the pine trees, and out of the universal semiconsciousness of the afternoon arouses a bristling uneasiness. The crowd is astir, looking at the sky. And sure enough, there is a great flat blackness reared up in the western sky, curled with white wisps and loose breast feathers. It looks very sinister, as only the elements still can look. Under the sudden weird whistling of the upper pine trees there is a subdued babble and calling of frightened voices.

They want to get down, the crowd wants to get down off the hill of Mercury before the storm comes. At any price to get off this hill! They stream toward the funicular, while the sky blackens with incredible rapidity. And as the crowd presses down toward the little station the first blaze of lightning opens out, followed immediately by a crash of thunder, and great darkness. In one strange movement the crowd takes refuge in the deep verandah of the restaurant, pressing among the little tables in silence. There is no rain, and no definite wind, only a sudden coldness which makes the crowd press closer.

They press closer, in the darkness and the suspense. They have become curiously unified, the crowd, as if they had fused into one body. As the air sends a chill waft under the verandah, the voices murmur plaintively, like birds under leaves, the bodies press closer together, seeking shelter in contact.

The gloom, dark as night, seems to continue a long time. Then suddenly the lightning dances white on the floor, dances and shakes upon the ground, up and down, and lights up the white striding of a man, lights him up only to the hips, white and naked and striding, with fire on his heels. He seems to be hurrying, this fiery man whose upper half is invisible, and at his naked heels white little flames seem to flutter. His flat, powerful thighs, his legs white as fire, stride rapidly across the open, in front of the verandah, dragging little white flames at the ankles, with the movement. He is going somewhere, swiftly.

In the great bang of the thunder the apparition disappears, the earth moves, and the house jumps in complete darkness. A faint whimpering of terror comes from the crowd, as the cold air swirls in. But still, upon the darkness, there is no rain. There is no relief: a long wait.

Brilliant and blinding, the lightning falls again; a strange bruising thud comes from the forest, as all the little tables and the secret tree trunks stand for one unnatural second exposed. Then the blow of the thunder, under which the house and the crowd reel as under an explosion. The storm is playing directly upon the Merkur. A belated sound of tearing branches comes out of the forest.

And again the white splash of the lightning on the ground; but nothing moves. And again the long, rattling, instantaneous volleying of the thunder, in the darkness. The crowd is panting with fear, as the lightning again strikes white, and something again seems to burst, in the forest, as the thunder crashes.

At last, into the motionlessness of the storm, in rushes the wind, with the fiery fling of bits of ice, and the sudden sea-like roaring of the pine trees. The crowd winces and draws back, as the bits of ice hit in the face like fire. The roar of the trees is so great, it becomes like another silence. And through it are heard the crashing and splintering of timber, as the hurricane concentrates upon the hill.

Down comes the hail, in a roar that covers every other sound, thrashing ponderously upon the ground and the roofs and the trees. And as the crowd surges irresistibly into the interior of the building, from the crushing of this ice fall, still amid the sombre hoarseness sound the tinkle and crackle of things breaking.

After an eternity of dread, it ends suddenly. Outside is a faint gleam of yellow light, over the snow and the endless débris of twigs and things broken. It is very cold, with the atmosphere of ice and deep winter. The forest looks wan, above the white earth, where the ice balls lie in their myriads, six inches deep, littered with all the twigs and things they have broken.

"Yes! Yes!" say the men, taking sudden courage as the yellow light comes into the air. "Now we can go!"

The first brave ones emerge, picking up the big hailstones, pointing to the overthrown tables. Some, however, do not linger. They hurry to the funicular station, to see if the apparatus is still working.

The funicular station is on the north side of the hill. The men come back, saying there is no one there. The crowd begins to emerge upon the wet, crunching whiteness of the hail, spreading around in curiosity, waiting for the men who operate the funicular.

On the south side of the outlook tower two bodies lay in the cold but thawing hail. The dark blue of the uniform showed blackish. Both men were dead. But the lightning had completely removed the clothing from the legs of one man, so that he was naked from the hips down. There he lay, his face sideways on the snow, and two drops of blood running from his nose into his big, blonde, military moustache. He lay there near the votive stone of the Mercury. His companion, a young man, lay face downward, a few yards behind him.

The sun began to emerge. The crowd gaped in dread, afraid to touch the bodies of the men. Why had they, the dead funicular men, come round to this side of the hill, anyhow?

The funicular would not work. Something had happened to it in the storm. The crowd began to wind down the bare hill, on the slippery ice. Everywhere the earth bristled with broken pine boughs and twigs. But the bushes and the leafy trees were stripped absolutely bare, to a miracle. The lower earth was leafless and naked as in winter.

"Absolute winter!" murmured the crowd, as they hurried, frightened, down the steep, winding descent, extricating themselves from the fallen pine branches.

Meanwhile the sun began to steam in great heat.

1928

UNIVERSITIES AND THEIR FUNCTION
by Alfred North Whitehead

THE universities are schools of education, and schools of research. But the primary reason for their existence is not to be found either in the mere knowledge conveyed to the students or in the mere opportunities for research afforded to the members of the faculty.

The justification for a university is that it preserves the connection between knowledge and the zest of life, by uniting the young and the old in the imaginative consideration of learning. The university imparts information, but it imparts it imaginatively. At least, this is the function which it should perform for society. A university which fails in this respect has no reason for existence. This atmosphere of excitement, arising from imaginative consideration, transforms knowledge. A fact is no longer a bare fact: it is invested with all its possibilities. It is no longer a burden on the memory: it is energizing as the poet of our dreams, and as the architect of our purposes.

Imagination is not to be divorced from the facts: it is a way of illuminating the facts. It works by eliciting the general principles which apply to the facts, as they exist, and then by an intellectual survey of alternative possibilities which are consistent with those principles. It enables men to construct an intellectual vision of a new world, and it preserves the zest of life by the suggestion of satisfying purposes.

Youth is imaginative, and if the imagination be strengthened by discipline this energy of imagination can in great measure be preserved through life. The tragedy of the world is that those who are imaginative have but slight experience, and those who are experienced have feeble imaginations. Fools act on imagination without knowledge; pedants act on knowledge without imagination. The task of a university is to weld together imagination and experience.

These reflections upon the general functions of a university can be at once translated in terms of the particular functions of a business school. We need not flinch from the assertion that the main function of such a school is to produce men with a greater zest for business.

In a simpler world, business relations were simpler, being based on the immediate contact of man with man and on immediate confrontation with all relevant material circumstances. To-day business organization requires an imaginative grasp of the psychologies of populations engaged in differing modes of occupation; of populations scattered through cities, through mountains, through plains; of populations on the ocean, and of populations in mines, and of populations in forests. It requires an imaginative grasp of conditions in the tropics, and of conditions in temperate zones. It requires an imaginative grasp of the interlocking interests of great organizations, and of the reactions of the whole complex to any change in one of its elements. It requires an imaginative understanding of laws of political economy, not merely in the abstract, but also with the power to construe them in terms of the particular circumstances of a concrete business. It requires some knowledge of the habits of government, and of the variations of those habits under diverse conditions. It requires an imaginative vision of the binding forces of any human organization, a sympathetic vision of the limits of human nature and of the conditions which evoke loyalty of service. It requires some knowledge of the laws of health, and of the laws of fatigue, and of the conditions for sustained reliability. It requires an imaginative understanding of the social effects of the conditions of factories. It requires a sufficient conception of the rôle of applied science in modern society. It requires that discipline of character which can say "yes" and "no" to other men, not by reason of blind obstinacy, but with firmness derived from a conscious evaluation of relevant alternatives.

The universities have trained the intellectual pioneers of our civilization — the priests, the lawyers, the statesmen, the doctors, the men of science, and the men of letters. The conduct of business now requires intellectual imagination of the same type as that which in former times has mainly passed into those other occupations.

There is one great difficulty which hampers all the higher types of human endeavor. In modern times this difficulty has even increased in its possibilities for evil. In any large organization the younger men, who are novices, must be set to jobs which consist in carrying out fixed duties in obedience to orders. No president of a large corporation meets his youngest employee at his office door with the offer of the most responsible job which the work of that corporation includes. The young men are set to work at a fixed routine, and only occasionally even see the president as he passes in and out of the building. Such work is a great discipline. It imparts knowledge, and it produces reliability of character; also it is the only work for which the young men, in that novice stage, are fit, and it is the work for which they are hired. There can be no criticism of the custom, but there may be an unfortunate effect — prolonged routine work dulls the imagination.

The way in which a university should function in the preparation for an intellectual career, such as modern business or one of the older professions, is by promoting the imaginative consideration of the various general principles underlying that career. Its students thus pass into their period of technical apprenticeship with their imaginations already practised in connecting details with general principles. The routine then receives its meaning, and also illuminates the principles which give it that meaning. Hence, instead of a drudgery issuing in a blind rule of thumb, the properly trained man has some hope of obtaining an imagination disciplined by detailed facts and by necessary habits.

Thus the proper function of a university is the imaginative acquisition of knowledge. Apart from this importance of the imagination, there is no reason why business men, and other professional men, should not pick up their facts bit by bit as they want them for particular occasions. A university is imaginative or it is nothing — at least nothing useful.

1929
POEMS
by Emily Dickinson

I

I RECKON, when I count at all,
First Poets — then the Sun —
Then Summer — then the Heaven of God —
And then the list is done.
But looking back — the first so seems

To comprehend the whole —
The others look a needless show,
So I write Poets — All.
This Summer lasts a solid year,
They can afford a sun.
The East would deem extravagant,
And if the final Heaven
Be beautiful as they disclose
To those who trust in them,
It is too difficult a grace
To justify the dream.

II

IT always felt to me a wrong
To that old Moses done,
To let him see the Canaan
Without the entering.

And though in soberer moments
No Moses there can be,
I'm satisfied the romance
In point of injury

Surpasses sharper stated
Of Stephen or of Paul,
For these were only put to death,
While God's adroiter will

On Moses seemed to fasten
In tantalizing play —
As Boy should deal with lesser Boy
To show supremacy.

The fault was doubtless Israel's;
Myself had banned the Tribes,
And ushered grand old Moses
In pentateuchal robes

Upon the broad possession
But titled him to see.
Old Man on Nebo! Late as this
One Justice bleeds for thee!

III

Through the dark sod
As education,
The Lily passes sure,
Feels her white foot
No trepidation,
Her faith no fear.

Afterward in the meadow
Swinging her beryl bell,
The mold-life all forgotten now —
In ecstasy and dell.

IV

And this of all my hopes —
This is the silent end;
Bountiful colored my morning rose,
Early and sere its end.

Never bud from a stem
Stepped with so gay a foot,
Never a worm so confident
Bored at so brave a root.

V

After great pain a formal feeling comes —
The nerves sit ceremonious like tombs;
The stiff Heart questions — was it He that bore?
And yesterday — or centuries before?

The feet mechanical
Go round a wooden way
Of ground or air or Ought, regardless grown,
A quartz contentment like a stone.

This is the hour of lead
Remembered if outlived,
As freezing persons recollect the snow —
First chill, then stupor, then the letting go.

VI

Of nearness to her sundered things
The Soul has special times,
When Dimness looks the Oddity,
Distinctness easy seems.

The shapes we buried dwell about.
Familiar in the rooms,
Untarnished by the sepulchre
Our moldering playmate comes

In just the jacket that he wore,
Long buttoned in the mold,
Since we, old mornings, children played,
Divided by a world.

The grave yields back her robberies,
The years are pilfered things,
Bright knots of apparitions
Salute us with their wings —

As we it were that perished,
Themselves had just remained
Till we rejoin them,
And 't was They, and not Ourselves
That mourned.

VII

It ceased to hurt me, though so slow
I could not see the trouble go —
But only knew by looking back
That something had obscured the track.

Nor when it altered, I could say —
For I had worn it every day
As constant as the childish frock
I hung upon the peg at night.

Nor what consoled it —
I could trace,
Except whereas 't was wilderness
It's better, almost Peace.

VIII

THE world feels dusty
When we stop to die;
We want the dew then,
Honors taste dry.

Flags vex a dying face,
But the least fan
Stirred by a friend's hand
Cools like the rain.

Mine be the ministry
When thy thirst comes,
Dews of thyself to fetch
And holy balms.

1930
ATMOSPHERE VERSUS ART
by Frank Jewett Mather, Jr.

WHAT is the duty of the museum toward the work of art?
First, obviously, to preserve it. Primarily a museum is simply a high-class storehouse — or, more politely, a treasure
house. Why preserve the work of art? Evidently that it may continue
to convey to the sympathetic spectator the creative ecstasy that went to
its marking. Thus it is a collateral duty to show the work of art and
show it well. Here difference of opinion arises. What, after all, is exhibiting well? Very few works of art, and those not the best, were
made in order to be exhibited in a museum. Most sculpture and most
painting were in one way and another associated with architecture; in
any case they were made for surroundings and eyes quite different
from ours. From those surroundings they have been torn; frequently
the original environment has been destroyed; their old home has gone
beyond recall; the museum provides on an artificial basis a new home.

Let us follow out what this making at home actually involves in
practice. A worried curator awakes to the fact that a fine big altarpiece
is homeless in his gallery. It was painted for an altar. So he buys an
altar of the period and sets the picture on it. I write feelingly, for I
have seen it done. But the altarpiece and its, at best, borrowed altar
are together mildly ridiculous in the gallery. What to do? Why, take

the further steps toward putting the altarpiece at its homely ease! If funds permit, buy a chapel of the period — they are, unhappily, for sale — and set up therein the altarpiece and the altar.

Now, according to approved museum practice, the picture is ideally at home. What a delusion! It stands over an altar and in a chapel for which it was not created; its being at home is an archæological fraud.

From the moment that a work of art made for a particular place is moved therefrom, an original set of associational values drops forever away from it. The attempt to recover them otherwise than through the historical imagination is entirely futile. It is the business of the museum to ascertain and exploit the values that remain. The picture, say, is now an exhibit in a museum; the task is to bring out to the full its museum values. It now is, or should be, in a neutral environment — in which, however, it is probably far better seen than it was in the gloom of its chapel. If it has lost by the move, it has also gained. And the museum value, while it lacks much that was important to the artist, also dispenses with much that was adventitious and confusing. The primary value is imperishable: the passing of a high creative impulse to an understanding soul — all this is intact. Indeed, through a degree of generalization and the dropping away of local associations, there has often come a new value of universality. It is by no means to be assumed that the Sistine Madonna was better seen in her chapel at Vicenza than she has been seen for generations in her museum sanctuary at Dresden. And it is even less to be supposed that she would be seen better at Dresden if the German Republic could persuade the Honorable Mussolini to cause the original chapel, still extant, to be taken down and set up again in the Dresden Gallery. In short, the way to run a museum successfully is to treat it as a museum and not as a congeries of antiquarian compilations.

II

A museum is properly a somewhat formidable place. One goes there to gain contact with personalities far greater than those we meet in ordinary life. It is no light matter to make the acquaintance of Rembrandt. All the museum really needs to offer is opportunity — and that means getting the right things and exhibiting them skillfully.

Good lighting, avoidance of obvious clashes, generous spacing, simple and neutral backgrounds — this is all that is necessary to enjoyment. The elaborately decorative appointment and hanging of an art gallery is largely labor lost. It is based on a false psychology — that the ensemble is highly important. It is really of very slight importance. The visitor, if he knows his business, makes an act of concentration by which he sees only one object at a time. Unless he is capable of such concentration, he is helpless in a museum, however exquisitely ar-

ranged. It really doesn't matter what is alongside or opposite the masterpiece he is contemplating, so long as he can isolate it for enjoyment.

But it will be argued that the period rooms are immensely liked, and
the readiest means of drawing a reluctant public to the museums. But
is it the business of the art museum to join the moving-picture theatre
in giving the public what it wants?

This question is best answered by indirection — by following out
what happens concretely when museums engage in this course. All our
art museums, with the possible exception of that of Newark, New Jersey, give a certain, however grudging, preference to the fine arts.
Practically that means that if they had a picture gallery and a Dutch
room, and came into possession of a fine Rembrandt, they would hang
it rather in the picture gallery than in the Dutch room. Why? Because
they know it would be better seen in the gallery that in the Dutch
room, and they deem a masterpiece of this sort worth the seeing. Now
suppose, instead of a Rembrandt, the museum bought a fine but not
great picture — say, a Metsu. Should it go into the Dutch room or into
the gallery? Evidently the decision would rest on the director's judgment of the picture. If it was a very fine Metsu that deserved to be
studied and contemplated, he would, if he had any sense at all, put it
in the gallery. If, on the contrary, it seemed to him just an ordinary
Metsu that deserved no concentrated observation, he would properly
make it a part of the decorative ensemble of his Dutch room.

Galleries by honored use and wont contain objects of the fine arts
for the purpose of delectation and contemplation. Period rooms contain such objects of the minor arts and such minor examples of the
fine arts as can be combined into an atmosphere which may be re-
spired and enjoyed without concentration, contemplation, or taking
thought of any kind. Here we capture the simple secret of the vogue
of the period room both with the public and with a certain type of
museum official: it can be enjoyed — nay, it can be created — by persons relatively without taste and too busy for reflection of any sort. For
the tired business man it is indeed the ideal art museum, and so it is
for the bewildered museum director at his wit's end.

III

It would be unfair to leave this matter without admitting that much
of the enthusiasm for atmosphere has had its causes in the frequently
preposterous management of our art museums. A city becomes ambitious. It helps a board of museum trustees to build an immense structure, which is put in the hands of an architect who, without guidance
from museum experts, builds himself an imposing and very costly
monument. As a museum, it will inevitably be a shocking and extravagant misfit. Many of our museums are of this sort; it is unnecessary to

name them. Tardily the trustees, with an enormous building on their hands, wake up to the fact that they haven't a director or collections. A director comes fairly easy — they hire him. Collections come hard. What is the director to do? His position depends on his making a prompt public impression. The empty halls haunt his dreams. Instead of thinking in terms of fine objects one after another, as a real director of fine arts must, he thinks in terms of galleries. There are many empty galleries, there are many periods of decoration — period rooms are the quick and easy solution. They are in the market; as compared with great works of art, they are both abundant and cheap. So, ho for period rooms, and the long-eared public behind you! In this fashion one might readily make a great art museum which would not contain a single great work of art.

Now the fact that this is a natural way of extricating one's self from certain awkward situations does not excuse it. If the aim of a museum is to extend culture through the understanding of great art, we have to do with a complete negation of its main purpose. At best we are dealing with a thoughtless sentimentality, at worst with a cynical disloyalty. I suppose that museum directors have to live, — I have to, — but I think some of them would be wise to let blundering trustees and overbearing architects stew in their own juice.

1931
THE NEW PILGRIM'S PROGRESS
An Odyssey of the Unemployed
by Robert Whitcomb

AFTER several months of riding freight trains, joining bread lines, sleeping in jails or Salvation Army "flophouses" or box cars, I began to realize that Wall Street had crashed and that unemployment was a national problem. At first I had no idea of the magnitude of the disaster; I saw it all purely in terms of my own personal difficulties. All that I knew was that I had been fired out of an unsatisfactory newspaper job in a suburb of New York City and would have to look for another berth.

After I had failed to find work in New York, I decided to "hit the road." I had seventeen dollars in my pocket and all I needed to do was to support myself.

United States Highway No. 1, which runs along the Atlantic Coast from Maine to Florida, was thronged with pedestrians in January of 1930 when I set out upon it, headed south. There was a sprinkling of adventurers, most of them posing as hatless college boys with Boston bags. Some were disappointed office workers on their way from New York to Miami. A few were obviously just graduating from the Boy Scouts and were indulging their *Wanderlust*. Nine tenths of them, however, were workmen in overalls. By the time I came to the short-leaf pines and open spaces south of Richmond, I had talked with a number of these men and learned that many were heads of families forced away from home by unemployment. Among them were skilled laborers, — carpenters, plasterers, operators of machines, — most of them willing enough to forgo their union status if they could only find some sort of work at any sort of wages. All of these wanderers were trying to hitch-hike their way along, but it was a discouraging business; their numbers had spoiled the sport, and most of them were doing more hiking than hitching.

I rode through South Carolina and Georgia in one lucky lift and then made for New Orleans. By this time I had exhausted my slender resources and found myself walking the streets of a strange city without a penny to my name.

I could not have hit upon a worse place than New Orleans at this time. I had arrived in the city at the height of that hysterical season which they call Mardi Gras. From all the corners and hollows of the earth tourists and sight-seers were pouring in, and they were followed by a ragged army of hoboes, bums, street fakers, and touts who converged upon the city from every point of the compass. While the carnival reigns it is always a problem for the New Orleans police to keep an eye on pickpockets, and this year the depression had made their task doubly difficult.

I had already had several brushes with the police and I knew their attitude. "No visible means of support" is the club they use in sending many an innocent victim to jail for weeks on end.

I heard that men were wanted on the banana wharf, unloading the heavy bunches of fruit at thirty-five cents an hour. I applied, only to be told that the jobs had all been taken. As I turned to leave the place, I observed a "No Smoking" sign and put my pipe in my pocket; but a "copper" had seen me and came running up excitedly. After so many weeks of tramping about, I presented anything but a prepossessing appearance. The cop was one of the kind to whom "orders is orders," and since I had been caught smoking on the sacred banana wharf of New Orleans there was nothing for it but that I must be arrested for investigation. While we were waiting for the patrol wagon, a well-dressed man in the company of a woman passed by smoking a cigarette; my captor politely informed him that smoking was not permitted.

This was the first time I had ever been arrested and it gave me my first introduction to a "bull pen." I was thrown into a large cell crowded with nearly a hundred prisoners. As I surveyed this pirate's crew, I tried to pick out the hardened criminals from the mere down-and-outers, and I could not. I was beginning to feel a mental kinship with these underdogs whose circumstances had placed them outside the law.

When my case came up, I was lucky to get a "floater" — a discharge with a warning to leave town within a few hours. Meanwhile I had heard about the Llano del Rio Colony in western Louisiana, near Leesville, which is run as a coöperative venture. There, I was told, I could earn food, clothing, and shelter; they had no unemployment. I determined to go there.

II

Fifteen years ago Llano was organized on a mud flat which was at that time the site of a deserted lumber camp. Since then hundreds have joined it and left it, but the population still manages to keep ahead of the original group. Everybody except the youngest children works eight hours a day, receiving no money but sharing all things in common. The work, which is not strenuous, allows for a wide range of aptitudes. There are a farm and a garden, a sawmill, an ice plant, a printing shop, a laundry, a general store, a tailor shop, a shoe shop, a library, and a garage. There are also a dance hall, an orchestra, and a rudimentary theatre.

In spite of the brave spirit of most of its people, Llano is an unhappy place. The community is full of elderly Middle-Western farmers who have sunk their last dollar in a Llano membership and are depressed by the feeling that they are married to the place, for better or for worse, until death do them part. Even the children are a joyless lot. I soon lost whatever enthusiasm I had worked up over their ideas, and in the end I left before I was kicked out.

From Llano I hitch-hiked to Fort Worth, Texas. I had now grown utterly despondent. Wherever I went I encountered the same stagnation of business. I had come two thousand miles in search of work, and the only things I had to show for my pains were tattered clothes and empty pockets. Moreover, my seedy appearance now made it almost impossible for me to get any lifts from motorists; when I signaled to a passing car, the driver would give one look at me and step on the gas. I had become a suspicious character. This drove me to "hopping" my first freight; it was either that or walk.

Hitch-hiking is a lonely business, but freight riding is full of companionship in misery. I was plunged at once into the mysteries of professional hobodom and learned to think in terms of railroad divisions, "brakies," "shacks," "dicks," "bulls," and "red-ball" and "manifest" expresses. I grew accustomed to approaching groups of hoboes as one of them, exchanging information about rumors of construction jobs and the intricacies of railroad yards. Little by little I came to realize that riding freights is like an exciting game, with the lost goals symbolized at best by a term in jail and at worst by an amputated leg or an unmarked grave in potter's field.

From Fort Worth I started toward Oklahoma City by rail. In Oklahoma City crowds of overalled and heavy-booted men stood about in the streets. I asked them what chance a man had in the oil fields. They told me that all the jobs had been filled long since, but that men were still pouring in from all over the world because they had heard about the oil boom. The city, they said, had been maintaining bread lines for local men out of work, but was unable to do anything for the army of "foreigners." Later that same day I rode west out of Oklahoma City.

III

At El Reno, Oklahoma, my next stop, I was held up several days by a railroad detective who had developed peculiar methods of his own for dealing with hoboes. At every railroad yard where valuable freight pauses temporarily, detectives are stationed to guard the property; but it is not an easy thing to do, for some of the yards are miles long. This bull at El Reno is an elderly man who takes the responsibilities of his job very seriously. By firing a pistol into the air, he frightens all the free "passengers" off the freights as they pass through. This, as it happens, works a great hardship on the town, because the hungry men collect there in large numbers, begging food; and if they cannot beg it they steal it. Once a week, however, the detective has his day off, and then all the accumulated hoboes hop the same train.

When we had caught another freight and were nearing Amarillo in the Panhandle of Texas, hoboes kept jumping on at each small division until our box car had accumulated fifty-odd. As our numbers increased our spirits rose and we gave vent to much smart talk. The President was roundly flayed as the prime cause of all evil, and a member of the train crew who stuck his head in at the side door was just as roundly booed. At one point the railroad tracks ran parallel to the highway and we passed one of those "Forward America" signs with its catchwords painted in huge letters: "Business Is Good — Keep It Good." Every man jack of us guffawed uproariously. We knew how to take a joke, even when it was on us.

I traveled for several divisions into New Mexico with one of this group. He was a six-foot Hollander, a plasterer by trade. Until a month prior to the time I met him he had been the affluent owner of an automobile; he had toured almost every state in the Union with his wife and daughter. Now he was willing to take any kind of job that would pay for his meals and leave him a dollar to send home — and he couldn't find it.

As we pulled into the small railroad town of Vaughn, New Mexico, we saw a carnival in full swing. This gave Dutch the bright idea that we might stage a prize fight and earn a stake. This would never have occurred to me in a million years, but with the proposition before me I accepted. We soon learned, however, that the carnival already had its quota of fighters. Then Dutch saw a plasterer's mixing board tied to the back of an automobile and nothing would do but that we must wait for the owner to appear; a plasterer might know of some work. When he came he turned out to be one of the carnival fighters. He knew about a temporary job for Dutch, but none for me, so I left them engaged in earnest conversation about plastering and fighting. Hoboes do not part sorrowfully; they have already parted too many times with too many people. But I remember Dutch particularly because he really was a fine example of a simple man.

IV

Even now, as I look back upon it in calm retrospect, I cannot trace the exact route of my vagabondage during those last dreadful months. I have a vivid recollection of my arrival in Cheyenne, Wyoming, in the teeth of a May snowstorm. Along with a dozen others, I had spent a cold night riding in a box car. We had lain on the floor in that attitude peculiar to hoboes — knees curled up, the right hand between them, and the left arm crooked under the head to serve as a pillow.

I remember, later, coming into the Mojave Desert from San Bernardino. It grew hotter and hotter until the temperature reached 120 degrees. There was a road job at Bagdad, between Barstow and Needles, and I got a place working on the bridge gang.

I shunted here and there along the California coast from San Diego to Eureka, in the redwood belt. I stayed a month in San Francisco and then took a trip to Seattle. Conditions, I found, were just as bad in Washington and Oregon as elsewhere. It was no good trying to go on. Without more ado I resolved to return to New York. Three weeks later I stepped off a moving van on the Manhattan side of the Holland Tunnel with fifty cents in my pocket.

The metropolitan newspapers were full of stories about unemployment. Economic articles were invading the Sunday feature sections and the literary reviews, and even the poets were singing about it. Nobody, however, seemed to know anything about the human side of unemployment. As if a conspiracy were afoot to hide the truth by subtle distortion, all the newspapers referred to the unemployed as "the idle." Well, maybe they were, but I doubt it. For ten months I was one of them and during that time I worked temporarily in gardens, in printing shops, in newspaper offices. I carried bricks, shoveled snow, worked on the highways, washed dishes, peeled potatoes, shelled garlic, cooked hamburgers. I was a packer, a checker, a tally man, a mess boy aboard ship. I mixed lime, covered doughnuts with sugar, acted as stevedore on the Seattle docks, planted corn, cucumbers, and other vegetables too numerous to mention. I helped a carpenter build an addition to a small house, scraped a motor boat, tinkered with Fords, fixed typewriters. And between whiles I was always on the move. Thus it was to be "idle"!

For me, all this is now a bad dream from which I have waked, but for countless others it remains the grimmest of realities. And as I walk about New York in a good "front," with neat clothes and a clean white shirt, I can still taste the peculiar flavor of mush and molasses; I can still hear the pounding of locomotives, and feel the coal dust in my eyes.

1932
THE WORLD'S ECONOMIC OUTLOOK
by John Maynard Keynes

THE immediate problem for which the world needs a solution to-day is different from the problem of a year ago. Then it was a question of how we could lift ourselves out of the state of acute slump into which we had fallen and raise the volume of production back toward a normal figure. But to-day our efforts are directed toward the attainment of more limited hopes. Can we prevent an almost complete collapse of the financial structure of modern capitalism?

The immediate causes of the world financial panic — for that is what it is — are obvious. They are to be found in a catastrophic fall in the money value, not only of commodities, but of practically every kind of asset. The "margins," as we call them, upon confidence in the maintenance of which the debt and credit structure of the modern world depends, have "run off." In many countries the assets of the banks are no longer equal, conservatively valued, to their liabilities to their depositors. Debtors of all kinds find that their securities are no longer the equal of their debts. Few governments still have revenues sufficient to cover the fixed money charges for which they have made themselves liable.

Moreover, a collapse of this kind feeds on itself. We are now in the phase where the risk of carrying assets with borrowed money is so great that there is a competitive panic to get liquid. And each individual who succeeds in getting more liquid forces down the price of assets in the process of getting liquid, with the result that the margins of other individuals are impaired and their courage undermined. And so the process continues.

The competitive struggle for liquidity has now extended beyond individuals and institutions to nations and to governments, each of which endeavors to make its internal balance sheet more liquid by restricting imports and stimulating exports by every possible means, the success of each one in this direction meaning the defeat of someone else. Moreover, each country discourages capital development within its own borders for fear of the effect on its international balance. Yet it will only be successful in its object in so far as its progress toward negation is greater than that of its neighbors.

II

We have here an extreme example of the *disharmony* of general and particular interest. Each nation, in an effort to improve its relative position, takes measures injurious to the absolute prosperity of its neighbors; and, since its example is not confined to itself, it suffers more from similar action by its neighbors than it gains by such action itself. Practically all the remedies popularly advocated to-day are of this internecine character. Competitive wage reductions, competitive tariffs, competitive liquidation of foreign assets, competitive currency deflations, competitive economy campaigns — all are of this beggar-my-neighbor description. For one man's expenditure is another man's income. Thus, whenever we refrain from expenditure, while we undoubtedly increase our own margin, we diminish that of someone else; and if the practice is universally followed everyone will be worse off. An individual may be forced by his private circumstances to curtail his normal expenditure, and no one can blame him. But let no one suppose that he is performing a public duty in behaving in such a way. The modern capitalist is a fair-weather sailor. As soon as a storm rises, he abandons the duties of navigation and even sinks the boats which might carry him to safety by his haste to push his neighbor off and himself in.

Unfortunately the popular mind has been educated away from the truth, away from common sense. The average man has been taught to believe what his own common sense, if he relied on it, would tell him was absurd. Even remedies of a right tendency have become discredited because of the failure of a timid and vacillating application of them. Now, at last, under the teaching of hard experience, there may be some slight improvement toward wiser counsels. But through lack of foresight and constructive imagination the financial and political authorities of the world have lacked the courage or the conviction at each stage of the decline to apply the available remedies in sufficiently drastic doses; and by now they have allowed the collapse to reach a point where the whole system may have lost its resiliency and its capacity for a rebound.

Meanwhile the problem of reparations and war debts darkens the whole scene. We all know that these are now as dead as mutton, and as distasteful as stale mutton. There is no question of any substantial payments being made. The problem has ceased to be financial and has become entirely political and psychological. If in the next six months the French were to make a very moderate and reasonable proposal in final settlement, I believe that the Germans, in spite of all their present protestations to the contrary, would accept it and would be wise to accept it. But to all outward appearances the French mind appears to be hardening against such a solution and in favor of forcing a situation in which Germany will default. French politicians (and in candid moments American politicians may confess to a fellow feeling) are conscious that it will be much easier for them, vis-à-vis the home political front, to get rid of reparations by a German default than to reach by agreement a moderate sum, most of which might have to be handed on to the United States. Moreover, this outcome would have what they deem to be the advantage of piling up grievances and a legal case against Germany for use in connection with the other outstanding questions created between the two countries by the Treaty of Versailles. I cannot, therefore, extract much comfort or prospective hope from developments in this sphere of international finance.

III

What elements of hope can we discern in the surrounding gloom? And what useful action does it still lie in our power to take?

The outstanding ground for cheerfulness lies, I think, in this — that the system has shown already its capacity to stand an almost inconceivable strain. This remarkable capacity is the best reason for hoping that we still have time to rally the constructive forces of the world.

Moreover, there has been a still recent and, in my judgment, most blessed event of which we have not yet had time to gain the full benefit. I mean Great Britain's abandonment of the gold standard. If Great Britain had somehow contrived to maintain her gold parity, the position of the world as a whole to-day would be considerably more desperate than it is, and default more general.

For Great Britain's action has had two signal consequences. The first has been to stop the decline of prices, measured in terms of national currencies, over a very considerable proportion of the world. Consider for a moment what an array of countries are now linked to the fortunes of sterling rather than of gold: Australasia, India, Ceylon, Malaya, East and West Africa, Egypt, and Scandinavia; and, in substance, though not so literally, South America, Canada, and Japan. France and the United States are the only remaining countries of major importance where the gold standard is functioning freely.

This means a very great abatement of the deflationary pressure which was existing six months ago. Over wide areas producers are now obtaining prices in terms of their domestic currencies which are not so desperately unsatisfactory in relation to their costs of production and to their debts. These events have been too recent to attract all the attention they deserve. There are several countries of which it could be argued that their economic and financial condition may have turned the corner in the last six months. It is true, for example, of Australia. I think it may be true of Argentina and Brazil. There has been an extraordinary improvement in India, where the export of gold previously hoarded, a consequence of the discount of sterling in terms of gold which no one predicted, has almost solved the financial problem.

As regards Great Britain herself, the number of persons employed to-day exceeds by 200,000 the number employed a year ago — which is true of no other industrial country. This has been achieved in spite of the fact that there has been, even during the past year, a further rise in real wages; for, while money wages have fallen by 2 per cent, the cost of living, in spite of the depreciation of the sterling exchange, has fallen by 4 per cent.

But there is a second major consequence of the partition of the countries of the world into two groups, on and off the gold standard respectively. For the two groups roughly correspond to those which have been exercising deflationary pressure on the rest of the world, by having a *net* creditor position which causes them to draw gold, and those which have been suffering this pressure. Now the departure of the latter group from gold means the beginning of a process toward the restoration of economic equilibrium. It means the setting into motion of natural forces which are certain in course of time to undermine and eventually destroy the creditor position of the two leading creditor gold countries. The process will be seen most rapidly in the case of France, whose creditor position is likely to be completely undermined before the end of 1932. The cessation of reparation receipts, the loss of tourist traffic, the competitive disadvantage of her export trades with non-gold countries, and the importation of a large proportion of the world's available gold, will, between them, do the work. In the case of the United States the process may be a slower one, largely because the reduction of tourist traffic, which costs France so dear, means for the United States a large saving. But the tendency will be the same. A point will surely come when the current release of gold from India and the mines will exceed the favorable balance of the gold countries.

Thus a process has been set moving which may relieve in the end the deflationary pressure. The question is whether this will have time to happen before financial organization and the system of international credit break under the strain. If it does, then the way will be cleared for a concerted policy, probably under the leadership of Great Britain, of capital expansion and price raising throughout the world. For without this the only alternative solution which I can envisage is one of the general default of debts and the disappearance of the existing credit system, followed by rebuilding on quite new foundations.

In the past, we have not infrequently had to wait for a war to terminate a major depression. I hope that in the future we shall not adhere to this purist financial attitude, and that we shall be ready to spend on the enterprises of peace what the financial maxims of the past would only allow us to spend on the devastations of war. At any rate, I predict with an assured confidence that the only way out is for us to discover *some* object which is admitted even by the deadheads to be a legitimate excuse for largely increasing the expenditure of someone on something!

This is not a crisis of poverty, but a crisis of abundance. It is not the harshness and the niggardliness of nature which are oppressing us, but our own incompetence and wrong-headedness which hinder us from making use of the bountifulness of inventive science and cause us to be overwhelmed by its generous fruits. The voices which — in such a conjuncture — tell us that the path of escape is to be found in strict economy and in refraining, wherever possible, from utilizing the world's potential production are the voices of fools and madmen.

Unluckily the traditional and ingrained beliefs of those who hold responsible positions throughout the world grew out of experiences which contained no parallel to the present, and are often the opposite of what one would wish them to believe to-day. In France the weight of authoritative opinion and public sentiment is genuinely and sincerely opposed to the whole line of thought which runs through what I have been saying. In the United States it is almost inconceivable what rubbish a public man has to utter to-day if he is to keep respectable. Serious and sensible bankers, who as men of common sense are trying to do what they can to stem the tide of liquidation and to stimulate the forces of expansion, have to go about assuring the world of their conviction that there is no serious risk of inflation, when what they really mean is that they cannot yet see good enough grounds for daring to hope for it. In Great Britain opinion is probably more advanced. I believe that the ideas of British statesmen and even of British bankers are on sounder lines than those current elsewhere. What we in London have to fear is timidity and a reluctance to act boldly.

Nothing could be a greater advantage to the world than that the United States should solve her own domestic problems, and, by solving them, provide the stimulus and the example to other countries.

CONFESSIONS OF A NOVELIST
by Edith Wharton

WHEN I first began to talk with novelists about the art of fiction I was amazed at the frequently repeated phrase, "I've been hunting about for months for a good subject." Hunting about for a subject! Good heavens! The truth is that I have never attached much importance to subject, partly because every incident, every situation, about me is perpetually presenting itself to me in the light of story-telling material, and partly from the conviction that the possibilities of a given subject are — whatever a given imagination can make of them.

In the birth of fiction, it is sometimes the situation, the "case," which first presents itself to the mind, and sometimes the characters who first appear, asking to be fitted into a situation. I have often speculated on the conditions likely to give the priority to one or the other, but I doubt if fiction can be usefully divided into novels of situation and of character, since a novel, if worth anything at all, is always both at once, in inextricable combination. I can only say that in my own case a situation sometimes occurs to me first, and in others a single figure suddenly walks into my mind. If the situation takes the lead, I leave it lying about, as it were, in a quiet place, and just wait till the characters creep stealthily up and wriggle themselves into it. All I seem to have done is to say, at the outset: "This thing happened — but to whom?" Then I wait, holding my breath, and one by one they appear and take possession of the case. When it befalls in the other way, I may be strolling about casually in my mind, and suddenly a character will start up before me, coming seemingly from nowhere; and again, but more breathlessly, I watch; and presently the character draws nearer, and seems to become aware of me, and to feel the shy but desperate need to unfold his or her tale. I cannot say in which way my subject will probably present itself — though perhaps in short stories the situation, in novels one of the characters, is most likely to appear first.

This, however, is not the most interesting point of the adventure. Compared with what follows it is not interesting at all, though it has, in my case, one odd feature I have not heard of elsewhere — that is, that my characters always appear with their names. Sometimes these names seem to me affected, sometimes almost ridiculous; but I am obliged to own that they are never fundamentally unsuitable. And the proof that they are not, that they really belong to the people, is the difficulty which arises when I try to substitute other names. For many years the attempt always ended fatally; any character I unchristened instantly died on my hands, as if it were some kind of sensitive crustacean, and the name it bore were its shell. Only very gradually, and in very few cases, have I gained enough mastery over them to be able to effect the change, and even now, when I do, I have to resort to *piqûres* and oxygen, and not always successfully.

These names are hardly ever what I call "real names" — that is, the current patronymics one would find in an address book or a telephone directory; and often it is their excessive oddness which makes me try to change them. When in a book by someone else I meet people called by current names I always say to myself, "Ah, those names were tied on afterward"; and I often find that the characters thus labeled are less living than the others. Yet there seems to be no general rule, for, in the case of certain famous novelists whose characters have out-of-the-way names, many are tied on too. But I often wonder how the novelist whose people arrive without names manages to establish relations with them!

II

A still more spectral element in my creative life is the sudden appearance of names without characters. Several times, in this way, a name to which I can attach no known association of ideas has forced itself upon me in a furtive shadowy way, not succeeding in making its bearer visible, yet hanging about obstinately for years in the background of my thoughts. The Princess Estradina was such a name. I knew nothing of its origin, and still less of the invisible character to whom it presumably belonged. Who was she, what were her nationality, her history, her claims upon my attention? She must have been there, lurking and haunting me, for years before she suddenly walked into *The Custom of the Country,* in high-colored flesh and blood, cool, dominant, and thoroughly at home.

But this is a mere parenthesis; what I want to try to hint at is the elusive moment when these people who haunt my brain actually begin to speak within me with their own voices. The situating of my tale, and its descriptive and narrative portions, I am conscious of conducting, though often unaware of how the story first came to me, pleading to be told; but when the dialogue begins, then I become merely a recording instrument, and my hand never hesitates because my mind has not to choose, but only to set down what these stupid or intelligent, lethargic or passionate, people say to each other in a language, and with arguments, that appear to be all their own. It is for this reason that I attach such importance to dialogue, and yet regard it as an effect to be so sparingly used. For by dialogue I do not mean the pages of "Yes" and "No," of platitudes and repetitions, of which most actual talk is composed, and which any writer with a photographic mind and a good memory can set down by the yard. The vital dialogue is that exchanged by characters whom their creator has really vitalized, and only the significant passages of their talk should be recorded, in high relief against the narrative, and not uselessly embedded in it.

In my case these moments of high tension, when the creature lives and its creator listens to it, have nothing to do with the "walking away with the subject," the "settling it in their own way," with which some novelists so oddly charge their characters. It is a necessity to me that the note of inevitableness should be sounded at the very opening of my tale, and that my characters should go forward to their ineluctable doom like the "murdered man" in *The Pot of Basil.* From the first I know exactly what is going to happen to every one of them; their fate is settled beyond rescue, and I have but to watch and record. When I read that great geniuses like Dickens and Trollope "killed off" a character, or changed the conclusion of a tale, in response to the request or the criticism of a reader, I am dumbfounded. What then was their own relation to their subject?

These people of mine, whose ultimate destiny I know, walk to it by ways unrevealed to me beforehand. Not only their speech, but what I might call their subsidiary action, seems to be their very own, and I am sometimes startled at the dramatic effect of a word or gesture which would never have occurred to me if I had been pondering over an abstract "situation," as yet uninhabited by its "characters."

The story-telling process, though it takes place in some secret region on the sheer edge of consciousness, is yet always illuminated by the clear light of my critical attention. What happens there is as real and as tangible as my encounters with my friends and neighbors, often more so, though it is entirely different in quality. It produces in me a great emotional excitement, quite unrelated to the joy or sorrow caused by real happenings, but as intense, and with as great an appearance of reality; and my two lives, divided between these equally real yet totally unrelated worlds, have gone on thus, side by side, equally absorbing, but wholly isolated from each other, ever since in my infancy I "read stories" aloud to myself out of Washington Irving's *Alhambra,* which I generally held upside down.

III

After writing *The Valley of Decision,* and my book on Italian villas, I felt that I had said my say about Italy, and the idea of attempting a novel of contemporary life in New York began to fascinate me. Still I hesitated. *The Valley of Decision* was not (in my sense of the term) a novel at all, but only a romantic chronicle, unrolling its episodes like the frescoed legends on the palace walls of its background; my idea of a novel was something very different, something far more compact and centripetal, and I doubted whether I should ever acquire enough constructive power to achieve anything beyond isolated character studies, or the stringing together of picturesque episodes. But my mind was full of my new subject, and, whatever else I was about, I went on, in Tyndall's brooding phrase, trying to "look into it till it became luminous."

Fate had planted me in New York, and it was always my instinct as a story-teller to use the material nearest to hand, and most familiarly my own. Novelists of my generation must have noticed, in recent years, as one of the unforeseen results of "crowd-mentality" and the general habit of standardizing, that the modern critic requires every novelist to treat the same kind of subject, and relegates to insignificance the author who declines to conform. At present the demand is that only the man with the dinner pail shall be deemed worthy of attention, and fiction is classed according to its degree of conformity to this rule.

There could be no greater critical ineptitude than to judge a novel according to *what it ought to have been about*. The bigger the imagination, the more powerful the intellectual equipment, the more different subjects will come within the novelist's reach; and Balzac spread his net over nearly every class and situation in the French social system. As a matter of fact, there are only two essential rules: one, that the novelist should deal only with what is within his reach, literally or figuratively, and the other that the value of a subject depends almost wholly on what the author sees in it, and how deeply he is able to see into it. Almost — but not quite; for there are certain subjects too shallow to yield anything to the most searching gaze. I had always felt this, and now my problem was how to make use of a subject — fashionable New York — which, of all others, seemed most completely to fall within the condemned category. There it was before me, in all its flatness and futility, asking to be dealt with as the theme most available to my hand, since I had been steeped in it from infancy, and should not have to get it up out of notebooks and encyclopædias — and yet!

The problem, of course, was how to extract from such a subject the typical human significance which is the story-teller's excuse for telling one story rather than another. In what aspect could a society of irresponsible pleasure seekers be said to have, on the "old woe of the world," any deeper bearing than the people composing such a society could guess? The answer to my musings was that a frivolous society can acquire dramatic significance only through what its frivolity destroys. Its tragic implication lies in its power of debasing people and ideals. The answer, in short, was my heroine, Lily Bart.

Once I had understood that, the tale rushed on toward its climax. I already had definite ideas as to how any given subject should be viewed, and from what angle approached; my trouble was that the story kept drawing into its web so many subordinate themes that to show their organic connection with the main issue, yet keep them from crowding to the front, was a staggering task for a beginner.

The novel was already promised to *Scribner's Magazine*, but no date had been fixed for its delivery, and between my critical dissatisfaction with the work, and the distractions of a busy and hospitable life, full of friends and travel, reading and gardening, I had let the months drift by without really tackling my subject. And then, suddenly, my friend Mr. Burlingame, then the editor of *Scribner's,* came to my rescue by asking me to come to his. It was found that a novel which was to have preceded mine would not be ready in time, and I was asked to replace it. The first chapters of my tale would have to appear almost at once, and it must be completed within four or five months! I have always been a slow worker, and was then a very inexperienced one, and I was to be put to the severest test to which a novelist can be subjected: my novel was to appear in print, and be exposed to public comment, before I had worked it out to its climax. What that climax was to be I had known before I began; nor have I ever understood the mental state of the novelist who starts out without knowing where or how he will end. To me the last page is always latent in the first, but the intervening windings of the way become clear only as I write; and now I was asked to gallop over them before I had even traced them out!

I hesitated for a day, and then accepted, and buckled down to my task; and I can only say that, of all the friendly turns that Mr. Burlingame ever did me, his exacting this effort was the most helpful. Not only did it give me what I most lacked, — self-confidence, — but it bent me to the discipline of the daily task. When the first chapters began to appear, I had written hardly fifty thousand words; but I kept at it, and finished and delivered my novel at the date appointed.

To be turned from a drifting amateur into a professional was a great advance; but it was as nothing compared to the effect on my imagination of a systematic daily effort. I was really like the servant who went out to find an ass, and came back with a kingdom — the kingdom of mastery over my tools. I remember saying to myself, when the book was done: "I don't yet know how to write a novel; *but I know how to find out how to.*"

From that day I went on trying systematically to exercise this faculty of "finding out how to"; but I wrote two or three novels without feeling that I had made much progress. It was not until I wrote *Ethan Frome* that I suddenly felt in full control of my *métier*, as an artisan should be of his tools.

All novelists who describe (whether from without or within) what is called "society life" are pursued by the idiotic accusation of putting "real people" (that is, persons actually known to the author) into their books.

It is discouraging to know that the books into the making of which so much of one's soul has entered will be snatched at by readers curious only to discover which of the heroes and heroines of the "society column" are to be found in it. But I long ago made up my mind that if one has sought the publicity of print, and sold one's wares in the open market, one has sold to the purchasers of one's books the right to think what they choose about them; and the novelist's best safeguard is to try to put out of his mind the quality of the praise or blame likely to be meted out to him by reviewers and readers, and to write only for that dispassionate and ironic critic who dwells within the breast.

1934
NURSERY CRIMES
by Bergen Evans

THAT the older generation is what it is surprises no one with any knowledge of psychology who has examined the pabulum upon which its members were nourished in their most impressionable years. In fact, it redounds to our credit that we are not more abandoned than we are when we consider that at a formative age we were taught to admire such things as Jack's murderous requital of the giant's hospitality, little Goldilocks' atrocious greediness, and the unscrupulous mendacity of little Hans! Who could estimate, for instance, the effect upon our infantile morality of such tales as that of Grimm's of the soldier who, by merely striking upon his tinder box, could have his dog, with eyes as big as saucers, convey to his bedroom whatsoever young lady pleased him and who, when finally detected by a sagacious counselor, thwarted justice by forcibly subverting the machinery of civic order?

These tales, however, do not generally reach us before the age of three or four. It is to the nursery rhymes, the very bases of our mental fabric and social attitudes, which are taught us much earlier, that we must look for the more dangerous influences. "Let me write a nation's songs," a sage observed, "and I care not who writes its laws." And certainly the forces which dictated the baneful ballads of our bassinets were sinister!

What objectionable practices, for instance, are condoned in "Higgledy-piggledy, my son John" and "Little Polly Flinders"! Surely the amused toleration of sleeping in one's trousers and sitting among the cinders could not be without a deleterious effect upon the child's later attitudes toward public sanitation and social hygiene! And in the latter there is a noticeable trace of that sadism which is all too common in these little poems. It is found again, for example, combined with hysteria, in "Three Blind Mice," where a foolish farmer's wife, after yielding to an absurd phobia, seeks satisfaction in mutilating the former objects of her terror. This inculcation of harmful fears is also observable in "Little Miss Muffet."

In so far, of course, as the attitudes and complexes engendered affect only the individual, they are the concern of the psychologist and the psychoanalyst, but there can be little doubt that in the subliminal depths of our nurseries forces are deliberately at work to condition the child's social attitudes. And these forces are directed and controlled by those to whose advantage it is to maintain the status quo and to continue the old system of capitalistic and bourgeois oppression of the masses. The evidence lies plainly before us in the nursery rhymes.

Is it merely the exigency of rhyme, think you, that compels Higgledy-piggledy, my black hen, to lay eggs but for *gentlemen?* Or is there not a direct implication that the proletariat is not entitled to a substantial breakfast?

And does not Simple Simon (simple indeed!) symbolically set forth the luckless unemployed? That the pieman, the capitalist, should be pictured as en route to a merrymaking at the very moment of his callous refusal is indicative of the coarse frankness with which the possessing classes avow their selfishness.

And what shall we say to the underhand manner in which the incompetence of the worker, and hence his lack of right to a share of this world's goods, are suggested in such verses as "Jack and Jill," "Little Boy-Blue," and "Little Bo-Peep"?

II

Perhaps it is as well to treat the subject in a purely scientific manner by quoting some of these rhymes, once in every child's mouth, and appending a brief note in which the underlying force and the psychological effect are considered.

The following are typical: —

> Goosie, goosie, gander, whither shall I wander?
> Upstairs and downstairs and in my lady's chamber.
> There I met an old man who wouldn't say his prayers —
> I took him by the left leg and threw him downstairs.

Here we see, held up for the delectation of the young, a representation of someone, apparently a member of the leisured classes, wandering about a house in a state of dangerous aimlessness and indolence, boldly disregarding all privacy. In the course of this peregrination he chances upon an elderly man upon whom he attempts to force his own religious practices and, not meeting with immediate and slavish acquiescence, proceeds to employ brutal violence.

Surely this is the nurture of fanaticism!

> Little Jack Horner sat in a corner
> Eating his Christmas pie.
> He put in his thumb and pulled out a plum,
> And said, "What a good boy am I!"

Obviously a picture of a sullen and inhibited child, who, conscious of his own greediness and execrable table manners, soothes himself with dangerous self-laudation. Students of the subject are undecided, but it is not unlikely that there is a sinister political suggestion in the approval expressed at the obtaining of the plum in a manner which openly defies convention.

That corruption in office is regarded with complacency by the majority of our citizens need no longer astonish us.

> Sing a song of sixpence, a pocket full of rye,
> Four and twenty blackbirds baked in a pie.
> When the pie was opened the birds began to sing,
> And wasn't that a dainty dish to set before a king?
>
> The king was in his counting-house, counting out his money.
> The queen was in the parlor, eating bread and honey.
> The maid was in the garden, hanging out the clothes,
> When by came a blackbird and pecked off her nose!

Passing over the vulgar ostentation of the first few lines and the intimation of the atrocious cuisine which would leave the birds so underdone, we find put forth for the amusement of the young an account of avarice and gluttony in high places. In neither king nor queen is there any suggestion of social responsibility, and the phrase "*his* money" is deliberately misleading. While the monarch gloats over extorted pelf, no doubt wrung from horny-handed peasants, and his degenerate consort pampers herself in greedy sloth, the worker, upon whose efforts their cleanliness and health depend, is foully mutilated by what was most probably an escaped victim of their bizarre appetites and barbaric cookery. And yet they manifest no concern!

Such literature is the food of young Harrimans and Romanoffs!

> Hey diddle diddle, the cat and the fiddle,
> The cow jumped over the moon.
> The little dog laughed to see such fun,
> And the dish ran away with the spoon.

This famous old rhyme belongs to a group which, though apparently innocuous, is really the most dangerous of all. Verses in this group, such as "The Man in the Moon came down too soon" and "Pease porridge hot," are composed of colossal masses of absurdity and are intended to destroy the last vestiges of the child's truth sense so that he may easily be led to regard the stock exchange as a safe road to wealth and the present state of society as in every way desirable.

Closely allied are other poems which encourage the young to indulge in those irrational hopes upon which the predatory members of society subsist. Here we would place "If wishes were horses" and "Bobbie Shaftoe." The latter is particularly illustrative in the confident manner in which it predicts that Shaftoe, despite the fact that common experience ascribes to seafaring men a course of conduct diametrically opposite, will fulfill his matrimonial obligations.

> There was an old woman who lived in a shoe;
> She had so many children she didn't know what to do.
> She gave them some gruel without any bread
> And whipped them all soundly and sent them to bed.

Here we see the crowded and unsanitary living conditions of the proletariat, their prolificity and their meagre diet, treated with a hardhearted levity. That the old woman did not know what to do about her excessive fecundity would only earn her the scorn of the inmates of any modern nursery. The suggestion of sadism, so often an accompaniment of the overstrained nerves and enfeebled constitutions of the poor, gives a macabre touch to the grim picture.

When this is the stuff of risibility for bourgeois juveniles we need not wonder at revolutions!

> Georgie Porgie, pudding and pie,
> Kissed the girls and made them cry.
> When the boys came out to play,
> Georgie Porgie ran away.

An interesting illustration of the state of affairs all too prevalent under the bourgeois sex morality. Here, instead of innocent and natural love play, we see the attitude engendered by the parental teaching of shame. Georgie, though from his cognomen we may assume him to be somewhat heavy and phlegmatic, is possessed of normal instincts and emotions. When, however, he proceeds to allow these their natural expression, the girls, warped by a perverse morality, pretend pain instead of pleasure. This, of course, has its effect upon Georgie, who, finding his natural feelings inhibited, becomes introverted and shuns the society of his playmates.

There is little doubt that we have here the root of much of the need for the expensive system of asylums and mental hospitals which our decadent society must support.

> See-saw, Margery Daw,
> Jenny shall have a new master.
> She shall have but a penny a day,
> Because she won't work any faster!

It is dreadful to think that this instance of the mistreatment of a worker is taught to babes as a merry song! Jenny's wages are to be cut below the level of subsistence because of her effort to maintain a rate of production that would ensure continued employment. There is much uncertainty regarding Margery Daw, but as "see-saw" carries an unmistakable suggestion of the fluctuations of dividends it is generally assumed that she was an irate stockholder whose greed initiated the oppressive measures.

> "Orange and lemons," say the bells of St. Clements;
> "I owe you five farthings," say the bells of St. Martins;
> "When will you pay me?" ask the bells of Old Bailey.
> "I don't know," says the big bell of Bow.

Or

> "When I get rich," say the bells of Shoreditch.

This attempt to suggest the sound of money in all things, even in the harmless ringing of the bells, may well account for the mercenary attitude so characteristic of the bourgeois. The inexorable demand for so trifling a sum is exceeded in baseness only by the flat refusal of the one version and the despicable evasion of the other.

That national obligations were repudiated and the gold standard abandoned by adults whose infancy had been thus conditioned should surprise no one who has made a study of psychology.

> Curlylocks, Curlylocks, wilt thou be mine?
> Thou shalt not wash dishes, nor yet feed the swine,
> But sit on a cushion and sew a fine seam,
> And feed upon strawberries, sugar and cream.

What a complete illustration of the unenlightened attitude toward women! The wooer, after tickling the young lady's vanity by an allu-sion to her coiffure, attempts to induce her to become his chattel by assuring her that, denied any share in their common labor and reduced to enervating indolence, she shall waste her time and ruin her eyesight on worthless needlework while she is pampered with a dangerous diet of fruit, sugar, and fat which will serve only to obviate in time the need for the cushion.

A dark picture indeed! And one that would deny all hope of emancipation were it not that the indomitable spirit of man has injected a ray of truth even into the profoundest depths of tyranny. "Old Mother Hubbard," for instance, infuses a salutary touch of economic realism into the nursery which has done much to counteract some of the pernicious doctrines alluded to above, while the bold application of Communism by the Knave of Hearts has, as many mothers can testify, stirred the more vigorous of the young to emulation. Even Tom the Piper's son, though his lack of technical proficiency is to be deplored, shows a splendid disregard of vested interests, and Little Tommy Tittlemouse, who, we are told, caught fishes in other men's ditches, deserves to be ranked among the village Hampdens for his brave struggle against feudal privilege. In these and a few others we see the beginnings of that glorious counter-propaganda which in our neo-nurseries is sweeping all before it.

1935
OFF STAGE AND ON
by Sacha Guitry

I WAS born on February 21, 1885. There is nothing in this revelation to move the reader to tears, but it must be agreed that for me this is a date.

When I came into the world I was exceedingly red. My parents looked at me with fright and then at each other with sadness. Finally, my father said to my mother, "It's a monster, but no matter; we'll love it just the same."

But I ought to tell you why I came into the world.

René de Pont-Jest, onetime officer of the French navy, novelist, journalist, distinguished in appearance, subtle in mind, a skillful blade, a lover of women and of gambling — a type of Parisian now vanished, with his white gaiters and checkered trousers, — used to give masked balls four times a season in his house in the rue Condorcet. Everybody who was anybody in Paris crowded to them. In the course of the evening Christine Nilsson would chant, Sarah Bernhardt would enchant, Serpette would be at the piano, Mounet-Sully would read verse, and

Coquelin the younger would recite his first monologues. One evening Mounet-Sully provided a surprise for the guests. He brought with him a young man still doing his military service who was not immediately recognized and who conquered them all by the fashion in which he recited *La Mort du Loup.*

"Who is that astonishing young man?"

"Why, that's Guitry. You know, the chap who played the lead in *Le Fils de Coralie.*"

"So it is!"

He was welcomed, acclaimed, he stayed to supper, and he was urged to come again the next furlough. He promised, and indeed he was ready to swear he'd come back. He came back in January; he came again in February; but when he asked for a fourth furlough, he was refused. He went absent without leave. The matter was serious, but René de Pont-Jest intervened in person. Several people bestirred themselves. Louise Abbéma knew Guitry's commanding officer. Sarah Bernhardt knew the Minister of War. The thing was arranged.

But for him to have gone absent without leave, to have risked imprisonment, there must have been a reason. All the intimates of the household — though not, of course, Monsieur de Pont-Jest — knew that the reason was Mademoiselle de Pont-Jest. She was twenty years old; she was beauty itself; they adored each other. When his military service was ended, he asked for her hand and was categorically refused, three times over. Monsieur de Pont-Jest did not want his daughter to marry an actor; he did not want her to, but in 1882 my father and mother were married at St. Martin's-in-the-Fields, in London.

Lucien Guitry had been on tour in England for four days with Sarah Bernhardt and her handsome husband, Damala, when Mademoiselle de Pont-Jest joined him. In his memoirs he says: —

"Oh, that trip to London, arriving on a Saturday night at six! Everything was shut, and the next day was Sunday! And the day after was Shrove Monday! Tuesday was the Queen's birthday! Thank God, on Wednesday I found something to do!"

That Wednesday was his wedding day. His witness was Sarah Bernhardt. Thirty-seven years later, when I married Yvonne Printemps, my witness was Sarah Bernhardt.

I ought to say a word about my father's situation at this time. Born in Paris in 1860, he matriculated at the Conservatoire at the age of fifteen years and emerged two years later with two prizes — neither of them a first. He won the second prize for tragedy and the second also for comedy. The firsts had been awarded that year to Théophile Barral, to that worthy Barral who played bits for years at the Comédie-Française and later character parts in the Boulevard theatres. He was a good enough actor, as a matter of fact, but still, we must agree that the Conservatoire is a rather comic place. No more comic than other schools, but not any less, really.

The Comédie-Française, having as a result the right to my father's services, called for them. Even in those days he declined the honor. He thus became subject to a fine of 10,000 francs, a verdict he accepted in order to enter the Gymnase, where he was engaged straight out of school to play the leading part in a new play, *Le Fils de Coralie*, which afforded him a brilliant début. He was playing at the same time the rôle of Armand Duval in *La Dame aux Camélias*, and embarking upon a magnificent career, when suddenly Montigny, the director of the theatre, died. My father, who had the warmest affection for Montigny and considered him a great producer, within a few months was able to leave the Gymnase. He had signed a contract with the imperial theatres of Russia so advantageous as to permit him to buy himself out of a contract with the Gymnase which had bound him against his will to continue with Montigny's antipathetic successor. Already in his twenties he displayed his characteristic inability to work with anybody he disliked.

In point of fact, the marriage he contracted at the age of twenty-two had something to do with his decision, for, though that decision condemned the young couple to nine years of exile in Russia, at least it ensured them a livelihood — ensured all four a livelihood, for there were soon four of us. When I came into the world my brother was already there waiting for me. True, he had not been waiting long: he was born on March 5, 1884, I on the twenty-first of February following. You can calculate for yourself that we were twins for twelve days every year.

There you have it — why I was born, why I was born in St. Petersburg, and why, during the first five years of my life, I spent my winters in Russia and my summers in France.

II

It was in St. Petersburg, in 1890, that I made my first appearance. I couldn't say exactly that I played a part. The truth is that I took part in a pantomime in one act which my father had got up in collaboration with a great Russian actor named Davidoff. This pantomime was performed at the imperial palace in the presence of Alexander III. My father played Pierrot; I was Pierrot junior.

It had been arranged that we should stay to supper with the Tsar after the show. I was put on his right. Opposite me sat a young man in a white uniform who was later to become Nicholas II. My father had coached me carefully for the supper: "Above all, you mustn't leave anything on your plate — therefore, don't let them serve you much."

But a terrible thing happened. When the cheese was passed, and it was my turn to help myself, I did it so awkwardly that there fell on my plate a lump of Gruyère as big as a box of dominoes. The servant was about to relieve me of this excessive portion when the Emperor nudged his elbow, and the cheese was left. I raised my eyes and met my father's pitiless glance, which seemed to say, "Remember what I told you: leave nothing on your plate." I attacked my Gruyère in the midst of a stubborn, frightening silence. At the fifth mouthful a great burst of laughter, led by the Emperor, put an end to my torture. I had learned my lesson.

When, after an interminable separation of thirteen years, my father came for the first time to see me act, I was playing in *Deburau* at the Vaudeville. Twenty-eight years had gone by since my début in St. Petersburg, and he had not seen me on the stage since that evening. Twenty-eight years — and here I was playing Pierrot again! But this time it was I who played the father.

If I were asked at what age I began to feel that my vocation lay in the theatre, I should answer that when I was five years old I was convinced that some day I would do what my father did — only, I didn't know what my father did. It goes without saying that I couldn't guess what a profession was, nor could I know the exact meaning of the word "career"; but I could not doubt that whatever my father did must be passionately interesting, and I was absorbed by the thought of it. He had had made for me copies of certain of his theatre costumes, and I loved to rig myself out in them. I had Louis the Eleventh's cloak and felt hat, Hamlet's doublet and hose, Tabarin's jacket, and a Punch as big — or as little — as myself. I would stand poor Punch up behind a towel rack and make him play Polonius, and I killed him so often that I ended by destroying him.

Dressed up in one of these costumes, nothing seemed to me more fun than to burst into the drawing-room with a terrible scowl on my face. It was my ambition to provoke laughter by surprise. I may say that in this I have not changed.

Those who witnessed these apparitions always laughed with my father and often cried out, "How much like you he looks!" The idea that I resembled my father obsessed me, and the desire I had to resemble him more and more led entirely naturally to the desire to do what he did when I grew up. But what *did* he do?

I used to watch him live with amazement. What was there about him that others lacked? It was simply that he was twenty years younger than anybody else. He was a very young man, and it is only now, thinking about it, that I realize it. But why did he seem so different from the others? What was there in him that was so precious? Obviously, his future!

He would rush to table, lunch in twelve minutes, and rush off, saying, "By God, I'm going to be late again!" He was always afraid of being late; yet I knew it was to his work he was going. When he came home in the evening he would sometimes say, "It's all right; I'm satisfied. I believe it's going to go very well."

Then we would dine, and at table he would speak of his friends. I knew them very well, had seen them often in our house; from time to time they had brought me toys. But the way he spoke of them bewildered me.

"I nearly died laughing at Hittemans in two. . . . Lina Munte is doing well now, but she was laying it on for a few days. . . . Lorteur's afraid he'll go up in his lines next Tuesday."

I had finally learned that there was something special about Tuesday. Later I discovered that it was the opening night at the Mikhailovsky Theatre. On those nights my father would dine even more hurriedly than usual. He was always nervous, but never depressed. Every now and again his face would change. His thick eyebrows would contract in a frown and he would cry out, "My lord, you are a nobleman and I am but a commoner, yet I dare tell you that any man who insults a woman is a coward!" A moment later he would be accusing himself aloud of abominable crimes, there before the servants; and the only thing that consoled me a little was that it did not seem to astonish them at all. Of a sudden his glance, which had been concentrated, terrifying, threatening, would become unbelievably gentle. He would look at me tenderly and say in a sweet voice, "Clementine, I would give my life for a kiss from your lips!"

Obviously, I could not understand that he was going over his lines, I had no notion that the most magnificent career the stage can offer was opening before this fortunate and enchanting man who had just kissed me and left; but how I loved him, how handsome I thought him, how much I liked him, this young man who was my father!

Once, as I was being put to bed, I said to my nurse, "Where is Papa going this evening?"

She answered, "He's going to work, and earn some money for you." Seeing my astonishment, she added, "Well, he's going to play this evening."

I fell asleep with the idea that a man could earn money by playing; and I grew up with the idea that "play" was a synonym for the word "work." I haven't changed my idea.

DECAY IN THE LANGUAGE
by Lord Dunsany

TO every complaint that one may utter about bad language one usually gets the answer, "A language must grow." This is particularly true when we have some new invention every year or so, needing a new name, but it is of vital importance that we should be able to distinguish between growth and decay. For the difference between growth and decay in language there is fortunately a convenient test, and that test is meaning, the purpose for which language was originally invented. The decay that is affecting our language is taking place among adjectives, so much so that many of these necessary things have already died. One cannot prove that an adjective is dead merely because in so many hundred pages it never appears; the proof is when the need of that particular adjective arises and it is not used, a noun being thrown in to take its place, as a sheet of paper may stop a hole in a window in the absence of a pane of glass.

If you read of "a strange man in an expensive car," that is no proof that other adjectives equally suitable are dead; but if you read of "a mystery man in a luxury car" that proves that the adjectives "mysterious" and "luxurious" have decayed away, for no one would otherwise use this lumber of nouns. There is, of course, no lack of meaning in "a mystery man in a luxury car"; only a lack of grace. I imagine that hundreds of things had names among savages a thousand years before those graces appeared by which the Romans, for instance, built their sentences; and I think that the deepness of the German forests, which the legions did not easily penetrate, is probably responsible for the German tendency to use heaps of nouns to this day, a clumsiness unknown in France and Italy.

When meaning disappears from modern sentences is the moment that a third noun is added to the heap, or even an honest adjective; for instance, if we were to write "a great luxury man," it would not be quite clear whether we were intending a man who lived in great luxury or whether a luxury man of large size. If instead of the adjective "great" we have yet another noun, the confusion is liable to be even worse. There are no landmarks to guide one through this confusion, for in a single copy of the *Times* I read two advertisements: the first of them spoke of "best position seats" — obviously the hyphen, which was not there, should be imagined between the first word and the second; but there are no rules for this clumsy game, because the other advertisement spoke of a "great equality myth," and in that case the hyphen had to be understood between the second word and the third.

It may not be quite clear to my readers why the hyphen should have come in each case where I have said that it should; but I have had the advantage of reading the context, and have worked it out in that way. The alternative to reading the context is to know exactly which of several ambiguities the writer intends with his row of nouns, and for this purpose you must obviously know just what he intends to say. Does not this mean that in the language of jumbled nouns you can only say what everyone knows already? Then the writer with something new to say will not be understood, even when he has got a hearing.

Two years ago, when a large body of Canadian writers visited London, I pointed out to them at a meeting in the Mansion House some of the symptoms of this decay, and the direction in which it was progressing. I pointed out that instead of speaking of the English Eleven, which was playing cricket then against the Australians, they spoke of the England Eleven, evidently finding some quality in the noun that they could not perceive in the adjective; and I added that they spoke of the captain of this team as the England Eleven Captain, and that his selection was liable to be described as England Eleven Captain Selection, and that any difficulty in this selection might be written of nowadays as an England Eleven Captain Selection Difficulty. I then warned this gathering of writers that, if they did not all exert themselves to put some check upon this particular decay, the time would come when people would be writing of an England Eleven Captain Selection Difficulty Rumor. I hope that this day has not yet come, but we are hovering upon the brink of it, and the careful investigator may very likely be able to discover in modern writers a case of six nouns jostling each other, like lost railway trucks without couplings bumping each other noisily on a hill.

Take the word "weather": it was well enough understood by our ancestors, and had a big share in shaping our destinies; but nowadays the word is never used without being propped up and supported by the ridiculous word "conditions." It makes me think of an old wall supported by a broom or a disused cupboard or the ruins of a rusty perambulator; yet you cannot harm a wall by propping it up with absurdities, whereas you can harm a word by such odds and ends. A people that has never seen the word "weather" used without that old clothes-prop leaning against it will soon be unable to recognize it when the rubbish is cleared away; and so a fine word will be lost to a people that surely has need of it. Or can anybody show me a case where the words "weather conditions" have ever been written by anyone in which the plain honest word "weather" did not say all that was needed?

A dead adjective that I lament perhaps more than any other is the word "hostile," the disappearance of which throws the word "enemy" from its place to do the work of the lost adjective. You read no more of the enemy's troops or the enemy's position; it would be the "enemy troops" and the "enemy position"; and such a line as Kipling's, —

> When the guns of the enemy wheel into line,

would no longer be written. One has only to read any history of any war prior to the Great War to see how a certain splendor has now been lost from such narratives by the disappearance of the enemy himself, his presence being denoted only by this false adjective, doing work that does not properly belong to it.

And then we have the form of sentence nowadays which rather resembles a wall with a bicycle wheel built into it, or a plum pudding in which a watch and chain has been included in the baking. For instance, such a sentence as "Lord Dunsany has sent an article to the editor of the *Atlantic Monthly*" would seem a bit bald to the ultramodern writer. He would rather say, "Lord Dunsany has sent an article — he was born when Queen Victoria was on the throne — to the editor of the *Atlantic Monthly*." The meaning is not hidden here, but it is jerky; it is the kind of thing to read in a motor going fast on a bad road, or in a swaying railway-carriage, whence the style probably originated.

1937
PLANNING IN AN ECONOMY OF ABUNDANCE
by Walter Lippmann

WAR provides an excellent climate for the administration of a planned economy. For, in wartime the control of economic activity is feasible because the plan is calculable. It is calculable because there is a specific purpose to be achieved, the supply of a military force of known size with known requirements out of known resources, and to this concrete objective all other needs must conform. The planners know definitely what goods are needed and in what amount. There is no problem of how much can be sold. There is only the problem of how much can be produced. There is no worry about the varying tastes of voluntary consumers; the consumer is rationed. There is no such thing as a choice of occupation; labor is conscripted. Thus, though war economies are notoriously inefficient, they can be administered by the method of overhead planning and control because, theoretically at least, there are no unknown factors, and there can be no resistance; it is possible, therefore, to calculate the relation of the means to the end and execute a plan whether people like it or not.

But the question whether an economy can be planned for abundance, for the general welfare, for the improvement of the popular standard of life, comes down to the question of whether concepts of this sort can be translated into orders for particular goods which are as definite as the "requisitions" of a general military staff. The general staff can tell the planner exactly how much food, clothing, ammunition, it needs for each soldier. But in time of peace who shall tell the planners for abundance what they must provide?

The answer given by Mr. Lewis Mumford, in *Technics and Civilization,* is that "a normal standard of consumption" can be defined by biologists, moralists, and men of cultured taste; that the goods necessary to support it can be "standardized, weighed, measured"; that they should be supplied to all members of the community. He calls this "basic communism." It is not quite clear to me whether he believes that the goods listed in this normal standard are to be furnished as they are to soldiers out of a public commissariat or whether he proposes to guarantee everyone a basic money income sufficient to buy a "normal" quantity of goods. If he has in mind the providing of rations of standard goods, then, of course, he has considerable confidence in his ability to determine what is good for the people, small respect for their varied tastes, and an implied willingness to make them like what they ought to like. Conceivably this could be done. But I should suppose it could be done only under the compulsion of necessity: that is, if goods were so scarce that the choice lay between the official ration and nothing. On the other hand, if he has in mind a guaranteed minimum income which may be spent freely, then he has no way of knowing whether the consumers will have his own excellent tastes, and go to the stores demanding what he thinks they should demand. But if they do not wish to buy what he would like them to buy, then his planners are bound to find that there is a scarcity of some goods and a glut of others.

The difficulty of planning production to satisfy many choices is the rock on which the whole conception founders. For, as productivity rises above the level of necessity the variety of choice is multiplied; and as choice is multiplied the possibility of an overhead calculation of the relation between demand and supply diminishes.

II

We may approximate an idea of the order of magnitudes in this field by remembering that during the year 1929 the American people spent approximately ninety billion dollars. Now, of the ninety billions spent, some twenty billions went into the purchase of food. This meant a highly varied diet. But even assuming that food is the most nearly calculable of human necessities, the one that can, by simplifying the public bill of fare, be rationed successfully among large bodies of men, there would have remained in 1929 variable expenditures of about seventy billions.

By what formula could a planning authority determine which goods to provide against the purchases of thirty million families with seventy billions of free spendable income? The calculation is not even theoretically possible. For, unless the people are to be deprived of the right to dispose of their incomes voluntarily, anyone who sets out to plan American production must first forecast how many units of each commodity the people would buy, not only at varying prices for that commodity, but in all possible combinations of prices for all commodities.

Let us suppose that the planning authority wishes to make a five-year plan for the production of automobiles, and that by means of the familiar mathematical curves used by economists it determines that at $500 a car the people will buy ten million new cars in five years. The planners could then calculate the amount of steel, wood, glass, leather, rubber, gasoline, oil, pipelines, pumps, filling stations, needed to manufacture and service that many additional automobiles. This would be theoretically feasible. The problem would not differ essentially from planning to supply an army; the industrial system would be planned to produce ten million automobiles. There would be a single, specific quantitative objective as the premise of the plan. But such a planned economy would be for monomaniacs.

So let us suppose that the authority has also to plan the construction of houses. The task immediately becomes more complicated. For now it is no longer possible to stop at determining how many houses the people will buy at, let us say, $3000 a piece. It is necessary also to decide how they will choose, and in what proportions, between a new car at $500 and a new house at $3000. With cheap houses available, some will prefer them to cars; others will prefer cheap cars to houses. The planners would have to predict the choice. They would then find, of course, that since houses also require steel, wood, glass, they would have to recalculate the plan drawn up when they had only automobiles in mind. Even if we make the fantastic hypothesis that the planning authority could draw up reliable estimates of what the demand would be in all combinations of prices, for all the thousands of articles that Americans buy, there is still no way of deciding which schedule would fit the people's conception of the most abundant life.

Out of all the possible plans of production some schedule would have to be selected arbitrarily. There is absolutely no objective and universal criterion by which to decide between better houses and more automobiles, between pork and beef, between the radio and the movies. In military planning one criterion exists: to mobilize the most powerful army that national resources will support. But civilian planning for a more abundant life has no definable criterion. It can have none.

The necessary calculations cannot, therefore, be made, and the concept of a civilian planned economy is not merely administratively impracticable; it is not even theoretically conceivable.

All the books which recommend the establishment of a planned economy in a civilian society paint an entrancing vision of what a benevolent despotism could do. They ask — never very clearly, to be sure — that somehow the people should surrender the planning of their existence to "engineers," "experts," and "technologists," to leaders, saviors, heroes. This is the political premise of the whole collectivist philosophy: that the dictators will be patriotic or class-conscious, whichever term seems the more eulogistic to the orator. It is the premise, too, of the whole philosophy of regulation by the state, currently regarded as progressivism. Though it is disguised by the illusion that a bureaucracy accountable to a majority of voters, and susceptible to the pressure of organized minorities, is not exercising compulsion, it is evident that the more varied and comprehensive the regulation becomes, the more the state becomes a despotic power as against the individual. For the fragment of control over the government that one man exercises through his vote is in no effective sense proportionate to the authority exercised over him by the government.

Benevolent despots might indeed be found. On the other hand, they might not be. They may appear at one time; they may not appear at another. The people, unless they choose to face the machine guns on the barricades, can take no steps to see to it that benevolent despots are selected and the malevolent cashiered. They cannot select their despots. The despots must select themselves, and, no matter whether they are good or bad, they will continue in office so long as they can suppress rebellion and escape assassination.

Thus, by a kind of tragic irony, the search for security and a rational society, if it seeks salvation through political authority, ends in the most irrational form of government imaginable — in the dictatorship of casual oligarchs, who have no hereditary title, no constitutional origin or responsibility, and who cannot be replaced except by violence.

1938
THE AESTHETICS OF EATING
by André Simon

THE Art of Good Living is a living art. Its body, that which all may see and many acquire, is called Gastronomy. Gastronomy speaks the language of common sense when it asks all, whether they be rich or poor, to make the unescapable daily business of eating and drinking an amusing and profitable hobby rather than let it become a dull duty. There is neither pleasure nor profit, hence no justification, in dealing with our daily food as mere coal shoveled into the boiler. Our meals should mean both physical restoration and intellectual relaxation.

It is not a matter of riches, but of the right attitude of mind, detached yet keen, of all who are capable of pursuing any branch of art or learning merely for the love and enjoyment of it. But unlike poetry, with poets upon a plane high above the heads of their admirers, Gastronomy bestows its choicest rewards upon the rank and file of its followers, upon you and me, upon men and women of taste who may have but little or no culinary talent. And the more numerous the people of taste, or the more fastidious their taste, the greater will be the professional skill of the cooks and the professional honesty of the vintners.

Gastronomy is sometimes associated in the minds of ill-informed people with excess, but excess is the hallmark of fast living, as sure a road to damnation as good living is to salvation. Nor must we confuse Gastronomy with high living. It is entirely opposed to it. High living is inseparable from extravagance, from rare and rich and costly foods and wines, from fatty hearts and enlarged livers. Gastronomy, on the contrary, teaches us to avoid not merely excess, quantitatively speaking, but hurried meals and unwise combinations.

When speaking of excess and moderation in the matter of both food and drink, there is a very important factor which is all too often overlooked. This is the time factor. Do not bolt your food and do not drink hastily. Gastronomy insists that sufficient time should be allowed for mastication and digestion, though it recognizes that both rules may be broken occasionally without real harm ensuing. But it does not admit any exception whatever to the most important rule of all, that of quality.

The quantity of food that we may eat and of wine that we may drink depends, naturally, upon age, sex, occupation, heredity, environment, and other factors. It is for each one of us to find out our own limitations, to stop when we have had enough, and to part in the shortest time possible with whatever we have been foolish enough to eat and drink in excess of our requirements. But there is no distinction of age or sex when it comes to the question of quality. Food may look beautiful and its taste may be very attractive, but that alone does not make it acceptable to Gastronomy. It must above all be absolutely sound and fresh.

There is also what is known as the important factor of suitability, the science of combining happily flavors and savors, liquids and solids. Instinct, here, is not always dependable as a guide, but it is a help. If one, even without being told, no more thinks of playing a funeral march at a wedding than of wearing tennis shoes with full evening dress, it is simply because one knows instinctively that it would be wrong. Yet lapses from good taste in the matter of dress cause no injury whatever to either kidneys or liver, or any of the other organs upon which our bodily health and sweetness of disposition depend to such a considerable extent. But sardines and cocoa, roast beef and strong tea, ice cream and claret, or any such unsuitable combinations, are lapses from good taste which are paid for in headaches, biliousness, sleepiness during the day and insomnia at night, and all manner of other ills which make our lives, and the lives of those with whom we live, miserable instead of joyful.

II

Without denying that every one of us is entitled to his or her taste, and while admitting willingly that there are a great many more exceptions than rules in the matter of the harmony that should exist between savors and flavors as between solids and liquids, there are certain basic rules which one should know, even if only to have the wicked satisfaction of breaking them willfully.

A meal should be constructed somewhat like a book — that is, with a foreword or introduction to begin with, then the story, the really important part, and lastly the epilogue or conclusion to bring it to a happy end. Translated into the language of Gastronomy, this means that we should begin our meals with hors d'œuvres or soup, by way of preface; then pass on to the meal proper, the most important part — short or long, as the case may be, but the part of the meal from which we are to derive the nourishment which we need; lastly, we finish with cheese or dessert, a pleasant and useful part of the meal, one that is intended to help us assimilate, or inwardly digest, the story.

Hors d'œuvres, in their modern form, have reached us from China by way of Russia. The Chinese are far too highly civilized to press their point of view upon their friends; they place before them all they have prepared for their refection and entertainment, be it fish, fruit, meat, or vegetables, all daintily arranged in small dishes which are promptly refilled as soon as necessary. Guests help themselves to whatever pleases their eye, just as they choose. The Russians have improved upon the Chinese way to this extent, that they have made a Chinese puzzle of all sorts of small canapés; all manner of appetizing mouthfuls or tidbits serve as an introduction to the real meal that is to follow. The danger is that the variety and excellence of the Russian hors d'œuvres may become too much of a temptation for the weak and hungry, leading them to indulge in a manner that will ruin their appetite for the meal proper.

Hors d'œuvres should never be substantial. They should be vinegary and spicy. They are intended to stimulate the flow of gastric juices necessary to deal adequately with the "story" that is to come. They should also include a fair allowance of olive oil or butter, in order that the walls of the stomach may receive an oily cover that will protect them from too rapid penetration by the volatile ethers of the alcohol in wines and spirits. Nordic peoples swallow a tot or two of vodka or aqua vitæ with their hors d'œuvres; Latin peoples drink a sharp, young white wine with theirs, a wine that will clean the palate and leave it expectant and appreciative, ready to receive the better wine coming with the meal proper. American people favor cocktails — and they also patronize grapefruit, melon, and all kinds of fruit, sweet or sweetened, which are not allowed as hors d'œuvres by orthodox Gastronomy.

Soups have the same mission as hors d'œuvres, but a different method of approaching it. They stimulate the salivary glands and the flow of gastric juices by their heat and seasonings, and they afford to the walls of the stomach the same oily protection through the cream and butter or fat in them. That is why cold soups are as much a heresy as iced melon, and this is also why it is quite wrong to serve at the same meal hors d'œuvres first and soup after. The classical method is hors d'œuvres for lunch and no soup; soup for dinner and no hors d'œuvres. With soup, which cannot be too hot, iced wine is both a gastronomical heresy and a real danger to internal peace. The wine served with soup should be at the temperature of the room and of fairly high alcoholic content, such as a brown sherry or an old Madeira.

After the preface of our hors d'œuvres or the introduction of our soup comes the story of our meal. It may be one of those short stories complete in one chapter or course — just one large grilled sole, for instance, with half a bottle of Chablis, or else a fair-sized broiled steak, with half a bottle of claret. Each is a complete meal in itself, and better than fiction. There are combinations of foods and wines beyond count, but what matters is to remember that harmony is made up of contrasts free from jarring notes, and that we should aim at well-balanced, harmonious meals.

If we are to succeed, we must remember that whenever there is to be more than one course the one that comes first should help as much as possible the one that is to follow. Boiled cod with egg sauce, for instance, may be quite acceptable and even enjoyable, but it can never be exciting; it should be served first, with an inexpensive white wine of no real merit; it calms the appetite but leaves the palate unimpressed. Then comes the roast duckling or lamb, with a mature claret or Burgundy, which we can enjoy at leisure. Reverse the order and the harmony is broken, the meal unthinkable.

The closing pages of the book and last stage of the meal, cheese and dessert, add really nothing to the story, but they are its pleasing summing up. They are not intended so much to supply further nourishment as to help the digestion of the meal — that is to say, its prompt dispatch, just as the hors d'œuvres and soup helped at the time of their arrival. Cheese is a digestive, and dessert is chiefly useful on account of the leisure which it introduces at the time when the stomach needs peace and quiet.

One last rule, which no disciple of true Gastronomy should ever overlook, is simplicity. Our senses of taste and smell are exceedingly delicate, and they are far more easily shocked or hurt than our other senses; they take longer to recover. We hear very distinctly even when not listening with attention, just as the light of day or vivid colorings force themselves upon our sight without our looking for or at them. But, curiously enough, food and drink that force their smell and flavor upon us without our looking for them are almost invariably objectionable. The taste of good food is always discreet. Highly spiced sauces are injurious to the delicate taste buds of the palate, and their only excuse is to cover the objectionable taste or else the total absence of any flavor in the food with which they are used.

Gastronomy can never countenance, for instance, the use of red pepper and highly seasoned sauces with fresh oysters, any more than it will permit any oysters to be eaten if they are not absolutely fresh. The nutritive value of the fresh oyster is one thing and its gastronomical merit another; both are closely allied, of course, but there is no reason why the second should be destroyed completely by condiments which will hide the fresh marine sapidity of the oyster without in the least enhancing its nutritive value.

Most gastronomical heresies are due to a desire to introduce some novelty and make it fashionable. Fashion cannot play with our food and drink quite the same tricks that it plays with woman's dress. A woman's head will wear any hat, but her stomach will turn if she takes the same liberties with it. Gastronomy is, of course, greatly influenced by social and economic changes. With the ever-rising rate of speed of living and the ever-rising tide of taxation, there is neither time nor money nowadays, even if there were the disposition, to indulge in the type of gastronomy which gladdened the hearts and stretched the waistcoats of our fathers.

Gastronomy is in no way dependent upon riches, nor is it the privilege of any class. It is within the reach of all who are fortunate in the possession of a fair share of common sense, and of a little imagination, who are capable of appreciating that which is good; whether they be rich or poor, they will always find a way of making the best of whatever happens to be at hand to eat and drink — of making it look its best, taste its best, and do most good.

---

¹939
THE BLOW THAT HURTS
by Gene Tunney

A PUNCH in the nose might seem to be an intensely personal thing — much more so, for example, than pushing the queen's rook's pawn on a board of checkered squares. Yet I have been astonished to hear of enmities and feuds in the game of chess, that epitome of abstract combat. The queen's rook's pawn seems to have occasioned a surprising lot of rancor and fury. I find it difficult to understand, but then I have been merely a boxer, a devotee of one of the most noted of all physical-contest sports.

Some years ago a great international chess tournament was staged in New York, with an imposing array of the grand masters of the game. Newspaper files will reveal that this tournament made the front pages in a spectacular way, though chess is hardly of headline popularity. The tournament was ornamented by the presence not only of Capablanca, then at the height of his genius, but also of Dr. Emanuel Lasker, the venerated adept who for so many years was the champion. Dr. Lasker had a peculiarity — he loved strong black cigars and smoked them always. Other grand masters charged that when they played him he would blow clouds of acrid and noxious smoke across the board and into their faces, thereby disconcerting them and throwing them off their game. Foul play, they roared. This state of affairs was only exacerbated by the popularity and honored regard that the almost legendary chess master enjoyed in New York. His admirers, knowing his love for strong black cigars, sent him many gifts of them — the strongest and the blackest. In consequence, the Doctor had an abundance of acrid and noxious smoke to blow into the faces of his opponents. The more deeply he became absorbed in profound combinations at the chessboard, the harder he would puff away and the more wrathfully other chess masters would protest to the officials. As for the merits of the case, I surely am not one to adjudicate at this late day, but I'd suppose that where there's smoke there's fire — or at any rate some heat.

By way of contrast, take prize fighting. Few human beings have fought each other more savagely or more often than Harry Greb and I. We punched and cut and bruised each other in a series of bouts, five of them. In the first Greb gave me a ferocious beating, closed both eyes, broke my nose, chipped my teeth, and cut my lips to pieces. He did everything but knock me out. In our last fight I beat him about as badly, so badly that he was helpless in the latter rounds. He seemed like a dead-game fighter, wanting to be spared the indignity of being knocked out. Pain meant nothing — he didn't want the folks back home to read of his being knocked out. From the beginning of our first to the end of our last bout, Greb and I went through the ferocious gamut of giving and taking, hitting and being hit. We were always the best of friends; never any ill will or anger. You see, we were not chess players.

Harry was bitter about one fight, our fourth. I won the decision, and this enraged him. He was sure he had beaten me, felt to the depths of his soul that he was the victor. It was one of those newspaper-decision affairs of the period, sports writers giving the verdict in their stories. Cleveland was the place; and Regis Welsh of the *Pittsburgh Post,* one of Greb's best friends, in his newspaper story the day after the fight gave the decision to me, putting my photo on the front page with the caption "Too Much for Our Boy." Greb never spoke to him again. They were enemies ever after. All the bitterness the battle had stirred in Greb was directed, not against me, not against the antagonist who had been in there hitting him, but against his newspaper friend who had merely tapped a few keys on a typewriter. He didn't resent the physical pain of being murdered, he resented losing — losing unjustly, as he thought.

It isn't physical pain that hurts so much, it's the blow to one's vanity. But what is vanity? What are we most proud of? A whole lot of things, among which physical prowess in a fight is by no means the most important. Intellectual pride, as any theologian will tell you, is the most damning; and the vanity of artists is famous in the literature of history and comedy alike. As a boxer I should say that it's in the realm of the intellectual and artistic that a blow is the most painful, where feelings are hurt the most. For example, I think the man I hit the hardest in my whole boxing career was onetime heavyweight champion of Europe, Erminio Spalla, but I never hurt Spalla's feelings. Yet I might have — I'm sure I could have turned him into a rancorous enemy, but he remains an excellent friend. I knocked him out in a bout at the Polo Grounds back in 1924. He was no boxing master; he was crude, but he could hit. I didn't want him to lay that powerful right of his on my chin — it might be uncomfortable, and so it was when it eventually landed. After being hit I boxed him carefully, waiting for a decisive opening, and then hit him with every ounce of strength I had. I knocked him out with what I imagine was the hardest blow I ever struck. But, as I have remarked, I never hurt his feelings.

One day last fall I was having dinner in New York at Christ Cella's place of unceremonious hospitality, and heard a couple of Italian waiters chattering about Spalla. He had been Italy's pride, and my presence made them recall him. But they were by no means talking about boxing — their topic was opera, the newest operatic star in Italy. They were discussing what they had read in their Mulberry Street newspapers — that prize fighter Spalla, former champion of Italy and all Europe, had just made a resounding success in his debut at La Scala in Milan singing "Amonasro" in Verdi's *Aïda*. This did not surprise me a bit, because the very point on which I remembered I had never hurt Spalla's feelings was his singing.

Several years before I fought him, he and I had trained together with other boxers in the same quarters in New Jersey — and he was always singing. He told me he was studying baritone, and when we were not sparring in training bouts he was caroling operatic arias. He had a rich and beautiful voice, and I used to ask him to sing for me, which he did with a lusty good will — *Pagliacci* and *Trovatore*. After we fought and the knockout brought Spalla's pugilistic career to an end, he went back to Italy. Later on he wrote to me, and told me that with the money he had earned in the prize ring he was pursuing his studies for an operatic career. I suspect he was grateful because that hardest punch I ever hit finished him in pugilism. We corresponded on and off, and he kept me informed how he was getting along with the arias and the high notes. Then came a letter in which he told me that he was soon to make his debut at La Scala — which he did with first-rate success.

Just a few days ago I had a letter from my old prize-ring antagonist. It's worth quoting: "Dear Gene: Following the hostiliti between America and Italy in the cinema world I was urgently called by the La Scalla Film Company to play the role in many of their films. And so to quote the old proverb — 'It is an ill wind that blows, etc. etc.' I am enclosing my autographed fotograph, and I trust you will send me yours, as I always want to see you in the best of health. My wife has had another son and so I am the father of five. And how is your family progressing?" Quite nicely, Erminio, quite nicely.

What I am quite sure of is this — if, instead of hitting Spalla so hard, I had made disparaging comment about his singing, he would have hated me. Remarks about faulty production, vibrato and flatting on the top notes — that's the sort of thing which creates those embittered vendettas in opera companies. I liked Spalla's singing, but even if I hadn't I should never have told him so. I would have punched him in the nose instead, for I don't like to make enemies.

Among people who have no contact with the boxing tradition of the English-speaking world, a blow in the face is a deadly insult — while a wound with a sword may be taken with equanimity. Our boxing tradition has ameliorated the innate combativeness of man, has taken much of the homicide out of fight and physical clash. The fistic exchange has become conventionalized. It's not good sportsmanship to resent with abiding rancor a punch in a fight. So a prize fight, being the epitome of the boxing tradition, is decidedly impersonal — a thing of abstraction.

I recall a scene the morning after my first fight with Jack Dempsey as one of the strangest I ever experienced. It had me disconcerted, as well as considerably embarrassed.

After that bout in the rain in Philadelphia it seemed to me proper to go and pay my respects to Jack. He had been severely punished, and must feel pretty blue after losing the championship. The next afternoon I went to his hotel. He had a suite of rooms, and when I got there Jack was in an inside bedroom. In the outer room were gathered the Dempsey entourage of manager, handlers, trainers, and disappointed followers. They greeted me with an instant bristling of hostility. I was the focus of scowls and angry, sullen glances. Gene Normile was in tears. Jerry the Greek came to me, shook his fist, and mumbled hoarsely, "You can't licka the 'Chump,' you can't licka the 'Chump.' " Jack Dempsey always inspired loyalty, and this was it. They bitterly resented my defeating him.

I had the nervous feeling of being in the camp of the enemy, surrounded by smouldering hatred. I had only one impulse — to get in there to Jack. I found him sitting on a bed, and then I realized how badly he had been battered in that downpour the night before. He put out his hand, and said, "Hello, Gene." It was as if we were visiting casually, in the course of commonplace acquaintance. Before that Jack and I had never been friends particularly. In fact, I think he rather resented me as a challenger. But after we had fought and I had defeated him for the championship — Jack was the only friend I had in the camp of the enemy.

Of all the sports, it is my opinion that boxing, though the most physically injurious, is the most impersonal. I indulge in golf, tennis, squash rackets, and shooting, and can conscientiously say that my resentment in defeat in any of them is far greater than anything I ever felt or experienced in a long career of boxing. There is a subconscious mutuality of respect engendered by the give-and-take of the prize fight that has a certain spiritual quality to it which leaves no room for rancor, resentment, or jealousy. It is true that prize fighting seems sheerly physical and elemental, but what other sport or art has as little bitterness or envy among its devotees? Could the answer be that the more elemental we become in sport and art, the closer to the spiritual we get?

1940
THE WINNER LOSES
A Picture of Occupied France
by Gertrude Stein

WE were spending the afternoon with our friends, Madame Pierlot and the d'Aiguys, in September '39 when France declared war on Germany — England had done it first. They all were upset but hopeful, but I was terribly frightened; I had been so sure there was not going to be war and here it was, it was war, and I made quite a scene. I said, "They shouldn't! They shouldn't!" and they were very sweet, and I apologized and said I was sorry but it was awful, and they comforted me — they, the French, who had so much at stake, and I had nothing at stake comparatively.

Well, that was a Sunday.

And then there was another Sunday and we were at Béon again that Sunday, and Russia came into the war and Poland was smashed, and I did not care about Poland, but it did frighten me about France — oh dear, that was another Sunday.

And then we settled down to a really wonderful winter.

We did not know that we were going to stay all winter. There is no way of heating this stone house except by open fires, and we are in the mountains, there is a great deal of snow, and it is cold; but gradually we stayed. We had some coal, enough for the kitchen stove, and one grate fire that we more or less kept burning day and night, and there is always plenty of wood here as we are in wooded mountains, so gradually we stayed the winter. The only break was a forty-eight-hour run to Paris to get our winter clothing and arrange our affairs and then we were back for the winter.

Those few hours in Paris made us realize that the country is a better place in war than a city. They grow the things to eat right where you are, so there is no privation, as taking it away is difficult, particularly in the mountains, so there was plenty of meat and potatoes and bread and honey and we had some sugar and we even had all the oranges and lemons we needed and dates; a little short in gasoline for the car, but we learned to do what we wanted with that little, so we settled down to a comfortable and pleasantly exciting winter.

I had not spent a winter in the country, in the real country, since my childhood in California and I did enjoy it; there was snow, and moonlight, and I had to saw wood. There was plenty of wood to be had, but no men to saw it; and every day Basket II, our new poodle, and I took long walks. We took them by day and we took them in the evening, and as I used to wander around the country in the dark — because of course we had the blackout and there was no light anywhere, and the soldiers at the front were indulging in a kind of red Indian warfare all that winter — I used to wonder how anybody could get near without being seen, because I did get to be able to see every bit of the road and the fields beside them, no matter how dark it was.

There were a number of people all around spending the winter unexpectedly in the country, so we had plenty of society and we talked about the war, but not too much, and we had hired a radio wireless and we listened to it, but not too much, and the winter was all too soon over. . . .

And so gradually spring came, a nice early spring, and all the men in the village had leave for agriculture and they all came home for a month, and nobody was very uneasy and nobody talked about the war, but nobody seemed to think that anything was going to happen. . . .

There were slight political disturbances and a little wave of uneasiness, and Paul Reynaud, as the village said, began to say that there were not to be any more Sundays. The post-office clerks were the first to have their Sundays taken away. The village said it as a joke, "Paul Reynaud says that there are not to be any more Sundays." As country people work Sundays anyway when there is work, they said it as a joke to the children and the young boys, "Paul Reynaud says that there are not to be any Sundays any more." By that time all the men who had had an agricultural leave were gone again, and April was nearly over.

The book of astrological predictions had predicted all these things, so we were all very well satisfied.

Beside these astrological predictions there were others, and the ones they talked about most in the country were the predictions of the curé d'Ars. Ars is in this department of the Ain, and the curé, who died about eighty years ago, became a saint; and he had predicted that this year there would be a war and the women would have to sow the grain alone, but that the war would be over in time for the men to get in the harvest; and so when Alice Toklas sometimes worried about how hot it would be all summer with the shutters closed all the evening I said, "Do not worry, the war will be over before then; they cannot all be wrong."

So the month of March and April went on. We dug in the garden, we had a lot of soldiers in Belley, the 13th Chasseurs and the Foreign

Legion being fitted out for Norway; and then Sammy Stewart sent us an American Mixmaster at Easter and that helped make the cakes which were being made then for the soldiers and everybody, and so the time went on. Then it was more troublesome, the government changed, — the book of prophecy said it would, so that was all right, — and the soldiers left for Norway; and then our servant and friend Madame Roux had her only son, who was a soldier, of course, dying of meningitis at Annecy, and we forgot everything for two weeks in her trouble and then we woke up to there being a certain uneasiness.

The book of prophecy said that the month of May was the beginning of the end of the Nazis, and it gave the dates. They were all Tuesdays — well, anyway they were mostly Tuesdays — and they were going to be bad days for the Nazis, and I read the book every night in bed and everybody telephoned to ask what the book said and what the dates were, and the month began.

The dates the book gave were absolutely the dates the things happened.

The first was the German attack on the new moon, the seventh, and that was a Tuesday.

Tuesdays had begun.

Everybody was quiet; one of the farmers' wives — the richest of the farmers and our town councilor — was the only one who said anything. She always said, *"Ils avancent toujours, ces coquins-là."* "The rascals are always coming on," she said.

There was nothing else to say and nobody said it, and then the Germans took Sedan.

That gave us all so bad a turn that nobody said anything; they just said how do you do, and talked about the weather, and that was all — there was nothing to say.

I had been in Paris as a child of five at school, and that was only ten years after the Franco-Prussian War and the debacle which began with Sedan, and when we children swung on the chains around the Arc de Triomphe we were told that the chains were there so that no one could pass under it because the Germans had, and so the name Sedan was as terrible to me as it was to all the people around us and nobody said anything. The French are very conversational and they are always polite, but when there is really nothing to say they do not say anything. And there was nothing to say.

The next thing was that General Weygand was appointed the head of the army and he said if they could hold out a month it would be all right. Nobody said anything. Nobody mentioned Gamelin's name — nobody.

I once said to a farmer that Gamelin's nose was too short to make a good general, in France you have to have a real nose, and he laughed; there was no secrecy about anything, but there was nothing to say.

We had the habit of going to Chambéry to do our shopping once a week; we always went on Tuesdays because that suited best in every way, and so it was Tuesday, and nobody was very cheerful. We had a drink in a café, Vichy for me and pineapple juice for Alice Toklas, and we heard the radio going. "What's the news?" we asked mechanically. "Amiens has fallen," said the girl.

"Let's not believe it," I said; "you know they never hear it straight." So we went to the news bulletin, and there it was not written up, and we said to the girl in charge, "You know, they are putting out false news in the town; they told us Amiens was taken." "No," she said, "but I will go and ask." She came back; she said, "Yes, it is true."

We did not continue shopping, we just hurried home.

And then began the series of Tuesdays in which Paul Reynaud in a tragic voice told that he had something grave to announce.

That was that Tuesday.

And the next Tuesday was the treason of the Belgian king.

And he always announced it the same way, and always in the same voice.

I have never listened to the radio since.

It was so awful that it became funny.

Well, not funny, but they did all want to know if next Tuesday Paul Reynaud would have something grave to announce.

And he did.

"Oh dear, what a month of May!" I can just hear Paul Reynaud's voice saying that.

Madame Pierlot's little granddaughter said not to worry, it was the month of the Virgin, and nothing begun in the month of the Virgin could end badly; and the book of prophecy had predicted every date, but exactly. I used to read it every night; there was no mistake, but he said each one of these days was a step on in the destruction of the Third Reich, and here we were. I still believed, but here we were, one Tuesday after another; the dates were right, but oh dear!

Of course, as they were steadily advancing, the question of parachutists and bombing became more active. We had all gotten careless about lights, and wandering about, but now we were strict about lights, and we stayed at home.

II

I had begun the beginning of May to write a book for children, a book of alphabets with stories for each letter, and a book of birthdays, — each story had to have a birthday in it, — and I did get so that I could not think about the war but just about the stories I was making up for this book. I would walk in the daytime and make up stories, and I walked up and down on the terrace in the evening and made up stories, and I went to sleep making up stories, and I pretty well did succeed in keeping my mind off the war except for the three times a day when there was the French communiqué, and that always gave me a sinking feeling in my stomach, and though I slept well every morning I woke up with that funny feeling in my stomach.

The farmers who were left were formed into a guard to wander about at night with their shotguns to shoot parachutists if they came. Our local policeman, the policeman of Belley, lives in Bilignin, and he had an up-to-date antiparachutist's gun. He did not look very martial and I said to him, "What are you going to do with it?" and he said, "I — I am not afraid." Well, Frenchmen are never afraid, but they do like peace and their regular daily life. So now nobody talked about the war; there was nothing to say about that. They talked about parachutists and Italy and that was natural enough — we are right here in a corner made by Italy and Switzerland.

The women did say, "They are advancing all the time, the rascals," but the men said nothing. They were not even sad; they just said nothing.

And so that month was almost over; and then one day, it was a Sunday, I was out walking with Basket just before lunch, and as I came up the hill Emil Rosset and the very lively servant they had, who had been with them for twenty-five years and had had a decoration and reward by the government for faithful service on a farm, and who in spite of all that is very young and lively, were standing pointing and said, "Mademoiselle! Mademoiselle! Did you see them?" "What?" I said. "The airplanes — the enemy airplanes! There they go, just behind the cloud!"

Well, I just did not see them; they had gone behind the clouds.

There were eight, they told me, and were flying very feebly.

We have a range of hills right in front of the terrace; on the other side of these hills is the Rhone, and that is where they had come from.

Of course we were all really excited; enemy airplanes in a city are depressing, but in the open country, with wooded hills all around, they are exciting.

We have several very religious families in Bilignin and one with four girls and a boy, and they all go into Belley to Mass, and Madame Tavel said to me, "I knew it," — it was her day to stay home with the animals, — "I knew it: they always come on Sunday and burn the church." She had been a young girl in French Lorraine in the last war and met her husband there, who had been a prisoner.

"But," she said, "of course we have to go to Mass just the same."

It was she who later on said to her little girl, who was to go out into the fields with the cows and who was crying, Madame Tavel said, "Yes, my little one, you are right to cry. Weep. But, little one, the cows have to go, and you with them all the same. *Tu as raison, pleures, ma petite.*"

We went over to Culoz, which is about twelve kilometres away, to see our friends and to hear the news. Culoz is the big railroad station in this part of the world where trains are made up for various directions, and there they had dropped bombs. All the veterans of Culoz turned out to see the bombs drop and they were disappointed in them; they found them to be bombs of decidedly *deuxième catégorie*, very second-rate indeed.

It was the only time we had bombs really anywhere near us, and one of the German airplanes was brought down near a friend's house not far away and a country boy seventeen years old brought in the aviators, and it was a pleasant interlude, and we could all talk again and we had something to talk about and the veterans all were very pleased for the first time in this war; one of our friends remarked that it really was a *fête pour les anciens combattants*.

The war was coming nearer. The mayor of Belley came to Bilignin to tell the mothers that two of their sons were killed.

It was sad; they were each one the only sons of widows who had lost their husbands in the last war, and they were the only ones, now the war is over we know, who were killed anywhere in this countryside.

They were both hard-working quiet fellows twenty-six years old, and had gone to school together and worked together and one of them had just changed his company so as to be near the other, and now one bomb at the front had killed them both.

That month was over and June was commencing.

I had finished the child's book and had settled down to cutting the box hedges. We have what they call a *jardin de curé*, with lots of box hedges and little paths and one tall box pillar, and I found that cutting box hedges was almost as soothing as sawing wood. I walked a great deal and I cut box hedges, and every night I read the book of prophecy and went promptly to sleep.

And none of us talked about the war because there was nothing to say.

The book of prophecy once more gave the significant days for June and they were absolutely the days that the crucial events happened, only they were not the defeat of Germany but the downfall of France.

It made me feel very Shakespearean — the witches' prophecy in *Macbeth* about the woods marching and Julius Cæsar and the Ides of March; the twentieth century was just like that and like nothing else.

And then Italy came into the war and then I was scared, completely scared, and my stomach felt very weak, because — well, here we were right in everybody's path; any enemy that wanted to go anywhere might easily come here. I was frightened; I woke up completely upset. And I said to Alice Toklas, "Let's go away." We went into Belley first and there there were quantities of cars passing, people getting away

from Besançon, both of us and all the Belleysiens standing and looking on; and I went to the garage to have my car put in order and there
were quantities of cars getting ready to leave, and we had our papers
prepared to go to Bordeaux and we telephoned to the American consul in Lyon and he said, "I'll fix up your passports. Do not hesitate —
leave."

And then we began to tell Madame Roux that we could not take
Basket with us and she would have to take care of him, but not to
sacrifice herself to him; and she was all upset and she said she wished
we were away in safety but that we would not leave, and she said the
village was upset and so were we, and we went to bed intending to
leave the next morning.

I read the book of predictions and went to sleep.

The next morning I said, "Well, instead of deciding let us go to see
the *préfet* at Bourg and the American consul at Lyon."

We went; it was a lovely day, the drive from Bourg to Lyon was
heavenly. They all said, "Leave," and I said to Alice Toklas, "Well, I
don't know — it would be awfully uncomfortable and I am fussy about
my food. Let's not leave." So we came back, and the village was happy
and we were happy and that was all right, and I said I would not hear
any more news — Alice Toklas could listen to the wireless, but as for
me I was going to cut box hedges and forget the war.

Well, two days after when I woke up, Alice Toklas said sooner or
later we would have to go.

I did not have much enthusiasm for leaving and we had not had our
passports visaed for Spain, and the American consul had told us we
could, so I said, "Let's compromise and go to Lyon again."

The car's tire was down and Madame Roux said, "You see, even the
car does not want to leave."

Just then Balthus and his wife came along; they had come down
from Paris, sleeping two days in their little car, and they were going to
their summer home in Savoy and after, if necessary, to Switzerland,
Madame Balthus being Swiss. Well, anyway we went to Lyon.

On the way back we were stopped every few minutes by the military;
they were preparing to blow up bridges and were placing anti-aircraft
guns and it all seemed very near and less than ever did I want to go on
the road.

And at the same time when Alice Toklas would say about some
place on the road, "Look, what a lovely house that is!" I said, "I do not
want to look at it — it is all going to be destroyed."

So just before we got to Belley, at a little village near a little lake,
there were Doctor and Madame Chaboux.

"What," said we, stopping, "are you doing here?"

"We are paying for our year's fishing rights," they said; "and you?"

said they. "Well," said we, "we are trying to make up our minds what to do, go or stay."

"Now," said I, "tell me, Doctor Chaboux, what shall I do?"

"Well, we stay," said they. "Yes," said I, "but a doctor is like a soldier — he has to stay."

"Yes," said they.

"But now how about us? Should we or should we not?"

"Well," said Doctor Chaboux, reflecting, "I can't guarantee you anything, but my advice is stay. I had friends," he said, "who in the last war stayed in their homes all through the German occupation, and they saved their homes and those who left lost theirs. No," he said, "I think unless your house is actually destroyed by a bombardment, I always think the best thing to do is to stay." He went on, "Everybody knows you here; everybody likes you; we all would help you in every way. Why risk yourself among strangers?"

"Thank you," we said, "that is all we need. We stay."

So back we came and we unpacked our spare gasoline and our bags and we said to Madame Roux, "Here we are and here we stay."

And I went out for a walk and I said to one of the farmers, "We are staying."

"*Vous faites bien*," he said, "*mademoiselle*. We all said, 'Why should these ladies leave? In this quiet corner they are as safe as anywhere,' and we have cows and milk and chickens and flour and we can all live and we know you will help us out in any way you can and we will do the same for you. Here in this little corner we are *en famille*, and if you left, to go where? — *aller, où?*"

And they all said to me, "*Aller, où?*" and I said, "You are right — *aller, où?*"

We stayed, and dear me, I would have hated to have left.

III

The Kiddie has just written me a letter from America and he says in it, "We have been wondering what the end of war in France will mean for you, whether you could endure staying there or the exact opposite, whether you could endure not staying there."

So I said to Alice Toklas, "I am cutting the hedges, even the very tall one on a ladder, and I am not reading the prediction book any more, and I am walking and I am not knowing what the news is," and Alice Toklas began making raspberry jam, — it was a wonderful raspberry year, — and the long slow days passed away. . . .

We went to Belley to buy food and the rest of the time I cut box hedges and Alice Toklas went on making raspberry jam; we had lots of raspberries; and as I did not listen to any news any more it was heavy but peaceful.

Then came the next Sunday.

I went out for a walk in the morning and stopped to talk with one of the farmers, Monsieur Tavel. "Well," said he, "the battle of Lyon has commenced." "What?" said I. "Are they at Lyon?" From then on they were always spoken of as "they"; they did not have any other name. "Yes," he said, "but it is all right; there are lots of soldiers there and it is all right." "But why is it all right?" I said. "Well," he said, "because there is an old prophecy which says that the day will come when France will be betrayed by a Catholic king, not her own king but another king — that another king will be crazy, and that all the Paris region will be occupied by the enemy and, in front of Lyon, France will be saved by a very old man on a white horse.

"Well," he said, "the king of the Belgians was a Catholic king and he betrayed us, the king of Italy has gone mad, and the Maréchal Pétain is a very old man and he always rides a white horse. So it is all right," said Monsieur Tavel.

Well, Lyon was awfully near and if there was going to be a great battle — well, anyway it was a bright sunny day, and I came back and I was tired and so I took out my deck chair and sat in the sun on the terrace and I went sound asleep. Then there was a half-past-twelve communiqué and I woke up just to hear that the Maréchal Pétain had asked for an armistice.

Well, then he had saved France and everything was over. But it wasn't, not at all — it was just beginning for us.

The village did not know what to say and nobody said anything; they just sighed; it was all very quiet.

We thought we could keep the shutters open and light the light, but they said no, not yet, the armistice was not signed and they, the Germans, might be anywhere.

The boys between sixteen and twenty — we have five of them in the village — were frightened lest they should be taken into the German army; they went to Belley to try to enlist in the French army, but naturally that could not be done. They came back with tears in their eyes and nervous. The peasants could not work — nobody did anything for a day or two. And then news commenced again; the man who bought the milk of Bilignin had met somebody who had seen the Germans and they had been quite kind — had given them gasoline for their car. They had been stuck somewhere without gasoline because, as the Germans advanced, the order had come that the gasoline should be poured away. Some did it and some did not. Belley is very law-abiding and so all the people who sold gasoline did.

The man who had the milk route which included Bilignin told them he would not come for the milk any more, nor would he pay them, but they could have three of his pigs. They had no way of getting them, so they asked me and I supplied the means of locomotion, and we brought back three pigs and somebody from Belley came out and butchered them and they gave us a beautiful big roast of pork, and with that and a ham we had bought and what there was to eat in the village we were very well fixed.

Everybody was getting more and more nervous and on Tuesday we went in to Belley; there was no armistice yet, but we thought we might get some soap and other things we needed.

We were in the biggest store in Belley, a sort of a bazaar, when all of a sudden the proprietor called out, "Go to the back of the shop!" Well, naturally we didn't, and we heard a rumbling noise and there two enemy machine-gun tanks came rushing through the street, with the German cross painted on them.

Oh my, it did make us feel most uncommonly queer. "Let's go home," we said, and we did not do any more shopping; we went back to Bilignin.

And there we waited. . . .

The only news we had about Belley or about anything, because the electricity and the post office were cut off, was by way of the policeman of Belley, who lives in Bilignin. He had to go back to sleep in Belley, but he always managed to get out once during the day to see his mother and give us the news — yes, the Germans were there in Belley; yes, so far they had behaved very correctly; no, nobody knew anything about the armistice.

I remember the last newspaper the postman brought to us. I went out and said, "It is nice to see you." "I wish," said he, "that I could bring you better news, and I do not think I will come again," and he did not, not for more than three weeks.

Basket and I had begun to walk again, the cows and the children began to go out again, and then we began to hear cannon.

Every day we heard the cannon; it seemed to be all around us, which, as it turned out, it was and in some strange way we all cheered up at the sound of the cannonade.

We all began to talk about hearing the cannon, we all began to try to locate the direction of the cannon; some of the *anciens combattants* thought it came from the Alps, others thought it came from right near by, and then one evening I smelt the brimstone, and the color of the earth in the setting sun was a very strange yellow green and there were clouds, strange clouds, the kind of clouds I had never seen before, thick yellow-green clouds rolling past the hills, and it reminded me of pictures of the Civil War, the battle of Lookout Mountain and that kind of thing — it looked like it and it smelled like it, and in a strange way it was comforting.

The policeman in his daily visit home told us that it was cannon and that it was all around us; the French had blown up the bridges of the Rhone all around us, some only about four kilometres away, and in all the places we knew so well there were machine guns and cannon and fighting and quantities of Germans; armored cars were going through Belley, and in all the villages around there were Germans and some motorcycle Germans came through our village.

And then came another bad Sunday; some of the children went in to Mass and came back with an exciting story that everybody that had any gasoline in their possession was going to be shot. Well, I had some extra gasoline besides what was in my car and I did not want to be shot. So, very nervous, I rushed off to the farmer, our neighbor, who is one of the municipal councilors of Belley, and asked what I should do. "Do nothing," he said; "unless they put up a notice here in Bilignin you do not need to do anything. Besides," said he, "I am going to Belley to find out all about it." And he came back and told us that what had happened was that Belley had gotten rid of all its gasoline and a German company had come along and they had had an accident and lost their gasoline tank, and they had asked at a garage for gasoline. Monsieur Barlet, our very gentle garage keeper, had said that he had none, and the Germans had not believed him and said they would shoot him if he did not produce it, and the mayor, who is also a gentle soul, but efficient, said he would put up a notice and have the town crier announce what was happening, and everybody who had any gasoline would bring it, and everybody in Belley did, and very soon the Germans had more than they needed and everybody went home with their gasoline and Monsieur Barlet was not shot. But he was and is our local hero, and he was quite pale for some days after and we all thanked him for not being shot, and he always carries around in his pocketbook the order that was posted that saved him from being shot.

That was absolutely the only unpleasant incident that happened in Belley, and that was on the Sunday when the Germans were very nervous; they were held up at the Rhone, and as the Rhone makes many bends, and the Chasseurs Alpins were fighting hard there, they thought they were caught in a trap.

IV

Well, then came Tuesday and Wednesday, and the rain poured and poured and the notice of the signing of the armistice was signed by the mayor of Belley and the German Colonel in command there, and posted up in Bilignin. . . .

When the Germans left, in Belley, in Yenne, in Lyon, and I imagine everywhere else in France, they thanked the mayors and congratulated them upon the extraordinary discipline of their populations. The Germans called it discipline, but it was not — it was the state of being civilized that the French call *retenue.* It was all not at all what we had feared and expected, and it all was very wonderful and very sad.

The days went on; everybody began to work in the fields, nobody had anything to say, and everybody was waiting, waiting for the Germans to go away — "they."

Everybody, when I went out walking and they were with the cows, would ask a little anxiously, "Is it eight o'clock yet?" Everybody was supposed to be at home and with the shutters closed by eight o'clock. We went into Belley quite often and it was always just that, neither more nor less than just that.

And then finally one day we went in and as we turned into the main road they whistled. We did not suppose it had anything to do with us and in a way it did not, except that nobody was supposed to be on the main roads for two days because they were leaving, and the roads were to be kept open for them. We had not stopped when they whistled, but they did not bother us; they did not, one might say, bother anyone.

And then miles and miles of them went away and they were gone.

Everybody breathed again.

Everybody began to talk again, not about anything in particular, but they all just began to talk again.

The post office was open again and everybody began to worry about everybody's husband and brother and father and nephew and son, everybody, and nobody had heard anything for so long.

Slowly they began to hear; some did not hear for a very long time, but more or less they all began to hear and they all began to write all the soldiers about coming home, and they said they were coming home and they did come home. . . . The curé d'Ars had said that the women would plant the grain and the men would harvest it and here they were — they are harvesting it, and it is all harvested.

He also said that when everything was at its worst, then it would turn out to be at its best.

v

It is very true that all the old predictions are that there will be a complete disaster; one said that the cock would completely lose its feathers and that afterwards its feathers would be more beautiful than ever. The French do naturally not like that life is too easy, they like, like the phœnix, to rise from the ashes. They really do believe that those that win lose. . . .

And so everybody is very busy accommodating themselves to everything, and I must say the French are really happy in combining and contriving and intriguing and succeeding, and above all in saving. This evening, in going out walking, I met the town's people bringing in as much wood as they could carry; of course there are lots of woods around here and fallen branches and everybody is carrying in some for autumn burning.

I have been talking to the young people and asking them how they like it all and they said they are very pleased. They say now they can begin to feel that they have their future to create, that they were tired of the weak vices that they were all indulging in, that if they had had an easy victory the vices would have been weaker and more of them, and now — well, now there is really something to do — they have to make France itself again and there is a future; and then there is to be lots of electricity and they want France to be self-sufficing, and they think it will be and they all think that French people were getting soft, and French people should not be soft. Well, anyway they are looking forward, and then besides they won't all just go into the bureaucracy the way they were doing; they will have to find other things to do. In short, they feel alive and like it.

The older people, once they have gotten over the shock, do not seem to mind either; nobody seems to mind, as Madeleine Rops said after having come all the way from Bordeaux to Belley. Really, you know, you would not think that it was a defeated country — not at all; they seem much more wide-awake than they were.

Well, yes, they do a little regret the predictions, but still all the predictions said that the cock would lose its feathers but would come out more crowing than ever, and they all said that when the worst was there the best would follow; and then there was Sainte Odile, who said that after her blood flowed in June, four months after, France would be more glorious than ever. Well, why not?

I had my own private prediction, and that was that when I had cut all the box hedges in the garden the war would be all over. Well, the box hedge is all cut now today, the eighth of August, but the war is not all over yet. But anyway our light is lit and the shutters are open, and perhaps everybody will find out, as the French know so well, that the winner loses, and everybody will be, too, like the French, that is, tremendously occupied with the business of daily living, and that that will be enough.

CLICHÉS ON THE AIR
by Frank Sullivan

Q. Hello, Mr. Arbuthnot.

A. Hello, young man. Does exercise tie your muscles into knots?

Q. Why, yes, it does.

A. Are you a slave to floors? Are your gums sore and tender to the touch?

Q. Now wait a second, Mr. Arbuthnot.

A. Do you inhale? Does the wrong soap rob you of a complexion like peaches and cream? Are you a washday wife — does washing leave you so "done in" you can't even drag yourself to a movie?

Q. Oh, I see, Arby. You're the fellow who writes the commercials for the radio programs.

A. Is your loveliness hidden by dull, mousy hair? Then why not try Shampine? You'll be amazed at the change.

Q. Will my hair glisten with a new beauty I'd never have believed possible? Is Shampine entirely different from any shampoo I've ever tried? Does it create a rich, creamy lather?

A. Just one treatment is all that is necessary. Now then, are your fingernails alluring?

Q. Oh, Mr. Arbuthnot, stop it! Have a cigar.

A. Is it a cigar in which only the finest Havana tobacco has been blended with choice domestic leaf?

Q. It is. It has that real Havana flavor.

A. Does it offer everything a discriminating smoker looks for in a cigar?

Q. It offers perfect smoking satisfaction. It is mild and smooth. The flavor lasts. Have one.

A. No, thanks. I never smoke cigars.

Q. Then have one of these cigarettes, made of the finest tobacco money can buy.

A. Are they the best cigarette value for my money?

Q. Indeed, yes. The price is only fifteen cents plus local taxes in certain states. Try one now.

A. No, thanks. I never use tobacco in any form. It gives me heartburn.

Q. Ah, you are a slave to stomach distress.

A. I am, and do you know what I should do?

Q. What?

A. I should do as thousands have done. Get a box of Blips, the new, scientific, anti-acid remedy. Why should I suffer any longer from that peculiar stinging sensation in the chest? Blips are really wonderful.

Q. Are they soothing, healing, and refreshing?

A. Ask your doctor. *He'll* tell you.

Q. Are they on sale at all drugstores throughout the United States and Canada?

A. They are, and they have given prompt relief to thousands.

Q. What have scientific tests shown?

A. Scientific tests have shown that Blips are the brand-new, sure-fire method of relief. Buy a box today. Remember the name — Blips, spelled C-h-o-l-m-o-n-d-e-l-e-y. . . . By the way, young man, you need a shave.

Q. I have determined not to shave until I can find the shaving cream that is kind to tender skins.

A. You mean the cream that creates a quick billow of de luxe, cooling lather?

Q. Yes, the one that conditions my skin for a cool, refreshing shave, and leaves my face young and more attractive.

A. Ah, then, you must use Blops shaving cream. It will give you that well-groomed look women admire.

Q. Shall I be delighted, pleased, and amazed?

A. You'll never regret it. Are your teeth alluring?

Q. Yes.

A. They look filmy to me. Now listen carefully. Here's the way to make your teeth gleam and sparkle. Use Blupps toothpaste.

Q. Will it stimulate the gums, cleanse the teeth to their natural brightness, and help remove acid film?

A. You'll never know how alluring your smile can be until you clean your teeth with Blupps.

Q. I shall buy a tube at my corner drugstore tonight, or at the very latest, tomorrow morning.

A. Insist on the genuine article. Be sure to look for the trademark.

Q. Never fear. I shall refuse all substitutes.

A. Whee-e-e!

Q. Why, Mr. Arbuthnot, you're sure full of pep this morning. Been eating yeast?

A. No, I've been drinking it. Bleeps yeast in tomato juice is simply divine. It is rich in wholesome, natural vitamins.

Q. Ka-choo-oo!

A. Young man, you are evidently suffering from a head cold. You've got that tired, achy feeling.

Q. It's nothing.

A. Nothing? Why, a simple cold is often the forerunner of pneumonia. Many a long and painful illness could be prevented by dissolving a tablet in a glass of water.

Q. I am subject to colds.

A. Then why keep on being miserable? Relieve your distress with Blapps.

Q. Do they shrink swollen membranes, soothe irritation, and help clear the nasal passages?

A. Just a few drops work wonders.

Q. I shall buy a box today, for they cost but a few cents.

A. You'll find they're really wonderful. By the way, have you discovered Blope's soup? The country's buzzing with talk about it.

Q. Yes, women everywhere are praising its smooth, nourishing qualities.

A. Ah, then you *have* heard. Was your coffee good this morning?

Q. It was rich, fragrant, satisfying, and delicious.

A. Then you had better switch to Bloops Coffee.

Q. Why?

A. Because it is rich, fragrant, satisfying, and delicious. Give your hair a chance.

Q. Why should I?

A. Because you too can be beautiful.

Q. Who? *Me!*

A. Just beneath your present skin is a younger, lovelier, brand-new skin.

Q. Really?

A. Learn beauty's secret. Soft hands are truly adorable, says lovely Mrs. Lippincott Rittenhouse, lovely Philadelphia matron.

Q. She did not say that. It was lovely Mrs. Huntington Van Rensselaer Carnegie, lovely Park Avenue matron, who said that. Lovely Mrs. Rittenhouse was the one who said that women are quick to appreciate the fine performance, luxurious new riding smoothness, and delightful handling ease of the new Blipler motorcar.

A. Blood lines count in cars as well as horses, I always say.

Q. *You* always say! It was lovely Priscilla Vanderbilt St. George, lovely Tuxedo debutante, who said that.

A. Okay, you know so much — who said this: "I am an athlete and have to keep up my strength. That is why I always ask for Blippety spark plugs."

Q. That was said by lovely Mrs. Cabot Winthrop Revere, lovely outfielder of the Boston Red Sox.

A. By cracky, you're right. Well, the name of the winner will be announced two weeks from tonight.

Q. The name of what winner?

A. Why, the winner of the big prize — who else? Here's all you do, folks.

Q. Enclose three wrappers.

A. Now stop interrupting. Just print your name and address plainly, folks.

Q. And get your entry blank from the nearest dealer.

A. This amazing offer is absolutely free to any housewife.

Q. For further details —

A. See your daily newspaper. "My husband and I will use the money for a real vacation which we could not otherwise afford," says Mrs. Ethel Soderblum, of No. 238 East 127th Street, Sitka, Alaska.

Q. I shall mail my entry not later than Thursday next.

A. Young man, do you know why it's a wonderful idea to start the day with a nice, big, rich, creamy dish of Cruncho?

Q. You bet I do! Because Cruncho is the super-American breakfast food, because it tastes super-good, and because it's super-good for me.

A. Isn't it wonderful to think that Cruncho tastes so super?

Q. M-m-m! I should say so. I shall go into the pantry this very minute to see if there is some of this marvelous, rich, creamy, juicy, delicious breakfast food, which creates such a billowy lather . . .

A. M-m-m!

Q. And opens up the pores . . .

A. M-m-m!

Q. And makes the hair glisten with new beauty.

A. M-m-m!

Q. And if there isn't any of this delicious, rich, etc., in the pantry, I shall ask Mother to get some from our corner grocer tonight.

A. Don't delay. If you put it off you may forget. Be sure to read . . . you'll enjoy . . . you'll never regret . . . just ask for . . . tune in again . . . with the compliments of your neighborhood . . . don't suffer any longer . . . you'll be amazed . . . see for yourself . . . ask your mother . . . ask your father . . . ask your sister . . .

Q. Hold on a moment, Mr. Arbuthnot. You're getting too excited. Control yourself!

A. Pleasant surprise . . . children need plenty . . . Folks, here's good news . . . on sale everywhere . . . favorite dish . . . no rub, no polish — just sprinkle . . . tastes better that way . . .

Q. Mr. Arbuthnot! What is the matter? Please stop! Somebody call a doctor!

A. You'll love it . . . light, flaky crackers . . . makes washing a pleasure . . . works like magic . . . used it for years . . . makes shaving a delight . . . a child can drive it . . .

Q. Arbuthnot! Stop!

A. My God, I can't stop! . . . Big news for women . . . all-round economy . . . dollar value . . . just think . . . now listen, men . . . give you the most for the least . . . for further details . . . try it . . . just say

Blub . . . insist . . . tune in . . . go to your nearest . . . don't forget . . . don't delay . . . don't wait . . . don't suffer . . . don't neglect . . ..

Q. Officer! Quick! Call an ambulance. Clinical tests show that radio commercials have driven our cliché expert, Mr. Arbuthnot, temporarily off his nut.

Officer. Medical authorities agree that they are apt to do that. A simple radio commercial is often the forerunner of dementia.

1942
FROM A FLYING TIGER
by J. Gilpin Bright

RANGOON, BURMA
September 6, 1941

DEAR MA AND PA: —

Last Saturday the Group commander, Colonel Chennault, got the bad dope that twelve pilots were wanted in Rangoon to ferry some new planes up here. We took the 9:30 train in the evening, which turned out to be an hour late, and arrived there at 8:00 in the morning after hitting every cattle crossing on the way — and maybe some of the cattle, too. When we arrived at the Minto Mansions Hotel and called up the field, it was discovered that there were no planes at all ready.

On Friday, the people at the airport said that they would have three planes ready the next morning. I went to the field, however, and as usual there were no planes ready. One was finally produced and my squadron adjutant (second in command) went off and at 4:00 in the afternoon, Pete and I got a couple and followed. After circling the town to look it over we headed back north towards the airport. Seeing the great gold 300-foot dome of the native temple ahead, I nosed over and went right past the thing at a hundred feet or so. It covers what in the city would be a city block. It consists of one lesser temple after another, building up to the large gold-leaf monster which is in the shape of a Hershey's Kiss. After passing the temple we went right over the airport and steered a course for Pegu, one of the larger towns on the Rangoon-Mandalay railway. From there we turned north and went straight to Toungoo by dint of compass and picking up the railway from time to time. This is certainly beautiful country to fly over. The earth is bright green — of varying intensity — in every direction, interlaced with many silvery winding streams that don't seem to go anywhere in particular. We flew through towering cumulus clouds part of the way, and also through dirty low-lying rain clouds. Cross-country flying is something the Navy should have done more of, I can see now.

TOUNGOO. *September* 9, 1941. — Once again I have paid my dues to the Caterpillar Club. Yesterday, just before lunch, I was cruising around north of the field when I came upon another plane. As the standard procedure has been to engage anyone you come across, I rocked my wings and we went to it in a mock battle. We had two little skirmishes and then flew apart to start another. As soon as I figured that we were far enough apart, I turned and started towards him. I had a theory that I wanted to try out, so I nosed down to give him the altitude advantage, though by doing so I would have the speed advantage. He, not getting the idea, nosed down too, to make a head-on attack instead of keeping his altitude.

There is nothing the matter with a head-on attack, even though the Army and Navy don't allow it, except that two diving planes would not get very far by using it. In level flight it has some sense to it, provided that the pilots give some indication of their intentions as far as avoiding the other person is concerned. In dogfighting there is no set rule, as there is on the highway, where two cars coming head-on always go to the right. Seeing he was following me down, I nosed over still more to let him know what was going on. Until this second nose-over of mine, I just thought he was trying to be fancy and give me a thrill, but then I realized that he was carrying it a bit far. On my second push over he nosed down again; so, not wanting to have any more to do with it, I pushed violently forward on the stick, because even then I figured that I was below him and could miss him all right. Just as I thought that everything was O.K., he nosed over again — right into my face, it seemed. The only way to miss then was for both to do a quarter-roll and pass with our wings at ninety degrees to the horizon. As I was a trifle to the left of him, I rolled to the right and our right wings struck together just outboard of the landing gear. He never started to roll at all. The collision sounded like a very loud chop. Since both planes had been going well over 200 m.p.h., there was very little shock; but of course, once the wing went off, the plane went crazy, rolling and spinning about. I rolled back the hood and opened the safety belt and was thrown clear as the plane was in an outside spin. Upon my leaving the plane it righted itself; and as I looked about, it was right beside me, not twenty feet away, floating down upside down. When I pulled the ripcord it went on ahead of me, of course, and I watched it crash in the woods below. Soon afterwards the sound came up to me. Over me was a lot of debris floating down. I never did see the other plane or another parachute, although I looked for both on the way down. The wind blew me into the woods, where I landed, the chute catching in the top of a big tree, leaving me dangling ten feet off the ground. To top it off, the harness release would not release, so I had to worm out of it by climbing up the risers and shaking off the leg straps.

After an hour in the swamps, I found the railroad track and was led to the highway by a coolie who, although he could not speak the language, seemed to know what the score was. He lent me his bicycle, on which I started to go to the airdrome, but before I had gone two hundred yards one of the Group cars came up the road and picked me up. Someone had called up to report the crash as it was some ten miles north of the airdrome and therefore too far away to be seen by them.

Back at the Group hospital where I went to get a few scratches fixed up, word finally arrived that the other pilot had not got out of his plane. They found him and his plane with the right wing cut off upside down in the woods. In the Navy, where he was before he came here, he was in Pete Wright's dive-bombing squadron on the *Ranger*. He was a fairly old hand, having some fourteen hundred hours in the air.

September 13, 1941. — I did not start flying again until Thursday. As my legs were very sore I have been down to the hospital having them rubbed every day, and that has done them good. I suppose that they hit the cross member above the rudder pedals when the wings hit.

One story that I keep forgetting to tell you is about Peter. Peter, it seems, went up through the clouds one day to do a little stunting practice. On coming down through them again he found the railroad but did not know whether he was north or south of the field. Of course he turned the wrong way. There would be no story if he hadn't. As his gas was looking very low and there is no place to land except in the rice field, he was quite worried. Suddenly a large field loomed up in the apparent wilderness, where he landed after making a few passes over it to chase the cows off. Immediately a car drew up and he was whisked away to the Colonel's house. The latter turned out to be a large stone affair on the Chestnut Hill order, with hardwood floors and the walls covered with old maps. The Colonel's lady added one to the lunch table, and they all went to it with the silver service. The Colonel's daughter appeared just about that time, and Peter nearly fell off his chair. The English have the right idea on this wilderness living.

Today my squadron commander and another fellow went up to have a "dog." It seems that in the course of the previous evening's chatter they had said they didn't think much of each other's dogfighting ideas and that furthermore they would like to fight each other. I went up with them to witness the thing and to fight with them between bouts with each other. Their idea was that I would provide comic relief for their serious business, because I was not an old hand and consequently could not seriously compete with them. They were good and would tell you if you wanted to know it. You know the type. You probably can guess the outcome. I beat them both in three straight fights apiece. (A fight is considered over when one man is on the other's tail and cannot be shaken.) We have had less chatter since then.

RANGOON. *November* 12, 1941. — At long last I have got out of the Ensign–Second Lieutenant class; not far, but still out of it. As the matter now stands there are four ranks among the pilots: Squadron Leader, Vice Squadron Leader, Flight Leader, and Wing Man. I was a wing man for a long time, but was made a flight leader last week along with a lot of others. I have always had definite ideas about how a flight should be led, so I am very glad to be able to lead. I have had two tries at it and found it quite nice to be out in front making the decisions instead of following someone else's. It's not nearly so tiring.

November 18. — Rangoon is getting to be a busier place every day with all the business that the Burma Road is drawing. All the hotels were full of Chinese with gold fillings in their teeth, American businessmen, and Army people in uniform. I went shopping Saturday morning for a few essentials and had lunch at the Savoy. The races in the afternoon were not too good as they were all flat races and not so interesting as a steeplechase would be. Besides, all the races were fixed, so that when you had bet your last rupee on the nose of a likely nag and saw the jockey fall off or rein in when he was miles in the lead you were likely to be a bit sulky. In the evening we listened to the gay, brittle banter of the smart set at the Silver Grill, and retired eventually to the Mayo Marine Club for the night. The latter is the Rangoon equivalent of a YMCA for the Officers and Men of the Navy and Merchant Marine.

Sunday afternoon we flew some new planes back to Toungoo without incident except when Wright darted out of formation to see if he could blow some sailboats over with his propeller blast. He was soon followed by two more of us, leaving the leader flying along by himself, wondering where his boys had gone. We soon joined up again and found the leader with oil streaming along his fuselage. He flew up beside me and pointed to it. I pointed to Rangoon, as it looked rather bad, and he peeled off and went back. Incidentally, we proved rather conclusively that sailboats are not to be tipped over by an airplane.

KUNMING, CHINA. *January* 31, 1942. — On December 15 two of our squadrons, mine included, went up to Kunming, while the remaining one went to the aid of the RAF at Rangoon. We arrived there late in the afternoon, to find that eight Jap bombers had been over that morning, without fighter escort, and had blown up a bit of the town. Most of us figured that they were just making a final gesture, knowing that we were arriving soon. We had the wrong dope, however, as the next day eight or nine bombers showed up — again without escort. Our first flight, with me flying wing on the squadron leader, saw them first. We went down on them out of the sun and surprised them, but after the first pass at them the skipper turned away, figuring that we were too far away (80 miles) and too few in number. Our other squadron met them a minute later and shot them all down but one. We lost a bit of "face" on that deal.

After the big doings in Rangoon on December 23 and 25, our people were in rather poor repair, so our squadron was sent down on December 28 to relieve them. You may have heard that on New Year's Day (maybe January 2 — I'm not sure) we lost three planes and no pilots, and the Japs one plane. I unfortunately was one of the casualties. Forty fighters jumped six of us. I turned to fight them instead of clearing out. One of the jokers shot up my motor and I had to make a wheels-up landing in a rice field. No injuries were received on this maneuver. Since then, we have had four or five brushes with them, besides a few strafing raids. On one of these they had eighteen single-engined bombers and about fifty fighters. I managed to get a bomber. I got a fighter a day or so later in another raid. On all these jobs, we have had only about fifteen planes in the air, which is a source of amazement to the correspondents. They think it great stuff that we, although greatly outnumbered, can knock off so many planes. The secret, of course, is in letting the enemy beat himself. With our faster planes we can let them mill around until they break their own formation up. Then we get the strays. The bombers never stay with their escort, so they don't make out very well either.

Kunming. *No date.* — While in Toungoo, we had been continually told of the splendors of Kunming. As it developed, we live in a stone building with charcoal braziers to heat each room. Every night it is touch and go whether the cold or the monoxide from the charcoal will get us first.

There is a girls' college in town where all the students were supposed to be just dying to see us. Unfortunately a bunch of mechanics got there before the pilots, and what with chasing the slant-eyed things around the dormitories and one thing and another the doors were closed to us after the first engagement. A little headway was made after we got eight bombers. One day there had been some talk of our being the saviors of Kunming. In fact they even went so far as to bring a brass band and a host of flower girls out to the field. After a speech, each pilot's name was to be read out, whereupon he would step forward and have a wreath put around his neck in the best "Man o' War winning the Kentucky Derby" manner. The hitch in the proceedings was that, just when the speaker was starting with something like "Friends of China, we in Yunnan Province," a guy came running out of the operations building and yelled at the Second Squadron to man their planes. As it turned out, it was a fake alarm but it broke up the party.

We have had numerous engagements. They have so many planes in the air that you can't take time to work on any *one*. I got a single-engined bomber one day and a fighter on another, for certain. Have damaged a few more, but can't claim any as they all have about a dozen friends who rush to their assistance and keep you from seeing what happens. Have been on several strafing raids to near-by fields and shot up two sitting on the ground. They are getting the word now though, as they have all kinds of anti-aircraft. The black puffs looked rather thick and fast on our last raid, so we conceded the day to them and went home.

For the past week there has been an influx of camera and newspaper men into the privacy of our alert-shack. Some of the lads are getting quite cocky as a result of our publicity, but it doesn't last. A bunch of Jap fighters will make a Christian out of anybody. One of our pilots, after overshooting the runway and whipping off through the bushes, demolishing his plane, announced that he had been "Christianized."

March 2, 1942. — My airplane score still stands at two in the air and two that I caught on the ground on strafing raids, which probably doesn't sound very good in view of the numbers of Japs shot down by us, but is just about average in my squadron. I have been in five combats and three strafing raids. In the first combat, I had to dive away when about thirty fighters surprised six of us. I turned to fight, but before I could down anything, one of them put two bullets through my intake manifold. The next time up, we ran into a bunch of single-engined bombers and I got one that burst into flames just before I pulled away to avoid a collision. Two days later a few twin-engined bombers arrived with fighter escort. Although I fired on them several times, their motors refused to catch fire as they were doing in some of the others I could see. The fourth time out, there were only fighters in the air. I managed to fire at eight, but only got one from dead stern. Like six others that I fired on, he was going home not watching out for planes. One stupe I surprised twice in the same way. Although he staggered about a lot, I never could get him cut off. He and a friend would separate when I came at them and come head-on.

No matter which one I would go for, the other would have a good shot at my side. I retired as gracefully as possible. The last time I caught up with some of these Japs there were only fighters again. My wing man and I dove through a light cloud on two of them, but they saw us and looped up, firing at us on their backs. I fired on one without success and then looked around for the wing man. Neither he nor the Japs were visible. Finally I saw a parachute far below and went down to investigate, as the Japs are not at all averse to shooting a man in a chute. It turned out to be my missing man. He said he was scared to death when I came down, as he thought the Japs were after him. I watched him hit the ground and then flew down low, waving my hand. He waved back, so I figured he was all right.

One thing in particular that these shootings have brought out is that those who have had aerial gunnery back in the States are much better for it. I should really like to take about a week or two off and do some. In the Navy I only fired twice, so you see that I am like a hunter who has never done any trapshooting. I do a lot of shooting, but it's all of questionable accuracy.

A couple of nights ago the Generalissimo and Madame Chiang Kai-shek gave us a big feed at our barracks. They both gave speeches — the former in Chinese (interpreted for us) and the latter in English. The Generalissimo was quite flowery in the traditional Chinese manner, and Madame gushed a bit. She thinks airplanes are just too-o-o romantic. One of the pilots from New England said she was just an old Wellesley girl that was on fire with the cause. Clichés like "wings of steel" and "intrepid airmen" were thick and fast.

Recreation hereabout is not very varied.

KUNMING. *May* 18, 1942. We are still based at Kunming, which would be a quiet spot as far as action is concerned, if it were not for the numerous offensive raids we have put on. Since the Japs won't come to us, we have been putting on a little harassing program intended to stir them up — like poking a hornet's nest with a stick and then running like mad, only on a larger scale. When the Japs were up to the Salween bridge on the Burma Road we went down every day and strafed and bombed them. I was only on one of those raids, because we take turns on such things; but we did manage to get a few trucks and one plane that was sitting in a field. We have also been carrying out some missions in Indo-China. The first one, which you probably read of in the papers, was done by six people who volunteered for the job; in fact they thought it up. They went down to Hanoi in broad daylight and bombed and strafed a whole field full of airplanes. One of them was brought down by anti-aircraft fire and crashed. The others were all O.K.

The next job down there was when I took four planes down to just past Lao-Kay, which is at the border on the Yunnan-Hanoi railroad. The idea was to blow up the daily train that comes up from the south, to look over the country and the airfield in particular, and to alert all the fighters based along the railway. We were too late for the train, so we went down the track twenty-five miles to make them think we were going to Hanoi, and then turned off into the mountains so that their net would get confused when the stations along the railroad stopped reporting us. A few days later some others caught the train and ruined it. They went back to catch the wrecking train the next day but, not finding it, they decided to blow up the freight yard at Lao-Kay. Peter was on the trip and in fact was flying on the leader (who was one of the fellows on the Hanoi trip) when the latter was hit by anti-aircraft and bailed out over enemy territory. That made two casualties among the heroic six. The next day I was about to take off on a bombing practice session when someone ran up and said that Jones, another of the six, had crashed near the bombing target. I saw his plane still burning in a field. It seems that he got a little confused, according to observers, and started to pull out of his dive too late. That made three of the original six left. They had all been promoted one rank by the Generalissimo and will probably be decorated; so it was even more tragic than it would have been anyway. If they were in the United States Army, they would probably get the Congressional Medal of Honor. The same six also had blown up an entire motorized column a few days before, — a feat which had been witnessed by the Chinese Army across the river, — so they were quite the fair-haired boys.

We are supposed to move to Chungking any day now, but as the weather continues to be disgustingly good we can't just haul out of here and let the town be blown up. The fair weather up there starts at about the same time that the rainy season gets under way here. Today is the first dirty weather we have had to date, so maybe that's a good sign. Most of us have seen about as much of Kunming as we want to, and will welcome any change.

The Army Air Forces are due to take us over on the Fourth of July. Or I can get a Navy commission and remain here on detached service with the Army. The General hasn't heard from the Navy Department on just what rank or chance for regular commission they will give us, so I can't say much on that. The Army plan as outlined by General Chennault to me is this: he wants about fifteen of us to join the Army out here and help him train the new men in the arts of fighting off the Japs (such as they are). After that is done, we will be sent back to the States for a job there. The time involved would be anywhere from a week to three months after the expiration of our contracts. (Mine is up

July 14, counting my accrued leave that I have never dipped into.)
The General said, "I will make you a second lieutenant," and my face
fell as I had figured on being a captain. "And the next day," he continued, "I will make you a major." I just about fell off my stool, as "a
major" conjures up pictures in my mind of a pretty big shot.

In just about every letter I get, you mention this absurd news that,
after my being shot up and making a forced landing, I was in a hospital for some time. Actually I had a day's rest and was back on duty the
next day. I have not tried to be the little soldier, hiding the horrors of
war from his anxious parents, but have passed over some of the super-
fluous news and nastiness that there is no point in mentioning. Leave
that stuff to Steinbeck and Hemingway — they love it.

July 24, 1942. — Once again I am stationed out in the sticks at one of
our regular advanced base fields. Since I am now in the Air Corps, I
am not supposed to say which one, although when I was in the AVG
I mentioned it several times. Officers are supposed to censor their own
mail — sort of an honor system.

So far the Army and I are hitting it off very nicely. The only thing
that they haven't got that the AVG had is quality in pilots. Everything
else seems to be run much better — because, I imagine, they have a lot
more people per squadron than the AVG. In the Army you have special
non-flying officers who handle messings, engineering, armament, and
all the details not pertaining to flying that pilots had to do in the AVG.
I still haven't got quite used to being addressed as "Sir" or "Major" by
lieutenants older than I. I think it's absurd and is mostly a hangover
from the peacetime army days when a major was an old fud and could
throw his weight around.

There is not much going on around here as the Japs have business
elsewhere evidently. Efforts to stir them up are not successful.

Love,
G<small>IL</small>

1943
MADEMOISELLE O
by Vladimir Nabokov

I HAVE often noticed that after I had bestowed on my characters
some treasured item of my past it would pine away in the artificial world where I had so abruptly placed it. Although it lingered
on in my mind its personal warmth, its retrospective appeal, had gone

and presently it became more closely identified with my novel than with the folds of my former self where it had seemed to be so safe from the intrusion of the artist. Houses have crumbled in my memory as soundlessly as they did in the silent films of yore, and the portrait of my old French governess whom I once lent to a youthful hero of mine is already hardly discernible, now that it is engulfed in the description of a childhood entirely unrelated to my own. The man in me revolts against the fictionist, and here is my desperate attempt to save what is left of poor Mademoiselle O.

This "O" oddly enough is by no means the abbreviation of something beginning with an "O." It is not the initial of Olivier or Oudinet, but actually the thing itself: a round and naked name which seems about to collapse without a full stop to support it; a loose wheel of a name rolling downhill, hesitating, wobbling; a toothless yawn; a melon; an egg; a lake. What lake? The lake near which she had spent most of her life, for she was born in Switzerland, of wholly French parents, as she proudly would add. But this did not improve matters. Very soon, as soon as she had rashly imparted to us the power of speaking her language, looping the loop of her name became the means of enraging her beyond measure. We squeezed every drop out of that vulnerable vowel; we inflated it till our cheeks all but cracked; we punned it, we punted it; we bounced it like a ball that leaves planet-like spots on the ceiling; we imagined Mademoiselle's father arriving in some watering place and people exclaiming: *"Oh! O au'eaux!"* In her favorite book, the squat, salmon-pink Larousse dictionary (with that red-curled maiden blowing the fluff off a dandelion on the cover), the first name listed under "O" happened to be that of "François, Marquis d'O, b. and d. in Paris, Superintendent of Finances under Henry III"; him we elected for Mademoiselle's ancestor, and she would have gladly adopted the legend herself had we not scoffed at the paradox of a nought handling millions.

A large woman, a very stout woman as round as her name, Mademoiselle rolled into our existence as I was about to be eight. There she is. I see her so plainly: her abundant dark hair which is covertly graying, the three wrinkles on her austere forehead, her beetling brows, the steely eyes behind a black-rimmed pince-nez, that vestigial mustache, that blotchy complexion which in moments of wrath assumes a purple flush in the region of the third and amplest chin, so regally spread over the frilled mountain of her blouse. And now she sits down, or rather she tackles the job of sitting down, the jelly of her jowl quaking, her prodigious posterior, with the three buttons on the side, lowering itself warily; then at the last she surrenders her bulk to God and to the wicker armchair, which, out of sheer fright, bursts into a salvo of crackling.

The winter she came was the only one of my childhood that I spent in the country. It was also a particularly severe one, incidentally producing as much snow as Mademoiselle O might have expected to find in the hyperborean gloom of remote Muscovy. When she alighted at the little station from which she still had to travel half a dozen miles by sleigh to our country house, I was not there to greet her, but I do so now, as I try to imagine what she saw and felt at that last stage of her fabulous journey. Her Russian vocabulary, I know, consisted of one short word — the same solitary word which seven years later she was to take back to Switzerland. This word, which in her case may be phonetically rendered as "giddy-ay," meant "Where?" And that was a good deal; uttered by her like the raucous cry of some lost bird, it accumulated such interrogatory force that it sufficed for all her needs. "Giddy-ay? Giddy-ay?" she would wail, not only to find out her whereabouts but also to express an abyss of misery: the fact that she was a stranger, shipwrecked, penniless, ailing, and that she was searching for the blessed land where at last she would be understood.

I can see her as she stands in the middle of the platform, and vainly my ghostly envoy offers her an arm which she cannot see. The door of the waiting room opens with the shuddering whine peculiar to nights of intense frost; a cloud of hot air rushes out almost as profuse as the steam from the great funnel-shaped stack of the panting engine; and now our coachman is attending to Mademoiselle: a burly man in sheepskin with the leather outside, his huge gloves protruding from his scarlet sash into which he has tucked them. I hear the snow crunching under his felt boots while he busies himself with the luggage, the jingling harness, and then his own nose, which he blows by means of a dexterous flip of finger and thumb as he trudges back round the sleigh. Slowly, with grim misgivings, Mademoiselle climbs in, clutching at her helper in mortal fear lest the sleigh move off before her vast form is securely encased. Finally she settles down with a grunt and thrusts her fists into her skimpy plush muff. At the juicy smacking of their driver's lips the horses strain their quarters, shift hoofs, strain again; and then Mademoiselle gives a backward jerk of the torso as the heavy sleigh is wrenched out of its world of steel, fur, flesh, to enter a frictionless medium where it skims along a ghostly road that it seems barely to touch.

For one moment, thanks to the sudden aura of a lone lantern at the turning, a grossly exaggerated shadow, also holding a muff, races beside the sleigh, climbs a billow of snow, and is gone, leaving Mademoiselle to be swallowed up by what she will later allude to with awe and gusto as "the Steppe." There, in the endless gloom, the changeable twinkle of remote village lights seems to her to be the yellow eyes of wolves. She is cold, she is frozen stiff — frozen "to the center of her brain," for she soars with the wildest hyperbole when not clinging to the safest old saw. Every now and then she looks back to make sure that, always at the same distance, like those companionable phantoms of ships in polar seas, the second sleigh bearing her trunk and hatbox is following. And now I notice that I have quite forgotten the moon; for surely there must be a moon, that full incredibly clear moon that goes so well with our lusty frosts — and with Mademoiselle's name. So there it comes, steering out of a medley of small dappled clouds which it tinges with a vague iridescence; and as it sails higher it glazes the runner-tracks left on the road where every sparkling lump of snow is emphasized by a swollen shadow.

Very lovely, very lonesome. But what am *I* doing here in the stereoscopic dreamland? Somehow those two sleighs have slipped away; they have left me behind on the blue-white road. No, even the vibration in my ears is not their receding bells, but my own blood singing. All is still, spellbound, enthralled by that great heavenly "O" shining above my Russian wilderness. The snow is real, and as I bend to it and scoop up a handful, thirty-five years crumble to glittering frost-dust between my tingling fingers.

II

An oil lamp is brought into the gloaming. Gently it soars and comes down; the hand of memory, now in a servant's white cotton glove, places it in the center of a round table. The flame is nicely adjusted, and a rosy silk-flounced lamp shade crowns the light.

A warm, bright room in a snow-muffled house, soon to be termed *le château*; built by my great-grandfather, who, being afraid of fires, had the staircase made of iron, so that when the house was burned to the ground during the Revolution, those fretted steps remained standing, still leading up. But this is neither here nor there: such a number of things fade away, while and because their owners grow, change, and forget them, that it would be unfair to lay all the blame on civic convulsions.

Some more about that room, please. The oval mirror. Hanging aslant on taut cords, its pure brow inclined, it strives to retain the falling furniture and a slope of sheeny floor that keep slipping from its embrace. The chandelier pendants. These emit a delicate tinkling whenever anything is moved in an upstairs room. Colored pencils. That tiny heap of emerald pencil dust on the oilcloth where a penknife has just done its recurrent duty. We are sitting at the table, my brother and I and Miss Jones, who now and then looks at her watch: roads must be dreadful with all that snow; and anyway, many professional hardships lie in wait for that vague French person who will replace her.

Those colored pencils — how I loved them. The green one by a whirl of the wrist could be made to produce so simply a ruffled tree or the smoke of a house where spinach was cooking. The blue by drawing a single horizontal line invited a distant sail. Somehow or other the brown was always broken, whereas the little purple chap, a special favorite of mine, had got worn down so short as to become scarcely manageable. The white one alone, that lanky albino among pencils, kept its length, or at least did so until I realized that, far from being a fraud, leaving no mark on the page, it was the ideal tool because I could imagine whatever I wished while I scrawled.

Alas, these pencils too have been distributed among the characters of my books to keep fictitious children busy; they are not quite my own now. Somewhere, in the apartment house of a chapter, in the hired room of a paragraph, I have also placed that tilted mirror, and the lamp, and the chandelier-drops. Few things are left, many have been squandered. Have I given away that old brown dachshund fast asleep on the sofa? No, I think he is still mine. His grizzled muzzle, with that wart at the puckered corner of the mouth, is tucked into the curve of his hock, and from time to time a deep sigh distends his ribs. He is so old and his sleep is so thickly padded with dreams (about chewable slippers and a few last smells) that he does not stir when faint bells jingle outside and a pneumatic door heaves and clangs in the vestibule. She has come after all; I had so hoped she would not.

In our childhood we know a lot about hands since they live and hover at the level of our stature; Mademoiselle's were unpleasant because of the froggy gloss on their tight skin besprinkled with brownish liver spots. Before her time no stranger had ever stroked my face. Mademoiselle, as soon as she came, took me completely aback by patting my cheek in sign of spontaneous affection. Later on this gesture went through a natural evolution, producing varieties which she classified according to their degree of strength as flick, slap, smack, and finally what may be translated as "the Great Volley" and which, indeed, resembled the backhand smash of a tennis ace.

All her mannerisms come back to me when I think of her hands. Her manner of peeling rather than sharpening a pencil, the point held towards her stupendous and sterile bosom swathed in green wool. The way she had of inserting her little finger into her ear and vibrating it very rapidly. The ritual observed every time she gave me a fresh copybook. Always panting a little, her mouth slightly open and emitting in quick succession a series of asthmatic purrs, she would open the copybook to make a margin in it; that is, she would trace a vertical line with her thumbnail, fold in the outer edge of the page, press, release, smooth it out with a final pat, after which the book would be briskly twisted around and placed before me ready for use.

A new pen followed; she would moisten the glistening nib with susur-
rous lips before dipping it into the baptismal ink font. Then, delight-
ing in every limb of every limpid letter (especially so because the preceding copybook had ended in utter sloppiness), with exquisite care I
would inscribe the word *Dictée* while Mademoiselle hunted through
her collection of spelling tests for a good hard passage.

III

Meanwhile the setting has changed. Hoarfrost and snow have been
removed by a silent property man. The summer afternoon is alive
with steep clouds breasting the blue. Eyed shadows move on the garden paths. Lessons are over and Mademoiselle is reading to us on the
veranda where the plaited chairs smell of vanilla in the heat. The sun
is everywhere — on the steps, on the mat, on the white window sills,
where it repeats the hues of the stained glass. This is the time when
Mademoiselle is at her very best.

What a number of volumes she read through to us on that veranda!
Her slender voice sped on and on, never weakening, without the
slightest hitch or hesitation, an admirable reading-machine wholly independent of her sick bronchial tubes. We got it all: the so-called
"Pink Library" — inventive Jules Verne, bombastic Hugo, romantic
Dumas the Elder. There she sat distilling her reading voice from the
still prison of her person. Apart from the lips, one of her chins, the
smallest but real one, was the only mobile detail of her Buddha-like
bulk. The black-rimmed pince-nez reflected eternity. Occasionally a fly
would light on her stern forehead and the three wrinkles would instantly leap up together like three runners over three hurdles. But
nothing whatever changed in the expression of her face — that face
which I so often tried to sketch, for its impassive and simple symmetry
offered an almost voluptuous temptation to my furtive pencil.

Presently my attention would wander still further, and it was then
perhaps that the rare purity of her rhythmic voice accomplished its
true purpose. I looked at a creamy cloud and years later was able to
visualize its exact shape. The gardener was pottering among the peo-
nies. A wagtail took a few steps, remembered something, and then
strutted on. Coming from nowhere, a comma butterfly settled on the
threshold, basked in the sun with its fulvous wings spread, suddenly
closed them just to show the tiny initial chalked on the under side, and
as suddenly darted away. But the most constant source of enchantment was the rhomboids of colored glass inset harlequinwise in the
crisscross panes of the side windows. The garden when viewed
through these magic panes grew strangely still and aloof. If one
looked through the blue glass the sand turned to cinders while inky-
black trees swam in a tropical sky. The yellow one led to Cathay and

tea-colored vistas. The red made the foliage drip ruby dark upon a
pink-flushed footpath. The green soaked greenery in a greener green.
And when after such richness one turned to a little square of normal
savorless glass with its lone mosquito or lame daddy longlegs, it was
like taking a draught of water when one is not thirsty, and one saw the
first withered leaf lying on yonder bench and the blandly familiar
birch trees. But of all the windows this is the pane through which
parched nostalgia would long to peer now.

Mademoiselle never found out how potent had been the even flow
of her voice. The claims she later put forward were quite different.
"Ah," she sighed, "didn't we love each other! Those good old days in
the château! The dead wax doll we once buried under the oak! (No —
a golliwog in red pants!) And that time you ran away and left me
stumbling and howling in the depths of the forest! (The grove just
beyond the old tennis court!) My, what a spanking you bad boys got!
(Not I — *I* managed to escape and find Mother!) And the Princess,
your aunt, whom you struck with your little fist because she had been
rude to me! (I don't remember.) And the way you whispered to me all
your childish troubles! (Never!) And the cozy nook in my room where
you loved to snuggle because you felt so warm and secure!"

Mademoiselle's room, both in the country and in town, was a weird
place to me — something like a dim hothouse sheltering a thick-leaved
plant imbued with a heavy, queerly acrid odor — and although next to
ours, it did not seem to belong to our pleasant, well-aired home. In
that sickening mist, reeking among other effluvia with the brown smell
of oxidized apple peels, the lamp burned low, and strange objects
glimmered upon the writing desk: a lacquered box with licorice sticks,
black segments of which she would hack off with her penknife and put
to melt under her tongue; a picture postcard of a lake and a castle
with prismatic spangles sublimating its windows; a bumpy ball of
tightly rolled and compressed bits of silver paper that came from all
those chocolates she used to consume at night; photographs of the
nephew who had died, of his mother who had signed hers "Mater
dolorosa," of a certain Monsieur de Marante who had been forced by
his family to marry a rich widow.

Lording it over the rest was one in a noble frame incrusted with
garnets; it showed in three-quarter view a slim young brunette clad in
a close-fitting checked dress, with a liquid glint in her eye and a great
roll of hair burdening her pale graceful neck. "A braid as thick as my
arm and reaching down to my ankles!" was Mademoiselle's melodramatic comment. For this had been she — but in vain did my eyes
probe and dig into her familiar form to try to extract the exquisite
creature it had engulfed. Such discoveries as I did make merely increased the difficulties of my task; and the grownups who during the

day beheld only a densely clothed Mademoiselle O never saw what we children saw when, roused from her sleep by one of us shrieking himself out of a bad dream, disheveled, candle in hand, a gleam of gilt lace on the blood-red dressing gown that could not quite wrap her quaking mass, the nightmare Jézabel of Racine's absurd play stamped barefooted into our bedroom.

All my life I have been a poor go-to-sleeper. No matter how great my weariness, the wrench of parting with consciousness is unspeakably repulsive to me. I loathe Somnus, that black-masked headsman binding me to the block; and if in the course of years I have got so used to my nightly ordeal as almost to swagger while the familiar axe is coming out of its great velvet-lined case, initially I had no such comfort or defense, nothing — save a door left ajar into Mademoiselle's room. That meek line of light was something I could cling to, since in absolute darkness my head would swim, just as the soul dissolves in the blackness of sleep.

Saturday night used to be a pleasurable prospect because that was the night Mademoiselle indulged in the luxury of a weekly bath, thus granting a longer lease to my tenuous gleam. But then a subtler torture set in. The bathroom was at the end of a Z-shaped corridor some twenty heartbeats distant from my bed, and between apprehending Mademoiselle's return and envying my brother's stolid snore, I could never really put my additional time to profit by deftly getting to sleep while a chink in the dark still bespoke a speck of myself in Nirvana. At length they would come, those inexorable steps, plodding along the passage and causing some little glass object, which had been secretly sharing my vigil, to tinkle in dismay on its shelf.

Now she has entered her room. A brisk interchange of light-values tells me that the candle on her bed table takes over the job of the lamp on her desk. My line of light is still there, but grown old and wan, and flickers whenever Mademoiselle makes her bed creak by moving. For I still hear her. Now it is a silvery rustle spelling "Suchard"; now the trk-trk-trk of a fruit knife cutting the pages of *La Revue des deux mondes;* I hear her panting slightly. And all the time I am in acute distress, desperately trying to coax sleep, opening my eyes every few seconds to check the faded gleam, and imagining paradise as a place where a sleepless neighbor reads an endless book by the light of an eternal candle.

The inevitable happens: the pince-nez case shuts with a click, the review shuffles onto the marble of the bed table, and gustily Mademoiselle's pursed lips blow; the first attempt fails, a groggy flame squirms and ducks; then comes a second lunge, and light collapses. In that pitchy blackness I lose my bearings, my bed seems to be slowly drifting, panic makes me sit up and stare; finally my dark-adapted eyes sift out, among entoptic floaters, certain more precious blurrings that roam in aimless amnesia until, half-remembering, they settle down as the dim folds of window curtains.

How utterly foreign to the troubles of the night were those exciting St. Petersburg mornings when the fierce and tender, damp and dazzling arctic spring bundled away broken ice down the sea-bright Neva! It made the roofs shine. It painted the slush in the streets a rich purplish-blue shade which I have never seen anywhere since. Mademoiselle, her coat of imitation seal majestically swelling on her bosom, sat on the back seat of the landau with my brother next to her and me facing them, joined to them by the valley of the velvety rug; and as I looked up I could see, strung on ropes from house to house high above the street, great semi-transparent banners billowing, their three wide bands pale red, pale blue, and merely pale — deprived by the sun and the flying shadows of any too blunt connection with a national holiday, but undoubtedly celebrating now, in the city of memory, that spring day, that drive, the swish of the mud, and the ruffled exotic bird on Mademoiselle's hat.

IV

The unusual aspect of her limbless and boneless name may have had something to do with the morbid touchiness that was perhaps her main characteristic. Being absolutely Russian-proof, she fortunately remained unaware of what native servants did to that name; but whenever she was being introduced to a guest and it rolled out, sounding somewhat like a terminal interjection in a doggerel rhyme, her look was a mixture of defiance and anxiety. Her obesity was another reason for her always being on the defensive, as if she were living among cannibals who licked their chops behind her back.

And as though nature had not wished to spare her anything that makes one supersensitive, she was hard of hearing. Sometimes at table we boys would suddenly become aware of two big tears crawling down Mademoiselle's ample cheeks. "Don't mind me," she would say in a small voice, and she kept on eating till the unwiped tears blinded her; then with a heartbroken hiccough she would rise and blunder out of the dining room. Little by little the truth would come out. The general talk had turned, say, on the subject of the warship my uncle commanded, and she had perceived in this a sly dig at her Switzerland that had no navy. Or else it was because she fancied that whenever French was spoken the game consisted in deliberately preventing her from directing and bejeweling the conversation. Poor lady, she was always in such a nervous hurry to seize control of intelligible table talk before it bolted back into Russian that no wonder she bungled her cue.

"And your Parliament, sir, how is it getting along?" she would suddenly burst out brightly from her end of the table, challenging my father, who, after a harassing day, was not exactly eager to discuss troubles of the State with a somehow unreal person who neither knew nor cared anything about them. Thinking that someone had referred to music, "But Silence, too, may be beautiful," she would bubble. "Why, one evening in a desolate valley of the Alps I actually *heard* Silence." Sallies like these, especially when growing deafness led her to answer a question none had put, resulted in a painful hush instead of touching off the rockets of a sprightly *causerie*.

And, really, her French was so lovely! Ought one to have minded the shallowness of her culture, the bitterness of her temper, the banality of her mind, when that pearly language of hers purled and scintillated, as innocent of sense as the alliterative sins of Racine's pious verse? My father's library, not her limited lore, taught me to appreciate authentic poetry; nevertheless something of her tongue's limpidity and luster has had a singularly bracing effect upon me, like those sparkling salts which are used to purify the blood. That is why it makes me so sad to imagine now the anguish Mademoiselle O must have felt at seeing how lost, how little valued was the nightingale voice which came from her elephantine body. She stayed with us long, much too long, obstinately hoping for some miracle that would transform her into a kind of Madame de Rambouillet holding a gold-and-satin salon of poets, princes, and politicians under her brilliant spell.

She would have gone on hoping had it not been for Leonidas Orlov. He was a Russian tutor, with mild blue eyes and strong political opinions, who had been engaged to coach us in winter and play tennis and ride with us during the summer holidays. He taught mathematics entrancingly, lost his stirrups, and lobbed every ball into the lilac bushes. While venerating my father, he could not quite stomach certain aspects of our household, such as footmen and French, which last he considered an aristocratic convention of no use in a liberal statesman's home. On the other hand Mademoiselle decided that if Orlov answered her point-blank questions only with short grunts (which he tried to Germanize for want of a better tongue), it was not because he could not understand French, but because he wished to insult her in front of everybody.

I can see and hear Mademoiselle requesting him in dulcet tones, but with an ominous tightening of the lips, to pass her the bread; and likewise I can hear and see Orlov unflinchingly going on with his soup; finally with a slashing "Pardon, Monsieur," Mademoiselle would swoop right across his plate, snatch up the breadbasket, and recoil again with a "Thank you, sir" so charged with irony that Orlov's downy ears would turn the color of geranium. "The brute! The cad! The Nihilist!" she sobbed later in her room — which was no longer next to ours though still on the same floor.

If Orlov happened to come tripping downstairs while, with an asthmatic pause after every ten steps or so, she was working her way up (for the little hydraulic elevator would constantly, and rather insultingly too, refuse to function), Mademoiselle maintained that he had viciously bumped into her, pushed her, knocked her down, and we already could see him trampling her prostrate body. More and more frequently she would leave the table, and the chocolate ice or *gâteau d'Artois* that she would have missed was diplomatically sent up in her wake. From her remote room she would write a sixteen-page letter to my mother, who, hurrying upstairs, would find her dramatically packing her trunk. And then one day she was allowed to go on packing

V

Because of the war she had some trouble in reaching Switzerland. "The Germans," she wrote with her usual emphasis, "stripped me to the skin, searching me for some secret message which, *hélas!* they did not find." Nor have I — at least up to this point of her life story. But some ten years later, in the middle twenties long after our correspondence had fizzled out, by some fluke move of life in exile I chanced to pass through Lausanne — so I thought I might as well look up Mademoiselle O if she was still alive.

She was. Stouter than ever, but quite gray and almost totally deaf, she welcomed me with a tumultuous outburst of affection. Instead of the Château de Chillon picture there was now one of a gaudy troika. She spoke as warmly of her life in Russia as if it were her own lost homeland. Indeed I found in the neighborhood quite a colony of such old Swiss governesses ousted by our Revolution. Clustering together in a constant seething of competitive reminiscences, they formed a small island in the midst of a country which had grown alien to them. One is always at home in one's past, no matter what its color, which partly explains those pathetic ladies' posthumous love for another land that they never really had known and where most of them had been continuously unhappy.

As no dialogue was possible because of Mademoiselle's deafness, I decided to bring her next day the appliance which I gathered she could not afford. No sooner had she adjusted the clumsy thing than she turned to me with a dazzled look of moist wonder and bliss in her eyes. She swore she could hear every word, every murmur of mine. She could not, for I had not spoken. Was it silence she heard, that Silence she had talked about in the past? No, she had been lying to herself then; now she was lying to me.

Before leaving for Basle and Berlin, I found myself somehow or other walking along the lake in the clammy and misty night. At one spot a lone arc light dimly diluted the darkness. In its nimbus the mist seemed transformed into a visible drizzle. *"Il pleut toujours en Suisse"* was one of those casual comments which formerly had made Mademoiselle weep. Below, a wide ripple, almost a wave, and something vaguely white happened to attract my eye. As I came quite close to the lapping water I saw what it was — an aged swan, a large and uncouth creature, making ridiculous efforts to hoist himself into a moored boat. He could not do it. The heavy, impotent flapping of his wings, that scaly, slippery sound against the rocking and plashing boat, the gluey glistening of the dark swell where it caught the light — all seemed for a moment laden with that strange significance which sometimes in our dreams is attached to a finger pressed to mute lips and then pointing to something we have not time to discern before waking with a shudder. But although I soon forgot that dismal night it was, oddly enough, that night, that compound image — shudder and swan and swell — which first came to my mind when a couple of years later I learned that Mademoiselle had died.

She had spent all her life in feeling miserable; this misery was her native element; its fluctuations, its varying depths, alone gave her the impression of moving and living. What bothers me is that a sense of misery, and nothing else, is not enough to make a permanent soul. My enormous and morose Mademoiselle O is all right on earth but impossible in eternity. Have I really salvaged her from fiction?

Just before the rhythm I hear falters and fades, I catch myself wondering whether, during the years I knew her, I had not kept utterly missing something in her that was far more she than her name or her chins or her ways or even her French — something perhaps akin to that glimpse of her, to the radiant deceit she used in order to have me depart pleased with my own kindness, or to that swan whose agony was so much more real than a drooping dancer's white arms; something in short which I could appreciate only after the things and beings that I had most loved in the security of my childhood had been turned to ashes or shot through the heart.

1944
WARTIME JOURNEY
by Jan Struther

THE westbound train is running four hours late.
A dozen times at least it's pulled into a siding,
And the passengers listen, and wonder,
And listen, and wait
For the growing thunder and then the dying thunder

Of troop train or freight
Taking the right of way.
The conductor's an old man, patient and gray:
He's ridden this road for thirty years or more,
And he knows the score.
"Yes, *Sir*,
Wartime riding's not like peacetime riding."

Five hours late, and crowded. At the end of the aisle
There's a girl with blonde hair and a tired smile,
Writing V-mail to a boy gone overseas.
There's a woman with a fretful baby on her knees:
His dad's not seen him; she's traveled a night and a day;
The Army camp is three nights more away.
Servicemen: a bunch of young trainees —
Through with their basic, but no insignia to show it
Except hands calloused, shoulders broadened by drill —
Eyeing with frank respect
The man in new civilians, whose chest is decked
With a ribbon, and his face with a fresh-healed scar.
He stares in front of him, not at the railroad car
But at jungles and fever-swamps in the South Seas.
For him it's over, but his buddies are there still,
Sweating, fighting, dying or dead. He is tall,
And walks with a limp when he fetches a drink of water.
He's the only one in the coach who has known slaughter,
But the others will know it, or their men will know it,
In a few months, less or more,
And *they* know the score.
"Yes, *Ma'am*.
This war, 't ain't just the menfolks' war."

Six hours late. The slim quicksilver bar
On the wall of the coach has climbed to 94°.
It isn't a real coach, but a baggage car
Hauled from retirement, fixed to meet the rush:
The seats are upright, covered in dirty plush;
The sides, windowless iron, vibrate with the heat.
In back, two businessmen unfasten their collars
And loosen their shoes to ease their swollen feet.
They missed the Limited — scrambled on at a run.
"This is a hell of a train," says the paunchy one.
"I wouldn't take it again for a thousand dollars."
But the thin one has a son

In Africa or the Arctic (he doesn't know which —
This is a crazy war),
And to him it doesn't matter any more
Whether he travels the poor man's way or the rich.
He knows the score.
"Yes, *Sir.*
Folks know things now they never knew before."

Seven hours late. The lamps begin to dim.
("This is a borrowed car from another road:
The lights don't jibe — they'll fold up pretty soon,"
The conductor says, when the fat man rails at him.)
"This is the damnedest train — let's sit in the diner."
But the other grins, retorting,
"We got no diner. This ain't the Streamliner."
So he pipes down. There's some Scotch in one of his grips,
And when it's reached his lips
Often enough, he nods, and begins to snore.
The baby's sleeping now, its head at rest
Against the chain-store rayon of its mother's breast;
And she too drowses, wondering whether her Joe
Will be somebody changed, or the guy she used to know.
The blonde girl sleeps, her high-heeled, open-toed,
Frail shoes lolling over.
She dreams about her lover —
An evening at the movies, a soda, a juke-box tune,
And back-porch good-night kisses under the moon.
She knows the score.
"Yes, *Ma'am.*
Wartime courting's not like peacetime courting."

Eight hours late: and now there's no more light
At all, and the trainees sleep,
Dreaming of the dropped rifle and the Top Kick,
K.P., the G.I. boots, the bucking jeep,
The latrine rumor, the chow-hound and the gold-brick.
The thin man dreams of his son, freezing or sweating.
The fat man dreams of wealth, but now and again
Something breaks into his dream like a thief in the night,
And instead of begetting
Money, he's killing men.
The tall man stares before him: it'll take
Longer for him to sleep. The things he's seen
Lurk still behind his eyelids. He dare not drop them

In case those pictures haunt him — he cannot stop them.
He'd sooner stay awake.
But even he, lulled by the train's noise,
Sleeps fitfully at last, dreaming of boys
He knew who will not any more
Discuss the double-header at the corner store.
All of these know the score.
"Yes, *Sir.* Yes, *Ma'am.*
This war — seems like it's everybody's war."

Nine hours late: and even that ill-matched couple
On the front seat — the lady with the blue-white hair
And the young Negro soldier, silent and supple —
Who, at the journey's start,
Sat ramrod straight, aware of one another
Beyond invisible bars, sister and brother,
Both ill at ease, yet both without escape
From a base-born, base-bred,
Nebulous, opposite yet identical dread
(He of a white folks' glance he's learned to fear,
She of a touch she feels is kin to rape) —
Even these two now sleep: they're drowned in peace,
White head and black head nodding an inch apart.

Exhaustion brings oblivion, lulls mistrust,
Falls blindly on the just and the unjust,
Quenches discrimination, gives release
From self-forged barriers to the human heart.
"Yes, *Sir.*
Seems like that's what's required.
I've ridden this road for thiry years or more
And I reckon I know the score.
Yes, *Ma'am.*
God keep us tired.
God keep us tired."

———————————————

WRITERS IN HOLLYWOOD
by Raymond Chandler

HOLLYWOOD is easy to hate, easy to sneer at, easy to lampoon. Some of the best lampooning has been done by people who have never been through a studio gate, some of the best sneering by egocentric geniuses who departed huffily — not forgetting to collect their last pay check — leaving behind them nothing but the exquisite aroma of their personalities and a botched job for the tired hacks to clean up.

I hold no brief for Hollywood. I have worked there a little over two years, which is far from enough to make me an authority, but more than enough to make me feel pretty thoroughly bored. That should not be so. The making of a picture ought surely to be a rather fascinating adventure. It is not; it is an endless contention of tawdry egos, some of them powerful, almost all of them vociferous, and almost none of them capable of anything much more creative than credit-stealing and self-promotion.

Hollywood is a showman's paradise. But showmen make nothing; they exploit what someone else has made. The publisher and the play producer are showmen too; but they exploit what is already made. The showmen of Hollywood control the making — and thereby degrade it. For the basic art of motion pictures is the screenplay; it is fundamental, without it there is nothing. Everything derives from the screenplay, and most of that which derives is an applied skill which, however adept, is artistically not in the same class with the creation of a screenplay. But in Hollywood the screenplay is written by a salaried writer under the supervision of a producer — that is to say, by an employee without power of decision over the uses of his own craft, without ownership of it, and, however extravagantly paid, almost without honor for it.

I am not interested in why the Hollywood system exists or persists, nor in learning out of what bitter struggles for prestige it arose, nor in how much money it succeeds in making out of bad pictures. I am interested only in the fact that as a result of it there is no such thing as an art of the screenplay, and there never will be as long as the system lasts, for it is the essence of this system that it seeks to exploit a talent without permitting it the right to be a talent. It cannot be done; you can only destroy the talent, which is exactly what happens — when there is any to destroy.

Granted that there isn't much. Some chatty publisher (probably Bennett Cerf) remarked once that there are writers in Hollywood making two thousand dollars a week who haven't had an idea in ten years. He exaggerated — backwards: there are writers in Hollywood making two thousand a week who never had an idea in their lives, who have never written a photographable scene, who could not make two cents a word in the pulp market if their lives depended on it. Hollywood is full of such writers, although there are few at such high salaries. They are, to put it bluntly, a pretty dreary lot of hacks, and most of them know it, and they take their kicks and their salaries and try to be reasonably grateful to an industry which permits them to live much more opulently than they could live anywhere else.

And I have no doubt that most of them, also, would like to be much better writers than they are, would like to have force and integrity and imagination — enough of these to earn a decent living at some art of literature that has the dignity of a free profession. It will not happen to them, and there is not much reason why it should. If it ever could have happened, it will not happen now. For even the best of them (with a few rare exceptions) devote their entire time to work which has no more possibility of distinction than a Pekinese has of becoming a Great Dane: to asinine musicals about technicolor legs and the yowling of night-club singers; to "psychological" dramas with wooden plots, stock characters, and that persistent note of fuzzy earnestness which suggests the conversation of schoolgirls in puberty; to sprightly and sophisticated comedies (we hope) in which the gags are as stale as the attitudes, in which there is always a drink in every hand, a butler in every doorway, and a telephone on the edge of every bathtub; to historical epics in which the male actors look like female impersonators, and the lovely feminine star looks just a little too starry-eyed for a babe who has spent half her life swapping husbands; and last but not least, to those pictures of deep social import in which everybody is thoughtful and grown-up and sincere and the more difficult problems of life are wordily resolved into a unanimous vote of confidence in the inviolability of the Constitution, the sanctity of the home, and the paramount importance of the streamlined kitchen.

And these, dear readers, are the million-dollar babies — the cream of the crop. Most of the boys and girls who write for the screen never get anywhere near this far. They devote their sparkling lines and their structural finesse to horse operas, cheap gun-in-the-kidney melodramas, horror items about mad scientists and cliffhangers concerned with screaming blondes and circular saws. The writers of this tripe are licked before they start. Even in a purely technical sense their work is doomed for lack of the time to do it properly. The challenge of screenwriting is to say much in little and then take half of that little out and still preserve an effect of leisure and natural movement. Such a technique requires experiment and elimination. The cheap pictures simply cannot afford it.

II

Let me not imply that there are no writers of authentic ability in Hollywood. There are not many, but there are not many anywhere. The creative gift is a scarce commodity, and patience and imitation have always done most of its work. There is no reason to expect from the anonymous toilers of the screen a quality which we are very obviously not getting from the publicized litterateurs of the best-seller list, from the compilers of fourth-rate historical novels which sell half a million copies, from the Broadway candy butchers known as playwrights, or from the sulky maestri of the little magazines.

To me the interesting point about Hollywood's writers of talent is not how few or how many they are, but how little of worth their talent is allowed to achieve. Interesting — but hardly unexpected, once you accept the premise that writers are employed to write screenplays on the theory that, being writers, they have a particular gift and training for the job, and are then prevented from doing it with any independence or finality whatsoever, on the theory that, being merely writers, they know nothing about making pictures; and of course if they don't know how to make pictures, they couldn't possibly know how to write them. It takes a producer to tell them that.

I do not wish to become unduly vitriolic on the subject of producers. My own experience does not justify it, and after all, producers too are slaves of the system. Also, the term "producer" is of very vague definition. Some producers are powerful in their own right, and some are little more than legmen for the front office; some — few, I trust — receive less money than some of the writers who work for them. It is even said that in one large Hollywood studio there are producers who are lower than writers; not merely in earning power, but in prestige, importance, and aesthetic ability. It is, of course, a *very* large studio where all sorts of unexplained things could happen and hardly be noticed.

For my thesis the personal qualities of a producer are rather beside the point. Some are able and humane men and some are low-grade individuals with the morals of a goat, the artistic integrity of a slot machine, and the manners of a floorwalker with delusions of grandeur. In so far as the writing of the screenplay is concerned, however, the producer is the boss; the writer either gets along with him and his ideas (if he has any) or gets out. This means both personal and artistic subordination, and no writer of quality will long accept either without surrendering that which made him a writer of quality, without dulling the fine edge of his mind, without becoming little by little a conniver rather than a creator, a supple and facile journeyman rather than a craftsman of original thought.

It makes very little difference how a writer feels toward his producer as a man; the fact that the producer can change and destroy and disregard his work can only operate to diminish that work in its conception and to make it mechanical and indifferent in execution. The impulse to perfection cannot exist where the definition of perfection is the arbitrary decision of authority. That which is born in loneliness and from the heart cannot be defended against the judgment of a committee of sycophants. The volatile essences which make literature cannot survive the clichés of a long series of story conferences. There is little magic of word or emotion or situation which can remain alive after the incessant bone-scraping revisions imposed on the Hollywood writer by the process of rule by decree. That these magics do somehow, here and there, by another and even rarer magic, survive and reach the screen more or less intact is the infrequent miracle which keeps Hollywood's handful of fine writers from cutting their throats.

Hollywood has no right to expect such miracles, and it does not deserve the men who bring them to pass. Its conception of what makes a good picture is still as juvenile as its treatment of writing talent is insulting and degrading. Its idea of "production value" is spending a million dollars dressing up a story that any good writer would throw away. Its vision of the rewarding movie is a vehicle for some glamorpuss with two expressions and eighteen changes of costume, or for some male idol of the muddled millions with a permanent hangover, six worn-out acting tricks, the build of a lifeguard, and the mentality of a chicken-strangler. Pictures for such purposes as these, Hollywood lovingly and carefully makes. The good ones smack it in the rear when it isn't looking.

III

There is no present indication whatever that the Hollywood writer is on the point of acquiring any real control over his work, any right to choose what that work shall be (other than refusing jobs, which he can only do within narrow limits), or even any right to decide how the values in the producer-chosen work shall be brought out. There is no present guarantee that his best lines, best ideas, best scenes will not be changed or omitted on the set by the director or dropped on the floor during the later process of cutting — for the simple but essential reason that the best things in any picture, artistically speaking, are invariably the easiest to leave out, mechanically speaking.

There is no attempt in Hollywood to exploit the writer as an artist of meaning to the picture-buying public; there is every attempt to keep the public uninformed about his vital contribution to whatever art the movie contains. On the billboards, in the newspaper advertisements, his name will be smaller than that of the most insignificant bit-player who achieves what is known as billing; it will be the first to disappear as the size of the ad is cut down toward the middle of the week; it will be the last and least to be mentioned in any word-of-mouth or radio promotion.

The first picture I worked on was nominated for an Academy award (if that means anything), but I was not even invited to the press review held right in the studio. An extremely successful picture made by another studio from a story I wrote used verbatim lines out of the story in its promotional campaign, but my name was never mentioned once in any radio, magazine, billboard, or newspaper advertising that I saw or heard — and I saw and heard a great deal. This neglect is of no consequence to me personally; to any writer of books a Hollywood by-line is trivial. To those whose whole work is in Hollywood it is not trivial, because it is part of a deliberate and successful plan to reduce the professional screenwriter to the status of an assistant picture-maker, superficially deferred to (while he is in the room), essentially ignored, and even in his most brilliant achievements carefully pushed out of the way of any possible accolade which might otherwise fall to the star, the producer, the director.

If all this is true, why then should any writer of genuine ability continue to work in Hollywood at all? The obvious reason is not enough: few screenwriters possess homes in Bel-Air, illuminated swimming pools, wives in full-length mink coats, three servants, and that air of tired genius gone a little sour. Money buys pathetically little in Hollywood beyond the pleasure of living in an unreal world, associating with a narrow group of people who think, talk, and drink nothing but pictures, most of them bad, and the doubtful pleasure of watching famous actors and actresses guzzle in some of the rudest restaurants in the world.

I do not mean that Hollywood society is any duller or more dissipated than moneyed society anywhere: God knows it couldn't be. But it is a pretty thin reward for a lifetime devoted to the essential craft of what might be a great art. I suppose the truth is that the veterans of the Hollywood scene do not realize how little they are getting, how many dull egotists they have to smile at, how many shoddy people they have to treat as friends, how little real accomplishment is possible, how much gaudy trash their life contains. The superficial friendliness of Hollywood is pleasant — until you find out that nearly every sleeve conceals a knife. The companionship during working hours with men and women who take the business of fiction seriously gives a pale heat to the writer's lonely soul. It is so easy to forget that there is a world in which men buy their own groceries and, if they choose, think their own thoughts. In Hollywood you don't even write your own checks — and what you think is what you hope some producer or studio executive will like.

Beyond this I suppose there is hope; there are several hopes. The cold dynasty will not last forever, the dictatorial producer is already a little unsure, the top-heavy director has long since become a joke in his own studio; after a while even technicolor will not save him. There is hope that a decayed and makeshift system will pass, that somehow the flatulent moguls will learn that only writers can write screenplays and only proud and independent writers can write good screenplays, and that present methods of dealing with such men are destructive of the very force by which pictures must live.

And there is the intense and beautiful hope that the Hollywood writers themselves — such of them as are capable of it — will recognize that writing for the screen is no job for amateurs and half-writers whose problems are always solved by somebody else. It is the writers' own weakness as craftsmen that permits the superior egos to bleed them white of initiative, imagination, and integrity. If even a quarter of the *highly paid* screenwriters in Hollywood could produce a completely integrated and photographable screenplay under their own power, with only the amount of interference and discussion necessary to protect the studio's investment in actors and ensure a reasonable freedom from libel and censorship troubles, then the producer would assume his proper function of coördinating and conciliating the various crafts which combine to make a picture; and the director — heaven help his strutting soul — would be reduced to the ignominious task of making pictures as they are conceived and written — and not as the director would try to write them, if only he knew how to write.

Certainly there are producers and directors — although how pitifully few — who are sincere enough to want such a change, and talented enough to have no fear of its effect on their own position. Yet it is only a little over three years since the major (and only this very year the minor) studios were forced, after prolonged and bitter struggle, to agree to treat the writers according to some reasonable standard of business ethics.

This struggle is still going on; in a sense it will always go on, in a sense it always *should* go on. But so far the cards are stacked against the writer. If there is no art of the screenplay, the reason is at least partly that there exists no available body of technical theory and practice by which it can be learned. There is no available library of screenplay literature, because the screenplays belong to the studios, and they will only show them within their guarded walls. There is no body of critical opinion, because there are no critics of the screenplay; there are only critics of motion pictures as entertainment, and most of these critics know nothing whatever of the means whereby the motion picture is created and put on celluloid. There is no teaching, because there is no one to teach. If you do not know how pictures are made, you cannot speak with any authority on how they should be constructed; if you do, you are busy enough trying to do it.

There is no correlation of crafts within the studio itself; the average — and far better than average — screenwriter knows hardly anything of the technical problems of the director, and nothing at all of the superlative skill of the trained cutter. He spends his effort in writing shots that cannot be made, or which if made would be thrown away; in writing dialogue that cannot be spoken, sound effects that cannot be heard, and nuances of mood and emotion which the camera cannot reproduce. His idea of an effective scene is something that has to be shot down a stair well or out of a gopher hole; or a conversation so static that the director, in order to impart a sense of motion to it, is compelled to photograph it from nine different angles.

In fact, no part of the vast body of technical knowledge which Hollywood contains is systematically and as a matter of course made available to the new writer in a studio. They tell him to look at pictures — which is to learn architecture by staring at a house. And then they send him back to his rabbit hutch to write little scenes which his producer, in between telephone calls to his blondes and his booze-companions, will tell him ought to have been written quite differently. The producer is probably correct; the scene ought to have been written differently. It ought to have been written right. But first it had to be written. The producer didn't do that. He wouldn't know how. Anyway he's too busy. And he's making too much money. And the atmosphere of intellectual squalor in which the salaried writer operates would offend his dignity.

I have kept the best hope of all for the last. In spite of all I have said, the writers of Hollywood *are* winning their battle for prestige. More and more of them are becoming showmen in their own right, producers and directors of their own screenplays. Let us be glad for their additional importance and power, and not examine the artistic result too critically. The boys make good (and some of them might even make good pictures). Let us rejoice together, for the tendency to become showmen is well in the acceptable tradition of the literary art as practiced among the cameras.

For the very nicest thing Hollywood can possibly think of to say to a writer is that he is too good to be only a writer.

WHAT'S WRONG WITH THE FAMILY?
by Della D. Cyrus

SOMETHING is wrong with the family. It is a subject on which almost everybody is ready to express an opinion in newspaper and pulpit, on platform and street corner. The trouble is the breakdown of character, they say. People nowadays think they should be happy. It's time they got back to the old-fashioned virtues of responsibility and adherence to duty. The trouble is with modern women. They should stay home and take care of their children. Alcohol is the key to it all. People don't believe in God and don't go to church. There aren't enough parks or playgrounds. The war accounts for it.

Everyone seems to know the answer, and almost everyone knows what should be done, but the symptoms continue to become more alarming, and actually nothing is done to stop the steady statistical disintegration of the family.

We are so fascinated just watching and denouncing the symptoms of family disease that we fail to see the source of the infection — the family itself. The family falls apart in modern urban life not because human nature is more depraved than it used to be, but because *the family* is out of harmony with the modern world and no longer meets the most vital needs of its members. The statistics which we all view with so much alarm reflect the simple fact that the family lets people down, and there is nothing else to supply the values and satisfactions which the family once supplied.

Family life was well adapted to the ways of Europe in the twelfth century, and even to the ways of the isolated American pioneer in the nineteenth century. Then it provided its members with work, food, clothing, shelter, education, love, companionship, religion, and social life. The family was the community and the community was the family. The family as a unit produced the things necessary for its life as a unit. A man without a wife was as crippled economically and as lonesome as a woman without a husband. The more children a couple had, the better living they could make and the more secure was their future. It was a life which set the family against the world, and for its survival it cultivated strong feelings of possessiveness within the family, and strong feelings of suspicion and hostility toward outsiders.

In the heyday of the family there was incompatibility, of course, and frustration and boredom, but these things were offset by a common cause and the knowledge that every member of the family was essential. If, in the past, families faced up to their problems and stuck together, it was not because they had more character or more religion than we have, though they did have more assurance about what they believed, but rather it was because they had no alternative.

Clearly the family is no longer an independent world of its own, but completely dependent on the rest of society for the necessities of its life as well as for most of its education, culture, and amusement. Nor is the individual any longer dependent on the family for the satisfaction of his own needs. Both men and women can live comfortable lives, filled with friendships, social activities, and even love, without ever taking on the responsibilities and restrictions of family living. Even children and the aged, if sufficiently neglected, will be taken care of at public expense in the modern city.

If the family has nothing distinctive to offer in the modern city, which cannot be obtained more cheaply and less painfully elsewhere, why do people still cling to it? The fact is that no adequate alternative to family living is available for the man and woman who love each other and who want to have children.

This then is the sole cohesive element in the modern family — the love of a man and a woman and their love for their children. Not economic necessity, not to produce together the means of staying alive — just love. This means that the modern family puts a burden on love which it was not compelled to carry in the past and one which it cannot carry now.

Since our sexual morality does not approve of love outside of marriage, the family automatically fails whenever love fails. The far greater number of divorces among childless couples than among couples with children indicates that many families keep operating just to protect their young. But the increasing number of divorces among couples with children shows that parental responsibility is not enough to save an institution which draws so small and tight a circle around its members.

We are still trying to maintain the isolation of the family in a world which makes that isolation impossible, and we are still trying to find values in the family which are no longer there. We still expect to find the world there, rich, warm, various, exciting, and alive. But the world is outside. We cannot understand why we feel so restless and so unfulfilled when we exercise the old family attitudes of exclusiveness, possessiveness, and suspicion toward outsiders, which suited so well the pioneer family of the past. By trying to pretend that the family is a world of its own, we only succeed in cutting it off from the world.

II

Let us look at some specific ways in which the family fails to meet our needs as individuals. Because women usually work within the limits of the family, they suffer most from its failures. It isolates them especially from any vital relationship with the world outside the family, and under modern conditions they cannot find an adequate sense of calling or purpose within the family. Not only are they forced into unhealthy dependence on their husbands and children for most of the satisfactions of their lives, but the family does not even provide them with a physical or spiritual environment in which they can be successful wives and mothers.

Modern conveniences plus modern high standards, while freeing women from the back-breaking physical labor of the pioneer woman, have increased enormously her petty cleaning-up tasks. If the pioneer woman had spent so much time on the luxury and boredom of cleanliness, she wouldn't have been paying her way.

The preparing of food has a little more status as important work and may have the virtue of saving some women from complete futility. But even this is very different from the role the pioneer woman played in providing a family with food. Then the preparing of a meal was an incidental task in the long process of growing, picking, processing, and storing in which she had taken an essential part. The modern woman, spending money earned by her husband to buy food already produced, canned, or tastelessly prepared by others, cannot have the same feeling of being an essential part of life.

But, we keep arguing, housekeeping and cooking are not the essential jobs of a woman. These jobs take time, of course, and involve a considerable amount of drudgery, but everyone has some drudgery — even business executives and college presidents. A woman's real job is the care and training of her children. No job is more important, more satisfying, more close to life, than the directing of young lives from infancy to maturity. A mother has a full-time job by definition. Any woman who can't be satisfied with a home and children should never get married. These are prevalent beliefs which amount to a national faith and sink so far into so many generations of feeling that many people are incapable of examining them at all.

If they are valid beliefs, why is there so much evidence that women are making a botch of motherhood?

The crucial years in the life of the family are the years during which there are children under school age. They are the years when the important groundwork of the child's personality is being formed. They are the years which convince everybody that a woman should never try to be anything but a mother, and they account for the fact that most women linger pointlessly at home long after their job as a mother is done. They are the years which place the heaviest burdens on marriage. Divorces are not so frequent during these years as they are later, but this is the period when many marriages in fact get broken, whether or not they end in divorce.

Why are these years so difficult and so often fatal? Exactly what takes place in a family of two or three small children? The mother in this family, whether she has a fourth-grade education or a Ph.D. in philosophy, has less freedom and less leisure than anyone else in our society. Even if she has a washing machine, mangle, vacuum cleaner, and Mixmaster (sometimes she doesn't have any of these things), she works hours which have long been illegal for anyone in industry. When her children are well, she works twelve hours a day, seven days a week. When they are ill or when there is a new baby, she works from fourteen to twenty hours, often going for months without an adequate period of unbroken sleep. And never, even in her deepest sleep, is she entirely free from her responsibility. Consequently, a woman is almost always tired during these years, if not actually ill, and this alone makes her an unhappy and unfit companion for her husband and children.

The mother's working day is divided between caring for the house and caring for the children, which, under modern conditions, is a simple neurosis-producing situation. The mother and her children are constantly at cross purposes, because the children, if they are normal, are bent on noise, mess, dirt, and destruction, while she is struggling to create quiet, order, and cleanliness. Her children, because of their lack of equipment and companionship, and because of their very youngness, need her attention, her time, and her help, while she needs more time and energy than she has, to accomplish the essential jobs of washing, cooking, cleaning, and putting away. In this contest, either the house or the child is bound to lose; and whichever happens, the mother is left with a feeling of incompetence and failure. Nor is there any time or place, from her children's waking in the morning until their going to bed at night, and sometimes not even then, which the mother can count on as her own to rest or read, to collect her thoughts, to regain her perspective and her self-respect and begin over again.

Most people recognize this period in a woman's life as a difficult but inevitable one. The typical remark made most often by older women is: "But it only lasts a few years and then you wish you had your children back again." This endlessly repeated bit of wisdom is, all unwittingly, the most devastating comment which could be made on the prevailing ideal for the mother. It amounts to smug acceptance of the fact that in those years the mother loses the value of her education and training for other work, loses touch with the large problems of a larger world, and loses confidence in herself as a mature citizen of the world who might have something of value to contribute to it.

"Only a few years" in the life of the child means the most crucial years of his development, during which he is cramped and lonely and pushed away and overwatched by a mother who is too tired and too busy and too unhappy to give him the kind of mothering he needs.

III

Meanwhile, what is happening to the marriage during these years? If the husband is a mature and sympathetic person who can throw himself into the spirit of the rough-and-tumble life of babies, diapers, chaotic meals, and sleepless nights; if he is vocationally adjusted, economically secure, hopeful for his future, not too overworked, and takes the attitude that things are temporarily a bit too tough for his wife, they can grit their teeth and pull through without irreparably damaging their relationship. When these favorable conditions prevail, they can, on occasion, laugh and have fun together. But obviously these are rare conditions.

Too many men in the modern city get too little satisfaction from their work, are worried about money, overworked, and apprehensive of the future. These are just the years when men are trying hardest to make a career or to make money. Far from being able to wade happily into the noisy discontent which is their homes, most men have too little energy for their children and almost none for the problems of their wives. Instead, they need someone to sympathize with *them,* someone to allay their fears and listen to their plans. Above all, they need someone to play with, laugh with, and relax with.

So they come home to a physically exhausted, nervously taut, emotionally dissipated woman who still has several hours of work to do. Both are so aware of their own needs that even when they understand the needs of the other, there is little they can do about it. Both know that somewhere there should be help for this situation, that somewhere in the world there should be rest and laughter and love. Almost in spite of themselves, they hit out at each other, because it was in their marriage that both had expected to find these things. Finally the marriage falls to pieces in fact, if not in court, or it settles down into the quietness of resignation and despair. Couples caught in this situation often feel that it could be saved if they could leave the home together and go somewhere to dance or drink or talk in a new atmosphere. But even this kind of shock treatment too often is unavailable, because it is too difficult and too expensive to get anybody to stay with the children.

Playing at home is more difficult still. If the children don't shatter the relationship between husband and wife — and very small children are capable of breaking into life's most poignant moments at any hour of the day or the night — still the home is the wife's eternal workshop and she, at least, cannot experience there the sense of freedom and new experience which she and her husband both need. Because playing together is so hard to arrange, a frequent solution is for the husband to go off to bowl or to work overtime, or to make love to someone who is available and will take him the way he is, while the wife stays home more lonely and resentful than ever.

Add to all of these difficulties of marriage and children the problems of emotionally warped individuals who demand an abnormal amount of love and consideration, the sexually repressed or maladjusted, the physically ill who cannot carry their share of the load, and it is hard to understand, not why so many families break up, but why so many still hang together.

Men are even less critical of the family than women and although men are aware of the disappointing contrast between what they want and what they get, they are so blinded by the traditional promises of home, love, food, and fireside that when these things are cold and unappetizing they look everywhere but at the family itself for the trouble.

That a man might find what he wanted in a very different kind of family life rarely occurs to him, and he resists changing the family pattern long after his wife is willing to do so or in fact has changed it by going to work outside their home. His resistance is not difficult to understand, because young mothers who work at outside jobs can almost never make arrangements for home and children which are satisfactory for everybody.

If a good nursery school is available for the children and the family can get and pay for a first-rate housekeeper, the woman may work at an outside job she likes, to the greater satisfaction of everybody, including her husband. But desirable housekeepers and nursery schools are available to only a select few. Most mothers must resort to makeshift arrangements which are bad for the children and leave the mother with most of the work to do at home in addition to her other job.

The young child, if he is still reasonably normal, is so happy to be in school and among his contemporaries that he takes life in his stride for several years without causing anybody too much anxiety. But what about the older child and particularly the adolescent? What does the family do for him? It may have disintegrated altogether, leaving him without any real ties to anybody. Or the parents may be hanging together by threads of grim duty or resigned boredom waiting for him to get old enough so that they can stop pretending to be a family. Or the mother may have thrown all of her longing for life into plans for her adolescent child so that he is unable to have any life of his own. But even if none of these frequent conditions exists, the very best family cannot meet all the needs of an adolescent in the modern world.

The adolescent suffers as much from the social isolation of the family as he does from its individual failures. Adolescents, by definition, are trying to outgrow the family and their problem is that they have nothing to grow into. Delinquents are not delinquent because their parents don't watch them, or because they haven't any place to play basketball, or because there are too many beer joints on every corner.

They are delinquent because, in addition to their tension over the individual failures of their individual families, they have no real part to play in the life of the world. They are boiling over with vitality and ability which our society does not want or need.

Instead of giving them an important and useful social function which their growing maturity demands, we tell them to stick to their studies, help their mothers, and stay out of trouble. We insist that they stop acting like children but refuse to let them act like adults. Juvenile Court judges and Community Welfare Councils talk about uniting community facilities for combating juvenile delinquency, or uniting delinquents to solve their own problems, but no one says anything about uniting families into the kind of communities which might give an adolescent something real to belong to.

Sporadic and timid beginnings have been made in interfamily coöperation. Families have coöperated in running nursery schools, tot yards, and victory gardens. Whole communities have built common heating and refrigeration systems. Housing projects have included common nurseries, laundries, and recreational halls. During the present housing shortage, groups of families have been forced to live together as one family in the same house — with conspicuous lack of success. The horror of anything faintly suggesting communal living prevents even timid and partial coöperative projects from being taken up generally. But the need is not for half-hearted coöperative projects or for communal living. The need is for effective communities. Must we always wait for bombs, fires, and floods to see in a tardy flash that we all live together in the same world? Can't we see now that that old bus, the family, has broken down on a lonely road at night and that we are all in it together?

IV

Suppose a group of families in the same neighborhood of a large city decided to pool their problems and their strength. If they began on the problems of young mothers and children, they could as a group establish a child center for children of all ages in their neighborhood, to be run for as many hours a day as the group wished, perhaps twenty-four. They could secure a spacious building with ground around it, — perhaps a school, — get equipment, and hire a trained staff, perhaps some of the mothers themselves, who might be assisted by untrained mothers who wished to assist. This center could provide everything which children need: outdoor and indoor space, things to make and do, physical care, companionship, social experience, and supervision. It could be near enough to everybody's house to make it convenient for children to come and go easily at whatever hours fitted into their particular family plan.

The objection that this takes the responsibility for children off the mother, where it belongs, and places it on the community, where it doesn't belong, is an irrational objection. Under our present lack of community, child welfare agencies, juvenile courts, reform schools, detention homes, and crèches testify to the fact that society is already taking unsatisfactory responsibility for too many children whose parents have given up entirely. Under a truly community plan, parents would not be relinquishing responsibility but would be pooling it. In a sense, all children would be the responsibility of all parents. Under such a plan, parents would be much less likely to give up entirely, because the burden would be shared by all. By freeing children for the kind of play and companionship which they need, a community plan would give mothers some time in which to use capacities of their own. And only when a mother has some satisfactory life of her own can she give her children the unmixed love and unselfish guidance which are her special gift.

The next step for a group of families to take in creating a community life might be a coöperative house-cleaning plan. Commercial house-cleaning companies are already in existence in some large cities, but a community might have its own, composed of some of its own members, or several communities might form such a company together. Thus all general house cleaning would become a community business, carried on by people especially trained for the job, abolishing it forever as the lonely, unpaid, soapy preoccupation of some twenty-five million women.

Another experiment for such communities could be a coöperative kitchen and dining building. Immediately, of course, the noxious ogre of communal eating raises its ugly head. But there is no reason why a community could not run, or hire to have run, a coöperative kitchen without eating in common. A central kitchen could be located near enough to everyone, so that meals could be delivered to private homes. Or a dining building could be so arranged to permit families to dine in private intimacy if they wished. Or, since it is to be a democratic community, families who wanted to could go on cooking their own meals in their own kitchens. Most families would discover that their children would heckle them into eating with other children as often as possible. And wives, whether the working kind or the staying at home kind, when offered the choice of cooking a meal or eating out, often choose the latter. Whatever inevitable objection and resistance there is to anything so strange and unproved should be weighed against the freeing of human beings for a life of meaning and hope.

If families coöperated on the problems of child care, house cleaning, and cooking, women immediately would be free and obliged to make some choices about their own lives. Some who like to be home-makers could go on being full-time homemakers. Some could work in the community enterprises themselves, while others could follow part-time or whole-time careers for which they had been trained. Some could develop talents which now atrophy. But all would have the freedom and the responsibility to do something valuable with their time. All would have the freedom and the responsibility to be part of a world larger than the family. Can anyone doubt that women so freed and so responsible would contribute more to the gracious living of the family as well as to the good living of the world?

Community coöperation need not stop with meeting these problems alone. The community could have a recreational building or buildings for children and adults. It could have a sitters bureau or a clinic or a theater. Adolescents could take an important part in group planning and administration. Many jobs could be the special responsibility of adolescents for which they would receive both pay and community status. Whatever common problems the group decided to meet, they would not be met by "resources" or by "facilities" applied from the outside, but by the people themselves working or paying in common.

Man has split the atom and communicated with the moon. The time is now past due for him to try something more difficult and more important — living with his fellow man.

1947
IN COUNTRY SLEEP
by Dylan Thomas

1

Never and never, my girl riding far and near
In the land of the hearthstone tales, and spelled asleep,
Fear or believe that the wolf in a sheepwhite hood
Loping and bleating roughly and blithely shall leap,
               My dear, my dear,
Out of a lair in the flocked leaves in the dew dipped year
To eat your heart in the house in the rosy wood.

Sleep, good, for ever, slow and deep, spelled rare and wise,
My girl ranging the night in the rose and shire
Of the hobnail tales: no gooseherd or swine will turn
Into a homestall king or hamlet of fire
               And prince of ice
To court the honeyed heart from your side before sunrise
In a spinney of ringed boys and ganders, spike and burn,

Nor the innocent lie in the rooting dingle wooed
And staved, and riven among plumes my rider weep.
From the broomed witch's spume you are shielded by fern
And flower of country sleep and the greenwood keep.
                              Lie fast and soothed,
Safe be and smooth from the bellows of the rushy brood.
Never, my girl until tolled to sleep by the stern

Bell believe or fear that the rustic shade or spell
Shall harrow and snow the blood while you ride wide and near,
For who unmanningly haunts the mountain ravened eaves
Or skulks in the dell moon but moonshine echoing clear
                              From the starred well?
A hill touches an angel. Out of a saint's cell
The nightbird lauds through nunneries and domes of leaves

Her robin breasted tree, three Marys in the rays.
Sanctum sanctorum the animal eye of the wood
In the rain telling its beads, and the gravest ghost
The owl at its knelling. Fox and holt kneel before blood.
                              Now the tales praise
The star rise at pasture and nightlong the fables graze
On the lord's-table of the bowing grass. Fear most

For ever of all not the wolf in his baaing hood
Nor the tusked prince, in the ruttish farm, at the rind
And mire of love, but the Thief as meek as the dew.
The country is holy: O bide in that country kind,
                              Know the green good,
Under the prayer wheeling moon in the rosy wood
Be shielded by chant and flower and gay may you

Lie in grace. Sleep spelled at rest in the lowly house
In the squirrel nimble grove, under linen and thatch
And star: held and blessed, though you scour the high four
Winds, from the dousing shade and the roarer at the latch,
                              Cool in your vows.
Yet out of the beaked, web dark and the pouncing boughs
Be you sure the Thief will seek a way sly and sure

And sly as snow and meek as dew blown to the thorn,
This night and each vast night until the stern bell talks
In the tower and tolls to sleep over the stalls
Of the hearthstone tales my own, last love; and the soul walks
                                                    The waters shorn.
This night and each night since the falling star you were born,
Ever and ever he finds a way, as the snow falls,

As the rain falls, hail on the fleece, as the vale mist rides
Through the haygold stalls, as the dew falls on the wind-
Milled dust of the apple tree and the pounded islands
Of the morning leaves, as the star falls, as the winged
                                                    Apple seed glides,
And falls, and flowers in the yawning wound at your side,
As the world falls, silent as the cyclone of silence.

                                    2

Night and the reindeer on the clouds above the haycocks
And the wings of the great roc ribboned for the fair!
The leaping saga of prayer! And high, there, on the hare-
                                                    Heeled winds the rooks
Cawing from their black bethels soaring, the holy books
Of birds! Among the cocks like fire the red fox

Burning! Night and the vein of birds in the winged sloe wrist
Of the wood! Pastoral beat of blood through the laced leaves!
The stream from the priest black wristed spinney and sleeves
                                                    Of thistling frost
Of the nightingale's din and tale! The upgiven ghost
Of the dingle torn to singing and the surpliced

Hill of cypresses! The din and tale in the skimmed
Yard of the buttermilk rain on the pail! The sermon
Of blood! The bird loud vein! The saga from mermen
                                                    To seraphim
Leaping! The gospel rooks! All tell, this night, of him
Who comes as red as the fox and sly as the heeled wind.

Illumination of music! the lulled black backed
Gull, on the wave with sand in its eyes! and the foal moves
Through the shaken greensward lake, silent, on moonshod hooves,
                                                    In the winds' wakes.
Music of elements, that a miracle makes!
Earth, air, water, fire, singing into the white act,

The haygold haired, my love asleep, and the rift blue
Eyed, in the haloed house, in her rareness and hilly
High riding, held and blessed and true, and so stilly
                              Lying the sky
Might cross its planets, the bell weep, night gather her eyes,
The Thief fall on the dead like the willynilly dew,

Only for the turning of the earth in her holy
Heart! Slyly, slowly, hearing the wound in her side go
Round the sun, he comes to my love like the designed snow.
                                And truly he
Flows to the strand of flowers like the dew's ruly sea,
And surely he sails like the ship shape clouds. Oh he

Comes designed to my love to steal not her tide raking
Wound, nor her riding high, nor her eyes, nor kindled hair,
But her faith that each vast night and the saga of prayer
                              He comes to take
Her faith that this last night for his unsacred sake
He comes to leave her in the lawless sun awaking

Naked and forsaken to grieve he will not come.
Ever and ever by all your vows believe and fear
My dear this night he comes and night without end my dear
                              Since you were born:
And you shall wake, from country sleep, this dawn and each first
    dawn,
Your faith as deathless as the outcry of the ruled sun.

1948
DEATH OF A PIG
by E. B. White

I SPENT several days and nights in mid-September with an ailing pig and I feel driven to account for this stretch of time, more particularly since the pig died at last, and I lived, and things might easily have gone the other way round and none left to do the accounting. Even now, so close to the event, I cannot recall the hours sharply and am not ready to say whether death came on the third night or the fourth night. This uncertainty afflicts me with a sense of personal deterioration; if I were in decent health I would know how many nights I had sat up with a pig.

The scheme of buying a spring pig in blossom-time, feeding it through summer and fall, and butchering it when the solid cold weather arrives, is a familiar scheme to me and follows an antique pattern. It is a tragedy enacted on most farms with perfect fidelity to the original script. The murder, being premeditated, is in the first degree but is quick and skillful, and the smoked bacon and ham provide a ceremonial ending whose fitness is seldom questioned.

Once in a while something slips — one of the actors goes up in his lines and the whole performance stumbles and halts. My pig simply failed to show up for a meal. The alarm spread rapidly. The classic outline of the tragedy was lost. I found myself cast suddenly in the role of pig's friend and physician — a farcical character with an enema bag for a prop. I had a presentiment, the very first afternoon, that the play would never regain its balance and that my sympathies were now wholly with the pig. This was slapstick — the sort of dramatic treatment which instantly appealed to my old dachshund, Fred, who joined the vigil, held the bag, and, when all was over, presided at the interment. When we slid the body into the grave, we both were shaken to the core. The loss we felt was not the loss of ham but the loss of pig. He had evidently become precious to me, not that he represented a distant nourishment in a hungry time, but that he had suffered in a suffering world. But I'm running ahead of my story and shall have to go back.

My pigpen is at the bottom of an old orchard below the house. The pigs I have raised have lived in a faded building which once was an icehouse. There is a pleasant yard to move about in, shaded by an apple tree which overhangs the low rail fence. A pig couldn't ask for anything better — or none has, at any rate. The sawdust in the icehouse makes a comfortable bottom in which to root, and a warm bed. This sawdust, however, came under suspicion when the pig took sick. One of my neighbors said he thought the pig would have done better on new ground — the same principle that applies in planting potatoes. He said there might be something unhealthy about that sawdust, that he never thought well of sawdust.

It was about four o'clock in the afternoon when I first noticed that there was something wrong with the pig. He failed to appear at the trough for his supper, and when a pig (or a child) refuses supper a chill wave of fear runs through any household, or icehousehold. After examining my pig, who was stretched out in the sawdust inside the building, I went to the phone and cranked it four times. Mr. Dameron answered. "What's good for a sick pig?" I asked. (There is never any identification needed on a country phone; the person on the other end knows who is talking by the sound of the voice and by the character of the question.)

"I don't know, I never had a sick pig," said Mr. Dameron, "but I can find out quick enough. You hang up and I'll call Henry."

Mr. Dameron was back on the line again in five minutes. "Henry says roll him over on his back and give him two ounces of castor oil or sweet oil, and if that doesn't do the trick give him an injection of soapy water. He says he's almost sure the pig's plugged up, and even if he's wrong, it can't do any harm."

I thanked Mr. Dameron. I didn't go right down to the pig, though. I sank into a chair and sat still for a few minutes to think about my troubles, and then I got up and went to the barn, catching up on some odds and ends that needed tending to. Unconsciously I held off, for an hour, the deed by which I would officially recognize the collapse of the performance of raising a pig; I wanted no interruption in the regularity of feeding, the steadiness of growth, the even succession of days. I wanted no interruption, wanted no oil, no deviation. I just wanted to keep on raising a pig, full meal after full meal, spring into summer into fall. I didn't even know whether there were two ounces of castor oil on the place.

II

Shortly after five o'clock I remembered that we had been invited out to dinner that night and realized that if I were to dose a pig there was no time to lose. The dinner date seemed a familiar conflict: I move in a desultory society and often a week or two will roll by without my going to anybody's house to dinner or anyone's coming to mine, but when an occasion does arise, and I am summoned, something usually turns up (an hour or two in advance) to make all human intercourse seem vastly inappropriate. I have come to believe that there is in hostesses a special power of divination, and that they deliberately arrange dinners to coincide with pig failure or some other sort of failure. At any rate, it was after five o'clock and I knew I could put off no longer the evil hour.

When my son and I arrived at the pigyard, armed with a small bottle of castor oil and a length of clothesline, the pig had emerged from his house and was standing in the middle of his yard, listlessly. He gave us a slim greeting. I could see that he felt uncomfortable and uncertain. I had brought the clothesline thinking I'd have to tie him (the pig weighed more than a hundred pounds) but we never used it. My son reached down, grabbed both front legs, upset him quickly, and when he opened his mouth to scream I turned the oil into his throat — a pink, corrugated area I had never seen before. I had just time to read the label while the neck of the bottle was in his mouth. It said Puretest. The screams, slightly muffled by oil, were pitched in the hysterically high range of pigsound, as though torture were being carried out, but they didn't last long: it was all over rather suddenly, and, his legs released, the pig righted himself.

In the upset position the corners of his mouth had been turned down, giving him a frowning expression. Back on his feet again, he regained the set smile that a pig wears even in sickness. He stood his ground, sucking slightly at the residue of oil; a few drops leaked out of his lips while his wicked eyes, shaded by their coy little lashes, turned on me in disgust and hatred. I scratched him gently with oily fingers and he remained quiet, as though trying to recall the satisfaction of being scratched when in health, and seeming to rehearse in his mind the indignity to which he had just been subjected. I noticed, as I stood there, four or five small dark spots on his back near the tail end, reddish brown in color, each about the size of a housefly. I could not make out what they were. They did not look troublesome but at the same time they did not look like mere surface bruises or chafe marks. Rather they seemed blemishes of internal origin. His stiff white bristles almost completely hid them and I had to part the bristles with my fingers to get a good look.

Several hours later, a few minutes before midnight, having dined well and at someone else's expense, I returned to the pighouse with a flashlight. The patient was asleep. Kneeling, I felt his ears (as you might put your hand on the forehead of a child) and they seemed cool, and then with the light made a careful examination of the yard and the house for sign that the oil had worked. I found none and went to bed.

We had been having an unseasonable spell of weather — hot, close days, with the fog shutting in every night, scaling for a few hours in midday, then creeping back again at dark, drifting in first over the trees on the point, then suddenly blowing across the fields, blotting out the world and taking possession of houses, men, and animals. Everyone kept hoping for a break, but the break failed to come. Next day was another hot one. I visited the pig before breakfast and tried to tempt him with a little milk in his trough. He just stared at it, while I made a sucking sound through my teeth to remind him of past pleasures of the feast. With very small, timid pigs, weanlings, this ruse is often quite successful and will encourage them to eat; but with a large, sick pig the ruse is senseless and the sound I made must have made him feel, if anything, more miserable. He not only did not crave food, he felt a positive revulsion to it. I found a place under the apple tree where he had vomited in the night.

At this point, although a depression had settled over me, I didn't suppose that I was going to lose my pig. From the lustiness of a healthy pig a man derives a feeling of personal lustiness; the stuff that goes into the trough and is received with such enthusiasm is an earnest of some later feast of his own, and when this suddenly comes to an end and the food lies stale and untouched, souring in the sun, the pig's imbalance becomes the man's, vicariously, and life seems insecure, displaced, transitory.

III

As my own spirits declined, along with the pig's, the spirits of my vile old dachshund rose. The frequency of our trips down the footpath through the orchard to the pigyard delighted him, although he suffers greatly from arthritis, moves with difficulty, and would be bedridden if he could find anyone willing to serve him meals on a tray.

He never missed a chance to visit the pig with me, and he made many professional calls on his own. You could see him down there at all hours, his white face parting the grass along the fence as he wobbled and stumbled about, his stethoscope dangling — a happy quack, writing his villainous prescriptions and grinning his corrosive grin. When the enema bag appeared, and the bucket of warm suds, his happiness was complete, and he managed to squeeze his enormous body between the two lowest rails of the yard and then assumed full charge of the irrigation. Once, when I lowered the bag to check the flow, he reached in and hurriedly drank a few mouthfuls of the suds to test their potency. I have noticed that Fred will feverishly consume any substance that is associated with trouble — the bitter flavor is to his liking. When the bag was above reach, he concentrated on the pig and was everywhere at once, a tower of strength and inconvenience. The pig, curiously enough, stood rather quietly through this colonic carnival, and the enema, though ineffective, was not as difficult as I had anticipated.

I discovered, though, that once having given a pig an enema there is no turning back, no chance of resuming one of life's more stereotyped roles. The pig's lot and mine were inextricably bound now, as though the rubber tube were the silver cord. From then until the time of his death I held the pig steadily in the bowl of my mind; the task of trying to deliver him from his misery became a strong obsession. His suffering soon became the embodiment of all earthly wretchedness. Along toward the end of the afternoon, defeated in physicking, I phoned the veterinary twenty miles away and placed the case formally in his hands. He was full of questions, and when I casually mentioned the dark spots on the pig's back, his voice changed its tone.

"I don't want to scare you," he said, "but when there are spots, erysipelas has to be considered."

Together we considered erysipelas, with frequent interruptions from the telephone operator, who wasn't sure the connection had been established.

"If a pig has erysipelas can he give it to a person?" I asked.

"Yes, he can," replied the vet.

"Have they answered?" asked the operator.

"Yes, they have," I said. Then I addressed the vet again. "You better come over here and examine this pig right away."

"I can't come myself," said the vet, "but McFarland can come this evening if that's all right. Mac knows more about pigs than I do anyway. You needn't worry too much about the spots. To indicate erysipelas they would have to be deep hemorrhagic infarcts."

"Deep hemorrhagic what?" I asked.

"Infarcts," said the vet.

"Have they answered?" asked the operator.

"Well," I said, "I don't know what you'd call these spots, except they're about the size of a housefly. If the pig has erysipelas I guess I have it, too, by this time, because we've been very close lately."

"McFarland will be over," said the vet.

I hung up. My throat felt dry and I went to the cupboard and got a bottle of whiskey. Deep hemorrhagic infarcts — the phrase began fastening its hooks in my head. I had assumed that there could be nothing much wrong with a pig during the months it was being groomed for murder; my confidence in the essential health and endurance of pigs had been strong and deep, particularly in the health of pigs that belonged to me and that were part of my proud scheme. The awakening had been violent and I minded it all the more because I knew that what could be true of my pig could be true also of the rest of my tidy world. I tried to put this distasteful idea from me, but it kept recurring. I took a short drink of the whiskey and then, although I wanted to go down to the yard and look for fresh signs, I was scared to. I was certain I had erysipelas.

It was long after dark and the supper dishes had been put away when a car drove in and McFarland got out. He had a girl with him. I could just make her out in the darkness — she seemed young and pretty. "This is Miss Owen," he said. "We've been having a picnic supper on the shore, that's why I'm late."

McFarland stood in the driveway and stripped off his jacket, then his shirt. His stocky arms and capable hands showed up in my flashlight's gleam as I helped him find his coverall and get zipped up. The rear seat of his car contained an astonishing amount of paraphernalia, which he soon overhauled, selecting a chain, a syringe, a bottle of oil, a rubber tube, and some other things I couldn't identify. Miss Owen said she'd go along with us and see the pig. I led the way down the warm slope of the orchard, my light picking out the path for them, and we all three climbed the fence, entered the pighouse, and squatted by the pig while McFarland took a rectal reading. My flashlight picked up the glitter of an engagement ring on the girl's hand.

"No elevation," said McFarland, twisting the thermometer in the light. "You needn't worry about erysipelas." He ran his hand slowly over the pig's stomach and at one point the pig cried out in pain.

"Poor piggledy-wiggledy!" said Miss Owen.

The treatment I had been giving the pig for two days was then repeated, somewhat more expertly, by the doctor, Miss Owen and I handing him things as he needed them — holding the chain that he had looped around the pig's upper jaw, holding the syringe, holding the bottle stopper, the end of the tube, all of us working in darkness and in comfort, working with the instinctive teamwork induced by emergency conditions, the pig unprotesting, the house shadowy, protecting, intimate. I went to bed tired but with a feeling of relief that I had turned over part of the responsibility of the case to a licensed doctor. I was beginning to think, though, that the pig was not going to live.

IV

He died twenty-four hours later, or it might have been forty-eight — there is a blur in time here, and I may have lost or picked up a day in the telling and the pig one in the dying. At intervals during the last day I took cool fresh water down to him and at such times as he found the strength to get to his feet he would stand with head in the pail and snuffle his snout around. He drank a few sips but no more; yet it seemed to comfort him to dip his nose in water and bobble it about, sucking in and blowing out through his teeth. Much of the time, now, he lay indoors half buried in sawdust. Once, near the last, while I was attending him I saw him try to make a bed for himself but he lacked the strength, and when he set his snout into the dust he was unable to plow even the little furrow he needed to lie down in.

He came out of the house to die. When I went down, before going to bed, he lay stretched in the yard a few feet from the door. I knelt, saw that he was dead, and left him there: his face had a mild look, expressive neither of deep peace nor of deep suffering, although I think he had suffered a good deal. I went back up to the house and to bed, and cried internally — deep hemorrhagic intears. I didn't wake till nearly eight the next morning, and when I looked out the open window the grave was already being dug, down beyond the dump under a wild apple. I could hear the spade strike against the small rocks that blocked the way. Never send to know for whom the grave is dug, I said to myself, it's dug for thee. Fred, I well knew, was supervising the work of digging, so I ate breakfast slowly.

It was a Saturday morning. The thicket in which I found the grave-diggers at work was dark and warm, the sky overcast. Here, among alders and young hackmatacks, at the foot of the apple tree, Lennie had dug a beautiful hole, five feet long, three feet wide, three feet deep. He was standing in it, removing the last spadefuls of earth while Fred patrolled the brink in simple but impressive circles, disturbing the loose earth of the mound so that it trickled back in. There had been no rain in weeks and the soil, even three feet down, was dry and powdery. As I stood and stared, an enormous earthworm which had been partially exposed by the spade at the bottom dug itself deeper and made a slow withdrawal, seeking even remoter moistures at even lonelier depths. And just as Lennie stepped out and rested his spade against the tree and lit a cigarette, a small green apple separated itself from a branch overhead and fell into the hole. Everything about this last scene seemed overwritten — the dismal sky, the shabby woods, the imminence of rain, the worm (legendary bedfellow of the dead), the apple (conventional garnish of a pig).

But even so, there was a directness and dispatch about animal burial, I thought, that made it a more decent affair than human burial: there was no stopover in the undertaker's foul parlor, no wreath nor spray; and when we hitched a line to the pig's hind legs and dragged him swiftly from his yard, throwing our weight into the harness and leaving a wake of crushed grass and smoothed rubble over the dump, ours was a businesslike procession, with Fred, the dishonorable pallbearer, staggering along in the rear, his perverse bereavement showing in every seam in his face; and the post mortem performed handily and swiftly right at the edge of the grave, so that the inwards which had caused the pig's death preceded him into the ground and he lay at last resting squarely on the cause of his own undoing.

I threw in the first shovelful, and then we worked rapidly and without talk, until the job was complete. I picked up the rope, made it fast to Fred's collar (he is a notorious ghoul), and we all three filed back up the path to the house, Fred bringing up the rear and holding back every inch of the way, feigning unusual stiffness. I noticed that although he weighed far less than the pig, he was harder to drag, being possessed of the vital spark.

The news of the death of my pig traveled fast and far, and I received many expressions of sympathy from friends and neighbors, for no one took the event lightly and the premature expiration of a pig is, I soon discovered, a departure which the community marks solemnly on its calendar, a sorrow in which it feels fully involved. I have written this account in penitence and in grief, as a man who failed to raise his pig, and to explain my deviation from the classic course of so many raised pigs. The grave in the woods is unmarked, but Fred can direct the mourner to it unerringly and with immense good will, and I know he and I shall often revisit it, singly and together, in seasons of reflection and despair, on flagless memorial days of our own choosing.

WHO WILL DO THE DIRTY WORK?
by David L. Cohn

LARGE numbers of us in the United States are corroded by resentments, conscious or subconscious. The worm of discontent, for all our riches, gnaws at our secret hearts. We are restless, dissatisfied, vaguely troubled; haunted by we know not what. Our cup runneth over with gadgets but we are not serene.

The source of our resentments, in my opinion, is that many of us are not what we should like to be, or what we think we ought to be. We do not occupy the place in business or society to which our merits "entitle" us. Saddest of all, having been "educated" for a higher (economic) place in life, through no fault of our own we are condemned to what we regard as a lower place.

Our dilemma is difficult. It is fraught perhaps with a certain inevitability, given the nation's needs, the manner of its growth, the quality of our industrial genius, the nature of men.

According to Seymour E. Harris, Professor of Economics at Harvard, "The need for executives does not increase in proportion to the growth of population. From 1910 to 1940, while the population was increasing 36 per cent, the number of openings for executives was increased only 8 per cent. And from 1929 to 1946 the number of active proprietors of unincorporated enterprises (roughly, the field of small business) actually declined 2.6 per cent."

This is also true, if to a lesser degree, of the land. The American farm has long been growing larger, and the larger farms, which are in reality farm-factories owned by corporations, account for a disproportionately large fraction of total farm output and income. Roughly speaking, 10 per cent of our farms produce 50 per cent of our food. This means the constant thinning of the ranks of the subsistence farmer — the "noble independent farmer" as he was called in the 1830's — while machinery has converted the once large farm family from an economic asset into a liability. Fewer people being needed on the land, they must turn to the cities and factories for a livelihood.

The remorseless process of the big becoming bigger is accompanied by a collateral process through which many corporations have expanded into fields foreign to those for which they were chartered. A paint company processes foods; an oil company manufactures cosmetics; recently a railroad-car manufacturer wanted to buy two rayon mills.

Yet, as the big grow bigger, we have continued to preach a doctrine valid perhaps during much of the American past for large numbers of men, but of increasingly dubious application since the turn of the century. It is: *Rise above your station.* At the same time, parents have been saying that their children must have advantages they did not have; the opportunity to get an education, to "amount to something," to do clean, white-collar work, instead of dirty handwork.

What does it mean to rise above your station in an industrial society dominated by giant corporations? What can it mean except the opportunity to acquire a managerial job with one of them? Yet how is one to win the grand prize of manager? The number of such positions is tiny compared with the number of aspirants, and the competition for the limited quantity of managerships is so fierce that usually they go only to the superlatively equipped. What of the rest of us? How are we to "amount to something" even when we have gone to college?

Our dilemma — the dilemma of those of us who would rise above our station — is the more cruel since it stems from the noblest instinct of our democratic society: the right of every man to have the opportunity to realize to the utmost his potentialities. This is the cornerstone of the nation. It is a concept so deeply ingrained within us as to become embodied in the folk saying that every American boy may expect to become President. Nor is this all. The right to rise above one's station has acquired a touching poignancy because millions of our citizens derive from communities overseas where a man was expected to stay in the place denominated for him by king, bishop, landlord, or even God. "Once a cobbler, always a cobbler" was a maxim almost as effective as law over wide reaches of the world.

Furthermore, we are faced with a melancholy paradox. It would almost seem that as the dimensions of the nation have widened in riches and power, the dimensions of opportunity for the individual have decreased; that, while we may be leader of the democratic world, we afford less and less room for business leaders here at home. The nobility of the instinct of which we have been speaking remains unsullied, the attractiveness of the aspiration undimmed. But the hard fact remains — let's face it unblinkingly — that most of us cannot now reasonably expect to rise above our station as the term and the opportunity were once understood in the United States, even though we may be the world's richest nation with much of our potential richness as yet unrealized. If this is true of the so-called average man, what of the better-equipped men and women, the college graduates? What are their prospects in the immediate future?

The President's Commission on Higher Education has proposed for 1960 — only eleven years hence — an enrollment of 4.6 million college students. This is almost double the present enrollment which, in turn, is ten times larger than the student body of 1900. We all agree that the wider the diffusion of education among us, the better for the nation. But we, more perhaps than most peoples, have a pathetic faith in the *cash* value of an education. Here, generally speaking, education is not a preparation for the good life but an allegedly almost infallible method of rising socially and financially. And in so doing, we tread increasingly unstable ground, for we are turning out more college graduates than the economy is prepared to receive.

While the President's Commission on Higher Education was proposing that we have more college students, the Veterans Administration addressed itself to a cold fact. There will soon be more college graduates than there are jobs for them in their chosen fields.

By 1950, for example, close to 50,000 engineers will be graduated, as against an annual replacement need of 7000. Lawyers will become a surplus commodity with few takers, yet they continue to flock to college although many members of the class of 1948 are jobless. There is still room for chemists and psychologists but only if they have a graduate degree. There are already too many personnel men. The fields of physical education, social science, and English are crowded. Recruits are badly needed in the ranks of medicine, dentistry, nursing, and grade-school teaching, but even here we could quickly reach the saturation point under a vigorously expanded program.

What to do? The Veterans Bureau suggests that more students ought to prepare themselves for the trades, or begin their careers as clerks and office workers. This suggestion flows inevitably from the facts, but will it commend itself to the aspirant? How stem the force of drives among a highly aggressive people? Will a man who thinks of himself as a potential engineer be content to run a lathe?

II

We resent physical labor for many reasons: the exaggerated claims of manufacturers and "science" that machines can give us all a push-button existence; the feeling that if we work with our hands we are less likely to "better ourselves"; and the effects of middle-class snobbishness which dictates that physical labor is not respectable.

What remedies are in sight?

If men's work attitudes are affected by snobbishness, we must make labor truly dignified, not in the sense of the bogus exaltation of the worker by Communism, but in the sense of evaluating a man for what he is and his usefulness to society rather than by his clothes or his occupation. This, however, is difficult to achieve. We do not truly believe in the dignity of labor — a concept mouthed by politicians and sung by poets who never sweated for a day in a Kansas wheat field. Nor will it be simple to knock the snobbishness out of the heads of many American mothers who would rather see Sister marry a white-collar moron than become the wife of a skillful, highly paid patternmaker.

Yet this change of point of view is the condition precedent to the next step. Since it is arithmetically demonstrable that many professional fields will soon be overcrowded, it is reckless for men to enter them unless they are extraordinarily gifted. Their only recourse under the circumstances is to fit themselves, as the Bureau of Labor suggests, for the trades however short this is of their aspirations.

The third step involves a realization by big business that the trend toward the obliteration of small operators and independent owners, the whittling down of the middle class, and the stultification of men's aspirations to rise economically may ultimately wreck the structure of present society. Here, fortunately, many enlightened businessmen are aware of what is happening; they are worried lest the American dream become a nightmare; and they know that men are more than statistical digits called consumers. But many sections of business are less enlightened, and numerous maladjustments in our society flow, not from the greed of businessmen, but from their social illiteracy, their lack of imagination and sensitivity, their unawareness of the hour, and a dangerous time-lag in their thinking.

"When two men ride a horse, one must go in the front," said Thomas Hobbes. The time has come when Americans must consider whether their countrymen will be long content to ride on the mare's rump.

1950
PEGGETY'S PARCEL OF SHORTCOMINGS
by John Hersey

I WELL remember," said Miss Peg, the pastry cook, with a coffee éclair hovering in her fingers, "the night I fell into the embrace of the United States Merchant Marine. I weighed scant two hundred eight pounds at that time. I was, you might say, thin as a shelf."

Probably Miss Peg meant to say "sylph." In fairness, you had to grant to Miss Peg that she was always willing to risk elegance, if there was any of it handy. Only sometimes her tongue slipped — especially if it was all lubricated to receive an éclair or a napoleon.

They were gathered — Miss Peg, Mrs. Manterbaum, and Johnny the second busboy — in the pantry locker down in the basement. As pastry chef, Miss Peg kept the key to the locker, and late each evening, about eleven o'clock, when the clubhouse was quite deserted and lay black and junky on the Florida beach, like a tremendous shipwreck, she would ghost in through the service entrance to the basement with one or two guests, unlock the wire mesh door to her locker, light up the single bare bulb that hung down from the ceiling, get out a few good things, seat the party on the wooden crates she kept her pans in, and then she would begin to talk. Mrs. Manterbaum, whose job was to keep the cabañas clean, was notorious among the help for her sweet tooth, a regular sugar-thief, and she had worked herself into the position of being invited by Miss Peg almost every night to taste a few "extra" pastries. Miss Peg used to ask Johnny the second busboy about once a week, because he was good-natured about pushing her pastry cart around to the Big People in the dining room for her. If there was one thing she hated in life, it was cart pushing. That, and bending down to slide her pans in and out of her ovens.

"I was twenty-three," Miss Peg said, "and I was then doing scullery for a certain Mrs. Charles Saunders in Old Bridge Harbor, on Long Island. Mr. Saunders was in asphalt and, as we used to say, he couldn't get out. Though in truth he was prosperous. Mrs. Saunders had fourteen in help. I remember one thing about Mr. Saunders, which was, he was very particular about the way his shoes were laid out in the mornings — the laces had to be real loose and the tongues lifted out and bent forward, so he could more or less walk right into his shoes. If Mr. Saunders had any difficulty about walking into his shoes, any morning, he was liable to a very bad state of mind at breakfast, and goodness knew who would feel the shock of it. You understand, I only heard these things. Small Peggety, as they called me — the 'Small' was belittling, you might say, considering my heft — never advanced beyond the Near Pantry, and had no occasion to see Mr. Saunders standing in his own shoes, laced or unlaced. Fact is, the first time I ever laid eyes on him, close by, was the day the United States Merchant Marine and I had our little heave-to.

"It happened in the following particulars. My cousin Bob, who never came across with the rest of us, lives some short distance outside Greenock, by Glasgow, and he being a familiar of certain public houses on the waterfront, travels, you might say, victoriously — by talking with those who go to sea."

"Vicariously," Johnny said.

"I beg your pardon?" Miss Peg said, very grand.

Johnny realized one of the reasons Miss Peg liked him was that he had gone through third year high school and was, in her words, "a bookish lad"; he did read a good bit. Miss Peg had never had any schooling, and her elegance had been picked up over the years of service while she was passing the peas, so to speak. Johnny dared, now and then, to catch her up on some of her errors of overreaching.

"Your cousin Bob," Johnny said, "travels vicariously."

"*Well?*" said Miss Peg, with rising tone, as if to ask why the young scoundrel felt it necessary to repeat something that had already been said. "So one evening," she went on, "Bob met this tidy, small-boned Yank, a Boatswain's Mate, Third Class, in the United States Merchant Marine, named Bufano. A swarthy sort. Talking of one big thing and another, they landed at last upon me, so it was necessary — Bob thought — to tell the fellow all about me. I will say, Bob has a straight tongue, he did not dangle any pretty marionette before this Bufano's eyes. To be blunt about it, he said his cousin Peggety was *fat*. 'So much the better,' says this Bufano. 'I always was squeamish about getting myself bruised against sharp and knobby things. I am glad to hear that you have a nice soft cousin.'

"The first thing *I* knew," said Peg, "I received a postcard written in a fine Eyetalian hand, all curlicues and scrolls on the capital letters, like a birthday cake, saying, *Meet me outside Ritz corner 46 and Mad six pm Thursday evening. Assume this is helps night out. I have grand news of your cousin Bob from other side. Bufano, Bsns Mate 3/c, S.S. Fanter.* This 'grand news' " — Miss Peg said, leaping ahead in her narrative, as she sometimes did — "was that our Bob was spending much time in the public houses and was a two-hump camel when it came to the ale: he could drink twice as much and hold it twice as long as anyone else. 'Grand news'!"

II

"The next Thursday," Miss Peg resumed, "I got myself all frilled up, smelling like a church on Easter morning, and Mason the chauffeur was just about to drive the help to the station, and me, sitting there, taking up half the back seat of the car, happy as a lintie thinking about my unknown sailor boy, when out from the quarters comes a message: 'Tell Small Peggety to stop by at Mr. Saunders' office, 30 Rockefeller Plaza. He has a wee errand for her.'

"Our Maggie, the cook, who if I was overweight she was a dried-up apricot of the fuzzy variety, said sarcastic, 'Write down the address. Our Peggety is in love, she's a bag of daydreams, she'll never remember.'

"Between the message and Maggie, it took quite some time for the others to dill me down to where I was calm again. Wasn't it just like Mr. Saunders to save his 'wee errand' for *that* day? Any other time, this command would have made me tingle with the fun of doing it — 'thistles in me thumbs,' as our Mum used to say when she had a thrill. But that day, it was all I could do to think of my seafaring man with the handwriting like Queen Victoria's Golden Jubilee fireworks.

"Nevertheless, when we reached the city, I went of course as directed to 30 Rockefeller Plaza and I shot up into the sky where Mr. Saunders did his work and up I went to the lady at the desk and I said, trying to be sort of saucy and mature, 'I am the Peggety. Mr. Saunders has a wee errand for me.'

"The lady looked at me and said, 'Sister, aren't you kind of dressed up for *this* errand?'

"So I replied, 'The nature of the work was not divulged, you might say.'

"The lady flicked a switch on a box, and I heard Mr. Saunders' voice come out of the box, only his voice sounded like his nose had been snipped off by a crow or was pinched with a clothespin; he said, 'What is it?'

" 'Your maid,' the lady said into the box, 'has come for the carcass.'

"This gave me the goose pimples all over, and since I was a thimber sort of girl, a large skin area, you might say, there was a considerable amount of puckering up to be got done with.

"Mr. Saunders kind of laughed a noseless laugh from the box and said, 'Send her in.'

"I walked into the office whither the lady nodded, and there he was, the master, looking very wild, but with his nose, thank the Lord, quite unharmed. It must have been merely the mechanics of the box that had taken away his nose from his voice. In general the master was very wild, however. He was in his shirt-sleeves and he was dressed in a big white apron and he had in his hand a butcher's knife of the largest sort, and I thought: Oh me, I thought asphalt was used to pave the roads, what *can* it be that the master does for a living?

"He said to me, 'Sit down, girl, I'll be ready in a few minutes.'

"It was then," Miss Peg said, "that I noticed another gentleman in the room, he was dressed in ordinary business clothes, though his look was rather ferocious, too, it seemed to me, but at the time, you must remember, I was only Small Peggety, twenty-three winters along, tipping the scales approximately two-o-eight, with no experience of the world beyond the Near Pantry, consequently this fierceness may have been imaginary on my part.

"I also noticed — and this hit me all of a sudden, like the sun coming out from under a cloud — a smell in the place like Fulton Street at the East River, in other words, fish in all its glory. And by following my senses, I tracked this scent to Mr. Saunders' desk, where lay, about as big as my upper arm, no, bigger yet, a whole salmon. A very substantial fish, I can assure you, Mrs. Manterbaum.

"Mr. Saunders grasped the butcher knife in both hands, and he began to stagger and struggle around the room, talking the while like that raddio fellow, Mr. Clem McCarthy, dealing with the Derby, in case you are interested in the horses, Mrs. Manterbaum — breathless he was and yet in command of the telling. I soon puzzled it out that Mr. Saunders was describing to his friend the capture of this particular salmon of his. He was using the butcher knife for his rod and reel, and I was fearful lest he would fish himself into total blindness with that sharp thing. And so we had game-fishing all up and down the office for the next half hour. They say that salmon do go up-river in order to make love, and to hear Mr. Saunders speak of the reluctance of this whopper to leave the headwaters of the Skampawam, or whatever the river would be named, in Nova Scotia, it was — to hear *him*, I believe this fish must have been engaged in the romance of the century in the salmon world. Really, the aquarium should be told about it. Well! I tell you! We *finally* landed the thing, but we were panting and giving off a deal of perspiration over it — and there the lecherous rascal was, big as life and ten times smellier, right on Mr. Saunders' desk, asphalt be damned.

" 'He's been thawing out all day,' Mr. Saunders said. 'We shipped him down in dry ice. His guts were cleaned up there, and now' — advancing on the salmon with the dreadful knife, he said this — 'now I'm going to lop off his head and tail so the girl here can manage him by hand and take him out home for us, and tomorrow night, Spencer, tomorrow *night!* Well, you'll just have to wait and taste him.'

"Our creature was thawed out, all right, and he gave up his head till there was salmon blood all over the newspapers on Mr. Saunders' desk. Likewise the tail, a smaller operation but also not without splashes and clots of red. By this time the odor of fish was almost a fog around us that you could see. Whew!

"More newspapers, a bundle, string; there we were. 'Now, girl,' said Mr. Saunders, who, never having been on *my* side of the Near Pantry, of course did not know me by name, 'now, girl, you may take it home. And have a care!'

"What a care I had, all that suffering night! And yet . . .

"It was now, you see, pushing six o'clock, because of the length of Mr. Saunders' description of his triumph over the poor hooked thing. Thus, if I was to meet my friend with the birthday-cake handwriting, I would have to rush right over there, with no time to park my bundle meanwhile. Right through the newspaper, through goodness knows how many layers of current events, you could not fail to smell my pink beheaded treat. Trembling I dashed to the Ritz, corner of Madison and Forty-sixth.

"I was on time but early. The Merchant Marine, being a man of the world, had decided to have a wee tease of Small Peggety, who knew nothing. So there I stood, before the most swoshy hotel in the land, waiting, with ladies going by in ermine and sapphires and curls right out of the permanent-wave machine, and me, under the marquee with all its sweet little light bulbs, me, embracing a two-and-a-half-foot stink. I was mortified to death, Mrs. Manterbaum.

III

"At last he came and worth waiting for. Short, stocky, and sort of pale Moorish-complected. His pants as tight as wedding gloves. He was a lovely, tiny creature. He strolled right up to me, with all the swagger of his cute bowlegs, and he said, raising his white cap, 'Miss Peggety, if I am not mistaken. I could have spotted you, my dear, from a mile away.'

"Well, he had my heart right then and there, though now in my calmer years I can see that his first remark — about kenning me from such a very impressive distance — left something to be desired as a compliment.

"Right there on the streetcorner, as he gazed up into my eyes, looking for my soul, you might say, and my heart like a moth by a sixty-watt lamp, I saw that the flanges of his nostrils were working away quite passionate, exactly like Mr. Rudolph Valentino's, but then I realized that it wasn't so much love at first sight as it was he had caught a whiff of something about my person. What he smelt, you already know, Mrs. Manterbaum.

"I had no doubt, in the next moments, that my Bufano was as packed full of gentility as his bell-bottoms were packed full of Bufano. Because without so much as muttering, 'Hm, fishy out tonight, ain't it, Miss Peggety?' — with no such remarks, without a flicker of his lovely waxen eyelids, without even moving to windward of me, he said, 'Well, my dear, what'll it be? Shall we dance? Or is food your pleasure? A steak, Miss Peggety?' You see how well bred he was? Steak! Any lesser man would have asked me if I was in the mood for a bite of sea food.

"Timid, I said, 'First off, Mr. Bufano, I'd like to run down to Grand Central and check this parcel for the evening.'

"I could see from the way my Bufano looked at the package in my arms that he knew what I was carrying. Jaunty as you please he swung around and offered me the crook of his arm.

"At the checking place in Grand Central, I just pushed the package across the brass-plated counter. The man there pulled it toward him and actually snapped the checking tag onto the string. Then (I guess his nose was tuned in by this time) he looked up and said, 'What's in here?'

" 'Just some laundry,' I said. My Bufano stiffened a little at that. The counterman thumped at the package with his fists, shook his head, unsnapped the tag, and shoved the thing back to me.

" 'Sorry, lady,' the counterman said, 'we ain't allowed to accept no carrion here.'

"I guess my feelings took a tumble that you could see and hear, because Bufano said, 'Cheer up, my dear, we'll just hurry over to Pennsylvania Station. We should have done that in the first place. You'll have to leave from there when our spree is over.'

"But the man in the parcel room at Penn Station was even quicker than our Grand Central fellow. Indeed, he looked at us at first with a dread look of suspicion, as if we were trying to dispose of the parts of a human body, one by one. I must confess, with the moisture and even some of the tint of corpuscles beginning to show through at the ends, my package might have been a man's thigh-piece, from groin to knee-cap. Except for the odor, which gave us an unmistakable alibi. All the man at the Penn Station counter said was, 'Uhn-uhn,' negative.

"My Bufano was a cheerful little rooster, he said we should try the Hotel Wentman, just a couple blocks over; they had a big check room, he said. No luck, they wouldn't take fish. We tried the Hotel Regina. No luck. We tried the Hampdon and the Marjoran. No and no. They wouldn't even let us all the way across the lobby at the St. Anselm. Mr. Bufano tried to rent a room at a little no-good place away over West, thinking we would put our salmon to bed in it, but they stopped us in the elevator.

"And so it was that a few minutes before eight o'clock in the evening, we stood on a windswept corner in western Manhattan, and the tears welled up in my eyes and not even my pigeon, my Bufano, could comfort me. For suddenly I had realized that this parcel was more than a cut-off salmon. This was all my troubles, wrapped up in shabby newsprint. This was all the things that kept me from all my desires. That package — I suddenly realized it, Mrs. Manterbaum — that package was all the unhappinesses I couldn't get rid of in this life: it was my fleshiness, my unbeatable appetite for chocolate things, and my being without any learning, and no friends to speak of, and teased by such spiteful old maids as our Maggie, and couldn't even be promoted past the Near Pantry, and what good was I anyhow? And I was embracing all these things in my arms like a dear beloved friend, and smelling to high heaven of the burden.

"Then it was that my Bufano said, 'Well, Miss Peggety, three's a crowd, but let's face facts, he goes where we go.'

"And I suddenly realized, you have to live with whatever it is you have to live with, so I dried up my eyes and said, 'Suits me, Mr. Bufano.'

" 'Well!' he beamed, and a gold tooth he had glistened like the planet Venus at the edge of night. 'What was it to be, steak or a little twinkletoes?'

"Now that I knew where I was, with my shortcomings folded up in a wee bundle of old papers, you might say, and my Bufano willing to accept them if I would, I grew bold suddenly and said, 'Couldn't we do both, Mr. Bufano? Eat and dance too?'

" 'Miss Peggety, you're a dear,' he said, and if I had cried this time, it would have been for other reasons than mere fishiness. My Bufano was so delicate!

"We had a grand time, I can tell you. My Bufano took me here and there, now dancing, now eating, now tippling a wee beer, now riding a Fifth Avenue bus just for the ride, as idle as you please. Soon we were used to our scaly friend and his consequences. What if everybody *did* turn and give us a stare, with tiny wrinkles at the bridge of the nose? In a way, it was gaudy, you might say. Surely Small Peggety had never in her life attracted so much attention, either from eye or nostril. I will go farther. Our salmon became more than a novelty: he was, at last, a handy thing to have about the person. In a crowded situation, we could always get passageway — the mob just opened up for us, real respectful. In the eating places (my Bufano took me to some of the basement ones, away to the fringes of the great city, where, either through kinship with the proprietor or a grand little tip, there was never a question of accepting us with our third party), we used it for a little extra table, beside us, to hold an ash tray or perhaps a wee pony of spirits. There it was, squared off at both ends, like a piece of log, and it stood up steady and true, very convenient by the knee for a reach. And there our hands did brush against one another: that was when I knew that my Bufano was the nicest one of all.

"Indeed, what except my parcel of shortcomings led to the bliss of the evening? I had to be back to the Near Pantry by seven in the morning, which meant, at the latest, the 5.13 from Penn Station. It was still only about three in the morning when my Bufano, with the gentlest way in the world, said, 'My dear, don't you think that your salmon needs a little ventilation? I should hate, for your Mr. Saunders' sake, to have it fester and decay. It wants aeration. I propose that we go up to Central Park, and fold back the newspapers, and give it the night air to keep it tasty.'

"That we did. We found a wee hillock, away from the paved walks — 'Asphalt!' my Bufano had remarked as we had gone along the walks. 'Your Mr. Saunders is everywhere' — and we set up our fish on the hill and peeled away the newsprint and let the sweet, damp night get at it. We moved away a little, to wait for the salmon to grow mellow, when, next thing I knew, as natural as the dew all around and the constellations winking up there, Bufano got his arms about me. He could just barely make it with his short little arms and my girth, which he praised. And he stood on tiptoe and kissed me."

Miss Peg's voice had fallen low; her eyelids shaded her jovial eyes in a modest downward look. Mrs. Manterbaum sighed.

"Did you catch your train?" Johnny the busboy asked.

"I caught my train, Johnny," Miss Peg said. "Yes, I caught my train." She paused. "I never saw my Bufano again, either. He was the hit-and-run sort, you might say. But I don't know, Johnny, it didn't matter. That night did something for me. You know, Mrs. Manterbaum, I have never been able to give sufficient worry to my faults since that night. Some would call me slack. . . . I don't know. . . . Yes, I caught the 5.13, Johnny."

"How was the fish next night?" Mrs. Manterbaum of the sugartooth wanted to know.

"When they brought it out to the Near Pantry, after the second serving," Miss Peg replied, "I dared to cut away a wee snippet. I put it in my mouth. Oh, heavens, Mrs. Manterbaum! It faded on the tongue. It put this angel cake of mine to shame. And as I rested the morsel against my palate and let it warm my throat, the way the men do with their brandy, I squeezed out a sob, Mrs. Manterbaum, I'm not ashamed to tell you that, and I said to myself, 'I'm not so bad as I thought, not half so bad.' . . . *Well!*" Miss Peg said abruptly and more briskly. "Time to lock up."

Miss Peg lifted the pan of delicacies and slid it onto the shelf where it belonged. She stood up and dusted the crumbs from the front of her dress, seeming to be rather pleased with herself.

1951
THE PARENTS AT COUNTRY DAY
by Charles W. Morton

ALL PARENTS *will report at the gymnasium at 7.30 a.m., Saturday, March 10, for assignment to work details. The child (or children) of any parent tardy or absent will be punished severely.* — NIRVANA HEIGHTS PARENTS ASSOCIATION. SIMONE J. LEGREE, PRESIDENT.

Such a notice — if the Nirvana Heights Country Day School were candid enough to couch its exactions in plain English — sums up in brief the relationship between parents and any good private school attended nowadays by their children. The better the school, the more frequent and terse the notice will be. A collect telegram, "Report gymnasium immediately — Legree," would be quite possible in a really successful school, and a Sunday or a business day would be just as likely as a Saturday. The school commands, the parent must jump to it: into those fatigues, get going, no excuses, and no nonsense about it, either.

The only worse thing than having children, in point of the unlimited liability thus imposed on the parent, is having children who attend a private school. There is nothing else quite like it, so expensive, so freighted with responsibility, so uncomfortable, tiring, incessant. Time was when maintenance of an ocean-going yacht or a racing stable or a big country place was one of the inescapable burdens of the rich. The really rich, who know they could never afford the demands of a private school and who intend to remain solvent, protect themselves by sending their children to public schools. But even the not so well-to-do are caught up in the private school's dragnet by the device known as the "Parents Association."

The Parents Association is what makes Country Day seem, to parents at any rate, like life in an ant palace: everyone tearing around madly — collecting, organizing, hoarding, working. It is all obligatory. Any parent, for instance, exempted (by presentation of a medical certificate) from folk dancing must nevertheless attend and feign a lively enjoyment in watching other parents folk-dance. Each parent must go to all meetings of the Association, remain awake throughout them,* and ask at least one question in the question period.

No parent is entitled to make any criticism of the school's affairs. On the contrary, the parent must affirm, loudly, the perfection of all that it undertakes. ("I've always liked *Iolanthe,* but I'm frank to say that these kids — and with only a piano accompaniment, too — were just as good as anything that the D'Oyly Carte crowd ever pulled off. . . .") I myself, for asking why the children were not being instructed in the elements of English grammar, was set upon by masked assailants on my way home from a Parents Association meeting, and I escaped only by vigorous use of my sword-cane.

At the bottom of the heap, archdupe of them all, is the luckless parent who has accepted for his spawn a "scholarship" at Nirvana Heights Country Day. For each $500 rebate on the fees, a scholarship parent must return to the school at least $5000 in goods and services. His must be the choicest offerings for the "bazaar," his the basic vehicle in the car pool, his the most skillful hand with paintbrush, floor-sander, or upholsterer's needle. Deprived of any time to earn his own living, the scholarship man remains permanently in need of the scholarship. Fifty scholarship parents, according to the recent report of a survey committee, are thus worth $225,000 a year to the school, equivalent to endowment income on some $6,000,000.

With fifty scholarship parents under its belt, the school moves in briskly on these and all others. There will be folk dancing (proceeds to the A.A.) Thursday at 8 — and decline if you dare. On Saturday, parents must attend the Big Game which Country Day will lose, traditionally, to detested Nirvana High School. Sunday morning at 11, a theologian conveniently borrowed from near-by Nirvana Junior College will lecture on Nature Worship in California (each parent must buy

---

*Strangely enough, few parents fall asleep on these occasions, ravaged as they are by the folding chairs and by hunger pains resulting from the dinner ($3.50) previously served by the Parents Association.

tickets for at least two guests, proceeds to apply on purchase of a new coffee urn for the Parents Association).

Throughout the week, all parents carry on their regular assignments of soliciting funds, door-to-door selling, chiseling wholesale prices for whatever the Parents Association is about to buy — prices that the Association's Purchasing Review Committee will report later on were altogether too high — and reshingling the Barn and Carriage House. Whenever these activities seem to be played out, the school will decide to hold its Twenty-seventh (or Thirty-first) Anniversary Celebration, and a new crusade is launched.

I know one mother who was ordered by her school to establish a literary agency to market the writings of other school parents, with the school getting a 50-50 split in the fees to the hard-driven authors. Another parent sells neckties. Some conduct sight-seeing tours. Still another was bidden to set up an "entertainment bureau" which would provide "entertainers" — that is, parents — for parties and such, but alas, the parents were not sufficiently entertaining. A lecture bureau fared more fruitfully, doubtless because no one expects lectures to be entertaining. Heartened by this success, Country Day made a husband-wife team establish a booking office for movie films. Many schools have a wood lot where the parents are kept busy felling, hewing, and sawing ("Fit parents make a fit school!"); they sell the firewood around town, and as often as not to themselves — after, of course, they have filled the school's bunkers.

The rummage sale is no longer quite the thing; it has been supplanted by a de luxe model in which parents — and others — are commanded to surrender such high-yield belongings as jewelry, furs, furniture, paintings, rare books, old gold and old cash. While one crew of parents is wresting these valuables from people in general, another is parading with placards advertising the sale.

For the children, as they confect their "mobiles" and daub their abstractions in the studio, it may very well be a Day School. But for the parents it seems to be a straightforward 24-hour proposition.

1952
MY HORSE BUCK
by J. Frank Dobie

ALL the old-time range men of validity whom I have known remember horses with affection and respect as a part of the best of themselves. After their knees have begun to stiffen, most men realize that they have been disappointed in themselves, in other men, in achievement, in love, in most of whatever they expected out of life; but a man who has had a good horse in his life — a horse beyond the play world — will remember him as a certitude, like a calm mother, a lovely lake, or a gracious tree, amid all the flickering vanishments.

I remember Buck. He was raised on our ranch and was about half Spanish. He was a bright bay with a blaze in his face and stockings on his forefeet. He could hardly have weighed when fat over 850 pounds and was about 14 hands high. A Mexican broke him when he was three years old. From then on, nobody but me rode him, even after I left for college. He had a fine barrel and chest and was very fast for short distances but did not have the endurance of some other horses, straight Spaniards, in our remuda. What he lacked in toughness, he made up in intelligence, especially cow sense, loyalty, understanding, and generosity.

As a colt he had been bitten by a rattlesnake on the right ankle just above the hoof; a hard, hairless scab marked the place as long as he lived. He traveled through the world listening for the warning rattle. A kind of weed in the Southwest bears seeds that when ripe rattle in their pods a good deal like the sound made by a rattlesnake. Many a time when my spur or stirrup set these seeds a-rattling, Buck's suddenness in jumping all but left me seated in the air. I don't recall his smelling rattlesnakes, but he could smell afar off the rotten flesh of a yearling or any other cow brute afflicted with screwworms. He understood that I was hunting these animals in order to drive them to a pen and doctor them. In hot weather they take refuge in high weeds and thick brush. When he smelled one, he would point to it with his ears and turn towards it. A dog trained for hunting out wormy cases could not have been more helpful.

Once a sullen cow that had been roped raked him in the breast with the tip of a horn. After that experience, he was wariness personified around anything roped, but he never, like some horses that have been hooked, shied away from an animal he was after. He knew and loved his business too well for that. He did not love it when, at the rate of less than a mile an hour, he was driving the thirsty, hot, tired, slobbering drag end of a herd, animals stopping behind every bush or without any bush, turning aside the moment they were free of a driver. When sufficiently exasperated, Buck would go for a halting cow with mouth open and grab her just forward of the tail bone if she did not move on. Work like this may be humiliating to a gallant young cowboy and an eager cow horse; it is never pictured as a part of the romance of the range, but it is very necessary. It helps a cowboy to graduate into a cowman. A too high-strung horse without cow sense, which includes cow patience, will go to pieces at it just as he will go to pieces in running or cutting cattle.

Buck had the rein to make the proverbial "turn on a two-bit piece and give back fifteen cents in change." One hot summer while we were gathering steers on leased grass about twelve miles from home, I galled his side with a tight cinch. I hated to keep on riding him with the galled side, but was obliged to on account of a shortage of horses. As I saddled up in camp one day after dinner, I left the cinch so loose that a hand might have been laid between it and Buck's belly. We had to ride about a mile before going through a wire gap into the pasture where some snaky steers ran. As we rode along, a vaquero called my attention to the loose cinch.

"I will tighten it when we get to the gap," I said.

"*Cuidado* (have care) and don't forget," he said.

At the gap, which he got down to open, I saw him look at me. I decided to wait until we struck something before tightening the girth. Two minutes later my father yelled and we saw a little bunch of steers high-tailing it through scattered mesquites for a thicket along a creek beyond. I forgot all about the cinch. Buck was easily the fastest horse ridden by the four or five men in our "cow crowd." He left like a cry of joy to get around the steers.

As we headed them, they turned to the left at an acute angle, and Buck turned at an angle considerably more acute. Sometimes he turned so quickly that the *tapadera* (toe-fender) of my stirrup raked the ground on the inside of the turn. This time when he doubled back, running full speed, the loose saddle naturally turned on him. As my left hip hit the ground, I saw stars. One foot was still in a stirrup and the saddle was under Buck's belly. I suppose that I instinctively pulled on the reins, but I believe that Buck would have stopped had he not been bridled. His stop was instantaneous; he did not drag me on the ground at all. He had provocation to go on, too, for in coming over his side and back, the spur on my right foot had raked him. He never needed spurs. I wore them on him just to be in fashion.

Sometimes in running through brush, Buck seemed to read my mind — or maybe I was reading his. He was better in the brush than I was. In brush work, man and horse must dodge, turn, go over bushes and under limbs, absolutely in accord, rider yielding to the instinct and judgment of the horse as much as horse yields to his.

Buck did not have to be staked. If I left a dragrope on him, he would stay close to camp, at noon or through the night. He was no paragon. Many men have ridden and remembered hardier horses. He was not proud, but carried himself in a very trim manner. He did the best he could, willingly and generously, and he had a good heart. His chemistry mixed with mine. He was good company. I loved to hear him drink water, he was so hearty in swallowing, and then, after he was full, to watch him lip the water's surface and drip big drops back into it.

Sometimes after we had watered and, passing on, had come to good grass near shade, I'd unsaddle and turn him loose to graze. Then I'd lie down on the saddle and, while the blanket dried, listen to his energetic cropping and watch the buzzards sail and the Gulf clouds float. Buck would blow out his breath once in a while, presumably to clear his nostrils but also, it seemed to me, to express contentment.

He never asked me to stop, unless it was to stale, and never, like some gentle saddle horses, interrupted his step to grab a mouthful of grass; but if I stopped with slackened rein to watch cattle, or maybe just to gaze over the flow of hills to the horizon, he'd reach down and begin cutting grass. He knew that was all right with me, though a person's seat on a grazing horse is not nearly so comfortable as on one with upright head. Occasionally I washed the sweat off his back and favored him in other ways, but nobody in our part of the country pampered cow horses with sugar or other delicacy.

While riding Buck in boyhood and early youth, I fell in love with four or five girls but told only one. She was right in considering the matter a joke and thereby did me one of the biggest favors of my life. All those rose-lipped maidens and all the light-foot lads with whom I ran in those days have little meaning for me now. They never had much in comparison with numerous people I have known since. Buck, however, always in association with the plot of earth over which I rode him, increases in meaning. To remember him is a joy and a tonic.

1953
DETECTIVES OF TIME
by N. J. Berrill

THE Atomic Age has started and explosions make more sound and fury than other atomic ventures. Yet if knowledge leads to wisdom as well as power, then one of the quieter projects may in the end be more potent. It concerns the discovery of an atomic clock which is built into everything that has been alive. Scientists are putting natural atomic energy to work to unravel distant human history and what has been and may be happening to this continent. When was the icecap farthest south? Did men come before or after? What has happened since, and what is the shape of things to come?

The new science is radiocarbon dating. Atoms are studied in connection with fossil elephants, ancient Peruvian architecture and customs, pollen grains in the beds of old filled-up lakes, and not least the charred wood and burned bones buried deep in wayside caves. Willard F. Libby of the Institute for Nuclear Studies of the University of Chicago was the first to see, in 1945, that radioactive carbon might be used for dating the past. Now there are radiocarbon laboratories not only at Chicago but at Yale, Columbia, Michigan, Pennsylvania, Cambridge, Copenhagen, and in New Zealand.

The discovery of the carbon clock goes back in part to the late thirties. At that time the scientists who were studying cosmic rays pouring in from outer space began to analyze what goes on in the upper atmosphere. They found that the rays set free neutrons which in their turn convert atmospheric nitrogen into radioactive carbon. Libby took this information and worked out the proportion of radiocarbon to ordinary carbon normally present in the air.

Both kinds of carbon join with oxygen to make carbon dioxide; carbon dioxide, both radioactive and normal, is absorbed by plants and by the animals that eat them.

That is the starting point. What makes it a clock is this: radiocarbon, like all radioactive atoms, has a limited life and is continually disintegrating. After 5568 years, on an average, only half an original store of radiocarbon atoms will be left. After another 5568 years only half of those will be left, and so on. By the time 25,000 years have passed, only about one thirtieth of the original store will be left; and since the proportion is low to begin with, it is difficult to estimate what the ratio is in material older than that.

All animals and plants while they are alive contain the two kinds of carbon in the same proportion as they occur in the air. The moment the plant or animal dies, no more carbon is taken in and the carbon clock begins to run down, ticking away the years until hardly any radiocarbon is left. But as long as some wood or charred bone remains which is less than 30,000 years old, the radiocarbon can be counted in a Geiger tube and the age of the piece determined. This is the tool. What it can do depends upon human ingenuity.

For a long time oceanographers have wanted to know the rate of turnover in the oceans. It is slow and difficult to measure, but all marine life, large and small, depends upon it: it brings certain salts in short supply continually to the surface. The water sinks in polar regions and moves in the depths toward the equator, where it may rise again. Once the water sinks, it is as cut off from fresh supplies of radiocarbon as though it were a plant or animal that died, and radiocarbon counts can give the age of oceanic carbon just as readily as the age of a piece of ancient charcoal. Guesses gave the travel time from polar to equatorial regions all the way from ten to thousands of years.

Radiocarbon has yielded the answer, but it has been hard to get. The difficulty is the small amount of carbon the water contains: 200

gallons of sea water are required for a single carbon count. Yet Laurence Kulp of the Lamont Geological Observatory of Columbia University and Maurice Ewing of the Oceanographic Institute at Woods Hole combined their experience and effort and have succeeded in solving many supposedly impossible problems concerning the ocean.

They designed an open tank which could be lowered to a depth of 3 or 4 miles. At the right moment large doors are closed and 200 gallons of ocean water of a particular depth and location are sealed within. The sample is brought up to the deck of the ship and the carbon extracted and eventually sent to the radiocarbon laboratory. The first samples of water came from the two sides of the mid-Atlantic ridge at the latitude of Newfoundland from depths of over a mile. And radiocarbon counts have given the ages at 1600 years and older. The water left the surface in Arctic regions at the time the Romans abandoned Britain, and even now is only halfway to the equator. The flow is remarkably slow — so slow that it tells something of the crust of the earth that lies beneath the ocean floor.

II

Two points catch the eye at once. At Two Creeks, Wisconsin, the trees of an ancient spruce forest lie shattered, all with splintered ends and all pointing in a southwestern direction. The evidence shows that the forest went down beneath the creeping edge of a glacier of the last advance of the continental icecap, and that the ice advanced only another 20 or 30 miles. It was the turning point of the last ice age, and according to radiocarbon the forest fell about 11,400 years ago — only half as long ago as earlier estimations had placed the start of the ice withdrawal. And only twice as far back in time as recorded human history.

The other point is this. Burned bison bone has been found in Texas, of a kind of bison now extinct, associated with man-made spear tips. The age according to radiocarbon is 9883 years. Several pairs of woven sandals found buried in Fort Rock Cave near Crater Lake in Oregon are 9053 years old. The exact figures may be larger or smaller, but these ages show that men were living and were hunting bison in North America when half the continent was still covered by ice. From here on the questions come faster than the answers.

One fact stands out. Fragments of skin and other tissue of an extinct superbison found in frozen muck near Fairbanks, Alaska, are older than 28,000 years according to the radiocarbon count. The permafrost must have been continuous in that region ever since the last major phase of the last ice age. Did men reach North America from Asia by traveling over the dry and frozen Bering Strait before the days of stone lamps and warm skin clothing? Did they get across in a warm interglacial period many thousand years before, or did they come in boats along the coastal waters?

There are few facts to go on; yet in a cave near the southern tip of South America the burned bones of the giant sloth, horses, and the South American camel have been found together with human bones and artifacts. Their radiocarbon age is about 9000 years, and as long ago as that men were cooking the flesh of animals 7000 miles to the south of the ice.

We are accustomed to thinking of Stone Age man as hunting mammoths and other extinct elephants in Europe. The superb paintings on the walls of Lascaux Cave in France prove it beyond all question. Charcoal found in the same cave has a radiocarbon age of a little more than 11,000 years, although there is nothing to show that the fires were lit by the same men that did the drawing. It is more startling to find evidence that men were hunting elephants in America as well, and at a time long before the ice began to melt.

Both at Tepexpan, Mexico, and at Clovis, New Mexico, burned bison bone, of a kind of bison now extinct, has been found with spear points of a certain kind. The radiocarbon age is about 10,000 years, and the period is that of Folsom man, the name given to the hunters who made their spear points in this particular way. But at each place the Folsom layer lies over a deeper one of a very different kind and greater age. This deeper layer contains no bison bones but does contain the bones of elephants — not of the existing kinds, but of mastodons and mammoths — and the remnants of man-made weapons. At Tepexpan in 1952, Mexican scientists found weapon points actually embedded in the ribs, with knives and scrapers lying around. The radiocarbon age of pine pollen in the surrounding muck is about 9000 years — pollen in the bone cavities is mixed pine and spruce and is probably older. It looks as if this particular hunting party were disturbed after the kill had been made: perhaps saber-toothed tigers, which also hunted elephants at that time and place, interfered with the process of dismemberment.

Human history on this continent begins somewhere in the age of ice or during an earlier interglacial period. Men hunted elephants, camels, horses, giant sloths, and armadillos as large as an ox, superbison, and giant beavers. They had dire wolves and saber-toothed tigers for unwanted company. All the animals were here before the ice age began more than half a million years ago, and all survived the alternating periods of hot and cold well into the present postglacial times. Remains of the giant sloth with a radiocarbon age of 10,000 to 11,000 years have been found in caves as far apart as the tip of Patagonia and Las Vegas, Nevada.

This is the beginning and the end of a story, for all of these mammals disappeared, except the llama — one of the smaller South American camels — and the horse, which was reintroduced by the Spaniards. Their going coincided with the presence of man, but it flatters the skill of these primitive hunters too much to suppose that they were the cause. There is a mystery here. Sometime after the continental ice began to withdraw, a rich fauna disappeared. Men witnessed the extinction, which makes it part of human experience and something more than just a matter of curiosity.

Giant sloths in Nevada are out of place. They were great beasts that stood 12 to 14 feet high; they plodded along on bearlike hind legs, feeding on the foliage of trees or grubbing for roots in the soft earth. Nevada territory in their day must have been very different from what it is now — more humid, with thick forests and semitropical undergrowth. Then something happened, and men may have been victims as well as the beasts.

III

The 9000-year-old sandals from the Oregon cave were worn by men long before Mount Mazuma blew up and covered the region with ashes and brimstone, leaving a hole where the mountain stood that is now Crater Lake. Radiocarbon dates the charcoal of a tree that was killed and buried by the eruption at 6453 years, or about 2500 years after the making of the sandals. The Newberry Crater, which took the place of the exploded mountain, went on erupting until 2000 years ago — again according to countings made of the charcoal recovered from the crater. Then the hole filled up and became the lake.

This is not the answer to the vanishing animals, but it does suggest climatic changes and some increase in aridity. And at this point pollen grains unite with radiocarbon dating to give a clearer picture.

Pollen grains survive in a recognizable form for thousands of years in the mud of ancient bogs and lake beds. After treatment they can be identified as spruce or pine, birch, oak, or whatever they happen to be. And either the pollen grains or associated wood can be dated by radiocarbon. When the information is put together we see the forest creeping northward in the wake of the retreating ice. More than that, we see the changing nature of the forest and the climate it belongs to.

The main retreat of the icecap began about 8000 B.C. Some 500 years later the belt of pines extending along the southern edge of the Arctic tundra lay on a line passing through West Virginia. By 7000 B.C. it had shifted north to Connecticut. In 6000 B.C. the line passed through southern Minnesota, in 5000 B.C. through northern Minnesota, and in 4000 B.C. through northern Maine. With extensive tundra to the north of the pine, the continental ice must by this time have virtually melted away.

During the several thousand years that it took the ice to melt, and while the pine belt was shifting slowly to the north, oak dominated the southern forests. Altogether the tree pollens of this period indicate a temperature and humidity much greater than at present. This is plausible in any case. A lot of heat was needed to melt the icecap, and as long as it was melting and running off the land, the humidity would be high.

At that time of humid warmth, men were hunting bison of a kind that no longer lives. The plains supported camels and horses, while what is now the southwestern desert region had deep forests and rivers, with at least three times the present rainfall — the haunts of the giant sloth and the men who laid traps for them. The elephants may have already gone — perhaps there was too much water or too much sticky heat.

Around 4000 B.C. — at about the time Mount Mazuma blew its top — the climate changed; not suddenly, but all too fast. From warm and moist it became warm and dry, and the reason is fairly clear. With no more ice to melt, the lakes and swamps and rivers dwindled, evaporation from shrinking water surfaces grew less, and the water table sank. The land grew dry, the hazy overcast gave way to bluer skies — and the vegetation changed. The forests thinned out and the plains became parched and hard — that much seems certain. During this period the long-familiar animals disappeared. They were too big, needed too much food, and couldn't get enough of it.

The time was critical and important, and a lot of the mystery remains. Long, warm interglacial periods have occurred at intervals through the whole of the ice age. The mammals now vanished survived them all. Our own species of man came into being early in this age but remained a primitive hunter for several hundred thousand years. Why should the great extinction and the first beginnings of human civilizations coincide with the onset of the hot, dry millennia?

Ice appears to be almost a thing of the past, but that may or may not be true. There is still a lot of it left in Greenland and Antarctica, and sooner or later it will grow again or melt entirely away. It spells discomfort either way. If it goes on melting until all is gone, the ocean level will rise by another 140 to 190 feet — high enough to drown New York and London and much of the best agricultural land in the world. Radiocarbon again has something to say. Cedar logs from an old drowned forest dredged with mud from the sea at Bermuda were alive in 9000 B.C., when the sea level was much lower. They were growing at the same time as the spruce in the Two Creeks forest in Wisconsin. Sediments of the same age dredged from the lower Mississippi show that the sea was 80 feet lower than at present; in 7000 B.C. it was 70 feet lower, in 5000 B.C. it was 50 feet, and in 1000 B.C. it was 25 feet lower than now. In the last twenty years it has risen by nearly half a foot — a pace that seems to bring the end in sight.

Yet somewhere there appears to be a catch. All radiocarbon counts of the age of peat in the Florida Everglades show that it started to form about 5000 years ago; earlier than that, the lower Florida peninsula was under water. This is the period known as the thermal maximum — the first thousand years of the warm dry spell. The sea level was higher than it has been since, implying that there was less ice in the icecap and more water in the ocean than there is at present. Perhaps the warm postglacial peak was reached between 6000 and 5000 years ago, and the ocean became lower as the ice began to grow again. The recent rise may well be only a minor fluctuation. For, in spite of the milder trend of the last few decades, the climate of the temperate earth has become comparatively cool and moist during the last two thousand years. The Norse colonies in Greenland were frozen out by expansion of the icecap, and many existing glaciers may be successors to and not descendants of the last ice age.

We may be two or three thousand years past the middle of a short interglacial period — and a further fall in average temperature of about 4.5 degrees Fahrenheit is all that is needed to bring the end. We seem to be caught between too much sea and too much ice. Atomic clocks may show which will be our fate.

1954
FROM US TO YOU
by William L. Copithorne

I THINK we ought to write a Christmas letter this year," my wife said at the breakfast table the other morning.

"A what?" I asked warily.

"A Christmas letter. You know, like the kind the Huggins send out to all their friends every year."

I recalled the Huggins' Christmas letters — five-page mimeographed reports on family activities for the preceding year, with the simple greetings of the season all but buried.

I hurried off to work before my wife could pursue the subject any further, but that evening she presented me with a packet of letters including not only the recent efforts of the Huggins but Christmas letters other families had sent us as well. My wife is a saver.

"Now you read these and see if you don't think it would be a good idea for us to do this instead of sending cards this Christmas," she said.

One would have been enough, for the letters were indistinguishable in style and content. Posing innocently as Christmas greetings, they were actually unabashed family sagas. The writers touched lightly on the misfortunes which their families suffered during the year, dwelt gladly on happy events, and missed no opportunity for self-congratulation.

I haven't the slightest intention of writing a Christmas letter myself, but once I'd put a red or green ribbon in my typewriter I'm sure I could turn one out in no time at all.

"A MERRY CHRISTMAS FROM OUR HOUSE TO YOURS!" is the standard beginning. Centered at the top of an 8½″ x 11″ sheet of paper, it spares the writer the nuisance of penning salutations on the hundred or more copies he will doubtless send out. The exclamation mark is the first of dozens that will be used. No Christmas letter averages fewer than eighteen "!'s," "!!'s," or "(!)'s" a page.

The opening sentence always starts with the word "Well." "Well, here it is Christmas again!" is a favorite; or, "Well, hard as it is to realize, Christmas has rolled round once more!" A somewhat more expansive opening is "Well, Christmas finds us all one year older, but young as ever in the spirit of the Season!" Actually what is said is unimportant as long as the sentence starts with "Well," and ends, of course, with an exclamation mark.

Having taken due note of the season, the Christmas letter-writer works immediately into his first main topic — the accidents which befell him and his family and the diseases they suffered during the year. He writes with cheerful fortitude. Broken arms and legs call forth the reminiscent chuckle, and childhood diseases open the way for humor of a sort. "As it must to all children," the Huggins wrote last Christmas, "the mumps came to Albert Jr. and to Susie. Fortunately they were taken sick during the spring vacation and didn't miss any school. We don't think they'd agree with our use of the word 'fortunately.' (Ha-ha!)" The parenthetical "Ha-ha!" or simply "Ha!" appears at least once in each paragraph of a Christmas letter.

The writer next reviews the unusual activities of the year — the family's annual vacation at Sunrise Lake, for example. The summer vacation looms large in Christmas letters. Golf scores, size of fish caught, and the successes of the children in swimming and boating contests are good for a page and a half.

A peculiarity of the Christmas letter which the reader may find disconcerting is its inconstant point of view. Most Christmas letters presume to be joint husband-and-wife efforts, but sudden shifts, sometimes within a sentence, to an outsider's point of view are frequent. Writing from his own and his wife Bea's point of view, Jim could say: "We drove to Sunrise Lake in the record time of seven hours and

fourteen minutes. Jim was trying to establish a record, and he succeeded, with the help, of course, of the new Mercury which Bea insisted that we have before taking another long trip."

One reason for the use of the shifting point of view is the partial
cover-up it affords the writer. Since he devotes a good part of the
letter to his achievements of the past year, he must take care to avoid
appearing boastful. "He succeeded" sounds better than "I succeeded."

The shifting point of view has its limitations, of course, and when
the writer wants to record an especially proud accomplishment he
makes use of the footnote. If properly handled, the footnote can actually make him seem to be self-effacing.

Should Jim, for example, want to tell about the big one he caught at
Sunrise Lake, he first says that his son, Joey, is the real fisherman in
the family — that Joey, in fact, caught a bigger trout than he did last
summer. He then writes the following footnote, signing it "Bea": "Jim
insists on being a devoted parent. Actually it was *he* who caught the
larger trout — a ten-pounder, the biggest, according to the people at
the grocery store, that anyone had caught at Sunrise Lake in six
years!"

On an average, three footnotes appear at the bottom of each page
of a Christmas letter.

The last section of the letter is devoted to such routine matters as
recent improvements the writer has made on his house ("With only
the part-time help of a chimney pointer, Jim built a fireplace this fall
on the north end of our living room") or activities in the community
("Jim is now Captain of our precinct in the Civil Defense program,
and Bea has been made Den Mother of Joey's Cub Scout troop. She
says she does not plan to hibernate for the winter, however").

An effort obviously is made to keep the tone of the letter humorous,
but the underlying seriousness is never lost sight of. If, for a moment,
it sinks from view, the writer is quick with a footnote or a "Ha-ha!" to
indicate the depth of his irony.

The concluding paragraph of the Christmas letter, like the opening,
always begins with the word "Well." "Well, that about sums up our
activities for the year" is what the Huggins invariably say, although
they make it clear that they have merely scratched the surface by adding: "Of course there was the time back in April when Susie won first
prize in the poetry-reciting contest, and in September when Albert Jr.
was elected president of his Junior High School class, but we really
must close."

Before signing their names, Christmas letter-writers usually succeed
in reminding themselves that their purpose, after all, has been to extend Christmas greetings. "And so, A Merry Christmas to you all!" is
the conventional ending, although a few, like the Huggins, prefer the

full-blown close. "All of us," they wrote last year, "Albert Sr., Evelyn, Susie, and Albert Jr., join with Tiny Tim in saying, 'God bless us, every one!' "

As I say, I have no intention of writing one of these letters myself. Come to think of it, though, I never did let old Bill Mason out in Seattle know about that 78 I shot last summer, and I'm sure the Potters down in Shreveport haven't heard how our David talked at nine months and was walking at ten and a half . . .

---

¹955
BANJO BOOMER
by Wallace Stevens

THE mulberry is a double tree.
Mulberry, shade me, shade me awhile.

A white, pink, purple berry tree,
A very dark-leaved berry tree.
Mulberry, shade me, shade me awhile.

A churchyard kind of bush as well,
A silent sort of bush, as well.
Mulberry, shade me, shade me awhile.

It is a shape of life described
By another shape without a word.
Mulberry, shade me, shade me awhile—

With nothing fixed by a single word.
Mulberry, shade me, shade me awhile.

HOW MR. HOGAN ROBBED A BANK
by John Steinbeck

ON the Saturday before Labor Day, 1955, at 9:04½ A.M., Mr. Hogan robbed a bank. He was forty-two years old, married, and the father of a boy and a girl, named John and Joan, twelve and thirteen respectively. Mrs. Hogan's name was Joan and Mr. Hogan's was John, but since they called themselves Papa and Mama that left their names free for the children, who were considered very smart for their ages, each having jumped a grade in school. The Hogans lived at 215 East Maple Street, in a brown-shingle house with white trim — there are two. 215 is the one across from the street light and it is the one with the big tree in the yard, either oak or elm — the biggest tree in the whole street, maybe in the whole town.

John and Joan were in bed at the time of the robbery, for it was Saturday. At 9:10 A.M., Mrs. Hogan was making the cup of tea she always had. Mr. Hogan went to work early. Mrs. Hogan drank her tea slowly, scalding hot, and read her fortune in the tea leaves. There was a cloud and a five-pointed star with two short points in the bottom of the cup, but that was at 9:12 and the robbery was all over by then.

The way Mr. Hogan went about robbing the bank was very interesting. He gave it a great deal of thought and had for a long time, but he did not discuss it with anyone. He just read his newspaper and kept his own counsel. But he worked it out to his own satisfaction that people went to too much trouble robbing banks and that got them in a mess. The simpler the better, he always thought. People went in for too much hullabaloo and hanky-panky. If you didn't do that, if you left hanky-panky out, robbing a bank would be a relatively sound venture — barring accidents, of course, of an improbable kind, but then they could happen to a man crossing the street or anything. Since Mr. Hogan's method worked fine, it proved that his thinking was sound. He often considered writing a little booklet on his technique when the how-to rage was running so high. He figured out the first sentence, which went: "To successfully rob a bank, forget all about hanky-panky."

Mr. Hogan was not just a clerk at Fettucci's grocery store. He was more like the manager. Mr. Hogan was in charge, even hired and fired the boy who delivered groceries after school. He even put in orders with the salesmen, sometimes when Mr. Fettucci was right in the store too, maybe talking to a customer. "You do it, John," he would say and he would nod at the customer, "John knows the ropes. Been with me — how long you been with me, John?"

"Sixteen years."

"Sixteen years. Knows the business as good as me. John, why he even banks the money."

And so he did. Whenever he had a moment, Mr. Hogan went into the storeroom on the alley, took off his apron, put on his necktie and coat, and went back through the store to the cash register. The checks and bills would be ready for him inside the bankbook with a rubber band around it. Then he went next door and stood at the teller's window and handed the checks and bankbook through to Mr. Cup and passed the time of day with him too. Then, when the bankbook was handed back, he checked the entry, put the rubber band around it and walked next door to Fettucci's grocery and put the bankbook in the cash register, continued on to the storeroom, removed his coat and tie, put on his apron, and went back into the store ready for business. If there was no line at the teller's window, the whole thing didn't take more than five minutes, even passing the time of day.

Mr. Hogan was a man who noticed things, and when it came to robbing the bank, this trait stood him in good stead. He had noticed, for instance, where the big bills were kept right in the drawer under the counter and he had noticed also what days there were likely to be more than other days. Thursday was payday at the American Can Company's local plant, for instance, so there would be more then. Some Fridays people drew more money to tide them over the week-end. But it was even Steven, maybe not a thousand dollars difference, between Thursdays and Fridays and Saturday mornings. Saturdays were not terribly good because people didn't come to get money that early in the morning, and the bank closed at noon. But he thought it over and came to the conclusion that the Saturday before a long week-end in the summer would be the best of all. People going on trips, vacations, people with relatives visiting, and the bank closed Monday. He thought it out and looked, and sure enough the Saturday morning before Labor Day the cash drawer had twice as much money in it — he saw it when Mr. Cup pulled out the drawer.

Mr. Hogan thought about it during all that year, not all the time, of course, but when he had some moments. It was a busy year too. That was the year John and Joan had the mumps and Mrs. Hogan got her teeth pulled and was fitted for a denture. That was the year when Mr. Hogan was Master of the Lodge, with all the time that takes. Larry Shield died that year — he was Mrs. Hogan's brother and was buried from the Hogan house at 215 East Maple. Larry was a bachelor and had a room in the Pine Tree House and he played pool nearly every night. He worked at the Silver Diner but that closed at nine and so Larry would go to Louie's and play pool for an hour. Therefore, it was a surprise when he left enough so that after funeral expenses there were twelve hundred dollars left. And even more surprising that he

left a will in Mrs. Hogan's favor, but his double-barreled twelve-gauge
shotgun he left to John Hogan, Jr. Mr. Hogan was pleased, although
he never hunted. He put the shotgun away in the back of the closet in
the bathroom, where he kept his things, to keep it for young John. He
didn't want children handling guns and he never bought any shells. It
was some of that twelve hundred that got Mrs. Hogan her dentures.
Also, she bought a bicycle for John and a doll buggy and walking-
talking doll for Joan — a doll with three changes of dresses and a little
suitcase, complete with play make-up. Mr. Hogan thought it might
spoil the children, but it didn't seem to. They made just as good marks
in school and John even got a job delivering papers. It was a very busy
year. Both John and Joan wanted to enter the W. R. Hearst National
"I Love America" Contest and Mr. Hogan thought it was almost too
much, but they promised to do the work during their summer vacation, so he finally agreed.

II

During that year, no one noticed any difference in Mr. Hogan. It was
true, he was thinking about robbing the bank, but he only thought
about it in the evening when there was neither a Lodge meeting nor a
movie they wanted to go to, so it did not become an obsession and
people noticed no change in him.

He had studied everything so carefully that the approach of Labor
Day did not catch him unprepared or nervous. It was hot that summer
and the hot spells were longer than usual. Saturday was the end of
two weeks heat without a break and people were irritated with it and
anxious to get out of town, although the country was just as hot. They
didn't think of that. The children were excited because the "I Love
America" Essay Contest was due to be concluded and the winners
announced, and the first prize was an all-expense-paid two days trip to
Washington, D.C., with every fixing — hotel room, three meals a day,
and side trips in a limousine — not only for the winner, but for an
accompanying chaperone; visit to the White House — shake hands
with the President — everything. Mr. Hogan thought they were getting their hopes too high and he said so.

"You've got to be prepared to lose," he told his children. "There're
probably thousands and thousands entered. You get your hopes up
and it might spoil the whole autumn. Now I don't want any long faces
in this house after the contest is over."

"I was against it from the start," he told Mrs. Hogan. That was the
morning she saw the Washington Monument in her teacup, but she
didn't tell anybody about that except Ruth Tyler, Bob Tyler's wife.
Ruthie brought over her cards and read them in the Hogan kitchen,
but she didn't find a journey. She did tell Mrs. Hogan that the cards
were often wrong. The cards had said Mrs. Winkle was going on a trip

to Europe and the next week Mrs. Winkle got a fishbone in her throat and choked to death. Ruthie, just thinking out loud, wondered if there was any connection between the fishbone and the ocean voyage to Europe. "You've got to interpret them right." Ruthie did say she saw money coming to the Hogans.

"Oh, I got that already from poor Larry," Mrs. Hogan explained.

"I must have got the past and future cards mixed," said Ruthie. "You've got to interpret them right."

Saturday dawned a blaster. The early morning weather report on the radio said "Continued hot and humid, light scattered rain Sunday night and Monday." Mrs. Hogan said, "Wouldn't you know? Labor Day." And Mr. Hogan said, "I'm sure glad we didn't plan anything." He finished his egg and mopped the plate with his toast. Mrs. Hogan said, "Did I put coffee on the list?" He took the paper from his handkerchief pocket and consulted it. "Yes, coffee, it's here."

"I had a crazy idea I forgot to write it down," said Mrs. Hogan. "Ruth and I are going to Altar Guild this afternoon. It's at Mrs. Alfred Drake's. You know, they just came to town. I can't wait to see their furniture."

"They trade with us," said Mr. Hogan. "Opened an account last week. Are the milk bottles ready?"

"On the porch."

Mr. Hogan looked at his watch just before he picked up the bottles and it was five minutes to eight. He was about to go down the stairs, when he turned and looked back through the opened door at Mrs. Hogan. She said, "Want something, Papa?"

"No," he said. "No," and he walked down the steps.

He went down to the corner and turned right on Spooner, and Spooner runs into Main Street in two blocks, and right across from where it runs in, there is Fettucci's and the bank around the corner and the alley beside the bank. Mr. Hogan picked up a handbill in front of Fettucci's and unlocked the door. He went through to the storeroom, opened the door to the alley, and looked out. A cat tried to force its way in, but Mr. Hogan blocked it with his foot and leg and closed the door. He took off his coat and put on his long apron, tied the strings in a bowknot behind his back. Then he got the broom from behind the counter and swept out behind the counters and scooped the sweepings into a dustpan; and, going through the storeroom, he opened the door to the alley. The cat had gone away. He emptied the dustpan into the garbage can and tapped it smartly to dislodge a piece of lettuce leaf. Then he went back to the store and worked for a while on the order sheet. Mrs. Clooney came in for a half a pound of bacon. She said it was hot and Mr. Hogan agreed. "Summers are getting hotter," he said.

"I think so myself," said Mrs. Clooney. "How's Mrs. standing up?"

"Just fine," said Mr. Hogan. "She's going to Altar Guild."

"So am I. I just can't wait to see their furniture," said Mrs. Clooney, and she went out.

III

Mr. Hogan put a five-pound hunk of bacon on the slicer and stripped off the pieces and laid them on wax paper and then he put the wax-paper-covered squares in the cooler cabinet. At ten minutes to nine, Mr. Hogan went to a shelf. He pushed a spaghetti box aside and took down a cereal box, which he emptied in the little closet toilet. Then, with a banana knife, he cut out the Mickey Mouse mask that was on the back. The rest of the box he took to the toilet and tore up the cardboard and flushed it down. He went into the store then and yanked a piece of string loose and tied the ends through the side holes of the mask and then he looked at his watch — a large silver Hamilton with black hands. It was two minutes to nine.

Perhaps the next four minutes were his only time of nervousness at all. At one minute to nine, he took the broom and went out to sweep the sidewalk and he swept it very rapidly — was sweeping it, in fact, when Mr. Warner unlocked the bank door. He said good morning to Mr. Warner and a few seconds later the bank staff of four emerged from the coffee shop. Mr. Hogan saw them across the street and he waved at them and they waved back. He finished the sidewalk and went back in the store. He laid his watch on the little step of the cash register. He sighed very deeply, more like a deep breath than a sigh. He knew that Mr. Warner would have the safe open now and he would be carrying the cash trays to the teller's window. Mr. Hogan looked at the watch on the cash register step. Mr. Kenworthy paused in the store entrance, then shook his head vaguely and walked on and Mr. Hogan let out his breath gradually. His left hand went behind his back and pulled the bowknot on his apron, and then the black hand on his watch crept up on the four-minute mark and covered it.

Mr. Hogan opened the charge account drawer and took out the store pistol, a silver-colored Iver Johnson .38. He moved quickly to the storeroom, slipped off his apron, put on his coat, and stuck the revolver in his side pocket. The Mickey Mouse mask he shoved up under his coat where it didn't show. He opened the alley door and looked up and down and stepped quickly out, leaving the door slightly ajar. It is sixty feet to where the alley enters Main Street, and there he paused and looked up and down and then he turned his head toward the center of the street as he passed the bank window. At the bank's swinging door, he took out the mask from under his coat and put it on. Mr. Warner was just entering his office and his back was to the door. The top of Will Cup's head was visible through the teller's grill.

Mr. Hogan moved quickly and quietly around the end of the counter and into the teller's cage. He had the revolver in his right hand now. When Will Cup turned his head and saw the revolver, he froze. Mr. Hogan slipped his toe under the trigger of the floor alarm and he motioned Will Cup to the floor with the revolver and Will went down quick. Then Mr. Hogan opened the cash drawer and with two quick movements he piled the large bills from the tray together. He made a whipping motion to Will on the floor, to indicate that he should turn over and face the wall, and Will did. Then Mr. Hogan stepped back around the counter. At the door of the bank, he took off his mask, and as he passed the window he turned his head toward the middle of the street. He moved into the alley, walked quickly to the storeroom, and entered. The cat had got in. It watched him from a pile of canned goods cartons. Mr. Hogan went to the toilet closet and tore up the mask and flushed it. He took off his coat and put on his apron. He looked out into the store and then moved to the cash register. The revolver went back into the charge account drawer. He punched No Sale and, lifting the top drawer, distributed the stolen money underneath the top tray and then pulled the tray forward and closed the register, and only then did he look at his watch and it was 9:07½.

He was trying to get the cat out of the storeroom when the commotion boiled out of the bank. He took his broom and went out on the sidewalk. He heard all about it and offered his opinion when it was asked for. He said he didn't think the fellow could get away — where could he get to? Still, with the holiday coming up —

It was an exciting day. Mr. Fettucci was as proud as though it were his bank. The sirens sounded around town for hours. Hundreds of holiday travelers had to stop at the roadblocks set up all around the edge of town and several sneaky-looking men had their cars searched.

Mrs. Hogan heard about it over the phone and she dressed earlier than she would have ordinarily and came to the store on her way to Altar Guild. She hoped Mr. Hogan would have seen or heard something new, but he hadn't. "I don't see how the fellow can get away," he said.

Mrs. Hogan was so excited, she forgot her own news. She only remembered when she got to Mrs. Drake's house, but she asked permission and phoned the store the first moment she could. "I forgot to tell you. John's won honorable mention."

"What?"

"In the 'I Love America' Contest."

"What did he win?"

"Honorable mention."

"Fine. Fine — Anything come with it?"

"Why, he'll get his picture and his name all over the country. Radio too. Maybe even television. They've already asked for a photograph of him."

"Fine," said Mr. Hogan. "I hope it don't spoil him." He put up the receiver and said to Mr. Fettucci, "I guess we've got a celebrity in the family."

Fettucci stayed open until nine on Saturdays. Mr. Hogan ate a few snacks from cold cuts, but not much, because Mrs. Hogan always kept his supper warming.

It was 9:05, or :06, or :07, when he got back to the brown-shingle house at 215 East Maple. He went in through the front door and out to the kitchen where the family was waiting for him.

"Got to wash up," he said, and went up to the bathroom. He turned the key in the bathroom door and then he flushed the toilet and turned on the water in the basin and tub while he counted the money. Eight thousand three hundred and twenty dollars. From the top shelf of the storage closet in the bathroom, he took down the big leather case that held his Knight Templar's uniform. The plumed hat lay there on its form. The white ostrich feather was a little yellow and needed changing. Mr. Hogan lifted out the hat and pried the form up from the bottom of the case. He put the money in the form and then he thought again and removed two bills and shoved them in his side pocket. Then he put the form back over the money and laid the hat on top and closed the case and shoved it back on the top shelf. Finally he washed his hands and turned off the water in the tub and the basin.

In the kitchen, Mrs. Hogan and the children faced him, beaming. "Guess what some young man's going on?"

"What?" asked Mr. Hogan.

"Radio," said John. "Monday night. Eight o'clock."

"I guess we got a celebrity in the family," said Mr. Hogan.

Mrs. Hogan said, "I just hope some young lady hasn't got her nose out of joint."

Mr. Hogan pulled up to the table and stretched his legs. "Mama, I guess I got a fine family," he said. He reached in his pocket and took out two five-dollar bills. He handed one to John. "That's for winning," he said. He poked the other bill at Joan. "And that's for being a good sport. One celebrity and one good sport. What a fine family!" He rubbed his hands together and lifted the lid of the covered dish. "Kidneys," he said. "Fine."

And that's how Mr. Hogan did it.

TWO TALES OF DARKNESS
by Ernest Hemingway

1. A Man of the World

The blind man knew the sounds of all the different machines in the saloon. I don't know how long it took him to learn the sounds of the machines but it must have taken him quite a time because he only worked one saloon at a time. He worked two towns though and he would start out of The Flats alone after it was good and dark on his way up to Jessup. He'd stop by the side of the road when he heard a car coming and their lights would pick him up and either they would stop and give him a ride or they wouldn't and would go on by on the icy road. It would depend on how they were loaded and whether there were women in the car because the blind man smelled plenty strong and especially in winter. But someone would always stop for him because he was a blind man.

Everybody knew him and they called him Blindy which is a good name for a blind man in that part of the country, and the name of the saloon that he threw his trade to was The Pilot. Right next to it was another saloon, also with gambling and a dining room, that was called The Index. Both of these were the names of mountains and they were both good saloons with old-days bars and the gambling was about the same in one as in the other except you ate better in The Pilot probably, although you got a better sizzling steak at The Index. Then The Index was open all night long and got the early morning trade and from daylight until ten o'clock in the morning the drinks were on the house. They were the only saloons in Jessup and they did not have to do that kind of thing. But that was the way they were.

Blindy probably preferred The Pilot because the machines were right along the left-hand wall as you came in and faced the bar. This gave him better control over them than he would have had at The Index where they were scattered on account it was a bigger place with more room. On this night it was really cold outside and he came in with icicles on his mustache and small pus icicles out of both eyes and he didn't look really very good. Even his smell was froze but that wasn't for very long and he started to put out almost as soon as the door was shut. It was always hard for me to look at him but I was looking at him carefully because I knew he always rode and I didn't see how he would be frozen up so bad. Finally I asked him.

"Where you walk from, Blindy?"

"Willie Sawyer put me out of his car down below the railway bridge. There weren't no more cars come and I walked in."

"What did he put you afoot for?" somebody asked.

"Said I smelled too bad."

Someone had pulled the handle on a machine and Blindy started listening to the whirr. It came up nothing. "Any dudes playing?" he asked me.

"Can't you hear?"

"Not yet."

"No dudes, Blindy, and it's a Wednesday."

"I know what night it is. Don't start telling me what night it is."

Blindy went down the line of machines feeling in all of them to see if anything had been left in the cups by mistake. Naturally there wasn't anything, but that was the first part of his pitch. He came back to the bar where we were and Al Chaney asked him to have a drink.

"No," Blindy said. "I got to be careful on those roads."

"What you mean those roads?" somebody asked him. "You only go on one road. Between here and The Flats."

"I been on lots of roads," Blindy said. "And any time I may have to take off and go on more."

Somebody hit on a machine but it wasn't any heavy hit. Blindy moved on it just the same. It was a quarter machine and the young fellow who was playing it gave him a quarter sort of reluctantly. Blindy felt it before he put it in his pocket.

"Thank you," he said. "You'll never miss it."

The young fellow said, "Nice to know that," and put a quarter back in the machine and pulled down again.

He hit again but this time pretty good and he scooped in the quarters and gave a quarter to Blindy.

"Thanks," Blindy said. "You're doing fine."

"Tonight's my night," the young fellow who was playing said.

"Your night is my night," Blindy said and the young fellow went on playing but he wasn't doing any good any more and Blindy was so strong standing by him and he looked so awful and finally the fellow quit playing and came over to the bar. Blindy had run him out but he had no way of noticing it because the fellow didn't say anything, so Blindy just checked the machines again with his hand and stood there waiting for someone else to come in and make a play.

There wasn't any play at the wheel nor at the crap table and at the poker game there were just gamblers sitting there and cutting each other up. It was a quiet evening on a week night in town and there wasn't any excitement. The place was not making a nickel except at the bar. But at the bar it was pleasant and the place had been nice until Blindy had come in. Now everybody was figuring they might as well go next door to The Index or else cut out and go home.

"What will yours be, Tom?" Frank the bartender asked me. "This is on the house."

"I was figuring on shoving."

"Have one first then."

"The same with ditch," I said. Frank asked the young fellow, who was wearing heavy Oregon Cities and a black hat and was shaved clean and had a snow-burned face, what he would drink and the young fellow took the same. The whisky was Old Forester.

I nodded to him and raised my drink and we both sipped at the drinks. Blindy was down at the far end of the machines. I think he figured maybe no one would come in if they saw him at the door. Not that he was self-conscious.

"How did that man lose his sight?" the young fellow asked me.

"I wouldn't know," I told him.

"In a fight," Frank told him.

"Him fight?" the stranger said. He shook his head.

"Yeah," Frank said. "He got that high voice out of the same fight. Tell him, Tom."

"I never heard of it."

"No. You wouldn't of," Frank said. "Of course not. You wasn't here, I suppose. Mister, it was a night about as cold as tonight. Maybe colder. It was a quick fight too. I didn't see the start of it. Then they come fighting out of the door of The Index. Blackie, him that's Blindy now, and this other boy Willie Sawyer, and they were slugging and kneeing and gouging and biting and I see one of Blackie's eyes hanging down on his cheek. They were fighting on the ice of the road with the snow all banked up and the light from this door and The Index door, and Hollis Sands was right behind Willie Sawyer who was gouging for the eye and Hollis kept hollering, 'Bite it off! Bite it off just like it was a grape!' Blackie was biting onto Willie Sawyer's face and he had a good holt and it give way with a jerk and then he had another good holt and they were down on the ice now and Willie Sawyer was gouging him to make him let go and then Blackie gave a yell like you've never heard. Worse than when they cut a boar."

Blindy had come up opposite us and we smelled him and turned around.

" 'Bite it off just like it was a grape,' " he said in his high-pitched voice and looked at us, moving his head up and down. "That was the left eye. He got the other one without no advice. Then he stomped me when I couldn't see. That was the bad part." He patted himself.

"I could fight good then," he said. "But he got the eye before I knew even what was happening. He got it with a lucky gouge. Well," Blindy said without any rancor, "that put a stop to my fighting days."

"Give Blackie a drink," I said to Frank.

"Blindy's the name, Tom. I earned that name. You seen me earn it. That's the same fellow who put me adrift down the road tonight. Fellow bit the eye. We ain't never made friends."

"What did you do to him?" the stranger asked.

"Oh you'll see him around," Blindy said. "You'll recognize him any time you see him. I'll let it come as a surprise."

"You don't want to see him," I told the stranger.

"You know that's one of the reasons I'd like to see sometimes," Blindy said. "I'd like to just have one good look at him."

"You know what he looks like," Frank told him. "You went up and put your hands on his face once."

"Did it again tonight too," Blindy said happily. "That's why he put me out of the car. He ain't got no sense of humor at all. I told him on a cold night like this he'd ought to bundle up so the whole inside of his face wouldn't catch cold. He didn't even think that was funny. You know that Willie Sawyer he'll never be a man of the world."

"Blackie, you have one on the house," Frank said. "I can't drive you home because I only live just down the road. But you can sleep in the back of the place."

"That's mighty good of you, Frank. Only just don't call me Blackie. I'm not Blackie any more. Blindy's my name."

"Have a drink, Blindy."

"Yes, sir," Blindy said. His hand reached out and found the glass and he raised it accurately to the three of us.

"That Willie Sawyer," he said. "Probably alone home by himself. That Willie Sawyer he don't know how to have any fun at all."

2. Get a Seeing-Eyed Dog

"And what did we do then?" he asked her. She told him.

"That part is very strange. I can't remember that at all."

"Can you remember the safari leaving?"

"I should. But I don't. I remember the women going down the trail to the beach for the water with the pots on their heads and I remember the flock of geese the toto drove back and forth to the water. I remember how slowly they all went and they were always going down or coming up. There was a very big tide too and the flats were yellow and the channel ran by the far island. The wind blew all the time and there were no flies and no mosquitoes. There was a roof and a cement floor and the poles that held the roof up, and the wind blew through all the time. It was cool all day and lovely and cool at night."

"Do you remember when the big dhow came in and careened on the low tide?"

"Yes, I remember her and the crew coming ashore in her boats and coming up the path from the beach, and the geese were afraid of them and so were the women."

"That was the day we caught so many fish but had to come in because it was so rough."

"I remember that."

"You're remembering well today," she said. "Don't do it too much."

"I'm sorry you didn't get to fly to Zanzibar," he said. "That upper beach from where we were was a fine place to land. You could have landed and taken off from there quite easily."

"We can always go to Zanzibar. Don't try to remember too much today. Would you like me to read to you? There's always something in the old *New Yorkers* that we missed."

"No, please don't read," he said. "Just talk. Talk about the good days."

"Do you want to hear about what it's like outside?"

"It's raining," he said. "I know that."

"It's raining a big rain," she told him. "There won't be any tourists out with this weather. The wind is very wild and we can go down and sit by the fire."

"We could anyway. I don't care about them any more. I like to hear them talk."

"Some of them are awful," she said. "But some of them are quite nice. I think it's really the nicest ones that go out to Torcello."

"That's quite true," he said. "I hadn't thought of that. There's really nothing for them to see unless they are a little bit nice."

"Can I make you a drink?" she asked. "You know how worthless a nurse I am. I wasn't trained for it and I haven't any talent. But I can make drinks."

"Let's have a drink."

"What do you want?"

"Anything," he said.

"I'll make a surprise. I'll make it downstairs."

He heard the door open and close and her feet on the stairs and he thought, I must get her to go on a trip. I must figure out some way to do it. I have to think up something practical. I've got this now for the rest of my life and I must figure out ways not to destroy her life and ruin her with it. She has been so good and she was not built to be good. I mean this sort of good. I mean good every day and dull good.

He heard her coming up the stairs and noticed the difference in her tread when she was carrying two glasses and when she had walked down barehanded. He heard the rain on the windowpane and he smelled the beech logs burning in the fireplace. As she came into the room he put his hand out for the drink a little too soon. But then he felt it tall and cold and closed his hand on it and felt her touch the glass with her own.

"It's our old drink for out here," she said. "Campari and Gordon's with ice."

"I'm certainly glad you're not a girl who would say 'on the rocks.' "

"No," she said. "I wouldn't ever say that. We've *been* on the rocks."

"On our own two feet when the chips were down and for keeps," he remembered. "Do you remember when we barred those phrases?"

"That was in the time of my lion. Wasn't he a wonderful lion? I can't wait till we see him."

"I can't either," he said.

"I'm sorry."

"Do you remember when we barred that phrase?"

"I nearly said it again."

"You know," he told her, "we're awfully lucky to have come here. I remember it so well that it is palpable. That's a new word and we'll bar it soon. But it really is wonderful. When I hear the rain I can see it on the stones and on the canal and on the lagoon, and I know the way the trees bend in every wind and how the church and the tower are in every sort of light. We couldn't have come to a better place for me. It's really perfect. We've got the good radio and a fine tape recorder and I'm going to write better than I ever could. If you take your time with the tape recorder you can get the words right. I can work slow and I can see the words when I say them. If they're wrong I hear them wrong and I can do them over and work on them until I get them right. Honey, in lots of ways we couldn't have it better."

"Oh Philip —"

"Shit," he said. "The dark is just the dark. This isn't like the real dark. I can see very well inside and now my head is better all the time and I can remember and I can make up well. You wait and see. Didn't I remember better today?"

"You remember better all the time. And you're getting strong."

"I am strong," he said. "Now if you —"

"If me what?"

"If you'd go away for a while and get a rest and a change from this."

"Don't you want me?"

"Of course I want you, darling."

"Then why do we have to talk about me going away? I know I'm not good at looking after you but I can do things other people can't do and we do love each other. You love me and you know it and we know things nobody else knows."

"We do wonderful things in the dark," he said.

"And we did wonderful things in the daytime too."

"You know I rather like the dark. In some ways it is an improvement."

"Don't lie too much," she said. "You don't have to be so bloody noble."

"Listen to it rain," he said. "How is the tide now?"

"It's way out and the wind has driven the water even further out. You could almost walk to Burano."

"All except one place," he said. "Are there many birds?"

"Mostly gulls and terns. They are down on the flats and when they get up the wind catches them."

"Aren't there any shore birds?"

"There are a few working on the part of the flats that only comes out when we have this wind and this tide."

"Do you think it will ever be spring?"

"I don't know," she said. "It certainly doesn't act like it."

"Have you drunk all your drink?"

"Just about. Why don't you drink yours?"

"I was saving it."

"Drink it up," she said. "Wasn't it awful when you couldn't drink at all?"

"No, you see," he said. "What I was thinking about when you went downstairs was that you could go to Paris and then to London and you'd see people and could have some fun and then you'd come back and it would have to be spring by then and you could tell me all about everything."

"No," she said.

"I think it would be intelligent to do," he said. "You know this is a long sort of stupid business and we have to learn to pace ourselves. And I don't want to wear you out. You know — "

"I wish you wouldn't say 'you know' so much."

"You see? That's one of the things. I could learn to talk in a non-irritating way. You might be mad about me when you came back."

"What would you do nights?"

"Nights are easy."

"I'll bet they are. I suppose you've learned how to sleep too."

"I'm going to," he told her and drank half the drink. "That's part of The Plan. You know this is how it works. If you go away and have some fun then I have a good conscience. Then for the first time in my life with a good conscience I sleep automatically. I take a pillow which represents my good conscience and I put my arms around it and off I go to sleep. If I wake up by any odd chance I just think beautiful happy dirty thoughts. Or I make wonderful fine good resolutions. Or I remember things. You know I want you to have fun — "

"Please don't say 'you know.' "

"I'll concentrate on not saying it. It's barred but I forget and let the bars down. Anyway I don't want you just to be a seeing-eyed dog."

"I'm not and you know it. Anyway it's seeing-eye not seeing-eyed."

"I knew that," he told her. "Come and sit here, would you mind very much?"

She came and sat by him on the bed and they both heard the rain hard against the pane of the window and he tried not to feel her head and her lovely face the way a blind man feels and there was no other way that he could touch her face except that way. He held her close and kissed the top of her head. I will have to try it another day, he thought. I must not be so stupid about it. She feels so lovely and I love her so much and have done her so much damage and I must learn to take good care of her in every way I can. If I think of her and of her only, everything will be all right.

"I won't say 'you know' all the time any more," he told her. "We can start with that."

She shook her head and he could feel her tremble.

"You say it all you want," she said and kissed him.

"Please don't cry, my blessed," he said.

"I don't want you to sleep with any lousy pillow," she said.

"I won't. Not *any* lousy pillow."

Stop it, he said to himself. Stop it right now.

"Look, *tu,*" he said. "We'll go down now and have lunch in our old fine place by the fire and I'll tell you what a wonderful kitten you are and what lucky kittens we are."

"We really are."

"We'll work everything out fine."

"I just don't want to be sent away."

But walking down the stairs feeling each stair carefully and holding to the banister he thought, I must get her away and get her away as soon as I can without hurting her. Because I am not doing too well at this. That I can promise you. But what else can you do? Nothing, he thought. There's nothing you can do. But maybe, as you go along, you will get good at it.

1958
HOW BIG IS ONE?
by Edward Weeks

MY late friend, the French writer Raoul de Roussy de Sales, who knew America intimately, used to tease me about our infatuation with bigness. "It's in your blood," he would say. "When I listen to Americans talking on shipboard, or in a Paris restaurant, or here in New York, it is only a question of time before someone will come out with that favorite boast of yours — 'the biggest in the world!' The New York skyline, or the Washington Monument, or the Chicago Merchandise Mart — the biggest in the world. You say it without thinking what it means." How right he was, yet until he prodded me about it, I had never realized that this was indeed our national boast. We take pride in being big, and in a youthful way we used to think that bigness was our own special prerogative. But now we know better; now we find ourselves confronted with nations or with groups of nations which are quite as big as we are and which have the potential of being considerably bigger. This calls for a new orientation; indeed, I think it might be timely if we examine this concept of bigness and try to determine how it has affected our private lives and our thinking.

We have been in love with bigness ever since the adolescence of our democracy. The courtship began on the frontier: the uncut virgin forests, so dense and terrifying; the untamed flooding rivers; the limitless prairies; the almost impassable Sierras — to overcome obstacles like these, man, so puny in comparison, had to outdo himself. He had to be bigger than Hercules. The English live on a small, contained island, and English humor is naturally based on understatement; but an American when he is having fun always exaggerates.

Our first hero of the frontier was a superman, Davy Crockett, who could outshoot, outfight, and outwoo anyone. One day he sauntered into the forest for an airing but forgot to take his thunderbolt along. This made it embarrassing when he came face to face with a panther. The scene is described in the old almanac, as Howard Mumford Jones says, "in metaphoric language which has all the freshness of dawn." The panther growled and Crockett growled right back — "He grated thunder with his teeth" — and so the battle began. In the end, the panther, tamed, goes home with Davy, lights the fire on a dark night with flashes from his eyes, brushes the hearth every morning with his tail, and rakes the garden with his claws. Davy did the impossible, and listening to the legends of his prowess made it easier for the little guy on the frontier to do the possible.

Davy Crockett had a blood brother in Mike Fink, the giant of the river boatmen, and first cousins in Tony Beaver and Paul Bunyan of the North Woods and Pecos Bill of the Southwest. They were ring-tailed roarers, and everything they did had an air of gigantic plausibility. Prunes are a necessary part of the lumberjack's diet, and Paul Bunyan's camp had such a zest for prunes that the prune trains which hauled the fruit came in with two engines, one before and one behind pushing. "Paul used to have twenty flunkies sweepin' the prunestones out from under the tables, but even then they'd get so thick we had to wade through 'em up over our shoes sometimes on our way in to dinner. They'd be all over the floor and in behind the stove and piled up against the windows where they'd dumped 'em outside so the cook couldn't see out at all hardly. . . . In Paul's camp back there in Wisconsin the prunestones used to get so thick they had to have twenty ox-teams haulin' 'em away, and they hauled 'em out in the woods, and the chipmunks ate 'em and grew so big the people shot 'em for tigers." Only an American could have invented that build-up, and I am grateful to Esther Shephard for having recaptured the legend so accurately in her *Paul Bunyan.*

Texas, with its fondness for bigness, preferred the living man to the legend: it provided the space for men like Richard King, the founder of the King Ranch. Richard King's story as told by Tom Lea is Horatio Alger multiplied by a thousand. The son of Irish immigrants, he ran off to sea at the age of eleven; a river boat captain in his twenties, he came ashore, married the parson's daughter, bought 15,000 acres of desert at two cents an acre, and went into the cattle business. His close friend and adviser was Lieutenant Colonel Robert E. Lee of the Second United States Cavalry, and it was Lee who gave King what has come to be the family slogan: "Buy land; and never sell." The King Ranch has grown to 700,000 acres in Texas — just about as big as a good ranch ought to be.

II

I entered publishing in the summer of 1923 as a book salesman in New York. As I look back over the thirty-five years of my working life, I recognize that a significant change has taken place in our business community. The motorcars which I used to covet as a young bachelor, the Stutz Bearcat, the Mercer, the Simplex, the Locomobile, the Pierce Arrow — all these beauties and hundreds of the lesser breeds, like the Hupmobile, the Maxwell, the Franklin, the Stanley Steamer, and the Moon — are museum pieces today. The beauty and the originality which went into their design have been melted down and vulgarized in the models of the five major companies which survive.

In the days I am speaking of, Mr. Potts was our family grocer, and he knew the exact cuts of roast beef and lamb which would bring joy to my father's heart, just as he was prepared for my mother's remonstrance when there was too much gristle. There used to be a family grocer, like Mr. Potts, in every American community. Then some genius in Memphis, Tennessee, came up with the Piggly-Wiggly, the first gigantic cash and carry where the customer waited on himself, and in no time there were chains of these supermarkets stretching across the country. Such consolidation as this has been going on in every aspect of business, and at a faster and faster tempo.

When I was a book salesman, an American book publisher who sold a million dollars' worth of his books in one year was doing quite a prosperous business. Today a publisher who sells only a million dollars' worth of books a year cannot afford to remain in business; he has to join forces with another and larger publisher so that their combined production will carry them over the break-even point.

In the nineteen-twenties almost every American city had two newspapers, and the larger ones had four or five, and there is no doubt that this competition for ideas, for stories, for the truth was a healthy thing for the community. Today most American communities are being served by a single paper.

Of the daily papers that were being published in this country in 1929, 45 per cent have either perished or been consolidated. This consolidation, this process of making big ones out of little ones, is a remorseless thing, and it may be a harmful thing if it tends to regiment our thinking.

We Americans have a remarkable capacity for ambivalence. On the one hand we like to enjoy the benefits of mass production, and on the other we like to assert our individual taste. Ever since the Civil War we have been exercising our genius to build larger and larger combines. Experience has taught us that when these consolidations grow to the size of a giant octopus, we have got to find someone to regulate them. When our railroads achieved almost insufferable power, we devised the Interstate Commerce Commission, and we eventually found in Joseph Eastman a regulator of impeccable integrity who knew as much as any railroad president. We have not had such good luck with our other regulatory agencies, as the recent ignoble record of the FCC makes clear. What troubles me most is their willingness to favor the pyramiding under a single ownership of television channels, radio stations, and newspapers. Isn't this the very monopoly they were supposed to avoid?

The empire builders, who were well on their way to a plutocracy, were brought within bounds by the first Roosevelt. Then under the second Roosevelt it was labor's turn, and in their bid for power they have raised the challenge of what regulations can be devised which will bring them to a clearer recognition of their national responsibility. In the not far future we can see another huge decision looming up: When atomic energy is harnessed for industrial use, will it be in the hands of a few private corporations or in a consolidation which the government will control? My point is that in the daily exposure to such bigness the individual is made to feel smaller than he used to be, smaller and more helpless than his father and grandfather before him.

In his book, *Reflections on America,* Jacques Maritain, the French philosopher, draws a sharp distinction "between the spirit of the American people and the logic of the superimposed structure or ritual of civilization." He speaks of "the state of tension, of hidden conflict, between this spirit of the people and this logic of the structure; the steady, latent rebellion of the spirit of the people against the logic of the structure." Maritain believes that the spirit of the American people is gradually overcoming and breaking the logic of their materialistic civilization. I should like to share his optimism, but first we have some questions to answer, questions about what the pressure of bigness is doing to American integrity and to American taste.

III

Henry Wallace has called this the century of the Common Man. Well, the longer I live in it the more I wonder whether we are producing the Uncommon Man in sufficient quantity. It seems to me regrettable that after a hundred years of public education we have produced such a demand for the lowest common denominator of emotionalism.

Am I, I sometimes wonder, a minority of one when I shudder at certain photographs in our pictorial magazines? The picture of a Negro being lynched; the picture of an airliner which has crashed and burned, with that naked body to the left identified as an opera singer whose voice we have all heard and loved; the picture of a grieving mother whose child has just been crushed in an automobile accident? Am I a minority of one in thinking that these are invasions of privacy, indecent and so shocking that we cringe from the sight?

Television, for which we once had such high hope, is constantly betrayed by the same temptation. It can rise magnificently to the occasion, as when it brought home to us the tragedy in Hungary, yet time and again its sponsored programs sink to a sodden level of brutality, shooting, and torture. And is there any other country in the world which would suffer through such incredible singing commercials as are flung at us? Does the language always have to be butchered for popular appeal, as when we are adjured to "live modern" and "smoke for real"? These are deliberate efforts to reduce a valuable medium to the level of the bobby-soxers.

There was a time when the American automobiles led the world in their beauty, diversity, and power, but the gaudy gondolas of today are an insult to the intelligence. In an era of close crowding when parking is an insoluble problem, it was sheer arrogance on the part of the Detroit designers to produce a car which was longer than the normal garage, so wasteful of gasoline, so laden with useless chromium and fantails that it costs a small fortune to have a rear fender repaired.

Is it inevitable in mass production that when you cater to the many, something has to give, and what gives is quality? I wonder if this has to be. I wonder if the great majority of the American people do not have more taste than they are credited with. The phenomenal increase in the sale of classical music recordings the moment they become available at mass production prices tells me that Americans will support higher standards when they are given the chance. I stress the aberration of taste in our time because I think it is something that does not have to be. The republic deserves better standards, not only for the elect, but straight across the board.

I wish that those who are dependent upon American taste would remember what Alexis de Tocqueville wrote a hundred and twenty-five years ago in his great book, *Democracy in America*. "When the conditions of society are becoming more equal," said Tocqueville, "and each individual man becomes more like all the rest, more weak and more insignificant, a habit grows up of ceasing to notice the citizens to consider only the people, and of overlooking individuals to think only of their kind."

It seems to me that our tastemakers have been guilty of this fallacy ever since the close of World War II. They have ceased to notice the citizens and consider only the people, just as Tocqueville warned. They no longer plan for the differences in individual taste, but think only of people in the mass.

In the years that followed the crash of 1929, Americans began to transfer their trust from big business to big government; if big business and banking, so ran the reasoning, could not be trusted to keep us out of depressions, perhaps big government could. Gradually in this emergency we began to shape up our version of the welfare state, a concept which was evolving in many parts of the Western world and to which both Democrats and Republicans are now committed.

A welfare state requires a big government with many bureaus, just as big government in its turn requires big taxes. We embarked on big government with the idea of safeguarding those segments of American society which were most in jeopardy, and now after twenty-five years of experimentation we are beginning to learn that the effects of big government upon the individual are both good and bad. It is good to provide the individual with security, and to give him the chance to adjust his special claims. But if we gain security, and sacrifice first venture and then initiative, we may find, as the Labor Party in England did, that we end with all too little incentive. As I travel this country since the war, I have the repeated impression that fewer and fewer young men are venturing into business on their own. More and more of them seek the safety of the big corporations. There are compelling reasons for this, the ever-shrinking margin of operating profit being the most insistent. But if we keep on trading independence and initiative for security, I wonder what kind of American enterprise will be left fifty years from now.

A subtle conditioning of the voter has been taking place during the steady build-up of big government. During the Depression and recovery we took our directives from Washington almost without question; so too during the war, when we were dedicated to a single purpose and when the leadership in Washington in every department was the best the nation could supply. But those in authority in these days are less sure. This administration has practiced a policy of nondisclosure toward the press and the electorate which has left the average citizen in a state of constant uncertainty. I have nothing but admiration for the dedication and stamina of Secretary Dulles, but I wish with all my heart that he had made our purpose and our commitments clearer for our allies and for our own people to understand. When we pulled that dam out from under Nasser's feet, we projected a crisis which must have come as a great shock to France and Britain. And how can we blame the young leaders of Hungary for misunderstanding the words "dynamic liberation" when we at home had no clear notion of what they meant? It was inexcusable not to have warned the American people that the Sputniks were coming and that greater exertions must be expected of us. This is no time for remoteness or for lulling slogans or for the avoidance of hard truths. The volume of material, the thousands of articles dealing with the great issues of today which are pouring into my office from unknown, unestablished writers, testifies to the conscientiousness and the courage of American thinking. The pity of it is that such people have not been taken more fully into the confidence of their own government.

IV

I have said that the concept of bigness has been an American ideal since our earliest times. I pointed to our propensity to build larger and larger combines ever since the Civil War, and how the process of consolidation has speeded up during the past thirty-five years. I suggested that we cannot have the fruits of mass production without suffering the effects of regimentation. And I ask that we look closely at what the pressure of bigness has done to American taste and opinion. Is the individual beginning to lose self-confidence and his independence? In short, how big is one?

One is as big as George F. Kennan, who believes that we cannot continue to live in this state of frozen belligerency in Europe.

One is as big as Omer Carmichael, the superintendent of schools in Louisville, Kentucky, who led the movement for voluntary integration in his border state.

One is as big as Frank Laubach, who believes in teaching the underdeveloped nations how to read their own languages, and then in supplying them with reading matter which will aid them to develop their farming and health.

One is as big as Linus Pauling, Harold C. Urey, and Robert Oppen-
heimer, who have never underestimated Russian scientific capacities,
who have always believed in the peaceful value of scientific exchange
and never ceased to struggle against fanaticism in secrecy and security.

One is as big as Edith Hamilton, the classicist, the lover of Greece
and of moderation; and as Alice Hamilton, her younger sister, who
pioneered in the dangerous field of industrial medicine.

One is as big as Sheldon and Eleanor Glueck, who for years have
been guiding lights in the resistant field of juvenile delinquency.

One is as big as Ralph Bunche and Eleanor Roosevelt.

One is as big as Louis M. Lyons, whose interpretation of the news
and whose judgment of the popular press have provided, in the words
of the Lauterbach Award, "a conscience for a whole profession."

One is as big as I. I. Rabi, a brilliant scientist and a passionate hu-
manist, who, on being asked how long it would take us to catch up to
Russia and to safeguard our long-range future, replied, "A generation. You know how long it takes to change a cultural pattern. The
growing general awareness of this need will help us, but nevertheless
we will have to work hard to succeed in a generation."

One is as big as Frederick May Eliot, president for twenty-one years
of the American Unitarian Association, who worked himself to the
bone for the deepening of faith and for reconciliation.

One is as big as you yourself can make it.

1959
THE PORCUPINES IN THE ARTICHOKES
by James Thurber

I HAVE writers the way other people have mice," a disturbed
hostess has written me. "What can I do to keep them from arguing, fighting, and throwing highball glasses after dinner? One
doesn't dare mention names, such as Herman Melville and Harold
Loeb, or the fight is on. What would you suggest?"

Well, now, it isn't easy to entertain writers and have any fun. You
might begin by saying, over the first cocktail, "I don't want any writers
to be mentioned this evening." Do not make the mistake of adding,
"From Washington Irving to Jack Kerouac," because that would instantly precipitate an argument about Washington Irving and Jack
Kerouac. You might begin by saying, "The porcupines are getting our
artichokes." This could, of course, lead to literary wrangling and jan-
gling, but everything is a calculated risk when writers are present,
even "My grandfather almost married a Pawnee woman," or "I won-

der if you gentlemen would help me put the handle back on my ice-box." A writer, of course, can turn anything at all into a literary dis-cussion, and it might be better not to say anything about anything.

I myself have found, or rather my wife has found, that you can sometimes keep writers from fighting by getting them into some kind of pencil-and-paper game. You could say, for example, "There are thirty-seven given names and nicknames, male and female, in the word 'miracle.' I want you all to see how many you can find." This almost always takes up a good hour, during which the writers are mercifully silent.

My wife, during a party in August, when writers are at their worst, brought out the pencils and paper and said, "I want you all to write down the names of as many animals and birds as you can think of with a double 'o' in their names." This worked fine for about half an hour, during which the literary men wrote down: moose, goose, mongoose, raccoon, baboon, loon, rook, coot, spoonbill, kangaroo, cockatoo, roos-ter, poodle, bloodhound, woodchuck, woodpecker, woodcock, whip-poorwill, and cuckoo.

The trouble started, as my wife should have known it would, when the papers were gathered up and the scoring began. Every writer, in a room full of writers, wants to be the best, and the judge, or umpire, or referee is soon overwhelmed and shouted down like a chickadee trying to take charge of a caucus of crows. Nobody can ever remember exactly what happened at any drinking party invaded and taken over by writers, because, as the bowl continues to flow, their eloquence and invention take on the sharp edge of temper and cussedness. My wife gave up the hopeless task of scoring and turned it over to a lawyer guest when the question of the validity of habitat names set all the crows to cawing at once. It was decided that brook trout, moor hen, stool pigeon, and the like were out. Then there turned up, on this paper and that, what the lawyer, raising his voice, called behavior names — whooping crane, which was allowed after near fisticuffs, hoot owl, which also made it, and moo cow, which was shouted down, along with brood mare. The lawyer-judge, full of Scotch and a love of definition, tried to put into separate categories saber-toothed tiger, hooded falcon, smooth-haired fox terrier, hookworm and bookworm, hoop snake and coon dog, and it was soon evident that the task of arbiter was too much for him.

There are always two or three writers, in this kind of game, who deliberately louse things up by taking and holding an untenable posi-tion. One of these obstinate fellows had written down pool shark, and another had come up with booze hound, and they defended their stand on the ground that my wife, in the beginning, had not stipulated *real* animals and birds. The shouting about this died down when micro-organism turned up on the paper of a stuffy textbook writer, who defended it on the ground that a double "o" is a double "o" whether hyphenated or not. Everybody turned on him, and somebody threw an ash tray.

At this point my wife drew me aside, which isn't easy to do at a yelling party, since I am a writer, too, and told me, "You'll simply have to get them to singing." I tried to get them to singing, but it was no good, because the whooping-crane man and the brook-trout man suddenly began attacking each other's books, viewpoint, style, and implementation. In a sense, the crane of whooping crane and the brook of brook trout saved the situation, if wreckage can be saved by further wreckage. All of a moment a whooping literary argument was on. It concerned the merits and demerits of Rupert Brooke, Stephen Crane, Tennyson's "The Brook" and Tennyson himself, Hart Crane, and Bret Harte; also *The Heart of the Matter, The Heart is a Lonely Hunter,* and *The Death of the Heart,* thus involving Graham Greene, Carson McCullers, Elizabeth Bowen, Kenneth Grahame, *The Wind in the Willows, Gone with the Wind,* Kenneth Tynan, Kenneth Burke, *A Biography of Kit Carson,* Burke's Speech on Conciliation with the Colonies, Marc Connelly, Mark Sabre, *If Winter Comes,* Robert Frost, W. H. Auden, J. D. Salinger, *J.B.,* A. E. Housman, AE, A. J. Liebling, *B.F.'s Daughter,* and, if my memory serves, Herman Melville, Harold Loeb, Washington Irving, and Jack Kerouac.

That night three highball glasses, two friendships, and a woman's heart were broken. There is really only one safe rule for a hostess to go by. Do not ask writers to your house, especially in the summer, and in three other seasons of the year — spring, autumn, and winter.

I was going to end my advice to hostesses on that wintry note, but after tossing and turning in bed for two or three minutes one night, which is all I can do at my age without falling asleep, I decided that I had not been helpful enough to the lady in distress who wrote me. She should, then, hide any flat package a writer brings to her party. It is likely to contain a long-playing record which he intends to plop on her phonograph when everybody else wants to argue, and there are things worse than writers' arguing, such as a recording, in Ooglala Sioux, of a group of Indian squaws chanting in an endless monotone, with a background of tom-toms, a dirge mourning the miscarriage of a chief's daughter or daughter-in-law. If it isn't that, it will be a recording of "The Waste Land" in Gaelic, or a recitation of "Evangeline" by the writer's five-year-old niece. Don't let your writer guests get their teeth into poetry, for God's sake. Prose is bad enough, but poetry is worse. Somebody is sure to misquote "Under a spreading chestnut tree," by changing the "a" to "the," and the hecklers will be at him like dogs on a bone. Somebody will then bet somebody else that he can't correctly finish "The light that never was . . ." and he will be right, because the challenged man will say, "on land or sea," when it is really "on sea or land." The hostess should conceal all flat packages and return them later, the later the better.

It is high time that a note of hope, or at least of wan cheerfulness, creep into this discourse. Don't get the idea that writers never agree about anything, because they do, approximately twice during the course of an eight-hour evening. Their form of agreement goes roughly like this: "You are right, you are right, you are absolutely right! The trouble is, you don't have the vaguest idea why you *are*." The writer who is thus agreed with will, of course, disagree with the agreer, like this: "You are completely wrong, and so was I. It is remarkable how you always reveal the weakness of a point by insisting that it is well taken." Here the point, whatever it may have been, is lost sight of in an exchange of what might be called abstract double talk, or backfiring Dada. Now nobody in the room knows what the writers are not talking about, including the two men themselves.

My experience of writers at parties goes back to the year that *Jurgen* was published and has been confined to endless talkers born between the years 1885 and 1905, the wives of some of whom have not got in more than ninety words edgewise since 1922 — at parties, that is. When the writer husband is hung over, the wife is allowed to talk, and she often does, though knowing full well that her spouse isn't paying any attention. The literary men roughly in my age group become more articulate, and less coherent, as the years go on, but their age does not keep them away from parties. Now and then those who are in their sixties or seventies confuse *Spoon River Anthology* with *Of Time and the River*, but otherwise it is hard to tell them from the younger men.

Among the American writers I have stayed up with all night were — to name only those who are, alas, no longer with us — Robert Benchley, Heywood Broun, Scott Fitzgerald, Thomas Wolfe, and Sinclair Lewis. Benchley was, as everybody knows who knew him, the Great Companion, who often talked about the mystery and lure of heaven when the bright stars were waning. Broun was usually in some area of politics, justice, and fair play. Once, around two in the morning, he asked me not to cross a picket line that had been set up in front of Twenty-One, and I had to tell him that that was where we were. "Under the circumstances then," he said in that unforgettable voice, "I think we should have another drink." Fitzgerald talked about the dear dead past, the Unattained and the Unattainable, for he was the romantic to the end, and the farthest removed of all male writers from such subjects as the conquest of an old-time movie actress in the back seat of a Hupmobile in the year when Teddy Roosevelt stood at Armageddon and battled for the Lord. Wolfe discoursed for twelve hours about love, and writing (his own), and Carolina. Lewis was all over the written and unwritten areas of his time, and went in for some excellent mimicry of his colleagues. All these unforgettable nights except one — I met the wondrous Sinclair Lewis in Bermuda — were spent in New York City. In London, the British writers have a strange way of going home from a party before daybreak, and the one whose early departure I always most regret is Compton Mackenzie, as good an actor and imitator as he is a writer, whose impersonation of Wordsworth I would go three thousand miles to see, and have more than once.

It was the late incomparable John McNulty who had the perfect answer to the problems of the writer-beleaguered hostess. McNulty was a piano-playing man, and he once said, "The thing to do in mixed company is play *Dear Old Girl.*" He would stop the fight about Jim Tully or James Branch Cabell by going to the piano and sliding into *Dear Old Girl* in his famous silent-movie-theater style, and every guy in the room between the ages of eighteen and eighty would lean on the piano and join in the chorus. That undying song, first published in 1903, I think, leads naturally into *Let Me Call You Sweetheart, I Want a Girl Just Like the Girl, Down by the Old Mill Stream,* and all the rest, with no space for rock and roll, or rockers and rollers, or for the voices of writers raised in argument instead of melody.

Let me, in conclusion, assure the distraught hostess that some of my best friends are writers, and adjure her, for God's sake, not to bring them and me together at a party at her house. We write such lovely letters to each other, it would be a shame to spoil it.

1960
THE COST OF SECRECY
by I. I. Rabi

THOSE of us who travel abroad and have the problem of representing the United States in one way or another are often taken aback at the degree and intensity of criticism which is directed both at our actions and at the statements of some of our political figures. No such intense criticism is directed at the Soviet Union for acts compared with which our own slips would seem to be minor. At first sight, the criticism which holds us to a stricter accounting seems unfair. However, if one probes more deeply, this attitude is quite natural.

We must understand that we occupy an entirely different position in the world from that of the Russians. Not only is the United States the leader of the Western world, but to an extent greater than we realize, the United States is the leader of the whole world. Beneath the scoffing, mocking, and hostility of the Communist world, there is nevertheless a deep respect. America is the ideal, not only materially but in most elements of existence which human beings share in common. If America were to disappear, there would be no embodiment of the Russian goal, no one to catch up with and surpass. For these reasons, when we fall short of the high standards which we and the world have set for us, the failure is felt very deeply. The elevated and rarefied moral atmosphere in which we are supposed to live may be a bit hard on us plain folks here at home, but it is the role which we have assumed and the role which we have to play.

If one can be certain of anything in the uncertain course of events in this decade of the sixties it is this: the moment the United States stops supplying leadership, the world as we know it will disintegrate and fragment into chaos, with no one but the Russians to pick up the pieces. We therefore have a moral obligation to be wise, in order to guide ourselves and others, and to be prosperous, so that we can spare from our own supplies to help others. We seem to have found a way to be prosperous, and now we ask ourselves, How can we cultivate wisdom in policy and action, especially in the field of atomic energy for war and peace, which is so central to all our problems?

As I review the fifteen years which have passed since the end of World War II, I am forced to the conclusion that many of our difficulties stem from one fundamental distortion of our natural habit: the distortion caused by the exaggerated secrecy in the military field, and in the atomic field especially. All will agree that these fields are central to our problems of foreign and domestic policy, but one may well ask why I regard secrecy, which seems so necessary, as being at the same time so very damaging.

The answer lies in our history and our tradition. We are a pluralistic society dedicated to a distribution both of authority and responsibility. We have always been against concentration of power in Washington, whether in the hands of the President or lesser public officials. The pressure of events has compelled a greater and greater concentration of power, but it has been granted most grudgingly. To some, the weakness of our central government is a source of regret, but there is no doubt as to the general public feeling. Washington is and always has been suspect.

Although the Constitution vests control of foreign policy firmly in the hands of the President, in actual fact the President does not operate in a vacuum. He must share his responsibilities with the Senate and with the House of Representatives. Agencies of the government, in addition to the Department of State, are directly concerned; the Department of Defense and the Atomic Energy Commission are the most important. Beyond these, there are other agencies, but almost as important are the press — the daily, weekly, and monthly periodicals — television, and radio. Behind these are the opinion makers in the universities, in the labor unions, in large and small business, and, of newer importance, the scientists and experts of every variety.

Policy comes out as a harmony produced by all these interacting forces, each contributing after its own unique fashion. This has been the American tradition and practice. Now, what happens when secrecy intervenes? Pathetic and profound ignorance of the facts in their proper context does not prevent the policy makers outside of government from carrying on in the field of atomic energy as if all were clear to them. They gather a rumor here, a leak there, and off they go. Ignorant or learned, they take a stand, and public opinion is formed.

Our government cannot act strongly without ample support from public opinion. For wise action, an informed public opinion is necessary. When secrecy intervenes, an informed public opinion can hardly exist. Too often we have, instead, a manipulated public opinion formed by leaks, half-truths, innuendoes, and sometimes by outright distortion of the actual facts.

One would think that the policy makers within the various departments and agencies of government would be free of the disabilities which afflict the unanointed without. Not at all. Under the sensible doctrine that a secret shared by many is no secret at all, a person is admitted to a share of classified information under the rubric "need to know." For years after the war, this doctrine was interpreted so as to keep information about atomic weapons from the military other than the highest officers, which often meant from the officers who did the actual planning. The difficulty of secrecy within the government is that, unless administered with the greatest wisdom, it furthers confusion, which comes from ignorance or partial knowledge, and often results in inaction or unwise acts. The farcical snafu of the U-2 incident with all its overtones of tragedy shows how great the costs of secrecy can be, even in the highest echelons of government.

We can now ask ourselves, What have we really gained from our exaggerated secrecy in the way of real security? Actually, very little. The Russians are not far behind us in atomic weapons, but our allies have been left way behind, after expending an enormous treasure in trying to rediscover facts and techniques already known to the Russians as well as to ourselves. The secrets of military technology must be as highly protected as any trade secrets, but only as long as they are real secrets. In most cases, this time is measured in years rather than in decades. Although most policy makers, amateur or professional, are not deeply interested in or capable of judging the technological situation, secrecy results in frustration, doubt, and timidity about the exercise of any independent judgment. The result has been that a number of less inhibited men of greater or lesser scientific or technical accomplishment, but with a low boiling point, have been gaining the public ear on the basis of prestige acquired through a technical accomplishment, quite limited in scope. Their policy statements are given weight on the basis of skills not necessarily relevant to the dread subjects of war and peace, which they discuss with easy confidence. Were it not for the secrecy which hides the hard core of the matter, the intelligent public would be quite capable of judging the questions under discussion. The fear of being guilty of a judgment based on a partial knowledge of the facts misleads many judicious people into accepting judgments by others whose knowledge is often even more partial but which extends into the dread domain of the top-secret.

The questions which should concern the informed nontechnical general opinion are such questions as: How many weapons do we actually have? What are their means of delivery? What are the effects of these weapons? What is the composition of the stockpile in the range of yields and sizes? How much do they cost? Who controls them, and by what means are they controlled? What are claimed to be the further needs for nuclear and other weapons, and what is the justification? What do we know about the state of weapons in other countries?

The answer to every one of these questions falls under a high degree of classification. Some of them have this classification for very good reasons, and others merely from force of habit. One can nevertheless ask, How can the publisher, editor, commentator, or editorial writer of an important organ influential in informing and shaping public opinion carry on in an intelligent way without a fairly full knowledge of these and other facts?

Most of the fog which surrounds these matters serves only to confuse the American citizenry. Actually, a great deal of information concerning the general questions I have raised is in the public domain. The general budget of the Atomic Energy Commission is known, and the ambitious newspaperman can learn a great deal from it. The services in their rival claims do, in the end, tell a great deal about their military secrets, and the practiced eye can discern this information. In the same way, other important secrets do leak out, bit by bit. It is hard to believe that foreign governments, friendly or hostile, have not given these matters, as they appear in public documents, very close study; they therefore must possess fairly reliable estimates. Our press could do likewise, but the fact is that it has not availed itself of the wealth of material which already exists. The reason for these inhibitions can best be discovered by members of the fourth estate.

We have been engaged in tripartite negotiations with the Soviets and the United Kingdom on a test suspension coupled with a system of inspection. Clearly, this is a most delicate matter, perhaps best left to the wisdom of the President and his most trusted advisers who have access to full information. Nevertheless, it was not left to the President, and public debate, which impairs the freedom of action of the President, has been raging over the land. This would be the right thing if the debate were well informed. Unfortunately, when the debate is not well informed it becomes a conflict of pressure groups rather than a quest for clarity and wisdom.

To live at peace with the atom, we must find our way back to the fundamental principles on which this republic was founded. We must again become a nation of free men informed by a free press. Since the very beginning, we have been told that this is a dangerous doctrine. In about a century and three quarters of national existence, we have learned to live dangerously in a dynamic society. Totalitarian countries preserve their secrecy by regimenting their people, giving them neither freedom of travel, freedom of the press, freedom of conscience, nor freedom of opinion. Some may envy their secrecy, but no one will envy their lives.

Our ancient freedoms also entail responsibilities and can be exercised successfully only by people who have learned how to handle freedom over a long period of time. We must not let this skill atrophy for want of use while pursuing the phantom of security through secrecy.

1961
THE NATURE OF THE ARTIST
by Catherine Drinker Bowen

MUSIC has been, and is, the happiest single factor of my life. More than once I have testified in print to the joys of sitting in the second fiddler's chair and following, under the lamp, players more skillful than I by far, but equal in their love of chamber music and their willingness to keep on playing until two in the morning. Star events in my life were playing Mozart string quintets with Piatagorsky, quartets with Sidney Griller and with Boris Croyt of the Budapest. I know why these brilliant players let me sit in with them, and it has little to do with the fact that I spent, long ago, four years at music school, two at the Peabody Institute in Baltimore and two at the Juilliard in New York. The reason I am made part of these delightful sessions is that the musicians have read my books. And they have not hesitated to tell me so: "I read your John Adams book and I wanted to see what you were like."

There is more than one road to Elysium, and, as Francis Bacon said, the fairer path is longer about. If musicians do me the honor to be curious about me, it is as nothing compared with my curiosity concerning musicians. Biographers, by their very nature, want to know everything about everybody, dead or alive. With me the appetite has centered on the genus lawyer and the genus musician. While I was writing the biographies of Tchaikovsky and the brothers Anton and Nicholas Rubinstein, I became familiar with many great musicians of the past — not only famous virtuosos, celebrated performers, and conductors of orchestras, but men and women of the profession who truly loved to make music, and said so. I think of Borodin, the composer who, when he was a medical student, played string quartets once a week, and used to walk seven Russian miles with his cello, not being able to afford cab fares. Then there was Paderewski's teacher, Theodor Leschetizky. To Leschetizky it was incomprehensible that a musician could be without music even for a day. (Incidentally, his dog was named Solo.) Leschetizky could not keep away from music. On entering the room he sometimes played a chord on the piano, as if to say good morning, and on leaving, to say good-by. Once, when a talented pupil and her sister were going away, after a visit to his house, Leschetizky helped them pack, then exclaimed, "But you haven't said good-by to the piano!" Seeing they were hurried, Leschetizky went to the piano himself and played a joyous little good-by, adding, "It will be several days before you can hear a piano again."

Musicians have a lighthearted way of identifying music with the events and associations of their daily lives. Take Karl Maria von Weber, who composed so many charming waltzes. Weber and his close friend, Gansbacher, when writing to each other, always referred to their several lady friends by musical keys: "I see or hear nothing of D minor; she is quite dead to me, which causes me heartfelt regret. F major has disappeared altogether." I think of Henry Purcell in the seventeenth century, who wrote such truly enchanting music. When Purcell published his book of *Sonatas a Tré* — those beautiful sonatas for two violins and harpsichord — he wrote in the preface, "The Author heartily wishes that his Book may fall into no other hands but theirs who carry musical Souls about them."

People who carry musical souls about them are, I think, more receptive than others. They smile more readily. One feels in them a pleasing propensity toward the lesser sins, a pleasing readiness also to admit the possibility that on occasion they may be in the wrong, they may be mistaken.

II

What is the motivation that lies behind great art? What propels the artist to his work? What keeps him on the track, that extraordinary track from which nothing can divert him? Is it circumstance; is it something in the original gene? While I was studying for the biographies of Tchaikovsky and the Rubinsteins, I read what material I could find about genius, from graphs drawn up in university laboratories to Santayana on aesthetics and to Freud and others in psychiatry. I found no satisfactory answer. So I turned to a study of the lives of artists, of the conditions under which men produce their best work and function at their highest and happiest. I noted especially the artist's concept of himself, his confessed estimate of his powers, his personal morality and outlook on his world.

Critics are prodigal with notions as to what motivated certain compositions of the masters. Brahms's biographers have said that he wrote such and such music because he was "grieving over Clara Schumann," Robert Schumann's wife, with whom Brahms was in love for years. Maybe the critics were right. But what Brahms himself said at the time was, "Some of my best ideas come to me while I am brushing my shoes before dawn."

I think he was serious when he said it. I heard a magnificent painter say that she got her best ideas while she was taking her bath before breakfast. Many years ago, Theodore Roethke, the distinguished poet, told me that in order to write poetry he had to have, when he got up in the morning, "a sense of well-being."

I think I know what he meant — a sense of his powers serving him, pulling together with all their native force. Whether a person is endowed with big powers or little powers, he has to feel confidence, complete and functioning. This sense of well-being has little to do with happiness, as the world counts happiness. Poets, novelists, even historians, sometimes write from a sense of desperation, pour it out, and thus get rid of it. Observe for a moment that gloomy Scotsman, Thomas Carlyle (I happen to be his fervent admirer). In 1835, Carlyle was in London working on his history of the French Revolution — two volumes filled with life, color, movement. "The great difficulty," Carlyle wrote in his diary, "is to keep oneself in right balance, not despondent, not exasperated, defiant, free and clear."

While I was writing *Yankee from Olympus,* I typed that out and tacked it over my desk. Now let me give you the rest of Carlyle's paragraph: "defiant, free and clear. . . . Nevertheless," he says, "it is now some three-and-twenty months since I have earned one penny by the craft of literature. I have been ready to work. I know no fault I have committed. To ask able editors to employ me will not improve but worsen matters. I am like a spinster, waiting to be married. . . . Write then and complain of nothing — defy all things. In this humour I write my book, without hope of it, except of *being done with it.*"

Now, I suspect that Carlyle was not quite as depressed after he wrote those lines as before. Artists have a way of making gloomy, desperate confessions in diaries, and writing gloomy, desperate letters to their friends, about how they will never be able to finish this book or this symphony. Then they go back to work with the greatest zest. There is excitement in the very act of composition. Some of you know this at first hand — a deep satisfaction when the thing begins to take shape. Actually, I wonder if life holds a deeper satisfaction. If Carlyle wrote his book "without hope of it, except of being done with it," that still gave room for quite a lot of hope. The time when an artist truly despairs is when in his work he falls short, knows himself blocked, stopped, helpless, and has no hope of "being done with it," almost as if breath itself had been cut off. One feels sorry for Rameau, the composer, as he grew old. "From day to day my taste improves," he said. "But I have lost all my genius."

III

I have noted that, barring accidents, artists whose powers wear best and last longest are those who have trained themselves to work under adversity. I am impressed by the really formidable discipline under which great artists operate. I do not refer here to moral discipline, or the pleasing virtues which lead to good citizenship. I mean artistic discipline — discipline with regard to working hours, a hoarding of themselves so they can pour it out where it really counts. Great artists treasure their time with a bitter and snarling miserliness. Tchaikovsky, for example, was a man of much charm and friendliness. People used to follow him around town. Everybody wanted him at parties, and Tchaikovsky liked parties. In 1937 I was in Russia and visited Klin, outside Moscow, where Tchaikovsky had a country villa. I saw a sign which used to hang outside the gate. It read: "P.I. Tchaikovsky. Receives Mondays and Thursdays, 3 to 5. Not at home. Please do not ring."

I think the world at large has little conception of how hard great artists work. You can say they are driven, you can say they are inspired. One thing is sure: from an early age they are aware of their natural endowments. I know of not one first-rate talent who was not — or is not — entirely conscious of his gifts. If anyone called him genius to his face, he would look uncomfortable and probably be rude. Stanislavsky, the great theatrical producer, said, "Only home-made geniuses boast of their nearness to Apollo, of their all-embracing inner fire." When Johann Sebastian Bach was asked the secret of his mastery, he replied, "I worked hard." Charles Darwin and Sir Isaac Newton had similar answers to that question. Some of the classic composers acknowledged their talent with a splendid simplicity. "I know," said Haydn, "that God has bestowed a talent upon me, and I thank Him for it." Someone protested the gaiety of Haydn's church music. "I cannot help it," Haydn replied. "I give forth what is in me. When I think of the Divine Being, my heart is so full of joy that the notes fly off as from a spindle. And as I have a cheerful heart, He will pardon me if I serve Him cheerfully."

Haydn had a personal habit, as a composer, which, when I read about it years ago, clarified a number of things for me. As a beginner, I was fearful of the act of writing. To sit down at the typewriter, alone in the room, and start a book or a chapter or a short story seemed to me a terrifying act of presumption, though a thrilling one. I used to get all dressed up, at eight o'clock in the morning or earlier, put on my good suit, good shoes, lipstick, everything, and sit solemnly down at my desk on the third floor. I remember one Saturday my daughter of eight dashed in and found me at the typewriter, thus accoutered. She said, "Ma, you going someplace this morning?" I told her I hoped so, I hoped so indeed. She understood, and laughed, and left the room.

It was during those early, tentative days that I read how Joseph Haydn, when he sat down to compose, used to put on full court regalia, gold-braided coat, buckled shoes, and a diamond ring which the Emperor had given him. It was certainly arguing from the sublime to the ridiculous. Yet if Joseph Haydn was awe-struck before the act of composition, then C. D. Bowen surely had a right to shake in her shoes. Haydn's character was like his music, the more intimately you know it, the more you love and admire. Before he was sixty, Haydn never traveled, but lived quietly on the estate of his patron, Prince Esterházy, and wrote innumerable pieces for water parties, balls, and family birthdays. But when Prince Esterházy died, Salomon, the violin virtuoso, hurried to Vienna and urged Haydn to tour Europe with him. They would play in every important city of the Continent — a dazzling prospect. Haydn's friends worried, because Haydn was an unworldly soul, and they wondered how he would handle himself. Mozart especially was uneasy. "Papa," Mozart said, "Papa Haydn, you have no training for the great world, and you speak few languages." "Ach!" Haydn said. "My language is understood all over the world."

When Haydn was an old man, he made his last public appearance. It was in Vienna, in 1808, and his choral work, *The Creation,* was given before a brilliant audience. When the singers reached the passage, "And there was light," the audience burst into applause. Haydn, overcome with excitement, exclaimed aloud, "Not I, but a power from above created that."

Artists, writers, even great philosophers, are sometimes quite ingenuous about their powers, indignantly surprised when someone does not recognize them for what they are. One of the stories I like best is about Schopenhauer. Not an endearing character, certainly, but hardly one to ignore. Apparently Schopenhauer ate, quantitatively, like an elephant. One day a young man, an admirer, came to lunch, and sat marveling at the philosopher's capacity. The young man stayed for supper, and the sage went at it as if he had not been fed in a week. Finally the young man said, "Sir, why do you eat so much?"

"I eat a great deal," Schopenhauer replied, "because I am a great man."

Your great artist looks on his talent as a responsibility laid on him by God, or perhaps a curse set on him by the devil. Whichever way he looks at it, while he is writing that book or composing that symphony, Doom hangs over him. He is afraid something will interfere to stop him. Tchaikovsky was forever writing to his friends, "I fear that I shall die with my music in me." Artists often think they are going to die before their time. They seem to possess a heightened sense of the passing of the hours. In psychiatric terms I have heard this described as guilt, under the theory that artistic creation is a lifelong, recurring act of expiation. This is hard for me to accept. I think rather that artists dread death because they love life. Artists have so much to do and so little time to do it! Joseph Conrad was convinced that he would die early, although there was nothing wrong with his health. He bemoaned this sad, oncoming fate — and lived to a ripe enough age. Do you remember the *New Yorker* profile of William Faulkner some years ago? Walking along New York city streets, Faulkner would look over his shoulder. "I got a Doom follerin' me," he said.

It is amusing to observe the ways and means used to ward off the evil eye. Tchaikovsky was convinced that he dare not let himself look for success at the next concert. He was aware that his new symphony was good; he did not doubt it. But at the first performance, something would surely go wrong. The audience would be filled with his sworn enemies, or the timpani player would be late with his roll, the cymbalist would let go two bars early. When Tchaikovsky conducted the orchestra himself, he suffered from a neurotic fear that his head would fall off. He had an awkward time, holding it down with one hand while he conducted with the other. I used to try it, while I was writing his biography.

Nineteenth-century romanticists indulged, I believe, in the loudest moans on record. Among these romantics, Wagner yelled more agonizingly than any. Have you read his letters to Liszt, written when Wagner was young, living in exile? Here is a sample: "Everything seems so waste, so waste, so waste! Dearest friend, art, with me, after all, is a pure stopgap, nothing else. A stopgap in order to live at all. It is therefore with genuine despair that I always resume art. The only thing I want is *money;* that, at least, one ought to be able to get. *Love* I abandon, and *art!*"

Now, guess how the next sentence reads: "Well, the *Rheingold* is ready, readier than I ever thought it would be. I went to this music with so much faith, so much joy. And with a true fury of despair I continued, and have at last finished it."

Your true artist, let us note, always does finish. Sometimes he rages, like Wagner. Sometimes he finishes in serenity, and writes at the bottom of his music paper, like Palestrina and Bach, the words *Soli Dei Gloria.* But he finishes. This is not to say that great artists are never blocked in their inspiration. On the contrary, they can be temporarily put off by failure, by success, by illness, by disappointment, or perhaps by some difficulty intrinsic to the composition itself, one of those snags, those compositional pitfalls that lie in wait on every page. Robert Frost once told me he could not write if he heard that somebody had said something mean about him.

IV

All artists quiver under the lash of adverse criticism. Rachmaninoff's first symphony was a failure. So Rachmaninoff took sick and lay around on sofas for a year, without writing one measure of music. He was twenty-two at the time. But he recovered, and wrote much music. When Beethoven heard that a certain conductor refused to perform one of his symphonies, he went to bed and stayed there until the symphony was performed. Charles Dickens was forever defending himself against criticism, writing letters to the press and protesting that he was misunderstood. Yet neither criticism nor misunderstanding stopped his output. "Dickens," said G. K. Chesterton, "was the character whom anybody can hurt and nobody can kill."

The recovery is what counts, not the illness. Certain artists work better when they are in rebellion against something or other — against the society in which they live, against their immediate boss if they have one, or their wife or their husband or their best friend. Such a person enjoys all the arrogance of opposition, with little to lose. That of course is one reason why success is a danger — it doubles the risk.

To do their best work, different personalities require differing degrees of hardship or ease. William James has pointed this out eloquently in his *Varieties of Religious Experience.* "Some men and women there are who can live on smiles and the word 'yes' forever," James says. "For others, this is too tepid and relaxed a moral climate. Some austerity and wintry negativity, some roughness, danger, stringency and effort, some no! no! must be mixed in, to produce the sense of an existence with character and texture and power. The range of individual difference," he says, "in this respect is enormous; but whatever the mixture of yesses and noes may be, the person is infallibly aware when he has struck it in the right proportion *for him.* 'This,' he feels, 'is my proper vocation, this is the *optimum*, the law, the life for me to live. Here I find the degree of equilibrium, safety, calm, and leisure which I need, or here I find the challenge, passion, fight and hardship without which my soul's energy expires.' "

As a biographer, I am always curious to see how a talented man reacts to his first great success. I once heard a psychiatrist say that he had seen more people break down after success than after failure. Woodrow Wilson remarked that many a man has been ruined by his secondary successes. Young artists in particular, I think, can be thus diverted, pushed off their true road by the praise of friends and neighbors. Brahms wrote to his publisher, concerning Max Bruch, the composer. "Bruch is shortsighted. He sees only to the next laurel wreath."

Johannes Brahms wrote enough string quartets, he said, to paper his room. Of these he submitted only three for publication, the three that we know. One night in a Vienna café, a young composer was complaining of the poor reception his first opera had had from the critics. "Ach!" Brahms said. "It is customary to drown the first litter."

Brahms had a right to say it; he had destroyed his own offspring when he considered them unworthy. The point to bear in mind, I think, is that, to hit the target, a man has to shoot off much ammunition. One of the marks of true genius is a quality of abundance. A rich, rollicking abundance, enough to give indigestion to ordinary people. Great artists turn it out in rolls, in swatches. They cover whole ceilings with paintings, they chip out a mountainside in stone, they write not one novel but a shelf full. It follows that some of their work is better than other. As much as a third of it may be pretty bad. Shall we say this unevenness is the mark of their humanity — of their proud mortality as well as of their immortality?

The stories I have told here are an illustration of the artist and his nature — of the artist's faith in himself, of his defiance of society when it does not serve his art, of his self-discipline, his self-indulgence, his golden humor, or his nervous lack of humor on occasion. Most of the men whom I mentioned lived in times past. Yet I cannot think the artist's nature has changed in a mere century or two, or that it will change. It is the environment that changes. If Picasso paints a *Guernica,* it is because Picasso lives in times of horror and despair. If sculptured man is distorted in iron and stone, it is because the artist has reason to see him as distorted. In the discord and formlessness of modern music we hear and feel the harshness of man's present fate.

These pictures and this music are not pretty. Let us take pride, however, that in America the artist is free to express reality as he sees it. But freedom for the artist, as for anyone else, is an evanescent thing. Overnight it can vanish. A sense of freedom, the sense of well-being that Theodore Roethke spoke of, is partly contingent on the poet's assurance that his environment *respects* his art, holds it high in estimation — as high, for instance, as it holds science, the launching of satellites, or important journeys to the moon.

1962
CANADIAN SPRING
by Sheila Burnford

OUR heralds of spring in northwest Canada bear no resemblance to the traditional and seldom inspire the poet within us: no primroses, lambs, or forsythia here, no tender green over the earth and soft unfolding buds. Instead we have the ice-breaker battering a channel through the ice cap, smelt running in snow-swollen creeks, frost boils erupting on the roads, municipal drains backing up, and finally an inch-by-inch clearing of the snow-drifts in the garden until the exhausted daffodils push their way through the ironbound earth at last — in June. One's whole soul cries out for spring hats and blossom, new-mown grass, the mayfly hatch, the first young tender morels; instead one pokes ineffectually with a stick at overflowing gutters, yearns over the etiolated narcissus brought up from the cellar, and plucks not primroses but long-lost overshoes and last year's oyster shells from the snow receding at the porch.

In the first week of May, Susan and I reach the peak of delayed-spring frustration, and on a morning when the returning geese fly low over the city in an exultant, baying, clamorous pack, we receive their message especially loud and clear, for we are on our way to Whitefish, to the little hunting cabin on the shore of a lonely, hill-ringed lake, peaceful and timeless: Susan to paint and I to potter; Raimie, my Labrador, to escort us and investigate possible strange noises in the night. We have discarded our families for the weekend.

The track down the hillside to the cabin turns into a fast-running creek at this time of year, carrying off the melting snow from the hills, but the ground is hard and frozen, and the car coasts down in a childishly satisfying welter of flying spray. We leave it in a clearing, load ourselves up like pack mules, then walk or stagger the last quarter of a mile. The trail winds through spruce and poplar, the branches interlaced overhead, and always I come upon the little cabin crouched by the water's edge long before I am prepared for it, so secretly does it seem to camouflage itself against the background of trees. Weather-beaten and gray, wearing its roof and chimney slightly askew, its one half-lidded eye bleary from the winter's gales, it huddles like some shabby, eccentric old woman on a park bench in spring, blinking in the sunshine; and around her skirts, instead of cheeping sparrows, the peaty brown snow creeks make little murmurous singing sounds.

We open the door, and then, as quickly as possible, the window, when the familiar stuffy, sunbaked smell of mouse nests, straw, waders, and mud-encrusted gunnysacks hits us. The boats are stored there, and we haul out the light punt, then the heavy freight canoe, and a tangled mass of decrepit reed blinds — all the paraphernalia of last fall's hunting; sweep out the first layer of powdered mud and little fluffy piles of duck and partridge feathers; then, lastly, after tossing for the victim, out go all the visible mouse corpses, hurled into the bush, from where they are conscientiously retrieved by the dog and returned to the steps. We leave the door and windows open to the cold sweet northern air; then, mutually unenthusiastic about housework at any time, we call it a day and sit on the wooden steps, at peace with the world, a bottle of beer apiece, so sheltered from the wind and warm in the noon sun that we take off our heavy sweaters and roll up our shirt sleeves.

Almost immediately the cabin's own particular chipmunk appears on the lower branches of an ash, rather leaner than usual after the winter, but recognizable at once by his unusually stubby tail and exuberant personality. He resumes the teasing of the dog from where he left off last November, chattering excitedly. Raimie rises to his baiting like a trout to a fly and is soon reduced to hysterical, impotent rage, until at last the chipmunk becomes a little too bold and is chased up a flue pipe lying under the cabin. A brief but blessed silence follows, until Raimie's eyes close and the next round starts. This has gone on for years.

II

The ice is going out on the lake, and there is open water before us for about a hundred yards from the shoreline, edged by a new high bank of turf and reeds built up through the winter by ice pressure. The marsh water close in reflects a sky pierced with reed stalks and patterned with a faint constant movement of infinitesimal bubble rings, but out beyond the channel little rippling waves lap greedily against the ice stretching across the lake to the far shore — gray, sodden ice, heavy with age, the darkness of the imprisoned water lying shadowlike a few inches below the surface. There is no hint of green yet in the hills beyond — rather, a quickening of purple; and the three long plumes of the waterfall are vivid and white even at this distance.

The first frog chorus tunes up in the bulrushes a few feet from where we sit, and the mallards who were disturbed at our coming return in quacking pairs to the open water. Four whistlers pass like children's bath toys drawn on a string, line astern, three drakes and a demure little hen leading. One drake is courting extravagantly, head bobbing and turning from side to side to a slow beat of six, then a fantastic arching of neck to twist his head back down the length of his body; but the little hen is not impressed by these contortions and swims on unheeding. The other two watch admiringly, then suddenly rise in unison and fly off with faint despondent cries; and so relieved by their departure apparently is the hen that she turns and acknowledges at last her exhibitionist suitor. They glide and posture in an endless fascinating ritual, the handsome drake in shining black and white, the drab little hen.

A long raft of ice and twigs sails by in a sudden gust of wind, with six mallard passengers aboard; sober and serious as priests on a cruise ship, they stare solemnly as they glide by, all heads turning together. The dog, inquisitive about our laughter, picks his way on heaving planks down to the water's edge, but is taken off guard by the sudden splash of an equally surprised muskrat and slips on the precarious plank, so that his hindquarters slide into the water and he hangs on with scrabbling forepaws. I help him up, because he is nine years old and not so agile, but I laugh so much that he is offended; he shakes his coat, soaking us with moody satisfaction, then disappears into the bush. I know that he will not go far, but will return stealthily and take up position concealed by some bush or tree so that he can keep me within range; and I know that if I turn suddenly I will be able to catch him at it, to his embarrassment — but not this time, for I am feeling a little guilty.

I make amends with a piece of cheese when we settle down on the steps again to eat our lunch — satisfying hunks of homemade bread and cheese, dill pickles, and another bottle of beer to celebrate our weekend emancipation. Redwings chatter in the mountain ash above, chatter in a desultory way, rather as we do ourselves, with long silences savored peacefully between their observations. The frog activity is dying down, but the muskrats are suddenly busy, the V of their wake spreading in the still water close to shore, preoccupied, bewhiskered little faces forging through the reeds. More ducks flight in and settle on the larger ice floes, preening themselves, their cheerful garrulity suddenly silenced when an osprey appears overhead and hovers watchfully. They rise in a body and circle, rising and falling uneasily, until the hawk drifts off down the shoreline on an eddy of wind, effortless as a feather.

Now the wind rises and falls too, sighing through the topmost pine branches, and all around is a chorus of protesting creaks and groans of trees bearing the chafing weight of others uprooted in the winter gales and fallen against them. I am very content; lambs, primroses, and sprays of blossom are suddenly revealed as banal, hackneyed manifestations before this northland subtlety. I find myself filled with pity for the unfortunate masses who must wait another year before picking their next daffodil.

Susan settles down in a protected dip with easel and paint box and all the colorful clutter of a painter. She will be lost to the world for the next three hours. I whistle to Raimie, and we strike off from the trail into the bush, where the snow has receded, walking softly on a carpet of damp brown leaves; through the willow and alder clumps, whippy with new life, striking like a lash across the unwary face; over the mossy, rotting deadfalls; and around the impenetrable branches of new-fallen jack pine, the needles still dark green, the last desperate growth of cones in rubbery clusters like brown sea snails; between towering spruce and white pine; through enchanting sunlit clearings of terraced rock slabs, covered in pinky-gray lichen and long trailing tendrils of twinflower — the stems and leaves are brown now, but at the angle of each geometrically perfect pair is a minuscule of green. The surrounding moss is ankle deep, beautiful hummocky moss, and however soggy it may be within, I cannot resist it; I throw myself down and try to count the uncountable flowerets in a quarter inch. My eyes are on a level with the ledge of rock; caught below an overhang is a papery garter-snake skin, old, yet still clearly patterned and wonderfully supple, over two feet long. I tie it in a neat bow on Raimie's tail; he is not amused, but suffers it as a collar instead.

I meander along the banks of a trout-brown creek, sun-dappled until it winds through the dark gloom of a cedar swamp, the twisted, agonized roots and branches of the giant fallen trees forming a dark dramatic frieze against the new vivid green of the living spruce beyond. The cold strikes suddenly, for the sun cannot penetrate the intertwined vaulting, and even the creek contributes to the brooding eeriness with weird shapes and fantastic grottoes sculptured from the overhanging ledges of ice.

Suddenly Raimie hurtles past, nearly knocking me into the creek, tail streaming, nose to the ground like a hound. He disappears into the thick undergrowth, his golden coat flashing momentarily in a patch of sun, and as I walk on, his quarry erupts from the bush across my path, then pauses to look back, upright on his haunches, still as a plaster rabbit on a suburban lawn, save for his twitching nose. A mighty crashing heralds Raimie's reappearance, and the rabbit bounds off with a flash of full white winter trousers, contrasting absurdly with his neat tan summer coat. My idiot dog will now make the full round of the rabbit's tracks before starting off on this new line, for he stubbornly refuses to hunt on anything but scent, and I have often wondered what would happen if a rabbit decided to run in ever-diminishing circles.

Of course, Raimie should not be hunting rabbits — or even his dearest enemy, the groundhog, for that matter — for he is a gundog, trained, with nine years' wisdom and experience. *He* knows that, and *I* know that, but after several argumentative years together, we long ago arrived at a mature and satisfactory compromise: in return for shouldering a few extra duties (watchdog, child-sitter, sled dog, juvenile circus performer, lost-hamster retriever, plus the full-time summer job of bear-scare on mushrooming expeditions), he may hunt for his own amusement, without let or hindrance, throughout the year until September 15, or such time as the upland game and wildfowl season opens, when he must immediately put aside all temptation and revert forthwith to his professional capacity of model gundog. It was his terrible misfortune to be born a scion of the great Shedd of Arden, to spring from a long illustrious line of field-trial champions and inherit the nose of an inspired cross between radar and a divining rod — and yet be subject for his lifetime to the whim of a woman-wielded gun. Any other dog would have a nervous breakdown, and because of his most generous acceptance of the inequalities of fate, I feel I must make allowances.

He never betrays our agreement, and would not acknowledge a rabbit if he fell over one during the shooting season; and even my hunting companions, critical field-trial purists though they are, admit that it would be difficult to find his equal as a retriever of lost and given-up birds, or a heart more eager and willing for work, whatever the conditions. Their only accusation, in fact, is that he smells faintly — but deliciously, I contend — of Schiaparelli's "Shocking," just behind the ears. He is the only dog I know who has been confronted with eleven mallards down in a treacherous, ice-fringed Manitoba slough and has set to work, systematically and entirely under his own directive, to bring them in (his mistress watching admiringly but uselessly, as her boots were leaking), then disappeared into the surrounding countryside, to reappear at ten-minute intervals with four more crippled birds. And only a woman owner could appreciate the gallantry of his compliment in bringing all fifteen birds to me, even though I had not fired a shot — a dogless companion being responsible for the massacre. And I know of no sight more fascinating than to watch him paddle painstakingly back and forth across a suspect area of water, submerging his head at intervals, until he finally dives straight down and comes up with a live but suicidally minded duck.

If I have digressed, it could be suspected that I dote on him.

III

I leave the creek to come out from the darkness of the bush at the edge of a field, part of a long-abandoned fox farm, and there, less than a hundred yards away, in a dip before the sagging barn, is a black bear. We stare at one another in mutual horror for a long second; then he turns and bolts across the field, galloping so fast that his back legs cross over his front ones, and disappears into the far trees. But that is the direction I want to go in as well, back to the lake, and I don't feel entirely happy about bears, and however antisocial this one may be, perhaps he has a mother or a cousin or a sister (with cubs) who isn't. I call my moral support away from his rabbit hunting and hear the reassuring sounds of his coming almost immediately. He arrives, panting, with beaming eyes and half a yard of pink tongue lolling out of a grinning mouth; I gather he has had a wonderful time. I am delighted, even more than usual, to see him. I am interested to see him sniff the wind as we cross the field, and the ridge of hair rise along his back, but he trots along beside me unconcerned; and so, of course, am I — now.

Susan has had a satisfying afternoon as well; two canvases are propped against the backs of chairs, she has found the glove she lost last fall in the bush, and has seen two deer, one mink, and a flock of geese. We sit on the steps again before dinner, loath to come in until the last possible moment, and watch a spectacular sunset flaming in wild, windblown ragged clouds. The air below is still and soft and full of evening sounds: wings whistling overhead, throbbing frog chorus from the reeds, chickadees, and the solitary falling cadence of a white-throated sparrow far back in the bush; little whispers of wind rustling the dead brown bulrush spikes; and always the soft melodious tinkling of shifting ice in the background; coy bridling giggles of mallard hens in the next bay, protesting their virtue to the hoarse excited quacks of their swains; the occasional caustic comment of a raven. We sit there until the loons cry in the gathering darkness and the cold drives us into the snug, stuffy warmth of the cabin.

We have partridge for dinner, succulent gamy partridge shot in a Saskatchewan bluff last fall, marinated and cooked in homemade wine from a local Italian producer; Burgundy jelly from the Trappists in Quebec; and wild rice that grew along these shores only last year, dark and fragrant with woodsmoke from the Indians' fires across the lake. We drink the remainder of the wine — a muscatel, says the sticking-plaster label on the gin bottle, with a surprisingly pleasant though elusive bouquet (a quality enhanced perhaps by the fact that our wine-glasses once contained anchovy paste).

We play featherheaded chess until our eyes will no longer stay open and we realize that we are dozing between moves. Raimie is already asleep on a sagging cot, muzzle resting on a headless decoy, his nostrils twitching — dreaming of rabbits, probably. I lie awake in the darkness for a while, zipped into the cocoon of my sleeping bag, listening to the sighs and creaks of the wooden framework; there is a soft, intermittent scratching on the roof, which I finally identify as a scraping branch; outside there are faint little plops in the water, and a closer, intensified tinkling of the ice, which must mean that the wind is shifting.

In the middle of the night I waken with a sudden wide-awake alertness, almost as though someone had called me by name, but I hear nothing — only the sound of Raimie's tail thumping on the cot when he hears me sit up. I get out of bed and stand by the open door, looking out across the lake; a star is hanging low over the hills, and when the moon appears from a bank of clouds the lake is bright before me, half a mile or more of shining water triumphing over the sinking ice. And as I stand there I realize that the wind is warm and soft and full of promise — the promise of the northland spring, fulfilled at last in the silent, vanquished ice.

1963
THE NEGRO IS YOUR BROTHER
by Martin Luther King, Jr.

From the Birmingham jail, where he was imprisoned as a participant in non-violent demonstrations against segregation, DR. MARTIN LUTHER KING, JR., *wrote in longhand the letter which follows. It was his response to a public statement of concern and caution issued by eight white religious leaders of the South.*

WHILE confined here in the Birmingham city jail, I came across your recent statement calling our present activities "unwise and untimely." Seldom, if ever, do I pause to answer criticism of my work and ideas. If I sought to answer all of the criticisms that cross my desk, my secretaries would be engaged in little else in the course of the day, and I would have no time for constructive work. But since I feel that you are men of genuine good will and your criticisms are sincerely set forth, I would like to answer your statement in what I hope will be patient and reasonable terms.

I think I should give the reason for my being in Birmingham, since you have been influenced by the argument of "outsiders coming in." I have the honor of serving as president of the Southern Christian Leadership Conference, an organization operating in every Southern state, with headquarters in Atlanta, Georgia. We have some eighty-five affiliate organizations all across the South, one being the Alabama Christian Movement for Human Rights. Whenever necessary and possible, we share staff, educational and financial resources with our affiliates. Several months ago our local affiliate here in Birmingham invited us to be on call to engage in a nonviolent direct-action program if such were deemed necessary. We readily consented, and when the hour came we lived up to our promises. So I am here, along with several members of my staff, because we were invited here. I am here because I have basic organizational ties here.

Beyond this, I am in Birmingham because injustice is here. Just as the eighth-century prophets left their little villages and carried their "thus saith the Lord" far beyond the boundaries of their hometowns; and just as the Apostle Paul left his little village of Tarsus and carried the gospel of Jesus Christ to practically every hamlet and city of the Greco-Roman world, I too am compelled to carry the gospel of freedom beyond my particular hometown. Like Paul, I must constantly respond to the Macedonian call for aid.

Moreover, I am cognizant of the interrelatedness of all communities and states. I cannot sit idly by in Atlanta and not be concerned about what happens in Birmingham. Injustice anywhere is a threat to justice everywhere. We are caught in an inescapable network of mutuality, tied in a single garment of destiny. Whatever affects one directly affects all indirectly. Never again can we afford to live with the narrow, provincial "outside agitator" idea. Anyone who lives inside the United States can never be considered an outsider.

You deplore the demonstrations that are presently taking place in Birmingham. But I am sorry that your statement did not express a similar concern for the conditions that brought the demonstrations into being. I am sure that each of you would want to go beyond the superficial social analyst who looks merely at effects and does not grapple with underlying causes. I would not hesitate to say that it is unfortunate that so-called demonstrations are taking place in Birmingham at this time, but I would say in more emphatic terms that it is even more unfortunate that the white power structure of this city left the Negro community with no other alternative.

In any nonviolent campaign there are four basic steps: collection of the facts to determine whether injustices are alive, negotiation, self-purification, and direct action. We have gone through all of these steps in Birmingham. There can be no gain-saying of the fact that racial injustice engulfs this community. Birmingham is probably the most thoroughly segregated city in the United States. Its ugly record of police brutality is known in every section of this country. Its unjust treatment of Negroes in the courts is a notorious reality. There have been more unsolved bombings of Negro homes and churches in Birmingham than in any other city in this nation. These are the hard, brutal, and unbelievable facts. On the basis of them, Negro leaders sought to negotiate with the city fathers. But the political leaders consistently refused to engage in good-faith negotiation.

Then came the opportunity last September to talk with some of the leaders of the economic community. In these negotiating sessions certain promises were made by the merchants, such as the promise to remove the humiliating racial signs from the stores. On the basis of these promises, Reverend Shuttlesworth and the leaders of the Alabama Christian Movement for Human Rights agreed to call a moratorium on any type of demonstration. As the weeks and months unfolded, we realized that we were the victims of a broken promise. The signs remained. As in so many experiences of the past, we were confronted with blasted hopes, and the dark shadow of a deep disappointment settled upon us. So we had no alternative except that of preparing for direct action, whereby we would present our very bodies as a means of laying our case before the conscience of the local and national community. We were not unmindful of the difficulties involved. So we decided to go through a process of self-purification. We started having workshops on nonviolence and repeatedly asked ourselves the questions, "Are you able to accept blows without retaliating?" and "Are you able to endure the ordeals of jail?" We decided to set our direct-action program around the Easter season, realizing that, with exception of Christmas, this was the largest shopping period of the year. Knowing that a strong economic withdrawal program would be the by-product of direct action, we felt that this was the best time to bring pressure on the merchants for the needed changes. Then it occurred to us that the March election was ahead, and so we speedily decided to postpone action until after election day. When we discovered that Mr. Conner was in the runoff, we decided again to postpone action so that the demonstration could not be used to cloud the issues. At this time we agreed to begin our nonviolent witness the day after the runoff.

This reveals that we did not move irresponsibly into direct action. We, too, wanted to see Mr. Conner defeated, so we went through postponement after postponement to aid in this community need. After this we felt that direct action could be delayed no longer.

You may well ask, "Why direct action, why sit-ins, marches, and so forth? Isn't negotiation a better path?" You are exactly right in your call for negotiation. Indeed, this is the purpose of direct action. Non-violent direct action seeks to create such a crisis and establish such creative tension that a community that has consistently refused to negotiate is forced to confront the issue. It seeks so to dramatize the issue that it can no longer be ignored. I just referred to the creation of tension as a part of the work of the nonviolent resister. This may sound rather shocking. But I must confess that I am not afraid of the word "tension." I have earnestly worked and preached against violent tension, but there is a type of constructive nonviolent tension that is necessary for growth. Just as Socrates felt that it was necessary to create a tension in the mind so that individuals could rise from the bondage of myths and half-truths to the unfettered realm of creative analysis and objective appraisal, we must see the need of having non-violent gadflies to create the kind of tension in society that will help men to rise from the dark depths of prejudice and racism to the majestic heights of understanding and brotherhood. So, the purpose of direct action is to create a situation so crisis-packed that it will inevitably open the door to negotiation. We therefore concur with you in your call for negotiation. Too long has our beloved Southland been bogged down in the tragic attempt to live in monologue rather than dialogue.

One of the basic points in your statement is that our acts are untimely. Some have asked, "Why didn't you give the new administration time to act?" The only answer that I can give to this inquiry is that the new administration must be prodded about as much as the outgoing one before it acts. We will be sadly mistaken if we feel that the election of Mr. Boutwell will bring the millennium to Birmingham. While Mr. Boutwell is much more articulate and gentle than Mr. Conner, they are both segregationists, dedicated to the task of maintaining the status quo. The hope I see in Mr. Boutwell is that he will be reasonable enough to see the futility of massive resistance to desegregation. But he will not see this without pressure from the devotees of civil rights. My friends, I must say to you that we have not made a single gain in civil rights without determined legal and nonviolent pressure. History is the long and tragic story of the fact that privileged groups seldom give up their privileges voluntarily. Individuals may see the moral light and voluntarily give up their unjust posture; but, as Reinhold Niebuhr has reminded us, groups are more immoral than individuals.

We know through painful experience that freedom is never voluntarily given by the oppressor; it must be demanded by the oppressed. Frankly, I have never yet engaged in a direct-action movement that was "well timed" according to the timetable of those who have not suffered unduly from the disease of segregation. For years now I have heard the word "wait." It rings in the ear of every Negro with a piercing familiarity. This "wait" has almost always meant "never." It has been a tranquilizing thalidomide, relieving the emotional stress for a moment, only to give birth to an ill-formed infant of frustration. We must come to see with the distinguished jurist of yesterday that "justice too long delayed is justice denied." We have waited for more than three hundred and forty years for our God-given and constitutional rights. The nations of Asia and Africa are moving with jetlike speed toward the goal of political independence, and we still creep at horse-and-buggy pace toward the gaining of a cup of coffee at a lunch counter. I guess it is easy for those who have never felt the stinging darts of segregation to say "wait." But when you have seen vicious mobs lynch your mothers and fathers at will and drown your sisters and brothers at whim; when you have seen hate-filled policemen curse, kick, brutalize, and even kill your black brothers and sisters with impunity; when you see the vast majority of your twenty million Negro brothers smothering in an airtight cage of poverty in the midst of an affluent society; when you suddenly find your tongue twisted and your speech stammering as you seek to explain to your six-year-old daughter why she cannot go to the public amusement park that has just been advertised on television, and see tears welling up in her little eyes when she is told that Funtown is closed to colored children, and see the depressing clouds of inferiority begin to form in her little mental sky, and see her begin to distort her little personality by unconsciously developing a bitterness toward white people; when you have to concoct an answer for a five-year-old son asking in agonizing pathos, "Daddy, why do white people treat colored people so mean?"; when you take a cross-country drive and find it necessary to sleep night after night in the uncomfortable corners of your automobile because no motel will accept you; when you are humiliated day in and day out by nagging signs reading "white" and "colored"; when your first name becomes "nigger" and your middle name becomes "boy" (however old you are) and your last name becomes "John," and when your wife and mother are never given the respected title "Mrs."; when you are harried by day and haunted by night by the fact that you are a Negro, living constantly at tiptoe stance, never quite knowing what to expect next, and plagued with inner fears and outer resentments; when you are forever fighting a degenerating sense of "nobodyness" — then you will understand why we find it difficult to wait. There comes a time when the cup of endurance runs over and men are no longer willing to be plunged into an abyss of injustice where they experience the bleakness of corroding despair. I hope, sirs, you can understand our legitimate and unavoidable impatience.

You express a great deal of anxiety over our willingness to break laws. This is certainly a legitimate concern. Since we so diligently urge people to obey the Supreme Court's decision of 1954 outlawing segregation in the public schools, it is rather strange and paradoxical to find us consciously breaking laws. One may well ask, "How can you advocate breaking some laws and obeying others?" The answer is found in the fact that there are two types of laws: there are just laws, and there are unjust laws. I would agree with St. Augustine that "An unjust law is no law at all."

Now, what is the difference between the two? How does one determine when a law is just or unjust? A just law is a man-made code that squares with the moral law, or the law of God. An unjust law is a code that is out of harmony with the moral law. To put it in the terms of St. Thomas Aquinas, an unjust law is a human law that is not rooted in eternal and natural law. Any law that uplifts human personality is just. Any law that degrades human personality is unjust. All segregation statutes are unjust because segregation distorts the soul and damages the personality. It gives the segregator a false sense of superiority and the segregated a false sense of inferiority. To use the words of Martin Buber, the great Jewish philosopher, segregation substitutes an "I — it" relationship for the "I — thou" relationship and ends up relegating persons to the status of things. So segregation is not only politically, economically, and sociologically unsound, but it is morally wrong and sinful. Paul Tillich has said that sin is separation. Isn't segregation an existential expression of man's tragic separation, an expression of his awful estrangement, his terrible sinfulness? So I can urge men to obey the 1954 decision of the Supreme Court because it is morally right, and I can urge them to disobey segregation ordinances because they are morally wrong.

Let us turn to a more concrete example of just and unjust laws. An unjust law is a code that a majority inflicts on a minority that is not binding on itself. This is difference made legal. On the other hand, a just law is a code that a majority compels a minority to follow, and that it is willing to follow itself. This is sameness made legal.

Let me give another explanation. An unjust law is a code inflicted upon a minority which that minority had no part in enacting or creating because it did not have the unhampered right to vote. Who can say that the legislature of Alabama which set up the segregation laws was democratically elected? Throughout the state of Alabama all types of conniving methods are used to prevent Negroes from becoming registered voters, and there are some counties without a single Negro registered to vote, despite the fact that the Negroes constitute a majority of the population. Can any law set up in such a state be considered democratically structured?

These are just a few examples of unjust and just laws. There are some instances when a law is just on its face and unjust in its application. For instance, I was arrested Friday on a charge of parading without a permit. Now, there is nothing wrong with an ordinance which requires a permit for a parade, but when the ordinance is used to preserve segregation and to deny citizens the First Amendment privilege of peaceful assembly and peaceful protest, then it becomes unjust.

Of course, there is nothing new about this kind of civil disobedience. It was seen sublimely in the refusal of Shadrach, Meshach, and Abednego to obey the laws of Nebuchadnezzar because a higher moral law was involved. It was practiced superbly by the early Christians, who were willing to face hungry lions and the excruciating pain of chopping blocks before submitting to certain unjust laws of the Roman Empire. To a degree, academic freedom is a reality today because Socrates practiced civil disobedience.

We can never forget that everything Hitler did in Germany was "legal" and everything the Hungarian freedom fighters did in Hungary was "illegal." It was "illegal" to aid and comfort a Jew in Hitler's Germany. But I am sure that if I had lived in Germany during that time, I would have aided and comforted my Jewish brothers even though it was illegal. If I lived in a Communist country today where certain principles dear to the Christian faith are suppressed, I believe I would openly advocate disobeying these anti-religious laws.

I must make two honest confessions to you, my Christian and Jewish brothers. First, I must confess that over the last few years I have been gravely disappointed with the white moderate. I have almost reached the regrettable conclusion that the Negro's great stumbling block in the stride toward freedom is not the White Citizens Councillor or the Ku Klux Klanner but the white moderate who is more devoted to order than to justice; who prefers a negative peace which is the absence of tension to a positive peace which is the presence of justice; who constantly says, "I agree with you in the goal you seek, but I can't agree with your methods of direct action"; who paternalistically feels that he can set the timetable for another man's freedom; who lives by the myth of time; and who constantly advises the Negro to wait until a "more convenient season." Shallow understanding from people of good will is more frustrating than absolute misunderstanding from people of ill will. Lukewarm acceptance is much more bewildering than outright rejection.

In your statement you asserted that our actions, even though peaceful, must be condemned because they precipitate violence. But can this assertion be logically made? Isn't this like condemning the robbed man because his possession of money precipitated the evil act of robbery?

Isn't this like condemning Socrates because his unswerving commitment to truth and his philosophical delvings precipitated the misguided popular mind to make him drink the hemlock? Isn't this like condemning Jesus because His unique God-consciousness and never-ceasing devotion to His will precipitated the evil act of crucifixion? We must come to see, as federal courts have consistently affirmed, that it is immoral to urge an individual to withdraw his efforts to gain his basic constitutional rights because the quest precipitates violence. Society must protect the robbed and punish the robber.

I had also hoped that the white moderate would reject the myth of time. I received a letter this morning from a white brother in Texas which said, "All Christians know that the colored people will receive equal rights eventually, but is it possible that you are in too great of a religious hurry? It has taken Christianity almost 2000 years to accomplish what it has. The teachings of Christ take time to come to earth." All that is said here grows out of a tragic misconception of time. It is the strangely irrational notion that there is something in the very flow of time that will inevitably cure all ills. Actually, time is neutral. It can be used either destructively or constructively. I am coming to feel that the people of ill will have used time much more effectively than the people of good will. We will have to repent in this generation not merely for the vitriolic words and actions of the bad people but for the appalling silence of the good people. We must come to see that human progress never rolls in on wheels of inevitability. It comes through the tireless efforts and persistent work of men willing to be coworkers with God, and without this hard work time itself becomes an ally of the forces of social stagnation.

You spoke of our activity in Birmingham as extreme. At first I was rather disappointed that fellow clergymen would see my nonviolent efforts as those of an extremist. I started thinking about the fact that I stand in the middle of two opposing forces in the Negro community. One is a force of complacency made up of Negroes who, as a result of long years of oppression, have been so completely drained of self-respect and a sense of "somebodyness" that they have adjusted to segregation, and, on the other hand, of a few Negroes in the middle class who, because of a degree of academic and economic security and because at points they profit by segregation, have unconsciously become insensitive to the problems of the masses. The other force is one of bitterness and hatred and comes perilously close to advocating violence. It is expressed in the various black nationalist groups that are springing up over the nation, the largest and best known being Elijah Muhammad's Muslim movement. This movement is nourished by the contemporary frustration over the continued existence of racial discrimination. It is made up of people who have lost faith in America, who have absolutely repudiated Christianity, and who have concluded that the white man is an incurable devil. I have tried to stand between these two forces, saying that we need not follow the do-nothingism of the complacent or the hatred and despair of the black nationalist. There is a more excellent way, of love and nonviolent protest. I'm grateful to God that, through the Negro church, the dimension of nonviolence entered our struggle. If this philosophy had not emerged, I am convinced that by now many streets of the South would be flowing with floods of blood. And I am further convinced that if our white brothers dismiss as "rabble-rousers" and "outside agitators" those of us who are working through the channels of nonviolent direct action and refuse to support our nonviolent efforts, millions of Negroes, out of frustration and despair, will seek solace and security in black nationalist ideologies, a development that will lead inevitably to a frightening racial nightmare.

Oppressed people cannot remain oppressed forever. The urge for freedom will eventually come. This is what has happened to the American Negro. Something within has reminded him of his birthright of freedom; something without has reminded him that he can gain it. Consciously and unconsciously, he has been swept in by what the Germans call the *Zeitgeist,* and with his black brothers of Africa and his brown and yellow brothers of Asia, South America, and the Caribbean, he is moving with a sense of cosmic urgency toward the promised land of racial justice. Recognizing this vital urge that has engulfed the Negro community, one should readily understand public demonstrations. The Negro has many pent-up resentments and latent frustrations. He has to get them out. So let him march sometime; let him have his prayer pilgrimages to the city hall; understand why he must have sit-ins and freedom rides. If his repressed emotions do not come out in these nonviolent ways, they will come out in ominous expressions of violence. This is not a threat; it is a fact of history. So I have not said to my people, "Get rid of your discontent." But I have tried to say that this normal and healthy discontent can be channeled through the creative outlet of nonviolent direct action. Now this approach is being dismissed as extremist. I must admit that I was initially disappointed in being so categorized.

But as I continued to think about the matter, I gradually gained a bit of satisfaction from being considered an extremist. Was not Jesus an extremist in love? — "Love your enemies, bless them that curse you, pray for them that despitefully use you." Was not Amos an extremist for justice? — "Let justice roll down like waters and righteousness like a mighty stream." Was not Paul an extremist for the gospel of Jesus Christ? — "I bear in my body the marks of the Lord Jesus." Was not Martin Luther an extremist? — "Here I stand; I can do no other so help me God." Was not John Bunyan an extremist? — "I will stay in jail to the end of my days before I make a mockery of my conscience." Was not Abraham Lincoln an extremist? — "This nation cannot survive half slave and half free." Was not Thomas Jefferson an extremist? — "We hold these truths to be self-evident, that all men are created equal." So the question is not whether we will be extremist, but what kind of extremists we will be. Will we be extremists for hate, or will we be extremists for love? Will we be extremists for the preservation of injustice, or will we be extremists for the cause of justice?

I had hoped that the white moderate would see this. Maybe I was too optimistic. Maybe I expected too much. I guess I should have realized that few members of a race that has oppressed another race can understand or appreciate the deep groans and passionate yearnings of those that have been oppressed, and still fewer have the vision to see that injustice must be rooted out by strong, persistent, and determined action. I am thankful, however, that some of our white brothers have grasped the meaning of this social revolution and committed themselves to it. They are still all too small in quantity, but they are big in quality. Some, like Ralph McGill, Lillian Smith, Harry Golden, and James Dabbs, have written about our struggle in eloquent, prophetic, and understanding terms. Others have marched with us down nameless streets of the South. They sat in with us at lunch counters and rode in with us on the freedom rides. They have languished in filthy roach-infested jails, suffering the abuse and brutality of angry policemen who see them as "dirty nigger lovers." They, unlike many of their moderate brothers, have recognized the urgency of the moment and sensed the need for powerful "action" antidotes to combat the disease of segregation.

Let me rush on to mention my other disappointment. I have been disappointed with the white church and its leadership. Of course, there are some notable exceptions. I am not unmindful of the fact that each of you has taken some significant stands on this issue. I commend you, Reverend Stallings, for your Christian stand this past Sunday in welcoming Negroes to your Baptist Church worship service on a nonsegregated basis. I commend the Catholic leaders of this state for integrating Springhill College several years ago.

But despite these notable exceptions, I must honestly reiterate that I have been disappointed with the church. I do not say that as one of those negative critics who can always find something wrong with the church. I say it as a minister of the gospel who loves the church, who was nurtured in its bosom, who has been sustained by its spiritual blessings, and who will remain true to it as long as the cord of life shall lengthen.

I had the strange feeling when I was suddenly catapulted into the leadership of the bus protest in Montgomery several years ago that we would have the support of the white church. I felt that the white ministers, priests, and rabbis of the South would be some of our strongest allies. Instead, some few have been outright opponents, refusing to understand the freedom movement and misrepresenting its leaders; all too many others have been more cautious than courageous and have remained silent behind the anesthetizing security of stained-glass windows.

In spite of my shattered dreams of the past, I came to Birmingham with the hope that the white religious leadership of this community would see the justice of our cause and with deep moral concern serve as the channel through which our just grievances could get to the power structure. I had hoped that each of you would understand. But again I have been disappointed.

I have heard numerous religious leaders of the South call upon their worshipers to comply with a desegregation decision because it is the law, but I have longed to hear white ministers say, follow this decree because integration is morally right and the Negro is your brother. In the midst of blatant injustices inflicted upon the Negro, I have watched white churches stand on the sidelines and merely mouth pious irrelevancies and sanctimonious trivialities. In the midst of a mighty struggle to rid our nation of racial and economic injustice, I have heard so many ministers say, "Those are social issues which the gospel has nothing to do with," and I have watched so many churches commit themselves to a completely other-worldly religion which made a strange distinction between bodies and souls, the sacred and the secular.

There was a time when the church was very powerful. It was during that period that the early Christians rejoiced when they were deemed worthy to suffer for what they believed. In those days the church was not merely a thermometer that recorded the ideas and principles of popular opinion; it was the thermostat that transformed the mores of society. Wherever the early Christians entered a town the power structure got disturbed and immediately sought to convict them for being "disturbers of the peace" and "outside agitators." But they went on with the conviction that they were "a colony of heaven" and had to obey God rather than man. They were small in number but big in commitment. They were too God-intoxicated to be "astronomically intimidated." They brought an end to such ancient evils as infanticide and gladiatorial contest.

Things are different now. The contemporary church is so often a weak, ineffectual voice with an uncertain sound. It is so often the arch supporter of the status quo. Far from being disturbed by the presence of the church, the power structure of the average community is consoled by the church's often vocal sanction of things as they are.

But the judgment of God is upon the church as never before. If the church of today does not recapture the sacrificial spirit of the early church, it will lose its authentic ring, forfeit the loyalty of millions, and be dismissed as an irrelevant social club with no meaning for the twentieth century. I meet young people every day whose disappointment with the church has risen to outright disgust.

I hope the church as a whole will meet the challenge of this decisive hour. But even if the church does not come to the aid of justice, I have no despair about the future. I have no fear about the outcome of our struggle in Birmingham, even if our motives are presently misunderstood. We will reach the goal of freedom in Birmingham and all over the nation, because the goal of America is freedom. Abused and scorned though we may be, our destiny is tied up with the destiny of America. Before the Pilgrims landed at Plymouth, we were here. Before the pen of Jefferson scratched across the pages of history the majestic word of the Declaration of Independence, we were here. For more than two centuries our foreparents labored here without wages; they made cotton king; and they built the homes of their masters in the midst of brutal injustice and shameful humiliation — and yet out of a bottomless vitality our people continue to thrive and develop. If the inexpressible cruelties of slavery could not stop us, the opposition we now face will surely fail. We will win our freedom because the sacred heritage of our nation and the eternal will of God are embodied in our echoing demands.

I must close now. But before closing I am impelled to mention one other point in your statement that troubled me profoundly. You warmly commended the Birmingham police force for keeping "order" and "preventing violence." I don't believe you would have so warmly commended the police force if you had seen its angry violent dogs literally biting six unarmed, nonviolent Negroes. I don't believe you would so quickly commend the policemen if you would observe their ugly and inhuman treatment of Negroes here in the city jail; if you would watch them push and curse old Negro women and young Negro girls; if you would see them slap and kick old Negro men and young boys; if you would observe them, as they did on two occasions, refusing to give us food because we wanted to sing our grace together. I'm sorry that I can't join you in your praise for the police department.

It is true that they have been rather disciplined in their public handling of the demonstrators. In this sense they have been publicly "nonviolent." But for what purpose? To preserve the evil system of segregation. Over the last few years I have consistently preached that nonviolence demands that the means we use must be as pure as the ends we seek. So I have tried to make it clear that it is wrong to use immoral means to attain moral ends. But now I must affirm that it is just as wrong, or even more, to use moral means to preserve immoral ends.

I wish you had commended the Negro demonstrators of Birmingham for their sublime courage, their willingness to suffer, and their amazing discipline in the midst of the most inhuman provocation. One day the South will recognize its real heroes. They will be the James Merediths, courageously and with a majestic sense of purpose facing jeering and hostile mobs and the agonizing loneliness that characterizes the life of the pioneer. They will be old, oppressed, battered Negro women, symbolized in a seventy-two-year-old woman of Montgomery, Alabama, who rose up with a sense of dignity and with her people decided not to ride the segregated buses, and responded to one who inquired about her tiredness with ungrammatical profundity, "My feets is tired, but my soul is rested." They will be young high school and college students, young ministers of the gospel and a host of their elders courageously and nonviolently sitting in at lunch counters and willingly going to jail for conscience's sake. One day the South will know that when these disinherited children of God sat down at lunch counters they were in reality standing up for the best in the American dream and the most sacred values in our Judeo-Christian heritage.

Never before have I written a letter this long — or should I say a book? I'm afraid that it is much too long to take your precious time. I can assure you that it would have been much shorter if I had been writing from a comfortable desk, but what else is there to do when you are alone for days in the dull monotony of a narrow jail cell other than write long letters, think strange thoughts, and pray long prayers?

If I have said anything in this letter that is an understatement of the truth and is indicative of an unreasonable impatience, I beg you to forgive me. If I have said anything in this letter that is an overstatement of the truth and is indicative of my having a patience that makes me patient with anything less than brotherhood, I beg God to forgive me.

Yours for the cause of Peace and Brotherhood,
MARTIN LUTHER KING, JR.

U.S.A. REVISITED
by John Dos Passos

Turnpike

Out of the Jersey truckfarms, the cornfields, the green slopes golden with Guernseys; cowbarns sporting a silo the way a church sports a steeple; bright watertanks, one a huge ball rolling through treetops; the toycolored plants of new industries . . .

SCENICRUISER FOR ECONOMY
Go Greyhound

. . . the sixlane highway
that arched the reedy rivers and skirted the fields of red clover,
now in whine of windfriction, hiss of tires, valve-chatter, grumble of diesels, drone of exhausts,
plunges under a rampaging bridge,
sixlane under sixlane.

HORSE TRANSPORTATION

To the right a square brick mansion with curved stone pediments, capped by a glassedin cupola,
(uncompromising as a tintype of General Ulysses S Grant, posed on a porch with his family, all in their stiff Sunday best),
stands up and is gone,
vanished like the haze of croplands bucolic with summer some long dead landowner viewed with pleasure from his cupola.

CITIES SERVICE

The turnpike speeds out of yesterday, mudguard to mudguard through sulphuric gusts into tomorrow's horizon:
intertwined tubing that curves round aluminum bottleshapes, distillators, retorts: a plumber's nightmare! Steel pylons supporting hightension powerlines stalk like H. G. Wells' Martians across the industrial plain.

DRIVE SLOW ACCIDENT AHEAD

This was three nights ago. You can still see where the shoulder's gouged. The night had been misty and after midnight the turnpike troopers set the signs putting the speedlimit at thirtyfive instead of sixty. As the fog thickened in the predawn chill, smoke from a smoldering dump reduced visibility to zero.

This is the time when the turnpike roars with produce trucks charging into town to make the early market.

The driver of the first tractortrailer to get into trouble told police afterwards he had already slowed down to thirtyfive when he saw a sign warning of fog ahead. Suddenly he found he couldn't see anything and stepped on his brakes and immediately another tractortrailer, driven by a young man from North Carolina, struck him in the rear. The impact pushed the first tractortrailer about seventyfive feet up the road into a car driven by a New Jersey man.

That car ended up safe in the ditch but the two tractortrailers jackknifed across the traffic lanes. Before anybody could lift a hand ten more tractortrailers and two cars had plowed into the wreckage. Five drivers were killed outright. One died on the way to the hospital and seven men were more or less seriously injured.

The last man to pile up, a man named Gautier from Port Huron, Michigan, who was bringing in a truckload of Great Lakes fish, told a reporter in the hospital he never saw the wreckage before he hit it. All he saw was a fogbank and the brakelights of the truck ahead, and then he crashed. He was lucky to get out of it with minor cuts about the head and hands and was released after treatment. The desk sergeant said it was the worst he'd ever seen. "No cars overturned but the trailers all split open. One was completely buried under wreckage."

The troopers sealed off the turnpike and deflected the traffic to route 1. Ambulance and rescue squads came in from Elizabeth. It took a fleet of wrecking trucks, bulldozers, a moveable crane and a train of flatcars to clear away enough wreckage so that they could remove the dead. It was twelve hours before the turnpike was completely reopened for traffic.

KEEP AWAKE

"Thank you for your patience" on a red ground.

Now there are trucks on every lane:
Suburban Propane
    Mason and Dixon   Flammable
      Liquid Sugar   Red Star Express
        Dog Food Pigeon Feeds
        U-Haul
      Continental Truckers
  Caution Airbrakes: The left arrow points "Home and Fireside"; the right arrow points "Kingdom Come."

Airport. Beyond a row of fatbellied yellow old planes of the Air Reserve a control tower glistens festive in the sun. Across the road wharfbuildings, masts, derricks, dance of light on waterways between the straight prows of oceangoing ships.

SERVICE AREA

Then smells of the Jersey salt meadows: sulphur, varnish, a whiff of dead apples, smoldering rags and paper ash, moldy bologny drenched in bay rum, ether ... obsolete crisco and the strangling stench of burned tires. One good swift reek of a pigpen and always

exhausts, petroleum essences and, like death immediate and undetectable, carbon monoxide.

Last Gasoline.

Through the afternoon haze, beyond the humdrum heights of Weehawken the buildings of Manhattan rise sunflecked in mirage. Empire State.

The sun through girderwork stipples the converging lanes of cars that clog an artery cut through the upthrust rock.

Brakes squeak, tires squeal. Pandemonium pours spiraling downward —

(breathless a lithograph: the old Erie depot, docks and the khaki-colored Hudson; seaport smells, tarry ropes, gulls screaming, steamboat whistles, tugs bleating, barges: the North River of my boyhood).

Immediately the traffic is sucked underground into the tranquil routine of the Lincoln Tunnel, interminable as officework, tiled like the bathrooms advertized by roadside motels ... The even measured lighting fades in harsh sunlight.

Cops.

It's New York.

Hall of Fame

Headlines are another sort of death. It was hard not to be reminded of the mortician's train of funeral cars as the somber limousines crawled past the portal of the fiftystory hostelry so discreetly discharging — black tie and the girls in glory — the invited guests who in some past incarnation had been the subjects of coverstories in this weekly magazine of national — nay international — circulation.

"I saw your picture in the paper."

Impeccably gladhanded the guests throng room after salmontinted room where waiters, who left their own faces behind in the pantry, deftly circulate cocktail trays. The aroma of luxury. Every alcoholic exhalation: gin, vermouth and zest of lemon, warmsweet of bourbon, smoky reek of scotch, all buoyed on rafts of toasted cheese, caviar canapes, fat gooseliver, anchovies, olives . . .

Camera men abound. The camera men neither eat nor drink. Tirelessly they snap famous faces, twisting in and out between eminent waistcoats, squirming with dervish whirls under brassiered bosoms, converge on politicians whose eyes roll come hither at the nearest lens.

The photographers are mad for angles. They crouch behind their cocked cameras, shoot up, shoot down, back off on all fours. They teeter on stepladders, they balance on mantels, they crawl up the walls.

The public image is the photograph.

A dozen cameras pin down each front page phiz. Lens stares into lens. Say cheese. Flashlight blanks out flashlight, making eyes blink behind the glare on glasses, picking out a swollen ear, shiny pores on a nose, creases in a woman's neck, or the peevish wrinkle at the corner of a mouth smiling that public smile.

In the flicker and flare, face stares into face. There's a phrase that freezes unspoken on every tongue: "By God I thought you were dead."

Can it be that the Arabs are right, and the dour pueblodwellers of our own Southwest, when they say the camera takes something away that can never be recovered, skims some private value off the soul?

The tactful greeters, the girls sorting indexcards at flowerscented tables, have managed, through their intricate engineering of mass hospitality, to find chairs for this multitude, placecards. Now we are grouped at tables in the grand ballroom that rises tier upon gilded tier into a dim empyrean.

Posycolored ladies and their whitefronted escorts throng every box. The dancefloor is all tables. While spotlights cut satin swaths through the smokeblue air, trays glitter as nimbly the waiters pass brook trout in aspic, some marvel of soup, rare roast beef veiled in sauce, pour just the right wine . . . Nebuchadnezzar never feasted so the day he spelled his doom off the Babylonian wall.

We must listen too. Public address. These tidings are all glad. Keep it light. Informal. Let's not get stuffy. Penguin figures talk and teeter behind the distant mike, extolling, explaining, wisecracking why and how

each of these poor humans:

bundles of nerves, hearts resolutely pumping blood, anguished tubs of guts, congeries of interacting braincells, suffering nocturnal despair, rejoicing in inexplicable morning aspirations,

became,
out of all the infinite possibilities of human kind,
Material for a Cover Story.

Palms sting from clapping. On a screen above the stage the enormous simulacrum shines while a tiny black and white figure
collared by an inquisitive spot
pops up to bumble and bow behind his table.

That simp on the screen can't be me. Where? When? A case of mistaken identity. No never. Least of all in a photograph redrawn and tinted by the art department. Maybe some inkling of a former self now long since scrapped. It is today's self that lives. The dead selves linger on as photographs.
"Wouldn't it be funny," I ask my neighbors, "if it turned out that we were really all dead, and this Hall of Fame was an ingenious Hell?"
Nobody seems the least amused by the suggestion.

The Greeks might have thought so. For the Greeks the spirits of the dead were simulacra, very like a photograph bereft of blood and brain and nerve. Those ghosts, that Odysseus, at another famous banquet in the royal hall of the rich Phaeacians, told Alcinous about, —
who crowded so fearfully around him when he cut the ram's throat on Ocean's shore that he had to draw his sword to cow them, —
were mere images of men, antique celebrities crowding out of Erebus to drink of the live blood. Achilles hissed he'd rather be a slave, a poor man's slave on earth, than king of all the celebrated dead. When Odysseus' own mother's ghost rose up before the pool of blood he tried to take her in his arms, but like smoke she drifted through his fingers: the image has no life.

The party lasted till long after midnight. Then we all went home to search out our pictures in the morning paper.

A Family Tragedy

The breeze drops with the sun. There's a hush. Standing with your legs apart to cast from one of the rock ribs of the island's shore, your feet tread the grooves the ice left in the granite. This time of day the colors run. Greens from emerald to olive-brown seep out from under the clustered spires of sprucewoods into the lake's sheen. The open reaches are still blue from the sky, and rosy buff and white from clouds reflected. As your lure comes twinkling towards you through the darkclear water the ripples catch a hundred hues.
The air is steeped in redolence of spruce and fir and the mossy

loamsmells of untrodden woods. There's silence now. Not an outboard. Not a plane. In the hush you feel the quiet of ten thousand
silent years since the last glacier melted back into the Arctic north and
left this immensity of pools and watercourses for the forest to take
over.

Silence. Except for the lapping of tiny waves and the sudden idiot
titter of a loon. It's startling at first. The lake is full of loons.

It was Jim Knox who taught us to feel at home with the loons. Jim
came from up north in the Canadian plains but he'd lived on this lake
from a boy. Summers he guided and took out fishing parties. Winters
he went in the woods for the lumbering. The lake was his life. His
pleasure in it was catching. He had a special feeling for the loons on
the lake.

He told us how they'd come back soon after the ice broke up and lay
their eggs and raise their brood. Both birds look after the young loon-
lets. Their enemy is the big pike, walleyes, northerns, that will come
up from under and swallow a baby loon or a duckling at one gulp.
When the brood is grown Jim says for the rest of the summer the
loons just play. They'll dive and sport and swim in circles; sometimes
it's like a kind of tag. Maybe that laugh really is when something
strikes them funny. At night the loon makes a different sound. That
sound at night we thought was owls was a loon crying. "They'll cry all
night, night after night if they've lost a wee one."

The last time we saw Jim he went into town before supper in the
skiff we used for trolling. We'd beached the houseboat cosily in a cove
of the big bay that skirted the Indian reservation, not too far from the
railroad bridge. He took along the frozen chickens we never got to eat
because we caught so much fish. They'd make supper for him and his
wife. He grinned happily when he said it. He was a man who enjoyed
his victuals. He was going to bring us some lures and leaders and a
bucket of minnows. He'd be back early for a last day's fishing.

In the morning we swam at sunup. Practiced casting but there were
no fish in the cove. We couldn't imagine what had become of Jim
Knox. We roamed in the rocky woods where we thought we found
some trace of the passing of a bear. Still no sign of Jim.

At last, when the sun was already high the skiff came shooting out
of the sun's sheen on the lake. Instead of Jim's rosy Scottish face there
was a dark face above the outboard.

He was Fergus, he said quietly as he tied the boat alongside. He said
his last name, an Indian name, but he said it so low we couldn't catch
it. He'd come instead. When we asked what had happened to Jim he
looked grave but all he would say was "A family tragedy."

Fergus was probably around twenty but the grave air seemed habitual. He may have had a little white blood but he looked like a full-blooded Indian, not the sort of man you asked questions. That didn't mean he wasn't friendly. He was just not talkative. The few English words he used were well chosen and carefully pronounced. We guessed he must at least have finished highschool. Something about him made us think he read books.

Fergus was knowledgeable about many things. He confirmed our hunch that some birds we'd been trying to imagine were halfgrown loons, were really grebes. He knew the European cormorant.

But when we decided to take the skiff out for some trolling his heart wasn't in it. He kept getting us tangled in the weeds. Fishing wasn't Fergus's meat.

Jim Knox, now, loved fishing. That was why he was such an excellent guide. He remembered every fish he ever caught, how the water looked, what time of day it was, what the weather was like. He knew where the northerns lay in the deeps under the steep rocks and how to steer the skiff round the fringes of the weeds to lure the big bass out to strike without tangling up the tackle. He'd grin all over when he scooped one up with the net. If he didn't find fish in one spot he'd find them in another.

He was a good cook too. He liked to eat well. He described dishes he had at home. He and his wife loved wild rice. He was a domestic sort of man in a backwoods way. Men who live a lot in the wilds have to know housekeeping.

Fish are so plentiful in these lakes nobody thinks of cleaning and scaling them the way we do at home. Jim would just cut a big fillet off each side with a sharp knife and throw the skeleton away. He liked to fry the fish in lard in a castiron skillet. He dipped the fillets in batter and cornflake crumbs and fried them a delicate brown. He laughed about the iron skillet. His wife had never seen an iron skillet before they were married. She came from away, from a place way south of here. Everything had been strange to her in this northwoods country. He guessed she'd get used to it in time.

Some of the best fishing was near a lumber camp where there was a sawmill in the woods. Jim and the man who ran the sawmill had married sisters. Jim often worked for him in the woods in winter. Jim had built himself a cabin there. When we went ashore Jim showed us a long trailerlike job, neatly carpentered. He was proud of his cabin. He pointed out how tight it was against the weather.

It was built that way so that you could move it on skids through the snow. All you needed to do was tow it with a pickup truck. Even the mess shack could be moved that way. This fall Jim's brotherinlaw was planning to shift the whole camp up into a fresh stand of timber. But

Jim said what he thought he'd do with his cabin when the ice was firm was haul it down the lake into town. Twenty miles — what's that? Winter was when transportation was really easy on the lake. Why you could almost tow it with a snow toboggan.

He showed us his snow toboggan propelled by small caterpillar treads. Hardly burned any more gas than a motorcycle, he said. In winter you could go anywhere on a snow toboggan. Winter on this lake was the big time for commercial fishing with nets under the ice. People who'd never lived in the northwoods couldn't guess how fine it was on the lake in winter.

Jim talked quite a lot about how he was going to move his cabin into town and weatherboard it for more insulation and join it onto his house. His wife said she felt cramped there. He showed even white teeth in a grin. Maybe one of these days they'd need more room for a family.

The last afternoon we had terrific fishing, trolling round the rocky point of an island. The rocks were white with the droppings of the gulls.

The lake abounded in gulls and terns, and on one outcropping we'd passed a row of gaunt black cormorants, with their wings stretched out in the sun. "Enough to scare yous," Jim said. "Look like something prehistoric don't they?"

Those northerns rose to the bait at a certain spot on every turn. We'd run out of minnows and were fishing with lures. We hauled in a beautiful small-mouthed bass. We always threw back the pretty little yellow perch. It got so that we had to throw the big northerns back too, because we already had more than we could eat for supper, and we'd run out of ice.

Jim was in high spirits. Every time we passed a small reedy inlet we caught a glimpse of a mallard duck with a flock of ducklings. He kept pointing out how she'd swim out from the shore each time the boat passed to hustle her ducklings back behind the reeds. He was delighted with the way that mallard cared for her ducklings. "Now ain't she the careful mother?"

When the time came to give up the houseboat back at the float on the edge of town the man who handled the rentals produced an envelope with the money we'd given Jim Knox to buy the minnows.

"What happened?"

"The poor guy." The man was so shaken up he could hardly talk. "The poor guy," he kept saying. "He comes home that night and finds his house door locked. Both doors locked. He breaks a window and goes in and finds his wife lying on the bed with her wrists slashed. The blood was already dry on the floor and the bedclothes. She did it herself. She'd been dead for three days."

Holiday Inn

VACANCY

Weary of the motor's purr, speed buzzing in the ears, the traffic's challenge, the slither on asphalt of rubber, the landscape's green flicker unrolling along roadsides, the slide past of billboards, the trees pirouetting, the glimpses of rivers, lakes, revolving hills, never quite thoroughly pictured because your eye's on the highway;

by the time the sun — August is the touring month, the family month — the dogday sun sultry in decline, that glares so hot off brightwork and sheening paint, is three quarters down the sky,

the vacationers are ready to turn in

to the nearest motel: stationwagons packed with camping equipment and little children's heads, convertibles, twodoors, fourdoors, Volkswagen busses, hunched trailers in a dozen shapes (Man like the Snail can drag his house with him wherever he goes), pickups mounted with bunks and a gas stove, the old gypsy wagon motorized and enamelled a delicate blue. There's a pet dog in every other car: even horses ride, a Chrysler with a brace of scotties on the back seat and a horsepullman in tow turns in right now.

Community housing. The motel's a latterday pueblo, a pueblo for transients, built, instead of adobe, of stuccoed cinderblock and glass. The travelling public — Dad and Mom and Aunt Susie and the kids — pack themselves into identical cubicles, only these are draped and air-conditioned and furnished with walltowall carpets and tiled baths. The men rush for the icecube machines — there's a bottle of bourbon in the travelling bag. The children raid the cold drink dispensers. Already, in sportshirts and madras shorts, the barelegged tourists exhibit, as they line up for the cafeteria, an assortment of knock knees and bandy legs, seats so tight they'll surely split. Why do the broadest-bottomed women sport the startlingest designs? Purple and green petunias. The baboon effect: Miss Mandril 1963! Bobbypins and serried curlers have reached the distinction of a formal hairdo, like the shock-heads of old time Hottentots. The teenage children, whose legs are more often brown and shapely, favor tornoff jeans. A lot go barefoot. Only the old people still dress like citizens.

Other families smelling of sunburn oil and insect repellent straggle towards the swimming pool. A swim, even in chlorinated water asquirm with kids, delightfully strips away fatigue.

We are all hung with cameras. Maybe it's not quite too late for kodachrome or to use up the few last feet of movie reel on Sister in a red bathingsuit poised on the springboard to dive, or Junior standing on his head: "Now everybody watch this."

NO VACANCY

Every cubicle is full.
Poocho is fed and bedded in the car.

The kids have been treated for sunburn and poison ivy, bandaids applied where needed, and tucked away. Their sleep's a little restless in anticipation of tomorrow.

Thoughtfully Dad and Mom put fresh rolls in their cameras. A wonderful day but the pleasure's too soon gone.

The way the children looked lined up against the balustrade in front of the great curl of water that hangs glassgreen over Niagara's thunderous fall before it's lost in the mist of the gorge, the twins up topside on the blockhouse of the old reconstructed fort, the whole gang grinning as they bite into Mom's sandwiches at the roadside table, or the littlest peering quaintly down into the clear spring behind the picnic ground. The hours go fast. None of us will ever be quite this way again.

Images of the fleeting world.

The sunny moment's fled, the pictures of a wonderful day have faded from the retina, the loved voice no longer sounds in the ear. Who can recapture the fragrance of swamp magnolia? Tomorrow's here before we had a chance to taste today, and death waits to rub it all out at the end of the road.

The snapshot stays. Click. The camera will peel a casual thin scrim of immortality off the fading scene. That's why we spend so much on film

and that's why

Mr. George Eastman, who slung all these cameras round everybody's neck and used to live in a big old stone house among marvelous flowergardens in the handsomest broad elmshaded street of Rochester New York,

made such an incredible amount of money.

The Kodak Man

George Eastman was born in 1854 in Waterbury, in one of those white frame houses, with a flavor of the classical revival about the porch, that give such elegance to the towns and villages of upstate New York.

His people were not well off but they were proud of their first settler stock. The father, George Washington Eastman, taught the lost art of penmanship. There were two girls but George was the only boy.

The year the Civil War broke out, when George was six, the family moved to Rochester. Mr. Eastman hoped to make a better living by setting up what was certainly one of the first commercial colleges. Besides the fine Spencerian pen, he taught his students double entry bookkeeping, the writing of business letters and the rudiments of office management. They were hardly settled in Rochester before Mr. Eastman died. The family had hard sledding. Mrs. Eastman took in boarders. Young George helped out by cutting walnut brackets for bookcases with a scrollsaw. At fourteen he had to go to work as an office boy. Whatever he could earn was sorely needed to make ends meet. He worked for an insurance firm. He was a conscientious lad. When at twenty he secured a position as bookkeeper with the Rochester Savings Bank, the family and friends thought his career was made; —

but George had a hobby. He was an amateur photographer. He improvised a dark room. He developed his own plates. His equipment didn't satisfy him. He coated his own plates. It took too long by hand. By the time he was twentyfive he had worked out a mechanical process for coating dry plates. He put through a patent, and managed to interest a local promoter, who ran a plant for the manufacture of wagoner's whips, in the factory production of photographic plates on a large scale.

George Eastman resigned from the bank. From that day on he hardly left his factory. He watched every process with an anxious eye. His equipment never satisfied him. Everything had to be improved. He experimented early and late. Trial and error. Many a night he slept in a hammock slung in a corner of his workshop.

In 1884 he patented a paperbacked film you could roll. He never forgot he was an amateur photographer. He wanted a product cheap and practical enough for everybody to use. He drove himself tirelessly.

He hired chemists. He drove them as hard as he drove himself. "The technical men," he wrote in an instruction manual, "must make a record to hold their jobs. If they do not they are no better than uneducated men: in fact not as good, because an educated man who is not efficient is a spoiled man."

In 1888 he marketed the first "Kodak," a fixed-focus box camera that took round pictures two and a half inches in diameter on a paperback roll of a hundred exposures. When you had exposed them all you mailed the box back to the factory for recharging. They developed the negatives and printed the pictures. "You press the button and we do the rest," was the salesman's slogan. He called it a kodak because that was what it sounded like when you clicked the shutter.

George Eastman's whole being was in his factories. Even after his company had several plants he personally supervised them all. He had no time for any life of his own. He remained a wifeless childless man. The kodak caught on so fast that when the company went through one of its periodic reorganizations in 1889 it was capitalized at a million dollars. Competitors he bought up or priced out of the market. By now the kodak was a folding camera equipped with a roll of transparent film you could load in daylight. It was Eastman's film that Edison used in his early experiments with the kinetoscope that foreshadowed motion pictures.

By the turn of the century the Eastman Kodak Company was capitalized at thirty five million dollars and had plants in Rochester; in Kingsport, Tennessee; in Harrow, England, and Vincennes, France; in Germany and Hungary and Australia, and agencies and subsidiaries in every city in the world. After twenty five years of unremitting work George Eastman found himself one of the richest men in America. He'd been too busy to know exactly how it happened.

All the paternal feelings he might have lavished on a family and children were spent on his company and on his home city of Rochester.

Childless, he had a pathetic concern for children and young people. He endowed Rochester University with thirty five million dollars for a medical department and a music school and a women's college and a theatre. He gave twenty millions to M.I.T. He financed a dental clinic in Rochester where school children could have their teeth attended to free, and tonsil and adenoid operations, and where hare lips and cleft palates could be remedied. When he saw what bad teeth English children had he started a dental dispensary in London.

His Eastman Kodak Company was the largest producer of photographic material in the world. Already known as one of the world's great philanthropists,

George Eastman remained a lonely unapproachable man.

He dreaded the public eye. Whenever possible he made his donations anonymous. He almost never talked to reporters. The master of mass photography rarely let his own photograph be taken. In the great age of public millionaires he was the least known of them all.

When war broke out in Europe he was concerned about the children left homeless and orphans. He spent weeks at a time at a sort of home orphanage he set up in the South of France which he called le Chateau des Enfants. A spare whitehaired man in steelrimmed spectacles, he would stand embarrassedly by watching the children play. The children hardly knew who he was.

At seventyone he retired as president of the company but continued as chairman of the board on the lookout for what he called "interesting new developments."

Even so time sometimes hung heavy. He had no family. He'd reached the age when a man's best friends are dying all around. He'd treasured his friends.

At seventytwo he got up a party to hunt big game in Africa. "With gun and camera." They joined the Martin Johnsons, who were the famous wild animal photographers of the time, and spent four months driving in trucks and touring cars around the great plains shooting lions and buffalo, rhinoceros and cheetah, impala and gazelle. He was still a pretty good shot and a tolerable camp cook. Camping out in wild country was one of his pleasures. In camp even on the African veldt he set up a private little kitchen of his own where he could turn out mince pies and ostrichegg omelets for his party.

As the trip neared its end he wrote home to his secretary: "We have travelled four thousand miles with motor car, camel and porter safaris without serious mishap or even discomfort ... Whether anybody is justified in killing a lot of wild animals (mostly harmless) just for the pleasure of taking home socalled 'trophies' to show his friends and bragging (inferentially at least) of his prowess as a hunter, is of course a matter that is open to the opinions of the onlookers, but from whatever viewpoint it is looked at, from that of the sportsman or that of the sentimentalist, the fact remains that the adventure is now over, and this adventurer with his mind filled with memories of many new things he has seen and experienced, now at the end, as always, is turning his face eagerly homeward, to a place where there is an abundance of pure water, where the great majority of the inhabitants are not hopelessly and unspeakably filthy, where the mosquitos are not allowed to spread disease, where the roads are smooth and the streets clean, where the four seasons follow each other in glorious sequence, where there is music, art and science, and boundless scope and unlimited opportunity for the development of all that is admirable in man, and above all where he hopes to enjoy the priceless privilege of a few more years of contact with the friends whom he has gathered about him during the course of a long, interesting and eventful life."

Old age hung heavy on his hands. He was a very solitary man.

Six years later, at his home in Rochester, when at the age of seventyeight he decided he had lived long enough, he prepared a short note before he killed himself, written in his firm regular hand: "To my friends: my work is done. Why wait?"

Wild Life in the Hills

After the long straight swoop across the pancakeflat prairies, hour after hour of harvested land streaked with yellow wheatstubble to the horizon, it's exciting to see hills ahead, dark hills under clouds against the west. For dwellers in the flatlands the hills are a tourist attraction. But on what a scale. The advertisers have gone mad. There's a sign on every fencepost. Billboards zigzag along the highway:

Marvels Ahead
Genuine Prairie Dog City
DOGTOWN RANCH STORE
They Are Alive
Show children wild prairie dogs
REPTILE GARDENS
free ice   free water
Born Lucky See Free Zoo
THINK TALL
Chuck Wagon Quartette
See the Thunder Mine
LOST INJUN MAKE RESERVATION
SIOUX MOTEL

Now the plains heave up into buffcolored slopes. Railroad lines converge. Watertanks glint above the distant checkboard of towns. Grain elevators ride the hills the way cathedrals do in Spain.

THE GATEWAY TO THE BLACK HILLS

In Rapid City the traffic is bumper to bumper. It's a shock after days of empty country under the spacious prairie sky. Camp trailers throng the road to Mt. Rushmore.

DIZZYLAND
Where Weight Turns Upside Down
Instructive   Educational   Exciting
Alligators   Crocodiles   Iguanas   Giant Lizards
Miss This Show and You'll be Sorry the Rest
of Your Life
THE GRAVITY SPOT
Wild Animal Cubs
Snakes

Inside the national park every parking lot is packed. Tents rub elbows with tents under the great black pines in every allotted campsite. Lakes are black with boats. The green upland meadows are dotted with hikers. The Black Hills are as crowded as Central Park on a fine Sunday.

The narrow road through the hills to Mount Rushmore turns out unbelievably winding. Can all these loops be necessary? The cars advance by inches bumper to bumper past marvelous outlooks through tall groves of pine poised above the cloudshadows that travel across the rusty plain.

At last they come into view, the enormous faces carved at such expense out of a cliff upthrust into the sky. The parking places are all full. Every viewpoint is dense with craning heads, brandished cameras, fieldglasses, pointing hands, tots held up so that they can see above the crowd. But it's not sculpture. Somehow the rockhewn faces look flat like old photographs badly reproduced on newsprint.

George Washington hasn't enough chin. He looks more like Susan B. Anthony. Teddy Roosevelt has lost his glasses. Poor Jefferson has the air of a female impersonator. Abe Lincoln at least has a profile. Sidewhiskers give his face some shape.

They don't look big at all way up there on that enormous cliff, under the vast sky and a threatening thunderstorm. "They'll stand out more at night," whispers someone hopefully. "The spotlights set them off."

Won't do us any good. By night we'll be a hundred miles to the west, out in the empty drylands of Wyoming.

The National Park Service must be proud of that road. It's a whimsical road. The touring cars are squeezed along it by the press of traffic like toothpaste out of a tube. It winds up and down the steep mountainside, makes figure eights and switchbacks and actually ties itself in knots. At the sharp curves underloops pass beneath ingenious bridges stoutly built of the great unpeeled trunks of the black pines of these mountains. There are tunnels through the cliff.

The final tunnel is most ingeniously contrived so that we get a last look at the effigies of The Four Great Americans framed in rock. They flicker in the distant sunlight as unsubstantial as faces painted on balloons. They have a dim forgotten look. Coming out of the tunnel there is a curve. The four spook faces slip out of sight behind a magnificent great stand of black pine. The rain pours.

We breast a final hill and wind down into sunlight again in a less crowded valley where every blade of grass glistens from the shower. The lodge we just passed was where Calvin Coolidge used to come on his vacations from the presidency. There's a lake and crowds of campers beside a hundred parked trailers.

The traffic is held up again. What can be wrong? The people on the incoming lane have a look of blank wonder on their faces. Incredulous wonder. It can't be an accident. They look pleased. Our lane's completely stalled.

We climb out of the car. "Goats," says someone in the car ahead. "Goats nothing," says a young man in a blue sedan with a Connecticut license, "they are bighorn sheep . . . there is nothing else they could be."

His wife reaches out a triscuit to a tall slender darkhoofed creature. The long dark muzzle munches. The eyes are dark, fringed with lashes, liquid as brooks.

There is this ewe and a lamb, and up on the slope, a big old ram with spiralled-back horns.

"They haven't any right to be so tame . . . They are the shyest animal that lives."

The ewe pokes her head into another car and backs off munching. The lamb seems shyer. Somebody hopefully produces a pretzel. The ram stands on the steep flank of the cutting a few feet above the two lanes of cars. His hoofs are firmly planted in the shale. Every camera whips out of its case. The mountain sheep hold their ground while shutters click all about them.

"Ovis canadiensis," insists the young man from Connecticut. His voice is shaky with excitement.

People begin to think of the mileage before them, the stalled cars behind. Cameras are shoved back into cases. Motorists climb back into their cars. Everybody drives very carefully as the two lanes of traffic start moving again.

The ewe and the lamb hold their ground, pushing their muzzles towards the passing cars for another cracker, while the ram looks on, for all the world like an old gypsy who's sent his women off to beg, from his post above the road.

1965
HEMINGWAY IN CUBA
by Robert Manning

WHO in my generation was not moved by Hemingway the writer and fascinated by Hemingway the maker of his own legend? "Veteran out of the wars before he was twenty," as Archibald MacLeish described him. "Famous at twenty-five; thirty a master." Wine-stained moods in the sidewalk cafés and roistering nights in Left Bank *boîtes*. Walking home alone in the rain. Talk of death, and scenes of it, in the Spanish sun. Treks and trophies in Tanganyika's green hills. Duck-shooting in the Venetian marshes. Fighting in, and writing about, two world wars. Loving and drinking and fishing out of Key West and Havana. Swaggering into Toots Shor's or posturing in *Life* magazine or talking a verbless sort of Choctaw for the notebooks of Lillian Ross and the pages of the *New Yorker*.

By the time I got the opportunity to meet him, he was savoring the highest moment of his fame — he had just won the Nobel Prize for Literature — but he was moving into the twilight of his life. He was fifty-five but looked older, and was trying to mend a ruptured kidney, a cracked skull, two compressed and one cracked vertebra, and bad burns suffered in the crash of his airplane in the Uganda bush the previous winter. Those injuries, added to half a dozen head wounds, more than 200 shrapnel scars, a shot-off kneecap, wounds in the feet, hands, and groin, had slowed him down. The casually comfortable Cuban villa [the Finca Vigía] had become more home than any place he'd had, and days aboard the *Pilar* were his substitute for high adventure abroad.

A big man. Even after allowing for all the descriptions and photographs, the first impression of Hemingway in the flesh was size. He was barefoot and barelegged, wearing only floppy khaki shorts and a checked sport shirt, its tail tumbling outside. He squinted slightly through round silver-framed glasses, and a tentative smile, the sort that could instantly turn into a sneer or snarl, showed through his clipped white beard. Idleness had turned him to paunch, and he must have weighed then about 225 pounds, but there was no other suggestion of softness in the burly, broad-shouldered frame, and he had the biceps and calves of an N.F.L. linebacker.

"Drink?" Hemingway asked. The alacrity of the reply pleased him, and the smile broadened into a laugh. "Thank God you're a drinking man. There was a photographer here for three days a while ago who didn't drink. He was the cruelest man I've ever met. Cruelest man in the world. Made us stand in the sun for hours at a time. And he didn't drink." With stiff caution, he sank into a large overstuffed chair which had been lined back, sides, and bottom with big art and picture books to brace his injured back.

Hemingway sipped and said, "I don't mind talking tonight, because I never work at night. There's a lot of difference between night thinking and day thinking. Night thoughts are usually nothing. The work you do at night you always will have to do over again in the daytime anyhow. So let's talk. When I talk, incidentally, it's just talk. But when I write I mean it for good."

The living room was nearly fifty feet long and high-ceilinged, with gleaming white walls that set off the Hemingways' small but choice collection of paintings (including a Miró, two by Juan Gris, a Klee, a Braque — since stolen from the villa — and five André Massons), a few trophy heads from the African safaris. In another room, near the entrance to a large tile-floored dining room, was an oil portrait of Hemingway in his thirties, wearing a flowing, open-collar white shirt. "It's an old-days picture of me as Kid Balzac by Waldo Pierce," said Hemingway. "Mary has it around because she likes it."

He rubbed the tight-curled white beard and explained that he wore it because when clean-shaven his skin was afflicted with sore spots if he spent much time in the sun. "I'll clip the damned thing off for Christmas so as not to run against Santa Claus," he said, "and if I rest the hide a couple of weeks at a time, I may be able to keep it off. Hope so anyway."

In one large corner of the living room stood a six-foot-high rack filled with dozens of magazines and newspapers from the States, London, and Paris. In casual piles, books littered windowsills and tables and spilled a trail into two large rooms adjacent. One was a thirty-by-twenty-foot library whose floor-to-ceiling shelves sagged with books. The other was Hemingway's large but crowded bedroom study — littered with correspondence in varied stages of attention or neglect. There were neat piles of opened letters together with stamped and addressed replies; cardboard boxes overflowing with the shards of correspondence that had been opened, presumably read, and one day might be filed; a couple of filing cabinets, whose mysteries probably were best known to a part-time stenographer the Hemingways brought in from Havana a day or two at a time when needed. There was also a large lion skin, in the gaping mouth of which lay half a dozen letters and a pair of manila envelopes. "That's the Urgent in-box," Hemingway explained.

Evening sounds grew strident in the soft tropical outdoors. Distant dogs yelped. Near the house, a hoot owl broke into short, sharp cries. "That's the Bitchy Owl," Hemingway said. "He'll go on like that all night. He's lived here longer than we have.

"I respect writing very much," he said abruptly, "the writer not at all, except as the instrument to do the writing. When a writer retires deliberately from life or is forced out of it by some defect, his writing has a tendency to atrophy, just like a man's limb when it's not used.

"I'm not advocating the strenuous life for everyone or trying to say it's the choice form of life. Anyone who's had the luck or misfortune to be an athlete has to keep his body in shape. The body and mind are closely coordinated. Fattening of the body can lead to fattening of the mind. I would be tempted to say that it can lead to fattening of the soul, but I don't know anything about the soul." He halted, broodingly, as if reflecting on his own aches and pains, his too ample paunch, a blood pressure that was too high, and a set of muscles that were suffering from too many weeks of disuse. "However, in everyone the process of fattening or wasting away will set in, and I guess one is as bad as the other."

He had been reading about medical discoveries which suggested to him that a diet or regimen or treatment that may work for one man does not necessarily work for another. "This was known years ago, really, by people who make proverbs. But now doctors have discovered that certain men need more exercise than others; that certain men are affected by alcohol more than others; that certain people can assimilate more punishment in many ways than others.

"Take Primo Carnera, for instance. Now he was a real nice guy, but he was so big and clumsy it was pitiful. Or take Tom Wolfe, who just never could discipline his mind to his tongue. Or Scott Fitzgerald, who just couldn't drink." He pointed to a couch across the room. "If Scott had been drinking with us and Mary called us to dinner, Scott'd make it to his feet, all right, but then he'd probably fall down. Alcohol was just poison to him. Because all these guys had these weaknesses, it won them sympathy and favor, more sometimes than a guy without those defects would get."

For a good part of his adult life Hemingway was, of course, a ten-goal drinker, and he could hold it well. He was far more disciplined in this regard, though, than the legend may suggest. Frequently when he was working hard, he would drink nothing, except perhaps a glass or two of wine with meals. By rising at about daybreak or half an hour thereafter, he had put in a full writing day by ten or eleven in the morning and was ready for relaxation when others were little more than under way.

As in his early days, Hemingway in the late years worked with painful slowness. He wrote mostly in longhand, frequently while standing at a bookcase in his bedroom; occasionally he would typewrite ("when trying to keep up with dialogue"). For years he carefully logged each day's work. Except for occasional spurts when he was engaged in relatively unimportant efforts, his output ran between 400 and 700 words a day. Mary Hemingway remembers very few occasions when it topped 1000 words.

He did not find writing to be quick or easy. "I always hurt some," he remarked.

Hemingway was capable of great interest in and generosity toward younger writers and some older writers, but as he shows in *A Moveable Feast,* he had a curious and unbecoming compulsion to poke and peck at the reputations of many of his literary contemporaries. Gertrude Stein, Sherwood Anderson, T. S. Eliot, not to mention Fitzgerald, Wolfe, Ford Madox Ford, James Gould Cozzens, and others, were invariably good for a jab or two if their names came up. As for the critics — "I often feel," he said, "that there is now a rivalry between writing and criticism, rather than the feeling that one should help the other." Writers today could not learn much from the critics. "Critics should deal more with dead writers. A living writer can learn a lot from dead writers."

Fiction-writing, Hemingway felt, was to invent out of knowledge. "To invent out of knowledge means to produce inventions that are true. Every man should have a built-in automatic crap detector operating inside him. It also should have a manual drill and a crank handle in case the machine breaks down. If you're going to write, you have to find out what's bad for you. Part of that you learn fast, and then you learn what's good for you."

What sort of things? "Well, take certain diseases. These diseases are not good for you. I was born before the age of antibiotics, of course. . . . Now take *The Big Sky* [by A. B. Guthrie]. That was a very good book in many ways, and it was very good on one of the diseases . . . just about the best book ever written on the clap." Hemingway smiled.

"But back to inventing. In *The Old Man and the Sea* I knew two or three things about the situation, but I didn't know the story." He hesitated, filling the intervals with a vague movement of his hands. "I didn't even know if that big fish was going to bite for the old man when it started smelling around the bait. I had to write on, inventing out of knowledge. You reject everything that is not or can't be completely true. I didn't know what was going to happen for sure in *For Whom the Bell Tolls* or *Farewell to Arms*. I was inventing."

Philip Young's *Ernest Hemingway*, published in 1953, had attributed much of Hemingway's inspiration or "invention" to his violent experiences as a boy and in World War I.

"If you haven't read it, don't bother," Hemingway volunteered. "How would you like it if someone said that everything you've done in your life was done because of some trauma. Young had a theory that was like — you know, the Procrustean bed, and he had to cut me to fit into it."

During dinner, the talk continued on writing styles and techniques. Hemingway thought too many contemporary writers defeated themselves through addiction to symbols. "No good book has ever been written that has in it symbols arrived at beforehand and stuck in." He waved a chunk of French bread. "That kind of symbol sticks out like — like raisins in raisin bread. Raisin bread is all right, but plain bread is better."

He mentioned Santiago, his old fisherman, in roughly these terms: Santiago was never alone because he had his friend and enemy, the sea, and the things that lived in the sea, some of which he loved and others he hated. He loved the sea, but the sea is a great whore, as the book made clear. He had tried to make everything in the story real — the boy, the sea, and the marlin and the sharks, the hope being that each would then mean many things. In that way, the parts of a story become symbols, but they are not first designed or planted as symbols.

The Bitchy Owl hooted the household to sleep. I was awakened by
tropical birds at the dawn of a bright and promising day. This was to
be Hemingway's first fishing trip on *Pilar* since long before his African
crash. By six thirty he was dressed in yesterday's floppy shorts and
sport shirt, barefooted, and hunched over his New York *Times,* one of
the six papers he and Mary read every day. From the record player
came a mixture of Scarlatti, Beethoven, Oscar Peterson, and a remake
of some 1928 Louis Armstrong.

At brief intervals Hemingway popped a pill into his mouth. "Since
the crash I have to take so many of them they have to fight among
themselves unless I space them out," he said.

While we were breakfasting, a grizzled Canary Islander named Gregorio, who served as the *Pilar's* first mate, chef, caretaker, and bartender, was preparing the boat for a day at sea. By nine o'clock, with a
young nephew to help him, he had fueled the boat, stocked it with
beer, whiskey, wine, and a bottle of tequila, a batch of fresh limes, and
food for a large seafood lunch afloat. As we made out of Havana
Harbor, Gregorio at the wheel and the young boy readying the deep-
sea rods, reels, and fresh bait-fish, Hemingway pointed out landmarks
and waved jovially to passing skippers. They invariably waved back,
occasionally shouting greetings to "Papa." He sniffed the sharp sea air
with delight and peered ahead for the dark line made by the Gulf
Stream. "Watch the birds," he said. "They show us when the fish are
up."

Mary Hemingway had matters to handle at the finca and in the city,
so she could not come along, but out of concern for Hemingway's
health she exacted a promise. In return for the long-missed fun of a
fishing expedition, he agreed to take it easy and come back early, in
time for a nap before an art exhibit to which he and Mary had promised their support. He was in a hurry, therefore, to reach good fishing
water. Gregorio pushed the boat hard to a stretch of the Gulf Stream
off Cojimar. Hemingway relaxed into one of the two cushioned bunks
in the boat's open-ended cabin.

"It's wonderful to get out on the water. I need it." He gestured
toward the ocean. "It's the last free place there is, the sea. Even Africa's about gone; it's at war, and that's going to go on for a very long
time."

The *Pilar* fished two rods from its high antenna-like outriggers and
two from seats at the stern, and at Hemingway's instruction, Gregorio
and the boy baited two with live fish carefully wired to the hooks, and
two with artificial lures. A man-o'-war bird gliding lazily off the coast
pointed to the first school of the day, and within an hour the *Pilar* had
its first fish, a pair of bonito sounding at the end of the outrigger lines.
Before it was over, the day was to be one of the best fishing days in

many months, with frequent good runs of bonito and dolphin and pleasant interludes of quiet in which to sip drinks, to soak up the Caribbean sun, and to talk.

Sometimes moody, sometimes erupting with boyish glee at the strike of a tuna or the golden blue explosion of a hooked dolphin, and sometimes — as if to defy or outwit his wounds — pulling himself by his arms to the flying bridge to steer the *Pilar* for a spell, Hemingway talked little of the present, not at all of the future, and a great deal of the past.

He recalled when Scribner's sent him first galley proofs of *For Whom the Bell Tolls*. "I remember, I spent ninety hours on the proofs of that book without once leaving the hotel room. When I finished, I thought the type was so small nobody would ever buy the book. I'd shot my eyes, you see. I had corrected the manuscript several times but still was not satisfied. I told Max Perkins about the type, and he said if I really thought it was too small, he'd have the whole book reprinted. That's a real expensive thing, you know. He was a sweet guy. But Max was right, the type was all right."

"Do you ever read any of your stuff over again?"

"Sometimes I do," he said. "When I'm feeling low. It makes you feel good to look back and see you can write."

"Is there anything you've written that you would do differently if you could do it over?"

"Not yet."

New York. "It's a very unnatural place to live. I could never live there. And there's not much fun going to the city now. Max is dead. Granny Rice is dead. He was a wonderful guy. We always used to go to the Bronx Zoo and look at the animals."

The Key West days, in the early thirties, were a good time. "There was a fighter there — he'd had one eye ruined, but he was still pretty good, and he decided to start fighting again. He wanted to be his own promotor. He asked me if I would referee his bout each week. I told him, 'Nothing doing,' he shouldn't go in the ring anymore. Any fighter who knew about his bad eye would just poke his thumb in the other one and then beat his head off.

"The fighter said, 'The guys come from somewhere else won't know 'bout my eye, and no one around here in the Keys gonna dare poke my eye.'

"So I finally agreed to referee for him. This was the Negro section, you know, and they really introduced me: 'And the referee for to-night, the world-famous millionaire, sportsman, and playboy, Mister Ernest Hemingway!' " Hemingway chuckled. "Playboy was the greatest title they thought they could give a man." Chuckle again. "How can the Nobel Prize move a man who has heard plaudits like that?"

Frequently a sharp cry from Gregorio on the flying bridge interrupted the talk. "Feesh! Papa, feesh!" Line would snap from one of the outriggers, and a reel begin to snarl. "You take him," Hemingway would say, or if two fish struck at once, as frequently happened, he would leap to one rod and I to the other.

He talked about the act of playing a fish as if it were an English sentence. "The way to do it, the style, is not just an idle concept. It is simply the way to get done what is supposed to be done; in this case it brings in the fish. The fact that the right way looks pretty or beautiful when it's done is just incidental."

Hemingway had written only one play, *The Fifth Column.* Why no others?

"If you write a play, you have to stick around and fix it up," he said. "They always want to fool around with them to make them commercially successful, and you don't like to stick around that long. After I've written, I want to go home and take a shower."

Almost absently, he plucked James Joyce out of the air. "Once Joyce said to me he was afraid his writing was too suburban and that maybe he should get around a bit and see the world, the way I was doing. He was under great discipline, you know — his wife, his work, his bad eyes. And his wife said, yes, it *was* too suburban. 'Jim could do with a spot of that lion-hunting.' How do you like that? A *spot* of lion-hunting!

"We'd go out, and Joyce would fall into an argument or a fight. He couldn't even see the man, so he'd say, 'Deal with him, Hemingway! Deal with him!'" Hemingway paused. "In the big league it is not the way it says in the books."

Hemingway was not warm toward T. S. Eliot. He preferred to praise Ezra Pound, who at that time was still confined in St. Elizabeth's mental hospital in Washington. "Ezra Pound is a great poet, and whatever he did, he has been punished greatly, and I believe should be freed to go and write poems in Italy, where he is loved and understood. He was the master of Eliot. I was a member of an organization which Pound founded with Natalia Barney in order to get Eliot out of his job in a bank so he could be free to write poetry. It was called Bel Esprit. Eliot, I believe, was able to get out of his job and edit a review and write poetry freely due to the backing of other people than this organization. But the organization was typical of Pound's generosity and interest in all forms of the arts regardless of any benefits to himself or of the possibilities that the people he encouraged would be his rivals.

"Eliot is a winner of the Nobel Prize. I believe it might well have gone to Pound, as a poet. Pound certainly deserved punishment, but I believe this would be a good year to release poets and allow them to continue to write poetry. . . . Ezra Pound, no matter what he may think, is not as great a poet as Dante, but he is a very great poet for all his errors."

Dusk was coming when the *Pilar* turned toward Havana Harbor, its skipper steering grandly from the flying bridge. What remained of the bottle of tequila and half of a lime rested in a holder cut into the mahogany rail near the wheel. "To ward off sea serpents," Hemingway explained, passing the bottle for a ceremonial homecoming swig.

Hemingway's good spirits on his return helped to diminish his wife's concern about his overextending himself. She served up a hot oyster stew, and later, clutching an early nightcap, Hemingway sprawled with pleased fatigue in his big armchair and talked of books he had recently read. He had started Saul Bellow's *The Adventures of Augie March,* but didn't like it. "But when I'm working," he said, " and read to get away from it, I'm inclined to make bad judgments about other people's writing." He thought Bellow's very early book, *Dangling Man,* much better.

One of the post-war writers who had impressed him most was John Horne Burns, who wrote *The Gallery* and two other novels and then, in 1953, died in circumstances that suggested suicide. "There was a fellow who wrote a fine book and then a stinking book about a prep school, and then he just blew himself up," Hemingway mused, adding a gesture that seemed to ask, how do you explain such a thing? He stared at nothing, seeming tired and sad.

"You know," he said, "my father shot himself."

There was silence. It had frequently been said that Hemingway never cared to talk about his father's suicide.

"Do you think it took courage?" I asked.

Hemingway pursed his lips and shook his head. "No. It's everybody's right, but there's a certain amount of egotism in it and a certain disregard of others." He turned off that conversation by picking up a handful of books. "Here are a few things you might like to look at before you turn off the light." He held out *The Retreat,* by P. H. Newby, Max Perkins' selected letters, *The Jungle is Neutral,* by Frederick S. Chapman, and Malcolm Cowley's *The Literary Situation.*

By seven the next morning a rabble of dogs yipped and yelped in the yard near the finca's small guesthouse. Hemingway, in a tattered robe and old slippers, was already half through the *Times.*

"Did you finish the Cowley book last night?" he asked. "Very good, I think. I never realized what a tough time writers have economically, if they have it as tough as Malcolm says they do."

He was reminded of his early days in Paris. "It never seemed like hardship to me. It was hard work, but it was fun. I was working, and I had a wife and kid to support. I remember, first I used to go to the market every morning and get the stuff for Bumby's [his first son, John] bottle. His mother had to have her sleep." Lest this should be taken as a criticism, he added, "That's characteristic, you know, of the very finest women. They need their sleep, and when they get it, they're wonderful."

Another part of the routine in the Paris days, to pick up eating money, was Hemingway's daily trip to a gymnasium to work as a sparring partner for fighters. The pay was two dollars an hour. "That was very good money then, and I didn't get marked up very much. I had one rule: never provoke a fighter. I tried not to get hit. They had plenty of guys they could knock around."

He reached for the mail, slit open one from a pile of fifteen letters. It was from a high school English teacher in Miami, Florida, who complained that her students rarely read good literature and relied for "knowledge" on the movies, television, and radio. To arouse their interest, she wrote, she told them about Hemingway's adventures and pressed them to read his writings. "Therefore, in a sense," she concluded, "you are the teacher in my tenth grade classroom. I thought you'd like to know it." Hemingway found the letter depressing: "Pretty bad if kids are spending all that time away from books."

The next fishing expedition was even better than the first — fewer fish, but two of them were small marlin, one about eighty pounds, the other eighty-five, that struck simultaneously and were boated, Hemingway's with dispatch, the second at a cost of amateurish sweat and agony that was the subject of as much merriment as congratulations. It was a more sprightly occasion, too, because Mary Hemingway was able to come along. A bright, generous, and energetic woman, Hemingway's fourth wife cared for him well, anticipated his moods and his desires, enjoyed and played bountiful hostess to his friends, diplomatically turned aside some of the most taxing demands on his time and generosity. More than that, she shared his love and the broad mixture of interests — books, good talk, traveling, fishing, shooting — that were central to Hemingway's life. His marriage to her was plainly the central and guiding personal relationship of his last fifteen years.

Hemingway gazed happily at the pair of marlin. "We're back in business," he said, and gave Mary a hug. "This calls for celebration," said Mary.

"Off to the Floridita," said Hemingway.

The Floridita was once one of those comfortably shoddy Havana saloons where the food was cheap and good and the drinking serious. By then, enjoying a prosperity that was due in no small part to its reputation as the place you could see and maybe even drink with Papa Hemingway, it had taken on a red-plush grandeur and even had a velvet cord to block off the dining room entrance. "It looks crummy now," Hemingway said, "but the drinking's as good as ever."

The Floridita played a special role in Hemingway's life. "My not living in the United States," he explained, "does not mean any separation from the tongue or even the country. Any time I come to the Floridita I see Americans from all over. It can even be closer to America in many ways than being in New York. You go there for a drink or two, and see everybody from everyplace. I live in Cuba because I love Cuba — that does not mean a dislike for anyplace else. And because here I get privacy when I write. If I want to see anyone, I just go into town, or the Air Force guys come out to the place, naval characters and all — guys I knew in the war. I used to have privacy in Key West, but then I had less and less when I was trying to work, and there were too many people around, so I'd come over here and work in the Ambos Mundos Hotel."

The Floridita's bar was crowded, but several customers obligingly slid away from one section that had been designated long before by the proprietor as "Papa's Corner." Smiles. "Hello, Papa." Handshakes all around. "Three *Papa Dobles*," said Hemingway, and the barkeep hastened to manufacture three immense daiquiris according to a Floridita recipe that relies more on grapefruit juice than on lemon or lime juice. The *Papa Doble* was a heavy seller in those days at $1.25, and a bargain at that.

Two sailors off a U.S. aircraft carrier worked up nerve to approach the author and ask for an autograph. "I read all your books," said one of them.

"What about you?" Hemingway said to the other.

"I don't read much," the young sailor said.

"Get started," Hemingway said.

The Floridita's owner appeared, with embraces for the Hemingways and the news that he was installing a modern men's room. Hemingway noted sadly that all the good things were passing. "A wonderful old john back there," he said. "Makes you want to shout: Water closets of the world unite; you have nothing to lose but your chains."

The Hemingways left Cuba in July of 1960 and went to Key West. From there, with luggage that filled a train compartment, they went to New York to live for a while in a small apartment. Later they moved to the new place Hemingway had bought in Ketchum, Idaho, close to the kind of shooting, fishing, walking that had beguiled him as a young boy in upper Michigan. He went to Spain for six weeks that summer to follow his friend Ordoñez and his rival, Dominguin, in their *mano a mano* tour of bullfights and to write *The Dangerous Summer*, bullfight pieces commissioned by *Life* magazine. I have the impression that he didn't think very much of them, but he didn't say. His spirits seemed low after that and ostensibly stayed that way, though he apparently kept at work out in Ketchum almost until the day his gun went off.

The rereading of the notes and letters from which these glimpses of Hemingway are drawn — for glimpses are all they are — induces a curious thought: It is possible that to have known him, at least to have known him superficially and late in his life, makes it more rather than less difficult to understand him.

He made himself easy to parody, but he was impossible to imitate. He sometimes did or said things that seemed almost perversely calculated to obscure his many gallantries and generosities and the many enjoyments and enthusiasms he made possible for others. He could be fierce in his sensitivity to criticism and competitive in his craft to the point of vindictiveness, but he could laugh at himself ("I'm Ernie Hemorrhoid, the poor man's Pyle," he announced when he put on his war correspondent's uniform) and could enjoy the pure pride of believing that he had accomplished much of what he set out to do forty-five years before in a Parisian loft.

1966
WHITE-COLLAR PILL PARTY
by Bruce Jackson

DRUGS, like chewing gum, TV, oversize cars, and crime, are part of the American way of life. No one receives an exemption.

Think for a moment: how many people do you know who cannot stop stuffing themselves without an amphetamine and who cannot go to sleep without a barbiturate (over *nine billion* of those produced last year) or make it through a workday without a sequence of tranquilizers? And what about those six million alcoholics, who daily ingest quantities of what is, by sheer force of numbers, the most addicting drug in America?

The publicity goes to the junkies, but these account for only a small portion of the American drug problem. Far more worrisome are the millions of people who have become dependent on commercial drugs. The junkie *knows* he is hooked; the housewife on amphetamine and the businessman on meprobamate hardly ever realize what has gone wrong.

Sometimes the pill-takers meet other pill-takers, and an odd thing happens: instead of using the drug to cope with the world, they begin to use their time to take drugs. Taking drugs becomes *something to do.* When this stage is reached, the drug-taking pattern broadens: the user takes a wider variety of drugs with increasing frequency. For want of a better term, one might call it the white-collar drug scene.

I first learned about it during a party in Chicago last winter, and the best way to introduce you will be to tell you something about that evening, the people I met, what I think was happening.

There were about a dozen people in the room, and over the noise from the record player scraps of conversation came through:

"Now the Desbutal, if you take it with this stuff, has a peculiar effect, contraindication, at least it did for me. You let me know if you . . ."

"I don't have one legitimate prescription, Harry, not *one!* Can you imagine that?" "I'll get you some tomorrow, dear."

". . . and this pharmacist on Fifth will sell you all the leapers [amphetamines] you can carry — just like that. Right off the street. I don't think he'd know a prescription if it bit him." "As long as he can read the labels, what the hell."

"You know, a funny thing happened to me. I got this green and yellow capsule, and I looked it up in the Book, and it wasn't anything I'd been using, and I thought, great! It's not something I've built a tolerance to. And I took it. A couple of them. And you know what happened? *Nothing!* That's what happened, not a goddamned thing."

The Book — the *Physicians' Desk Reference,* which lists the composition and effects of almost all commercial pharmaceuticals produced in this country — passes back and forth, and two or three people at a time look up the contents and possible values of a drug one of them has just discovered or heard about or acquired or taken. The Book is the pillhead's *Yellow Pages:* you look up the effect you want ("Sympathomimetics" or "Cerebral Stimulants," for example), and it tells you the magic columns. The pillheads swap stories of kicks and sound like professional chemists discussing recent developments; others listen, then examine the *PDR* to see if the drug discussed really could do that.

Eddie, the host, a painter who has received some recognition, had been awake three or four days, he was not exactly sure. He consumes between 150 and 200 milligrams of amphetamine a day, needs a large part of that to stay awake, even when he has slipped a night's sleep in somewhere. The dose would cause most people some difficulty; the familiar diet pill, a capsule of Dexamyl or Eskatrol, which makes the new user edgy and over-energetic and slightly insomniac the first few days, contains only 10 or 15 milligrams of amphetamine. But amphetamine is one of the few central nervous system stimulants to which one can develop a tolerance, and over the months and years Ed and his friends have built up massive tolerances and dependencies. "Leapers aren't so hard to give up," he told me. "I mean, I sleep almost constantly when I'm off, but you get over that. But everything is so damned boring without the pills."

I asked him if he knew many amphetamine users who have given up the pills.

"For good?"

I nodded.

"I haven't known anybody that's given it up for good." He reached out and took a few pills from the candy dish in the middle of the coffee table, then washed them down with some Coke.

The last couple to arrive — a journalist and his wife — settled into positions. The wife was next to me on the oversize sofa, and she skimmed through the "Product Identification Section" of the *PDR,* dozens of pages of pretty color photos of tablets and capsules. "Hey!" she said to no one in particular. Then, to her husband, "Look at the pretty hexagonal. George, get the Source to get some of them for me." George, across the table, near the fire, nodded.

I had been advised to watch him as he turned on. As the pills took effect something happened to the muscles of his face, and the whole assembly seemed to go rubbery. His features settled lower and more loosely on the bones of his head. He began to talk with considerably more verve.

A distractingly pretty girl with dark brown eyes sat at the edge of our group and ignored both the joint making its rounds and the record player belching away just behind her. Between the thumb and middle finger of her left hand she held a pill that was blue on one side and yellow on the other; steadily, with the double-edged razor blade she held in her right hand, she sawed on the seam between the two halves of the pill. Every once in a while she rotated it a few degrees with her left index finger. Her skin was smooth, and the light from the fireplace played tricks with it, all of them charming. The right hand sawed on.

I got the Book from the coffee table and looked for the pill in the pages of color pictures, but before I found it, Ed leaned over and said, "They're Desbutal Gradumets. Abbott Labs."

I turned to the "Professional Products Information" section and learned that Desbutal is a combination of Desoxyn (methamphetamine hydrochloride, also marketed as Methedrine) and Nembutal, that the pill the girl sawed contained 15 milligrams of the Desoxyn, that the combination of drugs served "to both stimulate and calm the patient so that feelings of depression are overcome and a sense of well-being and increased energy is produced. Inner tension and anxiety are relieved so that a sense of serenity and ease of mind prevails." Gradumets, the Book explained, "are indicated in the management of obesity, the management of depressed states, certain behavioral syndromes, and a number of typical geriatric conditions," as well as "helpful in managing psychosomatic complaints and neuroses," Parkinson's disease, and a hangover.

The girl, obviously, was not interested in all of the pill's splendid therapeutic promises; were she, she would not have been so diligently sawing along that seam. She was after the methamphetamine, which like other amphetamines "depresses appetite, elevates the mood, increases the urge to work, imparts a sense of increased efficiency, and counteracts sleepiness and the feeling of fatigue in most persons."

After what seemed a long while the pill split into two round sections. A few scraps of the yellow Nembutal adhered to the Desoxyn side, and she carefully scraped them away. "Wilkinson's the best blade for this sort of thing," she said. I asked if she didn't cut herself on occasion, and she showed me a few nicks in her left thumb. "But a single edge isn't thin enough to do it neatly."

She put the blue disk in one small container, the yellow in another, then from a third took a fresh Desbutal and began sawing. I asked why she kept the Nembutal, since it was the Desoxyn she was after.

"Sometimes I might want to sleep, you know. I might *have* to sleep because something is coming up the next day. It's not easy for us to sleep, and sometimes we just don't for a couple or three days. But if we have to, we can just take a few of these." She smiled at me tolerantly, then returned to her blade and tablet.

When I saw Ed in New York several weeks later, I asked about her. "Some are like that," he said; "they like to carve on their pills. She'll sit and carve for thirty or forty minutes."

"Is that sort of ritual an important part of it all?"

"I think it is. She seems to have gotten hung up on it. I told her that she shouldn't take that Nembutal, that I have been cutting the Nembutal off my pills. It only takes about thirty seconds. And she can spend a good half hour at it if she has a mind to. I told her once about the effect of taking a Spansule; you know, one of those big things with sustained release [like Dexamyl, a mixture of dextroamphetamine sulfate and amobarbital designed to be effective over a twelve-hour period]. What you do is open the capsule and put it in a little bowl and grind up the little pellets until it's powder, then stuff all the powder back in the pill and take it, and it all goes off at once. I'll be damned if I haven't seen her grinding away like she was making matzo meal. That's a sign of a fairly confirmed head when they reach that ritual stage."

Next to the candy dish filled with Dexedrine, Dexamyl, Eskatrol, Desbutal, and a few other products I hadn't yet learned to identify, near the five-pound box of Dexedrine tablets someone had brought, were two bottles. One was filled with Dexedrine Elixir, the other with Dexamyl Elixir. Someone took a long swallow from the latter, and I thought him to be an extremely heavy user, but when the man left the room, a lawyer told me he'd bet the man was new at it. "He has to be. A mouthful is like two pills, and if he was a real head, he'd have a far greater tolerance to the Dexedrine than the amobarbital, and the stuff would make him sleepy. Anyhow, I don't like to mess with barbiturates much anymore. Dorothy Kilgallen died from that." He took a drink from the Dexedrine bottle and said, "And this tastes better. Very tasty stuff, like cherry syrup. Make a nice cherry Coke with it. The Dexamyl Elixir is bitter."

Someone emptied the tobacco from a Salem and filled the tube with grass; he tamped it down with a Tinkertoy stick, crimped the tip, then lighted it and inhaled noisily. He immediately passed the joint to the person on his left. Since one must hold the smoke in one's lungs for several seconds to get the full effect, it is more economical for several people to turn on at once. The grass was very good and seemed to produce a quiet but substantial high. One doesn't notice it coming on, but there is a realization that for a while now the room has been a decidedly pleasant one, and some noises are particularly interesting for their own sake.

I leaned back and closed my eyes for a moment. It was almost 5 A.M., and in three hours I had to catch a plane at O'Hare. "You're not going to *sleep* are you?" The tone implied that this group considered few human frailties truly gauche, but going to sleep was surely one of them. I shook my head no and looked to see who had spoken. It was Ed's wife; she looked concerned. "Do you want a pill?" I shook my head no again.

Then, just then, I realized that Ed — who knew I was not a pill-user — had not once in the evening offered me one of the many samples that had been passed around, nor had anyone else. Just the grass, but not the pills. His wife suggested a pill not so that I might get high, but merely so that I could stay awake without difficulty.

"I'm not tired," I said, "just relaxing." I assured her I wouldn't doze off. She was still concerned, however, and got me a cup of coffee from the kitchen and offered some Murine from her purse.

The front door opened, and there was a vicious blast of winter off Lake Michigan. Ed kicked the door closed behind him and dumped an armful of logs by the fireplace, then went back into the kitchen. A moment later he returned and passed around a small dish of capsules. And this time it was handed to me. They looked familiar. "One a Days," he said. I had learned enough from the Book to see the need for them: the amphetamine user often does not eat for long periods of time (some days his only nourishment is the sugar in the bottles of soda which he drinks to wash down the pills and counter their side effect of dehydration of the mouth), and he not only tends to lose weight but also risks vitamin deficiencies. After a while, the heavy user learns to force-feed himself or go off pills every once in a while in order to eat without difficulty and to keep his tolerance level down.

Later, getting settled in the plane, I thought, What a wild party that was. I'd never been to anything quite like it, and I began making notes about what had gone on. Not long before we came into Logan, it suddenly struck me that there had been nothing wild about the party at all, nothing. There had been women there, some of them unaccompanied and some with husbands or dates, but there had been none of the playing around and sexual hustling that several years of academic and business world parties had led me to consider a correlative of almost any evening gathering of more than ten men and women: no meaningful looks, no wisecracks, no "accidental" rubbing. No one had spoken loudly, no one had become giggly or silly, no one had lost control or seemed anywhere near it. Viewed with some perspective, the evening seemed nothing more than comfortable.

There are various ways to acquire the pills, but the most common is also the most legal: prescriptions. Even though there is now a federal law requiring physicians and pharmacists to maintain careful records regarding prescriptions for drugs like Dexamyl, many physicians are careless about prescribing them, and few seem to realize that the kind of personality that needs them is often the kind of personality that can easily acquire an overwhelming dependency on them. Often a patient will be issued a refillable prescription; if the patient is a heavy user, all he needs to do is visit several physicians and get refillable prescriptions from each. If he is worried that a cross-check of druggists' lists might turn up his name, he can easily give some of his doctors false names.

There are dealers, generically called the Source, who specialize in selling these drugs; some give them away. They do not seem to be underworld types but professional people in various capacities who, for one reason or another, have access to large quantities of them. If one is completely without connections, the drugs can be made at home. One young man I know made mescaline, amphetamine, meth-

amphetamine, LSD, and DET and DMT (diethyl- and dimethyltryp-
tamine, hallucinogens of shorter duration and greater punch than
LSD) in his kitchen.

There was talk in Manhattan last winter, just before the new law
took effect, that some LSD factories were closing down, and I know
that some Sources stopped supplying. For a short time the price of
LSD went up; then things stabilized, competition increased, a new
packaging method developed popularity (instead of the familiar sugar
cubes, one now takes one's dose on a tiny slip of paper; like a spitball,
only you don't spit it out), and now the price for a dose of LSD is
about 20 percent *less* than it was a year ago.

Since most of the pillheads I'm talking about are middle-class and
either professional or semiprofessional, they will still be able to obtain
their drugs. Their drugs of choice have a legitimate use, and it is
unlikely that the government's attempt to prevent diversion will be
more than partially successful. If our narcotics agents have been unable to keep off the open market drugs which have no legitimate use
at all — heroin and marijuana — it hardly seems likely that they will
be able to control chemicals legitimately in the possession of millions
of citizens. I asked one amphetamine head in the Southwest how local
supplies had been affected by the new law. "I heard about that law,"
he said, "but I haven't seen anybody getting panicked." Another user
tells me prices have risen slightly, but not enough yet to present
difficulties.

There are marked differences between these drug-users and the
ones who make the newspapers. They're well educated (largely college
graduates), are older (25 to 40), and middle-class (with a range of
occupations: writers, artists, lawyers, TV executives, journalists, political aides, housewives). They're not like the high school kids who are
after a kick in any form (some of them rather illusory, as one psychosomatic gem reported to me by a New Jersey teen-ager: "What some
of the kids do is take a cigarette and saturate it with perfume or
hairspray. When this is completely soaked in and dry, they cup the
cigarettes and inhale every drag. Somehow this gives them a good
high"), or college students experimenting with drugs as part of a romantic program of self-location. The kids take drugs "because it's
cool" and to get high, but when you talk to them you find that most
ascribe the same general high to a wide range of drugs having quite
diverse effects; they're promiscuous and insensitive. There is considerable evidence to suggest that almost none of the college drug-users
take anything illegal after graduation, for most of them lose their connections and their curiosity.

It is not likely that many of the thousands of solitary amphetamine
abusers would join these groups. They take drugs to *avoid* deviance —
so they can be fashionably slim, or bright and alert and functional, or

so they can muster the *quoi que* with which to face the tedium of house-work or some other dull job — and the last thing they want is mem-bership in a group defined solely by one clear form of rule-breaking behavior. Several of the group members were first turned on by physi-cians, but a larger number were turned on by friends. Most were after a particular therapeutic effect, but after a while interest developed in the drug for its own sake and the effect became a cause, and after that the pattern of drug-taking overcame the pattern of taking a specific drug.

Some of the socialized amphetamine-users specialize. One takes Dexedrine and Dexamyl almost exclusively; he takes other combina-tions only when he is trying to reduce his tolerance to Dexamyl. Though he is partly addicted to the barbiturates, they do not seem to trouble him very much, and on the few occasions when he has had to go off drugs (as when he was in California for a few months and found getting legal prescriptions too difficult and for some reason didn't connect with a local Source), he has had no physiological trou-ble giving them up. He did, of course, suffer from the overwhelming depression and enervation that characterize amphetamine withdrawal. Most heads will use other drugs along with amphetamine — especially marijuana — in order to appreciate the heightened alertness they've acquired; some alternate with hallucinogens.

To the heroin addict, the square is anyone who does not use heroin. For the dedicated pillhead there is a slightly narrower definition: the square is someone who has an alcohol dependency; those who use nothing at all aren't even classified. The boozers do bad things, they get drunk and lose control and hurt themselves and other people. They contaminate their tubes, and whenever they get really far out, they don't even remember it the next day. The pillhead's disdain is sometimes rather excessive. One girl, for example, was living with a fellow who, like her, was taking over 500 milligrams of amphetamine a day. They were getting on well. One night the two were at a party, and instead of chewing pills, her man had a few beers; the girl was furious, betrayed, outraged. Another time, at a large party that sprawled through a sprawling apartment, a girl had been on scotch and grass and she went to sleep. There were three men in the room, none of them interested in her sexually, yet they jeered and wisecracked as she nodded off. It was 4 or 5 A.M. of a Sunday, not too unreasonable a time to be drowsy. When they saw she was really asleep — breaking the double taboo by having drunk too much scotch and been put to sleep by it — they muttered a goddamn and went into another room; she was too depressing to have around.

There is an important difference in the drug-use patterns of the pillhead and opiate dependent: the latter is interested only in getting his drug and avoiding withdrawal; the former is also interested in perceiving his drugs' effects. I remember one occasion attended by someone who had obtained a fairly large mixed bag. In such a situation a junkie would have shot himself insensible; this fellow gave most of his away to his friends. With each gift he said something about a particular aspect of the drug which he found interesting. The heroin-user is far less social. His stuff is too hard to get, too expensive, his withdrawal too agonizing. But the pillhead is an experimenter. Often he seems to be interested as much in observing himself experiencing reactions as he is in having the reactions.

A large part of the attractiveness may be the ritual associated with this kind of group drug abuse: the *PDR* (a holy book), the Source (the medicine man whose preparations promise a polychromatic world of sensory and mystical experiences), the sharing of proscribed materials in a closed community, the sawing and grinding, the being privy to the Pythian secrets of colors and milligrams and trade names and con-traindications and optimum dosages. And, of course, using drugs is something of a fad.

But there are costs. Kicks are rarely free in this world, and drugs are no exception. One risks dysfunction; one can go out of one's head; one may get into trouble with the police. Though the users are from a socioeconomic class that can most likely beat a first offense at almost anything, there is the problem that legal involvement of any kind, whether successfully prosecuted or not, can cause considerable embar-rassment; an arrest for taking drugs may be negligible to a slum dweller in New York, but it is quite something else for a lawyer or reporter. And there is always the most tempting danger of all: getting habituated to drugs to such a degree that the drugs are no longer something extra in life but are instead a major goal.

One user wrote me, "Lately I find myself wishing not that I might kick the lunatic habit — but simply that our drug firms would soon develop something NEW which might refresh the memory of the flash and glow of that first voom-voom pill." I had asked him why take them at all, and he wrote, "I don't know. Really. Why smoke, drink, drive recklessly, sunbathe, fornicate, shoot tigers, climb mountains, gamble, lie, steal, cheat, kill, make war — and blame it all largely on our par-ents. Possibly to make oneself more acceptable to oneself."

There is nothing *wrong* with using chemicals to help cope with life. That is one of the things science is supposed to do, help us cope, and the business of living can be rough at times. And we have the requisite faith: I am sure that far more Americans believe in the efficacy of a pill than believe in God. The problem arises when one's concern shifts so that life becomes primarily an exercise in coping with the chemicals.

THE DAY THE COMPUTERS GOT
WALDON ASHENFELTER
by Bob Elliott and Ray Goulding

A PRESIDENTIAL commission has recommended approval of plans for establishing a computerized data center where all personal information on individual Americans compiled by some twenty scattered agencies would be assembled in one place and made available to the federal government as a whole.

Backers of the proposal contend that it would lead to greater efficiency, and insist that the cradle-to-grave dossiers on the nation's citizens would be used only in a generalized way to help deal with broad issues. Opponents argue that the ready availability of so much confidential data at the push of a computer button could pose a dangerous threat to the privacy of the individual by enabling the federal bureaucracy to become a monstrous, snooping Big Brother.

Obviously, the plan elicits reactions that are emotional, and cooler heads are needed to envision the aura of quiet, uneventful routine certain to pervade the Central Data Bank once it becomes accepted as just another minor government agency.

Fade in:

Interior — Basement GHQ of the Central Data Bank — Night. (At stage right, 950 sophisticated third-generation computers may be seen stretching off into the distance. At stage left, the CDB graveyard-shift chargé d'affaires, Nimrod Gippard, is seated behind a desk. He is thirty-five-ish and attired in socks that don't match. At the open, Gippard is efficiently stuffing mimeographed extortion letters to Omaha's 3277 suspected sex deviates into envelopes. He glances up as Waldon Ashenfelter, an indoorsy type of questionable ancestry, enters.)

GIPPARD: Yes, sir?

ASHENFELTER (flashing ID card): Ashenfelter. Bureau of Indian Affairs. Like to have you run a check on a key figure named Y. Claude Garfunkel.

GIPPARD (reaching for pad and pencil): Sure thing. What's his Social Security number?

ASHENFELTER: I dunno.

GIPPARD: Hmmm. How about his zip code? Or maybe a cross-reference to some banks where he may have been turned down for a loan. Just any clue at all to his identity.

ASHENFELTER: Well, as I say, his name is Y. Claude Garfunkel.

GIPPARD (after a weary sigh): It's not much to go on, but I'll see what I can do.

(Gippard rises and crosses to the master data-recall panel. Ashenfelter strolls

to a nearby computer and casually begins checking the confidential reports on his four small children to learn how many are known extremists.)

ASHENFELTER: You're new here, aren't you?

GIPPARD: No. Just my first week on the night shift. Everybody got moved around after we lost McElhenny.

ASHENFELTER: Wasn't he that heavy-set fellow with beady eyes who drove the Hudson?

GIPPARD: Yeah. Terrible thing. Pulled his own dossier one night when things were quiet and found out he was a swish. Kind of made him go all to pieces.

ASHENFELTER: That's a shame. And now I suppose he's gone into analysis and gotten himself cross-filed as a loony.

GIPPARD: No. He blew his brains out right away. But having a suicide on your record can make things tough, too.

ASHENFELTER: Yeah. Shows a strong trend toward instability.

(The computer informs Ashenfelter that his oldest boy was detained by police in 1963 for roller-skating on municipal property, and that the five-year-old probably founded the Farmer-Labor Party in Minnesota.)

ASHENFELTER (cont.) (mutters in despair): Where did I fail them as a father?

GIPPARD: Didn't you tell me you're with Indian Affairs?

ASHENFELTER: Yeah. Why?

GIPPARD: I think I'm onto something hot. Is that like India Indians or whoop-it-up Indians?

ASHENFELTER: I guess you'd say whoop-it-up.

GIPPARD: Well, either way, no Indian named Garfunkel has ever complied with the Alien Registration Law.

ASHENFELTER: I never said he was an Indian. He's Jewish, and I think he's playing around with my wife.

GIPPARD: Gee, that's too bad.

ASHENFELTER (dramatically): Oh, I blame myself really. I guess I'd started taking LaVerne for granted and —

GIPPARD: No. I mean it's too bad he's only Jewish. The computers aren't programmed to feed back home-wreckers by religious affiliation.

ASHENFELTER: Oh.

GIPPARD: Can you think of anything kinky that's traditional with Jews? You know. Like draft dodging . . . smoking pot . . . something a computer could really hang its hat on.

ASHENFELTER: No. They just seem to feed each other a lot of chicken soup. And they do something around Christmastime with candles. But I'm not sure any of it's illegal.

GIPPARD: We'll soon see. If the curve on known poultry processors correlates geographically with a year-end upswing in tallow rendering

— Well, you can appreciate what that kind of data would mean to the bird dogs at the ICC and the FDA. They'd be able to pinpoint exactly where it was all happening and when.

ASHENFELTER: Uh-huh — Where and when what?

GIPPARD: That's exactly what I intend to find out.

(Gippard turns back to the panel and resumes work with a sense of destiny. Ashenfelter, whistling softly to himself, absently begins plunking the basic melody of "Mexicali Rose" on the keyboard of a nearby computer. The machine responds by furnishing him with Howard Hughes's 1965 income tax return and the unlisted phone numbers of eight members of a New Orleans wife-swapping club who may have known Lee Harvey Oswald. As Ashenfelter pockets the information, Major General Courtney ("Old Napalm and Guts") Nimshaw enters. He has a riding crop but no mustache.)

NIMSHAW: Yoohoo! Anybody home?

GIPPARD: Back here at the main console.

(Nimshaw moves to join Gippard, then sees Ashenfelter for the first time and freezes. The two stand eyeing each other suspiciously as Gippard re-enters the scene.)

GIPPARD: Oh, forgive me. General Nimshaw, I'd like for you to meet Ashenfelter from Indian Affairs.

(Nimshaw and Ashenfelter ad-lib warm greetings as they shake hands. Then each rushes off to pull the dossier of the other. Ashenfelter learns that Nimshaw was a notorious bed wetter during his days at West Point and that his heavy drinking later caused an entire airborne division to be parachuted into Ireland on D-Day. Nimshaw learns that Ashenfelter owns 200 shares of stock in a Canadian steel mill that trades with Communist China and that he had been considered a bad credit risk since 1949, when he refused to pay a Cincinnati dance studio for $5500 worth of tango lessons. Apparently satisfied, both men return to join Gippard, who has been checking out a possible similarity in the patterns of poultry-buying by key Jewish housewives and reported sightings of Soviet fishing trawlers off the Alaskan coast.)

ASHENFELTER: Working late tonight, eh, General?

NIMSHAW (nervously): Well, I just stumbled across a little military hardware transport thing. We seem to have mislaid an eighty-six-car trainload of munitions between here and the West Coast. Can't very well write it off as normal pilferage. So I thought maybe Gippard could run a check for me on the engineer and brakeman. You know. Where they hang out in their spare time. Whether they might take a freight train with them. What do you think, Gipp?

GIPPARD: Sure. Just have a few more things to run through for Ashenfelter first. He's seeking a final solution to the Jewish problem.

ASHENFELTER (blanching): Well, not exactly the whole —

NIMSHAW: Oh, has all that come up again?

(Two janitors carrying lunch pails enter and cross directly to the computer

programmed for medical case histories of nymphomaniacs. They pull several dossiers at random and then cross directly to a far corner, unwrapping bacon, lettuce, and tomato sandwiches as they go. They spread a picnic cloth on the floor and begin reading the dossiers as they eat. They emit occasional guffaws, but the others pay no attention to them.)

GIPPARD (as he compares graph curves): No doubt about it. Whatever those Russian trawlers are up to, it's good for the delicatessen business. This could be the break we've been hoping for.

NIMSHAW: Hating Jews been a big thing with you for quite a while, Ashenfelter?

ASHENFELTER (coldly): About as long as you've been losing government property by the trainload, I imagine.

(Nimshaw and Ashenfelter eye each other uneasily for a moment. Then they quickly exchange hush money in the form of drafts drawn against secret Swiss bank accounts as Gippard's assistant, Llewelyn Fordyce, enters. Fordyce is a typical brilliant young career civil servant who has been lost for several hours trying to find his way back from the men's room. He appears haggard, but is in satisfactory condition otherwise.)

FORDYCE: Are you gentlemen being taken care of?

(Ashenfelter and Nimshaw nod affirmatively. Fordyce hurriedly roots through the desk drawers, pausing only to take a quick, compulsive inventory of paper clips and map pins as he does so.)

FORDYCE (cont.) (shouts): Hey, Gipp! I can't find the registry cards for these two idiots out here.

GIPPARD (faintly, from a distance): I've been too busy to sign 'em in yet. Take care of it, will you?

(Fordyce gives a curt, efficient nod, inefficiently failing to realize that Gippard is too far away to see him nodding. Fordyce then brings forth two large pink cards and hands them to Nimshaw and Ashenfelter.)

FORDYCE: If you'd just fill these out please. We're trying to accumulate data on everybody who uses the data bank so we can eventually tie it all in with something or other.

(Nimshaw studies the section of his card dealing with maximum fines and imprisonment for giving false information, while Ashenfelter skips over the hard part and goes directly to the multiple-choice questions.)

FORDYCE (cont.): And try to be as specific as you can about religious beliefs and your affiliation with subversive groups. We're beginning to think there's more to this business of Quakers denying they belong to the Minutemen than meets the eye.

(Nimshaw and Ashenfelter squirm uneasily as they sense the implication. Ashenfelter hurriedly changes his answer regarding prayer in public schools from "undecided" to "not necessarily" as Nimshaw perjures himself by listing the principal activity at the Forest Hills Tennis Club as tennis. Meantime,

Gippard has rejoined the group, carrying four rolls of computer tape carefully stacked in no particular sequence.)

GIPPARD: I know I'm onto something here, Fordyce, but I'm not sure what to make of it. Surveillance reports on kosher poultry dealers indicate that most of them don't even show up for work on Saturday. And that timing correlates with an unexplained increase in activity at golf courses near key military installations. But the big thing is that drunken drivers tend to get nabbed most often on Saturday night, and that's exactly when organized groups are endangering national security by deliberately staying up late with their lights turned on to overload public power plants.

FORDYCE (whistles softly in amazement): We're really going to catch a covey of them in this net. How'd you happen to stumble across it all?

GIPPARD: Well, it seemed pretty innocent at first. This clown from Indian Affairs just asked me to dig up what I could so he'd have some excuse for exterminating the Jews.

(Ashenfelter emits a burbling throat noise as an apparent prelude to something more coherent, but he is quickly shushed.)

GIPPARD (cont.): But you know how one correlation always leads to another. Now we've got a grizzly by the tail, Fordyce, and I can see "organized conspiracy" written all over it.

FORDYCE: Beyond question. And somewhere among those 192 million dossiers is the ID number of the Mister Big we're after. Do the machines compute a cause-and-effect relationship that might help narrow things down?

GIPPARD: Well, frankly, the computers have gotten into a pretty nasty argument among themselves over that. Most of them see how golf could lead to drunken driving. But the one that's programmed to chart moral decay and leisure time fun is pretty sure that drunken driving causes golf.

(Nimshaw glances up from the job of filling out his registry card.)

NIMSHAW: That's the most ridiculous thing I ever heard in my life.

FORDYCE (with forced restraint): General, would you please stick to whatever people like you are supposed to know about and leave computer-finding interpretation to analysts who are trained for the job?

(Nimshaw starts to reply, but then recalls the fate of a fellow officer who was broken to corporal for insubordination. He meekly resumes pondering question No. 153, unable to decide whether admitting or denying the purchase of Girl Scout cookies will weigh most heavily against him in years to come.)

FORDYCE (cont.): Any other cause-and-effect computations that we ought to consider in depth, Gipp?

GIPPARD: Not really. Of course, Number 327's been out of step with the others ever since it had that circuitry trouble. It just keeps saying,

"Malcolm W. Biggs causes kosher poultry." Types out the same damned thing over and over: "Malcolm W. Biggs causes kosher poultry."

FORDYCE: Who's Malcolm W. Biggs?

GIPPARD: I think he was a juror at one of the Jimmy Hoffa trials. Number 327 was running a check on him when the circuits blew, and it's had kind of an obsession about him ever since.

FORDYCE: Mmmm. Well, personally, I've never paid much attention to the opinions of paranoids. They can get your thinking as screwed up as theirs is.

(Fordyce notices Ashenfelter making an erasure on his card to change the data regarding his shoe size from 9½ C to something less likely to pinch across the instep.)

FORDYCE (cont.) (shrieks at Ashenfelter): What do you think you're doing there? You're trying to hide something from me. I've met your kind before.

(Ashenfelter wearily goes back to a 9½ C, even though they make his feet hurt, and Fordyce reacts with a look of smug satisfaction.)

GIPPARD: Maybe if I fed this junk back into the machine, it could name some people who fit the pattern.

FORDYCE: Why don't you just reprocess the computations in an effort to gain individualized data that correlates?

(Gippard stares thoughtfully at Fordyce for a long moment and then exits to nail the ringleaders through incriminating association with the key words "drunk," "poultry," "golf," and "kilowatt.")

NIMSHAW: I think maybe I'd better come back sometime when you're not so busy.

(He slips his registry card into his pocket and starts toward the door, but Fordyce grabs him firmly by the wrist.)

FORDYCE: Just a minute. You can't take that card out of here with you. It may contain classified information you shouldn't even have access to.

NIMSHAW: But it's about me. I'm the one who just filled it out.

FORDYCE: Don't try to muddy up the issue. Nobody walks out of this department with government property. Let's have it.

(Nimshaw reluctantly surrenders the card. Fordyce glances at it and reacts with a look of horror.)

FORDYCE (cont.): You've filled this whole thing out in longhand! The instructions clearly state, "Type or print legibly." You'll have to do it over again.

(Fordyce tears up the card and hands Nimshaw a new one. Nimshaw, suddenly aware that a display of bad conduct could cost him his good conduct medal, goes back to work, sobbing quietly to himself.)

GIPPARD (faintly, from a distance): Eureka! Hot damn!

FORDYCE (happily): He's hit paydirt. I know old Gippard, and he hasn't cut loose like that since he linked Ralph Nader with the trouble at Berkeley.

(Gippard enters on the dead run, unmindful of the computer tape streaming out behind him.)

GIPPARD: It all correlates beautifully (ticks off points on his fingers). A chicken plucker. Three arrests for common drunk. FBI's observed him playing golf with a known Cuban. Psychiatric report shows he sleeps with all the lights on.

FORDYCE: All wrapped up in one neat bundle. Who is he?

GIPPARD: A virtual unknown. Never been tagged as anything worse than possibly disloyal until I found him. He uses the name Y. Claude Garfunkel.

ASHENFELTER: Y. Claude Garfunkel!

FORDYCE (menacingly): Touch a raw nerve, Ashenfelter?

(The two janitors, who are really undercover sophomores majoring in forestry at Kansas State on CIA scholarships, rise and slowly converge on Ashenfelter.)

GIPPARD: Want to tell us about it, Ashenfelter? We have our own methods of computing the truth out of you anyway, you know.

FORDYCE: No point in stalling. What's the connection? The two of you conspired to give false opinions to the Harris Poll, didn't you?

ASHENFELTER (pitifully): No! Nothing like that. I swear.

GIPPARD: Then what, man? What? Have you tried to sabotage the Data Bank by forging each other's Social Security numbers?

ASHENFELTER (a barely audible whisper): No. Please don't build a treason case against me. I'll tell. A neighbor saw him with my wife at a luau in Baltimore.

(The CIA men posing as college students posing as janitors react intuitively to jab Ashenfelter with a sodium-pentathol injection. Gippard rushes to a computer, where he begins cross-checking Garfunkel and Ashenfelter in the Urban Affairs file on "Polynesian power" advocates in Baltimore's Hawaiian ghetto and Interstate Commerce Commission reports on suspected participants in interstate hanky-panky. Fordyce grabs the red "hot line"' telephone on his desk and reacts with annoyance as he gets a busy signal. General Nimshaw, sensing himself caught up in a tide of events which he can neither turn back nor understand, hastily erases the computer tape containing his own dossier and then slashes his wrists under an assumed name.)

Fade Out.

1968
HOW COULD VIETNAM HAPPEN?
An Autopsy
by James C. Thomson, Jr.

As a case study in the making of foreign policy, the Vietnam War will fascinate historians and social scientists for many decades to come. One question that will certainly be asked: How did men of superior ability, sound training, and high ideals — American policy-makers of the 1960s — create such costly and divisive policy?

As one who watched the decision-making process in Washington from 1961 to 1966 under Presidents Kennedy and Johnson, I can suggest a preliminary answer by briefly listing some of the factors that seemed to me to shape our Vietnam policy during my years as an East Asia specialist at the State Department and the White House.

A first and central ingredient in these years of Vietnam decisions does involve history. The ingredient was *the legacy of the 1950s* — by which I mean the so-called "loss of China," the Korean War, and the Far East policy of Secretary of State Dulles.

This legacy had an institutional by-product for the Kennedy Administration: in 1961 the U.S. government's East Asian establishment was undoubtedly the most rigid and doctrinaire of Washington's regional divisions in foreign affairs. This was especially true at the Department of State, where the incoming Administration found the Bureau of Far Eastern Affairs the hardest nut to crack. It was a bureau that had been purged of its best China expertise, and of farsighted, dispassionate men, as a result of McCarthyism. Its members were generally committed to one policy line: the close containment and isolation of mainland China, the harassment of "neutralist" nations which sought to avoid alignment with either Washington or Peking, and the maintenance of a network of alliances with anti-Communist client states on China's periphery.

Another aspect of the legacy was the special vulnerability and sensitivity of the new Democratic Administration on Far East policy issues. The memory of the McCarthy era was still very sharp, and Kennedy's margin of victory was too thin. The 1960 Offshore Islands TV debate between Kennedy and Nixon had shown the President-elect the perils of "fresh thinking." The Administration was inherently leery of moving too fast on Asia. As a result, the Far East Bureau (now the Bureau of East Asian and Pacific Affairs) was the last one to be overhauled. Not until Averell Harriman was brought in as Assistant Secretary in December, 1961, were significant personnel changes attempted, and it took Harriman several months to make a deep imprint on the bureau because of his necessary preoccupation with the Laos settlement. Once he did so, there was virtually no effort to bring back the purged or exiled East Asia experts.

There were other important by-products of this "legacy of the fifties":

The new Administration inherited and somewhat shared *a general perception of China-on-the-march* — a sense of China's vastness, its numbers, its belligerence; a revived sense, perhaps, of the Golden Horde. This was a perception fed by Chinese intervention in the Korean War.

The new Administration inherited and briefly accepted *a monolithic conception of the Communist bloc*. Despite much earlier predictions and reports by outside analysts, policy-makers did not begin to accept the reality and possible finality of the Sino-Soviet split until the first weeks of 1962. The inevitably corrosive impact of competing nationalisms on Communism was largely ignored.

The new Administration inherited and to some extent shared *the "domino theory" about Asia*. This theory resulted from profound ignorance of Asian history and hence ignorance of the radical differences among Asian nations and societies. It resulted from a blindness to the power and resilience of Asian nationalisms.

Finally, the legacy of the fifties was apparently compounded by an uneasy sense of a worldwide Communist challenge to the new Administration after the Bay of Pigs fiasco. A first manifestation was the President's traumatic Vienna meeting with Khrushchev in June, 1961; then came the Berlin crisis of the summer. All this created an atmosphere in which President Kennedy undoubtedly felt under special pressure to show his nation's mettle in Vietnam — if the Vietnamese, unlike the people of Laos, were willing to fight.

In general, the legacy of the fifties shaped such early moves of the new Administration as the decisions to maintain a high-visibility SEATO, to back away from diplomatic recognition of Mongolia in the summer of 1961, and most important, to expand U.S. military assistance to South Vietnam that winter on the basis of the much more tentative Eisenhower commitment. It should be added that the increased commitment to Vietnam was also fueled by a new breed of military strategists and academic social scientists (some of whom had entered the new Administration) who had developed theories of counterguerrilla warfare and were eager to see them put to the test. To some, "counterinsurgency" seemed a new panacea for coping with the world's instability.

So much for the legacy and the history. But surely among the policy-makers of the Kennedy and Johnson Administrations there were men who would warn of the dangers of an open-ended commitment to the Vietnam quagmire?

This raises a central question, at the heart of the policy process: Where were the experts, the doubters, and the dissenters?

The answer is complex but instructive.

In the first place, the American government was sorely *lacking in real Vietnam or Indochina expertise*. Originally treated as an adjunct of Embassy Paris, our Saigon embassy and the Vietnam Desk at State were largely staffed from 1954 onward by French-speaking Foreign Service personnel of narrowly European experience. Such diplomats were even more closely restricted than the normal embassy officer — by cast of mind as well as language — to contacts with Vietnam's French-speaking urban elites.

In addition, the *shadow of the "loss of China"* distorted Vietnam reporting. Career officers in the Department, and especially those in the field, had not forgotten the fate of their World War II colleagues who wrote in frankness from China and were later pilloried by Senate committees for critical comments on the Chinese Nationalists. Candid reporting on the strengths of the Viet Cong and the weaknesses of the Diem government was inhibited by the memory. It was also inhibited by some higher officials, notably Ambassador Nolting in Saigon, who refused to sign off on such cables.

In due course, to be sure, some Vietnam talent was discovered or developed. But a recurrent and increasingly important factor in the decision-making process was *the banishment of real expertise*. Here the underlying cause was the "closed politics" of policy-making as issues become hot: the more sensitive the issue, and the higher it rises in the bureaucracy, the more completely the experts are excluded while the harassed senior generalists take over (that is, the Secretaries, Undersecretaries, and Presidential Assistants). The frantic skimming of briefing papers in the back seats of limousines is no substitute for the presence of specialists; furthermore, in times of crisis such papers are deemed "too sensitive" even for review by the specialists. Another underlying cause of this banishment, as Vietnam became more critical, was the replacement of the experts, who were generally and increasingly pessimistic, by men described as "can-do guys," loyal and energetic fixers unsoured by expertise.

Despite the banishment of the experts, internal doubters and dissenters did indeed appear and persist. Yet as I watched the process, such men were effectively neutralized by a subtle dynamic: *the domestication of dissenters*. Such "domestication" arose out of a twofold clubbish need: on the one hand, the dissenter's desire to stay aboard; and on the other hand, the nondissenter's conscience. Simply stated, dissent, when recognized, was made to feel at home. On the lowest possible scale of importance, I must confess my own considerable sense of dignity and acceptance (both vital) when my senior White House employer would refer to me as his "favorite dove." Far more significant was the case of the former Undersecretary of State, George Ball. Once Mr. Ball began to express doubts, he was warmly institutionalized: he was encouraged to become the inhouse devil's advocate on Vietnam. The upshot was inevitable: the process of escalation allowed for periodic requests to Mr. Ball to speak his piece; Ball felt good, I assume (he had fought for righteousness); the others felt good (they had given a full hearing to the dovish option); and there was minimal unpleasantness. The club remained intact; and it is of course possible that matters would have gotten worse faster if Mr. Ball had kept silent, or left before his final departure in the fall of 1966. There was also, of course, the case of the last institutionalized doubter, Bill Moyers. The President is said to have greeted his arrival at meetings with an affectionate, "Well, here comes Mr. Stop-the-Bombing . . ." Here again the dynamics of domesticated dissent sustained the relationship for a while.

A related point — and crucial, I suppose, to government at all times — was *the "effectiveness" trap,* the trap that keeps men from speaking out, as clearly or often as they might, within the government. And it is the trap that keeps men from resigning in protest and airing their dissent outside the government. The most important asset that a man brings to bureaucratic life is his "effectiveness," a mysterious combination of training, style, and connections. To preserve your effectiveness, you must decide where and when to fight the mainstream of policy; the opportunities range from pillow talk with your wife, to private drinks with your friends, to meetings with the Secretary of State or the President. The inclination to remain silent or to acquiesce in the presence of the great men — to live to fight another day, to give on this issue so that you can be "effective" on later issues — is overwhelming. Nor is it the tendency of youth alone; some of our most senior officials, men of wealth and fame, whose place in history is secure, have remained silent lest their connection with power be terminated. As for the disinclination to resign in protest: while not necessarily a Washington or even American specialty, it seems more true of a government in which ministers have no parliamentary back-bench to which to retreat. To exit is to lose even those marginal chances for "effectiveness."

Another factor must be noted: as the Vietnam controversy escalated at home, there developed *a preoccupation with Vietnam public relations as opposed to Vietnam policy-making.* And here, ironically, internal doubters and dissenters were heavily employed. For such men, by virtue of their own doubts, were often deemed best able to "massage" the doubting intelligentsia. My senior East Asia colleague at the White House, a brilliant and humane doubter who had dealt with Indochina since 1954, spent three quarters of his working days on Vietnam public relations: drafting presidential responses to letters from important critics, writing conciliatory language for presidential speeches, and meeting quite interminably with delegations of outraged Quakers, clergymen, academics, and housewives.

Through a variety of procedures, both institutional and personal, doubt, dissent, and expertise were effectively neutralized in the making of policy. But what can be said of the men "in charge"? It is patently absurd to suggest that they produced such tragedy by intention and calculation. But it is neither absurd nor difficult to discern certain forces at work that caused decent and honorable men to do great harm.

Here I would stress the paramount role of *executive fatigue*. Many of today's Vietnam policymakers have been on the job for from four to seven years. Complaints may be few, and physical health may remain unimpaired, though emotional health is far harder to gauge. But what is most seriously eroded in the deadening process of fatigue is freshness of thought, imagination, a sense of possibility, a sense of priorities and perspective.

Below the level of the fatigued executives in the making of Vietnam policy was a widespread phenomenon: *the curator mentality* in the Department of State. By this I mean the collective inertia produced by the bureaucrat's view of his job. At State, the average "desk officer" inherits from his predecessor our policy toward Country X; he regards it as his function to keep that policy intact — under glass, untampered with, and dusted — so that he may pass it on in two to four years to his successor. And such curatorial service generally merits promotion within the system. (Maintain the status quo, and you will stay out of trouble.) In some circumstances, the inertia bred by such an outlook can act as a brake against rash innovation. But on many issues, this inertia sustains the momentum of bad policy and unwise commitments — momentum that might otherwise have been resisted within the ranks. Clearly, Vietnam is such an issue.

To fatigue and inertia must be added the factor of internal confusion. Even among the "architects" of our Vietnam commitment, there has been persistent *confusion as to what type of war we were fighting* and, as a direct consequence, *confusion as to how to end that war.* (The "credibility gap" is, in part, a reflection of such internal confusion.) Was it, for instance, a civil war, in which case counterinsurgency might suffice? Or was it a war of international aggression? (This might invoke SEATO or UN commitment.) Who was the aggressor — and the "real enemy"? The Viet Cong? Hanoi? Peking? Moscow? International

Communism? Or maybe "Asian Communism"? Differing enemies dictated differing strategies and tactics. And confused throughout, in like
fashion, was the question of American objectives; your objectives depended on whom you were fighting and why. I shall not forget my
assignment from an Assistant Secretary of State in March, 1964: to
draft a speech for Secretary McNamara which would, *inter alia,* once
and for all dispose of the canard that the Vietnam conflict was a civil
war. "But in some ways, of course," I mused, "it *is* a civil war." "Don't
play word games with me!" snapped the Assistant Secretary.

Similar confusion beset the concept of "negotiations" — anathema
to much of official Washington from 1961 to 1965. Not until April,
1965, did "unconditional discussions" become respectable, via a presidential speech; even then the Secretary of State stressed privately to
newsmen that nothing had changed, since "discussions" were by no
means the same as "negotiations." Months later that issue was resolved. But it took even longer to obtain a fragile internal agreement
that negotiations might include the Viet Cong as something other than
an appendage to Hanoi's delegation.

Of course, one force — a constant in the vortex of commitment —
was that of *wishful thinking.* I partook of it myself at many times. I did
so especially during Washington's struggle with Diem in the autumn
of 1963 when some of us at State believed that for once, in dealing
with a difficult client state, the U.S. government could use the leverage
of our economic and military assistance to make good things happen,
instead of being led around by the nose by men like Chiang Kai-shek
and Syngman Rhee (and, in that particular instance, by Diem). If we
could prove that point, I thought, and move into a new day, with or
without Diem, then Vietnam was well worth the effort. Later came the
wishful thinking of the air-strike planners in the late autumn of 1964;
there were those who actually thought that after six weeks of air
strikes, the North Vietnamese would come crawling to us to ask for
peace talks. And what, someone asked in one of the meetings of the
time, if they don't? The answer was that we would bomb for another
four weeks, and that would do the trick. And a few weeks later came
one instance of wishful thinking that was symptomatic of good men
misled: in January, 1965, I encountered one of the very highest figures in the Administration at a dinner, drew him aside, and told him
of my worries about the air-strike option. He told me that I really
shouldn't worry; it was his conviction that before any such plans could
be put into effect, a neutralist government would come to power in
Saigon that would politely invite us out. And finally, there was the
recurrent wishful thinking that sustained many of us through the
trying months of 1965–1966 after the air strikes had begun: that

surely, somehow, one way or another, we would "be in a conference in six months," and the escalatory spiral would be suspended. The basis of our hope: "It simply can't go on."

As a further influence on policy-makers I would cite the factor of *bureaucratic detachment.* In quiet, air-conditioned, thick-carpeted rooms, such terms as "systematic pressure," "armed reconnaissance," "targets of opportunity," and even "body count" seemed to breed a sort of games-theory detachment. Most memorable to me was a moment in the late 1964 target planning when the question under discussion was how heavy our bombing should be, and how extensive our strafing, at some midpoint in the projected pattern of systematic pressure. An Assistant Secretary of State resolved the point in the following words: "It seems to me that our orchestration should be mainly violins, but with periodic touches of brass."

There is an unprovable factor that relates to bureaucratic detachment: the ingredient of *crypto-racism.* I do not mean to imply any conscious contempt for Asian loss of life on the part of Washington officials. But I do mean to imply that bureaucratic detachment may well be compounded by a traditional Western sense that there are so many Asians, after all; that Asians have a fatalism about life and a disregard for its loss; that they are cruel and barbaric to their own people; and that they are very different from us (and all look alike?). And I *do* mean to imply that the upshot of such subliminal views is a subliminal question whether Asians, and particularly Asian peasants, and most particularly Asian Communists, are really people — like you and me. To put the matter another way: would we have pursued quite such policies — and quite such military tactics — if the Vietnamese were white?

It is impossible to write of Vietnam decision-making without writing about language. Throughout the conflict, words have been of paramount importance. I refer here to the impact of *rhetorical escalation* and to the *problem of oversell.* In an important sense, Vietnam has become of crucial significance to us *because we have said that it is of crucial significance.*

The key here is domestic politics: the need to sell the American people, press, and Congress on support for an unpopular and costly war in which the objectives themselves have been in flux. To sell means to persuade, and to persuade means rhetoric. As the difficulties and costs have mounted, so has the definition of the stakes. This is not to say that rhetorical escalation is an orderly process; executive prose is the product of many writers, and some concepts — North Vietnamese infiltration, America's "national honor," Red China as the chief

enemy — have entered the rhetoric only gradually and even sporadic-
ally. But there is an upward spiral nonetheless. And once you have
said that the American Experiment itself stands or falls on the Vietnam outcome, you have thereby created a national stake far beyond
any earlier stakes.

Crucial throughout the process of Vietnam decision-making was a
conviction among many policy-makers: that Vietnam posed a *fundamental test of America's national will*. Time and again I was told by men
reared in the tradition of Henry L. Stimson that all we needed was the
will, and we would then prevail. Implicit in such a view, it seemed to
me, was a curious assumption that Asians lacked will, or at least that in
a contest between Asian and Anglo-Saxon wills, the non-Asians must
prevail. A corollary to the persistent belief in will was a *fascination with
power* and an awe in the face of the power America possessed as no
nation or civilization ever before. Those who doubted our role in Vietnam were said to shrink from the burdens of power, the obligations of
power, the uses of power, the responsibility of power. By implication,
such men were soft-headed and effete.

Finally, no discussion of the factors and forces at work on Vietnam
policy-makers can ignore the central fact of *human ego investment*. Men
who have participated in a decision develop a stake in that decision. As
they participate in further, related decisions, their stake increases. It
might have been possible to dissuade a man of strong self-confidence
at an early stage of the ladder of decision; but it is infinitely harder at
later stages since a change of mind there usually involves implicit or
explicit repudiation of a chain of previous decisions.

To put it bluntly: at the heart of the Vietnam calamity is a group of
able, dedicated men who have been regularly and repeatedly wrong —
and whose standing with their contemporaries, and more important,
with history, depends, as they see it, on being proven right. These are
not men who can be asked to extricate themselves from error.

The various ingredients I have cited in the making of Vietnam policy
have created a variety of results, most of them fairly obvious. Here are
some that seem to me most central:

Throughout the conflict, there has been *persistent and repeated miscalculation* by virtually all the actors, in high echelons and low, whether
dove, hawk, or something else. To cite one simple example among
many: in late 1964 and early 1965, some peace-seeking planners at
State who strongly opposed the projected bombing of the North urged
that, instead, American ground forces be sent to South Vietnam; this
would, they said, increase our bargaining leverage against the North
— our "chips" — and would give us something to negotiate about (the

withdrawal of our forces) at an early peace conference. Simultaneously, the air-strike option was urged by many in the military who were dead set against American participation in "another land war in Asia"; they were joined by other civilian peace-seekers who wanted to bomb Hanoi into early negotiations. By late 1965, we had ended up with the worst of all worlds: ineffective and costly air strikes against the North, spiraling ground forces in the South, and no negotiations in sight.

Throughout the conflict as well, there has been *a steady give-in to pressures for a military solution* and only minimal and sporadic efforts at a diplomatic and political solution. In part this resulted from the confusion (earlier cited) among the civilians — confusion regarding objectives and strategy. And in part this resulted from the self-enlarging nature of military investment.

Throughout the conflict, there have been *missed opportunities, large and small, to disengage ourselves from Vietnam on increasingly unpleasant but still acceptable terms.* Of the many moments from 1961 onward, I shall cite only one, the last and most important opportunity that was lost: in the summer of 1964 the President instructed his chief advisers to prepare for him as wide a range of Vietnam options as possible for post-election consideration and decision. He explicitly asked that all options be laid out. What happened next was, in effect, Lyndon Johnson's slow-motion Bay of Pigs. For the advisers so effectively converged on one single option — juxtaposed against two other, phony options (in effect, blowing up the world, or scuttle-and-run) — that the President was confronted with unanimity for bombing the North from all his trusted counselors. Had he been more confident in foreign affairs, had he been deeply informed on Vietnam and Southeast Asia, and had he raised some hard questions that unanimity had submerged, this President could have used the largest electoral mandate in history to de-escalate in Vietnam, in the clear expectation that at the worst a neutralist government would come to power in Saigon and politely invite us out.

Long before I went into government, I was told a story about Henry L. Stimson that seemed to me pertinent during the years that I watched the Vietnam tragedy unfold — and participated in that tragedy. It seems to me more pertinent than ever as we move toward the election of 1968.

In his waning years Stimson was asked by an anxious questioner, "Mr. Secretary, how on earth can we ever bring peace to the world?" Stimson is said to have answered: "You begin by bringing to Washington a small handful of able men who believe that the achievement of peace is possible.

"You work them to the bone until they no longer believe that it is possible.

"And then you throw them out — and bring in a new bunch who believe that it is possible."

1969
LOOKING FOR THE BUCKHEAD BOYS
by James Dickey

Some of the time, going home, I go
Blind and can't find it.
The house I lived in growing up and out
The doors of high school is torn
Down and cleared
Away for further development, but that does not stop me.
First in the heart
Of my blind spot are
The Buckhead Boys.   If I can find them, even one,
I'm home. And if I can find him   catch him in or around
Buckhead, I'll never die: it's likely my youth will walk
Inside me like a king.

First of all, going home, I must go
To Wender and Roberts' Drug Store, for driving through I saw it
Shining   renewed   renewed
In chromium, but still there.
It's one of the places the Buckhead Boys used to be, before
Beer turned teen-ager.
Tommy Nichols
Is not there.   The Drug Store is full of women
Made of cosmetics.   Tommy Nichols has never been
In such a place: he was the Number Two Man on the Mile
Relay Team in his day.
What day?
My day. Where was I?

Number Three, and there are some sunlit
pictures
In the Book of the Dead to prove it: the 1939
North Fulton High School Annual.   Go down,
Go down

To Tyree's Pool Hall, for there was more
Concentration of the spirit
Of the Buckhead Boys
In there, than anywhere else in the world.

Do I want some shoes
To walk all over Buckhead like a king
Nobody knows?   Well, I can get them at Tyree's;
It's a shoe store now. I could tell you where every spittoon
Ought to be standing.   Charlie Gates used to say one of these days
I'm gonna get myself the reputation of being
The bravest man in Buckhead.   I'm going in Tyree's toilet
And pull down my pants and take a shit.

Maybe
Charlie's the key: the man who would say that would never leave
Buckhead.   Where is he? Maybe I ought to look up
Some Old Merchants.   Why didn't I think of that
Before?

Lord, Lord! Like a king!

Hardware.   Hardware and Hardware Merchants
Never die, and they have everything on hand
There is to know. Somewhere in the wood screws Mr. Hamby may
have
My Prodigal's Crown on sale. He showed up
For every football game at home
Or away, in the hills of North Georgia. There he is, as old
As ever.
Mr. Hamby, remember me?

God A'mighty! Ain't you the one
Who fumbled the punt and lost the Russell game?

That's right.
How're them butter fingers?

Still butter, I say,
Still fumbling. But what about the rest of the team? What about
Charlie
Gates?

He the boy that got lime in his eye from the goal line
When y'all played Gainesville?

Right.

I don't know. Seems to me
I see . . .

See? See? What does Charlie Gates see in his eye burning
With the goal line? Does he see a middle-aged man from the Book
Of the Dead looking for him in magic shoes
From Tyree's disappeared pool hall?

                        Mr. Hamby, Mr. Hamby,
Where? Where is Mont Black?

                  Paralyzed. Doctors can't do nothing.
         Where is Dick Shea?

                   Assistant Sales Manager
Of Kraft Cheese.

          How about Punchy Henderson?

                        Died of a heart attack
           Watching high school football
          In South Carolina.

                 Old Punchy, the last
Of the wind sprinters, and now for no reason the first
Of the heart attacks.

                        Harmon Quigley?
          He's up at County Work Farm
Sixteen.   Doing all right up there; be out next year.

           Didn't anybody get to be a doctor
  Or lawyer?

         Sure. Bobby Laster's a chiropractor. He's right out here
         At Bolton; got a real good business.
         Jack Siple?

                Moved away.
         Gordon Hamm?

                   Dead
In the war.

               O the Book
Of the Dead, and the dead bright sun on the page
Where the team stands ready to explode
In all directions with Time.   Did you say you see Charlie
Gates every now and then?

                    Seems to me.
Where?

      He may be out yonder at the Gulf Station between here and
Sandy Springs.

Let me go pull my car out
Of the parking lot in back
Of Wender and Roberts'.   Do I need gas?   No; let me drive around
the block
Let me drive around Buckhead
A few dozen times   turning   turning in my foreign
Car till the town spins   whirls till the chrome vanishes
From Wender and Roberts'   the spittoons are remade
From the sun itself   the dead pages flutter the hearts rise up, that
lie
In the ground, and Bobby Laster's backbreaking fingers
Pick up a cue stick   Tommy Nichols and I rack the balls
And Charlie Gates walks into Tyree's un-
imaginable toilet.
I go north
Now, and I can use fifty
Cents' worth of gas.
It is Gulf.   I pull in and praise the Lord Charlie
Gates comes out.   His blue shirt dazzles
Like a baton-pass.   He squints he looks at me
Through the goal line.   Charlie, Charlie, we have won away from
We have won at home
In the last minute.   Can you see me?   You say
What I say: where in God
Almighty have you been all this time?   I don't know,
Charlie.   I don't know.   But I've come to tell you a secret
That has to be put into code.   Understand what I mean when I say
To the one man who came back alive
From the Book of the Dead   to the bravest man
In Buckhead   to the lime-eyed ghost
Blue-wavering in the fumes
Of good Gulf gas, "Fill 'er up."
With wine? Light? Heart-attack blood? The contents of Tyree's toilet?
The beer
Of teen-age sons?   No; just
"Fill 'er up. Fill 'er up, Charlie."

REVIEWMANSHIP AND THE
I-WROTE-A-BOOK DISEASE
by Herbert Gold

ANXIETY and paranoia are epidemic conditions in civilized life, but one of the most curious subdivisions of these maladies is the dreaded I-Wrote-A-Book Disease, a weakness and rage which spread throughout the limbs, affecting brain, spine, toes, scalp, conjunctiva, and wives. The initial symptoms appear just after the pleasure of the publisher's first enthusiasm subsides, and indeed, seem to bear some relationship to a previous condition known as I-Wrote-A-Book euphoria, during which your average novelist haunts the post office to see when the new six-cent commemorative stamps will appear, the ones with his portrait engraved upon them. Another symptom: the runny mouth.

Exchanges of special-delivery hints, telegraphic complaints, and long-distance telephone advices with the publisher characterize the onset of the disease. From instant pleasure the novelist tumbles to instant long-suffering over such matters as jacket design, misprints in the proof, and delays at the printer. His temperature increases as the tempo of injustice accelerates. By the time the Virginia Kirkus Service and *Publisher's Weekly* reports are in with their early reviews, the writer is unfit to be tied. In fact, he is fit only to be sprinkled with feathers, since he has already been doused with the hot tar of afterthought, misunderstanding, and Manhattan plotting against him. In days long gone, epilepsy was considered a divine ailment, bestowing secret pleasures upon the sufferer, plus the gift of prophecy. In the early stages of I-Wrote-A-Book, the writer twitches and similarly indulges in foretelling of the future. "I'll kill the sons of bitches. I'll change publishers. I'll print the goddamn thing myself next time." Like other fortune tellers, he infrequently keeps his promises.

I consider myself one of the world's great authorities on certain subjects of general import, ranging from survival in Haiti to the meaning of life, and also on this one of more special urgency. As the writer of a number of books, I have received on various occasions (a) almost all bad reviews, (b) mixed reviews, and (c) almost entirely good reviews. Oddly enough, the latter result, which would seem so much more desirable, doesn't eliminate the satyr's ache. I have observed about good reviews, of myself and others: OK, they're good, but they're not good enough. OK, they're great, but they're not the greatest. OK, the book is a masterpiece, but is it the *greatest* masterpiece? And why can't the critic (coward! hack!) admit it?

In other words, writing a public fantasy involves a sort of nymphomania of desire to delight, astonish, reveal, whelm, and over-whelm. Momentary joys are fraught with pervading anxieties. The worst reviews accompany, in personal life, desperate attempts at revenge, suicide, divorce, and marriage. And so do the best reviews. An enormously successful, world-famous novelist suffered a physical and nervous collapse when his first renown came flooding in on him. "Is that all?" he explained. "Is that all there is? And I've worked so much for this? Silly praise and baskets of mail and demands on me to fly around and stand in front of dinner tables? I've filled my life with obsession and vanity for merely *this?*"

A deep thought, it's true — whether so much sacrifice of feeling is necessary to bear the emblem of feeling for others — but depth of thought didn't prevent his attacking one critic in the snow and rolling with him in a West Side Manhattan gutter. His dream of mastery was as abraded, by renown, as the dream of the forgotten first novelist who sighed, gave up, and went back to his job at J. Walter Thompson.

Writers expect too much. They expect, like God, to begin with the word and end with the rest on the seventh day, which is the day when everybody reads the New York *Times Book Review.* Instead, they strike the rock like Moses, and run the risks of blindness. From afar a voice in a cloud says, Be happy with the Cleveland *Plain Dealer.*

Nonetheless, though I would like to blame the psychic vulnerability of writers for their excesses in the field of pain, it's also true that the reviewing of books is an ambiguous practice which tends to spread infection. Every writer can tell his own story about this; he may have amnesia about his childhood, the war, and his first three marriages, but he recalls his abuse in the press. I would like, abandoning caution, to suggest a few occasions for Saint-Beuve Flu, beginning with one in which I am clearly the villain.

Twenty years ago, in student days (Paris, GI Bill), I was writing a first novel when the editor of a little magazine asked me to review a new book by Nelson Algren. I read it with rage. I thought it trivial, windy, derogatory of the human species; it violated the principles I had learned from Aristotle and the Columbia College humanities program; I savaged the book in a hot, merciless, young-man's review. The book was *The Man With the Golden Arm,* and I have never forgotten it. The characters are still vivid and touching, the prose is heated, urban-weird, with disturbing rhythms. Years later I realized why I couldn't put the book out of my mind: *I had been moved by it.* True, it violated my principles, but my principles were wrong. I was writing a first book by principle, and Algren had written a book from his chaotic feelings. With all its crudities, the book has a mythic power.

Much later I learned to feel shame for an act of projection onto Algren of my own growing pains. I did my best to make it up to him.

When I met him a few years ago, I confessed my sin in Paris circa 1950 and apologized. He seemed to fall asleep in the middle of my touching little speech.

Saul Bellow once said about a heedless critic, "Over every one of his reviews stands a secret, invisible headline — *I have written three unpublished novels.*"

There is no doubt that principle is often a better guide to thinking than chaos, and many graduate students are smarter and more informed than most novelists. Nevertheless, there are things which even a graduate student in philosophy doesn't know, but which Nelson Algren knew. His drowsiness, for example, was a masterstroke of revenge.

Now perhaps I have earned a bit of revenge myself. When I asked Vladimir Nabokov which American writers he admired, he said, "Several," but then refused to specify by actually naming them. "Anonymous praise hurts nobody." And if anonymous dispraise hurts everybody, so much the more objective.

Reviewmanship taxes the integrity muscles. Once I sought to review a close friend's book — I admire both the man's character and the book — by beginning with a frank acknowledgment that it was a book whose progress I had followed in the way of a friend. I thought this might set a new standard for other reviewers, who would then be obliged by the mighty force of example to acknowledge the weight of friendship, repaid debts, enmities, rivalries, extraneous calculations implicated in their reviews. The book-review editor rejected my notice by saying, "We don't admit friendship plays any part in reviewing. If it does, we don't admit it." And it was also clear that he was rejecting *me* for betraying the charade of objectivity. Furthermore, in somewhat prim fashion, he was saying that readers would be put off by the truth and by the sense of personality, a real human being who gets wet in the shower, writing and responding to a book written by another person.

Corrupt democracy is a better form of government than Spartan rigor, I'm sure. But make-believe blind justice is not as good as honest avowal, and not as just. "I Speak the Truth," says the modest book-summarizer; "I Lay Down the Law," proclaims the anonymous critic; better neither an institutional, bureaucratic ukase nor a finicky pretense at justice reading in braille. Better that the reviewer speak in his own voice, indicating where he stands, so that the reader also knows where he stands. Orville Prescott, long the powerful daily reviewer for the New York *Times,* was a perfect critic for me. I knew that his liking a book meant that I would hate it, and conversely, when he said he hated a book, it was a good augury for my reading. He rarely missed my aim. When he described *Lolita* as dull and boring, I knew I would find it fascinating and thrilling. To be a good guide is the best thing a reviewer can do, and Mr. Prescott served this function for many book-buyers.

There are several prevalent institutional conceptions of book reviewing:

1. Sell the book. This is less commom than it used to be; an attempt to develop standards has gotten under way — or an attempt to abolish standards, as in camp, which amounts to the same moral seriousness.

2. De-sell the book; I'm smarter than the writer, which is why I don't have to undergo this neurotic experience of giving up real life for book writing, actually doing it. (What's the writer trying to prove? What's his problem?) This is more common than it used to be, a by-product of standard-developing in the light of shaky taste.

3. The Institutional Informational Review. You've read the review, you don't need the book. After all, we of this organ do our best to fill your reading time, we give essences and messages, we instruct fully, we try not to make you miss your stop on the commuter train. The I. I. Review sometimes combines (1) and (2) in a silky way. It is anonymous, as if written by a corporate computer. It has an air of cool omnipotence which a breathing and irascible human being cannot achieve naturally, subject as human beings are to fits of whim and responsibility.

There are other types of reviews, too: The Review of my Friend's Book, the English Review of a Colonial Work, the I'm-Writing/Have-Written-a-Similar-Book Review, and so forth. At various times, I've been asked to review from the point of view of: a Cleveland writer, a Jewish writer, a New York writer, an expatriate writer, a San Francisco writer, a beat/hip writer, a young writer, a middle-aged writer, a sometimes-married writer, a contributor-to-quarterlies writer, and-um-a writer who gets his reviews in on time.

The anonymous review, which suggests total judgment by an infallible institution, and in fact makes possible either cowardly assault or craven praise by the faceless keypuncher, has gradually slipped from favor with increasing sophistication. *Newsweek* abandoned it years ago; *Life* signs its effective notices; *Look* has Peter S. Prescott, a reviewer with a defined personal voice; perhaps *Time, Playboy,* and the brief *New Yorker* sideswipes are the chief remaining offenders. But even *Time* has experimented with revealing the names of its reviewers, leaving the institutional reports of *Playboy* and the *New Yorker* out front with the banner of inconsequent authority. (The *New Yorker* tends to free-form assassination or faint praise with faint breath; *Playboy* deals more responsibly with its own wieldy point of view, and oddly enough, confesses with quirkinesses of style that people, not overworked machines, have done the reviewing.)

In a class by itself stands the *New York Review of Books,* which is both serious and trivial ("No, Madame, quadrivial" — James Joyce). It is serious because it gives its group of writers space to discuss books and other matters in depth, and also because it is taken seriously. It risks irrelevance and frivolity because of persistent personal friendship-mongering and enemy-hatcheting. Friends often review friends, demolition experts the rest. A classic example is James Baldwin's ardent review of Elia Kazan's novel *The Arrangement,* which embarrassed even the editors of what one critic has named the *New York Review of Each Other's Books.* It has a well-defined point of view (earnest, elegant, radical), and that's a contribution. It serves the Each Other too assiduously, probably honestly convinced that Each Other is all that matters, but this limits its reliability. Persistent OK-ness lowers the moral tone.

The traditional justification for the anonymous review is aulde English practice in the *Times Literary Supplement.* In England they used to know each other; the thought was that a man could be honest — objective — if his identity was protected. He wouldn't have to apologize to his friends. But in fact even in England the reviewers tend to be identified — particularly in the case of the friend's review; and even in England the freedom of the anonymous put-down has traditionally been exercised with glee by liberated malice. What didn't work in England doesn't work in the United States, either. What worked badly in England works worse here. It turns out that the craftsman, signing and taking responsibility for his words, is more serious than the chap hiding behind the protection of a bureacratic enterprise. The surprise is that anyone expected a different psychology from reviewers than from other men working for hire. The spirit of the anonymous medieval cathedral-builders, laboring for the glory of God, is absent from the short notices of the *New Yorker.*

Signed assaults, while also painful, admit the suspicion that a fallible person has reacted to a book. Also they admit the possibility of carrying a grudge with an identifying ribbon tied to it. Professor Irwin Corey argues for the blessedness of hatred on the grounds that without hatred there is no joy in revenge.

My favorite abusive review (every novelist has his own collection, along with the remedying dolls and pins) began by stating that it was a good thing I look like Gregory Peck and play great tennis, because *Fathers* proved that I sure can't write. (In fact, my tennis is ardently mediocre, and Gregory Peck looks more like Zero Mostel than I look like him.) The review built from these items of inaccurate praise to a crescendo demonstration of my worthlessness, greed, and senility. A few years later a young man approached me at a party in New York, introduced himself, and took my hand; and by the time I could respond by removing my five best fingers, I had .already handed him half a handshake. "I know you must be bugged with me," he said, "but man, I apologize. Look, it was one of my first reviews, and I wanted to make a reputation for myself. I really apologize, man. Let me buy you a drink, OK?"

My friend George P. Elliott, who overheard the conversation, made his usual rigorous Protestant estimation of how to show repentance. He suggested that the man write his apology in the magazine where the nuisance had been committed. On our way out, the reviewer popped up again and asked to join us for a drink. "No," I said.

"But it's raining!" he said, and true, it was, and the only bar that was nearby was the one where we were heading.

Personal contact with a reviewer can make for much worse trouble than absence from the felicity. Once I remarked winningly, I thought — charmingly, lightly, bravely — about a long review which had treated me as the great menace to the American novel. "Why did she bother writing about my book that way? It's not even a best seller." Winning, charming, light, and brave, as remarks go, is it not? But then I was quoted thusly: "Herbert Gold whined that he was attacked even though he isn't popular."

Ah, I whine fruitlessly, that's not what my song said at all.

Another time I was touched by an unusually perceptive and responsive review in a daily newspaper; I wrote to the critic (note that he became a critic rather than a reviewer as soon as he began to appreciate me properly). His reply arrived a few days later in rapid, inaccurate typing on newspaper copy paper: "Schmuck, I only had a day to read your novel and write my notice. What makes you think I know anything about it? Just write books and leave me alone, please."

A curious reverse twist in the infinite variety of reviewmanship came to me not long ago in the form of a letter from an editor, along with galleys of a new novel, in which the editor asked for comment, statement, reviews, any help at all in selling the book. He introduced it by saying it was "by the frequent reviewer X," with a clear implication: Now your novelist to praise, tomorrow perhaps your very own reviewer.

I flung both letter and book aside with annoyance. Then it happened that I picked up the book, started reading, and liked it a great deal. Now what to do? I wrote to the editor along these lines: liked the book, hated your letter. Even though it might help me to get a good review from Mr. X, I'm willing to praise his book, because the book really is remarkable, but your blackmail is atrocious.

A Soviet legend has it that Stalin, in his last paranoid days, called Molotov in and said, "I hear a rumor that you're a Jew."

"But my friend!" cried Molotov. "You've known me all my life, you know my family, how can you say such a thing?"

Stalin puffed silently on his pipe. At last he said, "Well, think it over."

The letter about the "frequent reviewer" is that sort of comment. Would you like to like this book? it asks. Well, think it over.

When the publisher printed my comment on the book jacket, he deleted the accusation of blackmail.

There are the reviewers who never read a writer, but are always "rereading," even a book just published, because they like to think of themselves as culture critics permanently evaluating the totality of human experience. There are the counterphobic reviewers, who seek joy and renown by saying the opposite of what everyone else says (Harold Robbins is high American tragic camp; Bernard Malamud writes soap opera). There are the truth-trumpeters who bruit about the obvious with an air of chagrined satisfaction (the times are corrupt! many men fail in their best hopes!); there are the integrity-upholders who stand like the Atlas of Rockefeller Center with the burdens of history on their swelling backs (Nabokov's new novel disappoints a lover of Giraudoux, Homer, and Shchedrin). Those who tell us they have standards are often smug and abstract, have no eyes to see with, hear only the distant drum of vanity. But those who *really* have no standards are at the mercy of this year's fad, beat or hip or camp or pornographic or just the well-promoted product issued by a canny publisher. In this paragraph of denunciation, I have to include myself as occasionally truth-trumpeting, integrity-upholding, abstract, self-righteous, and maybe, worst of all, sometimes even trying to see virtue in that in which others have found virtue. But I am generally cautious, sometimes ardent. If you respect yourself, you can still have a drink with me while it rains outside.

What it comes down to, from the novelist's point of view, is this: he has delivered himself of a book, and it pangs him mightily. He is standing in the night and from his mouth — a cry. He is bowing toward the East, where Manhattan lies, and his voice is borne but dimly on the wind.

If the word from Manhattan is friendly, he issues forth a negligent "Thank you," and returns quietly into his fantasy of eternal truth and beauty.

But if the machine speaks harshly, he shakes his fist at the sky, and his howl can be heard all the way into the kitchen: "Plague, malediction, eternal war henceforward! May the Grand Wazir of Cleveland put a curse upon thy soul!"

WARNING: THE CHAIN SAW COMETH
by Paul Brooks

Unless there is a potent public outcry, the U.S. Forest Service is about to preside over the destruction of the largest stand of virgin forest in the United States.

SAY "Admiralty Island" to the man on the street and he will think vaguely of the South Pacific; mention the environmental crisis in Alaska and his mind will turn automatically to the oil pipeline. If you don't know about Admiralty Island, Alaska — as I didn't a few months ago — that is because the conservation battle now reaching its climax there has had little press coverage. The money involved, though considerable, is peanuts compared to the oil leases on Prudhoe Bay. There is no new technology, no spectacular engineering feat, to lend drama. On the contrary, what we have here is an old story.

In the grass bordering the main (and only) street of Angoon, the Indian village on Admiralty, lies a corroded ship's cannon salvaged from the beach, embossed with the imperial eagle of Russia. It is a reminder that Southeast Alaska has been subject to violence and exploitation since Captain Vitus Behring, in the service of Peter the Great, sighted this uniquely beautiful land over two centuries ago. In nearby Juneau, as you enter the elevator in the principal hotel, you are confronted with a bas-relief of the supreme exploiter of them all, Count Alexander Baranof, enslaver of Indians, first king of the fur trade that was to bring the fur seal and sea otter to the brink of extinction. With his tight lips and prizefighter's nose, Baranof makes General Patton look like a peacenik. Though the Russians are long since gone, this is still an embattled country, where entrenched economic interests and militant conservationists are locked in a bitter struggle. At stake is no less than the largest stand of virgin forest in the United States.

Over one hundred miles long, and averaging twenty-odd miles in width, Admiralty (so named by Captain Cook) is approximately the size of New York's Long Island, but there the resemblance ends. Its population consists of about four hundred Tlingit Indians and a handful of non-natives, concentrated in the ancient village of Angoon. The interior is mountainous and rugged, without roads or even trails; the coastline is broken here and there with deep, rocky inlets and sinuous bays. A blanket of evergreen forest, roughly two-thirds hemlock and one-third Sitka spruce, covers most of the island, varied only by an occasional small opening of muskeg, by mountain peaks with surrounding parklike meadows, and by a dozen or so freshwater lakes. Whales, porpoises, and seals feed in the coastal waters; waterfowl

breed in the salt marshes; trout flourish in the lakes and streams, and
— beginning in late summer — salmon fight their way upstream in
awesome numbers to spawn and die. Bald eagles and Alaska brown
bears abound. No wonder that, as far back as 1931, the island was
considered for a national park. But that dream has long since faded.
With the coming of statehood, Alaska's timber industry has gone into
high gear. Admiralty lies at the heart of the Tongass National Forest,
temptingly accessible to Juneau and Japan. It is about to become a
part of the largest timber sale in American history.

Southeast Alaska's coastal islands have, of course, already been
heavily logged. In fact, Admiralty is the *only* sizable island left in approximately pristine condition. With such vast forests available elsewhere, allegedly being harvested on a "sustained yield" basis, is it necessary to throw Admiralty into the pot — so precipitously and so
irrevocably? Or is it worth saving? If you want to make an unemo-
tional judgment, don't set foot on the island. You will return, as my
wife and I did after a week's visit, highly prejudiced. You may even
join the ranks of the "preservationists" — persons who got that way,
according to the Pacific Logging Congress *Handbook,* "because of too
few trips to the woodshed to be taught old-fashioned values."

From Juneau one reaches Admiralty Island by floatplane or by boat.
On our first trip we combined the two, cruising up the principal inlet
before settling at Angoon. The tide was dead low when we reached
the island, and the long dock had no float. Knapsacks on our backs, we
climbed up the thirty-foot ladder and then lowered a rope for our
suitcase. As we walked up the dirt road to our quarters near the
schoolhouse, ravens croaked and whooshed overhead. The frame
houses and even the white church on the hill — topped by the ancient
cross of Russian orthodoxy — were built on piles. (We noticed that the
family wash, in this land of little sun, was hung under the houses.)
The village appeared all but empty, for despite a diminishing salmon
run, three quarters of the families were away from home, working
briefly in the canneries. Jobs for these Indians are scarce, and experience elsewhere indicates that they would benefit little from a logging
operation on their doorstep. As their old way of life has disappeared,
the Indians have gone on relief. With the decline of the salmon, many
canneries have closed. Currency in the trading post is largely food
stamps. What hope there is for the future seems to lie in the modern,
well-run school, where talented young teachers from around the
country seek to introduce these children from another age — many of
whom have never been off the island — to the frighteningly complex
world around them.

As the clouds lifted that evening, we looked westward to the snow-capped, glaciated mountains of Baranof Island. At the water's edge, a man and boy were gutting several large halibut, while a circle of gulls and crows and ravens waited to move in. Among the rocky headlands at our feet, we found miniature wild gardens of bluebells and columbine and Queen Anne's lace; the slopes above were covered with blueberry, salmonberry, and huckleberry bushes, and bright patches of purple fireweed. The dark, round object drifting offshore turned out, in our binoculars, to be the head of a seal.

A week's time is barely enough to sample this vast roadless area. In memory, scene blends into scene: deep bays with porpoises plunging and families of young harlequin ducks volplaning over the surface; on the nearby shore, the dark, lithe form of a mink darting among the rocks; flocks of Canada geese honking in long V's, all against the backdrop of the centuries-old forest. From the broad grass flat bursts a flock of mallards; we hear a single, quavering cry of a loon.

And the bald eagles. To an Easterner, the sight of one of these great birds is landmark for the whole summer; here we could see several at a time, the white heads of the adults brilliantly visible against the dark trees on which they perched. We watched them fishing, and we learned to recognize their curiously high pitched scream. We saw a young bird being harassed by a mixed flock of ravens and crows. Where we come from, young eagles are ominously scarce. Perhaps only in Alaska is the future of the species assured.

Always we were aware of the tides, which ran to over twenty feet. One morning, under the skilled hand of our friend and navigator, the little outboard motorboat fought its way through a roaring, swirling tide rip, like a salmon snaking upstream through the rapids. One forgets that this is salt water; I almost stooped for a drink. But then we entered one of those magic tide pools, bright with swaying sea anemones and brilliant orange starfish. The stream at the head of the bay where we disembarked was packed with humpback and dog salmon, some swimming bravely against the current, others, already having spawned, flopping feebly in the shallows till they died or were taken by a bear. The tall grass along the bank was flattened by the bears' passing; rotting fish heads and backbones filled the air with their stink. We followed a bear trail along the shore, pausing now and then to peer far into the lush, dark woods — a virgin forest with wide spaces and long vistas between towering spruce and hemlock, dead limbs festooned with old-man's-beard, young seedlings on decaying trunks, spongy sphagnum moss carpeting the forest floor.

On another day we flew to a conservation area on the east side of the island where we could get a close-up view of bears feeding on the salmon. (Red-carpet air service in Alaska is pleasantly informal. Since our floatplane couldn't drift quite up to the beach, our pilot, in rubber boots, carried us ashore piggyback.) As we followed the forest trail upstream, screaming gulls and croaking ravens, who feed on the bear's leavings, showed that there was a bear around the bend. The Alaska brown bear is larger than his cousin the grizzly — averaging 800 to the latter's 600 pounds — and when he stands on his hind legs to look you over, the sight is impressive. Apparently ponderous, he moves like a flash as he seizes a fish from the water. One keeps one's distance, particularly when there are cubs.

Admiralty Island has always been a bear-hunter's (and more recently a bear-photographer's) paradise; today, the bear population outnumbers the human by about two to one. But they need wilderness to survive. Logging camps, logging roads — and even worse, the highway that is planned — would spell their eventual doom. Like wolves, they are still considered "bad" animals, and they do not coexist happily with man.

Many Alaskans — sportsmen as well as conservationists — feel that Admiralty Island is worth saving for its bears alone. An even stronger case can be made for preserving one of the last refuges of our national bird, the bald eagle, which we watched with such joy during our days on the island. Poisoned by slow accumulation of DDT, which inhibits the formation of eggshells (some eagles in the Central States are laying eggs with no shells at all), the bald eagle is an endangered species everywhere but in Alaska. On Admiralty Island the eagles flourish; the breeding population of between four and five hundred pairs is greater than that in all the "lower 48" states combined. Largest of its race, with a wingspan reaching up to eight feet, the Alaska bald eagle is not primarily a scavenger; it prefers fresh food, and it is oriented toward the sea. The eagles' nests on Admiralty, when plotted on a map, make a dotted line clear around the island, each nest in the first or second big tree from the shore.

Eagles need stalwart old trees to carry the nest mass. They will not return to a cutover area, even seventy-five or eighty years later. Yet if the logging proceeds as planned, these great coastal forests will be the first to go. The federal Fish and Wildlife Service does insist that a hundred-yard radius be saved around each nest, which might result in an almost continuous fringe of old-growth forest — at best, the minimum for precarious survival.

The growing public concern for the future of our national bird could have far-reaching effects on more than the eagles. The timber industry is not worrying much about the wildlife on Admiralty Island or anywhere else — neither about the Sitka deer, which during severe winters need the shelter of the old forest for survival, nor the economically important salmon, whose spawning would suffer from silt in the rivers and fluctuations in water temperature when the shade of the forest was gone. Small birds and mammals not suitable for sport killing are ignored. The bears get attention, because sportsmen have money and political muscle. But the eagles are in a category by themselves. Their nesting sites are protected on orders from Washington, and the loggers are forced to listen. How appropriate if these great birds should be instrumental in saving this priceless wilderness and its other wildlife.

The citizen ordinarily thinks that our national forests are already safe under the trusteeship of the U.S. Forest Service. He is right in theory, but he would be appalled if he knew the facts. The Service is in the business of timber production, through sale of logging rights. Here in Southeast Alaska it has just made the biggest deal ever. The statistics are staggering. Involved are nine *billion* board feet — enough lumber to build a plank road from the Arctic Circle to the tip of South America. But don't be deceived; the sale has nothing to do with the American housing shortage. The bulk of the harvest will be ground into pulp, and virtually all of it will be shipped to Japan. The Forest Service has made three fifty-year contracts for logging in Alaska. The first is with Georgia Pacific at Ketchikan, the second with the Japanese-owned Alaska Lumber and Pulp Company in Sitka — currently being sued by the Environmental Protection Agency for polluting and massive fish kills. The third, which has been challenged in court, is with U. S. Plywood-Champion, all of whose output goes to Kanzaki Paper Manufacturing Company Ltd., Tokyo. For reasons obscure to the outsider, this third sale was made *after* the Forest Service realized that it had grossly overestimated the amount of timber in the areas allotted to the first two companies — in the case of the second sale by 797 (seven hundred and ninety-seven, lest you think that was a misprint) percent. The probable result is that Southeast Alaska will be stripped bare of its virgin forests to fulfill all three contracts.

To some professional foresters, this is fine. They estimate that 95 percent of the "commercial" forests — that is, trees worth cutting — in Southeast Alaska are what they call "overage." The quicker they are felled the better, so that "thrifty, fast-growing young trees" may take their place. (In 1968, the *Regional Forester* said that 98.5 percent of commercial timber in the Tongass National Forest would ultimately be "harvested.") Well and good perhaps from the point of view of timber or pulp production alone, though other experienced foresters violently disagree. But technical arguments aside, is that the only legitimate use of a national forest? What about the much touted principle of multiple use, with which the Forest Service automatically puts down any critic of its policy?

The phrase "multiple use" is comforting but widely misunderstood. In a national forest you can designate some areas to be logged, some saved for recreation, some preserved as wilderness. Once you have clear-cut an old forest, however, you will never have that forest again. You can have a tree farm, on which you grow a crop of even-age trees as a farmer grows corn. In time, a tree farm may become quite photogenic. But those expensive full-color advertisements of the big timber companies, those paintings of squirrels perched on mossy stumps, are misleading. We need tree farms, as we need cornfields; but don't call them forests.

Experience in Alaska shows that the thicket of young trees that follows clear-cutting is initially impenetrable. When it's a little older, you can get through it on hands and knees. But by the time it has reached mature size, it is ready to be cut again. Talk of "multiple use" *within* such an area is less than convincing, which is not to say that the principle is wrong or that the Forest Service has ignored it. After all, the very concept of a "wilderness area" originated within the Service over forty years ago. Many areas of the national forests have been set aside for recreation, including the finest of the interior lakes on Admiralty Island. The Service has a high level of professional competence; many of its employees are outdoorsmen and naturalists committed to the cause of conservation. Yet everywhere one hears the criticism that the Service, like so many government agencies, has become the captive of the industry it is supposed to regulate. A committee from the School of Forestry at the University of Montana, formed at the request of Senator Lee Metcalf, reported that the U. S. Forest Service's dominant interest is "lumber production to the exclusion of delicate ecological and social concerns." It is manipulated by special interests who want to make a short-term killing. This approach, says the report, is "completely out of step with the interests and desires of the American people."

Can the voice of the people be heard on Admiralty Island? The Sierra Club believes that it can. To the fury of the local establishment, this national conservation organization has gone to court to try to invalidate the sale to Plywood-Champion. The reaction in some quarters of Juneau has been almost hysterical. On the road from the airport, one sees a sign on a motel: "Sierra Club News: More Alaska Jobs Killed." On July 21, 1971, the *Southeast Alaska Empire* ran an editorial with the banner headline: "Sierra Club Go Home!" The lawsuit was described as "another attempt by outside interests to stifle the economic progress of Alaska." The paper's "letters" column erupted with anger and weird metaphor. "Never have we been faced with a serpent so deadly . . . the serpent engulfs us in its coils by legal procedures . . .

encircling industry and citizen alike to feed its own stomach with un-employment. . . . It is time for the people to pick up their sticks and destroy this serpent commonly known as the Sierra Club."

In its suit before the Federal District Court, heard in November, 1970, the serpent was joined by the Sitka Conservation Society and Karl Lane, a professional guide in Juneau. Five other conservation groups, both national and local, sought to join as coplaintiffs, but were refused by the judge on the grounds that they lacked "standing." The plaintiffs claimed that the Plywood-Champion sale violated stat-utes governing use of our national forests, "in that the major purpose of the sale is to establish a new industrial enterprise [that is, a pulp mill near Juneau] a substantial portion of the production of which will not be used for the use and necessities of the citizens of the United States." They laid particular stress on the violation of the Multiple Use and Sustained Yield Act of 1960 in that the defendants had failed "prop-erly to consider and balance outdoor recreation, watershed, wildlife and fish uses with timber requirements." On the contrary they had "irrevocably committed themselves to an inflexible schedule of har-vesting substantially all the operable virgin growth forests in South-eastern Alaska to the exclusion of all other legitimate uses of such forests." The judge ruled against the plaintiffs on the ground that they had failed to exhaust administrative remedies before going to court — in other words, that they had acted too late. As to the claim that the Forest Service ignored the principle of multiple use, the judge pointed out that since the federal statutes contain no standards for assigning relative values to competing uses, "the court concludes that this determination is committed to agency discretion and therefore unreviewable."

The nationwide implications of this latter conclusion, and the vast power it seems to allow to a single administrative agency, would sug-gest that the statutes need strengthening. As Richard Cooley wrote five years ago in his *Alaska: A Challenge in Conservation:* "Bureau auton-omy cannot be tolerated in the field of natural resources." Meanwhile, the Sierra Club, strongly supported by local conservationists, has filed an appeal, to the apparent disgust of the Juneau business community. Two prominent retailers bought a double-page spread in the *Empire* denouncing the Club for interfering with "progress." It "should try to salvage the ecology in the populated parts of the U. S. where PLUN-DERING has been going on, and let Alaskans make their own decisions and enjoy the great land we love."

Though lacking in logic in the current situation (Tongass National Forest does not belong to Alaska any more than Grand Canyon Na-tional Park belongs to Arizona), this outcry represents a defensive atti-tude toward the "lower 48" that the visitor to Alaska may find puz-

zling, but which in the light of history is understandable. Until very
recent times, Alaska has been treated like a stepchild of the United
States. For seventeen years following the purchase in 1867, it had no
organized government at all, being administered successively by the
War, Treasury, and Navy Departments. It then became a "civil and
judicial district," but not till 1912 was it established as a U. S. territory,
with its own legislature. Finally, twelve years ago, it achieved statehood. Alaskans have not forgotten the days before statehood when
they had to pass through immigration to enter the United States.
"Southeastern" has not forgotten its economic bondages to San Francisco and Seattle, nor the disastrous overexploitation of its fisheries
under the management of the U. S. Fish and Wildlife Service. Now
that the gold rush is only a memory and the salmon run has declined,
the Southeast naturally looks to its forests to bolster the economy. The
oil strikes may have made the state rich, but they haven't made jobs in
Juneau. Anchorage may be booming, but Anchorage is two time zones
away. The trees are here: we'll do what we can for the wildlife, and
we'll get used to the stink of the pulp mill when the wind is from the
north. In any case, islands like Admiralty are too big to be logged off
all at once. It will take a long time. We'll save the east side for conservation — for a while anyway. "Sierra Club, go home!"

Those who label the Sierra Club an outsider forget that its interest
in Southeast Alaska dates back to the days of its founder, John Muir,
that it has been around longer than either the Forest Service or Plywood-Champion, and that its rapidly growing membership in Alaska is
already *at* home. In the current lawsuit, it is defending basic principles
of land use with which a vast number of Americans agree. After centuries of exploitation, we have now come to value wilderness for its
own sake. In 1964, Congress passed the Wilderness Act to give permanent protection to those "primitive" and "wilderness" areas within the
national forests that had already been set aside by administrative decree. Yet paradoxically our greatest surviving wilderness, in Alaska, is
wholly unprotected, since no such areas have ever been established
there. And the Forest Service flatly refuses to designate specific areas
for preservation before the logging begins. The sequence is clear: cut
now, plan later.

Twin shibboleth to "multiple use" is the magic phrase "sustained
yield." The logging cycle is optimistically set (trees grow slowly in
Alaska) at one hundred years. How can one reconcile this rate of
growth with a fifty-year contract, which will require most of the existing commercial timber for its fulfillment? Even in terms of dollars
alone, there is a fundamental contradiction in this immense timber
sale. State agencies, chambers of commerce, airlines, the tourist industry are inviting visitors to Alaska to "get away from it all," to enjoy

"pure wilderness," on "the nation's last frontier." In our overcrowded world, recreation may be Alaska's greatest long-term asset. Like the salmon run, it produces steady income, whereas an area once logged yields nothing for at least a century. But will tourists come to Alaska to stare at barren shores, to fish in polluted rivers, to hunt in tree farms? As one knowledgeable outdoorsman and author put it: "Alaskans . . . must now anticipate an era a generation hence when Southeast Alaska will have no operating pulp mills and no tourist industry — unless tourists of that day have learned to enjoy stumpland vistas."

The timber industry points out that much old-growth timber in the Tongass National Forest is too scattered or inaccessible to be worth cutting (at least for now) and is therefore available for recreation. In short, what they don't want will remain as wilderness. A perfectly natural view for the industry to take, as it is natural for the Japanese to buy their pulp where they can get it. This view has prevailed elsewhere throughout Southeast Alaska, as it has from earliest times on the American frontier. But as the passage of the Wilderness Act demonstrated, it is no longer the view of Congress or of the American people.

On Admiralty Island nature's cycle is as yet unbroken. But the chain saws are very close, ready to move in the moment legal roadblocks are removed. By chance or intent, the first areas to go will be the most scenic, the most valuable for conservation. The bears and the eagles, whose home this has been for thousands of years, have no direct voice in the matter. But they are powerful symbols of something priceless that we now realize we have all but lost: what Henry Thoreau called "the tonic of wildness." If enough voices are raised in their behalf, they may yet save this greatest of wilderness islands.

1972
LONELINESS
by W. H. Auden

GATE-crashing ghost, aggressive
invisible visitor,
tactless gooseberry, spoiling
my *tête-à-tête* with myself,
blackmailing brute, behaving
as if the house were your own,
so viciously pursuing
your victim from room to room,
monotonously nagging,

ungenerous jabberer,
dirty devil, befouling
fair fancies, making the mind
a quagmire of disquiet,
weakening my will to work,
shadow without shape or sex,
excluding consolation,
blotting out Nature's beauties,
grey mist between me and God,
pestilent problem that won't
be put on the back-burner,
hard it is to endure you:

Routine is the one technique
I know of that enables
your host to ignore you now:
while typing business letters,
laying the table for one,
gobbling a thoughtless luncheon,
I briefly forget you're there,
but am safe from your haunting
only when soundly asleep.

History counsels patience:
tyrants come, like plagues, but none
can rule the roost for ever.
Indeed, your totter is near,
your days numbered: to-morrow
Chester, my chum, will return.
Then you'll be through: in no time
he'll throw you out neck-and-crop.
We'll merry-make your cadence
with music, feasting and fun.

1973
THE DUBLIN SOCIAL SCENE
by Mary Manning

THE Dublin social scene around six o'clock is varied and unpredictable. At the moment there is a craze for forming committees and having meetings to save something or somebody.
The invitations, usually received the very morning of the meeting, are

so vaguely worded that you are quite uncertain what you're there to save until you get there and even then nobody is quite sure. The only thing you can be assured of is that nothing will come of it. I asked a member of the diplomatic corps what he thought of these meetings. He shook his head and murmured smiling enigmatically, "My dear lady it's a form of sadistic amusement."

The meetings always run true to form. There is invariably one drunk man present who insists on asking irrelevant questions until asked to leave. The other evening one of these boring agitators having been forcibly urged to the nearest exit turned at the door and shouted at the chairman: "Farewell, a long farewell. We'll meet again at Philipstown. Bet you can't say that in Irish." The chairman hardly hesitated before retorting quietly: "Yes I can. FUCK OFF." Some of the meetings got so fierce that the last Abbey Theatre conference served only coffee and sandwiches. This happened to be a particularly vague meeting about the necessity for joining in with International Theatre. A good many people deprived of their usual stimulant seized the opportunity to nap, except Mary O'Malley who had hastened down from war-torn Belfast to chair the meeting and has of course lost the power of sleep. *Conor Cruise O'Brien could not be present. He was in Haiphong.*[1]

Then there are the Openings. Art shows. Independent Artists. Living Art and a great deal of dead art. At one opening I attended we had to wade through pools of blood — brought down every evening in a bucket from the abattoir — meant to remind us of Bloody Sunday. My eardrums were seriously damaged by the deafening pop music. Red wine was served in paper cups. The girls were either dressed as Russian cavalry officers or Fanny Hill, and the fellas were covered with hair and flaunting their body odor. During this opening the Tinkers charged in, en masse, stole sculpture, small pictures, overcoats, purses, anything they could lay hands on, drank up all the wine and rushed out before they were identified as Tinkers.

And the Sales of Work; the Charity Auctions all in aid of various good works. Protestant Orphans; a mysterious organization called the Sick and Indigent Roomkeepers Society; the Distressed Irish Gentlewomen; the Broken Governesses; the Down and Out Nannies; the Cats' Home; the Dogs' Home; and the Hospice for the Dying. The latter would seem to be a discouraging welcome for those who enter its portals in a wheelchair or ambulance, but I am told by those who know that it is perfectly extraordinary what a challenge this is! People who have been given up for dead seem to take on a new lease of life

---

[1] Conor Cruise O'Brien runs like a melody through my report because he runs like a recurring theme through Dublin life.

and WILL NOT DIE. This of course is very disappointing and presents many monetary problems. Not only are the dead raised but money has to be raised to keep them raised. These charitable affairs are usually opened by the Minister for Finance. Does he suspect?

Dinner parties are not often held. Dublin when you really settle down in it is a most inhospitable city and very few people have the good manners or maybe the energy to return hospitality. The few bachelors here are singularly brutish in this respect; they behave like prize bulls. One of the few bachelors in the city who entertains is the poet-art dealer Sean O'Criadin who commutes between Dublin, New York, London, and Paris but when he *is* here you know it. He gave a dinner party for my sister-in-law Helen *(The Gentle Americans)* Howe when she was in Dublin the other day and it was one of those evenings you remember. We were surrounded by beautiful objets d'art and ate off Royal Worcester and the host cooked the dinner himself, emerging now and then from the kitchen to say a few words and disappearing again. Helen swears she saw him at one point kneeling carving an enormous roast on the floor — on a platter of course. She sat next to Niall Montgomery a famous Dublin wit. There were twelve of us and the conversation turned as it often does to an analysis of *Conor Cruise O'Brien's talents*. People had reached the shouting and pointing stage when during a pause for breath Niall Montgomery was heard murmuring plaintively to nobody in particular, "Yes I like *Uncle Vanya,* but I like *The Cherry Orchard* best." When challenged on the relevance he said, "I heard the sound of chopping." Sean's party was exceptionally civilized however. We sat down to eat at eight as programmed and we left sober and happy at a reasonable hour. It is not always thus. The grander the party the more pretentious the occasion the more uncivilized it becomes. When you're asked for around eight-thirty expect the worst. You will not see food until ten, by then there are quite a few stretcher cases and the heads will be rolling in the soup. At one very grand party given by a hostess who is breathlessly climbing (her husband is in the building trade and has Dublin in ruins), all the status symbols were in and around the mansion: the heated swimming pool and sauna, the Mercedes car, and an atrocious collection of modern art. Two teen-age footmen or servitors had been corralled from the village and popped into white coats. They wore bashful expressions and had exceptionally large feet. The fat lady near me wreathed in smiles and pearls murmured, "Be kerful! They look like IRA." At that moment one of the boys approached us with a platter of caviar. "Fishes eggs ma'am," he said helpfully; "these is the black but the reds is coming!" "What did I tell you," said the fat lady when he had moved on: "Bolshies." I sat between a deaf baronet (the hostess had been after him for a year) and a sleeping architect. "This dreadful General Anim," the lady on the other side addressed the baronet, "only stirs up more African violence." "All they need is a window with a northern exposure and don't water the leaves," was the peculiar reply. "I think he means violets dear," whispered the hostess encouragingly. At this moment the architect woke up, peered at his food, poked it with a fork and said loudly, "What's this — human flesh?" *Conor Cruise O'Brien was not mentioned.*

Dublin society is now swarming with got-rich-quick parvenus. Most of the money is made in land speculation, chain market stores, chain pubs, manure, and one thing and another. In spite of their thing for the Irish language (they name their children Naoise, Cormac, Finn, Fiona, Derbhla), they do seem to fall into Anglo-Irish attitudes. They keep horses, their children ride in pony shows and hunt. They buy old masters and quite blatantly keep young mistresses; they go through mysterious divorces and still stay within the Church. As they rise, or rather spread, socially, they move into the country buy large houses and stud farms and cultivate assiduously the very people whose houses their rebel fathers had burned forty-five years ago. This seems to me the final irony and one which Proust would have relished. The Dublin Grand Opera which functions once a year in the Gaiety Theatre brings out the nouveaus in their mink capes, long gloves and satins and me diamonds. Nobody but a handful of shabby music lovers and the two critics ever listens to the music. They're all much too busy taking inventories of each other's clothes and thereby evaluating the husband's intake for the year. The wife of a cabinet minister told me quite frankly she didn't even know the name of the opera. "We just subscribe dear and hope for the best." The genteel accent which Thackeray lampooned in *Vanity Fair* and his *Irish Sketch-Book* is still rampant. "Do be kerful Des," one tycoon's wife murmured to her husband who was looking exquisitely miserable in a dinner jacket, "I bought this in Pors [Paris] and you can't get anything like it hur." *Conor Cruise O'Brien was in a stage box with a veiled lady.*

The Kildare Street Club now in a condition of stately dilapidation remains the last stronghold of the gentry. Nobody in trade here, dear! Quite a few professionals, doctors, lawyers, are admitted but even their pedigrees are scrutinized. In spite of the fact that the club is only holding on by its Norman eyelashes, the nouveaus can't get in because the club doesn't like "that sort of money." It's impossible to buy your way into this consecrated ground. It is usually rather empty, but it's crowded when the bloodstock sales are on and everyone comes up to shop on Thursdays and meet and greet each other for lunch at the club. The conversation is carried on in well-bred shouts because a great many of them are hard of hearing but bloody well determined to be heard. Those voices have been barking out orders in Norman castles, Jacobean dwellings, Georgian mansions, and of course, the playing fields of Eton for centuries. "Saw Poopsey at Goodwood. Nice gal. Is she married?" "Oh, I think so. She nearly always is. Do order whitebait. Denis we'll have a bottle of that German stuff. Roger's leg's kicking up. His wife's foaled again. No I won't hush. Why the devil should I hush? WHAT? Oh! Roger's behind me. He can't hear. Deaf as a post . . ."

A very sporty old lady in high boots limps over and smacks one of the speakers on the shoulder: "Halloo Corky! What are you doing here?" "Bloodstock. You look blooming Pugsy." "I'm not. Up for an operation. Me guts. Awful bore! Have to have the wretched things out. So I came up to have Whatshisname do a whatyoumaycallit." "Damn bore. I always say to the girls keep your crotch warm and you won't have any of those female troubles. Ha! Ha!"

Over there at that table in the corner sits the lone American member O. Z. Whitehead, but then he's a "nice" American (St. Mark's and Harvard) with an impeccable Edith Whartonish New York background. "Even allowing for the fact that he's an American — poor fella — he *is* one of us." The American Ambassador is always an honorary member, in fact this applies to the corps diplomatique in general, which means — oh dear — the club swallowing all those foreigners. The most endearing thing about the club is the close bond between the staff and the members. Paternalistic of course and I guess somewhat on the lines of the old Southern plantations, but nevertheless warm and genuine. Consequently they have the best service in Dublin. Nan who presides over the unisex bar (the gents have their own) knows everyone by name and I suspect knows even more than the name. She can keep her cool under the most trying circumstances. That evening for instance when Colonel Blank rushed in, thumped on the bar, and shouted: "What the devil is going on here? There's a fellow downstairs wandering around in a dinner jacket and WHITE TIE."

"Gracious Colonel I'll ask Hickey." Nan reached for the house phone. "It can't be a new waiter."

"SOMEBODY SHOULD TELL THE FELLA," shouted the colonel dashing down a double Scotch.

"It's all right sir." Nan put down the phone. "It's a member of the Edmund Burke Society; they're meeting here tonight."

"Edmund Burke who the devil is he?"

"I don't know sir but I'm sure he's a member. Soda sir?" *Nobody in this joint has ever heard of Conor Cruise O'Brien!*

First nights at the Abbey also afford an opportunity for social showoff. Here it is intellectual celebrities and oh what a holocaust! The curtain is hardly down, the play having been given a tumultuous re-ception, author appearing flushed with success and drink, thanking everybody and everyone, then the evisceration begins — in supper places and bars all over the city and you daren't turn your back be-cause of the knives flashing. "Never sat through such shit in my life." "What's the Abbey coming to?" "Beautiful did you say? Every time she opens her mouth I can only think of the Black Hole of Calcutta." "I know they all have to speak Irish in the Abbey but why the hell can't they learn to speak English?" "After tonight they're going to play the second act first." "Wouldn't make any difference if they played them both together." "Des, I am being perfectly sincere when I say this — you all know I'm sincere, if I'm nothing else I'm sincere but I'm just asking in all sincerity what the hell the goddamn play was about?" A few minutes later author drifts in, Miss Sincerity addresses him effu-sively: "Oh, Tom darling, I was just saying in all sincerity how wonder-ful your play was. Super, simply super darling. Your health." She lifts the cup of cold poison.

"Sorry I can't ask you to dinner darling," murmured Micheal Mac Liammoir, holding on to me at some meeting or other. "Not dear until the run of *The Ideal Husband* is over because all our furniture is on the stage of the Gate Theatre. We finish about Christmas and then we'll celebrate with oysters and champagne." He lowers his voice: "Darling can you tell me why we're here?" "Hilton," he turns to his partner, "Hilton why are we here dear?"

"Don't be funny Micheal," is the brisk response. "Our Georgian Heritage."

"Ah! There's Desmond Guinness. Yes, it must be Georgian. Hasn't he extraordinary eyes?" He moves off and a few minutes later delivers an impassioned speech on behalf of a lost cause — Georgian Dublin.

The dinner parties in the Harcourt Terrace residence of Hilton and Micheal are famous and you haven't lived until you have experienced one. The one essential is to plan to spend the next morning in bed, for you do not sit down to dinner until eleven, sometimes twelve mid-night. Your presence is not requested, is indeed openly resented be-fore ten. The habit of after-the-show eating still hangs on, but the cooks don't. There is a perpetual turnover in cooks. The last one whom Micheal described as an Irish-speaking giantess from Conne-mara disappeared without leaving a trace. There was a rumor they had now acquired a Lebanese dwarf but you never know till you get there. Be that as it may the food is always varied and rich, the conver-sation is loud merry and uninhibited and it's very bad form to go home before two. Stormy discussions, usually concerned with the past, often take place between the two hosts, and the guests are naturally drawn into the maelstrom. Scenes have occurred when guests have stormed downstairs to the hall and ordered taxis. "Can't stand another minute of this. Hilton is simply impossible! No I will not go upstairs and apologize. Let him come down here to me and go on his knees." A compromise is usually reached and reconciliation does take place and Micheal who never fights with anyone suddenly becomes Mrs. Pat Campbell or Maud Gonne. Oh but they're wonderful unique evenings and who would miss the happy chance. *Conor Cruise O'Brien loves them.*

One subject you must not drag into the open is the NORTH. It has become so dangerous that if you value your life you do not discuss the NORTH unless you are with people whose opinion coincides with yours. I was at a very enjoyable dinner the other evening, until the NORTH came up and then all hell broke loose. A glass was broken one lady threw her napkin in her host's face and ran crying from the room and my hostess who was handing round vegetables emphasized her point by knocking me on the head with a heavy silver serving spoon. She explained she thought it was the table. However someone cleverly brought the conversation round to *Conor Cruise O'Brien — knave or genius?* — and the demolition squad moved in: all was well.

Dulled by decades of the Fianna Fáil regime's dominance the Dublin-after-six set voted in the December referendum (on whether to abolish the Catholic Church's special constitutional status in Eire) like the rest of the country, "Yes" in its sleep. Owing to the intervention of heavenly power for once they were right.

Eccentricity coupled with inefficiency is so widespread you begin to accept anything. It's not peculiar at all to see a chamberpot as a table center holding a flower arrangement, or to eat your dinner with a pet dog beside you seated on a child's high chair. Show no surprise if your hostess is one hundred and seven years old and lively as a cricket and had her knee patted by Parnell. This same old lady gave us a delicious tea, but the house did have a peculiar smell which I found out emanated from an immensely fat fox terrier, who shared a bed with our hostess. She still played bridge and "did" the flower arrangements in church. I since learned that when the old terrier died she had a nervous breakdown and had to be removed to a Home where she perked up wonderfully and is now teaching the other inmates to play bridge. Another very handsome old lady who lives near me boasts of being ninety-eight. She also plays bridge, makes her own jam, and serves you a gossamer sponge cake. She spent thirty years in Kenya and knew the Baroness Blixen well. "Here I sit my dear," she said to me the other day, "knitting dishcloths I who used to hunt lions in Africa. I who ran my own coffee plantation high up in the hills and never saw a white face for weeks on end. After a while my dear you find white faces rather boring."

Why does my gardener change his boots before entering the kitchen for his dinner but does *not* remove his hat? Why does my housekeeper only wear her dentures after six in the evening? Who is that white-faced hatless man wearing three raincoats and carrying two carpetbags who runs past my house at least twice a week heading for the sea?

I phoned the local police station the other night and reported my Persian cat missing. Rang again the next morning to report him safely returned. The guard on duty exclaimed: "Thank God you called me ma'am. I had on the report pad Persian gentleman missing from his home." The conductor of the number 5 bus which passes the end of my road told me quite frankly he had absolutely no idea of their time schedule and they just did the run when they felt like it. It is a colorful scene this Dublin social pageant. There are so many big frogs puffing away in the small pond, dotty nonconformists, pseuds and nouveaus, but here and there some perfect darlings. The inefficiency is so deeply rooted in the national character one feels that the other Common Market nations are taking a grave risk. Might it not be infectious? I *know* I've become very odd since I returned. The only rock I cling to is that I *know* I'm odd. Still . . . Oh I just want to tell you that Major Hogan Eliot drew me aside in the supermarket and whispered, "If you find a dead kingfisher and dry it and keep it in your wardrobe your house will never be struck by lightning and it will keep away the moths." He is quite batty, poor love, but one must always pretend: "But I thought kingfishers were extinct Major." "I know," he smiled sadly, "but that makes it all the more interesting." And the *Irish Times* this morning reported "eight dead in Belfast, three of them seriously. . . ." And somebody has written "God is Love" all over my library book. You see what I mean and this happens day after day.

1974
INT'L JET SET HITS WATKINS GLEN
by L. E. Sissman

I'M glad I was born soon enough to have seen the American small town, if not at its height, at least in the early days of decline into its present forlorn status as a conduit for cars and people, all headed for some Big City over the horizon. The small town was not always a stultifying trap for bright young people to escape from; in the years before wartime travel ("How're you gonna keep 'em down on the farm/After they've seen Paree?") and the scorn of the Menckens and Sinclair Lewises made the cities a magnet for farm boys and girls,

the town of five to twenty thousand was a self-sufficient little city-state
of its own.

The main street of those Midwestern towns I remember from the
thirties varied little from one place to another: there were always a
number of brick Victorian buildings, labeled "Richards Block" or
"Denman Block," which housed, downstairs, the chief emporia of the
town — the stores which made it a shire town for the surrounding
farmlands. Each of these stores was run according to a very exact idea
of the rules of its particular game. A hardware store, for instance, had
to be densely hung inside with edged tools — scythes, sickles, saws —
of all descriptions. It had to smell like oil, like metal, and often like the
sacks of fertilizer stacked in the back room. It had to have unstained
wood floors, sometimes sprinkled with sawdust, and high cabinets of
small drawers containing bolts, screws, nails, and small plumbing accessories. It had to be owned and run by a middle-aged man in a blue
apron, assisted by one up-and-coming young man and one part-time
boy in his middle teens. It had to sell for cash on the barrelhead, and
it did.

The drugstore was a horse of a different color (and odor), but it was
circumscribed by equally strict rules. Often, in the thirties, it boasted
one of the few neon signs seen on Main Street, usually a blazing ver-
milion vertical down the side of the building, spelling out "Nyal" or
"Rexall" and sometimes the pharmacist's name as well. The window
displays, as opposed to the workaday pumps and pipe fittings of the
hardware store's unchanging (and fly-specked) windows, were quasi
works of art. Loose swags and taut diagonals of pleated crêpe paper in
jungle hues formed a nest for the product of the month, often a patent medicine or a new tooth powder; over the crêpe and cardboard
burned the store's invariable trademark, a pair of glass urns filled with
red and blue colored water and lighted from behind. Inside, the store,
except in the poorest towns, was rather splendid: after you recovered,
reeling slightly, from the rich, mingled fumes of iodoform, chocolate
soda syrup, and the essence of a thousand biologicals, you strode
across the marble floor to the marble soda fountain (for a malt or
phosphate) or to the pharmacist's counter at the back, behind which
were ranged multiple rows of functional apothecary jars. Here you
would ask the white-coated (and often rimless-spectacled) druggist for
aspirin or Four-Way Cold Tablets or Bromo-Seltzer, or perhaps for
paramedical advice, which he was glad to give. (When "a lady" fainted
"right on the street" in those days, she was carried directly to the
drugstore and ministered to by the druggist, who was often known as
"Doc.")

And the grocery store. Tan-and-white striped awnings outside, even
in the winter. White Salada Tea lettering on the windows. Inside

them, pyramids of cans and sometimes fresh grapefruit in tea-rose tissue wrappers. Inside the store itself, dark oiled softwood floors, a central space surrounded by counters, pickle barrels, cookie and cracker bins. Behind the counters, tall shelves of canned goods, dry groceries, and perhaps a white-enameled butcher's cold case across the back. Baskets of fresh fruits and vegetables (in season). Behind the counters, the grocer, in a striped apron, the butcher, in a bloody white one (and sometimes a surviving straw hat, yellow with age and perspiration), and two or three assistants, rushing like mad to pull the customers' orders down with long, spring-loaded hooks from the top shelves. On the phone — a tall black upright one with a newfangled dial on the base — the grocer himself or an assistant, taking a telephone order from a nearby customer. Standing by, the boy (in sweater and knickers) who would deliver it. Over all, the smell of coffee grinding and maybe a whiff of fresh celery, too.

Down the street, the other shops and offices that made the town sufficient unto itself and to its trading area: upstairs, behind gold signs in windows, lawyers', doctors', and dentists' offices, as well as Odd Fellows', Elks', and Red Men's halls. Free-standing, in a small grass plot ringed by a black iron fence, the spired and turreted Town Hall, or Town Hall-cum-Courthouse. And, oh yes, the Civil War statue and two gape-throated cannon with their pyramid of cannonballs. Down by the tracks, the depot and freight house, the angular feed-and-grain, topped by a checkered Purina Chow sign, and the turpentine-scented lumberyard. And then a long double row of neat white houses, often with large gingerbread carriage sheds behind, extending out Main Street to the end of town. Three or four blocks, perhaps.

These towns are by and large gone in 1974, their old stores shut up with dusty windows, or combined, two or three at a time, to make a superette, a W. T. Grant store, or a sub-and-pizza parlor. The business has moved to the big shopping center on the Interstate or to the city over the horizon, and the depopulated old towns drift along toward oblivion, centers of nothing in the middle of nowhere.

But I can think of one exception. Watkins Glen, New York, a nineteenth-century town at the foot of Seneca, the longest of the Finger Lakes, has suddenly been moved through a hundred years of time and plunked down, willy-nilly, in the middle of the seventies. Watkins, as it is called by natives (visitors, for some reason, refer to it as The Glen), enjoyed a modest Victorian fame as a honeymoon resort, largely because of the spectacular gorge on the outskirts of town from which it takes its name. Though it sits in beautiful country — the high, rolling plateaus between the lakes, studded with vineyards and commanding fine views of the lakes themselves — it is a pawky, homely town. Most of the buildings on the main street (which is also New York State Route 414, connecting Geneva to the north with Elmira to the south) were built between 1850 and 1890; they are unambitious piles of brick two stories high, and they still — even unto the 1970s — house such small-town throwbacks as an old-time soda parlor (complete with a tall sign picked out in individual electric bulbs), a storefront bakery, a yellow-clapboard Red Men's Hall, and a tiny Dodge dealership crammed into one small store, not to mention an equally tiny dime store and an old-fashioned grocery across the street from the ancient (but thriving) Hotel Jefferson.

What happened to give Watkins Glen a new lease on its old life was neither suburbanization (there is no large city near enough) nor the location of a new plant in the town, but the location of a major auto race on a course laid out on the plateau above the town. In 1948, the first so-called Watkins Glen Grand Prix — a sports-car race featuring a motley bunch of hybrid cars — was run on a course which included the town's main street. After an accident in which a spectator was killed in 1952, the event was moved to an impromptu course on back roads west of town. Later, as The Glen became an important annual event in the Sports Car Club of America's calendar, the course was redesigned and made both faster and safer. By the early sixties, earnest lobbying by the local organizers — and a lack of other suitable facilities — made Watkins Glen the venue for the Grand Prix of the United States, the most important auto race, except for Indy, run in this country. At that point, all hell broke loose. Attracted by substantial purses, the heroes of Europe's Formula One racing circus, accompanied by team managers, mechanics, wives, mistresses, and glamorous Riviera groupies, made en masse for Watkins Glen the first week in October every year. Correspondingly, the unheard-of opportunity to see stars like Graham Hill, Jim Clark, Stirling Moss, and Dan Gurney racing Lotuses, BRM's, Ferraris, and Porsches right in their own backyard brought tens of thousands of Canadian and American enthusiasts streaming into Watkins Glen in sports cars, on motorcycles with blanket rolls on the pillion, in hearses, in trailers, in campers of all shapes and sizes.

A city of a million would have been stymied — and paralyzed — by such an onslaught. Watkins Glen, however, is apparently made of sterner stuff. The town fathers, organized in efficient committees, parceled out the town's better sleeping spaces in hotels and motels to the various racing teams and the horde of journalists; mere spectators were also helped to find rooms in private houses, or, if they preferred, allowed to camp out up at the course. Somehow, everybody got fed and bedded down; on race day, a large and happy crowd watched a well-run event, and everybody drifted home again without riot or rebellion, leaving the burghers of Watkins some million dollars richer for their pains.

Toward the end of the sixties, when the purse for the Grand Prix had jumped to six figures, along with the crowds, there was a short outburst of bottle-breaking by some youths on the main street; this was soon quelled by the local police and sheriff's deputies, and everything went on as scheduled. There was some rowdiness up at the track, too: in a sea of camping kids estimated at over 100,000, there were bound to be a few fistfights, bad trips, and general disturbances. But again, the cheerful cops coped, and nothing got badly out of hand. I haven't been back for the last couple of years, but I hear that the crowds have continued to grow as well as the take. I intend to return — gasoline permitting — though, because there is nothing remotely like The Glen in race week.

After you get off the New York State Thruway in Geneva, you follow a long, straight road down along the lakeside. When you arrive within the precincts of Watkins Glen, you begin to notice that both lines of traffic are made up of sports cars. In the town itself, the main street is as serene and aloof as ever — but the noise of unmuffled exhausts is slightly deafening. If you stop into Paradiso's restaurant for hot cakes and coffee (a specialty), you hear the chatter of scores of race fans, speculating on the outcome of this year's race. If you check into the Hotel Jefferson (known familiarly to its regulars as The Jeff), you enjoy a surprisingly good meal (roast beef carved to order) and listen to the English, Australian, Argentinian, and Italian nasalities of drivers, girlfriends, and mechanics as they rehash the triumphs and disasters of that day's practice session. Out on the street, you see Stirling Moss, a regular visitor though no longer an active driver, lost in conversation with a spectacular English girl.

The international jet set has indeed hit Watkins Glen. And Watkins Glen, being York State, shrewd, and sensible, has remained exactly what it was: a slightly forlorn American small town. But quite a rich one now.

1975

AUGUSTINE'S CONCUBINE
by John Updike

To Carthage I came, where there sang all around me in my ears a cauldron of unholy loves . . . I sought what I might love, in love with loving, and safety I hated, and a way without snares.

She was, in that cauldron of the dark and slim, fair, fair enough to mock, with a Scythian roundness to her face, and in her curious stiff stolidity vulnerable, as the deaf and blind are vulnerable, standing expectant in an agitated room. "Why do you hate me, Aurelius?" she asked him at a party preceding a circus.

"I don't," he answered, through the smoke, through the noise, through the numbness her presence even then worked upon his heart. "Rather the contrary, as a matter of fact." He was certain she heard this last; she frowned, but it may have been an elbow in her side, a guffaw too close to her ear. She was dressed compactly, in black, intensifying her husband's suit of dark gray, suiting her female smallness, which was not yet slimness, her waist and arms and throat being, though not heavy, rounded, of substance, firm, pale, frontal. She had, he felt, no profile; she seemed always to face him, or to have her back turned, both positions expressive of not hostility (he felt) but of a resolution priorly taken, either to ignore him, or to confront him, he was baffled which. She was, he sensed, *new,* new, that is, to life, in a way not true of himself, youth as he was (*aet.* eighteen), or of the Carthaginians boiling about them.

"Love your dress," he said, seeing she would make no reply to his confession of the contrary of hatred.

"It's just a dress," she said, with that strange dismissive manner she had, yet staring at him as if a commitment, a dangerous declaration, had been made. They were to proceed by contradiction. Her eyes were of a blue pale to the whiteness of marble, compared with the dark Mediterranean glances that upheld them like the net of a conspiracy, beneath the smoke and laughter and giddying expectation of a circus.

"Absolute black," he said. "Very austere." Again meeting silence from her, he asked, a touch bored and *ergo* reckless, "*Are* you austere?"

She appeared to give the question unnecessarily hard thought, the hand accustomed to holding the cigarette (she had recently given up smoking) jerking impatiently. Her manner, contravening her calm body, was all stabs, discontinuous. "Not austere," she said. "Selective."

"Like me," he said, instantly, with too little thought, automatically teasing his precocious reputation as a rake, her manner having somehow saddened him, sharpened within him his hollow of famine, his hunger for God.

"No," she replied, seeming for the first time pleased to be talking with him, complacent as an infant who has seized, out of the blur of the world, a solid toy, "not like you. The opposite, in fact."

For this space . . . we lived seduced and seducing, deceived and deceiving, in divers lusts; openly, by sciences which they call liberal; secretly, with a false named religion; here proud, there superstitious, every where vain!

At their first trysts, the pressure of time, which with his other con-
quests had excited him to demonstrations of virile dispatch, unac-
countably defeated him; her calm pale body, cool and not supple compared to the dark warm bodies he had known, felt to exist in a slower
time, and to drag him into it, as a playful swimmer immerses another.
What was this numbness? Her simplicity, it crossed his mind, missed
some point. She remained complacent through his failures, her infant's smile of seizure undimmed. Her waist was less voluptuously in-
dented than he had expected, her breasts smaller than they appeared
when dressed. She offered herself unembarrassed. There was some
nuance, of shame perhaps, of sin, that he missed and that afflicted
him, in the smiling face of her willingness, with what amounted to loss
of leverage. Yet her faith proved justified. She led him to love her with
a fury that scourged his young body, that terrified the empty spaces
within him.

Strangely, he did not frighten her. She met his lust frontally,
amused and aroused, yet also holding within her, companion to her
wanton delight, the calm and distance of the condemned.

In those years I had one, — not in that which is called lawful marriage, but
whom I had found out in a wayward passion, void of understanding; yet but
one, remaining faithful even to her; in whom I in my own case experienced,
what difference there is betwixt the self-restraint of the marriage-covenant, for
the sake of issue, and the bargain of a lustful love, where children are born
against their parents' will, although, once born, they constrain love.

Her husband, dark gray shadow, she did not forsake; nor did she,
under questioning, reveal that love between them had been abandoned. Rather, she clave to this man, in her placid and factual manner, and gave him what a man might ask; that her lover found this
monstrous, she accepted as another incursion, more amusing than not,
into this her existence, which she so unambiguously perceived as having been created for love.

"You love him?" However often posed, the question carried its accents of astonishment.

Her hand, small and rounded as a child's, though cleaner, made its
impatient stab in air, and an unintended circlet of smoke spun away.
She had resumed the habit, her one concession to the stresses of her
harlot's life. "We make love."

"And how is it?"

She thought. "Nice."

"Perhaps you were right. I do hate you."

"But he's my husband!"

The word, religious and gray, frightened him. "Is it like," he asked
numbly, "with me?"

"No. Not at all." Her white eyes stared. Was she sincere?

How often do you do it? In what positions? Are you silent, or do the two of you speak throughout? What do you say? The litany, attempting to banish the mystery of her rounded limbs so simply laid open for another, won from her more tears than answers; it appeared, to this amorous youth whose precocious and epochal intuition it already was to seek truth and truth's Lord, not in mathematics nor the consensus of the *polis* but in reverent examination of one's own unique and uniquely configured self, that the details eluded her, she had forgotten, they didn't matter. Incredible! His jealousy would not rest, kept gnawing at this substantial shadow, her husband. He permitted the scandal to become open, and her husband faded a little, out of pride. The man's attentions, sensed through the veil of her, became indifferent, ironical; still he lived with her, shared her nights, could touch her at whim, shared the rearing of their children, a sacred sharing. This could not be borne. Aurelius made her pregnant.

And the husband did vanish, with their common goods. The lover and his concubine traveled to Rome, and then to Milan. Their child they called Adeodatus. The name, surprisingly, came from her; it subtly displeased him, that she fancied herself religious.

. . . time passed on, but I delayed to turn to the Lord; and from day to day deferred to live in Thee, and deferred not daily to die in myself. Loving a happy life, I feared it in its own abode, and sought it, by fleeing from it. I thought I should be too miserable, unless folded in female arms . . .

Her compliance disturbed him. Her love seemed unreasoning, demonic in its exemption from fatigue. Years after she should have wearied of his body, he would wake and find that in their sleep she had crowded him to the edge of the bed, her indistinct profile at rest in the curve of his armpit. The city's night traffic gleamed and glittered below; traveling torchlight shuddered on the walls. A cry arose, close to them. She would rise and smother the child with her breasts, that the father might sleep. Lying nevertheless awake, he felt her merge with the darkened room, in which there was this unseen horizon, of smallness and limit, of the coolness with which she assumed any position, placated any need, however sordid. Her spirit was too bare, like her face when, each morning, for coolness in the humid Italian heat, she pulled back her hair with both hands to knot it; her face gleamed taut and broad, perspiring, a Scythian moon of a face. She had grown plump in her years of happiness. He remembered her smoking, and wished she would begin again. He wished she would die. The blanched eyes, the blunt nose, the busy plump self-forgetful hands. Her lips, pouting in concentration, were startled to a smile by sudden awareness of his studying her; she would come forward and

smother him as if he, too, had been crying. *Concupiscentia.* Its innocence disturbed him, the simplicity of her invitation to descend with
her into her nature, into Nature, and to be immersed. Surely such
wallowing within Creation was a deflection of higher purposes. Like
bubbles, his empty spaces wanted to rise, break into air, and vanish.
Their bodies would become one, but his soul was pulled back taut, like
the hair at the back of her skull.

*Meanwhile my sins were being multiplied, and my concubine being torn from
my side as a hindrance to my marriage, my heart which clave unto her was torn
and wounded and bleeding. And she returned to Afric, vowing unto Thee
never to know any other man, leaving with me my son by her.*

She had been, the mother of Adeodatus, strangely calm in receiving
the news, anxious foremost to understand, to avoid misunderstanding;
her quest for clarity, which had made her appear rigid, frontal, iconic,
brusque at the party more than a decade ago, had tunneled through
all their intervening ecstasies. She was in his arms, her face tear-blurred
but held back from his, contemplating his naked shoulder as if the
truth might rest upon it like a butterfly. "Monica has found you a
wife?"

"My mother deems it crucial to my salvation that I marry."

"And the betrothed —?"

"Is two years under the fit age."

"Not fit, but beautiful?" she asked. *De pulchro et apto* had been the
title of his first dissertation, composed in Carthage and read aloud to
her there. She was illiterate. Since, he had ceased to share his compositions, with their shameful titles *De vita beata* or *De immortalitate animae.*
He had felt these subjects as betrayals of her, prefatory to this great
betrayal.

"Not beautiful, but sufficiently pleasing," he factually answered, unprepared for the sirocco of her grief. "But not you, not like you," were
all the words he could call into her weeping, repeating, "Not like you
at all," recognizing, at last, her firmness and smallness so close yet
remote in his arms as that of a child, an unformed person. The recognition hardened his heart. His cruelty as he held her heightened him.
He saw over her head, where gray hairs had come, scarcely distinguishable, to mingle with the fair, back to the fact that she had had a
husband and had accepted that husband and her lover as if they were
kindred manifestations of the same force, as if he himself were not
incomparable, unique, with truth's Lord within him. For this she was
rightly punished. Punished, nay, obliterated, as a heresy is obliterated,
while love for the heretic burns in the heart of the condemner. Aurelius grew immortally tall against her grieving; he felt in her, who had
so often sobbed in love's convulsion against his body, the benign en-

emy he was later to find in Pelagius, who held that Adam's sin touched only Adam, that men were born incorrupt, that unbaptized infants did not go to Hell. Such liberal plausibilities poisoned the water of life as it sprang from the stricken rock. So with her softness, her stolid waist and child's small eager hands, the austerity of her dress, the brazen circlets she wore as earrings, the halo of fine white hairs her skin bore everywhere; the sum was ease, and ease was deception, and deception evil. So with her perfect love for him. There was more. There must be more.

Nor was my wound cured, which had been made by the cutting away of the former, but after inflammation and most acute pain, it mortified, and my pains became less acute, but more desperate. To Thee be praise, glory to Thee, Fountain of Mercies. I was becoming more miserable, and Thou nearer.

In Africa, the sky never shows a cloud. The heat the desert bestows upon its green shore is severe but not oppressive, like that heavy Milanese heat wherein she had pulled back her hair from damp temples. She, too, could taste the dry joy of lightness, of renunciation. She cut off her hair. She forgot her son. Nor would she ever make love again; there was no moderation in what mattered.

Among the women of the cenobium she entered, she moved not as one with a great grief behind her but as one who, like a child, had yet to live. Blue was the color of the order, her color, between Hellenic white and medieval black. *The beautiful and the fitting:* this, the first of Augustine's dissertations, and the only one of which she was the substance, stayed in her memory and conspired, among these whispering gowned women and these sun-dazed walls of clay, to refine that aesthetic of rite and symbol with which half-formed Christianity, amid its renunciations, was to enrich the vocabulary of beauty. Though illiterate, she drew to herself, from these her sisters — the maimed and fanatic and shy — authority. Her limbs, veiled in blue, became emblems. Her complacence, that had never doubted the body's prerogatives, seemed here, in these corridors cloistered from the sun, to manifest Grace. Her shamelessness became pride. Her placid carriage suggested joy. It was as if her dynamic and egocentric lover, whom she had never failed to satisfy, in his rejection of her had himself failed, and been himself rejected, even as his verbal storms swept the Mediterranean and transformed the world.

She was a saint, whose name we do not know. For a thousand years, men would endeavor to hate the flesh, because of her.

1976
BREED
by John Sayles

BRIAN woke on the lee side of a hill with a buffalo licking his face. At first he was only aware of the tongue, sticky and thick as a baby's arm, lapping down to sample his ears and cheeks. He had laid his sleeping bag out in the dark, snuggling it at the foot of what he took to be a drift fence, to have at least some shelter from the grit-blasting Wyoming wind. If it *was* still Wyoming; he hadn't been awake enough during the last part of the ride to look out for signs.

As he squirmed away from whatever the big thing mopping at his face was he glimpsed through half-sleep that each of the posts in the fence was painted a different color. Cherry-red, lime-green, lemon-yellow. He was in a carny-colored corral with a live bull bison.

No.

He tried to go back under, thinking it was only the effects of the three-day power-hitch across the country from New Jersey, all that coffee and all those miles talking with strangers. But then the rich brown smell dawned on him and he knew. He knew. He had never seen a live buffalo before but he was sure this was what they smelled like. It smelled like The West.

The buffalo retreated a few steps when Brian sat up, fixing him with swimming brown walleyes. There were bare patches worn in the wool of its flanks and hump, shiny black leather showing through. Its beard was sugared with dust and meal of some kind, and Brian could hear the flop of its tail chasing flies.

"Morning, Buffalo."

The animal snorted through its flat nose for an answer, made munching quivers with its jaw. Brian fingered matter from his eyes and peered out over the fence to where he remembered the road. There were cut-out letters hung from a crossbar like the ranches he'd seen in southern Wyoming had. Brian read them backward. CODY SPRAGUE'S WILD WEST BUCKIN' BISON RIDE, it said, FOOD — GAS — SOUVENIRS. Brian didn't understand how he could have missed the sign and the flapping pennants strung from it, even in the dark. The buffalo licked its nose.

Brian pulled on his sweat-funky road clothes and packed his sleeping bag away. The buffalo had lowered its eyelids to half-mast, no longer interested. Brian stood and walked around it. A shifting cloud of tiny black flies shadowed its ass, an ass cracked and black as old inner-tube rubber. There was something not quite real about the thing, Brian felt as if stuffing or springs would pop out of the seams any moment. He eased his hands into the hump wool. Coarse and greasy, like a mat for scuffing your feet clean on. The buffalo didn't move but for the twitching of its rump skin as insects lit on it. Brian gave it a couple of gentle, open-palmed thumps on the side, feeling the solid weight like a great warm tree stump.

"Reach for the sky!"

Brian nearly jumped on the animal's back as a cold cylinder pressed the base of his neck.

"Take your mitts off my buffalo and turn around."

Brian turned himself around slowly and there was a little chicken-necked man pointing an empty Coke bottle level with his heart. "One false move and I'll fizz you to pieces." The little man cackled, showing chipped brown teeth and goosing Brian with the bottle. "Scared the piss outa *you*, young fella. I seen you there this morning, laid out. Didn't figure I should bother to wake you till you woke yourself, but Ishmael, he thought you was a bag a meal. He's kind of slow, Ishmael."

The buffalo swung its head around to give the man a tentative whiff, then swung back. The man was wearing a fringed buckskin jacket so stained it looked freshly ripped off the buck. He had a wrinkle-ring every other inch of his long neck, a crooked beak of a nose, and dirty white hair that shot out in little clumps. Of the three of them the buffalo seemed to have had the best sleep.

Brian introduced himself and stated his business, which was to make his way to whatever passed for a major highway out here on the lone prairie. Thumbing from East Orange to the West Coast. He had gotten a bum steer from a drunken oil-rigger the other night and was dumped out here.

"Cody Sprague," said the little man, extending his hand. "I offer my condolences and the use of my privy. Usually don't open till nine or ten," he said, "but it don't seem to make a difference either whichway."

He led Brian across the road to where there was a metal outhouse and an orange-and-black painted shack about the size of a Tastee-Freeze.

"People don't want to come," he said, "they don't want to come. Just blow by on that Interstate. That's what you'll be wantin to get to, isn't but five miles or so down the way. They finished that last stretch a couple years back and made me obsolete. That's what they want me. Obsolete."

Sprague clucked away at Brian's elbow, trotting a little to stay close as if his visitor would bolt for freedom any second. He called through the door of the little Sani-Port as Brian went in to wash and change to fresh clothes.

"You got any idee what it costs to keep a full-grown American bison in top running condition? Not just a matter of set im loose to graze, oh no, not when you've got a herd of one. Got to protect your investment, the same with any small businessman. Dropping like flies they are. That's an endangered species, the small businessman. Anyhow, you don't let him out there to graze. Don't know *what* he might pick up. You got five hundred head, you can afford to lose a few to poisnin, a few to varmint holes, a few to snakes and whatnot. Don't make a dent. But me, I got everything I own riding on Ishmael. He don't dine on nothin but the highest-protein feed. He's eaten up all my savings and most of the last bank loan I'm likely to get. You ever ridden a buffalo?"

"No," said Brian over the running water inside, "I've never even been on a horse."

"Then you got a treat coming, free a charge. You'll be my ice-breaker for the weekend, bring me luck. I'd offer you breakfast, but confidentially speakin, the grill over here is out of commission. They turned off my lectricity. You might of noticed the lamp in there don't work. How they expect a buffalo to keep up its health without lectric-ity I'll never understand. It's that kind of thinking put the species on the brink of extinction."

Brian came out with fresh clothes and his teeth finger-brushed, and Cody Sprague hustled him back into the corral with Ishmael.

"Is there a saddle or anything? Or do I just get on?"

"Well, I got a blanket I use for the little girls with bare legs if it makes them nervous, but no, you don't need a thing. Like sitting on a rug. Just don't climb up too high on the hump is all, kind of unsteady there. Attaboy, hop aboard."

The buffalo didn't seem to mind, didn't seem to notice Brian crawl-ing up on its back. Instead it lifted its head toward a bucket nailed to a post on the far side of the corral.

"How do I make him go?" asked Brian. There was no natural seat on a buffalo's back, he dug his fingers deep in the wool and pressed his knees to its flanks.

"That's my job, making him go, you just sit tight." Sprague scooted out of the corral, then returned with a half-empty sack of meal. He poured some in the far bucket, then clanged it with a stone. Ishmael began to move. He was in no hurry.

"Ridem cowboy!" yelled Sprague.

Brian felt some movement under him, distantly, a vague roll of muscle and bone. He tried to imagine himself as an eight-year-old kid instead of seventeen, and that helped a little. He tried to look pleased as the animal reached the bucket and buried its nose in the feed.

"This part of the ride," said Cody apologetically, "is where I usually

give them my little educational spiel about the history of the buffalo
and how the Indians depended on it and all. Got it from the library up
to Rapid. Got to have something to keep them entertained at the half-
way point while he's cleaning out that bucket. You know the Indian
used every part of the beast. Meat for food, hide for clothes and blankets, bone for tools, even the waste product, dried into buffalo chips,
they used that for fuel. There was a real — real *affin*ity between the
buffalo and the Plains Indian. Their souls were tied together." He
looked to Brian and waited.

"He sure is big." Brian threw a little extra enthusiasm into it. "I
didn't realize they were this big."

Sprague spat on the ground, sighing, then looked up to see what
was left in the bucket. "Pretty sorry attraction, that's what you mean,
isn't it?"

"Well, I wouldn't say — "

"I mean *isn*'t it? If he don't eat he don't move." Cody shook his
head. "The kids, well, they pick up on it right away. Least they used to
before that Interstate swept them all off. What kind of ride is it where
the animal stops and chows down for five minutes at a time? Got so
bad he'd commence to drool every time he seen a human under twelve
years of age. Feed, that's all they understand. Won't mind kindness
and he won't mind cruelty but you talk straight to his belly and oh
Lord will he listen. That's how they got extinct in the first place,
they seen their colleagues droppin all around them but they were too
involved with feeding their faces to put two and two together. They'd
rather be shot and scalped than miss the next mouthful. Plain stupid is
all." He gave Ishmael a thump in the side. "You'd just as soon name a
rock or a lump of clay as give a title to this old pile of gristle." He
squatted slightly to look the buffalo in the face. "A damn sorry attraction, aren't you? A damn sorry fleabag of an attraction."

He straightened and hefted the meal. "Might as well be stuffed, I
figure. Put him on wheels. The few people I get anymore all want to
snip a tuft of wool offen him for a souvenir. I had to put a stop to it,
wouldn't of been a thing left. Cody Sprague's Bald Buckin' Bison."

Ishmael lifted his head and flapped his tongue in the air a couple of
times.

"Got to fill the other bucket now. He expects it. Took me the longest
time to figure the right distance, long enough so it's two bits' worth of
ride but not so long that the thoroughbred here thinks it's not worth
the hike. The kids can tell though. I never been able to fool them.
They feel left out of it, feel gypped. Um, if you don't mind, would you
stay on him for the rest of the ride?" Cody was hustling across the
corral toward another hanging bucket, with Ishmael swinging a liquid
eye after him. "He needs the exercise."

Brian sat out the slow plod across the corral and slid off when it reached the bucket. He brushed his pants and got a stick to scrape his sneakers clean of the buffalo stool he'd stepped in. The rich brown smell was losing its charm.

"You'll be going now, I suppose," said Sprague coming up behind him.

"Uh, yeah. Guess so." It was a little creepy, the multicolored corral in the middle of all that open range. "Thanks for the ride, though."

"Nothing to keep you here, Lord knows." He was forcing a smile. "S'almost nine now, business should pick up. Ought to build a fire, case anybody stops for a hot dog." He gave a weak cackle. "I could use it for part of my pitch — frankfurters cowboy style. Call em prairie dogs."

"Yuh."

"You'll be wantin that Interstate I suppose, get you out of here. Five miles or so north on the road and you'll smack right into it."

"Thanks." Brian shouldered his duffel bag. "Hope the trade improves for you."

"Oh, no worry, no worry. I'll make out. Oh, and here, take one of these." He fished an aluminum star from his pocket and presented it to Brian. "Souvenir for you and good advertising for me."

"Deputy Sheriff," said the badge, "Issued at Cody Sprague's Wild West Buckin' Bison Ride." There was a picture of a cowboy tossed high off the back of an angrily kicking buffalo. Brian pinned it on his shirt and Cody brightened a bit.

"Who knows," he said, "maybe today's the day. Maybe we'll get discovered by the tourist office today and be written up. You get your attraction in one of those guidebooks and you got a gold mine. Wall-to-wall customers, turn em away at the gate. I could save up an maybe afford an opposite number for Ishmael. Don't know if or what buffalo feel but I suppose everything gets lonely for its own kind, don't you?"

"I suppose."

"Say, I wasn't kidding about that fire. If you're hungry I could whip us up a late breakfast in no time. There's stock I got to use before it goes bad so it'd be on the house."

"I really got to get going. Sorry."

"Well, maybe you brought me luck. Yessir, maybe today will be the day."

Brian left him waving from the middle of the corral, buckskin fringes blowing in the quickening breeze. When he was out of sight around the bend he unpinned the aluminum star and tossed it away, it dug into his chest too much. Then the signs appeared, the backs of them first, then the messages as he passed by and looked behind. Every thousand yards there was another, starting with Whoa! Here It

Is! and progressing to more distant warnings. When Brian got to FOR
THE RIDE OF YOUR LIFE, STOP AT CODY SPRAGUE'S he couldn't hold
out anymore, he dropped his bag and trotted back to where he'd
chucked the star. He found it without too much trouble and put it in
his back pocket.

He went through the land of blue-green sage clumps, leaning into the
wind whipping over low hills, walking alone. There weren't any cars or
people. More sage, more hills, more wind, but no human trace but the
road beneath him like a main street of some vanished civilization.
Open range, there were no fences or water tanks. He looked at his
Road Atlas and guessed that he was a little ways up into South Dakota,
a little below the Bear in the Lodge River with the Rosebud Indian
Reservation to the east and the Pine Ridge to the north. He tried to
remember who it was he'd seen in the same situation. Randolph Scott?
Audie Murphy? Brian checked the sun's position to reassure himself
that he was heading in the right direction. There was nothing else to
tell by. A patch of hill suddenly broke free into a butternut cluster of
high-rumped antelope, springing away from him. He was in The
West.

He had been walking on the road for over an hour when an old
Ford pickup clattered to a halt next to him. A swarthy, smooth-faced
man wearing a green John Deere cap stuck his head out.

"Who you workin for?" he called.

"Huh?"

"Who you workin for? Whose place you headed?"

"I'm not working for anybody," said Brian. "I'm trying to hitch
west."

"Oh. I thought you were a hand. S'gonna give you a ride over to
whatever outfit you're headed for."

Brian tried not to look too pleased. Thought he was a hand. "No,
I'm just hitching. I was walking up to the Interstate."

"You got a hell of a walk. That's twenty miles up."

"But the guy said it was only five."

"What guy?"

"The old guy back there. He's got a buffalo."

"Sprague? You can't listen to him, son. A nice fella, but he's a little
bit touched. Got a sign up on 90, says it's only five miles to his place.
Figured nobody's gonna bother, they know the real story, and he's
right. Guess he's started to believe his own publicity."

"Oh."

"But you hop in anyway, I'm goin up that area in a while." Brian
tossed his duffel bag in the back and got in with the man. "J. C.
Shangreau," he said, offering his hand. "I'll get you north surer than

most anything else you're likely to catch on this road. If you don't mind a few side trips."

Brian had to kick a shotgun wrapped in burlap under the seat to make room for his legs. "Don't mind at all."

"Got to pick up some hands to help me work my horses." Shangreau had quite a few gold teeth in his mouth and very bloodshot eyes. "Got me a couple sections up there, I run seventy-five head. Gonna have ourselves a cuttin bee if I can roust out enough of these boys."

They turned off left on one of the access roads and began to pass clusters of small trailer houses propped on cinder block. Shangreau stopped at one, went to the door and talked a bit, then came back alone.

"Hasn't recovered from last night yet. Can't say as I have either. There was nothin to celebrate, cept it being another Friday, but I did a job of it. You know when your teeth feel rubbery in the morning?"

Brian wasn't used to adults asking him hangover questions. "Yeah."

"That's the kind of bag I got on. Rubber-toothed."

He stopped at another trailer with no luck. This one hadn't come home overnight.

"Hope he's feelin good now, cause there's an ambush waitin at home for him. I had a big one like that in the kitchen I'd think twice about carryin on. She'll just squeeze all the good time right out of that man."

"Many of these people around here Indian?" Brian asked it non-committally, fishing. The drill-rigger the night before had gone on and on about how the Indians and the coyotes should have been wiped out long ago.

"Oh sure," said Shangreau, "most of em. Not many purebred though, things being what they are. Most of these boys I'm after is at least half or more Indian. You got your Ogalala around here, your Hunkpapa and the rest. I'm a good quarter Sioux myself. Old Jim Crow who we're headin after now is maybe seven-eights, fifteen-six-teenths, something like that. It's hard to keep count. Jim has got three or four tribes to start with, his mother was part Flathead as I recall, and then he's got white and I wouldn't be surprised if one of them buffalo soldiers didn't slip in a little black blood way back when. But you won't see too many purebred, less we catch Bad Heart at home, and he's another story altogether. What are you?"

"Irish."

"Me too, a good quarter. Monaghans."

They came to a pair of trailer houses that had been butted up to-gether. A dozen fat little children wearing glasses ran barefoot out front. An older fat boy with extra-thick glasses and a silver-sprayed cowboy hat chased them, tossing a lasso at their legs. Brian got out of the pickup with Shangreau and a round, sad-looking man met them at the door to the first trailer.

"I see you're bright-eyed an bushy-tailed as everyone else is this mornin," said J. C. "Them horses don't have much competition today, it looks like. Jim Crow, this here's Brian."

"Hey."

Jim Crow nodded. He was wearing nothing but flannel pajama bottoms and his belly hung over. His slant eyes and mournful expression made him kind of Mongoloid-looking.

"You know anyone else could join us? Couple of my possibilities crapped out on me."

"My brother-law's here from over the Rosebud. Sam. I'll ask him. And Raymond could come along. Raymond!"

The boy in the silver cowboy hat turned from where he had just cut a little sister out from the herd.

"You're coming along with us to work J. C.'s horses. Go tell your ma."

Raymond left the little sister to untie herself and ran off looking happy.

Sam was a little older and a little heavier than Jim Crow and had blue eyes. Brian sat in front between J. C. and Crow while Raymond and Sam were open in the back. Raymond's hat blew off almost immediately and they had to stop for him to run get it. His father told him to sit on it till they got to J. C.'s.

They stopped next at a lone trailer still on its wheels to pick up a young man called Jackson Blackroot. All the men got out and went to the door to try and catch a glimpse of Blackroot's new wife, who was supposed to be a looker. She obliged by coming out to say Hello boys and offer to make coffee. They turned it down, suddenly shy. She was dark and thin and reasonably pretty though Brian didn't see anything outstanding. Jackson was a friendly young guy with a big white smile who looked like an Italian. He shook Brian's hand and said he was pleased to meet him.

Bad Heart's trailer was alone too, a little box of a thing sitting on a hill. J. C. stopped out front and honked once.

"Be surprised if he's there," whispered Crow.

"If he is I be surprised if he shows himself."

They waited for a few minutes with the motor running and Shangreau had the pickup in gear when a short, pock-scarred man emerged from the trailer and hopped in the rear without a greeting.

It was a long bumpy way up to Shangreau's ranch and he did most of what little talking went on. The other men seemed to know each other and about each other but weren't particularly comfortable riding together.

"Brian," asked J.C., "you in any big hurry to get up there?"

Brian shrugged.

"I mean if you're not you might's well stop for lunch with us, look on when we work the horses. Hell, you can join the party if you're careful, can always use an extra hand when we're cutting."

"Sure." Brian was willing to follow just about anything at this point if there was food in it. He hadn't eaten since yesterday morning. He wondered exactly what cutting was going to be.

The J. C. Ranch wasn't much. A side-listing barn surrounded by a wood-and-wire corral and a medium-sized unpainted shack in a couple of thousand acres of dry-looking open range. The shack squatted on a wood platform, there was a gas tank and a hot water heater on the front porch. J. C. explained that this was the working house, they had another aluminum-sided place further west on the property. There were wide cracks in the floorboard inside, blankets hung to separate the rooms. Shangreau's broad-faced wife grunted a hello and went back to pouring cornstarch into her stewpot. She had the biggest arms Brian had ever seen on a woman.

The men took turns washing their hands in a pail and sat around the kitchen table. Lunch was a tasteless boiled beef and potato stew that the men loaded with salt and shoveled down. There was little talk at the table.

"Well now," said J. C., pushing back in his chair when everyone seemed finished, "let's get at them horses."

The men broke free into work. They readied their ropes and other gear while Brian and Raymond collected wood, old shack boards, and dead scrub for the branding fire. They built up the fire in a far corner of the corral, Jim Crow nursing it with a scuffed old hand bellows. When there were bright orange coals at the bottom and the irons were all laid out, the men spread with ropes in hand, forming a rough circle around the narrow chute that led into the corral from the barn, what Shangreau called the squeezer.

"And now, pilgrim," he said waving Brian back a little, "you gonna see some *masc*ulatin."

Raymond went up and started the first horse out through the squeezer and things began to happen fast, Brian struggling to keep up. The horse was not so huge, its back about chin-high to Brian, but it was thick and barrel-chested, its mottled gray sides working fast with suspicion. Raymond flapped his hat and clucked along the chute rail beside it till it was in the open and the men were swinging rope at its hooves, not picture-book lassoing but dropping open nooses on the ground and jerking up when it stepped in or near them. It took a while, plenty of near misses and times when the horse kicked free or the rope just slipped away, and Bad Heart was closest to Brian cursing a constant chant low on his breath, fuckin horse, goddamn horse, hold im, bust the fucker, and Raymond was in the corral trying to get his rope untangled and join the fun and Brian was hustling not to be trampled or roped.

"Bust im! Bust im!" J. C. was yelling and the stocky horse wheeled and crow-hopped but was met in every direction by another snapping rope. Finally Sam forefooted him cleanly and Jim jumped in quick to slip one over the head and jumped back to be clear as they hauled the animal crashing down onto its side.

"Choke im down! Choke im down!" yelled J. C. and they held its head into the ground with the rope while Bad Heart, cursing louder now and grimacing, wrestled its hind legs bent, one at a time, and strapped them back against its belly. They held it on its back now, writhing and lathered, eyes bugged hugely and nostrils wide, the men adding a rope here and there to help them muscle it still. Shangreau motioned Brian up with his head and handed him a rope end.

"Choke im," he said, "don't let him jerk. You let him jerk he's gonna hurt himself."

J. C. went to where the tools were laid out on a tarp and returned with a long, mean-looking jack-knifey thing. The horse rested between spurts of resistance now, its huge chest heaving, playing out in flurries like a hooked fish. The men used the pauses to dig in their heels and get a stronger grip. J. C. waved the blade through the branding fire a few times, then knelt between the stallion's pinioned legs.

"Hold him tight, boys, they're comin off!"

The horse farted and screamed and shot a wad of snot into the blanket Bad Heart held its head with all at once, its spine arched clear off the ground and whumped back down, but J. C. had them in his fist and wouldn't be shook. He aimed and he hacked and blood covered his wrists till they cut free in his hands, a loose, sticky mess that he heaved into the far corner of the corral. He wasn't through. The horse rested quivering and Brian shifted the rope from where it had scored its image in his palms and J. C. brought what he had pointed out before as the masculator, a pair of hedge clippers that gripped at the end instead of cut.

"Ready?" he called, and when they were straining against the horse he worked the masculator inside and grabbed it onto what he wanted and yanked. There was blood spurting then, flecking the horse and the men and staining solid one leg of J. C.'s work pants. The rest was relatively easy, the branding and the tail-bobbing, the horse too drained to do much more than try to wave its head under Bad Heart's knee. With the smell of burnt flesh and fear around them, the men shortened their holds, worked in toward the horse, quiet now, Bad Heart's stream of abuse almost soothing. Each man grabbed a rope at some strategic point on the horse, J. C. taking over for Brian, and when each nodded that he was ready, they unlooped and jumped back in one quick motion. The horse lay still on its back for a moment, as if it had fallen asleep or died, then slowly rolled to its side and worked its legs underneath. It stood woozily at first, snorted and shook its head a few times, groin dripping thinly into the dirt, and then Raymond opened the corral gate to the range beyond and hat-flapped it out. It trotted a hundred yards off and began to graze.

"Forget he ever had em in a couple minutes," said J. C. He thumped Brian on the back, his hand sticking for a moment. "Gonna make a cowboy out of you in no time."

The men sat near each other, leaning on the corral slats, resting.

"What's it for?" Brian decided there was no cause to try to seem to know any more than he did. "Why can't you leave them like they are?"

"It's a matter of breed." J. C. was working a little piece of horse from the masculator jaws. "You leave them stallions be, they don't want a thing but fight and fuck all day long. You don't want your herd to inbreed. Let them inbreed and whatever it is strange in them comes to the surface, gets to be the rule rather than the exception."

Bad Heart sat alone across the corral from them, over by where the genitals had been thrown. Raymond tried to do tricks with his rope.

"Don't want em too wild," said Jackson Blackroot.

"Or too stunted and mean," said Sam. "Or too high-strung."

"And you don't want any candy-assed little lap ponies. Like I said, it's a matter of breed. We keep one, maybe two stallions isolated, and trade them between outfits to crossbreed. You stud my herd, I'll stud yours. What we want is what you call your hybrid vigor. Like all the different stock I've got in me. Irish and Indian and whatnot. Keeps one strain from takin over and going bad."

"But you do keep a stud horse?"

"Oh yeah. Now I know what you're thinking, these sod-pounders up here haven't heard of artificial insemination. We know all right, it's a matter of choice. I been up to county fairs and whatnot, seen the machines they got. The mechanical jackoff machine and the dock syringe and all that. If that's your modern rancher, well you can have him. If God meant beasts to fuck machines he would of given em batteries. It's like that ASPCA bunch, always on our backs about the modern rancher and the proper way to masculate. Now there isn't but one way to do it. Ours. Horses know they been *cut.*"

Cutting and branding and bobbing took about a half-hour per horse. It was tense, hard work and Brian got numbed to where only the burnt-hair smell when the brand was seared on bothered him. He liked the shouting and sweating and the physical pull against the animals, and supposed the rest, the cutting and all, was necessary. They didn't seem to mind much after it was done.

The men seemed to loosen and touch more often as they got deeper into work, breaks between cuttings grew longer and more frequent. They sat on a little rise to the side of the corral passing dripping ice-chest beers and a bottle of Johnnie Walker J. C. had provided, gazing over at the string of fresh-cut geldings. Gimme a hit a that coffin varnish, they would say, and the bottle would be passed down, bloody hand to bloody hand, all of them half-shot with liquor but soon to work it off on the next horse.

"Must be some connection with their minds," said Sam. "Once you lop their balls off, whatever part of their mind that takes care of thinking on the fillies must turn off too. So they don't even remember, don't even think like a stallion anymore. They forget the old ways."

"They turn into cows, is what. Just strong and dumb."

"But you got to do it," said J. C. "Otherwise you might's well let them run wild, run and fuck whenever they want, tear down all the fences and keep territory all to themselves. Nosir, it's got to be done."

The afternoon wore on in tugs and whinnies. Raymond forefooted a big roan all by himself and Brian caught a stray hoof in his thigh that spun him around. One of the horses, a little scab-colored animal, turned out to be a real bad one, kicking all red-eyed and salty, running at the men instead of away until Bad Heart up with a branding iron, swinging at its head and spitting oaths but only managing to herd it right on out of the half-open corral door. It scampered up the rise with the others, kicking its heels and snorting.

"Raymond, dammit!" yelled Jim Crow. "You sposed to latch that damn gate shut!"

"I *did!*" Raymond had the look of the falsely accused; he took his silver hat off to plead his innocence. "I closed it right after that last one."

"Then how'd it get open?"

"It wasn't me."

"Don't worry about it," said J. C. "We'll have to go catch him to-morra. He's a tricky sumbitch to bring in. Just a wrong-headed animal, is all. That's the one you give me," he said to Bad Heart, "pay back that loan."

Bad Heart grunted.

It was turning to evening when they finished. A cloud of fat black flies gloated over the heap of testicles in the corner. Brian had a charley-horse limp where he'd been kicked. They sprawled on the rise and pulled their boots off, wiggled red, sick-looking toes in the air, and sucked down beer in gasping pulls. Still-warm sweat came tangy through their denim, they knocked shoulders and knees, compared injuries, and debated over who would be sorest in the morning. Bad

Heart coiled the rope he had brought and lay down alone in the back of the pickup. They pondered on what they should do next.

"The way I see it," said Jim Crow, "it's a choice between more of Minnie's cooking and goin out for some serious drinking."

They were silent then, it was up to J. C. to pass the verdict on his wife's cooking.

"Sheeit," he said, "if that's all that's keepin us here let's roll. What's open?"

"Not much. Not much legal, anyways. There is that whatsisname's place, up to Interior."

"Then let's get on the stick. Brian, you a drinkin man?"

"I suppose."

"Well you will be after tonight. Interior, what's that, fifty mile or so? Should be able to get there afore dark and then it's every man for himself. No need to change but we'll have to go round and tell the women. Let's ride, fellas."

In the pickup they talked about horses and farm machinery and who used to be a bad hat when they were young and who was still capable of some orneriness on a full tank and about drunks they'd had and horses they'd owned and about poor old Roger DuPree whose woman had the roving eye. They passed liquor front seat to truck-bed, taking careful, fair pulls of the remaining Johnnie Walker and the half-bottle of Mogen David J. C. had stashed under the barn floor. Brian closed one eye the way he did when he drank so they wouldn't cross and Bad Heart carefully wiped the neck when it was his turn. They banged over the yellow-brown land in the long plains twilight, holding the bottles below sight-line as they stopped at each trailer to say they wouldn't be out too late. Raymond started to protest when it was time for him to be left off, but Jim Crow said a few growling words and his mournful face darkened even sadder; it would just *kill* him if he had to smack the boy. Raymond didn't want a scene in front of the guys and scooted off flapping the rump of an imaginary mount with his silver hat. The liquor ran out and Sam's belly began to rumble so they turned out of their way to hunt some food.

They reached a little kitchen emporium just before it closed up and J. C. sprang for a loaf of Wonder Bread and some deviled ham spread. The old woman in the store wore a crucifix nearly half her size and wouldn't sell alcoholic beverages. FOR PEACE OF MIND, said a faded sign over the door, INVESTIGATE THE CATHOLIC FAITH.

"Sonsabitches damnwell ought to be investigated," said Jim Crow. "Gotten so I can't but give a little peep of colorful language around the house and she's off in the bedroom on her knees mumbling an hour's worth of nonsense to save my soul. What makes her think I'd trust that bunch with my soul escapes me."

"Now they mean well enough, Jim, it's just they don't understand Indian ways. Think they dealin with a bunch of savages up here that haven't ever heard of religion. Think that somebody's got to get their-selves nailed to a tree before you got a religion."

"Fuck religion!" shouted Bad Heart from the back, and that ended the conversation.

A sudden rain hit them with a loud furious slap, drenching the men in the back instantly and smearing the windshield so thick that J. C. lost sight and the pickup sloughed sideways into the shoulder ditch. It only added to their spirits, rain soothing them where the sweat had caked itchy, not cold enough to soak through their layer of alcohol. It gave them a chance to show they didn't give a fart in a windstorm how the weather blew, to pile out and hunker down in the mud and slog and heave and be splattered by the tires when the pickup finally scrambled up onto the road. The flash downpour cut dead almost the moment the truck was free, just to make its point clear. J. C. spread a blanket over the hood and the men stood together at the side of the road waiting for Jackson Blackroot to slap them down a sandwich with his brand-new Bowie knife. The ham spread was a bit watery but nobody kicked, they hurried to stuff a little wadding down to soak up more liquor. They pulled wet jeans away from their skin and stomped their boots free of mud on the road pavement. J. C. came over to Brian.

"Don't you worry about the delay, son. We'll show you a real cowboy drunk soon enough."

"No rush."

"Damn right there's no rush. Got time to burn out here. Time grows on trees. Well, bushes anyway, we're a little short on trees. There isn't a picture show or a place with live music in some hundred miles, the Roman Church is about the only organization has regular meetings and you can have that. Isn't much cause for people to get together. Workin horses like we done is something though. A little excitement, even if it is work. Hell, it's better that it is work, you feel good about it even after it's over, not like a drunk where it takes a couple years of selective memory to make it into something you like to talk about."

"Doesn't seem so bad."

"Oh, there's worse. I'm sure. But I see you're passing through, not staying. Nobody lives here unless they were born here and can't hack it anywhere else. It's why most of the land around here was made into reservation, nobody else wanted it. Oh, the Badlands, up by Interior, they're striking to look at so the Park Service took them for the tour-ists, but the rest — hell, even the migrating birds don't come back anymore."

"Where you traveling to, Brian?" It was old Sam that asked.

"California."

He frowned. "You best be careful. That California is wild. Had a brother was killed there."

"I'll watch myself."

"I'd steer clear of it if it was me. They say it's wild."

J. C. laughed. "When was this brother killed, Sam?"

"Just around the start of the war. Got himself caught in something called the Zoot Suit Riots and that was all she wrote. Just plain wild."

"You know where I found Brian?" said J. C. "He was walkin up Six-Hat Road there by Petrie's, sayin he's gonna walk to the Innerstate. Seems he got his directions from old Cody Sprague there."

The men laughed. "Be better off gettin em from the buffalo," said Jackson Blackroot, "at least he's a native."

"Sprague isn't from around here?"

"He come out from some city back east, what was it, Philadelphia — ?"

"Pittsburgh."

"Right. He come out from Pittsburgh on his vacation one summer and he sees all these roadside attractions up there on 90, the prairie dog village, reptile farms, Wall Drug Store, all that, and he thinks he's found his calling. He worked in some factory all his life and always had something about bein his own boss, owning his own business. So he takes his savings, which couldn't of been much, and buys himself two acres down on Six-Hat, the most worthless two acres in the whole state probly, and somewhere he gets ahold of that animal. Gonna build a dude ranch with the money he makes selling rides. Well it's been six, seven years now and I don't know how the hell he survives but he still hasn't got but them two acres and that animal."

"He's a nice old guy though," said J. C. "Talk your ear off, a little crazy, but a nice old guy."

"He's a character all right," said Jackson.

"He's an asshole." Bad Heart climbed into the rear of the pickup.

They had eaten all the bread and were talking about Sam's brother getting killed in Los Angeles when Jackson remembered something.

"Hey," he said, "what we gonna do about that wake they're having over there for Honda Joe? Suppose we ought to go?"

"Just slipped my mind," said J. C. "Live just five mile away from us, no way I can't make an appearance, and it slipped my mind. Listen, as long as there's all of us together and we got the truck — "

"I suppose we ought to go."

"Damn shame it is, young kid like that. Goes through all that Vietnam business with hardly a scratch, gets himself a Silver Star, then comes back to smash hisself up on a goddamn motorsickle. Young kids like that seem bent on it. I remember I couldn't talk my brother out of his plan for all the world, nosir, he had to have his California."

"It wasn't this it would have been some other," said Jackson.

"If it wasn't the bike maybe he would of drunk himself to death like some others around here."

"No, I don't think so. Honda Joe was always in a hurry to get there."

"Well he got there all right. In a couple pieces maybe, but he got there."

"We ought to go look in on him, for his mother's sake. What say, fellas?"

"I never liked Honda Joe," said Bad Heart.

"Well then, dammit, you can stay in the truck."

"If there's one thing I can't stand," said Jim Crow very quietly when they were on their way to Honda Joe's wake, "it's a sulky Indian."

It was still twilight when they passed by the access road to J. C.'s place again. He didn't offer to drop Bad Heart home before they went on. They crossed Six-Hat Road. Brian was just able to make out one of Cody Sprague's signs to the right, and then a half-mile further along they were stopped by a horse standing in the middle of the road, facing them.

J. C. turned on the headlights and they saw it was the scab-colored one that had escaped in the afternoon.

"The hell's he doin out here?" said J. C. He turned the engine off and got out quietly. He left the door open and walked slowly toward the horse, talking soft. "Good horse," he said, "nice horse. Come to papa. Attaboy."

The horse stood for a moment, nostrils wide open, then bolted off the road and out of sight. J. C. slammed back into the truck. Only Bad Heart dared laugh.

The trailer was alone and far away from the blacktops, far even from the oiled road that serviced most of the other places around. It sat as if run aground next to the dry streambed that cut through a gently sloping basin. Young men's cars, Pintos and Mavericks, Mustangs and Broncos, surrounded it, parked every whichway. To the rear was an orderly block where the family men had pulled in their Jeeps and pickups. J. C. slipped in among these and the men eased out. They had sobered, what with the food and the surprise rain and the knowledge of the work cut out ahead of them. They shuffled and stuffed their hands in their pockets, waiting for J. C. to lead. The mud and blood had stiffened again on their clothes, they tried to get all their scratching done before they had to go in. Bad Heart stretched out in the rear, glaring out into space. J. C. sighed and fished under the seat, behind the shotgun, and came out with a pint of gin. "I was saving this for an emergency," he said, and tossed it to Bad Heart. "Entertain yourself."

They were met at the door by two dark old Indians wearing VFW hats. Evening, gentlemen, glad you could come. There was a visitor's book to sign and no place to sit, the trailer was crammed to its aluminum gills. There were nods and hullos from the men already inside, crop and stock and weather conversations to drift into, and womannoise coming from back in the bedrooms. Drink was offered and declined, for the moment anyway. A knot of angry-looking young men leaned together against one wall, planning to make yet another wine run up to Interior and back. Suspicious eyes lingered on Brian, coming hardest and hairiest from the young men. Brian felt extra uncomfortable in his sun-lightened hair and three-day road stubble in the midst of all the smooth, dark people. He was glad for the stains of horse-cutting left on him, as if having shared that gave him some right of entry.

Mrs. Pierce was on them before they could get their bearings. She smelled of tears and Four Roses and clutched at their elbows like she was drowning.

"J. C.," she said, "you come, I knew you would. And Jim. Boys. I knew you'd all come, I knew everybody'd come for my Joey."

She closed one eye when she had to focus on somebody. She squinted up to Brian. "Do I know you?"

"This is Brian, Mrs. Pierce," said J. C. "He's been workin horses over to my place."

"Well Brian," she said sober-faced, talking slow as if explaining house rules to a new kid in the neighborhood, "you just make yourself at home. Joey had him a lot of white friends, he was in the Army."

The woman had straight black hair with streaks of iron-gray, she stood up to Brian's shoulders, her face flat and unwrinkled. She could have been anywhere from thirty-five to fifty. She was beautiful. Brian told her not to worry about him.

"You come to stay a while, J. C.? You have something to drink? We got plenty, everybody brang for my Joey. We'll go right through the night into tomorrow with him. Will you stay, J. C.?"

"Well, now, Mrs. Pierce, we'd really like to, we all thought high of young Joseph there, but like I said we been workin horses all day and these boys are just all *in*. I promised their women I'd get them home early and in one piece. You know how it is."

The woman gave a little laugh. "Oh, I do, I surely do. We'll get him home in one piece, that's what the recruiters said, come onto Rosebud when we were over there. Make a man of him and send him back in better shape than when he left. Well, he's back, I suppose. Least I know where he is, not like some that are missing or buried over there. Don't figure anyone'll want to borrow him anymore." She stopped a moment and turned something over in her mind with great effort, then looked to J. C. again. "We're havin a service Tuesday over to the Roman. Appreciate it if you all could be there."

"We'll make every effort, Ma'am. And if there's anything you need help with in the coming weeks — "

"Oh no, J. C., save your help. Won't need it. After the service I'll just hitch up and drive on out of here. Go up north, I got people. I put two husbands and four sons in this country now and I'll be damned if it gets a drop more outen me. No, I'm to go up north."

"It's hard livin up there, Mrs. Pierce."

"Well it aint no bed a goddamn roses down here neither, is it?"

The men hung on in the main room a bit more for courtesy, swapping small talk and trying to remember which of the wild Pierce boys had been responsible for which piece of mischief, trying to keep out of the way of the women, who seemed to know what they were there for. Mrs. Pierce weaved her way through the somber crowd assuring and being assured that her poor Joey was a good boy and would be sorely missed by all. Brian noticed she was wearing the boy's Silver Star on a chain around her neck.

It took a good hour to get through the crowd, the people didn't seem to see much of each other and there was a lot of catching up to do, but they were herded steadily, inevitably, toward the bedroom where they knew Honda Joe would be laid out. They shied and shuffled at the doorway a little, but there was no avoiding it. A steady, humming moan came from within, surrounded by other, soothing sounds, J. C. took a deep breath and led the way.

Whoever did the postmortem on Honda Joe must have learned the trade by mail. The corpse, tucked to the chin under an American flag, looked more like it should have been leaning against a stuffed pony at the Wall Drug Store than like something that had lived and breathed. The skin had a thick look to it and a sheen like new leather, and even under the flag you could tell everything hadn't been put back where it belonged. The men went past the Murphy bed on both sides, up on their toes as if someone was sleeping. They clasped their hands in front of them and tried to look properly mournful. Jackson Blackroot muttered a few words to the corpse. Brian took his turn and concentrated on a spot on the boy's hairline till he felt he'd put in his time. He was moving away when he heard the whooping from outside.

"Yee-haaaaa!" somebody was yelling. "Yipyipyeeeeee!"

There was the sound of hooves then, and the whooping grew distant. The men emptied out into the night range to see what it was.

"Yeow! Yeow! Yeow!" called a voice over to the left. Someone was riding a horse out there in the pitch black, someone pretty loaded from the sound of him.

"Goddamn Indians," grumbled one of the old men wearing a VFW hat. "Got no sense a dignity."

"Yee-hahaaaa!" called the rider as a gray shape galloped by on the right.

"Sounds a bit like Bad Heart," said J. C. "Sounds a whole lot like him."

They went to J. C.'s pickup and Bad Heart was gone. There was some gear missing too, some rope, a bridle. They checked in the front. J. C.'s shotgun was still there but Jackson's Bowie knife was gone.

"He loses it I'll wring his goddamn neck," said Jackson.

The men all got in their cars and pickups then and put their headlights on. The beams criss-crossed out across the little basin, making eerie pockets of dark and light.

"Yah-haaaaa!"

A horse and rider appeared at the far edge of the light, disappeared into shadow, then came into view again. It was Bad Heart, bareback on the little scab-colored stallion. It strained forward as if it were trying to race right out from under him. There was something tied with rope to its tail, dragging and flopping behind, kicking up dust that hung in the headlights' arc. Bad Heart whacked its ribs and kneed it straight for the dry streambed. It gathered and leaped, stretching out in the air, and landed in perfect stride on the far bank.

"Fucker can ride," said Jim Crow.

"Fucker could always ride," said J. C. "Nobody ever denied that. Like he's born on horseback."

Bad Heart lay close to the line of the stallion's back, seemed to flow with its every muscle. With the day's blood staining his old tan Levis and the scabby red-brown of the horse it was hard to tell where one began and the other left off.

"Yee-yeeheeeeeeeee!"

Bad Heart circled the trailer a few more times before a couple of the young men commandeered Jeeps and lit out after him. It was a good chase for a while, the Jeeps having more speed but the little stallion being able to cut and turn quicker. They honked and flicked their lights and kept Bad Heart pinned in view of the trailer but couldn't land him till he tried to make the horse jump the streambed one time too many. It just pulled up short and ducked its head, sending him flying over, tumbling through the air till he hit halfway up the opposite bank.

The horse trotted off out of all the lights and Bad Heart lay wailing.

He was pretty scraped up when they got to him, one side of his face

all skinned and his left leg bent crooked from midway up the thigh.
He cursed as they made a splint from a rake handle, cursed as they
carried him in on a blanket, cursed when they laid him out on the
Murphy bed next to Honda Joe.

"Wait'll the fucker wakes up in the mornin," he kept saying while
they tried to calm him down. "Gonna have a big surprise. Wait'll he
wakes up. Big fuckin surprise."

Jackson found his Bowie knife tucked in Bad Heart's boot when
they pulled it off. The knife was bloody up to the hilt.

Brian went out with J. C. and Jackson to see about the horse. Everyone had turned their headlights off so J. C. got his flashlight from the
pickup. They walked out in the dark a bit and then they heard whuff-
ing up ahead and J. C. shined at it.

The stallion held its head up high, eyes shining back amber in the
beam, bridle dangling, chest and sides lathered and heaving. It stood
and looked at them as Jackson whispered his way up and took the
bridle.

J. C. came up and took the Bowie knife from Jackson. He cut the
rope free from the stallion's tail. Brian went back with him to see what
had been dragging behind.

It was a blood-sticky hide. The hair coarse and greasy, like something you'd scuff your feet clean on. It had a sad, lonely smell. It
smelled like The West.

J. C. played the light off away from it. "I suppose we best take this
thing over, break the news to old Sprague. You wanna come along for
the ride?"

"Sure."

"Spose we'll call it a night after that. Get you up to 90 in the morning." He turned the flashlight on the stallion, limping a bit as it followed Jackson toward the trailer. "There isn't all that much to do in
Interior anyways."

———————

1977

CHILDREN OF AFFLUENCE
by Robert Coles

IT won't do to talk of *the* affluent in America. It won't do to say that in
our upper-middle-class suburbs, or among our wealthy, one observes clear-cut, consistent psychological or cultural characteristics.
Even in relatively homogeneous places there are substantial differences
in homelife, in values taught, hobbies encouraged, beliefs advocated or
sometimes virtually instilled. But it is the obligation of a psychological

observer like me, who wants to know how children make sense of a certain kind of life, to document as faithfully as possible the way a common heritage of money and power affects the assumptions of particular boys and girls.

I started my work with affluent children by seeing troubled boys and girls; they were the ones I saw as a child psychiatrist *before* I began my years of "field work" in the South, then Appalachia, then the North, then the West. There are only a few hundred child psychiatrists in the United States, and often their time is claimed by those who have money. After a while, if one is not careful, the well-off and the rich come to be seen exclusively through a clinician's eye: homes full of bitterness, deceit, snobbishness, neuroses, psychoses; homes with young children in mental pain, and with older children, adolescents and young adults, who use drugs, drink, run away, rebel constantly and disruptively, become truants, delinquents, addicts, alcoholics, become compulsively promiscuous, go crazy, go wild, go to ruin.

We blame the alcoholism, insanity, meanness, apathy, drug usage, despondency, and, not least, cruelty to children we see or are told exists in the ghetto or among the rural poor upon various "socioeconomic factors." All of those signs of psychological deterioration can be found among quite privileged families, too — and so we remind ourselves, perhaps, that wealth corrupts.

No — it is not that simple. Wealth does not corrupt nor does it ennoble. But wealth does govern the minds of privileged children, gives them a peculiar kind of identity which they never lose, whether they grow up to be stockbrokers or communards, and whether they lead healthy or unstable lives. There is, I think, a message that virtually all quite well-off American families transmit to their children — an emotional expression of those familiar, classbound prerogatives, money and power. I use the word "entitlement" to describe that message.

The word was given to me by the rather rich parents of a child I began to talk with almost two decades ago, in 1959. I have watched those parents become grandparents, and have seen what they described as "the responsibilities of entitlement" handed down to a new generation. When the father, a lawyer and stockbroker from a prominent and quietly influential family, referred to the "entitlement" his children were growing up to know, he had in mind a social rather than a psychological phenomenon: the various juries or committees that select the Mardi Gras participants in New Orleans's annual parade and celebration. He knew that his daughter was "entitled" to be invited.

He wanted, however, to go beyond that social fact. He talked about what he had received from his parents and what he would give to his children, "automatically, without any thought," and what they too would pass on. The father was careful to distinguish between the social entitlement and "something else," a "something else" he couldn't quite define but knew he had to try to evoke if he was to be psychologically candid: "I mean they should be responsible, and try to live up to their ideals, and not just sit around wondering which island in the Caribbean to visit this year, and where to go next summer to get away from the heat and humidity here in New Orleans."

He was worried about what a lot of money can do to a personality. When his young daughter, during a Mardi Gras season, kept *assuming* she would one day become a Mardi Gras queen, he realized that his notion of "entitlement" was not quite hers. Noblesse oblige requires a gesture toward others.

He was not the only parent to express such a concern to me in the course of my work. In homes where mothers and fathers profess no explicit reformist persuasions, they nevertheless worry about what happens to children who grow up surrounded by just about everything they want, virtually on demand. "When they're like that, they've gone from spoiled to spoiled rotten — and beyond, to some state I don't know how to describe."

Obviously, it is possible for parents to have a lot of money yet avoid bringing up their children in such a way that they feel like members of a royal family. But even parents determined not to spoil their children often recognize what might be called the existential (as opposed to strictly psychological) aspects of their situation. A father may begin rather early on lecturing his children about the meaning of money; a mother may do her share by saying no, even when yes is so easy to say. And a child, by the age of five or six, has very definite notions of what is possible, even if it is not always permitted. That child, in conversation, and without embarrassment or the kind of reticence and secretiveness that come later, may reveal a substantial knowledge of economic affairs. A six-year-old girl I spoke to knew that she would, at twenty-one, inherit half a million dollars. She also knew that her father "only" gave her twenty-five cents a week, whereas some friends of hers received as much as a dollar. She was vexed; she asked her parents why they were so "strict." One friend had even used the word "stingy" for the parents. The father, in a matter-of-fact way, pointed out to the daughter that she did, after all, get "anything she really wants." Why, then, the need for an extravagant allowance? The girl was won over. But admonitions don't always modify the quite realistic appraisal children make of what they are heir to; and they don't diminish their sense of entitlement — a state of mind that pervades their view of the world.

In an Appalachian home, for instance, a boy of seven made the following comment in 1963, after a mine his father owned had suffered an explosion, killing two men and injuring seriously nine others: "I heard my mother saying she felt sorry for the families of the miners. I feel sorry for them, too. I hope the men who got hurt get better. I'm sure they will. My father has called in doctors from Lexington. He wants the best doctors in all Kentucky for those miners. Daddy says it was the miners' fault; they get careless, and the next thing you know, there's an explosion. It's too bad. I guess there are a lot of kids who are praying hard for their fathers. I wish God was nice to everyone. He's been very good to us. My daddy says it's been hard work, running the mine, and another one he has. It's just as hard to run a mine as it is to go down and dig the coal! I'm glad my father is the owner, though. I wouldn't want him to get killed or hurt bad down there, way underground. Daddy has given us a good life. We have a lot of fun coming up, he says, in the next few years. We're going on some trips. Daddy deserves his vacations. He says he's happy because he can keep us happy, and he does."

Abundance is this boy's destiny, he has every reason to believe, abundance and limitless possibility. He may even land on the stars. Certainly he has traveled widely in this country. He associates the seasons with travel. In winter, there is a trip south, to one or another Caribbean island. He worries, on these trips, about his two dogs, and the other animals — the guinea pigs, hamsters, rabbits, chickens. There is always someone in the house, a maid, a handyman. Still, it is sad to say goodbye. Now if the family owned a plane, the animals could come along on those trips!

The boy doesn't really believe that his father will ever own a Lear jet; yet he can construct a fantasy: "I had this dream. In it I was walking through the woods with Daddy, and all of a sudden there was an open field, and I looked, and I saw a hawk, and it was circling and circling. I like going hunting with Daddy, and I thought we were hunting. But when I looked at him, he didn't have his gun. Then he pointed at the hawk, and it was coming down. It landed ahead of us, and it was real strange — because the hawk turned into an airplane! I couldn't believe it. We went toward the plane, and Daddy said we could get a ride anytime we wanted, because it was ours; he'd just bought it. That's when I woke up, I think."

Four years after the boy dreamed that his father owned a plane, the father got one. The boom of the 1970s in the coal fields made his father even richer. The boy was, of course, eager to go on flying trips; eager, also, to learn to fly. At thirteen he dreamed (by day) of becoming an astronaut, or of going to the Air Force Academy and afterwards becoming a "supersonic pilot."

He would never become a commercial pilot, however; and his reasons were interesting. "I've gone on a lot of commercial flights, and there are a lot of people on board, and the pilot has to be nice to everyone, and he makes all these announcements about the seat belts, and stuff like that.

My dad's pilot was in the Air Force, and then he flew commercial. He was glad to get out, though. He says you have to be like a waiter; you have to answer complaints from the customers, and apologize to them, just because the ride gets bumpy. It's best to work for yourself, or work for another person, if you trust him and like him. If you go commercial, like our pilot says, you're a servant."

Many of the children I have worked with are similarly disposed; they do not like large groups of people in public places — in fact, have been taught the value not only of privacy but of the quiet that goes with being relatively alone. Some of the children are afraid of those crowds, can't imagine how it would be possible to survive them. Of course, what is strange, unknown, or portrayed as unattractive, uncomfortable, or just to be avoided as a nuisance can for a given child become a source of curiosity, like an event to be experienced at all costs. An eight-year-old girl who lived on a farm well outside Boston wanted desperately to go to the city and see Santa Claus — not because she believed in him, but because she wanted to see "those crowds" she had seen on television. She got her wish, was excited at first, then became quite disappointed, and ultimately uncomfortable. She didn't like being jostled, shoved, and ignored when she protested.

A week after the girl had gone through her Boston "adventure" (as she had called the trip *before* she embarked upon it), each student in her third-grade class was asked to draw a picture in some way connected to the Christmas season, and the girl obliged eagerly. She drew Santa Claus standing beside a pile of packages, presents for the many children who stood near him. They blended into one another — a mob scene. Watching them but removed from them was one child, bigger and on a higher level — suspended in space, it seemed, and partially surrounded by a thin but visible line. The girl wrote on the bottom of the drawing, "I saw Santa Claus." She made it quite clear what she had intended to portray. "He was standing there, handing out these gifts. They were all the same, I think, and they were plastic squirt guns for the boys and little dolls for the girls. I felt sorry for the kids. I asked my mother why kids wanted to push each other, just to get that junk. My mother said a lot of people just don't know any better. I was going to force my way up to Santa Claus and tell him to stop being so dumb! My mother said he was probably a drunk, trying to make a few dollars so he could spend it in a bar that evening! I don't want to be in a store like that again. We went up to a balcony and watched, and then we got out of the place and came home. I told my mother that I didn't care if I ever went to Boston again. I have two friends, and they've never been in Boston, and they don't want to go there, except to ride through on the way to the airport."

She sounded at that moment more aloof, condescending, and snobbish than she ordinarily is. She spends her time with two or three girls who live on nearby estates. Those girls don't see each other regularly, and each of them is quite able to be alone — in fact, rather anxious for those times of solitude. Sometimes a day or two goes by with no formal arrangement to play. They meet in school, and that seems to be enough. Each girl has obligations — a horse to groom, a stall to work on. They are quite "self-sufficient," a word they have heard used repeatedly by their parents. Even within one's own social circle there is no point surrendering to excessive gregariousness!

Once up on her own horse, she is (by her own description) in her "own world." She has heard her mother use that expression. The mother is not boasting, or dismissing others who live in other worlds. The mother is describing, as does the child, a state of progressive withdrawal from people, and the familiar routines or objects of the environment, in favor of a mixture of reverie and disciplined activity.

Nothing seems impossible, burdensome, difficult. There are no distractions, petty or boring details to attend to. And one is closer to one's "self." The mother talks about the "self," and the child does, too. "It is strange," the girl comments, "because you forget yourself riding or skiing, but you also remember yourself the way you don't when you're just sitting around watching television or reading or playing in your room."

None of the other American children I have worked with have placed such a continuous and strong emphasis on the "self" — its display, its possibilities, its cultivation and development, even the repeated use of the word *self*. A ten-year-old boy who lived in Westchester County made this very clear. I met him originally because his parents were lawyers, and active in the civil rights movement. His father, a patrician Yankee, very much endorsed the students who went south in the early 1960s, and worked on behalf of integrated schools up north. The boy, however, attended private schools — a source of anguish to both father and son, who do not lend themselves to a description that suggests hypocrisy.

The boy knew that he, also, *would* be (as opposed to *wanted* to be) a lawyer. He was quick to perceive and acknowledge his situation, and as he did so, he brought his "self" right into the discussion: "I don't want to tell other kids what to do. I told my father I should be going to the public schools myself. Then I could say anything. Then I could ask why we don't have black kids with us in school. But you have to try to do what's best for your *own* life, even if you can't speak up for the black people. When I'm grown up I'll be like my father; I'll help the black people all I can. It's this way: first you build *yourself* up. You learn all you can. Later, you can *give of yourself*. That's what Dad says: you can't help others until you've learned to help *yourself*. It's not that you're being selfish, if you're going to a private school and your parents have a lot of money. We had a maid here, and she wasn't right in the head. She lost her temper and told Daddy that he's a phony, and he's out for himself and no one else, and the same goes for my sister and me. Then she quit. Daddy tried to get her to talk with us, but she wouldn't. She said that's all we ever do — talk, talk. I told Daddy she was contradicting herself, because she told me a few weeks ago that I'm always doing something, and I should sit down and talk with her. But I don't know what to say to her! I think she got angry with me, because I was putting on my skis, for cross-country skiing, and she said I had too much, that was my problem. I asked her where the regular skis were, and she said she wouldn't tell me, even if she knew! It's too bad, what happened to her.

"I feel sorry for her, though. It's not fun to be a maid. The poor woman doesn't look very good. She weighs too much. She's only forty, my mother thinks, but she looks as if she's sixty, and is sick. She should take better care of herself. Now she's thrown away this job, and she told my mother last year that it was the best one she'd ever had, so she's her own worst enemy. I wonder what she'll think when she looks at herself in the mirror."

This boy was no budding egotist. If anything, he was less self-centered at ten than many other children of his community and others like it. He was willing to think about those less fortunate than himself — the maid, and black people in general. True, he would often repeat uncritically his father's words, or a version of them. But he was trying to respond to his father's wishes and beliefs as well as his words. It was impossible for him, no matter how compassionate his nature, to conceive of life as others live it — the maid and, yes, millions of children his age, who don't look in the mirror very often, and may not even own one; who don't worry about how one looks, and what is said, and how one sounds, and how one smells.

It is important that a child's sense of entitlement be distinguished not only from the psychiatric dangers of narcissism but from the less pathological and not all that uncommon phenomenon known as being "spoiled." It is a matter of degree; "spoiled" children are self-centered all right, petulant and demanding — but not as grandiose or, alas, saddled with illusions (or delusions) as the children clinicians have in mind when using the phrase "narcissistic entitlement." The rich or quite well-to-do are all too commonly charged with producing spoiled children. Yet one sees spoiled children everywhere, among the very poor as well as the inordinately rich.

In one of the first wealthy families I came to know there was a girl who was described by both parents as "spoiled." At the time, I fear, I was ready to pronounce every child in New Orleans's Garden District spoiled. Were they not all living comfortable, indeed luxurious, lives, as compared to the lives of the black or working-class white children I was getting to know in other sections of that city?

Nevertheless, I soon began to realize that it wouldn't do to characterize without qualification one set of children as spoiled, by virtue of their social and economic background, as against another set of children who were obviously less fortunate in many respects. One meets, among the rich, restrained, disciplined, and by no means indulged children; sometimes, even, boys and girls who have learned to be remarkably self-critical, even ascetic — anything but "spoiled" in the conventional sense of the word. True, one can find a touch and more of arrogance, or at least sustained self-assurance, in those apparently spartan boys and girls who seem quite anxious to deny themselves all sorts of presumably accessible privileges if not luxuries. But one also finds in these children a consistent willingness to place serious and not always pleasant burdens on themselves— to the point where they often struck me, when I came to their homes fresh from visits with much poorer age-mates, as remarkably *less* spoiled: not so much whining or crying; fewer demands for candy or other sweets; even, sometimes, a relative indifference to toys, however near at hand and expensive they may have been; a disregard of television — so often demanded by the children that I was seeing.

A New Orleans black woman said to me in 1961: "I don't know how to figure out these rich white kids. They're something! I used to think, before I took a job with this family, that the only difference between a rich kid and a poor kid is that the rich kid knows he has a lot of money and he grows up and becomes spoiled rotten. That's what my mother told me; she took care of a white girl, and the girl was an only child, and her father owned a department store in McComb, Mississippi, and that girl thought she was God's special creature. My mother used to come home and tell us about the 'little princess'; but she turned out to be no good. She was so pampered, she couldn't do a thing for herself. All she knew how to do was order people around.

"It's different with these two children. I've never seen such a boy and such a girl. They think they're the best ones who ever lived — like that girl in McComb — but they don't behave like her. They're never asking me to do much of anything. They even ask if *they* can help *me*! They tell me that they want to know how to do everything. The girl says she wants to learn how to run the washing machine and the dishwasher. She says she wants to learn all my secret recipes. She says she'd like to give the best parties in the Garden District when she grows up, and she'd like to be able to give them without anyone's help. She says I could serve the food, but she would like to make it. The boy says he's going to be a lawyer and a banker, so he wants to know how much everything costs. He doesn't want to waste anything. He'll see me throw something away, and he wants to know why. I only wish that my own kids were like him!

"But these children here are special, and don't they know it! That's what being rich is: you know you're different from most people. These two kids act as if they're going to be tops in everything, and they're pleased as can be with themselves, because there is nothing they can't do, and there's nothing they can't get, and there's nothing they can't win, and they're always showing off what they can do, and then before you can tell them how good they are, they're telling the same thing to themselves. It's confusing! They're not spoiled one bit, but oh, they have a high opinion of themselves!"

Actually, children like the ones she speaks of don't allow themselves quite the unqualified confidence she describes, though she certainly has correctly conveyed the appearance they give. Boys and girls may seem without anxiety or self-doubt; they have been brought up, as the maid suggests, to feel important, superior, destined for a satisfying, rewarding life — and at, say, eight or nine they already appear to know all that. Yet there are moments of hesitation, if not apprehension. An eleven-year-old boy from a prominent and quite brilliant Massachusetts family told his teachers, in an autobiographical composition about the vicissitudes of "entitlement": "I don't always do everything right. I'd like to be able to say I don't make any mistakes, but I do, and when I do, I feel bad. My father and mother say that if you train yourself, you can be right *almost* 100 percent of the time. Even they make mistakes, though. I like to be first in sports. I like to beat my brothers at skiing. But I don't always go down the slopes as fast as I could and I sometimes fall down. Last year I broke my leg. When I get a bad cold, I feel disappointed in myself. I don't think it's right to be easy on yourself. If you are, then you slip back, and you don't get a lot of the rewards in life. If you really work for the rewards, you'll get them."

A platitude — the kind of assurance his teachers, as a matter of fact, have rather often given him. In the fourth grade, for instance, the teacher had this written on the blackboard (and kept it there for weeks): "Those who want something badly enough get it, provided they are willing to wait and work." The boy considers that assertion neither banal nor unrealistic. He has been brought up to believe that such is and will be (for him) the case. He knows that others are not so lucky, but he hasn't really met those "others," and they don't cross his mind at all. What does occur to him sometimes is the need for constant exertion, lest he fail to "measure up." One "measures up" when one tries hard and succeeds. If one slackens or stumbles, one ought to be firm with oneself — but not in any self-pitying or self-excusing or self-paralyzing way. The emphasis is on a quick and efficient moment of scrutiny followed by "a fast pick-up."

Such counsel is not as callous as it may sound — or, ironically, as it may well have been intended to sound. The child who hears it gets, briefly, upset; but unless he or she stops heeding what has been said, quite often "a fast pick-up" does indeed take place — an effort to redeem what has been missed or lost, or only somewhat accomplished. Again, it is a matter of feeling entitled. A child who has been told repeatedly that all he or she needs to do is try hard does not feel inclined to allow himself or herself long stretches of time for skeptical self-examination. The point is to feel *entitled* — then act upon that feeling. The boy whose composition was just quoted from used the word "entitled" in another essay he wrote, this one meant to be a description of his younger (age five) brother. The writing was not, however, without an autobiographical strain to it: "I was watching my brother from my bedroom window. He was climbing up the fence we built for our corral. He got to the top, and then he just stood there and waved and shouted. No one was there. He was talking to himself. He was very happy. Then he would fall. He would be upset for a few seconds, but he would climb right back up again. Then he would be even happier! He was entitled to be happy. It is his fence, and he has learned to climb it, and stay up, and balance himself."

1978
RAILROADS
Aboard the Ghost Trains
by Tracy Kidder

AS recently as the mid-1950s you could still travel almost anywhere in the United States on a train, and usually do it in comfort, arriving on time. But in fact, intercity passenger trains were in deep, long-standing trouble. The causes were as obvious as highways and airplanes and as obscure as the accounting and marketing practices of the New York Central Railroad.

Within about fifteen years the once vast and efficient national passenger system was a ruin. The government took over what was left. In 1971 the old romantic names — such passwords to travel as Atchison, Topeka & Santa Fe, Illinois Central Gulf, Milwaukee Road, Southern Pacific — disappeared from the sides of coaches and most of what was left of intercity passenger trains fell under the hegemony of the publicly financed corporation called Amtrak. This could have been the name of a new luncheon meat or CIA project. In fact, it represented the worst passenger railroad in the industrialized world.

Mismanaged and inadequately financed, Amtrak was forced to rely for maintenance, operating crews, and tracks on private railroads, several of which were in decline while others were hostile toward this federal interloper. Some of the best private railroads tried hard to make Amtrak's trains respectable in their own territories. But over most of the system, battered equipment, demoralized crews, and ruined tracks made for slow trains, late trains, trains bossed by rude conductors, trains that broke down, trains that pitched as if at sea.

Some trains do have obvious promise. Most transportation experts agree that swift new Amtrak coaches, operating in a rebuilt northeast corridor between Boston, New York, and Washington, would attract a host of riders and might even turn a profit. Yet the corridor could as easily become all there is of the railroad. Fast trains traveling on short schedules through other busy regions may prosper. But I fear that graveyard runs await the trains that I like best — the few remaining "long hauls" that ramble across the great American distances towing real bedrooms, real restaurants, and real lounges equipped with easy chairs. They are little towns on wheels.

For those who want to recollect or imagine what American passenger trains used to be, it is time to obey the conductor's venerable command and climb aboard.

Not long ago I went traveling on trains again. One afternoon in late October, while walking through a woods near my small New England town, I came upon an abandoned stretch of railroad track. I balanced on one rust-caked rail awhile. Birds were flocking. Woodsmoke hung in the air. When I got home, I spent the afternoon gazing at the yellowed map of the United States on my wall.

The best way to go would be south, like the birds. I could catch the Transcontinental Sleeping Car when it was hitched to the Southern Railway's *Southern Crescent*. I found the necessary instructions, in fine print, inside my Amtrak timetable: "Thru passengers may occupy the Transcontinental Sleeping Car during overnight layover in New Orleans." What a good idea! Two days out of Washington, D.C., at roughly 8 P.M., I'd ride into New Orleans on the sleeper. There I might climb off and eat some gumbo. The following noon I'd be back on the coast-to-coast sleeper when it departed for Los Angeles, attached to the *Sunset Limited*.

In many places in the United States, the world of the passenger train lies hidden, behind shabby, neglected façades, in abandoned parts of cities and towns. This time I entered through South Station in Boston. It was dank and gloomy. Men leaned in corners clutching bottles wrapped in paper bags. One could catch a glimpse of a grand old building under the grit, behind the various plywood partitions. All along the route the scene was the same: pillared, porticoed, generously marbled stations, now empty and unkept, with neat little Amtrak ticket counters off in the corners near the pinball machines.

I rode down the northeast corridor to Washington first. One vision, widely shared, fancies this stretch of railroad completely reconstructed and populated with dozens of new 120-mph trains. Inside, the seats would be filled with bankers from Boston, ladies from Baltimore, and New Yorkers with attaché cases open on their laps. Through the windows of those speeding trains, one would see blurs of traffic jams on the so-called expressways, while overhead jet planes would circle as usual, waiting for their moments to land.

Work on this dream started in the spring of 1977, after many delays. And I could see the change beginning. Although my train to Washington ran the old slow schedule, over tracks yet to be repaired, the equipment was brand new. It was a train of freshly minted "Amfleet" coaches. I didn't like their tiny windows, a legacy from Amtrak's first president, who was "an airlines man." The stand-up diner served prepackaged food from which all taste had been expunged. And I missed the sound of the conductor's voice singing out the stops; a public-address system has usurped that function inside the Amfleet cars. Yet the new cars were clean and their motion smooth. They did represent a great improvement over the filthy, dimly lit, rocking-rolling train that I had suffered on two years before, between Boston and D.C. If Amfleet was the future, it seemed acceptable.

I was instructed in this point of view by a well-informed stranger whom I met on board. A mechanical engineer in his fifties, enamored of obsolete steam locomotives, my new acquaintance said he had loved railroads ever since he was old enough to line up a string of toys beneath his parents' kitchen table and pretend that he had made a train.

"It don't seem like railroading," he said, looking around our Amfleet coach. "But I guess they don't run railroads just to seem like railroading. I would say that this car here rides comparable to a Union Pacific coach in the 1950s."

I laughed disdainfully, betraying my ignorance.

My knowledgeable companion looked at me from over the tops of his glasses. "That was a compliment, you know."

After Washington, I transferred from Amfleet to older sorts of trains, from the future to the past. I found myself on an excursion into memories, mostly other peoples':

"When I got out of the service in '46 there was forty-two schedules a day through here and now there's just the *Crescent*," said the Southern Railway agent as he made up my ticket for the Transcontinental Sleeper in the all but empty, small cinderblock building that now serves as Southern's Birmingham station. "And there was seventeen clerks in the ticket office then, and I'm the last of them. I don't believe they count on this train or me bein' around here much longer."

The elderly, slow-moving agent opened up a cluttered drawer and pulled out a bar of soap, which he handed to me. The wrapper read: "You're safe and sure when you travel by PULLMAN."

"Now that," said the agent, "is a real souvenir. You have a nice trip and hurry back, hear?"

A few days later, on the *Sunset Limited,* I struck up a conversation about baked potatoes, then and now, with a dining-car steward named Ike Houston. It took him back. "We gotta forget the old days," he insisted. In a moment, however, he was remembering the ride he had taken on the *Sunset* many years ago, when the train made its maiden voyage west.

It sounded like a trip that had been worth taking. "Was the food good then?" I asked.

"Oh, man," said Houston. He shook his head at me, it was such a stupid question. "Ooooh, man!"

Train windows look out on the oldest parts of cities and towns, cross-sectioned by the tracks. You glide beside landscapes that no automobile has ever visited. From Washington, I rode down to Georgia, past many little towns whose names I didn't catch, the train rumbling through them as if it meant to knock them flat. From Atlanta I went to Birmingham, then to Louisville (a stormy voyage on Amtrak's wretched *Floridian,* over the ruined tracks of the Louisville and Nashville), then back to Birmingham, and at last I was lying by my window on the coast-to-coast sleeping car, going to New Orleans on the Southern.

The Southern Railway is one of three that stayed out of the Amtrak pact. It runs the *Crescent* by itself and pays the losses. The new management does not love passenger trains. At present it is maneuvering to rid itself of this last, unprofitable piece of "varnish." A Texan, very fond of trains, summarized this general problem for me. "It is *en*tirely possible to love railroads," he drawled, "and not love railroad companies." Yet during the era of Amtrak, the *Crescent* has been a plug for private enterprise in general and for the Southern Railway in particular. The cars on my train were old and some of the upholstery threadbare, but the only dirty car in the whole train was the Transcontinental Sleeper, which belongs to Amtrak. The porters, who wore starched white coats with holes in them and fraying cuffs, were almost painfully polite. (The porters seemed to be in mourning for the trains of yesterday. Many railroad men are thus afflicted. One veteran dining-car steward who works for Amtrak could not bear to serve his customers with Amtrak's ordinary table settings. So he purchased a set of old railroad silver. Now he carries on board his own gleaming pitchers, forks, and knives. He cannot bring back the fancy menus, but he does make sure that in his car passengers still eat in the traditional style.)

The *Crescent* rolled down across low trestles, through that swampy region which natives call "L.A." (meaning "Lower Alabama"), over brown rivers, past small red-roofed stations with ancient baggage carts by their front doors and weeds sprouting up through the cracks in their platforms. In Mississippi, a delicate black and green steam engine, wearing the inscription "Hattiesburg & Bonhomie Southern" on its side, sat by the tracks, looking ready to roll. In the dusk, Purvis, Poplarville, Slidell slipped past. We crossed Lake Pontchartrain in the dark, and then New Orleans lit the sky.

Late that night, just before I fell asleep, I felt my car being moved around in the New Orleans yards. When I awoke in the morning and stepped outside, I saw that my sleeper had been hitched to the *Sunset,* just in front of a remarkable, a wonderful old railroad car. It sat there at the end of the train, shining, like a gift. "Silver Lookout" was its name.

The "Lookout" would be the *Sunset*'s first-class lounge car. It would belong to me and my fellow passengers all the way to Los Angeles. It was early, hours before departure, but I took possession right away. I climbed aboard the enormous car and prowled around inside.

At the front end, I found four huge bedrooms, equipped with showers that no longer worked. Next, I discovered a pleasant-looking barroom; the seats were very soft. At the back of the car was a spacious lounge, flanked by tall windows. A stairway led from there to an observation deck, but I did not climb up to investigate that wonder, because a couple of Amtrak maintenance men were sitting up there talking.

"I hear this car will be gone next year," one of them remarked.

"Yup," said the other, yawning.

I sat down in one of the lower lounge's swivel chairs and practiced gazing out the "Silver Lookout's" rounded stern.

The "Lookout" was never crowded on that trip. Counting its empty seats when we pulled out of New Orleans, I felt both pleased and sorry. I believe most fans of travel by railroad have shared these emotions. An empty train is a bad omen, promising a bleak, trainless future, but it often makes for pleasant riding. In my experience, crowds on trains have usually meant dirty floors, bad smells, and squalling babies. Crowded trains can lead to enmity among the passengers. But on a train with less than half of its seats filled — as was the case with the *Sunset* — friendliness invariably prevails.

The journey from New Orleans to Los Angeles lasts for two and a half days, time for an ephemeral community to form inside the "Silver Lookout." Surely we had the best of Amtrak's new generation of porters, a young black man named Richard Ruffin, who told me that he always met interesting people in this car. Aboard were the Atterburys, Kirby and Renee, restaurateurs and seasoned travelers riding just to enjoy the "Silver Lookout" once again, for they feared its imminent retirement. There was also "Big Bill," a bartender from New Orleans, a very heavyset young man whose calling card described him aptly as "Dilettante Extraordinaire" and as "barman, entertainer, counselor." He was just traveling. Apparently just traveling, too, were several unaccompanied elderly women. There was a soft-spoken blind girl, and a woman who was drunk on sweet gin drinks most of the way to the coast. Her hair was dyed yellow. She had a hoarse, loud laugh.

When we reached El Paso and the train stopped for awhile, we all climbed out for the touch of stationary ground. I was strolling down the platform, admiring the train, when the hard-drinking woman from the "Lookout" came rushing toward me, her pocketbook bouncing, her arms outstretched.

"Greet me!" she cried, breathing sweetish odors of the barroom. "Pretend you're greeting me."

She was upon me before I could open my arms and deliver the welcoming hug. She pulled up short. She made a sour face. "Ahhh, you're no fun," she said, and she climbed back on the train.

Perhaps the most robust inhabitant of that fine and ancient lounge car was the shoe salesman. I met him on the second day out. We were riding through West Texas then. It is mostly sand hills, mesquite, and stubby telephone poles strung with single wire. You have to peer through the glass to notice the changes in the landscape. From time to time we passed a dirt road with the name of a ranch hung over it. The road would stretch off to the horizon. I was sitting in the lower lounge, occupying myself with thoughts of life out there, thinking that one could die of thirst on some of those ranches' driveways, when from the corner of my eye I saw a man sit down beside me. He started making sounds, clearing his throat, stirring about in his chair. So I turned to him. He was tall and bony-looking, all elbows and knees, with a wrinkled face and a large pitted nose, a quite elderly Ichabod Crane. He said something about the weather, and then I noticed his shoes.

They didn't match. On his left foot he was wearing a very shiny blue loafer and on his right a black brogan — "an attractive arch-preserver brogan," he would tell me later.

I showed an interest in his footgear, and the fellow pounced. He must have used that trick before.

Would I like to buy some shoes? Perhaps I'd like to be a salesman. Well, anyway, he would like to show me some of his samples. They were on display back in his tiny roomette, a dozen shoes lined up next to a paper plate of hors d'oeuvres, peanut butter and jelly on Ritz crackers.

Shoes, of course, led to other topics, and so it was that I heard a great deal about my new friend's days as an optometrist in a rural Massachusetts town. A year ago he sold his office equipment and hit the road. Now he was traveling, selling shoes on the side.

The sixty-five-year-old woman occupying the roomette across from the shoe salesman's confided to me one evening that the man was driving her mad. "He won't leave me alone! I think he watches in the morning and as soon as I get out of bed and he sees my feet, he's poking his head in through the curtain." In El Paso, the shoe salesman marched around the station singing the Harvard fight song — in order, I think, to tell us a piece of his life history. It was obvious why he was riding the rails: trains are notoriously sociable places.

On the last night of the voyage, a party was held inside the "Silver Lookout." One of the few young women on the train was having a birthday. Richard, most excellent of porters, arranged for a cake. Afterward, we sat around the lower lounge and played a get-acquainted game. One had to affix an alliterative adjective to one's given name, and repeat all the other names that had gone before. It was interesting to hear the names that people chose for themselves. A demure young woman told us she was "Lascivious" Lele and a rather opinionated fellow admitted that he thought of himself, or feared that others thought of him, as "Inane" Irving. The shoe salesman had dressed for the party in a necktie, gray flannels, and a yellow smoking jacket that looked suspiciously like a bathrobe. He styled himself "Daring" Dick.

We were rolling in the dark now through Arizona, sipping drinks. The shoe salesman tried to repeat the names that had preceded his, and misspoke every one of them. Someone near me whispered, "He's doing it on purpose." But everyone else laughed, in a very friendly, indulgent manner, and the shoe salesman's cheeks began to glow. As the ghost train rattled on, he turned his face away. Then he made a remark as mournful as the sound of those famous old whistles blowing across the prairie. "I wish this train would never end," he said.

1979
DR. CAHN'S VISIT
by Richard Stern

"HOW far is it now, George?"

The old man was riding next to his son, Will. George was his brother, dead the day after Franklin Roosevelt.

"Almost there, Dad."

"What does 'almost' mean?"

"It's Eighty-sixth and Park. The hospital's at Ninety-ninth and Fifth. Mother's in the Klingenstein Pavilion."

"Mother's not well?"

"No, she's not well. Liss and I took her to the hospital a couple of weeks ago."

"It must have slipped my mind." The green eyes darkened with sympathy. "I'm sure you did the right thing. Is it a good hospital?"

"Very good. You were on staff there half a century."

"Of course I was. For many years, I believe."

"Fifty."

"Many as that?"

"A little slower, pal. These jolts are hard on the old man."

The cabbie was no chicken himself. "It's your ride."

"Are we nearly there, George?"

"Two minutes more."

"The day isn't friendly," said Dr. Cahn. "I don't remember such — such — "

"Heat."

"Heat in New York." He took off his gray fedora and scratched at the hairless, liver-spotted skin. Circulatory difficulty left it dry, itchy. Scratching had shredded and inflamed its soft center.

"It's damn hot. In the nineties. Like you."

"What's that?"

"It's as hot as you are old. Ninety-one."

"Ninety-one. That's not good."

"It's a grand age."

"That's your view."

"And Mother's eighty. You've lived good, long lives."

"Mother's not well, son?"

"Not too well. That's why Liss and I thought you ought to see her. Mother's looking forward to seeing you."

"Of course. I should be with her. Is this the first time I've come to visit?"

"Yes."

"I should be with her."

The last weeks at home had been difficult. Dr. Cahn had been the center of the household. Suddenly, his wife was. The nurses looked after her. And when he talked, she didn't answer. He grew angry, sullen. When her ulcerous mouth improved, her voice was rough and her thought harsh. "I wish you'd stop smoking for five minutes. Look at the ashes on your coat. Please stop smoking."

"Of course, dear. I didn't know I was annoying you." The ash tumbled like a suicide from thirty stories, the butt was crushed into its dead brothers. "I'll smoke inside." And he was off, but, in two minutes, back.

Lighting up. Sometimes he lit two cigarettes at once. Or lit the filtered end. The odor was foul, and sometimes his wife was too weak to register her disgust.

They sat and lay within silent yards of each other. Dr. Cahn was in his favorite armchair, the *Times* bridge column inches from his cigarette. He read it all day long. The vocabulary of the game deformed his speech. "I need some clubs" might mean "I'm hungry." "My spades are tired" meant he was. Or his eyes were. Praise of someone might come out "He laid his hand out clearly." In the bedridden weeks, such mistakes intensified his wife's exasperation. "He's become such a penny-pincher," she said to Liss when Dr. Cahn refused to pay her for the carton of cigarettes she brought, saying, "They can't charge so much. You've been cheated."

"Liss has paid. Give her the money."

"Are you telling me what's trump? I've played this game all my life."

"You certainly have. And I can't bear it."

In sixty marital years, there had never been such anger. When Will came from Chicago to persuade his mother into the hospital, the bitterness dismayed him.

It was, therefore, not so clear that Dr. Cahn should visit his wife. Why disturb her last days? Besides, Dr. Cahn seldom went out anywhere. He wouldn't walk with the black nurses (women whom he loved, teased, and was teased by). It wasn't done. "I'll go out later. My feet aren't friendly today." Or, lowering the paper, "My legs can't trump."

Liss opposed his visit. "Mother's afraid he'll make a scene."

"It doesn't matter," said Will. "He has to have some sense of what's happening. They've been the center of each other's lives. It wouldn't be right."

The hope had been that Dr. Cahn would die first. He was ten years older, his mind had slipped its moorings years ago. Mrs. Cahn was clearheaded, and, except near the end, energetic. She loved to travel, wanted especially to visit Will in Chicago — she had not seen his new apartment — but she wouldn't leave her husband even for a day. "Suppose something happened." "Bring him along." "He can't travel. He'd make an awful scene."

Only old friends tolerated him, played bridge with him, forgiving his lapses and muddled critiques of their play. "If you don't understand a two bid now, you never will." Dr. Cahn was the most gentlemanly of men, but his tongue roughened with his memory. It was as if a lifetime of restraint were only the rind of a wicked impatience.

"He's so spoiled," said Mrs. Cahn, the spoiler.

"Here we are, Dad."

They parked under the blue awning. Dr. Cahn got out his wallet — he always paid for taxis, meals, shows — looked at the few bills, then handed it to his son. Will took a dollar, added two of his own, and thanked his father.

"This is a weak elevator," he said of one of the monsters made to drift the ill from floor to floor. A nurse wheeled in a stretcher and Dr. Cahn removed his fedora.

"Mother's on eight."

"Minnie is here?"

"Yes. She's ill. Step out now."

"I don't need your hand."

Each day, his mother filled less of the bed. Her face, unsupported by dentures, seemed shot away. Asleep, it looked to Will as if the universe leaned on the crumpled cheeks. When he kissed them, he feared they'd turn to dust, so astonishingly delicate was the flesh. The only vanity left was love of attention, and that was part of the only thing that counted, the thought of those who cared for her. How she appreciated the good nurses, and her children. They — who'd never before seen their mother's naked body — would change her nightgown if the nurse was gone. They brought her the bedpan and, though she usually suggested they leave the room, sat beside her while, under the sheets, her weak body emptied its small waste.

For the first time in his adult life, Will found her beautiful. Her flesh was mottled like a Pollock canvas, the facial skin trenched with the awful last ditches of self-defense; but her look melted him. It was human beauty.

Day by day, manners that seemed as much a part of her as her eyes — fussiness, bossiness, nagging inquisitiveness — dropped away. She was down to what she was.

Not since childhood had she held him so closely, kissed his cheek with such force. "This is mine. This is what lasts," said the force.

What was she to him? Sometimes, little more than the old organic scenery of his life. Sometimes she was the meaning of it. "Hello, darling," she'd say. "I'm so glad to see you." The voice, never melodious, was rusty, avian. Beautiful. No actress could match it. "How are you? What's happening?"

"Very little. How are you today?"

She told her news. "Dr. Vacarian was in, he wanted to give me another treatment. I told him, 'No more.' And no more medicine." Each day, she had renounced more therapy. An unspoken decision had been made after a five-hour barium treatment which usurped the last of her strength. (Will thought that might have been its point.) It had given her her last moments of eloquence, a frightening jeremiad about life dark beyond belief, nothing left, nothing right. It was the last complaint of an old champion of complaint, and after it, she had made up her mind to go. There was no more talk of going home.

"Hello, darling. How are you today?"

Will bent over, was kissed and held against her cheek. "Mother, Dad's here."

To his delight, she showed hers. "Where is he?" Dr. Cahn had waited at the door. Now he came in, looked at the bed, realized where he was and who was there.

"Dolph, dear. How are you, my darling? I'm so happy you came to see me."

The old man stooped over and took her face in his hands. For seconds, there was silence. "My dearest," he said; then, "I didn't know. I had no idea. I've been so worried about you. But don't worry now. You look wonderful. A little thin, perhaps. We'll fix that. We'll have you out in no time."

The old man's pounding heart must have driven blood through the clogged vessels. There was no talk of trumps.

"You can kiss me, dear." Dr. Cahn put his lips on hers.

He sat next to the bed and held his wife's hand through the low rail. Over and over he told her she'd be well. She asked about home and the nurses. He answered well for a while. Then they both saw him grow vague and tired. To Will he said, "I don't like the way she's looking. Are you sure she has a good doctor?"

Of course Mrs. Cahn heard. Her happiness watered a bit, not at the facts, but at his inattention. Still, she held on. She knew he could not sit so long in a strange room. "I'm so glad you came, darling."

Dr. Cahn heard his cue and rose. "We mustn't tire you, Minnie dear. We'll come back soon."

She held out her small arms, he managed to lean over, and they kissed again.

In the taxi, he was very tired. "Are we home?"

"Almost, Dad. You're happy you saw Mother, aren't you?"

"Of course I'm happy. But it's not a good day. It's a very poor day. Not a good bid at all."

1980
THE TROUBLE WITH ARCHITECTS
The Bird's-eye Syndrome
by Andrew Ward

A woman I know worked for a time in one of those prestigious sweatshops in which the imposing abodes of America's corporations are designed. A mean woman with an X-Acto knife, she was given the job of constructing the little presentation models with which her firm coaxed its clients even further into the frontiers of modern architecture. But she could stand the subsistence pay, the stiff neck, and the enforced veneration for the firm's presiding genius only long enough to complete a single model: a one-inch-to-one-foot cardboard and Mylar prototype of a huge building slated for construction somewhere in downtown Houston.

A few years after she quit the firm she found herself at the Houston airport and decided to kill the two hours she had between planes by taking a cab downtown and finding the building over whose embryo she had labored so long. Though she couldn't remember what company had commissioned it, she figured she had been so intimately acquainted with its design that she could spot it without any trouble.

But after an hour's search up and down the city streets, she could not for the life of her find it, and had to assume, as she boarded her plane, that the design had been changed or the project had been canceled just after she had quit. Then, suddenly, looking down at the retreating city as her plane rose in the sky, she saw her building standing right smackdab in the middle of Houston. During her search she must have passed it half a dozen times, but only now, with a bird's-eye view of it on a cardboard and Mylar scale, could she recognize it.

I think my friend may have stumbled upon what's wrong with modern architecture: it is best appreciated from a couple of thousand feet off the ground. It is conceived from an aerial point of view, from the Olympian perspective of a god, an angel, a chairman of the board.

I visited a firm a while ago whose work is on such a scale and whose aesthetic is so grandiose that I only wish Albert Speer could have tagged along to give me some guidance. Crammed atop fifty waist-high tables in the center of the main studio were thousands of dollars' worth of presentation models representing millions of dollars' worth of buildings. Some were of structures that are already towering over us; others were of headquarters still rising out of the doomed woodlands of suburban Connecticut; still more were of buildings that shall forever remain a gleam in the architect's eye.

As I wandered through the studio, my natural perspective was from above. During presentations, executives must have had to stoop pretty far down to get some earthbound notion of what the buildings were going to look like, and stooping does not come naturally to your upper-echelon corporate exec. Getting up close to models can wreck the illusion, anyway; you see a flap of Mylar peeling away, a fleck of rubber cement, the little everyday defects that have no place in a meeting where traffic flow patterns, image, and executive toiletry are up for discussion. No, it is far preferable to maintain one's posture and keep one's distance.

What struck me about the models with their breakaway roofs was that they contained some pretty ingenious notions, some intricate and innovative problem-solving, but that none of these could be appreciated by someone trying to walk along a building's barren and wind-whipped façade, or heading for the restroom along one of its dizzying, sloping corridors, or reading back issues in a brass and glass lobby five stories high.

That we are but grains of sand on the beach of time, droplets in the ocean of life, is a notion worth considering now and then, but it isn't something sane people want to dwell upon, or in. Nature has been doing a fine job of reminding us of our insignificance without a lot of architects seconding the motion. The hitch, of course, is that the men who commission these buildings don't tend to feel as insignificant as the rest of us (maybe because they aren't as insignificant as the rest of us). And it may even be that they don't really mean to make the rest of us feel insignificant. It's just that the same building that makes a visitor feel puny makes its proprietor, whose experience is charged with the thrill of ownership, feel like a giant.

Architecture, especially institutional architecture, may always have been designed and bestowed from above, but since the invention of the airplane the aerial perspective has been given disproportionate validity. Have you ever noticed how exalted our downtown areas appear from the clouds? At some altitudes you could mistake the new convention centers and condo complexes for Utopia. But down on the ground the same places are oppressive, depressing, downright crummy. Part of this effect is a function of distance; from thousands of feet in the air you can't see the litter and the bag ladies. But that can be only part of it, because sometimes the reverse is true.

I lived for a while in Cornwall, Connecticut, conceivably the loveliest town in the nation. Most of the houses were built by country carpenters in the eighteenth and nineteenth centuries, and they coexist in absolute harmony (in marked contrast to their occupants). As one walks along the streets, it seems that everyone's lawn stretches for acres and every grove of trees extends into miles of forest, as if, over time, the town grew organically out of the countryside. But I was once shown some aerial photographs of Cornwall in which the town, stripped of its mystery, looked like a condemned stretch of southern New Jersey. You could see the abandoned cars just beyond the Cotters' back fence, the bald lots gleaned for firewood on the Franklins' hill.

An architect would no more have recreated such a scheme and proposed it to a developer than he would serve Kool-Aid to Harold Geneen. He would have tidied up those uneven, impracticably distanced houses into evenly staggered modules, pruned the woodlots, landscaped the pastures, gutted the hardware store to make way for a wok outlet and a quiche parlor, unified the churches, consolidated the schools, and tied the whole thing together with pedestrian walkways and bike paths. Only then could his clients, standing over the one-inch-to-ten-feet mock-up like titans 300 feet tall, come to grips with the theme, the continuity, the concept, at a glance.

Maybe the grandiose style is just an outgrowth of the grandiosity of the institutions it services. And perhaps the young turks of modern architecture have already turned their backs on the ostentatious. I don't know. The last young turk I met designed his parents' solar house on the Cape last year; has been reduced to making installation estimates for a carpet warehouse this year; and, if things don't pick up next year, may join his buddy the English major in a cabinetmaking business in Vermont. A look at the major commissions under way just beyond New York's city limits indicates to me that the grandiose is getting grander all the time.

I suppose I won't be satisfied until architects return to Asher Benjamin and the golden mean, but if they have any interest in designing buildings to accommodate people, they should at least design structures in the same way they're built: from the ground up.

1981
CATHEDRAL
by Raymond Carver

THIS blind man, an old friend of my wife's, he was on his way to spend the night. His wife had died. So he was visiting the dead wife's relatives in Connecticut. He called my wife from his in-laws'. Arrangements were made. He would come by train, a five-hour trip, and my wife would meet him at the station. She hadn't seen him since she worked for him one summer in Seattle ten years ago. But she and the blind man had kept in touch. They made tapes and mailed them back and forth. I wasn't enthusiastic about his visit. He was no one I knew. And his being blind bothered me. My idea of blindness came from the movies. In movies, the blind moved slowly and never laughed. Sometimes they were led by seeing-eye dogs. A blind man in my house was not something I looked forward to.

That summer in Seattle she had needed a job. She didn't have any money. The man she was going to marry at the end of the summer was in officer's training school. He didn't have any money, either. But she was in love with the guy, and he was in love with her, etc. She'd seen something in the paper: Help Wanted — Reading for Blind Man, and a telephone number. She phoned and went over, was hired on the spot. She'd worked with this blind man all summer. She read stuff to him, case studies, reports, that sort of thing. She helped him organize his little office in the county social service department. They'd become good friends, my wife and the blind man. How do I know these things? She told me. And she told me something else. On her last day in the office, the blind man asked if he could touch her face. She agreed to this. She told me he ran his fingers over every part of her face, her nose — even her neck! She never forgot it. She even tried to write a poem about it. She was always writing a poem. She wrote a poem or two every year, usually after something really important had happened to her.

When we first started going out together, she showed me the poem. In the poem she recalled his fingers and the way they had moved around over her face. In the poem she talked about what she had felt at the time, about what went through her mind as he touched her nose and lips. I can recall I didn't think much of the poem. Of course I didn't tell her that. Maybe I just don't understand poetry. I admit it's not the first thing I reach for when I pick up something to read.

Anyway, this man who'd first enjoyed her favors, the officer-to-be, he'd been her childhood sweetheart. So okay. I'm saying that at the end of the summer she let the blind man run his hands over her face, said good-bye to him, married her childhood etc., who was now a commissioned officer, and she moved away from Seattle. But they'd kept in touch, she and the blind man. She made the first contact after a year or so. She called him up one night from an Air Force base in Alabama. She wanted to talk. They talked. He asked her to send him a tape and tell him about her life. She did this. She sent the tape. On the tape she told the blind man about her husband and about their life together in the military. She told the blind man she loved her husband but she didn't like it where they lived and she didn't like it that he was a part of the military-industrial complex. She told the blind man she'd written a poem and he was in it. She told him that she was writing a poem about what it was like to be an Air Force officer's wife in the Deep South. The poem wasn't finished yet. She was still writing it. The blind man made a tape. He sent her the tape. She made a tape. This went on for years. My wife's officer was posted to one base and then another. She sent tapes from Moody AFB, McGuire, McConnell, and finally Travis, near Sacramento, where one night she got to feeling lonely and cut off from people she kept losing in that moving-around life. She balked, couldn't go it another step. She went in and swallowed all the pills and capsules in the medicine cabinet and washed them down with a bottle of gin. Then she got into a hot bath and passed out.

But instead of dying she got sick. She threw up. Her officer — Why should he have a name? He was the childhood sweetheart, and what more does he want? — came home from a training mission, found her, and called the ambulance. In time, she put it on the tape and sent the tape to the blind man. Over the years she put all kinds of stuff on tapes and sent the tapes off lickety-split. Next to writing a poem every year, I think it was her chief means of recreation. On one tape she told the blind man she'd decided to live away from her officer for a time. On another tape she told him about her divorce. She and I began going out, and of course she told her blind man about this. She told him everything, or so it seemed to me. Once she asked me if I'd like to hear the latest tape from the blind man. This was a year ago. I was on the tape, she said. So I said okay, I'd listen to it. I got us drinks and we settled down in the living room. We made ready to listen. First she inserted the tape into the player and adjusted a couple of dials. Then she pushed a lever. The tape squeaked and someone began to talk in this loud voice. She lowered the volume. After a few minutes of harmless chitchat, I heard my own name rasped out by this stranger, this man I didn't even know! And then this: "From all you've said about him, I can only conclude — " But we were interrupted, a knock at the door, something, and we didn't get back to the tape. Maybe it was just as well. I'd heard enough, anyway.

Now this same blind stranger was coming to sleep in my house.

"Maybe I could take him bowling," I said to my wife. She was at the draining board doing scalloped potatoes. She put down the knife she was using on the onion and turned around.

"If you love me," she said, "you can do this for me. If you don't love me, okay. But if you had a friend, any friend, and the friend came to visit, I'd make him feel comfortable." She wiped her hands with the dish towel.

"I don't have any blind friends," I said.

"You don't have *any* friends," she said. "Period. Besides," she said, "goddammit, his wife's just died! Don't you understand that? The man's lost his wife!"

I didn't answer. She'd told me a little about the blind man's wife. The wife's name was Beulah. Beulah! That's a name for a colored woman.

"Was his wife a Negro?" I asked.

"Are you crazy?" my wife said. "Have you just flipped or something?" She picked up the onion. I saw it hit the floor, then roll under the stove. "What's wrong with you?" she said. "Are you drunk?"

"I'm just asking," I said.

Right then my wife filled me in with more detail than I cared to know. I made a drink and sat at the kitchen table to listen. Pieces of the story began to fall into place.

Beulah had gone to work for the blind man the summer after my wife had stopped working for him. Pretty soon Beulah and the blind man had themselves a church wedding. It was a little wedding — Who'd be anxious to attend such a wedding in the first place? — just the two of them, and the minister and the minister's wife. But it was a church wedding just the same. What Beulah had wanted, he'd said. But even then Beulah must have been carrying cancer in her lymph glands. After they had been inseparable for eight years — my wife's word, "inseparable" — Beulah's health went into a rapid decline. She died in a Seattle hospital room, the blind man sitting beside the bed and holding on to her hand. They'd married, lived and worked together, slept together — had sex, sure — and then the blind man buried her. All this without his having ever seen what the goddamned woman looked like. It was beyond my understanding. Hearing this, I felt sorry for the blind man for a minute. And then I found myself thinking what a pitiful life this woman must have led. Imagine a woman who could never see herself reflected in the eyes of her loved one. A woman who could go on day after day and never receive the smallest compliment from her beloved. A woman whose husband would never read the expression on her face, be it misery or something better. Someone who could wear makeup or not — what difference to him? She could, if she wanted, wear green eye shadow around one eye, a straight pin in her nostril, yellow slacks and burgundy pumps, no matter. And then to slip off into death, the blind man's hand on her hand, his blind eyes streaming tears — I'm imagining now — her last thought maybe this: that her beloved never knew what she looked like, and she on an express to the grave. Robert was left with a small insurance policy and half of a twenty-peso Mexican coin. The other half of the coin went into the box with her. Pathetic.

So when the time rolled around, my wife went to the rail station. With nothing to do but wait — and sure, I blamed him for that — I was having a drink and watching TV when I heard the car pull into the drive. I got up from the sofa with my drink and went to the window to have a look.

I saw my wife laughing as she parked the car. I saw her get out of the car and shut the door. She was still wearing a smile. Just amazing. She went around to the other side of the car to where the blind man was already starting to get out. This blind man, feature this, he was wearing a full beard! A beard on a blind man! Too much, I say. The blind man reached into the back seat and dragged out a suitcase. My wife took his arm, shut the car door, and, talking all the way, moved him down the drive and then up the steps to the front porch. I turned off the TV. I finished my drink, rinsed the glass, dried my hands. Then I went to the door.

My wife said, "I want you to meet Robert. Robert, this is my husband. I've told you all about him." She closed the porch screen. She was beaming. She had this blind man by his coat sleeve.

The blind man let go of his suitcase and up came his hand.
I took it. He squeezed hard, held my hand, and then he let it go.
"I feel like we've already met," he boomed.
"Likewise," I said. I didn't know what else to say. Then I said, "Welcome. I've heard a lot about you." We began to move then, a little group, from the porch into the living room, my wife guiding him by the arm. He carried his suitcase in his other hand. My wife said things like, "To your left here, Robert. That's right. Now watch it, there's a chair. That's it. Sit down right here. This is the sofa. We just bought this sofa two weeks ago."

I started to say something about the old sofa. I'd liked that old sofa. But I didn't say anything. Then I wanted to say something else, small talk, about the scenic Hudson River. How going *to* New York, sit on the right-hand side of the train, and coming *from* New York, the left-hand side.

"Did you have a good train ride?" I said, "Which side of the train did you sit on, by the way?"

"What a question, which side!" my wife said. "What's it matter which side?" she said.

"I just asked," I said.

"Right side," the blind man said. "For the sun. Until this morning," the blind man said, "I hadn't been on a train in nearly forty years. Not since I was a kid. With my folks. That's been a long time. I'd nearly forgotten that sensation. I have winter in my beard now," he said. "So I've been told, anyway. Do I look distinguished, my dear?" he said to my wife.

"You look distinguished, Robert," she said. "Robert," she said. "Robert, it's just so good to see you." My wife finally took her eyes off the blind man and looked at me.

I had the distinct feeling she didn't like what she saw. I shrugged.

I've never met or personally known anyone who was blind. This blind man was late forties, a heavyset, balding man with stooped shoulders, as if he carried a great weight there. He wore brown slacks, brown cordovan shoes, a light-brown shirt, a tie, a sports coat. Spiffy. He also had this full beard. But he didn't carry a cane and he didn't wear dark glasses. I'd always thought dark glasses were a must for the blind. Fact was, I wished he had a pair. At first glance, his eyes looked like anyone else's eyes. But if you looked close there was something different about them. Too much white in the iris, for one thing, and the pupils seemed to move around in the sockets without his knowing it or being able to control it. Creepy. As I stared at his face, I saw the left pupil turn in toward his nose, while the other made a futile effort to keep in one place. But it was only an effort, for that eye was on the roam without his knowing it or wanting it to be.

I said, "Let me get you a drink. What's your pleasure? We have a little of everything. It's one of our pastimes."

"Bub, I'm a scotch man myself," he said fast enough, in this big voice.

"Right," I said. Bub! "Sure you are. I knew it."

He let his fingers touch his suitcase, which was sitting alongside the sofa. He was taking his bearings. I didn't blame him for that.

"I'll move that up to your room," my wife said.

"No, that's fine," he said loudly. "It can go up when I go up."

"A little water with the scotch?" I said.

"Very little," he said.

"I knew it," I said.

He said, "Just a tad. The Irish actor, Barry Fitzgerald? I'm like that fellow. When I drink water, Fitzgerald said, I drink water. When I drink whiskey, I drink whiskey." My wife laughed. The blind man brought his hand up under his beard. He lifted his beard slowly and let it drop.

I did the drinks, three big glasses of scotch with a splash of water in each. Then we made ourselves comfortable and talked about Robert's travels. First the long flight from the West Coast to Connecticut, we covered that. Then from Connecticut up here by train. We had another drink concerning that leg of the trip.

I remembered having read somewhere that the blind didn't smoke because, speculation had it, they couldn't see the smoke they exhaled. I thought I knew that much and that much only about blind people. But this blind man smoked his cigarette down to the nubbin and then lit another one. This blind man filled his ashtray and my wife emptied it.

When we sat down to the table for dinner we had another drink. My wife heaped Robert's plate with cube steak, scalloped potatoes, green beans. I buttered him up two slices of bread. I said, "Here's bread and butter for you." I swallowed some of my drink. "Now let us pray," I said, and the blind man lowered his head. My wife looked at me, her mouth agape. "Pray the phone won't ring and the food doesn't get cold," I said.

We dug in. We ate everything there was to eat on the table. We ate like there was no tomorrow. We didn't talk. We ate. We scarfed. We grazed that table. We were into serious eating. The blind man had right away located his foods, he knew just where everything was on his plate. I watched with admiration as he used his knife and fork on the meat. He'd cut two pieces of meat, fork the meat into his mouth, and then go all out for the scalloped potatoes, the beans next, and then he'd tear off a hunk of buttered bread and eat that. He'd follow this up with a big drink of milk. It didn't seem to bother him to use his fingers once in a while, either. He used his bread to scoop beans.

We finished everything, including half of a strawberry pie. For a few moments we sat as if stunned. Sweat beaded on our faces. Finally, we got up from the table and left the dirty plates. We didn't look back. We took ourselves into the living room and sank into our places again. Robert and my wife sat on the sofa. I took the big chair. We had us two or three more drinks while they talked about the major things that had transpired for them in the past ten years. For the most part, I just listened. Now and then I joined in. I didn't want him to think I'd left the room, and I didn't want her to think I was feeling left out. They talked of things that had happened to them — to them! — these past ten years. I waited in vain to hear my name on my wife's sweet lips: "And then my dear husband came into my life" — something like that. But I heard nothing of the sort. More talk of Robert. Robert had done a little of everything, it seemed, a regular blind jack-of-all-trades. But most recently he and his wife had had an Amway distributorship, from which, I gathered, they'd earned their living, such as it was. The blind man was also a ham radio operator. He talked in his loud voice about conversations he'd had with fellow operators in Guam, the Philippines, Alaska, even Tahiti. He said he'd have a lot of friends there if he ever wanted to go visit those places. From time to time he'd turn his blind face toward me, put his hand under his beard, ask me something. How long had I been at my present position? (Three years.) Did I like my work? (I didn't.) Was I going to stay with it? (What were the options?)

Finally, when I thought he was beginning to run down, I got up and turned on the TV.

My wife looked at me with irritation. She was heading toward a boil. Then she looked at the blind man and said, "Robert, do you have a TV?"

The blind man said, "My dear, I have two TVs. I have a color set and a black-and-white thing, an old relic. It's funny, but if I turn the TV on, and I'm always turning it on, I turn the color set on. Always. It's funny."

I didn't know what to say to that. I had absolutely nothing to say about that. No opinion. So I watched the news program and tried to listen to what the announcer was saying.

"This is a color TV," the blind man said. "Don't ask me how, but I can tell."

"We traded up a while ago," I said.

The blind man had another taste of his drink. He lifted his beard, sniffed it, and let it fall. He leaned forward on the sofa. He positioned his ashtray on the coffee table, then put the lighter to his cigarette. He leaned back on the sofa and crossed his legs at the ankles.

My wife covered her mouth, and then she yawned. She stretched. She said, "I think I'll go upstairs and put on my robe. I think I'll change into something else. Robert, you make yourself comfortable," she said.

"I'm comfortable," the blind man said.

"I want you to feel comfortable in this house," she said.

"I am comfortable," the blind man said.

After she'd left the room, he and I listened to the weather report and then to the sports roundup. My wife had been gone so long I didn't know if she was going to come back. I thought she might have gone to bed. I wished she'd come back downstairs. I didn't want to be left alone with a blind man. I asked him if he wanted another drink, and he said sure. Then I asked if he wanted to smoke dope with me. I said I'd just rolled a number. I hadn't, but I planned to do so in about two shakes.

"I'll try some with you," he said.

"Damn right," I said. "That's the stuff."

I got our drinks and sat down on the sofa with him. Then I rolled us two fat numbers. I lit one and passed it. I brought it to his fingers. He took it and inhaled.

"Hold it as long as you can," I said. I could tell he didn't know the first thing.

My wife came back downstairs wearing her robe and pink slippers. "What do I smell?" she said.

"We thought we'd have us some cannabis," I said.

My wife gave me a purely savage look. Then she looked at him and said, "Robert, I didn't know you smoked."

He said, "I do now, my dear. First time for everything," he said. "But I don't feel anything yet."

"This stuff is pretty mellow," I said. "This stuff is mild. It's dope you can reason with. It doesn't mess you up."

"Not much it doesn't, bub," he said, and laughed.

My wife sat on the sofa between the blind man and me. I passed her the number. She took it and inhaled and then passed it back to me. "Which way is this going?" she said. Then she said, "I shouldn't be smoking this. I can hardly keep my eyes open as it is. That dinner did me in. I shouldn't have eaten so much."

"It was the strawberry pie," the blind man said. "That's what did it," he said, and he laughed his big laugh. Then he shook his head.

"There's more strawberry pie," I said.

"Do you want some more, Robert?" my wife asked.

"Maybe in a little while," he said.

We gave our attention to the TV. My wife yawned again. She said, "Your bed is made up when you feel like going to bed, Robert. I know you must have had a long day. When you're ready to go to bed, say so." She pulled his arm. "Robert?"

He came to and said, "I've had a real nice time. This beats tapes, doesn't it?"

I said, "Coming at you," and I put the number between his fingers. He inhaled, held the smoke, and then let it go. It was like he'd been doing it since he was nine years old.

"Thanks, bub," he said. "But I think this is all for me. I think I'm beginning to feel it," he said. He held the burning roach out for my wife.

"Same here," she said. "Ditto. Me too." She took the roach and passed it to me. "I may just sit here for a while between you two guys with my eyes closed. But don't let me bother you, okay? Either one of you. If it bothers you, say so. Otherwise, I may just sit here with my eyes closed until you're ready to go to bed," she said. "Your bed's made up, Robert, when you're ready. It's right next to our room at the top of the stairs. We'll show you up when you're ready. You wake me up now, you guys, if I fall asleep." She said that and then she closed her eyes and went to sleep.

The news program ended. I got up and turned the channel. I sat back down on the sofa. I wished my wife hadn't pooped out. Her head lay across the back of the sofa, her mouth open. She'd turned so that her robe had slipped away from her legs, exposing a juicy thigh. I reached to draw her robe over the thigh, and it was then I glanced at the blind man. What the hell! I flipped the robe open again.

"You say when you want some strawberry pie," I said.

"I will," he said.

I said, "Are you tired? Do you want me to take you up to your bed? Are you ready to hit the hay?"

"Not yet," he said. "No, I'll stay up with you, bub. If that's all right. I'll stay up until you're ready to turn in. We haven't had a chance to talk. Know what I mean? I feel like me and her monopolized the evening." He lifted his beard and he let it fall. He picked up his cigarettes and his lighter.

"That's all right," I said. Then I said, "I'm glad for the company." And I guess I was. Every night I smoked dope and stayed up as long as I could before I fell asleep. My wife and I hardly ever went to bed at the same time. When I did go to sleep, I had these dreams. Sometimes I'd wake up from one of them, the heart going crazy.

Something about the church and the middle ages, narrated by an Englishman, was on the TV. Not your run-of-the-mill TV fare. I wanted to watch something else. I turned to the other channels. But there was nothing on them, either. So I turned back to the first channel and apologized.

"Bub, it's all right," he said. "It's fine with me. Whatever you want to watch is okay. I'm always learning something. Learning never ends. It won't hurt me to learn something tonight. I got ears," he said.

We didn't say anything for a time. He was leaning forward with his head turned at me, while his right ear was aimed in the direction of the set. Very disconcerting. Now and then his eyelids drooped and then they snapped open again. Now and then he put his fingers into his beard and tugged, as if thinking about something he was hearing on the television.

On the screen a group of men wearing cowls was being set upon and tormented by men dressed in skeleton costumes and men dressed as devils. The men dressed as devils wore devil masks, horns, and long tails. This pageant was part of a procession. The Englishman said it all took place in Málaga, Spain, once a year. I tried to explain to the blind man what was happening.

"Skeletons," he said. "I know about skeletons," he said, and he nodded.

The TV showed Chartres Cathedral. Then there was a long slow look at Sainte Chapelle. Finally the picture switched to Notre Dame, with its flying buttresses, its spires reaching toward clouds. The camera pulled away to show the whole of the cathedral rising above the skyline.

There were times when the Englishman who was telling the thing would shut up, would simply let the camera move around over the cathedrals. Or else the camera would tour the countryside, men in fields walking behind oxen. I waited as long as I could. Then I felt I had to say something. I said, "They're showing the outside of this cathedral now. Gargoyles. Little statues carved to look like monsters. Now I guess they're in Italy. Yeah, they're in Italy. There's fresco paintings on the walls of this one church.

"What's fresco painting, bub?" he asked, and he sipped from his drink.

I reached for my glass. But it was empty. I tried to remember what I could remember about frescoes. "You're asking me what are frescoes?" I said. "That's a good question. I don't know."

The camera moved to a cathedral outside Lisbon, Portugal. The differences in the Portuguese cathedral compared with the French and Italian were not that great. But they were there. Mostly the interior stuff. Then something occurred to me and I said, "Something has occurred to me. Do you have an idea what a cathedral is? What they look like, that is? Do you follow me? If somebody says *cathedral* to you, do you have any notion what they're talking about? Do you know the difference between that and a Baptist church, say? Or that and a mosque, or synagogue?"

He let the smoke issue from his mouth. "I know they took hundreds of workers fifty or a hundred years to build," he said. "I just heard the man say that, of course. I know generations of the same families worked on a cathedral. I heard him say that, too. The men who began their life's work on them, they never lived to see the completion of their work. In that wise, bub, they're no different from the rest of us, right?" He laughed. Then his eyelids drooped again. His head nodded. He seemed to be snoozing. Maybe he was imagining himself in Portugal. The TV was showing another cathedral now. This one was in Germany. The Englishman's voice droned on. "Cathedrals," the blind man said. He sat up and rolled his head back and forth. "If you want the truth, bub, that's about all I know. What I just said. What I heard him say. But maybe you could describe one to me? I wish you'd do it. I'd like that. If you want to know, I really don't have a good idea."

I stared hard at the shot of the cathedral on the TV. It held a minute. Then it was gone, and the view was of the inside with rows of benches and high windows. How could I even begin to describe it? But say my life depended on it. Say my life was being threatened by an insane Turkish bey.

They took the camera outside again. I stared some more at the cathedral before the picture flipped off into the countryside. There was no use. I turned to the blind man and said, "To begin with, they're very tall. Very, very tall." I was looking around the room for clues. I tried again. "They reach way up. Up and up. Toward the sky. They soar. They're like poetry, that's what they're like. They're so big, some of them, they have to have these supports. To help hold them up, so to speak. These supports are called buttresses. They remind me of viaducts for some reason. But maybe you don't know viaducts, either? Sometimes the cathedrals have devils and such carved into the front. Sometimes great lords and ladies. Don't ask me why this is," I said. He was nodding. The whole upper part of his body seemed to be moving back and forth. "I'm not doing so good, am I?" I said.

He stopped nodding and leaned forward on the edge of the sofa. As he listened to me, he was running his fingers through his beard. I wasn't getting through to him though, I could see that. But he waited for me to go on just the same. He nodded, as if trying to encourage me. I tried to think what else I could say. "They're really big. They're massive. They're built of stone. Marble, too, sometimes. In those old days, when they built cathedrals, men aspired to be close to God. In those days God was an important part of everyone's life. This was reflected in their cathedral-building. I'm sorry," I said, "but it looks like that's the best I can do for you. I'm just no good at it."

"That's all right, bub," he said. "Hey, listen. I hope you don't mind my asking you. Can I ask you something? Let me ask you a simple question, yes or no. I'm just curious and there's no offense. You're my host. But let me ask if you are in any way religious? You don't mind my asking?"

I shook my head. He couldn't see that, though. A wink is the same as a nod to a blind man. "I guess I'm agnostic or something. No, the fact is, I don't believe in it. Anything. Sometimes it's hard. You know what I'm saying?"

"Sure, I do," he said.

"Right," I said.

The Englishman was still holding forth. My wife sighed in her sleep. She drew a long breath and continued with her sleep.

"You'll have to forgive me," I said. "But I can't tell you what a cathedral looks like. It just isn't in me to do it. I can't do any more than I've done." The blind man sat very still, his head down, as he listened to me. "The truth is, cathedrals don't mean anything special to me. Nothing. Cathedrals. They're something to look at on late-night TV. That's all they are."

It was then he cleared his throat. He brought something up. He took a handkerchief from his back pocket. In a minute he said, "I get it, bub. It's okay. It happens. Don't worry about it," he said. "Hey, listen to me. Will you do me a favor? I got an idea. Why don't you find us some heavy paper? And a pen. We'll do something. An experiment. Sure, you can do it. You can. We'll draw one together. Get us a pen and some heavy paper. Go on, bub, get the stuff," he said.

So I went upstairs. My legs felt like they didn't have any strength in them. They felt like they did sometimes after I'd run a couple miles. In my wife's room I looked around. I found some ballpoints in a little basket on her table. And then I tried to think where to look for the kind of paper he was talking about.

Downstairs, in the kitchen, I found a shopping bag with onion skins in the bottom of the bag. I emptied the bag and shook it. I brought it into the living room and sat down with it near his legs. I moved some things, smoothed the wrinkles from the bag, spread it out on the coffee table. The blind man got down from the sofa and sat next to me on the carpet.

He ran his fingers over the paper. He went up and down the sides of the paper and the edges, top and bottom. He fingered the corners. "All right," he said. "All right. Let's do her."

He found my hand, the hand with the pen. He closed his hand over my hand. "Go ahead, bub, draw," he said. "Draw. You'll see. I'll follow along with you. It'll be all right. Just begin now, like I'm telling you. You'll see. Draw," he said.

So I began. First I drew a box that resembled a house. It could have been the house I lived in. Then I put a roof on the house. At either end of the roof I drew spires. Crazy.

"Swell," he said. "Terrific. You're doing fine," he said. "Never thought anything like this could happen in your lifetime, did you? Well, it's a strange life, bub, we all know that. Go on now. Keep it up."

I put in windows with arches. I drew flying buttresses. I hung great doors. I couldn't stop. The TV station went off the air. I put down the pen and closed and opened my fingers. The blind man felt around over the paper. He moved the tips of his fingers slowly over the paper, over what I'd drawn, and he nodded. "Doing fine," he said.

I took up the pen, and he found my hand once more. I kept at it. I'm
no artist. But I kept drawing just the same.
   My wife opened her eyes and gazed at us. She sat up on the sofa, her
robe hanging open. She said, "What in the world are you doing?"
   I didn't answer her. The blind man said, "We're drawing a cathedral,
dear. Me and him are working on something important. Press hard
now," he said to me. "That's right. That's good," he said. "Sure. You got
it, bub. I can tell. You didn't think you could. But you can, can't you?
You're cooking with Crisco now. You'll see. Know what I'm saying?
We're going to have us something here in a minute. How's the old arm?
Put some people in there now. What's a church without people, bub?"
   "What's going on?" my wife said. "Robert, what are you doing? What's
going on?"
   "It's all right," he said to her. "Close your eyes now, bub," he said.
   I did that. I closed them just like he said.
   "Are they closed?" he said. "Don't fudge."
   "They're closed," I said.
   "Keep them that way," he said. He said, "Don't stop now." So we kept
on with it. His fingers rode my fingers as my hand went over the rough
paper. It was like nothing else in my life up to now.
   In a minute he said, "I think that's enough. I think you got the idea,"
he said. "Take a look. What do you think?"
   But I had my eyes closed. I thought I'd keep them closed a little
longer. I thought it was something I ought not to forget.
   "Well?" he said. "Are you looking?"
   My eyes were still closed. I was in my house and I knew that. But I
didn't feel inside anything.
   "It's really something," I said.

1982
THE WELLFLEET WHALE
by Stanley Kunitz

1. You have your language too,
       an eerie medley of clicks
       and hoots and trills,
    location-notes and love calls,
       whistles and grunts. Occasionally,
       it's like furniture being smashed,
    or the creaking of a mossy door,
       sounds that all melt into a liquid
       song with endless variations,

as if to compensate
for the vast loneliness of the sea,
Sometimes a disembodied voice
breaks in, as if from distant reefs,
and it's as much as one can bear
to listen to its long mournful cry,
a sorrow without name, both more
and less than human. It drags
across the ear like a record
running down.

2. No wind. No waves. No clouds.
Only the whisper of the tide,
as it withdrew, stroking the shore,
a lazy drift of gulls overhead,
and tiny points of light
bubbling in the channel.
It was the tag-end of summer.
From the harbor's mouth
you coasted into sight,
flashing news of your advent,
the crescent of your dorsal fin
clipping the diamonded surface.
We cheered at the sign of your greatness
when the black barrel of your head
erupted, ramming the water,
and you flowered for us
in the jet of your spouting.

3. All afternoon you swam
tirelessly round the bay,
with such an easy motion,
the slightest downbeat of your tail,
an almost imperceptible
undulation of your flippers,
you seemed like something poured,
not driven; you seemed
to marry grace with power.
And when you bounded into air,
slapping your flukes,
we thrilled to look upon
pure energy incarnate
as nobility of form.
You seemed to ask of us
not sympathy, or love,

or understanding,
but awe and wonder.

That night we watched you
swimming in the moon.
Your back was molten silver.
We guessed your silent passage
by the phosphorescence in your wake.
At dawn we found you stranded on the rocks.

4. There came a boy and a man
and yet other men running, and two
schoolgirls in yellow halters
and a housewife bedecked
with curlers, and whole families in beach
buggies with assorted yelping dogs.
The tide was almost out.
We could walk around you,
as you heaved deeper into the shoal,
crushed by your own weight,
collapsing into yourself,
your flippers and your flukes
quivering, your blowhole
spasmodically bubbling, roaring.
In the pit of your gaping mouth
you bared your fringework of baleen,
a thicket of horned bristles.
When the Curator of Mammals
arrived from Boston
to take samples of your blood
you were already oozing from below.
Somebody had carved his initials
in your flank. Hunters of souvenirs
had peeled off strips of your skin,
a membrane thin as paper.
You were blistered and cracked by the sun.
The gulls had been pecking at you.
The sound you made was a hoarse and fitful bleating.

What drew us to the magnet of your dying?
You made a bond between us,
the keepers of the nightfall watch,
who gathered in a ring around you,
boozing in the bonfire light.
Toward dawn we shared with you

your hour of desolation,
    the huge lingering passion
      of your unearthly outcry,
as you swung your blind head
    toward us and laboriously opened
      a bloodshot, glistening eye,
in which we swam with terror and recognition.

5.   Voyager, chief of the pelagic world,
    you brought with you the myth
      of another country, dimly remembered,
where flying reptiles
    lumbered over the steaming marshes
      and trumpeting thunder lizards
wallowed in the reeds.
    While empires rose and fell on land,
      your nation breasted the open main,
rocked in the consoling rhythm
    of the tides. Which ancestor first plunged
      head-down through zones of colored twilight
to scour the bottom of the dark?
    You ranged the North Atlantic track
      from Port-of-Spain to Baffin Bay,
edging between the ice-floes
    through the fat of summer,
      lob-tailing, breaching, sounding,
grazing in the pastures of the sea
    on krill-rich orange plankton
      crackling with life.
You prowled down the continental shelf,
    guided by the sun and stars
      and the taste of alluvial silt
on your way southward
    to the warm lagoons,
      the tropic of desire,
where the lovers lie belly to belly
    in the rub and nuzzle of their sporting;
      and you turned, like a god in exile,
out of your wide primeval element,
    delivered to the mercy of time.
    Master of the whale-roads,
let the white wings of the gulls
    spread out their cover.
    You have become like us,
disgraced and mortal.

MAGIC
The Gathering®

WALK THE BLIND ETERNITIES

They are the heroes of the Multiverse. United by their ability to bridge the chaotic gap between worlds, and set apart by that same unfathomable power, planeswalkers wander the Blind Eternities in an endless quest for knowledge and power.

TEST OF METAL
Matthew Stover

Tezzeret rises from the ashes of defeat, seeking that secret source of power he needs to reinvent himself.

OCTOBER 2010

Be there as destiny unfolds.

ALSO AVAILABLE AS E-BOOKS!

MAGIC
The Gathering®

Walk the Blind Eternities...

Discover the Planeswalkers in their travels across
the endless planes of the Multiverse...

AGENTS OF ARTIFICE
BY ARI MARMELL

Jace Beleren, a powerful sorcerer and Planeswalker whose rare
telepathic ability opens doors that many would prefer remain
closed, is at a crossroads: the decisions he makes now will forever
affect his path.

TEST OF METAL
BY MATTHEW STOVER

From the ashes of defeat, Tezzeret rises again. Beaten to within
an inch of his life and left for dead by the psychic sorcerer Jace
Beleren, Tezzeret is revived by the ancient dragon Planeswalker,
Nicol Bolas, who has plans for the embattled artificer: Find
Crucius the Mad Sphinx, and with him the secret of etherium.

ALARA UNBROKEN
BY DOUG BEYER

The fierce leonine Planeswalker Ajani Goldmane unwittingly
uncovers the nefarious agency behind the splintered planes of
Alara and their realignment. Meanwhile, fellow Planeswalker
Elspeth Tirel struggles to preserve the nobility of the first plane
she has ever wanted to call home. And the dragon shaman
Sarkhan Vol finds the embodiment of power he has always sought.

ZENDIKAR: IN THE TEETH OF AKOUM
BY ROBERT B. WINTERMUTE

Zendikar is a land of danger and adventure, a world of deadly
perils and priceless treasures. It is also a prison to one of the
most deadly threats the Multiverse has ever known: the dreaded
Eldrazi. When the Eldrazi escape their arcane prison, it falls to
Nissa Revane, a proud elf warrior and native of Zendikar, and a
mysterious Planeswalker named Sorin Markov to re-imprison the
titans of the æther before the plane is lost.

MAGIC
The Gathering

A PLANESWALKER NOVEL

THE PURIFYING FIRE
laura resnick

The Purifying Fire
©2010 Wizards of the Coast LLC

Published by Wizards of the Coast LLC

MAGIC: THE GATHERING, WIZARDS OF THE COAST, their respective logos and PLANESWALKER are trademarks of Wizards of the Coast LLC in the U.S.A. and other countries.

Printed in the U.S.A.

Cover art by Michael Komarck

First Printing: May 2010

9 8 7 6 5 4 3 2 1

ISBN: 978-0-7869-5559-6
620-21050000-001-EN

U.S., CANADA, ASIA, PACIFIC, & LATIN AMERICA	EUROPEAN HEADQUARTERS
Wizards of the Coast LLC	Hasbro UK Ltd
P.O. Box 707	Caswell Way
Renton, WA 98057-0707	Newport, Gwent NP9 0YH
+1-800-324-6496	GREAT BRITAIN
	Save this address for your records.

Visit our web site at www.wizards.com

THE PURIFYING FIRE

CHAPTER ONE

Is that the scroll the monks are talking about?" Brannon asked.

"Yes, it is." Chandra Nalaar smiled at the ginger-headed boy as she held out the scroll, neatly rolled up and encased in an ancient leather sheath. "The brothers are done with their work, so I thought I'd take a look at it, see what all the excitement is about."

"I heard it has strange writing that only a few of the monks can read," the boy said.

"That's right," Chandra said, sitting next to Brannon. "I can't read it, but the monks will tell me what is says."

The two of them were in a common room at Keral Keep, a place of learning and study for the fire mages of Regatha.

Brannon asked, "Where did you get the scroll?"

"Far away." Chandra was used to dodging questions about her travels throughout the Multiverse. It was easier for most people to accept lies than to understand what it meant to move back and forth among the infinite planes of reality. "Do you want to look at it with me?"

She had looked at the scroll before, but that was on a plane called Kephalai where she had

"liberated" it from the Sanctum of the Stars. Once back on Regatha, she had handed the scroll over to the monks at Keral Keep.

The scroll was said to be unique, the only record of a fire spell more powerful than any known. Its origin was utterly mysterious, and it had been fiercely protected on Kephalai. Chandra might not be able to interpret its meaning on her own, but she was curious enough to want another look.

The monks in the monastery's scriptorium were very interested in the scroll, enough that young Brannon was curious about it too.

"Yes," he said eagerly, "let's look at it. Unroll it!"

"All right. But remember," she cautioned. "It's very old and fragile, so—"

"Uh, Chandra?"

"—we have to be careful not to—"

"*Chandra*." Brannon was looking past her, his eyes wide with alarm.

She turned to look at whatever had captured his attention and shot to her feet when she saw a tall, menacing stranger standing at one end of the room.

"Chandra Nalaar, give me that scroll!" he said, his tone as much a demand as the words.

How does he know my name?

"Brannon, get out of here!" she said. "*Now*."

"But—"

"*Go!*"

Recognizing her tone, the boy turned and ran, seeking the safety of the stone halls of the monastery and the presence of others.

"Give me the scroll," said the stranger, "and no one gets hurt."

Chandra's attention was immediately drawn to the cold, cerulean intensity of his eyes, glowing in the shadow of his cowled cloak. She could sense his intrusion into her thoughts. *A telepath.*

Chandra had only just returned to this plane, and her comings and goings at the monastery passed without fanfare. No one on Regatha knew about the scroll unless one of the monks had renounced his vows and become loose-lipped. This stranger, she realized with a hot flood of surprise, must have come from Kephalai.

"You're a Planeswalker," she breathed.

"I'm not going to ask again," he warned her. "And you won't live long enough to be sorry you resisted."

If he had followed her æther trail through the Blind Eternities, he must be very skilled. A trick like that wasn't for beginners.

But he had picked the wrong person to follow.

"I see there's only one of you," she said, feeling her blood heat for combat.

"One is all it will take," he replied.

With hair-trigger speed, Chandra's fists lit up like torches as she thrust them toward the stranger, hurling a pair of fireballs like meteors.

But the mage was ready. As if he knew what she would do even before she did it, he met the fireballs with an ice-blue liquid mass that issued from his outstretched arms.

The counter attack was followed by a surge of power that flowed forth and encircled Chandra, glowing with the same cerulean intensity of his eyes. With Chandra momentarily paralyzed, the mind mage started mapping her consciousness, looking for the lynchpin he could use to disable her.

Chandra loathed mind mages. What could be more despicable than poking around in another person's private thoughts and feelings? The violation, along with the stranglehold of the spell, kindled her rage like phosphorous.

By now, conscious thought was no longer an option for Chandra. The world around her slowed to a geological pace, and she could feel the power of the mountain inside her. Immovable, dominating, volcanic in its fury, it grew from that darkest part of herself, that diamond of rage deep in her core until . . .

Boom.

An incomparable concussive blast left Chandra at ground zero, leveling everything around her and blasting a hole in the wall where the mind mage had been.

An eerie quiet pervaded the room. Sparks flickered and died in the dead air. "Didn't mean to blow my top like that," she muttered to no one in particular, as she surveyed the damage.

Chandra was sure he wasn't dead, though. She knew it wouldn't be that easy to kill an experienced Planeswalker.

"Chandra!" Brannon cried from beyond the hole in the outer wall.

"Brannon! What are you doing out there?" she shouted. "Get inside the monastery. *Now!*"

Instead of listening to her, the boy turned and ran again. What is the matter with him, she wondered.

Not daring to leave it behind, Chandra took the scroll and went after him. She couldn't leave it unprotected with a mind mage running around.

As she stepped through the hole, she saw the stranger standing on a rocky ledge that overlooked

her position, holding the small ginger-haired boy by the throat. Just like a kid to get in middle of things, she thought.

Brannon struggled to breathe, his feet dangling just above the ground.

"No!" Chandra's stomach knotted with fear at the sight of her young friend in the Planeswalker's powerful grip.

"Don't make me kill the child," the stranger said.

Brannon kicked and gasped in pain even as he tried to speak. "Let me g . . . *aaagh* . . ." The phrase trailed off in a choked gurgle. Tears of pain and fear rolled down his reddened cheeks.

Chandra hated to lose. She absolutely *hated* it!

But she knew the scroll in her hand, however unique, wasn't worth Brannon's life. She held it up as an offering and called, "Don't hurt him! You can have the scroll."

Chandra heard how hoarse with dread her voice sounded. She watched the mind mage give Brannon a sharp shake, to make him stop squirming.

"That's all I came for," the Planeswalker said. "As long as I get it right now, he's fine."

He looked cold, but not cruel. She believed that capturing Brannon was business, not pleasure.

So she tossed the scroll up to him.

It landed a few feet in front of him. "A wise decision. My impression is that you don't make many."

But before he could turn the boy over, Chandra heard her name called from the monastery. She turned to see Brannon looking out from the hole she had blasted in the wall.

"Chandra! What's happening?" he shouted from a distance.

An illusion!

"All right, mindbender . . . You want to play?"

With a quickness to match her temper, Chandra leaped into the air, an aura of flame surrounding her as she recited a spell. Spreading her arms and expanding her chest like a bellows, all the air in a thirty foot radius went dead as she sapped the oxygen she needed as fuel for her fire. She paused at the top of her breath until it felt like she would explode with the effort, and when she let go, explode she nearly did. With all her might she exhaled, eyes wide, tongue extended like some primal totem. Her breath had the force of a cannon and burned with chemical intensity.

The stranger balled up, shielding his body with his cloak. The force of the blast unsteadied him, but he obviously had been able to conjure some protection. He emerged merely singed when everything around him had been reduced to charcoal. The scroll had fallen from his grasp, but lay out of both their reaches.

"Nice trick," he mocked. "I bet you're a big hit with the boys."

Jokes? This guy has to go down, Chandra thought.

But he was just getting started. The mage's eyes glowed brightly, and his skin changed, newly streaked blue-grey. Chandra knew something was coming but she didn't know what. Still, she should have known this guy wouldn't fight his own fights. He summoned an massive cloud elemental that swooped down to knock Chandra off her feet before veering to where the scroll lay on the ground.

Two can play at that game, thought Chandra as she summoned her own fire elemental to meet the cloud. The two titans collided with a sharp hiss, flame and vapor locked in a mercurial embrace.

With the elementals occupied, the mind mage made a move to recover the scroll himself, but Chandra was on point as she raised a wall of fire between him and his quarry.

"You're going to have to work for it, mind-bender." Chandra was just starting to have fun.

Still, the stranger was undeterred. He ran down the wall to where he had last seen the scroll and stepped through the flame, an icy corona surrounding him. Chandra was waiting, though, her fist cocked, blazing hot. She hit him with a left cross that had the weight of the world behind it, and sent the mage flying backward, his body like a rag doll's as he tumbled over the rocks.

As the flames died down, Chandra surveyed the scene. She had done well. The elementals had died fighting and there was plenty of scorched earth, but she had done well.

"Chandra, that was amazing!"

She turned to see Brannon. "You shouldn't be out here, kiddo."

"What happened to him?"

"He took a nasty spill. He won't be back again."

"Are you sure?" he asked pointing in the direction of the mage. There were several cloaked figures, all exactly alike, moving in different directions.

"He's just trying to trick me. He doesn't want me to know which one is actually him," said Chandra pointing to the illusions. "Look, he's running away."

"I don't think so," said the boy in a strange voice. "I think he's going to get that scroll."

When she turned back, Chandra saw the familiar eerie blue glow in Brannon's eyes and she

knew . . . But right in that moment of realization, the mage hit her with a mental attack that caught her completely off-guard. She crumpled as her vision faded to black.

✶ ✶ ✶ ✶ ✶

"Chandra, are you all right?" The real Brannon reached her side and started helping her rise from the ground. "What happened? I saw your fire elemental. Wow, I've never seen anything that big! Not even Mother Luti can make 'em that big." The boy was nearly ecstatic. "And then there was a sort of . . . a blue wave of light or something. What *was* that?"

"That was the stranger," Chandra said grumpily. "Being . . . *clever*."

"The scroll!" Brannon said, seeing that her hands were empty. "Where's the scroll?"

"What are you talking about, Brannon?"

"He got it. He must have taken it!"

"The scroll?"

"I know you said the monks finished their work. But don't we need it any more?" he asked.

"What do you mean?"

"Did they copy it in their workshop? Is that what you said?"

"Kiddo, this is crazy talk. Everything is all right. He's not coming back," she assured him.

"Well I hope so, 'cause he was creepy." Brannon asked, eyeing their surroundings a little anxiously.

"Yes," she said. "But he's gone."

Chandra tried to clear her head. Something was missing. Why did that fight just happen? Who was that guy?

But the more she tried to think about it, the more it hurt. What is that kid talking about with the scroll?

CHAPTER TWO

Chandra was mad. And when she got mad, she liked to set things on fire.

Call it her little weakness.

She felt heat racing through her, turning her blood into curling flames of power that sparked out through her fingertips, her eyes, and the auburn tendrils of her long hair.

"You're saying you copied down the scroll *wrong*?" she demanded of Brother Sergil. "After all the trouble I went through to steal it? After how important I told you it was? You're saying that you and the other brothers made a mess of *your* part of the job? After I nearly got killed doing *my* part right?"

Brother Sergil, who evidently didn't feel deeply attached to his mortal existence, snapped, "Perhaps if you hadn't let someone steal the scroll *back* so soon after you brought it here, we wouldn't have a problem now!"

"Oh, *really*?" Chandra could feel her skin glowing with the power that her anger unleashed. True, she had lost the scroll, but that mage had been good. "And if anyone had bothered to *help* me fight off that mage, maybe the scroll would still be at the monastery, instead of who-knows-where?" Her memory of the scroll had not come

back. The mind mage had been thorough in cleansing it from her mind. She remembered everything she had done retrieving it, everything about the fight . . . But he had cut the scroll out with artisanal precision.

"All right, that's enough," said Luti, the mother mage of Keral Keep. "From *both* of you."

Chandra said, "What's the point of my bringing you something so valuable if you can't even—"

"*Stop*," said Luti.

"We've done our part as well as anyone could expect!" Brother Sergil said. "All I'm saying is—"

"Not as well as *I* expected! How did you—" Chandra stepped back with a sharp intake of breath as a small fireball exploded between her and Brother Sergil. The monk staggered backward, too, stumbling on the rough red stones that paved the monastery courtyard.

They both looked at Mother Luti in surprised silence.

"That's better," Luti said, her fingers glowing with the lingering effect of forming and throwing that fiery projectile between them. Her glance flickered over Chandra. "Quench your hair, young woman."

"What? Oh." Chandra became aware of the haze of fiery heat and pulsating flames surrounding her head. It wasn't a roaring blaze, but it was certainly a loss of control. She took a calming breath and brushed her palms over her hair, smoothing the dancing flames back into her auburn mane until Luti's nod indicated they had disappeared altogether.

"Until you can master your power better," Luti said, "it would be a good idea to learn to manage your temper."

Chandra let the comment pass without protest. She didn't like orders or reprimands, but she had come to the Keralian Monastery to *learn* to master her power, after all. And she had once again just demonstrated how little control over it she had.

"You have an extraordinary gift," Luti said. "Tremendous power. But as it is with our passions, it is with the fire you wield; they are good servants, but bad masters."

"It would help," Chandra said, glaring at Brother Sergil, "if people wouldn't—"

"Nothing will help," Luti said. "Certainly not other people. Only *you* can change the way your power manifests. Only within yourself can you find a way to master it in a reality which will, after all, always contain annoyances, distractions, fears, and sorrows."

"Right." Hoping to avoid another of Luti's lectures on the nature of life, Chandra hastened to change the subject. "Now what about the scroll?"

⁂ ⁂ ⁂ ⁂ ⁂

The pyromancers, scholars, and initiates at Keral Keep had no idea where the scroll had come from. And neither did Mother Luti, for that matter, but she alone did know where Chandra got it. Luti ran the haven for pyromancers and firemages, who came to study and practice in the monastery on Mount Kerlia, a potent source of power. She knew a lot.

There was wisdom to be learned from her, to be sure, but the great stone walls of the fortress that crowned the summit of Mount Keralia pulsed with mana as red as the rock it was built upon. This was why mages came from all over Regatha.

The most skilled fire mages on the entire plane dwelled within the stony halls of the monastery,

but none of them, including Luti, were as powerful as Chandra.

Perhaps Luti would have suspected the truth about Chandra even if she hadn't been told: Chandra was a Planeswalker.

Luti was well-versed in the legend of Jaya Ballard, the bombastic fire mage whose long-ago sojourn on Regatha had inspired the founding of this monastery. Jaya was a Planeswalker, too. And Planeswalkers were . . . different.

When she witnessed, first-hand, the magnitude of Chandra's power, Luti could only think of the celebrated pyromancy of Jaya Ballard, stories she assumed had grown like mushroom clouds with the passage of time. In any case, Chandra chose to privately reveal her nature to Luti soon after coming to Regatha, after deciding it wouldn't make sense to seek instruction in controlling her power while concealing what she could do.

It was a choice, Luti later told her, that demonstrated Chandra was capable of reasoned decisions when she applied herself.

Luti kept Chandra's secret mostly out of a desire that fire remain the most tangible of the visible mysteries on Regatha. She feared the acolytes at Keral Keep would look for answers in Chandra, rather than find their own path. To everyone else at the monastery, Chandra was simply an unusually powerful young mage who came from somewhere else. And since Chandra, like so many others, didn't want to talk about her past, no one pried.

Apart from Luti, none of the Keralians knew that Chandra had traveled the Blind Eternities, bridging that chaotic interval between the planes of the Multiverse, to steal that scroll on Kephalai,

a world they'd never heard of and could never visit themselves.

Chandra had heard of the scroll in her travels, and she was intrigued by its reputation. So, after some time studying and practicing at the Keep had improved her erratic control of pyromancy, Chandra decided to find and steal the scroll, which turned out to be a little better guarded than she had anticipated. That was a wild ride, to be sure. Still, she made it out with the scroll.

Since the scroll was fragile, the brothers' first act had been to make a few working copies of it. They had laboriously replicated the ancient writing by hand on fresh parchment.

Consdiering what had happened next, it was lucky they had done so. If she ever saw that mage again, she told herself, she would be ready. He would not trick her again.

Meanwhile, she knew from Luti's expression that she had better remain silent while Brother Sergil explained the problem the monks were having with their copies of the scroll.

"The script is archaic, a variant we have not seen before, so it's taken us some time to interpret its meaning. We are *sure*, though," Sergil said, with a dark glance at Chandra, "that we copied it correctly. The value of multiple brothers each making a copy means, of course, that we can compare all our results from the process and arrive at a consensus on the exact contents of the original. Right down to the tiniest brushstroke."

"Uh-huh." Chandra folded her arms and didn't attempt to conceal her boredom.

Mother Luti, who was a full head shorter than Chandra and triple her age, gave her a quelling look.

"The language of the scroll is a variant that our scholars haven't encountered, so our conclusions aren't as firm as one might wish. But it seems to be describing something of immense power, much as Chandra believed." Brother Sergil made the grudging concession to her with a little nod.

"An artifact? A spell? What?" Chandra was surprised.

"It could be either . . . or something else entirely."

"I could have told you that," said Chandra exasperated.

"You mean you could have told us that had you a memory—"

Mother Luti raised a hand to stop Brother Segril from going further, her head tilted in a gesture of contemplation. Her white hair shone brightly in the sunlight of the monastery courtyard where the three of them stood. "What kind of power?" she asked when she had their attention.

"The scroll describes either an extraordinary source of mana, or it's the key to accessing mana with extraordinary results. Either way, according to the scroll, it is something that will confer enormous power upon whomever unleashes it." He shrugged. "It's not clear to us if the text of the scroll declares this as a promise or as a warning. The intention of the author, like the its origin, is a mystery, Mother."

"And does the text strike you as fact or as fancy?" Luti asked.

"Well . . ." He cast a glance at Chandra. "That might be easier to answer if we still had the original."

Chandra scowled. "If you're blaming *me* because—"

"No, I just mean," the monk interrupted, "that the text seems to be saying the scroll itself contains the key to unlocking the mystery."

"But the location isn't in the text you've got?" Luti asked.

"No."

"And you copied the entire scroll?"

"Yes."

"So you're saying that part of the scroll was missing?" Chandra guessed.

"I don't think so," Brother Sergil said. "We're still discussing it . . . but the text seems to be complete. And, physically, the scroll itself was certainly complete. It was fragile, but it wasn't torn, or singed, or moth-eaten."

"So what *are* you saying?" Chandra asked.

"The purported location of this powerful artifact seems to be concealed in an internal puzzle," the monk said. "The answer *may* be in the text itself, it could be obfuscated by layers of magic, but . . ." He trailed off, clearly reluctant to continue.

"But?" Luti prodded.

"We've tried multiple ways of interpreting the text, various ways of scrambling the words and the letters, and numerous methods of translating the characters into numbers, various decryption spells . . ." He shook his head. "But so far, we only get gibberish. Of course, we'll keep trying, because if whatever this is does exist—if the text has any basis in fact—then this is very important information. Whoever possesses the power it speaks of could rule worlds. However . . . well, it's really starting to look as if, when the text says the key to under-standing is contained in the scroll itself . . ."

"You think it means the *physical* scroll?" Luti said. "The original?"

"Perhaps, yes. We are increasingly drawn to that possibility," Brother Sergil said.

"Oh, that *is* disappointing," Luti said.

Chandra said, "Look, I did everything I could to stop the scroll from being tak—"

"I didn't mean it that way, Chandra," Luti said. "We wouldn't even have known about the scroll, if not for you, and we'd certainly never have seen it or had a chance to study it. Believe me, I'm well aware of how hard you fought to keep it from the, er, intruder. Indeed, the vegetable garden on the southern side of the monastery may never recover from your struggle with him. Well, not this year, anyhow." She shrugged. "I just mean that it's frustrating to discover something so intriguing . . . and now face the possibility of never solving the puzzle.

"Since the stranger who took the scroll from us did not have the courtesy to identify himself," Luti said to Sergil, "we'll probably never know who sent him. If, indeed, anyone did send him. He may have been a free agent acting on his own behalf, after all."

"But we might be able to better estimate the veracity of the text if we knew more about its origins," said Sergil. "That is to say, where Chandra found it."

"Where she found it and where it comes from may be completely different things, Brother. That's a subject best left alone," Luti said, "for the sake of everyone's safety. We have all witnessed first hand the destruction that so closely followed the scroll's arrival," Luti paused, letting her words sink in. "We must make do with what we have. Please continue

studying the text. The answer to the puzzle may well be in our possession and just temporarily eluding us."

Looking dissatisfied, but clearly not prepared to fight about it with Luti, Brother Sergil bowed his head. "Yes, Mother."

After he had left the sunny courtyard, Luti turned to Chandra. "Well?"

Chandra shrugged. "If you're wondering whether I noticed anything unusual about the scroll when it was in my possession, I can't really answer that. And I swear by everything that burns, if I ever see that bastard again, I'll blow him so high into the sky, his ashes won't fall back down until people have forgotten he was ever born."

Luti didn't smile at her pledge. "Guard yourself, Chandra. The fire you kindle for your enemy may burn you more than him."

"Is that Jaya?"

"No, it is Luti. Listen, the Multiverse is a very big place," Luti said. "It is probable that you will never run into that mage again. It is better to think about what you can control . . ."

Chandra's attention waned as Luti went on. She was grateful for her wisdom, but she could be tedious at times.

"In a battle with another Planeswalker, it's said that Jaya cunningly defeated her opponent by—"

"That stinking rat made me believe he was going to kill Brannon," Chandra said.

Luti broke off. She knew Chandra had not been listening at all, but she had hoped to penetrate the Planeswalker's obvious disinterest. "As soon to kindle a fire with snow as to quench the fire of rage with words," she said, more to herself that to Chandra.

"What does that have to do with Brannon or what I said?" asked Chandra, unable to see the relevance of Luti's words.

Brannon lived at the monastery. His parents, ordinary peasant folk, had sent him here upon realizing they were increasingly unable to cope with the fiery power he had been exercising since early childhood. Because he needed instruction and supervision from people who understood his gift, his family had consigned him to the Keralians' care several years ago.

Chandra had also been a powerful child with parents who'd felt ill-equipped to deal with her explosive gifts. She felt some kinship with the boy and had become fond of him during her sojourn here.

It had been a terrible shock to see him in the clutches of the other Planeswalker. And it had been a relief as much as it was an infuriating surprise to discover that it was merely an illusion.

Chandra was disgusted by the subterfuge of that Planeswalker's ploys. She understood how his tactics were ultimately successful, but she didn't have to respect them. Chandra was used to dealing with conflict openly.

"Anyway, as many times as I replay the fight in my head, I don't even know if that jackass also managed to erase any other memories. If I had seen or felt anything special about the scroll, I have no memory of it now." She shrugged. "I don't even know what to think about what Brother Sergil said. I wish I remembered the scroll at all."

"I take it, then, that you don't even remember where you heard about the scroll? That you have no idea what you thought you were going after in the first place?"

"No." Chandra asked. "What do you think?"

"I believe what Brother Sergil told us. I believe that it tells of a great power, and I believe that it is old. And despite its supposed age, I'm also inclined to believe that the scroll, if it we are able to interpret it, could lead to the whatever it is."

"You really think something like this exists? That it can be found?" Chandra asked eagerly.

"Oh, yes. After all, if the text is just some ancient scribe's fancy, or if the power it speaks of has long since been seized or destroyed . . ." Luti shrugged. "Then why would the scroll be kept in a place as secure and heavily guarded as you described when you returned? What was it called again? The Sanctum of Stars?"

"Yes."

"Full of extremely valuable objects?"

"It sure looked that way to me." Chandra was not a thief by trade, however, so the valuation of objects was hardly familiar to her, particularly in the rush of stealing the scroll.

"It sounds as if they were quite prepared to kill to retrieve the scroll—and, indeed, to tear their own realm apart to find it . . . Well, their behavior certainly confirms that the scroll is important." Luti paused. "And whether the previous owners of the scroll employed that Planeswalker to come after it, or whether he followed you and retrieved it for his own reasons . . ."

Chandra said, "I see your point."

"Sometimes thinking things through logically is beneficial." Luti's voice was dry.

"Yes, Mother."

⁂ ⁂ ⁂ ⁂ ⁂

That night, Chandra dreamed of fire.

Not the fire that exploded from her in the battle

with the mind mage. And not the intoxicating heat she drew from the red stones of Mount Keralia.

The fire in her dreams tonight wasn't the flickering seduction of a new spell. It wasn't the spine-tingling flame of her growing skill that lapped at the edges of her mind tonight. And it certainly wasn't the heart-pounding art of boom she loved so much, with its showers of fire and light.

This was the fire of sorrow and grief, the fire of shame and regret. This was the fire that consumed the innocent.

In her sleep, she could hear their screams, as clearly as if it were happening all over again. She could see their writhing bodies. She whimpered as the stench of burning flesh assailed her nostrils. Her throat burned with sobs that wouldn't come out. She tried to move, but her limbs were immobile. She wanted to scream, but her lips moved without sound.

And when the blade of a sword swept down to her throat, she awoke with a gurgled scream of horror and shot upright, gasping.

She was trapped in smothering darkness. She instinctively threw up her right hand and called forth flame, to ward off danger and illuminate her surroundings.

Squinting against the sudden light of her fire magic, Chandra looked around in confusion.

Then she realized where she was; her bed chamber in Keral Keep. Her heart was pounding. Her skin was slick with sweat. She was shaking. For a moment, she thought she would vomit. Her teeth chattered a little as she focused on breathing.

In, two, three. Out, two, three. In, two, three. Out . . .

She shook her hand to douse the flames before she wrapped her arms around her knees.

She swallowed. She would not cry. She would not think.

She would not remember.

As she rocked back and forth, trying to calm herself, she started reciting her favorite passages from the Regathan sagas, at first just in her mind, the words flowing through her brain in a rapid tumble.

Then, as she regained some control of herself, she started saying them aloud, and after a while, it worked, as it usually did. Her heart slowed to a normal rhythm. Her hands stopped shaking. Her teeth stopped chattering. Tears stopped threatening to fill her eyes.

But she wouldn't sleep again. Not tonight.

So she rose from her bed, removed her simple linen shift, and started donning her clothes as if the garments were armor against her dreams.

Chandra put on her leggings and her thigh-high boots. She pulled her calf-length tunic over her head. It was split from hip to hem to allow her free movement. Her clothes were reddish-brown, the material simple. They were the working garments of a woman with too much magical power and too much serious intent to waste time on fripperies and frills. But since it was nighttime and she wasn't going anywhere, she left off her gauntlets and the leather vest she usually wore. The armor she needed right now was mental, not physical.

Her bed chamber was small and simple, like everyone else's at the monastery. It had a narrow wooden bed with linen sheets and rough wool blankets, a small table, a single chair, and a modest trunk. And this was all she needed. People at the Keralian Monastery, whether they were visitors

or permanent residents, came here in search of wisdom, knowledge, and power, not the creature comforts of material wealth.

The mountain air was cool at night, even at this time of year when the days were especially warm. Chandra welcomed the slight chill on her skin as she stepped out of her chamber, into the night air, and closed the door behind her. She moved quietly along the walkway, passing other chambers without waking anyone, until she reached the broad terrace on the eastern side of the monastery.

The moon was full tonight and shone brightly. To the west of the monastery's mountain were more mountains, but from this terrace, she gazed across the woodlands that lay peacefully below the imposing heights of Mount Keralia. And further east, past the forests, were the plains and the city of Zinara. When the air was this clear and still at night, she could see the tiny specks of light in the distance that were the flaming torches atop the great city's watch towers.

"Sleep soundly, little lambs," she murmured contemptuously.

The city was completely dominated by the Order of Heliud, a sect of mages whose dedication to an ordered society and strict adherence to law was becoming dictatorial. The city was prosperous under the Order's influence, but the number of laws had tripled under their governance so that one was scarcely able walk down a street without breaking a rule or two. And when it came to magic, licenses to practice even the simplest of spells became necessary. Eventually, the Order became so bold as to outlaw many forms of magic, deeming anything other than their own brand of heiromancy—peacekeeping magic, as they liked

to say, that emphasized law and order—as delete-rious to the public health. It was even rumored that the practice of fire magic in Zinara would result in imprisonment, and any violent act involving fire magic was punishable by death.

Needless to say, these stories from the city did little to foster relations between Keral Keep and the Order of Heliud.

Chandra had been told that, during Mother Luti's lifetime, the Order had gone from being merely an influential sect in Zinara and a few other cities, to dominating the entire plains region of Regatha. Under the current rule of Walbert III and his policy of "civilization for civil welfare", it was even said their influence was spreading across the seas. But more to the point, the Order was aggressively seeking to "civilize" the moun-tain and woodland regions. It was clear to all that Walbert—dwelling in the massive, marble-pillared Temple of Heliud, the heart of the Order's temporal and mystical power—aspired to control the entire plane.

According to reports from Samir Mia Kauldi, a village chief of good standing among the many races of the Great Western Wood, Zinaran soldiers were patrolling the forests between Mount Keralia and the plains. Samir said that two human druids had recently been arrested for summoning creatures that the Order had recently declared "enemies of order." Creature summoning—especially for the ritual combat that settled disputes among tribes—was an accepted and eons-old practice for the woodlanders, but the Heliuds believed that the path to civilization was paved with law, and that the law was equal before all. There were inviolate truths, objective

standards of right and wrong, and it was for the Order of Heliud to see that all sapient beings on Regatha benefited from the application of such standards.

To Chandra, this was so unreasonable as to seem insane. How could a group of people be so blind as to not see the shades of grey between the black and white truths they held so sacred? Surely a more relative approach was needed to accommodate the breadth of racial and cultural diversity on this great plane. However, as Samir had morosely reported to Luti, it wasn't that easy to talk sense to well-armed soldiers on horseback.

Just let them try that nonsense up here, Chandra thought. She'd send them fleeing back to Zinara with their horses' tails on fire.

In any event, the soldiers who patrolled the Great Western Wood were lucky that Samir had not been among those arrested. It would be amusing, though, if the soldiers took an elf prisoner next time they were meddling where they didn't belong. Chandra imagined the storm that such a move would precipitate. The elves would never allow their way of life to be compromised by the Order.

Oh, yes, that would be worth seeing.

"Don't mess with elves," she muttered, gazing down at the darkened forest below Mount Keralia.

CHAPTER THREE

Ghost warden?" Chandra said. "What's a ghost warden?"

"Normally, it's a spirit from the land of the dead summoned to protect the living," said her host, Samir Mia Kauldi.

Brannon cried, "I've heard of ghost wardens! They've got flowing white hair, and white armor, and no real legs, just wispy trails of magic dust where their feet should be! They float around in silence, spying on their masters' enemies!"

Chandra looked to Samir for confirmation of this description as they walked through the forest, the dry twigs and leaves crackling under their feet.

He nodded. " 'Spying' might be an exaggeration. As I said, they normally serve to protect, but the Order uses them to monitor the forest."

"They have arms without hands, and white lightning bolts shoot out of the place where their fingers should be!" Brannon said.

"I'm told that it feels more like a sharp sting than a lightning bolt," Samir said. "It startles more than anything else."

Samir Mia Kauldi was one of Keral Keep's staunchest allies in the Great Western Wood. He was well-respected among his fellow elves

and shared Keralian values concerning personal freedom and the right to self determination, but, most importantly, he understood the consequences of the Order of Heliud's ever-increasing influence on the plane of Regatha. If the Heliuds were allowed to continue asserting their "civilization" agenda on the rest of Regatha, it would, sooner or later, mean an end to the elves' way of life. Their tribes would be broken up and individuals would be relocated to the camps where they would be "trained" as productive members of society. The forests, stripped of the protectors, would become resources for the cities, the trees a commodity to be managed by ministers. Samir had heard how some of the smaller forests in the distant east had been clear-cut and used for lumber, only to be replanted in neat rows so that their next harvest might be more efficient. The geometry of their placement, and the flat grid of roads laid down, cut the living spine of those groves and all but stopped the once-rich flow of mana. The elves who were able to flee the camps and cities returned to unrecognizable terrain, pine barrens, monocultures of ash or spruce. The Order had broken these forests into pieces and made sure they would not go back together.

Samir had told all of this to Mother Luti, but for years there had only been stories from far away. Now it was becoming a reality everywhere. But Luti, however her fighting spirit raged, was not getting any younger. Because the journey down the mountain to the forest below was physically demanding, she seldom made the trip herself anymore. She did insist on regular contact with the races of the woodlands that surrounded Mount Keralia, and often sent others in her place. They

had to keep the Order's power in check, especially since the mountains seemed to be next in line for the Order's civilizing practices.

It was true that the Keralian pyromancers and the races of the Great Western Wood led independent existences, but they all shared this desire to limit the Order's influence to the plains and the cities of Regatha. As Luti said, they must be taught that fire and forest, much like their government, knew nothing of mercy.

Alone among the woodlanders, Samir Mia Kauldi actively agreed with Luti about this. He realized that the ghost wardens and mounted patrols were only the beginning of what was to come, but many in the forest remained unconvinced and dismissed the Order's encroachment as border skirmishes. Most believed that the stories of entire forests razed and replanted in the east would be impossible in an area as vast as the Great Western Wood.

Samir was short for an elf, with smooth skin the color of freshly-turned soil. He had a lithe build, a soft voice, and a round face that looked older than his years, possibly because of the perpetually harassed look that he carried with him like a empty coin purse: that is to say, without enthusiasm. Although he was a respected tribal chief and skilled summoner, his exhortations against the Order were met with little acceptance by other inhabitants of the woodlands. That wasn't to say he did not have support. Samir was known far and wide to summon the greatest beasts of Regatha. His status as chief had remained unchallenged because of this, and no tribe would dare question his authority, but might did not necessarily make right among the woodlanders. Much as it was with

the Keralians, tribes—and the individuals who made them up—were given the right determine their own future, whether for good or bad, so long as it was not disruptive to the harmony of life in the forest.

Samir first came to the monastery as a supplicant. Since then the Keralians had been prepared to offer whatever assistance necessary. Chandra relished the opportunity to leave the monastery, so often volunteered to act as a liason to Samir and his loose association of druids, elves, and oufes.

It had been two days since her heated discussion with Brother Sergil about the scroll, and Chandra had decided to bring Brannon along as company on the long trek to Samir's small village deep in the woods.

The boy was clearly excited by the news that ghost wardens had been seen in the Great Western Wood.

"So what does a ghost warden do besides float around and sting people?" Chandra asked Samir.

"It only stings," Samir said, "if threatened."

"Whatever," Chandra said. "What good are they if they don't do anything?"

"The order uses them as spies," Samir said. "Rather than have them protect a living being, as was originally the intention of a ghost warden, they have them watch over the forest in general. The summoners share a psychic link with the warden and so are able to sense when things are out of the ordinary."

"Its summoners? You mean the Order of Heliud?"

"Yes. It is said that the summoner, once alerted by the ghost warden, will dispatch a patrol to the area in question."

"You're sure about these sightings?"

"*So* sure," Samir said, "that I have recently returned from Zinara, where I went to speak to Walbert himself. And I tell you Chandra, a more ridiculous place you will never find. They put plants in pots to decorate windows that look out on other windows with still more potted plants. They contrive *fountains*, which are absurd stone structures that trickle water in a meek imitation . . ."

"Wait, I know what a fountain is. The high priest of the Order agreed to see you?" Chandra asked in surprise. Walbert III wasn't reputed to be a very accessible man.

"Only after I spent two days insisting I would not leave the grounds of the Temple until I was granted an audience. It was a harder task than you can imagine sitting on flagstones amid those tortured trees. Can you believe they top the trees to stunt their growth? Imagine the arrogance that imposes Heliudic aesthetic values on nature. Even flowers are made to look like wounds on their hideously stripped stalks."

"So you confronted him?" Chandra said with relish.

"Yes. I demanded to know by what right the Order sent soldiers into our land to arrest us, and I said these ghost wardens must be withdrawn from the Great Western Wood."

"What did Walbert say?"

Samir made a disgusted sound. "It was infuriating, my friend. Walbert claimed that, in the interest of 'unity' throughout these lands, the laws which govern the cities and the plains are being extended to govern the woodlands, too. The ghost wardens have been summoned to patrol this vast woodland for our protection."

His tone twisted the final word into an epithet. "And the soldiers are only enforcing fair and just laws that have been passed in the interest of preserving safety and . . . *order*. As if they have any understanding of protection, let alone fairness and justice."

Chandra was appalled. "Walbert is claiming the Order has authority over the woodlands?"

Samir nodded. "And he's enforcing that claim with the might of his soldiers and the skill of the Temple mages."

"He can't do that!"

"I said that to him." Samir shook his head. "In response, he offered me some pompous title in exchange for encouraging my people to abide by the laws of the plains. That, or I could remain in violation of some law and he would jail me. I decided to retreat and fight another day."

"So he's trying to take over the Great Western Wood." Chandra said in outrage. "That's unbelievable!"

"He will find it a more difficult task than he supposes," Samir said darkly. "The other tribes have been reluctant to enter into conflict with the Order, but if they continue to arrest druids for summoning hunters, perhaps I can bring others to my side."

"What will they want next?" Chandra said with contempt. "Control over Keral Keep? Do they imagine that the rule of the Order can spread to the mountains?"

"That may not be beyond the scope of their ambitions," Samir warned her. "They see the monastery as a threat. They think the Keralians are destructive and their teachings dangerous."

"It wasn't enough for them to outlaw fire magic

in their own lands? They think they can outlaw it on Mount Keralia?" Chandra shook her head. "They'd have to be crazy to believe that."

"Why do they hate fire?" Brannon's red eyebrows creased in a frown on his young, freckled face. "I like it. And everyone needs it, after all."

"They hate it because fire takes no holiday, kiddo," Chandra said, but the boy only looked confused. Truth be told, Chandra was confused by the statement too, but she had heard Mother Luti say it so often that it seemed appropriate here.

"They don't hate fire, precisely," Samir said to the boy. "I'm not even sure they hate fire magic."

"Of course they do," Chandra said. "Why else would they punish pyromancy with *death* in Zinara?"

"They punish it with imprisonment," said Samir. "You only get executed if you commit violence with your fire magic."

"Whatever," she said. "Either way, they obviously do hate fire magic. Or more likely, they're *afraid* of it."

"I think what they don't like," said Samir, "is the nature of those who wield it. The Order of Heliud believes that no one is above the law. The law equalizes." He shrugged. "Isn't it true that you Keralians believe there is no law greater than the will of fire? You believe fire burns the criminal and the prosecutor equally, yes? The Heliuds believe that the righteous may pass through fire unscathed."

Chandra frowned. "What are you talking about?"

"I am talking about the Purifying Fire."

"The what?"

"The Purifying Fire." When Chandra and Brannon just stared at him blankly, he said,

"Oh. Of course. Neither of you has ever been to Zinara?" They shook their heads. "And probably few members of the monastery have been there, either. Or know much about the Order of Heliud."

"Mother Luti tells us that relations between the monastery and the city have been tense for years." said Chandra. She knew that the woodlanders had been on civil terms with the people of the plains and the city until Walbert's ambitions had become too evident to ignore any longer.

"Yes." Samir nodded. "Those who feel the lure of Mount Keralia have little in common with those for whom order and structure are paramount. It's a very . . . *different* sort of perspective."

"It certainly is," Chandra said with distaste. "So what does fire have to do with the Order of Heliud?"

"The Order's power is said to come from something called the Purifying Fire. No one I know has ever seen it, and it is said that only a very select few within the Order have access to it, but it is believed to be a source of pure mana that dances perpetually like a flame in the ancient caverns beneath the Temple. The legend says that Heliud was a holy figure in the city of Thold across the Great Sea. He was accused of heresy, crimes against Thold, or some such thing. Regardless, Heliud was exiled along with his followers who believed his promise of a founding a shining city was indeed guidance from the Divine Will. The journey across the sea was long—they lost many of their number to sickness, and when they made landfall many more were lost to the vagaries of the wild.

"When they finally arrived at the site where Zinara was founded, Heliud's followers were

beginning to doubt his plan, or even if he had one. He was facing opposition by one of his followers, a man named Zin who believed they could go no further. They should settle. Heliud was unfit to lead them. The promised land he spoke of was a fever dream. Zin had the support of the majority and Heliud, emaciated and weak from the journey, was facing exile again."

"You seem to know a lot about this, Samir," said Chandra. "You got some sympathies you aren't telling us about?" She grinned to take away the sting of the words.

"During the time I spent in protest on the grounds of the temple, an acolyte would come out and educate me on the history of Heliud. Anyway, to get to the point, Heliud returned to camp some days later. He had returned to peak physical form except that his once-lustrous black hair had gone as grey as the silver fox. When questioned about his transformation, Heliud said that he had found the physical manifestation of the Divine Will in a flickering white flame in some nearby caverns. He had thrown himself into it as penitence for failing to recognize the signs he'd been given, but rather than dying as expected, he emerged revived, stronger even than he had been before, proof of his righteousness. He claimed the fire had cleansed him of error and chosen him as the sole arbiter of Divine Law on Regatha.

"Zin still had loyal followers, many of whom believed that Heliud's revitalization was somehow demonic in its origin. Heliud challenged Zin, saying that the Fire would be the judge of right and wrong. They had to go, one and the other, to face the Purifying Fire. As you might imagine, only Heliud emerged."

"What happened to Zin?" asked Brannon.

"It's interesting that you ask, Brannon, because I wondered the same thing. Heliud told his followers that Zin's body had vaporized in the flame. The followers of Zin did not believe this explanation, but they never found his body, for as long as they searched the caverns. They were eventually mollified when Heliud named their settlement in Zin's honor. They hold Zin sacred still, saying that his opposition was divinely inspired to test the truth of Heliud's leadership."

He paused, seemingly unwilling to finish the tale, but finally added, "Walbert is the successor to this legacy and the custodian of the Purifying Fire."

"Well, doesn't that just figure," said Chandra in disgust. "The members of the Order have forbidden fire magic to everyone in their land while drawing their *own* power from fire? Or from something that's just barely similar to fire?"

A flame that was cold and white didn't sound much like fire to her. It sounded as rigid and deadly dull as she imagined the members of the Order were.

Chandra was passionate about the heat and fury of fire magic. She loved the gold, orange, yellow of explosions, the blood-red blazes of pyromancy. What was the point of something cold, white, and hidden underground? Surely there was no beauty in that. No glory, or passion, or thrill.

"The Order has forbidden fire magic in their lands," Samir agreed, "and now they want to restrict our way of life in the Western Wood, too. Certain practices are still allowed, Walbert told me, because he says the laws issued by the Order are not, in his judgment, unreasonable. But now

other supposedly-dangerous practices such as summoning are forbidden to us." Samir's normally gentle expression grew thunderously angry. "And the ghost wardens are the Order's means of spying on us in our own land!"

"They have no right," Chandra said.

"None!" Samir rarely raised his voice, but he did so now.

"But at least a ghost warden doesn't sound like it can be a very *good* spy," Chandra said with a frown. "I mean, I'd sure notice it sneaking up on me, if it looks like what Brannon described."

"Me too!" said Brannon.

"Actually, it's more effective than you suppose," Samir said. "It's completely silent, after all. No feet or hands. We have many unusual things in the forest—"

"No argument there," said Chandra.

"—but we're not used to entities without any limbs. Well, apart from snakes, but you get my meaning."

"I don't like snakes," Chandra said frankly.

The shadowy forest felt claustrophobic to Chandra, who was much more used to the scenic vistas of mountain living. The woods were teeming with life, much of it strange and unnerving: carnivorous flowers whose sweet scent lured the unsuspecting, poisonous insects that posed as plants, ill-tempered beasts that resembled moss-covered rocks, and monsters that looked like trees, among many others. Dirt, noise, fungus. None of it appealed to Chandra, but it did offer time away from the other Keralians, who could become quite boring in their devotion.

Even so, sitting on the dry ground outside Samir's leafy hut, and politely pretending to

Φ

drink some insipid beverage flavored with mashed plant roots, Chandra felt eager to return to the monastery and tell Mother Luti what she had learned today. If creatures of the Order were roaming the woods now, how much longer would it be before the Order tried to intrude onto Mount Keralia?

"Hardly anything moves through the forest without making a sound," Samir said. "But these creatures do. Lately, numerous woodlanders have been surprised to notice a ghost warden watching them without having any idea how long it had been there."

"That would be creepy," said Brannon.

"For example," Samir said calmly, "ever since you arrived and we sat down here together, I haven't glanced at those bushes to our left until just a moment ago." Now he turned his head and stared hard at the lush shrubbery. "So I don't know how long that ghost warden has been listening to our conversation."

Brannon gasped. Chandra jumped as if she had been bitten, leaping to her feet in the same motion as she whirled to face the bushes Samir was looking at.

She saw a white creature there, as as motionless as a rock. It didn't breathe. Its pale eyes didn't blink. It didn't even react to Chandra's sudden movement, nor to Brannon pointing at it and crying out. And its long white hair remained still, despite the breeze that made the leaves rustle gently on the bush obscuring it from Chandra's view.

She circled around the clearing, moving to get a better view of the creature. From her new position, Chandra saw that, exactly as Brannon

had described, it had no hands or feet, although four appendages were attached to its torso in a disturbing suggestion of arms and legs that trailed off into whirls of glittering white dust where toes and fingers should have existed.

"How does it work?" Chandra asked Samir.

The ghost warden turned its head toward her when she spoke. Somehow, the movement was even more disturbing than the creature's stillness had been. Its motion was fluid and refined, like the passage of time.

"Work?" Samir, too, had risen to his feet. Now he pushed Brannon behind his body, shielding the boy from the creature.

"Can its master see through its eyes and hear through its ears?" Chandra asked, still staring at the ghost warden. "Does its creator see and hear us right now? Or does this thing have to return to its master to convey what it has witnessed?"

"I'm not sure," Samir said. "But, as I said, they are said to trigger an alert to patrols."

"I don't think they can do that," Chandra said decisively. "We should kill it to test the theory."

Now the creature displayed an almost eerily human reaction. It shrank away from her in recognition of the threat she posed.

"Chandra . . ." Samir said uneasily. "That might be unwise at this juncture."

But the very thought of a fight elevated Chandra's heartbeat. As her pulse quickened, so did the fire inside her. She could feel it bloom in the base of her skull as her hair became a mane of flame, and moved down her spine and out to her hands, lighting like torches.

"Be careful," Samir warned. "It has been unseasonably dry this year."

The ghost warden pointed a wispy limb toward Chandra, and a bolt of white light shot forth from the floating, shiny particles in its fingerless tendrils.

"Ouch!" Chandra staggered backward as it hit her in the stomach. The blow was enough to quench the fire that burned around her.

She doubled over, trying to catch her breath, and heard Brannon shouting her name. A moment later, she felt a hand on her back and heard Samir asking if she was all right.

"I'm fine," she croaked. "I feel like I've been . . . stung by the biggest wasp that ever lived, but I'm fine. Never mind me! *Get* that thing!"

"It's gone!" Brannon cried.

"Gone?" Chandra raised her head and looked toward the bushes. There was nothing there now but greenery. "Damn!"

"I see it!" Samir, whose eyes were far more accustomed than theirs to the shadowy forest, had spotted the creature as it fled through the trees. He pointed. "Over there!"

"Let's go!" Clutching her throbbing stomach, Chandra ran in the direction that Samir had indicated.

"*Can* we kill it?" he shouted, running after her.

"Let's find out!" she shouted back. Ghost or no ghost, Chandra thought she should be able to turn anything into a pile of ashes if she got it hot enough.

"This way!" Samir shouted behind her, veering off to the right and disappearing into the greenery.

Chandra turned to follow him. There was a broad thicket of bushes in her way, but it didn't look very thick. Rather than waste time going around it, she forced her way through it. This proved to be a mistake. The clinging shrubs and

their thorns clutched at her clothes and scratched her skin. Within moments, she found she was stuck, unable to move forward. The harder she tried to free herself, the more entangled she became.

"I see it!" Samir cried, his voice significantly farther away now. "Come on!"

"I'm . . . *coming*!" Chandra winced as she struggled to free herself.

She was panting, she was in pain, she was falling behind, and, worst of all, she was trapped by a damn *bush*. Exasperated, her temper flared as a burning heat rushed through her body, erupting in an aura of flame that set the thicket alight and turned the offending bush into a charred remnant.

She had only taken a few steps when she heard shrill screeching and chattering overhead. Something heavy fell down onto her back from the overhanging branches of a tree, wrapped its limbs around her neck, and bit her shoulder.

"*Agh!*" Chandra dived to the ground and rolled over on top of her attacker. She struck the small, struggling combatant with her elbow and, as soon as she felt its grip loosen, leaped to her feet and turned to face it.

An oufe? Chandra stopped cold. She didn't like the small woodland creatures, but she had no quarrel with them either.

Graceful green limbs, tiny features, and rather immodest rough clothing blurred in a tangle of movement as her attacker jumped to its feet and launched itself at her again, baring its sharp little teeth in a growl of rage.

Chandra instinctively threw a bolt of fire at the oufe. It leaped back, shrieking in fear and pain, which made her feel guilty. The little creature was barely half her size, and the bush she had just

destroyed might have been its place of worship or something. Oufes were a little strange that way.

Seeing that the frantic little creature wasn't seriously injured by her fire strike, though, Chandra said, "I'm sorry about your bush! But I don't have time for this!"

She turned and ran in the direction of Samir's distant shouts urging her to *hurry*. She heard more shrill chattering behind her and risked looking over her shoulder. Chandra saw that her attacker was being joined by two more, but tripped over a tree root and decided to keep her eyes on where she was going.

"Samir!" she shouted.

"Over here!" he shouted back.

"Chandra!" Brannon cried. "I can see it now! Hurry!"

Chandra heard more screeching behind her, but she didn't look back again, not even when the noises got more ear-splitting. She ran through a tight-knit grove of trees, jumping over fallen branches and toppled tree trunks, following the sounds of her friends' voices as they screamed for her to catch up.

When she catch up to Brannon and Samir, they were at the edge of a glade.

"There! Crossing the stream!" Samir cried. "It's just ahead of us now!"

He was breathing hard, and turned to look at Chandra as she drew up alongside him. Then he looked past her, and his sweat-beaded face underwent the most astonishing transition.

"Why," he said, "is there a load of oufes chasing you?"

"What?" Chandra looked over her shoulder. "Oh, *no*."

"Gosh," Brannon said. "They look really mad."

There appeared to be about twenty of them bearing down on her, screeching with murderous fury as they brandished sticks, spears, and daggers. Their eyes glowed with feral rage, their sharp teeth were bared, and their skin was flushed dark green with anger.

"What *is* it with oufes?" she muttered.

"This could be a problem," Samir said.

"What are they going to do?" Chandra said dismissively. "Nibble on my ankles?"

Samir said, "Well, given the opportunity . . ."

"I'm stopping that ghost warden!" Chandra spotted it floating above a narrow stream as it fled across the glade.

Samir said, "But what about—"

"You're a chief! You deal with it!"

Chandra closed the distance between herself and the ghost warden, spreading her arms wide as she felt power flow freely through her, answering her summons with satisfying heat. She shaped her will into a burning projectile and threw it at the ghost warden.

The creature flinched to escape a direct hit, a sign, in Chandra's estimation, that it could indeed be destroyed. It wouldn't expend energy fleeing or defending itself if it weren't vulnerable to her attacks. Chandra leaped over the narrow stream that her floating quarry had crossed only moments ago.

She heard a horse whinny somewhere beyond the glade as she threw another fireball that missed the ghost warden. Her next two also went wide into the underbrush that lay at the edge of the glade, where the tangle of dead twigs and leaves burst into flames.

"Hold still, damn you," Chandra muttered, trying again even as she heard thundering hooves approaching her on one side while oufes shrieked noisily on the other.

The ghost warden truly seemed to fear the fire, its entire form sliding horizontally away from the flaming projectiles with only a scant moment to spare. Then it abruptly returned two beams of white light in quick succession. Chandra dodged the first one and met the other with a deflective ball of flame.

"Oh no you don't!" She threw another fireball, and another, and another after that. The area surrounding the glade was a wall of flame by now, each successive explosion of fire adding to the blazing fury. The oufes were in hysterics, and Samir was shouting words she couldn't quite hear.

Moving at a run, Chandra circled the glade to block the ghost warden's only remaining escape route. It hovered uncertainly, facing Chandra, surrounded on all other sides by fire.

The approaching horses were now so close that Chandra could hear the jingle of their bridles directly behind her as she threw three more fireballs at the creature in quick succession. Its rapid, evasive movements managed to dodge the assaults, but the result was a bonfire that could not be avoided and the ghost warden was soon consumed in flames.

Over the roar of the fire and the shrieking of oufes, Chandra became fully aware of the rattling bridles and snorting horses behind her, as well as the sharp exclamations of male voices. She was already turning toward the sounds when she realized what Brannon was frantically screaming at her.

"Chandra! *Soldiers!* Behind you! Soldiers on horseback!"

There were four of them. Their horses were dancing nervously, frightened by the fire. The soldiers, all wearing boiled-leather armor over pale blue tunics, looked stunned as they gazed at her. Three of them had their swords drawn. One appeared to have entirely forgotten he was armed, and just stared at Chandra with his mouth hanging open.

She grinned as she raised her arms high, a mane of fire swirling around her head and shoulders. Flames licked across her skin, surrounding her body in a flaming aura. The torches at the end of her arms grew immense as she shouted, "Leave this forest! Never come back! Tell Walbert what you have seen! The Order is finished here!"

Since they seemed to need a little encouragement, she threw a fireball over their heads. One of the horses pranced sideways, its eyes rolling with fear. Another reared up, nearly unseating its rider.

When Chandra threw a second fireball, letting this one come a little closer to hitting one of the men, they all four turned and fled. The sight of their horses galloping away made her grin with exultation.

She watched until the green woodland swallowed them up, hiding them from her view as they fled, she supposed, in the direction of the plains. She felt someone tugging at her sleeve.

"Chandra," Brannon said, his eyes wide as he looked up at her. He was still a boy, and she was tall for a woman. "Samir says we should leave before the oufes strip your flesh from your bones and feed it to wolves."

"What?" Chandra frowned as she glanced over her shoulder in Samir's direction. "*Oh*."

The mage was holding back a mass of the woodland creatures with an undulating green net of tangled, writhing vines that he had conjured between them and the glade, Some of them were flinging themselves at the barrier, squealing as they got tangled up in it, while others were trying to climb it, in an attempt to go over the top and proceed from there.

All around them the glade burned. She had started a forest fire, one that was raging completely out of control.

"Oops."

Oufes, she knew, could be very touchy about this sort of thing. Indeed, Samir was taking quite a risk with his own people by interceding to protect her. However, she had destroyed a ghost warden and chased away four of Walbert's armed soldiers. Hopefully, when the oufes calmed down, they'd realize that she had acted for the best.

At the moment, though . . .

Chandra started toward Samir, intending to help him.

He glanced in her direction, and an expression of horror contorted his face when he saw her approaching him. "*Go!*" he ordered. "Go *now!*"

Brannon grabbed her by the shirt. "Chandra . . ."

Samir was right, she realized. These oufes were pointing at her and screaming. Her presence was only increasing their frenzy. She hated leaving Samir to deal with this alone, but that was the best choice available at the moment.

"All right, yes," Chandra said, grasping Brannon's hand. "Let's go. This way."

They ran across the glade together, their footsteps carrying them into a wall of fire. Knowing that no forest-dweller would follow them this way, they fled through the welcoming embrace of the flames.

CHAPTER FOUR

The first attack came the following night.

Chandra was lying awake in her narrow bed, torn between anger over Luti's latest lecture on self-control and a certain reluctant awareness that the mother mage had a valid point.

Fortunately, Chandra's fire—as she had been quick to remind Luti earlier tonight—had only burned down a *small* portion of the Great Western Wood. Samir had sent one of his many relatives to the monastery earlier to inform them that Chandra's forest fire had been contained and quelled after nightfall. The rains had been sporadic this year, but the elves' magic had kept the fire confined to the the glade where Chandra had destroyed the ghost warden.

"Nonetheless," Luti had said to her earlier tonight, "you did far more damage than good, Chandra."

"But I—"

"Eliminating one ghost warden may have been helpful—"

"*May* have been? That thing was a spy for the Order!"

"—or it may have been ill-advised. In either case—"

"Ill-advised *how*?" Chandra demanded.

"*In either case*," Luti said, clearly losing patience with her. "The possible benefit of eliminating one ghost warden from the forest cannot balance the catastrophe of *burning down* the forest."

More admonishments had followed. "Playing with fire is bad for those who burn themselves," said Luti quoting some sage or another. "But for the rest of us it is a great pleasure. I want you to be able to experience this pleasure as I do, Chandra, but until you learn to control your impulses, you will continue to burn yourself and those around you."

Chandra lay wide awake in bed thinking about that last statement and wrestling with the emotions it stirred.

She *hated* being reprimanded and lectured. It made her want to leave Regatha, Keral Keep, and Mother Luti far behind her. She was seething with indignation and felt like setting something on fire, even though that was precisely what had gotten her into this trouble in the first place.

On the other hand . . .

Chandra heaved a breath as she lay on her back, staring up into the darkness.

On the other hand, she had indeed destroyed part, however small, of the forest, enraged a tribe of oufes, and no doubt caused a lot of trouble for Samir. The woodlanders hadn't ever done her any harm. Samir considered her a friend, and the Keralians sought cooperation with the forest races against the encroaching power of the Order. It wasn't entirely unreasonable for Luti to say that making enemies in the woods by wreaking destruction had been a bad decision, or, rather, to quote her, "a stupid misstep." The actual decision had

been to rid the woodlands of a spy for the Order. That was a good idea, thought Chandra.

However, given the way things had turned out, it was possible that the woodlanders found a single ghost warden among many to be slightly less disruptive to their daily routine than she had been.

Chandra kept reviewing the events of that day and wondering what she should have done differently. Capture the ghost warden instead of kill it? How could she have done that? The creature was so fast and elusive, she had barely been able to get close enough to throw fireballs at it. Should she have just let it spy on her and then go its merry way? *Out of the question!* Instead of killing it in the woods, should she have chased it to the plains and thereby accidentally set the farmlands on fire? Would Luti be less exasperated with her now if farmers were enraged instead of woodlanders?

Chandra rolled over on her side and tried to punch some shape into her flat pillow.

And why might killing a ghost warden be ill-advised, anyway? Surely Luti didn't think it was a *good* thing to have those creepy creatures roaming the woods and spying for the Order? To hear Samir talk, it wasn't long before they started appearing in the mountains to protect the Keralians from themselves and anything they might do that the Order didn't like.

Tired of chasing this subject around and around in her head, Chandra closed her eyes and tried to will herself to relax and get some sleep. She forced herself to clear her mind, focus on her breathing, and let the darkness absorb the clamoring voices in her head.

But then she realized the voices weren't all in her head. She frowned irritably as she recognized

the sound of whispering directly outside her door. It was very late, but some of the Keralian acolytes were night owls who preferred to study and practice until dawn and then sleep all morning. Life at the monastery was pretty unstructured, and the residents seldom interfered with each other's habits, as long as they didn't impinge on the rights or comforts of anyone else.

Whispering and muttering outside her door, Chandra decided, especially while she was trying to sleep, counted as impinging on her rights and comforts. She heard two lowered voices. They sounded like they were arguing. She wished they'd go argue somewhere *else*. She was about to get out of bed and tell them so when the door to her chamber creaked open.

Chandra opened her eyes as her body went tense. Who was entering her room in the middle of the night?

She heard the same two voices again, now in her doorway. Chandra's room opened directly onto an outdoor walkway with a view of the mountains to the south and the sky overhead. Squinting through the dark, she saw two figures standing in her there, faintly illuminated by the moonlight.

The two intruders were short—shorter than Brannon certainly, whose head only came up to Chandra's shoulder. They were also broad and squat, with misshapen heads, and they moved in an odd, lumbering way, as if trying to keep their balance on the deck of a ship in rough waters. But it wasn't until Chandra saw their brightly glowing orange eyes that she realized what they were.

"Goblins?" she asked incredulously, so startled she forgot to feign sleep..

The closer one stumbled back in surprise when she spoke, careening into the other. The second goblin gave a muffled shriek, hopping around on one foot—his other, it seemed, had been stomped on by his staggering companion.

Chandra tilted her head back and blew a fiery breath straight upward. The resultant flame flew up to the ceiling and bounced tentatively there for a moment before it attached itself, burning like a torch to illuminate Chandra's room.

She got out of bed and looked at the intruders with unconcealed revulsion. "*Goblins.*"

The red skin that covered their misshapen, bald heads had the texture of lumpy dough. Hair sprouted from their fungal ears and their scaly hands had claws as long as the yellow fangs that protruded from their mouths, dripping with saliva.

"You're drooling on my floor!" Chandra said in disgust.

They also, she noticed, smelled *terrible*.

The goblin hopping around on one foot gibbered at its companion in a tongue Chandra didn't recognize. The other goblin hissed at her.

"I'll say this just once," she told them, letting flames ripple boldly along her skin in an effort to intimidate them. "Get out of my room. Get out *now*."

The goblin that had hissed at her nudged its companion, who was still obsessed with the pain in his foot. Getting no reaction, the hissing goblin nudged again. This annoyed the second goblin, who put down his aching foot and irritably swatted the first goblin. The first one growled in annoyance, turned around, and hit him back.

As if oblivious to Chandra's presence, they were suddenly clobbering each other with vehemence,

growling and gibbering. Chandra watched them for a few moments, but her amusement quickly palled, and she interrupted them with a stinging bolt of fire that got their attention.

"What in the Multiverse are you two doing here?" she demanded.

They blinked, as if startled to be reminded that they had invaded a woman's bedchamber in a monastery where they had no business being. Although goblins practiced fire magic, they were unwelcome here. The Keralians had no interest in studying and working alongside creatures who had the manners, values, and sanitary habits of rabid animals.

One of the goblins, evidently remembering the business at hand, bared its chipped yellow fangs and snarled, *"Kill woman."*

In unison, the two goblins gave a guttural little war cry, before launching themselves at Chandra.

She moved her hands forward, calling golden heat into her palms, and warded off her attackers' claws by throwing a large fireball into their faces. However, the goblins were perhaps more competent then they'd originally appeared. It was clear they had some moderate protection against fire, whether from a charm or spell. Chandra's opening salvo left them unsinged, though slightly disoriented.

Taking advantage of that moment, Chandra picked up the lone chair in her room, and brought it crashing down on the confused goblins. One of them screamed and clutched his bald head, staggering. Apparently rethinking his commitment to murder, he dashed out the door.

The other goblin merely seemed to be enraged by the heavy blow. It snarled viciously and,

doubling over, flew straight into Chandra's knees. The chair flew out of Chandra's grasp as she lost her balance and fell against the wall, propelled by the speed and surprising weight of her attacker.

The goblin tried to tear out her throat with its fangs, but Chandra gouged the beast's fiery orange eyes with one hand and pulled its hairy ear as hard as she could with the other, trying to pull its head away from her neck. While the beast was temporarily blinded, she balled her fist and transferred all her energy there. Her knuckles superheated like molten lava and she punched the goblin in the stomach. As the wind and a considerable amount of spittle was knocked out of her assailant, she pushed with her fist again, twisting it from side to side in an effort to cook the thing from the inside out.

She squirmed beneath her adversary, trying to shift her weight so that the goblin's dripping saliva and revolting breath weren't in such close proximity to her face.

"Chandra? Chandra!"

She risked glancing away from her opponent and saw Brother Sergil standing in the doorway, blinking at her. There were a couple of other Keralians behind him, also attracted by the commotion.

"There's a second goblin!" Chandra shouted. "It got away! Stop it! Get it!"

"A second . . ." Sergil gasped, still staring at her. "Fires above! What are you doing to that *goblin*?"

"Get the other one!" Chandra shouted, as the goblin took advantage of her distraction to throw its weight. She was suddenly rolling around on the floor with her gruesome opponent.

"Do you want some help with that?"

"*Sergil!* Get the . . . *Agh!*" She cried out in sudden pain when the beast's claw drew blood from her thigh. ". . . other one!"

"There's *another* one?" Brother Sergil said, sounding appalled, but he and the other monks disappeared before she could reply.

Trying to keep the goblin's fangs away from her throat, Chandra kept pressing her molten fist into its muscular belly. Her magic was much stronger than anything claimed by this stinking *thing*, she knew. She just needed a little more time . . . And, sure enough, a moment later, she felt the goblin's skin start to sizzle. The stench of burning cloth arose from the spot, followed by the sickly smell of roasting flesh. The goblin quivered, snarled again . . . then let out a howl of pain and released its hold on Chandra, intent now on getting away from her. She tried to cling to it, telling herself to take it captive, but really wanting to kill it. However, its fight or flight instinct had taken a distinct turn toward flight and Chandra released it rather than have her arm chewed off.

The goblin scrambled to its feet and ran out the door. Chandra leaped up and followed it out of the room. The claw wound on her thigh stung sharply now, slowing her down. She tried not to think about what sort of horrible, festering infection she would get from a filthy goblin claw.

On the walkway outside, the goblin barreled into a startled woman, who screamed, but the collision didn't stop the goblin's flight. Other Keralians were running around and shouting, apparently looking for the goblin that had previously fled. Chandra followed *this* goblin down the walkway and toward the eastern terrace.

"Chandra!" a familiar voice cried.

She looked over her shoulder and saw Brannon running toward her, trying to catch up. "Stay back!" she ordered.

"I'll help you!"

"Stay *back!*" Chandra doubted the goblin would have any scruples about killing a child.

"Brannon!" Brother Sergil shouted. "Stay with me!"

Chandra kept after the goblin.

Moving awkwardly, but quite fast nonetheless, the hideous assassin ran across the eastern terrace and straight for the stairway that led down to the herb garden below, from which it could escape over the red stone wall and into the dark night.

Chandra stretched out her arms, incredibly angry that this whole thing was happening. But anger was good for Chandra. Anger tapped that part of her that made the fire hot. Anger was the accelerant that took fire to inferno. That little beast was not getting away. Chandra raised a wall of fire around the fleeing goblin. He tried to run through it, but the wall grew thicker, moving with him as he ran, the circle shrinking in on him so that he couldn't escape. Shrieking in panic now, the goblin hesitated, unsure if any direction were better than another. And the flames closed in on him, no matter which direction he turned as he sought to flee the fire's destructive hunger.

Chandra's magic was much stronger than whatever pathetic power this lumpish assassin could claim. She only needed another moment . . . And sure enough, the goblin screamed in pain as he was consumed by the fire, his thrashing discernible even through the shifting wall that closed on him like a molten iron maiden.

When the glowing remnants of the dying goblin vanished and all that remained was her own fire, Chandra let go of her spell. The flames calmed, no longer moving and shifting to imprison her enemy. With nothing fueling it, the fire she had called forth began to die. Within a few moments, it would disappear altogether.

Chandra was breathing heavily, but she was no longer angry. Only her throbbing leg served as a reminder of the rage that had beaten so furiously in her heart moments ago. She wiped perspiration from her face, smoothed away the lingering flames from her long red hair, and leaned over, resting her hands on her knees as she tried to catch her breath.

Her head turned quickly when she heard footsteps approaching her, but she relaxed when she saw Luti, wearing a long, copper-colored robe. The mother mage's white hair was loosely braided and hanging over one shoulder. Her dark eyes were alert as she gazed at Chandra's dying fire on the eastern terrace.

"A goblin attack, they're saying," Luti said.

Chandra nodded. "Two of them."

"Yes, I heard. Unfortunately, no one can find the other one. It must have got away."

"Oh." Chandra steadied her breathing and stood upright again. "I don't think it'll come back. It didn't seem to be the persistent type."

Luti noticed her bleeding leg. "You're hurt."

"Goblin claw."

Luti grimaced. "We'll have to clean it and keep an eye on it. Fortunately, it doesn't look serious. But it'll sting for a few days."

"Chandra!" Brannon called, running toward her. "Are you all right?"

LAURA RESNICK

"I'm fine," she assured him as he reached her side.

"Was that really a goblin, like they're saying?" he asked eagerly.

"Yes."

"I wish I had gotten a good look. I've never seen one!"

"They're disgusting," she said. "I can't believe that female goblins actually . . . well . . . whatever they do."

Luti asked her, "Did you know your attackers?"

"Know them?" Chandra blinked. "They were *goblins*."

"You never saw them before?"

"You've seen one, you've seen 'em all, I guess."

"I wish you'd take this seriously, Chandra," Luti said. "But if you don't think they were personal enemies of yours, and considering we haven't had a goblin attack here in many years . . . I think we can guess who sent them."

"Who sent . . ." Chandra realized what she meant. "You mean the oufes? They can sure carry a grudge for little guys."

"Yes," Luti said. "Even though it was, of course, only a *small* portion of the forest."

❋ ❋ ❋ ❋

"No, no," Samir said, sitting in Mother Luti's private workshop in the monastery five days later. "Not *all* the woodlanders. There's some ill feeling about the fire among other factions, of course, but it's only the oufes who are calling for your execution, Chandra."

Samir, who looked more harassed than usual, had made the trip up the mountain that day to update Mother Luti and Chandra on the situation in the Great Western Wood.

"Only the oufes," Chandra repeated, shifting her position to stretch her sore leg. The claw wound was healing well, but it still ached a little.

Luti said, "I suppose we can regard that as good news."

"Actually, it's one particular tribe of oufes." Samir added wearily, "A big tribe."

"Presumably the tribe in whose territory the fire occurred?" Luti said.

"Yes. I've tried reasoning with them. To explain that Chandra was fighting a ghost warden who had invaded our lands to spy on us." Samir sighed. "But you know what oufes are like."

Luti said, "Not amenable to reason."

"Not really." He shrugged and added, "To them, the forest is sacred. What happened in the woods that day has offended them deeply. Imagine what the Keralians would do if some came in and set your monastery on fire . . . Okay, bad example, but you get what I mean.

"They insist that nothing less than Chandra's death will atone for the destruction of the forest. They're calling for her assassination."

"We supposed so," Luti said, "since as of now there have been three energetic attempts on Chandra's life."

Samir said, "And since those attempts failed, this morning the tribe increased the size of the reward they're offering for her death."

"What sort of reward do oufes offer?" Chandra said with a frown. "Most of the killers I've met aren't so keen on pussy willow trees."

"Well, I wouldn't know what they are offering," Samir said. "But you've seen the caliber of assassin they are attracting."

"Thank goodness for small mercies," Luti said

dryly. "Even so, we must resolve this matter."

Chandra said, "Maybe if I talked to them—"

"*No*," said Luti and Samir in unison.

Chandra blinked.

Samir said more gently, "Oufes don't leave the forest, so they certainly won't come here. And if you entered the forest, my friend, there's nothing I can say or do that would protect you from the tribe's wrath. Not in their current frame of mind, anyway."

"I can handle a little oufe wrath," Chandra said dismissively.

"And burn down *more* of the forest?" Luti said. "*No*."

"Mother Luti is right, Chandra," said Samir. "While the tribe remains this angry, I feel sure that a confrontation would only worsen the situation. We don't want that. Especially not at a time when cooperation between the monastery and the woodlanders is vital."

"So what's the solution?" Chandra said in frustration. "I just keep fighting off the assassins that come after me every day or two?"

"No, of course not," Samir said. "We must find a way to resolve this matter peaceably. You mentioned there were other attacks?"

"Yes," Luti said, "and you know about the goblins. But there was also a very large man with an axe outside the walls of the monastery. Luckily, he was more accustomed to chopping wood than people or he might have hurt Brannon."

"Brannon was attacked?" Samir repeated, clearly horrified.

"Perhaps not intentionally, but he was with Chandra when the idiot tried to take her down. Then, most recently, an archer sent a few arrows from that rock outcropping near the west wall.

Fortunately," Luti said, "the archer had poor aim and lacked stealth, so he didn't survive even until midday. But what next? How many attempts on her life must Chandra endure? And how long before someone *else* gets injured in one of these attacks? Or even killed?"

"That's an excellent point," Samir said with a nod. "I will appeal to the tribe on the basis of justice. If they persist in their quest for vengeance, they could be responsible for the death of an innocent person. Even a child!"

"Will that argument sway them?" Luti asked.

"Not immediately," Samir admitted. "Empathy is not an oufe characteristic."

Luti shook her head in exasperation. "*Oufes.* Even the smallest spark left unattended can make a fire."

"Have patience for now," Samir urged, "and give me time. I believe I can persuade them to call off these attacks. Oufes also tend to have short memories."

Luti sighed, then nodded. "All right, Samir. I have faith in your leadership and your powers of persuasion. We will try to be patient. Meanwhile . . ." She frowned down at her folded hands.

"Meanwhile?" Chandra prodded.

"Meanwhile, inform the tribe that Chandra has left the monastery."

Samir shook his head. "If I tell them a falsehood and they find out, then I will lose—"

"It's not a falsehood," Luti said. "At least, it won't be by this time tomorrow."

"I'm not running away!" Chandra said.

"Of course you're not," said Luti. "You are, at my request, leaving on a mission on behalf of the monastery."

"I am?" Chandra said suspiciously.

"Yes. A mission that only you can accomplish." Their eyes met. "We'll discuss the details later."

A mission that only you can accomplish . . .

Did Luti want her to planeswalk? Chandra's curiosity was kindled, but planeswalking wasn't something they could discuss in front of Samir, so she nodded in acceptance of Luti's statement.

"So . . ." Samir looked from Luti to Chandra, then back to Luti. "If I tell the tribe tomorrow that Chandra has left the monastery, I will be speaking the truth?"

Luti nodded. "And if you think it will help cool their rage, tell them Chandra has been sent away as punishment for what happened. That's not our way here, of course, but I rather doubt that oufes know—or care—what our ways are."

"Tell them I'm being *punished*?" Chandra was insulted. "I don't want a bunch of oufes thinking—"

"Does it really matter what oufes think of you, Chandra?" Luti said impatiently. "If it means these disruptive attacks cease, so be it. I just want to resolve this matter as quickly as possible, so that we can give our full attention to dealing with the Order!"

Chandra shrugged and folded her arms. She didn't like it, but Luti had a point, so she let it go.

"And speaking of the Order," Luti continued. "Killing that ghost warden has attracted Walbert's attention."

"What?" Chandra said in surprise.

"How do you know?" asked Samir.

"The soldiers from Zinara who saw you in the forest," Luti said to Chandra, "reported what they

saw. And the tale was carried all the way to the ears of the high priest of the Temple."

"To Walbert?"

Luti nodded. "I received a letter this morning from Walbert himself, brought by courier." She gestured to a sheaf of papers sitting on the table next to her. "A *long* letter."

"What does he want?" Chandra asked.

"His ultimate goal is to shut down Keral Keep and to outlaw fire magic as we practice it throughout Regatha."

"He wants *what*?" Chandra said in outrage.

"Of course that's what he wants," Samir said. "The rule of the Order can't spread to the mountains while Keral Keep stands."

"Precisely," said Luti. "Oh, Walbert's letter— which is so long-winded that one can only pity his scribes—he goes on about wanting peace, harmony, and unity; seemingly harmless aspirations. But his righteous language can't hide the fact that what he really wants is unchallenged rule over all the lands of Regatha. What he wants is total power." Luti scowled as she added, "He wants power over *us*."

"And us," Samir added.

"Yes," Luti agreed. "Over everyone."

"And to have such power," Samir said, "to rule over all of Regatha unopposed, to ensure that the Order holds sway over the forests and the mountains, as well as the plains . . . Walbert must eliminate all *other* power. Or at least nullify it."

"Particularly fire magic?" Chandra guessed.

"Yes," Luti said. "If Walbert can quell fire magic, then all the other undesirable practices— the ones he doesn't like—will become easier for him to control, too."

"What about this Purifying Fire that you told me about, Samir?" Chandra asked. "Is it really that important to the Order?"

"So people say, in Zinara."

"Can it be . . . I don't know—destroyed? Damaged? Eliminated?"

"What is created that cannot be destroyed? I suppose the answer is yes, but that would mean entering the Temple of Heliud and infiltrating the caverns. One would assume that it is heavily guarded. I can't imagine they let just anyone in there."

"It was just a question," Chandra muttered.

"You're not going to Zinara," Luti said firmly.

"What else does the letter say?"

"Exactly what you might expect. Walbert decries the 'irresponsible' teachings of the monastery and the 'dangerous reign' of pyromancy in the mountains."

"All because I killed a ghost warden?" Chandra said.

"His letter goes on at some length about the *undisciplined* nature of fire mages and the *destructive* influence of pyromancy in magic." Luti scowled, her intonation emphasizing those of Walbert's words that she particularly disagreed with. "Well, if I may paraphrase the great Jaya Ballard: others have criticized destruction, and you know what? They're all dead."

Chandra asked, "Is Walbert's reaction what you meant when you said that destroying the ghost warden might have been ill-advised?"

"Yes," said Luti. "I've never seen one, but I know those creatures are supposed to be hard to eliminate. I thought you might attract Walbert's attention when you killed it. But I've changed my mind about that being ill-advised."

"Why?"

"Walbert has been looking for an excuse to confront the Keralians openly." Luti shrugged. "Now that he has found one . . . I realize that it's a relief. The growing tension has been exhausting. I, too, am ready for confrontation."

"But will this . . ." Chandra frowned. "Mother, have I endangered the monastery?"

"No. Oh, you've burned down part of the Great Western Wood, turned the monastery into a target for inept assassins, and made Samir's life a nightmare of frenzied oufes and disgruntled woodlanders," Luti said. "But if Walbert didn't have the destruction of that ghost warden to use as an excuse, then he'd find something else. So I don't believe that *this*—" Luti picked up Walbert's letter from the table beside her and waved it at Chandra. "—is your fault. It was going to happen eventually."

Samir said, "I agree, Chandra. Walbert has been preparing to challenge the monastery for years. If he didn't feel ready to try to impose the rule of the Order here, he wouldn't have used the ghost warden's demise as an excuse." He added, "Remember, I've met Walbert. Nothing he does is done without a great deal of thought."

"What's he like?"

"He's about Luti's age, tall, gray-haired, thin. He holds himself erect and is very well-groomed. His smile is cold, like his eyes. He speaks in a calm, civilized tone, yet manages to be threatening." Samir thought for a moment. "The things he says are outrageous and self-serving, but listening to him talk, I'm sure he really believes what he's saying."

Luti made a sound of disgust. "Then he must believe that that I can be moved by the transparent

posturing in his letter. Does he imagine that the mountain cares, for even one moment, about the shade it casts on the plain? If he supposes that his absurd rhetoric will somehow curb our belief in the power of fire, then he is in for a rude awakening."

"Oh, I doubt Walbert thinks a letter will cause you to cooperate with his demands," said Samir. "Instead, I think he hopes the letter will incite you to rash behavior."

Luti's angry frown changed to a look of surprise. And then she smiled ruefully. "This is why you're such a valuable friend, Samir." She nodded. "Yes. Of course you're right. Walbert isn't just arrogant and power-hungry. He's also shrewd and manipulative. He will need popular support so he is trying to provoke us."

"But it's important," Samir said, "to give careful thought to your next move. Because careful thought is not what he's hoping for."

"Actually, my next move doesn't really call for that much thought," Luti said.

"Oh?"

"Walbert demands that I turn over Chandra to him—or, rather, 'the red-haired female pyromancer who attacked four soldiers of the Order after criminally destroying a ghost warden.'" Luti looked at Chandra as she added, "Which is why I think the first thing I should do is send you away for a while. Someplace where Walbert won't look for you."

"So it's not the oufes you were worried about, after all," Chandra said.

"Oh, I'm worried about them, too," Luti said. "Never underestimate just how vengeful an oufe can be."

CHAPTER FIVE

"There actually *is* a mission I'm asking you to go on for the monastery," Luti said to Chandra as they strolled through the herb garden, having just said farewell to Samir at the eastern gate. "Considering the danger that I suspect is involved, I'd be reluctant to send you, under normal circumstances. But since it's obviously a good idea for you to be absent for a while . . ."

"You want me to planeswalk?" Chandra guessed. "That's not dangerous."

"According to Jaya," Luti said, "it *is* rather dangerous. There aren't roads or signs or maps among the planes of the Multiverse, are there? There are no convenient doors indicating where to enter and leave the Blind Eternities. And I assume there aren't any heralds helpfully crying things like, 'Welcome to Regatha!'"

"Well, I guess it's a *little* dangerous," Chandra said with a shrug. "But nothing I can't handle."

"A place without time or logic. Without physical form or substance. No ordinary person can survive in the æther that exists between the planes. Only a Planeswalker can," Luti mused. "And they say that a Planeswalker can only survive there for a limited time. If you become disoriented and

get lost in the Blind Eternities, you might never emerge. Before long, you'd be consumed there and die."

"*They* say? *They*, who?" Chandra said dismissively. "Besides you, who around here knows anything about Planeswalkers?"

"Is it true?" Luti demanded.

Chandra looked out over the vast forest below the mountain, and to the plains that lay further east. "All right, yes. I could get lost and die in the Blind Eternities. So what? You, or Brannon, or Samir, could get lost and die in the mountains. The first time you sent me to meet with Samir, I thought I'd get lost and die in the Great Western Wood!"

"Yes, I remember. When you finally made your way back here, you were . . . irritable about your misadventure in the woods."

"But the only alternative to taking that sort of risk is to stay home all your life."

"And staying home isn't that safe these days, either," Luti said dryly as she sat on a bench under one of the garden's ancient olive trees. Her glance surveyed the vegetation. "Goodness, that rosemary really needs trimming! It's taking over the whole place."

Not remotely interested in gardening, Chandra sat next to her and asked, "So where do you want me to go?"

Luti folded her hands in her lap. "Kephalai. Which is also part of the danger I'm worried about."

"Keph . . ." Chandra laughed. "I get to steal the scroll again?"

"That all depends."

"On what?"

"On you, I suppose." She frowned again at the overgrown rosemary, then said, "Brother Sergil and the other monks working on the scroll believe they've solved the riddle. I don't suppose you remember the decorative border surrounding the text in the original scroll?"

"No. Like I said . . ."

"Yes, the Planeswalker who stole it from us played tricks on your memory." Luti nodded. "Well, after more days of studying the text, the brothers believe that the decorative border— which they did not copy or study during the brief time that we had the original here—contains the clue to where the artifact can be found."

"The border? In what way?"

"They're not sure. It may be a map, it may be hidden text, it may be a spell . . ." Luti shrugged. "So if you can *look* at the scroll again, you may be able to see the information concealed within the decorative border."

"And to look at the scroll, I need to go back to Kephalai."

"If it's still there. If the Planeswalker who stole it from us didn't take it somewhere else entirely."

"Even if the scroll is back on Kephalai now, I might not be able to interpret what's in the border," Chandra said.

"In that case, the monks would like an opportunity to study it themselves. So you'll need to bring it back here again, if you can." Luti looked at her. "If the scroll is back in the Sanctum of Stars now, it will certainly be under increased security. Stealing it a second time will be very dangerous."

"Fortunately," Chandra said, "I enjoy a challenge."

"Yes, I thought you'd say that. Even so, please be careful. If only for the sake of an old woman who has become rather fond of you, even though you're an awful lot of trouble to have around."

"Yes, Mother."

"I think it would be——" But Luti's comment ended on a shocked gasp as the rosemary plant lifted itself from the soil and attacked them.

Chandra saw claws and fangs hiding amidst the plant's spiky leaves as it suddenly turned into a tall, moving creature, with arms and legs that ended in the same spikes.

Heat flowed through her in immediate response to the danger, and she amputated one of the plant's attacking limbs with a bolt of fire that she swept downward as she was assaulted. The creature hissed in pain, swayed, then doubled over and re-formed itself into some sort of small, leafy wolf-looking thing.

"How did it do *that*?" Chandra blurted, staring in surprise.

Luti gasped again. "Watch out!" She hurled a fireball at the creature as it crouched to attack. The projectile hit the growling four-legged bush in the face, but the leafy wolf easily shook off the blow and leaped for Chandra.

Her fireball was considerably more powerful than Luti's, and when it hit the creature, the thing fell back with a screech, rolled over into a ball, and reshaped itself into the form of a giant spider.

"I *hate* spiders," Chandra said with feeling.

She raised her hands to call forth a hot flow of lava, and dumped it all over the disgusting creature that was scuttling toward her with murderous intent. The massive spidery *thing* was smothered beneath the lava and incinerated by the liquid fire.

The two women stared at the glowing pile of cooling lava that had destroyed their attacker.

"Well." Luti was panting. "That was . . . different."

"Ugh! Did you say you know what that thing was?"

"Yes. I'm pretty sure it was a woodland shape-shifter," Luti said, still breathless. "I've heard of them . . . but this is the first one . . . I've ever . . ." She sat down shakily on the bench again. "I'm too old for a shock like that."

"Even *I'm* too old for a shock like that." Chandra's heart was pounding after the brief fight.

"No *wonder* the rosemary looked so overgrown," Luti murmured.

"That was pretty clever, I have to admit."

"Not that we won't miss you, Chandra," Luti said, her hand resting over her heart on her heaving chest, "but how soon can you go?"

⋇ ⋇ ⋇ ⋇ ⋇

Chandra talked with Brother Sergil that evening, trying to get some idea of what to look for in the decorative border if she saw the scroll again. She didn't learn much. As Luti had already told her, it might be a pattern, it might be artfully concealed text, it might be an ornate map. Or it might be none of those. But he did tell her enough so that she would be able to identify the scroll, considering she had no memory of it.

Wonderful.

She decided to go to Brannon's room while he was getting ready for bed to tell him she was going away again, but that she would be back before long.

"You're not running away from *oufes*, are you?" he demanded.

"No, of course not," she assured him.

"Because we're better sorcerers than a bunch of elves and weird woodland creatures."

"Yes, we are." She tucked him into bed and said, "But the brothers want to know more about the scroll I brought back—you remember the scroll?"

"Yes. The one that the stranger stole."

"Right. So Mother Luti asked me to try to find it."

"I should come with you." He started to get out of bed. "I can help you!"

"I need you to stay here and protect the monastery," she said firmly, nudging him back onto his narrow cot. "There was another attack today. That's the fourth one. And if I hadn't been there, something awful might have happened to Mother Luti."

"I heard! A woodland shapeshifter!" Brannon's eyes glowed with excitement. "I kind of wish you hadn't killed it right away, Chandra. Mother Luti's never seen one before, and she's really *old*, so maybe I'll never get another chance to see one."

"I'm sorry about that," she said. "It was pretty interesting."

"But you weren't scared?"

"I was a little scared," she admitted. "Especially when it shaped itself like a *spider*."

"Ooh! I wish I'd seen that! Was Mother Luti scared?"

"Yes, I think she was pretty scared. And now, even though I won't be here after tonight, it might take Samir a little while to convince that oufe tribe to stop sending assassins to the monastery. So who knows what could happen next?"

"They might even send a spitebellows!" he said eagerly.

Chandra didn't know what that was, but she said, "*Exactly*. So while I'm away looking for the scroll, I need to know that someone is here protecting Mother Luti and the monastery. Someone I *trust*. Someone I can count on."

Brannon sighed, the weight of the world on his shoulders. "Oh, all right. I'll stay."

"Good. Thank you."

"But just this time. Next time, I'm coming, too."

"We'll see, kiddo."

"*Chandra*." The unfairness of her equivocation clearly incensed him.

"It's getting late," she said hastily. "Try to get some sleep."

"When will you be back?"

"Soon," she promised. "Goodnight."

"Here, take this." Brannon handed Chandra a small piece of flame quartz on a string. "It's for luck."

"Thanks, kiddo."

Chandra left Brannon, knowing he'd lie awake for a while thinking about the exciting things that had happened and that might happen again. She went back to her own room and began preparing to planeswalk.

Ideally, she'd rather do this outside, alone in the mountains. That was where she felt the most centered and focused, the best prepared for planeswalking. But it would be a little difficult to concentrate on entering the æther if she had to keep both eyes peeled for assassins outside the comparative safety of the monastery walls.

Even *inside* the walls, she needed to be alert, considering that goblins had invaded her room and a small bush had tried to kill her in the herb garden.

73

A death sentence from oufes was a nuisance, she decided.

But alone in her room, with the door closed and the table pushed in front of it to keep out intruders, she could prepare in safety and depart unseen.

Of course, in an emergency, she could planeswalk without as much preparation, but it was dangerous. Also pretty nauseating. The first time had been like that. She hadn't known what was happening, and the disorientation had been like some horrific combination of being poisoned, beaten, dropped down a well, and scalded. With no idea what was happening or where she was going, she'd thought she was dying. Indeed, she nearly *had* died. It was just luck, survival instinct, and some innate, previously unrecognized talent that had led her through the Blind Eternities to find the relative safety of another plane.

There, she learned what she really was, and had also learned how to travel more safely between the planes of the Multiverse. And, with practice, she was getting better at it.

She sat down on the floor of her dark room and began by focusing on her breathing.

In, out. Slow. Even. Relaxed. Inhale, exhale.

Each time a thought intruded, she banished it and focused again on her breathing.

Innnnnn. Outtttt.

With each cycle of her slow, rhythmic breathing, her bond grew stronger with the eternal flow of mana throughout the Multiverse and its infinite planes. Her bond to mana, that ethereal fuel for all magic, was strong on Regatha, and she would use it to carry her through, but there were other planes and other sources of mana ready for those who understood the use of the power.

Chandra felt a welcome tingle of heat begin to flow through her. She opened herself further, accepting the intense flow. She felt fire in her blood, in her bones, in her belly. She heard the roar of flames around her, and she felt their glow all through her body.

Still concentrating on maintaining a deep, relaxed breathing pattern, she sensed her physical presence on Regatha beginning to dissolve into flames as she slipped into the Blind Eternities. As she disappeared from her humble bedchamber into the hot blaze of a fiery chasm, she recognized the formless void that existed outside of time and space.

Green, blue, white, red, black. Undulating rivers of vibrant, multi-colored mana swirled around her in a dizzying whirlwind. Overhead. Underfoot. On all sides. Tumbling like waterfalls, twining like ribbons. Vibrating like the strings of a harp, filling her senses, flowing endlessly . . .

She moved as if swimming in invisible lava, pushing her way through something rich and heavy that she could neither see nor touch, but which surrounded her, engulfed her, and melded itself to her. Its fiery heat both energized and drained her, consorting with that Spark inside her, that innate quality that kept her from being devoured by the void.

She spread her hands wide, palms facing outward, and concentrated, trying to sense the energy of the planes echoing throughout the Multiverse. She had been to Kephalai once before, so this journey was easier than the other. Even though there was no path, she recognized the way. She sensed where Kephalai lay in the tumult of her surroundings, and she willed herself to journey

toward it. There was no herald, no marker. She sensed the energy flowing from a particular source, and she recognized it with comforting certainty as Kephalai.

She sought entry to the plane, a way through the shifting veils in her path, coming between her and her goal. Calling on all her power, she propelled herself toward the plane like a flaming arrow, shooting herself into physical reality once more.

"*Ungh!*" Chandra grunted as she was flung physically against something very *hard*, flat, and broad. She bounced off it and fell down to an equally hard surface. She lay there limp, breathless, trying not to pass out.

All right, the journey had gone well, but the arrival was a little bumpy.

She lay facedown on the stony ground, her ribs heaving as she gasped for breath, and a chill creeping across her sweat-drenched back and arms as the cool air of Kephalai washed over her.

She opened one eye and saw that she had bounced off a stone wall. No wonder it had hurt. The building nearby and the stone paving beneath her cheek were both a cool, pale gray. She thought she smelled dead fish, an odor so rank that even the gulls she saw circling overhead might decline a free meal.

"Mummy, look!" cried a child.

"No, dear, stay away from her," said a woman's voice.

Chandra rolled over and looked up at the woman and small child who were walking past her. They were both fair-skinned, with the blonde hair and blue eyes that were common on Kephalai. The woman was holding the little boy's hand, and

she had a well-bundled sleeping baby nestled in her other arm. She and the boy both wore cloaks over their clothing.

"Is it morning or afternoon?" Chandra asked, shivering a little. The cloud cover made it impossible to tell.

The woman scowled at her. "Women like *you* should stay off the streets by day and leave them safe for decent folk and innocent children!"

Chandra stared after the woman as she stomped away, dragging her little boy with her. "Some things don't change, wherever you go," she muttered.

She took a steadying breath and slowly hauled herself to her feet, wincing a little as she did so. She'd definitely have some bruises as souvenirs of her arrival on this plane. She rubbed a hand over her thigh and was glad that the claw wound there hadn't split open as a result of her crash landing. It might leave a scar, but it was still healing well.

Chandra looked around to get her bearings. She recognized the place, having been there before. Rising above the water on the other side of the harbor was the bridge where she'd had to seriously blow some things up so that she could leave Kephalai. She grinned when she saw there was still a heap of tumbled stone from the damage she'd done, including some hideous statue she'd destroyed. That hadn't been intentional, but there was no denying that Kephalai was a better looking place without it.

Chandra tensed when she heard screeching overhead. Looking into the sky, she relaxed when she saw only birds flying above. One of the nastier surprises of her previous adventure here had been the gargoyles from the Prelate's palace. Two of

them had captured Chandra and carried her above the city, hauling her off to captivity. If she was going to steal the scroll again, she'd need to do something about those creatures.

Getting her bearings, Chandra turned away from the harbor and started making her way along the city's crowded flagstone streets. The first order of business, obviously, was to see if the scroll was back in the Sanctum of Stars. Then she could decide what to do next.

The Sanctum of Stars was a sort of combined museum and treasury in the heart of the city. It was a repository of such rich, diverse, and rare objects that its renown extended beyond the plane. She spotted the Sanctum easily, though she was still some distance from it. Its pale stone spire rose majestically above the domed buildings surrounding it. Chandra crossed another bridge that stretched over one of the city's many canals. While walking in the direction of her goal, she considered how to approach this situation.

She had been seen by some of the Prelate's guards when she eluded capture during her previous visit there. And for all she knew, that tricky mage who'd followed her to Regatha could be lurking under a rock somewhere near. Obviously, she should avoid being recognized by anyone who had seen her before, or to whom a description could have been circulated. The problem was how to know who that might be. Chandra's appearance was distinctive, especially on Kephalai. She was taller than most of the inhabitants of Kephalai and her red hair, golden skin, and amber-flecked eyes stood out in a society where most of the people were fair-skinned, blue-eyed, and blonde-haired.

Since the air was chilly, she decided to confiscate a hooded cloak. If she covered her hair with a hood and kept her eyes shyly downcast, she ought to be able to enter the Sanctum of Stars without arousing much suspicion. It was a much-visited place, after all—and although her height and coloring were unusual here, Chandra didn't think these features alone would attract attention.

She found the garment-makers' district by asking a passing stranger for directions. Once there, she soon found her opportunity to acquire a cloak when a couple of careless lads took a break while loading up a cart with garments. Chandra didn't want to waste a whole day earning enough local coin to *buy* a cloak by performing fire tricks in a city square. With silent apologies to the merchant from whom she was stealing, she stealthily took a cloak from the back of the cart.

As she approached the Sanctum of Stars on foot, Chandra scraped the hair away from her face, tucked it under her collar as best she could, and pulled the hood of her cloak over her head. She was glad for its warmth in the chilly air.

If there were extra security here now, it wasn't obvious from the outside. The building still looked exactly the way it had looked before. Chandra admired the round stained-glass window in the center of the pale gray spire. The sapphire-blue glass had a large, glowing, eight-pointed white star embedded in it. She looked warily at the gargoyles squatting strategically around the spire, since it seemed likely that they, too, could turn into dangerous pursuers if given the command. But at the moment, at least, they were still.

She knew from previous reconnaissance that admission to the Sanctum of Stars was open to

all by day, though visitors were prohibited from bringing weapons into the building. There was no body search at the door, just a death penalty and prompt execution for anyone who violated the rule, a deterrent that had kept the Sanctum murder-free for nearly a century.

Keeping her eyes downcast, Chandra added a slight stoop to her posture and started limping a little. Overall, it was a weak diguise, but her hair was covered and she might be taken for an invalid of sorts.

She limped up to the entrance and, with her gaze on the stone steps at her feet, spoke in a bashful, age-weary voice to ask for permission to enter to the museum. The bored guard at the door granted it and let her enter. She went inside and, rather than make a beeline for the display case where she hoped to find the scroll again, she made herself meander around the exhibits for a while, pretending to admire the many exotic objects and rare artifacts in which she had no interest.

Moving slowly and maintaining the outward appearance of a bashful invalid, she gradually made her way to the big glass case where, on her last visit, four precious scrolls had been displayed. Originally, she had simply smashed the case and removed the scroll she'd wanted. She could see as she approached that the case had been replaced and that there were four scrolls inside it.

Chandra's heart thudded. *Yes.* The scroll was there! With Brother Segril's description, she could identify it easily. There was also a distinctive scorch mark on the leather casing, and a big dent in the gold end piece.

Unfortunately, she still had no idea what it contained. Given that it was rolled up, its contents

firmly hidden, she could not understand why it was displayed to the public. What was interesting about a rolled piece of paper? It could be some scribe's to-do list for all anyone knew.

Still, there was no question: she'd have to steal it a second time.

She was still gazing at it, trying to think of a plan, when two pairs of strong hands seized her from behind—one assailant for each arm—and a deep, booming voice said, "Chandra Nalaar, by the authority vested in me, I arrest you for crimes against the Prelate, the Sanctum of Stars, and the people of Kephalai!"

CHAPTER SIX

Chandra was stunned speechless. She raised her head as her two captors whirled her around with brute force; her hood fell back, and a rough hand yanked her long red hair out of her collar so that it fell freely around her shoulders.

There was a fairly good-sized crowd of visitors here. Most of them were staring in surprised fascination at Chandra, who was held firmly by two guards, one of whom had pressed the blade of his sword against her throat. She stared in bemusement at the third guard, a stocky, middle-aged man who didn't look remotely familiar. He had just *used her name* when arresting her.

How could he possibly know . . .

Oh, no.

The Planeswalker who had come to Regatha! He had known her name, too. Had she really thought he'd have just returned the scroll and left again?

She looked quickly around the Sanctum, but she didn't see the Planeswalker. She froze in appalled surprise, though, when she *did* see . . .

"Telepaths?" she guessed.

There were two of them. Both women. They emerged from their concealment walking arm

in arm. Their bald heads reflected the lights of the Sanctum as their hairless brows cast shadows over unnaturally bright eyes. She saw that their skin was eerily white, and they wore identical pale blue robes with an unfamiliar dark blue symbol embroidered on the left shoulder. They stared hard at Chandra.

She nodded, answering her own question. "Telepaths."

Chandra realized that her physical disguise had been pointless. These two had probably been reading everyone who entered the building!

Fine, read this: drop dead you creepy, bald hags!

The two women blinked in unison.

Well, this was just *great*. The intruder had returned the scroll to the Sanctum of Stars, told them her name, and told them she might be back. They had obviously prepared for this. She had just as obviously walked into a trap.

That fact became even clearer as about two dozen soldiers now poured into the hall, moving with swift, well-rehearsed efficiency.

Damn, damn, damn.

Eight of the soldiers took charge of organizing the departure of the gawking visitors. The rest of them surrounded Chandra, weapons drawn. In addition to swordsmen, there were six archers among them who drew their bows and pointed their arrows directly at her.

"Now, now, let's all stay calm," she said. "I'm sure we can discuss our differences like reasonable adults."

One of the mind mages warned the guards, "She intends to fight."

Chandra scowled and tried to block their probing. She knew she was stronger, if she could

LAURA RESNICK

concentrate. But for Chandra it was actually the opposite. Her mind was racing with possibility. Thoughts were moving in her head with such imprecision, that *she* barely knew she was thinking. She did know, however, that this whole situation was making her very mad.

They sensed it, or rather they sensed that Chandra's fuse was short. The telepath who had spoken before told the head guard, "We can't read her. She's too erratic."

The other one said, "Keep hold of her."

The head guard said impatiently to one of his men, "Where are the Enervants? They're supposed to be here!"

"Enervants?" Chandra said. "That's some nerve showing up late for the party." This was no time for jokes, but she couldn't help it.

"The Prelate told me you'd be back," the head guard said. "I said no one was that reckless, but she said that *you* might be.

So the Prelate of Kephalai had indeed enlisted the Planeswalker to retrieve the scroll from Regatha. And he'd reported to the Prelate.

"All right, so I've come back," Chandra said, assessing the situation. "Now what?"

"Now I turn you over the Enervants."

"Sounds like fun."

"Actually," the guard said, "I don't think you'll like them. They are particularly suited to breaking the will of even the most headstrong. It is said they enjoy torturing their subjects in the way most would enjoy a fine meal. They savor it. They take time over the courses, but are not so gluttonous that they don't leave a helping for the rats. I should imagine they will have a particularly good time with you."

There were more than twenty armed guards, a closed space, no visible exits, a scroll to liberate, a couple of mind mages who might have other tricks up their floppy blue sleeves . . . And whoever the Enervants were, they didn't sound like a crowd Chandra really wanted to meet.

"You're right," she said. "The Enervants are late. I don't like anyone who isn't punctual."

She was worried about the fragility of the scroll. She hadn't come all the way to Kephalai to destroy it by accident. However, like it or not, she only saw one viable option now.

"Have you ever heard of Jaya Ballard? No? No, of course not. My teacher's always quoting her, and I get a little tired of it. But I have to admit, once in a while, there's some good advice there."

She made her decision. Fire, scroll, fire.

"For example," Chandra said, feeling heat pour through her. "Jaya said, 'when in doubt . . .'" Fire licked her veins, her skin, her fingertips. "'Use the biggest boom you know.'"

The sound of steel being drawn from scabbards was decisive. The guards were poised for attack, arrows were knocked and drawn, but they hesitated as a small ball of white-hot flame emanated from Chandra's core. It didn't seem like much to them.

Chandra, meanwhile, concentrated on the on the ball as best as she could. As magical energy flowed into her, the ball expanded rapidly to the size of a human head and Chandra sagged a bit, as if the spell had failed. The ball remained where it was, quivering impotently like a mass of gelatin.

"That's not much of a boom," said one of the guards and the tension drained from the room, as many lowered their weapons laughing.

As they did so, Chandra sharpened her focus and the ball collapsed into an infinitesimal point before exploding with such force that it knocked everyone in the room off their feet. Arrows were incinerated, clothing set afire, and the swords of the guards were suddenly searing the flesh of their palms. Luckily the telepaths had no hair to burn, but the stench from the others in the room was more than Chandra had bargained for.

Immune to the blast herself, Chandra turned to smash the glass case but saw that her blast had already done so. She reached inside and grabbed the scroll, which seemed unharmed.

She heard screams all around her. People in panic, burning. People in pain.

"Kill her! *Kill* her!" someone shouted hoarsely.

Calling on all of her power, on everything she had left, Chandra formed another ball of fire in her free hand and cast it at the wall. The fiery explosion blew out an entire wall of the Sanctum. She squinted against the flying dust and debris, coughing as she inhaled. She ran through the burning chaos and out of the building. Four guards who had survived the explosions were hot on her heels, shouting, "*Stop that woman!*"

People in the crowded streets were screaming, too terrified by the explosion to pay any attention to one fleeing woman and the bloody, dirty soldiers running after her.

The Sanctum's structure was more precarious than it looked. Without that wall supporting its fourth side, the building began to cave in on itself.

Chandra heard the tremendous crack of splintering stone and the crash of collapsing walls and floors. Despite the soldiers right behind her, she turned to look. What she saw was so startling, she

stopped running and just stood there and stared in shock at her handiwork. So did the soldiers who, moments ago, had been so intent on killing her.

The tall spire of the Sanctum, high overhead, had started to sway. The gargoyles that squatted around it reacted slowly, their wings shuddering uncertainly as they unfolded from their hunched positions and prepared to take flight. Inside the building, all the soldiers and both mind mages were probably already dead; if not, then they would die within moments.

The massive spire toppled and fell. The Sanctum of Stars completely collapsed. It seemed to happen with a horrific slowness. The immense weight of cracking, falling stone created a terrifying roar. People in the streets were screaming in panic and fleeing to safety. Chandra turned and fled, too.

The enormous impact of the Sanctum collapsing on itself hurled rocks, flames, ashes, dust, and debris across the main square and down the length of every surrounding street. Chandra was knocked off her feet when the ground shook and a wave of rock and ash hurled her forward. Someone trampled her prone body as they ran headlong from the disaster. Winded and in pain, Chandra was lying face down in the street, debris still showering down on her as the dust of pulverized stone filled her lungs.

Coughing and bleeding, she lay there in a daze.

Fire above, the whole thing! The whole building! I didn't mean to do that.

The screams of children filled her ears. She heard a woman wailing. A horse was whinnying in terror.

She had just wanted to escape alive with the scroll.

Dead soldiers? Sure. Dead telepaths? Fair game.

But she hadn't meant to destroy a whole section of the city, terrorizing all of its citizens and perhaps killing innocents.

Pull yourself together. Come on! Get up. Get out of here—or you'll be joining the dead.

Coughing and shaking, she rose to her feet. The scroll was still in her hand. She looked down at it, trying to think.

She couldn't planeswalk. Not under these circumstances. And not with her strength so depleted. She didn't have anything left right now. She needed to regroup and get a handle on things.

Still coughing, she staggered down the street, away from the Sanctum, going in the same direction as the fleeing crowd. By the time she felt she really needed to sit down, she was well beyond the dust, debris, and milling panic. Many people were filling the market street where she stopped to rest. News of the disaster, as well as varied explanations for it, circulated quickly.

Someone who saw her sitting in a dazed slump on the street kindly offered her food and water. Chandra realized she was shaking with fatigue, and accepted gratefully. She hadn't really thought she was hungry, but once she started eating, she discovered she was ravenous. She consumed the food as greedily as a growing boy who hadn't eaten in two days. She was thirsty, too, after all the dust that had coated her throat when the Sanctum collapsed. She drank her fill, then poured water over her head, neck, and hands, washing away blood, dust, and filth.

Only then did she look skyward and realize that the hunt was already on for her.

She saw gargoyles flying overhead, their big wings spread wide and their spindly legs trailing behind their pudgy bodies as they patrolled the sky. She could see two of them directly above. Just as one would expect from creatures made of stone, they were remarkably thorough and methodical in their work. The two of them moved back and forth across the sky in an even, intersecting pattern, switching each other's route to double-check a section of ground with another implacable set of eyes.

Chandra moved slowly, so as not to attract their attention as she scooted beneath a street merchant's canopy to shield herself from their view.

She wondered just how well those gargoyles could see; if they could spot her red hair from overhead. She needed to cover it up again even if they did they have some other means of detecting her. How many of them were hovering over the city? She was too weak right now to deal with them if they plucked her off the street.

Within moments, she noticed something even more alarming. The woman who had given her food a little while ago was now pointing her out to a man. Or, rather, pointing to the spot where Chandra had been sitting a moment ago. The woman was frowning in perplexity as she scanned the street, looking for where she might have gone.

"She was *just* there, so she can't have gone far," is what Chandra guessed the woman said to the man as she searched the street with her eyes.

He wasn't wearing the uniform of a Sanctum guard, or of the Prelate's soldiers, but he looked far from innocuous.

He was older than Chandra, but he was still young, late twenties, maybe thirty. He was taller than average, but only by a little. He had fair skin, blue eyes, and black hair. When he turned his head, she saw that his hair was long and wavy, and tied neatly at the back of his neck. He was dressed simply—tan pants and top, with scuffed leather boots and a well-worn dark leather vest. There was a small coin purse attached to his belt, along with something else that looked like a tool or a weapon. It was shiny, like metal, and coiled like rope—or a like a whip.

He looked lithe, agile, and fit. More than that, he looked as alert as a wild animal scenting prey. His movements were economical—even something as simple as the turn of his head, when his gaze sought her out under the merchant's canopy. He didn't waste motion or squander energy.

And his face didn't give away any reaction when he saw her.

He nodded politely to the other woman without taking his gaze off Chandra, as if aware she'd use the slightest opportunity to bolt. His eyes held hers as he approached her. He didn't hurry, but his walk was direct and purposeful.

She rose to feet, her heart racing as she tried to summon the power to defend herself. But she was still too weak right now. She hadn't paced herself or conserved any strength. Back there in the Sanctum of Stars, she had thought only about living through her confrontation. She hadn't thought about what she would do afterwards.

Several oft-repeated lectures of Mother Luti's floated briefly through her mind. She needed to pace herself, control her power, and manage her emotions with more discipline. She needed to learn

the limits of her strength and ration it intelligently in her magic.

And not just the limits. She needed to learn the extent of her power, too, and how to master it. She thought of the collapsing Sanctum and the chaos in the streets of Kephalai, and she felt the weight of that deed.

Chandra's gaze remained locked with that of the approaching stranger. She couldn't enter the æther and escape him that way. She couldn't call forth fire and fight him. She felt naked as he stopped and stood before her.

His gaze released hers as he took in her appearance, looking her over from head to toe. It wasn't insolent, insulting, or sympathetic. He simply seemed to acknowledge her bedraggled condition and the event that had caused it.

Then he said, "Chandra Nalaar." It wasn't a question.

She shifted her weight. Since he was obviously looking for her, she wasn't really surprised that he knew her name. It seemed everyone did these days. But it made her uneasy, even so.

She asked, "Who are you?"

"My name is Gideon."

"And what's that to me?"

"I think we should get you out of here."

"What?" she said.

He glanced around. Just a slight turn of his chin, a quick flicker of his eyes to encompass the street scene and the gargoyle guardians overhead. "This situation is volatile. We should leave."

"Who are you?"

"We have very little time."

"Then answer my question quickly," she snapped.

"What happened back there," he said quietly, tilting his head to indicate the disaster at the Sanctum of Stars. "That was you."

She didn't respond.

He prodded, "Wasn't it?" When she remained unresponsive, he said, "Of course it was. Who else *could* have done it?"

"You'd better back up and tell me how you even know who I am." She was starting to think he wasn't working for the Prelate, or the ruined Sanctum.

"You've been making yourself conspicuous," he said.

"Maybe so. But *you* haven't. So I suggest you start explaining."

"What was it?" He lowered his voice so they wouldn't be overheard, but some emotion showed now. Tension? Disdain? She wasn't sure. "A explosion of that size? Inside the Sanctum?" She didn't deny it, and he whispered, "What were you *thinking*?"

She admitted wearily, "I was just thinking about surviving."

His gaze dropped to the scroll clutched in her hand. "And also about stealing?"

"All right, fine, so I'm a bad person," she said. "I had a troubled youth."

"You're *still* having a troubled youth."

"All the more reason to stay away from me, Gideon." She turned to go.

His grip on her arm stopped her. "Hunting you down has been troublesome. I don't intend to go through it twice."

She stared at him. "Why have you been hunting me down?"

He looked past her and, though he didn't move, she sensed his tension increase sharply. "Never

mind that now. I think we both know why *they're* hunting you down."

She turned to follow his gaze and saw half a dozen soldiers heading this way. She turned to escape in the other direction, only to see soldiers approaching from there, too.

"Are you their scout?" she demanded.

"No, *I* was hoping to avoid this." He looked up at the gruesome sky patrol. "And I think you may have been spotted from above, as well."

"Now what?"

"They're going to take you into custody." He added, "I hope you have a high threshold for pain."

Adrenaline surged through her, and she felt herself getting her second wind. "I think I can fight."

"No!"

"Will you help?"

"*No.*"

"Then get out of the way!"

Chandra felt stronger. She was thinking about survival again, and fear had a wonderfully energizing effect.

As the soldiers approached her from both sides in the crowded street, she felt heat start to flow through her, welcome and inspiring. She felt the fire moving through her blood once more.

Gideon moved swiftly. He grabbed the thing hanging from his belt—that coil of metal. It unfurled in his hand, glowing so brightly that Chandra was distracted. He swung his arm, and then the thing was twining around her.

"No!" she said, shocked and caught off guard. "Stop!"

It had broad, flexible blades and sharp edges, and it was cold . . . so *cold.* It tightened around

her, constricting her, stifling her breath. And its terrible cold trapped her fire, contained her heat, smothered her rage . . . As she struggled for air and shivered with cold, the weapon robbed her of consciousness.

But just before everything went black, she thought she heard him say, "I'm sorry."

CHAPTER SEVEN

When Chandra opened her eyes, she found herself staring into the beady eyes of a black snake.

Its tongue flicked out at her.

She flinched and tried to move back, but couldn't.

Her back was flat against a wall, her limbs uncomfortably chained in a spread-eagle position. Bound by her wrists and ankles, her movement was almost totally restricted.

As the snake's big face moved even closer, Chandra turned her head and made a stifled sound of protest. She really didn't like snakes.

"Ah." Someone spoke in a low, breathy voice. "It'sss awake."

She gaped at the snake. "Excuse me?" Her voice was a dry croak.

But the snake said nothing more for the moment.

Chandra blinked and tried to focus her vision. That was when she realized the "snake" was standing upright on a set of legs and wearing a black robe with a hood.

"Oh." She groaned as the realization penetrated her confusion. "You must be one of the Enervants I've heard so much about?"

"Yesss."

Her mistake was understandable. It was standing so close to her that its head almost entirely filled her field of vision. And from the neck up, this thing looked exactly like a snake. A *big* one.

She looked down and saw that it had hands; hands that were thin, almost delicate, and scaly black with long wrinkled fingernails. Strangely a snake with hands made sense to Chandra at this point. *Actual* snakes were pretty limited in their activities, after all; and none, so far as she knew, spoke or practiced magic.

Chandra wasn't sure what to make of these creatures, but she was sure they wouldn't like the inferno she was going to bring. But as she struggled against her bonds, she realized that she could barely move. And it wasn't because the chains were that tight. She felt absolutely exhausted, as if she hadn't eaten or slept for days.

Blinking a few times to clear her foggy vision, she looked at her surroundings. She was clearly being held in a dungeon. Stone walls, floor, and ceiling. No windows. No torches, either. No candles, no fire, no flames of any kind.

The only illumination in the room came from slimy-looking phosphorescent things clinging to the walls here and there. Chandra guessed that the snakelike sorcerers had brought them here from whatever swamp they called home.

With such faint light and no windows, the room was dark, stuffy, and dank. And it stank.

The odor of damp decay, she suspected, was coming from her companions. There were seven Enervants in the room with her. One was still peering into her face; its tongue flicked in and out every few moments, as if testing Chandra's scent.

The other six, who all looked just like the first one, were gliding silently around the room in a figure eight. Their bodies were evenly spaced as they followed the pattern at a steady pace. Their paths steadily intersected without ever bumping into each other or pausing in their flow.

Chandra found it eerie. "What are they doing?"

She coughed a little as she spoke. Her throat was dry and she was dying of thirst. But she'd be damned if she'd ask for anything.

To her surprise, her captor answered her. "Gathering ssstrength."

"Oh. Can't they do that elsewhere?"

The Enervant didn't answer. It just kept staring at her.

She tried another question. "Where am I? The Prelate's dungeon?"

The snake nodded, its head moving on its muscular neck in a slow, sinewy motion.

She tried to think of what else she wanted to ask, but she was so tired. It was hard to pull her thoughts together or make the effort to speak.

Chandra tried to remember what had happened to put her in this position.

She remembered the man, Gideon, and his weapon. She had never seen anything like it, but she was reasonably certain that he had used some form white-mana based magic to subdue her. Even in her weakened state, the weapon alone could not have pulled her into unconsciousness like that.

As if the Order back on Regatha weren't burden enough, she was in a dungeon on Kephalai because of some interfering heiromancer? But why would he be in league with these creatures? It didn't seem right.

Chandra remembered the feel of those coldly glowing white blades wrapping around her, constricting her, and trapping the flow of her fire. Imprisoning her power within her, so that she couldn't fight or defend herself. Or even breathe . . .

It surprised her that this Gideon wielded magic. She hadn't taken him for a mage. He looked like a warrior to her. Or maybe a tracker of some kind; one with special skills for an unusual quarry.

Chandra frowned, puzzled.

In that case, where was he now? Had he given her over, or had he abandoned his prey to superior forces?

Admittedly, Chandra hadn't been at her best just then, but Gideon's strength was impressive. Given that he was powerful, as well as quick with his hands, surely he didn't have to back down in the face of a few soldiers?

Perhaps he had decided he couldn't take on the soldiers *and* the gargoyles at the same time.

As Chandra watched the Enervants silently gliding through their pattern over and over in the dark dungeon, she realized that if Gideon had been ordered to kill her, then letting the Prelate's men have her might accomplish his goal.

But she wasn't sure he would leave such a thing to chance.

Chandra tugged against her chains, testing their strength as well as her own, and started thinking about how to get out of there.

She reached out with her senses, hoping to tap into the flow of mana. Even though she could feel its presence, she was having trouble concentrating enough to establish a solid bond.

What was *wrong* with her?

The Enervant who was guarding her suddenly hissed and turned its head away from her, which was something of a relief. She didn't enjoy being the object of its unwavering, beady-eyed stare. Its attention was focused on the narrow metal door across the room. Chandra looked that way, too, wondering what had drawn its interest.

A moment later, the hinges whined a little as the door opened.

"Oh, goody," Chandra said. "Visitors."

Two of the Prelate's soldiers entered, accompanied by another who she assumed was a telepath. Based on her physical appearance, Chandra assumed the woman belonged to the same order as the two mages who had died in the Sanctum of Stars earlier that day. Or had it been the day before? Come to think of it, Chandra had no idea how long she had been chained unconscious in this room, although the stiffness in her limbs suggested it had been a while.

The Enervants didn't look up at the newcomers, didn't even pause in their perambulations. They just kept moving back and forth silently, tracing their figure eight on the floor, over and over and over.

"Just watching them makes me tired," Chandra said as the mage, moving around the snake-headed wizards, approached her.

"No," said the woman. "It is not the watching. It is what you are watching."

"That is not a very encouraging start to this conversation," Chandra muttered.

"We are not here to encourage. Quite the opposite, really."

Chandra eyed her.

"They are Enervants." The mage nodded toward the six individuals moving steadily in their pattern. "This is their work."

"Yes, I've been told. They're gathering sssstrength," said Chandra imitating her captor. "I don't see why they have to gather it *here*, though."

The woman nodded. "They are gathering *your* strength."

"I thought they were having a little snake dance in my honor." Chandra scowled.

But Chandra understood. This was dark magic. These strange creatures were sapping her strength. She could feel the direct assault on her energy now that she knew about it.

And they were effective. Considering how exhausted she felt, she suspected they could quickly turn an ordinary mage into a useless husk.

Chandra glared at the telepath. "Your friends tried to read me, and they died for their efforts. Quit while you're ahead."

"I can be patient," the woman said coldly. "You may still be strong enough to resist now. You may even be strong enough to resist on my next visit. But you're much weaker now than you were yesterday, and tomorrow you will be weaker still. And when you are weak enough, we will succeed. You will not be able to conceal it from me then. I *will* find out what you did with the scroll."

"The scroll? That's what you want? I don't . . ." Cold surprise washed through Chandra.

The scroll.

"I don't know where it is," Chandra said, baffled by how they couldn't know this.

"You seem convinced of that, yes. But there are many corners in the mind, many places for things

to hide," said the telepath, her clear blue eyes radiating in the dark of the room. "You didn't succeed in killing everyone who was in the Sanctum of Stars, you know. Four soldiers survived. They saw you flee into the city streets with the scroll."

"Uh-huh." She wouldn't let herself think about what had happened. Truth be told, she was too tired to think about it, anyway.

"If you want the scroll back," Chandra said, "why not talk to the man who got it back last time?"

"The Prelate says he's gone." It was obvious the woman was only answering because she was curious to see what Chandra's reaction would be.

"Gone where?"

"I do not question the Prelate."

"No, *of course* not," said Chandra, using the same tone of voice the telepath had used moments before.

"Where is the scroll?" the mage demanded, realizing she was being mocked.

"Why does it matter so much to you?"

"You risked death *twice* to acquire it. Why does it matter so much to *you*?"

"If I tell you where the scroll is," Chandra said, "what then?"

"You destroyed the Sanctum of Stars, a holy place filled with Kephalai's most precious artifacts. You killed soldiers, guards, and mages dedicated to its protection. You damaged more than property. You damaged the will of the people of Kephalai. You created a city-wide panic. The death toll has not yet been measured." The mage's gaze was hostile. "But if you cooperate now and tell us where the scroll is, your sentence will be lenient."

"*How* lenient?"

"You will be executed. Quickly and humanely. Otherwise, we will leave you to the Enervants, and they are not know for their humanity."

"Well," Chandra said. "It's always nice to have choices."

"If you do not cooperate," the mage said, "if you force me to wait until you are weak enough for me to probe your mind for the answers we seek, then you will no longer have a choice. We will learn all that we want to know. I, personally, hope you decide to help us find the scroll. The Enervants' ways are are repellant to me. No one deserves what they have in store for you."

"*All* that you want to know?" Chandra said. "What answers are you looking for, besides the location of the scroll?"

"For starters, who are you, and what did you plan to do with the scroll?"

"I don't really like to talk about myself," Chandra said.

"Where were you born? Who are your people?"

"And I especially don't talk about my past."

The mage looked at her for a moment longer, then said, "It doesn't matter. Soon, I will know all that I want to know."

"You won't find out where the scroll is," Chandra said truthfully.

"Yes, I will. But, in any event, you have made your choice. I will inform the Prelate: death by slow torture."

"I look forward to it."

"I'm sure you do," she looked at Chandra with what seemed to be pitty. "These guards will remain outside the door should you decide to give us the answers we seek."

"How will they know when to come in?"

"This one is Dirk," she said indicating one of the guards. "Call his name, and he will come."

Only after the mage left the dungeon did Chandra risk dwelling on what the woman had told her.

They don't know where the scroll is.

It had been in Chandra's hand when she lost consciousness in the city streets, and she had woken up in captivity. She had assumed her captors had reclaimed possession of the scroll.

There was obviously more to Gideon than she thought. She'd seen for herself that he was fast, that he moved quickly. So he must have had time to conceal the scroll from the soldiers after incapacitating her.

Things were in chaos at the time, after all. Perhaps Gideon had claimed, when turning her unconscious carcass over to them, that she didn't have the scroll on her, and had planted the notion that she had hidden it somewhere.

Was that why he had let them capture her? So he could make off with the scroll?

I will kill *him for this.*

The rage felt good. It woke her up, cleared her head, and refreshed her senses.

She focused on her anger, on the fury in her heart at being duped by that man. She berated herself for the way he had taken her by surprise and overpowered her. She imagined him enjoying himself somewhere now, with her scroll, having a good laugh over her predicament.

Because of *him*, she was chained to a wall in a dungeon and being drained of energy by these snakes! *Get mad, this is good. Anger is accelerant. Rage is fuel. Fury is fire.*

She had to escape. Death by slow torture was

no way for a Planeswalker to die. More to the point, she couldn't hunt him, she couldn't get revenge on Gideon, if she died here.

A big boom would go a long way toward solving her current problem. But even with the reassuring glow of rage coursing through her now, she knew there was no way she could summon that kind of power. Not until she recovered from the sapping sorcery of the Enervants. And she'd only start recovering once she got away from them.

She had to act now. Immediately. The longer she was in their custody, the weaker she would get.

Chandra closed her eyes and focused on her breathing, concentrating, centering herself on the rage. She embraced the anger, nurtured the hot thirst for retribution. With each steady inhalation, she felt her tenuous mana bond become a little stronger, a little more within her reach. With each inhalation, she felt power coil firmly within her.

She targeted her attention on the seventh Enervant. He had moved to the side of the room where he was reaching into a box. From it he pulled what seemed to be a black, wriggling string. It was about a foot long and thin. He held it out with one hand and came close enough that Chandra could see that it was actually a snake.

"What are you going to do with that?" she asked.

The Enervant's eyes seemed to glitter in response.

"It's going to take more than that to crack me." Chandra was trying to put up a brave front, but, truthfully the snake was terrifying. Suspended by its tail, it moved purposefully, as though it was slithering toward the ground, its sharp head intent on reaching a target. The Enervant held

the snake higher and pinched it again beneath his other hand. He slowly drew his hand down the snake, stretching it taut. When he got to the head and let go, it remained as straight and stiff as a splinter of wood.

The black wizard held it out again, showing Chandra what he had done, perhaps taunting her with it, the dim phosphorescent light reflecting sickly in his eyes.

"Now we begin," he said with obvious pleasure.

Chandra steeled herself, not knowing what to expect. The Enervant went to her right hand and inspected it for a moment, his tongue flickering gently from his mouth. Chandra balled up a fist in response, but in retrospect it was the wrong thing to do. The creature leveled the straightened snake at her knuckles, placed its head directly between her index and forefinger, and pushed. The thing's head cut into her flesh easily, burning with a pain more intense than anything she had ever known.

Chandra screamed as the entire snake went into her hand, its form bulging beneath her skin as it began to slither up her arm. The pain was like nothing she had ever known.

"DIRK!" she screamed as loudly as she could. "Get in here now!"

Without any further promting, the two guards entered the room. "Get this thing out of my arm," she cried. "I'll tell you anything you want to know."

The guard called Dirk gave the command to the Enervant to do as she said. He produced a knife and made a small incision just above the snake's head, which emerged without prompting. The Enervant took hold of it with his withered nails

and pulled it out, spilling blood and interstitial fluid heedlessly. Both guards' faces went ashen. Chandra was sure the one behind Dirk was on the verge of fainting. For her own part, the only thing that kept Chandra conscious was a fury as pure the heart of the volcano. But she knew she could not let this show. Instead she let her head drop as though she'd fainted.

The guard called Dirk collected himself. "Well, out with it, then. Where's the scroll?" When Chandra didn't answer he nudged her, but she still gave no response. "Get some water," he told the other.

Dirk unshackled her right wrist and let her wounded arm hang. Although it was throbbing, Chandra didn't feel like there was lasting damage. She remained motionless with her head hanging until the guard came back with a pail and ladle. At that, Chandra raised her head weakly and looked at the guard. He held the full ladle out to her and she cupped the bowl in her hand, bending her head over it as though to drink, her hair falling around it to obscure the ladle from view.

Chandra focused her rage on the water and called on her power to heat it. Within seconds, the small amount of water had come to a boil, and she threw it into the guard's face, blinding him and scalding his flesh. He stumbled back into the Enervant, who dropped his knife and fell back, disrupting the path of the other enervants. The effect was immediate. Chandra could feel her strength returning, her power blossoming like a flower at the base of her skull and racing out to her extremities.

When the fire came to her like this, it was as if time slowed for Chandra. Everything around

LAURA RESNICK

her moved in slow motion, while she was able to think and move freely. Even as the others in the room were still trying to make sense of what was happening, Chandra grabbed the knife on the ground with her free hand and used it to pry the shackles on her left arm loose. Before the Enervant knew what was happening, she had released herself and was on top of it, driving the knife into his neck in the soft spot beneath its jaw. The snakeman went slack like a bag of grain.

She turned to deal with the other soldier, but he was was on his knees like a penitent, pleading for his life. Chandra ignored him and shifted her attention to the remaining six Enervants.

They were hissing noisily, their heads weaving and bobbing on necks that were much longer than they had originally seemed. They were moving to surround her, but Chandra noticed they were regulating their spacing and their movements were synchronizing again. She sensed they were trying to begin another ritual to drain her of her power. She had to act fast.

Chandra realized she was sweating and panting. The brief use of her power had already tired her far more than it should have, thanks to the Enervants' work. Searching for one act that would affect six adversaries, Chandra called on her remaining power to produce a sheet of fire between herself and the hissing snakes. As she had hoped, it halted their advance toward her.

However, they were still between her and the door. Not only could they prevent her escape, they could also leave the room and summon help. Fortunately, they were wholly focused on her, and they were obviously unwilling to pass through her fire. She needed to move quickly, though, before

they were able to act in concert again to sap her strength.

Fighting exhaustion and struggling hard to call forth more power in her weakened condition, Chandra spread her arms, then uttered a short spell that Mother Luti had taught her. She simultaneously clapped her hands together as she stared hard at the six wizards, keeping them all in focus. Her sheet of fire sprang around them like a trap, coiling to encircle them.

Their menacing hissing grew panicky as the fire closed in on them. Chandra clasped her hands together and squeezed hard, commanding her flames to embrace and consume her enemies. As the giant hooded snakes and their robes caught fire, their bodies writhed frantically. They clawed at each other, and their gaping jaws opened wide in agony, exposing their terrible fangs. The stench was unbelievable, and Chandra found it somehow disturbing that they didn't scream or make any noise beside that tortured hissing.

The burned soldier was still howling in pain, and the cowed one wept, openly terrified. The Enervants were still alive, but writhing in their death throes as the flames consumed them.

With her captors all but vanquished, Chandra fled past her fatal fire and out the door of her cell. Fortunately, the soldiers had left it unlocked when they entered.

Beyond the door was a narrow corridor that led in two directions. She looked to her right and could see a dead end. She had no choice but to go left. When she reached a corner, she was spotted by two soldiers standing guard in the intersecting hallway.

"Prisoner escaped!" one of them cried.

She ran straight into them, hurtling her full body weight at them before they could unsheathe their swords. Her best chance of staying alive now was to planeswalk out of Kephalai, and she needed to conserve what was left of her power if she was to enter the æther. She knocked one of them against the wall as hard as she could, and stomped on the other's stomach when he fell. Hoping that would at least slow them down, she ran onward.

She saw a stone staircase at the end of the corridor where four more guards waited.

Behind her, the soldiers she had just knocked down were shouting, "Prisoner escaping! Prisoner escaping!"

The soldiers she was approaching clearly heard. One of them, at the top of the stairs, shouted this same phrase through the bars of the door up there and called for help.

Another of the soldiers guarding the stairs saw her and warned her in a loud voice, "Within moments, thirty soldiers will come through that door! Surrender *now*!"

He was wrong. It didn't take moments. He had barely finished speaking when the door opened and armed soldiers began pouring through it.

And, if anything, he had underestimated their number.

Chandra turned around and ran back the way she had just come.

CHAPTER EIGHT

Fortunately, the two soldiers she had just knocked down hadn't expected her to turn back and trample them again. This time their feeble interference barely slowed her down as she dashed past.

Chandra knew she couldn't deal with all those reinforcements. As Gideon so obviously had understated, she had made herself conspicuous. She had to assume this was just the first wave. Now that the alarm had been sounded, the Prelate's entire army would be devoted to keeping her a prisoner or dispatching her. And in her current condition, they would succeed—not immediately and not without pain, but they would succeed.

She didn't have time to search for another way out of the prison. There might well not be one. And even if there were another way out, she had no chance of evading dozens of soldiers while she looked for it.

Her only remaining choice wasn't a good one, but at least there was a chance she would survive.

She turned a corner and ran back to the large cell where she had been held captive. Behind her, she could hear the footsteps, rattling swords, and shouts of a lot of soldiers.

In front of her, blocking the door to the cell, were the the two original guards, the coward supporting Dirk. When the coward saw her, a new look of horror washed across his puffy, sweating face.

"Out of my way!" Chandra snapped as she moved forward. They might have fully obliged had she not reached them before the two could move, shoving them to the floor outside the door.

Once inside she slammed the door shut. No lock on this side. Of course not. Dungeons were built to lock prisoners in, not to lock soldiers out.

A fetid cloud of smoke hung in the cell. The Enervants were dead, but their smoldering remains filled the room with an odor so foul Chandra could scarcely bear to breathe.

Coughing as the smoke and stench assaulted her, Chandra pressed her back against the door and heard heavy footsteps approaching. She had only moments now. A short controlled burst of fire welded the door to its jam. It wouldn't hold for long, but it would have to do.

She concentrated with all her might as she forged a path to the æther. The soldiers were pounding on the door, but Chandra was able to reach the meditative state she needed. *Breathe steadily and regularly.* At her first glimpse of the void, she hurled herself recklessly into it.

Behind her, on Kephalai, two guards—one an emotional wreck, the other gruesomely burned—would insist they had seen her enter the chamber. Their account would be dismissed as attempt to cover up incompetence when she wasn't found inside the cell. Nevertheless, there would be a thorough search of the whole prison, and that would take time. In the end, they'd never know

how she had disappeared. And when the Prelate received the report of Chandra's escape, she'd only be able to guess what had happened. In any case, without the mage who had followed Chandra back to Regatha last time, they'd never find her. She was out of their reach the moment she entered the æther.

Which wasn't the same thing as being *safe*.

Chandra fell through a tunnel of flame. And, having had no time to prepare herself for planeswalking, she was unprotected from the raw, red, furious force of this fire. It scalded her so brutally that she cried out in agony, feeling it burn through her flesh, her blood, her bones, and sink into her soul with angry, destructive heat.

Disoriented and in pain, she kept plummeting through the endless reaches of the void between the planes of the Multiverse. Her whole body felt consumed by fire and torn apart by her relentless fall. She had entered the Blind Eternities in sudden desperation, without sufficient power or focus, and now she was paying the price for such a rash act.

She had only entered the æther without preparation once before—the very first time she walked—and it had come close to killing her. Then, as now, she was fleeing death. But now, at least, she knew what was happening. This time, she didn't feel the blind, animal terror she had felt then. This time, she struggled to take charge of her planeswalk, rather than simply succumbing in helpless fear to its effects.

Chandra tried to focus on her breathing, her heartbeat, her body's rhythms . . . but the air in her lungs felt like boiling water, fire scorched her belly, and ice filled her veins. She tried to concentrate on her mana bonds to maintain her power, but

the Blind Eternities flowed around her with the brilliance of a billion suns, blinding and stunning her, while at the same time soaking her in dark fatigue. She tried to reach out and sense the energy of different planes, to seek out a physical reality where she could anchor herself, but everything around her tumbled in a multicolored chaos.

The channel through which Chandra plunged became fearfully black, an entropic void sucking at her life force. Just as she thought she would lose consciousness, fire became water, cold and viscous. Chandra panicked as a drowning sensation enveloped her before everything became white, binding and smothering, and surrounded her like an unbearable weight. A shift to green created pain she didn't understand, as if her bones were trying to push through her skin. And when fire engulfed her again, she welcomed the familiar agony.

When the pain became so familiar that it ceased to register, Chandra was so disoriented and exhausted, she couldn't move or think or react. She floated erratically in the whirling mana storm that surrounded her, dazed and inert for what seemed a very long time. Consciousness had become a relative state: it was becoming harder for her to separate herself from her surroundings. She told herself many times to gather her senses and find a way out of here before she died, yet she remained still, unable to move, as if her mind had become disconnected from her body. She had to focus on something tangible.

Kephalai . . .

Memory penetrated the haze of chaos. Chains on her hands and feet. Combat with other beings. Running. Panting.

She focused on these memories, coaxing them into vivid life in her scattered, confused mind.

Kephalai . . . Sanctum of Stars . . .

Knowledge of her physical reality, of her life on the planes of the Multiverse, started returning to her. And with this knowledge came the fervent, forceful desire to rejoin the dimensions of physical existence. To overcome her gradual absorption into the æther. To escape the Blind Eternities and find a plane on which to reclaim her power, her physical life, and her mental coherence.

She concentrated on the most vivid of the memories that were dancing around the edge of her consciousness. Memories of fear, anger, pain, urgency. She didn't remember the details now, but she vaguely knew she had lost the scroll, had failed to achieve her goal. This infuriated her, and she welcomed the rage, letting it warm her blood and sharpen her senses.

But she still wasn't strong enough. She instinctively recognized that she needed even more visceral connection to her physical life. So, with foreboding, she opened herself to the old memories, to her past, to the sensations she had banished to the realm of nightmare, to the events she never thought about, recalled, or acknowledged.

She opened herself to the fire of sorrow and grief, of shame and regret, to that which consumes innocence.

In the echoing corridors of her memory, she listened to their screams, hearing their agonized cries now as clearly as if it were happening all over again. In her mind's tormented eye, she watched their writhing bodies now, just as she had watched them then. Helpless. Horrified. Consumed by guilt. She forced herself to dwell on the memory

of what their burning flesh had smelled like. She felt the pain of the sobs that wouldn't come out of her mouth.

And when the blade of a sword swept down to her throat, to end her life . . .

Chandra sprang into awareness.

How long had she been wandering here, falling and floating between the physical planes of the Multiverse?

She banished the question. All she must think about was escaping the chaotic, sense-warping maze of the Blind Eternities. Until she was safely on a physical plane again, nothing else mattered, and no other thought could be allowed to penetrate her vulnerable focus.

She spread her senses and tried to find something familiar to orient her. She felt the flow of mana, which was reassuring, but it mingled with so many other forces in a bewildering whirlwind of color that she felt wrung out and frustrated as she tried to bond with it. Still, with no other way to survive and escape, she concentrated, summoning all her will, all her rage and heat and passion, and focused on channeling the magical energy.

When she finally felt ready, Chandra propelled herself through the undulating, swirling colors that consumed her, seeking the solid energy of a physical plane. She was vaguely aware that there was someplace she wanted to return, a place where she had a community and a purpose . . . but she couldn't even recall it well enough to look for it, let alone control this planeswalk to that extent. Right now, *all* that mattered was finding a plane, any plane at all. Later, she would think about where exactly in the Multiverse she wanted to be.

Then she sensed it. A dark, bitter energy . . .

but blessedly physical, solid, and tangible. And because she could sense it, because her will drew her toward it, a path to it began opening before her in the æther.

She hesitated. The plane she was approaching didn't feel at all familiar, and it certainly didn't feel welcoming.

Should she travel further? The next plane might be a better choice.

No. The next plane she encountered might just as easily be a worse choice. Or, in her weakness and confusion, she might not find another plane at all. Not before she succumbed to the consuming whirlwind she was trying to escape.

It must be now. Here. Go.

She moved through the æther, following the path that beckoned her to the physical plane she sensed. She let the plane's sullen energy lure her forward as she focused with all her might on making the transition away from the eternal flow surrounding her to the finite, solid reality that lay ahead of her.

Her body, her senses, her mind, all felt torn apart, stretched to the breaking point between two realities. She fought fear and struggled for control. She reached for the dark plane she sensed, stretching toward it with all her will.

Chandra's feet touched solid ground.

The sensation was so startling, the weight of her own body so unexpected, that she fell down, collapsing into an awkward heap with a choked gasp.

Then she lay there, eyes closed, her face pressed into the damp earth with grateful relief. She spread her palms against the ground, reveling in its solid, unyielding presence.

I'm alive. Alive!

The worst was over. She had escaped Kephalai and the Prelate's dungeon; escaped death by slow torture at the hands of the Enervants.

Right now, being lost on some wholly unfamiliar plane that radiated dark energy didn't matter. Even losing the scroll to that mage didn't matter. She was just very, very happy she wasn't dead.

Lying on the ground, soaking up the wonderful feeling of being alive, Chandra gradually became aware of a scuffling, scurrying sound nearby. When she opened her eyes to see what had made the noise, she realized that it was nighttime. She pushed herself to a sitting position and looked around, blinking as her eyes adjusted to the dark shadows of her surroundings.

High overhead, a full moon glowed white in the endless, starless black of the night sky. Its cool, silvery light shone down brightly on an eerie landscape of twisted trees, squatting bushes, dark expanses of emptiness, and the tumbled ruins of crumbling stone structures. The trees and bushes that Chandra could make out in the moonlight looked strangely stark and bony.

She realized none of them had any leaves.

That seemed odd. The temperature was mild. The air was cool, but not uncomfortably so— certainly not enough to suggest winter or a season of dormancy. The damp ground suggested precipitation. Indeed, the air itself felt humid. Obviously, drought hadn't caused the absence of leaves on all of the trees and bushes around here.

She wondered what *had* caused it. Had there been a fire here recently?

Curious, she rose to her feet, intending to examine some of the denuded branches more

closely. The act of rising, however, made her so dizzy she almost fell down again. Her vision swam darkly, and she felt light-headed.

That was when she realized she was desperately thirsty. She recalled now that she had been thirsty even back in the dungeon on Kephalai. And who knew how long ago that was? What seemed like days could also have been minutes—or even longer. Regardless, her physical needs were reasserting themselves now.

Chandra took a steadying breath and realized she must find water. Her stomach rumbled, and she realized that finding something to eat would be a good idea, too.

The air was heavy with damp and decay. Not the fetid odor of the Envervants in her cell back on Kephalai, but the rich, dark smell of sodden soil, of decomposing vegetation mingling with fog. This seemed like a plane where quenching her thirst shouldn't be too difficult. There must surely be substantial water here.

She heard scuffling again in the nearby undergrowth. The rustling sound of dead plants being brushed aside by some small creature's passing struck her as strange. Like the barren trees and naked bushes, the rustling of dead vegetation didn't seem to go with the damp richness of the soil and the air.

With her curiosity reawakened, Chandra walked past the tumbled, moss-covered stone walls surrounding the spot where she had entered this plane, and went over to a dark, twisted tree that was silhouetted by the moonlight. Her feet encountered a denser, softer surface as she got close to the tree, and she looked down.

Mulch, she realized, all around the tree where the leaves had once fallen. She wrapped her fingers

around a slender tree branch and gave it a slight squeeze. She was no expert, but the wood didn't feel right. It was slightly soft, as if the tree were rotting.

Chandra wondered whether the tree had become diseased and shed its leaves in its initial stages of dying.

She looked around at the moon-swept landscape, where all she saw were bare branches drooping in the silvery light.

It seemed that all the trees in the area had become infected with the same disease. Chandra started to wonder whether this was a local phenomenon, or whether the whole plane was covered with dying vegetation.

She started to feel uneasy, increasingly aware of the dark, bitter energy that permeated this place. Instinct warned her that whatever was killing the plant life here, the cause was more likely magical than mundane.

With her senses restored and her mind functioning again, Chandra realized that she was more than ready to return to Keral Keep. She would report that she had failed to get the scroll and didn't even know where it was now.

Well, presumably it's in the hands of some opportunist on Kephalai, she thought with a scowl.

She found this *infuriating*.

It would also be difficult for her to return to Kephalai and hunt down Gideon. Impossible, really. She might not be a shrewd strategic planner, and she *hated* losing, but she wasn't a fool. She knew that she had very little chance of moving freely on Kephalai ever again. *No* chance, actually. She had destroyed the Sanctum of Stars, wreaked havoc in the city, and stolen the scroll a second time.

Because of her actions, she would be hunted on Kephalai for a long time. There would certainly be a price on her head. Descriptions of her would circulate. If there were any tall, red-headed women in the Prelate's realm, they'd be harassed. She might even become the most notorious criminal they had ever known. In spite of what she knew was right, this gave Chandra a giddy feeling. She would go down in legend, or at least she hopped so.

Chandra moved over to a hedge of bushes and absently examined their branches, wondering whether she could have escaped with the scroll if that black-haired mage with his glowing, dagger-tail whip hadn't interfered. She'd never know for sure, but it was easier to blame him for the way things had gone. And she reveled for a few moments in a vision of roasting him alive in the fires of retribution.

Acknowledging that this dream would likely never be realized, she sighed. Meanwhile, her examination of the bushes revealed that they, too, were dying.

She decided that, ravenous though she was, if she came across any trees or bushes bearing fruit, she wouldn't eat it. Whatever was killing these plants could have easily infected other, seemingly healthy, foliage.

Chandra gazed around the darkened land-scape again and realized that, in fact, she was skeptical about finding any healthy-looking plants, at all. The sullen shroud of dark magic she sensed earlier seemed to stretch far and wide across this place.

She needed to get out of here and return to Regatha. There were problems to be faced

and solved back there. Hopefully, the oufe tribe that wanted her dead had calmed down a bit by now. And as for the Order of Heliud, and Walbert's demand that Chandra be turned over to his custody . . . Well, just let Walbert's soldiers *try* to come take her from the mountains. She'd make sure it didn't take long for them to rethink *that* plan.

Even so, as much as she wanted to leave this plane immediately, she knew—particularly after her recent experience—that she needed to recoup some of her strength before trying to re-enter the Blind Eternities. She had to search for some water, then get some rest. The syrupy darkness of the night sky and the full brilliance of the moon suggested that morning was still a long way off. By then, Chandra should be ready to planeswalk back to Regatha.

"All right," she said, looking around at the eerie landscape. "Water."

Despite her driving thirst, her surroundings were so creepy that it was with some reluctance that she set out in *any* direction. Although it was unquestionably better than being chained to a wall with her power being sucked away by seven giant snakes as a prelude to death by torture, wandering alone through the darkness was still a less-than-enjoyable endeavor.

She had not gone far when she heard noise coming from a cluster of bushes that she was passing, the rustle of dead vegetation under stomping footsteps, some faint, high-pitched squealing, some growling.

Chandra crouched down and crept closer to the commotion. The intensity of the squealing increased sharply, scraping at her senses. The

growling was replaced by satisfied grunting and the noisy smacking of . . . robust chewing?

Chandra pushed further into the thicket, taking care to move silently. Peering between leafless branches, she spotted her quarry.

She found herself looking at some sort of goblin. It was squat and ungainly, with lumpy gray skin, hairy legs, and arms so long they would surely drag along the ground when it stood up and walked. Its bald head was immense, and its long, pointy ears flopped sideways in a ridiculous manner. It was hunched over and grunting, while something in its grasp squealed. Chandra saw a tail and flailing little paws . . .

When she realized the beast was eating a small animal *alive*, she gasped aloud in revulsion.

The goblin heard her and whirled around to face her. Its fangs dripped with blood and entrails as it growled at her. The little animal in its grasp continued squealing in agony. Chandra's appalled gaze flashed to the animal's eviscerated torso and wiggling paws.

"Ugh! What are you *doing*?" she demanded. "Even for a goblin, this is unbelievable!"

The goblin stared at her for a moment, crouching frozen while its agonized prey flailed and squealed. Then, as if afraid Chandra would try to steal its treat, the creature stuffed the entire mole into its mouth and crunched down hard. Chandra winced at the mole's final, shrill scream, followed closely by the sound of its splintering bones. The goblin's cheeks bulged as it chewed, still staring at Chandra.

Then the creature swallowed its meal in one huge gulp and went completely still. The goblin and Chandra stared at each other in silence.

Ⴔ

"Well," she said at last. "That may not be the single most disgusting thing I've ever seen, but it's definitely on the list."

"List?" The goblin's voice was deep and husky.

"Never mind."

"Don't kill," it said.

"Agreed. You don't kill me, and I won't kill you."

It nodded. Its ears flopped a little.

"Where are we?" Chandra asked.

The goblin looked around for a moment, then returned its gaze to Chandra. "Bushes."

"I meant, what's the name of this realm?"

"Diraden."

"Never heard of it."

The goblin pointed at her. "What name?"

"Chandra. And you?"

"Jurl."

"Jurl, show me where there's water." When the goblin didn't move, just continued to stare at her, she added, "I don't like to brag, Jurl, but I'm a powerful fire mage. If you take me to water, I'll be nice. If you don't, I'll be mean."

"Water." The goblin looked over its shoulder. "Maybe not safe."

"Not safe? Is the water bad?" That might explain why everything around here was dying.

Jurl shook his head. "Water good."

"Then what's the problem?"

"Maybe guarded."

"By who?"

"Prince Velrav. Sometimes."

"A prince guards the water?" Chandra said skeptically.

"Servants."

"Oh, *servants* of the prince guard the water." That made a little more sense. But not much.

"Why guard water in a place as wet as Diraden?"

"See who come. Maybe take."

"Take? You mean, the prince's servants capture those who come to the water?"

"Sometimes."

"Do they take everyone? Or just goblins?"

"Everyone."

"So far, you're the only, er, person that I've met. Who else lives on Diraden?"

"Some like me. Some like . . ." Jurl shrugged. "Others. Many others. And some like you."

"And Prince Velrav's servants take them all?"

"Take *some* of all."

"Why?" Chandra asked.

"Hunger."

That was disconcerting. "They're taken when they're near the water?"

The goblin shrugged. "Near water. Near wood. Near ruins. Near hill. Near village. Near castle. Near—"

"So you're saying that the prince's servants have taken individuals from everywhere?" What a lovely plane she had stumbled onto.

"Yes."

"In that case, I might as well get water." And then maybe she'd try leaving Diraden straight away, without bothering to pause for rest. The situation here sounded deranged and deadly—and perfectly in keeping with the atmosphere she had sensed. If she felt better after drinking her fill, then perhaps leaving while she was still fatigued—but with proper preparation this time—would be better than sticking around here until she felt stronger. "Jurl, I'll bet you know this place well. Do you know how to get water without being bothered by Prince Velrav's servants?"

The goblin stared at her silently. Although its grotesque face showed no expression, she sensed it was suspicious of her request.

"If you take me there," Chandra said, "I won't tell anyone. I won't betray you. I'm thirsty. I just want to get water, and then go away."

"Go away?"

"Yes. You'll never see me again." It was a promise she intended to keep.

Jurl studied her. "Go away soon?"

"*Very* soon."

"How soon?"

"By morning."

"No." The goblin shook its head.

Chandra frowned. "Why not?"

"No morning."

"What?"

"Morning never come," Jurl said. "Not here."

✳ ✳ ✳ ✳ ✳

After some discussion, Chandra guessed that Prince Velrav was some sort of necromancer who had pulled a veil of eternal night across this plane. There was presumably a good reason for this, but Jurl didn't know what it was. Nor did Jurl remember an era when things had been different, so this had apparently been going on for quite some time.

When Chandra asked how long the trees had been naked and dying, he said, "Always."

She supposed perpetual darkness explained *why* they were dying. And black magic probably explained why they were dying so slowly that, as far back as Jurl could remember, they had looked exactly the way they looked right now.

But it was possible that this was just what normal trees looked like on the dark plane of

Diraden, swamped in black magic and ruled by a demented mage who occasionally had his subjects captured and brought back to his castle to satisfy "hunger." Jurl seemed to know no more than that about the "taking" of various individuals over the years; nor did he seem to think anything more *needed* to be known about it.

A goblin's life revolved around pretty simple interests, after all: hunt, eat, drink, reproduce, make merry, fight, kill, be killed. It seldom got more complicated than that.

It was a welcome relief that the water that Jurl led her to wasn't far away. They passed through a moonlit copse of tall, thin, trees with thick, spidery roots that had snaked across the surface of ground, covering the path in long, lumpy twists of rotting wood and thick, sickly vines. Beyond the wood, they came to a lagoon. Silvery light from the moon glinted off the still surface of the water, which was rimmed by a dense thicket of vegetation.

Chandra surveyed the sinister-looking pool of water. "How long have you been coming here?"

"Always."

Because some species of goblin matured fast, growing to adulthood within a couple of years of their birth, "always" might only mean a year or two. On the other hand, some goblins lived a very long time. Chandra was unsure which category Jurl fell into, but couldn't bring herself to ask.

"Water good," Jurl said encouragingly. He lay face down beside the lagoon, stuck his head into the water, and began drinking.

Chandra walked a few judicious steps away from his noisy gulping, then knelt down, reached a cupped hand into the lagoon, and scooped up a small quantity of water, which she studied in the

Φ

moonlight. It was clear and cold. When she brought it close to her nose, it had no odor. She bent over her hand to cautiously take a sip. It tasted fine.

With a shaky sigh of relief, she lay face down at the edge of the lagoon, bracing her hands by her shoulders, and drank her fill. After slaking her thirst, she rested briefly, then drank some more. When she was done, she realized how dehydrated she had been. Already, thanks to the water, Chandra's thoughts felt clearer, her body more responsive, her senses sharper. She was still tired, but she was in complete command of herself again.

Suddenly, the goblin made a hissing sound.

Chandra glanced at him and saw that he was frozen in position and staring across the lagoon. She followed his gaze, but she didn't see anything, which wasn't surprising. Jurl's eyes were probably better accustomed to this dim light than hers.

She whispered, "What's wrong?"

"Bog Wraith," the goblin growled. "*Bad*."

Chandra froze, peering into the darkness and trying to see the creature that Jurl saw. "Is that what takes people?"

"No. Can't take. Can tell."

"Can tell?" Chandra repeated. "It will tell its master it saw us here?"

"Yes."

And presumably its master was Prince Velrav. "Great."

"Kill," said Jurl.

"Kill it? I can't even see it."

"There." One long, lumpy arm pointed to a twisted tree that leaned out over the water, its barren branches touching the surface of the lagoon.

Staring hard, Chandra was able to make out something that looked like pale white skin gleaming in the moonlight. Then she realized that some of the shapes she had assumed were branches were actually the long, dark tendrils of the Bog Wraith's hair, floating eerily in the still air. The creature itself floated, too; a pale, transparent figure veiled in black shadows.

"Bad," Chandra agreed, aware of a chill in her blood as she studied the silently watchful creature.

"*Kill*," Jurl repeated.

This thing seemed familiar . . . She realized that it reminded her of the ghost warden she had destroyed on Regatha.

That wasn't the sort of incident she wanted to repeat here. She intended to leave Diraden unnoticed, not create a commotion and attract attention. And she wanted to enter the æther in a sane and steady manner, not to reenact her frantic and nearly fatal departure from Kephalai.

"No," she said to Jurl. "I won't kill it. All that thing has seen is a woman and a goblin drinking water. So what if it tells? Let's go quietly now."

As she turned to go, the goblin grunted, obviously dissatisfied.

When they had traveled some distance, Jurl said, "Now eat?"

She thought of his recent meal, which she had interrupted, and said truthfully, "I'm not that hungry."

"Sleep?"

"No, I'm going to leave," she said decisively. Diraden was no place to linger.

"Leave where?"

"It's complicated."

"Leave now?"

"Soon." And since she didn't want the goblin asking questions while she prepared to planeswalk, it was time to bid him farewell. "Thank you for taking me to water, Jurl. You've been, um, a good host."

"Still hungry." Jurl nodded at some nearby bushes. "Hunt."

"Enjoy." She tried not to think about it. "Goodbye."

"Wait here. Jurl bring food."

Jurl turned and entered the nearby thicket. Chandra had been wrong in her initial assumption that his long arms would drag on the ground. He walked with them bent sharply at the elbows, shoulders wide and forearms dangling at his sides, and he could move with surprising speed and silence.

Chandra turned away and continued walking as she considered her options. Not wanting to be there if the Jurl did return, she decided it would be best to return to the ruins where she had arrived, since the crumbling walls offered a little cover. It also made sense to her to open a path to the Blind Eternities at same spot she had entered the plane.

Fortunately, the journey to water had not taken her very far from the place she sought. She retraced her steps without difficulty and arrived back at the ruins before long. The crumbling, lichen-covered walls looked stark and foreboding in the eerie, eternal night.

As her gaze traveled over her stony destination, Chandra was surprised to see a flash of bright white light explode silently from within the ruins, although she couldn't see what had caused it. A stone wall stood between her and the source of the sudden, bold flare.

She froze in her tracks. She didn't think this source of bright light had anything to do

LAURA RESNICK

with this dark Prince Velrav, but wanted to be cautious, none the less.

She stretched out her senses in order to call on the mana of the Keralian Mountains as a means to protect herself. A flash of panic washed through her when she realized she could scarcely feel it.

Breathe, she told herself, smothering the fear. Breathe.

She concentrated. She focused on her memory of other planes, of other sources, but she still couldn't feel that flow of red mana. How was that possible? She was feeling stronger, better than she had a while ago, but she couldn't establish a mana bond.

Stop. Think.

She squared her shoulders and moved forward, her footfalls silent on the damp ground. Whatever was going on inside these stony ruins, she needed this space to commence her planeswalk back to Regatha. And, if necessary, she would make her temporary claim on these ruins clear to others. With or without the use of magic.

She crept up to the walls of the ruins, stepped quietly over some fallen stones, and peered around a corner, looking to the spot where the burst of light seemed to have originated.

She saw a man rising slowly to his feet as he seemed to gather himself and reconnoiter his surroundings.

Chandra saw two dark smudges on his tan leggings where he had been kneeling in the mud. His long, tousled hair hung in his face as he turned toward Chandra.

When the man saw her staring at him, he went still.

After a brief pause, he said, "Hello, Chandra."

Cold shock washed through her. "*Gideon.*"

CHAPTER NINE

I wasn't sure you'd still be alive. That was some walk you took." Gideon's voice was dry.

"How did you . . ." Chandra's heart was pounding as she realized what the answer had to be. "You *followed* me? You followed my trail through the Blind Eternities?"

He nodded. Just one small, downward movement of his chin. No motion wasted.

"*Planeswalker*," she breathed, still stunned. She hadn't forgotten the promises she'd made to herself about what she'd do if she ever found him again, but this revelation changed things a bit.

There was no wonder he had been able to catch her off guard and capture her so easily in that street back on Kephalai. *A Planeswalker!* He would be at least as powerful as she was. And he was a little older than she, so he was probably more experienced, more skilled at using his power, given that he'd had more time to learn and practice.

Gideon's gaze traveled over her. "I see that you're all right now."

Apart from looking like he'd taken a tumble when he entered this plane, his appearance was exactly the same as it had been.

She said, "Apparently that walk didn't do you any harm."

He gave a small, dismissive shrug. "I had time to prepare."

And he evidently knew that she hadn't.

Chandra was impressed that he had been able to follow the erratic trail of her confused wandering through the Blind Eternities. That had certainly taken skill.

Impressed—and disturbed. Why had he bothered?

She doubted she'd like his reasons, whatever they were.

"Where are we?" Gideon asked.

"You don't know?"

"I was following *you*," he reminded her.

"I got lost," she said irritably.

"I could tell." He looked around. "So you don't know where we are?"

"It's called Diraden. What are you doing here?"

He walked past her, moving beyond the ruined stone walls to look out over the landscape. "Like I said, I followed you."

"Why?"

"Everything's dying here," he observed.

"Where's my scroll?" Chandra demanded, noticing that he didn't have it on him in any obvious place.

"It's not your scroll." Gideon walked over to a tree, examined the naked branches, and used his foot to brush aside some loose dirt.

"It's not yours, either!" Chandra said.

"No," he agreed absently as he knelt down to touch the ground. He picked up a handful of damp soil, closed his fist around it, and inhaled deeply as he looked up at the sky.

"Where *is* it?" Chandra demanded.

Gideon was scarcely paying attention to her, which irked her. He stood upright again, looked into the distance, and said quietly, "Everything is wrong here."

"I asked you a question," she said with gritted teeth.

Ignoring her comment, he brushed past her and walked back into the ruins. Chandra followed him. When she started to speak again, he held up a hand to silence her. He was circling the spot where he had arrived on this plane. There was a frown of concentration on his face.

Chandra decided she'd had *enough*. "You tricked me! You helped the Prelate's soldiers capture me! You *stole* my scroll—"

"You stole it, too," he said dismissively, still frowning as he looked up at the sky again. "And it's not yours."

"I was imprisoned because of you! Enervants tried to drain all my power!"

"Enervants?" That got his attention for a moment. He glanced in her direction. "Do they smell as bad as people say?"

"Yes."

"Enervants," he murmured. "That explains why your planeswalk went so badly. You were weakened."

"In part," she snapped. "The other part is that I had to enter the æther just moments ahead of dozens of soldiers! They tortured me to find out where the scroll was, and they would have done it until I died because I didn't know where it was!"

"Yes, I heard." Gideon seemed lost in thought, his mind scarcely on the conversation as he said,

"All things considered, you did well to survive. But it's a pity you chose *this* place to end your walk."

"So sorry you don't like it," Chandra said acidly. "But since you weren't invited in the first place, why don't you just leave?"

He looked at her. "You haven't figured it out."

His face was in shadows and his expression guarded, but something about his bland tone infuriated her.

"If you followed me to take me prisoner and drag me back to Kephalai, then you made a big mistake, Gideon!" She threw her hands out to encircle him with a ring of fire . . .

And nothing happened.

He stood there calmly, not moving a muscle, not reacting physically at all. His voice sounded faintly amused when he said, "Indeed."

Chandra stared at her hands in bewildered shock, turning them over and studying her palms as if she could read the answer there to her sudden absence of power.

"But I feel much better now," she muttered. "So what . . ."

"You may feel better," Gideon said, "but surely there's something you *don't* feel?"

"I . . ." She frowned, realizing what he meant. "*Mana.*" Suddenly, her difficulty in feeling it earlier made sense.

He nodded. "Something's blocking our access to mana.

She stared at him in surprise. "Blocking mana?"

"It's not completely effective," he said. "That's why you feel *something*. But it's effective enough to be a serious problem for us."

"Us?" She realized the full import of what he was telling her. "You're without power, too?"

L A U R A   R E S N I C K

"As much as you are," he confirmed.

"I noticed it was hard to feel the flow," she said, thinking back. "Hard to bond. But I thought that was because I was still weak."

"No." He shook his head. "If you concentrate long and hard, you can probably call on enough mana here to start a small cooking fire. But that's about all, while it's being blocked so well."

Chandra had never heard of such a thing. "What could do this?"

"I'm not sure. Something very powerful, obviously."

"Or some*one*?" She thought of the hungry prince.

Gideon shrugged. "It would take constant focus and a lot of strength. The effort would be enormous. A big drain on just one person."

"So he probably has help," she mused.

"He?" Gideon repeated.

"There's a necromancer named Prince Velrav who rules here."

"Of course," Gideon said. "Black mana would be abundant here."

"Is that why it's always nighttime here?"

He looked at her sharply. "Always?"

She told him what she had learned from Jurl.

"A goblin," Gideon mused. "I suppose you couldn't get any sense from him of whether this phenomenon is recent or has been going on for centuries?"

"No."

Jurl had been pretty typical of goblins, in Chandra's experience: neither bright, nor articulate.

Gideon looked up at the night sky. "No clouds. But no stars."

"I noticed that, too," she said. "I've never seen that before."

"I doubt that's the normal night sky here."

"You think Velrav pulled a . . ." Chandra shrugged. "A *shroud* over this plane?"

"That's one way of putting it," Gideon said.

"Is that what's restricting the mana?"

"I don't know. But I've never experienced anything like this, and I've never been anywhere where *that* had happened." He jerked his chin skyward. "Perpetual night attributed to the local necromancer king . . ."

"Prince."

"My guess is, the two things are related. What else did your goblin friend tell you?"

"'Friend' would be an exaggeration."

"He led you to water. He didn't try to kill you. For a goblin, that sounds pretty friendly."

"Yes," she said pensively, reflecting on the encounter. Her first impression of Jurl, when she saw him eating his squealing prey alive, was that he was like all other goblins she had encountered— only more so. "He *was* surprisingly nice to me. I wonder why?"

"I don't suppose you threatened to set fire to him?" Gideon said dryly.

"Oh, yeah. Maybe that's why."

"What else did he tell you about Velrav?"

Chandra recounted Jurl's vague comments about Velrav's servants abducting individuals from every race living on Diraden, in order to satisfy the "hunger." She concluded by describing the encounter with the Bog Wraith.

Gideon said, "So you didn't kill it and alert Velrav's entire army to your presence?"

"No," she said stonily.

"It's nice to see you're learning from your mistakes."

"What do *you* know about my—"

"Before we go to all the trouble of destroying this . . . yes, *shroud* is a good word for it, we should make sure—"

"Hold on, what do you mean 'we'?" she said. "If you're determined to meddle in local problems, that's your choice. Enjoy yourself! But this has nothing to do with me. All *I* want to do is get the blazes *off* this creepy plane and . . . " The full weight of the problem facing them hit Chandra like a physical blow. She swayed a little as she realized exactly what this meant.

"Ah," Gideon said. "Therein lies the rub."

"We can't leave," she said, appalled by the realization.

"Not until we can establish proper mana bonds. As long as it's restricted . . ."

"We're stuck here."

Fleeing Kephalai in a weakened state, Chandra had risked dying in the Blind Eternities. And here, without access to any real power, she risked living the rest of her days in perpetual night.

"I'm stranded." She gazed at her handsome companion in horror. "With *you*."

"Well, if you get bored with me," he said, "there's always Jurl."

"I suppose you're going to suggest that you and I . . ." She swallowed, so revolted by the idea that she had trouble even saying it. "That we . . . work together. To get out of here."

"I can manage alone, if you'd rather just give in and settle down here. But, yes, I—"

"Give *in*?"

"I imagine it will be easier to escape this plane

if both of us are working on the problem." His lips relaxed momentarily into what might have been a slight smile. "Together."

She thought it over. "There are certain conditions, if you want my help."

"By all means, let's pause to negotiate the terms under which we'll cooperate."

"*I* didn't ask you to come here," she reminded him. "Your being here is entirely your own fault. You shouldn't have followed me. While we're on the subject, you also shouldn't have stolen my scroll or helped the Prelate's soldiers capture me!"

"I think we're digressing."

Chandra said, "My conditions are as follows."

"Go on."

"I won't return to Kephalai. You will not take me back there. You will not trick me or manipulate me into going there again."

"Agreed."

"Nor will you inform the Prelate, her forces, or any other inhabitants of Kephalai where I go when I leave here."

"Agreed," he said.

"You will not betray me to Prince Velrav or his minions in order to secure your own escape, and you will not prevent me from leaving this plane."

His black brows rose. "You *do* have a low opinion of me."

"If you don't like my terms," she said, "that's fine. We don't have to work together."

"No, your terms are fine. I agree to them."

She searched his face to see if she trusted his word on this. His expression gave away little. But she refused to be afraid of him . . . and she recognized, however reluctantly, that it made more

sense for them to cooperate here than to be at odds with each other.

He said, "As long as we're negotiating our partnership . . ."

"We're not partners," Chandra said sharply. "We're just . . . um . . ."

"I have some conditions, too."

"Oh?"

"You will—at least, insofar as you are capable of it—*think* before you act, while we are here."

"How dare—"

"I don't want to spend the rest of my life here— and probably a very short life, at that—because you didn't use your head." When she just glowered at him, he prodded, "Well?"

"Insofar as I am *capable*," she said darkly, "I will think before I act."

"Good. Next condition: You will not kill anyone who isn't a danger to us."

"How are we deciding who is or isn't a danger?" she asked suspiciously.

"Let's agree you'll trust my judgment on that."

"*No*." She turned away.

His hand on her arm stopped her. "Chandra."

She turned her head. Their eyes met. His were very serious. To her surprise, he didn't look angry. She wasn't quite sure what she saw there, though.

He said softly, "We could die here."

Gideon was a little taller than she. Chandra tilted her head up and said, "Then I'll die because of *my* judgment. Not *yours*."

His hand still held her arm. "I don't want to kill any innocents while I'm trying to get out of here."

The thought of innocents bothered her.

"I don't, either," she said, aware of how close together they were standing. So close that she

noticed now he needed to shave. The dark shadow starting to darken his jaw would become more obvious by morning . . . which wouldn't come, of course. Not on Diraden.

Gideon said, "You can be a little . . . reckless that way."

His gaze dropped, and his dark lashes lowered. Chandra had a feeling he was staring at her lips. She licked them, and she felt the grip on her arm tighten ever so slightly.

"I was trying to survive. They'd have killed me on Kephalai." She heard the breathlessness in her voice and didn't like it. She jerked her arm out of his hold and stepped away. "Anyhow, what makes you think we'll meet innocents? So far, I've talked to a goblin, seen a Bog Wraith, and heard about a black mage with a sinister appetite."

"The night is still young."

He looked at her impassively, as if that odd moment hadn't happened between them.

Maybe it hadn't for him.

She scowled at him. "So. Are we working together?"

"Yes."

"Fine," she said. "Since you're an advocate of *thinking* before you act, what's your plan?"

"First," he said, "I think we should find out who's watching us."

"Watching us?" She frowned. "What makes you think we're being w—"

"*Yaaagggh!*"

The wordless bellow was accompanied by something big and heavy careening into Chandra's back. At that same moment, she saw Jurl leap over a tumbled stone wall and attack Gideon, who whirled around to defend himself.

LAURA RESNICK

Chandra hit the ground with considerable force, and had the wind knocked out of her. She heard snarling right by her ear and felt a heavy body lying on top of her. Then a powerful grip seized her shoulders and started banging her against the ground. Over and over. *Hard.*

She called on fire, intending to incinerate her attacker . . . and then realized that she couldn't.

Damn, damn, damn.

While she fought to retain consciousness, Chandra saw a hairy, clawed hand out of the corner of her eye. Lumpy, gray skin. Another goblin.

Jurl? she wondered in confusion.

It kept banging her into the ground, as if trying to tenderize her.

That does it!

Without enough physical strength to gain the advantage, in her current position, she tried a different tactic. "I . . ." Fortunately, the ground wasn't hard: but even so, this was painful. ". . . surrender!" She was smashed into the ground again. "I surrender! I surrender!"

"What?" the goblin said, pausing in its assault.

"I surrender!" Now that she wasn't being pummeled against the ground, she could hear the grunts and blows of Gideon and the other goblin fighting each other.

"Surrender?" the goblin said, breathing on her neck.

"Yes! I surrender! I give up!" Chandra cried. "You win!"

The goblin's weight shifted. It was evidently surprised, and perhaps a little confused. Since goblins weren't known for their mercy, it might never have encountered this reaction to an attack

before. Typically, a fight with a goblin was a fight to the death.

The pause in the goblin's assault and the shifting of its weight was all Chandra needed. She used the muscles of her legs to buck the goblin off of her with a powerful scissor kick, before she rolled over and reached for one of the rocks lying at the base of a nearby ruined wall. Rock in hand, she threw herself at the goblin and smashed its massive head. The goblin shrieked and stumbled backward. Chandra jumped up and hit it in the head again right at the temple. The beast hit the ground hard. Unmoving, blood trickling from its ear, Chandra left the it where it lay and staggered away, unsure if it was dead.

"*Ugh!* I hate goblins! I *hate* them!"

Chandra turned around, intending to go help Gideon. He and the other goblin were rolling around on the ground together, their bodies wallowing frantically in the mud around the stone walls.

Chandra picked up another rock and moved toward them. The goblin lost its hold on Gideon, who rolled away and raised his foot to kick the goblin in the face with considerable force. It fell backward, then staggered in a circle and turned toward Gideon, who rolled across the ground rapidly and stretched out his arm, reaching for something. The goblin saw Chandra approaching them and froze. It turned its head and saw its companion lying prone on the ground.

The goblin gave a shrill little cry—then turned and fled.

"Stay back!" Gideon ordered as Chandra dashed across the ground.

"It's getting away!"

"Get down!" Gideon raised an arm to make wide, rapid circles over his head.

Chandra saw something glint brightly in the moonlight as it spun over Gideon's head, making a menacing *whooshing* sound. She realized it was that daggertail of his, unfurled and swirling above them with deadly speed.

Remembering that the thing had three very long, sharp blades, Chandra threw herself to the ground and covered her head. Without his magic guiding the weapon's steely tendrils, who knew whether Gideon's aim was any good.

She heard the *whooshing* sound change to a long steel sigh as Gideon unleashed the whip. She peeked between her fingers and saw that he had released the entire weapon, letting it sail through the dark night, handle and all. The goblin was speedy and had already covered some distance, but it couldn't outrun the flying weapon.

As Chandra rose to her knees, gaze fixed intently on the fleeing goblin, Gideon set off at a run. Chandra saw something glint briefly in the moonlight, then she saw the goblin fall down. She rose to her feet and ran after him, too.

When she reached Gideon's side, the goblin was lying on the ground, grunting and snarling as it struggled in the sharp tangle of flexible blades that were constraining its short legs.

"I shouldn't have doubted your aim," Chandra said to Gideon, breathing hard from her exertions.

"Lucky shot," Gideon said. "To be honest, I could scarcely see him."

"Chandra!" the goblin said in a familiar-sounding voice. "Don't kill!"

She sighed. "Hello, Jurl. We meet again."

Φ

CHAPTER TEN

Gideon seized the handle of the whip and jerked it sharply. Jurl's eyes bulged and he made a horrible groaning sound from the pain inflicted on his trapped limbs.

Chandra asked Gideon, "How did you know they were watching us?"

"The one that attacked you was casting a shadow on the stone wall near you. I realized it when he moved."

She hadn't seen the realization dawn on Gideon's face. She should remember that he was good at hiding things.

Gideon gave Jurl a light tap with his foot. "But I didn't know there was one behind me, too. They move quietly, don't they?"

"Don't kick!" Jurl said.

"Explain why you just attacked us," Gideon said to the goblin.

"Chandra go away soon."

Gideon glanced at Chandra, then said, "You attacked her because she was leaving?"

"Because no time."

"I think he means," Chandra said, "he attacked *now* because I had told him I was leaving very soon."

"Yes!" Jurl was apparently pleased with her interpretation. "No time."

"Why attack her at all?" Gideon asked the goblin.

"Take to Prince Velrav."

"What?" Chandra scowled. "You were going to turn me over to Velrav? To feed the hunger?"

"Yes."

"Now I see why you were so helpful, Jurl. You wanted me for yourself."

"Yes," Jurl confirmed.

"To think I was beginning to like you," she muttered.

"So you're one of Velrav's takers?" Gideon asked Jurl.

"Yes."

"I see," Gideon said. "Why?"

"Take gift to Velrav. Velrav give something."

"Ah. And if you took a beautiful fire mage to Velrav," Gideon said, "you'd get something good, wouldn't you?"

"Yes." Jurl looked as crestfallen as a writhing, captive goblin could look. "But not now." He looked at Gideon and added, "Don't kill."

"Why not?" Gideon gave the handle of his weapon another sharp tug.

Jurl gasped. "Give me life. I give you."

"Give us *what*?"

"Tell me what," Jurl said. "I get."

"What I want," Gideon said, "is someone who can answer all my questions."

"Questions?" Jurl repeated.

"My questions about Velrav. About Diraden. About why morning never comes."

Jurl thought it over, then suggested, "Wise woman?"

"Yes," Gideon agreed. "I want to speak to a wise woman."

"Village wise woman," Jurl said eagerly. "Know things."

"How far?" Gideon asked

"Not far. I bring you."

Gideon said to the goblin, "I'm going to remove the *sural* from your legs."

"What?"

"The weapon."

"Good!"

"And then I'm going to use it to tie your hands behind your back."

"*Bad.*"

"If you resist or try to get away while I'm doing this," Gideon said, "I will catch you again, but I won't be nice."

"You could end up like your friend, Jurl. You don't want that, do you?" Chandra prodded.

"Not friend," Jurl said dismissively.

"Then why did you bring him along?" she asked. "Wouldn't you have to share with him whatever Velrav gave you?"

"Need help now," Jurl said. "Kill later."

"No honor among goblins," Chandra muttered.

"I guess the prospect of attacking a woman alone was too daunting," Gideon said dryly.

"Intimidated by my beauty, no doubt," she said, recalling Gideon's earlier comment.

"Maybe so." There was no mockery in his voice. He was looking down at the goblin as he began untangling his weapon from its legs. His expression was hidden in shadows. Chandra stared at him in bemusement. Until he said, "Hold the rock where he can see it."

Gideon finished removing the sural from Jurl's legs. "Roll over."

Jurl said, "Don't tie hands."

"Roll over," Chandra said, "or you'll die right now, exactly the way your friend died."

"Not frien—"

"Shut up and do as you're told," she snapped.

With blatant reluctance, Jurl rolled over and allowed Gideon to seize his arms and start binding his hands together with the flexible blades of the sural.

When the goblin cried out in pain and protested, Gideon advised him to stop resisting. "This will hurt less if you cooperate."

When Gideon was satisfied that the restraint was secure enough, he rose to his feet, holding the handle of the sural. The lengths of steel that stretched between the handle and the goblin's bound wrists served as a sort of leash.

"Get up," Gideon said.

"Cannot," Jurl said.

Chandra moved to put her hands under the prostrate goblin's shoulders, and pushed him—with some effort—up to a kneeling position. From there, she and Gideon each took one arm and hauled Jurl to his feet.

"Now take us to the wise woman," Gideon said.

"Yes."

"Oh, one more thing." Gideon twitched the handle of the sural. Jurl protested as the sharp bands of steel tightened around his wrists and pulled his arms backward at a painful angle. "If you try to trick us, or betray us, or take us to anyone else . . ." Gideon tugged the handle again. "I'll pull on this thing so hard, it will cut off your hands."

"No!"

"Without hands, the rest of your life will be helpless and miserable. On the bright side," Gideon added, "it will no doubt also be very, very short."

"No trick!" Jurl promised. "Just wise woman!"

"Good," said Gideon.

"This way," Jurl said.

They left the stone ruins behind and set off in a different direction than Chandra had gone before. As they walked through the quiet, dying landscape, following their reluctant guide, Gideon said, "You're pretty useful when there's trouble, even without the fire magic."

So was he. But she was reluctant to pay him compliments. Instead she asked, "Where did you get your . . ." She pointed to the weapon whose handle he held.

"The sural?"

"Yes, your sural."

"My teacher gave it to me."

"Did he . . ." She hesitated, then asked, "Did he know about you?"

He didn't have to ask what she meant. "Yes."

"Was he a . . ." Chandra glanced at the goblin trudging ahead of them. "Was your teacher one of us?"

"No, but he knew about our kind."

"How?"

"His teacher was one." Gideon added, "And his teacher gave him the sural."

"Where did it originally come from?" She had never seen anything like it.

"I don't know." Beside her in the dark, Gideon said quietly, "His teacher died without telling him where he'd gotten it."

"Do you know how he died?" For a Planeswalker, there were so many possibilities.

"A pyromancer killed him." His voice was calm, without expression.

There was a long silence between them.

The ground they were walking over was particularly damp. It squished under Chandra's feet as she kept pace beside Gideon in the dark, neither of them speaking.

Ahead of them, Jurl trudged along, his shoulders stooped. He started to pant a little, and his steps got slower. Apparently the goblin was feeling fatigued. At one point, he asked to rest. Gideon refused the request.

The continuing cool silence between her and Gideon gradually got on Chandra's nerves. After all, it wasn't *her* fault that his teacher's teacher had been killed by a fire mage. For all she knew, he deserved what happened to him.

"So did you know him?" she asked abruptly.

"Know who?" He sounded mildly puzzled, as if he'd been thinking about something else entirely.

"The pla—" But before she could finish the word, she recalled that Jurl could hear them. The goblin was stupid and ignorant, but nonetheless capable of plotting and scheming. The less he learned by eavesdropping, the better. "The one who owned the sural. The one who died."

"No. He died many years before I met my teacher."

"How did you meet your teacher?" she asked.

Chandra had encountered very few Planeswalkers. In her experience, they were a rare breed, and they were loners. They didn't congregate, and they weren't necessarily friendly to each other.

LAURA RESNICK

"He . . . found me," Gideon said.

"After you . . ." She phrased it in a way that would make no sense to the goblin, in case the creature was feigning fatigue and listening to them. "Crossed over?"

"You mean after I traveled?" Gideon sounded a little amused by her attempt to question him without being understood by their captive.

"Yes."

"No, we met before that."

"How did he find you?"

"Jurl, you said it wasn't far," Gideon reminded the goblin. "This seems far."

"Yes," Jurl agreed wearily. "Seems far."

"If you've lied . . ."

"No." Jurl added, "Don't take hands."

"Well, maybe I'm just little tired," Gideon admitted to Chandra. "Does it seem far to you?"

She couldn't see his expression. Instead of answering him, she prodded, "You were about to tell me how you met your teacher."

"Was I?"

"Yes."

"Why do you want to know?"

"I'm bored." When he didn't respond, she said, "Of course, we could talk about something else. The scroll, for example."

"Then *I'd* be bored."

"So how did your teacher find you?"

"Well, *you'll* identify with this," he said. "I was a criminal."

"Somehow that doesn't surprise me." She asked, "What did you do? Attack women and take away their valuables?"

"Very funny. As a matter of fact, we sacrificed the cutest animals we could find and drank

their blood from our victims' skulls by the light of the moon."

"Then this place should bring you back to your roots."

"To be serious, we mostly broke into rich people's homes—"

"We?"

"There was a group of us. I was the leader, more or less. We stole money, goods, valuables. And, uh . . ."

He seemed reluctant to continue his story. "Yes?" she prodded.

"Then we gave it away." When she didn't respond, he added, "To the poor."

She frowned. "Why?"

"We were . . ." He seemed to search for the right word. "Idealistic."

"That's a far cry from drinking animal blood."

"I was very young. I wanted to change things," he said. "But I didn't know how. I was good at stealing. Good at fighting. Pretty good at handling a group of wild boys my own age."

"That's easy to believe."

"But I had a lot to learn."

"Where were your parents? Didn't they try to rein you in?" Her own parents had certainly tried, back when she was a girl.

"My mother was dead by then," he said.

"And your father?"

"Who knows?" He sounded indifferent. "I never met him."

They all walked in silence for a while. Chandra really started to feel, deep in her bones, how helpless she was here without her power. Even if they did get some answers from this wise woman Jurl was taking them to, what would they

do to get away from this plane? She tried to stop thinking it.

Finally she broke the silence: she had to find something to distract her from these thoughts.

"Your teacher," she said suddenly.

"What?" She could tell by Gideon's reaction that he had been far away. Perhaps lost in thoughts similar to her own.

"How did your teacher find you?" she said urgently. "How did he get you to give up your life as an outlaw?"

There was a pause. Then he said, "What makes you think I gave it up?"

She released her breath on a puff of surprise. Then she smiled—and felt grateful to him for making her smile. "I stand corrected."

In fact, for all she knew, he *was* an outlaw. She had assumed he followed her here to capture her and take her back to Kephalai. She had vaguely supposed he was some sort of inter-planar bounty hunter. The Prelate had employed someone with extraordinary abilities to go after Chandra last time. Why not this time?

But since the Prelate's forces didn't know where the scroll was, *this* Planeswalker obviously hadn't returned it to them.

Perhaps Gideon was still an outlaw. Or at least playing all the angles and working on both sides of the fence. The thought warmed him to her.

"As long as you stick to our bargain and don't try to deliver me to the Prelate," she said aloud, "I make no judgments about the path you have chosen in life."

"That's very kind of you."

"So were did your teacher find you?"

"I was in prison," he said.

"We *do* have a lot in common."

"He was respected, and the prison wasn't well equipped to hold someone with my abilities," Gideon said. "So I was released into his custody."

"And that's how your education began?"

"Yes," Gideon said. "More easily than he expected, I suppose. After my initial resistance—and an attempt to escape his custody—I became a dedicated student. Eager."

"You liked the power," she said, remembering her own obsession with it when she had started discovering some of the things she could do, things that no one in her community had understood or condoned.

"Yes, I liked the power. I liked developing and honing it. Mostly, though . . ." Gideon paused pensively. "Mostly, I realized that my teacher was the first person I'd ever met who could help me find what I was looking for."

"Which was?"

"Direction. Focus. A path for my life."

"Direction . . ." Chandra hadn't thought about direction before. She had gone to the Keralian Monastery to learn more about her power. How to access more of it, but also how to control it better. And her recent experiences demonstrated that she still had much to learn in that respect.

She didn't want to think about any of that now. Besides, she didn't even have access to her full power at the moment. And that wasn't a subject she wanted to dwell on, either, just now. So she asked Gideon, "When did you find out what you really were?"

"When the time came," he said. "When my Spark was ignited."

The Spark, Chandra had been taught, was

a suffusion of the Blind Eternities within a Planeswalker's soul. It was what gave an individual protection against the entropic forces of the æther. Although it happened differently for everyone, the ignition of a Planeswalker's Spark was the trigger for their first walk.

Gideon added, "But my teacher knew before I did."

"How did he know?"

"Because of my power. As I dedicated myself to my training, my strength grew. To me, it just seemed to be the result of studying and learning. But later, after I knew the truth about myself, he said that he had known for some time, because he'd only ever seen one other hieromancer as powerful as I was."

"Ah. The one who had given him the sural all those years ago."

"Yes. A long time before it happened, he believed my Spark would be ignited and I would become . . . what I became." Gideon said, "So he prepared me."

"He told you what you were?" she asked.

"No. He told me about our kind, and about the one that he had known. He related what he knew about the Multiverse, the æther, and the Blind Eternities. How to prepare for a walk. How to survive it."

"So you knew what was happening?"

"Yes. I was fully conscious of what was happening."

"Did you know *before* it happened?" she asked in astonishment.

"Not exactly. But when I *felt* my Spark ignite, I understood. It was . . ." He hesitated. "I killed someone," he said quietly. "Someone very powerful.

Very dangerous. I knew I shouldn't have lived through that confrontation. Not logically. I was shocked at how much power I had accessed. I sensed a clarity in the world around me. I felt an intensity of experience, an awareness of simply being that I had never known. I had a moment, however fleeting, where I understood everything around me. I understood the Multiverse on a fundamental level, if you can imagine such a thing, so that when I slipped into the æther I knew where to go."

"Is it like that every time?"

"No," he said. "As soon as I had landed on another plane, it was gone. I have tried to achieve that state of awareness for most of my life since then, but I have yet to come close." He let out a slow breath. "But the planeswalk worked. Very much the way my teacher had described it. And also by following his teachings, I found my way back. So that I could tell him what I was."

Chandra felt a mingled surge of wonder and envy. "I can't imagine . . ."

"Imagine what?" he asked.

"What my first walk would have been like, if I had known those things. If someone had told me."

"You didn't have any idea what was happening to you?"

"None," she said. "I'd never even heard of a planeswalk."

Chandra blinked as she realized they'd become indiscreet. She looked uneasily at the goblin walking ahead of them, its hands bound behind its back. But Jurl seemed to be paying no attention to them. Instead, he seemed jumpy, anxious, and wholly focused on their surroundings, as if expecting an ambush at any moment.

"That must have been hard," Gideon said.

"I didn't experience anything like you. I thought I was dying," she admitted. "Or dead. Or . . . I don't know. It was very painful. And, um, terrifying."

She didn't know why she was telling him this. She had never told anyone, not even Mother Luti. She'd never had a teacher except for Luti, and she had not known her long. Chandra had never even met another Planeswalker before her most recent encounters. All that she knew about planeswalking, she'd taught herself, and all that she learned about her kind, which wasn't a lot, she learned from Mother Luti.

"Some combination of desperation, survival instinct, and . . ." Chandra shrugged. "Sheer luck, I suppose, helped me find my way out of the æther and onto a physical plane that first time."

"And will," he said.

"What?"

"Will," Gideon said. "You have a very strong will. That makes a difference in who survives a walk like your first. And also like the one that brought you here."

"How did you follow me?" She knew it couldn't have been easy.

"Actually, you leave a pretty bright trail."

She supposed that was why that mind mage with the cerulean cloak had been able to find her on Regatha.

"But the trail was erratic and seemed to . . ." He searched for the right word ". . . *bounce* all over the place. I could tell it had been a rough journey." He added, "And to come *here* of all places . . ."

"I didn't exactly choose it," she said.

"I knew even as I approached that it was a bad destination."

"So why did you follow?"

"Why did you steal that scroll?" he countered. "*Twice?*"

"Why did *you* steal it?"

"I didn't exactly steal it."

"Then where *is* it?" she demanded.

"I don't know," he said. "Now that there is no Sanctum of Stars to keep it in, I suppose it's somewhere in the Prelate's palace, under lock and key."

"No, it's not," Chandra said. "The Prelate's pets were going to torture me to find it."

"That was before you escaped. Since then, the scroll has been found."

"*What?*"

"Don't even think about it, Chandra," he said. "If it's in the palace, you *might* get inside alive, but you'd never get back out. Not even you. They'll be watching for you. And now they know they made a mistake by not killing you the moment they identified you. They won't be that careless again."

"You *gave back* the scroll?"

"Yes."

"I don't believe you!"

They walked along in silence for a few paces.

"You gave it back?" she demanded.

"Yes."

"No, you didn't!"

He said nothing.

Her thoughts whirling, she said, "*Why* did you give it back?"

"It seemed like the most sensible thing to do. You know, to calm things down after you left."

"That's *it*?"

"More or less," he said.

"More or less of a reward?"

"Well, there was a reward."

"So *that's* why."

"Not exactly."

"What do you mean?"

"Well, I didn't precisely *give* it back."

"If you didn't give it back, then what did you do. *Precisely?*"

"I left it where it would be found by someone who would recognize it and turn it in for the reward."

"I don't understand," she said. "You stole it from me. You didn't keep it. You didn't sell it. You didn't take credit for retrieving it, and you didn't collect the reward."

"Actually, you seem to understand perfectly."

"If you didn't want it," she said, "why take it in the first place?"

"I thought that if the Prelate didn't have the scroll and didn't know where it was, then she wouldn't execute you immediately. She'd want to find it before she killed you. And since *you* didn't know where it was, there would be some delays." Gideon concluded, "I thought that would give you time to try to escape."

"You *wanted* me to escape?" She felt bewildered. "Why didn't you help me instead of manipulating me with your passive little ploy?"

"I didn't know about the Enervants," he said. "Or I might have been a bit more proactive."

"If you didn't want them to execute me, then why did you help them capture me?"

"Because you were about to start a battle with those soldiers in a street full of innocent people."

"In a . . . I was . . ." She realized what he was saying.

"You were thinking about yourself," he said. "I was thinking about the dozens of people who might get killed."

"Whatever." After a few long moments of tense silence, she said, "So you didn't want the scroll." When he didn't bother responding, she said, "And you don't want me to go back to Kephalai."

"I think it would be stupid." He added, "And fatal."

"Then what are you doing here?" she demanded. "Why did you follow me? Why were you looking for me on Kephalai? Who *are* you?"

Jurl said, "Stop talking."

"What?" Chandra snapped.

The goblin raised his head, his pointy ears perked alertly.

"He hears something," Gideon said in a low voice.

Their captive raised his head and sniffed the damp night air, apparently oblivious to their presence.

Chandra looked at Gideon. The grove of twisted, leafless trees that they were walking through cast so many shadows in the silvery light that she couldn't see his face well. But she sensed that he was as tense as she was.

Then Jurl's demeanor abruptly changed. He flinched, crouched low, and turned toward them, panting and making little noises of distress.

"What's wrong?" Gideon asked in a low voice.

"Riders," the goblin rasped.

"Riders?"

A moment later, Chandra heard the distant pounding of hooves. Approaching fast.

"*Bad*," Jurl said, "Hide!"

CHAPTER ELEVEN

Jurl scurried toward a thicket of bushes. The steel leash prevented him from going more than a few steps before he stopped, grunting in pain.

"*Hide.*" The goblin sounded terrified.

Gideon took Chandra's arm. "Come on."

Moving fast, they followed Jurl into the bushes. The thundering hoof beats were already much closer. As the three of them crouched down low behind the bushes' naked branches, Chandra was grateful for the dark. These shrubs were thick, even without leaves, but she knew that she and her companions would be visible in the light of day.

She leaned forward and looked off to the left, past Gideon, where the hoof beats were coming from. As she swayed slightly in that direction, unsteady in her crouching position, her shoulder came into contact with Gideon's.

He turned toward her. It was too dark to see his expression, but she could see his eyes looking directly into hers. Neither spoke. Then he, too, looked in the direction of the approaching riders.

Chandra heard a sharp whinny as the galloping horses entered the grove. Peering into the darkness, Chandra could see them faintly

now. Fortunately, they weren't coming this way. They passed through the withered grove at some distance from where they crouched in the bushes, moving diagonally away. She counted three riders . . . No, four, she realized, as they galloped into a pool of moonlight.

They were racing through a dense, low cloud of fog . . .

No, she realized a moment later, the fog moved *with* them, surrounding them and traveling in their company, flowing swiftly across the landscape. It made the horses look as if they were running atop a shifting white cloud, galloping through the air rather than on the ground. Yet their hooves must be touching soil, because they made a sound louder than thunder.

Watching this spectacle, Chandra felt chilled. The horses were all dark, and they galloped through the night with heedless speed. Perhaps, like Jurl, their eyes were well accustomed to this perpetual night. Or perhaps, she thought, as she watched the fog move with them, they didn't really need to see where they were going.

The lead horse appeared to be carrying two riders, one of whom was struggling, seemingly held captive by the other. She saw pale limbs fighting for freedom and dark-clad arms restraining them. Chandra thought she could hear a terrified wailing as the horses galloped out of sight. A few moments later, the sound of the riders had faded completely.

Now she heard only the pounding of her heart and Gideon's rapid breathing.

"What *was* that?" she asked Jurl.

"Fog Riders."

"Good name," she muttered.

"Who are they?" Gideon's voice was low. His body, so close to Chandra's, was still tense. "What are they doing?"

"Someone run away," Jurl said. "They find. Bring back."

"Back where?" Chandra asked.

"Velrav Castle."

She listened to Gideon's breathing and knew they were both thinking about the captive on that horse.

After a long moment, Gideon said, "Let's keep moving."

"Fog Riders, bad," Jurl said with feeling.

"Yes, I think we grasped that." Gideon rose to his feet and turned to help Chandra extract herself from the clinging arms of the thicket.

Something tugged on her hair. She winced as she pulled against it.

"Wait," Gideon said softly. He reached out to untangle her hair from a slender branch. Then he smoothed the rescued strand over her shoulder. "There."

"Thanks."

Feeling somber and sickened after what she had just witnessed, Chandra turned in the direction they had been heading before hearing the Fog Riders. Jurl grumbled a bit, but then he did the same. Gideon seemed preoccupied and didn't even bother tugging on the goblin's makeshift leash to get him to pick up his heel-dragging pace.

After a few moments walking in silence, Jurl nodded. "Village, near. You walk first," the goblin said.

"Why?" Gideon asked suspiciously.

"Not like goblin," Jurl explained, nodding in the direction of the village.

"What a mystery." Chandra said to Gideon, "I'll walk ahead. You keep a tight hold of his leash. If anything happens to me, cut off his hands." She added, "Did you hear that, Jurl?"

"Yes." He sounded morose.

Chandra moved past Jurl and walked ahead of him. Within moments, she saw a thatched hut. Then several others. They were part of a small village, nestled in the side of a hill and bathed in moonlight. It looked like there were about twenty dwellings here.

As she drew closer, she saw several people standing in the doorways of their huts, peering at her. By the time she reached the first few huts, she heard gasps and excited voices exchanging muffled comments. People were coming out of their huts and standing in the moonlight.

She thought at first that the gasps and the excitement were because of the goblin entering the village. But then she realized, as she stood surrounded by people, that they were all staring at *her*. And she thought she could guess why.

Although no one here looked like Gideon—they were too frail and hollow-eyed to resemble him—they had similar coloring: dark hair, dark eyes, fair skin. As Chandra looked around at the dozens of people who were emerging from their huts and gathering to stare at her, she saw, even in the light of the moon, that she was the only redhead present. Perhaps the only redhead they had ever seen.

"Hello," Chandra said, looking around at the gathering crowd. "We've come to speak to the wise woman."

A young woman, a girl by some standards, stepped forward, separating herself from the

crowd. She approached Chandra hesitantly, and slowly reached out a hand to touch her red hair.

Her voice was soft and shy as she said, "You're so beautiful!"

"Thank you," said Chandra.

Behind her, Jurl said, "Wise woman."

"My name is Gideon. We'd like to speak with the wise woman."

The girl said, "You're welcome here."

Gideon said, "Thank you."

Jurl said, "Wise woman."

"Yes," Chandra said, "if someone would tell the wise woman we've come to see her? It's important."

Sounding impatient now, Jurl repeated, "*Wise woman.*"

"Oh." Gideon said, "Chandra..."

"Yes," she said slowly. "I think I understand." Chandra looked at the girl standing before her. "You're the wise woman?"

She smiled sweetly. "Yes, I am the village menarch. Why have you come to see me?"

≈ ≈ ≈ ≈ ≈

The wise woman told them her name was Falia, and she led them to a hut where they could sit and talk.

As they entered the doorway of the small thatched hut, Jurl hung back, tugging a little on his leash.

"Free Jurl," he insisted.

"So you can attack us again?" said Chandra. "And trade us to your hungry prince in exchange for goblin goodies? No."

"Jurl bring here. Now set free." The goblin added with reproach, "You *promise*."

"No," said Gideon, "I promised I wouldn't kill

you if you brought us here. *Freeing* you is a whole different subject."

Jurl snarled in outrage.

Looking bored, Gideon tugged the leash sharply.

Jurl gasped in pain, went silent, and trudged into the hut with them. The interior was lighted by short, thick candles.

"Sit in the corner and be quiet," Gideon told the goblin.

Jurl's gaze searched the round hut. "No corner."

Gideon sighed. "Sit out of the way."

"Hungry," Jurl said sullenly.

The wise woman said in her soft, high voice, "We can provide food and drink for all of you."

"What food?" Jurl asked, sounding skeptical.

"Oh, don't pretend you're fussy," Chandra said.

"Thank you," Gideon said to Falia. "Whatever you offer us will be much appreciated."

The girl's gaze traveled over Chandra's bloodied, smeared appearance, the mud on Gideon's clothes, and his darkening jaw. "It seems you've had a long and difficult journey. After we talk, perhaps you would also like to wash, and then to rest."

Wash, Chandra thought with longing. Since they were stuck here, rest was obviously a good idea, too, even though she didn't relish the thought of closing her eyes on this grim and sinister plane.

"Yes, thank you," Gideon said. "We're grateful for your hospitality."

Falia's gaze went back to Gideon and lingered there. The expression of dawning fascination Chandra saw on her face belied Falia's

girlish appearance. Gideon was a handsome man, beautiful without being pretty, strong without being bulky. His predatory grace was evident in every movement, and his expression was friendly and reassuring as he returned the girl's unwavering gaze.

But Chandra didn't see a frightened girl in need of reassurance looking back at him. Falia wore the expression of a woman encountering an attractive stranger in her drab little village where everyone knew everyone else, and where the choice of marriage partners was very limited.

Falia gave a little start, evidently realizing she'd been staring, and said to them, "Please, sit now." The girl stuck her head outside the door of the hut to give instructions to someone while Gideon and Chandra helped Jurl sit.

"Free hands," said Jurl.

"Don't be ridiculous," said Chandra.

"He can't help it," said Gideon. "He's a goblin."

The two of them sat down side by side on the woven mats that covered the earthen floor.

Falia re-entered the hut and sat down facing them. Despite her frail appearance and sickly pallor, she was a pretty girl, with a delicate, ethereal quality. Her dark, hollow eyes seemed too sad and haunted for someone so young, but they gave her a world-weary hint of tragic beauty and inner wisdom.

Looking at her now, Chandra thought it seemed a bit less strange that this girl was the village wise woman.

Gideon said, "Please believe that I mean no insult or disrespect when I say that you seem very young to be a wise woman."

Falia looked puzzled. "I do?"

Gideon asked, "How is the wise woman—I mean menarch chosen here?"

"It's the calling of my family," she said. "When I showed first blood, my mother knew that I was ready. Someday I will marry and bear children. My daughter will one day assume this duty."

"That seems like a pretty short time in which to gain wisdom," Chandra said.

Gideon glanced at her, but didn't tell her to be quiet. So apparently he had a little wisdom, too.

"My wisdom was passed to me by my mother. Her wisdom is mine. She was given hers by her mother, and so it has been for generations within us."

"How do you pass it?" Chandra asked.

"We share our blood in the ritual passing of our power," the girl said pleasantly.

Chandra decided she didn't want details. This wasn't what they had come here to talk about.

"Ah, here is your meal," Falia said.

A woman entered the hut, carrying a large pot. A boy followed behind her, carrying wooden bowls and spoons. The woman smiled kindly at Gideon and Chandra as she set the pot down in front of them. Falia ladled soup into the two bowls the boy had brought, then handed the bowls to Chandra and Gideon.

The boy, who also placed his wares in front of them, paused to gape with wide-eyed curiosity until Falia put a hand on his shoulder to get his attention.

"Please give the goblin food. We must show him our appreciation." The boy picked up the pot, and carried it over to Jurl. He set it down in front of him, turned away, and left the hut.

With his hands still bound behind his back, Jurl

wiggled around into a kneeling position, then stuck his whole head into the pot and started slurping noisily.

Chandra looked down into her bowl. It contained a translucent, pale gray broth with lumpy, white things floating in it. It didn't look remotely appetizing, not even to someone as hungry as she was.

"How nice," Chandra said politely, trying not to let her face contort when she took a whiff. The stuff smelled ghastly. "What is this dish?"

"Grub soup," said Falia.

Chandra focused on keeping her expression courteous. "Ah."

No wonder everyone here was so thin! Who would ever eat more than they absolutely had to, if this was a typical local dish? She suddenly missed Regatha.

"It looks delicious," Gideon said in an admirably sincere tone. "Thank you."

"You're our guests, and guests are a gift from the gods!" Falia said with a bright smile as she rose to her feet. "That silly boy forgot to bring water for you. I'll go get it."

As soon as the girl disappeared through the doorway, Chandra said quietly, "I don't think I can eat this."

"It may be all we'll get for some time," Gideon said, looking into his bowl without enthusiasm. "And when was the last time you ate?"

"I can't even remember," she said. "But suddenly I'm not as hungry as I thought I was."

"Listen, it's meat. More or less." He sounded as if he was trying to convince himself. "It'll give you strength."

"I don't suppose many things grow in a land of

constant darkness," she said, noting the absence of vegetables in the soup. Chandra filled her spoon with the broth, which was much more viscous than she had anticipated, and lifted it to take a sip. The closer she brought it to her lips, the harder it was was. She dropped the spoonful back into her bowl, untasted.

"Eat. We have been given this food. We can't refuse it," Gideon said, also lifting a spoonful of soup from his bowl.

Chandra reflected irritably that Jurl's noisy slurping wasn't making the soup seem any less disgusting, either. She said loudly, "I think I'd have preferred roasted goblin."

"The village looks poor," Gideon said, "so they probably only serve goblin on special occasions."

Jurl gave a surly grunt before he returned to gobbling the grub soup.

Gideon said to her, "Eat."

"You first," she said.

He sniffed the thick, shiny, gray broth filling his spoon and evidently decided that inhaling was a mistake. Looking like he was holding his breath now, he took a sip. "It's . . . fine."

She knew he was lying, but Chandra used her spoon to scoop up a boiled grub. Gideon was right on one thing. It was meat. She needed strength. Summoning her will, she put it in her mouth and chewed on the rubbery morsel.

Falia re-entered the hut, carrying a clay pitcher and two cups. "Are you enjoying the soup?"

"It's excellent." Gideon took a big spoonful.

Falia smiled. "Good!"

"We have some questions, Falia," Gideon said.

"Eat first," Falia said. "Then we'll talk."

"Of course." Gideon nodded.

Chandra steeled her resolve and ate some more grub worms, washing them down with a generous quantity of water. Since Gideon was sipping the broth without expiring on the spot, she consumed some of it, too. The texture was disgusting, and the flavor could best be described as aquatic. She wondered what the grubs might have grown into.

The thought nearly made her gag, so she tried to empty her mind, and continued eating in silence—all while Jurl kept eating in noisy, voracious gulps.

The goblin finished his meal first. He gave a satisfied sigh, and shifted his position so that he could lean against the wall of the hut. After a few minutes, he fell into a peaceful doze. Chandra knew this because he snored.

When she could endure no more of the grub soup, Chandra set her bowl aside and looked at Falia, intending to thank her. That was when she realized that the girl was staring at Gideon again—this time, with a look that could only be longing.

From what Chandra had seen, there were few men in the village. Undoubtedly, Falia was evaluating Gideon's fitness as a mate. Though seemingly young for it, Falia clearly was ready for marriage. Chandra realized abruptly that the girl could well be several years older than she looked. Who knew what effects this blood ritual for the passing of wisdom had on an individual, to say nothing of her diet.

Even supposing that Falia was the same age at which girls on Chandra's native plane typically married, it was unsettling to see how she looked at Gideon.

Chandra wondered whether he was aware of her keen interest in him. Gideon simply ate, his gaze lowered all the while on the food. If he was aware of the girl's perusal, he didn't acknowledge or return it.

When he finished eating, he set aside his bowl, and thanked Falia, who seemed to awaken from a trance.

She smiled. "Now what have you come here to ask me?"

"Has it always been nighttime on Diraden?" Gideon asked. "Forever?"

"Ah." She nodded. "You've come to ask about Prince Velrav's rule."

"Yes. Did the endless night begin with him?"

"It did."

"What happened?"

"When my grandmother was a child," Falia said, "there was day *and* night here. King Gelidor ruled Diraden. He had three sons. The youngest, Prince Velrav, was wild and dissolute."

The girl was a good storyteller, and the tale flowed smoothly, but the heart of the story was simple. The young Prince Velrav had engaged in various scandalous and destructive indulgences until his father banished him from castle and court.

Furious over his exile, and more ambitious and vengeful than anyone had ever guessed, Prince Velrav studied black magic and consorted with the darkest blood demons of the realm to plot against his father.

"You tell the story well," Chandra said when Falia paused.

"Thank you," said Falia, smiling at Gideon as if *he* had delivered the compliment.

Jurl snored peacefully as the girl continued her story.

"When he felt ready to carry out his nefarious plan, Velrav returned to his father's castle. He presented himself as a humbled, penitent son, reformed in his ways and seeking forgiveness. The king welcomed home his wayward son, and never thought to protect himself from him."

"Which was evidently a mistake?" said Chandra.

Falia nodded. "In the dead of night, while the whole castle slept, the prince crept into his two brothers' bed chambers and murdered them both, along with their wives. Then he went into the nursery and slaughtered the three children whom his brothers had sired."

"He slaughtered the children?" Chandra repeated.

"Then he went to his parents' chamber," Falia said, "where he beheaded his mother with one heavy blow of his sword."

"He killed his *mother*?" Chandra blurted.

"He's very wicked," the girl said prosaically.

"He beheaded her," Gideon mused. "Interesting."

"It's not *interesting*," Chandra said. "It's disgusting! His own mother!"

"And then he murdered the king?" Gideon asked.

"No." Falia shook her head. "He fed on the king."

"He *ate* his father?" The grub soup churned unpleasantly in Chandra's stomach.

"No, he fed on him," Falia said.

Chandra said, "What's the diff—"

"And that didn't kill the king?" Gideon asked.

"It might have, of course," the girl said. "But he also fed the king of himself."

"Fed him of himself?" Chandra said with a frown. "What does that mean?"

Gideon asked, "Is the king still alive?"

"Of course not," Chandra said dismissively. "This happened when Falia's grandmother was a child." A man who'd had grown sons and grandchildren that long ago wouldn't still be alive now.

"Yes." Ignoring Chandra, Falia nodded, holding Gideon's gaze. "The king lives still. And since the night Prince Velrav killed his family and turned his father into a sickly shadow of what he himself had become," Falia said, "daylight has never again come to Diraden."

"How can the king still be alive after all this time?" Chandra wondered.

"Blood magic," Gideon said.

"*Fierce* blood magic," Falia said, her nostrils flaring. "Wicked. *Dark*." She made the words sound . . . seductive.

Gideon said to her, "That's what the 'hunger' is."

They looked to Falia for confirmation. She nodded.

"Why did he feed his father his own blood?" Gideon asked. "He'd killed the rest of the family. Why keep the king alive?"

"To curse him," said Falia. "The king lives in the darkest, deepest dungeon of the castle. He is fed only blood. He is left alone, in terrible solitude. No one speaks to him or sees him, except for Velrav, who visits him once in a great while and tells him about all the torment and suffering he is inflicting on the king's realm."

"And this has been going on since your grandmother was a child?" Chandra asked, appalled.

"So that's why Velrav made it perpetual night here," Gideon mused.

"I don't understand," Chandra said.

"Some blood drinkers don't like daylight," he said.

"You mean they don't want to be *seen* drinking blood?" she said in puzzlement.

"No, I mean the sunlight burns them," he said. "Like fire. Those who choose blood magic, those who decide to embrace the power it holds must guard themselves at all cost against the powers of light."

Fire. The word reminded Chandra of their predicament.

"They don't like fire, either," Gideon said. "They're vulnerable to it."

"So he uses the veil of false night to block sunlight *and* red mana," she mused.

"And that same sorcery winds up blocking *all* mana, except black," Gideon said.

Falia said, "Yes, my grandmother says there once used to be other mana here. Other colors in the æther. Other kinds of magic." She gave them both an assessing gaze. "You are not from Diraden, are you?"

They both went still.

After a moment, Gideon said, "No."

"Where did you come from?"

"Someplace very far away," Gideon said. "And we can't go back there while Velrav's power holds."

"And you would *like* to go back there? Together?"

"Yes," said Gideon. "We would."

Falia said with certainty, "The prince will not help you or give you permission to go."

"No, I didn't think so," Gideon said. "Tell me about this veil of night, Falia, this shroud. It

blocks mana and light, but it also keeps things alive, doesn't it?"

"Yes," she said. "Just enough that many things aren't really alive here anymore, yet they don't really die."

"That's a tremendous amount of power. Can he do that all alone?"

"No," the girl said, "his companions work with him to maintain the veil."

"His companions?" Gideon asked.

"They are the blood demons who helped him develop the power."

"And blood is what feeds their power?" Chandra asked.

"Yes," Falia said. "When they feel the hunger, they seek more blood to sustain them. To empower their dark work."

"How often do they get hungry?" Chandra asked.

"Often."

"And then people are taken." Gideon said.

"People. Goblins. Creatures. Animals." Falia paused. "They like people best. But any blood will feed the hunger. People, though . . . those thrill them."

Gideon studied her. "Do people with power thrill them in particular?"

Falia nodded.

"People with power," Chandra said, "such as a menarch?"

She lowered her eyes. "Yes."

"You're in danger?" Gideon asked quietly.

"Always," Falia said.

CHAPTER TWELVE

Falia offered them water to wash their skin and damp cloths to wipe away the worst of the grime and dirt from their garments. She loaned them a comb and got one of the village men to lend Gideon his razor. After they were clean and tidy, she suggested they all get some rest.

She was willing to share her hut with them . . . but not with Jurl.

"Goblins are treacherous," she said. "Even with his hands bound, I wouldn't feel safe sleeping in the same dwelling with him. We should put him in a secure place."

Chandra thought that made perfect sense, so they woke Jurl, who was cranky about being disturbed, but became more so at the prospect of being locked up while the rest of them slept in relative comfort.

One of the huts in the village had originally been built to protect livestock at night. However, most of the livestock on Diraden had long since died and now the building was empty. There was also a large, sturdy cage in the hut, which Falia said had formerly been used to keep wild boars being fattened for the annual harvest feast. There had been no harvests since Prince Velrav came to

power, obviously, and it had been some time since the villagers had even seen a wild boar.

They locked Jurl in the cage. He was hotly opposed to the idea, and it took Gideon some effort to get the goblin into the thing. Afterwards, Falia took Gideon back to her hut to clean the scratches that Jurl's claws had left on his skin.

Chandra remained behind in the livestock hut and said to the goblin, "Stop that snarling! We can't let you go, and that's your own fault."

"Bad," said Jurl.

"Nonsense. You'll be perfectly comfortable in here."

"Village eat goblin," he said ominously.

"What?" She realized Jurl must have heard her dinner conversation with Gideon. "Don't be silly. We were joking. They won't roast you."

"Stranger," Jurl said bitterly. "Stupid."

"I consider the source," Chandra said, "and feel unmoved by the insult."

She left him sulking and made her way back to Falia's hut.

Predictably, perhaps, the girl had convinced Gideon to remove his tunic, and she was making a lengthy and intimate task out of tending what were only a few negligible goblin scratches on his chest. Chandra gave the two of them a dismissive glance, then went over to the bedroll that had been provided for her, smoothed it out on the floor, and lay down. While doing so, she noticed in passing that Gideon had a broad, hard, mostly hairless chest, and his arms were well muscled. There were several scars on his left arm, and another on his stomach.

At length, Falia ministered to his wounds. Then she offered to comb his hair for him, which was still rather tousled.

Chandra snorted.

Giving no sign that he had noticed Chandra's derision, Gideon smiled kindly at Falia and assured her he was accustomed to doing it himself. "But thank you for the offer."

Rosy-cheeked and glowing from within now, Falia looked quite different from the pale, hollow-eyed girl whom they had first met. "Please make yourself comfortable in the other bedroll," she said to Gideon. "I must go and get another."

"Am I taking yours?" he said. "I don't want to deprive you of your bed, Falia."

"Please, you're my guest. It's my pleasure that you should sleep in my bed!"

I'll *bet* it is, Chandra thought.

"I'll get another bedroll for myself from my aunt's hut," the girl said. "I'll be back shortly."

As soon as she left, Chandra said reprovingly to Gideon, "She's a *child*."

"Actually, she's probably older than either of us, Chandra."

"You think?" She propped herself up on her elbows and looked at him in perplexity.

"One of the typical effects of blood magic is that it slows or even halts the normal aging process."

"But surely she's not a blood drinker?" Chandra said.

"No, I think she's exactly what she says she is: the village menarch. You heard what she said. The wise woman passes her wisdom to her successor through a blood ritual."

"Yes, I did hear that." Chandra lay down again and stared at the flickering light from the candles as it bounced off the ceiling. "The wise woman passes along knowledge and wisdom through her

blood, and maybe some power. And part of the power involves ensuring that the next wise woman remains the exact same age she is at the time of initiation . . . until it's time for her to turn the duty over to her successor?"

"It seems necessary," Gideon said. "She remains young so that she can marry and bear children, but that could take a long time considering how few people are in the village. I imagine mortality rates among infants is high in this kind of environment."

"I think she sees you as a potential mate." Chandra thought it over. "How old do you think she is?"

"We'd probably be able to make a better guess if we met the aunt who was the wise woman before her."

"Well," Chandra said, "no wonder Falia seems so, er, ready for marriage."

"That's a surprisingly tactful way for you to put it. You must be tired." He stepped over her prone body and started laying his bedroll in the narrow space between hers and the wall.

"What are you doing?" she demanded. "You're *not* sleeping this close to me."

"Yes, I am. I want you lying between me and her," he said firmly. "You're my protection."

Chandra snorted again. "Oh. All right. Fine."

She rolled over on her side, with her back to him, and closed her eyes. She assumed Falia wouldn't be pleased with this arrangement when she returned to the hut, but Chandra was much too tired to care.

❈ ❈ ❈ ❈ ❈

She dreamed of fire.

Not the hot power that had mingled with

her fear and fury when she killed the Enervants. And not the wild flames that had scalded her in the Blind Eternities as she made her escape from the Prelate's dungeon.

The fire in her dreams wasn't the seduction of a boom spell, or the fragile sparks of a new enchantment. No, this was the fire of sorrow and grief, of shame and regret.

"I don't want to kill any innocents," Gideon said in that calm, impassive voice he often used. White flames danced around him as he said it. Pure white.

And in those flames, she could hear their screams clearly. Their bodies writhed in the fire, and the stench of their burning flesh made her want to vomit, as it always did. Her throat burned with sobs that wouldn't come out.

But the sobs *must* be coming out, because she could hear them. Choked, desperate, tearful gasps.

"Chandra," he whispered, his voice cool against the heat of the agonized screams of the innocents dying in the fire.

She tried to move, but her limbs were immobile. She wanted to scream, but only a helpless moan emerged from her throat.

"Chandra."

And when the blade of a sword swept down to her throat, she awoke with a strangled gasp of horror.

It was dark. No candles were burning. And Chandra had no fire to call upon here.

"Shhh, it's a dream, just a dream," Gideon whispered. His arms came around her. "Shhh."

She struggled against the imprisoning arms.

"It's me," he whispered. "You had a nightmare."

Her heart was pounding. Her temples throbbed.

Ⴔ

She was sweating. A strangled sob escaped her throat, humiliating her.

His body was pressed up against her side as she lay on her back. One hard arm encircled her shoulders, the other curled around to cradle her face. "Shhh. You're fine. It was just a dream."

Chandra raised her hand to the hand that cupped her cheek. She intended to reject that intrusive, offending caress. To fling off his hand . . . But somehow, instead, she found herself grasping it. He returned her grip and squeezed gently.

"Just a dream," he said again.

She focused on her breathing, trying to steady it.

"Maybe going to bed on a belly full of grub worms wasn't such a good idea," he whispered.

A choke of surprised laughter escaped her.

Then she felt queasy. "You had to mention that," she murmured. "I'd actually forgotten."

"Sorry," he breathed against her ear.

She took a deep breath, then let it out slowly. She could still hear her heart thudding with terror and guilt.

Gideon said, "Do you want to tell me what you dreamed?"

"No."

He accepted this, and they lay quietly together. After a while, he lifted his head. Then he whispered, "It's too dark to see, but I think she's still asleep."

Chandra was glad she hadn't disturbed the girl. Having woken Gideon was embarrassing enough.

He lowered his head again, letting it rest close to hers. "I can't tell how long we've been asleep. The light's always exactly the same here."

"The moonlight, you mean."

"Mmm."

She tried to get her mind off the shadows of her past. It was better to think about the present—even *this* present. "Now that we know more about Velrav and this place . . . I don't feel we're any closer to knowing what to do about it. How to get out of here, I mean." She kept her voice soft, so as not to wake Falia.

"Widespread rebellion would be handy," Gideon said, "but I doubt it'll happen."

"Because it hasn't happened yet?" she whispered. "In all these years of suffering?"

"And also because this whole plane is steeped in dark magic."

"Including our hostess?" Chandra guessed.

"That blood ritual? Yes." Lying entwined with him like this, she could feel him shake his head slightly. "They won't unite. The different groups here won't help anyone but themselves. And however tormented the situation may be, it's got a sort of consistency and balance that they're used to by now."

"You'd think the food alone would be cause enough to rebel. *Grub soup?*"

She felt his soft puff of laughter against her cheek in the dark.

"If they *would* rebel," Gideon said after a moment, "then the flow of blood to Velrav and his companions might be reduced. Even cut off."

"So that's our plan?" she said doubtfully. "Lead an uprising?"

"No. It would take too long. Years, if it worked at all. Which it probably wouldn't." He added, "Besides, it might also take a while for Velrav to feel the effects of going hungry and start weakening. We need a faster plan."

"Yes. Faster is better."

"I thought you'd think so."

"But in our current condition," she whispered, "how can we attack someone that powerful?"

Gideon sighed and shifted his position a little. "I don't know."

Instead of rolling away from him, she shifted her position, too, getting more comfortable in his arms. The feel of his body was comforting. The whisper of his breath along her cheek, his voice soft in her ear . . . For now, he was a safe place to hide from her nightmares.

"You said blood drinkers are vulnerable to fire," she whispered. "Maybe we should burn down the castle. The normal way, I mean. With torches and that sort of thing."

"We'd have to go see the place to get an idea of what it would take to burn it down without magic. But stone walls added to a damp climate . . ."

The prospect wasn't promising. Chandra tried to think of another plan. "Jurl captures people and delivers them to Velrav. Actually, he probably captures goblins, too. He's obviously not sentimental about his own race."

"You think Jurl may know more about Velrav than we've learned so far?" Gideon guessed.

"But whether what he says will make much sense . . ."

"Well, we can try in the morning." He paused. "Or, uh, when it's time to get up, I mean."

The night was so still and silent, the villagers must all still be sleeping.

His hand brushed her hair as he whispered, "Try to get some more sleep."

Chandra's lids felt heavy, but she was afraid to go back to sleep. Afraid of what her dreams might

hold. She'd rather stay here, with him. "I'm not sleepy," she lied.

She was sure he heard the fatigue in her voice, but he didn't argue. Instead, he stroked her hair in silence for a while.

Finally he said, "I'm wondering . . ."

"Hmm?" She didn't move or open her eyes.

"Will you . . ." He hesitated and again, then said quietly, "What happened to your mother?"

Chandra drew in a sharp breath and went tense all over. She knew he felt it. The stroking hand on her hair became still.

"What?" Her voice was cold.

"You cried out for her. In your dream—your nightmare. It seemed like . . . What happened to her?"

She sat up, tearing herself out of his embrace. When she felt his hand on her arm, she flung it off.

He sat up, too, but he didn't try to touch her again. "Chandra . . ."

She started to speak, then changed her mind. Anything she might say now would reveal too much—even if only how forbidden the subject was.

"I apologize." His voice was calm. Trying to make *her* calm. "I shouldn't have asked."

Chandra inhaled deeply. *In, two, three.* Then exhaled. *Out, two, three.*

She could feel him peering at her, and was glad the darkness hid her face, as it hid his.

When she thought she had control of her voice—of her words, and thoughts—she said, "You're right, we should get some more sleep. I'm still tired."

There was a pause. "Of course."

His voice had that impassive tone he often used.

Chandra lay down on her bedroll with her back to him. She felt him move away from her, returning to his own bedroll, where he should have stayed in the first place.

She lay awake for a long time in the dark, with her eyes wide open, forbidding herself to think about anything. *Anything.*

⚹ ⚹ ⚹ ⚹ ⚹

Although she didn't expect it to happen, Chandra drifted off eventually, and she slept soundly. When she awoke, Gideon had already risen and gone back out into the night. Falia said some of the men had taken him to speak to someone who could tell him more about the Fog Riders that they had seen earlier.

"The rest of the villagers are all doing their work." Falia said to her, "There is no one to guide you to where he is. You must remain here."

The girl's manner toward her now was noticeably cool. It was all too easy to guess why, given where Gideon had chosen to place his bedroll when they all went to sleep. Chandra might have told Falia that she had no interest in Gideon, let alone in competing for his affections. But that seemed like too absurd a conversation to have with someone who looked so young.

Not wanting to stay on Diraden—or in Gideon's company—one moment longer than she had to, Chandra decided to tackle a task that she and Gideon had talked about: questioning Jurl. So she went into the livestock hut to see him.

The cage was empty. The goblin was gone.

Chandra turned around, intending to go alert the villagers. She found Falia in the doorway behind her. The girl had followed her here.

"He's escaped!" Chandra said.

"No," Falia said.

"Then were is he?"

"Being skinned and roasted."

"*What?*"

"Goblins make good eating." Falia gave Chandra's horrified reaction a look of cool amusement.

"You've *killed* him?"

"We've butchered him."

"You're going to *eat* him?" Chandra couldn't believe this was happening.

"Of course."

"Oh, *no.*" Chandra covered her face with her hands, swamped with guilt. "No wonder he was so angry at me! He *knew* you might do this! And Gideon and I locked him in here! We made him helpless!"

"He was a *goblin.*" The girl's voice was contemptuous.

"But he was my . . ."

Actually, friend would be wildly inaccurate. Jurl had tried to kill her and Gideon; and they had taken him prisoner and brutalized him when he resisted their questions or orders.

Such behavior, on either side, wasn't exactly the basis of friendship.

Chandra knew full well the goblin was treacherous, amoral, and vicious. She had no doubt that, given a chance, he'd have fed her to Velrav without the slightest hesitation or pang of regret. She had also known that a situation might arise where she or Gideon would have to kill Jurl.

But she had never intended to turn him into a helpless, caged victim that the villagers could skin and skewer at their leisure.

But that was exactly what she had done.

Chandra stared at the smirking girl in the doorway. "How can you eat someone you've *talked* to? Someone you've given food to?"

"I fed him because his skin looked a little too loose when you got here. A well-fed goblin is juicier."

Chandra was aghast that she had slept in the same small hut with this revolting, sneering, deceitful child! "I think I'm going to be sick."

She was so angry she felt dizzy. She also thought she felt a sudden headache coming on. There was a pounding in her ears, a harsh, uneven drumming that echoed around her . . .

Chandra frowned, realizing the sound wasn't inside her head. And it was, she realized with a creeping chill, familiar.

"If you plan to vomit, get it over with." The girl's voice was hard. Her eyes were narrow and her lips tight with loathing. "The riders are coming for you."

"What?" Chandra breathed.

"The Fog Riders are coming to take you to Prince Velrav." Falia's tone dripped with dark satisfaction.

Chandra heard the echoing beat of approaching horses, their hooves thundering against the ground. "Me?" Chandra felt the hut closing in on her. "But . . . why? I mean, how do they know I'm here?"

"Because I summoned them."

"You?"

"I told you, people thrill him. Power thrills him. Why do you suppose he has not fed on *me*?"

"Power," Chandra murmured. "*Power.*" She tried to call on mana. Any amount. Any feeble flow that she could use to power her fire.

"Because I trade with him for my life." Falia looked much older than she had before. Perhaps even older than her true age. In that moment, she looked hard, ruthless, and casually cruel. "I find special things for him. A fire mage, such as you . . . Oh, my. *Very* exotic, Chandra."

She looked at the girl sharply. "Did you drag that out of Jurl with your skinning and roasting tools?" She knew Falia hadn't heard it from her or Gideon.

"He traded the information for his life. But goblins are stupid. He was still caged when he gave up your secret, you see. He didn't even realize there was no reason not to kill him once he'd told us. If only more goblins were merchants."

"So you're one of the takers," Chandra said, calling on her fury, calling on fire . . . and scarcely even able to feel her chilled blood warm a little bit.

"This is Diraden." The girl's voice was flat. "*Everyone* is a taker. Some of us are just better at it than others."

Chandra decided they had chatted long enough. Fire magic wouldn't work. Velrav had seen to that. She'd have to evade those Fog Riders the old-fashioned way—by running, hiding, and finding a means to fight them even without her power. And the first step was to get out of this hut and away from this smirking *brat*.

Chandra ran, straight into Falia, driving the flat of her palm against the girl's face and striking upward. Falia shrieked in pain and fell backward. Chandra dashed past her . . . and found herself running straight into about a dozen spears.

She barely managed to stop her headlong rush into the ambush without skewering herself on the sharp metal points. She stood, frozen on the spot,

looking down at the spear blades pressed against the vulnerable flesh of her throat, her breasts, and her belly.

The hoof beats were getting closer. The riders would be here in moments.

Falia arose from her sprawled position on the ground. Her nose was gushing blood. It flowed down her face and into her mouth, coating her teeth with red as she snarled at Chandra. Her dark eyes blazing with fury, the girl walked over, spat in Chandra's face, and then slapped her, hard.

Chandra gave very serious though to retaliating . . . but she didn't favor dying of a dozen spear wounds in exchange for the pleasure of hitting the brat. Instead, she demanded, "What have you done with Gideon, you warped little bitch?"

"Gideon is where I told you he was."

"Is he alive?"

"Of course!"

Chandra studied her. "Ah, I see. You got him out of the way so you could have me carried off without his interference."

"When he returns, I'll tell him you disappeared. I'll be very convincing." Falia wiped her bloody face with her sleeve, but this only succeeded in smearing the blood all over her skin. "He'll never know what happened to you. And he'll forget about leaving here. Once you're gone, he'll stop thinking about going back to wherever you came from."

"And, of course, you'll comfort him tenderly while he grieves for me?" Chandra said.

"He will forget you," the girl said with malicious satisfaction. "You are *nothing*."

"I thought I was special enough to be a life-saving treat for your dark prince?" Chandra shrugged. "Listen, you sickly, demented, venomous *child*, if you think Gideon will *ever* notice you, then you're even sillier than I thought you were."

"He has already noticed me. I have more at my disposal than you may think. He will be mine," the girl said furiously, her blood-smeared, sallow face going an unbecoming shade of puce. "If I am ever to be allowed to live, and better, to die, I need to produce a healthy successor. Gideon will help me do that."

In that moment Chandra understood. Falia was as trapped as she was, perhaps even more so.

The noise of galloping hooves became too loud for further conversation, which was something of a relief.

The first thing Chandra saw was that fast-moving cloud of white fog traveling across the ground, glowing in the moonlight. Then she was able to see the riders, their looming black shapes rising out of the fog as they raced toward her.

They looked so terrifying that, for a moment, she couldn't move. It was like being trapped in one of her nightmares. She wanted to scream, to flee, to weep, and she couldn't do any of these things.

Then her wits came back to her in a welcome rush.

Spears! she thought. That ought to be an effective weapon against a rider.

And *fire*. Gideon had said that blood drinkers didn't like it.

The four riders entered this part of the village and cantered around Chandra and her captors, circling them like a pack of predators. The thick mist swirled around the villagers and amongst

them. Chandra felt as if icy snakes were twining around her knees when the fog reached her.

Perpetual nighttime worked in her favor on this occasion. Several of the men surrounding her were carrying torches.

She simulated terrified hysteria—which wasn't that big of a leap—and staggered to her right, feigning confusion and panic as she shrieked. The men broke position, some of them falling back, others stepping to one side. She found her opening and seized a torch from one of them. She swung it around like a club, using the fire to keep her captors away.

"Seize her!" Falia shouted.

Chandra shoved the torch into the face of one of the men. He staggered backwards, lost his footing, and dropped his spear. Chandra caught it with her foot and kicked it up to her other hand. Warding off her captors with the spear, she used the torch to set fire to thatched roofs of two nearby huts. With the light wind, there as a good chance the fire would spread to more huts. Meanwhile, it was already distracting the villagers and sparking some panic among them. She hoped that, beneath the dark pall that covered Diraden, a big enough fire would be visible from far away. It would alert Gideon, if he saw it.

She had never used a spear before, but she assumed that sticking the pointy end into soft flesh would be effective. Turning suddenly, she dashed toward one of the riders and shoved the spear into his guts.

The force of her blow almost unseated him, but he was a skilled rider and clung to his mount. She could see the rider's face as he moved away, the spear lodged in his belly. It was a bony and

ghastly white visage, with black eyes, and lips so dark they looked black, too.

The villagers had backed off to the edge of the fray, but Falia was screaming for them to seize her. They apparently thought it was a challenge best left to the Fog Riders. They were more concerned about their burning village.

Chandra turned with her torch to attack another of the four riders. As he came toward her, she shoved the torch into the dark horse's face. The animal whinnied, reared up, and danced sideways. She was about to follow up her attack and go after the rider when instinct warned her to look behind her.

The rider she had stabbed had withdrawn the spear from his guts and was swinging the long wooden handle straight toward her head.

In the moment before it hit her, Chandra thought irritably that Gideon hadn't warned her that blades wouldn't kill blood drinkers.

CHAPTER THIRTEEN

Chandra gradually became aware of a weight on her head. So heavy it hurt. Hurt *terribly*.

It felt as if an enormous rock was pounding *into* her skull, over and over. It hurt to move, it even hurt to groan. She lay there in dazed silence, wishing the pain would go away.

She heard unfamiliar voices, echoing noises, laughter, growls. Sometimes she heard sighs or sobbing and felt wetness on her face.

"There, there," said a deep, melodious voice.

For some reason, the voice frightened her. She hoped it would go away and never come back.

But it did come back.

"You look better, my dear."

There was a groan. Chandra thought she had made the noise. To test this theory, she deliberately tried to repeat the sound.

Yes! She heard it again. *She* was groaning.

But the effort was exhausting, and she sank back into oblivion.

"Yes, I think you may surprise us and survive," said the voice, some unknown time later. "I love surprises. Are you waking up?" the voice asked, dripping with amusement. "That's it. Open those eyes wide. Surely it's time for us to meet?"

Chandra squinted even in the dim light of the room. She heard a feeble moan and was embarrassed that *she* had made that pathetic sound.

Her vision adjusted and she gradually recognized that she was lying in a bed, with a red, silken canopy overhead. The opulent room was large and lighted with candles.

The pain in her head gave her a dazed feeling that she at first attributed to her unfamiliar surroundings.

"Ah, she lives," said the deep, melodious voice that had become so familiar to her recently.

Chandra didn't like the sound of it any more now than when she had been out of her senses. Moving carefully, she turned her head in the direction the voice had come from.

A young man stood next to a dormant fireplace on the far side of the room. He was tall, slim, and fair-skinned, with black hair that gleamed as if it had been polished, and red-rimmed dark eyes. His lips were so dark, they looked almost purple.

Chandra did not find him an attractive example of manhood.

"I've won," he said.

"Won?" she tried to say.

Her tongue wasn't quite working yet, but the man seemed to understand what she meant.

"The wager," he said. "Some bet you would die shortly after you were brought here. Others gambled that you'd linger for a bit, then quietly expire. I, however, knew that you would make a full recovery."

"Recover?"

"Do you remember what happened?"

"I . . ." Chandra had a feeling, despite the relative comfort of her bed, that this was not a good place to be.

She started wading through the debris in her mind. Abruptly, the details of her capture came back to her.

Where is Gideon?

She groaned.

"Oh, dear," said the young man. "That tragic?"

"Price Velrav," she croaked with certainty.

"At your service!" He swooped down in an elaborate genuflection. "May I call you Chandra?" He added, "Since you've been lying in my bed for so long, I feel like conventional formalities would be absurd."

She ignored the throbbing in her head, and looked under the sheet that covered her. "Where are my clothes?"

Her throat was so dry, she choked a little from the effort of speaking.

"I had them taken away to be cleaned. They were filthy." He crossed the room to sit on the bed beside her prone body. "I didn't want them soiling my sheets."

She glared at him. "This is *your* bed?"

"Well, *all* the beds here are mine, but for now it's yours," he said, leaning forward as he reached out to trail his pale fingers along her naked shoulder.

"Touch me and I'll break your fingers," she snapped, knocking his hand away.

"There's water on the bedside table, it sounds as though you need it. Please," he gestured to a pitcher, his movements light, almost feline. "Drink, you will feel better."

Chandra jerked her chin at him. "Off the bed."

"As you wish, my dear." He rose with an amused look on his face.

She held the sheet in place as she laboriously

pushed herself into a sitting position, always aware of the prince's red-rimmed gaze. She turned and poured herself a cup of water; she drank and felt better, pouring another glass as soon as she'd finished. Only after drinking a third glass did she look at him again.

"I like a woman who's that concentrated on fulfilling her needs," Velrav purred.

"I don't care what you like." Her voice sounded more normal now. She must have been unconscious for quite some time.

He grinned. Chandra steeled herself so as not to react to the eerily white teeth that were filed to sharp points revealed by his broad smile.

"The story the riders told me is easier to believe now." Velrav shrugged. "Lying there unconscious, you looked lovely, despite the bruises, and certainly very, er, *healthy*." His lascivious gaze traced her body up and down. "Even, one might say, robust."

"I attribute my good health to a steady diet of grub soup," she said sourly.

"That's a very nasty scratch on your thigh, though it's healing well. What did that to you?"

"A goblin," she said.

"Ugh. Nasty creatures," Velrav said fastidiously.

"And yet you eat them."

"*I* don't, my dear." He sounded appalled. "That's peasant food! Goblins are brought here only to feed some of my, er, less refined companions. What about that cut on your arm? It was festering nicely when you arrived."

She said nothing; it took her a moment to realize he was referring to the incision made by the Enervant to remove the burrowing snake.

"Hmmm, the red hair is exotic. Just as I

hoped." Velrav tilted his head, studying her. "And now that your eyes are open, I find their color intriguing. Almost amber . . . fiery . . .

"When they brought you to me I was unimpressed. Despite your unusual coloring, you seemed like any other woman offered as a tithe."

He grinned again. "Now that you're awake, however . . . Yes, *now* I see the woman they told me about!"

"Get my clothes," she said coldly. "I want to get dressed."

"A lone woman who fought off a dozen villagers and four Fog Riders? It sounded too improbable! I thought perhaps the riders were trying to save their own lives by inventing the tale."

She frowned, distracted. "How would telling you I fought them save their lives?"

"Ah, it would satisfactorily explain the messy condition you were in when you arrived! Unconscious. Pulse faint. Breath shallow. Face bruised. Your head split open and bleeding," he said. "Of course, I had the servants clean you up."

Chandra ran a hand over her head and found a gash on her temple. She explored it delicately with her fingers. It was tender and swollen, but healing.

"The spear handle," she murmured, remembering. Evidently the rider had come close to killing her with that blow.

"Mortal bodies are so fragile," Velrav said sadly. "Yours is obviously stronger than most—remarkably strong, I would say. But nonetheless vulnerable."

"Yes, well, why did you care what condition I arrived in? Does blood taste better to you when the victim is awake and screaming?" she said scathingly.

"My dear! Vitality is of the utmost importance! I was positively enthralled by the description of such a healthy and vivacious young woman when the Fog Riders were summoned." He sighed. "I rarely get such a special treat. Life is so . . . *dispirited* here. Naturally, I wanted you in perfect condition. And I gave orders to that effect." He folded his arms and smiled pleasantly at her. "The Fog Riders know how dangerous it is to disobey my orders."

"Well, sunlight can do a lot for morale," she said, not really interested. "You should look into it."

"Yes . . . Sunlight . . . You do say the most interesting things. Wherever did you get such an idea? I can't help but wonder. And wonder, I like to say, is the first of all passions."

"Listen here, Prince," Chandra said. "If you think I'm going to kindle anything but your funeral pyre, you are sadly mistaken."

"I can't tell you how happy that makes me, Chandra," he said with true glee. "Things have been so dull here for the past half-century."

Chandra wasn't sure how to react to that. Velrav just stood there looking at her, smiling, waiting.

"Maybe I could have my clothes now?" Chandra asked after what seemed forever.

The Prince's smile vanished. "How very boring," Velrav said, crestfallen. "The conversation was going so well for a minute . . . Mother always told me to temper my expectations."

"I suppose that's why you cut her head off?"

"Ah . . . Witty *and* well informed. You are a gift, Chandra. What could I have done to deserve this?"

"I'm sure you'll come up with something, but the clothes would be nice while you consider it."

"Yes, in due time. But I am curious about you. A *fire mage*, the girl claimed, although I can't imagine how this could be." Velrav said with evident fascination. "Is it true?"

"No need to ask me. Just release the enchantment you have on this plane, and you'll find out for yourself whether it's true."

"How rare and wonderful!" he said. "A fire mage! I haven't seen anyone who practiced fire magic since . . . Well, since before I murdered my family."

"I'd be happy to show you what I can do," she said.

"Oh, how I would enjoy that!"

"In that case, why don't y—"

"If only it were as easy for you as it is for me, eh?" he said with regret. "But how could I do so in good conscience? I do have to look out for my best interests, after all. And since there has been no fire magic on Diraden for quite some time," he said, "nor anyone of such enchantingly good health here for many years . . . Perhaps you'd like to tell me where you come from?"

"What does it matter? You can't go there."

"What makes you so sure?" he said. "You came here, after all. So why can't I go there?"

"I didn't come here on purpose." Staying somewhat close to the truth, she added, "And I don't know how to go back."

"Then fortune is mine."

"And the past doesn't matter."

"Oh, but it does," he said as he moved to a window to look out. "The past is what created who

we are now, after all. But you will tell me in time. And if you don't, then perhaps your lover will."

"My lover?"

"The girl claims the man who came to the village with you is your lover. She saw proof of this." He added, "I, of course, didn't intrude on her delicate feelings by asking what she meant by that."

"He's a bounty hunter. I was his prisoner," she said, hoping that Gideon was not in Velrav's custody.

"And now you're mine . . . The menarch was quite upset when we took her prize."

"Her prize?"

"Yes, your *bounty hunter*," said Velrav, still looking down at something from his position at the window. "And she objected. So forcefully that the riders considered killing her." He glanced over his shoulder at Chandra. "But they knew they couldn't do that without asking me first. And I certainly would have said no."

He returned his gaze to something outside, beyond the window. "If the menarch is going to die, then *I'll* be the one to kill her. But, in truth, I have no wish for that. She finds such interesting treats for me, after all."

"Treats." The word was flat. His arrogance was astonishing.

Pulling the sheet with her, Chandra rose slowly from the bed. She was light-headed and her legs felt shaky. She wrapped the sheet around herself.

"Besides," Velrav said, "she's such a puny thing, I don't think she'd satisfy my hunger. No, it's far better to let her live as long as she keeps giving me wonderful gifts."

Walking on bare feet across the cool stone floor, Chandra asked, with a growing feeling of dread, "What about the bounty hunter?"

Velrav met her gaze, then he nodded in the direction of the window. "See for yourself."

Chandra tried to brace herself for whatever was coming, but her heart was pounding and she suspected Velrav could see that she was breathing a little too fast. She approached the window and looked down, trying to see what Velrav had been gazing at.

She found herself looking into a courtyard, which was surrounded by the wings of the castle on three sides. On the fourth side was a huge gate, bordered by a gate house and stables for a dozen or so horses. There were no trees or plants in sight, and the whole area was well-lit by torches that were positioned along the surrounding walls.

The courtyard was empty apart from one man.

Chandra clenched her teeth together as she stared at him in horror, willing herself not to cry out or satisfy Velrav with a shocked reaction.

Gideon stood between two tall, thick wooden posts. His arms were stretched out and securely tied to the posts. His long black hair was tangled and matted, and his head hung down. But since his legs were supporting him—albeit just barely— she knew he wasn't unconscious or dead. Not yet, anyway.

His torso was naked. The wounds that Jurl had left there had reopened and bled anew. The claw marks gaped wide, red, and angry, and rivulets of dried blood stuck to Gideon's fair skin. But Chandra didn't remember there being so *many* wounds, nor that they were that severe . . .

She drew in a sharp breath through her nostrils.

Most of those marks could not have been from Jurl, she realized. Someone had been deliberately cutting him.

207

Aware of Velrav's amused gaze on her, she kept her expression stony. When she was sure she could control her tone, she said, "The bounty hunter."

"He appeared—out of nowhere, I gather—as the riders were about to carry you out of the village. And he interfered." Velrav made a *tsk tsk* sound. "Most unwise. We would have never known about him if he hadn't."

Chandra ground her teeth together and focused on her breathing. She knew it was too loud, knew that Velrav heard it.

"He had the most remarkable weapon," Velrav continued. "It's mine now, and I adore it! You've seen it, I assume? It's sort of a three-bladed whip. He killed one of the Fog Riders with it."

Since running one of them through with a spear hadn't worked, that surprised her. "How?"

Velrav ignored the question. "After we captured him, Falia sent a message asking me to meet her. A very bold thing to do, don't you agree? Naturally, I was curious."

"Did she throw another tantrum?"

"No, evidently she had resigned herself to her loss. Instead, she offered me more treats." When Chandra glanced at him with a frown, he nodded toward Gideon and said, "Information about him."

"Ah." So the girl continued making herself more valuable to Velrav alive than dead. And she also ensured, by telling the cheerfully vindictive prince that Gideon and Chandra were lovers, that their supposed relationship would be remade now into a source of suffering and torment, rather than comfort and satisfaction. "What a nasty little girl."

"This man is, like you, unusually healthy and strong. Also tall." Velrav concluded, "You both come from the same place?"

"He followed me."

"And then he tried to rescue you."

She suspected where this conversation was going. "Rescue? No, I guess he was trying to keep *his* prize." Chandra tore her gaze away from Gideon to look at Velrav. "He's a bounty hunter. No prisoner, no reward."

"What crime did you commit?" the Prince asked with interest.

"It's a long story." She allowed herself a deep breath. "And I am not going to tell it."

"Oh, I hope you will someday," he said. "I suspect it must be a very engaging tale. That man down there—Gideon?"

"Uh-huh."

"Gideon killed a Fog Rider, which no one has ever done before, and he gave the other three riders quite a fight." Velrav sighed voluptuously as he gazed down at his bloody captive. "You must have committed a *very* impressive crime, for a man like that to come after you."

"Has he been tied up there the whole time I've been lying in here?"

"More or less. And I believe he's been looking forward to this moment!" Velrav knocked hard on the window.

"Don't!" she said reflexively. The sound would carry well in the empty courtyard.

"Why ever not?" Velrav knocked harder.

As she had feared, Chandra lost control of her composure as Gideon's head slowly lifted. She pressed her palms against the window and looked down at him, distressed and appalled.

He looked up at the window. The torchlight illuminated his face, which was pale from blood loss and darkened by a thick shadow of hair on his jaws, chin, and upper lip. His left eye was blackened and swollen shut.

Gideon's weary, impassive expression didn't change, but she knew he saw her, silhouetted in the candlelight that shone on her unmistakable red hair.

"You look heartbroken, my dear," Velrav said smoothly. "I thought he was hunting you?"

"He was." She kept her gaze locked with Gideon's, though she doubted he could see her face clearly in this light. "That was just . . . business. What you're doing though . . ." She shook her head. "This is *disgusting*."

"I suppose it's a little . . . ostentatious," Velrav admitted. "But I assure you it's not our normal custom. We usually have some sport with our captives—"

"Sport?" she repeated with loathing.

"—and then feed on them. On rare occasions, we might bring someone into the fold. Someone like you, for example. But the rest die soon after arriving."

"So why is he . . . on *display* like this?"

"He killed a Fog Rider." Velrav's tone suggested the reason should be obvious, even to her. "So a certain amount of extraordinary treatment is expected. And I couldn't disappoint my companions and loyal servants, now could I? They deserve this."

She didn't try to continue speaking.

"You know, he's not looking at you like a hunter," Velrav observed, gazing down at Gideon. "No, indeed. The *hunt* is not what's in those lovely blue eyes of his."

"What do *you* know about hunting?" she said contemptuously. "You sit in this castle and have victims brought to you."

"Actually, I do still hunt a little," Velrav said, not sounding at all bothered by her disdain. "But not often, I must admit. Not anymore. Like everything else, I find it so *boring* by now."

"You've been alive for a long time." As she gazed at Gideon, Chandra remembered what he had told her about blood magic.

"Yes," he said. "Yes, I have."

"You've had total power, with no challengers, feeding on the blood of your people to stay young. You've had no purpose except to satisfy your own hunger." Chandra continued staring down at Gideon. "Night never turns to morning. The seasons never change. Even the moonlight never changes."

She could see Gideon's gaze growing more alert and intent as his exhausted, pain-fogged mind started to focus. She doubted he had known until this moment whether she was still alive. Even so, he maintained his control. She envied him that ability.

"What could possibly make your existence worthwhile anymore?" Chandra said to Velrav. "What could make your pointless existence still worth living?"

The prince was silent.

Someone entered the courtyard below. Like Velrav and the Fog Riders, this individual was male, slim, sickly pale, black-haired, with those unnaturally dark lips. He appeared to be in a hurry, going from one wing of the castle to another. As he passed Gideon, he withdrew a dagger from its sheathe on his belt and, with a casualness

that shocked Chandra, slashed the blade across Gideon's back. He bent down and licked at the flow of blood.

She gasped and slapped her palms against the window.

Gideon grimaced and closed his eyes for a few moments. He lowered his head, and even from here, Chandra could see his chest heaving with his rapid breaths as he tried to master the pain.

"I've sometimes wondered the same thing myself," Velrav said somberly. "Why go on? Why not just end it? The weight of my boredom sometimes becomes so *unbearable*, I think I'll go mad."

"You *are* mad." She couldn't take her eyes off Gideon.

"I have indeed wondered, from time to time, what could possibly make my life worth living again."

Gideon tilted his head up again and looked for her in the window. She balled her hands into fists against the glass and didn't bother to try hiding how enraged and upset she was. Velrav knew, anyhow. Of course he knew.

"And then you both arrived," Velrav said, "and now I know."

"Know what?" she asked absently as she leaned her throbbing head against the window. Her heart was beating like it wanted to escape her chest.

"Know what would make this existence bearable again," the dark prince said. "Know what can make this tedious life as exciting as it used to be, long ago."

She tore her gaze away from Gideon and turned to frown quizzically at the prince. "Not that I care," she said, "but what are you talking about?"

"Now I know there is more beyond Diraden." he said. "So much more, in fact, that I am eager to explore it. And somehow, you and your bounty hunter will help me."

CHAPTER FOURTEEN

That's his plan? To become a Planeswalker?" Gideon's voice was weary.

"Yes," Chandra said.

"What have you been telling him?"

"He kept pressing me about things and really I just got tired of it. I felt like if I told him the truth he would leave me alone."

"Well, it's really the least of our worries. It'll never happen."

"Well, there's a little more to the plan. He's going to use you to do it. He has some blood ritual that he's preparing with the court magi. He thinks he can transmute your essence, or something."

They were talking through the door of Gideon's dungeon cell. He had been moved from the scene of his public bloodletting in the courtyard once the Prince had come to a decision. That had been some days ago.

From the next cell over, an old man's demented laughter rang out intermittently.

"Has that been going on the whole time?" she asked. Chandra had been given leave to move about the castle unsupervised. Velrav was so confident in his enchantment that he felt he had little to fear. Nevertheless, Chandra's feet and

hands were shackled so that every where she went, she did it by taking mincing little steps. She didn't go many places. Still, she had been able to bribe one of the castle guards with a small bit of fire quartz that Brannon had given her on her last night at Keral Keep. That a simple rock was so exotic was a testament to Diraden's charm. She was grateful it had gotten her down here to see Gideon.

"Yes. If our man is to be believed, that's the king."

"Oh, yes indeed! I am the king and my rule would be absolute had my rule had not been absolved," he said, before breaking into uncontrolled laughter.

"That's not even a good play on words," said Chandra.

"It's better than some. Most of the time he doesn't make sense," said Gideon, over the ever-louder howls of laughter. "But the story Falia told us was more or less true. In between his laughing fits, he has told me a little about the prince's power, and his own. It seems that magical power here is based on lineage."

"What do you mean?"

"I'm not sure exactly, but all of this, the pall, the dampening spells, he achieves it all through rituals using the king's blood. It seems the prince's only true power comes from the king. That's why he has kept him alive for all these years.

"Indeed! The whelp knows he's nothing without me. If he ever wants total power, I must give it to him and he knows I never will." The maniacal laughter followed again. "And if I die without passing it to him, another will be born. He will have nothing. So he keeps me here, the

L A U R A   R E S N I C K

next best thing, prolonging my life with blood magic."

Silence followed for a few moments, one of the rare lulls in his laughter.

"If it's your power, why can't you use it against him?" asked Chandra.

"He has cursed me. Imagine that! Cursed me with the help of demons. He thinks he paid with the blood of his family. He thinks he will live forever, but there is more to come, and they will have their payment."

"Lovely," was all Chandra could think to say. The vitriol in the old man's voice made her skin crawl. There was little doubt for her that this was the king.

"All lovely things have an ending . . . *ha!*" Whatever was funny about this was lost on the two of them.

"This is how it goes," said Gideon. "A moment or two of lucidity and then he moves from word to word. If there is a point I don't see it."

"Gideon, things are really looking bad. I mean, I may just be stuck here. He says the two of us will explore the Multiverse together, but he's going to kill you. Why did you have to come after me when the Fog Riders came?" she asked.

"You were slung over their saddle like a sack of grain. There was so much blood pouring from your head, I wasn't sure you'd live." He gaze went to the healing wound on her temple. "It looks a lot better now."

"It is. But why did you fight them for me? You could be on the outside trying to figure something out."

"I guess I didn't think. I thought they were going to kill you. I panicked."

ℂℙ

"You weren't thinking?" Chandra asked, despite everything, unable to conceal a hint of enjoyment.

"You don't reserve the right to act irrationally, Chandra. Let's remember I'm the one imprisoned in a dungeon. You're the one sleeping in a nice bed and being offered a life spent trapsing across the planes of the Multiverse."

"I don't think his offer is reliable," she said. "He seems a little . . . cracked."

"It seems to run in the family," Gideon said dryly.

"Look, we made a deal when you got to Diraden, and you've stuck to your part of the bargain, so I'll stick to mine. We'll keep working together to get out of here."

He looked at her through the barred opening in the door, his gaze impassive. She knew that this was the face he offered to people when he wanted to conceal something. It made her feel impatient with him, even angry. He had nothing to conceal from her, not if they were going to escape.

"Why did you risk your life twice to steal the scroll on Kephalai?" he asked.

"You knew the scroll was precious," she said irritably. "You had it in your possession. Are you trying to tell me you didn't even look at it?"

"I looked at it."

"And?"

"And *what*?" He shrugged, then winced a little as his fresh wounds protested. "A spell written in a text I'm guessing you can't read—"

"Can *you*?"

"No, I can't read it. But I know where it is from."

"Don't mess with me Gideon."

"It's old, which explains what it was doing in the Sanctum of Stars. But that doesn't explain why *you* want it so badly."

"What does anyone want with anything? It's old, yeah. But it's unique. There's nothing else like it in the whole Multiverse, is what I've been told. It's a spell, yeah. But the monks back on Regatha think it could lead to something of immense power. Something way bigger than you or me." She paused while the king entered into another round of hysterics. "I don't know, Gideon. I wanted it for the glory. Something to make the Blind Eternities see."

"Never rely on the glory of morning, nor on the smile of a mother-in-law. Ah, ha, ha . . ."

As they waited for this latest laughing jag to subside, Gideon considered what Chandra had said, the passion she'd showed.

"It's from Zendikar," he said. "A plane of some repute. It is said to be host to some of the most powerful mana sources in the Multiverse, but it is also unpredictable, irratic. Violent and pacific in the same moment."

"Have you ever been there?"

"Never, but in my youth I searched."

Chandra stared at Gideon without seeing him, her mind fixed on what the scroll could lead to.

She wrapped her fingers around the bars that separated them. "You're sure the plane exisits?"

"I can't be certain, but, yes, reasonably sure."

"Do you know what this means, Gideon?" A light burned in Chandra's eyes. "If we could get to Zendikar and find this thing that the monks talk about? Think of the things we could do. Think of the power! The adventure!"

"Chandra, you don't even know what it is. It

could be anything. It could be the darkest power you've ever known. It could kill you. It could . . ."

"You said it, Gideon. It could be anything. And we'll never know until we find it."

After a moment, Gideon looked into Chandra's eyes. They sparkled with a clarity he had never seen before. There was hope there, to be sure, but there was something more. To say that it was fire would be obvious. To say that it was life would be an understatement.

"We can't do anything until we get out of here," he said in a monotone.

Chandra hung her head. There was silence in the dungeon.

"If I may say so," said the king in a remarkably clear voice. "I believe I can help."

CHAPTER FIFTEEN

The plan was a little crazy. So many things could go wrong, she was sure Gideon would never go for it, preferring instead to sacrifice himself so that she could live, or some ridiculous thing like that. But the king said he could help. He told them he still had some tricks up his sleeve.

This was how he told them they could beat the prince and escape the shroud that held Diraden in darkness and restricted their connection to mana. The king would need some of Gideon's blood. Not much, maybe a spoonful and he would offer a similar amount of his own. He would use a bit of childhood magic he'd learned to confound his parents so many centuries ago. He and his siblings had often traded a bit of their blood in order to assume one another's appearance and so get out of lessons. The king was a bit hard to stop once he started on his reminiscence. Chandra had to be diligent in keeping him focused.

The king said he could make himself look like Gideon and vice versa. The old man had been alive too long, he said. It was time for him to die, especially if his death were vexing to the ungrateful whelp sitting on his throne. He would go in Gideon's place to be killed. When the prince

221

mistakenly killed him, the shroud would be lifted. The prince would be powerless before them.

"But what about this transmutation he hopes to achieve? What if he is able to incorporate your essence?" Gideon asked, still skeptical of the plan.

"If it were possible, he would have tried. Don't you think?" asked Chandra. She had been in the dungeon for some time now. She couldn't rely on the guard to let her stay forever, or even be at the door when she tried to leave.

"The boy knows nothing. It is impossible," said the king. "My time has come and he cannot stop it."

"I am not filled with confidence," said Gideon.

"What else are we going to do?" asked Chandra. "I don't see a lot of options."

"Okay, but how are we going to move the blood between cells?"

"It must be in the woman's mouth!" shouted the king before entering into the first round of laughter in quite some time.

The thought was ridiculous to Chandra. Was this all an old crank's plan to put his tongue in her mouth? For the first time she moved down the hallway to the cell the king occupied and looked inside. What she saw nearly made her faint. Sitting cross-legged on the floor of his cell, the old man looked so pallid as to be translucent. Light blue veins covered his naked body like the veins of some gelid mineral. He was unbearably thin. He laughed with his toothless mouth wide, his tongue dryly avian. His black eyes were as lusterless as the surrounding stone.

"Gideon. We have to do this, but I'm not using my mouth."

✳ ✳ ✳ ✳ ✳

In the hours, perhaps days, following her conspiratorial meeting with Gideon and the king, she thanked that shred of humanity that allowed a cup and pail of water in Gideon's cell.

She had ferried the blood back and forth and the the two had both drunk their portion. The king said the effect of the transmogrification would last indefinitely, but once he were killed, the effect would disappear. Putting their faith in the old man was risky, to say the least, but what other choice did they have?

Velrav had decided that he wanted Chandra present for the ritual. She assumed that was for no better reason than to enjoy her reaction to Gideon's death.

She'd been passing the time unwillingly in her room, where she could remain unshackled, waiting. She didn't think she had ever been this anxious. She went over all sorts of scenarios even when she had no idea what to expect. The image of the laughing king burned into her mind so that every time she closed her eyes, she saw him there, like a malevolent idol.

It was a relief when one of the nameless castle guards finally came to escort her to a wing of the castle she had never seen. He led her into an oval room without appointment save a long stone table at one end. The plane of the table slanted toward the middle of the oval at a sharp angle. Four straps were positioned at the corners, presumably to hold something, or somebody, in place. She was placed at the opposite end of the room and made to stand in a slight depression covered with a metal grate.

Her wrists and feet shackled, Chandra stood wondering what she was supposed to do as the guard went around the room lighting sconces. Next

Gideon—she hoped it was the king—was escorted into the room by two guards. He was hunched slightly and his hair hung over his face; his naked torso, criss-crossed with wounds and mottled with bruises, was deathly pale. She hadn't noticed some of the wounds before. *Were the bruises new?* The guards picked him up, turned him upside down and strapped him to the table so that he faced up, his head pointing toward the floor. He offered no resistance. When his hair fell away from his face Chandra could see that he wore the stony expression, the impassive look she had come to know from him.

Chandra felt a little relief. At least they had gotten this far. But just then, another set of guards entered the room, carrying the king's body into the room. What was Gideon doing here? Did Velrav know the truth? The guards placed Gideon equidistant between Chandra and the king, at the wall so that the three of them formed a triangle, and left the room. Chandra was worried by this latest development, but there was nothing she could do.

And in walked Velrav. As tense as she felt, Chandra had to keep herself from laughing. He was wearing a lush and obviously expensive cloak, but he also wore a long conical hat with a broad brim and chin strap. The effect, though doubtlessly intended to make him look imposing, made him look like a fool, a sad minstrel imitating the pomp of royalty.

Velrav turned to Chandra. "I believe you know my father, the king? Are you surprised? No, of course not. Could you believe that I wouldn't know about your little clandestine visit? I thought I would let you visit your bounty hunter one last time."

Chandra couldn't respond. Her mind was racing. The whole situation was getting really annoying. Not a single thing had gone right since she got to this forsaken plane, and by now it was really going wrong. She could feel her skin begin to flush, all the familiar feelings of anger and frustration, but there was something missing. The bloom at the base of her skull, that power that she normally felt coursing down her spine and into her limbs wasn't there—but her blood was moving and that, at least, felt good.

"I brought him to bear witness to his only living son's transformation."

The old man began to laugh, that unmistakable laugh. Chandra balled her fists and clenched her jaw. Her mind raced uncontrollably. She tried to calm her mind down, tried to breathe, but she couldn't do it. Everything she knew, everything she'd done, nothing mattered. She felt it all fall away from her as the rage took control.

"I'm sorry, Chandra. He knows," said Gideon, from the table. "He came soon after you left and beat me within an inch of my life. With the body of the old man, I couldn't do a thing to defend myself."

The old man laughed still, rocking back and forth.

"Quiet, you old fool!" shouted Velrav as he pulled Gideon's sural from beneath his cloak and whipped at him clumsily, but it did nothing to stop the laughing. If anything, it only served to make the king laugh harder.

The fire in the sconce burned more brightly as Velrav kept whipping his laughing father, and Chandra felt it. She felt the mountain inside her. She was the volcano.

Everything slowed down when she got this way. She felt like she was moving outside of time as the power bloomed in the base of her skull, as the fierce flower she'd been missing filled her head and her hair became a raging halo of fire. Her fists became torches, her feet lit with alchemical intensity. She spread her arms wide, her shackles a molten puddle on the floor beneath her as she began to levitate.

Velrav turned to look at her, his mouth agape. The king's laugh raised to a fever pitch, his eyes gaining life as he reveled in Chandra's inferno.

Boom! Chandra brought her hands together in a thunderous clap as her feet returned to the floor, and a blade of fire rose from her hands. She turned to her right, spinning and swinging the flaming blade in order to carry through with all her momentum. When she came full circle she struck the prince in the neck, cleaving his head and opposite shoulder from his body. The cauterized flesh smoldered as the body fell to the side and Velrav's right arm and head landed in the laughing king's lap. It did nothing to quiet him.

The king patted the face of his son, and moved the head to the floor. He stood and crossed to Chandra, who was beginning to register what she had just done. Her flaming sword still burning brightly, and the old man only stopped laughing when he grabbed the blade. His flesh sizzled and burned immediately, the hideous hissing sound of the water in his body boiling away. With amazing resolve he impaled himself on the blade, even as Chandra tried to pull it back, but her shock made her too slow. The flames died, but not before the king. His body slumped on top of his son's.

L A U R A   R E S N I C K

Chandra turned to Gideon, who still lay upside-down on the table, blood coloring his once-pale face.

"Help me off," he said.

She turned and went to him. "Can you feel it? Mana!"

"Yes, I can feel it."

She wanted to revel in the flow of red mana that was suddenly *there*, had been there. She felt giddy, almost light-headed. She undid the straps holding him to the table and helped him off it.

"Let's leave. I'm sure I can planeswalk. Can you?" she asked him.

"I think I can, yes." He was looking at her in astonishment. "Chandra, what was that?"

"It was a blade of fire. I've never done that before."

"But how? I thought you were going to incinerate all of us. I've never seen anything like that."

She thought about it for a moment, then laughed with pleasure. "I feel *strong*." Her gaze wandered over his damaged, haggard appearance. "What about you?"

He looked down at his wounded, blood-streaked body. "I've been better." Gideon's eyes were wary, as though he was witnessing magic for the first time.

"We've got to get out of here, before someone comes, things are sure to be getting different out there," she said.

"You're right." His face resumed the confident calm she knew. "We need to planeswalk."

"Regatha?"

"I'm following you," said Gideon as he went and gathered his weapon.

After several minutes of concentration they left Diraden.

Φ

✳ ✳ ✳ ✳ ✳

They entered Regatha gently, landing on soft grass in a sunlit meadow.

Chandra lay on her back in the grass, looking up into the familiar sky. Gideon was stretched beside her. The sun came peeking through the lush trees at the edge of the meadow at an angle.

She touched his wounded, bloody chest. "Does it hurt very badly?"

His gaze dropped to her mouth. "Does what hurt?"

The trees overhead . . .

Chandra suddenly sat up.

Shoved aside, he lay looking up at her quizzically. "Is something wrong?"

"We're in the Great Western Wood," she said. "I'm, uh, not sure I should be here."

He sat up, too, and looked around. "Ah."

"We should go," Chandra said.

And then she realized she wasn't sure what to do with Gideon. She wanted to take him with her . . . but she thought it likely that the Keralians, though generally tolerant, would object to her bringing a mage with Gideon's particular talent. Especially given how tense things were between Keral Keep and the Order.

Chandra stood up, looked around, and got her bearings . . . and then realized where she could take Gideon.

"A friend of mine lives near here," she said. "We'll go to his home."

Samir would be distressed to see her in the forest, but she was confident he would nonetheless welcome them with sincere warmth and hospitality.

"This way," she said to Gideon, leading him toward Samir's nearby compound in the lush, green woodlands.

"Actually, Chandra, there's something . . ."

His voice trailed off and they both stood still, listening intently.

Chandra heard the rustle of a bush, then the crackling of a twig underfoot.

"Someone's coming," she whispered unnecessarily.

Oufes rarely made that much noise when moving through the forest, but she felt tense until she saw who it was. When a lithe, familiar figure came out of the dense greenery a few moments later, Chandra relaxed.

"Samir!"

"Chandra!" He smiled and waved. "You're *back*?" He looked around, as if fearing a hoard of angry oufes might instantly drop out of the trees and attack. "You shouldn't be here!"

"I know," she said. "And I'm leaving. But first—"

Samir's horrified gasp distracted her, as did the expression of shocked dismay on his face. "What *happened*?"

"What? Oh." She realized he was looking at Gideon. And as she glanced at her wounded, bloody, bearded, unwashed, unkempt, half-naked companion, Chandra realized that Samir's reaction was understandable.

"Chandra!" Samir said sharply, coming closer as he gazed at Gideon with appalled concern. "What did you *do* to him?"

"*I* didn't do anything to him! It was . . . uh, never mind. Listen, Samir, I would appreciate it if—"

"Young man, you're badly injured! You need healing!"

"It looks worse than it is," Gideon said.

Samir blinked. "Wait a moment. Have we . . ." He frowned and studied Gideon's face more closely. "I know you, don't I?"

Chandra said, "No, he's—"

"Yes!" Samir said. "Of course I do! It's Gideon, isn't it?"

Chandra froze.

"We met . . ." Samir's face clouded with dawning realization. "We met at the Temple of Heliud."

There was a tense silence as Chandra turned her stunned, appalled gaze on Gideon.

"Yes, that's right," Gideon said, his voice calm, his expression impassive. "I hope you've been well since then, Samir?"

CHAPTER SIXTEEN

"You're from Regatha?" Chandra said in blank shock.

Gideon's blue eyes met hers. She couldn't read his expression.

"From Regatha?" Samir repeated, sounding puzzled. "Er, where else *would* he be from, Chandra?"

Her gaze flashed to Samir. She blinked stupidly at him, abruptly remembering that he didn't know she was a Planeswalker. Indeed, she doubted Samir had ever even *heard* of Planeswalkers. And this was no time to start explaining the concept to him.

"I mean, you're from *here*?" she said to Gideon, feeling dumbfounded. Why had he never said so?

"I'm from Zinara." Gideon's voice was clear and firm. There was a flicker of warning in his eyes, reminding her to guard her tongue until they had a chance to talk alone together. Then he turned to Samir and said, by way of explanation for Chandra's puzzling remark, "As you can see, we've been through an ordeal. Chandra's disoriented."

"I am not!" she snapped.

Both men looked at her, then at each other. There was a brief, silent moment of commiseration

between them that she found infuriating.

"Chandra . . ." Samir approached her, his expression concerned, and laid a gentle hand on her arm. "You're covered in blood."

"What?" Chandra looked down and realized he was right. Almost every part of herself that she could see was messily splattered with blood—most of it Prince Velrav's, she supposed. Cutting off his head had been messy, though that had not been her concern at the time. Chandra realized how grisly her face must look right now.

"I'm fine, Samir," she said dismissively.

"But your friend is not," said the woodland mage. "He needs—"

"We're not friends," she said, glaring at Gideon.

The truth about her mysterious companion was dawning on her with a deluge of appalling implications.

"You *followed* me," she said accusingly to Gideon.

The two men looked at each other again.

"We should go to my home immediately," Samir said to Gideon. "It's nearby."

"I'm not going anywhere!" Chandra said.

Even after learning he was a Planeswalker, she had assumed that his business with her had originated on Kephalai and had something to do with the scroll. He'd been following her all along.

She said to him, "You lying, treacherous, *cowardly*—"

"Chandra!" Samir shook her shoulders. "We must go to my home. We can't stay here."

"I'm *not* staying here!" she said, contradicting her earlier assertion that she wasn't going anywhere. "Not with *him*. I'm going to Keral Keep."

LAURA RESNICK

"You can't," said Samir. "Not by day."

"Of course I can!"

"No, it's not safe."

Gideon looked sharply at Samir. "What do you mean?"

Samir said to Chandra, "A great deal has happened while you've been away. Come home with me, and I'll explain, while you wash and I look after Gideon."

"He doesn't need looking after!"

"He can't go all the way to Zinara like this," Samir said reasonably. "Those wounds should be cleaned and tended immediately." Samir glanced at Gideon's pale, haggard face. "He obviously needs food and drink, too."

"You're going to *feed* him?" she said. "You're going to feed this scheming . . ."

"I'm going to feed you, too," Samir said. "Perhaps then you'll make more sense."

"Samir," Gideon said, "what changes are you talking about?"

"Not here." Samir looked around nervously. "If Chandra is seen here now, I fear she may not live until sundown."

She said dismissively, "I can handle a few angry oufes."

"The problem has grown much bigger than that, Chandra," Samir said. "Much more serious."

"How serious?" asked Gideon.

"Two days ago," said Samir, "the inter-tribal council of the Great Western Wood agreed to capture Chandra and turn her over to the Order."

She stared at him in shock. She'd expected the situation would blow over, not worsen.

⁂ ⁂ ⁂ ⁂ ⁂

With mingled reluctance and resentment,

Chandra agreed to accompany the two men to Samir's family compound. As soon as they reached it, Samir showed her and Gideon into a small, fragrant hut that was primarily used for drying herbs.

"Wait here," he instructed them. "I'll get you some water for washing and some balm for those wounds. And I'll ask my wife to prepare some food."

"Oh, don't fuss over *him*, Samir," Chandra said. "He doesn't deserve your kindness."

"He's my guest," the village chief said.

And that, Chandra knew, settled the matter as far as Samir was concerned. She shrugged and folded her arms, knowing it was her anger that was letting her say things that risked letting Samir know their secrets, but not caring enough to stop herself. "Fine. Suit yourself. I just hope he doesn't give you cause to regret it."

Gideon's expression was so blank, it was as if he didn't even hear her speaking.

"I'll be back shortly," Samir said as he left the hut.

They stood alone together in the shadowy interior, staring at each other.

"You followed me to Kephalai!" she said as soon as Samir was out of earshot.

"Yes."

"From here!"

"Yes."

"Why?"

"Maybe we should sit down," Gideon suggested.

"Answer me!"

"Well, *I'm* sitting down," he said. "I think half my blood is lying on the pavement of Velrav's courtyard."

"How did you know I was going after the Scroll?" she demanded, watching him ease himself onto a wooden stool.

Gideon looked light-headed, probably because he had indeed lost a lot of blood and was certainly in need of food and water. He also looked as if the pain of his wounds had returned now that the excitement of escape had worn off.

It served him right.

"I *didn't* know," he said. "I'd never heard of the scroll. I'd never heard of Kephalai, either. I was just following you."

"*Why?*"

"Like I told you on Kephalai, you'd made yourself conspicuous."

"Yes, but that was on K——"

"Actually, I meant you'd made yourself conspicuous *here*," he said. "You misunderstood, of course, because you had just made yourself even *more* conspicuous on Kephalai."

"Did you follow me there so you could lecture me about my behavior?" she snapped.

"I followed you there," he said patiently, "to take you into custody."

"*Custody?* For who? Walbert?" When he nodded, she said, "So you *are* a bounty hunter."

"No, I'm more like a . . ." he shrugged. "A soldier."

"A soldier," she repeated.

"Yes."

"For the Order?"

He nodded again.

"Are you from Regatha?" she asked. "Originally, I mean?"

"No. I've only been here a short time." He added, "Even less time than you've been here."

She frowned. "How do you know how long I've

(p

been here?"

"Because not long ago, someone started practicing extreme fire magic in the mountains."

"How do you know about that?" she asked in surprise.

"You're not exactly discreet, Chandra," he said with a touch of exasperation. "And no one on Regatha had ever seen anything like that before. Except for *one* person, Walbert said. A Planeswalker who was here long ago, according to legend, and whose power and, uh, personality inspired the establishment of Keral Keep."

"Walbert knows about Planeswalkers?"

"Yes. Doesn't the mother mage of the monastery know? I mean, if it was founded because of a—"

"Yes, she knows. It's her monastery. But how does Walbert know about Jaya Ballard?"

"That's the name of the Planeswalker who was here?" Gideon said with a shrug, "Walbert knows a lot of things. He's well educated, well informed, and well organized."

"He's also arrogant, interfering, overbearing—"

"When he became aware of the spells being practiced," Gideon said, speaking as if he hadn't heard her at all, "he suspected that another Planeswalker had come to Mount Keralia after all these years. So he kept an eye on the situation. He soon learned that there was a brand new resident at the monastery, a woman who had arrived right before all that big magic started being let loose in the mountains." After a pause, he added, "And no one seemed to know anything about this woman, except the she was unusually powerful. She had simply . . . arrived one day, and she never talked about her past or where she came from."

LAURA RESNICK

"How did he learn this?"

"I told you. Walbert's well informed and well organized." Gideon added, "Besides, gossip travels faster than galloping horses. Even if it wasn't malicious, there was bound to be talk, Chandra."

"Hmph. So why did *you* come to Regatha? To sit at Walbert's feet in admiration?"

"I came for the Purifying Fire," he said.

"Ah. I've heard of it." She tilted her head and studied him. "You came to Regatha to increase your power."

"Yes." He'd evidently decided, once Samir blew his cover, not to hold anything back, and she was distantly pleased that she was going to, finally, get some honest answers from him, but more than that, she was still enraged at what he'd done.

Chandra thought it over and said skeptically, "So did Walbert simply give you free access to this mysterious source of white mana that people say is what has made the Order *so* powerful here?"

"He wanted something in exchange," Gideon said.

"You mean, he wanted you to go after the Planeswalker that he suspected had come to the Keralian Monastery."

"Yes."

"And do what?" she said, feeling her blood heat. "Kill me?"

"Just take you into custody."

"What does *that* mean?"

Silence.

"Gideon?" she prodded. "What did Walbert plan to do once he had me in custody?"

"I don't know." There was a pause. "I didn't ask. At the time, I didn't particularly care."

"Of course not," she said. "You just wanted

access to the Purifying Fire."

"Yes," he agreed. "But then you chased down a ghost warden and killed it for no reason—"

"No *reason*?" She couldn't believe her ears.

"It was harmless," he said. "It had minimal defenses, and it only used them when directly threatened."

"It was a *spy* for the Order!"

"You also *burned down* part of the Western Wood—"

"Which is not your concern! Or Walbert's!"

"—and you attacked four peacekeepers without provocation."

"Peacekeepers? Without provocation?" Now she was truly enraged; she could feel the fire igniting in her blood. "I chased away four *invading soldiers* who had no business being here! And Walbert has no right to try to impose his will on the woodlanders!"

"You imposed *yours* there when you set fire to their lands," Gideon pointed out. "I'd say that turned out a lot worse for them than Walbert trying to govern some of their excesses."

"What *excesses*?"

"Summoning dangerous creatures, engaging in deadly tribal feuds—"

"How is any of that Walbert's concern? Or yours?" Chandra challenged.

He said tersely, "It became Walbert's concern when some of those creatures—which, hard as this may be to imagine, Chandra, aren't always well supervised after they're summoned—started terrorizing farmers and villagers on the plains."

"If their farms and villages border the woodlands, then they've got to expect—"

"*What* do they have to expect, Chandra? To

see their children stolen? Their crops destroyed? Their livestock eaten? Their villages rampaged?"

"Problems like that don't give the Order a right to interfere in the forest!"

"Of course it does! But what gave *you* the right to interfere here?"

"*I* was protecting the woodlanders!"

"*That's* your idea of protecting them?" Gideon unleashed his anger. "Killing a harmless creature that was summoned here for their own good, and setting fire to their forest?"

"*For their own good?*" she shouted.

"If the excesses practiced in the forest don't cease, what do you suppose the farmers and towns-people will do, Chandra?" He didn't give her a chance to respond. "It will be a bloodbath!"

"And you think that gives Walbert a right to try to dictate how people live in the woodlands? And in the mountains?"

"Yes." Gideon looked tired again. His voice was calmer when he said, "Look, do you think you're the only person that the woodland oufes have decided to kill lately because they got angry about something? You're not." He added irritably, "You just happen to *deserve* it. But it goes on all the time now, Chandra."

"So?"

"You must have noticed how often innocent people wind up in harm's way when the local oufes decide someone has to die?" he said. "It's too dangerous."

Chandra thought of Mother Luti, Brannon, and the others at the monastery who'd been endangered by the attempts on her life. But she just glared silently at Gideon.

"Things have to change on Regatha," he said.

"Walbert's trying to bring peace and order to this plane. Life has become dangerously chaotic here. It can't go on any longer."

"Things were *fine* here until Walbert started interfering in lands where he has no right to intrude!"

He sighed. "So after the mysterious pyromancer that Walbert was concerned about incinerated a ghost warden, burned down part of the forest, incited a call for assassination from a tribe of hysterical oufes, and attacked four peacekeepers, I agreed with Walbert when he said you had to be contained.

"After that, this wasn't just about the Purifying Fire for me," Gideon said. "Not anymore. Because I realized you were too dangerous to leave on the loose here."

"So Walbert sent a letter to Mother Luti demanding she turn me over to him? Did he really think that would work?" Chandra said contemptuously.

"No," Gideon said. "He thought it might determine for certain whether you were a Planeswalker."

"What?"

"All things considered, he thought his demand might be the final push that the mother mage needed to decide that you should disappear for a while."

For a moment, Chandra felt as if she couldn't breathe. "It was a *trick*? To get me to planeswalk?"

"Yes," he said. "It was the only way I could be sure you were exactly what Walbert feared you were."

A red blaze of fury burned through her. "You manipulated me!"

"Chandra." His gaze followed the glow of flames moving along her skin as rage coursed through her, turning her blood into fire. "Don't."

"Don't *what*?"

"Don't make me fight you."

"Whyever *not*?" she snarled.

"Because I don't want to," he said wearily. "A lot has happened since we each left Regatha."

His gaze locked with hers.

She remembered that he had turned her over to the Prelate's soldiers, to be violated by the Enervants and probed by mind mages. She should kill him for that alone!

And then she remembered that he had hidden the scroll from them, to buy her time to escape . . .

"Please stop," he said quietly, remaining motionless while fire raced down to her hands and through the tendrils of her hair.

She remembered that, without his power to protect him, he had fought the Fog Riders for her.

"All so you could bring me back to Regatha?" she breathed.

"No." He thought it over. "Well . . . On Kephalai, yes," he admitted. "Walbert seemed certain you'd come back here. I was supposed to make sure you came back to *him*, incapacitated, instead of returning to the monastery to cause more trouble."

That renewed her rage. "If Walbert wanted me to stop causing *trouble*, then why didn't you just let me die on Kephalai?"

"If it had been strictly up to me," Gideon said, "I would have."

His honesty disarmed her. She was still furious . . . but she felt the flames of uncontrolled rage subsiding.

And in truth, looking at him, she knew she couldn't bring herself to kill Gideon. Not after everything that had passed.

"I don't know why," Gideon said, "but Walbert *wanted* you back on Regatha. In his custody, rather than roaming free."

"So that's why you created circumstances for me to escape from the Prelate's prison?"

He nodded. "That's why I followed you to Diraden, too."

"And then?"

They looked at each other for a long, silent moment.

"Things changed," he said at last.

Yes. Things had changed.

Chandra shifted her gaze away from him. "And then, when we escaped, I said I wanted to come back here." Her tone was sullen. "That certainly made things easier for you."

"I wasn't thinking about that," he said. "I was thinking about being alive and together and getting away."

She glanced at him.

A slight smile curved his mouth. "I never mentioned it, but I thought all along that the chances of getting out of there alive were pretty remote."

Feeling suddenly exhausted, Chandra sat down on the other wooden stool in this humble hut. "So we're alive and both back on Regatha. Now what?"

"Now . . . I don't know."

They were silent again.

Chandra heard footsteps approaching and she stiffened with tension for a moment, but relaxed when Samir came bustling into the hut.

He set down a pitcher of water, a basin, two small clay pots, and some soft cloths. "My wife has taken the children to stay with another family

while you're here, so that there won't be any risk of them seeing Chandra. They're good children, but they're too young for me to be sure they'll remember not to say anything to anyone."

"It's risky for you to have me here," Chandra realized. "I'm sorry."

"*I'm* sorry, Chandra," Samir said, pouring water into the basin. "I spoke against Walbert and the Order . . . Er, no offense intended," he said to Gideon.

"None taken."

"But I failed to persuade the other members of the council. Most voted in favor of cooperating with Walbert."

Gideon asked, "What's been happening here?"

Samir picked up one of the two small pots he had brought with him and poured some pale yellow powder into the basin of water. While stirring it around to dissolve it, he said, "Shortly after Chandra left on her journey, the Order's intrusion on the woodlands increased. More soldiers, more patrolling, more spies."

With the powder dissolved, Samir soaked a cloth in the water, then began cleaning the savage cuts on Gideon's chest and arms. "This will sting," Samir warned, "but it will fight infection."

Gideon made no sound as the liquid soaked into his open cuts. But Chandra could tell from his focused expression that it was painful.

Samir continued with his story as he worked. "Most of the woodlanders blamed the escalation of these impositions on Chandra's, er, encounter with the Ghost Warden and the soldiers. They felt we were suffering for her rash act."

Chandra was incensed by this . . . but since she knew Gideon condemned what she had done, and

since Samir had endured a great deal of trouble because of it, she kept her mouth shut.

"Then Walbert made his proposal to the inter-tribal council." Samir explained, "The council has one representative from every tribe or clan in the forest. It only meets when there is a problem or decision to be discussed that affects all the inhabitants of the Great Western Wood."

Chandra realized there was a gash on her left hand that she didn't remember getting. She picked up one of the cloths Samir had brought into the hut, dipped it into the basin of water, and applied it to her hand.

She drew in a sharp breath through her nostrils. It *did* sting.

"What was his proposal?" Gideon asked.

"You don't know?" Samir said in surprise. "When I met you at the temple, I had the impression you were in Walbert's confidence."

"I've been away. With Chandra. Whatever the proposal is, Walbert must have decided on it after I left."

"He has offered the races of the Western Wood a treaty," Samir said. "If we cooperate with the Order on certain matters, then all Ghost Wardens, all soldiers, and all forms of intrusion or interference will be completely withdrawn from the forest. And they will remain outside our land so long as we continue abiding by the terms of the treaty."

"What are the terms?" Chandra asked.

"There are some restrictions on summoning creatures. There will be penalties if our way of life affects the people of the plains. And there's a requirement that all grievances that have formerly led to violent reprisals hereafter are presented to an arbiter of the Order for judgment."

"And the council agreed to this?" she said in surprise.

"Well, it remains to be seen how sincere some of the council members are in their agreement," Samir admitted. "And some other members, of course, don't habitually think long-term."

"You mean," Chandra guessed, "that some woodlanders think they can bend the new rules once they're not being watched by ghost wardens and pestered by soldiers in their own territory. And the oufes are focused on getting the Order out of the forest *now*, rather than on what will happen next time they send assassins after someone who lives beyond the woods."

"Indeed." Samir finished cleaning Gideon's wounds and now picked up the second small pot he had brought with him, which contained some green balm. "This will be soothing, and it will help prevent further bleeding until you return to the Temple—where I imagine the mages can heal you better than my humble efforts."

"Thank you for your help," Gideon said. "It would have been hard to make it back to Zinara without any treatment."

While applying the balm, Samir said, "So the members of the council see a way to make all the trouble here stop . . . if they also agree to the final term. Which is to turn you over to the Order, Chandra."

"I suppose that after the fire I started here, it's not surprising that they agreed."

"Not everyone agreed," he assured her. "But, alas, enough of them did. And that's why you're not safe in the Western Wood anymore. You're too easy to recognize, and such interesting news travels fast. So you must stay hidden here until

nightfall. Then we'll cover your hair and make our way out of the forest."

"But why did Walbert make my capture a condition in his treaty with the inter-tribal council of the forest?" she asked in puzzlement. "I live with the Keralians, not with the woodlanders."

"The Keralians have received the same offer," Samir said. "Mother Luti rejected it. Rather emphatically."

Chandra nodded. She would have expected that.

"And now that the woodlanders have decided to accept the proposal . . ." Samir sighed. "It has put us on a different path."

"Walbert probably knew the Keralians would refuse," Gideon said pensively. "By getting your people to agree to his terms, he eliminates any alliance against the Order that might have existed between the woodlanders and the Keralians."

"Yes," said Samir sadly.

"He also gains partners in trying to secure Chandra's capture, and he reduces the places where she can hide—"

"Hide?" she repeated, affronted.

"—or roam freely." Gideon paused before continuing, "And since he knows the woodlanders have long been friendly with the monastery, he also counts on Samir's people to urge the monastery to accept the same treaty and surrender Chandra to the Order."

"The Keralians will never cooperate," Samir said with certainty. "They despise the Order, and they place a very high value on independence and freedom. If Walbert is determined to capture Chandra, he'll only succeed one way."

"By destroying the Keralians," Gideon said.

"Will he really go that far?" Samir asked.

The woodland mage and Chandra both looked at Gideon, awaiting his answer.

"Yes," he said, finally.

"You seem certain," Samir noted.

Gideon nodded. "Walbert will do whatever is necessary to achieve his goals. Including destroying Keral Keep."

CHAPTER SEVENTEEN

I don't understand," Chandra said to Gideon after Samir had left them alone in the hut again. "Walbert knows I planeswalked, doesn't he?"

"He must. I followed you, and he knew I planned to do that." Gideon added, "I didn't exactly say goodbye, but he knows."

"Then why is he trying to get others to capture me?" she said. "Why doesn't he just wait for you to bring me back?"

"Because we've been gone a lot longer than he expected. A lot longer than *I* expected."

"Oh. Right." She hadn't expected to be gone this long, either.

"He thinks I failed." Gideon said, "He probably thinks I'm dead."

"And that I killed you?" she said.

"Yes."

"But all this effort to capture me . . . He was *that* certain that I would return to Regatha?"

Gideon nodded. "Yes, he seemed sure you'd come back. And he wanted your return to be under his control."

"But *why* was he sure I'd come back?"

"I don't know." Gideon's expression was impossible to read as he met her gaze in the shadows of

the hut. "But you did come back, didn't you? And he knew you would."

"If Walbert thinks I killed you, then he must also think I'm very dangerous."

"You *are* very dangerous," Gideon said. He didn't sound like he was joking.

"And yet he's encouraging woodlanders like Samir to try to capture me." She said disdainfully, "He doesn't seem to have a problem with risking other people's lives, does he?"

"Neither do you," Gideon pointed out. "How many people died in the Sanctum of Stars because of you?"

"I didn't plan on that," she snapped.

"How many were inside when it collapsed, Chandra?" he persisted. "Ten? Twenty?"

"I don't know," she said tersely. "I was fleeing for my life, at the time."

"And the people you were fleeing from died because it was their duty to protect the Prelate's property from you," he said.

She was about to reply when she heard Samir's footsteps again. He entered the hut carrying a basket that held food, as well as a fresh pitcher of water for them.

"I hope you'll enjoy this," Samir said to them. "My wife is a wonderful cook!"

In truth, Chandra had never enjoyed anything she'd eaten at Samir's home, always finding the food bland and overcooked. But given how revolting the food on Diraden had been, this meal today tasted like one of the finest feasts of her life. Gideon evidently felt the same way. They both ate voraciously and spoke very little.

After the meal, Samir gave Gideon a threadbare tunic to wear, saying, "It's old and much-mended,

LAURA RESNICK

but it will hold together until you reach Zinara."

"Thank you." Gideon pulled it over his head. "For *all* your hospitality."

"A guest brings good luck," Samir said with a smile.

"Not necessarily," Chandra said gloomily.

Samir asked Gideon, "Are you returning to the Temple?"

"Yes."

"I'm *not* coming with you," Chandra warned him.

"No." He assured Samir, "Walbert will never know anything about today."

Samir glanced at Chandra, then smiled at Gideon. "I don't understand you, but I do believe you."

"I hope we meet again," Gideon said politely to him.

Samir glanced between them. "You two probably have a few things to say before you part. I'll wait outside, Gideon. When you're ready, I'll guide you to a path that leads east out of the forest. You can find the road to Zinara easily from there. And with so many of the Order's soldiers patrolling here now, you may encounter, er, colleagues on horseback soon after you leave here. Perhaps they'll help you get back to the Temple."

"Thank you, Samir." When he was alone again with Chandra, Gideon said to her, "You have to leave Regatha immediately."

"I just got back," she pointed out.

"No one is safe while you're here."

"Given how certain Walbert is that I'll come back, I don't think anyone will be safe after I *leave*, either," she said. "He'll just keep looking for me."

"This will only end if you go and never come back."

"I won't run away," she said. "Not while the Keralians have to deal with Walbert's obsession with capturing me."

"I'm letting you go free now," Gideon said, "but—"

"*Letting* me?" she repeated. "Do you imagine you could possibly—"

"—this is as far as I'll go for you," he said. "You've committed wrongs, Chandra."

"So has Walbert!"

"You'll only make it worse if you stay," Gideon said. "If you leave Regatha *now*, I'll lie to Walbert. I'll say you never came back here, that you died on another plane. But I won't do more than that for you."

"You don't even have to do *that* much."

"If you stay, I won't help you," he warned.

"I don't want your help!"

"I won't betray the Order." He took her by the shoulders, "Do you understand me?"

"Take your hands off me," she said through gritted teeth.

His grip on her tightened. "I won't turn away from my duty."

"What duty?" She frowned. "What does any of this have to do with you? You're not from here. You've been here even less time that I have!"

"The Order of Heliud isn't limited to just one plane, Chandra," he said. "Walbert's Order is . . . a local unit, you might say, of something much bigger. Something that extends across other planes of the Multiverse."

She drew in a long breath, her head spinning as she realized what he was saying. "So that's how

Walbert knows about Planeswalkers? He would have to know, wouldn't he, if he's part of something that exists on multiple planes?"

"Yes. Walbert knows. So does his designated successor. No one else, though."

"And if you're part of this thing, too, then that must be how you knew about the Purifying Fire before you ever came here. Because . . ." She gave him a quizzical look. "How did you put it? Gossip travels faster than galloping horses. Even across planes, it seems."

"And to places only a Planeswalker can travel."

And as a Planeswalker, she realized, Gideon would be highly important in a movement that existed on more than one plane. She asked, "So what *is* your duty?"

"I serve the Order. My duty is whatever is needed of me."

"And what purpose does the Order have?" she said. "Pestering people in every dimension until they behave the way you want them to?"

"Its purpose is to bring harmony, protection, and law to the Multiverse."

That statement awoke old ghosts. She smothered them and said nastily, "Oh, then it's a good thing you ate a hardy meal to keep your strength up."

He let go of her. "Well, it's not easy to keep up with a fire mage who thinks nothing of murder, pillage, and destruction."

"How *dare*—"

"I have to return to Zinara," he said. "Will you leave Regatha now?"

"No."

He looked momentarily sad. "Then I can't help you."

"I told you, I don't *want* your help."

"I won't let your choice become my weakness," he said firmly.

Chandra folded her arms and glared at him. "As long as you keep your word not to implicate Samir in anything, then what you do when you leave here is no concern of mine."

He looked at her for a long moment, saying nothing. Then he raised his hand to touch her cheek.

She intended to pull away and tell him again not to touch her . . . but as their eyes met, she found that she couldn't.

"Chandra . . ."

He didn't say more. What was there to left to say, after all?

She remembered wanting to kill him back on Kephalai when she was imprisoned in the Prelate's dungeon. She longed to feel that kind of rage toward him again. Chandra missed the clarity of that hot, simple hatred. She missed the familiarity and sharp-edged certainty of those old feelings so much, she almost wanted to weep for their loss.

And now, instead of killing Gideon, or fighting him, or telling him not to touch her . . . she listened in sorrowful silence to her erratic breathing and felt her aching heart beat too fast while they stood close together, their gazes locked, his fingers brushing her cheek so lightly that his touch almost tickled.

Then Gideon let out his breath and turned away. In the doorway of the hut, with his back to her and his hand resting on the coiled sural that hung from his belt, he said quietly over his shoulder, "You saved my life on Diraden."

Feeling a weight on her chest, she admitted,

"I may only be alive now because you were there with me."

"Goodbye, Chandra." He left.

❋ ❋ ❋ ❋ ❋

With a cloak covering her red hair and with Samir as her guide, Chandra escaped the green wood that night by the silvery light of the waxing moon.

The branches of trees and bushes clawed at her as she walked, she could scarcely see where she was going, and she knew that all manner of mundane and mystical creatures roamed the forest after dark; Chandra nonetheless found the Great Western Wood by night so much more pleasant and healthy a place than Diraden had been. There was life here, in all its robust and changing variety. And even in the current situation, at least not *everything* in the forest wanted to kill her, eat her, torment her, or betray her. So after recently surviving Diraden, sneaking out of the forest on Regatha by night just didn't provoke that much anxiety in her breast.

Samir, on the other hand, was *extremely* anxious. While Chandra was in his lands, he felt responsible for her safety. And once they reached the edge of the dense woodlands and arrived at the rocky path that led up to Keral Keep, Samir's anxiety didn't ease.

"You must push hard to reach safety before sunrise," he advised her. "The forces of the Order are patrolling the lower slopes of Mount Keralia now, too. If they see you, they may attack."

"Then they'll be sorry," she said grimly.

"With the Order tightening its noose around the monastery," Samir said, "trade and communications are both becoming difficult for

the Keralians." He handed her a small scroll. "Please give this message to Mother Luti. I will not endanger my people by openly violating the decision of the inter-tribal council, but I am Luti's friend—and yours—and so I will do what I can to help you, if my help is needed."

"Thank you, Samir." She clasped his hand warmly after taking the scroll from him.

"What would be best for everyone," he said, "is for all the factions of Regatha to re-establish balance and once again live in tolerance of one another."

Actually, Chandra thought that Walbert's death in a raging bonfire would be best for everyone, but she said only, "Yes, you're right."

"Now go quickly," he said. "You need to be inside the monastery's walls before dawn."

Despite recent hardships, Chandra was energized by rest, a decent meal, and the return to a plane that wasn't warped and twisted by Velrav's dark curse, so she was able to travel quickly as she ascended Mount Keralia.

Unfortunately, though, her speed wasn't enough to save her from discovery. The moon's position in the sky had scarcely changed since her parting from Samir when a sharp male voice in the dark said, "Halt! Who goes there?"

Chandra froze in her tracks, wondering whether the stranger could see her.

Another voice said, "Identify yourself!"

She remained silent and motionless in the dark, waiting to see what would happen.

A moment later, her course of action became clear. A small white orb appeared in the shadowy darkness of her rocky surroundings. It grew quickly in size. As it floated up into the air and

began circling the immediate area, she saw it briefly illuminate the figures of two men. If she moved again on the rocky path, they would hear her. And in another moment, that floating orb, which was coming her way, would shed light on her, and they'd see her.

Filled with the rich red mana that permeated the mountains of Regatha, Chandra called forth fire and sent a bolt of flame flying straight at the orb, to destroy it. It exploded in a pleasing shower of mingled white and golden light, then scattered itself on the mountain breeze. The two men were shouting.

"Did you see who that is? Is it her?"

"I'm not sure!"

Another glowing orb appeared. This one came straight toward Chandra, followed by the two armed mages as they quickly advanced on her with swords drawn, ready for combat.

She moved, scrambling off the path and through a gap in some boulders nearby, praying she wasn't about to disturb a sleeping snake or bad-tempered fox. The fabric of Samir's cloak caught on something, and pebbles rumbled noisily as Chandra yanked it free.

"What's that? There!" cried one of the soldiers. "Just off the path. Do you see?"

Her hood fell off as Chandra whirled around. She was bathed in the white light of the floating orb as she called flames into her hands again. She felt her hair catch fire.

"It *is* her! Seize her!"

One of the men fell back, screaming in agony as a huge fireball hit him in the chest and ignited his clothing. He staggered backward and fell from the path, down the steep slopes in the dark, his

body consumed by flames. The screaming ceased when Chandra heard his body bouncing off rocks far below this steep path.

"Wait! No! Don't!" the other soldier shouted at Chandra. "I'm not going to kill you!"

"Damn *right* you're not going to kill me," she said, forming another fireball.

"Our orders are to take you into custody!"

Chandra heard the fear in his voice at the same moment she realized he was backing away from her. That was when she noticed, in the light cast by the glowing orb, how young this soldier was. He looked barely eighteen. And scared.

She realized she didn't want to kill a frightened boy.

Holding the fireball poised for deadly action, she said, "If you don't want the same fate as your companion, then go. Go *now*. And don't come back."

He licked his lips, looking uncertain. "I have orders," he said breathlessly. "You have to come with me."

"Do you really want to die tonight?"

The young man slowly shook his head.

"Then go. Right now. Before I change my mind."

Looking devastated by his failure, he turned around, moving awkwardly, and began heading down the mountain.

Chandra threw her fireball at the slowly sinking white orb he had left behind, destroying it.

Then she heard more shouts and the voices of other soldiers. They had heard the commotion here. They were heading to this spot and would scour the mountainside in search of her.

She realized with frustration that she'd have to

abandon the path she was on. They'd be looking for her there and would chase her all the way up to the monastery.

Fortunately, she knew of a seldom-used, older trail that was not too far from here. But getting to it, in the dark and trying not to be heard by her pursuers, would be a laborious scramble over rough terrain.

With an exasperated sigh, Chandra turned and started making her way carefully in that direction. Samir was right. She must push hard to reach the monastery before daybreak.

❋ ❋ ❋ ❋ ❋

Within days of Chandra's nighttime encounter on Mount Keralia, Walbert's forces laid siege to the monastery.

Soldiers swarmed up the mountain and established base camps nearby, just beyond the range of the aggressive fire magic that the Keralians attempted to use on the intruders in their land.

The mages of the Order surrounded the monastery with an insubstantial but efficient white barrier. No one could sneak into the monastery or escape from it without passing through this mystical ward, which would capture the individual and instantly alert the hieromancers. It effectively cut off the Keralians from all access to the world beyond their red stone walls.

To preserve their supplies for as long as possible, Mother Luti organized a system of rationing for the monastery's food, ale, wine, and medicine. Fortunately, the deep well within the monastery walls could supply them with plentiful water for as long as the siege lasted. But, even with rationing, all other essential supplies would run out before long. The monastery had been built as a sheltered

place for study and learning; it had never been intended to withstand a long siege by determined enemies.

Chandra knew this stalemate must be resolved. And soon. She just didn't know how.

"I've had another message from Walbert," Mother Luti told her one evening, after Chandra responded to her request to come to Luti's workshop. "It arrived, rather dramatically, wrapped around an arrow that was shot into the south tower."

"Did it hurt anyone?" Chandra asked with concern.

"Fortunately, no." Mother Luti took a seat and gestured for Chandra to do the same. "And I suppose we'll have to expect similarly unconventional means of communication hereafter."

Their eyes met, and Chandra nodded. An angry pyromancer had killed a courier from the Order who had come to the monastery two days earlier. Obviously, Walbert wasn't going to risk sending another one.

Luti said, "Brannon has claimed the arrow as a war prize. The boy has become interested in archery since you were nearly killed by that bowman the oufe tribe sent after you. He's been practicing while you were away, and I must say, he's become rather good at it."

Chandra asked, "Is there anything new in Walbert's latest message?"

"No, it's the same as the previous one. You were seen ascending the mountain by night, Walbert knows you're here, he demands that we surrender you to him. He doesn't wish to destroy the monastery, but he will do it unless we deliver you. If we cooperate, we'll be left in peace, so long as we abide by certain terms. And so on and so forth."

Luti sounded bored and disgruntled. "The terms he proposes are similar to the ones that Samir told you the woodlanders had accepted."

Chandra rubbed her hands over her face and wondered what to do. The Keralians were united in their absolute, unconditional, unanimous rejection of Walbert's demands. Mother Luti had held two meetings at which the matter was discussed and voted on; one immediately after Chandra's recent return, and another last night, by which time it was clear how devastating the siege was going to be.

Not one single Keralian was willing to turn Chandra over to the Order.

It wasn't personal. Well . . . maybe in a few instances, it was; several of the Keralians, including Mother Luti herself, as well as the boy Brannon, were fond of Chandra. But, mostly, the refusal was based in the Keralians' way of life.

Being who and what they were, they would not bow down to anyone, give in to any ultimatum, surrender to any threat, or back down in the face of any challenge. They would not secure the safety of their monastery at the cost of Chandra's individual freedom. And nothing could induce them to abide by rules or conditions set by the Order—or by anyone else.

"What I still find puzzling," Luti said, "is Walbert's obsession with you."

"I'm puzzled, too," Chandra said.

"I've been thinking about it. It has to be because you're a Planeswalker," Luti said. "Walbert's reasons for pursuing you—and planning to execute you, I suppose—are presumably the fire in the Western Wood, the attack on the ghost warden, and your encounters with his men.

But none of that really explains all *this*." Luti waved a hand toward the window, indicating the siege that lay beyond the monastery's sheltering walls. "And since this man you've described to me, Gideon, is also a Planeswalker . . ." The mother mage shook her head. "Well, it's obviously not as if Walbert believes you're the only Planeswalker on Regatha. So whatever it is that Walbert fears or wants from you, it must be due to something about *you* in particular."

"But he doesn't *know* anything about me in particular."

"Well, he knows one thing," Luti said. "So I deduce that it must be the *crucial* thing: Unlike Gideon, *you* wield fire magic."

"So what?" Chandra said. "I still don't understand what he wants with a planeswalking fire mage or why he's doing all this."

"I don't it understand, either. Is his obsession with you a symptom of madness? In which case, can we hope he'll be assassinated soon and replaced by someone who'll end the siege and go home?"

"Gideon knows him, and Samir has met him," Chandra said, "and neither of them seems to think he's mad."

"Oh, well. Wishful thinking on my part." Luti added, "You *could* just planeswalk out of this problem, you know."

"No," said Chandra firmly. "I won't flee to safety and abandon you to deal with the consequences of my having been here. Besides, what will that accomplish? Will Walbert be merciful to you because you let me escape rather than surrendering me to him?"

"It's very interesting," Luti said pensively.

"*What's* interesting?"

"Walbert was convinced you would come back, and you did," the mother mage mused. "Now he's evidently convinced you won't leave . . . and, indeed, you won't."

That gave Chandra a chill. Did Walbert know more about her than she realized? Gideon hadn't seemed to think so . . . but that might only mean that Walbert hadn't confided fully in him.

For the first time, Chandra wondered if she *should* leave Regatha.

But then she thought of the Keralians, who'd be left in the middle of this mess, and of Samir, who had risked so much to protect her . . . and she couldn't believe that abandoning them all was the right course of action. Even though her being here didn't really seem to be right for them, either.

"I don't know what to do," she said to Mother Luti.

"Neither do I," Luti admitted. "Not about this, anyhow. But I have come to a decision about something else."

"Oh?"

"I have decided not to tell Brother Sergil what you've told me about the scroll."

"Why not, Mother?"

"Because I don't want the monks to pursue this any further."

"You don't?" Chandra said in surprise.

"No. It's much too dangerous." Luti frowned thoughtfully as she continued, "An ancient scroll that was *that* fiercely protected? A mysterious plane—which may or may not exist—where mana works differently than anywhere else in the Multiverse? And an artifact of such immense power that it will certainly be sought, coveted,

and fought over by people far more ruthless than any Keralian . . ." Luti shook her head. "If there is such a place as Zendikar, and if the artifact described in the scroll really can be found there . . . No," she said with finality. "I *don't* want it brought back here. I don't want anyone ever coming here to look for it. And I don't want Keral Keep to be involved with an object as dangerous as I believe that artifact must be." She gave a brief sigh and shrugged. "So I will tell the brothers that you couldn't find the original scroll and believe it has been destroyed. They'll study the copied text a little while longer . . . and then get frustrated or bored, set it aside, and move on."

They'd only move on if they survived this siege, Chandra thought. But she didn't say it. "As you wish, Mother."

Luti studied her. "But *you're* still interested in the artifact, aren't you?"

"Yes," Chandra admitted.

"I thought so." Luti nodded. "Fair enough. Individuals must pursue their own choices and destinies. My decision is made only with regard to what's best for this monastery."

"And if I someday find the artifact," Chandra said, "you're sure you don't want me to bring it here?"

"Chandra, if you ever find that artifact, I don't even want to *know* about it," Luti said with certainty. "Nor would I encourage you to tell my successor, whoever that may be."

And Chandra thought again that they were talking about the future as if the monastery definitely had one. Which wasn't at all certain at the moment.

✳ ✳ ✳ ✳ ✳

Chandra awoke from her nightmares sweating and breathing hard, with a scream on her lips.

The death of innocents was on her head. Because of her rash acts, her impulsive nature, and her reckless deeds.

She looked around her darkened bedchamber in Keral Keep and understood, for the first time in all the years she had been having this dream, why she had had it *tonight*.

The Keralians had welcomed her as one of their own kind when she first arrived here, and they had shared their home, their humble comforts, and their teachings and knowledge with her ever since then.

Now, as a result of that, soldiers and white mages were massed outside their walls, laying siege to their home, intent on destroying their way of life, and threatening to kill them.

All because of her.

Chandra swung her legs over the side of her narrow bed and, feeling nauseated, rested her head between her knees and concentrated on taking slow, steady breaths.

It's happening again. Because of *me*.

She must prevent it this time. She *must*.

Chandra knew she couldn't live with something like that happening twice. Indeed, she couldn't even live with what *had* happened—she was always running away from it.

I can't outrun two memories like that. I can't.

And suddenly, sitting here in the dark, breathing hard, sweating, shaking, hunched over her knees and trying not to be sick . . . She knew exactly what she must do.

Ⲫ

She had been confused and uncertain ever since returning to Keral Keep. Ever since things here had instantly spiraled into this crisis upon her return. She had floundered and vacillated. She had guiltily avoided eye contact with her fellow mages. She had expressed outrage when she mostly felt consuming guilt. She had considered fleeing and rejected it, and she had resolved to stay and then wondered if that was a mistake.

And all to avoid *this*, she now realized.

All to avoid the decision she knew she must make now—the one thing she could do to prevent the Keralians from meeting the fate that others had met because of her.

For a moment, she felt terribly sad as she hought about what would happen shortly. She was still young. There was still so much she hadn't seen or experienced. And now she never would.

Then a kind of peaceful resignation settled over her. Perhaps this was her fate. Perhaps she had been heading toward this choice ever since the nightmares began.

She stood up, walked over to the simple table and chair that were in the corner, and sat down there to write a brief message on a short sheet of parchment. Then she got dressed and left her chamber, heading for Brannon's bedroom. When she got there, she shook the boy awake.

Chandra indicated the parchment in her hand. "I have to send a message. I need your help."

He blinked sleepily. "Huh?"

"Bring your bow and arrow." She pulled back his covers and hauled him out of his bed.

He stumbled after her, following her out of his room and along the corridors of the monastery. By

LAURA RESNICK

the time they reached the south tower, he seemed to be awake.

"We're sending a message to them?" he asked, looking down at the mountainside with her. The moon was full tonight, casting a glow over the landscape. "The way they sent one to us?"

"Yes." She rolled the piece of parchment tightly around the arrow Brannon had brought, then tied it with a thin piece of twine she had brought from her room. "Here."

He looked at her handiwork and nodded. "Yes, this will fly."

"If they shot an arrow into the south tower . . ." She looked down at the rugged landscape below the tower. She could see the white glow of illumination from a base camp. "Yes, there they are. Can you shoot that far?"

"What am I aiming at?"

"That white glow. It's probably there to help a sentry keep watch in the night. If the arrow goes that far, they'll find it."

Brannon took a deep breath and nodded. "Yes, I can do that. I've been practicing."

"Mother Luti told me. And to make sure they see it . . ." She filled her breath with fiery heat, then blew gently on the head of the arrow. It caught fire. "Here. Quickly now."

He took the arrow with a nod, his talented young fingers comfortably handling the burning head as he prepared to shoot. Brannon raised the bow, drew back his arm, and aimed. After several steady breaths, he drew back a little further on the bow, his whole body taut with the strain, his gaze focused intently on his target. When he loosed the arrow, Chandra heard it sing through the air as it left the quivering bow behind. The small flame

sailed through the night, landing at the edge of the base camp.

There wasn't enough light for her to see any figures in the distant camp. But she was able to see that the flaming arrow was lifted off the ground and its fire doused.

"They've got it!" Brannon said. "Now what?"

"Now we wait for a reply."

❈ ❈ ❈ ❈ ❈

Chandra waited anxiously all the next day for a response to her message, but it didn't arrive until the day after that. And then she understood why it had taken so long.

She was playing with Brannon, trying to help relieve the natural restlessness of an adventurous boy now forbidden to go beyond the walls of the monastery. Brother Sergil came looking for her, to tell her she was wanted in Mother Luti's workshop. Brannon followed her there, but waited outside the door, as instructed.

When she entered the workshop, Mother Luti said to her, "Chandra, you have a visitor."

Her stunned gaze was already fixed on him. *"Gideon?"*

He nodded to her in silent greeting.

Gideon looked considerably better than he had the last time she'd seen him. His thick black hair was neatly braided down his back, and his face was clean-shaven and free of bruises. His pale brown tunic and leggings were clean and tidy, and he looked healthy and alert. The healing magic of the Order was obviously effective.

He did not have his sural with him; as a member of the Order, he would not have been admitted to the monastery while carrying a weapon.

And Chandra, though surprised to see him,

ⓒⓟ

specifically, wasn't at all surprised that he had agreed to come here alone and unarmed, even after a pyromancer had killed one of his colleagues at the gate the other day. She knew by now that Gideon did what others wouldn't or couldn't do.

"What are you doing here?" she asked.

"Walbert accepts your terms," he said. "I've come to take you into custody."

"Terms?" Luti repeated, looking quizzically at Chandra.

"He accepts?" When Gideon nodded, Chandra took a deep breath. "Good. I'm glad."

"*What* terms?" Luti asked.

"I'm turning myself in," Chandra told her. "Once I am in custody, Walbert will withdraw his forces from the mountain." She looked at Gideon. "Will he keep his word?"

"Yes."

She nodded, believing him—his promise confirmed what she expected of Walbert from what others had said of the man. Then she said to Mother Luti, "There are no other conditions. The Keralians will not be expected to abide by any terms or rules."

"Chandra," Luti said with concern, "are you sure this is what you want to do?"

"I'm sure." She looked at Gideon. "And I'm ready to leave."

"No!" Brannon burst into the workshop. "You can't go!"

Chandra turned around to look at the boy. She should have realized he would eavesdrop. "I have to go," she said to him. "Mother Luti will explain it to you."

"Something bad will happen to you there," Brannon said with certainty.

"Maybe," she said, "but I have to go."

"I'm coming with you!"

"No." She shook her head.

"But you promised! You said that the next time you left, I could come with you."

"I did *not* promise," she said firmly. "Anyway, I feel certain that you'd be very unhappy in the Temple."

"Why?"

"It doesn't suit people like us," Chandra said.

The boy looked to Mother Luti for a second opinion, but it was Gideon who spoke. "Chandra's right. You wouldn't like it there."

"*You* won't like it there, either," Brannon said to Chandra.

"No, but that doesn't matter anymore," Chandra said. "This is my choice, Brannon."

He looked angry and sad. "When are you coming back?"

She didn't answer, not knowing what to say.

"Soon?" he prodded.

"No," she said truthfully. "I don't think I'll be coming back soon."

CHAPTER EIGHTEEN

Chandra walked through the large front gate and beyond the monastery walls with Gideon at her side. When the gate closed behind them, she let out her breath in a rush.

Her decision was made, accepted, and enacted. She had committed herself to her fate, however unpleasant—and perhaps *short*—it might be. The Keralians wouldn't suffer or die the way others had indeed suffered and died because of her. She had prevented it from happening again.

Mother Luti had dealt with Walbert at a distance for years, and she knew his reputation was good, though she disliked what he intended to see in the world. She would not have let Chandra leave if she suspected Walbert of treachery or dishonesty in this matter. And Gideon had said Walbert would keep his word, and Chandra believed him.

Now she stood between the walls of the monastery and the mystical white barrier that had surrounded it for days. Beyond the barrier, a dozen armed soldiers awaited her.

Not quite knowing how to proceed, she glanced at Gideon.

He was looking straight ahead, wearing the impassive expression he relied on when he wanted to conceal things from others.

"Gideon?" she prodded, wondering what to do.

"Walbert asked me to come," he said quietly, without looking at her, "because he wanted to send someone you couldn't ambush. In case your offer wasn't sincere."

"It *is* sincere," she said.

"I know." Now he looked her at her. "Why?"

She wasn't going to answer. But then she glimpsed some of the concern that his cool expression masked, and she shrugged. "Ghosts, you might say."

"Ghosts?"

"I can't carry any more of them."

"I don't understand," he said.

"No, I don't suppose you do."

Gideon looked ahead again, his gaze on the translucent white barrier that separated them from the soldiers. "I didn't come to help you get out of this."

"I didn't think you had," she said.

"If you were counting on—"

"I'm not."

"You've made your choice," Gideon said firmly.

"Yes. And now that I have . . ." She gestured to the white barrier that separated her and the monastery from the world. "I think it might create the wrong impression if I blasted a fiery hole in this thing. So how do I get through it?"

"Just walk through it," he said.

"Just . . ."

"You'll be fine."

She shrugged again and walked forward. As soon as she entered the shimmering wall

of white, she felt the binding weight of ice surrounding her. She took a breath, trying not to panic or let fire start glowing along her skin in defensive reaction . . . until the white barrier began collapsing and contracting, moving in on her from all directions with alarming rapidity.

Startled, she called forth fire and tried to blow her way out of the smothering blanket of white that was enfolding her.

"Don't," Gideon said calmly, approaching her as she struggled within the shrinking wall of light and power. "It won't hurt you."

White magic was surrounding her, moving in on her, and covering her. It doused her fire as soon as she called flames to life. She tried again, and it happened again. Her hands, her hair, her arms all were smoking with her futile efforts to defend herself.

A trap!

The barrier was shrinking into a cloak that draped over every bit of Chandra's body. She struggled against it in horror, trying to tear it off or punch a hole through it, but it just kept folding in on her and shrinking. Then it started molding itself to her, following the contours of her body, the curve of her breast, the line of her thigh, and even the tapered shape of each individual finger.

"Gideon?" She heard how breathless her voice was and realized she was panting.

"It won't hurt you," he repeated. "It's just to prevent . . . accidents."

The thing settled all over her body and finally stopped moving. It didn't affect her vision, but she could see that it covered her entirely, like a second skin. It even covered her hair. The enchanted

sheath didn't hurt, tingle, or sting, and it didn't impede her physical movement in any way. But another failed attempt to create fire revealed to her exactly what it was.

"My very own portable prison," she said grimly. Her power was trapped inside this close-fitting shell of magic, just as she was.

"They thought it was for the best." Gideon nodded toward a place further down the hill, where the white mages who had created and maintained the barrier around the monastery were still camped. "They were a little concerned about what you might do in Zinara."

"You didn't do this to me?" she asked with a frown. "They did?"

"Yes," he said. "They're afraid of you."

"And you're not?" she challenged.

He gave her a bland look.

"But you *knew* about this," she said with certainty. And he had told her to step into it.

"Yes." His eyes held hers. "I told you to leave Regatha. You should have listened."

✖ ✖ ✖ ✖ ✖

Under other circumstances, Chandra would have found her entrance into Zinara interesting. It was an attractive city of tidy, pale stone buildings, spiraling towers, neatly-paved streets, and red-tiled roofs.

However, as she rode through the city gates with her armed escort, she was uncomfortable with the attention that she immediately attracted. She seemed to be entering the city via a major commercial street, and it was a busy afternoon. As Chandra, Gideon, and the soldiers of the Order rode slowly through the crowded area, people stopped what they were doing to stare openly

at her, point her out to others, and exchange speculations about her.

She could tell from their puzzled expressions, as well as from the bits of conversation that she overheard, that nothing had been said about her beyond the walls of the temple. The common people staring and pointing at her seemed only to wonder who she was, and whether she was a dangerous prisoner or, instead, an important visitor. Either circumstance could have accounted for her impressive escort.

Above all, people were curious about the way she glowed white all over. Because of this effect, she noticed, many of the people she was passing seemed to conclude that she was an important hieromancer. Some of them even bowed respectfully as she rode past them.

It was amusing, but Chandra wasn't in a mood to laugh about it.

The soldiers and mages of the Order had begun packing up and preparing to withdraw from the mountain as soon as Chandra had been taken into custody. She saw them making preparations even as she left the monastery behind her and followed Gideon down the mountain. The long ride across the plains to Zinara had happened in silence. She wasn't feeling talkative, and Gideon seemed preoccupied.

It was late in the day now. Chandra was tense as she rode through the city and approached the Temple of Heliud, but it was a relief to get here at last. She was ready to find out what fate awaited her, and to get on with it. She had never been any good at waiting, and she'd been wondering what the outcome would be ever since making her decision two nights ago.

Chandra assumed Walbert was going to execute her. Since he knew she was a Planeswalker, he knew how easily she could escape imprisonment, after all. She couldn't planeswalk at the moment, of course, not with this shimmering white shell entrapping her. But it would make no sense for Walbert to keep her power ensnared for many years to come, rather than simply eliminating her altogether. Even if he kept her imprisoned and guarded, the threat of mayhem or escape would always exist while she remained alive. Executing her was Walbert's only sensible choice.

In any event, she had achieved her goal. The Keralians were out of danger now and free of Walbert's demands and interference. Chandra had gotten what she wanted, and she would pay the price for that, as she had promised in the message that she had sent flying through the night on a burning arrow.

Her docile horse followed the mounted soldiers to the end of this busy street, around a corner, and into a large square. On the far side of the square sat a massive palace of marble with tall, thick, white pillars. Broad steps led up to a large set of carved doors. About twenty soldiers stood guard outside the building.

"The Temple of Heliud," she said. It was as impressive as the descriptions she had heard.

"Yes." It was the first time Gideon had spoken since they'd left Mount Keralia.

"Oh, so you still have a tongue?" Chandra said. "I was beginning to wonder."

He didn't react or respond.

When they reached the other side of the broad plaza, they dismounted. Chandra stood at the foot

of the broad steps and, for a long moment, gazed up at the massive white edifice where she was going to die.

"Walbert is waiting," Gideon said.

She nodded and started ascending the steps. He made no attempt to take her elbow or touch her.

When she reached the top of the steps and started crossing the wide marble landing, two soldiers moved to open one of the massive doors so she could enter the palace.

She walked into an enormous hall of polished white marble with pale blue veins running through it. Beautiful tapestries hung on the walls, and elegantly carved stone benches sat along the outskirts of the hall at regular intervals. Two long staircases curved together to the balcony overhead. She looked up at it and saw a man looking down at her.

"Walbert," she said with certainty.

He was exactly as Samir had described him: tall, slim, well-groomed, gray-haired, and about Luti's age. His blue eyes were bright with interest, but chilly.

His lean face broke into a sudden smile. Samir had said that even his smile was cold; but evidently something filled Walbert with unprecedented pleasure now, because his smile looked surprisingly warm.

"Hello, Chandra. Welcome to the Temple of Heliud."

He gazed down at her for another moment.

Then Walbert said pleasantly to Gideon, who stood beside her, "Let her refresh herself from the journey, then bring her to my study."

※ ※ ※ ※ ※

Walbert's study was grander than Mother Luti's workshop, which Chandra had expected, but it was nonetheless a workmanlike room, rather than a showplace. He had a large desk that was covered in parchments, scrolls, inkpots, and books. The walls were also lined with books. All of the furnishings in here were obviously chosen for durability and comfort, rather than just to look elegant.

Chandra entered the room, followed by Gideon. Four soldiers, who had shown her to a private chamber where she had "refreshed" herself, remained in the corridor now, just outside Walbert's door. The high priest of the Temple was sitting at his desk, signing a parchment that he handed to a young man, who nodded and left the room without speaking.

As soon as the door closed behind the young man, leaving the three of them in privacy, Chandra said to Walbert, "Gideon says you'll keep your word to withdraw your forces completely from Mount Keralia and leave the monastery alone from now on. Will you?"

Walbert looked amused. "No wasting time, I see! I like that, Chandra."

"I don't care what you like," she said. "I want to know——"

"Yes, I will keep my word." His amusement vanished, and he looked serious and intent. "As long as you remain in my custody, then I will leave the Keralians alone to destroy themselves however they please."

She ignored the provocative comment. "Then I won't try to escape execution."

"Execution?" He lifted his brows. "Oh, I'm not going to execute you, Chandra."

"What do you plan to do, then? Keep me like *this* the rest of my life?" She made a gesture that indicated the glowing second skin that imprisoned her.

"No," he said, "that's just a temporary measure. After tonight, there'll be no need for it."

She frowned. "Why? What's going to happen tonight?"

"Tonight, my visions will be fulfilled at long last."

"Visions?" Chandra repeated.

"The visions I have had for years," Walbert said, "when meditating in communion with the Purifying Fire."

Gideon's head moved. It was a very small motion, but he had been so still until now, it caught Chandra's attention. She glanced at him and saw that, although nothing showed in his expression, he was staring intently at Walbert now.

Evidently Walbert had never mentioned the visions to him.

"What are your visions about?" Chandra asked.

"Mostly, Chandra, they're about you."

"*Me?*" she blurted.

Walbert smiled again, and his expression was warm and serene as he gazed at her, his enemy and prisoner. "For years I have believed you would come during my lifetime. For years, I have awaited you."

She glanced at Gideon. He kept his face under control, but she could tell from the redoubled intensity of the gaze still focused on Walbert that he was as stunned as she was.

"You are the herald of the chaos that's on the verge of overwhelming this plane," Walbert said.

"Your arrival on Regatha threatens to usher in an era of ungoverned madness here."

"I just came here to study and learn," Chandra said. "Not to, er, herald and usher."

"I knew you would come, and you did," Walbert said. "I knew you would return, with or without Gideon, and you did. I knew you wouldn't leave again, even though you could have left—and, indeed, should have." He nodded. "You are the one whom I have seen in my visions, and it's your destiny to change everything here."

"No, it's not," she said firmly. "We each make our own destiny, and the only destiny *I* ever intended to have here—"

"Intended? You aren't in control of your destiny," Walbert said contemptuously. "You flow with your impulses and bounce erratically off your own emotions. I have seen you in the Purifying Fire, and I know who you are."

"Fine," she said in exasperation, "so your visions told you a fire-wielding Planeswalker would come to Regatha and cause trouble."

"No, an earthquake is *trouble*, Chandra," Walbert said. "You are a cataclysm."

"A cataclysm? Oh, for—"

"I have known ever since I first bonded with the power of the Purifying Fire that this day must come. I have seen in my visions how dangerous you are, what a deadly threat you are to the Order and our goals."

"Goals like ruling the forests and the mountains?" she said sharply. "Dominating all the mages of Regatha with your own rules, your own—"

"You came to Regatha to destroy everything I have built," Walbert said darkly. "You came here

LAURA RESNICK

to prevent me from bringing peace and harmony to this plane."

"I told you why I came here," she snapped.

"You are the kindling of the cataclysm that I have foreseen," he said with solemn certainty, "and I must stop you."

"Your notion of a cataclysm sounds like other people's idea of restoring balance to Regatha," she said. "Or being left alone to pursue their *own* goals instead of submitting to yours."

"I have prepared for this day for many years," Walbert said, "and tonight I will begin a new era on Regatha. One that is free of the destruction that threatens us here."

Gideon asked, "What are you going to do?"

He had been silent for so long, they both reacted as if one of the chairs had spoken.

Then Walbert recovered his composure and said, "I will give her to the Purifying Fire."

CHAPTER NINETEEN

Fire won't kill her." Gideon's voice was quiet and without expression.

"As I said, I don't intend to kill her," said Walbert.

"What will happen in the Purifying Fire?" Gideon asked.

"It will cleanse her."

"Cleanse me of *what*?" said Chandra.

"Of your power. It will purify you," Walbert said with evident devotion. "The Purifying Fire will eliminate the destructive poison of fire magic from your existence. It will forever sever your bond with the corrupting force of red mana."

"You're taking away my power?" Chandra said, appalled. "I don't understand. Why don't you just kill me?"

"Because once you're stripped of your power, you'll be an example for others."

"An *example*?" she repeated.

"You are the most powerful fire mage on this plane," Walbert said. "And *I* will take away your power."

"She'll be bound to this plane," Gideon said.

"Yes," said Walbert, holding Chandra's gaze. "No more planeswalking. You'll spend the rest of

your life on Regatha. Powerless. Defeated. Subject to my will."

"*No,*" Chandra said, a sick dread washing through her. She had anticipated death, not being stranded for life on just one plane, robbed of her power and with no reason to live.

He ignored her outburst. "I won't have to challenge the Keralians or invade the mountains again. They will *see* you stripped of all power and utterly impotent, and they will realize what they risk by continuing to oppose me. And so they will submit to the rule of the Order."

"No, they won't!"

"They *will.* I have foreseen it," he said with cold satisfaction. "The woodlanders will see you, too, vanquished and humbled, and they will understand that the Order must not be thwarted or disobeyed any longer."

"I thought I was coming here to die!" Chandra said angrily. "I agreed to be *executed,* not . . . violated, humiliated, and put on display!"

"Your message didn't mention execution as a condition of our agreement," Walbert said. "As far as your part of our bargain goes, you said you would surrender to my custody. And that was *all* you said."

"I *didn't* say that I'd allow you to feed me to the Purifying Fire!"

"The ceremony will take place tonight," Walbert said. "I have a great deal to do before then, so this conversation is over."

"I won't let you do this me, Walbert!"

He ignored her again as he shouted, "Guards!"

"*No!*" As the door behind her opened, Chandra leaped forward and threw herself across the desk at the old mage.

Alarmed, Walbert tried to evade her, but the speed and force of her attack shoved him back into his chair as he started to rise from it. She punched him in the face as footsteps thundered into the room. Chandra got her fingers on his throat and began squeezing just as several pairs of hands seized her. She kicked, bit, punched, and screamed threats as the soldiers pulled her off the high priest and subdued her.

Walbert tried to speak. He choked, coughed, and tried again, successfully. "Bring her hands together," he instructed the soldiers.

They did—with some difficulty, since Chandra continued struggling violently.

Walbert covered her wrists with his hands and closed his eyes, breathing deeply. Chandra felt something cool encircling her flesh, and she looked down to see a thick, shining white coil binding her wrists together, in addition to the shimmering sheath that already covered her flesh.

With her wrists bound together and four men holding her back, she tried to attack Walbert again. It was futile, but she was too enraged to give up.

Walbert turned to Gideon, who still hadn't moved, and said angrily, "Were you just going to stand there and watch her kill me?"

Gideon shrugged. "You've got guards."

Chandra was still kicking, struggling, and shouting when they dragged her from the room.

✼ ✼ ✼ ✼ ✼

She was alone in a locked chamber, with her wrists still bound, when he came to her.

Chandra's stomach clenched when the door to the chamber opened. Were they coming to get her for Walbert's ceremony? There was one small

window in this room, high up on the wall, so she knew that night had fallen some time ago.

When he entered the darkened room and closed the door behind him, she asked, "Is it time?"

"Not yet," Gideon said. "Soon, though."

"If you've come to tell me you didn't know what he would do," Chandra said coldly, "I'm not in—"

"That's not why I came."

"Then why *are* you here?"

"To tell you there may be a way out," he said.

She blinked. "You'll help me escape?"

"No," he said. "That's not possible."

"Of course it's possible," she snapped. "All we have to do is—"

"It's not possible without killing a lot of people," he said. "So the answer is *no*, Chandra."

She looked at the faintly glinting metal of the sural that was coiled at his belt. "Then kill me now."

In the dim light, she could see him shake his head.

"*Please*, Gideon." She heard the pleading in her voice and hated it, so she didn't say more.

He shook his head again.

She looked away.

"I'm sorry," he said. "I just . . . can't."

Chandra shrugged, gazing at the floor. "Maybe someone else will." And she would do her best to encourage them.

"There may be another way," he said.

When he didn't continue, she looked at him again. "Well?"

"I'd have come sooner, but I've been with the Keepers. And since I didn't want to arouse their suspicion, it took time. I had to be . . . circumspect about my questions."

"The Keepers?"

L A U R A   R E S N I C K

"Of the Purifying Fire," Gideon said. "It's never left unguarded."

She sat down on the narrow cot, which was the only item of furniture in the room, and looked at him in silence.

He said, "There may be a way to enter the Fire but keep your power."

"*May* be? You're not certain?"

"No one is certain," he said. "No one has tried it in this lifetime."

"Why not?"

"They're afraid of being cleansed of their power if they enter the flames." He added, "That's why no one in the Order has ever entered the Purifying Fire. Not Walbert, not the Keepers, not anyone."

Gideon crossed the room and sat beside her on the cot. "The Fire is very ancient, much older than the Order. Before the Temple was built, there was another temple that existed on this spot. Smaller, humbler. This place has been a holy site as far back as Heliud. The priests and priestesses of the old faith here, long ago, worshipped the Purifying Fire, and people came from all over Regatha to give themselves to it."

She frowned. "Give themselves? As sacrifices?"

"No. To prove they were worthy," he said. "Some died. Others survived. And if you survived the Purifying Fire, then you could become a priest or priestess of the faith. Because you had proved your soul was clean."

"Clean," she repeated flatly.

"That's how they survived the flames," Gideon said. "Not with magic, not with special protection. They entered the flames with a . . . a clean soul. And they didn't die."

She shook her head. "But I'm not going to die in the flames."

"Yes, you are."

Their eyes met in the shadowy room, illuminated now only by the glow emanating from her shimmering white body sheathe and the bright white coils that bound her wrists.

And she knew he was right. What would happen to her in the Purifying Fire would be, for her, the same as dying.

No, it would be worse than dying. Much worse.

"I can't bear it." Her voice broke.

"I know." He put his hand over both of hers, which were clenched together on her lap. "So we need to prevent it."

"But how does someone clean their soul?"

"You face the things you've done," he said, "and accept the weight of your responsibility for your deeds, without lies or excuses."

"That's it?" she said skeptically.

"That's what the Keepers said."

"And if I do that, then I won't . . . *my power* won't die in the Purifying Fire?"

He didn't answer, and she knew it was because he couldn't guarantee it. He had searched for a solution, for a way to save her. This was what he had been able to find. It wasn't perfect, but it was all that he could offer.

You face the things you've done . . .

"But I've done so *many* things," she said pensively.

"What did you do that gives you nightmares?"

She drew in a sharp breath and stared at him, her heart thudding with sudden fierceness.

He asked, "What did you do that left you with ghosts to carry?"

She tilted her head back and closed her eyes. "I don't talk about that. I *can't* talk about that." After a moment, she said, "I can't even think about it."

"But you dream about it." It wasn't a question.

She was silent.

His voice was kind when he said, "If you need some time alone now—"

"No," she said.

He waited patiently, not moving at all. His hand remained resting on both of hers. His breathing was steady.

"I . . ." She stopped, feeling sick. Her heart was racing. She forced herself to tell him. "I caused the deaths of my family and my whole village."

Gideon didn't move or speak.

Her breath came out in a rush. "I've never told anyone that. No one alive knows."

"That's what happened to your mother? You . . . caused her death?"

She nodded. He had asked her about it on Diraden, after she had cried out for her mother in her sleep. In the burning stench of her nightmares. Now she could give him an answer.

"I was raised in a traditional mountain village," she said, "on a plane I'll never go back to. My family were ordinary people. Decent people. My father was gentle. My mother was strict. I had two younger sisters who irritated me, and an older brother who I adored. He taught me to ride, and to fight, and . . . well, a lot of things. He was killed in the war. By then I had already discovered . . ."

"That you had power?"

"Yes. I played with fire in secret, going off alone into the hills to practice, even though it was forbidden."

"By whom?"

"By everyone. My parents forbade it, because they didn't understand it and were afraid. The elders of our village told me I had to stop, because it was against the law. And the law forbidding fire magic had been passed by the new ruler, when our lands were occupied at the end of the war."

She paused for a moment, then said, "But I didn't stop. I couldn't. It was like . . . Well, *you* know what it's like to discover you have that much power. That kind of talent. It's not something you can quit or give up."

"No."

"The more my parents and the village elders tried to get me to stop practicing and experimenting, the more suffocated I felt. Even though I was too young for it, they started talking about marrying me off, thinking that maybe that a husband and children would solve the problem." She shook her head. "But, of course, the problem was who I was. I didn't yet have any idea *what* I was, but I knew for certain I was never going to settle down to village life. I wasn't ever going to be one of them. With every passing day, I felt more and more . . . different. Separate."

She looked down at his hand, resting on hers, and remembered how alien she had felt in her own birthplace.

"Finally, my parents, under pressure from the village elders, talked seriously to another family about getting me married to their son. When I found out, I was *furious*. I wanted to run away. To leave home. But . . ." She shrugged. "I'd never been anywhere. I had no idea where I would go. And the whole realm was under martial law. I knew I wouldn't get far from our village before

I'd be stopped by soldiers. I felt trapped there. Imprisoned in that narrow, smothering life."

Chandra paused again. Gideon waited.

"I had been manifesting greater and greater power. Getting careless. Not hiding what I was doing, even though I knew I should. And now that I was so *angry* . . ." She started breathing harder. "I set off a huge explosion of fire on the outskirts of our village. I . . . yes, I wanted to frighten the village elders. And my parents. And the family who had just agreed to have their son marry me—I wanted them to change their minds, to refuse! I wanted *him* to refuse. I wanted to be set free."

When she stopped again, Gideon asked, "What happened?"

"The explosion attracted soldiers. They didn't know that one stupid, angry adolescent had done this. They thought the people in my village had to be rebels. They assumed the men had been practicing fire magic, in violation of the law, and were planning to use this secret power to attack the occupying forces." Her voice was breathless and uneven as she continued, "So they rounded up everyone in the village, forced them into the cottages that were closest to the fire—which was spreading—and barricaded the doors." Tears started welling up in her eyes. "The fire spread to those cottages . . . and everyone inside . . . burned."

The tears spilled over and rolled down her cheeks.

Gideon asked, "Where were you?"

"I had gone off to be by myself after starting the fire. I came running back to the village when I heard the soldiers attacking. When I saw what was happening, I fought them." She took shaky a breath and wiped her eyes. "It was the first time

I'd ever used my power that way. For fighting. It was the first . . ." Tears fell again. "First time I ever killed." She tried to steady her breathing.

"And your family?"

"They burned alive inside our home. I heard their screams. I saw my mother at the window, begging the soldiers to let my little sisters out of the burning building." Her voice broke. "I smelled their burning flesh . . ." She closed her eyes and wiped her face. "They all died because of me. My parents, my sisters, and everyone in the village. Because of *me*. Because I played with fire."

Gideon's gentle clasp on her hands became a firm grip. With his other hand, he stroked her hair.

"No one was left alive," she said. "No one. And it's my fault. I brought that fate down on them."

"And that's what haunts your dreams."

"Yes." She took a deep breath. "Those are my ghosts."

"How did you live through it?"

"When everyone was dead inside the burning buildings and the screams stopped, I didn't have the will to keep fighting. So the soldiers captured me easily then. They made me get down on my knees, so they could behead me on the spot. And when I saw the blade of that sword coming down to my neck . . . suddenly I wanted to live. I was *terrified*. And then . . ." She shrugged. "My spark was ignited. I planeswalked. One moment, I was kneeling in the dirt of my village with the smell of burning flesh in my nostrils and my head about to be cut off. And the next moment . . . I was in the Blind Eternities—with no idea where I was or what was happening." She gave a watery sigh. "And that's when my next life began. My life as a Planeswalker."

She took a few steadying breaths. "Sometimes since then, I've wanted to burn down the whole Multiverse."

"And you never went back?"

"No. I never wanted to."

Chandra felt his silent acceptance of everything she had told him. She supposed, from that, he understood the full weight of what she had done, but he didn't withdraw from her or condemn her. It was a surprise to find that he might not.

"I came to the Temple because I couldn't live with something like that happening again," she said. "I couldn't live with causing suffering and death at the monastery, to the people who had taken me in and treated me as one of their own."

"You did the right thing." His voice was very soft.

"And have I done the right thing now?" she wondered. "Telling you this?"

"Are they as heavy to carry as they were before?" he asked. "Your ghosts?"

She closed her eyes, feeling the load she carried. She felt the tears on her cheek and the hand that clasped hers. "No," she said at last, a little surprised. "No, not as heavy as before." The sorrow was as deep as ever, but the burden was lighter now that she had admitted what she had done.

They sat quietly together for a while.

Finally he said, "I have to go. Walbert is busy, but he's going to start wondering where I am. Especially since . . ."

"Since it's almost time?"

"Soon," he said.

She squared her shoulders. "I think I'm ready."

"How do you feel?"

She searched her soul. "I don't know if this is what it's like to feel clean," she said, "but I feel *better*. I feel I can face what will happen tonight."

CHAPTER TWENTY

Chandra remained alone in her dark chamber for longer than she had expected. Nothing in her life matched the sorrow of what had happened to her family and village because of her, but there were certainly other things she regretted, other things she had done that weighed on her. Indeed, there were enough such memories to keep her thoughts occupied until someone opened the door of her chamber and ordered her to come out. And then she wondered if she had remembered everything and taken responsibility for it.

She blinked as she entered the well-lit hallway where candles burned brightly in sconces that were spaced at regular intervals along the walls.

The four soldiers who were escorting her led her from this corridor on the upper level of the Temple down various flights of stairs until she finally thought they must be below ground level by now. There were no windows anywhere along this corridor, and the ceiling here was so low that the tallest soldier in her escort had to duck his head in a few places.

As they approached the end of the corridor, she saw Gideon waiting for her. He was holding a torch and standing beside an open doorway. He

gave a brief nod to the soldiers as they turned her over to him. Then they stood guard at the door.

Chandra paused in the doorway, looked down, and said without enthusiasm, "*More* stairs?"

"We're going to the caverns beneath the palace. Beneath Zinara," Gideon said.

Samir had told her that the Purifying Fire was said to burn in ancient caverns under the city, arising out of a powerful source of white mana that ran deep beneath the plains.

"They're waiting," he said quietly.

She nodded. With Gideon at her side, she began descending the steep marble stairs that led down into the belly of Regatha, below the bustling streets of Zinara and the imposing pillars of the Temple of Heliud.

The passage was narrow, barely wide enough for Gideon to descend beside her as her held her elbow to steady her. The stairs were ancient and uneven, and the flickering torch in Gideon's other hand created deceptive shadows. A misstep would be easy, and with her hands bound, she probably couldn't save herself from a headlong tumble. The ceiling of the tunnel was so low in places that Gideon had to lower the torch, holding it out in front of them while their heads brushed the stone ceiling. Chandra focused on her footsteps and her breath as she fought the feeling of being closed in, oppressed and smothered by stone.

After what must have been two hundred steps, they reached a broad, rough-hewn landing. It was made of the same marble as the stairs, but this surface was uneven and unpolished. The low ceiling of the steep tunnel gave way here to a spacious cavern. Chandra took a deep breath, glad to be out of the dark, stony embrace of the

tunnel. Gideon released her elbow and turned to set his torch in a niche carved into the stone wall. There were other torches there already, no doubt set there by those who awaited Chandra's arrival.

The landing overlooked the chamber of the Purifying Fire. The high-domed cavern was immense, probably as big as the temple that sat above it.

Hundreds of white, crystal-encrusted stalactites hung down from the ceiling. Some were as slender as a wand, others as thick as the trunks of young trees. Some were so long they nearly reached the floor of the cave. Stalagmites rose up from the rough white-marble floor of the cavern, reaching skyward like the spiraling towers of some fabled city. In several instances, they met and embraced the massive icicles of stone that dripped down toward them from the ceiling, twining together like lovers—or like enemies frozen together in the writhing throes of mortal combat. All of the vaguely menacing shapes glowed from within with mystical light, illuminating the cavern so brightly that Chandra found herself squinting.

At the very center of this extraordinary underground world was a pure white bonfire rising out of a deep cauldron of jagged white rock that was speckled with thousands of shiny crystal shards. Many members of the Order surrounded it—at least forty of them—dressed in plain tunics and leggings. They encircled the Fire, facing it, with their hands held up, palms turned toward their faces. They were still and silent as they . . . communed with the Purifying Fire? Drew strength from it? Probably both, Chandra guessed.

The Purifying Fire was twice as tall as a man, and so big around that Chandra estimated it would

take eight people, with their arms spread wide, to fully surround it. Its white flames licked and flickered like those of a regular fire, but it created no smoke and it made no sound. It was utterly silent.

And even from here, halfway across this vast space, Chandra could feel its cool power undulating in silent waves throughout the cavern. It quivered now, as if sensing her presence in the chamber, and seemed to lean toward her. Chandra felt sure its dancing white coolness responded to the red heat that was trapped within her by the shimmering second-skin that still covered her.

"The Purifying Fire," Gideon said.

"Impressive," she admitted.

"Come." He took her elbow and led her to the left edge of the landing.

"And still *more* stairs," she grumbled. Roughly chiseled into the bedrock, these steps looked lumpy, primitive, and dangerously uneven. "Did you people carve these stairs with a spoon?"

"They're old," Gideon said mildly.

With a firm hand on her elbow, he helped her down the rough, ancient steps to the main floor of the cavern. As their bodies touched, she could feel his tension and realized he was anxious about what would happen here tonight.

Chandra was surprised to realize that she was *not* anxious.

Not any longer.

Tonight, she had already faced the thing she feared most. After all these years of running from it, after the sickening nightmares, the chills and sweats in the dark, the refusal to think about it, the evasions and denials . . . tonight she had faced the one thing in the Multiverse that she had long thought she could *never* face. She had

stopped running at last from her ghosts, had turned around and accepted them. She had looked directly into the face of what she had done to her loved ones and admitted it—to herself, and to another.

She had confronted that, and it was something she had feared more than she feared the Purifying Fire.

If she could survive that rending of her soul tonight, then she could survive this. Whatever was going to happen inside the Purifying Fire, Chandra was ready for it.

When they reached the circle of white mages, priests, and Keepers standing around the silent flames with their eyes closed, Gideon came to a halt and waited respectfully for them to finish their . . . prayers? Meditation? Whatever.

Chandra saw no reason to emulate his courtesy. "Can we get on with it?" she said loudly. "It's been a long day for me."

Gideon closed his eyes and his lips twitched briefly. She couldn't tell if he was annoyed or amused.

Walbert flinched, glared at Chandra over his shoulder . . . then relaxed and offered her a smile.

Samir was right. It was *cold*.

"By all means, Chandra," the high priest of the Order of Heliud said. "I've waited a long time for this. Let's not wait any longer."

At a signal from Walbert, the circle of worshippers around the Purifying Fire shifted position, creating an opening for Chandra to walk through so that she could approach the dancing white flames. Then six of the men stepped forward, looking directly at her. Chandra saw that they were well armed.

Walbert said to her, "I would rather perform the ceremony in a way that lends itself to your

dignity, as well as mine. But if necessary, I will have you forcibly thrown into the Fire."

Out of the corner of her eye, she saw Gideon's chest start rising and falling faster.

"No," Chandra said. "It's not necessary. I have no desire to lose my dignity as well as . . . whatever else I'm about to lose."

Walbert smiled again. "I'm glad to hear that, Chandra. I don't want this to be needlessly unpleasant. For *any* of us."

"If you really want me to have a pleasant night," she said, "then let me go. Now."

Walbert's smiled broadened as he shook his head. "Alas, I'm afraid I can't do that."

"Oh, right," Chandra said. "*Destiny.*"

"Yes," he said seriously.

"Whatever."

"Shall we begin?" Walbert said to her.

"All right." Chandra took a step forward, then felt a hand on her shoulder.

"Wait," Gideon said, his voice subdued.

She turned her head to meet his gaze. What she saw there almost weakened her resolve. She said suddenly, "Don't stay."

He frowned a little. "Chandra . . ."

"Please don't stay to watch this," she said urgently. "*Please*, Gideon. Go now."

He came to a decision and nodded. His hand tightened briefly on her shoulder before he turned away. Chandra watched as he ascended the rough steps leading up to the landing, reclaimed the torch he had left perched in a sconce there, and disappeared into the tunnel that led back up to the palace.

Then Chandra turned back to Walbert. She saw that he was gazing at her with speculative

interest, but ignored it and said only, "I'm ready now."

Walbert nodded, and turned to the gathered mages, priests, and Keepers. "Let's begin."

Except for Walbert and Chandra, everyone present started chanting, and it sounded as if they had practiced well for this occasion. The chant was harmonious and their voices were clear and blended well. But as the sound echoed around the cavern and bounced off the walls and high ceiling, it was so loud that Chandra had to shout at Walbert to be heard.

"What now?" she asked.

Bizarrely, the old mage took Chandra by the shoulders and kissed her forehead. He did it so quickly, she didn't even have time to flinch away from the touch of his thin, dry lips, which she could feel even through the magical barrier that covered her skin.

Walbert did not shout the reply. He merely said, mouthing the words clearly, "Walk into the Fire."

"That's it?"

She hadn't shouted this question, and she was sure he couldn't have heard her words over the head-spinning echo of all those chanting voices. But he obviously understood her meaning. He gave a firm nod and gestured for her to enter the bonfire.

Chandra turned toward the Purifying Fire and started walking forward. The chanting grew even louder, as if her approach to the pure white flames gave strength to the voices of those watching her. When she was close enough to touch the blaze, she started shivering, covered with a piercing chill. She wasn't sure if this came

Ⓟ

only from the Purifying Fire, or if her own fear contributed to it.

She stretched out a hand and touched the Fire. The flames didn't burn, of course. Not with heat, not even with cold. They were chilly to the touch, but bearable. And they curled delicately around her wrist and seemed to tug gently, as if encouraging her to enter the silent, shimmering flames and prove herself there.

As Chandra stepped into the Fire, she felt the coiled magical binding around her wrists liquefy and melt away. Then the sheath that had covered her skin peeled away, too, freeing her. She didn't know if Walbert was releasing the spells, confident that the Purifying Fire would make her powerless now, or if the Fire itself was commencing its work of eliminating the magic that had entered its flames with her.

Chandra raised her arms and turned in a circle, whirling slowly inside the head-clearing chill of the white blaze, discovering the experience was not at all what she had expected. Rather than frightened, she felt empowered. Rather than defeated, she felt energized.

She tilted her head back, looking up through the translucent, undulating light embracing her and she surrendered—to her deeds, her past, her guilt, her sorrow. She felt the weight of the things she had done and the things she had failed to do. She accepted the burden . . . and then let it go. She abandoned her heavy load to the Fire, accepting whatever it might do with the regrets and the ghosts that she had brought with her into its purifying chill.

The blaze that surrounded her increased in its cold intensity, closing in on her, embracing

LAURA RESNICK

and engulfing her. It grew denser and became opaque, blocking Walbert and the other mages from Chandra's view. The Fire stroked along her flesh and seeped inside her body, exploring her inside and out, searching out her secrets, her guilt, the stains on her soul, discovering all that she might have tried to hide from its exploration—all that she had once tried to hide from herself.

The impact of this search was so forceful, Chandra couldn't breathe, couldn't think, couldn't even fear. She couldn't evade the intimate exploration of Purifying Fire, and she didn't try. She spread herself upon the cool white arms of this merciless embrace and gave herself to it without reserve or inhibition.

And when the Fire rewarded her courage by accepting her, she knew. She felt it. The searching intensity of the blaze transformed into a tender flood of welcome. Its piercing chill became a soothing coolness.

As the opacity cleared and the dancing flames again became translucent, Chandra knew that she was free. Golden heat flowed through her blood with rich, reassuring familiarity as she turned toward Walbert.

Her sorrow would always be with her, but there would be no more haunting nightmares. No more screams and acrid smoke pursuing her through her dreams.

Chandra stepped out of the Fire, out of the mysterious flow of white mana that had embraced so many souls for so long. She knew now that Walbert had misinterpreted what he had seen in the flickering white blaze. And if she did indeed have a destiny on Regatha, if there truly was a

reason that she had been meant to come to this plane . . . now she knew what it was.

The harsh glow of victory was in Walbert's pale blue eyes as he watched her walk out of the Fire and stand before him.

"Things had to be this way, Chandra," he said confidently. "It's for the best."

She considered this. "Perhaps."

There was no need to prepare further. She had found such focus, such strength, such certainty of intent in the Purifying Fire, all she had to do now was inhale deeply, spread her arms wide, and reach with her will for the rich red mana of Regatha.

Walbert understood an instant before it happened. "No!"

Chandra unleashed a spell that exploded with golden fire and fury throughout the entire cavern.

"You were right," she said to Walbert, raising her voice to be heard about the thundering roar of her spell. "I guess it is my destiny to change everything here, after all. I *am* the cataclysm you foresaw."

"*No!*" Walbert staggered backward, shock and horror contorting his face.

Above them, the ceiling of the cavern started caving in, in response to the power of Chandra's spell as it pushed skyward with boundless fury.

The mages of the Order were screaming and racing toward the steep tunnel that led back up to the palace and a chance of survival. Some of them would make it to safety. Others certainly wouldn't. Too many of them had come down here to watch Chandra be stripped of her power so that their Order could commence an era of unchallenged domination over Regatha.

"Bad decision," she said to their fleeing back-sides as they stampeded past her.

"You can't!" Walbert cried, too appalled by the destruction of his dreams and plans to run for his life now.

"I can," she said. "And I'm pretty sure I'm actually *meant* to."

Walbert had gone too far. He had tried to use the Purifying Fire to disrupt the balance on Regatha, to trample on the practices of other mages and other ways of life. He had disrespected and dismissed the value of all mana except that which empowered *him*. And now the white mana flow that ran deep beneath the plains of Regatha had embraced and then freed the fire-wielding Planeswalker whom Walbert had brought into these ancient caverns to become the key to his conquest.

Now everything would indeed change.

The madness of sudden, agonizing, unforeseen loss twisted Walbert's face now, and he attacked Chandra, who was off-guard, watching the celebrants run. He was stronger than he looked, and she staggered backward under the weight of his enraged assault.

Overhead, the ceiling of the cavern split open with a terrible crash, and a portion of the Temple, which had sat high overhead, plunged into the far end of the cavern. Moonlight pierced the big, ragged hole that was growing above the chamber, and dust, rocks, and boulders flew recklessly across the cavern at deadly speed. The walls and floor shook, and the hysterical screams coming from the world above were scarcely loud enough to carry through the thundering roar down here of crashing stone and groaning rock face.

A raging burst of red-and-orange heat roared across the chamber. It flowed over Chandra, mingling with the fire that sparked along her skin and the flames that raged in her hair.

Walbert screamed as the fire that engulfed the two of them consumed him. He tried to fight it off with his power, but Chandra could see that none came to him now when he called on it. The white mana that had spared her had also, it seemed, abandoned the high priest of the Temple. Chandra watched dispassionately as Walbert died like any common man.

⚕ ⚕ ⚕ ⚕ ⚕

"Chandra? *Chandra?*"

The sound of her named brought Chandra to her senses. She opened her eyes and wondered why she was lying on the hard stone ground.

The blood that trickled down her face when she sat up, as well as the sharp, blood-smeared rock lying nearby, answered her question. Now she remembered something falling onto her head—*hard*—only moments after she watched Walbert die.

She looked up and saw Gideon stepping through rubble and rock fragments as he approached her. Moonlight shone down on the far end of the cavern, but this portion still relied mainly on the glowing spires of rock for illumination. Chandra looked around and noticed that some of those spires had been destroyed in the cataclysm.

The Purifying Fire, however, glowed white and strong, enduring, as it always had.

"What happened?" Gideon's voice was hoarse.

Chandra touched her bloody forehead. "Falling rocks from overhead. I got knocked out."

"No, I meant . . ." He leaned down, seized her shoulders, hauled her roughly to her feet, and gave

her a hard shake. Her neck snapped back and her aching head protested as he shouted into her face, "*What did you do?*"

When she didn't say anything, he shook her again. "*Chandra!* What did you *do* here?"

"You can see what I did," she said, feeling worn out now. "It was a boom spell."

He shoved her away so violently that she bounced off the wall behind her and nearly fell back down.

"I didn't tell you how to save yourself so that you could do *this*!" His face was white with anger, pale and stark against the coal black of his hair.

Chandra looked around at the devastation she had wrought. The fire had been so hot, it had turned bodies to ashes, so it was hard to tell how many members of the Order had died here. She knew it must be at least a dozen. Perhaps more. There might also have been people in the portion of the Temple that had caved in and fallen when part of the cavern ceiling collapsed.

"The temple is ruined," she guessed. "And the Order . . ." She took a breath and thought it over. "Well, in disarray, certainly. Destroyed?" She shrugged. "I don't know. The mana flow is still strong here. They'll regroup in time. But perhaps they'll remember what happened here when their reach exceeded their grasp."

Gideon grabbed her again, and he looked so enraged, she thought he was going to strike her. She didn't resist or try to stop him. She knew he felt betrayed. In his position, she'd want to lash out, too.

But he let her go and turned away, breathing hard. "How could you do it?" he asked in a low voice.

"In a way, I think Walbert was right," she said. "I was meant to come here."

He gave her an incredulous look. When he saw that she was serious, he said, "You don't believe in destiny. Neither do I."

"I don't really believe in visions, either, and yet Walbert had them, and I was in them." She shrugged. "And even if none of that is true . . . it *is* true that someone had to stop him, and I was the one who could."

"I shouldn't have helped you." Gideon wasn't looking at her. He almost seemed to be talking to himself.

"Why *did* you help?"

For a moment, she didn't think he would answer. Then he said wearily, "Because I learned on Diraden what it was like to be without my power, and to think I might be stuck on one plane for the rest of my life." He met her gaze. "And because I saw there what that was like for *you*." He looked away again. "I couldn't see you like that permanently. I . . . couldn't."

"What Walbert wanted to do was wrong, Gideon," she said.

"No." He shook his head. "What you've done is wrong. And I . . ." He sighed and closed his eyes. "I helped you." After a moment, he said heavily, "You planned this. It's why you asked me to leave." It wasn't a question.

"I knew what I would do if I came out of the Fire with my power intact," she said. "And I didn't want to kill you."

He was silent for a long moment. Then he said, "I almost wish you had."

"No," she said. "I . . . can't."

He let out a long, slow, shaky breath. "You'd

better go. No one else was willing to come down here so soon after the . . . after *that*. But they'll come soon. They'll attack if you're still here. And I don't want any more deaths here tonight."

She looked in the direction of the steep tunnel of stairs that led out of here, knowing that soldiers would probably be waiting at the top. "I can't leave that way."

And it was the only exit—unless she grew wings and flew out of the gaping hole in the ceiling, high over the far end of the cavern.

"Were you planning to stay on Regatha?" he asked skeptically. "After *this*?"

"No," she realized, "I suppose not. If the remnants of the Order think I'm alive and at the monastery, there'll just be more trouble."

It would be better if everyone on Regatha thought she had died in the incinerating blaze that had swept through the cavern.

"You should leave now," Gideon said.

"You mean planeswalk?" she guessed.

"Start preparing," he corrected. "After you're gone, I'll convince them you died here and your body is ashes."

Chandra hadn't thought this far ahead and, for a moment, she had no idea where to go.

Then she realized which plane she most wanted to find now. And, despite her weary, bloody, head-spinning, thirsty condition, she suddenly looked forward to the journey.

"Gideon . . ."

"I know where you're going," he said. "I know what you want." He shook his head. "You won't find it. But that won't stop you from trying, will it?" He gazed at her without warmth. "You're a fool."

Anger flashed through her. She welcomed its simple, familiar heat. "There's something I didn't tell you about the night my family were burned alive in front of me."

"I'm not interested." He turned away from her.

She grabbed his arm. "The soldiers who killed them belonged to an order of mages that vowed to bring harmony, protection, and law to the land."

He froze.

"Does that sound familiar, Gideon?" she prodded in a venomous voice.

He turned his head to look at her. His expression was a mixture of suspicion, shock, and revelation.

"I have faced what I did," Chandra said, "and laid my ghosts to rest. But I will never forgive those men for what *they* did that night. And anyone who believes in the things they believed in is my enemy. Now and forever."

His breathing was faster as he stared at her, taking in what she was telling him.

"I acted on that here, and I will act on it wherever I go. Do you understand me?" she said through gritted teeth.

"I understand," he said at last, "what you're telling me."

"Then don't get in my way." She let go of his arm and turned away, eager to leave this place. Eager to leave him.

"Chandra."

"What?" she snapped over her shoulder, afraid she would weaken if she looked at him again.

"We will meet again."

She couldn't tell if it was a threat or a promise. Either way, and against her will, she held it to her heart.

Chandra heard Gideon's footsteps behind her, echoing softly in the ruined, charred cavern as he walked away. She didn't turn around or look back. And when the echo of his footsteps ascending the stairs that led back up to the devastated Temple faded away into silence, she prepared to planeswalk again.

The threat of domination by the Order was ended on Regatha, and balance was restored. There would still be some friction among the hieromancers of the city, the fire mages of the mountains, and the green mages of the woodlands. But there would be no more threat of one group dominating the others. Not in this lifetime.

Now, as she sat down on the charred stone floor of the chamber of the Purifying Fire, Chandra turned her thoughts to the future. She closed her eyes, concentrating on her breathing as she prepared to planeswalk, and she imagined the rich and mysterious plane of Zendikar . . . which in her heart, she *knew* must surely exist somewhere in the vast and wondrous Multiverse.